EXPLORING MARKETING RESEARCH

TENTH EDITION

William G. Zikmund

Barry J. Babin
Louisiana Tech University

SOUTH-WESTERN
CENGAGE Learning™

Australia • Brazil • Japan • Korea • Mexico • Singapore • Spain • United Kingdom • United States

SOUTH-WESTERN
CENGAGE Learning

Exploring Marketing Research, 10th Edition
William G. Zikmund, Barry J. Babin

VP/Editorial Director: Jack W. Calhoun

Executive Editor: Michael Roche

Editor-in-Chief: Melissa Acuña

Developmental Editors: Elizabeth Lowry, Jennifer Thomas

Editorial Assistant: Shanna Shelton

Executive Marketing Manager: Kimberly Kanakes

Senior Marketing Coordinator: Sarah Rose

Marketing Communications Manager: Sarah Greber

Director, Content and Media Production: Barbara Fuller-Jacobsen

Content Project Manager: Emily Nesheim

Media Editor: John Rich

Production Service: Macmillan Publishing Solutions

Senior Art Director: Stacy Jenkins Shirley

Internal Designer: Craig Ramsdell

Cover Designer: Craig Ramsdell

Cover Image: © Getty Images/Digital Vision

Text Permissions Manager: Mardell Glinski Schultz

Text Permissions Researcher: Lisa Nelson

Senior Permissions Manager, Images: Deanna Ettinger

Photo Permissions Researcher: Susan Lawson

Senior First Print Buyer: Miranda Klapper

For product information and technology assistance, contact us at
Cengage Learning Customer & Sales Support, 1-800-354-9706
For permission to use material from this text or product, submit all requests online at **www.cengage.com/permissions**
Further permissions questions can be emailed to
permissionrequest@cengage.com

ExamView® is a registered trademark of eInstruction Corp. Windows is a registered trademark of the Microsoft Corporation used herein under license. Macintosh and Power Macintosh are registered trademarks of Apple Computer, Inc. used herein under license.

Library of Congress Control Number: 2008940385

ISBN-13: 978-0-324-59376-1
ISBN-10: 0-324-59376-7
PKG ISBN-13: 978-0-324-78844-0
PKG ISBN-10: 0-324-78844-4

South-Western Cengage Learning
5191 Natorp Boulevard
Mason, OH 45040
USA

Cengage Learning products are represented in Canada by Nelson Education, Ltd.

For your course and learning solutions, visit **www.cengage.com**
Purchase any of our products at your local college store or at our preferred online store **www.ichapters.com**

Printed in Canada
1 2 3 4 5 6 7 12 11 10 09

To my wonderful children:
my dear little girl, Amie,
and that awesome dude, James.

BRIEF CONTENTS

CONTENTS

CONTENTS

PART 2: BEGINNING STAGES OF THE RESEARCH PROCESS

PART 3: RESEARCH DESIGNS FOR COLLECTING PRIMARY DATA

PART 4: MEASUREMENT CONCEPTS

PART 5: SAMPLING AND FIELDWORK

PART 6: DATA ANALYSIS AND PRESENTATION

PART 7: COMPREHENSIVE CASES WITH COMPUTERIZED DATABASES

PREFACE

Marketing research is a little like searching for a needle in a haystack. Researchers search for answers but forming the questions can be just as important. The "search" cannot be removed from "research." Following this analogy, the researcher must address questions such as these: How do you find the needle? Where does the search start? How do you translate recorded data into intelligence that can be used to answer managerial questions? Clearly, it would be helpful if you could discover better places to start searching and better techniques to help direct the search. When it works right, marketing research is a win-win proposition. The process enables a company to identify its customers and design products that maximize the value they receive from a purchase. In return, the company receives value as the customers spend their hard-earned money. The result: customers win and businesses win! All are better off.

Like searching for a needle in a haystack, imagine trying to find a single piece of market information from the Internet. This information may well be hidden beneath piles and piles of irrelevant stuff! Or how about trying to find a key piece of market information that may be hidden in the mind of a consumer or an employee who isn't consciously aware of all his or her reasons for some preference or behavior and, consequently, can't identify or talk about it? How do you go about finding this information that could be so crucial to making a good market decision?

Using an X-ray monitor would be a great way to find the needle. But your real-world success is probably more dependent on the ability to wield an effective research process than an X-ray monitor. And that's where this text comes in: *Exploring Marketing Research* equips students with the knowledge and skills involved in this basic research process that will simplify and provide more accuracy to their search for market intelligence.

Chapter 3 introduces this process, which includes six stages. Researchers must first work together with decision makers to decide why they are looking for that metaphorical needle; the next two stages plot out the way to go about finding the needle. Next are two stages that focus on the actual search for the needle. The process concludes when the market researcher communicates the benefits of finding "pointed" information that can help mend problems or create something really new and special to the decision maker. Success in this process usually merits the researcher a reward that is a bit more valuable than that needle!

New to *Exploring Marketing Research*

To ensure that students are able to conduct market research with an understanding of all the latest theories and techniques available to them, the tenth edition is substantially revised and updated. Certainly, the field of marketing research is dynamic both in terms of the demands placed on it by business and in terms of the technological advances that provide more tools for the researcher's toolbox.

The Internet is revolutionizing information systems, ways of gathering secondary data, survey processes, sampling, questionnaire design, qualitative analysis, and communication of results. Practically every chapter includes significant coverage of Internet-related topics, and most chapters also include review questions and activities that get students involved with the Internet in a relevant way. The Survey This! feature gets students and instructors directly involved with one important way that the Internet has changed research. This particular feature provides firsthand experience with the advantages and disadvantages of using online questionnaires. Additionally, students can then analyze data that they actually helped to provide.

In addition to greater currency and attention given to the Internet, key features added to the tenth edition include:

- Survey This!—Students respond to an online questionnaire using Qualtrics software. The questionnaire involves students' opinions, activities, and interests regarding numerous everyday behaviors ranging from study habits to involvement with social networking. The resulting data are made available to instructors and students. In the early chapters, this feature is useful for critiquing the way questionnaires are constructed and how research hypotheses are addressed in a questionnaire. In later chapters, students can use the data to respond to real research questions about other students. Students also get access to Qualtrics to design their own questionnaires.

- Tips of the Trade—Each chapter contains a useful list of important tips that correspond to the particular stage of the research process discussed in the chapter. The tips provide information addressing practical questions such as interview length, question wording, interviewer involvement, sample size requirements, and guides for data reliability and validity, as well as useful tips for testing hypotheses using inferential statistics.

- Chapter Vignettes—Each chapter opens with a story relevant to the material featured in that particular chapter. Some of these vignettes involve famous brands and companies, so the reader may well be familiar with some of the topics. Other vignettes involve "slice of life" stories describing a businessperson's struggle to make smart decisions and demonstrate how research is intertwined with this struggle. The ninth edition included all new vignettes and the tenth edition includes about one-third new vignettes with updates to the others.

- A Simplified Approach and Style—The boxed material, chapter objectives, and end-of-chapter materials are now presented in a simplified form that allows greater focus on the truly important information. Boxed materials highlight Research Snapshots that cover ethical angles of research, provide illustrations of research in practice, and offer relevant tips or detailed examples. The chapter learning objectives ensure an important coherence and structure to the chapters that culminate with the end-of-chapter materials.

  This deliberate approach has been taken to emphasize significant content material and issues, which will reinforce positive student learning outcomes. Moreover, this simplified approach continues into the analytical chapters, which deemphasize detailed statistical theory and focus more on how statistics are applied and used in marketing research. Homework and cases provide students with an opportunity to gain firsthand experience in these applications.

- Increased Coverage on International Business Issues—The examples and illustrations make much greater use of international business. Readers of this book may end up working outside the United States or Canada, so the increased international examples will increase awareness of research issues beyond North America and open up domestic students to global dynamics. This is a particularly important addition to the text since cultural and language barriers often present challenges for the researcher.

- Greater Attention to Qualitative Research—More and more companies are benefitting from qualitative research. In response to this important phenomenon, Chapter 6 was rewritten in the ninth edition to focus more exclusively on qualitative research. Phenomenology, grounded theory, ethnography, and case study approaches are now all covered. Several other chapters now emphasize qualitative research to a greater extent. For example, the Internet is not just a way of collecting quantitative data. Qualitative research is dramatically being changed by the Internet as consumers leave more and more artifactual data behind on social networking Web sites, company chat rooms, blogs, micro-blogs (such as tweets left on Twitter), and more.

Organization of the Book ⬅

The organization of the tenth edition of *Exploring Marketing Research* follows the logic of the marketing research process itself. The book is organized into seven parts, and each part presents the basic research concepts for one of the stages in the research process; each part also discusses how these concepts relate to decisions about conducting specific projects.

Part 1: Introduction emphasizes the interplay between research and business and how the importance and scope of research varies with the type of business orientation that characterizes a company. Included in this discussion is an overview of computerized data management and information systems, an overview of the entire marketing research process, and an explanation of how all of this is changing due to the Internet.

Without high ethical standards, no business is good. Thus, the introductory materials also include an emphasis on business ethics and the special ethical problems associated with marketing research.

Part 2: Beginning Stages of the Research Process covers the essentials involved in starting to study business problems. This part emphasizes decision making, problem definition, and the process of how the business problem must be translated into research questions and/or research hypotheses. Research proposals are covered in some detail, and the reader is encouraged to see these as the written agreement that helps put the decision maker and the researcher on the same page.

Chapter 6 emphasizes qualitative research applications. One role played by qualitative research is helping to separate business problem symptoms from true issues that can be attacked with marketing research. However, qualitative research extends far beyond problem definition; it allows greater potential for discovery as well as deeper and potentially more meaningful explanations in marketing research.

Part 2 concludes with a detailed discussion of secondary data and emphasizes its increasing importance in an increasingly data-rich world.

Part 3: Research Designs for Collecting Primary Data examines some topics most closely associated with marketing research. For example, the chapters describe issues related to planning, conducting, and administering surveys. Surveys remain a mainstay for collecting consumer and employee opinion.

Additionally, Part 3 includes two chapters that deal specifically with market experiments. As such, this part emphasizes test-marketing, which is also synonymous with marketing research in many ways.

Part 4: Measurement Concepts gives readers working knowledge of building blocks that are absolutely critical to effective research. This part describes the basics of measurement theory. Key topics include descriptions of the different levels of scale measurement and how this affects the interpretation of results. Basic ways to measure human attitudes and practical matters dealing with questionnaire design are also discussed. An increased emphasis is placed on the use of new technologies for conducting interviews. For instance, how does asking a question in an electronic format change options for respondents and the researcher? Topics such as these are highlighted in Part 4. Students can again get firsthand experience with state-of-the-art questionnaire design and surveying tools with the Qualtrics assignments.

Part 5: Sampling and Fieldwork explains the difference between a population and a sample. The reasons why sampling is needed and why it can be used to confidently allow predictions about larger numbers of people are covered. The fieldwork process is also discussed including the importance of supervision of fieldwork. Sloppy sampling and a lack of field supervision lead to error.

Part 6: Data Analysis and Presentation covers important processes necessary in translating raw data into market intelligence. Included among these topics, the data must be edited and coded. The coded data are then ready for analysis. Some of the most commonly used methods for analyzing data are also presented. For instance, basic descriptive statistics are discussed as ways of portraying key results like central tendency.

Inferential statistics are also discussed, including often-used univariate and bivariate approaches such as *t*-tests. Multivariate statistical approaches are also introduced so that the reader has an awareness of techniques that can analyze many variables simultaneously. Some hands-on experience with basic multivariate procedures is also provided. Additionally, this part discusses communication both in the form of a written report and an oral communication. Here again is another area that is being shaped by technological advances.

Part 7: Comprehensive Cases with Computerized Databases makes up the last section of the book. These cases provide materials that challenge students to apply and integrate the concepts they have learned throughout the text. Instructors will find that these cases provide some flexibility either to expand or simplify the assignment to suit the demands of varying course assignments.

The cases provide more variety and include some that involve analysis of internal marketing problems as well as an opportunity to use qualitative research. When quantitative data are included, they can be easily analyzed with basic statistical tools like SPSS. Excel files are also included with the same data. These files can be read directly by statistical programs like SAS or other programs. A new comprehensive case has been added to the tenth edition.

Superior Pedagogy

More than other marketing research textbooks, the tenth edition of *Exploring Marketing Research* addresses students' need to comprehend all aspects of the marketing research process. The following features facilitate learning throughout the book:

- **Learning Objectives.** Each chapter begins with a concise list of learning objectives that emphasize the major areas of competency the student should achieve before proceeding to the next chapter. The key is to avoid labeling everything a major learning objective and to provide the instructors with flexibility for emphasizing additional material from each chapter as they see fit.
- **Major Headings Keyed to Learning Objectives.** All first-level headings, with the exception of those labeled "Introduction," are keyed to learning objectives. This should be an aid in developing assessment rubrics and makes the book more user friendly in terms of identifying key material. Example assessment rubrics are available in the instructional resources.
- **Research Snapshots.** All of the box materials share a common title, Research Snapshots. Each chapter contains three Research Snapshots. The boxes explore marketing research processes in a variety of modern businesses situations, ranging from international considerations to research ethics. Some boxes also illustrate research techniques and applications in a step-by-step fashion. Every attempt is made to make the box material lively and relevant to the subject matter of the chapters.
- **Writing Style.** An accessible, interesting writing style continues as a hallmark of this book. With a careful balance between theory and practice and a sprinkling of interesting examples and anecdotes, the writing style clarifies and simplifies the market research process. In addition, the text offers a comprehensive treatment of important and current topics.
- **Statistical Approach.** A short review of statistical theory in Chapter 17 provides students with an overview of the basic aspects of statistics. Because this text stresses managerial applications more than statistical theory, students are given some basic tools to perform common data analysis. More sophisticated data analysis approaches are left for further reference. Thus, the readers can learn how to test simple hypotheses involving differences between means or relationships among variables. Cross-tabulation, *t*-tests, ANOVA, and regression are covered in sufficient depth to allow a student to use these techniques. The text includes screen shots to get students started running statistics using EXCEL, SAS or SPSS, which is available with this text.

    In addition, easy-to-follow, click-through sequences can walk a student through a few of the most basic approaches to producing statistical results.
- **Key Terms.** Learning the vocabulary of marketing research is essential to understanding the topic, and *Exploring Marketing Research* facilitates this with key terms. First, key concepts are boldfaced and completely defined when they first appear in the textbook. Second, all key terms and concepts are listed at the end of each chapter, and many terms are highlighted in a marginal glossary. Third, a glossary summarizing all key terms and definitions appears at the end of the book for handy reference. A glossary of frequently used symbols is also included.
- **Ethics Questions.** Identified by a special icon, ETHICS, ethics questions are included in most chapters. Among the compelling issues students are asked to explore is redefining the right to privacy in light of new technology. The ethical issues also provide a great opportunity for building critical thinking skills.

- **Internet Questions.** Internet questions also are identified by a special icon, **'NET**. Nearly all chapters include multiple questions and research activities that illustrate advances in Internet applications common to marketing research.
- **Research Activities.** The end-of-chapter materials include a few real-world research activities intended to provide actual research experience for the student. Most provide an opportunity for the student to gain experience with multiple content areas. Some involve ethical aspects of research, and some involve Internet usage.
- **Cases.** Extensive cases taken from real-life situations illustrate marketing research concepts and build knowledge and research skills. These cases offer students the opportunity to participate actively in the decision-making process, one of the most effective forms of learning. Video cases are also available via the instructor section of the book's Web site (**www.cengage.com/marketing/zikmund**).

Resources for Students

To promote learning and competency, it is also important to provide students with well-crafted resources. In addition to covering the latest information technology (described above), the tenth edition includes the following student resources:

- The Dedicated Website **www.cengage.com/marketing/zikmund**, developed especially for the new edition, includes chapter quizzes that allows you to test and retest your knowledge of chapter concepts. Each chapter has a quiz to encourage retesting. In addition, the Web site features downloadable flashcards of keyterms, the very best online marketing research resources available, and much more.
- The Qualtrics Research Suite was built for researchers by researchers. Enclosed with each new copy of *Exploring Marketing Research* is an access code that gives you access to a tool that makes survey creation easy enough for a beginner while at the same time sophisticated enough for the most demanding academic or corporate researcher. Qualtrics allows you to create and deploy surveys, and provides data for analysis. A survey included in the book in the Survey This! box on page 4 has you fill out an initial survey. Then the survey data collected from students using *Exploring Marketing Research* around the globe are used throughout the rest of the book in a variety of ways, from critiquing questionnaire construction to using the data to respond to real research questions about other students. Access to Qualtrics requires an access code that is provided with each new copy of the book.

Acknowledgments

Certainly, no list of acknowledgments will be complete. So many people have assisted in this project. Chief among these would be to the late Bill Zikmund for carrying the weight of this project for each of the first eight editions. I am privileged to be able to carry the project along into hopefully many more editions as the premier marketing research text. Also, thanks go to some of my team. My graduate assistants Kevin James, David Shows, Melanie Gardner, and Christina Chung have helped with research for this text and helped share some of the workload on other endeavors freeing up time for me to spend on this project. David was particularly helpful in getting the Survey This! feature underway. Thanks also to Julia Callaway for helping to manage my crazy schedule. I would be remiss not to also mention the support and patience of my family. All have contributed to the project and my kids are particularly helpful in judging the relevance of vignettes and examples. Also, thanks go to all the great faculty who mentored me during my days in the Ph.D. program at LSU. Most notable among these are Joseph F. Hair, Jr. and the late William R. Darden.

Special thanks go to all the good people at Cengage Learning who helped make this project possible. Thanks to my publishers, Neil Marquardt and Mike Roche, for motivating the whole team to stay on schedule. Thanks to Kimberly Kanakes for creative inspirations and marketing support. Also, a special thanks to Elizabeth Lowry, Emily Nesheim, Jennifer Thomas, and Jill Traut. They provided tremendous support through the writing and production process, including assistance with proofing, permissions, photos, and exhibits.

Many colleagues contributed ideas for this book. They made many suggestions that greatly enhanced this book. For their insightful reviews of the manuscript for the tenth or previous editions of *Exploring Marketing Research*, I would like to thank the following:

Karen Goncalves
Nichols College

Carol Bienstock
Radford University

Steven V. Cates
Averett University

Stephanie Noble
The University of Mississippi

Bob Lauman
Webster University

Natalie Wood
St. Joseph's University

Robert Jaross
Florida International University

Terry Paul
The Ohio State University

Mike Parent
Utah State University

Stephen Batory
Bloomsburg University

Michael R. Hyman
New Mexico State University

Rick Saucier
St. John's University

Xin Zhao
University of Utah

Gerald Albaum
University of Oregon

William Bearden
University of South Carolina

Joseph A. Bellizzi
Arizona State University–West

James A. Brunner
University of Toledo

F. Anthony Bushman
San Francisco State University

Thomas Buzas
Eastern Michigan University

Roy F. Cabaniss
Huston-Tillotson College

Michael d'Amico
University of Akron

Ron Eggers
Barton College

H. Harry Friedman
City University of New York–Brooklyn

Ron Goldsmith
Florida State University

Larry Goldstein
Iona College

David Gourley
Arizona State University

Jim Grimm
Illinois State University

Christopher Groening
University of Missouri

Al Gross
Robert Morris College

Don Heinz
University of Wisconsin

Craig Hollingshead
Texas A&M University–Kingsville

Victor Howe
University of Kentucky

Roy Howell
Texas Tech University

Rhea Ingram
Columbus State University–Georgia

P. K. Kannan
University of Maryland

Susan Kleine
Arizona State University

David B. Klenosky
Purdue University

C. S. Kohli
California State University–Fullerton

Jerome L. Langer
Assumption College

James H. Leigh
Texas A&M University

Larry Lowe
Bryant College

Karl Mann
Tennessee Technological University

Charles R. Martin
Wichita State University

Marlys Mason
Oklahoma State University

Tom K. Massey
University of Missouri–Kansas City

Sanjay Mishra
University of Kansas

G. M. Naidu
University of Wisconsin–Whitewater

Charles Prohaska
Central Connecticut State University

Alan Sawyer
University of Florida

Robert Schaffer
California State University–Pomona

Leon G. Schiffman
City University of New York–Baruch

David Shows
Louisiana Tech University

K. Sivakumar
Lehigh University

Mark Speece
Central Washington University

Harlan Spotts
Western New England College

Wilbur W. Stanton
Old Dominion University

Bruce L. Stern
Portland State University

James L. Taylor
University of Alabama

Gail Tom
California State University–Sacramento

Deborah Utter
Boston College

David Wheeler
Suffolk University

Richard Wilcox
Carthage College

Margaret Wright
University of Colorado

Clifford E. Young
University of Colorado–Denver

William Lee Ziegler
Bethune-Cookman College

Thanks also to all of the students who have inspired me and reinforced the fact that I made a great career decision about two decades ago. Thanks also to my close colleagues Mitch Griffin, Dave Ortinau, and Jim Boles for their continued support and insight.

Barry J. Babin
Louisiana Tech University
November 2008

In Remembrance

William G. Zikmund (1943–2002)

A native of the Chicago area, William G. Zikmund was a professor of marketing at Oklahoma State University and died shortly after completing the eighth edition. He received a Ph.D. in business administration with a concentration in marketing from the University of Colorado.

Before beginning his academic career, Professor Zikmund worked in marketing research for Conway/Millikin Company (a marketing research supplier) and Remington Arms Company (an extensive user of marketing research). Professor Zikmund also has served as a marketing research consultant to several business and nonprofit organizations. During his academic career, Professor Zikmund published dozens of articles and papers in a diverse group of scholarly journals, ranging from the *Journal of Marketing* to the *Accounting Review* to the *Journal of Applied Psychology*. In addition to *Exploring Marketing Research*, Professor Zikmund authored *Essentials of Marketing Research*, *Business Research Methods*, *Marketing*, *Effective Marketing*, and a work of fiction, *A Corporate Bestiary*.

Professor Zikmund was a member of several professional organizations, including the American Marketing Association, the Academy of Marketing Science, the Association for Consumer Research, the Society for Marketing Advances, the Marketing Educators' Association, and the Association of Collegiate Marketing Educators. He served on the editorial review boards of the *Journal of Marketing Education, Marketing Education Review, Journal of the Academy of Marketing Science*, and *Journal of Business Research*.

Part 1
Introduction

© PHIL KNOTT/PYMCA/JUPITER IMAGES

CHAPTER 1
THE ROLE OF MARKETING RESEARCH

LEARNING OUTCOMES

After studying this chapter, you should be able to

1. Know what marketing research is and what it does for business
2. Understand the difference between basic and applied marketing research
3. Understand how the role of marketing research changes when a firm is truly marketing oriented
4. Integrate marketing research results into the strategic planning process
5. Know when marketing research should and should not be conducted
6. Appreciate the way that technology and internationalization are changing marketing research

Chapter Vignette: "The Dude Looks Like a Lady"

© AP PHOTO/ROBERT E. KLEIN

Picture the typical car company. Now, picture the typical car customer. What do you see? Put those two images together and most people imagine one of the Big Three (GM, Ford, or Chrysler), selling an SUV to a middle-aged man. The idea of men selling cars to men may have once been accurate. But times change and many of the assumptions that underlie the car industry can be questioned. Perhaps one reason many car companies are struggling today is the failure to read these changes in the marketplace. Is the typical car customer a man? Is the typical car sold in the United States an SUV? Are men better at selling cars?

Toyota surpassed General Motors as the number one selling car brand in 2008. Toyota has earned this position by successfully selling to many types of customers, but they have been particularly successful in designing cars that appeal to women. Women buy about 6 out of every 10 Toyota cars sold in the United States. This is no accident. Toyota works hard to know their customers better than the competition.

Recently, Toyota placed an emphasis on conducting marketing research that addressed the key question: What features create the most value for female car consumers? The results were particularly revealing and helped Toyota make important design changes. For example, research revealed that women, in contrast to men, are more interested in the car interior and less interested in the car exterior. Women want a car that is easy to get in and out of, easy to put things like children's car seats into, and ergonomic controls that are easily adjustable even for a driver who is less than six feet tall. Safety and security are also key benefits that create relatively high value for women. Women also show more interest in fuel economy and the Toyota Prius appeals to this desire to save fuel! Although men generally find value in features like these too, men are still more often first concerned with exterior styling and power. Even the Toyota Yaris, Toyota's lowest-priced model, contains a driver's seat that can be adjusted not only forward and back, but up and down as well.

Toyota's status as the leading car company has other manufacturers playing catch-up. But, General Motors and Volvo, among others, are also gearing up by aiming marketing research more squarely at women. For example, General Motors made the decision to make its OnStar communication system standard on all vehicles. This added feature helps create a sense of security by automatically contacting help in the event of a crash. Volvo's research also suggests that women are more concerned than men with easy parking and a car that does not need frequent maintenance. Volvo has put an exclamation point on the emphasis on women in the marketplace by naming Anne Belec as president of Volvo Cars of North America. Now, research has put the "lady" squarely in the center of the auto industry and Aerosmith could say "the dude looks like a lady" for a good reason![1]

Introduction

Changes in the automobile industry like those discussed in the vignette clearly demonstrate how beneficial the right information can be in making informed marketing and managerial decisions. Marketing research can provide that information. Without the input that research provides, key business decisions including those shaping product and brand promotion, pricing, distribution, and product design are made in the dark.

We open with two examples illustrating how business decisions require intelligence and how research can provide that intelligence. The following illustrations focus specifically on how marketing research encourages innovation in the form of new products or improvements in existing goods and services. Imagine yourself in the role of brand manager as you read these examples and think about the information needs you may have in trying to build a successful brand.

Jelly Belly brand traditionally offered fifty official jelly bean flavors. However, research input from customers has helped that number grow and now Jelly Belly even has a variety of specialty beans. Consumers willingly submitted new flavor ideas as part of the Jelly Belly Dream Bean Contest (http://www.dreambeancontest.com). In return, the consumers received an opportunity to win prizes. The company receives some really off-the-wall flavor ideas.

Among the strangest are flavors such as Dill Pickle, Rotten Egg, Taco, Burned Bacon, and Cream of Wheat.[2] Top suggestions were put back on the Web so that people could vote for the flavor they most wanted to see introduced. In 2008, the winning flavor was Acai Berry which beat out other finalist flavors such as Sublime Chili Lime, Thai Iced Tea, and Mojito.

More recently, Jelly Belly is trying to capitalize on consumers' desires for sports performance products. Survey research suggests that consumers would respond favorably to food and drink products providing benefits that improve one's ability to exercise.[3] As a result, Jelly Belly has introduced Sport Beans. Sport Beans contain added electrolytes, carbohydrates, and vitamins designed to provide added energy and alertness. In addition, all the strange flavor suggestions also have spawned a new

Jelly Belly brand's market research has capitalized on consumers' desires to produce fifty varieties of jelly beans as well as recipes on how to create snacks with them.

product offering for the entire jelly bean market. Bean-Boozled Jelly Beans combines a traditional flavor with an exotic flavor so consumers can decide if they really prefer a buttered-popcorn jelly bean to a rotten egg. The product provides added value through the fun that comes with all the potential surprises. A Skunk Spray bean looks exactly like a Licorice bean. So, the bean lover never is sure when the bean will bamboozle! Successful companies are constantly scanning ideas in the hope of providing ways of adding value. Jelly Belly's Sports Beans and Bean-Boozled Beans offer two different ways of adding value.[4]

This book introduces the reader to the world of marketing research. Marketing research represents the eyes and the ears of a competitive business firm. The researcher's job includes determining what information is needed so that data can be analyzed and become intelligence. Consumers play a crucial role in this process.

They often are used as research participants and, with or without their knowledge, they provide the information. One way that consumers (and sometimes employees or managers) take part is by participating in surveys. Most readers have probably participated in surveys previously. Here is another chance to do so, only this time, you will first play the role of a research participant. Later, you will fill the role of a research analyst and even a key marketing decision maker as you try to make sense of data provided by the many users of this textbook.

Your first interaction with the "Survey This!" feature is simply to play the role of respondent and respond to the entire survey as honestly and completely as possible. Go to the URL provided in the preface and by your instructor, and simply participate. Your answers will be anonymously stored in the database. Once you've completed the survey, you can visit the course Web site and get a copy of the questions contained in the questionnaire.

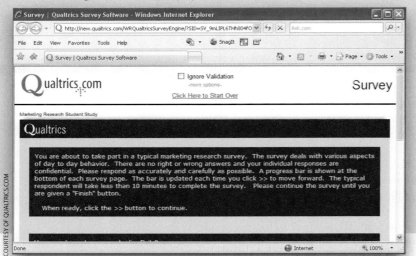

The coffee industry, after years of the "daily grind," has proved quite dynamic over the past decade. After years of steady decline, research on consumers' beverage purchases shows that coffee sales began rebounding around 1995. Telephone interviews with American consumers estimated that there were 80 million occasional coffee drinkers and 7 million daily upscale coffee drinkers in 1995. By 2001, estimates suggested there were 161 million daily or occasional U.S. coffee drinkers and 27 million daily upscale coffee drinkers.[5] By 2007, research indicates that although practically all coffee drinkers visit gourmet coffee shops, younger coffee consumers, particularly those under the age of 30, drink most of their coffee the *gourmet* way.[6]

Coffee drinking habits have also changed. In 1991 there were fewer than 450 coffeehouses in the United States. Today, places such as Starbucks, Second Cup, The Coffee Bean, Tea Leaf, and Gloria Jean's are virtually everywhere in the United States and Canada. There are more than 11,000 Starbucks stores alone today.[7] While locating these outlets requires significant formal research, Starbucks also is market testing new concepts aimed at other ways a coffee shop can provide value to consumers. One concept that has survived testing thus far is the addition of free, in-store high-speed wireless Internet access. Thus, you can have hot coffee in a hot spot! After Starbucks *barristas* began reporting that customers were asking clerks what music was playing in the stores, Starbucks began testing the sales of CDs containing their in-store music. Concepts still being tested include a lunch menu and limited wine service. The research that underlies the introduction of these value-added concepts could first include simply asking a consumer or a small group of consumers for their reaction to the concept. Survey research and then actual in-store tests may follow. However, had Starbucks simply asked consumers the question, "Are you willing to pay three dollars for a cup of coffee?" back in 1985, we would likely not be discussing them today. So, the research underlying such decisions can be multilayered.

These examples illustrate the need for market research in making informed business decisions. Jelly Belly provides consumers with the incentive of free samples of jelly beans in return for ideas about desirable new bean flavors. The statistics about coffee demonstrate how research can track trends that may lead to new business opportunities. Also, it is clear to see how research can be used to examine new concepts in progressively more complex stages, setting the stage for a more successful product introduction. These are only the tip of the iceberg when it comes to the types of marketing research that are conducted every day. This chapter introduces basic concepts of marketing research and describes how research can play a crucial role in successful marketing and business success in general.

What Is Marketing Research?

Part of business involves studying the different things that come together to create a business environment. Marketing research would not exist if business didn't exist. Thus, understanding marketing research requires at least a cursory understanding of business.

Business and Marketing Research

In its essence, business is very simple. Companies need to produce benefits that people want to buy. That means that consumers view the company as providing valuable bundles of benefits. There are many factors that can affect perceived value, and successful companies are those that understand the value equation. With this in mind, there are several key questions, the answers to which help provide this understanding.

1. *What do we sell?*
   This includes not only the benefits that are easily seen, but also the more emotional benefits such as the comfort and relaxation of enjoying a cup of gourmet coffee in a pleasant atmosphere or the novelty of trying a rotten egg jelly bean.
2. *How do consumers view our company?*
   All too often, companies define themselves too narrowly based only on the physical *product* they sell. A key question involves whom the customers will do business with if they do not choose your company. For instance, how is Starbucks viewed relative to its competitors? Who are the competitors? Does Starbucks compete more directly with Maxwell House, Seattle Drip, or something completely outside the coffee arena like a local lounge? Are we viewed more or less favorably relative to the competition?
3. *What does our company/product mean?*
   What knowledge do people have of the company and its products? Do they know how to use them? Do they know all the different needs the company can address? What does the packaging and promotion communicate to consumers?
4. *What do consumers desire?*
   How can the company make the lives of its customers better, and how can it do this in a way that is not easily duplicated by another firm? Part of this lies in uncovering the things that customers truly desire, but which they can often not put into words.

Answering these questions requires information. Marketing research's function is to supply information that helps provide these answers, thereby leading to more informed and more successful decision making. Managers that use this information reduce the risk associated with decision making.

In a way, "every business issue ultimately boils down to an information problem":[8] Can the right information be obtained and delivered? Research thus seeks to deliver accurate and precise information that can make marketing strategy and management more effective.[9] Marketing research attempts to supply accurate information that reduces the uncertainty in decision making. Very often, decisions are made with little information for various reasons, including insufficient time to conduct research or management's belief that enough is already known. Relying on seat-of-the-pants decision making—decision making without research—is like betting on a long shot at the racetrack because the horse's name is appealing. Occasionally there are successes, but in the long run uninformed decision making is unwise. Marketing research helps decision makers shift from intuitive information gathering to systematic and objective investigating.

Marketing Research Defined

Marketing research is the application of the scientific method in searching for the truth about marketing phenomena. Research applications include defining marketing opportunities and problems, generating and evaluating marketing ideas, monitoring performance, and generally understanding the marketing process. Marketing research is more than conducting surveys.[10] This process includes

marketing research

The application of the scientific method in searching for the truth about marketing phenomena. These activities include defining marketing opportunities and problems, generating and evaluating marketing ideas, monitoring performance, and understanding the marketing process.

Good Fat and Bad Fat

American consumers can be seen every day scouring nutrition labels. Most likely, the item they show the most interest in recently is the amount of fat. The Food and Drug Administration (FDA) is concerned that consumers get information that is not only accurate, but that also conveys the proper message to achieve a healthy diet. But all fat is not created equal. In particular, dieticians warn of the dangers associated with excess amounts of trans fats; diet nutrition labels break fats into saturated and unsaturated fats. Among numerous factors that complicate the interpretation of the nutrition label, trans fat (hydrogenated) is technically a nonsaturated fat, but it acts more like a saturated fat when consumed. So, where should it be placed? The FDA cannot address this problem intelligently without marketing research addressing questions such as the following.

1. If trans fats are listed as saturated fats, would consumers' beliefs about their consumption become more negative?

2. If the saturated fat amount includes a specific line indicating the amount of "saturated fat" that is really trans fat, would consumers become more confused about their diet?

3. If all amounts of fat are given equal prominence on the label, will consumer attitudes toward the different types of fats be the same?

4. Will consumers interpret foods free of trans fats as healthy?

Making this even more complicated is the fact that some consumer segments, such as teenagers in this case, may actually use the nutrition labels to select the brands that are least nutritious rather than most nutritious. So, they may actually seek out the one with the worst proportion of trans fats! The FDA specifically addressed trans fats in labeling regulations that took effect in 2006. Under these regulations, the FDA allows labels to claim zero trans fat as long as less than half a gram of hydrogenated oil per serving is contained. Simple?

Sources: "Health Labels are in the Eye of the Beholder," *Food Management*, 40 (January 2005), 80; Hunter, B. T., "Labeling Transfat is Tricky," *Consumers' Research Magazine*, 86 (July 2003), 8–10; Weise, E., "Food Labels Now Required to Mention Trans Fat, Allergens," *USA Today* (January 2, 2006), H1.

idea and theory development, problem definition, searching for and collecting information, analyzing data, and communicating the findings and their implications.

This definition suggests that marketing research information is not intuitive or haphazardly gathered. Literally, *research* (re-search) means "to search again." The term connotes patient study and scientific investigation wherein the researcher takes another, more careful look to try and know more about the subject. Ultimately, all findings are tied back to marketing theory.

The definition also emphasizes, through reference to the scientific method, that any information generated should be accurate and objective. The researcher should be personally detached and free of bias attempting to find truth. Research isn't performed to support preconceived ideas but to test them. If bias enters into the research process, the value of the research is considerably reduced. We will discuss this further in a subsequent chapter.

Clearly, our definition makes it clear that marketing research is relevant to all aspects of the marketing mix. Research can facilitate managerial decision making in all aspects of the firm's marketing mix: product, pricing, promotion, and distribution. By providing the necessary information on which to base marketing mix decisions, marketing research can decrease the risk of making a wrong decision in each area.

Finally, this definition of marketing research is limited by one's definition of *marketing*. Although one could hardly argue that research aimed at designing better products for a for-profit corporation like Toyota is clearly marketing research, marketing research also includes efforts that assist nonprofit organizations such as the American Heart Association, the San Diego Zoo, or a parochial elementary school. Each of these organizations exists to satisfy societal needs, and each requires marketing skills to produce and distribute their products and services. The federal government performs many of the same functions as for-profit business organizations. Governments can use research in much the same way as managers at Starbucks or General Motors. For instance, the FDA is an important user of marketing research, employing it to address the way people view and use various food and drugs. The FDA commissioned and funded research to address the question of how consumers used the risk summaries that are included with all drugs sold in the United States.[11] The Research Snapshot above describes a typical FDA market research project. This book explores marketing research as it applies to all organizations and institutions engaging in some form of marketing activity.

Applied and Basic Marketing Research

One useful way to describe research is based on the specificity of its purpose. Is the research intended to address a very specific problem or is it meant to describe some overall marketing phenomenon?

Applied Marketing Research

Applied marketing research is conducted to address a specific marketing decision for a specific firm or organization. The opening vignette describes a situation in which companies like Toyota and General Motors use applied marketing research to decide how to best create knowledge leading to better-designed products for particular market segments. Applied research is quite specific and a big part of this research is identifying exactly what issue a business needs to address.

applied marketing research

Research conducted to address a specific marketing decision for a specific firm or organization.

Basic Marketing Research

Basic marketing research is conducted without a specific decision in mind, and it usually does not address the needs of a specific organization. It attempts to expand the limits of marketing knowledge in general, and as such it is not aimed at solving a particular pragmatic problem. Basic research can be used to test the validity of a general marketing theory (one that applies to all of marketing) or to learn more about some market phenomenon. For instance, a great deal of basic marketing research addresses the ways in which retail atmosphere influences consumers' emotions and behavior.[12] From such research, we can learn how much the physical place creates value for consumers relative to the actual product consumed. This basic research does not examine the problem from any single retail or service provider's perspective. However, Starbucks' management may become aware of such research and use it to design applied research studies examining questions about its store designs. Thus, the two types of research are not completely independent.

Sometimes researchers use different terms to represent the same distinction. Some reserve the term *marketing* research to refer to basic research. Then, the term *market* research is used to capture applied research addressing the needs of a firm within a particular market. While the distinction is very useful in describing research, there are very few aspects of research that apply to only basic or only applied research. In addition, we will use the term *marketing research* more generally to refer to either type of research.

basic marketing research

Research conducted without a specific decision in mind that usually does not address the needs of a specific organization. It attempts to expand the limits of marketing knowledge in general and is not aimed at solving a particular pragmatic problem.

The Scientific Method

All marketing research, whether basic or applied, involves the scientific method. **The scientific method** is the way researchers go about using knowledge and evidence to reach objective conclusions about the real world. The scientific method is the same in social sciences such as marketing and in physical sciences such as physics. In this case, it is the way we come to understand marketing phenomena.

Exhibit 1.1 on the next page briefly illustrates the scientific method. In the scientific method, there are multiple routes to developing ideas. When the ideas can be stated in researchable terms, we reach the hypothesis stage. The next step involves testing the hypothesis against empirical evidence (facts from observation or experimentation). The results either support a hypothesis or do not support a hypothesis. From these results, new knowledge is acquired.

In basic research, testing these prior conceptions or hypotheses and then making inferences and conclusions about the phenomena leads to the establishment of general laws about the phenomena. Use of the scientific method in applied research ensures objectivity in gathering facts and testing creative ideas for alternative marketing strategies. The essence of research, whether basic or applied, lies in the scientific method. Much of this book deals with scientific methodology. Thus, the techniques of basic and applied research differ largely in application rather than in substance.

the scientific method

The way researchers go about using knowledge and evidence to reach objective conclusions about the real world.

EXHIBIT 1.1
A Summary of the Scientific Method

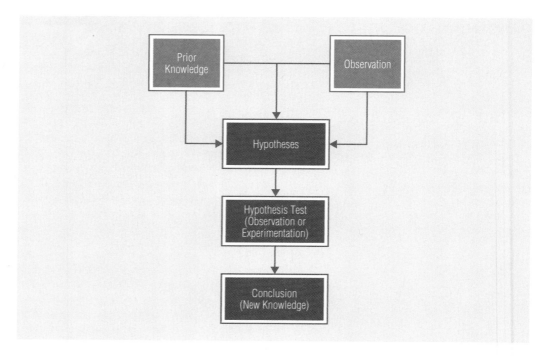

Marketing Research and Strategic Management Orientation

product-oriented

Describes a firm that prioritizes decision making in a way that emphasizes technical superiority in the product.

production-oriented

Describes a firm that prioritizes efficiency and effectiveness of the production processes in making decisions.

marketing concept

A central idea in modern marketing thinking that focuses on how the firm provides value to customers more than on the physical product or production process.

marketing orientation

The corporate culture existing for firms adopting the marketing concept. It emphasizes customer orientation, long-term profitability over short-term profits, and a cross-functional perspective.

customer-oriented

Describes a firm in which all decisions are made with a conscious awareness of their effect on the consumer.

In all of business strategy, there are only a few business orientations (see Exhibit 1.2). A firm can be **product-oriented**. A product-oriented firm prioritizes decision making in a way that emphasizes technical superiority in the product. Thus, input from technicians and experts in the field are very important in making critical decisions. A firm can be **production-oriented**. Production orientation means that the firm prioritizes efficiency and effectiveness of the production processes in making decisions. Here, input from engineers and accounting becomes important as the firm seeks to drive costs down. Production-oriented firms are usually very large firms manufacturing products in very large quantities. In both of these orientations, marketing research may take a backseat.

In contrast, marketing research is a primary tool enabling implementation of a marketing orientation.[13] The **marketing concept** is a central idea in modern marketing thinking that focuses more on how the firm provides value to customers than on the physical product or production process. It has evolved over time as product- and production-oriented firms respond to changes in the competitive and economic environments. When a firm adapts the marketing concept, it develops a **marketing orientation**. A marketing-oriented firm exhibits several key aspects including:

1. Be **customer-oriented**—meaning that all firm decisions are made with a conscious awareness of their effect on the consumer
2. Emphasize long-run profitability rather than short-term profits or sales volume
3. Adopt a cross-functional perspective, meaning that marketing is integrated across other business functions

Customer Orientation

According to the marketing concept, the consumer is at the center of the operation, the pivot point about which the business moves to achieve the balanced best interests of all concerned. According to this philosophy, the firm creates products and services with consumers' needs in mind. Many marketing theorists and marketing managers believe that the creation of value for consumers is the justification for a firm's existence. Therefore, unlike the other two orientations, marketing research addressing consumer desires, beliefs, and attitudes becomes essential.

EXHIBIT 1.2
Business Orientations

Product-Oriented Firm	**Example**
Prioritizes decision making that emphasizes the physical product design, trendiness, or technical superiority	The fashion industry makes clothes in styles and sizes that few can adopt.

Little consumer research

Production-Oriented Firm	**Example**
Prioritizes efficiency and effectiveness of the production processes in making decisions	U.S. auto industry's assembly-line process is intent on reducing costs of production as low as possible.

Little consumer research

Marketing-Oriented Firm	**Example**
Focuses on how the firm provides value to customers	Well-known hotel chains serve by addressing the needs of travelers, particularly business travelers.

Much consumer research

Yoplait Go-Gurt, yogurt packaged in a three-sided tube designed to fit in kids' lunchboxes, had more than $100 million in sales its first year on the market. The development of Go-Gurt clearly illustrates a consumer orientation. The company's consumer research about eating regular yogurt at school showed that moms and kids in their "tweens" wanted convenience and portability. Some brands, like Colombo Spoon in a Snap, offered the convenience of having a utensil as part of the packaging and delivery system. However, from what Yoplait marketers learned about consumers, they thought kids would eat more yogurts if they could "lose the spoon" and eat yogurt anywhere, anytime. Moms and kids participating in a taste test were invited to sample different brand-on-the-go packaging shapes—long tubes, thin tubes, fat tubes, and other shapes—without being told how to handle the packaging. One of the company's researchers said, "It was funny to see the moms fidget around, then daintily pour the product onto a spoon, then into their mouths. The kids instantly jumped on it. They knew what to do."[14] Squeezing Go-Gurt from the tube was a big plus. The kids loved the fact that the packaging gave them permission to play with their food, something parents always tell them not to do. Go-Gurt is a fun, convenient product that allows consumers the freedom to eat whenever and wherever they want. Yoplait realized that knowledge of consumers' needs, coupled with product research and development, leads to successful marketing strategies and that industry leadership—indeed, corporate survival—depends on satisfying consumers.

TO THE POINT

The aim of marketing is to know your customer so well that when your prospects are confronted with your product, it fits them so exactly that it sells itself.

—Peter Drucker

Long-Run Profitability

Customer orientation does not mean slavery to consumers' every fleeting whim. Implicit in the marketing concept is the assumption of the continuity of the firm. Thus, the firm must eventually experience profitability to survive (see Exhibit 1.3 on the next page). High fuel prices have stifled the market for large SUVs and trucks. This has contributed to troubles at most automotive companies. GM is now carefully considering which brands should be part of its portfolio. Surprisingly, one of the brands that GM is considering dropping is Saturn. Saturn produces economy cars that generally get great gas mileage, are recognized as innovative by automotive experts, and that display among the highest average customer satisfaction among GM brands. However, Saturn has yet to become profitable.[15] Pricing the cars higher is not a good option because Saturn consumers show too much price sensitivity and thus, they would likely switch to other brands.

The second aspect of the marketing concept argues against profitless volume or sales volume for the sake of volume alone. Sometimes, the best decision for a customer and the best decision in the long run for the firm is the sale that is not made. For instance, a parts supplier might be able to mislead a customer about the relative quality of the parts he or she sells and make an immediate sale. However, when the parts begin to fail sooner than expected, the customer will almost certainly not do business with this firm again. If instead the salesperson had been honest and suggested another supplier, he or she might have been able to find another opportunity to do business with that firm.

EXHIBIT 1.3
Long-Run Profitability

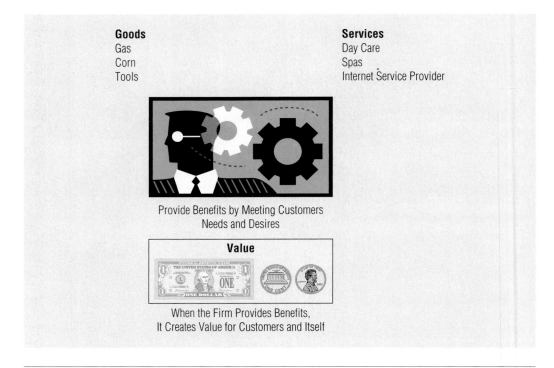

A Cross-Functional Effort

Marketing personnel do not work in a vacuum, isolated from other company activities. The actions of people in areas such as production, credit, and research and development may affect an organization's marketing efforts. Similarly, the work of marketers will affect activities in other departments. Problems are almost certain to arise from lack of an integrated, company-wide effort. The marketing concept stresses a cross-functional perspective to achieve consumer orientation and long-term profitability. The first panel of Exhibit 1.4 illustrates a firm in which every department works independently; it is not cross-functional and, consequently, not marketing-oriented. The

EXHIBIT 1.4
Isolation versus Cross-functionality of Marketing in a Firm

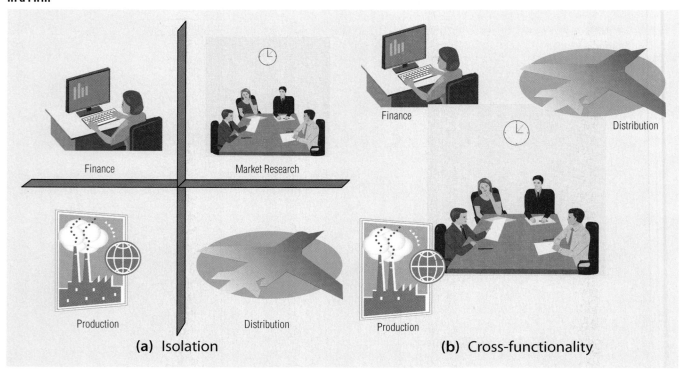

second panel illustrates a firm in which marketing personnel work cross-functionally with other departments to achieve long-term profitability.

Problems occur when the marketing department views focusing on consumer needs as its sole responsibility. Indeed, other functional areas' goals may conflict with customer satisfaction or long-term profitability. For instance, the engineering department may want long lead times for product design, with simplicity and economy as major design goals. Marketing, however, may prefer short lead times and more complex designs with custom components and optional features for multiple models. The finance department may want fixed budgets, strict spending justifications, and prices that cover costs, whereas the marketing department may seek flexible budgets, liberal spending rationales, and below-cost prices to develop markets quickly.

Similar differences in outlook may be found in other functional areas of the organization, and these may be sources of serious conflicts. When a firm lacks organizational procedures for communicating marketing information and coordinating marketing efforts, the effectiveness of its marketing programs will suffer. Marketing research findings produce some of the most crucial marketing information; thus, such research is management's key tool for finding out what customers want and how best to satisfy their needs. It is vital, then, that management conduct marketing research, that researchers produce valid and reliable results, and that those results be communicated to decision makers so that they can help shape the firm's marketing strategy.

Marketing-oriented firms visualize a chain of customers within the production and delivery system.[16] An accountant who prepares a report for a sales manager should view the manager as a customer who will use the information to make decisions that will benefit external customers who buy the company's products. Every employee should contribute to quality improvement and providing value to customers.

Keeping Customers and Building Relationships

Marketers often talk about getting customers, but keeping customers is equally important. Effective marketers work to build long-term relationships with their customers. The term **relationship marketing** communicates the idea that a major goal of marketing is to build long-term relationships with the customers contributing to the firm's success. Once an exchange is made, effective marketing stresses managing the relationships that will bring about additional exchanges. Effective marketers view making a sale not as the end of a process but as the start of the organization's relationship with a customer. Satisfied customers will return to a company that has treated them well if they need to purchase the same product in the future. If they need a related item, satisfied customers know the first place to look. Harley-Davidson is a company that over time has developed a familial type bond with its loyal customers. Now, they are seeking to expand their offering to new parts of the world. The Research Snapshot on the next page describes some of the issues arising from this investigation.

Total quality management is a business philosophy that has much in common with the marketing concept. It embodies the belief that the management process must focus on integrating customer-driven quality throughout the organization. The philosophy underlying the implementation of total quality management was clearly articulated by a Burger King executive: "The customer is the vital key to our success. We are now looking at our business through the customers' eyes and measuring our performance against their expectations, not ours."[17] A company that employs a total quality strategy must evaluate itself through the eyes of the customer.

Obviously, the marketing concept and total quality management are closely intertwined. In a company that practices total quality management, manufacturing's orientation toward lowest-cost productivity should harmonize with marketing's commitment to quality products at acceptable prices. For example, if Ford Motor Company advertises that "Quality Is Job One," the production department must make sure that every automobile that comes off the assembly line will meet consumers' quality specifications. The notion that quality improvement is every employee's job must be integrated throughout the organization so that marketing and production will be in harmony. If this notion conflicts with manufacturing's desire to allow for variations from quality standards, the firm must implement statistical quality controls and other improvements in the manufacturing operation to improve its systems and increase productivity.

Chapter 8 discusses the measurement of quality, customer satisfaction, and value in detail. Throughout this book, however, we will explain how marketing research can help a company achieve the goal of creating valuable experiences for customers.

relationship marketing
Communicates the idea that a major goal of marketing is to build long-term relationships with the customers contributing to the firm's success.

total quality management
Total quality management is a business philosophy that has much in common with the marketing concept.

Harley-Davidson Goes Abroad

Before Harley-Davidson goes overseas, it must perform considerable research on that market. It may find that consumers in some countries, such as France or Italy, have a strong preference for more economical and practical motor bikes. There, people may prefer a Vespa Wasp to a Harley Hog! Other times, they may find that consumers have a favorable attitude toward Harley-Davidson and that it could even be a product viewed as very prestigious. Harley recently considered doing business in India based on trend analysis showing a booming economy. Favorable consumer opinion and a booming economy were insufficient to justify distributing Harleys in India. The problem? Luxury imports would be subject to very high duties which would make them cost-prohibitive to nearly all Indian consumers and India has strict emission rules for motor bikes. Thus, although research on the market was largely positive, Harley's research on the political operating environment eventually determined its decision. Even after considerable negotiation, India refused to budge on tariffs although they were willing to give on emission standards. Instead, Harley may direct its effort more toward the U.S. women's market for bikes. Research shows that motorcycle ownership among U.S. women has nearly doubled since 1990 to approximately 10 percent. Product research suggests that Harley may need to design smaller and sportier bikes to satisfy this market's desires. Perhaps these new products would also be easier to market in India. Research will tell.

Sources: "Harley Davidson Rules Out India Foray for Near Future," *Asia-Africa Intelligence Wire* (September 2, 2005); "Women Kick it Into Gear," *Akron Beacon Journal* (May 22, 2005); "No Duty Cut on Harley Davidson Bikes, India to US," *The Financial Express* (February 24, 2008), www.financialexpress.com/news/No-duty-cut-on-Harley-Davidson-bikes-India-to-US/276635, accessed July 7, 2008.

© MICHAEL NEWMAN/PHOTOEDIT

© GEORGE DOYLE & CIARAN GRIFFIN

Marketing Research: A Means for Implementing the Marketing Concept

Home building used to be a business completely dominated by local construction contractors. If a customer wanted a home that would provide maximum satisfaction, a custom home at a custom price was the only option. Today, there is another option. Several home builders are going national. In doing so, they have implemented market-driven design processes that integrate research into the home designs. The research tracks consumers' actual living patterns to build homes with maximum livability. Thus, rather than "wasting space" on things like hallways that add little or even distract from a home's livability, that space is cannibalized, allowing more space allocated to the places where families really "live." In addition, research shows that consumers will make use of outdoor living areas if they are properly designed. Thus, the homes often include covered porches or lanais in place of less used indoor space like a formal living room.[18]

Marketing research can also help prevent commercialization of products that are not consumer oriented. Sometimes ideas that look like technological breakthroughs in the laboratory fall flat when presented to consumers. For example, a powdered pain reliever was supposed to be a soothing remedy because it was to be mixed with milk. It did not soothe customers, however. Research showed that the public thought this great

Fun in the snow depends on weather trends, equipment, and clothing—all subjects for a market researcher.

© AGEFOTOSTOCK /SUPERSTOCK

step forward was actually a step backward in convenience. Someone forgot to consider how consumers would actually use the product.

By improving efficiency, research also facilitates profitability. For instance, during the introduction of a new product, accurate forecasting of the product's potential sales volume is an essential basis for estimating its profitability. A firm considering the introduction of a cat snack that contains hairball medicine might rely on a test market experiment to determine the optimal price for this new concept. Extensive testing should be done to ensure that the marketing program is fine-tuned to maximize the firm's profitability while satisfying consumers.

Analysis of data may also be a form of marketing research that can increase efficiency. Marketing representatives from Exxon Chemical Company used laptop computers to present a complex set of calculations to sales prospects to show them the advantage of Exxon products over competitors' products. Such analysis of research data improves the salesperson's batting average and the firm's efficiency.

Because of the importance of integrating company efforts, a marketing researcher must be knowledgeable not only about marketing research but about the entire spectrum of marketing activities.

Marketing Research and Strategic Marketing Management

Effective marketing management requires research. DirectTV, the direct-broadcast satellite television service, uses marketing research to determine which kinds of programming to add to its lineup of channels. A company executive says, "Research has driven every aspect of our business decisions."[19] At Ford Motor Company, research is so fundamental that the company hardly makes any significant decision without the benefit of some kind of marketing research. The prime managerial value of marketing research comes from the reduced uncertainty that results from information and facilitates decision making about marketing strategies and tactics to achieve an organization's strategic goals.

Developing and implementing a marketing strategy involves four stages:

1. Identifying and evaluating market opportunities
2. Analyzing market segments and selecting target markets
3. Planning and implementing a marketing mix that will provide value to customers and meet organizational objectives
4. Analyzing firm performance

Exhibit 1.5 on the next page illustrates the integration of research and marketing strategy and the way they come together to create value in the marketplace.

> **TOTHEPOINT**
>
> *The secret of success is to know something nobody else knows.*
>
> —Aristotle Onassis

■ IDENTIFYING AND EVALUATING MARKET OPPORTUNITIES

One job that marketing research can perform is monitoring the competitive environment for signals indicating a business opportunity. A mere description of some social or economic activity, such as trends in consumer purchasing behavior, may help managers recognize problems and identify opportunities for enriching marketing efforts. In some cases, this research can motivate a firm to take action to address consumer desires in a way that is beneficial to both the customers and to the firm.

At times, evaluating opportunities may involve something as mundane as tracking weather trends. Consumers have a physical need to maintain some degree of physical comfort. Thus, changes in the temperature patterns may create business opportunities for utility companies, appliance companies, and even beverage companies as more consumers will select a hot beverage like hot chocolate when the weather is cold and dreary. Companies can also adjust their logistic distribution patterns based on the weather. When Hurricane Katrina hit the Gulf Coast of the United States, several chainsaw companies (such as Poulan) and companies that manufacture generators (such as Honda) began directing inventory toward those areas even before the hurricane actually

EXHIBIT 1.5
**Marketing Research Cuts
Decision Risk with Input that
Leads to Value**

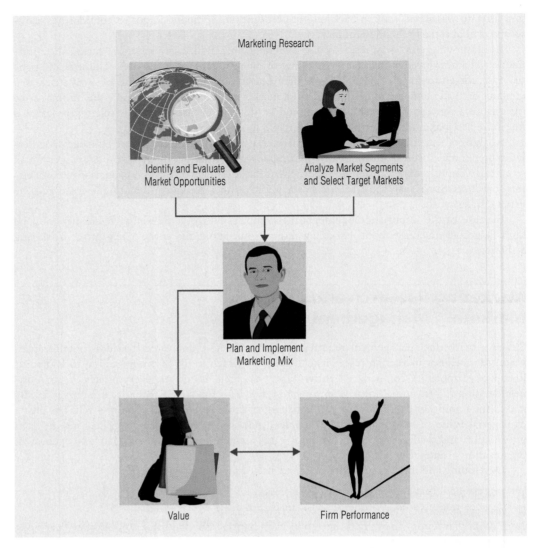

EXHIBIT 1.5
Marketing Research Cuts Decision Risk with Input that Leads to Value

struck. As a result, many home supply stores like Home Depot and Lowe's were able to maintain inventories of these vital products despite an increase in demand of over 1,000 percent! Thus, the misfortune of a hurricane created a business opportunity that also provided real value to consumers. In this case, the businesses and the consumers all benefited from the fact that firms scan the environment for opportunities.

Another opportunity was presented by a research study on running shoes was to investigate the occasions or situations associated with product use—that is, when individuals wore running shoes. The researchers found that most owners of running shoes wore the shoes while walking, not running. Also, most of this walking was part of a normal daily activity like shopping or commuting to work. Many of the people who wore running shoes for routine activities considered the shoes an alternative to other casual shoes. This research ultimately led to a shift in design and production toward walking shoes designed for comfortable, everyday walking and casual wear.[20]

Market opportunities may be evaluated using many performance criteria. For example, the performance criterion of market demand typically is estimated using marketing research techniques. Estimates of market potential or predictions about future environmental conditions allow managers to evaluate opportunities. Accurate sales forecasts are among the most useful pieces of planning information a marketing manager can have. Complete accuracy in forecasting the future is not possible, because change is constantly occurring in the marketing environment.

Nevertheless, objective forecasts of demand or changing environments may be the foundations on which marketing strategies are built.

■ ANALYZING AND SELECTING TARGET MARKETS

The second stage of marketing strategy development is to analyze market segments and select target markets. Marketing research is a major source of information for determining which characteristics of market segments distinguish them from the overall market. Such research can help "locate" or describe a market segment in terms of demographic and characteristics. Geo-demographics can be important to study and track in this effort. **Geo-demographics** refers to information describing the demographic profile of consumers in a particular geographic region. The company may learn that consumers in a particular postal code within a region tend to be middle-aged, have multiple children over the age of twelve, and have college degrees and white-collar jobs. Once the company knows the geo-demographics of a market segment, it can effectively communicate with those customers by choosing media that reach that particular profile. For example, *Architectural Digest* is a magazine that is read predominantly by consumers with very high social status in the most exclusive zip codes in the United States.

geo-demographics

Refers to information describing the demographic profile of consumers in a particular geographic region.

Planning and Implementing a Marketing Mix

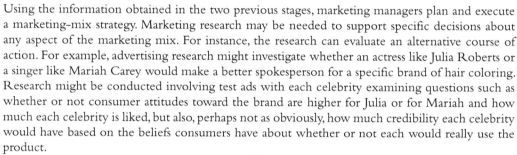

Using the information obtained in the two previous stages, marketing managers plan and execute a marketing-mix strategy. Marketing research may be needed to support specific decisions about any aspect of the marketing mix. For instance, the research can evaluate an alternative course of action. For example, advertising research might investigate whether an actress like Julia Roberts or a singer like Mariah Carey would make a better spokesperson for a specific brand of hair coloring. Research might be conducted involving test ads with each celebrity examining questions such as whether or not consumer attitudes toward the brand are higher for Julia or for Mariah and how much each celebrity is liked, but also, perhaps not as obviously, how much credibility each celebrity would have based on the beliefs consumers have about whether or not each would really use the product.

It is essential that an overall research plan involve all elements of marketing strategy. In other words, once the research identifies a target market and media that can be used in promotion, it needs to determine what benefits are required to create value for the customers, what price is most appropriate and, not to be overlooked, what channels of distribution will best reach the consumer. The integration of all of this research leads to effective brand management.[21] The following examples highlight selected types of research that might be conducted for each element of the marketing mix.

Product Research

Product research takes many forms and includes studies designed to evaluate and develop new products and to learn how to adapt existing product lines. Concept testing exposes potential customers to a new product idea to judge the acceptance and feasibility of the concept. Product testing reveals a product prototype's strengths and weaknesses or determines whether a finished product performs better than competing brands or according to expectations. Brand-name evaluation studies investigate whether a name is appropriate for a product. Package testing assesses size, color, shape, ease of use, and other attributes of a package. Product research encompasses all applications of marketing research that seek to develop product attributes that will add value for consumers.

Before Cheetos became the first major brand of American snack food to be made and marketed in China, product taste tests revealed that traditional cheese-flavored corn puffs Cheetos did not appeal to Chinese consumers. So the company conducted consumer research with 600 different flavors to learn which flavors would be most appealing. Among the flavors Chinese consumers tested and disliked were ranch dressing, nacho, Italian pizza, Hawaiian barbecue, peanut satay, North Sea crab, chili prawn, coconut milk curry, smoked octopus, caramel, and cuttlefish.

Research did show that consumers liked other flavors. So, when Cheetos were introduced in China, they came in two flavors: savory American cream and zesty Japanese steak.[22] So, the result was essentially cheeseless Cheetos.

Pricing Research

pricing

Involves finding the amount of monetary sacrifice that best represents the value customers perceive in a product after considering various market constraints.

In many ways, pricing research represents typical marketing research. Many test markets address the question of how consumers will respond to a product offering two different prices. **Pricing** involves finding the amount of monetary sacrifice that best represents the value customers perceive in a product after considering various market constraints. Most organizations conduct pricing research. Starbucks may seem expensive now, but if the price doubled, would Starbucks lose many customers? How much more are Toyota customers willing to pay for each extra mile per gallon? How much is too much to pay for gas? Pricing research also investigates the way people respond to pricing tactics. How do consumers respond to price reductions in one form or another? How much are people willing to pay for some critical product attribute? Do consumers view prices and/or quantity discounts as fair in a given category?[23] Do price gaps among national brands, regional brands, and private labels exist?[24] Most importantly, research also addresses the way consumers determine perceived value.

Pricing research addresses consumer quality perceptions by its very nature. A great deal of research addresses consumer reactions to low prices and documents the fact that, in quite a few instances, prices can actually be too low. In other words, sales can actually decrease with lower prices instead of increasing.[25]

Recently, Wal-Mart test marketed a Starbucks-type coffee shop called Medina's Kicks.[26] A Kicks coffee shop was set up in a Texas Wal-Mart store. They are testing prices relative to the nearby Starbucks. At prices 25 percent below Starbucks, sales remain relatively low while Starbucks remains popular. By lowering the price, they may also have lowered the perceived product quality. By raising the price, might quality perceptions improve and get consumers to think the coffee may be more similar to Starbucks? These are typical pricing questions.

Distribution Research

marketing channel

A network of interdependent institutions that perform the logistics necessary for consumption to occur.

supply chain

Another term for a channel of distribution, meaning the link between suppliers and customers.

Distribution involves the marketing channels that will physically "distribute" products from a producer to a consumer. A **marketing channel** is a network of interdependent institutions that perform the logistics necessary for consumption to occur. Some channels are very short and involve only a producer and a consumer, and some are very long involving much transportation and wholesale and retail firms. It may be somewhat obvious why the term **supply chain** is sometimes used to refer to a channel of distribution. Distribution is necessary to remove the physical separations between buyers and sellers (see Exhibit 1.6).

Distribution research is typified by studies aimed at selecting retail sites or warehouse locations. A survey of retailers or wholesalers may be conducted because the actions of one channel member can greatly affect the performance of other channel members. Distribution research often is needed to gain knowledge about retailers' and wholesalers' operations and to learn their reactions to a manufacturer's marketing policies. It may also be used to examine the effect of just-in-time ordering systems or exclusive distribution on product quality. Research focused on developing and improving the efficiency of marketing channels is extremely important.

Golden Books traditionally distributed its small hardcover children's books with golden spines to book retailers like Waldenbooks or B. Dalton Booksellers. When it researched where its customers would prefer to purchase Golden Books, the company learned that mass merchandisers, grocery stores, and drug stores would be just as popular as the upscale stores as distribution channels. Today, publishing companies like Golden Books face the possibility of new and shorter marketing channels that would allow home delivery via the Internet. Not only does this mean reduced time from production to consumption, but it also allows the books to come alive through interactivity. Should Golden Book abandon its more traditional marketing channels and focus its resources on this new delivery option?

EXHIBIT 1.6
Distribution Channels

Similarly, other companies are faced with key decisions involving distribution in a new and more technologically advanced operating environment. Television technology has advanced greatly. As a result, more and more consumers are building home theaters. These home theaters include increasingly more affordable technologies such as flat-screen, high-definition televisions and sound systems that rival those found in movie theaters. How will this affect the traditional channels of distribution for motion pictures, such as production studios, entertainment companies, theater groups or cooperatives, and individual theaters? Also, prescription drugs can now be purchased via the Internet. For the consumer, this marketing channel bypasses the traditional doctor's visit and local pharmacy. For the pharmaceutical firm, is it wise to take advantage of this channel? By removing the family doctor from the channel of distribution, does the drug seem to be less effective, and if so, is the brand's reputation harmed? Marketing research is needed to examine related issues including whether or not the product is equally effective through both the new and traditional marketing channel. Research results may both help firms make the distribution decision and help policy makers decide on the limits that should be placed on prescription drug distribution options.

Promotion Research

Promotion is the communication function of the firm responsible for informing and persuading buyers. **Promotion research** investigates the effectiveness of advertising, premiums, coupons, sampling, discounts, public relations, and other sales promotions. However, among all of these, firms spend more time, money, and effort on advertising research.

The marketing research findings of Zales, a large jewelry retailer, helped in the creation of advertising with large, one-word headlines that simply asked, "Confused?," "Nervous?," or "Lost?" The advertisements overtly acknowledged the considerable emotional and financial risks that consumers face in jewelry purchases. Research had shown that typical consumers felt unable

promotion

The communication function of the firm responsible for informing and persuading buyers.

promotion research

Investigates the effectiveness of advertising, premiums, coupons, sampling, discounts, public relations, and other sales promotions.

to determine the relative quality of various jewelry items, believed jewelry purchases were expensive, and needed reassurance about their purchases, especially because they often purchased jewelry for someone else. This promotion helped communicate an effective message of empathy with the consumer.

Similarly, a business in transition must effectively communicate its meaning. As AT&T's business shifts from that of a pure long-distance provider into that of a distanceless cable, Internet, and wireless communication specialist, it is trying to make sure its image changes too. But research showed its brand name still conjured up the image of an old-fashioned telephone company.[27] Marketing research also indicates great familiarity with the blue-and-white striped globe that served as AT&T's logo. A survey found 75 percent unaided recognition among the broad consumer market, 77 percent recognition among 18- to 24-year-olds, and 80 percent recognition among "high-value, active networkers"—consumers spending seventy-five dollars or more per month on long-distance and wireless services. Because of this high level of recognition, AT&T produced numerous TV commercials featuring an animation of the logo bouncing around, giving fun, high-intensity demonstrations of the various ways the company is transforming itself in the broadband-enabled world, accompanied by voice-over explanations of these new services. Future research may even consider placing the logo on iPod sites or even as a product placement in video games as a way of further transforming AT&T's image from "Ma Bell" into a modern technology service provider.[28]

Media research helps businesses make decisions about whether television, newspapers, magazines, or other media alternatives are best suited to convey the intended message. Choices among media alternatives may be based on research that shows the proportion of consumers in each market segment that a particular advertising vehicle can reach.

integrated marketing communication

All promotional efforts (advertising, public relations, personal selling, event marketing, and so forth) should be coordinated to communicate a consistent image.

integrated marketing mix

The effects of various combinations of marketing-mix elements on important outcomes.

Best Buy has reinvented the traditional Geek image and made it work for them.

The Integrated Marketing Mix

Marketing today focuses increasingly on the fact that different promotional decisions should not be made in isolation. Instead, the concept of **integrated marketing communication** is adopted, meaning that all promotional efforts (advertising, public relations, personal selling, event marketing, and so forth) should be coordinated to communicate a consistent image. Likewise, marketing firms realize that the elements of the marketing mix itself must work together. For instance, a change in price can affect the quality of the product, which may also influence decisions about distribution. From a research standpoint, the **integrated marketing mix** means that research studies often investigate effects of various combinations of marketing mix elements on important outcomes like sales and image. Research suggests that consumer-oriented firms are particularly oriented toward integrating all aspects of their marketing into a single message.[29]

Best Buy, a U.S.-based electronic and appliance retailer, recently showed the success of integrating sales and service with promotion. You'll find a Geek in every Best Buy. The Geeks are technology experts (i.e., "computer geeks") that provide knowledgeable sales advice and technical service. To be a Geek, you have to look like a Geek! Their attire is carefully coordinated: white socks with black shoes, black pants that are just a little too short, a white sport shirt, and a narrow black tie. Today, the Geeks have become prominent in Best Buy television ads, and they even provide in-home setup and technical service. The Geeks are transforming Best Buy in the minds of consumers.[30] Companies that integrate the use of consistent spokespeople, such as the Geeks, across marketing elements enjoy more favorable brand images among consumers and are better able to communicate relevant information.[31]

Analyzing Marketing Performance

After a marketing strategy has been implemented, marketing research may serve to inform managers whether planned activities were properly executed and are accomplishing what they were expected to achieve. In other words, marketing research may be conducted to obtain feedback for evaluation and control of marketing programs. This aspect of marketing research is especially important for successful **total value management**, which attempts to manage the entire process by which a consumer receives benefits from a company.

Performance-monitoring research refers to research that regularly, sometimes routinely, provides feedback for evaluation and control of marketing activity. For example, most firms continuously monitor wholesale and retail activity to ensure early detection of sales declines and other anomalies. In the grocery and drug industries, sales research may use Universal Product Codes (UPCs) on packages read by electronic cash registers and computerized checkout counters to provide valuable market-share information to store and brand managers interested in the retail sales volumes of their products. Market-share analysis and sales analysis are the most common forms of performance-monitoring research. Almost every organization compares its current sales with previous sales and with competitors' sales. However, analyzing marketing performance is not limited to the investigation of sales figures.

Marketing metrics refer to quantitative ways of monitoring and measuring marketing performance. Research is needed to determine marketing metrics that allow a firm to know whether the resources invested in marketing activities have met their quantitative business goals. Marketing metrics allow the firm to assess the return on investment (ROI) associated with marketing activities. Performance monitoring research conducted by the ACNielsen firm suggests that only 18 percent of television commercials return a positive ROI for the companies advertised.[32]

When analysis of marketing performance indicates that things are not going as planned, marketing research may be required to explain why something went wrong. Detailed information about specific mistakes or failures is frequently sought. If a general problem area is identified, breaking down industry sales volume and a firm's sales volume into different geographical areas may explain specific problems. Exploring problems in greater depth may indicate which managerial judgments were erroneous.

total value management

The management and monitoring the entire process by which consumers receive benefits from a company.

performance-monitoring research

Refers to research that regularly, sometimes routinely, provides feedback for evaluation and control of marketing activity.

marketing metrics

Quantitative ways of monitoring and measuring marketing performance.

When Is Marketing Research Needed?

The need to make intelligent, informed decisions ultimately motivates marketing research. Not every decision requires marketing research. Thus, when confronting a key decision, a marketing manager must initially decide whether or not to conduct marketing research. The determination of the need for marketing research centers on (1) time constraints, (2) the availability of data, (3) the nature of the decision to be made, and (4) the value of the research information in relation to costs.

Time Constraints

Systematic research takes time. In many instances management believes that a decision must be made immediately, allowing no time for research. Decisions sometimes are made without adequate information or thorough understanding of market situations. Although making decisions without researching a situation is not ideal, sometimes the urgency of a situation precludes the use of research. The urgency with which managers often want to make decisions often conflicts with the marketing researchers' desire for rigor in following the scientific method.

Availability of Data

Often managers already possess enough information to make sound decisions without additional marketing research. When they lack adequate information, however, research must be considered. This means that data need to be collected from an appropriate source. If a potential source of data exists, managers will want to know how much it will cost to get the data.

If the data cannot be obtained, or it cannot be obtained in a timely fashion, this particular research project should not be conducted. For example, many African nations have never conducted a population census. Organizations engaged in international business often find that data about business activity or population characteristics that are readily available in the United States are nonexistent or sparse in developing countries. Imagine the problems facing marketing researchers who wish to investigate market potential in places like Uzbekistan, Yugoslavian Macedonia, and Rwanda.

Nature of the Decision

The value of marketing research will depend on the nature of the managerial decision to be made. A routine tactical decision that does not require a substantial investment may not seem to warrant a substantial expenditure for marketing research. For example, a computer company must update its operator's instruction manual when it makes minor product modifications. The research cost of determining the proper wording to use in the updated manual is likely to be too high for such a minor decision. The nature of the decision is not totally independent of the next issue to be considered: the benefits versus the costs of the research. In general, however, the more strategically or tactically important the decision, the more likely it is that research will be conducted.

Benefits versus Costs

There are both costs and benefits to conducting marketing research. Earlier we discussed some of the managerial benefits of marketing research. Of course, conducting research to obtain these benefits requires an expenditure of money. In any decision-making situation, managers must identify alternative courses of action and then weigh the value of each alternative against its cost. Marketing research can be thought of as an investment alternative. When deciding whether to make a decision without research or to postpone the decision in order to conduct research, managers should ask three questions:

1. Will the payoff or rate of return be worth the investment?
2. Will the information gained by marketing research improve the quality of the marketing decision enough to warrant the expenditure?
3. Is the proposed research expenditure the best use of the available funds?

For example, *TV-Cable Week* was not test-marketed before its launch. Although the magazine had articles and stories about television personalities and events, its main feature was program listings, channel by channel, showing the exact programs a particular subscriber could receive. To produce a custom magazine for each individual cable television system in the country required developing a costly computer system. Because that development necessitated a substantial expenditure, one that could not be scaled down for research, conducting research was judged to be an unwise investment. The value of the research information was not positive because its cost exceeded its benefits. Unfortunately, pricing and distribution problems became so compelling after the magazine was launched that the product was a marketing failure. Nevertheless, without the luxury of hindsight, managers made a reasonable decision not to conduct research. They analyzed the cost of the information (that is, the cost of test-marketing) relative to the potential benefits of the information. Exhibit 1.7 outlines the criteria for determining when to conduct marketing research.

EXHIBIT 1.7 Determining When to Conduct Marketing Research

Time Constraints		Availability of Data		Nature of the Decision		Benefits versus Costs		
Is sufficient time available before a decision will be made?	Yes →	Can the decision be made with what is already known?	Yes →	Is the decision of considerable strategic or tactical importance?	Yes →	Does the value of the research information exceed the cost of conducting research?	Yes →	Conduct Marketing Research
No ↓		No ↓		No ↓		No ↓		
				Do Not Conduct Marketing Research				

Marketing Research in the Twenty-First Century

Marketing research, like all business activity, continues to change. Changes in communication technologies and the trend toward an ever more global marketplace have played a large role in many of these changes.

Communication Technologies

Virtually everyone is "connected" today. Increasingly, many people are "connected" nearly all the time. Within the lifetime of the typical undergraduate college senior, the way information is exchanged, stored, and gathered has been revolutionized completely. Today, the amount of information formally contained in an entire library can rest easily in a single personal computer.

The speed with which information can be exchanged has also increased tremendously. During the 1970s, exchanging information overnight from anywhere in the continental United States was heralded as a near miracle of modern technology. Today, we can exchange information from nearly anywhere in the world to nearly anywhere in the world almost instantly. Internet connections are now wireless, so one doesn't have to be tethered to a wall to access the World Wide Web. Our mobile phones and handheld data devices can be used not only to converse, but also as a means of communication that can even involve marketing research data. In many cases, technology also has made it possible to store or collect data for lower costs than in the past. Electronic communications are usually less costly than regular mail—and certainly less costly than a face-to-face interview—and cost about the same amount no matter how far away a respondent is from a researcher. Thus, the expressions "time is collapsing" and "distance is disappearing" capture the tremendous revolution in the speed and reach of our communication technologies.

Changes in computer technology have made for easier data collection and data analysis. As we discuss in a later chapter, many consumer household panels now exist and can be accessed via the Internet. Thus, there is less need for the time and expense associated with regular mail survey approaches. Furthermore, the computing power necessary to solve complicated statistical problems is now easily accessible. Again, as recently as the 1970s, such computer applications required expensive mainframe computers found only in very large corporations, major universities, and large governmental/military institutions. Researchers could expect to wait hours or even longer to get results from a statistical program involving 200 respondents. Today, even the most basic laptop computers can solve complicated statistical problems involving thousands of data points in practically a nanosecond.

"Jacques" Daniels

Sales of U.S. distilled spirits declined over the last 10 to 15 years as more Americans turn to wine or beer as their beverage of choice. As a result, companies like Bacardi and Brown-Forman, producers of Jack Daniels, pursued market development strategies involving increased efforts to expand into international markets. The Brown-Forman marketing budget for international ventures includes a significant allocation for marketing research. By doing research before launching the product, Brown-Forman can learn product usage patterns within a particular culture. Some of the findings from this research are indicated as follows.

1. Japanese consumers use Jack Daniels (JD) as a dinner beverage. A party of four or five consumers in a restaurant will order and drink a bottle of "JD" with their meal.
2. Australian consumers mostly consume distilled spirits in their homes. Also in contrast to Japanese consumers, Australians prefer to mix JD with soft drinks or other mixers. As a result of this research, JD launched a mixture called "Jack and Cola" sold in 12-ounce bottles all around

Australia. The product has been very successful.
3. British distilled spirit consumers also like mixed drinks, but they usually partake in bars and restaurants.
4. In China and India, consumers more often chose counterfeits or "knock-offs" to save money. Thus, innovative research approaches have addressed questions related to the way the black market works and how they can better educate consumers about the differences between the real thing and the knock-offs.
5. Chinese consumers enjoy JD mixed with green tea.

The result is that more than half of all Jack Daniels made is now consumed outside of the United States. The global sales increase has contributed to impressive sales growth of over 40 percent since 2002. Indeed, sales of Jack Daniels are looking up as of 2009.

Sources: Swibel, Mathew, "How Distiller Brown-Forman Gets Rich by Exploiting the Greenback's Fall—and Pushing its Brands Abroad," *Forbes*, 175, no. 8 (2005), 152–155. Kiley, D. "Jack Daniel's International Appeal," Businessweek (October 10, 2007), accessed at http://www.businessweek.com/innovate/content/oct2007/id20071010_651037.htm, September 14, 2008.

Global Marketing Research

Marketing research has become increasingly global as more and more firms take advantage of markets that have few, if any, geographic boundaries. Some companies have extensive international marketing research operations. Upjohn conducts marketing research in 160 different countries. ACNielsen International, known for its television ratings, is the world's largest marketing research company. Two-thirds of its business comes from outside the United States.[33] Starbucks can now be found in nearly every developed country on the earth. Toyota offers its products on all continents and truly represents today's global corporation. The Research Snapshot above demonstrates how even a company rich with American heritage is adopting to a global market with the benefit of marketing research.

Companies that conduct business in foreign countries must understand the nature of those particular markets and judge whether they require customized marketing strategies. For example, although the fifteen nations of the European Union share a single formal market, marketing research shows that Europeans do not share identical tastes for many consumer products. Marketing researchers have found no such thing as a typical European consumer; language, religion, climate, and centuries of tradition divide the nations of the European Union. Scantel Research, a British firm that advises companies on color preferences, found inexplicable differences in Europeans' preferences in medicines. The French prefer to pop purple pills, but the English and Dutch favor white ones. Consumers in all three countries dislike bright red capsules, which are big sellers in the United States. This example illustrates that companies that do business in Europe must research throughout Europe to adapt to local customs and buying habits.[34]

Even companies that produce brands that are icons in their own country are now doing research internationally. The Research Snapshot above discusses how Brown-Forman, the parent company of Jack Daniels (the classic American "Sour Mash" or Bourbon Whiskey), are now interviewing consumers in the far corners of the world.[35] The internationalization of research places greater demands on marketing researchers and heightens the need for research tools that allow us to **culturally cross-validate** research results, meaning that the empirical findings from one culture also exist and behave similarly in another culture. The development and application of these international research tools are an important topic in basic marketing research.

cultural cross-validate

To verify that the empirical findings from one culture also exist and behave similarly in another culture.

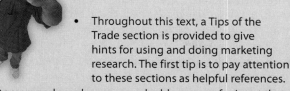

TIPS OF THE TRADE

- Throughout this text, a Tips of the Trade section is provided to give hints for using and doing marketing research. The first tip is to pay attention to these sections as helpful references.
- Customers and employees are valuable sources for input that leads to innovation in the marketplace and in the workplace.
- Business problems ultimately boil down to information problems because with the right information, the business can take effective action.
- Good marketing research is as rigorous as good research in other fields, including the physical sciences.

- Research plays a role before, during, and after key marketing decisions.
  - Research helps design marketing strategies and tactics before action is taken.
  - Once a plan is implemented, research monitors performance with key metrics providing valuable feedback.
  - After a plan is implemented, research assesses performance against benchmarks and seeks explanations for the failure or success of the action.
- Research that costs more than it could ever return should not be conducted.

Summary

There were six learning objectives in this chapter. After reading the chapter, the student should be competent in each area described by a learning objective.

1. Know what marketing is and what it does for business. Marketing research is is the application of the scientific method in searching for the truth about marketing phenomena. Thus, it is the intelligence-gathering function in business. The intelligence includes information about customers, competitors, economic trends, employees, and other factors that affect marketing success. This intelligence assists in decisions ranging from long-range planning to near-term tactical decisions. While many business decisions are made "by the seat of the pants" or based on a manager's intuition, this type of decision making carries with it a large amount of risk. By first researching an issue and gathering intelligence on customers, competitors, and the market, a company can make a more informed decision. The result is less risky decision making.

2. Understand the differences between basic and applied marketing research. Applied marketing research seeks to facilitate managerial decision making. Basic or pure research seeks to increase knowledge of theories and concepts. Both are important. Applied research examples are emphasized in this text although practically all of the tools and techniques that are discussed are appropriate to either type of research. Some use the term market research to refer to applied research and marketing research to refer to basic research.

3. Understand how the role of marketing research changes when a firm is truly marketing oriented. Every company has a particular operating orientation. Production-oriented companies emphasize producing outputs as efficiently as possible. Generally, this leads to an emphasis on low-cost production and low-cost positioning in the marketplace. Product-oriented companies emphasize producing a sophisticated product that is also technologically advanced. Firms that are oriented around the marketing concept become very consumer oriented. Consumer-oriented companies have to have close contact with customers on a regular basis because providing a high value experience is the central focus of the entire firm. On the other hand, a low-cost orientation typical to a production orientation does not require a great deal of consumer-oriented research. Marketing oriented companies, therefore, tend to do more marketing research and emphasize marketing research more than do other firms.

4. Integrate marketing research results into the strategic planning process. Marketing research is a means of implementing the marketing concept, the most central idea in marketing. The marketing concept says that a firm must be oriented both toward consumer satisfaction and toward long-run profitability (rather than toward short-run sales volume). Organizations need to focus both on creating and on keeping customers. Marketing research can help implement the marketing concept by identifying consumers' problems and needs, improving efficiency, and evaluating the effectiveness of marketing strategies and tactics. The development and implementation of a marketing strategy consist of four stages: (1) identifying and evaluating opportunities, (2) analyzing market segments and selecting target markets, (3) planning and implementing a marketing mix that will provide value to customers and meet the objectives of the organization, and (4) analyzing firm performance. Marketing research helps in each stage by providing information for strategic decision making. In particular, marketing research aimed at the marketing mix seeks information useful in marking better decisions about product design, promotion, distribution, and pricing.

5. Know when marketing research should and should not be conducted. Marketing managers determine whether marketing research should be conducted based on (1) time constraints, (2) availability of data, (3) the nature of the decision to be made, and (4) the benefit of the research information versus its cost. Research should only be conducted when time is available, data can be found, the decision can be shaped by information, and the benefits outweigh the cost of doing the research.

6. Appreciate the way that technology and internationalization are changing marketing research. Technology has changed almost every aspect of marketing research. Modern computer and communications technology makes data collection, study design, data analysis, data reporting, and practically all other aspects of research easier and better. Furthermore, as more companies do business outside their own borders, companies are doing research in an international marketplace. This places a greater emphasis on research that can assess the degree to which research tools can be applied and interpreted the same way in difference cultures. Thus, research techniques often must cross-validate results.

Key Terms and Concepts

applied marketing research 7
basic marketing research 7
cultural cross-validate 22
customer-oriented 8
geo-demographics 15
integrated marketing communication 18
integrated marketing mix 18
marketing channel 16

marketing concept 8
marketing metrics 19
marketing orientation 8
marketing research 5
performance-monitoring research 19
pricing 16
product-oriented 8
production-oriented 8

promotion 17
promotion research 17
relationship marketing 11
the scientific method 7
supply chain 16
total quality management 11
total value management 19

Questions for Review and Critical Thinking

1. Is it possible to make sound marketing decisions without marketing research? What advantages does research offer to the decision maker over seat-of-the-pants decision making?
2. Define a marketing orientation and a product orientation. Under which strategic orientation is there a greater need for marketing research?
3. Name some products that logically might have been developed with the help of marketing research.
4. Define *marketing research* and describe its task.
5. Which of the following organizations are likely to use marketing research? Why? How?
   a. Manufacturer of breakfast cereals
   b. Manufacturer of nuts, bolts, and other fasteners
   c. The Federal Trade Commission
   d. A hospital
   e. A company that publishes marketing textbooks
6. An automobile manufacturer is conducting research in an attempt to predict the type of car design consumers will desire in the year 2020. Is this basic or applied research? Explain.

7. What is the definition of an *integrated marketing mix*? How might this affect the research a firm conducts?
8. Comment on the following statements:
   a. Marketing managers are paid to take chances with decisions. Marketing researchers are paid to reduce the risk of making those decisions.
   b. A marketing strategy can be no better than the information on which it is formulated.
   c. The purpose of research is to solve marketing problems.
9. List the conditions that help a researcher decide when marketing research should or should not be conducted.
10. How have technology and internationalization affected marketing research?
11. **'NET** How do you believe the Internet has facilitated research? Try to use the Internet to find the total annual sales for Starbucks and for Toyota. You might start by using a general search engine like ask.com. University libraries also generally have access to business resources that may contain industry level data.
12. What types of tools does the marketing researcher use more given the ever increasing internationalization of marketing?

Research Activities

1. **'NET** Suppose you owned a jewelry store in Denton, Texas. You are considering opening a second store just like your current store. You are undecided on whether to locate the new store in another location in Denton, Texas, or in Birmingham, Alabama. Why would you decide to have some marketing research done before making the decision? Should the research be conducted? Go to http://www.census.gov. Do you think any of this information would be useful in the research?

2. Use the Internet to find recent examples of news articles involving the use of marketing research in making decisions about each element of the marketing mix.
3. Find an article illustrating an example of an applied marketing research study involving some aspect of technology. How does it differ from a basic research study also focusing on a similar aspect of technology?

CHAPTER 2
INFORMATION SYSTEMS AND KNOWLEDGE MANAGEMENT

After studying this chapter, you should be able to

1. Know why concepts like data, information, and intelligence represent value
2. Understand the four characteristics that describe data
3. Know what a decision support system is and does
4. Describe marketing research's role in predictive analytics
5. Recognize the major categories of databases

Chapter Vignette: That Ding Is Lifting Me Higher!

In just over a decade, online technologies have dramatically changed the way we shop for airline tickets. Most transactions can be conducted without any person-to-person contact. These changes mean that airline consumers spend a lot of time online. At any given time, a major airline is serving approximately 1,000 customers through its Web site. In a typical day, that means over 1 million customers have *touched* the company. Each touch leaves behind a record that researchers and managers can use to guide decision making.

Even occasional flyers probably know that airline prices can be difficult to predict. A roundtrip flight from Atlanta to Tampa may well cost more than a roundtrip flight from Tampa to San Francisco! A direct flight from New York to Paris may cost less than an indirect flight from New York to Paris with a two-hour layover in Houston! Airline pricing doesn't always make sense to consumers, but does make sense to managers interested in the bottom line. Pricing like this takes a great deal of research on who is flying to where. At times, the airline's attempt to maximize yield can lead to very attractive price offers to consumers. In fact, airline travel can sometimes compete with or even beat the price of driving, particularly when a consumer is targeted by an airline with a special fare between specific locations.

© PURESTOCK/JUPITER

Airlines use sophisticated yield management systems which try to maximize the revenue realized on any given flight and by the airline overall. An empty seat is the worst thing for a positive yield. However, how can an airline predict how many consumers will be on each flight? When someone books a flight online, a lot of information is recorded beyond the fact that one more seat is unavailable on a particular flight. Information can be taken from the consumer's Web cookies so that the company knows what cities the consumer searched for, how long it took for a decision to be made, how the ticket was paid for and much more. All of which may be useful to yield management. Empty seats can be minimized by offering price promotions on specific flights for which a lot of unsold seats remain beyond some date determined by patterns of purchasing.

Southwest Airlines prices often ring a bell! Consumers can opt to download Southwest's Ding software, which uses information input into a questionnaire along with customer patterns of behavior to trigger special offers tailored specifically to a particular consumer. For example, a college student in College Station, Texas may wish to visit parents in Orange County, California. The student has flexibility to visit on any of a number of weekends. Ding retains this information and integrates it with anticipated load. When Ding anticipates flights from Houston, Texas to Orange County Airport that will not be at full load, the student is notified with an audible "ding" on her computer which is followed up with an e-mail containing a link showing very low fares for that customer. From a profitability standpoint, allowing someone to fly for a ridiculously low price is better than having an empty seat on the airplane. Although it may seem strange to consumers, the results of yield management systems like these show that airlines actually increase profits when the disparity between the lowest prices and highest prices that passengers pay is greatest.

Now, why are some airlines charging you to check a bag and charging you several hundred dollars to make small changes in your reservations? Remember, these systems are designed to maximize profits, not customer value or customer loyalty![1]

Introduction

Southwest Airlines' use of Ding to manage its pricing illustrates the sophisticated way in which modern marketing firms often integrate real-time data into their decision processes. Many of the decisions that used to be made with guesswork are now supplemented with intelligence either automatically delivered by computer software or drawn from a data warehouse.

Airlines aren't alone in this effort. Imagine all the information that passes through a single Home Depot store each day. Every customer transaction, every empty shelf, every employee's work schedule—right down to the schedule to clean restrooms—creates potentially valuable information that can be used by researchers and decision makers. Considering that Home Depot operates thousands of stores, obviously, Home Depot needs a data depot!

Like many firms, Home Depot has outsourced the storage and management of data inventories. In this case, IBM manages the data, allowing it to be integrated into management strategy and tactics. Data from cash registers, time clocks, shelf counts, and much more are all compiled, analyzed, and either fed automatically into management systems or supplied in the form of a research report. In a way, this type of marketing research is automatic![2]

This chapter discusses knowledge management and the role decision support systems and predictive analytics play in helping firms make informed marketing decisions. The chapter also introduces the concept of global information systems that exist beyond the walls of any business. Marketing research plays an important role in making sense out of the glut of data now available. Today, data technology allows businesses to more easily integrate research findings into marketing strategy and operations.

Data, Information, and Intelligence Equal Value

In everyday language, terms like *information* and *data* are often used interchangeably. Researchers use these terms in specific ways that emphasize how useful each can be. Marketing managers may not be as intimately involved in finding and analyzing data; however, the decisions that they make based on the input received from research will make or break the firm. In this way, data, information, and intelligence all have the potential to create value to the firm through better decision making. One way in which these terms are not interchangeable lies in how closely linked they are to creating value for consumers and businesses.

Data are simply facts or recorded measures of certain phenomena (things or events). **Information** is data formatted (structured) to support decision making or define the relationship between two facts. **Market intelligence** is the subset of data and information that actually has some explanatory power enabling effective decisions to be made. So, there is more data than information, and more information than intelligence. Most data are irrelevant to any specific decision making situation and therefore not always valuable. When data becomes information, its relevance is examined more closely through some analytical procedure. Conclusions are drawn from the structured data or information to actually shape marketing decisions. The result is market intelligence and this should enable better decision making, better value provided to customers in that their desires are more closely met and thereby, more value for the firm in the form of improved performance.[3]

The chapter vignette revealed the tremendous amount of data recorded through airline customers' interactions with airline Web sites. Think again about the thousands upon thousands of unsummarized facts recorded by Home Depot each day. Each time a product is scanned at

data

Facts or recorded measures of certain phenomena (things).

information

Data formatted (structured) to support decision making or define the relationship between two facts.

market intelligence

The subset of data and information that actually has some explanatory power enabling effective decisions to be made.

S U R V E Y T H I S !

Go back and review the questionnaire that you responded to last chapter. Later, you'll be asked to analyze data with the hope of predicting and explaining some important outcomes with marketing implications. Now, which sections do you think would provide the most value to a firm that provides online access to Blu-ray videos of late release movies and television specials? How could the information be used by a DSS that included a predictive analytics component? How would the question change if instead of an online provider of video files, the client was a private university seeking to increase admissions from students with strong prospects for success?

checkout, that fact is recorded and becomes data. Each customer's transactions are simultaneously entered into the store's computerized inventory system. The inventory system structures the data in such a way that a stocking report can be generated and orders for that store can be placed. Thus, the automated inventory system turns data into information. Further, the information from each store's sales and inventory records may be harvested by analysts tracking sales trends. The analysts may analyze the trends and prepare reports that help Home Depot buyers get the right products into each store or to even suggest places for new Home Depot locations. Thus, the analyst has now completed the transformation of data into intelligence. Exhibit 2.1 on the next page helps to illustrate the distinction between data, information, and intelligence.

The Characteristics of Valuable Information

Not all data are valuable to decision makers. Useful data become information and help a marketing manager make decisions. Useful data can also become intelligence. Altogether, data, information, and intelligence can create knowledge.

Data Characteristics

Four characteristics help determine how valuable data may be: relevance, quality, timeliness, and completeness.

■ RELEVANCE

Relevance is the characteristics of data reflecting how pertinent these particular facts are to the situation at hand. Put another way, the facts are logically connected to the situation. Unfortunately, irrelevant data and information often creep into decision making. One particularly useful way to

relevance

The characteristics of data reflecting how pertinent these particular facts are to the situation at hand.

27

EXHIBIT 2.1
**Data, Information,
Intelligence**

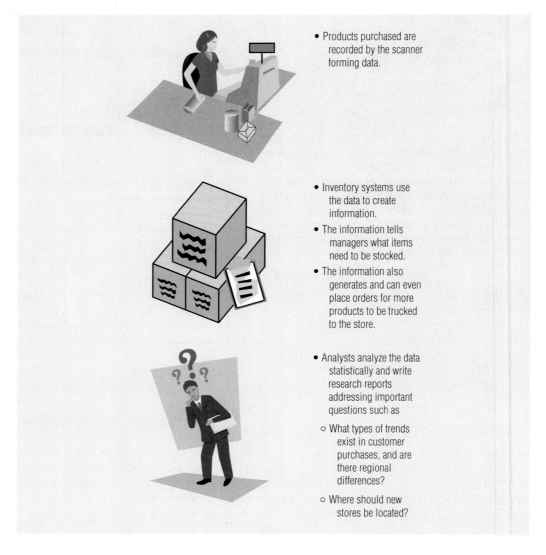

- Products purchased are recorded by the scanner forming data.

- Inventory systems use the data to create information.
- The information tells managers what items need to be stocked.
- The information also generates and can even place orders for more products to be trucked to the store.

- Analysts analyze the data statistically and write research reports addressing important questions such as
  - What types of trends exist in customer purchases, and are there regional differences?
  - Where should new stores be located?

distinguish relevance from irrelevance is to think about how things change. Relevant data are facts about things that will materially alter the situation if they change. So, this simple question becomes important:

Will a change in the data coincide with a change in some important outcome?

American consumers' dietary trends are relevant to Krispy Kreme Doughnuts. If American diets become more health-conscious, then it can be expected that sales of doughnuts will be affected. This may lead Krispy Kreme to rethink its product offering. However, information on the height of Mount Washington is irrelevant because it isn't going to change any time soon and even if it did, it would not affect U.S. doughnut preferences.

■ QUALITY

data quality

The degree to which data represent the true situation.

Data quality is the degree to which data represent the true situation. High-quality data are accurate, valid, and reliable. High-quality data represent reality faithfully. If a consumer were to replace the product UPC from one drill at Home Depot with one from a different drill, not only would the consumer be acting unethically, but it would also mean that the data collected at the checkout counter would be inaccurate. Therefore, to the extent that the cash register is not actually recording the products that consumers take out of the stores, its quality is lowered. Sometimes, researchers will try to obtain the same data from multiple data sources as one check on its quality.[4] Data quality is a critical issue in marketing research, and it will be discussed throughout this text.

■ TIMELINESS

Marketing is a dynamic field in which out-of-date information can lead to poor decisions. Marketing information must be timely—that is, provided at the right time. Computerized information systems can record events and dispense relevant information soon after the event. A great deal of marketing information becomes available almost at the moment that a transaction occurs. **Timeliness** means that the data are current enough to still be relevant.

Computer technology has redefined standards for timely information. For example, if a marketing executive at Home Depot wishes to know the sales volume of any store worldwide, detailed information about any of thousands of products can be instantly determined. At Home Depot, the point-of-sale checkout system uses UPC scanners and satellite communications to link individual stores to the headquarters' computer system, from which managers can retrieve and analyze up-to-the-minute sales data on all merchandise in each store.

timeliness

Means that the data are current enough to still be relevant.

■ COMPLETENESS

Information completeness refers to having the right amount of information. Marketing managers must have sufficient information about all aspects of their decisions. For example, a researcher investigating Eastern European markets may plan to analyze four former Soviet-bloc countries. Population statistics and information on inflation rates may be available on all four countries. However, information about disposable personal income may be available for only three of the countries. If information about disposable personal income or other economic characteristics cannot be obtained, the information is incomplete. Often incomplete information leads decision makers to conduct marketing research.

information completeness

Having the right amount of information.

Managing Data, Information, and Intelligence

Who has the best pizza in town? The answer to this question requires knowledge. Indeed, you, as a consumer, have stored knowledge about many products. You know the best restaurants, best theaters, best movies, and so forth. All of this knowledge helps you make decisions as a consumer. Much of it is based on personal research involving product trials or searches for information. From a consumer's perspective, knowledge is simply what you have stored in memory. It helps you, as a consumer, make decisions.

Organizations can use knowledge in a similar way. Knowledge is accumulated not just from a single individual, however, but from salespeople, managers, customer reports, and custom-ordered research. All of this *data* forms the organization's memory. Put another way, this is the firm's knowledge. From a company's perspective, **knowledge** is a blend of previous experience, insight, and *data* that forms organizational memory. It provides a framework that can be thoughtfully applied when assessing a marketing problem. Marketing researchers and decision makers use this knowledge to help create solutions to strategic and tactical problems. Thus, knowledge is a key resource and a potential competitive advantage.[5] Modern technology is greatly expanding marketers' ability to aquire data.

Knowledge management is the process of creating an inclusive, comprehensive, easily accessible organizational memory, which can be called the organization's *intellectual capital*.[6] The purpose of knowledge management is to organize the intellectual capital of an organization in a formally structured way for easy use. Knowledge is presented in a way that helps employees comprehend and act on that information and make better decisions in all areas of the marketing mix. Knowledge management systems are particularly useful in making data available across the functional areas of the firm. Thus, marketing knowledge and financial knowledge can be integrated. Recent research demonstrates how knowledge management systems are particularly useful in new product development and introduction.[7]

The firm's sales force plays a particularly useful role in the knowledge management process. Salespeople are in a key position to have a lot of knowledge about customers and the firm's capabilities. Thus, they are tools both for accumulating knowledge and for turning it into useful

knowledge

A blend of previous experience, insight, and data that forms organizational memory.

knowledge management

The process of creating an inclusive, comprehensive, easily accessible organizational memory, which is often called the organization's *intellectual capital*.

RFID Technology Gets Cheaper—Marketing Knowledge Grows

Radio frequency identification (RFID) tags have been used by large organizations for several years now. The U.S. military makes great use of RFIDs in tracking the whereabouts of virtually all kinds of products both big and small. Logistics officers can instantly track the whereabouts of Humvees and MREs (Meals Ready to Eat). Information from the tag is transmitted to computer servers and then directly into a GTN (Global Tracking Network). Equipment and supplies can then be ordered and dispatched to needed locations with a minimal of human contact. Product consumption (ammunition, food, water, computer printers, and so forth) can also be tracked in real time. The Marines can know in real time if personnel in a desert use more food and water than personnel in a jungle.

Wal-Mart is pushing suppliers to adopt the technology. Not only can Wal-Mart use them in logistical operations, but the potential exists to "go into" consumers' homes and track how much and the way consumers actually consume products. Potentially, decision support systems (DSS) could tie ordering to customer consumption. However, the costs of RFIDs make it impractial for many suppliers.

Alien Technology Corporation recently announced a drop in the price of RFID tags. Now, when a company orders a million or more, the unit cost for an RFID is 12.9¢. Although this is a "basic" RFID tag, it still can store 96 bits of information. Analysts predict that the price of RFID tags will continue to drop, opening up the avenue for more and more applications. RFID technology is even contributing to a drop in shoplifting around the USA due to the ability to better track product whereabouts both in and out of the store.

Sources: Clark, Don, "Alien Cuts Radio ID Tag Price to Spur Adoption by Retailiners," *The Wall Street Journal* (September 12, 2005), D4; Fergueson, R. B., "Marines Deploy RFID," *e-Week*, 21 (November 15, 2004), 37. *Business Wire*, "Correcting and Replacing Shoplifting and Retail Loss Continue Six Year Decline According to Survey," (June 24, 2008), Retrieved July 14, 2008, from ABI/INFORM Dateline database (document ID: 1500093791).

COURTESY, DIVISION OF PUBLIC AFFAIRS, UNITED STATES MARINE CORPS, DEPARTMENT OF DEFENSE, USA

© GEORGE DOYLE & CIARAN GRIFFIN

---

global information system

An organized collection of computer hardware, software, data, and personnel designed to capture, store, update, manipulate, analyze, and immediately display information about worldwide business activity.

TO THE POINT

An immense and ever-increasing wealth of knowledge is scattered about the world today; knowledge that would probably suffice to solve all the mighty difficulties of our age, but it is dispersed and unorganized. We need a sort of mental clearing house for the mind: a depot where knowledge and ideas are received, sorted, summarized, digested, clarified and compared.[9]

—H. G. Wells

information.[8] Market-oriented organizations generally provide both formal and informal methods through which the knowledge gained by salespeople can be entered into a data warehouse to assist all decision makers, not just the sales force.

Global Information Systems

Increased global competition and technological advances in interactive media have given rise to global information systems. A **global information system** is an organized collection of computer hardware, software, data, and personnel designed to capture, store, update, manipulate, analyze, and immediately display information about worldwide business activities. A global information system is a tool for providing past, present, and projected information on internal operations and external activity. Using satellite communications, high-speed microcomputers, electronic data interchanges, fiber optics, data storage devices, and other technological advances in interactive media, global information systems are changing the nature of business.

Consider a simple example. At any moment, United Parcel Service (UPS) can track the status of any shipment around the world. UPS drivers use handheld electronic clipboards called delivery information acquisition devices (DIADs) to record appropriate data about each pickup or delivery. The data are then entered into the company's main computer for record-keeping and analysis. A satellite telecommunications system allows UPS to track any shipment for a customer. Consumers also can get near real time information on the status of a delivery as information from the DIADs is eventually made available through www.ups.com.

RFID stands for radio frequency identification. This relatively new technology is in a tiny chip, which can be woven onto a fabric, placed in packaging, or otherwise attached to virtually any product, allowing it to be tracked anywhere in the world. This can provide great insight into the different distribution channels around the world and, potentially, to the different ways consumers acquire and use products. The U.S. military uses RFID technology to assist in its logistics, and Wal-Mart is one of the leading proponents of the technology as it can greatly assist in its global information system.[10] The Research Snapshot above describes in more detail how RFID technology is used by the United States Marine Corps and by Wal-Mart.

Decision Support Systems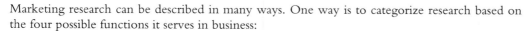

Marketing research can be described in many ways. One way is to categorize research based on the four possible functions it serves in business:

1. Foundational—answers basic questions such as what consumer segments should be served and with what types of products.
2. Testing—addresses things like new product concepts or promotional ideas. How effective will they be?
3. Issues—examines how specific issues impact the firm. The way organizational structure impacts employee outcomes or the impacts of advertising spending are issues that can be researched.
4. Performance—this type of research monitors specific metrics including financial statistics like profitability and delivery times. They are critical in real-time management and in "what-if" and sensitivity types of analyses examining the potential impact of a change in policy.

The performance category is most relevant in decision support systems. The metrics that are monitored can be fed into automated decision-making systems, or they can trigger reports that are delivered to managers. These form the basis of a decision support system and best typify the way marketing research assists managers with day-to-day operational decisions.

A marketing **decision support system (DSS)** is a system that helps decision makers confront problems through direct interaction with computerized databases and analytical software programs. The purpose of a decision support system is to store data and transform them into organized information that is easily accessible to marketing managers. Doing so saves managers countless hours so that decisions that might take days or even weeks otherwise can be made in minutes using a DSS.

Modern decision support systems greatly facilitate **customer relationship management (CRM)**. A CRM system is the part of the DSS that addresses exchanges between the firm and its customers. It brings together information about customers including sales data, market trends, marketing promotions and the way consumers respond to them, customer preferences, and more. A CRM system describes customer relationships in sufficient detail so that managers, salespeople, customer service representatives, and perhaps the customers themselves can access information directly, match customer needs with satisfying product offerings, remind customers of service requirements, and know what other products a customer has purchased.

Casinos track regular customers' behavior via "player's cards" that are swiped each time a consumer conducts a transaction. This information is fed automatically into a CRM system that creates tailor-made promotional packages. The promotion may be unique to a specific customer's preferences as tracked by their own pattern of behavior. You may notice when visiting certain Web sites that they seem to be able to predict your behavior. Casino customers arrive to the resort and are greeted with their favorite beverage and coupons for their favorite restaurants. This information is found in the CRM system and is based on behavior tracked on previous visits.

Exhibit 2.2 illustrates a decision support system. Raw, unsummarized data are input to the DSS. Data collected in marketing research projects are a major source of this input, but the data may be purchased or collected by accountants, sales managers, production managers, or company employees other than marketing researchers. Effective marketers spend a great deal of time and effort collecting information for input into the decision support system. Useful information is the output of a DSS. A decision support system requires both databases and software. For firms operating across national borders, the DSS becomes part of its global information system.

decision support system (DSS)

A computer-based system that helps decision makers confront problems through direct interaction with databases and analytical software programs.

customer relationship management (CRM)

Part of the DSS that addresses exchanges between the firm and its customers.

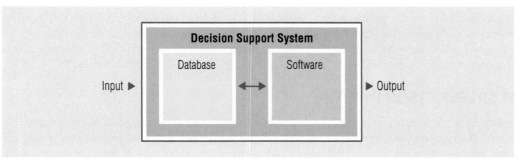

EXHIBIT 2.2
Decision Support System

Databases and Data Warehousing

database

A collection of raw data arranged logically and organized in a form that can be stored and processed by a computer.

A **database** is a collection of raw data arranged logically and organized in a form that can be stored and processed by a computer. A customer mailing list is one type of database. Population characteristics may be recorded by state, county, and city in another database. Modern computer technology makes both the storage and retrieval of this information easy and convenient. The population data needed to do a retail site analysis may have meant days, possibly weeks, in a library. Today, the information is just a few clicks away.

data warehousing

The process allowing important day-to-day operational data to be stored and organized for simplified access.

Data warehousing is the process allowing important day-to-day operational data to be stored and organized for simplified access. More specifically, a **data warehouse** is the multitiered computer storehouse of current and historical data. Data warehouse management requires that the detailed data from operational systems be extracted, transformed, placed into logical partitions (for example, daily data, weekly data, etc.), and stored in a consistent and secure manner. Organizations with data warehouses may integrate databases from both inside and outside the company. Managing a data warehouse effectively requires considerable computing power and expertise. As a result, data warehouse companies exist that provide this service for companies in return for a fee.[11] Data warehousing allows for sophisticated analysis, such as data mining, discussed in Chapter 7.

data warehouse

The multitiered computer storehouse of current and historical data.

Input Management

How does data end up in a data warehouse where it can be used by a decision support system? In other words, how is the input managed? Input includes all the numerical, text, voice, and image data that enter the DSS. Systematic accumulation of pertinent, timely, and accurate data is essential to the success of a decision support system.

DSS managers, systems analysts, and programmers are responsible for the decision support system as a whole, but many functions within an organization provide input data. Marketing researchers, accountants, corporate librarians, sales personnel, production managers, and many others within the organization help to collect data and provide input for the DSS. Input data can also come from external sources.

Exhibit 2.3 shows six major sources of data input: internal records, proprietary marketing research, salesperson input, behavioral tracking, Web tracking, and outside vendors and external distributors of data. Each source can provide valuable input.

■ INTERNAL RECORDS

Internal records, such as accounting reports of sales and inventory figures, provide considerable data that may become useful information for marketing managers. An effective data collection system establishes orderly procedures to ensure that data about costs, shipments, inventory, sales, and other aspects of regular operations are routinely collected and entered into the computer.

■ PROPRIETARY MARKETING RESEARCH

proprietary marketing research

The gathering of new data to investigate specific problems.

Marketing research has already been defined as a broad set of procedures and methods. To clarify the DSS concept, consider a narrower view of marketing research. **Proprietary marketing research** emphasizes the company's gathering of new data. Few proprietary marketing research procedures and methods are conducted regularly or continuously. Instead, research projects conducted to study specific company problems generate data; this is proprietary marketing research. Providing managers with nonroutine data that otherwise would not be available is a major function of proprietary marketing research. Earlier, we discussed four categories of research. Proprietary marketing research may involve either or both of the "testing" and "issues" types of research.

■ SALESPERSON INPUT

Salespeople work in firms' external environments, so they commonly provide essential marketing data. Sales representatives' reports frequently alert managers to changes in competitors' prices and new product offerings. It also may involve the types of complaints salespeople are hearing from

EXHIBIT 2.3 **Six Major Sources of Marketing Input for Decision Support Systems**

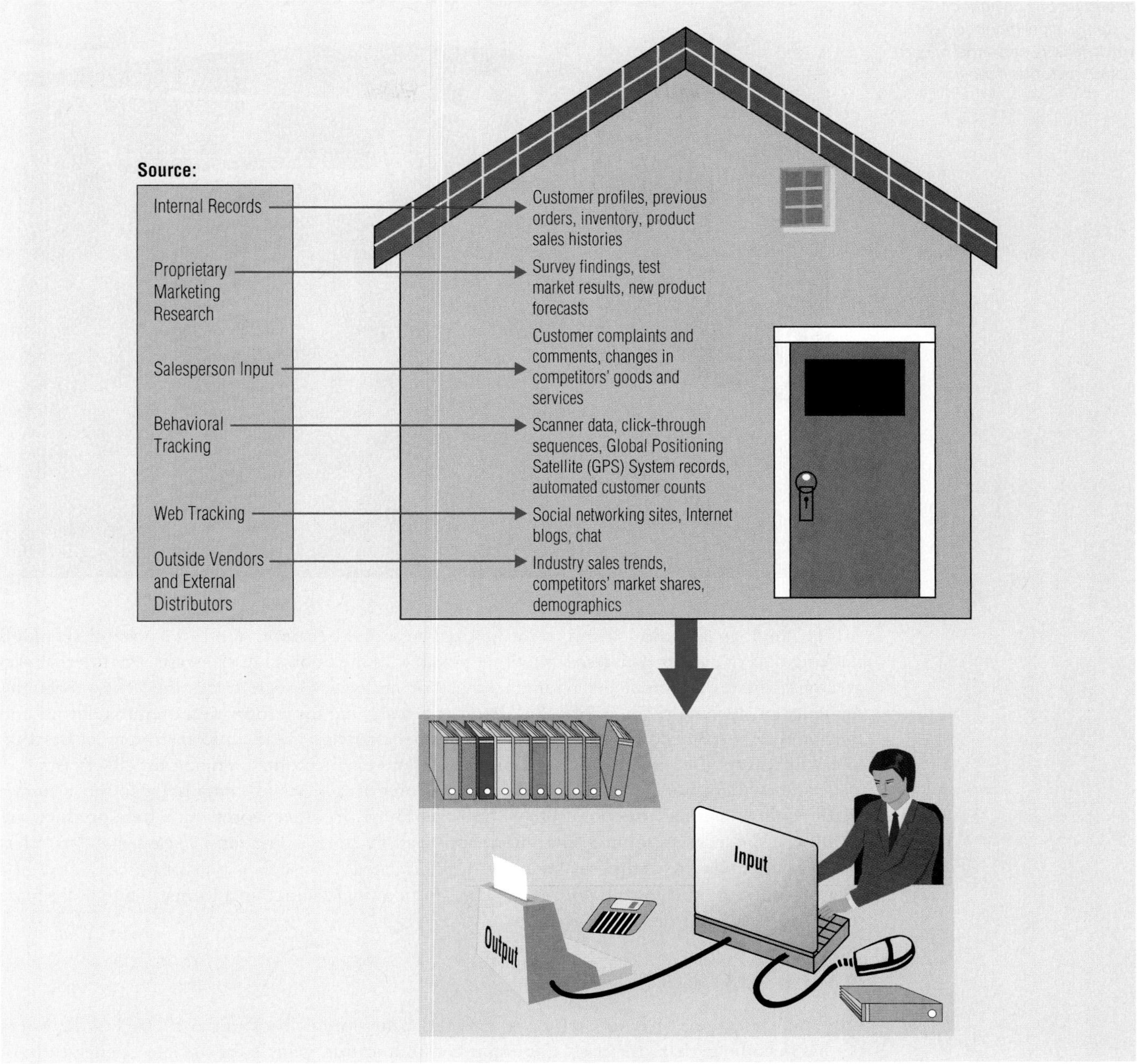

Source:

Internal Records → Customer profiles, previous orders, inventory, product sales histories

Proprietary Marketing Research → Survey findings, test market results, new product forecasts

Salesperson Input → Customer complaints and comments, changes in competitors' goods and services

Behavioral Tracking → Scanner data, click-through sequences, Global Positioning Satellite (GPS) System records, automated customer counts

Web Tracking → Social networking sites, Internet blogs, chat

Outside Vendors and External Distributors → Industry sales trends, competitors' market shares, demographics

Input

Output

customers. As trends become evident, this data may become marketing intelligence, leading to a change in product design or service delivery.

■ BEHAVIORAL TRACKING

Modern technology provides new ways of tracking human behavior. Global positioning satellite (GPS) systems allow management to track the whereabouts of delivery personnel at all times. This is the same system that provides directions through an automobile's navigation system. For example, if your delivery person takes a quick break for nine holes of golf or decides to stop at Neil's Bar for a couple of beers mid-afternoon, management can spot these as deviations from the appropriate delivery route are noted. Thus, it can help track which employees are doing their jobs well.

GPS devices, like those used in automobile navigation systems, allow management to track delivery personnel or even actual customer behavior.

© CREATAS IMAGES/JUPITER IMAGES

Technology also allows firms to track actual customer behavior. While it's possible that GPS tracking data of customers is also sometimes possible, as the photograph suggests, the Internet also greatly facilitates customer behavior tracking. For instance, Google tracks the "click-through" sequence of customers. Therefore, if a customer is searching for information on refrigerators, and then goes to BestBuy.com, Google can track this behavior and use the information to let BestBuy know how important it is to advertise on Google and even automate pricing for advertisers.[12]

scanner data
The accumulated records resulting from point of sale data recordings.

Purchase behavior can also be tracked at the point of sale. **Scanner data** refers to the accumulated records resulting from point of sale data recordings. In other words, each time products are scanned at a checkout counter, the information can be stored. The term *single-source* data refers to a system's ability to gather several types of interrelated data, such as type of purchase, use of a sales promotion, or advertising frequency data, from a single source in a format that will facilitate integration, comparison, and analysis.

■ WEB TRACKING

Little did the original inventors of the Internet probably foresee back in the 1960s, but the Internet has become perhaps the most important communication vehicle for the latest generations of teens. Web tracking is performed by marketing researchers to monitor trends and information posted by consumers that pertains to the company's brand or products. MySpace.com logged nearly 70 million unique visitors in December 2007 and is one of the top 10 most visited web sites in America.[13] Marketing researchers monitor postings and create vehicles such as contests which invite consumers to leave ideas and feedback about the brand. The Research Snapshot on the next page demonstrates how publishing and production companies use input from social networking sites. Other sources for information include Internet blogs and chat rooms where consumers share information about their own experiences, including complaints that serve as a type of warning to other consumers.

■ OUTSIDE VENDORS AND EXTERNAL DISTRIBUTORS

Outside vendors and external distributors market information as their products. Many organizations specialize in the collection and publication of high-quality information. One outside vendor,

MySpace Means My Data

Social networking sites have become perhaps the most important marketing tool for companies wanting to reach youth markets. Information gathered from these Web sites has become input into product designs including music, movies, and books aimed at teen markets. The publishers of the Clique series of teen books such as Twilight Saga create MySpace pages and encourage fans to visit the sites and leave input. Fans can even give input that will shape the content of the novels. The publishers set up polls asking questions such as who Bella should choose. The polls record thousands of votes and the publishers use the information to help keep authors in tune with the teen markets.

Another benefit of Web tracking is international access. For example, nearly 1 million Indian consumers have a Facebook account. The popularity of Facebook over more regional networking sites like Hi5 or Orkut is thought to lie in a simple fact—Indian consumers find Facebook fun! By creating entertaining activities and experiences, consumers become practically addicted. The more time consumers spend, the more information they leave behind. Thus, social networking is an inexpensive way to take in data from international sources.

Sources: Sellers, J., "Teen Marketing 2.0," *Publishers' Weekly*, 254, no. 35 (2007), 27; Srivasta, P., "The Gregarious Web: What Are Senior Indian Execs Doing Hanging Around at Social Networking Site, Facebook.com?" *Business Today*, (October 21, 2007), 226.

the ACNielsen Company, provides television program ratings, audience counts, and information about the demographic composition of television viewer groups. Other vendors specialize in the distribution of information. Public libraries have always purchased information, traditionally in the form of books, and they have served as distributors of this information.

Media representatives often provide useful demographic and lifestyle data about their audiences. *Advertising Age, The Wall Street Journal, Sales and Marketing Management,* and other trade- and business-oriented publications are important sources of information. These publications keep managers up-to-date about the economy, competitors' activities, and other aspects of the marketing environment.

Companies called *data specialists* record and store certain marketing information. Computer technology has changed the way many of these organizations supply data, favoring the development of computerized databases.

Computerized Data Archives

Historically, collections of organized and readily retrievable data were available in printed form at libraries. The *Statistical Abstract of the United States,* which is filled with tables of statistical facts, is a typical example. In recent years, the *Statistical Abstract* has become available electronically. Users can purchase it via CD-ROM or access it via the Internet. The entire 2000 census as well as projections through the current year are available in print, CD-ROM, and via the Internet at **http://www.census.gov**. More and more data are available in digitized form every day.

Numerous computerized search and retrieval systems and electronic databases are available as subscription services or in libraries. Just as a student can query the school library to find information for a term paper without leaving home, data acquisition for businesses has also become far more convenient in recent years. Today, business people access online information search and retrieval services, such as Dow Jones News Retrieval and Bloomberg Financial Markets, without leaving their offices. In fact, some information services can be accessed from remote locations via digital wireless devices.

Modern library patrons can command a computer to search indexes and retrieve databases from a range of vendors. Just as wholesalers collect goods from manufacturers and offer them for sale to retailers who then provide them to consumers, many information firms serve as data wholesalers. **Data wholesalers** put together consortia of data sources into packages that are offered to municipal, corporate, and university libraries for a fee. Information consumers then access the data through these libraries. Some of the better known *databases* include Wilson Business Center, Hoovers, PROQUEST, INFOTRAC, DIALOG (Dialog Information Services, Inc.),

data wholesalers

Companies that put together consortia of data sources into packages that are offered to municipal, corporate, and university libraries for a fee.

LEXIS-NEXIS, and Dow Jones News Retrieval Services. These databases provide all types of information including recent news stories and data tables charting statistical trends.

DIALOG, for example, maintains more than 600 databases. A typical database may have a million or more records, each consisting of a one- or two-paragraph abstract that summarizes the major points of a published article along with bibliographic information. One of the DIALOG databases, ABI/INFORM, abstracts significant articles in more than 1,000 current business and management journals. Many computerized archives provide full-text downloads of published articles about companies and various research topics.

Exhibit 2.4 illustrates the services provided by two popular vendors of information services that electronically index numerous databases. For a more extensive listing, see the *Gale Directory of Databases*.[14]

Several types of databases from outside vendors and external distributors are so fundamental to decision support systems that they deserve further explanation. The following sections discuss statistical databases, financial databases, and video databases in slightly more detail.

■ STATISTICAL DATABASES

Statistical databases contain numerical data for market analysis and forecasting. Often demographic, sales, and other relevant marketing variables are recorded by geographical area. Geographic information systems use these *geographical databases* and powerful software to prepare computer maps of relevant variables. Companies such as Claritas, Urban Decision Systems, and CACI all offer geographic or demographic databases that are widely used in industry.

One source for these huge data warehouses is scanner data. Substituting mechanized record-keeping like optical scanners for human record-keeping results in greater accuracy and more rapid feedback about store activity.

One weakness of scanner data is that not all points of sale have scanner technology. For instance, many convenience stores lack scanner technology, as do most vending machines. Thus,

EXHIBIT 2.4
Vendors of Information Services and Electronic Indexing

Vendors	Selected Databases	Type of Data
DIALOG	ABI/INFORM	Summaries and citations from over 1,000 academic management, marketing, and general business journals with full text of more than 500 of these publications
	ASI (American Statistics Index)	Abstracts and indexes of federal government statistical publications
	PROMT (The Predicast Overview of Markets and Technologies)	Summaries and full text from 1,000 U.S. and international business and trade journals, industry newsletters, newspapers, and market research studies; information about industries and companies, including the products and technologies they develop and the markets in which they compete
	Investext	Full text of over 2 million company, industry, and geographic research reports written by analysts at more than 600 leading investment banks, brokerage houses, and consulting firms worldwide
Dow Jones News Retrieval	Business Newsstand	Articles from *New York Times, Los Angeles Times, Washington Post,* and other leading newspapers and magazines
	Historical Market Data Center	Historical data on securities, dividends, and exchange rates
	Web Center	Information obtained from searches of corporate, industry, government, and news Web sites

those purchases go unrecorded. The Universal Product Code, or UPC, contains information on the category of goods, the manufacturer, and product identification based on size, flavor, color, and so on. This is what the optical scanner actually reads. If a large percentage of a brand's sales occur in environments without the ability to read the UPC code, the marketer should be aware that the scanner data may not be representative.

■ FINANCIAL DATABASES

Competitors' and customers' financial data, such as income statements and balance sheets, may interest managers. These are easy to access in financial databases. CompuStat publishes an extensive financial database on thousands of companies, broken down by industry and other criteria. To illustrate the depth of this pool of information, CompuStat's Global Advantage offers extensive data on approximately 7,000 companies in more than thirty countries in Europe, the Pacific Rim, and North America.

■ VIDEO DATABASES

Video databases and streaming media are having a major impact on the marketing of many goods and services. For example, movie studios provide clips of upcoming films and advertising agencies put television commercials on the Internet (see AdCritic at http://www.creativity-online.com, for example). McDonald's maintains a digital archive of television commercials and other video footage to share with its franchisers around the world. The video database enables franchisers and their advertising agencies to create local advertising without filming the same types of scenes already archived. Videos on practically every type of product consumption or brand can be found on YouTube.com. In 2008, both major political campaigns produced advertisements meant solely for distribution through YouTube and other Web video sources. Just imagine the potential value of digital video databases to advertising agencies' support systems as firms can monitor the number of hits on different videos and even know for how long most people view a video. They can also monitor the buzz (Internet chatter) created by provocative videos.

electronic data interchange (EDI)

Type of exchange that occurs when one company's computer system is integrated with another company's system.

Networks and Electronic Data Interchange

Electronic data interchange (EDI) systems integrate one company's computer system directly with another company's system. Much of the input to a company's decision support system may come through networks from other companies' computers. Companies such as Computer Technology

YouTube provides a digital archive that can be mined for data or used as a vehicle to test ideas and concepts.

Corporation and Microelectronics market data services that allow corporations to exchange business information with suppliers or customers. For example, every evening Wal-Mart transmits millions of characters of data about the day's sales to its apparel suppliers. Wrangler, a supplier of blue jeans, for instance, shares the data and a model that interprets the data. Wrangler also shares software applications that act to replenish stock in Wal-Mart stores. This DSS lets Wrangler's managers know when to send specific quantities of specific sizes and colors of jeans to specific stores from specific warehouses. The result is a learning loop that lowers inventory costs and leads to fewer stockouts.

© AP PHOTO/CAMERON BLOCK

How Did They Know That?

Major state universities have thousands and thousands of alumni. But, typically, the university has limited resources to personally call on alumni to financially support the university. Historically, only one out of every hundred or so alumni would provide gifts sufficient to balance the average unit costs of marketing to all alums. What if the university could improve the hit ratio and better target relatively expensive marketing approaches like personal meetings to those who are 50 percent likely to give a major gift instead of 5 percent likely. This is exactly what modern predictive analytic tools can do. Using all the information on alumni, much of it gathered through various touchpoints with the university, a statistical model can be built which predicts responsiveness to appeals and places a potential donor value on each alumnus. So, perhaps an alum with football season tickets who also attends at least three orchestra performances and who majored in marketing becomes registered as a donor with high value. More marketing efforts can be directed their way and in this way, marketing is made much more efficient.

Similarly, pharmaceutical firms use data mining approaches based on volumes of input on physicians in their directories to better predict the types of drugs each doctor is likely to prescribe. When a doctor switches prescriptions for a patient, the program identifies a probable reason such as side effects, insurance coverage, cost, and so on; and this feedback allows them to adjust production and marketing accordingly. In this manner, they can design products that doctors are more likely to prescribe. Predictive outcomes of programmed research of this type truly represent win-win propositions. The physicians (customers) get products that more closely match their desires and the company performs better through increased sales. Modern technology enhances firms' ability to be opportunistic in their relationships in a good way.

Sources: Crosno, J. L. and R. Dahlstrom, "A Meta-Analystic Review of Opportunism in Exchange Relationships," *Journal of the Academy of Marketing Science*, 36 (June 2008), 191–201; Goldman, L., "Web 2.0 Brings Web Analytics 2.0," *DM Review*, 17 (March 2007), 28; "SAS Helps ImpactRX Provide Real Time Marketing Intelligence to Pharma Companies," *Business Wire*, (March 17, 2008), retrieved July 14, 2008 from ABI/INFORM Dateline database (document ID: 1447327611); "SPSS Text Mining Reveals Greater Customer Insights as Organizations Worldwide Tap into Unstructured Data," *Business Wire*, (June 16, 2008), retrieved July 15, 2008 from ABI/INFORM Dateline database (document ID: 1495884601).

Predictive Analytics

predictive analytics

A system linking computerized data sources to statistical tools allowing more accurate forecasts of consumers' opinions and actions.

The term predictive analytics did not exist prior to the widespread usage of the Internet. In fact, no other facet of business better illustrates how the Internet can be leveraged for business success than predictive analytics. Broadly speaking, **predictive analytics** refers to linking computerized data sources to statistical tools that can search for predictive relationships and trends which allow more accurate forecast of consumers' opinions and actions. Predictive analytics also eliminates manual scanning of data. Software companies like SPSS and SAS offer products that both look for data and then use statistical tools to reveal key predictive relationships. We'll learn more about SPSS and specific statistical tools later in the book.

The airline systems described in the opening vignette represent a type of predictive analytics. Information taken from consumers' actual archived behavior along with preference data provided by direct input from the consumer is used to model sales levels that can be achieved with various amounts of discounts. Airlines may be expected to use the latest research technologies like predictive analytics, but other industries including some that are much smaller and seemingly less significant are taking advantage of this new tool. Monterey Mushrooms, the nation's leading mushroom producer, used to arm its salesforce with volumes of paper reports showing sales data for hundreds and hundreds of vendors over several quarters.[15] Spotting trends was much like finding a needle in a hastack! The company now integrates information about vendors and cost information including shipping and packaging cost to predict which sales calls will be most profitable. The company can allocate resources accordingly (see the Research Snapshot above for an illustration). Beats finding a needle in a haystack!

The marketing researchers' job in predictive analytics is twofold. First, identify the key sources of information that may create predictive intelligence and second, use analytic tools to build predictive models. Although the information can come from many varied places, the Internet is a prime source for key information. In the following pages we discuss the World Wide Web and how to use the Internet for research. However, keep in mind that the Internet is constantly changing.

How Is the Internet Useful in Research?

The Internet is useful to researchers in many ways. In fact, more and more applications become known as the technology grows and is adopted by more and more users. The Internet is particularly useful as a source of available data and as a way of collecting data.

■ ACCESSING AVAILABLE DATA

The Internet allows instantaneous and effortless access to a great deal of information. Non-commercial and commercial organizations make a wealth of data and other resources available on the Internet. For example, the U.S. Library of Congress provides full text of all versions of House and Senate legislation and full text of the *Congressional Record*. The Internal Revenue Service makes it possible to download an income tax form. Cengage learning (**www.cengage.com**) and its South-Western college division (**www.cengage.com/southwestern**) have online directories that allow college professors to access information about the company and its textbooks. The Gale Research Database (**http://www.gale.cengage.com/**) provides basic statistics and news stories on literally thousands of companies worldwide. Thus, information that formerly took a great deal of time and effort to obtain is now available with a few clicks. Further, since it can often be electronically downloaded or copied, it is not necessary for a person to transcribe the data. Therefore, it is available in a more error-free form.

■ COLLECTING DATA

The Internet is also revolutionizing the way researchers collect data. Later in this text, we discuss in more detail the use of Web-based surveys. In other words, questionnaires can be posted on a Web site and respondents can be invited to go to the particular URL and participate in the survey. This cuts down on the expense associated with traditional mail surveys and also reduces error since the data can be automatically recorded rather than transcribed from a paper form into an electronic format.

Furthermore, when a consumer uses the World Wide Web, his or her usage leaves a record that can be traced and observed. For instance, we can know how many pages were visited at some shopping site before a purchase was made. We can know if products were abandoned in the "virtual cart" without a purchase being made. Online auctions provide another mechanism to track consumers' behavior. Prototype products can be offered for sale in an online auction to help assist with product design, forecasting demand, and setting an appropriate price.[16]

■ NAVIGATING THE INTERNET

Parties that furnish information on the World Wide Web are called **content providers**. Content providers maintain Web sites. A Web site consists of one or more Web pages with related information about a particular topic; for example, a university Web site might include pages about its mission, courses, and faculty (see **http://www.gsu.edu**, for example). The introductory page or opening screen is called the home page because it provides basic information about the purpose of the document along with a menu of selections or links that lead to other screens with more specific information. Thus, each page can have connections, or hyperlinks, to other pages, which may be on any computer connected to the Internet. People using the World Wide Web may be viewing information that is stored on a host computer or on a machine halfway around the world.

Most Web browsers also allow the user to enter a **Uniform Resource Locator (URL)** into the program. The URL is really just a Web site address that Web browsers recognize. Many Web sites allow any user or visitor access without previous approval. However, many commercial sites require that the user have a valid account and password before access is granted.

One of the most basic research tools available via the Internet is a search engine. A **search engine** is a computerized directory that allows anyone to search the World Wide Web for information based on a keyword search. A **keyword search** takes place as the search engine searches

---

TOTHEPOINT

The Net is 10.5 on the Richter scale of economic change.

—Nicholas Negroponte

content providers

Parties that furnish information on the World Wide Web.

Uniform Resource Locator (URL)

A Web site address that Web browsers recognize.

search engine

A computerized directory that allows anyone to search the World Wide Web for information using a keyword search.

keyword search

Takes place as the search engine searches through millions of Web pages for documents containing the keywords.

through millions of Web pages for documents containing the keywords. Some of the most comprehensive and accurate search engines are:

Ask Jeeves	http://www.ask.com
Yahoo!	http://www.yahoo.com
Dogpile	http://www.dogpile.com
Google	http://www.google.com
Hotbot	http://www.hotbot.com
Go network	http://go.com
Excite	http://www.excite.com
Lycos	http://www.lycos.com
WebCrawler	http://www.webcrawler.com

Google revolutionized search engines by changing the way the search was actually conducted. It searches based on a mathematical theory known as *graph theory*.[17] Google greatly improved the accuracy and usefulness of the search results obtained from a keyword search. Exhibit 2.5 illustrates the Google interface and expanded Google options. For instance, if one clicks on Google Scholar, a search of basic research papers on any given topic indicated by the keywords can be performed.

A Boolean search is a search that combines relevant key words by operators that refine the search. The operators include words like and, or, and not. So, a search of Churchill will bring up thousands of hits. For example, Churchill Downs the home of the Kentucky Derby will surface. However, enter "war" and "Churchill" and the search becomes quickly limited to sites that contain both words. As a result, a student doing a paper on Winston Churhill's leadership during WWII has just become easier. Modern data mining approaches can actually automate Web searches using Boolean operators. Researchers may wish to monitor negative information about a brand.

EXHIBIT 2.5
The Google Web Interface

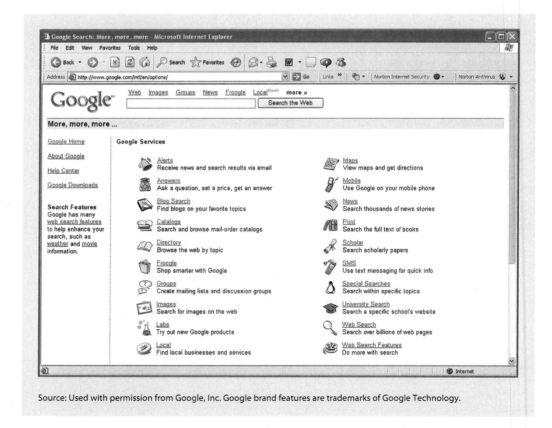

Source: Used with permission from Google, Inc. Google brand features are trademarks of Google Technology.

Environmental Scanning

The Internet is an especially useful source for scanning many types of environmental changes. **Environmental scanning** entails all information gathering designed to detect changes in the external operating environment of the firm. Even things beyond the control of the firm can have a significant impact on firm performance.

Ford Motor Company maintains an Internet-based relationship marketing program that, among other things, helps the automaker scan its environment using the Internet. Its dealer Web site creates a centralized communication service linking dealers via an Internet connection. Its buyer Web site allows prospective buyers to visit a virtual showroom and to get price quotes and financial information. Its owner Web site allows an owner who registers and supplies pertinent vehicle information to get free e-mail and other ownership perks. A perk might be a free Hertz upgrade or an autographed photo of one of the Ford-sponsored NASCAR drivers. In return, Ford collects data at all levels, which allows managers to scan for trends and apply what they learn at a local level.

PHOTO COURTESY OF VICKI BEAVER

Here is the result of a Boolean search for "Ford and Feedback." The URL is shown but can be reached by navigating to ask.com and then searching the key phrase.

Information Technology

Data and information can be delivered to consumers or other end users via either **pull technology** or **push technology**. Conventionally, consumers request information from a Web page and the browser then determines a response. Thus, the consumer is essentially asking for the data. In this case, it is said to be pulled through the channel. The opposite of pull is push. Push technology sends data to a user's computer without a request being made. In other words, software is used to guess what information might be interesting to consumers based on the pattern of previous responses. Push technology allows personalized information to be delivered to consumers without the need for them to even be physically at their Internet device.[18] When airline customers go to a Web site to search for flights from Columbus to Riverside, they are pulling information. When those same customers get "Dinged" with a special on flights from Columbus to Riverside, they have had the information pushed to them based on their previous behavior.

Today's information technology uses "smart agents" or "intelligent agents" to deliver customized content to a viewer's desktop. **Smart agent software** is capable of learning an Internet user's preferences and automatically searching out information and distributing the information to a user's computer. My Yahoo! and MyExcite are portal services that personalize Web pages. Users can get stock quotes relevant to their portfolios, news about favorite sports teams, local weather, and other personalized information. Users can customize the sections of the service they want delivered. With push technology, pertinent content is delivered to the viewer's desktop without the user having to do the searching.

Cookies, in computer terminology, are small data files that record a user's Web usage history. If a person looks up a weather report by keying in a zip code into a personalized Web page, the fact that the user visited the Web site and the zip code entered are recorded in the cookie. This is a clue that tells where the person lives (or maybe where he or she may be planning to visit). Web sites can then direct information to that consumer based on information in the cookie. So, someone in College Station, Texas, may receive pop-up ads for restaurants in College Station.

environmental scanning

Entails all information gathering designed to detect changes in the external operating environment of the firm.

pull technology

Consumers request information from a Web page and the browser then determines a response; the consumer is essentially asking for the data.

push technology

Sends data to a user's computer without a request being made; software is used to guess what information might be interesting to consumers based on the pattern of previous responses.

smart agent software

Software capable of learning an Internet user's preferences and automatically searching out information in selected Web sites and then distributing it.

cookies

Small data files that a content provider can save onto the computer of someone who visits its Web site.

- Researchers should focus on relevance as the key characteristic of useful data.
  - Do so by asking, "Will knowledge of some fact change some important outcome?"
- Focus more on getting managers the right data than the most data.

- The Internet is a valuable source of data.
  - The Internet is:
    - A useful information collection vehicle
    - An exhaustive information repository
    - A great place for data mining

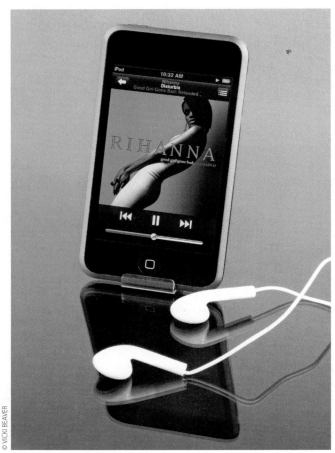

The iPod offers one example of how modern technology makes it possible to store and deliver information. Various models can capture, store, and deliver hundreds of songs to their owners.

intranet

A company's private data network that uses Internet standards and technology.

Information technology is having a major impact on the nature of marketing research. We will explore this topic in several places throughout this book.

Intranets

An **Intranet** is a company's private data network that uses Internet standards and technology.[19] The information on an Intranet—data, graphics, video, and voice—is available only inside the organization or to those individuals whom the organization deems as appropriate participants. Thus, a key difference between the Internet and an Intranet is that security software programs, or "firewalls," are installed to limit access to only those employees authorized to enter the system. Intranets then serve as secure knowledge portals that contain substantial amounts of organizational memory and can integrate it with information from outside sources. The challenge in designing an Intranet is making sure that it is capable of delivering relevant data to decision makers. Research suggests that relevance is a key in getting knowledge workers to actually make use of company Intranets.[20]

The Intranet can be extended to include key consumers as a source of valuable research. Their participation in the Intranet can lead to new product developments. Texas Instruments has successfully established an Intranet that integrates communications between customers and researchers leading to the introduction and modification of its calculators.[21] An Intranet lets authorized users, possibly including key customers, look at product drawings, employee newsletters, sales figures, and other kinds of company information.

Internet2

As sophisticated as the Internet and Intranets are today, new technologies, such as Internet2, may dramatically enhance researchers' ability to answer marketing problems in the future. Internet2 (http://www.internet2.edu/) is a collaborative effort involving just over 200 universities, government entities including the military, and sixty corporate organizations in the United States. The project hopes to re-create some of the cooperative spirit that created the Internet originally. Internet2 users are limited to those involved with the affiliate organizations. The hope is to create a faster, more powerful Internet by providing multimodal access, employing more wireless technologies, and building in global trading mechanisms. Right now, the Internet2 is a research tool for the universities and organizations involved in its development.[22]

Summary

1. Know why concepts like data, information, and intelligence represent value. Increased global competition and technological advances in interactive media have spurred development of global information systems. A global information system is an organized collection of computer hardware, software, data, and personnel designed to capture, store, update, manipulate, analyze, and immediately display information about worldwide business activity.

From a research perspective, there is a difference between data, information, and intelligence. Data are simply facts or recorded measures of certain phenomena (things); information is data formatted (structured) to support decision making or define the relationship between two facts. Market intelligence is the subset of data and information that actually has some explanatory power enabling effective decisions to be made. The proper use of data, information, and intelligence means better decision making and better decision making means greater value for the firm.

2. Understand the four characteristics that describe data. The usefulness of data to management can be described based on four characteristics: relevance, quality, timeliness, and completeness. Relevant data have the characteristic of pertinence to the situation at hand. The information is useful. The quality of information is the degree to which data represent the true situation. High-quality data are accurate, valid, and reliable. High-quality data represent reality faithfully and present a good picture of reality. Timely information is obtained at the right time. Computerized information systems can record events and present information soon after a transaction takes place, improving timeliness. Complete information is the right quantity of information. Marketing managers must have sufficient information to relate all aspects of their decisions together.

3. Know what a decision support system is and does. A database is a collection of raw data arranged logically and organized in a form that can be stored and processed by a computer. Marketing data come from four major sources: internal records, proprietary marketing research, marketing intelligence, and outside vendors and external distributors. Each source can provide valuable input. Because most companies compile and store many different databases, they often develop data warehousing systems. Data warehousing is the process allowing important day-to-day operational data to be stored and organized for simplified access. More specifically, a data warehouse is the multitiered computer storehouse of current and historical data. Data warehouse management requires that the detailed data from operational systems be extracted, transformed, and stored (warehoused) so that the various database tables from both inside and outside the company are consistent. All of this feeds into the decision support system that automates or assists business decision making.

4. Describe marketing research's role in predictive analytics. Predictive analytics refers to linking computerized data sources to statistical tools that can search for relationships and trends which allow more accurate prediction of consumers' opinions and actions. Thus, it combines automated data mining with multivariate statistical tools to enhance prediction. The marketing researcher's job in predictive analytics is twofold. First, identify the key sources of information that may create predictive intelligence and second, use analytic tools to build predictive models.

5. Recognize the major categories of databases. The Internet is a worldwide network of computers that allows users access to information and documents from distant sources. It is a combination of a worldwide communication system and the world's largest public library. The World Wide Web is a system of thousands of interconnected pages, or documents, that can be easily accessed with Web browsers and search engines.

An Intranet is a company's private data network that uses Internet standards and technology. The information on an Intranet—data, graphics, video, and voice—is available only inside the organization. Thus, a key difference between the Internet and an Intranet is that "firewalls," or security software programs, are installed to limit access to only those employees authorized to enter the system.

A company uses Internet features to build its own Intranet. Groupware and other technology can facilitate the transfer of data, information, and knowledge. In organizations that practice knowledge management, Intranets function to make the knowledge of company experts more accessible throughout their organizations.

Key Terms and Concepts

content providers *39*
cookies *41*
customer relationship management
  (CRM) *31*
data *26*
database *32*
data quality *28*
data warehouse *32*
data warehousing *32*
data wholesalers *35*
decision support system (DSS) *31*

electronic data interchange (EDI) *37*
environmental scanning *41*
global information system *30*
information *26*
information completeness *29*
intranet *42*
keyword search *39*
knowledge *29*
knowledge management *29*
market intelligence *26*
predictive analytics *38*

proprietary marketing research *32*
pull technology *41*
push technology *41*
relevance *27*
scanner data *34*
search engine *39*
smart agent software *41*
timeliness *29*
Uniform Resource Locator (URL) *39*

Questions for Review and Critical Thinking

1. What is the difference between data, information, and intelligence?
2. What are the characteristics of useful information?
3. What is the key question distinguishing relevant data from irrelevant data?
4. Define *knowledge management*. What is its purpose within an organization?
5. What types of databases might be found in the following organizations?
   a. Holiday Inn
   b. A Major University Athletic Department
   c. Anheuser-Busch
6. What type of operational questions could a delivery firm like FedEx expect to automate with the company's decision support system?
7. What makes a decision support system successful?
8. What is data warehousing?
9. **'NET** How does data warehousing assist decision making? Visit http://www.kbb.com. While there, choose two cars that you might consider buying and compare them. Which do you like the best? What would you do now? What are at least three pieces of data that should be stored in a data warehouse somewhere based on your interaction with *Kelly Blue Book*?

10. **'NET** Give three examples of computerized databases that are available at your college or university library.
11. **'NET** What is predictive analytics? Think about the three Web sites that you interact with most. List at least 10 pieces of information that you exchange with these Web sites that you believe have potential to become useful data that can be made into intelligence through predictive analytics.
12. Suppose a retail firm is interested in studying the effect of lighting on customer purchase behavior. Which of the following pieces of information is the least relevant and why?
    a. Amount of natural light in the store
    b. The compensation system for store salespeople
    c. The color of the walls in the store
    d. The type of lighting: fluorescent or incandescent
13. **'NET** Imagine the data collected by eBay each day. List at least five types of data that are collected through the daily operations. Describe how each type illustrates in it data, information, or intelligence. Make sure you list at least one example of each.
14. How could New Balance, a maker of athletic shoes, use RFID technology to collect data?
15. **'NET** The Spider's Apprentice is a Web site that provides many useful tips about using search engines. Go to http://www.monash.com/spidap.html to learn the ins and outs of search engines.

Research Activities

1. **'NET** To learn more about data warehousing, go to http://www.dwinfocenter.org. How could a company that provides music and video files via the Internet use a data warehouse?
2. **'NET** Use the Internet to see if you can find information to answer the following questions:

   a. What is the weather in Denver today?
   b. What are four restaurants in the French Quarter in New Orleans?
   c. What is the most popular novel among teenage girls age 14–16?

Case 2.1 Harvard Cooperative Society

From his office window overlooking the main floor of the Harvard Cooperative Society, CEO Jerry Murphy can glance down and see customers shopping.[23] They make their way through the narrow aisles of the crowded department store, picking up a sweatshirt here, trying on a baseball cap there, checking out the endless array of merchandise that bears the Harvard University insignia.

Watching Murphy, you can well imagine the Co-op's founders, who started the store in 1882, peering through the tiny windowpanes to keep an eye on the shop floor. Was the Harvard Square store attracting steady traffic? Were the college students buying enough books and supplies for the Coop to make a profit? Back then, it was tough to answer those questions precisely. The owners had to watch and wait, relying only on their gut feelings to know how things were going from minute to minute.

Now, more than a hundred years later, Murphy can tell you, down to the last stock-keeping unit, how he's doing at any given moment. His window on the business is the PC that sits on his desk.

All day long it delivers up-to-the-minute, easy-to-read electronic reports on what's selling and what's not, which items are running low in inventory and which have fallen short of forecast. In a matter of seconds, the computer can report gross margins for any product or supplier, and Murphy can decide whether the margins are fat enough to justify keeping the supplier or product on board. "We were in the 1800s, and we had to move ahead," he says of the $55 million business.

Questions

1. What is a decision support system? What advantages does a decision support system have for a business like the Harvard Cooperative Society?
2. How would the decision support system of a business like the Harvard Cooperative Society differ from that of a major corporation?
3. Briefly outline the components of the Harvard Cooperative Society's decision support system.

CHAPTER 3
THE MARKETING RESEARCH PROCESS

After studying this chapter, you should be able to

1. Understand the role marketing research plays in making decisions
2. Classify marketing research as either exploratory research, descriptive research, or causal research
3. List the major stages of the marketing research process and the steps within each
4. Understand the concepts of theory and hypothesis and the critical role they play in research
5. Know the difference between a research project and a research program

Chapter Vignette: Changing for Wired Students

It has been said that today's students are wired differently than their predecessors. Well, in today's high-tech world, students don't even need a wire to be different.[1] The changing educational technologies and environment mean today's students enjoy many more choices than did their parents. Universities offer new degree programs in varied and specific fields including areas like sports marketing and gaming management, and graduate degrees can be obtained without ever physically stepping foot on an actual university campus. Options for nontraditional students who have difficulty attending day classes or devoting years of study to obtaining a degree have grown exponentially. The University of Phoenix, Strayer University, and Nova Southeast typify institutions that specifically cater to those seeking a nontraditional degree program. These competitive pressures have led even the most traditional universities to rethink the traditional "sage on the stage" approach and conventional academic calendars.

Students pursue their MBA either traditionally, in weekend-only programs, at night school, online, or in some combination. Over a quarter of a million U.S. students alone attend MBA classes of one form or another at any given time. In urban areas, such as the Dallas-Fort Worth, Texas area, there are sometimes a dozen or more institutions offering an MBA. It is clear that the market for the MBA degree is particularly competitive and the fact is that those universities that offer a market-oriented program are most attractive to students. Marketing research can help accomplish this by addressing questions such as the following:

- How do consumers trade off convenience with quality perceptions?
- Will offering courses online expand the pool of MBA program applicants?
- Who are the key sources of competition?

- When is the best time to offer classes? Should schools offer a weekend program?
- Where is the best place to hold classes? Should classes be offered in multiple locations? Should a program be offered overseas?
- How are nontraditional vis-à-vis traditional MBA programs viewed in terms of value, quality, and prestige?
- Is demand sufficient? That is, are there enough potential students to make this financially feasible?
- How can a particular MBA program be differentiated from competing schools?
- Can a business school better accomplish the mission of the university with an online MBA program?

The competitive MBA market typifies the landscape of many marketing firms. Clearly, universities could benefit from marketing research addressing some of these key questions. Each university maintains its own academic standard while still trying to attract enough students to make its MBA program feasible. The competitive landscape is filled with both potential opportunities and potential problems. Decisions made by university faculty and administrators will determine how successfully each school deals with the changing marketplace.

Introduction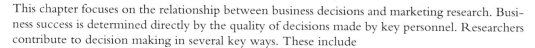

This chapter focuses on the relationship between business decisions and marketing research. Business success is determined directly by the quality of decisions made by key personnel. Researchers contribute to decision making in several key ways. These include

1. Helping to better define the current situation
2. Defining the firm—determining how consumers, competitors, and employees view the firm
3. Providing ideas for product improvements or possible new product development
4. Testing ideas that will assist in implementing the marketing mix strategy for the firm
5. Examining how correct a certain marketing theory is in a given situation

The chapter introduces the types of research that allow researchers to provide input to key decision makers. Product design is also discussed because effective design depends on marketing research. Last but not least, the chapter discusses stages in the marketing research process.

Decision Making and Marketing Research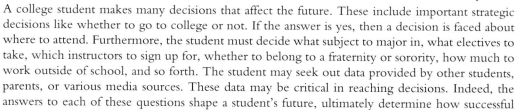

A college student makes many decisions that affect the future. These include important strategic decisions like whether to go to college or not. If the answer is yes, then a decision is faced about where to attend. Furthermore, the student must decide what subject to major in, what electives to take, which instructors to sign up for, whether to belong to a fraternity or sorority, how much to work outside of school, and so forth. The student may seek out data provided by other students, parents, or various media sources. These data may be critical in reaching decisions. Indeed, the answers to each of these questions shape a student's future, ultimately determine how successful he or she will be, and shape the way he or she is viewed by others.

Likewise, businesses face decisions that shape the future of the organization, its employees, and its customers. In each case, the decisions are brought about as the firm either seeks to capitalize on some opportunity or to lessen any potential negative impacts related to some market problem. Formally defined, **decision making** is the process of developing and deciding among alternative ways of resolving a problem or choosing from among alternative opportunities. A decision maker must recognize the nature of the problem or opportunity, identify how much information is currently available and how reliable it is, and determine what information is needed to better deal with the situation.

Every decision-making situation can be classified based on whether it best represents a problem or an opportunity and on whether it represents a situation characterized by complete certainty or absolute ambiguity. A **market opportunity** is a situation that makes some potential competitive advantage possible. Thus, the discovery of some underserved market segment presents such an opportunity. For example, eBay capitalized on the opportunity presented by technological advances to do much the same thing that is done at a garage sale but on a very, very large scale. A **market problem** is a business situation that makes some significant negative consequence more likely. The situation is due to some force acting in or on the firm's market.

decision making

The process of developing and deciding among alternative ways of resolving a problem or choosing from among alternative opportunities.

market opportunity

A situation that makes some potential competitive advantage possible.

market problem

A situation that makes some significant negative consequence more likely.

Now that you've been through the Cengage Zikmund and Babin Web survey (which you responded to in Chapter 1 and which you will view results for later), you can use it to help better learn course concepts. In later chapters, you'll analyze actual data to address key research questions and hypotheses. In this chapter, you will learn the basic research process which is composed of six stages. List each stage in the basic research process. Try to describe activities that went on or are going on or will go on based on this survey project that correspond to each of the six stages. Use Exhibits 3.5 and 3.6 to help with this task. Also, provide a list of deliverables that you will be able to produce for a client aiming at better understanding the college student market. Finally, comment on how well you believe the sample that will be obtained (marketing research students using this book all around North America and a few from other parts of the world will be responding to the survey).

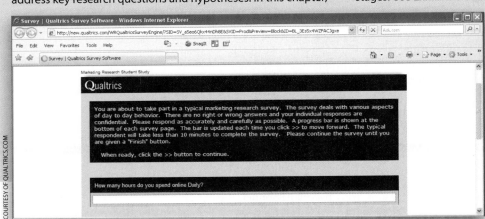

COURTESY OF QUALTRICS.COM

© GEORGE DOYLE

An impending natural disaster can present a problem for many firms as they face potential loss of property and personnel and the possibility that their operations, and therefore their revenue, will be interrupted. Problems are usually not as obvious as they may seem. In fact, they usually are not easily observable. Instead, problems are inferred from **symptoms**, which are observable cues that serve as a signal of a problem because they are caused by that problem. A drop in market share is generally only a symptom of a market problem and not the problem itself. Research may help identify what is causing this symptom so that decision makers can actually attack the problem, not just the symptom. Patients don't usually go to the doctor and point out their problem (like an ulcer). Instead, they point out symptoms (upset stomach). Similarly, decision makers usually hear about symptoms and often need help from research to identify and attack problems. Whether facing an opportunity or a problem, businesses need quality information to deal effectively with these situations. Decision situations are also characterized by how much certainty or ambiguity exists.

symptoms

Observable cues that serve as a signal of a problem because they are caused by that problem.

Can you identify symptoms that may indicate problems for these businesses? What market problems might they signify?

© SUSAN VAN ETTEN

Certainty

Complete certainty means that the decision maker has all information needed to make an optimal decision. This includes the exact nature of the marketing problem or opportunity. For example, an advertising agency may need to know the demographic characteristics of subscribers to magazines in which it may place a client's advertisements. The agency knows exactly what information it needs and where to find the information. If a manager is completely certain about both the problem or opportunity and future outcomes, then research may not be needed at all. However, perfect certainty, especially about the future, is rare.

Uncertainty means that the manager grasps the general nature of desired objectives, but the information about alternatives is incomplete. Predictions about forces that shape future events are educated guesses. Under conditions of uncertainty, effective managers recognize that spending additional time to gather data that clarify the nature of a decision is needed. For instance, a university may understand that there is an objective of increasing the number of MBA students, but it may not know whether an online, weekend, or off-site MBA program is the best way to accomplish the objective. Marketing decisions generally involve uncertainty, particularly when a company is seeking different opportunities.

Ambiguity

Ambiguity means that the nature of the problem itself is unclear. Objectives are vague and decision alternatives are difficult to define. This is by far the most difficult decision situation, but perhaps the most common.

Marketing managers face a variety of problems and decisions. Complete certainty and predictable future outcomes may make marketing research a waste of time. However, under conditions of uncertainty or ambiguity, marketing research becomes more attractive to the decision makers. Decisions also vary in terms of importance, meaning that some may have great impact on the welfare of the firm and others may have negligible impact. The more important, ambiguous, or uncertain a situation is, the more likely it is that additional time must be spent on marketing research.

■ CLASSIFYING DECISION SITUATIONS

Exhibit 3.1 depicts decision situations characterized by the nature of the decision and the degree of ambiguity.[2] Under problem-focused decision making and conditions of high ambiguity, symptoms may not clearly point to some problem. Indeed, they may be quite vague or subtle, indicating only

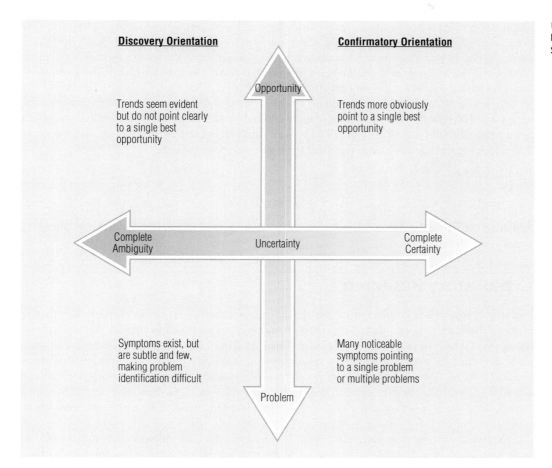

EXHIBIT 3.1
Describing Decision-Making Situations

small deviations from normal conditions. For instance, a fast-food restaurant may be experiencing small changes in the sales of its individual products, but no change in overall sales. Such a symptom may not easily point to a problem situation such as a change in consumer tastes. As ambiguity is lessened, the symptoms are clearer and are better indicators of a problem. A large and sudden drop in overall sales may suggest the problem that the restaurant's menu does not fare well compared to competitors' menus. Thus, a menu change may be in order.

Similarly, in opportunity-oriented research, ambiguity is characterized by marketplace and environmental trends that do not suggest a clear direction. As the trends become larger and clearer, they are more diagnostic, meaning they point more clearly to a single opportunity.

Types of Marketing Research

Marketing research can reduce uncertainty. It also helps focus decision making. Sometimes marketing researchers know exactly what their marketing problems are and can design careful studies to test specific hypotheses. A university may face a problem with an out-of-date curriculum. Awareness of this problem could be based on input from employers, students, and alumni. The problem could even be contributing to low enrollment. How should the faculty and administration decide to address this problem? They may devise a careful test exploring which of three new curricula can be implemented to improve this perception. This type of research is problem-oriented and seems relatively unambiguous. The marketing research may culminate with researchers preparing a report suggesting the relative effect of each alternative curriculum on enrollment. The decision should follow relatively directly from the research.

In more ambiguous circumstances, management may be totally unaware of a marketing problem. Alternatively, the company may be scanning the environment for opportunities. For example, a small undergraduate university in a mid-sized Colorado town may consider adding an online MBA program. University administrators may have little idea as to how this would affect the image of their school among current students, employers, alumni, or faculty. They also may not know exactly what programs would be most desired by its current or potential customer bases. Some preliminary research may be necessary to gain insights into the nature of such a situation. Without it, the situation may remain too ambiguous to make more than a seat-of-the-pants decision. Marketing research is almost certainly needed.

Marketing research can be classified on the basis of either technique or purpose. Experiments, surveys, and observational studies are just a few common research techniques. Classifying research by its purpose shows how the nature of a decision situation influences the research methodology. The following section introduces the three types of marketing research:

1. Exploratory
2. Descriptive
3. Causal

Matching the particular decision situation with the right type of research is important in obtaining useful research results.

Exploratory Research

exploratory research

Conducted to clarify ambiguous situations or discover ideas that may be potential business opportunities.

Exploratory research is conducted to clarify ambiguous situations or discover ideas that may be potential business opportunities. Exploratory research is *not* intended to provide conclusive evidence from which to determine a particular course of action. In this sense, it is not an end unto itself. Researchers usually undertake exploratory research with the full expectation that more research will be needed to provide more conclusive evidence. Using exploratory research can sometimes also make the difference in determining the relevance of follow-up research. Rushing into detailed surveys before it is clear exactly what decisions need to be made can waste time, money, and effort by providing irrelevant information.

Exploratory research is particularly useful in new product development.[3] Sony and Honda have each been instrumental in developing robot technology.[4] Making a functional robot that

Cute, Funny, or Sexy? What Makes a Mascot Tick?

Has the Pillsbury Doughboy ever changed? How old should the Brawny (paper towel) man be? What should the M&Ms characters be named? Why is Aflac synonymous with a duck? Does a country need a mascot? In truth, a lot of research goes into these kinds of questions beginning with exploratory research. For instance, focus groups involving female consumers revealed a considerable amount of intimate discussion about the Brawny man. Thus, it seemed that a sexy Brawny man would yield a better response than a humorous or intelligent Brawny man. When England developed an official mascot in conjunction with the World Cup, the desire to cultivate children's affinity led to more of a cute Sir George.

Mr. Peanut, the icon for Planter's Peanuts, has actually changed very little since his introduction in the 1920s. He looks good for his age. Again, exploratory research suggests generally positive comments about Mr. Peanut, so only minor changes

in the color scheme have been introduced. A few years ago, exploratory research led to some further tests of a Mr. Peanut in Bermuda shorts, but the tests proved overwhelmingly negative, sending Planters back to a more original peanut!

Similarly, simple exploratory research merely asked a few consumers for their reactions to the Mars M&M characters. Mars was interested in discovering names for the characters. They found that most consumers simply referred to them by their colors. This piece of information became useful in shaping future research and marketing strategy.

Sources: Voight, Joan, "Mascot Makeover: The Risky Business of Tampering with Brand Icons," *Adweek* (July 7, 2003), 20–26; Elliot, Stuart, "Updating a venerable character, or tarnishing a sterling reputation?" *The New York Times*, (March 19, 2004), C5; "A Mascot for All Seasons: Arise, Sir George," *License! Europe*, (January 31, 2006).

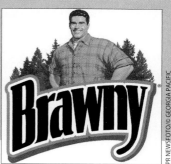

© GEORGE DOYLE & CIARAN GRIFFIN

PR NEWSFOTO/© GEORGIA PACIFIC

can move around, perform basic functions, carry out instructions, and even carry on a conversation isn't really a problem. What Sony and Honda have to research is what market opportunities may exist based on robot technology. Research can allow consumers to interact with robots as a form of exploratory research. The observational research suggest that consumers interact much more when the robot has human qualities, including the ability to walk on two legs. Researchers noticed that people will actually talk to the robot (which can understand basic oral commands) more when it has human qualities. In addition, consumers do seem entertained by a walking, talking, dancing robot. Thus, this has allowed each company to form more specific research questions focusing on the relative value of a robot as an entertainment device or as a security guard.

In our university example, it could be that exploratory research is needed to help identify concerns about nontraditional course delivery for business classes. This exploratory research should include open-ended interviews with faculty, students, and alumni. By doing so, specific hypotheses can be developed that test the relative attractiveness of alternative curricula to students and the effect of online instruction on job satisfaction and on alumni quality perceptions.[5] These hypotheses may be tested by either or both of the remaining two research types. The Research Snapshot above describes how exploratory research helps companies understand what a mascot like the Aflac duck or a pair of M&Ms can do for their performance.

Descriptive Research

Descriptive research, as the name implies, describes characteristics of objects, people, groups, organizations, or environments. Put more simply, descriptive research tries to "paint a picture" of a given situation. Marketing managers frequently need to determine who purchases a product, portray the size of the market, identify competitors' actions, and so on. Descriptive research addresses *who, what, when, where, why,* and *how* questions.

Descriptive research often helps describe market segments. For example, marketing researchers used simple descriptive surveys to describe consumers who are heavy consumers (buy a lot) of organic food products. The resulting report showed that these consumers tend to live in coastal cities with populations over 500,000, with the majority residing on the West Coast. The most frequent buyers of organic foods are affluent men and women ages 45–54 (36 percent) and 18–34 (35 percent).[6] Interestingly, consumers who buy organic foods are not very brand-oriented—81 percent of them cannot name a single organic brand. Research such as this helps high-quality supermarkets such as Whole Foods make location decisions. Over half of Whole Foods' food products are organic.

descriptive research

Describes characteristics of objects, people, groups, organizations, or environments; tries to "paint a picture" of a given situation.

The Squeaky Wheel Gets ...

Marketing problems are often people problems. Disgruntled marketing employees can lack creativity and lose the motivation that drives a strong work ethic. What appears to be a marketing problem can reallly be an internal people problem. With this in mind, what kind of things do coworkers do that irritate other coworkers? Several descriptive research studies address this by surveying employees and having them rate potentially problematic behaviors based on how annoying they actually are. Perhaps the resulting list isn't surprising, but some of the most problematic coworker habits and practices include the following.

- Slacking—the perception that a coworker is simply not pulling his or her share of the work is one of the most frequently mentioned annoying behaviors.
- Abusing the printer or copier—printing things unnecessarily, wasting paper, occupying the printer or copier or both with personal documents and slowing down the work.
  - Leaving used tea bags in the office sink.
  - Currying favor with the boss.

- Constantly eating and leaving behind crumbs and warming things in the microwave that leave behind strong odors (i.e., pickled cabbage, fish, popcorn, etc.)
- Over air-conditioning the office making it cold as a meat locker.
- Being fortunate enough to have a window and then keeping the shade closed all day.
- Coming in late but leaving on time.
- Noisiness—squeaky chairs, loud laughter, loud phone calls, annoying body noises.

The question becomes how these annoying habits should be dealt with. Should employees confront each other or should management create policies that restrict all possible annoying behavior? Is that possible? Maybe this calls for more research.

Sources: "What Your Workers Find Most Annoying," *Legal Alert for Supervisors*, 3, no. 64 (2008) 3; Piccolo, C. "Irritating Coworkers," *Medhunters.com*, (2008), http://www.medhunters.com/articles/irritatingCoworkers.html, accessed July 20, 2008; "Xerox Survey Reveals Environmental Pet Peeves Among Office Workers," *Graphic Arts Online* (April 17, 2008), www.graphicartsonline.com, accessed June 18, 2008; Nudd, T., "Pet Peeves," *Adweek*, 46 (September 26, 2005), 33.

Similarly, the university considering the addition of an online MBA program might benefit from descriptive research profiling the market and the potential customers. Online customers are not identical to the traditional MBA student. They tend to be older than the average 24-year-old traditional student, instead averaging about 30 years of age. Also, they tend to live in rural communities, be more introverted, and expect a higher workload than traditional students. Another key statistic is that the dropout rate for online students is significantly higher than for traditional MBA students. Nearly 14 percent of online students drop before completing a course as compared to 7.2 percent for traditional in-class students. For this and other reasons, online students are much more costly to serve.[7] What makes a coworker irritating? The Research Snapshot above describes this phenomenon using descriptive research results.

Accuracy is critically important in descriptive research. If a descriptive study misestimates a university's demand for its MBA offering by even a few students, it can mean the difference between the program sustaining itself or being a drain on already scarce resources. For instance, if a cohort group of twenty-five students is predicted, but only fifteen students actually sign up, the program will likely not generate enough revenue to sustain itself. Therefore, it is easy to see that descriptive research forecasting sales revenue and costs or describing consumer attitudes, satisfaction, and commitment must be accurate or decision making will suffer.

Descriptive research about consumers who buy organic food has paid off for the Whole Foods chain of stores.

Unlike exploratory research, descriptive studies are conducted with a considerable understanding of the situation being studied. This understanding, which may have been developed in part from exploratory research, directs the study toward specific issues. Later, we will discuss the role of research questions and hypotheses. These statements help greatly in designing and implementing a descriptive study. Without these, the researcher would have little or no idea of what questions to ask.

Survey research typifies a descriptive study. Many surveys try to answer questions such as "Why are brand A's sales lower than brand B's sales?" In other words, a **diagnostic analysis** seeks to diagnose reasons for market outcomes and focuses specifically on the beliefs and feelings consumers have about and toward competing products. A research study trying to diagnose slumping French wine sales might ask consumers their beliefs about the taste of French, Australian, and American wines. The results might indicate a deficiency in taste, suggesting that consumers do not believe French wines taste as fruity as do the others. Descriptive research can sometimes provide an explanation by diagnosing differences among competitors, but descriptive research does not provide direct evidence of causality.

diagnostic analysis

Seeks to diagnose reasons for market outcomes and focuses specifically on the beliefs and feelings consumers have about and toward competing products.

Causal Research

If a decision maker knows what causes important outcomes like sales and employee satisfaction, then he or she can shape firm decisions in a positive way. Causal inferences are very powerful because they lead to greater control. **Causal research** allows causal inferences to be made. That is, causal research seeks to identify cause-and-effect relationships to show that one event actually makes another happen. Rain causes grass to get wet. Rain is the cause and wet grass is the effect.

Exploratory and/or descriptive research usually precedes causal research. In causal studies, researchers typically have a good understanding of the phenomena being studied. Because of this, the research can make an educated prediction about the cause and effect relationships that will be tested. Although greater knowledge of the situation is a good thing, it doesn't come without a price. Causal research designs can take a long time to implement. Also, they often involve intricate designs that can be very expensive. Thus, even though managers may often want the assurance that causal inferences can bring, they are not always willing to spend the time and money it takes to get them.

causal research

Allows causal inferences to be made; seeks to identify cause-and-effect relationships.

■ CAUSALITY

Ideally, managers want to know how a change in one event (say, using a new product logo) will change another event of interest, like sales. Causal research attempts to establish that when we do one thing, another thing will follow. A **causal inference** is just such a conclusion. While we use the term "cause" all the time in everyday language, scientifically establishing something as a cause is not so easy and even researchers sometimes confuse causality with correlation. A causal inference can only be supported when very specific causal evidence exists. Three critical pieces of causal evidence are

causal inference

A conclusion that when one thing happens, another specific thing will follow.

1. Temporal Sequence
2. Concomitant Variance
3. Nonspurious Association

Temporal Sequence

Temporal sequence deals with the time order of events. In other words, having an *appropriate causal order of events,* or temporal sequence, is one criterion for causality. The cause must occur before the effect. It would be difficult for a restaurant manager to blame a decrease in sales on a new chef if the drop in sales occurred before the new chef arrived. If advertising causes sales, the advertising must appear before the change in sales.

temporal sequence

One of three criteria for causality; deals with the time order of events—the cause must occur before the effect.

Concomitant Variation

Concomitant variation occurs when two events "covary," meaning they vary systematically. In causal terms, concomitant variation means that when a change in the cause occurs, a change in the outcome also is observed. Correlation, which we discuss in a later chapter, is often used to represent concomitant variation. Causality cannot possibly exist when there is no systematic variation between the variables. For example, if a retail store never changes its employees' vacation policy,

concomitant variation

One of three criteria for causality; occurs when two events "covary," meaning they vary systematically.

then the vacation policy cannot possibly be responsible for a change in customer satisfaction. There is no correlation between the two events. On the other hand, if two events vary together, one event may be causing the other. If a university increases its number of online MBA course offerings and experiences a decrease in enrollment in its traditional in-class MBA offerings, the online course offerings may be causing the decrease. But, the systematic variation alone doesn't guarantee it.

Nonspurious Association

nonspurious association

One of three criteria for causality; means any covariation between a cause and an effect is true and not simply due to some other variable.

Nonspurious association means any covariation between a cause and an effect is indeed due to the cause and not simply due to some other variable. A spurious association is one that is not true. Often, a causal inference cannot be made even though the other two conditions exist because both the cause and effect have some common cause; that is, both may be influenced by a third variable. For instance, a city worker notices an alarming trend. On days when a large number of ice cream cones are sold at Virginia Beach, more people drown. So, when ice cream sales go up, so does drowning. Should the city decide to ban ice cream? This would be silly because the concomitant variation observed between ice cream consumption and drowning is spurious. On days when the beach is particularly crowded, more ice cream is sold and more people drown. So, the number of people at the beach, being associated with both, may cause both. Exhibit 3.2 illustrates the concept of spurious association.

Establishing evidence of nonspuriousness can be difficult. If a researcher finds a third variable that is related to both the cause and effect, causing a significant drop in the correlation between the cause and effect, then a causal inference becomes difficult to support. Although the researcher would like to rule out the possibility of any alternative causes, it is impossible to observe the effect of all variables on the correlation between the cause and effect. Therefore, the researcher must use theory to identify the most likely "third" variables that would relate significantly to both the cause and effect. The research must control for these variables in some way, as we will see in Chapter 11. In addition, the researcher should use theory to make sure that the cause-and-effect relationship truly makes sense.

In summary, causal research should do all of the following:

1. Establish the appropriate causal order or sequence of events
2. Measure the concomitant variation (relationship) between the presumed cause and the presumed effect
3. Examine the possibility of spuriousness by considering the presence of alternative plausible causal factors

EXHIBIT 3.2 Ice Cream is a Spurious Cause of Drowning

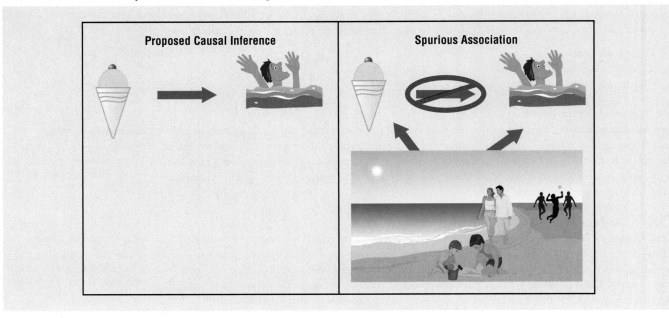

■ DEGREES OF CAUSALITY

In everyday language, we often use the word "cause" in an absolute sense. For example, a warning label used on cigarette packages claims "smoking causes cancer." Is this true in an absolute sense? **Absolute causality** means the cause is necessary and sufficient to bring about the effect. Thus, if we find only one smoker who does not eventually get cancer, the claim is false. Although this is a very strong inference, it is impractical to think that we can establish absolute causality in the behavioral sciences.

Why do we continue to do causal research then? Well, although managers may like to be able to draw absolute conclusions, they can often make very good decisions based on less powerful inferences. **Conditional causality** means that a cause is necessary but not sufficient to bring about an effect. This is a weaker causal inference. One way to think about conditional causality is that the cause can bring about the effect, but it cannot do so alone. If other conditions are right, the cause can bring about the effect. We know there are other medical factors that contribute to cancer. For instance, lifestyle and diet are also both plausible causes of cancer. Thus, if one smokes and has a diet and lifestyle that promote cancer, smoking could be a considered a conditional cause of cancer. However, it we can find someone who has contracted cancer and never smoked, the causal inference would be proven wrong.

Contributory causality may be the weakest form of causality, but it is still a useful concept. A cause need be neither necessary nor sufficient to bring about an effect. However, causal evidence can be established using the three types of evidence shown on the previous page. For any outcome, there may be multiple causes. So, an event can be a contributory cause of something so long as the introduction of the other possible causes does not eliminate the correlation between it and the effect. This will become clearer when we discuss ways to test relationships later in the text. Smoking then can be a contributory cause of cancer so long as the introduction of other possible causes does not cause both smoking and cancer.

absolute causality

Means the cause is necessary and sufficient to bring about the effect.

conditional causality

Means that a cause is necessary but not sufficient to bring about an effect.

contributory causality

Means that a cause need be neither necessary nor sufficient to bring about an effect.

■ EXPERIMENTS

Marketing *experiments* hold the greatest potential for establishing cause-and-effect relationships. An **experiment** is a carefully controlled study in which the researcher manipulates a proposed cause and observes any corresponding change in the proposed effect. An **experimental variable** represents the proposed cause and is controlled by the researcher who manipulates its value. **Manipulation** means that the researcher alters the level of the variable in specific increments. So, managers often want to make decisions about the price and distribution of a new product. In other words, both price and the type of retail outlet in which a product is placed are considered potential causes of sales. A study can be designed which manipulates both the price and distribution.

Suppose a company produces a new video game console called the Wee Station. They may manipulate price by offering it for $100 among some consumers and $300 among others. Retail distribution may be manipulated by selling the Wee Station at discount stores in some consumer markets and at specialty electronic stores in others. The retailer can examine whether price and distribution cause sales by comparing the sales results in each of the four conditions created. Exhibit 3.3 on the next page illustrates this study. We will say much more about manipulations and experimental designs in Chapters 11 and 12.

An experiment like the one described above may take place in a test-market. Test-marketing is a frequently used form of marketing experimentation. A **test-market** is an experiment that is conducted within actual market conditions. Anheuser-Busch test-marketed a "not-so-soft soft drink" named Chelsea. The two experimental variables manipulated were the alcohol level and degree of sweetness. Anheuser-Busch first introduced Chelsea to the test-market as a sweet drink with a slight alcoholic content—about 0.4 percent. A Virginia nurses' association and some religious groups strongly criticized the company and the new product. These critics suggested that Anheuser-Busch had introduced a product that might encourage children to become beer drinkers. They contended that Chelsea was packaged like beer and looked, foamed, and poured like it. Later, Anheuser-Busch reintroduced the product in another test market as a soft drink with only "a trace of alcohol" as a "natural alternative" to soft drinks, with not-so-sweet and stylish attributes. Similar problems occurred in the second experiment. Therefore, the reduction in alcohol did not cause a more favorable impression of Chelsea.

experiment

A carefully controlled study in which the researcher manipulates a proposed cause and observes any corresponding change in the proposed effect.

experimental variable

Represents the proposed cause which the researcher controls by manipulating its value

manipulation

Means that the researcher alters the level of the variable in specific increments.

test-market

An experiment that is conducted within actual market conditions.

EXHIBIT 3.3
Testing for Causes with an Experiment

	Wee Station Sales by Condition	
	High Price	**Low Price**
Specialty Distribution	Peoria, Illinois: Retail Price: $300 Retail Store: Best Buy	Des Moines, Iowa: Retail Price: $100 Retail Store: Best Buy
General Distribution	St. Louis, Missouri: Retail Price: $300 Retail Store: Big Cheap-Mart	Kansas City, Missouri: Retail Price: $100 Retail Store: Big Cheap-Mart

Assuming that Wee Station consumers are the same in each of these cities, the extent to which price and distribution cause sales can be examined by comparing the sales results in each of these 4 conditions.

Most basic scientific studies in marketing (for example, the development of consumer behavior theory) ultimately seek to identify cause-and-effect relationships. One often associates science with experiments. To predict a relationship between, say, price and perceived quality of a product, causal studies often create statistical experiments with controls that establish contrast groups.

Uncertainty Influences the Type of Research

The most appropriate type and the amount of research needed are determined in part by how much uncertainty surrounds the marketing situation motivating the research. Exhibit 3.4 contrasts the types of research and illustrates that exploratory research is conducted during the early stages of decision making. At this point, the decision situation is usually highly ambiguous and management is very uncertain about what actions should be taken. When management is aware of the problem but lacks some knowledge, descriptive research is usually conducted. Causal research requires sharply defined problems.

Each type of research also produces a different type of result. In many ways, exploratory research is the most productive since it should yield large numbers of ideas. It is discovery-oriented and as such, unstructured approaches can be very successful. Too much structure in this type of research may lead to more narrowly focused types of responses that could stifle creativity. Thus, although it is productive, its results usually need further testing and evaluation before they can be made actionable. At times, managers do take managerial action based only on exploratory

EXHIBIT 3.4 **Characteristics of Different Types of Marketing Research**

	Exploratory Research	**Descriptive Research**	**Causal Research**
Amount of Uncertainty Characterizing Decision Situation	Highly ambiguous	Partially defined	Clearly defined
Key Research Statement	Research question	Research question	Research hypothesis
When Conducted?	Early stage of decision making	Later stages of decision making	Later stages of decision making
Usual Research Approach	Unstructured	Structured	Highly structured
Examples	"Our sales are declining for no apparent reason" "What kinds of new products are fast-food customers interested in?"	"What kind of people patronize our stores compared to our primary competitor?" "What product features are most important to our customers?"	"Will consumers buy more products in a blue package?" "Which of two advertising campaigns will be more effective?"
Nature of Results	Discovery oriented, productive, but still speculative. Often in need of further research.	Can be confirmatory although more research is sometimes still needed. Results can be managerially actionable.	Confirmatory oriented. Fairly conclusive with managerially actionable results often obtained.

research results. Sometimes, management may not be able to or may not care to invest the time and resources needed to conduct further research. Decisions made based only on exploratory research can be more risky since exploratory research does not test ideas among a scientific sample.[8] For instance, a business school professor may ask a class of current MBA students for ideas about an online program. Although the students may provide many ideas that sound very good, even the best of them has not been tested on a sample of potential online MBA students.

Descriptive research is usually focused around one or more fairly specific research questions. It is usually much more structured, and for many common types of marketing research, it can yield managerially actionable results. For example, descriptive research is often used to profile a market segment both demographically and psychographically. Results like this can greatly assist firms in deciding when and where to offer their goods or services for sale.

Causal research is usually very tightly focused around a small number of research hypotheses. Experimental methods require tight control of research procedures. Thus, causal research is highly structured to produce specific results. Causal research results are often managerially actionable since they suggest that if management changes the value of a "cause," some desirable effect will come about. So, by changing a package's color, i.e., the cause, from orange to blue, higher sales occur.

Stages in the Research Process ◀

Marketing research, like other forms of scientific inquiry, involves a sequence of highly interrelated activities. The stages of the research process overlap continuously, and it is somewhat of an oversimplification to state that every research project has exactly the same ordered sequence of activities. Nevertheless, marketing research often follows a general pattern. The stages are

1. Defining the research objectives
2. Planning a research design
3. Planning a sample
4. Collecting the data
5. Analyzing the data
6. Formulating the conclusions and preparing the report

Exhibit 3.5 portrays these six stages as a cyclical or circular-flow process. The circular-flow concept is used because conclusions from research studies can generate new ideas and

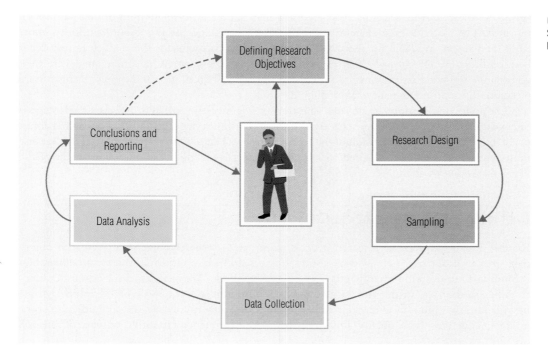

EXHIBIT 3.5
Stages of the Research Process

PHOTODISC/GETTY IMAGES

Research is sometimes directly actionable. The results may also suggest ideas for new studies.

forward linkage

Implies that the earlier stages of the research process influence the later stages.

backward linkage

Implies that later steps influence earlier stages of the research process.

research objectives

The goals to be achieved by conducting research.

deliverables

The term used often in consulting to describe research objectives to a research client.

knowledge that can lead to further investigation. Thus, there is a dashed connection between *conclusions and reporting* and *defining the research objectives*. Notice also, though, that management is in the center of the process. The research objectives cannot be properly defined without managerial input. After all, it is the manager who ultimately has to make the decision. It is also the manager who may ask for additional research once a report is given.

In practice, the stages overlap somewhat from a timing perspective. Later stages sometimes can be completed before earlier ones. The terms *forward linkage* and *backward linkage* reflect the interrelationships between stages. **Forward linkage** implies that the earlier stages influence the later stages. Thus, the research objectives outlined in the first stage affect the sample selection and the way data are collected. The sample selection question affects the wording of questionnaire items. For example, if the research concentrates on respondents with low educational levels, the questionnaire wording will be simpler than if the respondents were college graduates.

Backward linkage implies that later steps influence earlier stages of the research process. If it is known that the data will be collected via e-mail, then the sampling should include those with e-mail access. A very important example of backward linkage is the knowledge that the executives who will read the research report are looking for specific results. The professional researcher anticipates executives' needs for information throughout the planning process, particularly during the analysis and reporting.

Alternatives in the Research Process

The researcher must choose among a number of alternatives during each stage of the research process. The research process can be compared to a map. There is no single right or best path for all journeys. The road one takes depends on where one wants to go and the resources (money, time, labor, and so on) available for the trip. The map analogy is useful for the marketing researcher because there are several paths that can be followed at each stage. When there are severe time constraints, the quickest path may be most appropriate. When money and human resources are plentiful, the appropriate path may be quite different.

The following sections briefly describe the six stages of the research process. (Each stage is discussed in greater depth in later chapters.) Exhibit 3.6 shows the decisions that researchers must make in each stage. This discussion of the research process begins with research objectives, because most research projects are initiated to remedy managers' uncertainty about some aspect of the firm's marketing program.

Defining the Research Objectives

Exhibit 3.6 shows that the research process begins with **research objectives**. Research objectives are the goals to be achieved by conducting research. In consulting, the term **deliverables** is often used to describe the objectives to a research client. The genesis of the research objectives lies in the type of decision situation faced. The objectives may involve exploring some new product within a new market. Alternatively, they may involve testing the effect of some policy change on service quality. Different types of objectives lead to different types of research designs.

EXHIBIT 3.6 **Flowchart of the Marketing Research Process**

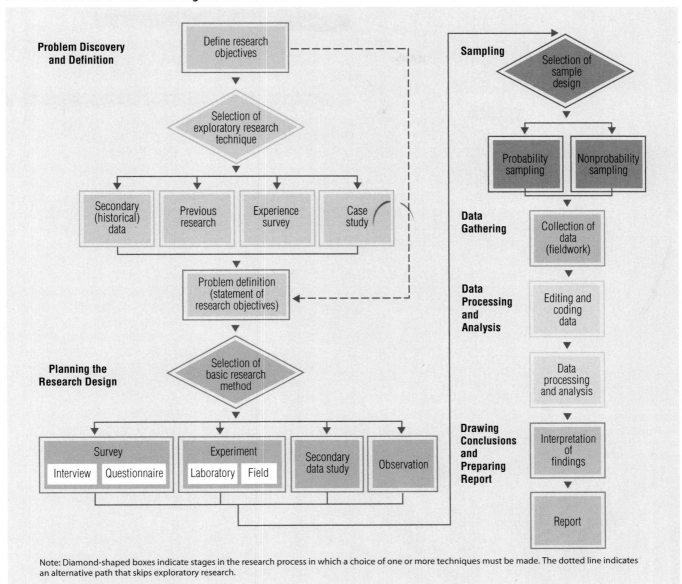

Note: Diamond-shaped boxes indicate stages in the research process in which a choice of one or more techniques must be made. The dotted line indicates an alternative path that skips exploratory research.

In applied or market research, the objectives cannot be listed until there is an understanding of the decision situation. This understanding must be shared between the actual decision maker and the lead researcher. We often describe this understanding as a problem statement. In general usage, the word *problem* suggests that something has gone wrong. This isn't always the case before research gets started. Actually, the research objective may be to simply clarify a situation, define an opportunity, or monitor and evaluate current operations. The research objectives cannot be developed until managers and researchers have agreed on the actual business "problem" that will be addressed by the research. Thus, they set out to "discover" this problem through a series of interviews and through a document called a research proposal.

It should be noted that this process is oriented more toward *discovery* than *confirmation*. Managers and researchers alike may not have a clear-cut understanding of the situation at the outset of the research process. Managers may only be able to list symptoms that could indicate a problem. Sales may be declining, but management may not know the exact nature of the problem. Thus, the problem statement often is made only in general terms; what is to be investigated is not yet specifically identified.

■ DEFINING THE MANAGERIAL DECISION SITUATION

In marketing research, the adage "a problem well defined is a problem half solved" is worth remembering. This adage emphasizes that an orderly definition of the research problem lends a sense of direction to the investigation. Careful attention to problem definition allows the researcher to set the proper research objectives. If the purpose of the research is clear, the chances of collecting necessary and relevant information and not collecting surplus information will be much greater.

Albert Einstein noted that "the formulation of a problem is often more essential than its solution."[9] This is good advice for marketing managers. Managers naturally concentrate on finding the right answer rather than asking the right question. They also want one solution quickly rather than having to spend time considering many possible solutions. Properly defining a problem can be more difficult than solving it. In marketing research, if data are collected before the nature of the marketing problem is carefully thought out, they probably will not allow useful results.

Marketing research must have clear objectives and definite designs. Unfortunately, little or no planning goes into the formulation of many research problems. Consider the case of the Ha-Pah-Shu-Tse brand of Indian fried bread mix (the name "Ha-Pah-Shu-Tse" comes from the Pawnee Indian word for red corn). The owner of the company, Mr. Ha-Pah-Shu-Tse, thought that his product, one of the few Native American food products available in the United States, was not selling because it was not widely advertised. He wanted a management consulting group to conduct some research concerning advertising themes. However, the management consultants pointed out to the Ha-Pah-Shu-Tse family that using the family name on the bread mix might be a foremost source of concern. They suggested that consumer behavior research investigating the brand image might be a better initial starting point rather than advertising copy research. Family management agreed.

Defining the decision situation must precede the research objectives. Frequently the marketing researcher will not be involved until line management has discovered that some information about a particular aspect of the marketing mix is needed. Even at this point the exact nature of the situation may be poorly defined. Once a problem area has been discovered, the marketing researcher and management together can begin the process of precisely defining it.

Frequently, research is conducted without a clear definition of the research's objectives. Too many researchers forget that the best place to begin a research project is at the end. Knowing what is to be accomplished determines the research process. An error or omission in problem objectives is likely to be a costly mistake that cannot be corrected in later stages of the process. Chapter 5 discusses problem objectives in greater detail.

The library contains a wealth of information. Studies forming a literature review can be found in the library.

© DIGITAL VISION/GETTY IMAGES

■ EXPLORATORY RESEARCH

Exploratory research can be used to help identify the decisions that need to be made. The preliminary activities undertaken can yield results that place the situation into a more easily researched context. Exploratory research can progressively narrow the scope of the research topic and help transform ambiguous problems into well-defined ones that yield specific research objectives. By investigating any existing studies on the subject, talking with knowledgeable individuals, and informally investigating the situation, the researcher can progressively sharpen the concepts. After such exploration, the researcher should know exactly which data to collect during the formal phases of the project and how to conduct the project. Exhibit 3.6 indicates that researchers must decide whether to use one or more exploratory research techniques or bypass this stage altogether.

The marketing researcher can employ techniques from four basic categories to obtain insights and gain a clearer idea of the problem: previous research, pilot studies, case studies, and experience surveys. These are discussed in detail in Chapter 6. This section will briefly discuss previous research and focus group interviews, the most popular type of pilot study.

■ PREVIOUS RESEARCH

As a general rule, researchers should first investigate previous research to see whether or not others may have addressed the same research problems previously. Previous research reports should be searched within the company's archives. In addition, some firms specialize in providing various types of research reports, such as economic forecasts. The *Census of Population* and the *Survey of Current Business* are each examples of previous research conducted by an outside source.

Literature Review

Previous research may also exist in the public domain. A **literature review** is a directed search of published works, including periodicals and books, that discusses theory and presents empirical results that are relevant to the topic at hand. A literature survey is common in applied market research studies but it is a fundamental requirement of a basic (i.e., marketing) research report. Literature reviews are conducted using traditional Internet and library research tools. Modern electronic search engines available in most university libraries have made literature reviews simpler and faster.

Suppose a real estate developer is interested in developing a piece of commercial property. In particular, the site has been identified as a location for a lifestyle center containing places for people to shop, be entertained, dine, work and live—all in one location. Success will depend on attracting people to this place and creating the right feel. The decision to move forward with the project involves many dimensions including the location, tenant mix, the physical design or atmosphere of the place, which is affected by things like color, scents, and architecture. Obviously, prudence calls for more than a cursory study of the feasibility of this project and the implications for different types of designs. Before launching an exhaustive study, the researcher can first look through research journals and find hundreds of studies that address the different decision dimensions.[10] This may, for example, give some idea on what type of architecture will work best to create the right atmosphere and enable a smaller set of possibilities to be studied further.

A business endeavor this big is best done with a lot of research. Luckily, there is a lot of previous research in the form of previous literature and reports to provide a start.

literature review

A directed search of published works, including periodicals and books, that discusses theory and presents empirical results that are relevant to the topic at hand.

Pilot Studies

Almost all consumers take a test drive before buying a car. A pilot study serves a similar purpose for the researcher. A **pilot study** is a small-scale research project that collects data from respondents similar to those that will be used in the full study. It can serve as a guide for a larger study or examine specific aspects of the research to see if the selected procedures will actually work as intended. Pilot studies are critical in refining measures and reducing the risk that the full study will be fatally flawed. This is particularly true for experimental research, which depends critically on valid manipulations of experimental variables.[11] Pilot studies also often are useful in fine-tuning research objectives. Pilot studies are sometimes referred to as pretests. A **pretest** is a very descriptive term indicating a small-scale study in which the results are only preliminary and intended only to assist in design of a subsequent study.

Focus group interviews are sometimes used as a pilot study. A **focus group** interview brings together six to twelve people in a loosely structured format. The technique is based on the assumption that individuals are more willing to talk about things when they are able to do so within a group discussion format. Focus group respondents sometimes feed on each other's comments to develop ideas that would be difficult to express in a different interview format. Focus groups are discussed much more in Chapter 6.

pilot study

A small-scale research project that collects data from respondents similar to those to be used in the full study.

pretest

A small-scale study in which the results are only preliminary and intended only to assist in design of a subsequent study.

focus group

A small group discussion about some research topic led by a moderator who guides discussion among the participants.

For example, suppose a consultant is hired by Carrefour to research the way consumers react to sales promotions. Carrefour is second in size only to Wal-Mart, operating nearly 11,000 stores in twenty-nine countries (www.carrefour.fr). Carrefour began in France over forty-five years ago and pioneered the discount hypermarket format. More specifically, the researcher may be asked to help management decide whether or not the size of promotions should vary with national culture. In other words, the basic research question is whether or not culture influences consumer perceptions of sales promotions.[12] A pretest may be needed to examine whether or not differences in currency might interfere with these perceptions, or whether or not the different terms that refer to promotions and discounts can be translated into the languages of each culture. For example, is a discount expressed in Korean won interpreted the same way as a discount expressed in euros? Using mid 2008 exchange rates, each euro equals about $1.60, whereas a single dollar is worth about 1,020 won.[13] As a result, a €1 (1 Euro) discount means a savings of over 1,600 won!

Exploratory research need not always follow a structured design. Because the purpose of exploratory research is to gain insights and discover new ideas, researchers may use considerable creativity and flexibility. Some companies perform exploratory research routinely as part of environmental scanning. If the conclusions made during this stage suggest marketing opportunities, the researcher is in a position to begin planning a formal, quantitative research project.

■ STATING RESEARCH OBJECTIVES

After identifying and clarifying the problem, with or without exploratory research, the researcher must formally state the research objectives. This statement delineates the type of research that is needed and what intelligence may result that would allow the decision maker to make informed choices. The statement of research objectives culminates the process of clarifying the managerial decision into something actionable.

A written decision statement expresses the business situation to the researcher. The research objectives try to directly address the decision statement or statements, as the case may be. As such, the research objectives represent a contract of sorts that commits the researcher to producing the needed research. This is why they are expressed as deliverables in applied market research. Research objectives drive the rest of the research process. Indeed, before proceeding, the researcher and managers must agree that the objectives are appropriate and will produce relevant information.

■ WHAT IS A THEORY?

theory

A formal, logical explanation of some events that includes predictions of how things relate to one another.

Ultimately, theory plays a role in determining the appropriate research objectives. A **theory** is a formal, logical explanation of some events that includes descriptions of how things relate to one another. A theory is built through a process of reviewing previous findings of similar studies, simple logical deduction, and knowledge of applicable theoretical areas. For example, if a web designer is trying to decide what color the background of the page should be, the researcher may first consult previous studies examining the effects of color on package design and retail store design. He or she may also find theories that deal with the wavelength of different colors or theories that explain retail atmospherics. This may lead to specific predictions that predict blue as a good background color.[14]

While it may seem that theory is only relevant to academic or basic marketing research, theory plays a role in understanding practical research as well. Before setting research objectives, the researcher must be able to describe the business situation in some coherent way. Without this type of explanation, the researcher would have little idea of where to start. Ultimately, the logical explanation helps the researcher know what variables need to be included in the study and how they may relate to one another. The Research Snapshot on the next page illustrates how theory and practice come together in marketing research.

■ WHAT IS A HYPOTHESIS?

hypothesis

A formal statement explaining some outcome.

A **hypothesis** is a formal statement explaining some outcome. Hypotheses (pl.) must be testable. In other words, when one states a hypothesis, it should be written as a proposition. For example,

Nothing So Practical As Theory?
Theory and marketing practice do come together. First, students learn theory in their formal education. Business professors consider it good practice to blend theory and practice in their teaching. Business professionals use these theories to help shape their thinking about different business situations.

Neurology, psychobiology, anthropology, economics, and social psychology all offer relevant theories that can help explain marketing problems. Recently, structuration theory has been proposed as a way of explaining marketing communication outcomes. The theory suggests that more focus should be placed on the communication exchanges between buyers and sellers and that if one can understand the goals of the buyer and seller involved in a communication interaction, then the outcome of the interaction can be predicted. Studies using theory of this type may assist electronic communication design in better placements of pop-up ads and hyperlinks and can also assist face-to-face sales exchanges in better predicting when a consumer is actually ready to buy.

Sources: Green, Paul E., "Theory, Practice Both Have Key MR Roles," *Marketing News*, 38 (September 15, 2004), 40–44; Schultz, Don, "Accepted Industry Truths Not Always Acceptable," *Marketing News*, 39 (October 15, 2005), 6; Stewart, D. T., "Traditional Ad Research Overlooks Interactions," *Marketing News*, 39 (November 15, 2005), 26–29.

using our opening vignette as an example, the researcher may use theoretical reasoning to develop the following hypothesis:

H1: The more hours per week a prospective MBA student works, the more favorable the attitude toward online MBA class offerings.

In its simplest form, a hypothesis is a guess. A sales manager may hypothesize that the salespeople who are highest in product knowledge will be the most productive. An advertising manager may hypothesize that if consumers' attitudes toward a product change in a positive direction, there will be an increase in consumption of the product.

We often apply statistics to data to empirically test hypotheses. **Empirical testing** means that something has been examined against reality using data. When the data are consistent with a hypothesis, we say the hypothesis is *supported*. When the data are inconsistent with a hypothesis, we say the hypothesis is *not supported*. We are often tempted to say that we prove a hypothesis when the data conform to the prediction; this isn't really true. Because our result is based on statistics, there is always the possibility that our conclusion is wrong. Now, at times we can be very, very confident in our conclusion, but from an absolute perspective, statistics cannot prove a hypothesis is true.

Exhibit 3.7 illustrates how decision statements are linked to research objectives, which are linked to research hypotheses. Although the first two objectives each have one hypothesis, notice that the third has two. In reality, most research projects will involve more than one research objective, and each of these may often involve more than one hypothesis. Think about how you might go about trying to test the hypotheses listed in Exhibit 3.7.

empirical testing
Means that something has been examined against reality using data.

EXHIBIT 3.7
Example Decision Statements, Research Objectives, and Research Hypotheses

Decision Statement	Research Objectives	Hypotheses
What should be the retail price for product X?	Forecast sales for product X at three different prices.	Sales will be higher at $5.00 than at $4.00 or at $6.99.
In what ways can we improve our service quality?	Identify the top factors that contribute to customers' perceptions.	Cleanliness is related positively to customers' service quality service perceptions.
		Crowding is related negatively to customers' service quality perceptions.
Should we invest in a training program to reduce employee role conflict among our employees?	Determine how much role conflict influences employee job satisfaction.	Role conflict is related positively to job satisfaction.

Planning the Research Design

research design

A master plan that specifies the methods and procedures for collecting and analyzing the needed information.

After the researcher has formulated the research problem, he or she must develop the research design as part of the research design stage. A **research design** is a master plan that specifies the methods and procedures for collecting and analyzing the needed information. A research design provides a framework or plan of action for the research. Objectives of the study determined during the early stages of research are included in the design to ensure that the information collected is appropriate for solving the problem. The researcher also must determine the sources of information, the design technique (survey or experiment, for example), the sampling methodology, and the schedule and cost of the research.

■ SELECTION OF THE BASIC RESEARCH METHOD

Here again, the researcher must make a decision. Exhibit 3.6 shows four basic design techniques for descriptive and causal research: surveys, experiments, secondary data, and observation. The objectives of the study, the available data sources, the urgency of the decision, and the cost of obtaining the data will determine which method should be chosen. The managerial aspects of selecting the research design will be considered later.

survey

A research technique in which a sample is interviewed in some form or the behavior of respondents is observed and described in some way.

The most common method of generating primary data is the survey. Most people have seen the results of political surveys by Gallup or Harris Online, and some have been respondents (members of a sample who supply answers) to marketing research questionnaires. A **survey** is a research technique in which a sample is interviewed in some form or the behavior of respondents is observed and described in some way. The term *surveyor* is most often reserved for civil engineers who describe some piece of property using a transit. Similarly, marketing researchers describe some market segment using a questionnaire. The task of writing a list of questions and designing the format of the printed or written questionnaire is an essential aspect of the development of a survey research design.

Research investigators may choose to contact respondents by telephone or mail, on the Internet, or in person. An advertiser spending nearly $3 million for thirty seconds of commercial time during the Super Bowl may telephone people to quickly gather information concerning their responses to the advertising. A forklift truck manufacturer trying to determine a cause for low sales in the wholesale grocery industry might choose a mail questionnaire because the appropriate executives are hard to reach by telephone. A manufacturer of a birth control device for men might determine the need for a versatile survey method wherein an interviewer can ask a variety of personal questions in a flexible format. While personal interviews are expensive, they are valuable because investigators can use visual aids and supplement the interviews with observations. Each of these survey methods has advantages and disadvantages. A researcher's task is to find the most appropriate way to collect the needed information.

The objective of many research projects is merely to record what can be observed—for example, the number of automobiles that pass by a proposed site for a gas station. This can be mechanically recorded or observed by humans. Research personnel known as mystery shoppers may act as customers to observe actions of sales personnel or do comparative shopping to learn prices at competing outlets. A mystery shopper is paid to pretend to be a customer and gather data about the way employees behave and the way they are treated in general. How often are store policies followed? How often are they treated courteously? Mystery shoppers can be valuable sources for observational data.

The main advantage of the observation technique is that it records behavior without relying on reports from respondents. Observational data are often collected unobtrusively and passively without a respondent's direct participation. For instance, the ACNielsen Company uses a "people meter" attached to television sets to record the programs being watched by each household member. This eliminates the possible bias of respondents stating that they watched the president's State of the Union address rather than a situation comedy on another station.

Observation is more complex than mere "nose counting," and the task is more difficult than the inexperienced researcher would imagine. Several things of interest, such as attitudes, opinions, motivations, and other intangible states of mind, simply cannot be observed.

■ THE "BEST" RESEARCH DESIGN

It is argued that there is no single best research design. As such, the researcher often has several alternatives that can accomplish the stated research objectives. Consider the researcher who must forecast sales for the upcoming year. Some commonly used forecasting methods are surveying executive opinion, collecting sales force composite opinions, surveying user expectations, projecting trends, and analyzing market factors. Any one of these may yield a reliable forecast.

The ability to select the most appropriate research design develops with experience. Inexperienced researchers often jump to the conclusion that a survey methodology is usually the best design because they are most comfortable with this method. When Chicago's Museum of Science and Industry wanted to determine the relative popularity of its exhibits, it could have conducted a survey. Instead, a creative researcher familiar with other research designs suggested a far less expensive alternative: an unobtrusive observation technique. The researcher suggested that the museum merely keep track of the frequency with which the floor tiles in front of the various exhibits had to be replaced, indicating where the heaviest traffic occurred. When this was done, the museum found that the chick-hatching exhibit was the most popular. This method provided the same results as a survey but at a much lower cost.

> **TO THE POINT**
>
> *You cannot put the same shoe on every foot.*
>
> —Publius Syrus

Sampling

Although the sampling plan is outlined in the research design, the sampling stage is a distinct phase of the research process. For convenience, however, we will treat the sample planning and the actual sample generation processes together in this section.

If you take your first bite of a steak and conclude that the entire steak needs salt to taste good, you have just conducted a sample. **Sampling** involves any procedure that draws conclusions based on measurements of a portion of the entire population. In other words, a sample is a subset from a larger population. In the steak analogy, the first bite is the sample and the entire steak is the population. If certain statistical procedures are followed, a researcher need not select every item in a population because the results of a good sample should have the same characteristics as the population as a whole. Of course, when errors are made, samples do not give reliable estimates of the population. So, should the first bite come from the edge or the center of a steak?

A famous example of error due to sampling is the 1936 *Literary Digest* fiasco. The magazine conducted a survey and predicted that Republican Alf Landon would win over Democrat Franklin D. Roosevelt by a landslide in that year's presidential election. This prediction was wrong—and the error was due to sample selection. The post-mortems showed that *Literary Digest* had sampled its readers as well as telephone subscribers. In 1936, these people were not a representative cross-section of voters, because a disproportionate number of them were Republicans.

In 2004, early "exit polls" led many to believe that John Kerry would win the U.S. Presidential election.[15] The "exit polls" were performed early on election day and done mostly in highly urban areas in the Northeast, areas that are predominantly democratic. The resulting sample of voters responding to the early exit polls did not represent the entire U.S. population, and Kerry lost to Bush by over 3 million votes, or about 3 percent of all votes cast. Thus, the accuracy of predictions from research depends on getting a sample that really matches the population.

The first sampling question to ask is "Who is to be sampled?" The answer to this primary question requires the identification of a *target population*. Defining this population and determining the sampling units may not be so easy. If, for example, a savings and loan association surveys people who already have accounts for answers to image questions, the selected sampling units will not represent *potential* customers. Specifying the target population is a crucial aspect of the sampling plan.

The next sampling issue concerns sample size. How big should the sample be? Although management may wish to examine every potential buyer of a product or service, doing so may be unnecessary as well as unrealistic. Typically, larger samples are more precise than smaller ones, but proper probability sampling can allow a small proportion of the total population to give a reliable measure of the whole. A later discussion will explain how large a sample must be in order to be truly representative of the universe or population.

The final sampling decision is how to select the sampling units. Simple random sampling may be the best known type, in which every unit in the population has an equal and known chance

sampling

Involves any procedure that draws conclusions based on measurements of a portion of the population.

of being selected. However, this is only one type of sampling. For example, a cluster-sampling procedure may reduce costs and make data gathering procedures more efficient. If members of the population are found in close geographical clusters, a sampling procedure that selects area clusters rather than individual units in the population will reduce costs. Rather than selecting 1,000 individuals throughout the United States, it may be more economical to first select twenty-five counties and then sample within those counties. This will substantially reduce travel, hiring, and training costs. In determining the appropriate sampling plan, the researcher will have to select the most appropriate sampling procedure for meeting the established study objectives. Chapter 16 provides a full discussion of sampling.

Gathering Data

The data gathering stage begins once the sampling plan has been formalized. Data gathering is the process of gathering or collecting information. Data may be gathered by human observers or interviewers, or they may be recorded by machines as in the case of scanner data.

Obviously, the many research techniques involve many methods of gathering data. Surveys require direct participation by research respondents. This may involve filling out a questionnaire or interacting with an interviewer. In this sense, they are obtrusive. **Unobtrusive methods** of data gathering are those in which the subjects do not have to be disturbed for data to be collected. They may even be unaware that research is going on at all. For instance, a simple count of motorists driving past a proposed franchising location is one kind of data gathering method. However the data are collected, it is important to minimize errors in the process. For example, the data gathering should be consistent in all geographical areas. If an interviewer phrases questions incorrectly or records a respondent's statements inaccurately (not verbatim), major data collection errors will result.

unobtrusive methods

Methods in which research respondents do not have to be disturbed for data to be gathered.

Processing and Analyzing Data

■ EDITING AND CODING

After the fieldwork has been completed, the data must be converted into a format that will answer the marketing manager's questions. This is part of the data processing and analysis stage. Here, the information content will be mined from the raw data. Data processing generally begins with editing and coding the data. Editing involves checking the data collection forms for omissions, legibility, and consistency in classification. The editing process corrects problems such as interviewer errors (an answer recorded on the wrong portion of a questionnaire, for example) before the data are transferred to the computer.

Before data can be tabulated, meaningful categories and character symbols must be established for groups of responses. The rules for interpreting, categorizing, recording, and transferring the data to the data storage media are called codes. This coding process facilitates computer or hand tabulation. If computer analysis is to be used, the data are entered into the computer and verified. Computer-assisted (online) interviewing is an example of the impact of technological change on the research process. Telephone interviewers, seated at computer terminals, read survey questions displayed on the monitor. The interviewer asks the questions and then types in the respondents' answers. Thus, answers are collected and processed into the computer at the same time, eliminating intermediate steps that could introduce errors.

■ DATA ANALYSIS

data analysis

The application of reasoning to understand the data that have been gathered.

Data analysis is the application of reasoning to understand the data that have been gathered. In its simplest form, analysis may involve determining consistent patterns and summarizing the relevant details revealed in the investigation. The appropriate analytical technique for data analysis will be determined by management's information requirements, the characteristics of the research design, and the nature of the data gathered. Statistical analysis may range from portraying a simple frequency distribution to more complex multivariate analyses approaches, such as multiple regression. Later chapters will discuss three general categories of statistical analysis: univariate analysis, bivariate analysis, and multivariate analysis.

- Extra effort spent distinguishing symptoms from problems usually pays off. Tracking symptoms to root causes proves very difficult in many cases. Managers generally are focused on symptoms. Make sure the managers are interviewed with the thought in mind that the research should focus on relevant issues. Here are two tips to keep in mind.
  - Use exploratory research tools in the interviews with managers. Later in the text, we'll discuss ways to probe during an interview that may help get the discussion beyond symptoms.
  - A diagnostic analysis can be helpful at sorting relevant issues from symptoms.
- Vague research questions usually call for exploratory research. Very specific research questions usually call for a causal design. For example:
  - In what ways can Oracle leverage its brand name into new industries? Because this is a broad and relatively vague question, some exploratory research addressing the way consumers view the Oracle brand is a potential starting place for research.

- The use of an animated character in a pop-up help window will lead consumers to be more satisfied with the information they receive from the www.edmunds.com Web site than will the use of a videotaped person. This is actually stated in hypotheses form and is very specific. It is relatively easy for the researcher to visualize the details of the study needed to test this question. A causal design seems appropriate.
- Don't overlook the first stage of the research process—defining research objectives. The deliverables are in many ways the most important part of a research proposal. Make sure that management agrees with the deliverables by securing official approval prior to moving forward with the research. Just as importantly, do not promise deliverables that cannot be fulfilled. Researchers should try to state deliverables in terms of research outcomes not in terms of decision outcomes:
  - Good deliverable: Provide a measure of consumer shopping value perceptions for Anthopolgie consumers (both store and online shoppers) and its major competitor, Urban Outfitters.
  - Poor deliverable: Increase profitability at Anthropologie by luring customers from Urban Outfitters.

Drawing Conclusions and Preparing a Report

One of the most important jobs that a researcher performs is communicating the research results. This is the final stage of the research project, but it is far from the least important. The conclusions and report preparation stage consists of interpreting the research results, describing the implications, and drawing the appropriate conclusions for managerial decisions. These conclusions should fulfill the deliverables promised in the research proposal. In addition, it's important that the researcher consider the varying abilities of people to understand the research results. The report shouldn't be written the same way to a group of PhDs as it would be to a group of line managers.

All too many applied market research reports are overly complicated statements of technical aspects and sophisticated research methods. Frequently, management is not interested in detailed reporting of the research design and statistical findings, but wishes only a summary of the findings. If the findings of the research remain unread on the marketing manager's desk, the study will have been useless. The importance of effective communication cannot be overemphasized. Research is only as good as its applications.

Now that we have outlined the research process, note that the order of topics in this book follows the flowchart of the research process presented in Exhibit 3.4. Keep this flowchart in mind while reading later chapters.

The Research Program Strategy

Our discussion of the marketing research process began with the assumption that the researcher wished to collect data to achieve a specific marketing objective. When the researcher has only one or a small number of research objectives that can be addressed in a single study, that study is referred to as a **research project**. We have emphasized the researcher's need to select specific techniques for solving one-dimensional problems, such as identifying market segments, selecting the best packaging design, or test-marketing a new product.

However, if you think about a firm's marketing mix activity in a given period of time (such as a year), you'll realize that marketing research is not a one-shot activity—it is a continuous process.

research project

A single study that addresses one or a small number of research objectives.

An exploratory research study may be followed by a survey, or a researcher may conduct a specific research project for each aspect of the marketing mix. If a new product is being developed, the different types of research might include market potential studies to identify the size and characteristics of the market; product usage testing to record consumers' reactions to prototype products; brand name and packaging research to determine the product's symbolic connotations; and test-marketing the new product. Thus, when numerous related studies come together to address issues about a single company, we refer to this as a **research program**. Because research is a continuous process, management should view marketing research at a strategic planning level. The program strategy refers to a firm's overall plan to use marketing research. It is a planning activity that places a series of marketing research projects in the context of the company's marketing plan.

The marketing research program strategy can be likened to a term insurance policy. Conducting marketing research minimizes risk and increases certainty. Each research project can be seen as a series of term insurance policies that makes the marketing manager's job a bit safer.

research program

Numerous related studies that come together to address multiple, related research objectives.

Summary

1. Understand the role marketing research plays in making decisions. Decision making occurs when managers choose among alternative ways of resolving problems or pursuing opportunities. Decision makers must recognize the nature of the problem or opportunity, identify how much information is available, and recognize what information they need. Every marketing decision can be classified on a continuum ranging from complete certainty to absolute ambiguity. Research is a way that managers can become informed about the different alternatives and make an educated guess about which alternative, if any, is the best to pursue.

2. Classify marketing research as either exploratory research, descriptive research, or causal research. Exploratory, descriptive, and causal research are three major types of marketing research projects. The clarity with which the decision situation is defined determines whether exploratory, descriptive, or causal research is most appropriate. When the decision is very ambiguous, or the interest is on discovering ideas, exploratory research is most appropriate. Descriptive research attempts to paint a picture of the given situation by describing characteristics of objects, people, or organizations. Causal research identifies cause-and-effect relationships. Or, in other words, what change in "Y" will occur when there is some change in "X"? Three conditions must be satisfied to establish evidence of causality: 1) temporal sequence—the cause must occur before the effect; 2) concomitant variation—a change in the cause is associated with a change in the effect; and 3) nonspurious association—the cause is true and not eliminated by the introduction of another potential cause.

3. List the major stages of the marketing research process and the steps within each. The six major stages of the research process are 1) defining the research objectives, 2) planning the research design, 3) sampling, 4) data gathering, 5) data processing and analysis, and 6) drawing conclusions and report preparation. Each stage involves several activities or steps. For instance, in planning the research design, the researchers must decide which type of study will be done and, if needed, recruit participants and design and develop experimental stimuli. Quite often research projects are conducted together as parts of a research program. Such programs can involve successive projects that monitor an established product or a group of projects undertaken for a proposed new product to determine the optimal form of various parts of the marketing mix.

4. Understand the concepts of theory and hypothesis and the critical role they play in research. A *hypothesis* is a formal statement explaining some outcome. It is stated in a way that it is testable. A *theory* is a formal, logical explanation of some events that includes predictions of how things relate to one another. A theory is built through a process of reviewing previous findings of similar studies, simple logical deduction, and knowledge of applicable theoretical areas. The explanations in a theory are often in the form of hypotheses. They are extremely useful in research because they give the research an idea of what to expect prior to testing. As such, they also help to identify the variables that need to be included in the study. Often, certain types of hypotheses point to the need for a specific type of research design.

5. Know the difference between a research project and a research program. A *research project* addresses one of a small number of research objectives that can be included in a single study. In contrast, a *research program* represents a series of studies addressing multiple research objectives. Many marketing activities require an ongoing research task of some type.

Key Terms and Concepts

absolute causality *55*
backward linkage *58*
causal inference *53*
causal research *53*
concomitant variation *53*
conditional causality *55*
contributory causality *55*
data analysis *66*
decision making *47*
deliverables *58*
descriptive research *51*
diagnostic analysis *53*
empirical testing *63*

experiment *55*
experimental variable *55*
exploratory research *50*
focus group *61*
forward linkage *57*
hypothesis *62*
literature review *61*
manipulation *55*
market opportunity *47*
market problem *47*
nonspurious association *54*
pilot study *61*
pretest *61*

research design *64*
research objectives *58*
research program *68*
research project *67*
sampling *65*
survey *64*
symptoms *48*
temporal sequence *53*
test-market *55*
theory *62*
unobtrusive methods *66*

Questions for Review and Critical Thinking

1. List five ways that marketing research can contribute to effective business decision making.

2. Define *market opportunity, market problem,* and *symptoms.* Give an example of each as it applies to a university business school.

3. Consider the following list, and indicate and explain whether each best fits the definition of a problem, opportunity, or symptom:
   a. A 12.5 percent decrease in store traffic for a children's shoe store in a medium-sized city mall.
   b. FedEx's fuel costs increase 200 percent between 2005 and 2009.
   c. A furniture manufacturer and retailer in North Carolina reads a research report indicating consumer trends toward Australian Jara and Kari wood. The export of these products is very limited and very expensive.
   d. Marlboro reads a research report written by the U.S. FDA. It indicates that the number of cigarette smokers in sub-Saharan Africa is expected to increase dramatically over the next decade.
   e. The Starwood Hotel group faces exchange rates between the US and Europe, Great Britain, and Canada that have changed dramatically between 2004 and 2009.

4. What are the three types of marketing research? Indicate which type each item in the list below illustrates. Explain your answers.
   a. Establishing the relationship between advertising and sales in the beer industry
   b. Identifying target market demographics for a shopping center located in Omaha, Nebraska
   c. Estimating the 5-year sales potential for Cat-Scan machines in the Ark-La-Tex (Arkansas, Louisiana, and Texas) region of the United States
   d. Testing the effect of the inside temperature of a clothing store on sales of outerwear
   e. Discovering the ways that people who live in apartments actually use vacuum cleaners, and identifying cleaning tasks for which they do not use a vacuum

5. Describe the type of research evidence that allows one to infer causality.

6. What is an experimental manipulation? A marketing researcher is hired by a specialty retail firm. The retailer is trying to decide what level of lighting and what temperature it should maintain in its stores. How can the researcher manipulate these experimental variables within a causal design?

7. A market researcher gives a presentation to a music industry executive. After considering the results of a test-market examining whether or not lowering the price of in-store CDs will lower the number of illicit downloads of the same music, the executive claims: "The test-market was conducted in eight cities. In two of the cities, lowering the price did not decrease illicit downloading. Therefore, lowering the price does not decrease this behavior, and we should not decide to lower prices based on this research." Comment on the executive's conclusion. What type of inference is being made? Will the decision not to lower prices be a good one?

8. Do the stages in the research process seem to follow the scientific method?

9. Why is the "define research objectives" of the research process probably the most important stage?

10. Suppose Auchan (http://www.auchan.fr), a hypermarket chain based out of France, was considering opening three hypermarkets in the midwestern United States. What role would theory play in designing a research study to track how the shopping habits of consumers from the United States differ from those in France and from those in Japan? What kind of hypothesis might be examined in a study of this topic?

11. Define research project and research program. Referring to the question immediately above, do you think a research project or a research program is needed to provide useful input to the Auchan decision makers?

12. What type of research design would you recommend in the situations below? For each applied market research project, what might be an example of a "deliverable"? Which do you think would involve actually testing a research hypothesis?
   a. The manufacturer and marketer of flight simulators and other pilot training equipment wish to forecast sales volume for the next five years.

b. A local chapter of the American Lung Association wishes to identify the demographic characteristics of individuals who donate more than $500 per year.

c. A major petroleum company is concerned with the increased costs of producing and marketing regular leaded gasoline and is considering dropping this product.

d. A food company researcher wishes to know what types of food are carried in brown-bag lunches to learn if the company can capitalize on this phenomenon.

e. A researcher wishes to explore the feasibility of a casino in a community where gaming had previously been banned.

Research Activities

1. **'NET** Look up information about the online MBA programs at the University of Phoenix (http://business.phoenix.edu/business/graduate.aspx). Compare it to the traditional MBA program at your university. Suppose each was looking to expand the numbers of students in their programs. How might the research design differ for each?

2. **'NET** Use a web browser to go to the Gallup Organization's home page (http://www.gallup.com). The Gallup home page changes regularly. However, it should provide an opportunity to read the results of a recent poll. For example, a poll might break down Americans' sympathies toward Israel or the Palestinians based on numerous individual characteristics such as political affiliation or religious involvement. After reading the results of a Gallup poll of this type, learn how polls are conducted (hint: see "About Gallup" for "FAQs"). You may need to click on the Frequently Asked Questions List (FAQ) to find this information. List the various stages of the research process and how they were (or were not) followed in Gallup's project.

3. Any significant business decision requires input from a research project. Write a brief essay either defending this statement or refuting it.

Case 3.1 A New "Joe" on the Block

© GETTY IMAGES/
PHOTODISC GREEN

Joe Brown is ready to start a new career. After spending 30 years as a market researcher and inspired by the success of Starbucks, he is ready to enter the coffee shop business. However, before opening his first shop, he realizes that a great deal of research is needed. He has some key questions in mind.

• What markets in the United States hold the most promise for a new coffee shop?
• What type of location is best for a coffee shop?
• What is it that makes a coffee shop popular?
• What coffee do Americans prefer?

A quick trip to the Internet reveals more previous research on coffee, markets, and related materials than he expected. Many studies address taste. For example, he finds several studies that in one way or another compare the taste of different coffee shop coffees. Most commonly, they compare the taste of coffee from Starbucks against coffee from McDonald's, Dunkin' Donuts, Burger King, and sometimes a local competitor. However, it becomes difficult to draw a conclusion as the results seem to be inconsistent.

• One study had a headline that poked fun at Starbucks' high-priced coffee. The author of this study personally purchased coffee to go at four places, took them to his office, tasted them, made notes and then drew conclusions. All the coffee was tasted black with no sugar. Just cups of joe. He reached the conclusion that McDonald's Premium Coffee (at about $1.50 a cup), tasted nearly as good as Starbucks House Blend (at about $1.70 a cup), both of which were much better than either Dunkin' Donuts (at about $1.20) or Burger King (less than $1). This study argued that McDonald's was best, all things considered.

• Another study was written up by a good critic who was simply interested in identifying the best-tasting coffee. Again, he tasted them all black with nothing added. Each cup of coffee was consumed in the urban location near the inner city center in which he lived. He reached the conclusion that Starbucks' coffee had the best flavor although it showed room for improvement. McDonald's premium coffee was not as good, but better than the other two. Dunkin' Donuts coffee had reasonably unobjectionable taste but was very weak and watery. The Burger King coffee was simply not very good.

• Yet another study talked about Starbucks becoming a huge company and how it has lost touch with the common coffee shop coffee customer. The researchers stood outside a small organic specialty shop and interviewed 100 consumers as they exited the shop. They asked, "Which coffee do you prefer?" The results showed a preference for a local coffee, tea, and incense shop, and otherwise put Starbucks last behind McDonald's, Burger King, and Dunkin' Donuts.

• Still another study compared the coffee-drinking experience. A sample of 50 consumers in St. Louis, Missouri were interviewed and asked to list the coffee shop they frequented most. Starbucks was listed by more consumers than any other place. A small percentage listed Dunkin' Donuts but none listed McDonald's, despite their efforts at creating a premium coffee experience. The study did not ask consumers to compare the tastes of the coffee across the different places.

Joe also wants to find data showing coffee consumption patterns and the number of coffee shops around the United States, so he spends time looking for data on the Internet. His searches don't reveal anything satisfying.

As Joe ponders how to go about starting "A Cup of Joe," he wonders about the relevance of this previous research. Is it useful at all? He even questions whether he is capable of doing any primary research himself and considers hiring someone to do a feasibility study for him. Maybe doing research is easier than using research.

Sources: Shiver, J., "Taste Test: The Little Joes Take on Starbucks," *USA Today*, (March 26, 2008), http://www.usatoday.com/money/industries/food/2006-03-26-coffee_x.htm, accessed July 20, 2008; Associated Press, "McDonald's Coffee Beats Starbucks, Says Consumer Reports," *The Seattle Times*, (February 2, 2007), http://seattletimes.nwsource.com/html/businesstechnology/2003553322_webcoffeetest02.html, accessed July 20, 2008; "Coffee Wars: Starbucks v McDonald's," *The Economist* 386, (January 10, 2008), 58.

Questions

1. What are the top three key decisions faced by Joe?
2. What are the key deliverables that an outside researcher should produce to help Joe with the key decisions?
3. How relevant are the coffee taste studies cited above? Explain.
4. What flaws in the coffee taste studies should Joe consider in trying to weigh the merits of their results?
5. Briefly relate this situation to each of the major stages of the marketing research process.
6. Try to do a quick search to explore the question: "Are American consumer preferences the same all across the United States?"
7. Would it be better for Joe to do the research himself or have a consultant perform the work?
8. If a consultant comes in to do the job, what are three key deliverables that would likely be important to Joe in making a decision to launch the Cup of Joe coffee shop.

CHAPTER 4
THE HUMAN SIDE OF MARKETING RESEARCH: ORGANIZATIONAL AND ETHICAL ISSUES

After studying this chapter, you should be able to

1. Know when research should be conducted externally and when it should be done internally

2. Be familiar with the types of jobs, job responsibilities, and career paths available within the marketing research industry

3. Become sensitive to the often conflicting relationship between marketing management and researchers

4. Define ethic and understand how it applies to marketing research

5. Appreciate the rights and obligations of a) research respondents—particularly children, b) research clients or sponsors, and c) marketing researchers

6. Avoid situations involving a conflict of interest in performing marketing research

Chapter Vignette: The Longest Drive or the Tallest Tale?

© (REVIEW)/JUPITER IMAGES

Pick up a golf magazine, watch the Golf Channel, or view some golf-related Web sites, and no doubt you will see a lot of claims by companies who say they can help golfers lower their scores. Even a golf novice can see how a longer golf shot is usually better than a shorter golf shot. Thus, the claims include slogans such as Callaway's "designed to be the longest ball in all of golf," Bridgestone's "distance technology," and balls with names such as Precept Distance iQ, and Nike Juice with "Ginormous Hugantic Distance!" Obviously, these companies do a great deal of product research to produce golf balls that will conform to the rules of golf while gaining a yard or two over the competitors. Perhaps not quite as obviously, they do equal amounts of marketing research to understand just what it is that makes a golfer believe they have the longest ball in the game.

Now, imagine a young marketing researcher who leaves her job as a research analyst for a mid-sized firm to start a small firm of her own. The mid-sized firm that she worked for previously had been involved in a project for Maxfli so she had some insight into how consumers perceive golf technology. Her first big break comes when a polymer company that wants to leverage their brand into the golf ball business approaches her about a research project. The project is related to golfer perceptions of the technological advantage and perceived distance of golf balls and how this would relate to sales. The owner of the company is adamant that he wants to know how to make golfers "think they are hitting the longest drives of their lives." The company has invested millions of dollars in new polymer coatings that enhance the energy of the ball when struck at high speeds. From her previous project, she knows that perceived distance is the number one concern of golfers when purchasing golf balls. She also knows that the company has already gone forward with plans to build a production facility. The only deliverable the owner is interested in is "how to make people believe this is the longest ball."

Golf ball companies traditionally have tested golf ball performance with mechanical robots called Iron Byron and by surveying actual golfers about the golf balls they use. In this case, the robot tests reveal two things: (1) the top 10 or so longest golf balls all go approximately the same distance, and (2) the golf balls that deliver the longest drives for professional golfers do not deliver the longest drives for average golfers. The young researcher really needs the business and would like to deliver a report that the owner will like and do so with the least cost. Based on her research with Maxfli, she believes that this new technology will be best suited to weaker golfers with slower swing speeds (who cannot swing a club as fast as others). She thinks about a possible study. She can get a sample of golfers with slower swing speeds, tell them that the golf ball they will be testing will be the most expensive on the market, and have them compare it to a Maxfli ball that she knows is best for golfers with a high swing speed. The group should both really hit and believe that the new ball goes further than the Maxfli. Then, she would be able to deliver the results the owner of the company wants and have a successful big break.

Sources: For information on golf ball testing and research, see "Flying High and Far," Golf.com, http://www.golf.com/golf/features/flash/ballguide3.html, accessed July 21, 2008; Sauerhaft, R., "How We Did It: The Best Golf Ball for You," *Golf Magazine*, (February 1, 2008), http://www.golf.com/golf/equipment/article/0,28136,1695805,00.html, accessed July 21, 2008; Tannar, K., "The Longest Golf Ball Testing for 2007 Balls," http://probablegolfinstruction.com/longest_golf_ball.htm, accessed July 21, 2008.

Introduction

The vignette describes a situation that involves marketing research and in particular, the human side. A company is looking for research to help sell a new product, in this case a golf ball. Rather than doing the research itself, an outside agency is hired. The owner, given this is a small agency, is faced with a number of dilemmas. Some of these introduce business ethic into the arena of marketing research. This chapter focuses on the social element of marketing research by discussing the people who do use and participate in research and the situations that they sometimes find themselves in.

Who Does the Research?

The vignette described in this chapter involves one company hiring an outside company to conduct and provide results from a research project. Although this is very typical, many companies have their own employees perform research projects and research programs. Thus, research is sometimes performed in-house, meaning that employees of the company that will benefit from the research project actually perform the research. In other cases, the research is performed by an **outside agency**, meaning that the company that will benefit from the research results hires an independent, outside firm to perform a research project. While it would seem that **in-house research** would usually be of higher quality because of the increased knowledge of the researchers conducting the studies, there are several reasons why employees of the firm may not always be the best people to do the job.

outside agency
An independent research firm contracted by the company that actually will benefit from the research.

in-house research
Research performed by employees of the company that will benefit from the research.

Do It Yourself or Let Your Fingers Do the Walking?

When the firm facing a decision encounters one of the following situations, they should consider having the research performed by an outside agency.

- An outside agency often can provide a fresh perspective. Creativity is often hindered by too much knowledge. When a firm is seeking new ideas, particularly in discovery-oriented research, an outsider is not constrained by the groupthink that often affects a company employee. In other words, employees who spend so much time together in their day-to-day work activities begin to act and think alike to a large degree. History is filled with stories of products that remained unsuccessful commercially for years until someone from outside the company discovered a useful application. The technology for a microwave oven was invented in the 1940s by a company called Raytheon. Raytheon worked on radar systems for the Allied military in World War II. Not until someone from another company, Amana, tested the concept of using microwaves in a kitchen appliance did it become a commercial success.

TO THE POINT

To manage a business is to manage its future; and to manage the future is to manage information.

—Marion Harper

By now, you are becoming familiar with the student question-naire that accompanies this book. Examine the items in the ques-tionnaire and the questionnaire overall for the following issues.

1. Were you required to identify yourself by name in completing the survey?

2. Can the results (you can access the results through your instructor) be linked to respondents by name?
3. Do any items need to be tied to a name to be useful to the researcher?
4. Consider the portion of the survey shown below. What if another instructor asked for the results from this particular section of the survey but was only interested in them if the names of the students also can be provided? The instructor believes that he can use the results to encourage particular students to change their study habits. Take the role of the researchers who implemented this research. Should you provide the information this instructor is asking for? Why or why not?

Please read each of the following statements. After reading each, click on the the circle that best describes how much you agree with each statement.

	Strongly Agree	Agree	Neutral	Disagree	Strongly Disagree
I make time to study every day.	O	O	O	O	O
I know the material better after I study.	O	O	O	O	O
I can't study when it's quiet.	O	O	O	O	O
I prefer to not be around others when I study.	O	O	O	O	O
I can study the night before and be ready for a test.	O	O	O	O	O
I like to study with others.	O	O	O	O	O
I arrange time to study with others.	O	O	O	O	O

COURTESY OF QUALTRICS.COM

© GEORGE DOYLE

- An outside agency often can be more objective. When a firm is facing a particularly sensitive situation that may even impact a large number of jobs within the company, it may be difficult for researchers to be objective. Alternatively, if a particular chief executive within the firm is in love with some new idea, researchers may feel a great deal of pressure to present results that are supportive of the concept. In these cases, outside researchers may be a good choice. Since they don't have to work for the company and interact with the players involved on a daily basis, they are less concerned about presenting results that may not be truly welcome.

- An outside agency may have special expertise. When a firm needs research requiring a par-ticular expertise that some outside agency specializes in, it may be a good idea to use that firm to conduct the research. For example, if a company is searching for new ideas about how to use its Web site, an online focus group interview may be needed. While this is a skill that may not be prevalent within the company, there are several research firms that specialize in this particular type of research. Thus, the outside agency may have greater competency in this specific area.

- An outside agency will have local knowledge and expertise and may specialize in research from its home area. When a company needs consumer research from that particular country or even from a particular part of a country, the outside agency becomes advantageous because of its knowledge of customs and values in that particular area plus the acceptable ways with which to get information from consumers. For example, a research agency based here in the United States would probably not strongly consider a door–to–door survey for consumer research. However, in other parts of the world, particularly with less developed communica-tion infrastructure, this may be a viable and accepted option.

Likewise, there are conditions that make in–house research more attractive as well, as in the following situations.

- If the research project needs to be completed very quickly, chances are that in-house research-ers can get started more quickly and get quicker access to internal resources that can help get the project done in short order.

- If the research project will require the close collaboration of many other employees from diverse areas of the organization, then in-house research may be preferable. The in-house research firms can usually gain cooperation and can more quickly ascertain just who needs to be interviewed and where those people can be found.
- A third reason for doing a project in-house has to do with economy. In-house research can almost always be done more cheaply than that done by an outside research firm.
- If secrecy is a major concern, then the research is best done in-house. Even though the outside firm might be trusted, it may take slightly less care in disguising its research efforts. Thus, other companies may pick up on signals in the marketplace that suggest the area of research for a firm. (See Exhibit 4.1.)

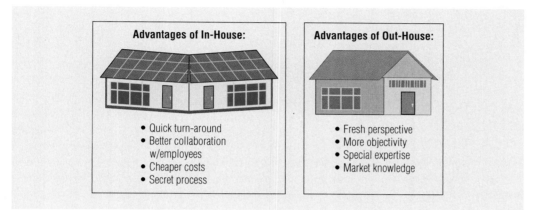

EXHIBIT 4.1
Should Research be Done In-House or "Out-House"?

Working in the Marketing Research Field

About three-fourths of all U.S. organizations have a department or individual responsible for marketing research. Consumer products companies, manufacturers, service firms, health-care organizations and retailers are most likely to have an in-house marketing research department. Marketing research clearly has a presence and this is particularly true for larger firms. The amount of companies doing research is likely increasing because as times get tough or as competition increases, firms actually become more attuned to marketing research. The insurance industry has been tuned into marketing research in a big way as competition increased over the last decade. A large research company may well be staffed with dozens or even hundreds of people involved with marketing research in some way. MetLife has been singled out as a role model for exemplary performance and integration of its marketing research team into decision making. The marketing research team has helped MetLife:[1]

- Build stronger relationships with customers
- Integrate customer and competitor information into decision processes
- Have better working relationships with vendors
- Become more entrepeneurial and marketing oriented

The placement of marketing research within a firm's organizational structure and the structure of the research department itself vary substantially, depending on the firm's degree of marketing orientation and research sophistication. A marketing research department can easily become isolated with poor organizational placement. Researchers may lack a voice in executive committees when they have no continuous relationship with marketing management. This can occur when the research department is positioned at an inappropriately low level. Given the critically important nature of the intelligence coming out of a research department, it should be placed relatively high in the organizational structure to ensure that senior management is well informed. Research departments should also be linked with a broad spectrum of other units within the organization. Thus, they should be positioned to provide credible information both upstream and downstream within the marketing organization—as is the case at MetLife.

Thousands of people work for large global research firms like Nielsen. Marketing research truly presents a world of opportunity for careers. [http://www2.acnielsen.com/careers/]

research suppliers

Commercial providers of marketing research services.

syndicated service

A marketing research supplier that provides standardized information for many clients in return for a fee.

Research departments that perform a staff function must wait for management to request assistance. Often the term "client" is used by the research department to refer to line management for whom services are being performed. The research department responds to clients' requests and is responsible for the design and execution of all research.

Research Suppliers and Contractors

As mentioned in the beginning of the chapter, sometimes obtaining marketing research from an outside organization makes good sense. In these cases, marketing managers must interact with **research suppliers**, who are commercial providers of marketing research services. Marketing research is carried out by firms that may be variously classified as marketing research consulting companies, such as Burke or the Walker Information Research Company; advertising agencies, such as JWT Worldwide; suppliers of syndicated research services, such as The Nielsen Company; as well as interviewing agencies, universities, and government agencies, among others. Research suppliers provide varied services which can be classified into several types.

■ SYNDICATED SERVICE

No matter how large a firm's marketing research department is, some projects are too expensive to perform in-house. A **syndicated service** is a marketing research supplier that provides standardized information for many clients in return for a fee. They are a sort of supermarket for standardized research results. For example, J. D. Power and Associates sells research about customers' ratings of automobile quality and their reasons for satisfaction. Most automobile manufacturers and their advertising agencies subscribe to this syndicated service because the company provides important industry-wide information it gathers from a national sample of thousands of car buyers. By specializing in this type of customer satisfaction research, J. D. Power gains certain economies of scale.

Syndicated services can provide expensive information economically to numerous clients because the information is not specific to one client but interests many. Such suppliers offer standardized information to measure media audiences, wholesale and retail distribution data, and other forms of data. The world's largest marketing research company, The Nielsen Company, is a leader in providing standardized data across many industries including retailing, consumer behavior, and media. They also provide services beyond syndicated information, but this is a core of their business. Nearly 40,000 people work for The Nielsen Company worldwide.

■ STANDARDIZED RESEARCH SERVICES

standardized research service

Companies that develop a unique methodology for investigating a business specialty area.

Standardized research service providers develop a unique methodology for investigating a business specialty area. Several research firms, such as Retail Forward (http://www.retailforward.com), provide location services for retail firms. The Research Snapshot on the next page illustrates an interesting application for which an outside location service company may be particularly useful. Research suppliers conduct studies for multiple individual clients using the same methods.

The Nielsen Company (http://www2.acnielsen.com) collects information throughout the new-product development process, from initial concept screening through test-marketing. The BASES system can evaluate initiatives relative to other products in the competitive environment.

RESEARCH SNAPSHOT

Finding Häagen-Dazs in China

Ice cream lovers needn't worry if they are sent on a business trip to China. Häagen-Dazs ice cream shops first appeared in Shanghai, China, in 1996 and now there are dozens of Häagen-Dazs ice cream shops in coastal China, with plans for many more. Clearly, many firms would like to follow Häagen-Dazs into China. China is expected to be the world's largest consumer market by 2020. However, where should an ice cream shop be located in China? While location decisions can be difficult enough within the borders of one's own country, imagine trying to decide where to put a shop in a huge, unfamiliar country.

Fortunately, standardized research companies like Retail Forward have resources deployed all around the world that can synthesize Geographic Information Systems (GIS) information with survey research and other information to assist firms with location decisions in China and in other developing countries.

Since U.S.-based retail firms may lack the necessary connections and knowledge (expertise) to efficiently conduct research in faraway places, the use of an outside research provider not only saves time and money, but also yields higher quality results than an in-house study. Imagine how difficult language barriers could be when dealing with the Chinese consumer market.

And, as difficult as identifying good retail locations seems in China, other top emerging retail nations include India, Russia, and the Ukraine. As in China, American and European firms may find that using a research supplier to help with retail location issues in these countries is wiser than doing the research themselves.

Sources: "Häagen-Dazs in China," *China Business Review*, 31 (July/August 2004), 22; Hall, Cecily, "Spanning the Retail Globe," *WWD: Women's Wear Daily*, 190 (July 21, 2005), 11. www.haagen-dazs.com, accessed September 15, 2008.

For example, a client can compare its Day-After Recall scores with average scores for a product category.

Even when a firm could perform the research task in-house, research suppliers may be able to conduct the project at a lower cost, faster, and relatively more objectively. A company that wishes to quickly evaluate a new advertising strategy may find an ad agency's research department is able to provide technical expertise on copy development research that is not available within the company itself. Researchers may be well advised to seek outside help with research when conducting research in a foreign country in which the necessary human resources and knowledge to effectively collect data are lacking. The Research Snapshot above illustrates this situation.

Doing research in a foreign country is often better done by an outside agency with resources in those places.

Limited Research Service Companies and Custom Research

Limited-service research suppliers specialize in particular research activities, such as syndicated service, field interviewing, data warehousing, or data processing. Full-service research suppliers sometimes contract these companies for ad hoc marketing research projects. The client usually controls these marketing research agencies or management consulting firms, but the research supplier handles most of the operating details of **custom research** projects. These are projects that are tailored specifically to a client's unique needs. A custom research supplier may employ individuals with titles that imply relationships with clients, such as *account executive* or *account group manager,* as well as functional specialists with titles such as *statistician, librarian, director of field services, director of tabulation and data processing,* and *interviewer.*

Exhibit 4.2 on the next page lists the top twenty suppliers of global research in calendar year (CY) 2007. Most provide multiple services ranging from designing activities to fieldwork. The services they can provide are not covered in detail here because they are discussed throughout the book, especially in the sections on fieldwork. Clearly, the exhibit reveals that research is big business. Its growth will continue as data availability increases and as

custom research

Research projects that are tailored specifically to a client's unique needs.

77

EXHIBIT 4.2 **The Largest Research Firms in the World**

Rank	Company	Home Country	Web site	Number of Employees	Approximate Revenue (millions)
1	The Nielsen Company	USA	www.nielsen.com	39,500	3,696
2	IMS Health Inc.	USA	www.imshealth.com	7,400	2,000
3	TNS	UK	www.tns-global.com	14,600	1,850
4	The Kantar Group	UK	www.kantargroup.com	6900	1400
5	GfK AG	Germany	www.gfk.com	9000	1400
6	Ipsos Group	France	www.ipsos.com	6500	1100
7	Synovate	UK	www.synovate.com	6000	750
8	IRI	USA	www.infores.com	3600	700
9	Westat Inc.	USA	www.westat.com	2000	425
10	Arbitron	USA	www.arbitron.com	1050	350
11	INTAGE Inc	Japan	www.intage.co.jp	1600	265
12	JD Power	USA	www.jdpa.com	850	230
13	Harris Interactive Inc	USA	www.harrisinteractive.com	1100	220
14	Maritz Research	USA	www.maritzresearch.com	800	215
15	The NPD Group	USA	www.npd.com	950	190
16	Video Research	Japan	www.videor.co.jp	400	175
17	Opinion Research Corp.	USA	www.opinionresearch.com	675	155
18	IBOPE	Brazil	www.ibope.com.br	1700	105
19	Lieberman Research Worldwide	USA	www.lrwonline.com	300	80
20	Telephia Inc	USA	www.telephia.com	250	70

Sources: "Top 50 US Market Research Firms," *Marketing News*, (June 15, 2008), H4; "Top 25 Global Research Organizations," *Marketing News*, August 15, 2007), H4.

businesses desire more precision in their decision making. Therefore, attractive career opportunities are numerous for those with the right skills and desires.

A look at the top 20 shows that marketing research also is a global enterprise. Marketing research is conducted all around the world although given roots within the United States; American firms are numerous. Other large firms based in the United States that don't make the top 20 global list include:

Burke, Inc. with revenue of nearly $50 million.
Walker Research (Information) at just over $20 million in revenue.
Savitz Research with revenue of about $15 million.

Each of these firms is within the top 50 largest market research firms in the United States.

Size of the Marketing Research Firm

Marketing research organizations themselves consist of layers of employees. Each employee has certain specific functions to perform based on his or her area of expertise and experience. A look at these jobs not only describes the potential structure of a research organization, but it also provides insight into the types of careers available in marketing research.

■ SMALL FIRMS

While it is difficult to precisely define the boundaries between small firms, mid-sized firms, and large firms, generally speaking, government statistics usually consider firms with fewer than 100 employees to be small. In small firms, the vice president of marketing may be in charge of all significant marketing research. This officer generally has a sales manager collect and analyze sales histories, trade association statistics, and other internal data. Small marketing companies usually have few resources and special competencies to conduct large-scale, sophisticated research projects. An advertising agency or a firm that specializes in marketing research will be contracted if a large-scale survey is needed. Small businesses will generally have fewer than five employees regularly involved in marketing research.

Some small firms are small marketing research firms. Small marketing research firms are less likely to have major corporate clients, rather, they will probably work for other small firms and in particular, start-up firms. Typical studies involve feasibility studies and assessing consumer attitudes and the relationship between customer satisfaction and customer loyalty.[2] A small firm can be a good place to start a career or to start your own business. Researchers working for a small firm will probably have to be involved in many, if not all, of the stages of research.

■ MID-SIZED FIRMS

Mid-sized firms can be thought of as those with between 100 and 500 employees. In a mid-sized marketing firm, the research department might be organized as shown in Exhibit 4.3. Someone usually holds the position of **director of marketing research**. This person provides leadership in research efforts and integrates all staff-level research activities. (This position will be discussed in greater detail in the next section.)

A **research analyst** is responsible for client contact, project design, preparation of proposals, selection of research suppliers, and supervision of data collection, analysis, and reporting activities. Normally, the research analyst is responsible for several projects simultaneously covering a wide spectrum of the firm's organizational activities. He or she works with product or division management and makes recommendations based on analysis of collected data.

© ANDREW HOLT/ALAMY

When market research departments grow, they begin to specialize by product or business unit. This happened in the Marriott Corporation, which now has a specific director of marketing research for its lodging facilities.

EXHIBIT 4.3
Structure of a Medium-Sized Research Department

director of marketing research

This person provides leadership in research efforts and integrates all staff-level research activities into one effort. The director plans, executes, and controls the firm's marketing research function.

research analyst

A person responsible for client contact, project design, preparation of proposals, selection of research suppliers, and supervision of data collection, analysis, and reporting activities.

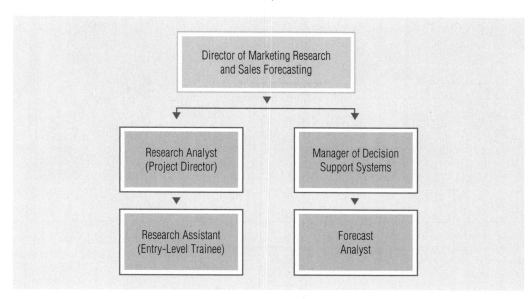

research assistants

Research employees who provide technical assistance with questionnaire design, data analyses, and similar activities.

manager of decision support systems

Employee who supervises the collection and analysis of sales, inventory, and other periodic customer relationship management (CRM) data.

forecast analyst

Employee who provides technical assistance such as running computer programs and manipulating data to generate a sales forecast.

Research assistants (or associates) provide technical assistance with questionnaire design, data analyses, and so forth. Another common name for this position is *junior analyst*. The **manager of decision support systems** supervises the collection and analysis of sales, inventory, and other periodic customer relationship management (CRM) data. Sales forecasts for product lines usually are developed using analytical and quantitative techniques. Sales information is provided to satisfy the planning, analysis, and control needs of decision makers. The manager of decision support systems may be assisted by a **forecast analyst** who provides technical assistance, such as running computer programs and manipulating data to forecast sales.

Personnel within a planning department may perform the marketing research function in a mid-sized firm. At times, they may outsource some research functions. The planner may design research studies and then contract with outside firms that supply research services such as interviewing or data processing. They can combine the input from these outside agencies with their own work to write research reports.

■ LARGE FIRMS

As marketing research departments grow, they tend to specialize by product or strategic business unit. Major firms can be thought of as those with over 500 employees. Marriott Corporation has a director of marketing research for lodging (for example, Marriott Hotels and Resorts, Courtyard by Marriott, and Fairfield Inn) and a director of marketing research for contract services (for example, Senior Living Services). Each business unit's research director reports to the vice president of corporate marketing services. Many large organizations have managers of customer quality research who specialize in conducting surveys to measure consumers' satisfaction with product quality.

Exhibit 4.4 illustrates the organization of a major firm's marketing research department. Within this organization, the centralized marketing research department conducts research for all

EXHIBIT 4.4 Organization of the Marketing Research Department in a Large Firm

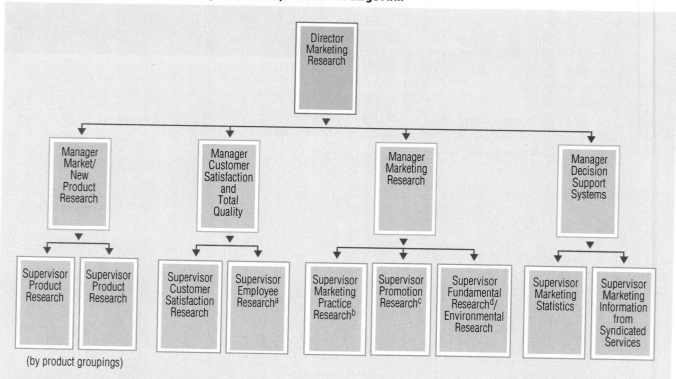

(by product groupings)

[a]Conducts research to improve total quality management in production.
[b]Conducts research that cuts across product lines or involves competitive marketing practices or characteristics of customer groups.
[c]Conducts research that cuts across product lines to measure the effectiveness of promotional activities.
[d]Conducts research aimed at gaining a basic understanding of various elements of the marketing process.

the division's product groups. This is typical of a large research department that conducts much of its own research, including fieldwork. The director of marketing research reports to the vice president of marketing.

Other positions within a major firm's research department may include director of data collection (field supervisor), manager of quantitative research, focus group moderator, and manager of data processing. These are not shown in Exhibit 4.4. Even large firms sometimes outsource some research functions or even an entire project from time to time. For now, we turn our attention to the job of director of marketing research and the interface between the marketing research department and other departments.

The Director of Marketing Research as a Manager

A director of marketing research plans, executes, and controls the firm's marketing research function. This person typically serves on company executive committees that identify competitive opportunities and formulate marketing strategies. The various directors from each functional area generally make up this committee (such as finance, sales, production, and so forth). The director of marketing research provides the research perspective during meetings. For instance, the researcher can provide input as to what types of market intelligence can be feasibly obtained given the decision being discussed. Marketing research directors typically face problems like these:

- Skilled research professionals like conducting research better than managing people. They pride themselves on being hands-on researchers. However, a director is a manager and spends more time in meetings and managing than actually conducting research.
- The research management role often is not formally recognized.
- Outstanding research professionals often have trouble delegating responsibility. The pride that comes with being a knowledgeable researcher makes it difficult to give up control. They may genuinely feel "I can do it better myself." As a result, they delegate only elementary or tedious tasks to subordinates. The subordinates can sometimes become disenchanted and thus become unhappy with their work.
- Finally, research is often seen as a hodgepodge of techniques available to answer individual, unrelated questions. According to this view, a research operation encompasses an array of more or less equal projects, each handled by a project director. Hence, many firms view a full-time director as unnecessary.[3]

Marketing research jobs range across a large spectrum of activities and salaries. Jobs are available practically all over the world. The Research Snapshot on the next page gives a rough idea of what marketing research salaries are like internationally.

Conflict between Marketing Management and Marketing Research

In principle, the functions of marketing research should merge harmoniously with the objectives of marketing management for the benefit of both parties. In practice, the relationship between the marketing research department and the users of marketing research frequently is characterized by misunderstanding and conflict.

Research That Implies Criticism

A product manager who requests a survey of dealer loyalty will not be happy if the survey finds that the dealers are extremely critical. Similarly, a sales manager who informally projects a 5 percent increase in sales will not like hearing from the research department that the market potential indicates sales volume should be up by 20 percent. In each of these situations, marketing research presents information that implies criticism of a line executive's decision. In personal life, a sure way to lose a friend is to be openly critical of him or her. Things are no different in business.

Marketing Research Pays

Marketing research can pay! Careers in marketing research can be very lucrative. This is particularly true if one has the right attributes. These attributes include being a good people person as well as having good quantitative skills and a good education. The fastest career tracks in marketing research are for those with at least a master's degree.

The prospects of finding a job remain good. Marketing researchers have long been in greater demand than the supply can address. The salaries also can be very lucrative. The 2006 U.S. Department of Labor Salary Survey suggests that marketing research analysts' salaries are generally between $40,000 and $85,000 although some analysts have salaries well over $100,000 per year. These are for actual research analysts and not research directors. Beginning research employees, with little or no experience, generally enter the firm as a survey researcher. Those salaries are considerably less, generally between $22,500 and $45,000. However, they require no significant work experience.

Job opportunities in marketing research exist outside the United States as well. The salaries also are lucrative in other countries. The chart in next column shows typical salary ranges for non-managerial marketing research positions in the United States, Australia, Japan, and the United Kingdom. For comparison purposes, salaries for non-managerial sales employees also are provided. The salaries are expressed in thousands of U.S. dollars and reflect the latest available statistics. As can be seen, research jobs compare very favorably. In addition, researchers that move into research director positions see a substantial increase in pay. Perhaps you'll give marketing research a try?

Common Currency ($)	Australia	UK	Japan	United States
Sales Executive				
High	97.32	89.88	74.89	55.00
Low	38.92	49.93	46.81	35.00
Marketing Research				
High	116.78	89.88	93.59	85.76
Low	38.92	37.95	46.81	41.23

Sources: Enright, A., "Carve out a Niche," *Marketing News* (November 15, 2005), 17; "Occupational Employment and Wages," U.S. Department of Labor, (2008), http://www.bls.gov/oes/current/oes193021.htm accessed September 15, 2008; Walters, Robert, "Market Research Search Results," (2008), http://www.robertwalters.com, accessed July 20, 2008.

© PHOTODISC/GETTY IMAGES

© GEORGE DOYLE & CIARAN GRIFFIN

Money

Research budgets are a source of conflict between management and researchers. Financial managers often see research as a cost rather than as an investment or a way of lowering risk. Successful decisions that are supported by research are seldom attributed to the marketing researcher. Thus, as is often true in many areas of business, managers often want to spend as little as possible on research. In contrast, researchers often vigorously resist cutting corners in conducting research. For instance, they may feel that a large random sample is necessary to adequately address a research question using descriptive research. This approach can be very expensive and sometimes time consuming. Inevitably, management's desire to save money and the researcher's desire to conduct rigorous research conflict. Successful research projects often are those that are based on compromise. This may involve working within a budget that will produce meaningful results and sacrifice precision and rigor minimally.

Time

Researchers say, "Good research takes time!" Managers say, "Time is money!" Like oil and water, these two views do not go together easily. A look back at the research process in the last chapter makes it clear that it can take some time to complete a research project. Simply planning one can involve days, if not weeks, of study and preparation. For instance, conducting a literature review or a review of previous studies can take weeks. Without them, the researcher may not be able to develop specific research hypotheses that would direct the project very specifically toward the current issue. Other times, the researcher may wish to interview more people than time can allow or take the time to use a more sophisticated data analysis approach.

The more quickly the research project is done, the less likely it is to be successful. This doesn't mean it can't provide valuable information. It simply is not as certain that a quickly put-together study will provide valuable answers as would a more deliberately planned project. When studies are rushed, the following sources of error become more prominent than they would be otherwise.

- Conducting a study that is not needed. Taking more time to perform a literature search, including through company and industry reports, may have provided the needed intelligence without a new study.
- Addressing the wrong issue. Taking more time could help make sure the decision statement is well defined and that the research questions that follow will truly address relevant issues, lessening the chance that the research goes in the wrong direction.
- Sampling difficulties. Correctly defining, identifying, and contacting a truly representative sample is a difficult and time-consuming task. However, in some types of research, the quality of results depends directly on the quality of the sample.
- Inadequate data analysis. The researcher may analyze the data quickly and without the rigor that would otherwise be taken. Therefore, certain assumptions may not be considered, and important information within the data is simply not discovered.

Sometimes a marketing researcher will have to submit to the time pressure and do a quick-and-dirty study. A sudden event can make it necessary to acquire data quickly—but rush jobs can sometimes be avoided with proper planning of the research program. Researchers are sometimes backed into a corner where a study simply must be conducted under severe time limitations. When this happens, the researcher is obligated to disclose this limitation to management. The research report and presentation should include all the study limitations, including those that resulted from a shortage of time or money.

TO THE POINT

Someone's sitting in the shade today because someone planted a tree a long time ago.

—Warren Buffett

Intuitive Decision Making

The fact of the matter is that managers are decision makers. They are action-oriented, and they often rely on gut reaction and intuition. Many times their intuition serves them well, so it isn't surprising that they sometimes do not believe a research project will help improve their decision making. At other times, they resist research because it just may provide information that is counter to their intuition or their desires. They particularly abhor being held back while waiting for some research report. Thus, decision makers think more questions, more probing, and more studying can simply become annoying.[4] Sometimes, decision makers learn the hard way that informed decisions are usually better.

When managers do use marketing research, they often want simple projects yielding concrete and certain results. Researchers tend to see problems as complex questions that can be answered only within probability ranges. One aspect of this conflict is the fact that a research report provides findings, but cannot make decisions. Decision-oriented executives may unrealistically expect research to make decisions for them or provide some type of guarantee that the action they take will be correct. While research provides information for decision making, it does not remove all the uncertainties involved in complex decisions. Certain alternatives may be eliminated, but the research may reveal new aspects of a problem. Although research is a valuable decision-making tool, the executive is not freed from the decision-making task altogether but is simply able to perform the task in a more informed manner.

Presentation of the right facts can be extremely useful. However, decision makers often believe that researchers collect the wrong facts. Many researchers view themselves as technicians who generate numbers using sophisticated mathematical and statistical techniques; they may spend more time on technical details than on satisfying managerial needs. Each person who has a narrow perspective of another's job is a partial cause of the problem of generating limited or useless information.

The following illustrations typify poor decision-making that could have been avoided through focused research.

1. A manufacturing company lured by promotion of low production costs in a developing nation decides to relocate production facilities from the United States. Sales and customer satisfaction plummet afterwards. However, research on the customer decision-making process may have revealed that customers find value in the personal contact with technicians and services that originate at the production facilities. Language and cultural barriers diminished the quality of these particular touchpoints.

2. Intuition may suggest that longtime customers are the best customers. In other words, someone who will purchase things over a period of years is more valuable than someone who will only purchase things for a couple of years. Thus, a supplier of airplane parts shuns new customers seeking to purchase products on a short-term basis in favor of old, steady customers. However, marketing research on potential new customer segments that examines not only the potential length of the relationship, but the pattern of spending over the relationship, might well reveal that a customer who front-end loads (buys more things early in a relationship) over a short period of time could be worth more than a customer buying the same amount over the same or even a longer period of time.[5]

3. An Internet retailer (Send.com) used a television ad to try to stimulate more gift purchasing among its customers. The spot centers on several men on the golf course drinking champagne. The "punch line" comes when one of the guys is hit in the groin. The voice-over exclaims, "He just got hit in the little giver!" Simply concept testing would have likely revealed that the ad was failing to communicate and even offensive to some consumers. The concept was flawed for a broad based market. This is the type of punch line that a male ad executive may find funny and entertaining; however, the audience for these ads is not all male. Had research been used to test this idea prior to spending the money to produce the ad and buy the spots, it would have revealed that men didn't respond as favorably as expected to the ads and women found them boorish.[6]

Thus, intuition has its limits as a replacement for informed market intelligence.[7]

Future Decisions Based on Past Experience

Managers wish to predict the future, but researchers measure only current or past events. In 1957, Ford introduced the Edsel, one of the classic business failures of all time. One reason for the Edsel's failure was that the marketing research conducted several years before the car's introduction indicated a strong demand for a medium-priced car for the "man on his way up." By the time the car was introduced, however, consumer preference had shifted to two cars, one being a small import for the suburban wife. Not all research information is so dated, but all research describes what people have done in the past. In this sense, researchers use the past to predict the future.

Reducing the Conflict between Management and Researchers

Given the conflicting goals of management and research, it is probably impossible to completely eliminate the conflict. However, when researchers and decision makers work more closely together, there will be less conflict. The more closely they work together, the better the communication between decision makers and researchers. In this way, business decision makers will better understand the information needs and work requirements of researchers. It will allow for better planning of research projects and a greater appreciation for the role that research plays in minimizing the riskiness of business decision making. Exhibit 4.5 lists some common areas of conflict between research and management. Many of these can be avoided through improved understanding of the other's position.

With closer cooperation, managers are more involved with projects from the beginning. Early involvement increases the likelihood that managers will accept and act on the results. Researchers' responsibility should be made explicit by a formal job description. Better planning and an annual statement of the research program for the upcoming year will help minimize emergency assignments, which usually waste resources and demoralize personnel.

EXHIBIT 4.5 **Areas of Conflict Between Top Management and Marketing Researchers**

Area of Potential Conflict	Top Management's Position	Marketing Researcher's Position
Research responsibility	Marketing researchers lack a sense of accountability. The sole function of the marketing researcher is to provide information.	The responsibility for research should be explicitly defined, and this responsibility should be consistently followed. The researcher should be involved with top management in decision making.
Research personnel	Marketing researchers are generally poor communicators who lack enthusiasm, skills, and imagination.	Top managers are anti-intellectual. Researchers should be hired, judged, and compensated on the basis of their research capabilities.
Budget	Research costs too much. Since the marketing research department's contribution is difficult to measure, budget cuts in the department are defensible.	"You get what you pay for." Research must have a continuing, long-term commitment from top management.
Assignments	Projects tend to be overengineered and not executed with a sense of urgency. Researchers have a ritualized, staid approach.	Top managers make too many nonresearchable or emergency requests and do not allocate sufficient time or money.
Problem definition	The marketing researcher is best equipped to define the problem; it is sufficient for the top manager to give general direction. Top managers cannot help it if circumstances change. The marketing researcher must appreciate this and be willing to respond to changes.	Researchers are often not given all the relevant facts about situations, which often change after research is under way. Top managers are generally unsympathetic to this widespread problem.
Research reporting	Most reports are dull, use too much jargon and too many qualifiers, and are not decision-oriented. Reports too often are presented after a decision has been made.	Top managers treat research reports superficially. Good research demands thorough reporting and documentation. Top managers give insufficient time to prepare good reports.
Use of research	Top managers should be free to use research as they see fit. Changes in the need for and timing of research are sometimes unavoidable.	Top managers' use of research to support a predetermined position or to confirm or excuse past decisions represents misuse. Also, it is wasteful to request research and then not use it after it has been conducted.

Based on John G. Keane, "Some Observations on Marketing Research in Top Management Decision Making," *Journal of Marketing*, October 1969, p. 13.

Marketing researchers likewise will come to understand management's perspective better. Researchers enhance company profits by encouraging better decisions. The closer together managers and researchers work, the more researchers realize that managers sometimes need information urgently. Thus, they should try to develop cost-saving research alternatives and realize that sometimes a quick-and-dirty study is necessary, even though it may not be as scientifically rigorous as might be desired. Sometimes, quick-and-dirty studies still provide usable and timely information. In other words, they should focus on results.

Perhaps most important is more effective communication of the research findings and research designs. The researchers must understand the interests and needs of the users of the research. If the researchers are sensitive to the decision-making orientation of management and can translate research performance into management language, organizational conflict will diminish.

A **research generalist** can effectively serve as a link between management and the research specialist. The research generalist acts as a problem definer, an educator, a liaison, a communicator, and a friendly ear. This intermediary could work with specialists who understand management's needs and demands. The student of marketing research who has a business degree seems most suited for this coordinating function.

Several strategies for reducing the conflict between management and research are possible. Managers generally should plan the role of research better, and researchers should become more decision-oriented and improve their communication skills (see Exhibit 4.6 on the next page).[8]

research generalist

An employee who serves as a link between management and research specialists. The research generalist acts as a problem definer, an educator, a liaison, a communicator, and a friendly ear.

EXHIBIT 4.6
Improving Two-Way Communication to Reduce Conflict

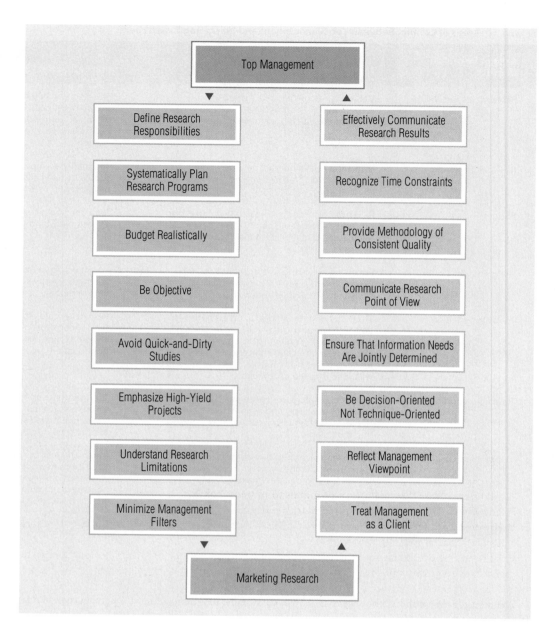

Cross-Functional Teams

Marketing orientation was discussed in Chapter 1. In a truly marketing-oriented organization, all employees are involved in the intelligence-gathering and dissemination process. Therefore, employees from different areas of the organization are more likely to communicate and act on marketing information in marketing-oriented firms.

cross-functional teams

Employee teams composed of individuals from various functional areas such as engineering, production, finance, and marketing who share a common purpose.

Thus, employees are more likely to discuss market information between different functional areas in a marketing-oriented firm. **Cross-functional teams** are composed of individuals from various functional areas such as engineering, production, finance, and marketing who share a common purpose. Cross-functional teams help organizations focus on a core business process, such as customer service or new-product development. Working in teams reduces the tendency for employees to focus single-mindedly on an isolated functional activity. Cross-functional teams help employees increase customer value since communication about their specific desires and opinions are better communicated across the firm.

At trendsetting organizations, many marketing research directors are members of cross-functional teams. New-product development, for example, may be done by a cross-functional team of engineers, finance executives, production personnel, marketing managers, and marketing researchers who take an integrated approach to solve a problem or exploit opportunities. In the old days, marketing research may not have been involved in developing new products until long after many key decisions about product specifications and manufacturing had been made. Now marketing researchers' input is part of an integrated team effort. Researchers act both as business consultants and as providers of technical services. Researchers working in teams are more likely to understand the broad purpose of their research and less likely to focus exclusively on research methodology.

The effective cross-functional team is a good illustration of the marketing concept in action. It reflects an effort to satisfy customers by using all the organization's resources. Cross-functional teams are having a dramatic impact on views of the role of marketing research within the organization.

Ethical Issues in Marketing Research

As in all human interactions, ethical issues exist in marketing research. This book considers various ethical issues concerning fair business dealings, proper research techniques, and appropriate use of research results in other chapters. The remainder of this chapter addresses society's and managers' concerns about the ethical implications of marketing research.

Ethical Questions Are Philosophical Questions

Ethical questions are philosophical questions. There are several philosophical theories that address how one develops a moral philosophy and how behavior is affected by morals. These include theories about cognitive moral development, the bases for ethical behavioral intentions, and opposing moral values.[9] While ethic remains a somewhat elusive topic, what is clear is that not everyone involved in business, or in fact involved in any human behavior, comes to the table with the same ethical standards or orientations.[10]

Marketing ethic is the application of morals to business behavior related to the exchange environment. Generally, good ethic conforms to the notion of "right," and a lack of ethic conforms to the notion of "wrong." Highly ethical behavior can be characterized as being fair, just, and acceptable.[11] Ethical values can be highly influenced by one's moral standards. **Moral standards** are principles that reflect beliefs about what is ethical and what is unethical. More simply, they can be thought of as rules distinguishing right from wrong. The Golden Rule, "Do unto others as you would have them do unto you," is one such ethical principle.

An **ethical dilemma** simply refers to a situation in which one chooses from alternative courses of actions, each with different ethical implications. Each individual develops a philosophy or way of thinking that is applied to resolve the dilemmas they face. Many people use moral standards to guide their actions when confronted with an ethical dilemma. Others adapt an ethical orientation that rejects absolute principles. Their ethic are based more on the social or cultural acceptability of behavior. If it conforms to social or cultural norms, then it is ethical.

■ RELATIVISM

Relativism is a term that reflects the degree to which one rejects moral standards in favor of the acceptability of some action. This way of thinking rejects absolute principles in favor of situation-based evaluations. Thus, an action that is judged ethical in one situation can be deemed unethical in another.

■ IDEALISM

In contrast, **idealism** is a term that reflects the degree to which one bases one's morality on moral standards. Someone who is an ethical idealist will try to apply ethical principles like the Golden Rule in all ethical dilemmas.

marketing ethic

The application of morals to behavior related to the exchange environment.

moral standards

Principles that reflect beliefs about what is ethical and what is unethical.

ethical dilemma

Refers to a situation in which one chooses from alternative courses of actions, each with different ethical implications.

relativism

A term that reflects the degree to which one rejects moral standards in favor of the acceptability of some action. This way of thinking rejects absolute principles in favor of situation-based evaluations.

idealism

A term that reflects the degree to which one bases one's morality on moral standards.

For example, a student may face an ethical dilemma when taking a test. Another student may arrange to exchange multiple choice responses to a test via electronic text messages. This represents an ethical dilemma because there are alternative courses of action each with differing moral implications. An ethical idealist may apply a rule that cheating is always wrong and therefore would not be likely to participate in the behavior. An ethical relativist may instead argue that the behavior is acceptable because a lot of the other students will be doing the same. In other words, the consensus is that this sort of cheating is acceptable, so this student would be likely to go ahead and participate in the behavior. Marketing researchers, marketing managers, and even consumers face ethical dilemmas practically every day. The following sections describe how this can occur.

General Rights and Obligations of Concerned Parties

Everyone involved in marketing research can face an ethical dilemma. For this discussion, we can divide those involved in research into three parties:

1. The people actually performing the research, who can also be thought of as the "doers"
2. The research client, sponsor, or the management team requesting the research, who can be thought of as "users" of marketing research
3. The research participants, meaning the actual research respondents or subjects

Each party has certain rights and obligations toward the other parties. Exhibit 4.7 diagrams these relationships.

Like the rest of business, research works best when all parties act ethically. Each party depends on the other to do so. A client depends on the researcher to be honest in presenting research results. The researcher depends on the client to be honest in presenting the reasons for doing the research and in describing the business situation. Each is also dependent on the research participant's honesty in answering questions during a research study. Thus, each is morally obligated toward the other. Likewise, each also has certain rights. The following section elaborates on the obligations and rights of each party.

Rights and Obligations of the Research Participant

Most marketing research is conducted with the research participant's consent. In other words, the participation is active. Traditional survey research requires that a respondent voluntarily answer questions in one way or another. This may involve answering questions on the phone, responding to an e-mail request, or even sending a completed questionnaire by regular mail. In these cases, **informed consent** means that the individual understands what the researcher wants him or her to do and consents to the research study. In other cases, research participants may not be aware that

informed consent

When an individual understands what the researcher wants him or her to do and consents to the research study.

EXHIBIT 4.7

Interaction of Rights and Obligations Informed

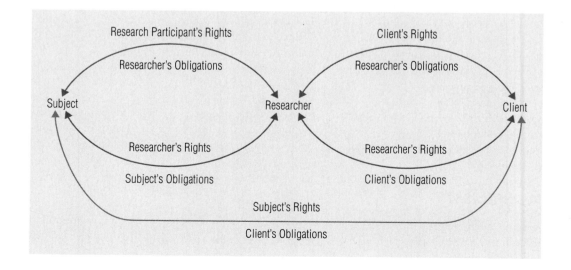

they are being monitored in some way. For instance, a research firm may monitor superstore purchases via an electronic scanner. The information may assist in understanding how customers respond to promotions. However, no consent is provided since the participant is participating passively. The ethical responsibilities vary depending on whether participation is active or passive.

■ THE OBLIGATION TO BE TRUTHFUL

When someone willingly consents to participate actively, it is generally expected that he or she will provide truthful answers. Honest cooperation is the main obligation of the research participant. In return for being truthful, the subject has the right to expect confidentiality. **Confidentiality** means that information involved in the research will not be shared with others. When the respondent truly believes that confidentiality will be maintained, then it becomes much easier to respond truthfully, even about potentially sensitive topics. Likewise, the researcher and research sponsor also may expect the respondent to maintain confidentiality. For instance, if the research involves a new food product from Nabisco, then they may not want the respondent to discuss the idea for fear that the idea may fall into the competition's hands. Thus, confidentiality is a tool to help ensure truthful responses.

confidentiality
The information involved in a research will not be shared with others.

■ PARTICIPANT'S RIGHT TO PRIVACY

Active Research

Americans relish their privacy. Hence, the right to privacy is an important issue in marketing research. This issue involves the participant's freedom to choose whether to comply with the investigator's request. Traditionally, researchers have assumed that individuals make an informed choice. However, critics have argued that the old, the poor, the poorly educated, and other underprivileged individuals may be unaware of their right to choose. They have further argued that an interviewer may begin with some vague explanation of a survey's purpose, initially ask questions that are relatively innocuous, and then move to questions of a highly personal nature. It has been suggested that subjects be informed of their right to be left alone or to break off the interview at any time. Researchers should not follow the tendency to "hold on" to busy respondents. However, this view definitely is not universally accepted in the research community.

The privacy issue is illustrated by these questions:

- "Is a telephone call that interrupts family dinner an invasion of privacy?"
- "Is an e-mail requesting response to a 30-minute survey an invasion of privacy?"

Generally, interviewing firms practice common courtesy by trying not to interview late in the evening or at other inconvenient times. However, the computerized random phone number interview has stimulated increased debate over the privacy issue. As a practical matter, respondents may feel more relaxed about privacy issues if they know who is conducting the survey. Thus, it is generally recommended that field interviewers indicate that they are legitimate researchers and name the company they work for as soon as someone answers the phone. For in-person surveys, interviewers should wear official name tags and provide identification giving their name and the names of their companies.

Research companies should adhere to the principles of the "do-not-call" policy and should respect consumers' "Internet privacy." **Do-not-call legislation** restricts any telemarketing effort from calling consumers who either register with a no-call list in their state or who request not to be called. Legislators aimed these laws at sales-related calls. However, legislation in several states, including California, Louisiana, and Rhode Island, has extended this legislation to apply to "those that seek marketing information." Thus, the legislation effectively protects consumers' privacy from researchers as well as salespeople.[12]

do-not-call legislation
Restricts any telemarketing effort from calling consumers who either register with a no-call list or who request not to be called.

Consumers often are confused about the difference between telemarketing efforts and true marketing research. Part of this is because telemarketers sometimes disguise their sales efforts by opening the conversation by saying they are doing research. The resulting confusion contributes to both increased refusal rates and lower trust. In 1980, a public opinion poll found that 19 percent of Americans reported having refused to participate in a marketing survey within the past year. Today, that number approaches 50 percent. In 2001, only 40 percent of Americans either agreed or strongly agreed that marketers will protect their privacy. That number is down from 50 percent in 1995.[13]

Companies using the Internet to do marketing research also face legislative changes. Much of this legislation is aimed at making sure consumers are properly notified about the collection of data and to whom it will be distributed. Researchers should make sure that consumers are given a clear and easy way to either consent to participation in active research or to easily opt out. Furthermore, companies should ensure that the information consumers send via the Internet is secure.[14]

Passive Research

Passive research involves different types of privacy issues. Generally, it is believed that unobtrusive observation of public behavior in places such as stores, airports, and museums is not a serious invasion of privacy. This belief is based on the fact that the consumers are indeed anonymous in that they are never identified by name nor is any attempt made to identify them. They are "faces in the crowd." As long as the behavior observed is typical of behavior commonly conducted in public, then there is no invasion of privacy. In contrast, recording behavior that is not typically conducted in public would be a violation of privacy. For example, hidden cameras recording people (without consent) taking showers at a health club, even if ultimately intended to gather information to help improve the shower experience, would be considered inappropriate.

Technology has also created new ways of collecting data passively that have privacy implications. Researchers are very interested in consumers' online behavior. For instance, the paths that consumers take while browsing the Internet can be extremely useful in understanding what kinds of information are most valued by consumers. Much of this information can be harvested and entered into a data warehouse. Researchers sometimes have legitimate reasons to use this data, which can improve consumers' ability to make wise decisions. In these cases, the researcher should gain the consumers' consent in some form before harvesting information from their Web usage patterns. Furthermore, if the information will be shared with other companies, a specific consent agreement is needed. This can come in the form of a question to which consumers respond yes or no, as in the following example:

> From time to time, the opportunity to share your information with other companies arises and this could be very helpful to you in offering you desirable product choices. We respect your privacy, however, and if you do not wish us to share this information, we will not. Would you like us to share your information with other companies?

- *Yes, you can share the information*
- *No, please keep my information private*

Not all of these attempts are legitimate. Most readers have probably encountered spyware on their home computer. **Spyware** is software that is placed on your computer without consent or knowledge while using the Internet. This software then tracks your usage and sends the information back through the Internet to the source. Then, based on these usage patterns, the user will receive push technology advertising, usually in the form of pop-up ads. Sometimes, the user will receive so many pop-up ads that the computer becomes unusable. The use of spyware is illegitimate because it is done without consent and therefore violates the right to privacy and confidentiality.

spyware

Software placed on a computer without consent or knowledge of the user.

Kid's Stuff Is Complicated

Children are involved in at least half of all spending in the United States. Thus, researchers need input from them to be able to deliver high-value products. However, legislators rightly have special concern for privacy when business interacts with children in some way. Researchers have a special obligation to ensure the safety of children. COPPA, the Children's Online Privacy Protection Act, defines a child as anyone under the age of thirteen. Anyone engaging in contact with a child through the Internet is obligated to obtain parental consent and notification before any personal information or identification can be provided by a child. Therefore, a researcher collecting a child's name, phone number, or e-mail address without parental consent is violating the law. While the law and ethic do not always correspond, in this case, it is probably pretty clear that a child's personal information shouldn't be collected.

Issues involving consent and confidentiality are complicated by a child's increased vulnerability. For instance, should a child be allowed to consent to participating in research without parental consent? Even something as innocuous as offering a child a cupcake for participating in research might not meet all parents' approval. Clearly, children under a certain age should only be interviewed in the presence of a parent. However, will the child respond the same way when a parent is present as when alone? Imagine asking a fourteen-year-old if he or she enjoys smoking cigarettes. How might a parent's presence change the response?[15] The age of consent for marketing research isn't clear even when research is within the guidelines of COPPA. To be safe, most standard research conducted with children under the age of sixteen should only be done with parental consent. When the research involves matters that are for "mature audiences," such as human sexuality or alcohol consumption, then parental consent should be sought for anyone under the age of eighteen.

Doing research with children can yield extremely useful information. However, it is also more risky than doing research with adults. When in doubt, researchers should consider how they would like to see their own child treated and then go even further to make sure that there are no ethical problems with the use of children in research.

■ DECEPTION AND THE RIGHT TO BE INFORMED

Experimental Designs

Experimental manipulations often involve some degree of deception. In fact, without some deception, a researcher would never know if a research subject was responding to the actual manipulation or to their perception of the experimental variable. This is why researchers sometimes use a placebo.

A **placebo** is a false experimental effect used to create the perception of a true effect. Imagine two consumers, each participating in a study of the effect of a new herbal supplement on hypertension. One consumer receives a packet containing the citrus-flavored supplement, which is meant to be mixed in water and drunk with breakfast. The other also receives a packet, but in this case the packet contains a mixture that will simply color the water and provide a citrus flavor. The second consumer also believes he or she is drinking the actual supplement. In this way, the psychological effect is the same on both consumers, and any actual difference in hypertension must be due to the actual herbs contained in the supplement. Interestingly, experimental subjects often display some placebo effect in which the mere belief that some treatment has been applied causes some effect.

This type of deception can be considered ethical. Primarily, researchers conducting an experiment must generally (1) gain the willful cooperation of the research subject and (2) fully explain the actual experimental variables applied following the experiment's completion. Every experiment should include a **debriefing** session in which research subjects are fully informed and provided a chance to ask any questions that they may have about the experiment.

Mystery Shopper Research

Researchers sometimes will even withhold the actual research questions from respondents in simple descriptive research. A distinction can thus be made between deception and discreet silence. For instance, sometimes providing the actual research question to respondents is simply providing them more information than they need to give a valid response. A researcher may ask questions about the perceived price of a product when his or her real interest is in how consumers form quality impressions.

placebo

A false experimental effect used to create the perception that some effect has been administered.

debriefing

Research subjects are fully informed and provided with a chance to ask any questions they may have about the experiment.

Research aimed at marketing employees also sometimes involves deception. For instance, employees are sometimes passive respondents in observational research involving a mystery shopper. **Mystery shoppers** are employees of a research firm that are paid to "pretend" to be actual shoppers. A mystery shopper would rarely identify him- or herself as anything other than a customer. However, since most employees perform their jobs in public, and perform behaviors that are easily observable, research using mystery shoppers is not considered an invasion of an employee's privacy.

mystery shoppers

Employees of a research firm that are paid to pretend to be actual shoppers.

■ PROTECTION FROM HARM

Researchers should do everything they can to make sure that research participants are not harmed by participating in research. Most marketing research does not expose participants to any harm. However, the researcher should consider every possibility. For example, if the research involves tasting food or drink, the possibility exists that a research participant could have a severe allergic reaction. Similarly, researchers studying retail and workplace atmospherics often manipulate odors by injecting certain scents into the air.[16] The researcher is sometimes in a difficult situation. He or she has to somehow find out what things the subject is allergic to, without revealing the actual experimental conditions. One way this may be done is by asking the subjects to provide a list of potential allergies ostensibly as part of a separate research project.

Other times, research may involve some potential psychological harm. This may come in the form of stress or in the form of some experimental treatment that questions some strongly held conviction. For instance, a researcher studying helping behavior may lead a subject to believe that another person is being harmed in some way. In this way, the researcher can see how much a subject can withstand before doing something to help another person. In reality, the other person is usually a research confederate simply pretending to be in pain. Three key questions that can determine whether a research participant is being treated unethically as a result of experimental procedures are:

1. Has the research subject provided consent to participate in an experiment?
2. Is the research subject subjected to substantial physical or psychological trauma?
3. Can the research subject be easily returned to his or her initial state?

The issue of consent is tricky in experiments because the researcher cannot reveal exactly what the research is about ahead of time or the validity of the experiment will be threatened. In addition, experimental research subjects are usually provided some incentive to participate. We will have more on this later in the book, but ethically speaking, the incentives should always be noncoercive. In other words, a faculty member seeking volunteers should not withhold a student's grade if he or she does not participate in an experiment. Thus, the volunteer should provide consent without fear of harm for saying no and with some idea about any potential risk involved.

If the answer to the second question is yes, then the research should not be conducted. If the answer to the second question is no and consent is obtained, then the manipulation does not present an ethical problem, and the researcher can proceed.

The third question is really helpful in understanding how far one can go in applying manipulations to a research subject. If the answer to the third question is no, then the research should not be conducted. The Research Snapshot on the next page discussed the use of hypnosis in marketing research. If the hypnotic state would cause the participant severe trauma, or if he or she cannot be easily returned to the prehypnotic state, then the research procedure should not be used. If, for instance, the consumer makes a large number of purchases under hypnosis, going deeply into debt, returning him or her to the original state may be difficult. If so, the application of hypnosis is probably inappropriate. If the answer to this question is yes, then the manipulation is ethical.

human subjects review committee

Carefully reviews proposed research design to try to make sure that no harm can come to any research participant. Otherwise known as an Institutional Review Board or IRB.

Institutional Review Board

Another name for a human subjects review committee.

Many research companies and practically all universities now maintain a **human subjects review committee**. This is a committee that carefully reviews a proposed research design to try to make sure that no harm can come to any research participant. A side benefit of this committee is that it can also review the procedures to make sure no legal problems are created by implementing the particular design. Sometimes, the name **Institutional Review Board** (IRB) is used to refer to this committee.

Must Win Auction! Must Win Auction!

Auctions are certainly not new. However, auctions are no longer relegated to estate sales, livestock yards, or art sales; eBay and competing Web sites have brought the consumer auction to the masses. Consumers can bid on practically any product imaginable. The NCAA BCS Football Championship Game is sold out each year. But, you can always bid for tickets on eBay. A lucky owner of tickets for this game can sell tickets to the highest bidder. In 2004, loyal Louisiana State University Tiger fans were willing to bid and pay more than $600 for a ticket with a face value of about $60. Four years later, some of those same fans paid over $1,000 for a ticket to watch the Tigers win the national championship again.

Recently, there has been considerable interest in understanding why consumers have flocked to online auctions in such large numbers. The research can help Web designers and online auction companies decide how to design their sites to enhance the experience for consumers. When questioned, consumers often talk about how they can get a good price by participating in an auction, or they can get something they might not be able to otherwise. However, could it be that emotional reasons involved in competing to "win" the auctions are equally as important?

When consumers are unable or unwilling to voice their emotional or psychological reasons for behavior, some researchers have turned to hypnosis. Hypnosis relaxes the inhibitions of consumers and can get them to behave in a manner that may more accurately reflect their true thoughts, emotions, and behavior. A researcher may consider using hypnosis to study online auctions.

Research participants could be recruited and asked to participate in a real online auction on eBay. Half of the participants will participate in the auction while a researcher looks on. The other half will do the same thing, but only after being induced into a hypnotic state by a member of the research team.

When preparing the report, the researcher notices that, indeed, those in the hypnotic state reported experiencing more emotions and more feelings of competitiveness than did other participants. Hypnotized respondents also placed more bids, purchased more goods, and had higher average price offers than did the others. Although the results appear to be valuable to the client, the researcher is beginning to have some reservations about the research approach used. Is the use of hypnosis ever ethical marketing research? If so, would this situation qualify as one in which there are no ethical issues in the use of hypnosis? Questions like these continue to plague the researcher. Compounding this problem is the fact that the research client wanted the research report completed by yesterday. The researcher suspects that the company already has a tactical plan for redesigning their Web operations. It isn't clear that the research results would ever be used anyway.

Sources: Wood, Charles M. and Tracy A. Suter, "Making Marketing Principles Tangible: Online Auctions as Living Case Studies," *Journal of Marketing Education*, 26 (August 2004), 137–144; Weinberg, Bruce D. and Lenita Davis, "Exploring the WOW in Online-Auction Feedback," *Journal of Business Research*, 58 (November 2005), 1609–1621. Fellman, M. W., "Mesmerizing Method Gets Results," *Marketing News*, 32 (July 20 1998), 1–38; McDonald, W. J., "Consumer Decision Making and Altered States of Consciousness: A Study of Dualities," *Journal of Business Research*, 42 (July 1998), 287–294; Handerson, Naomi R., "Good Research Tools Never Go Out of Style and Don't Shift in the Winds of Whatever Is New and Trendy," *Marketing Research*, 17 (Spring 2005), 39–40.

Rights and Obligations of the Client Sponsor (User)

■ ETHICAL BEHAVIOR BETWEEN BUYER AND SELLER

The general business ethic expected between a purchasing agent and a sales representative should hold in a marketing research situation. For example, if a purchasing agent has already decided to purchase a product from a friend, it would be unethical for that person to solicit competitive bids from others because they have no chance of being accepted. Similarly, a client seeking research should only seek bids from firms that have a legitimate chance of actually doing the work. In addition, any section on the ethical obligation of a research client would be remiss not to mention that the user is obligated to pay the provider the agreed-upon wage and pay within the agreed-upon time.

■ AN OPEN RELATIONSHIP WITH RESEARCH SUPPLIERS

The client sponsor has the obligation to encourage the research supplier to objectively seek out the truth. To encourage this objectivity, a full and open statement of the decision situation, a full disclosure of constraints in time and money, and any other insights that assist the researcher should be provided. This means that the researcher will be provided adequate access to key decision makers. These decision makers should agree to openly and honestly discuss matters related to the situation. Finally, this means that the client is open to actually using the research results. Time is simply too valuable to ask a researcher to perform a project when the results will not be used.

■ AN OPEN RELATIONSHIP WITH INTERESTED PARTIES

Conclusions should be based on data—not conjecture. Users should not knowingly disseminate conclusions from a research project in a manner that twists them into a position that cannot be supported by the data. Twisting the results in a self-serving manner or to support some political position poses serious ethical questions. A user may also be tempted to misrepresent results while trying to close a sale. Obviously, this is also morally inappropriate.

advocacy research

Research undertaken to support a specific claim in a legal action or represent some advocacy group.

Advocacy research—research undertaken to support a specific claim in a legal action or to represent some advocacy group—puts a client in a unique situation. Researchers often conduct advocacy research in their role as an expert witness. For instance, a researcher may be deposed to present evidence showing that a "knock-off" brand diminishes the value of a better known name brand. In conventional research, attributes such as sample size, profile of people actually interviewed, and number of questions asked are weighed against cost in traditional research. However, a court's opinion on whether research results are reliable may be based exclusively on any one specific research aspect. Thus, the slightest variation from technically correct procedures may be magnified by an attorney until a standard marketing research project no longer appears adequate in a judge's eyes. How open should the client be in the courtroom?

The ethic of advocacy research presents a number of serious issues that can lead to an ethical dilemma:

- Lawyers' first responsibility is to represent their clients. Therefore, they might not be interested as much in the truth as they are in evidence that supports their client's position. Presenting accurate research results may harm the client.
- A researcher should be objective. However, he or she runs the risk of conducting research that does not support the desired position. In this case, the lawyer may ask the researcher if the results can somehow be interpreted in another manner.
- Should the lawyer (in this case a user of research) ask the researcher to take the stand and present an inaccurate picture of the results?

Ethically, the attorney should certainly not put the researcher on the stand and encourage an act of perjury. The attorney may hope to ask specific questions that are so limited that taken alone, they may appear to support the client. However, this is risky because the opposing attorney likely also has an expert witness that can suggest questions for cross-examination. Returning to our branding example, if the research does not support an infringement of the known brand's name, then the brand name's attorney should probably not have the researcher take the stand.

Advocacy researchers do not necessarily bias results intentionally. However, attorneys rarely submit advocacy research evidence that does not support their clients' positions.

The question of advocacy research is one of objectivity: Can the researcher seek out the truth when the sponsoring client wishes to support its position at a trial? The ethical question stems from a conflict between legal ethic and research ethic. Although the courts have set judicial standards for marketing research methodology, perhaps only the client and individual researcher can resolve this question.

Privacy

People believe the collection and distribution of personal information without their knowledge is a serious violation of their privacy. The privacy rights of research participants create a privacy obligation on the part of the research client. Suppose a database marketing company is offering a mailing list compiled by screening millions of households to obtain brand usage information. The information would be extremely valuable to your firm, but you suspect those individuals who filled out the information forms were misled into thinking they were participating in a survey. Would it be ethical to purchase the mailing list? If respondents have been deceived about the purpose of a survey and their names subsequently are sold as part of a user mailing list, this practice is certainly unethical. The client and the research supplier have the obligation to maintain respondents' privacy.

Consider another example. Sales managers know that a marketing research survey of their business-to-business customers' buying intentions includes a means to attach a customer's name to each questionnaire. This confidential information could be of benefit to a sales representative calling on a specific customer. A client wishing to be ethical must resist the temptation to identify those accounts (that is, those respondents) that are the hottest prospects.

Privacy on the Internet

Privacy on the Internet is a controversial issue. A number of groups question whether Web site questionnaires, registration forms, and other means of collecting personal information will be kept confidential. Many marketers argue that their organizations don't need to know who the user is because the individual's name is not important for their purposes. However, they do want to know certain information (such as demographic characteristics or product usage) associated with an anonymous profile. For instance, a Web advertiser could reach a targeted audience without having access to identifying information. Of course, unethical companies may violate anonymity guidelines. Research shows that consumers are sensitive to confidentiality notices before providing information via a Web site. Over 80 percent of consumers report looking for specific privacy notices before they will exchange information electronically. In addition, over half believe that companies do not do enough to ensure the privacy of personal information.[17] Thus, research users should not disclose private information without permission from the consumers who provided that information.

Rights and Obligations of the Researcher

Marketing research firms and marketing research departments should practice good business ethic. Researchers are often the focus of discussions of business ethic because of the necessity that they interact with the public. Several professional organizations have written and adopted codes of ethic for their researchers, including the American Marketing Association, the European Society for Opinion and Market Research, and the Marketing Research Society.[18] Many of these codes are lengthy and the full contents can be found at the associations' Web sites. Key code components, most of which are described further in this chapter, directly relevant to marketing research prohibit:

- Representing a sales pitch as marketing research
- Providing the name of respondents who were promised anonymity for some purpose other than the research
- Breaching the confidentiality of the research client or research participant
- Doing research for multiple firms competing in the same market
- Disseminating false or misleading results
- Plagiarizing the work of other researchers
- Violating the integrity of data gathered in the field

In addition, the researchers have rights. In particular, once a research consulting firm is hired to conduct some research, they have the right to cooperation from the sponsoring client. Also, the researchers have the right to be paid for the work they do as long as it is done professionally. Sometimes, the client may not like the results. But not liking the results is no basis for not paying. The client should pay the researcher for competent work in full and in a timely manner.

■ THE PURPOSE OF RESEARCH IS RESEARCH

Mixing Sales and Research

Consumers sometimes agree to participate in an interview that is purported to be pure research, but it eventually becomes obvious that the interview is really a sales pitch in disguise. This is unprofessional at best and fraudulent at worst. The Federal Trade Commission (FTC) has indicated that it is illegal to use any plan, scheme, or ruse that misrepresents the true status of a person seeking admission to a prospect's home, office, or other establishment. No research firm or basic marketing researcher should engage in any sales attempts. Applied market researchers working for the sponsoring company should also avoid overtly mixing research and sales. However, the line is becoming less clear with increasing technology.

Research That Isn't Research

Consider the following typical exchange between a product manager and a marketing researcher. The manager wants to hire the firm to do a test-market for a new product:

Researcher:	*What if the test results are favorable?*
Product manager:	*Why, we'll launch the product nationally, of course.*
Researcher:	*And if the results are unfavorable?*
Product manager:	*They won't be. I'm sure of that.*
Researcher:	*But just suppose they are.*
Product manager:	*I don't think we should throw out a good product just because of one little market test.*
Researcher:	*Then why test?*
Product manager:	*Listen, Smith, this is a major product introduction. It's got to have some research behind it.*

It's probably pretty easy to see what is actually going on here. The product manager really wants research that will justify a decision that already has been made. If the test-market's results contradict the decision, the product manager will almost certainly disregard the research. This isn't really research so much as it is **pseudo-research** because it is conducted not to gather information for marketing decisions but to bolster a point of view and satisfy other needs.

The most common type of pseudo-research is performed to justify a decision that has already been made or that management is already strongly committed to. A media company may wish to sell advertising space on Internet search sites. Even though they strongly believe that the ads will be worth the rates they will charge advertisers, they may not have the hard evidence to support this view. Therefore, the advertiser's sales force may provide feedback indicating customer resistance to moving their advertising from local radio to the Internet. The advertising company may then commission a study for which the only result they care to find is that the Internet ads will be effective. In this situation, a researcher should walk away from the project if it appears that management strongly desires the research to support a predetermined opinion only. While it is a fairly easy matter for an outside researcher to walk away from such a job, it is another matter for an in-house researcher to refuse such a job. Thus, avoiding pseudo-research is a right of the researcher but an obligation for the manager.

Occasionally, marketing research is requested simply to pass blame for failure to another area. A product manager may deliberately request a research study with no intention of paying attention to the findings and recommendations. The manager knows that the particular project is in trouble but plays the standard game to cover up for his or her mismanagement. If the project fails, marketing research will become the scapegoat. The ruse may involve a statement something like this: "Well, research should have identified the problem earlier!"

pseudo-research
Conducted not to gather information for marketing decisions but to bolster a point of view and satisfy other needs.

Push Polls

Politicians have concocted and specialize in a particular type of pseudo-research as a means of damaging opposing candidates' reputations and protecting their own. A **push poll** is telemarketing under the guise of research. Its name derives from the fact that the purpose of the poll is to push consumers into a pre-determined response. For instance, thousands of potential voters can be called and asked to participate in a survey. The interviewer then may ask loaded questions that put a certain spin on a candidate. "Do you think that candidate X, who is involved with people known to be linked to scandal and crime, can be trusted with the responsibility of office?" This is a push poll. An honest question may simply ask how much candidate X can be trusted.

Push polling has pushed beyond politics. For example, during the summer of 2008, famous Green Bay Packer quarterback Brett Favre, who had announced his retirement earlier in the year, changed his mind and expressed a desire to play the 2008–09 season. However, the Packers were less than receptive. Several polls on the Internet and even via the telephone were conducted. Most of the polls were intended to get the Packers to welcome Brett back more than they were intended to provide a true picture of the population. The questions were often phrased in a leading fashion such as: "Do you believe that a proven, experienced quarterback who has led his team to the Super Bowl in the past gives the Packers the best chance of winning this year?" Obviously, this is a leading question because it frames the choice so that a yes response is very likely.

push poll
Telemarketing under guise of research.

Service Monitoring

Occasionally, the line between research and customer service isn't completely clear. For instance, Toyota may survey all of its new car owners after the first year of ownership. While the survey appears to be research, it may also provide information that could be used to correct some issue with the customer. For example, if the research shows that a customer is dissatisfied with the way the car handles, Toyota could follow up with the specific customer. The follow-up could result in changing the tires of the car, resulting in a smoother and quieter ride, as well as a more satisfied customer. Should a pattern develop showing other customers with the same opinion, Toyota may need to switch the original equipment tires used on this particular car.

In this case, both research and customer service are involved. Since the car is under warranty, there would be no selling attempt. Researchers are often asked to design satisfaction surveys. These may identify the customer so they may be contacted by the company. Such practice is acceptable as long as the researcher allows the consumer the option of either being contacted or not being contacted. In other words, the customer should be asked whether it is okay for someone to follow up in an effort to improve their satisfaction. There are actually situations in which a customer could be made more satisfied by purchasing some product.

Push polls, selling under the guise of research, and pseudo-research are all misrepresentations of the true purpose of research and should be avoided. It is important that researchers understand the difference between research and selling.

Push polls are often used to sway public opinion rather than measure it. Were they helpful to Brett Favre in 2008? Not really! He turned up as a Jet!

■ OBJECTIVITY

The need for objective scientific investigation to ensure accuracy is stressed throughout this book. Researchers should maintain high standards to be certain that their data are accurate. Furthermore, they must not intentionally try to prove a particular point for political purposes. The conclusions should be based on the data not the desires of the researchers, the clients/managers or even the participants.

■ MISREPRESENTATION OF RESEARCH

It should go without saying, but research results should not be misrepresented. This means, for instance, that the statistical accuracy of a test should be stated precisely and the meaning of findings should not be understated or overstated. Both the researcher and the client share this obligation. There are many ways that research results can be reported in a less than full and honest way. For example, a researcher may present results showing a relationship between advertising spending and sales. However, the researcher may also discover that this relationship disappears when the primary competitors' prices are taken into account. In other words, the relationship between advertising spending and sales is made spurious by the competitors' prices (see Chapter 3). Thus, it would be questionable to say the least to report a finding suggesting that sales could be increased by increasing ad spending without also mentioning the spurious nature of this finding.

Honesty in Presenting Results

Misrepresentation can also occur in the way results are presented. For instance, charts can be created that make a very small difference appear very big. Likewise, they can be altered to make a meaningful difference seem small. Exhibit 4.8 on the next page illustrates this effect. Each chart presents exactly the same data. The data represent consumer responses to service quality ratings and satisfaction ratings. Both quality and satisfaction are collected on a 5-point strongly-disagree-to-strongly-agree scale. In frame A, the chart appears to show meaningful differences between men

TOTHEPOINT

He uses statistics as a drunken man uses a lamppost—for support rather than illumination.

—Andrew Lang

EXHIBIT 4.8
**How Results Can Be
Misrepresented in a Report
or Presentation**

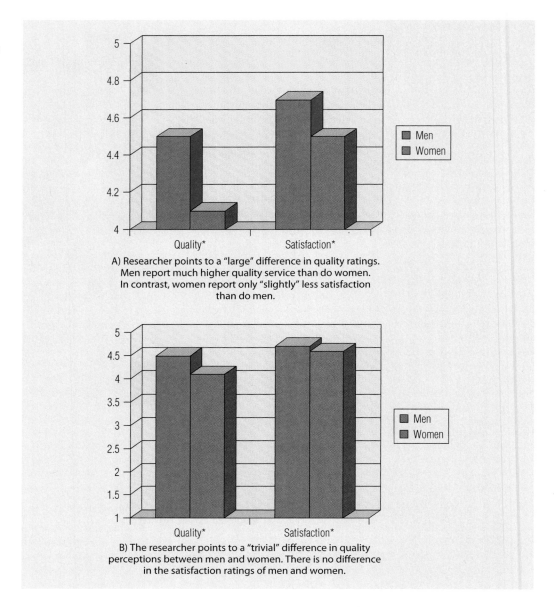

A) Researcher points to a "large" difference in quality ratings.
Men report much higher quality service than do women.
In contrast, women report only "slightly" less satisfaction
than do men.

B) The researcher points to a "trivial" difference in quality
perceptions between men and women. There is no difference
in the satisfaction ratings of men and women.

and women, particularly for the service-quality rating. However, notice that the scale range is
shown as 4 to 5. In frame B, the researcher presents the same data but shows the full scale range
(1 to 5). Now, the differences are reported as trivial.

All charts and figures should reflect fully the relevant range of values reported by respondents.
If the scale range is from 1 to 5, then the chart should reflect a 1 to 5 range unless there is some
value that is simply not used by respondents. If no or only a very few respondents had reported a
1 for their service quality or satisfaction rating, then it may be appropriate to show the range as 2
to 5. However, if there is any doubt, the researcher should show the full scale range.

The American Marketing Association's marketing Code of Ethic states that "a user of research
shall not knowingly disseminate conclusions from a given research project or service that are inconsistent with or not warranted by the data." A dramatic example of a violation of this principle
occurred in an advertisement of a cigarette smoker study. The advertisement compared two brands
and stated that "of those expressing a preference, over 65 percent preferred" the advertised brand to
a competing brand. The misleading portion of this reported result was that most of the respondents
did *not* express a preference; they indicated that both brands tasted about the same. Thus, only a
very small percentage of those studied actually revealed a preference, and the results were somewhat
misleading. Such shading of results violates the obligation to report accurate findings.

■ HONESTY IN REPORTING ERRORS

Likewise, any major error that has occurred during the course of the study should not be kept secret from management or the sponsor. Hiding errors or variations from the proper procedures tends to distort or shade the results. Similarly, every research design presents some limitations. For instance, the sample size may be smaller than ideal. The researcher should point out the key limitations in the research report and presentation. In this way, any factors that qualify the findings can be understood. The decision maker needs this information before deciding on any risky course of action.

■ CONFIDENTIALITY

Confidentiality comes into play in several ways. The researcher must abide by any confidentiality agreement with research participants. For instance, a researcher conducting a descriptive research survey may have identified each participant's e-mail address in the course of conducting the research. After seeing the results, the client may ask for the e-mail addresses as a logical prospect list. However, as long as the researcher assured each participant's confidentiality, the e-mail addresses cannot ethically be provided to the firm. Indeed, a commitment of confidentiality also helps build trust among survey respondents.[19]

The marketing researcher often is obligated to protect the confidentiality of the research sponsor. In fact, business clients value marketing researchers' confidentiality more than any other attribute of a research firm.[20] Researchers must honor all implied and expressed promises of confidentiality whether they are made to a research participant or research client. This brings us to the topic of conflicts of interest which should be avoided, but doing so isn't always as easy as it may seem.

The Researcher and Conflicts of Interest

Imagine a researcher conducting a test market for a new high-tech Apple iPhone device that allows interactive video. Just after conducting the research, the same researcher is contacted by Samsung. Samsung, who has yet to develop video capability, wants research that addresses whether or not there is a market for iPphone interactive video. The researcher is now in a difficult position. Certainly, an ethical dilemma exists presenting multiple choices to the researcher, including the following.

- Agreeing to do the research for Samsung and using some results from the Apple study to prepare a report and recommendation for Samsung
- Agreeing to sell the new concept to Samsung without doing any additional research. In other words, provide Apple's company secrets to Samsung
- Conducting an entirely new project for Samsung without revealing any of the results or ideas from the Apple study
- Turning down the chance to do the study without revealing any information about Apple to Samsung

Which is the best choice? Obviously, both of the first two options violate the principle of maintaining client confidentiality. Thus, both are unethical. The third choice, conducting an entirely new study, may be an option. However, it may prove nearly impossible to do the entire project as if the Apple study had never been done. Even with the best of intentions, the researcher may inadvertently violate confidentiality with Apple. The last choice is the best option from a moral standpoint. It avoids any potential **conflict of interest**. In other words, actions that would best serve one client, Samsung, would be detrimental to another client, Apple. Generally, it is best to avoid working for two direct competitors.

This would be a good time to revisit the opening chapter vignette. Does the situation present the researcher with any potential conflicts of interest? How can they be addressed?

conflict of interest

Occurs when one researcher works for two competing companies.

A Final Note on Ethics

Certainly, there are researchers who would twist results for a client or who would fabricate results for personal gain. However, these are not professionals. When one is professional, one realizes that one's actions not only have personal implications, but also implications for one's field. Indeed, just

- A good way to get started in the marketing research industry is to target either a large marketing research firm or a local research firm with offers to serve as an intern. An internship will provide insight and experience that can provide a leg up on others in getting the job.
- When a company faces a very emotional decision, it is usually better to have the research needed to address the related research questions done by an outside firm.
- The potential for conflict between a client/manager and a researcher can be minimized with better communication and by making sure that both parties agree on the deliverables of a research project before that project is conducted.

- Those involved in research should consider the position of others involved in the process. When considering conducting or using research in some manner, one way to help ensure fair treatment of others involved in research is to consider whether you would like to be treated in this manner or whether you would like someone to treat a close member of your family in such a manner.
- Research with particularly vulnerable segments such as children involves special care. When doing research with children under the age of 16, parental consent is nearly always needed.

© GEORGE DOYLE & CIARAN GRIFFIN

a few unscrupulous researchers can give the field a bad name. Thus, researchers should maintain the highest integrity in their work to protect our industry. Research participants should also play their role, or else the data they provide will not lead to better products for all consumers. Finally, the research users must also follow good professional ethic in their treatment of researchers and research results. When all three parties participate with integrity, consumers in general, and society overall, gain the most benefit from professional marketing research.

Summary

1. Know when research should be conducted externally and when it should be done internally. The company who needs the research is not always the best company to actually perform the research. Sometimes it is better to use an outside supplier of some form. An outside agency is better when a fresh perspective is needed, when it would be difficult for inside researchers to be objective, and when the outside firm has some special expertise. In contrast, it is better to do the research in-house when it needs to be done very quickly, when the project requires close collaboration of many employees within the company, when the budget for the project is limited, and when secrecy is a major concern. The decision to go outside or stay inside for research depends on these particular issues.

2. Be familiar with the types of jobs, job responsibilities, and career paths available within the marketing research industry. A marketing research function may be organized in any number of ways depending on a firm's size, business, and stage of research sophistication. Marketing research managers must remember they are managers, not just researchers. Marketing research offers many career opportunities. Entry-level jobs may involve simple tasks such as data entry or performing survey research. A research analyst may be the next step on the career path. This position may involve project design, preparation of proposals, data analysis, and interpretation. Whereas there are several intermediate positions that differ depending on whether one works for a small or large firm, the director of marketing research is the chief information officer in charge of marketing information systems and research projects. The director plans, executes, and controls the marketing research function.

3. Become sensitive to the often conflicting relationship between marketing management and researchers. Researchers and managers have different and often conflicting goals. Some of the key sources of conflict include money, time, intuition, and experience. Managers want to spend the least amount of money on research possible, have it done in the shortest period of time conceivable, and believe that intuition and experience are good substitutes for research. Researchers will exchange greater expense for more precision in the research, would like to take more time to be more certain of results, and are hesitant to rely on intuition and experience. Better communication is a key to reducing this conflict. One tool that can be useful is the implementation of cross-functional teams.

4. Define ethic and understand how it applies to marketing research. Marketing ethic is the application of morals to behavior related to the exchange environment. Generally, good ethic conforms to the notion of "right" and a lack of ethic conforms to the notion of "wrong." Those involved in marketing research face numerous ethical dilemmas. Researchers serve clients or, put another way, the doers of research serve the users. It is often easy for a doer to compromise professional standards in an effort to please the user. After all, the user pays the bills. Given the large number of ethical dilemmas involved in research, ethic is highly applicable to marketing research.

5. Appreciate the rights and obligations of a) research respondents—particularly children, b) research clients or sponsors, and c) marketing researchers. Each party involved in research has certain rights and obligations. These are generally interdependent in the sense that one party's right often leads to an obligation for another party. While the rights and obligations of all three parties are important, the obligation of the researcher to protect research participants is particularly important. Experimental manipulations can sometimes expose subjects to some form of harm or involve them in a ruse. The researcher must be willing to fully inform the subjects of the true purpose of the research during a debriefing. The researcher must also avoid subjecting participants to undue physical or psychological trauma. In addition, it should be reasonably easy to return an experimental subject to his or her original, pre-experiment condition.

6. Avoid situations involving a conflict of interest in performing marketing research. A marketing research conflict of interest occurs when a researcher is faced with doing something to benefit one client at the expense of another client. One situation where this occurs is when a researcher could use results obtained in a study done for Brand A to prepare a report for its primary competitor Brand B. The researcher might consider recollecting the data anew for Brand B, but even this opens up the researcher to the appearance of a conflict of interest. The best way to avoid a conflict of interest is to avoid getting involved with multiple projects involving competing firms within some market.

Key Terms and Concepts

advocacy research, *94*
confidentiality, *89*
conflict of interest, *99*
cross-functional teams, *86*
custom research, *77*
debriefing, *91*
director of marketing research, *79*
do-not-call legislation, *89*
ethical dilemma, *87*
forecast analyst, *80*
human subjects review committee, *92*

idealism, *87*
informed consent, *88*
in-house research, *73*
Institutional Review Board, *92*
manager of decision support systems, *80*
marketing ethic, *87*
moral standards, *87*
mystery shoppers, *92*
outside agency, *73*
placebo, *91*
pseudo-research, *96*

push poll, *96*
relativism, *87*
research analyst, *79*
research assistants, *80*
research generalist, *85*
research suppliers, *76*
spyware, *90*
standardized research service, *76*
syndicated service, *76*

Questions for Review and Critical Thinking

1. What are the conditions that make in-house research preferable? What are the conditions that make outside research preferable? Would the company in the opening vignette have been better off to do the marketing research desired in-house rather than out-house?

2. Read a recent news article from *The Wall Street Journal* or other key source that deals with a new-product introduction. Would you think it would be better for that firm to do research in-house or to use an outside agency? Explain.

3. What might the organizational structure of the research department be like for the following organizations?
    a. A large advertising agency
    b. A founder-owned company that operates a 20-unit restaurant chain
    c. Your university
    d. An industrial marketer with four product divisions
    e. A large consumer products company

4. What problems do marketing research directors face in their roles as managers?

5. What are some of the basic causes of conflict between management and marketing research?

6. Comment on the following situation: A product manager asks the research department to forecast costs for some basic ingredients (raw materials) for a new product. The researcher asserts that this is not a research job; it is a production forecast.

7. What is the difference between research and pseudo-research? Cite several examples of each.

8. **ETHICS** What is marketing ethic? How is marketing ethic relevant to research?

9. **ETHICS** What is the difference between ethical relativism and ethical idealism? How might a person with an idealist ethical philosophy and a person with a relativist ethical philosophy

differ with respect to including a sales pitch at the end of a research survey?

10. **ETHICS** What obligations does a researcher have with respect to confidentiality?

11. How should a marketing researcher help top management better understand the functions and limitations of research?

12. **ETHICS** List at least one research obligation for researcher participants (respondents), marketing researchers, and research clients (sponsors).

13. **ETHICS** What is a conflict of interest in a research context? How can such conflicts of interest be avoided?

14. **ETHICS** What key questions help resolve the question of whether or not research participants serving as subjects in an experiment are treated ethically?

15. Identify a research supplier in your area and determine what syndicated services and other functions are available to clients.

16. **'NET** Use the internet to find at least five marketing research firms that perform survey research. List and describe each firm briefly.

17. What actions might the marketing research industry take to convince the public that marketing research is a legitimate activity and that firms that misrepresent their intentions and distort findings to achieve their aims are not true marketing research companies?

18. **ETHICS** Comment on the ethic of the following situations.

   a. A food warehouse club advertises "savings up to 30 percent" after a survey showed a range of savings from 2 to 30 percent below average prices for selected items.

   b. A radio station broadcasts the following message during a syndicated rating service's rating period: "Please fill out your diary" [which lists what media the consumer has been watching or listening to].

   c. A sewing machine retailer advertises a market test and indicates that the regular price will be cut to one-half for three days only.

   d. A researcher tells a potential respondent that an interview will last ten minutes rather than the thirty minutes he or she actually anticipates.

   e. A respondent tells an interviewer that she wishes to cooperate with the survey, but her time is valuable and, therefore, she expects to be paid for the interview.

   f. When you visit your favorite sports team's home page on the Web, you are asked to fill out a registration questionnaire before you enter the site. The team then sells your information (team allegiance, age, address, and so on) to a company that markets sports memorabilia via catalogs and direct mail.

19. **ETHICS** Comment on the following interview:

Interviewer:	*Good afternoon, sir. My name is Mrs. Johnson, and I am with Counseling Services. We are conducting a survey concerning Memorial Park. Do you own a funeral plot? Please answer yes or no.*
Respondent:	*(pauses)*
Interviewer:	*You do not own a funeral plot, do you?*
Respondent:	*No.*
Interviewer:	*Would you mind if I sent you a letter concerning Memorial Park? Please answer yes or no.*
Respondent:	*No.*
Interviewer:	*Would you please give me your address?*

20. **ETHICS** Try to participate in a survey at a survey Web site such as http://www.mysurvey.com or http://www.themsrgroup.com. Write a short essay response about your experience with particular attention paid to how the sites have protections in place to prevent children from providing personal information.

Research Activities

1. **'NET** Find the mission statement of at least 3 of the top research firms described earlier in the chapter (see Exhibit 4.2). What career opportunities exist at these firms? Would you consider each firm a small, mid-sized, or large firm? How might a job with one of these firms differ from starting your own research business?

2. **'NET—ETHICS** One purpose of the United Kingdom's Market Research Society is to set and enforce the ethical standards to be observed by research practitioners. Go to its Web site at http://www.mrs.org.uk. Click on its code of conduct and evaluate it.

Case 4.1 Global Eating

Barton Boomer, director of marketing research for a large research firm, has a bachelor's degree in marketing from Michigan State University. He joined the firm nine years ago after a one-year stint as a marketing research trainee at the corporate headquarters of a western packing corporation. Barton has a wife and two children. He earns $60,000 a year and owns a home in the suburbs. He is typical of a marketing research analyst. He is asked to interview an executive with a local restaurant chain, Eats-R-Wee. Eats-R-Wee is

expanding internationally. The logical two choices for expansion are either to expand first to other nations that have values similar to those in the market area of Eats-R-Wee or to expand to the nearest geographical neighbor. During the initial interviews, Mr. Big, Vice President of Operations for Eats-R-Wee, makes several points to Barton.

- "Barton, we are all set to move across the border to Ontario and begin our international expansion with our neighbor to the north, Canada. Can you provide some research that will support this position?"

- "Barton, we are in a hurry. We can't sit on our hands for weeks waiting to make this decision. We need a comprehensive research project completed by the end of the month."
- "We are interested in how our competitors will react. Have you ever done research for them?"
- "Don't worry about the fee; we'll pay you top money for a 'good' report."

Marla Madam, Barton's Director of Marketing Research, encourages Barton to get back in touch with Mr. Big and tell him that the project will get underway right away.

Question

Critique this situation with respect to Barton's job. What recommendations would you have for him? Should the company get involved with the research? Explain your answers.

Case 4.2 Big Brother is Watching?

© GETTY IMAGES/ PHOTODISC GREEN

Technology is making our behavior more and more difficult to keep secret. Right at this very moment, there is probably some way that your location can be tracked in a way that researchers could use the information. Do you have your mobile phone with you? Is there an RFID (sometimes pronounced Rfid) tag in your shirt, your backpack, or some other personal item? Are you in your car, and does it have a GPS (Global Positioning Satellite) device? All of these are ways that your location and movements might be tracked.

For instance, rental cars can be tracked using GPS. Suppose a research firm contracts with an insurance firm to study the way people drive when using a rental car. A customer's every movement is then tracked. So, if the customer stops at a fast-food restaurant, the researcher knows. If the customer goes to the movie when he or she should be on a sales call, the researcher knows. If the customer is speeding, the researcher knows.

Clearly, modern technology is making confidentiality more and more difficult to maintain. While legitimate uses of this type of technology may assist in easing traffic patterns and providing better locations for service stations, shopping developments, and other retailers, at what point does the collection of such information become a concern? When would you become concerned about having your whereabouts constantly tracked?

Question

Suppose a GIS (Geographic Information Systems) research firm is approached by the state legislature and asked to provide data about vehicle movement within the state for all cars with a satellite tracking mechanism. Based on the movement of the cars over a certain time, the police can decide when a car was speeding. They intend on using this data to send speeding tickets to those who moved too far, too fast. If you are the research firm, would you supply the data? Discuss the ethical implications of the decision.

Part 2
Beginning Stages of the Research Process

CHAPTER 5
Problem Definition:
Jump-Starting the Research Process

CHAPTER 6
Qualitative Research Tools

CHAPTER 7
Secondary Data Research
in a Digital Age

LEARNING OUTCOMES

After studying this chapter, you should be able to

1. Explain why proper "problem definition" is essential to useful marketing research
2. Know how to identify and refine problems using a problem definition process
3. Translate managerial decision statements into relevant research objectives
4. Translate research objectives into research questions and/or research hypotheses
5. Outline the components of a research proposal
6. Construct dummy tables as part of a research proposal

Chapter Vignette: Mario Lagasto's "Advertising" Problem

James Michael, owner of a small market research firm in Columbus, Ohio, sits over a bowl of spaghetti and meatballs and a glass of Chianti Classico at Mario Lagasto's Italian Restaurant. James isn't there just for lunch; he is there discussing Lagasto's current business situation with Mario Lagasto, the restaurant's owner. James finishes only about a third of the spaghetti and half of the wine, and says, "Thanks for the lunch. It seems that I remember the house red being a lovely Barbera d'Asti."

Mario replies, "Ah, yes, from Cascina Ballarin to be exact. But, we had to move that to our reserve list. Our new comptroller has really helped us control our costs."

James asks, "Well, let's get down to business. What seems to be the problem? People certainly love Italian food."

Mario explains that his sales, which have grown every year since he opened the restaurant in 1990, have actually dropped over the last twelve months. Yet, the suburban neighborhood has continued to grow. "I was sitting at home and I realized that all the downtown restaurants have dramatically increased their television advertising and on top of this, the city's downtown revival campaign is everywhere!" He continued, "I've been using the same advertising for years: a few spots on local radio, an occasional newspaper spot, and a billboard on the main highway across from the restaurant. When I see the fancy advertising run by my competitors, it is clear that I have an advertising problem. I want you to tell me what I can do to make my advertising more effective!"

Once the interview is complete, James informs Mario that he will go back and prepare a proposal that will describe how he may be able to help Lagasto's get back on track.

Once back in the office, James begins to scribble some notes. He begins to study the advertising of both Lagasto and his competitors. He realizes that some of the neighborhood competitors, including the big chain Italian restaurants like Olive Garden, have always had a large promotional budget, including television ads. The advertising deficit isn't new. He tries to identify all the things that have changed since Lagasto's sales trends turned downward. Does Mario really have an advertising problem? Is it a problem with competitive positioning? Is it a problem with a change in the external operating environment? Has Mario just missed out on some growth opportunities? Then, just as hunger starts to set in, he remembers the rather average spaghetti and meatballs and red wine he had for lunch. He thinks about how it is has changed from what he remembers. Maybe James' hunger has led to a discovery!

Introduction

Chapter 3 discussed some basics of translating a business situation into specific research objectives. Thus, it is the first stage in the research process introduced in Chapter 3. While marketing managers and even researchers may be tempted to skip this step and go directly to designing the research project, the odds that a research project will prove useful are directly related to how well the research objectives correspond to the true business "problem." Clearly, the easiest thing for James to do in the opening vignette is to start designing a study of Lagasto's advertising effectiveness. This seems to be what Mario wants. Is an advertising study what Mario needs, however?

This chapter looks at this important step in the research process more closely. Some useful tools are described that can help translate the business situation into relevant, actionable research objectives. Research too often takes the blame for business failures when the real failure was really management's view of its own company's situation. The Research Snapshot on page 108 describes some classic illustrations involving companies as big and successful as Coca-Cola, RJ Reynolds, and Ford. While the researcher has some say in what is actually studied, remember that the client (either management or an outside sponsor) is the research customer and the researcher is serving the client's needs through research. In other words, when clients fail to understand their situation or insist on studying an irrelevant problem, the research is very likely to fail, even if it is done perfectly.

Good Decisions Start with a Good Problem Definition

decision statement

A written expression of the key question(s) that the research user wishes to answer.

Translating a business situation into something that can be researched is somewhat like translating one language into another. A good problem definition results when managers and researchers reach a consensus on a decision statement or question. A **decision statement** is a written expression of the key question(s) that a manager—that is, a research user—wishes to answer. The statement captures the true reason that research is being considered at all and therefore, it must be relevant, clear, and goal oriented. As discussed in Chapter 3, the researcher translates this into research terms by rephrasing the decision statement into one or more research objectives. These are expressed as deliverables in the research proposal. The researcher then further expresses these in precise and scientific research terminology by creating research hypotheses from the research objectives.

Opportunities and Problems

problem definition

The process of defining and developing a decision statement and the steps involved in translating it into more precise research terminology, including a set of research objectives.

In this chapter, we use the term *problem definition*. Realize that sometimes research can be used in opportunity seeking and a true troubling situation that epitomizes a problem doesn't truly exist. For simplicity however, the term **problem definition** is adapted here to refer to the process of defining and developing a decision statement and the steps involved in translating it into more precise research terminology, including a set of research objectives. If this process breaks down at any point, the research will almost certainly be useless or even harmful. Research will be useless if it presents results that simply are deemed irrelevant and do not assist in decision making. It can be harmful both because of the wasted resources and because it may misdirect the company in a poor direction. Thus, we use the term problem definition as one that translates either troubling situations or business opportunities into research terms.

Ultimately, it is difficult to say that any one step in the research process is most important. However, formally defining the problem to be attacked by research by developing decision statements and translating them into actionable research objectives must be done well or the rest of the

Take a look at the portion of the survey shown.

Consider the following questions as you think about this section of the survey and other sections of the survey not shown here.

- What kinds of decision statements might be involved using the information collected in this portion of the survey? Think about the types of companies who might be interested in this information.
- Would any nonprofit institutions be interested in this data?
- Translate a decision statement from above into a research question and the related research hypothesis or hypotheses.
- What would a dummy table look like that might provide the data for these hypotheses?

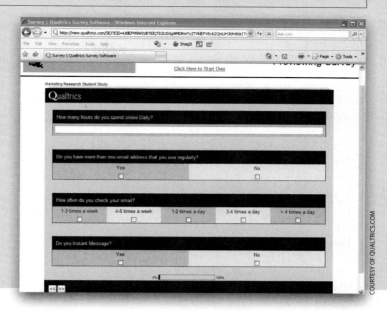

research process is misdirected. Even a good road map is useless unless you know just where you are going. All of the roads can be correctly drawn, but they still don't get you where you want to be. Similarly, even the best research procedures will not overcome poor problem definition.

Problem Complexity

Ultimately, the quality of marketing research in improving business decisions is limited by the quality of the problem definition stage. This is far from the easiest stage of the research process. Indeed, it can be the most complex. Exhibit 5.1 helps to illustrate factors that influence how complex the process can be.

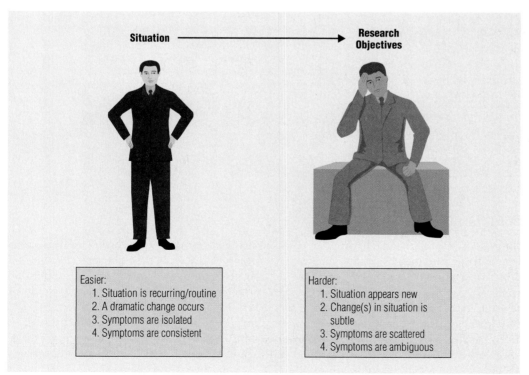

Situation ⟶ **Research Objectives**

Easier:
1. Situation is recurring/routine
2. A dramatic change occurs
3. Symptoms are isolated
4. Symptoms are consistent

Harder:
1. Situation appears new
2. Change(s) in situation is subtle
3. Symptoms are scattered
4. Symptoms are ambiguous

EXHIBIT 5.1
Defining Problems Can Be Difficult

© GEORGE DOYLE & CIARAN GRIFFIN

COURTESY OF QUALTRICS.COM

Good Answers, Bad Questions?

It's amazing, but sometimes even the most successful companies make huge blunders. These blunders often are based on a mis-understanding of exactly what the brand and/or product means to consumers. Some of the famous, or infamous, examples of such blunders include RJR's introduction of Premier "Smokeless" Cigarettes, Ford's introduction of the Edsel in the 1950s, and most famous (or infamous) of all, Coca-Cola's introduction of New Coke as a replacement for regular "old" Coke.

Volumes have been written about each of these episodes. One does have to wonder, how did these great companies do such apparently dumb things? The blame is often placed at the foot of marketing research: "Research should have revealed that product was a loser." However, researchers address the questions they are asked to address by management. Certainly, the researchers play a role in framing any decision situation into something that can be addressed by a pointed research question. The decision makers, management, almost always start the process by asking research for input. Hopefully, the dialogue that results will lead to a productive research question that will provide useful results, but it isn't always the case.

Hindsight certainly is clearer than foresight. It seems almost unthinkable that Coke could have based its decision to replace a product with a century-long success record without considering the emotional meaning that goes along with drinking a "Coke." However, management considered Coke to be a beverage, not a brand. Thus, the focus was on the taste of Coke. Thus, researchers set about trying to decide if New Coke, which was more similar to Pepsi, tasted better than the original Coke. A great deal of very careful research suggested clearly that it did taste better. If the key question was taste, New Coke was preferred over old Coke by more consumers. In fact, there was considerable evidence that already showed a taste preference for Pepsi over old Coke. Interestingly, Coke appeared to view itself as its primary competitor. At least two very important questions were never asked or were addressed insufficiently:

1. Do consumers prefer New Coke over Pepsi?
2. When people know what they are drinking, do they still prefer New Coke to old Coke?

For a taste test to be valid, it is should be done "blindly," meaning that the taster doesn't know what he or she is drinking. Only then can one assess taste without being psychologically influenced by knowing the brand. So, Coke and Pepsi conducted a blind taste test. This is certainly a good research practice—if the question is taste. The Coke research correctly answered the taste question. The big problem is that since management didn't realize that most of the meaning of Coke is psychological, and since they were so convinced that their old product was "inferior," the dialogue between management and researchers never produced more useful questions.

In the case of Ford's Edsel, a postmortem analysis suggests that research actually indicated many of the problems that ultimately led to its demise. The name, Edsel, was never tested by research, even though hundreds of other possibilities were.

Similarly, the idea of a smokeless cigarette seemed appealing. Marketing research addressed the question, "What is the attitude of smokers and nonsmokers toward a smokeless cigarette?" Nonsmokers loved the idea. Smokers, particularly those who lived with a nonsmoker, also indicated a favorable attitude. However, as we know, the product failed miserably. If you take the "smoke" out of "smoking," is it still the same thing? This question was never asked. Would someone who would try a smokeless cigarette replace their old brand with this new brand? Again, this wasn't asked.

Businesses will continue to make mistakes as long as people are involved in decision making. Consider Macy's. Clearly, Macy's is a very recognizable name brand that brings with it considerable "equity." However, in its recent acquisitions, Macy's has taken over well-known regional and local retail "institutions," and renamed them Macy's. Is this name change a good thing? Given that Macy's is replacing the names of local institutions, a backlash is clearly possible in some locations. Yahoo revamped its home page in an effort to provide more news and financial information. However, they did so despite click-through evidence showing that stories about Britney Spears drew the most interest. So, is Yahoo better positioned to deliver serious news or titillating pop stories? Certainly, questions that define the brand deserve research that is conducted thoroughly and involves more than superficial analyses. Even further, when research uncovers evidence, that evidence should be seriously considered before making a decision.

Sources: Kohno, S., "gia Design," *Gourment Retailer*, 29 (May 2008), 116–117; Gibson, Larry, "Why the New Coke Failed," *Marketing Research*, 15 (Summer 2003), 52; "Is Macy's the New Coke?" *Advertising Age*, 76 (September 26, 2005), 24.

■ SITUATION FREQUENCY

Business situations are often cyclical. Cyclical business situations lead to recurring business problems and opportunities. These problems can even become routine. In these cases, problem definition can be easy and identifying the types of research that are needed should likewise be somewhat familiar. In some cases, problems are so routine that they can be solved without any additional research. Recurring problems can even be automated through a company's DSS.

Pricing problems often occur routinely. Just think about how the price of gas fluctuates when several stations are located within sight of each other. One station's prices definitely affect the sales of the other stations as well as of the station itself. Similarly, automobile companies, airline companies, and computer companies, to name just a few, face recurring pricing issues. Because these situations recur so frequently, addressing them becomes routine. Decision makers know how to communicate them to researchers and researchers know what data are needed.

Most pricing decisions in the airline industry are automated based on sophisticated demand models. The models take into account fluctuations in travel patterns based on the time of the year, time of the day, degree of competition for that particular route, and many other factors. At one time, these decisions were based on periodic research reports. Now, the information is simply fed into a decision support system that generates a pricing schedule. It is interesting that one factor that is not very important in many of these pricing decisions is the cost involved in flying someone from point A to point B. Indeed, some passengers pay a fare much higher than the actual costs and others pay a fare much lower than the actual costs involved in getting them to their desired destination.

Dramatic Changes

When a sudden change in the business situation takes place, it can be easier to define the problem. For example, if Lagasto's business had fallen sharply in a two-month period, the key factors to study could be isolated by identifying other factors that have changed in that same time period. For example, it could be that road construction began on a nearby feeder road just over two months ago. This may lead to questions about how much traffic time and patterns influence sales at the restaurant.

In contrast, when changes are very subtle and take effect over a long period of time, it can be more difficult to define the actual decision and research problems. Consumer tastes often change slowly. The American diet evolves slowly. Detecting trends that would permanently affect one particular food market segment can be difficult. If Americans are slowly increasing their preference toward a lighter diet, traditional Italian foods may be selected less often. However, it may be difficult to detect the beginning of such a trend and even more difficult to know whether such a trend is relatively permanent or simply a temporary fad.

■ HOW WIDESPREAD ARE THE SYMPTOMS?

The more scattered any symptoms are, the more difficult it is to put them together into some coherent problem statement. In contrast, firms may sometimes face situations in which multiple symptoms exist, but they are all pointing to some specific business area. For instance, an automobile manufacturing company may exhibit symptoms such as increased complaints about a car's handling, increased warranty costs due to repairs, higher labor costs due to inefficiency, and lower performance ratings by consumer advocates such as *Consumer Reports*. All of these symptoms point to production as a likely problem area. This may lead to research questions that deal with supplier-manufacturer relationships, job performance, job satisfaction, supervisory support, and performance. Although having a lot of problems in one area may not sound very positive, it can be very helpful in pointing out the direction that is most in need of attention and improvement.

In contrast, when the problems are more widespread, developing useful research questions can prove extremely difficult. If consumers complain about the handling and appearance of a specific car model, and these complaints are accompanied by other symptoms including consumer beliefs that gas mileage could be better and that the dealerships have an unpleasant environment, researchers may have difficulty putting all these scattered symptoms together into one or a few related research questions. Later in the chapter, we'll discuss some tools for trying to analyze symptoms with an eye toward identifying some potential common cause.

■ SYMPTOM AMBIGUITY

Ambiguity is almost always unpleasant. People simply are uncomfortable with the uncertainty that comes with ambiguity. Similarly, an environmental scan of a business situation may lead to many symptoms, none of which seem to point in a clear and logical direction. In this case, the problem area, or perhaps even problem areas, remains vague and the alternative directions are difficult to ascertain.

A retail store may face a situation in which sales and traffic are up, but margins are down. They may have decreased employee turnover, but lower job satisfaction. In addition, there may be several issues that arise with their suppliers, none of which is clearly positive or negative. In this case, it may be very difficult to sort through the evidence and reach a definitive decision statement or list of research objectives.

Identifying Problems and the Problem-Definition Process

Problems Mean Gaps

A **problem** occurs when there is a difference between the current conditions and a more preferable set of conditions. In other words, a gap exists between the way things are now and a way that things could be better. The gap can come about in a number of ways:[1]

1. Actual business performance is worse than expected business performance. For instance, sales, profits, and margins could be below targets set by management. This is a very typical type of problem analysis. Think of all the new products that fail to meet their targeted goals. Trend analysis would also be included in this type of problem. Management is constantly monitoring key performance variables. Previous performance usually provides a benchmark forming expectations. Sales, for example, are generally expected to increase a certain percentage each year. When sales fall below this expectation, or particularly when they fall below the previous year's sales, management usually recognizes that they have a potential problem on their hands.

2. Actual business performance is less than possible business performance. Realization of this gap first requires that management have some idea of what is possible. This may form a research problem in and of itself.[2] Opportunity-seeking often falls into this type of problem-definition process. Many American and European Union companies have redefined what possible sales levels are based upon the expansion of free markets around the world. China's Civil Aviation Administration has relaxed requirements opening the Chinese air travel market to private airlines.[3] Suddenly, the possible market size for air travel has increased significantly, creating opportunities for growth.

3. Expected business performance is greater than possible business performance. Sometimes, management has unrealistic views of possible performance levels—either too high or too low. One key problem with new product introductions involves identifying realistic possibilities for sales. While you may have heard the old adage that 90 percent of all new products fail, how many of the failures had a realistic sales ceiling? In other words, did the company know the possible size of the market? In this case, the problem is not with the product but with the plan. Some product "failures" may actually have been successful if management had a more accurate idea of the total market potential. The Research Snapshot on page 108 illustrates this point.[4] Management can close this gap through decision making. Researchers help managers make decisions by providing relevant input.

Using a Problem-Definition Process

The problem-definition process involves several interrelated steps as shown in Exhibit 5.2. Sometimes, the boundaries between each step aren't exactly clear. But generally, completing one step leads to the other and by the time the problem is defined, each of these steps has been addressed in some way. The steps are

1. Understand the business situation—identify key symptoms
2. Identify key problem(s) from symptoms
3. Write managerial decision statement and corresponding research objectives
4. Determine the unit of analysis
5. Determine the relevant variables
6. Write research questions and/or research hypotheses

A separate section deals with each stage below.

Understand the Business Decision

A **situation analysis** involves the gathering of background information to familiarize researchers and managers with the decision-making environment. It is a way of formally documenting the problem-definition process. Gaining an awareness of marketplace conditions and an appreciation

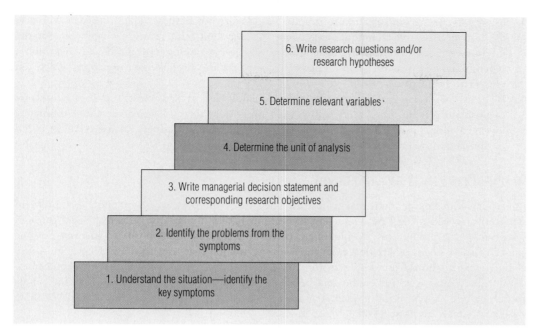

EXHIBIT 5.2
The Problem-Definition Process

of the situation often requires exploratory research. Some qualitative research techniques covered in Chapter 6 can be helpful in problem definition. The situation analysis begins with an interview between the researcher and management.

■ INTERVIEW PROCESS

The researcher must enter a dialogue with the key decision makers in an effort to fully understand the situation that has motivated a research effort. This process is critical and the researcher should be granted access to all individuals who have specific knowledge of or insight into this situation. Researchers working with marketing managers who want the information "yesterday" often get little assistance when they ask, "What are your objectives for this study?" Nevertheless, even decision makers who have only a gut feeling that marketing research might be a good idea benefit greatly if they work with the marketing researcher to articulate precise research objectives.[5] Even when there is good cooperation, seldom can key decision makers express the situation in research terms. Thus, the researcher's job is to sort through the discussion and narrow down the discussion to issues that can be changed and that can be researched.

Researchers are often tempted to accept the first plausible problem statement offered by management. For instance, in the opening vignette, Mario clearly believes an advertising problem exists. However, it is very important that the researcher not blindly accept a convenient problem definition for expediency's sake. In fact, research demonstrates that people who are better problem solvers generally reject problem definitions as given to them. Rather, they take information provided by others and re-associate it with other information in a creative way. This allows them to develop more innovative and more effective decision statements.[6]

Problems and opportunities can be discovered through many, many ways. The initial interview between researcher and manager represents a discovery-oriented process. There is certainly much art involved in translating scattered pieces of evidence about some business situation into relevant problem statements and then relevant research objectives. Some helpful hints that can be useful in the interview process include the following.

1. Develop many alternative decisions and problems. These can emerge from the interview material or from simply rephrasing decision statements and problem statements. Run ideas by different people at different levels of the organization to get fresh perspectives.
2. Think about possible solutions to the problem.[7] Ultimately, for the research to be actionable, some plausible solution must exist. After pairing decision statements with research objectives, think about the solutions that might result. This can help make sure any research that results is useful.

3. Make lists. Use free-association techniques to generate lists of ideas. The more ideas, the better. Use interrogative techniques to generate lists of potential questions that can be used in the interview process. **Interrogative techniques** simply involve asking multiple what, where, who, when, why, and how questions. They can also be used to provoke introspection, which can assist with problem definition.

4. Be open-minded. It is very important to consider all ideas as plausible in the beginning stages of problem solving. One sure way to stifle progress is to think only like those intimately involved in the business situation or only like those in other industries. Analogies can be useful in thinking more creatively.

interrogative techniques
Asking multiple what, where, who, when, why, and how questions.

■ IDENTIFYING SYMPTOMS

Interviews with key decision makers also can be one of the best ways to identify key problem symptoms. Recall that all problems have symptoms just as human disease is diagnosed through symptoms. Once symptoms are identified, then the researcher must probe to identify possible causes of these changes. **Probing** is an interview technique that tries to draw deeper and more elaborate explanations from the discussion. This discussion may involve potential problem causes. This probing process will likely be very helpful in identifying key variables that are prime candidates for study. Applications of qualitative research tools in probing can be very helpful.[8] Probing should take place along several key dimensions.

probing
An interview technique that tries to draw deeper and more elaborate explanations from the discussion.

1. Clarification—ask the decision maker to explain exactly what certain phrases or terms mean.
2. Free form thinking—ask for top of the mind associations by saying "What does __ make you think of."
3. Pause—the researcher can sometimes pause and not say anything. The silence may motivate the decision maker to elaborate in a meaningful way.
4. Contrast—ask the decision maker to describe how events discussed are similar or different to other events.
5. Meaning—ask the decision maker to "tell me something," or elaborate on an interesting point.
6. Most important, the researcher should ask, "What has changed?" Then, the researcher should probe more deeply to identify potential causes of the change.

At the risk of seeming repetitive, it is important that the researcher repeatedly probe to make sure that some important change has not been left out.

In addition, the researcher should look for changes in company documents, including financial statements and operating reports. Changes may also be identified by tracking down news about competitors and customers. Exhibit 5.3 provides a summary of this approach. The Research Snapshot on the next page describes a changing marketplace for autos presenting opportunities and problems.

EXHIBIT 5.3
What Has Changed?

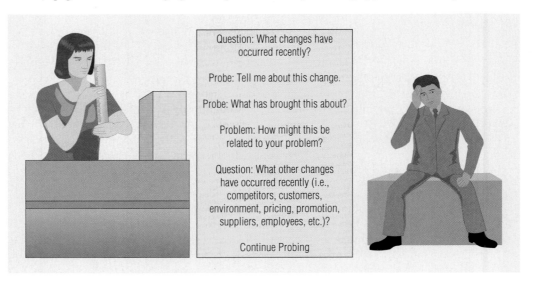

Question: What changes have occurred recently?

Probe: Tell me about this change.

Probe: What has brought this about?

Problem: How might this be related to your problem?

Question: What other changes have occurred recently (i.e., competitors, customers, environment, pricing, promotion, suppliers, employees, etc.)?

Continue Probing

Opportunity Is a "Fleeting" Thing

Have non-European automotive companies missed out on European opportunities? Europe represents a nearly $17 million annual market for new automobiles. Traditionally, the thinking is that European's prefer smaller or "light-cars." Thus, European car companies like BMW and Audi were slow to enter the SUV market. Mercedes entered the SUV market rather early on, but the emphasis was on the American market. American and Japanese companies offered little more than a token effort at selling SUVs in Europe. Thus, the SUV wars were fought in America where total volume reached 4 million shortly after 2000. Europeans were left with fewer choices if an SUV struck their fancy.

As a result, pre-2000 SUV sales in Europe were almost nonexistent. However, SUV sales in Europe have increased dramatically since then. By 2004, European SUV sales reached 16.5 million units, about one in twenty of all new autos sold in Europe. Today, Nissan, Toyota, Land Rover, and Suzuki are major players in the European SUV market. However, sales expectations for new entries from Opel, Renault, Volkswagen, Mercedes, and Audi are sluggish through 2008 with so many SUVs to choose from coupled with

high fuel prices. In hindsight, could it be that several prominent automobile companies missed opportunities in Europe because they failed to know how big the market truly was?

Looking at this from the opposite direction, the tiny (by U.S. standards) two-seater SMART (http://www.smartusa.com) car is being introduced in the United States. Approximately 30,000 U.S. consumers have put down $99 to reserve the right to buy a SMART car upon introduction. SMART is poised to take advantage of an opportunity created by high gas prices while GM scrambles to turn production away from large SUVs like HUMMER toward new entries like the GM Volt. The relative success of these new entries against European minis like the SMART may also depend on the exchange rate which presently makes European entries expensive in the U.S. Word is there may even be a SMART SUV—a miniature version of an American icon. What is the SMART future?

Sources: "The Business Week," *Business Week*, 4008 (June 16, 2008), 6-10; Crain, K. C., "Analyst Sees Sales Decline for Light Vehicles in 2005," *Automotive News*, 79 (January 24, 2005), 111; Meiners, Jena, "SUV Sales in Europe will Peak in 2008," *Automotive News Europe*, 9 (June 28, 2004); Marquand, R., "Euope's Little Smart Car to Hit U.S. Streets," *Christian Science Monitor* (2008), http://www.csmonitor.com/2008/0109/p01s01-woeu.html, accessed July 31, 2008.

Think back to the opening vignette. Often, multiple interviews are necessary to identify all the key symptoms and gain a better understanding of the actual business situation. On a follow-up interview, the dialogue between James and Mario may proceed as follows:

A "smart" marketing researcher may spot an opportunity if consumers are becoming more concerned about high fuel costs—alternatively, they may have to deal with consumer perceptions that such a small car would not be safe.

James: Mario, as you suggested, the downward sales trend began twelve months ago. Aside from the advertising you mentioned earlier, what other changes have occurred inside of your business within the past year?

Mario: Just a few things. Although sales are down, our profits haven't suffered very much. Since we hired the comptroller just over a year ago, we've effectively managed our costs by changing suppliers and dropping some of the more costly items from our menu.

James (probing): Such as changing the house red? Tell me, what led to this decision?

Mario: The Barbera d'Asti that we served costs us almost $15 per bottle. Customers don't like to pay more than $5 per glass for a house wine, so we were doing little more than breaking even on it. Besides, the Olive Garden and Macaroni Grill serve a jug wine for their house red. They always have.

James: Have you noticed changes in your customers?

Mario: Other than the fact that they are coming less often, no! They are the same faces that I have seen for years. They tend to come from the nearby neighborhoods.

James: Have the complaints or comments changed?

Mario: Not to speak of. A few commented on removing an item or two from the menu. A couple about the wine change, but they can still get the Barbera on our reserve list for just $42 a bottle.

James: Has there been a change in personnel?

Mario: Yes, we've had more than the usual share of turnover. I've turned over most personnel decisions to the comptroller. We've had trouble maintaining good kitchen help.

James: Have you noticed any changes to the competitors that you have not already mentioned?

Mario: Most of the nearby places are doing the same things they have done for years. The chain Italian restaurants have the same promotions each year and their menu doesn't change very much.

In *change interviewing*, the researcher is trying to identify possible changes in the customers, the competitors, the internal conditions of the company, and the external environment. The interplay between things that have changed and things that have stayed the same can often lead to key research factors. Before preparing the proposal, James and Mario agree that the real decision faced is not as narrow as an advertising problem; rather, the decision involves finding ways in which Mario can return sales to their previous level. In this case, James is beginning to suspect that one key factor is that the food and beverage quality have suffered as a result of cost-cutting measures. Perhaps this has been noticed by more than a few customers.

Almost any situation can be framed from a number of different perspectives. A pricing problem may be rephrased as a brand image problem. People expect high quality products to have higher prices. A quality problem may be rephrased as a packaging problem. For example, a potato chip company thought that a quality differential between their potatoes and their competitors was the cause for the symptom showing sliding market share. However, one of the research questions that eventually resulted dealt with consumer preferences for packaging. In the end, research suggested that consumers prefer a foil package because it helps the chips stay fresher longer. Thus, the key gap turned out to be a package gap![9]

Researchers should make sure that they have uncovered all possible relevant symptoms and considered their potential causes. Perhaps more interview time with key decision makers asking why people choose Coke would have helped identify some of the less tangible aspects of the Coke-Pepsi-New Coke battle. It can help avoid mistakes later.

Identifying the Relevant Issues from the Symptoms

Anticipating all the many influences and dimensions of a problem is impossible for any researcher or executive. The interview process above is extremely useful in translating the decision situation into a working problem definition by focusing on symptom identification. However, the researcher needs to be doubly certain that the research attacks real problems and not superficial symptoms.

For instance, when a firm has a problem with advertising effectiveness, the possible causes of this problem may be low brand awareness, the wrong brand image, use of the wrong media, or perhaps too small a budget. Certain occurrences that appear to be the problem may be only symptoms of a deeper problem. Exhibit 5.4 illustrates how symptoms can be translated into a problem and then a decision statement.

EXHIBIT 5.4 **Symptoms Can Be Confusing**

	Firm's Situation	Symptoms	Probable Problem	Decision Statement
Research Action	Conduct Situation Analysis including interviews with key decision makers		Consider results of probing and apply creative processes	Express in actionable terms and make sure decision makers are in agreement
Situation 1	22-year-old neighborhood swimming association seeks research help	• Declining Membership for 6 years • Increased attendance at new water park • Less frequent usage among members	Swim facility is outdated and does not appeal to younger families. Younger families and children have a negative image of pool. Their "old market" is aging.	What things can be done to energize new markets and create a more favorable attitude toward the association?
Situation 2	Manufacturer of palm-sized computer with wireless Internet access believes B2B sales are too low	• Distributors complain prices are too high • Business users still use larger computers	• Business users do not see advantages of smaller units • Advantages are not outweighed by costs • Transition costs may be a drawback for B2B customers more than for B2C customers	What things can be done to improve competitive positioning of the new product in B2B markets?
Situation 3	A new micro-brewery is trying to establish itself	• Consumers seem to prefer national brands over the local microbrew products • Many customers order national brands within the microbrew itself • Some customers hesitant to try new microbrew flavors	Is there a negative flavor gap? Do consumers appreciate the micro-brew approach and the full beer tasting (as opposed to drinking) experience?	How can we encourage more consumers to come to the microbrew and try our products? Should we redesign the brewery to be more inviting?

Translating Managerial Decision Statements into Corresponding Research Objectives

The situation analysis ends once researchers have a clear idea of the managerial objectives from the research effort. Decisions statements capture these objectives in a way that invites multiple solutions. Multiple solutions are encouraged by using plural nouns to describe solutions (i.e., ways instead of way). In other words, a decision statement that says in what "ways" a problem can be solved is better than one that says in what "way" a problem can be solved. Thinking like this produces many possible approaches.

Information Needs

Decision statements must be translated into research objectives. At this point, the researcher is starting to visualize what will need to be measured and what type of study will be needed. Exhibit 5.5 extends the examples from Exhibit 5.4, showing research objectives that correspond to each decision statement. Note that each research objective states a corresponding, potential result(s) of the research project. Thus, in some ways, it is stating the information that is needed to help make the decision. Once the decision statement is written, the research essentially answers the question, "What information is needed to address this situation?" Later, research questions will be distinguished from hypotheses in more detail, for now, just consider how they are linked all the way to the decision statement.

Referring back to the opening vignette, the analysis of the symptoms has led to the conclusion that there is a loyalty problem. Perhaps customers used to eat at the restaurant more frequently because it was seen as more unique and of higher quality than the chain restaurants. In other words,

EXHIBIT 5.5 **Translating Decision Statements**

	Decision Statement	Research Objectives	Research Questions	Research Hypotheses
Research Action	Express in actionable terms and make sure decision makers are in agreement	Expresses potential research results that should aid decision-making	Ask a question that corresponds to each research objective	Specific statement explaining relationships, usually involving two variables, and including the direction of the relationship
Situation 1	What things can be done to energize new markets and create a more favorable attitude toward the association?	Determine reasons why families may choose to join or not join a "swim club."	How do the type of facilities and pricing relate to family attitudes toward a swim facility?	Child-friendly *pool designs* are positively related to *attitudes toward the facility*. Flexible *pricing policies* are positively related to *attitudes toward the facility*.
Situation 2	What product features can be improved and emphasized to improve competitive positioning of the new product in B2B markets?	List actions that may overcome the objections (switching costs) of B2B customers toward adoption of the new product.	What are the factors that most lead to perceptions of high switching costs?	*Perceived difficulty* in learning how to use the new device is related to *switching costs*. *Price* is positively related to *switching costs*. Knowledge of new product is positively related to *switching costs*.
Situation 3	How can we encourage more consumers to come to the microbrew and try our products? Should we redesign the brewery to be more inviting?	Describe how situational factors influence beer consumption and consumer attitudes toward beer products. List factors that will improve attitudes toward the microbrewery.	Do situational factors (such as time of day, food pairings, or environmental factors) relate to taste perceptions of beer?	Microbrew beer is *preferred* when consumed *with food* more than when consumed alone. An exciting *atmosphere* will improve consumer *attitudes toward the microbrew*.

there is gap between how frequently we expect good customers to return and how often they have been returning over the past year. They eventually agree on the following decision statement:

In what ways can Mario Lagasto's Restaurant build customer loyalty *so that revenues increase through more frequent* patronage *and* higher average tickets?

What information or data will be needed to help answer this question? Obviously, we'll need to study customer loyalty, restaurant patronage, and customer spending behavior. James needs to find out what things might cause customer loyalty, patronage, and spending to increase. Thinking back to the interview, James knows that there have been several changes in the restaurant itself, many related to saving costs. Saving costs on food preparation and quality sounds like a good idea; however, if it harms customer loyalty even slightly, it probably isn't worthwhile. Thus, the corresponding research objectives are stated as follows.

- Determine what key variables relate to customer loyalty among competing restaurants, meaning 1) how committed the customer is emotionally to the restaurant and 2) how frequently the customer visits one restaurant relative to the competition.
- Profile customers that spend significantly more money than average each time they visit Lagasto's restaurant.

These research objectives are the deliverables of the research project. A research study will be conducted that (1) shows how much each of several key variables relates to customer commitment and patronage frequency and (2) provides a description of the type of customer that spends the most money.

The researcher should reach a consensus agreement with the decision maker regarding the overall decision statement(s) and research objectives. If the decision maker agrees that the statement captures the situation well and understands how the research objectives, if accomplished, will help address the situation, then the researcher can proceed. The researcher should make every effort to ensure that the decision maker understands what a research project can deliver. If there is no agreement on the decision statement or research objectives, more dialogue between decision makers and researchers is needed.

Determine the Unit of Analysis

unit of analysis

A study that indicates what or who should provide the data and at what level of aggregation.

The **unit of analysis** for a study indicates what or who should provide the data and at what level of aggregation. Researchers specify whether an investigation will collect data about individuals (such as customers, employees, and owners), households (families, extended families, and so forth), organizations (businesses and business units), departments (sales, finance, and so forth), geographical areas, or objects (products, advertisements, and so forth). In studies of home buying, for example, the husband/wife dyad typically is the unit of analysis rather than the individual because many purchase decisions are made jointly by husband and wife. Similarly, sales problems may not be due to either the sales manager or the salesperson individually, but they could be due to the specific pairing of sales managers and salespeople. In this case, the dyad consisting of a sales manager and a salesperson becomes the unit of analysis.[10]

Researchers who think carefully and creatively about situations often discover that a problem can be investigated at more than one level of analysis. For example, a marketing researcher may be interested in the relationship between service quality and customer satisfaction. This relationship could be studied at the individual level meaning individual customers. However, it could also be studied at the store level. In this case, a store could have consistent service quality across all employees and thus whatever the store is doing to create this would be driving consistent customer satisfaction relationships as well. The problem could also be studied at the company level where it may be something about the entire company that is most responsible for particular relationships between quality and satisfaction. In some instances, some things may be measured at the company level with outcomes measured at the individual employee or customer level.[11] Analyses like these are called **multi-level** and are becoming more prevalent as software for doing these types of analyses becomes more widely available. Determining the unit of analysis, although relatively straightforward in most projects, should not be overlooked during the problem-definition stage of the research.

multi-level analysis

Research studying variables measured at more than one unit of analysis

Determine Relevant Variables

■ WHAT IS A VARIABLE?

What things should be studied to address a decision statement? Researchers answer this question by identifying key variables. A **variable** is anything that varies or changes from one instance to another. Variables can exhibit differences in value, usually in magnitude or strength, or in direction. In research, a variable is either observed or manipulated, in which case it is an experimental variable.

The converse of a variable is a **constant**. A constant is something that does not change. Constants are not useful in addressing research questions. Since constants don't change, management isn't very interested in hearing the key to the problem is something that won't or can't be changed. In causal research, it can be important to make sure that some potential variable is actually held constant while studying the cause and effect between two other variables. In this way, a spurious relationship can be ruled out. At this point however, the notion of a constant is more important in helping to understand how it differs from a variable.

■ TYPES OF VARIABLES

There are several key terms that help describe types of variables. The *variance* in *variables* is captured either with numerical differences or by a symbol indentifying category membership. In addition, different terms describe whether a variable is a potential cause or an effect.

A **continuous variable** is one that can take on a range of values that correspond systematically to some quantitative amount. Consumer attitude toward different airlines is a variable that would generally be captured by numbers, with higher numbers indicating a more positive attitude than lower numbers. Each attribute of airlines' services, such as safety, seat comfort, and baggage handling can be numerically scored in this way. Sales volume, profits, and margin are common business metrics that represent continuous variables. Strictly speaking, continuous variables could take on an infinite range of values, but practically speaking, survey research usually produces responses with a finite range of scale values such as 1–7.

A **categorical variable** is one that indicates membership in some group. The term **classificatory variable** is sometimes also used and is generally interchangeable with *categorical variable*. Categorical variables take on only a small number of values (one, two, or three) or simply identify membership in a group (A, B, or C).

For example, people can be categorized as either male or female. A variable representing biological sex describes this important difference. The variable values can be an "M" for membership in the male category and an "F" for membership in the female category. Alternatively, the researcher could assign a "0" for men and a "1" for women. In either case, the same information is represented.

A common categorical variable in consumer research is adoption, meaning the consumer either did or did not purchase a new product. Thus, the two groups, purchase or not purchase, comprise the variable. Similarly, turnover, or whether an employee has quit or not, is a common organizational variable.

In descriptive and causal research, the terms *dependent variable* and *independent variable* describe different variable types. This distinction becomes very important in understanding how business processes can be modeled by a researcher. The distinction must be clear before one can correctly apply certain statistical procedures like multiple regression analysis. In some cases, however, such as when only one variable is involved in a hypothesis, the researcher need not make this distinction.

A **dependent variable** is a process outcome or a variable that is predicted and/or explained by other variables. An **independent variable** is a variable that is expected to influence the dependent variable in some way. Such variables are independent in the sense that they are determined outside of the process being studied. That is another way of saying that dependent variables do not change independent variables.

For example, average customer loyalty may be a dependent variable that is influenced or predicted by an independent variable such as perceptions of restaurant food quality, service quality, and customer satisfaction. Thus, a process is described by which several variables together help create and explain how much customer loyalty exists. In other words, if we know how a customer rates the food quality, service quality, and satisfaction with a restaurant, then we can predict that customer's loyalty toward that restaurant. Note that this does not mean that we can predict food quality or service quality with customer loyalty.

variable

Anything that varies or changes from one instance to another; can exhibit differences in value, usually in magnitude or strength, or in direction.

constant

Something that does not change; is not useful in addressing research questions.

continuous variable

A variable that can take on a range of values that correspond systematically to some quantitative amount.

categorical variable

A variable that indicates membership in some group.

classificatory variable

Another term for a categorical variable because it classifies units into categories.

dependent variable

A process outcome or a variable that is predicted and/or explained by other variables.

independent variable

A variable that is expected to influence the dependent variable in some way.

Several variables describe child consumers. Their biological sex is a categorical variable; how much they weigh and how often they go out to eat are continuous variables.

Dependent variables are conventionally represented by the letter Y. Independent variables are conventionally represented by the letter X. If research involves two dependent variables and two or more independent variables, subscripts may also be used to indicate Y_1, Y_2 and X_1, X_2, and so on.

Ultimately, theory is critical in building processes that include both independent and dependent variables (see Chapter 3). Managers and researchers must be careful to identify relevant and actionable variables. *Relevant* means that a change in the variable matters and *actionable* means that a variable can be controlled by managerial action. Superfluous variables are those that are neither relevant nor actionable and should not be included in a study. Theory should help distinguish relevant from superfluous variables.

The process of identifying the relevant variables overlaps with the process of determining the research objectives. Typically, each research objective will mention a variable or variables to be measured or analyzed. As the translation process proceeds through research objectives, research questions, and research hypotheses, it is usually possible to emphasize the variables that should be included in a study (as in Exhibits 5.5 and 5.6). The Research Snapshot on the next page dealing with pricing turbulence identifies the variables that must be measured to test hypotheses involved in research questions whose answers produce the key deliverables promised.

Exhibit 5.6 includes some common marketing research hypotheses and a description of the key variables involved in each. In the first case, a regional grocery chain is considering offering a delivery service that would allow consumers to purchase groceries via the store Web site. They have conducted a trial of this in one market and have conducted a survey in that area. In the second case, a Korean automobile company is considering offering one of its models for sale in Europe. The company has also conducted a survey in two key European auto markets.

EXHIBIT 5.6 **Common Marketing Problems, Corresponding Research Hypotheses, and Variable Descriptions**

Managerial Decision	Research Question(s)	Research Hypotheses	Categorical Variable(s)	Continuous Variable(s)
Retail grocer considering web-based delivery service	Is there sufficient demand? Will delivery influence customer perceptions of quality? Will delivery service (new retail form) cannibalize current business?	*Projected sales volume* will exceed $5 M annually. *Retail form* influences *quality perceptions* such that Web (in-store) customers perceive lower (higher) quality. Web customers express lower *intentions to visit store* than other customers.	Retail Form (independent variable)—classifies respondents based on whether they shopped (1) in-store or (2) via the Web (delivery).	Sales Volume—dollar amount based on a test trial in one geographic market (i.e., Phoenix/ Scottsdale). Intentions to visit store (dependent variable)—the percentage likelihood that a survey respondent would visit the store within the next 7 days.
What market segments should be served?	Does nationality matter? Will French and German consumers express interest in our product? Does the attitude toward Korean companies influence purchase intentions?	*French* consumers have more *interest in purchasing our product* than *German* consumers. *Attitude toward Korean companies* is related positively to *product purchase interest.*	Nationality (independent variable)—represents which country a survey respondent lives in: (1) France (2) Germany	Attitude toward Korean companies (independent variable)— ratings scale that describes how favorably survey respondents view Korean companies (quality, reputation, value; higher scores mean better attitude) Product purchase interest—ratings scale that shows how interested a consumer is in buying the Korean product (higher scores = more interest)

RESEARCH SNAPSHOT

Pricing Turbulence

A heavy equipment distributor sought out research because it believed there was an opportunity to increase revenues by raising prices. After several weeks of discussion, interviews, and proposal reviews, they settled on a decision question that asked, "In what ways could revenues be increased by altering pricing policies across customers?" A research project was conducted that offered the following deliverables: (1) demonstrate how much customer characteristics and environmental characteristics influence price elasticity and (2) identify market segments based on price elasticity. This led to several hypotheses including the following.

H1: The desired delivery time for equipment is negatively related to price sensitivity.
H2: The degree of market turbulence is negatively related to price sensitivity.

In addition, a research question specifically addressing market segments was asked.

RQ1: Are there market segments that can be identified based on customers' desired benefits or environmental characteristics?

In other words, the more critical a piece of heavy equipment is to a company, the less concerned they are with the price.

Similarly, customers are less concerned with price in markets that are more turbulent, meaning there are ever-changing environmental, competitive, and political pressures.

A study of heavy equipment purchasers around the world supported both hypotheses. For business segments where delivery time is of critical importance, higher prices can be charged without the fear of losing business. Similarly, in turbulent international markets, customers have other important concerns that make them less sensitive to equipment price and more sensitive to reliability and service. In the end, the heavy equipment company was able to build customer characteristic data into a DSS (Decision Support System) system that automated prices.

Interestingly, management did not express any concerns about either market segments or market turbulence in the initial interviews. Thus, this research succeeded because good research objectives, questions, and hypotheses were developed before any study was implemented.

Sources: Smith, M. F., I. Sinha, R. Lancianai, and H. Forman, "Role of Market Turbulence in Shaping Pricing," *Industrial Marketing Management*, 28 (November 1999), 637–649; Peters, G., "Combating Too Much Information," *Industrial Distribution*, 94 (December 2005), 22.

Writing Research Questions from Research Objectives

Both managers and researchers expect problem–definition efforts to result in statements of research questions and research objectives. At the end of the problem–definition stage, the researcher should prepare a written statement that clarifies any ambiguity about what the research hopes to accomplish. This completes the translation process.

Research questions express the research objectives in terms of questions that can be addressed by research. For example, one of the key research questions involved in the opening vignette is "Are *consumer perceptions* of food quality, price, and atmosphere related to *customer loyalty*?" Hypotheses are more specific than research questions. One key distinction between research questions and hypotheses is that hypotheses can generally specify the direction of a relationship. In other words, when an independent variable goes up, we have sufficient knowledge to predict that the dependent variable should also go up (or down as the case may be). One key research hypothesis for Lagasto's is:

research questions

Express the research objectives in terms of questions that can be addressed by research.

Food quality perceptions *are related positively to* customer commitment *toward a restaurant*.

At times, a researcher may suspect that two variables are related but have insufficient theoretical rationale to support the relationship as positive or negative. In this case, hypotheses cannot be offered. At times in research, particularly in exploratory research, a proposal can only offer research questions. Research hypotheses are much more specific and therefore require considerably more theoretical support. In addition, research questions are interrogative, whereas research hypotheses are declarative.

Clarity in Research Questions and Hypotheses

Research questions make it easier to understand what is perplexing managers and to indicate what issues have to be resolved. A research question is the researcher's translation of the marketing problem into a specific inquiry.

A research question can be too vague and general, such as "Is advertising copy 1 better than advertising copy 2?" What does better mean? Advertising effectiveness can be variously measured by sales, recall of sales message, brand awareness, intention to buy, recognition, or knowledge, to name a few possibilities. Asking a more specific research question (such as, "Which advertisement has a higher day-after recall score?") helps the researcher design a study that will produce useful results. Research question answers should provide input that can be used as a standard for selecting from among alternative solutions. Problem definition seeks to state research questions clearly and to develop well-formulated, specific hypotheses.

A sales manager may hypothesize that salespeople who show the highest job satisfaction will be the most productive. An advertising manager may believe that if consumers' attitudes toward a product are changed in a positive direction, consumption of the product also will increase. Hypotheses are statements that can be empirically tested.

A formal hypothesis has considerable practical value in planning and designing research. It forces researchers to be clear about what they expect to find through the study, and it raises crucial questions about data required. When evaluating a hypothesis, researchers should ensure that the information collected will be useful in decision making. Notice how the following hypotheses express expected relationships between variables.

- There is a positive relationship between *buying on the Internet* and the presence of *younger children* in the home.
- *Sales* are lower for salespeople in regions that receive less *advertising support*.
- Consumers will experience *cognitive dissonance* after the decision to *adopt* a TiVo personal video recorder.
- *Opinion leaders* are more affected by mass media communication *sources* than are non-leaders.
- Among non-exporters, the degree of perceived importance of overcoming barriers to exporting is related positively to general interest in exporting (export intentions).[12]

Management is often faced with a "go/no go" decision. In such cases, a research question or hypothesis may be expressed in terms of a meaningful barrier that represents the turning point in such a decision. In this case, the research involves a **managerial action standard** that specifies a specific performance criterion upon which a decision can be based. If the criterion to be measured (for example, sales or attitude changes) turns out to be higher than some predetermined level, management will do *A*; if it is lower, management will do *B*.[13] In Exhibit 5.6, the specified sales volume of $5 million represents a managerial action standard for the retail grocery chain.

managerial action standard

A specific performance criterion upon which a decision can be based.

Research objectives also should be limited to a manageable number. Fewer study objectives make it easier to ensure that each will be addressed fully. It becomes easy to lose focus with too many research objectives.

Exhibit 5.7 summarizes how a decision statement (corresponding to a marketing problem) leads to research objectives that become a basis for the research design. Once the research has been conducted, the results may show an unanticipated aspect of the problem and suggest a need for additional research to satisfy the main objective. Accomplished researchers who have had the experience of uncovering additional aspects of a marketing problem after finishing fieldwork recommend designing studies that include questions designed to reveal the unexpected.

How Much Time Should Be Spent on Problem Definition?

Budget constraints usually influence how much effort is spent on problem definition. Marketing situations can be complex and numerous variables may be relevant. Searching for every conceivable cause and minor influence is impractical. The more important the decision faced by management, the more resources should be allocated toward problem definition. While not a guarantee,

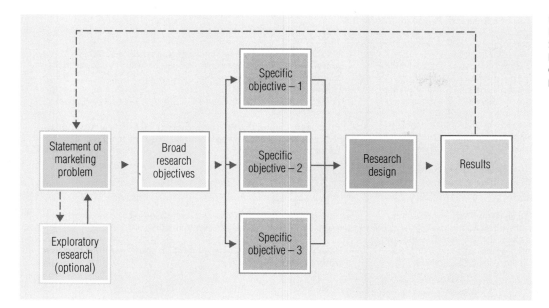

EXHIBIT 5.7
Influence of Decision Statement of Marketing Problem on Research Objectives and Research Designs

allowing more time and spending more money will help make sure the research objectives that result are relevant and can demonstrate which influences management should focus on.

Marketing managers, being responsible for decision making, may wish the problem-definition process to proceed quickly. Researchers who take a long time to produce a set of research objectives can frustrate managers. However, the time taken to identify the correct problem is usually time well spent.

The Research Proposal

The **research proposal** is a written statement of the research design. It always includes a statement explaining the purpose of the study (in the form of research objectives or deliverables) and a definition of the problem, often in the form of a decision statement. A good proposal systematically outlines the particular research methodology and details procedures that will be used during each stage of the research process. Normally a schedule of costs and deadlines is included in the research proposal. The research proposal becomes the primary communication document between the researcher and the research user.

Exhibit 5.8 on the next page illustrates an abbreviated proposal for a short research project conducted for the Internal Revenue Service (IRS) that explores public attitudes toward a variety of tax-related issues.

research proposal
A written statement of the research design.

The Proposal as a Planning Tool

Preparation of a research proposal forces the researcher to think critically about each stage of the research process. Vague plans, abstract ideas, and sweeping generalizations about problems or procedures must become concrete and precise statements about specific events. Data requirements and research procedures must be specified clearly so others may understand their exact implications. All ambiguities about why and how the research will be conducted must be clarified before the proposal is complete.

The researcher submits the proposal to management for acceptance, modification, or rejection. Research clients (management) evaluate the proposed study with particular emphasis on whether or not it will provide useful information, and whether it will do so within a reasonable resource budget. Initial proposals are almost always revised after the first review.

EXHIBIT 5.8 **An Abbreviated Version of a Research Proposal for the IRS**

Current Situation

Public perception of the IRS appears to be extremely negative. The IRS is the brunt of jokes, and the public avoids contact with any IRS entity. As a result, taxpayers are more inclined to cheat on their returns and many services provided by the IRS to assist taxpayers in preparing their tax returns and to help them understand ways they can avoid paying unnecessary taxes and penalties go unused. In addition, negative attitude lessens the Service's ability to effectively lobby for policy changes. The key decision faced by the IRS due to this situation can be stated as,

What steps could be taken to effectively improve consumer perceptions of the IRS and help design more user-friendly services?

Purpose of the Research

The general purpose of the study is to determine the taxpaying public's perceptions of the role of the IRS in administering the tax laws. In defining the limits of this study, the IRS identified the study areas to be addressed. A careful review of those areas led to the identification of the following specific research objectives:

1. To identify the extent to which taxpayers cheat on their returns, their reasons for doing so, and approaches that can be taken to deter this kind of behavior
2. To determine taxpayers' experience and level of satisfaction with various IRS services
3. To determine what services taxpayers need
4. To develop an accurate profile of taxpayers' behavior relative to the preparation of their income tax returns
5. To assess taxpayers' knowledge and opinions about various tax laws and procedures

Research Design

The survey research method will be the basic research design. Each respondent will be interviewed in his or her home. The personal interviews are generally expected to last between 35 and 45 minutes, although the length will vary depending on the previous tax-related experiences of the respondent. For example, if a respondent has never been audited, questions on audit experience will not be addressed. Or, if a respondent has never contacted the IRS for assistance, certain questions concerning reactions to IRS services will be skipped.

Some sample questions that will be asked are

Did you or your spouse prepare your federal tax return for (year)?

☐ Self
☐ Spouse
☐ Someone else

Did the federal income tax package you received in the mail contain all the forms necessary for you to fill out your return?

☐ Yes
☐ No
☐ Didn't receive one in the mail
☐ Don't know

If you were calling the IRS for assistance and no one was able to help you immediately, would you rather get a busy signal or be asked to wait on hold?

☐ Busy signal
☐ Wait on hold
☐ Neither
☐ Don't know

During the interview a self-administered questionnaire will be given to the taxpayer to ask certain sensitive questions, such as

Have you ever claimed a dependent on your tax return that you weren't really entitled to?

☐ Yes
☐ No

Sample Design

A survey of approximately 5,000 individuals located in 50 counties throughout the country will provide the database for this study. The sample will be selected on a probability basis from all households in the continental United States.

Eligible respondents will be adults over the age of 18. Within each household an effort will be made to interview the individual who is most familiar with completing the federal tax forms. When there is more than one taxpayer in the household, a random process will be used to select the taxpayer to be interviewed.

Data Gathering

The fieldworkers of a consulting organization will conduct the interviews.

Data Processing and Analysis

Standard editing and coding procedures will be utilized. Simple tabulation and cross-tabulations will be utilized to analyze the data.

Report Preparation

A written report will be prepared, and an oral presentation of the findings will be made by the research analyst at the convenience of the IRS.

Budget and Time Schedule

Any complete research proposal should include a schedule of how long it will take to conduct each stage of the research and a statement of itemized costs.

Based on *A General Taxpayer Opinion Survey*, Office of Planning and Research, Internal Revenue Service, March 1980.

The proposal helps managers decide if the proper information will be obtained and if the proposed research will accomplish what is desired. If the marketing problem has not been adequately translated into a set of specific research objectives and a research design, the client's assessment of the proposal will help ensure that the researchers revise it to meet the client's information needs.

An effective proposal communicates exactly what information will be obtained, where it will be obtained, and how it will be obtained. For this reason, it must be explicit about sample selection, measurement, fieldwork, and data analysis. For instance, most proposals involving descriptive research include a proposed questionnaire (or at least some sample questions).

The format for the IRS research proposal in Exhibit 5.8 follows the six stages in the research process outlined in Chapter 3. At each stage, one or more questions must be answered before the researcher can select one of the various alternatives. For example, before a proposal can be completed, the researcher needs to know what is to be measured. A simple statement like "market share" may not be enough; market share may be measured by auditing retailers' or wholesalers' sales, using trade association data, or asking consumers what brands they buy. What is to be measured is just one of many important questions that must be answered before setting the research process in motion. This issue will be addressed in greater detail in Chapter 13. For now, Exhibit 5.9 presents an overview of some of the basic questions that managers and researchers typically must answer when planning a research design.

The Proposal as a Contract

When the research will be conducted by a consultant or an outside research supplier, the written proposal serves as that person's bid to offer a specific service. Typically, a client solicits several competitive proposals, and these written offers help management judge the relative quality of alternative research suppliers.

A wise researcher will not agree to do a research job for which no written proposal exists. The proposal also serves as a contract that describes the product the research user will buy. In fact, the

EXHIBIT 5.9 **Basic Points Addressed by Research Proposals**

Decisions to Make	Basic Questions
Problem definition	What is the purpose of the study? How much is already known? Is additional background information necessary? What is to be measured? How? Can the data be made available? Should research be conducted? Can a hypothesis be formulated?
Selection of basic research design	What types of questions need to be answered? Are descriptive or causal findings required? What is the source of the data? Can objective answers be obtained by asking people? How quickly is the information needed? How should survey questions be worded? How should experimental manipulations be made?
Selection of sample	Who or what is the source of the data? Can the target population be identified? Is a sample necessary? How accurate must the sample be? Is a probability sample necessary? Is a national sample necessary? How large a sample is necessary? How will the sample be selected?
Data gathering	Who will gather the data? Where and how will the data be collected? What types of scales will be used? How long will data gathering take? How much supervision is needed? What procedures will data collectors need to follow?
Data analysis and evaluation	Will standardized editing and coding procedures be used? How will the data be categorized? Will computer or hand tabulation be used? What is the nature of the data? What questions need to be answered? How many variables are to be investigated simultaneously? What are the criteria for evaluation of performance? What statistical tools are appropriate?
Type of report	Who will read the report? Are managerial recommendations requested? How many presentations are required? What will be the format of the written report?
Overall evaluation	How much will the study cost? Is the time frame acceptable? Is outside help needed? Will this research design attain the stated research objectives? When should the research begin?

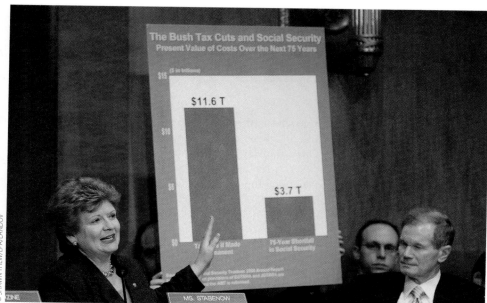

The Bush Tax Cuts and Social Security
Present Value of Costs Over the Next 75 Years

$11.6 T

$3.7 T

© SHAWN THEW/EPA/LANDOV

Congress fights about everything . . . including how to spend taxpayers' money on federal research grants.

proposal is in many ways the same as the final research report without the actual results. Misstatements and faulty communication may occur if the parties rely only on each individual's memory of what occurred at a planning meeting. The proposal creates a record, which greatly reduces conflicts that might arise after the research has been conducted. Both the researcher and the research client should sign the proposal indicating agreement on what will be done.

The proposal then functions as a formal, written statement of agreement between marketing executives and researchers. As such, it protects the researcher from criticisms such as, "Shouldn't we have had a larger sample?" or "Why didn't you use a focus group approach?" As a record of the researcher's obligation, the proposal also provides a standard for determining whether the actual research was conducted as originally planned.

Suppose in our Italian restaurant case, following the research, Mario is unhappy with the nature of the results because they indicate that customers report higher loyalty toward other restaurants. This is something that Mario may not wish to face. In his despair, he complains to James saying,

"What I really wanted was an advertising study, yet you provide results indicating my food is no good! Why should I pay you?"

James can refer back to the research proposal, which is signed by Mario. He can point right to the deliverables described above showing that Mario agreed to a study involving customer loyalty and the restaurant characteristics that lead to loyalty. The proposal certainly protects the researcher in this case. In most cases like this, after the initial emotional reaction to unflattering results, the client comes around and realizes the report contents include information that will be helpful. Realize too that the proposal protects Mario in case James produced a study that addresses only research objectives not included in the proposal.

In basic research efforts, a formal proposal serves much the same purpose. **Funded marketing research** generally refers to basic research usually performed by academic researchers and supported by some public or private institution. Most commonly, researchers pursue federal government grants. A very detailed proposal is usually needed for federal grants, and the agreement for funding is predicated on the research actually delivering the results described in the proposal.

One important comment needs to be made about the nature of research proposals. Not all proposals follow the same format. A researcher can adapt his or her proposal to the target audience or situation. An extremely brief proposal submitted by an organization's internal marketing research department to its own marketing executives bears little resemblance to a complex proposal submitted by a university professor to a federal government agency to research a basic consumer issue.

funded marketing research

Refers to basic research usually performed by academic researchers that is financially supported by some public or private institution as in federal government grants.

Anticipating Outcomes

As mentioned above, the proposal and the final research report will contain much of the same information. The proposal describes the data collection, measurement, data analysis, and so forth, in future tense. In the report, the actual results are presented. In this sense, the proposal anticipates the research outcome.

Experienced researchers know that research fails more often because the problem-definition process breaks down or because the research client never truly understood what a research project could or couldn't do. While it probably seems as though the proposal should make this clear, any shortcoming in the proposal can contribute to a communication failure. Thus, any tool that helps communication become as clear as can be is valued very highly.

Using Dummy Tables to Clarify Research Objectives

One tool that is perhaps the best way to let management know exactly what kind of results will be produced by research is the *dummy table*. **Dummy tables** are placed in research proposals and are exact representations of the actual tables that will show results in the final report with one exception: The results are hypothetical. They get the name because the researcher fills in, or "dummies up," the tables with likely but fictitious data. Dummy tables include the tables that will present hypothesis test results. In this way, they are linked directly to research objectives.

A research analyst can present dummy tables to the decision maker and ask, "Given findings like these, will you be able to make a decision?" If the decision maker says yes, the proposal may be accepted. However, if the decision maker cannot see how results like those in the dummy tables will help make the needed decision(s), it may be back to the drawing board. In other words, the client and researcher need to rethink what research results are necessary to solve the problem. Sometimes, examining the dummy tables may reveal that a key variable is missing or that some dependent variable is really not relevant. In other words, the marketing problem is clarified by deciding on action standards or performance criteria and recognizing the types of research findings necessary to make specific decisions.

dummy tables

Tables placed in research proposals that are exact representations of the actual tables that will show results in the final report with the exception that the results are hypothetical (fictitious).

Example Dummy Table

Exhibit 5.10 shows a dummy table taken from the research proposal for Mario Lagasto's Italian Restaurant. From it, Mario can see that it shows what things most determine how often a customer chooses a restaurant over its top competitors. If the results turn out as shown in the dummy table, it would suggest that Mario needs to emphasize food quality, a pleasant atmosphere, service quality, and wine and beverage quality to restore loyalty. In contrast, results like these would suggest that customers are not price sensitive. Price would not determine loyalty according to results like these.

EXHIBIT 5.10 A Dummy Table for Mario Lagasto

Regression Table: Results Showing which Variables Determine Restaurant Customer's Loyalty (Patronage Frequency)

Independent Variable	Standardized Regression Coefficient	Rank (Importance in Determining Frequency)	Mean Score Rank (How Lagasto's Ranks Compared to Ten Closest Competitors)
Food Quality	.50**	1	6
Pleasant Atmosphere	.45**	2	7
Service Quality	.30**	3	5
Wine and Beverage Quality	.25**	4	8
Convenience of Location	.15*	5	3
Advertising	.05	6	4
Menu Prices	−.05	7	2

* P-VALUE < .001
** P-VALUE < .05

- Researchers should allocate a substantial amount of time toward identifying and refining decision statements, research problems and questions, and research hypotheses. This is a way that the relevance of the research can be increased.
- Use qualitative research tools to probe the key decision makers during early interviews.
  - Ask what has changed.
  - Ask the decision maker to tell more about situations for clarification.
  - Ask the decision maker to compare and contrast situations.
- Express decision statements in creative terms whenever possible. For example, state them in plural form by using terms such as "what ways" might solve a problem rather than trying to find "the way" to solve a problem.
- Research questions and research hypotheses clearly identify the variables that need to be studied.
- Dummy tables are a very effective way to communicate exactly how a research problem might be linked to better decision making.

Such results would indicate that the emphasis on cost control—to the extent that it lowers prices, reduces food or beverage quality, or harms the atmosphere and service quality—is misplaced and harmful. In addition, results like these would suggest that Mario's strengths are things that are not very important. Although these results would suggest Mario is second overall in terms of consumer price perceptions, this variable does not determine loyalty. Looking at the table, Mario can see how the results could be used.

While some tables may require some additional explanation from the researcher, every effort should be made to allow tables to stand alone and be interpreted by someone who is not an experienced researcher. In other words, the user should be able to understand the results and surmise implications that the results imply. When the final report is compiled, these tables will be included with the results replaced with the actual research results.

Summary

1. Explain why proper "problem definition" is essential to useful marketing research. Problem definition is the process of defining and developing a decision statement and the steps involved in translating it into more precise research terminology, including a set of research objectives. While it is difficult to point to any particular research stage as the most important, a strong case can be made for this, the first stage. If this step falls apart, the entire research design is misguided. Effective problem definition helps make sure the research objectives are relevant and useful—meaning the results will actually be used. If problem definition is glossed over or done poorly, the results are likely irrelevant and potentially harmful.

2. Know how to identify and refine problems using a problem definition process. Problems and opportunities are usually associated with differences. The differences can occur because of changes in some situation, or they can occur because expectations were unrealistic. Problems occur when there is a difference, or gap, between the current situation and a more ideal situation. One very common type of gap is when business performance does not match the expectations of performance in that dimension. In addition, opportunities exist when actual performance in some area does not match the potential performance. Research can supply information to help close the gap. Thus, problems are noticed by spotting these gaps. While many of these gaps may just be symptoms, further steps are taken to make sure that research addresses relevant issues, not just symptoms.

3. Translate managerial decision statements into relevant research objectives. The problem-definition process outlined in the chapter can help make sure that the research objectives are relevant. A situation analysis is helpful in this regard. In particular, interviews that identify symptoms and then probe the respondent for potential causes of these symptoms are helpful. One tool to help in this process is the "what has changed?" technique. The research objectives, once written, also indicate what variables are likely needed in the study.

4. Translate research objectives into research questions and/or research hypotheses. Research questions simply restate the research objectives in the form of a question. When the researcher has sufficient theoretical reasoning to make a more specific prediction that includes the direction of any predicted relationship, the research question can be translated into one or more research hypotheses.

5. Outline the components of a research proposal. The research proposal is a written statement of the research design that will be followed in addressing a specific problem. The research proposal allows managers to evaluate the details of the proposed research and determine if alterations are needed. Most research proposals include the following sections: decision description, purpose of the research including the research objectives, research design, sample design, data gathering and/or fieldwork techniques, data processing and analysis, budget, and time schedule.

6. Construct dummy tables as part of a research proposal. Dummy tables are included in research proposals and look exactly like the real tables that will be included in the final research report. However, they cannot actually contain results since the study has not yet been done. So, they include hypothetical results that look as much as possible like the actual results. These tables are a very good tool for communicating the value of a research project to management because they provide a real sense for implications that may result from the research.

Key Terms and Concepts

categorical variable, *117*
classificatory variable, *117*
constant, *117*
continuous variable, *117*
decision statement, *106*
dependent variable, *117*
dummy tables, *125*

funded marketing research, *124*
independent variable, *117*
interrogative techniques, *112*
managerial action standard, *120*
multi-level analysis, *116*
probing, *112*
problem, *110*

problem definition, *106*
research proposal, *121*
research questions, *119*
situation analysis, *110*
unit of analysis, *116*
variable, *117*

Questions for Review and Critical Thinking

1. What is a *decision statement?* How does the focus on an irrelevant decision affect the research process?
2. Define *problem recognition.* How is this process like translating text from one language into another? What role does "probing" play in this process?
3. List and describe four factors that influence how difficult the problem-definition process can be.
4. What are three types of gaps that exist, indicating that research may be needed to assist a business in making some decision?
5. Examine an article in *The Wall Street Journal* or a similar source that discusses a business situation of a company in the electronics or defense industry. Identify a problem that exists with the company. Develop some research objectives that you believe correspond to the problem.
6. What is a situation analysis? How can it be used to separate symptoms from actual problems?
7. Define *unit of analysis* in a marketing research context.
8. Recall the concept of marketing orientation from the first chapter. If a company was conducting research investigating whether companies that are marketing-oriented outperformed companies that were production-oriented, what would the appropriate unit of analysis be?
9. Find some business journal articles that deal with culture and international expansion. Find one that lists some hypotheses. What kinds of decisions might be assisted by the results of testing these hypotheses?

10. List and describe at least four terms that can describe the nature of a variable.
11. For each of the following variables, explain why it should be considered either continuous or categorical:
    a. Whether or not a university played in a football bowl game during 2006
    b. The average wait time a customer has before being served in a full-service restaurant
    c. Letter grades of A, B, C, D, or F
    d. The job satisfaction of a company's salespeople
    e. A consumer's age
12. Write at least three examples of hypotheses that involve a managerial action statement. Provide a corresponding decision statement for each.
13. What are the major components of a research proposal? How does a research proposal assist the researcher?
14. The chapter provides an example dummy table for the Lagasto's restaurant vignette. Provide another example dummy table that corresponds to this same situation.
15. Evaluate the following statements of marketing problems. For each provide a decision statement and corresponding research objectives:
    a. A farm implement manufacturer: Our objective is to learn the most effective form of advertising so we can maximize product line profits.
    b. An employees' credit union: Our problem is to determine the reasons why employees join the credit union, determine

members' awareness of credit union services, and measure attitudes and beliefs about how effectively the credit union is operated.

c. The producer of a television show: We have a marketing problem. The program's ratings are low. We need to learn how we can improve our ratings.

d. A soft-drink manufacturer: The marketing problem is that we do not know if our bottlers are more satisfied with us than our competitors' bottlers are with them.

e. A women's magazine: Our problem is to document the demographic changes that have occurred in recent decades in the lives of women and to put them in historical perspective; to examine several generations of American women through most of this century, tracking their roles as students, workers, wives, and mothers and noting the changes in timing, sequence, and duration of these roles; to examine at what age and for how long a woman enters various stages of her life: school, work, marriage, childbearing, divorce. This will be accomplished by analyzing demographic data over several generations.

f. A manufacturer of fishing boats: The problem is to determine sales trends over the past five years by product category and to determine the seasonality of unit boat sales by quarters and by region of the country.

g. The inventor of a tension-headache remedy (a cooling pad that is placed on the forehead for up to four hours): The purpose of this research is (1) to identify the market potential for the product, (2) to identify what desirable features the product should possess, and (3) to determine possible advertising strategies/channel strategies for the product.

16. Comment on the following statements and situations:

a. "The best marketing researchers are prepared to rethink and rewrite their proposals."

b. "The client's signature is an essential element of the research proposal."

17. You have been hired by a group of hotel owners, restaurant owners, and other people engaged in businesses that benefit from tourism on South Padre Island, Texas. They wish to learn how they can attract a large number of college students to their town during spring break. Define the marketing decision statement.

18. You have been hired by a local Big Brothers and Big Sisters organization to learn how they can increase the number of males who volunteer to become Big Brothers to fatherless boys. Define your research objectives.

19. How might research questions differ in multilevel analysis as opposed to studies involving only a single level as the unit of analysis?

Research Activities

1. **'NET** Examine the Web site for International Communications Research (http://icrsurvey.com).[14] What services do they seem to offer that fall into the problem-definition process?

2. Consider the current situation within your local university music department. Assuming it stages musical productions to which audiences are invited and for which tickets are sold, describe the marketing situation it faces. Prepare a research proposal that would help it address a key decision. Make sure it includes at least one dummy table.

Case 5.1 E-ZPass

© GETTY IMAGES/
PHOTODISC GREEN

In the 1990s, a task force was formed among executives of seven regional transportation agencies in the New York–New Jersey area.[15] The mission of the task force was to investigate the feasibility and desirability of adopting electronic toll collection (ETC) for the interregional roadways of the area. Electronic toll collection is accomplished by providing commuters with small transceivers (tags) that emit a tuned radio signal. Receivers placed at tollbooths are able to receive the radio signal and identify the commuter associated with the particular signal. Commuters establish ETC accounts that are debited for each use of a toll road or facility, thus eliminating the need for the commuter to pay by cash or token. Because the radio signal can be read from a car in motion, ETC can reduce traffic jams at toll plazas by allowing tag holders to pass through at moderate speeds.

At the time the New York and New Jersey agencies were studying the service, electronic toll collection was already being used successfully in Texas and Louisiana. Even though several of the agencies had individually considered implementing ETC, they recognized that independent adoption would fall far short of the potential benefits achievable with an integrated interregional system.

The task force was most interested in identifying the ideal configuration of service attributes for each agency's commuters, and determining how similar or different these configurations might be across agencies. The task force identified a lengthy list of attributes that was ultimately culled to six questions.

• How many accounts are necessary and what statements will be received?

• How and where does one pay for E-ZPass?

• What lanes are available for use and how they are controlled?

• Is the tag transferable to other vehicles?

• What is the price of the tag and possible service charge?

• What are other possible uses for the E-ZPass tag (airport parking, gasoline purchases, and so forth)?

From a marketing researcher's perspective, it also seemed important to assess commuter demand for the service. However, the task force was not convinced that it needed a projection of demand, because it was committed to implementing ETC regardless of initial commuter acceptance. The task force considered its primary role to be investigating commuters' preferences for how the service should be configured *ideally*.

Questions

1. Evaluate the problem-definition process. Has the problem been defined adequately so that a relevant decision statement can be written?
2. What type of research design would you recommend for this project?
3. What research questions might be tested?
4. What might a dummy table include in this research proposal?

Case 5.2 Cane's Goes International

© GETTY IMAGES/
PHOTODISC GREEN

Raising Cane's is a fast-food chicken finger establishment based in Baton Rouge, Louisiana. Cane's restaurants are popular throughout the Gulf South. Cane's recently has been approached by people interested in opening Cane's restaurants in other countries. The best contact is an Australian. However, Cane's has also been approached about outlets in Montreal, Quebec, and in Monterey, Mexico. Cane's prepares high-quality fried chicken fingers and has a limited menu consisting of fingers, fries, slaw, and lemonade (http://www.raisingcanes.com).

1. Write a decision statement for Raising Cane's situation.
2. Write corresponding research objectives and research questions.
3. What role would a proposal play in assisting this research effort and in assisting Cane's in improving their business situation?

Case 5.3 Mario Lagasto's Italian Restaurant

© GETTY IMAGES/
PHOTODISC GREEN

Based on the case scenario described throughout this chapter, prepare a research proposal that addresses this situation.

CHAPTER 6
QUALITATIVE RESEARCH TOOLS

After studying this chapter, you should be able to

1. Compare and contrast qualitative research and quantitative research
2. Understand the role of qualitative research in exploratory research designs
3. Describe the basic orientations of qualitative research
4. Recognize common qualitative research tools and know the advantages and limitations of their use
5. Prepare a focus group interview outline
6. Recognize technological advances in the application of qualitative research approaches
7. Appreciate the role of exploratory qualitative research in *scientific* decision making

Chapter Vignette: What's in the Van?

Is this shoe too cool? That was really the question asked by VF Corporation when they acquired Vans, the company that makes the shoe shown here.[1] Vans traditionally are synonymous with skateboarding and skateboard culture. Readers that are unfamiliar with skateboarding may well have never heard of the company. However, a reader that is part of the skateboard culture is probably looking down at his or her Vans right now!

Former Vans CEO Gary Schoenfeld points out that a decade before the acquisition (a $396 million deal), Vans was practically a dead brand.[2] However, he hoped to capitalize on a revival in skateboard interest that began in the 1990s. If Vans could remain the number one skateboard shoe provider, the shoe segment of their business would grow with this trend. Beyond this, the incoming management team was given the task of deciding how to raise Vans sales to $500 million per year.

Where would the growth come from? The trend in skateboard growth alone cannot support this goal. Should the company define itself as a "skateboard footwear" company, a "lifestyle" company, or as the icon for the skate culture? How would a core customer react to seeing Vans products in department stores like JCPenney? Answering this question requires a deeper interpretation of the meaning of the "Van."

Skateboarding is a dynamic activity. A study by Board-Trac suggests that today over one in four skateboarders is female, as opposed to fewer than one in ten as recently as 2000.[3] So, what exactly is in the mind and heart of a "boarder"? In 2008, the first "Goofy versus Regular" Skateboarding Competition was held and illustrates the carefree attitude of skaters.[4] In contrast, some of the growth is attributable to both men and women who simply find skateboarding a good alternative to more mundane exercise routines. Two important research questions involve "What is the meaning of a pair of Vans?" and "What things define the skateboarding experience?"

Questions like these call for qualitative research methods.[5] Not just any researcher is "fit" for this job. One way to collect this data is to hire young, energetic research employees to become "boarders" and immerse themselves into the culture.

They may have to "Kasper" like a "flatland techer" while probing for meaning among the discussion and activities of the other boarders. Here, Vans may find that their brand helps identify a boarder and make them feel unique in some ways. If so, Vans may want to investigate increasing their product line beyond shoes and simple apparel. The Vans Web site is much more than a place to find a pair of shoes (http://www.vans.com). Here, the lifestyle of the Vans fan is epitomized.

Depth interviews of Vans wearers can describe in detail why a consumer wears Vans. Vans shouldn't be surprised if they find a significant portion of their shoes are sold to people like Mr. Samuel Teel, a retired attorney from Toledo, Ohio. Sam is completely unaware of the connection between Vans and skateboarding. He likes Vans because he doesn't have to bend to tie his shoes! Maybe there are some secondary segments that could bring growth to Vans. Distribution through more general merchandisers like Kohl's and JCPenney provides ready access to secondary markets like these. But, will openly marketing to them complicate things? Time will tell.

Introduction: What Is Qualitative Research?

Describing Qualitative Research

Chemists sometimes use the term *qualitative analysis* to mean research that determines what some compound is made of. In other words, the focus is on the inner meaning of the chemical—its *qualities*. As the word implies, qualitative research is interested more in *qualities* than quantities. Therefore, qualitative research is not about applying specific numbers to measure variables or using statistical procedures to numerically specify a relationship's strength.

Qualitative marketing research is research that addresses marketing objectives through techniques that allow the researcher to provide elaborate interpretations of market phenomena without depending on numerical measurement. Its focus is on discovering true inner meanings and new insights. Qualitative research is very widely applied in practice. There are many research firms that specialize in qualitative research.

Qualitative research is less structured than most quantitative approaches. Unlike the marketing research that most people are most familiar with, qualitative research does not rely on self-response questionnaires containing structured response formats. Instead, a qualitative approach is more **researcher-dependent** in that the researcher must extract meaning from unstructured responses, such as text from a recorded interview or a collage representing the meaning of some experience, such as skateboarding. The researcher interprets the data to extract its meaning and converts it to information.

■ USES OF QUALITATIVE RESEARCH

Mechanics can't use a hammer to fix everything that is broken. Instead, the mechanic has a toolbox from which a tool is matched to a problem. Marketing research is the same. The researcher has many tools available and the research design should try to match the best tool to the research objective. Also, just as a mechanic is probably not an expert with every tool, each researcher usually has special expertise with a small number of tools. Not every researcher has expertise with tools that would comprise qualitative research.

Generally, the less specific the research objective, the more likely that qualitative research tools will be appropriate. Also, when the emphasis is on a deeper understanding of motivations or on developing novel concepts, qualitative research is very appropriate. The following list represents common situations that often call for qualitative research.[6]

1. When it is difficult to develop specific and actionable decision statements or research objectives. For instance, if after several interviews with the research client the researcher still can't determine what needs to be measured, then qualitative research approaches may help with problem definition. Perhaps several previous studies of the same topic have not proven particularly useful.

qualitative marketing research

Research that addresses marketing objectives through techniques that allow the researcher to provide elaborate interpretations of market phenomena without depending on numerical measurement; its focus is on discovering true inner meanings and new insights.

researcher-dependent

Research in which the researcher must extract meaning from unstructured responses such as text from a recorded interview or a collage representing the meaning of some experience.

Qualitative researchers can learn about the skating experience by becoming immersed in the culture.

© SKY BONILLO/PHOTOEDIT

Although we most often think of surveys as ways of collecting quantitative data, we can also use them to collect qualitative data. Take a look at the question that was part of the in-class survey at left in the screenshot.

Find at least three responses from students in the data and try to interpret the results. What approach best fits your attempt to interpret this data? What do you think (what theory) can be learned from the responses to this question? Compare your interpretation to those of other students. How much do you agree with other students and what do you think is the source of disagreement if any?

2. When the research objective is to develop an understanding of some phenomena in great detail and in much depth. Qualitative research tools are aimed at discovering the primary themes indicating human motivations and the documentation of activities is usually very complete.

3. When the research objective is to learn how consumers use a product in its natural setting or to learn how to express some concept in colloquial terms. A survey can probably ask many useful questions, but watching how someone actually experiences a product will usually be more insightful. Qualitative research produces many product improvement ideas.

4. When some behavior the researcher is studying is particularly context-dependent—meaning the reasons something is liked or some behavior is performed depends very much on the particular situation surrounding the event. Understanding why Vans are liked so much is probably difficult to understand properly outside the skating environment.

5. When a fresh approach to studying some problem is needed. This is particularly the case when quantitative research has been less than satisfying. Qualitative tools can yield unique insights, many of which may lead to new product ideas.

Each situation also describes a situation that may require an exploratory orientation. In Chapter 3, we defined exploratory research as appropriate in ambiguous situations or when new insight is needed. In the last chapter, we indicated that exploratory research approaches are sometimes needed just to reach the appropriate decision statement and research objectives. While equating qualitative research with exploratory research is an oversimplification, the application of qualitative tools can help clear up ambiguity and provide innovative ideas.

Qualitative "versus" Quantitative Research

In social science, one can find many debates about the superiority of qualitative research over quantitative research or vice versa.[7] We'll begin by saying that this is largely a superfluous argument in either direction. The truth is that qualitative research can accomplish research objectives that quantitative research cannot. Similarly truthful, but no more so, quantitative research can accomplish objectives that qualitative research cannot. The key to successfully using either is to match the right approach to the right research context.

Many good research projects combine both qualitative and quantitative research. For instance, developing valid survey measures requires first a deep understanding of the concept to be measured and a description of the way these ideas are expressed in everyday language. Both of these are tasks best suited for qualitative research. However, validating the measure formally to make sure it can reliably capture the intended concept will likely require quantitative research.[8] Also, qualitative research may be needed to separate symptoms from problems and then quantitative research may follow to test relationships among relevant variables. The Research Snapshot on the next page describes one such situation.[9]

Quantitative marketing research can be defined as marketing research that addresses research objectives through empirical assessments that involve numerical measurement and analysis approaches. Qualitative research is more apt to stand on its own in the sense that it requires less interpretation. For example, quantitative research is quite appropriate when a research objective involves a managerial action standard. For example, a salad dressing company considered changing its recipe.[10] The new recipe was tested with a sample of consumers. Each consumer rated the product using numeric scales. Management established a rule that a majority of consumers rating the new product higher than the old product would have to be established with 90 percent confidence before replacing the old formula. A project like this can involve both quantitative measurement in the form of numeric rating scales and quantitative analysis in the form of applied statistical procedures.

quantitative marketing research

Marketing research that addresses research objectives through empirical assessments that involve numerical measurement and analysis.

Contrasting Qualitative and Quantitative Methods

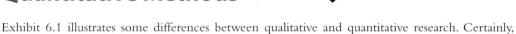

Exhibit 6.1 illustrates some differences between qualitative and quantitative research. Certainly, these are generalities and exceptions may apply. However, it covers some of the key distinctions.

Quantitative researchers direct a considerable amount of activity toward measuring concepts with scales that either directly or indirectly provide numeric values. The numeric values can then be used in statistical computations and hypothesis testing. As will be described in detail later, this

EXHIBIT 6.1
Comparing Qualitative and Quantitative Research

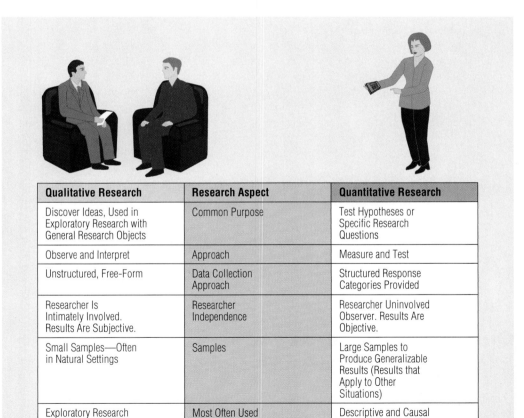

Qualitative Research	Research Aspect	Quantitative Research
Discover Ideas, Used in Exploratory Research with General Research Objects	Common Purpose	Test Hypotheses or Specific Research Questions
Observe and Interpret	Approach	Measure and Test
Unstructured, Free-Form	Data Collection Approach	Structured Response Categories Provided
Researcher Is Intimately Involved. Results Are Subjective.	Researcher Independence	Researcher Uninvolved Observer. Results Are Objective.
Small Samples—Often in Natural Settings	Samples	Large Samples to Produce Generalizable Results (Results that Apply to Other Situations)
Exploratory Research Designs	Most Often Used	Descriptive and Causal Research Designs

My Friends at P&G

With literally thousands of products to manage, Procter & Gamble (P&G) finds itself in the situation to conduct qualitative research almost daily. P&G doesn't introduce a product that hasn't been reviewed from nearly every possible angle. In-depth input on all aspects of business is part of the recipe for success. Before taking a product to a new country, P&G combines qualitative research techniques to discover potential problems or opportunities for marketing the product. So we can be sure that a product modification like Tide Kick or a laundry detergent made just for the French market, Le Croix Plus, has been "focus grouped." Today, P&G takes advantage of the Internet and the social networking phenomenon with a MySpace page dedicated to collecting qualitative research input. Here, they can float ideas about new products and collect criticisms and praise for their old products. Interestingly, P&G is among the companies actively blocking social networking Web sites in the workplace out of concerns for productivity and computer security.

At times, P&G seeks outside help to conduct research. Such was the case when P&G wanted a study of its marketing problems. The selected researchers began by applying qualitative research techniques including depth interviews, observational techniques (shadowing), and focus groups on P&G managers and marketing employees. These interviews gave the researchers the idea that perhaps P&G was suffering more from a management problem than from a marketing problem. It helped form a general research question that asked whether any marketing problems were really due to low morale among the marketing employees. After a lot of qualitative interviews with dozens and dozens of P&G employees, a quantitative study followed up these findings and supported this idea and led to suggestions for improving marketing morale! P&G quality begins with qualitative research.

Sources: Cornwell, L., "P&G Launches Two Social Networking Sites," *Marketing News*, 41 (February 1, 2007), 21; Nelson, Emily, "Focus Groupies: P&G Keeps Cincinnati Busy with all its Studies," *The Wall Street Journal* (Eastern Edition), 239 (January 24 2002), A1; Stengel, J. R., A. L. Dixon, and C. T. Allen, "Listening Begins at Home," *Harvard Business Review* (November 2003), 106–116; Lynch, C., "More Companies Ban Social Networks," *CIO*, 21 (April 15, 2008), 14.

process involves comparing numbers in some way. In contrast, qualitative researchers are more interested in observing, listening, and interpreting. As such, the researcher is intimately involved in the research process and in constructing the results. For these reasons, qualitative research is said to be more **subjective**, meaning that the results are researcher-dependent. Different researchers may reach different conclusions based on the same interview. In contrast, when a survey respondent provides a commitment score on a quantitative scale, it is thought to be more objective because the number will be the same no matter what researcher is involved in the analysis.

subjective
Results are researcher-dependent, meaning different researchers may reach different conclusions based on the same interview.

Qualitative research seldom involves samples with hundreds of respondents. Instead, a handful of consumers are usually the source of qualitative data. This is perfectly acceptable in discovery-oriented research. All ideas would still have to be tested before adopted. Does a smaller sample mean that qualitative research is cheaper than quantitative? Perhaps not. Although fewer respondents have to be interviewed, the greater researcher involvement in both the data collection and analysis can drive up the costs of qualitative research.

Given the close relationship between qualitative research and exploratory designs, it should not be surprising that qualitative research is most often used in exploratory designs. Small samples, interpretive procedures that require subjective judgments, and the unstructured interview format all make traditional hypotheses testing difficult with qualitative research. Thus, these procedures are not best suited for drawing definitive conclusions such as results from causal designs involving experiments. These disadvantages for drawing inferences, however, become advantages when the goal is to draw out potential explanations because the researcher spends more time with each respondent and is able to explore much more ground due to the flexibility of the procedures.

Qualitative Research and Exploratory Research Designs

When researchers have limited experience or knowledge about a research issue, exploratory research is a useful step. Exploratory research, which often involves qualitative methods, can be an essential first step to a more rigorous, conclusive, confirmatory study by reducing the chance of beginning with an inadequate, incorrect, or misleading set of research objectives.

Philosophically, research can be considered as either exploratory or confirmatory. Confirmatory research tests hypotheses. The results of these tests help decision making by suggesting a specific course of action. Exploratory research, on the other hand, takes a different approach. For instance, exploratory research may well be needed to develop the ideas that lead to research hypotheses in the first place.

Most exploratory research designs produce **qualitative data**. These data are not characterized by numbers and instead are textual, visual, or oral. The focus of qualitative research is not on numbers but on stories, visual portrayals, meaningful characterizations, interpretations, and other expressive descriptions. Exploratory designs do not usually produce **quantitative data**, which represent phenomena by assigning numbers in an ordered and meaningful way.

For example, a quantitative researcher may search for numbers that indicate economic trends. This may lead to hypothesis tests concerning how much the economy influences movie consumption. An exploratory researcher is more likely to adopt a qualitative approach that might involve trying to develop a deeper understanding of how families are impacted by changing economic times and why people suffering economically spend scarce resources on movie consumption. This may lead to the development of a hypothesis, but would not test one.

Some types of qualitative studies can be conducted very quickly. Others take a very long time. For example, a single focus group analysis involving a large bottling company's sales force can likely be conducted and interpreted in a matter of days. This would provide faster results than most descriptive or causal designs. However, other types of qualitative research, such as a participant-observer study aimed at understanding skateboarding, could take months to complete. A qualitative approach can, but does not necessarily, save time.

Idea Generation

Exploratory research plays a big role in new product development, including developing and screening new product ideas. Exhibit 6.2 on the next page shows the new product development process and describes how marketing research is involved at each step.[11] Exploratory research is particularly useful in idea generation and screening by producing multiple ideas and then narrowing the choices down to a small number of alternatives. In this process, exploratory research may indicate that some new product ideas are unworkable.

Qualitative research can generate ideas for new products, advertising copy, promotional ideas, and product improvements in numerous ways. Researchers using qualitative approaches can ask consumers to describe their product experiences in great detail. This data can reveal the consumer needs that a product can truly address. For example, a consumer may be asked to describe their dog food experiences. When a customer is asked what he or she wants in a dog food, the reply likely will be "Something that is good for the dog." Once the consumer is encouraged to continue, however, we may learn that the dog food "smells bad in the refrigerator" and "is messy to clean up." Thus, the interview reveals that needs related to dog food are not entirely centered on the dog.

Technology can also assist in this effort. For example, automobile marketers have consumers design their dream cars using computerized design systems similar to those used by automotive designers. This exploratory research might generate ideas that would never have occurred to the firm's own designers.[12]

Concept Testing

Research's main role in idea screening is concept testing. **Concept testing** is a frequently performed type of exploratory research representing many similar research procedures all having the same purpose: to screen new, revised, or repositioned ideas. Although the term *testing* is used, concept testing approaches are largely qualitative. Typically, respondents are presented with a written statement, pictorial representation, or some other idea description form and asked for comments. The questions almost always include whether the idea is likable, whether it would be useful, and whether it seems new. Respondents then are provided an opportunity to elaborate on the idea orally, in

qualitative data

Data that are not characterized by numbers, and instead are textual, visual, or oral; focus is on stories, visual portrayals, meaningful characterizations, interpretations, and other expressive descriptions.

quantitative data

Represent phenomena by assigning numbers in an ordered and meaningful way.

TOTHEPOINT

The cure for boredom is curiosity. There is no cure for curiosity.

—Dorothy Parker

concept testing

A frequently performed type of exploratory research representing many similar research procedures all having the same purpose: to screen new, revised, or repositioned ideas.

EXHIBIT 6.2
**The Role of Research in the
New Product Development
(NPD) Process**

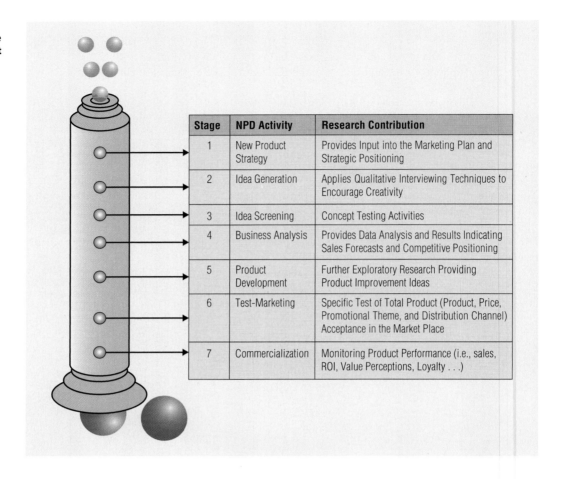

Stage	NPD Activity	Research Contribution
1	New Product Strategy	Provides Input into the Marketing Plan and Strategic Positioning
2	Idea Generation	Applies Qualitative Interviewing Techniques to Encourage Creativity
3	Idea Screening	Concept Testing Activities
4	Business Analysis	Provides Data Analysis and Results Indicating Sales Forecasts and Competitive Positioning
5	Product Development	Further Exploratory Research Providing Product Improvement Ideas
6	Test-Marketing	Specific Test of Total Product (Product, Price, Promotional Theme, and Distribution Channel) Acceptance in the Market Place
7	Commercialization	Monitoring Product Performance (i.e., sales, ROI, Value Perceptions, Loyalty . . .)

writing, or through some visual communication. Concept testing allows an initial evaluation prior to the commitment of any additional research and development, manufacturing, or other company resources. Perhaps just as importantly, the qualitative analysis of respondent comments provides themes that can be used to improve the product.

Concept testing processes work best when they not only identify ideas with the most potential, but they also lead to important refinements. Beiersdorf, the German company that produces Nivea skin care products (**http://www.beiersdorf.com**, http://www.nivea.com), like all consumer product firms, is constantly developing and screening new product ideas. One idea included a blemish-hiding skin crème that worked by reflecting light from the blemish causing it to "disappear." During concept testing, most consumers were interested but asked questions about its moisturizing abilities. As a result, the product was introduced by emphasizing both its ability to hide blemishes and to moisturize the skin.[13]

Likewise, if Vans introduces snowboarding and biking products as a way of increasing sales revenues, those products will have to undergo concept screening. Will consumers respond favorably to the ideas of a Vans Cushioned Snowboard or Vans Biking Shoes? What does the Vans idea mean to snowboarders or bikers? Clearly, concept testing including probing interview techniques will be helpful in this effort.

Many ideas may not get evaluated unfavorably overall, but may contain flaws pointed out through concept-testing procedures. Aside from vanishing skin crème, Procter & Gamble marketed Enviro-Paks first in Europe and Canada. Enviro-Paks are a soft plastic refill pouch of detergents, fabric softeners, and other cleaning products. Given the successful introduction in these important markets, they decided to consider introducing the product in the United States. Concept testing with American consumers, however, indicated that they preferred refill packaging that was different and that would be more convenient to use.

Exhibit 6.3 shows excellent concept statements for two new alternative chain restaurant concepts. Each is being floated by a national franchise that operates various chain restaurants that compete with the likes of Hooters and Outback Steakhouse. The statements portraying the intangibles (brand image, product appearance, name, and price) and a description of the product simulate reality. The product idea is clearly conveyed to the research participant who is then asked to respond in some way. Their comments become the key information gleaned from the study.

Component	Concept	
	Havana's	**Bekkah**
Brand Image	Family oriented, Cuban themed, with generous portions of modestly priced food	Upscale hangout for on-the-go individuals looking for a change of pace
Atmosphere	Bright colors, Cuban music all day and every day with every restaurant built around a bar featuring genuine '57 Chevys	Muted colors and stone walls giving the appearance of an oasis in an arid climate
Product Assortment	Traditional Cuban slow-cooked meats with generous sides like black beans and fried plantains. Cuban sangria and a wide assortment of beer are featured.	Lebanese meats sliced very thin with traditional Middle Eastern seasonings, a variety of pita breads, feta cheese, and yogurt relishes. Lebanese wines are featured and supplement an otherwise domestic collection.
Price Points	Average ticket per customer is projected to be around $14.	Average ticket per customer is projected to be around $26.
Location	Suburban location around the top 10 largest metropolitan areas in the United States and Canada	Major SMSAs (standard metropolitan statistical areas) across the southern United States from San Diego, CA to Jacksonville, FL

EXHIBIT 6.3
Testing New Product Concepts

Qualitative Research Orientations

Qualitative research can be performed in many ways using many techniques. Orientations to qualitative research are very much influenced by the different fields of study involved in research. These orientations are each associated with a category of qualitative research. The major categories of qualitative research include

1. Phenomenology—originating in philosophy and psychology
2. Ethnography—originating in anthropology
3. Grounded theory—originating in sociology
4. Case studies—originating in psychology and in business research

Precise lines between these approaches are difficult to draw and a particular qualitative research study may involve elements of two or more approaches. However, each category does reflect a somewhat unique approach to human inquiry and approaches to discovering knowledge. Each will be described briefly, followed by a description of some of the more common qualitative techniques used to generate qualitative data.

Phenomenology

■ WHAT IS A PHENOMENOLOGICAL APPROACH TO RESEARCH?

Phenomenology represents a philosophical approach to studying human experiences based on the idea that human experience itself is inherently subjective and determined by the context in which people live.[14] The phenomenological researcher focuses on how a person's behavior is shaped by the relationship he or she has with the physical environment, objects, people, and situations. Phenomenological inquiry seeks to describe, reflect upon, and interpret experiences.

phenomenology

A philosophical approach to studying human experiences based on the idea that human experience itself is inherently subjective and determined by the context in which people live.

Researchers with a phenomenological orientation rely largely on conversational interview tools. When conversational interviews are face to face, they are recorded either with video- or audiotape and then interpreted by the researcher. The phenomenological interviewer is careful to avoid asking direct questions when at all possible. Instead, the research respondent is asked to tell a story about some experience. In addition, the researcher must do everything possible to make sure a respondent is comfortable telling his or her story. One way to accomplish this is to become a member of the group (for example, becoming a skateboarder in the scenario described earlier in this chapter). Another way may be to avoid having the person use his or her real name. This might be particularly necessary in studying potentially sensitive topics including smoking, shoplifting, or employee theft.

Therefore, a phenomenological approach to studying the meaning of Vans may require considerable time. The researcher may first spend weeks or months fitting in with the person or group of interest to establish a comfort level. During this time, careful notes of conversations are made. If an interview is sought, the researcher would likely not begin by asking a skateboarder to describe his or her shoes. Rather, asking for favorite skateboard incidents or talking about what makes a skateboarder unique may generate productive conversation. Generally, the approach is very unstructured as a way of avoiding leading questions and to provide every opportunity for new insights.

■ WHAT IS HERMENEUTICS?

hermeneutics

An approach to understanding phenomenology that relies on analysis of texts through which a person tells a story about him- or herself.

The term hermeneutics is important in phenomenology. **Hermeneutics** is an approach to understanding phenomenology that relies on analysis of texts in which a person tells a story about him- or herself.[15] Meaning is then drawn by connecting text passages to one another or to themes expressed outside the story. These connections are usually facilitated by coding the key meanings expressed in the story. While a full understanding of hermeneutics is beyond the scope of this text, some of the terminology is used when applying qualitative tools. For instance, a **hermeneutic unit** refers to a text passage from a respondent's story that is linked with a key theme from within this story or provided by the researcher.[16] These passages are an important way in which data are interpreted.

hermeneutic unit

Refers to a text passage from a respondent's story that is linked with a key theme from within this story or provided by the researcher.

Computerized software exists to assist in coding and interpreting texts and images. ATLAS. ti is one such software package that adopts the term hermeneutic unit in referring to groups of phrases that are linked with meaning. Hermeneutic units and computerized software are also very appropriate in grounded theory approaches. One useful component of computerized approaches is a word counter. The word counter will return counts of how many times words were used in a story or recorded interview. Often, frequently occurring words suggest a key theme and greatly assist the researcher in developing an interpretation. Additionally, qualitative software provides an easy way to record field notes and remove the clerical tasks of transcribing or otherwise manually recording large volumes of text or other qualitative input.[17] The Research Snapshot on the next page demonstrates the use of hermeneutics in interpreting a story about a consumer shopping for a car.

Ethnography

■ WHAT IS ETHNOGRAPHY?

ethnography

Represents ways of studying cultures through methods that involve becoming highly active within that culture.

Ethnography represents ways of studying cultures through methods that involve becoming highly active within that culture. **Participant-observation** typifies an ethnographic research approach. Participant-observation means the researcher becomes immersed within the culture that he or she is studying and draws data from his or her observations. A *culture* can be either a broad culture, like American culture, or a narrow culture, like urban gangs or skateboarding enthusiasts.[18]

participant-observation

Ethnographic research approach where the researcher becomes immersed within the culture that he or she is studying and draws data from his or her observations.

Organizational culture would also be relevant for ethnographic study.[19] At times, researchers have actually become employees of an organization for an extended period of time. In doing so, they become part of the culture and over time other employees come to act quite naturally

RESEARCH SNAPSHOT

"When Will I Ever Learn?"

A hermeneutic approach can be used to provide insight into car shopping experiences. The approach involves a small number of consumers providing relatively lengthy stories about recent car shopping experiences. The goal is trying to discover particular reasons why certain car models are eliminated from consideration. The consumer tells a story of comparing a Ford and a GM (General Motors) minivan. She describes the two vehicles in great detail and ultimately concludes, "We might have gone with the Ford instead because it was real close between the Ford and the GM." The Ford was cheaper, but the way the door opened suggested difficulties in dealing with kids and groceries and the like, and so she purchased the GM model. The researcher in this story goes on to interpret the plotline of the story as having to do with her responsibility for poor consumption outcomes. Consider the following passage.

"It has got GM defects and that is really frustrating. I mean the transmission had to be rebuilt after about 150 miles . . . and it had this horrible vibration problem. We took a long vacation where you couldn't go over sixty miles an hour because the thing started shaking so bad. . . . I told everybody, 'Don't buy one of these things.' We should have known because our Buick—the Buick that is in the shop right now—its transmission lasted about 3,000 miles. My husband's parents are GM people and they had one go bad. I keep thinking, When I am going to learn? I think this one has done it. I don't think I will ever go back to GM after this."[20]

The research concludes that a hermeneutic link exists between the phrase "When I am going to learn?" and the plot of self-responsibility. The resulting behavior including no longer considering GM products and the negative word-of-mouth behavior are ways of restoring esteem given the events.

Source: *Journal of Marketing Research* by/Winer, Russ. Copyright 1997 by Am Marketing assn (AMA) (CHIC). Reproduced with permission of Am Marketing Assn (AMA) (CHIC) in the format Textbook via Copyright Clearance Center; Thompson, Craig J., "Interpreting Consumers: A Hermeneutical Framework for Deriving Marketing Insights from the Tests of Consumers' Consumption Stories," *Journal of Marketing Research*, 34 (November 1997), 438–455 (see pp. 443–444 for quotation).

around the researcher. The researcher may observe behaviors that the employee would never reveal otherwise. For instance, a researcher investigating the ethical behavior of salespeople may have difficulty getting a car salesperson to reveal any potentially deceptive sales tactics in a traditional interview. However, ethnographic techniques may result in the salesperson letting down his or her guard, resulting in more valid discoveries about the car-selling culture.

Ethnographic (participant-observation) approaches may be useful to understanding how children obtain value from their experiences with toys.

139

■ OBSERVATION IN ETHNOGRAPHY

Observation plays a key role in ethnography. Researchers today sometimes ask households for permission to place video cameras in their home. In doing so, the ethnographer can study the consumer in a "natural habitat" and use the observations to test new products, develop new product ideas, and develop marketing strategies in general.[21]

Ethnographic study can be particularly useful when a certain culture is comprised of individuals who cannot or will not verbalize their thoughts and feelings. For instance, ethnography has advantages for discovering insights among children since it does not rely largely on their answers to questions. Instead, the researcher can simply become part of the environment, allow the children to do what they do naturally, and record their behavior.[22]

The opening vignette describing a participant-observer approach to learning about skateboarding culture represents an ethnographic approach. Here, the researcher would draw insight from observations and personal experiences with the culture. Kodak used in-home ethnographic research in developing the "Pass Along" advertisement campaign.[23] The research revealed that consumers, particularly younger consumers, enjoyed passing disposable cameras around to friends and these images became a prominent part of the campaign.

TO THE POINT

I never predict. I just look out the window and see what is visible—but not yet seen.

—Peter Drucker

Grounded Theory

■ WHAT IS GROUNDED THEORY?

Grounded theory is probably applied less often in business research than is either phenomenology or ethnography.[24]

grounded theory
Represents an inductive investigation in which the researcher poses questions about information provided by respondents or taken from historical records; the researcher asks the questions to him- or herself and repeatedly questions the responses to derive deeper explanations.

Grounded theory represents an inductive investigation in which the researcher poses questions about information provided by respondents or taken from historical records. The researcher asks the questions to him- or herself and repeatedly questions the responses to derive deeper explanations. Grounded theory is particularly applicable in highly dynamic situations involving rapid and significant change. Two key questions asked by the grounded theory researcher are "What is happening here?" and "How is it different?"[25] The distinguishing characteristic of grounded theory is that it does not begin with a theory but instead extracts one from whatever emerges from an area of inquiry.

■ HOW IS GROUNDED THEORY USED?

Consider a company that approaches a researcher to study whether or not its sales force is as effective as it has been over the past five years. The researcher uses grounded theory to discover a potential explanation. A theory is inductively developed based on text analysis of dozens of sales meetings that had been recorded over the previous five years. By questioning the events discussed in the sales interviews and analyzing differences in the situations that may have led to the discussion, the researcher is able to develop a theory. The theory suggests that with an increasing reliance on e-mail and other technological devices for communication, the salespeople do not communicate with each other informally as much as they did five years previously. As a result, the salespeople had failed to bond into a close-knit "community."[26]

Computerized software also can be useful in developing grounded theory. In our Vans example, the researcher may interpret skateboarders' stories of good and bad skating experiences by questioning the events and changes described. These may yield theories about the role that certain brands play in shaping a good or bad experience. Alternatively, grounded theorists often rely on visual representations. Thus, the skateboarder could develop collages representing good and bad experiences. Just as with the text, questions can be applied to the visuals in an effort to develop theory.

Case Studies

■ WHAT ARE CASE STUDIES?

case studies
The documented history of a particular person, group, organization, or event.

Case studies simply refer to the documented history of a particular person, group, organization, or event. Typically, a case study may describe consumers' acceptance or rejection of a particular product.

Alternatively, case studies may describe the events of a specific company introducing a new product or dealing with some management crisis. Textbook cases typify this kind of case study. Clinical interviews of individual consumers can represent a case study. These may focus on their experiences with certain brands or products.

The case studies can then be analyzed for important themes. **Themes** are identified by the frequency with which the same term (or a synonym) arises in the narrative description. The themes may be useful in discovering variables that are relevant to potential explanations.

■ HOW ARE CASE STUDIES USED?

Case studies are commonly applied in business. For instance, case studies of brands that sell "luxury" products helped provide insight into what makes up a prestigious brand. A marketing researcher carefully conducted case studies of higher-end wine labels (such as Penfold's Grange) including the methods of production and marketing. This analysis suggested that a key ingredient to a prestige brand may well be authenticity. When consumers know something is authentic, they attach more esteem to that product or brand.[27]

A primary advantage of the case study is that an entire organization or entity can be investigated in depth with meticulous attention to detail. This highly focused attention enables the researcher to carefully study the order of events as they occur or to concentrate on identifying the relationships among functions, individuals, or entities. Conducting a case study often requires the cooperation of the party whose history is being studied. This freedom to search for whatever data an investigator deems important makes the success of any case study highly dependent on the alertness, creativity, intelligence, and motivation of the individual performing the case analysis.

©PHOTO CUISINE/CORBIS

Qualitative research reveals that products that are perceived as "authentic" offer more value for consumers.

Common Techniques Used in Qualitative Research

Qualitative researchers apply a nearly endless number of techniques. These techniques overlap more than one of the categories previously discussed, although each category may display a preference for certain techniques. Exhibit 6.4 on the next page lists characteristics of some common qualitative research techniques. Each is then described.

themes

Identified by the frequency with which the same term (or a synonym) arises in the narrative description.

Focus Group Interview

The focus group interview is so widely used that many advertising and research agencies do nothing but focus group interviews. In that sense, it is wrongly synonymous with qualitative research. A **focus group interview** is an unstructured, free-flowing interview with a small group of people, usually between six and ten. Focus groups are led by a trained moderator who follows a flexible format encouraging dialogue among respondents. Common focus group topics include employee programs, brand meanings, problems with products, advertising themes, or new-product concepts.

The group meets at a central location at a designated time. Participants may range from consumers talking about hair coloring, petroleum engineers talking about problems in the "oil patch,"

focus group interview

An unstructured, free-flowing interview with a small group of around six to ten people. Focus groups are led by a trained moderator who follows a flexible format encouraging dialogue among respondents.

EXHIBIT 6.4   Common Qualitative Research Tools

Tool	Description	Type of Approach (Category)	Key Advantages	Key Disadvantages
Focus Group Interviews	Small group discussions led by a trained moderator	Ethnography, Case Studies	• Can be done quickly • Gain multiple perspectives • Flexibility	• Results do not generalize to larger population • Difficult to use for sensitive topics • Expensive
Depth Interviews	One-on-one, probing interview between a trained researcher and a respondent	Ethnography, Grounded Theory, Case Studies	• Gain considerable insight from each individual • Good for understanding unusual behaviors	• Results not meant to generalize • Very expensive per each interview
Conversations	Unstructured dialogue recorded by a researcher	Phenomenology, Grounded Theory	• Gain unique insights from enthusiasts • Can cover sensitive topics • Less expensive than depth interviews or focus groups	• Easy to get off course • Interpretations are very researcher-dependent
Semi-Structured Interviews	Open-ended questions, often in writing, that ask for short essay-type answers from respondents	Grounded theory, ethnography	• Can address more specific issues • Results can be easily interpreted • Cost advantages over focus groups and depth interviews	• Lack the flexibility that is likely to produce truly creative or novel explanations
Word Association/ Sentence Completion	Records the first thoughts that come to a consumer in response to some stimulus	Grounded theory, case studies	• Economical • Can be done quickly	• Lack the flexibility that is likely to produce truly creative or novel explanations
Observation	Recorded notes describing observed events	Ethnography, grounded theory, case studies	• Can be inobtrusive • Can yield actual behavior patterns	• Can be very expensive with participant-observer series
Collages	Respondent assembles pictures that represent their thoughts/feelings	Phenomenology, Grounded theory	• Flexible enough to allow novel insights	• Highly dependent on the researcher's interpretation of the collage
Thematic Apperception/ Cartoon Tests	Researcher provides an ambiguous picture and respondent tells about the story	Phenomenology, Grounded theory	• Projective, allows to get at sensitive issues • Flexible	• Highly dependent on the researcher's interpretation

children talking about toys, or employees talking about their jobs. A moderator begins by providing some opening statement to broadly steer discussion in the intended direction. Ideally, discussion topics emerge at the group's initiative, not the moderator's. Consistent with phenomenological approaches, moderators should avoid direct questioning unless absolutely necessary.

■ ADVANTAGES OF FOCUS GROUP INTERVIEWS

Focus groups allow people to discuss their true feelings, anxieties, and frustrations, as well as the depth of their convictions, in their own words. While other approaches may also do much the same, focus groups offer several advantages.

1. Relatively fast
2. Easy to execute
3. Allow respondents to piggyback off each other's ideas
4. Provide multiple perspectives

5. Flexibility to allow more detailed descriptions
6. High degree of scrutiny

Speed and Ease

In an emergency situation, three or four group sessions can be conducted, analyzed, and reported in a week or so. The large number of research firms that conduct focus group interviews makes it easy to find someone to conduct the research. Practically every state in the United States contains multiple research firms that have their own focus group facilities. Companies with large research departments likely have at least one qualified focus group moderator so that they need not outsource the focus group.

Piggybacking and Multiple Perspectives

Furthermore, the group approach may produce thoughts that would not be produced otherwise. The interplay between respondents allows them to **piggyback** off of each other's ideas. In other words, one respondent stimulates thought among the others and, as this process continues, increasingly creative insights are possible. A comment by one individual often triggers a chain of responses from the other participants. The social nature of the focus group also helps bring out multiple views as each person shares a particular perspective.

piggyback

A procedure in which one respondent stimulates thought among the others; as this process continues, increasingly creative insights are possible.

Flexibility

The flexibility of focus group interviews is advantageous, especially when compared with the more structured and rigid survey format. Numerous topics can be discussed and many insights can be gained, particularly with regard to the variations in consumer behavior in different situations. Responses that would be unlikely to emerge in a survey often come out in group interviews: "*If* it is one of the three brands I sometimes use and *if* it is on sale, I buy it; otherwise, I buy my regular brand" or "*If* the day is hot and I have to serve the whole neighborhood, I make Kool-Aid; otherwise, I give them Dr Pepper or Coke."

If a researcher is investigating a target group to determine who consumes a particular beverage or why a consumer purchases a certain brand, situational factors must be included in any interpretations of respondent comments. For instance, in the situation above, the fact that a particular beverage is consumed must be noted. It would be inappropriate to say that Kool-Aid is preferred in general. The proper interpretation is situation-specific. On a hot day the whole neighborhood gets Kool-Aid. When the weather isn't hot, the kids may get nothing, or if only a few kids are

Focus group facilities typically include a comfortable room for respondents, recording equipment, and a viewing room via a two-way mirror.

around, they may get lucky and get Dr Pepper. Thus, Kool-Aid can be interpreted as appropriate for satisfying large numbers of hot kids while Dr Pepper is a treat for a select few.

Scrutiny

A focus group interview allows closer scrutiny in several ways. First, the session can be observed by several people, as it is usually conducted in a room containing a two-way mirror. The respondents and moderator are on one side, and an invited audience that may include both researchers and decision makers is on the other. If the decision makers are located in another city or country, the session may be shown via a live video hookup. Either through live video or a two-way mirror, some check on the eventual interpretations is provided through the ability to actually watch the research being conducted. Second, focus group sessions are generally recorded on audio- or videotape. Later, detailed examination of the recorded session can offer additional insight and help clear up disagreements about what happened.

■ FOCUS GROUP ILLUSTRATION

Focus groups often are used for concept screening and concept refinement. The concept may be continually modified, refined, and retested until management believes it is acceptable. While RJR's initial attempts at smokeless cigarettes failed in the United States, Philip Morris is developing a smokeless cigarette for the U.K. market. Focus groups are being used to help understand how the product will be received and how it might be improved.[28] The voluntary focus group respondents are presented with samples of the product and then they discuss it among themselves. The interview results suggest that the key product features that must be conveyed are the fact that it produces no ashes, no side smoke, and very little odor. These beliefs are expected to lead to a positive attitude. Focus group respondents show little concern about how the cigarette actually functioned. Smokers believe they will use the product if nonsmokers are not irritated by being near someone using the "electronic cigarette." Thus, the focus groups are useful in refining the product and developing a theory of how it should be marketed.

■ FOCUS GROUP RESPONDENTS

What is a research supplier's responsibility when recruiting individuals to participate in a focus group? Practically every focus group interview requires that respondents be screened based on some relevant characteristic. For example, if the topic involves improving parochial school education, the group

Imagine the differences in reactions to legislation further restricting smoking behavior that would be found among a group of smokers compared to a group of nonsmokers.

should probably not include non-parents or parents with no plans of having children. The respondents in this case should be parents who are likely to put or are currently putting a child through school.

Even after careful screening, some consumers that fit the desired profile make poor focus group participants because they are unwilling to express their views or from the other extreme, because they are overbearing. When a researcher finds good focus group participants, he or she may be tempted to use them over and over again. Is this appropriate? Should respondents be recruited because they will freely offer a lot of discussion without being overbearing or because they have the desired characteristics given the focus group topic? This is a question the focus group planner may well face. Consider a research client viewing videotapes of a series of six focus groups conducted about new kitchen appliance designs. The client realizes that four respondents appeared in more than one of the six focus group interviews and that ten respondents appeared in focus groups performed by the same researcher on another topic six months previous. Whenever diversity of opinion is needed, relying on what essentially become professional focus group respondents is not likely appropriate. The researcher should take the extra effort to find new respondents rather than relying on conveniently available and appropriately talkative respondents.

Group Composition

The ideal size of the focus group is six to ten people. If the group is too small, one or two members may intimidate the others. Groups that are too large may not allow for adequate participation by each group member.

Homogeneous groups seem to work best because they allow researchers to concentrate on consumers with similar lifestyles, experiences, and communication skills. This lessens the chance for an overly confrontational focus group but it also matches the fact that so much marketing is directed toward market segments than to all consumers. From an ethnographic perspective, qualitative research respondents should all be members of a unique and identifiable culture. Vans may benefit from a focus group interview comprised only of skateboard enthusiasts. Perhaps participants can be recruited from a local skate park.

When the Center for Disease Control and Prevention tested public service announcements about AIDS through focus groups, it discovered that single-race groups and racially diverse groups reacted differently. By conducting separate focus groups, the organization was able to gain important insights about which creative strategies were most appropriate for targeted versus broad audiences.

For example, a typical homogeneous group might be made up of married, full-time homemakers with children at home. The researcher may find that including first-time mothers in a group with women who have three or four children reduces the new mothers' participation. Instead of giving their opinion, they become more interested in listening to the more experienced mothers for advice. Although they may differ in their opinions, they defer to the more experienced mothers. Therefore, researchers may consider interviewing first-time mothers and experienced mothers in separate groups.

Researchers who wish to collect information from different types of people should conduct several focus groups. A diverse overall sample may be obtained by using different groups even though each group is homogeneous. For instance, in discussing household chores, four groups might be used.

1. Married Men
2. Married Women
3. Single Men
4. Single Women

Although each group is homogenous, by using four groups, researchers obtain opinions from a wide degree of respondents. Similarly, a rule of thumb is that four focus group sessions, each in a different city, can satisfy exploratory research needs dealing with common consumer product or possible employee development issues.

■ ENVIRONMENTAL CONDITIONS

A focus group session may typically take place at the research agency in a room specifically designed for this purpose. Research suppliers that specialize in conducting focus groups operate from commercial facilities that have videotape cameras in observation rooms behind two-way mirrors and microphone systems connected to tape recorders and speakers to allow greater scrutiny as discussed above. Refreshments are provided to help create a more relaxed atmosphere conducive to a free exchange of ideas. More open and intimate reports of personal experiences and sentiments can be obtained under these conditions.

■ THE FOCUS GROUP MODERATOR

moderator
A person who leads a focus group interview and ensures that everyone gets a chance to speak and contribute to the discussion.

Exhibit 6.5 is a partial transcript of a focus group interview. Notice how the **moderator** ensures that everyone gets a chance to speak and how he or she contributes to the discussion.

There are several qualities that a good moderator must possess.

1. The moderator must develop rapport with the group to promote interaction among all participants. The moderator should be someone who is really interested in people, who listens carefully to what others have to say, and who can readily establish rapport, gain people's confidence, and make them feel relaxed and eager to talk.
2. The moderator must be a good listener. Careful listening is especially important because the group interview's purpose is to stimulate spontaneous responses. Without good listening skills, the moderator may direct the group in an unproductive direction.
3. The moderator must try not to interject his or her own opinions. Good moderators usually say less rather than more. They can stimulate productive discussion with generalized follow-ups such as, "Tell us more about that incident," or "How are your experiences similar or different from the one you just heard?" The moderator must be particularly careful not to ask leading questions such as "You do like cornflakes, don't you?"
4. The moderator must be able to control discussion without being overbearing. The moderator's role is also to focus the discussion on the areas of concern. When a topic is no longer generating fresh ideas, the effective moderator changes the flow of discussion. The moderator does not give the group total control of the discussion, but he or she normally has prepared questions on topics that concern management. However, the timing of these questions in the discussion and the manner in which they are raised are left to the moderator's discretion. The term *focus group* thus stems from the moderator's task. He or she starts out by asking for a general discussion but usually *focuses* in on specific topics during the session.

EXHIBIT 6.5
What Happens in a Focus Group

"My company is interested in finding out how people feel about different products and services," the moderator tells the semicircle of women. "In this group situation, what we're doing is exploring how you feel. Today we're interested in talking about restaurants and eating out."

The women have been told that someone "from a market research company" is listening to them, but they don't know which franchiser is the sponsor.

When the moderator displays the first card on the easel beside her, a card reading "McDonald's, Jack in the Box, Carl's Jr., Burger King, Wendy's," she asks, "What do you think of these restaurants?"

"The only one I really enjoy going to is Carl's Jr.," says Anne, a bright-faced woman in her early twenties who wears athletic shorts and flip-flops. "I don't know what Burger King does to their hamburgers, but I always get indigestion."

"You get indigestion at Burger King?" the moderator asks solicitously.

Anne nods. "It looks great when they bring it to you, but as soon as I start eating it, and especially when I finish, I get this awful feeling. . . ."

"I think it looks great on TV," says Nancy, whose hair has been frosted with two colors, for a total of three. "The lettuce is so crispy, you know—"

"Oh yeah, and it's these huge hamburgers," says Laura.

"But then you get it and it's all crushed together," Anne says ruefully.

"I think the worst is Jack in the Box," says Victoria, a very thin woman who lives in Reseda, near a block that she contends houses one of every food franchise in the world. "The meat doesn't taste like meat. It tastes . . . low-grade. Fatty. The last time I ate there—I had a coupon for it and we were close by and this friend of mine hadn't tried it—" she explains quickly, "it was terrible. I've heard that Wendy's—I haven't been there yet, but everybody who goes there thinks it's terrific."

"Really?" Nancy looks a little funny at Victoria. "Wendy's?"

"I've been there," Anne says. "It's terrible."

"Is it terrible?" Victoria asks sheepishly, retreating from the group's conclusion that she's been taking restaurant advice from a pack of cretins out there in Reseda.

"Oh, my daughter is the hamburger addict of the world, and she couldn't finish it," Nancy says. "It ran all down—it was so greasy—"

"I like Burger King," says Marlene, who has had nine children during her 25-year marriage, "and I like Carl's Jr." She smiles nicely, relishing the impending heresy: "McDonald's I could vomit from." The women laugh. "I like Jack in the Box Super Tacos."

"Charlie Hass on Advertising," *New West Magazine*, November 5, 1979, pp. 32–39.

■ FOCUS GROUPS AS DIAGNOSTIC TOOLS

Focus groups are perhaps the predominant means by which marketing researchers implement exploratory research designs. Focus groups also can be helpful in later stages of a research project, particularly when the findings from surveys or other quantitative techniques raise more questions than they answer. Managers who are puzzled about the meaning of survey research results may use focus groups to better understand what consumer surveys indicate. In such a situation, the focus group supplies diagnostic help after quantitative research has been conducted.

Focus groups are also excellent diagnostic tools for spotting problems with ideas. For instance, idea screening is often done with focus groups. An initial concept is presented to the group and then they are allowed to comment on it in detail. This usually leads to lengthy lists of potential product problems and some ideas for overcoming them. Mature products can also be "focused-grouped" in this manner.

Depth Interviews

An alternative to a focus group is a depth interview. A **depth interview** is a one-on-one interview between a professional researcher and a research respondent. Depth interviews are much the same as a psychological, clinical interview, but with a different purpose. The researcher asks many questions and follows up each answer with probes for additional elaboration. An excerpt from a depth interview is given in Exhibit 6.6. The interviews allowed the reserachers to develop a theory of the way children react to product advertisements. In each case, the child was elaborating on their reactions to or memories of advertisements.

Like focus group moderators, the interviewer's role is critical in a depth interview. He or she must be a highly skilled individual who can encourage the respondent to talk freely without influencing the direction of the conversation. Probing questions are critical.

Laddering is a term used for a particular approach to probing, asking respondents to compare differences between brands at different levels. A repertory grid interview is an approach developed in the mid-twentieth century to conduct interviews that drew out the way people distinguished concepts. Laddering is derived from the repertory grid approach and is very useful in identifying

depth interview

A one-on-one interview between a professional researcher and a research respondent conducted about some relevant business or social topic.

laddering

A particular approach to probing asking respondents to compare differences between brands at different levels that produces distinctions at the attribute level, the benefit level, and the value or motivation level. Laddering is based on the classical repertory grid approach.

EXHIBIT 6.6 **Example Results from a Depth Interview**

Respondent Comments	Interpreted Meaning
"I like to watch [Barbie ads] because I like to see how pretty the Barbies are and if there is going to be, like, a new kind of Barbie. There is one Barbie . . . that comes with some little lipstick-type thing on a towel. You dip it in water and put the lipstick on the Barbie. The Barbie's lipstick turns darker."	Children look forward to seeing some advertisements and take value from viewing them.
"It's like a fairy tale on the commercial, I mean people can't really be thin. And they can't just pop out of it like that. That's not real."	Children are not detached from reality when viewing the ads.
"The Honey Comb commercial has never left my head because it's got all those details in it. It's got bright colors, and music and kids with interesting things in it. That's what makes it stay in my head. I don't like that kind of cereal or the new kinds. I don't like sweet cereal. I just like the commercials though."	Children appreciate the hedonic value aspects of viewing advertisements.
"I don't like that one (Chip's Ahoy ad) because it made me too hungry. Cookies are my favorite. And we're not allowed to have snacks."	Signifies the role of parents in facilitating the consumption of children.

© ELENA ELISSEEVA/SHUTTERSTOCK

Source: Adapted from Moore, E. S. and R. J. Lutz, "Children, Advertising, and Product Experiences: A Multimethod Inquiry," *Journal of Consumer Research*, 27 (June 2000), 31–48.

the potential meaning of brand names. What usually results with laddering is that respondents first distinguish things using attribute-level distinctions, second are benefit-level distinctions, and third are distinctions at the value or motivation level. Laddering, for example, can then distinguish two brands of skateboarding shoes based on a) the materials they are made of, b) the comfort they provide, and c) the excitement they create.

Each depth interview may last more than an hour. Thus, it is a time-consuming process if multiple interviews are conducted. Not only does the interview have to be conducted, but each interview produces about the same amount of text as does a focus group interview. This has to be analyzed and interpreted by the researcher. A third major issue stems from the necessity of recording both surface reactions and subconscious motivations of the respondent. Analysis and interpretation of such data are highly subjective, and it is difficult to settle on a true interpretation.

Depth interviews provide more insight into a particular individual than do focus groups. In addition, since the setting isn't really social, respondents are more likely to discuss sensitive topics than are those in a focus group. Depth interviews are particularly advantageous when some unique or unusual behavior is being studied. For instance, depth interviews have been usefully applied to reveal characteristics of adolescent behavior, ranging from the ways they get what they want from their parents to shopping, smoking, and shoplifting.[29]

Depth interviews are similar to focus groups in many ways. The costs are similar if only one to two interviews are conducted. However, if a dozen or more interviews are included in a report, the costs are higher than focus group interviews due to the increased interviewing and analysis time.

Conversations

conversations

An informal qualitative data-gathering approach in which the researcher engages a respondent in a discussion of the relevant subject matter.

Holding **conversations** in qualitative research is an informal data-gathering approach in which the researcher engages a respondent in a discussion of the relevant subject matter. This approach is almost completely unstructured and the researcher enters the conversation with few expectations. The goal is to have the respondent produce a dialogue about his or her lived experiences. Meaning will be extracted from the resulting dialogue.

A conversational approach to qualitative research is particularly appropriate in phenomenological research and for developing grounded theory. In our Vans experience, the researcher may simply tape-record a conversation about becoming a "skater." The resulting dialogue can then be analyzed for themes and plots. The result may be some interesting and novel insight into the consumption patterns of skaters, for example, if the respondent said,

> "I knew I was a real skater when I just had to have Vans, not just for boarding, but for wearing."

This theme may connect to a rite-of-passage plot and show how Vans play a role in this process.

Technology is also influencing conversational research. Online communications such as the reviews posted about book purchases at http://www.barnesandnoble.com can be treated as a conversation. Companies may discover product problems and ideas for overcoming them by analyzing these computer-based consumer dialogues.[30]

A conversational approach is advantageous because each interview is usually inexpensive to conduct. Unlike depth interviews or focus groups, respondents need not be paid because they are enthusiasts in a product area. Often, the conversation takes place spontaneously, with little set up or with little need for any formal setting such as a focus group studio. They are relatively effective at getting at sensitive issues once the researcher establishes a rapport with them. Conversational approaches, however, are prone to produce little relevant information since little effort is made to steer the conversation. Additionally, the data analysis is very much researcher-dependent.

■ SEMI-STRUCTURED INTERVIEWS

Semi-structured interviews usually come in written form and ask respondents for short essay responses to specific open-ended questions. Respondents are free to write as much or as little as they want. The questions would be divided into sections, typically, and within each section, the opening question would be followed by some probing questions. When these are performed face to face, there is room for less structured follow-ups.

The advantages to this approach include an ability to address more specific issues. Responses are usually easier to interpret than other qualitative approaches. Since the researcher can simply prepare the questions in writing ahead of time, and if in writing, the questions are administered without the presence of an interviewer, semi-structured interviews can be relatively cost-effective.

Some researchers interested in studying car salesperson stereotypes used qualitative semi-structured interviews to map consumers' cognitions (memory). The semi-structured interview began with a free-association task.

List the first five things that come into your mind when you think of a "car salesman."

This was followed up with a probing question.

Describe the way a typical "car salesman" looks.

This was followed with questions about how the car salesperson acts and how the respondent feels in the presence of a car salesperson. The results led to research showing how the information that consumers process differs in the presence of a typical car salesperson, as opposed to a less typical car salesperson.[31]

Free-Association and Sentence Completion Methods

Free-association techniques simply record a respondent's first cognitive reactions (top-of-mind) to some stimulus. The Rorschach or inkblot test typifies the free-association method. Respondents view an ambiguous figure and are asked to say the first thing that comes to their mind. Free-association techniques allow researchers to map a respondent's thoughts or memory.

The sentence completion method is based on free-association principles. Respondents simply are required to complete a few partial sentences with the first word or phrase that comes to mind. For example:

People who drink beer are _____.
A man who drinks a dark beer is _____.
Imported beer is most liked by _____.
The woman in the phone commercial _____.

Answers to sentence-completion questions tend to be more extensive than responses to word-association tests. Although the responses lack the ability to probe for meaning as in other qualitative techniques, they are very effective in finding out what is on a respondent's mind. They can also do so in a quick and very cost-effective manner. Free-association and sentence-completion tasks are sometimes used in conjunction with other approaches. For instance, they can sometimes be used as effective icebreakers in focus group interviews.

free-association techniques

Record respondents' first (top-of-mind) cognitive reactions to some stimulus.

■ OBSERVATION

Throughout this chapter, we have described how observation can be a very important qualitative tool. The participant-observer approach typifies how observation can be used to explore various issues. Meaning is extracted from field notes. **Field notes** are the researchers' descriptions of what actually happens in the field. These notes then become the text from which meaning is extracted.

Observation may also take place in visual form. Researchers may observe consumers in their home, as mentioned above, or try to gain knowledge from photographic records of one type or another. Observation can either be very inexpensive, such as when a research associate sits and simply observes behavior, or it can be very expensive, as in most participant-observer studies. Observational research is keenly advantageous for gaining insight into things that respondents cannot or will not verbalize.

Field notes

The researcher's descriptions of what actually happens in the field; these notes then become the text from which meaning is extracted.

■ COLLAGES

Marketing researchers sometimes have respondents prepare a collage to represent their experience with some good, service, or brand. The collages are then analyzed for meaning much in the same manner as text dialogues are analyzed. Computer software can even be applied to help develop potential grounded theories from the visual representations.

Harley-Davidson commissioned research in which collages depicting feelings about Harley-Davidson were compared based on whether the respondent was a Harley owner or an owner of a competitor's brand. The collages of "Hog" owners revealed themes of artwork and the freedom of the great outdoors. These themes did not emerge in the non-Hog groups. This led to confirmatory research which helped Harley continue its growth, appealing more specifically to its diverse market segments.[32]

Like sentence completion and word association, collages are often used within some other approach, such as a focus group or a depth interview. Collages offer the advantage of flexibility but are also very much subject to the researcher's interpretations.

■ THEMATIC APPERCEPTION TEST (TAT)

thematic apperception test (TAT)

A test that presents subjects with an ambiguous picture(s) in which consumers and products are the center of attention; the investigator asks the subject to tell what is happening in the picture(s) now and what might happen next.

A **thematic apperception test (TAT)** presents subjects with an ambiguous picture(s) in which consumers and products are the center of attention. The investigator asks the subject to tell what is happening in the picture(s) now and what might happen next. Hence, themes (*thematic*) are elicited on the basis of the perceptual-interpretive (*apperception*) use of the pictures. The researcher then analyzes the contents of the stories that the subjects relate.

The picture or cartoon stimulus must be sufficiently interesting to encourage discussion but ambiguous enough not to disclose the nature of the research project. Clues should not be given to the character's positive or negative predisposition. A pretest of a TAT investigating why men might purchase chainsaws used a picture of a man looking at a very large tree. The research respondents were homeowners and weekend woodcutters. They almost unanimously said that they would get professional help from a tree surgeon to deal with this situation. Thus, early in pretesting, the researchers found out that the picture was not sufficiently ambiguous. The tree was too large and did not allow respondents to identify with the tree-cutting task. If subjects are to project their own views into the situation, the environmental setting should be a well-defined, familiar problem, but the solution should be ambiguous.

Frequently, the TAT consists of a series of pictures with some continuity so that stories may be constructed in a variety of settings. The first picture might portray two people discussing a product in a supermarket; in the second picture, a person might be preparing the product in the kitchen; the final picture might show the product being served at the dinner table. A TAT might include several ambiguous pictures of a skateboarder and then show him or her heading to the store. This might reveal ideas about the brands and products that fit the role of skateboarder.

picture frustration

A version of the TAT using a cartoon drawing in which the respondent suggests a dialogue in which the characters might engage.

A **picture frustration** version of the TAT uses a cartoon drawing in which the respondent suggests a dialogue in which the characters might engage. Exhibit 6.7 is a purposely ambiguous illustration of an everyday occurrence. The two office workers are shown in a situation and the respondent is asked what the woman might be talking about. This setting could be used for discussions about products, packaging, the display of merchandise, store personnel, and so on.

■ PROJECTIVE RESEARCH TECHNIQUES

projective technique

An indirect means of questioning enabling respondents to project beliefs and feelings onto a third party, an inanimate object, or a task situation.

A TAT represents a projective research technique. A **projective technique** is an indirect means of questioning enabling respondents to project beliefs and feelings onto a third party, an inanimate object, or a task situation. Projective techniques usually encourage respondents to describe a situation in their own words with little prompting by the interviewer. Individuals are expected to interpret the situation within the context of their own experiences, attitudes, and personalities and to express opinions and emotions that may be hidden from others and possibly themselves. All projective techniques are particularly useful in studying sensitive issues.

There is an old story about asking a man why he purchased a Mercedes. When asked directly why he purchased a Mercedes, he responds that the car holds its value and does not depreciate much, that it gets better gas mileage than you'd expect, or that it has a comfortable ride. If you ask the same person why a neighbor purchased a Mercedes, he may well answer, "Oh, that status seeker!" This story illustrates that individuals may be more likely to give true answers (consciously or unconsciously) to disguised questions, and a projective technique provides a way of disguising just who is being described.

EXHIBIT 6.7
Picture Frustration Version of TAT

Preparing a Focus Group Outline

Focus group researchers use a discussion guide to help control the interview and guide the discussion into product areas. A **discussion guide** includes written introductory comments informing the group about the focus group purpose and rules and then outlines topics or questions to be addressed in the group session. Thus, the discussion guide serves as the focus group outline. Some discussion guides will have only a few phrases in the entire document. Others may be more detailed. The amount of content depends on the nature and experience of the researcher and the complexity of the topic.

A cancer center that wanted to warn the public about the effects of the sun used the discussion guide in Exhibit 6.8 on the next page. The marketing researchers had several objectives for this question guide:

- The first question was very general, asking that respondents describe their feelings about being out in the sun. This opening question aimed to elicit the full range of views within in the group. Some individuals might view being out in the sun as a healthful practice, whereas others view the sun as deadly. The hope is that by exposing the full range of opinions, respondents would be motivated to fully explain their own position. This was the only question asked specifically of every respondent. Each respondent had to give an answer before free discussion began. In this way, individuals experience a nonthreatening environment encouraging their free and full opinion. A general question seeking a reaction serves as an effective icebreaker.
- The second question asks whether participants could think of any reason they should be warned about sunlight exposure. This question was simply designed to introduce the idea of a warning label.
- Subsequent questions were asked and became increasingly specific. They were first asked about possible warning formats that might be effective. Respondents are allowed to react to any formats suggested by any other respondent. After this discussion, the moderator will introduce some specific formats the cancer center personnel have in mind.

discussion guide

A focus group outline that includes written introductory comments informing the group about the focus group purpose and rules and then outlines topics or questions to be addressed in the group session.

EXHIBIT 6.8 Discussion Guide for a Focus Group Interview

Thank you very much for agreeing to help out with this research. We call this a focus group; let me explain how it works, and then please let me know if something isn't clear.

This is a discussion, as though you were sitting around just talking. You can disagree with each other, or just comment. We do ask that just one person talk at a time, because we tape-record the session to save me from having to take notes. Nothing you say will be associated with you or your church—this is just an easy way for us to get some people together.

The subject is health risk warnings. Some of you may remember seeing a chart in a newspaper that gives a pollen count or a pollution count. And you've heard on the radio sometimes a hurricane watch or warning. You've seen warnings on cigarette packages or cigarette advertising, even if you don't smoke. And today we're going to talk about warnings about the sun. Before we start, does anybody have a question?

1. OK, let's go around and talk about how often you spend time in the sun, and what you're likely to be doing. (FOR PARENTS): What about your kids—do you like them to be out in the sun?

2. OK, can you think of any reason that somebody would give you a warning about exposure to the sun?

(PROBE: IS ANY SUN EXPOSURE BAD, OR ONLY A CERTAIN DEGREE OF EXPOSURE, AND IF SO, WHAT IS IT? OR IS THE SUN GOOD FOR YOU?)

3. What if we had a way to measure the rays of the sun that are associated with skin problems, so that you could find out which times of the day or which days are especially dangerous? How could, say, a radio station tell you that information in a way that would be useful?

4. Now let me ask you about specific ways to measure danger. Suppose somebody said, "We monitored the sun's rays at noon, and a typical fair-skinned person with unprotected skin will burn after 40 minutes of direct exposure." What would you think?

5. Now let me ask you about another way to say the same kind of thing. Suppose somebody said, "The sun's rays at noon today

measured 10 times the 8 A.M. baseline level of danger." What would you think?

6. OK, now suppose that you heard the same degree of danger expressed this way: "The sun's rays at noon today measured 8 on a sun danger scale that ranges from 1 to 10." What would you think?

7. What if the danger scale wasn't in numbers, but words? Suppose you heard, "The sun's rays at noon showed a moderate danger reading," or "The sun's rays showed a high danger reading." What would you think?

8. And here's another possibility: What if you heard "Here's the sun danger reading at noon today—the unprotected skin of a typical fair-skinned person will age the equivalent of 1 hour in a 10-minute period."

9. OK, what if somebody said today is a day to wear long sleeves and a hat, or today is a day you need sunscreen and long sleeves? What would you think?

10. OK, here's my last question. There are really three things you can do about sun danger: You can spend less time in the sun, you can go out at less dangerous times of day, like before 10 in the morning or after 4 in the afternoon, and you can cover your skin by wearing a hat or long sleeves, or using protective sunscreen lotion. Thinking about yourself listening to the radio, what kind of announcement would make you likely to do one or more of those things? (PARENTS: WHAT WOULD MAKE YOU BE SURE THAT YOUR CHILD WAS PROTECTED?)

11. And what would you be most likely to do to protect yourself? (YOUR CHILD?)

12. Before we break up, is there anything else you think would be useful for M. D. Anderson's people to know? Do you have any questions about any aspect of this interview?

OK, thank you very much for your help.

Betsy D. Gelb and Michael P. Eriksen, "Market Research May Help Prevent Cancer," *Marketing Research*, September 1991, p. 46. Published by American Marketing Association. Reprinted with Permission.

- Finally, the "bottom-line" question is asked: "What format would be most likely to induce people to take protective measures?" There would be probing follow-ups of each opinion so that a respondent couldn't simply say something like "the second one." All focus groups finish up with a catch-all question asking for any comments including any thoughts they wanted passed along to the sponsor (which in this case was only then revealed as the Houston-based cancer center).

Researchers who planned the outline established certain objectives for each part of the focus group. The initial effort was to break the ice and establish rapport within the group. The logical flow of the group session then moved from general discussion about sunbathing to more focused discussion of types of warnings about danger from sun exposure.

In general, the following steps should be used to conduct an effective focus group discussion guide.

1. Welcome and introductions should take place first. Respondents begin to feel more comfortable after introducing themselves.

2. Begin the interview with a broad icebreaker that does not reveal too many specifics about the interview. Sometimes, this may even involve respondents providing some written story or their reaction to some stimulus like a photograph, film, product, or advertisement.

3. Questions become increasingly more specific as the interview proceeds. However, the moderator will notice that a good interview will cover the specific question topics before they have to be asked. This is preferable as respondents are clearly not forced to react to the specific issue; it just emerges naturally.

4. If there is a very specific objective to be accomplished, such as explaining why a respondent would either buy or not buy a product, that question should probably be saved for last.

5. A debriefing statement should provide respondents with the actual focus group objectives and answer any questions they may have. This is also a final shot to gain some insight from the group.

■ DISADVANTAGES OF FOCUS GROUPS

Focus groups offer many advantages. Like practically every other research technique, the focus group has some limitations and disadvantages too. Problems with focus groups include those discussed as follows.

First, focus groups require objective, sensitive, and effective moderators. It is very difficult for a moderator to remain completely objective about most topics. In large research firms, the moderator may be provided only enough information to effectively conduct the interview, no more. The focus group interview shouldn't reduce to only the moderator's opinion. Also, without a good moderator, one or two participants may dominate a session, yielding results that are really the opinion of one or two people, not the group. The moderator has to try very hard to make sure that all respondents feel comfortable giving their opinions and even a timid respondent's opinion is given due consideration. While many people, even some with little or no background to do so, conduct focus groups, good moderators become effective through a combination of good people skills (which cannot be taught), training (in qualitative research), and experience.

Second, some unique sampling problems arise with focus groups. Researchers often select focus group participants because they have similar backgrounds and experiences or because screening indicates that the participants are more articulate or gregarious than the typical consumer. Such participants may not be representative of the entire target market. Thus, focus group results are not intended to be representative of a larger population.

Third, although not so much an issue with online formats where respondents can remain anonymous, traditional face-to-face focus groups may not be useful for discussing sensitive topics. A focus group is a social setting and usually involves people with little to no familiarity with each other. Therefore, issues that people normally do not like to discuss in public may also prove difficult to discuss in a focus group.

Fourth, focus groups do cost a considerable amount of money, particularly when they are not conducted by someone employed by the company desiring the focus group. As research projects go, there are many more expensive approaches, including a full-blown mail survey using a national random sample. This may costs thousands of dollars to conduct and thousands of dollars to analyze and disseminate. Focus group prices vary regionally, but the following figures provide a rough guideline.

Renting Facilities and Equipment	$ 700
Paying Respondents ($100/person)	$ 1,000
Researcher Costs	
• Preparation	$ 800
• Moderating	$ 1,000
• Analysis and Report Preparation	$ 1,500
Miscellaneous Expenses	$ 300

Thus, a client can expect a professional focus group to cost around $5,000 or more. However, most marketing topics will call for multiple focus groups. There is some cost advantage in this, as some costs will not change proportionately just because there are multiple interviews. Preparation costs may be the same for one or more interviews; the analysis and report preparation will likely only increase slightly because two or three interviews are included instead of one.

Modern Technology and Qualitative Research

Technological advances have greatly improved researchers ability to perform all aspects of marketing research. Modern statistical packages and easy to use software packages enable quantitative analyses to be easily and quickly conducted. Technological advances are perhaps changing qualitative marketing research even more. The Internet and data warehouses make volumes and volumes of data available, only a small portion of which is numerical. Software is increasingly able to identify text data and group it in some way. This section focuses on how technology enables and facilitates modern qualitative research.

Facilitating Interviewing

■ VIDEOCONFERENCING AND STREAMING MEDIA

The videoconferencing industry has grown dramatically in recent years. As our ability to communicate via telecommunications and videoconferencing links has improved in quality, the number of companies using these systems to conduct focus groups has increased. With videoconference focus groups, marketing managers can stay home and watch on television rather than having to take a trip to a focus group facility.

Focus Vision Network of New York is a marketing research company that provides videoconferencing equipment and services. The Focus Vision system is modular, allowing for easy movement and an ability to capture each group member close up. The system operates via a remote keypad that allows observers in a far-off location to pan the focus group room or zoom in on a particular participant. Managers viewing at remote locations can even send the moderator messages during the interview. For example, while new product names were being tested in one focus group, an observant manager contacted the moderator with an idea and the moderator then asked respondents for a reaction to the new name on the spot.[33]

streaming media

Consist of multimedia content such as audio or video that is made available in real time over the Internet or a corporate Intranet.

Streaming media consist of multimedia content such as audio or video that is made available in real time over the Internet or a corporate Intranet. This new technology for digital media delivery allows researchers to "broadcast" focus groups that can be viewed online. Offsite managers view the focus group using a media player like Microsoft Media Player. Like videoconferencing, this saves a trip to a focus group facility. Traditionally, the quality of streaming video has been far lower than videoconferencing. However, the quality difference is fast disappearing as streaming technology improves.

■ INTERACTIVE MEDIA AND ONLINE FOCUS GROUPS

Internet applications of qualitative exploratory research are growing rapidly and involve both formal and informal applications. Formally, the term **online focus group** refers to a qualitative research effort in which a group of individuals provides unstructured comments by entering their remarks into an electronic, Internet display board of some type. Participants use a keyboard and mouse to make their remarks during a chat-room session or in the form of a blog. Because respondents enter their comments into the computer, transcripts of verbatim responses are available immediately after the group session. Online groups can be quick and cost-efficient. However, because there is less interaction between participants, group synergy and snowballing of ideas may be diminished.

online focus group

A qualitative research effort in which a group of individuals provides unstructured comments by entering their remarks into an electronic Internet display board of some type.

Several companies have established a form of informal, "continuous" focus group by establishing an Internet blog for that purpose.[34] We might call this technique a **focus blog** when the intention is to mine the site for business research purposes. General Motors, P&G, American Express, Fandango and Lego all have used ideas harvested from their focus blogs. Lego blogs can be found at http://www.thenxtstep.blogspot.com and http://www.legoblog.co.uk. While real life, in-person focus group respondents are generally paid $100 or more to show up and participate for ninety minutes, bloggers and online focus group respondents often participate for absolutely no fee at all! Thus, technology provides some cost advantages over traditional focus group approaches.[35]

focus blog

A type of informal, "continuous" focus group established as an Internet blog for the purpose of collecting qualitative data from participant comments.

■ ONLINE VERSUS FACE-TO-FACE FOCUS GROUP TECHNIQUES

A research company can facilitate a formal online focus group by setting up a private, electronic chat room for that purpose. Participants in formal and informal online focus groups feel that their anonymity is very secure. Often respondents will say things in this environment that they would never say otherwise. For example, a lingerie company was able to get insights into how it could design sexy products for larger women. Online, these women freely discussed what it would take "to feel better about being naked."[36] One can hardly imagine how difficult such a discussion might be face to face. Increased anonymity can be a major advantage for a company investigating sensitive or embarrassing issues.

Because participants do not have to be together in the same room at a research facility, the number of participants in online focus groups can be larger than in traditional focus groups. Twenty-five

TO THE POINT

Necessity, mother of invention.

—William Wycherley

participants or more is not uncommon for the simultaneous chat-room format. Participants can be at widely separated locations, even in different time zones, because the Internet does not have geographical restrictions. Of course, a major disadvantage is that often the researcher does not exercise as much control in precisely who participates. In other words, a person could very easily not match the desired profile or even answer screening questions in a misleading way simply to participate.

A major drawback with online focus groups is that moderators cannot see body language and facial expressions (bewilderment, excitement, interest, and so forth). Thus, they cannot fully interpret how people are reacting. Also, moderators' ability to probe and ask additional questions on the spot is reduced in online focus groups. Research that requires focus group members to actually touch something (such as a new easy-opening packaging design) or taste something is not generally suitable for an online format.

■ SOCIAL NETWORKING

Social networking is one of the most impactful trends in recent times. For many consumers, particularly younger generations, social networking sites like MySpace, Second Life, Zebo, and others, have become the primary tool for communicating with friends both far and near and known and unknown. Social networking has replaced large volumes of e-mail and many would say, face–to-face communications as well. While the impact that social networking will eventually have on society is an interesting question, what is most relevant to marketing research is the large portion of this information that discusses marketing and consumer-related information.

Companies can assign research assistants to monitor these sites for information related to their particular brands. The information can be coded as either positive or negative. When too much negative information is being spread, the company can try to react to change the opinions. In addition, many companies like P&G (see the Research Snapshot on page 134) and Ford maintain their own social networking sites for the purpose of gathering research data. In a way, these social networking sites are a way that companies can eavesdrop on consumer conversations and discover key information about their products.

■ SOFTWARE DEVELOPMENT

Interpretive Software

Computerized qualitative analysis is now commonly used. Two commonly used programs are ATLAS.ti and NVivo. These can save a lot of time by helping to identify themes and connections within text. In fact, today's programs can even assist in interpreting videotapes and photographs for meaning.

Computerized analysis of depth interviews with service providers and their customers revealed interesting key themes dealing with the friendship or bond that forms between them. Some of the themes that emerged included the feeling that meetings were more like get-togethers with a friend, the feeling that the service provider wants to give something back to a client, and the belief that one can share one's true thoughts and feelings with a client. On the not-so-positive side, a theme that also emerged was that sometimes the friendships are not mutual. Comments like, "I thought she would never leave" or "Won't he give me a break?" would be consistent with that theme.[37]

There are many other software programs that can assist with basic qualitative interpretation. Some are available as freeware. AnSWR is available from the U.S. Centers for Disease Control and Prevention (http://www.cdc.gov/hiv/software/answr.htm) as is EZ-Text (http://www.cdc.gov/hiv/software/ez-text.htm). Transana will read video and audio tape data and is available from the Wisconsin Center for Education Research (http://www.transana.org). Commercial programs will normally have a student or trial version available free of charge or at reduced rates.

Text Mining

Generally, when managers think of data mining capabilities, they think of statistical analyses of large volumes of quantitative data. However, modern predictive analytic software enables text data to be mined from various sources including social networking sites, recorded conversations from call centers, e-mail contacts, and many more sources. Large companies including Sikorsky Aircraft, one of the largest helicopter companies in the world, and Cablecom, a Swiss telecommunications firm, have used

Research Knows Almost No Boundaries!

Qualitative research knows *almost* no boundaries! Well, at least not for Ford. Large companies like Ford are increasingly using qualitative research including phenomenology, ethnography, and grounded theory. Ford now relies on qualitative input to help with ideas for product design, marketing campaign design, concept testing and even relationships with suppliers. The advances in technologies have helped make automakers more willing to base decisions on consumer input. Some feel that, for perhaps the first time, companies like Ford may now place consumer input above cost cutting in making key decisions.

Ford used information posted online, in-home ethnography, and traditional focus groups to refine a global marketing campaign centered around the Ford Mustang. Marketing researchers interpreted all of this input in a way that placed great emphasis on the feelings associated with driving a Mustang. As a result, Ford developed a slogan and campaign built around "No boundaries!" However, early concept testing showed that this slogan did not create a positive impression in some Asian cultures. Thus, after a few adjustments and further testing, they settled on "Make Every Day Exciting!" Additionally, grounded theory approaches are helping companies better see into the future by building predictive theories about what characteristics might create value for consumers into the future.

Sources: Flint, D. and B. Woodruff, "The Initiators of Changes in Customers' Desired Values: Results from a Theory Building Study," *Industrial Marketing Management*, 30 (2008), 321–330; "Market Research Drives Product Development at Ford," *RP News Wire* (2008), www.reliableplant.com/article.asp?articleid=3802, accessed June 30, 2008; "Changan Ford's Focus Finishes First and Second at China Circuit Championship Beijing Race," *Ford Motor Company Press Release* (2006), http://media.ford.com/newsroom/release_display.cfm?release=24292, accessed August 4, 2008.

© TRANSTOCK/JUPITER IMAGES

© GEORGE DOYLE & CIARAN GRIFFIN

---

text mining software to help reveal and interpret issues related to customer churn.[38] Leading statistical analysis companies such as SAS and SPSS offer advanced text mining capabilities. Although these programs can be expensive, they offer companies the ability to extract meaning from the tremendous amounts of verbal information generated by their customers, partners and competitors.

Exploratory Research in Science and in Practice

Any research tool, qualitative or quantitative, can be misapplied. Some people believe that a good statistician can support practically any argument. Well, this may be part urban legend but certainly statistics can be misleading. For instance, a statistician may leave a key variable out of an analysis as a way of not presenting the entire picture. Qualitative research and exploratory research also can be used improperly and produce misleading results. Hopefully, the researcher has simply errored when this occurs. Intentionally misleading others with research results is blatantly unprofessional. A big part of correctly applying any tool is knowing when to use it.

Misuses of Exploratory Qualitative Research

Exploratory research, whether qualitative or quantitative, cannot take the place of conclusive, confirmatory research. Because many qualitative tools are applied in exploratory design, they are likewise limited in the ability to draw conclusive inferences—test hypotheses. One of the biggest drawbacks is the subjectivity that comes along with "interpretation." In fact, the term *interpretive* research is sometimes used synonymously with qualitative research. When only one researcher interprets the meaning of what a single person said in a depth interview or similar technique, one should be very cautious before major marketing decisions are made based only on these results. Is the result **replicable**, meaning the same conclusion is intersubjectively certifiable—another researcher's interpretation would match (or they would get the same result by conducting the same research procedures)? The temptation is to act on one interpretation because having other researchers interpret things like depth interviews takes resources that are not always readily available.

Indeed, some qualitative methodologies were generally frowned upon for years based on a few early and public misapplications during what became known as the "motivational research" era. While many of the ideas produced during this time had some merit, as can sometimes be the case, too

replicable

Something is intersubjectively certifiable meaning the same conclusion would be reached based on another researcher's interpretation of the research or by independently duplicating the research procedures.

few researchers did too much interpretation of too few respondents. Compounding this, marketers were quick to act on the results, believing that the results peaked inside one's subliminal consciousness and therefore held some type of extra power. Thus, often the research was flawed based on poor interpretation, and the decision process was flawed because the deciders acted prematurely. Projective techniques and depth interviews were frequently used in the late 1950s and early 1960s, producing some interesting and occasionally bizarre reasons for consumers' purchasing behavior:

- A woman is very serious when she bakes a cake because unconsciously she is going through the symbolic act of giving birth.
- A man buys a convertible as a substitute mistress and a safer (and potentially cheaper) way of committing adultery.
- Men who wear suspenders are reacting to an unresolved castration complex.[39]

Decades later, researchers for McCann-Erickson and other advertising agencies interviewed women about roaches. Among other qualitative techniques, a form of TAT involving story completion regarding attitudes toward insecticides is often used in understanding the meanings of insects in consumers' lives. Research like this revealed themes including:

- The joy of victory over roaches (watching them die or seeing them dead)
- Using the roach as a metaphor through which women can take out their hostility toward men (women generally referred to roaches as "he" instead of "she" in their stories).
- A pervasive fear and hatred of roaches. When Orkin tested ads depicting roaches running on the television screen, viewers actually threw things at the screen before even thinking about whether the bugs were real. Although viewers felt real fear during the ads, Orkin decided to run the ads and even started a contest for people who could tell stories about damaging a television during the ad.[40]

Certainly, some useful findings resulted. Even today, we have the Pillsbury Doughboy as evidence that useful ideas were produced. In many of these cases, interpretations were either misleading or too ambitious (taken too far). However, many companies became frustrated when decisions based upon motivational research approaches proved poor. Thus, marketing researchers moved away from qualitative tools during the late 1960s and 1970s. Today, however, qualitative tools have won acceptance once again as researchers realize they have greater power in discovering insights that would be difficult to capture in typical survey research (which is limited as an exploratory tool).

■ SCIENTIFIC DECISION PROCESSES

Objectivity and replicability are two characteristics of scientific inquiry. Are focus groups objective and replicable? Would three different researchers all interpret focus group data identically? How should a facial expression or nod of the head be interpreted? Have subjects fully grasped the idea or concept behind a nonexistent product? Have respondents overstated their interest because they tend to like all new products? Many of these questions reduce to a matter of opinion that may vary from researcher to researcher and from one respondent group to another. Therefore, a focus group, or a depth interview, or TAT alone does not best represent a complete scientific inquiry.

However, if the thoughts discovered through these techniques survive preliminary evaluations and are developed into research hypotheses, they can be further tested. These tests may involve survey research or an experiment testing an idea very specifically (for example, if Diet Cherry Dr. Pepper is liked better than Diet Pepsi, and so forth). Thus, exploratory research approaches using qualitative research tools are very much a *part* of *scientific* inquiry.

An exploratory research design is the most productive design, meaning the tools used produce more discoveries than do other research designs. A company cannot determine the most important product benefits until all benefits obtained from consuming the product are known.

Before making a *scientific* decision, a research project should include a confirmatory study using objective tools and an adequate sample in terms of both size and how well it represents a population. But, is a *scientific* decision approach always used or needed?

In practice, many marketing decisions are based solely on the results of focus group interviews or some other exploratory result. Given that some decisions involve relatively small risk, a scientific

- Qualitative research tools are most helpful when
  - Research questions are not very specific
  - Some specific behavior needs to be studied in depth
  - When the value of a product changes dramatically from situation to situation or consumer to consumer
  - When exploring a research area with the intent of studying it further
  - Concept testing
- The focus group moderator is key to a successful interview. Not just anyone can moderate a focus group. Generally speaking, a good moderator can get more out of a respondent by saying less.
  - Focus group questions should start with more general questions and work to the more specific.
  - Don't be afraid to use props such as advertisements, photos, or actual products to get respondents talking.

- Modern technology makes a tremendous amount of qualitative information available via the Internet. Formal interviews can sometimes be replaced by data pulled from blogs and social networking sites. Consumers can also be interviewed using Internet video technology.
- Exploratory research designs do not lend themselves well to hypothesis testing or scientifically concluding that one alternative is better than another.
- The overall value of a research tool is not determined by whether it is quantitative or qualitative but by the value that it produces. Qualitative tools are irreplacable for many, many marketing research situations.

decision process is not always justified. However, as risk increases, the confidence that comes along with a rigorous research and decision process becomes well worth the investment. The primary barriers to scientific decisions are (1) time, (2) money, and (3) emotion.

■ TIME

Sometimes, researchers simply are not given enough time to follow up on exploratory research results. Marketing companies feel an increasingly urgent need to get new products to the market faster. Thus, a seemingly good idea generated in a focus group (like Diet, Vanilla, or Cherry Dr Pepper) is simply not tested with a more conclusive study. The risk of delaying a decision may be seen as greater than the risk of proceeding without completing the scientific process. Thus, although the researcher may wish to protest, there may be logical reasons for such action. The decision makers should be aware, though, that the conclusions drawn from exploratory research designs are just that—exploratory. Thus, there is less likelihood of good results from the decision than if the research process had involved further testing.

■ MONEY

Similarly, researchers sometimes do not follow up on exploratory research results because they believe the cost is too high. Realize that thousands of dollars may have already been spent on qualitative research. Managers who are unfamiliar with research will be very tempted to wonder, "Why do I need yet another study?" and "What did I spend all that money for?" Thus, they choose to proceed based only on exploratory results. Again, the researcher has fulfilled the professional obligation as long as the tentative nature of any ideas derived from exploratory research has been relayed through the research report.

Again, this isn't always a bad approach. If the decision itself does not involve a great deal of risk or if it can be reversed easily, the best course of action may be to proceed to implementation instead of investing more money in confirmatory research. Remember, research shouldn't be performed if it will cost more than it will return.

■ EMOTION

Time, money, and emotion are all related. Decision makers sometimes become so anxious to have something resolved, or they get so excited about some novel discovery resulting from a focus group interview, they may act rashly. Perhaps some of the ideas produced during the motivational research era sounded so enticing that decision makers got caught up in the emotion of the moment and proceeded without the proper amount of testing. Thus, as in life, when we fall in love with something, we are prone to act irrationally. The chances of emotion interfering in this way are lessened, but not eliminated, by making sure multiple decision makers are involved in the decision process.

In conclusion, we began this section by suggesting that exploratory, qualitative research cannot take the place of a confirmatory study. However, a confirmatory study cannot take the place of an exploratory, qualitative study either. While confirmatory studies are best for testing specific ideas, a qualitative study is needed to develop ideas and practical theories.

Summary

1. Compare and contrast qualitative research and quantitative research. The chapter emphasized that any argument about the overall superiority of qualitative versus quantitative research is misplaced. Rather, each approach has advantages and disadvantages that make it appropriate in certain situations. The most noticeable difference is the relative absence of numbers in qualitative research. Qualitative research relies more on researchers' subjective interpretations of text or other visual material. In contrast, the numbers produced in quantitative research are objective in the sense that they don't change simply because someone else computed them. Qualitative research involves small samples while quantitative research usually uses large samples. Qualitative procedures are generally more flexible and produce deeper and more elaborate explanations than quantitative research.

2. Understand the role of qualitative research in exploratory research designs. The high degree of flexibility that goes along with most qualitative techniques makes it very useful in exploratory research designs. Therefore, exploratory research designs most often involve some qualitative research technique. Many of the things that some criticize qualitative research for, such as lack of structure, actually are advantageous in an exploratory design.

3. Describe the basic orientations of qualitative research. Phenomenology is a philosophical approach to studying human experiences based on the idea that human experience itself is inherently subjective and determined by the context within which a person experiences something. It lends itself well to conversational research. Ethnography represents ways of studying cultures through methods that include high involvement with that culture. Participant-observation is a common ethnographic approach. Grounded theory represents inductive qualitative investigation in which the researcher continually poses questions about a respondent's discourse in an effort to derive a deep explanation of their behavior. Collages are sometimes used to develop grounded theory. Case studies simply are documented histories of a particular person, group, organization, or event.

4. Recognize common qualitative research tools and know the advantages and limitations of their use. Two of the most common qualitative research tools include the focus group interview and the depth interview. The focus group has some cost advantage per respondent because it would take ten times as long to conduct the interview portion(s) of a series of depth interviews compared to one focus group. However, the depth interview is more appropriate for discussing sensitive topics. Researchers today though have a wide variety of tools at their disposal aside from the focus group and depth interview. Exhibit 6.4 describes many of these approaches.

5. Prepare a focus group interview outline. A focus group outline should begin with introductory comments followed by a very general opening question that does not lead the respondent. More specific questions should be listed until a blunt question directly pertaining to the study objective is included. It should conclude with debriefing comments and a chance for question-and-answers with respondents.

6. Recognize technological advances in the application of qualitative research approaches. Videoconferencing and online chat rooms are more economical ways of trying to do much the same as traditional focus group interviews. Some companies have even established a focus blog that is a source for continuous commentary on a company. Others have their own social networking sites intended to collect information about their brand and products. While they are certainly cost advantageous, there is less control over who participates. Modern software also enables much more power to mine and aid in the interpretation of non-numeric data.

7. Appreciate the role of exploratory qualitative research in scientific decision making. Qualitative research has a rightful place in scientific discovery and the idea that qualitative research is somehow lacking in rigor because it is not quantitative is simply misplaced. Risks do come with using exploratory research procedures in general to make scientific decisions. While not all decisions require a scientific decision process, companies sometimes do make major decisions using only exploratory research. There are several explanations for this behavior that involve time, money and emotion. A lack of time, a lack of money and strong emotions to move on all represent barriers to a scientific decision process. Ultimately, the researcher's job is to make sure that decision makers understand the increased risk that comes along with basing a decision only on exploratory research results.

Key Terms

Questions for Review and Critical Thinking

1. Define *qualitative* and *quantitative* research. Compare and contrast the two approaches.

2. Why do exploratory research designs rely so much on qualitative research techniques?

3. Why do causal designs rely so much on quantitative research techniques?

4. What are the basic categories (orientations) of qualitative research?

5. Of the four basic categories of qualitative research, which do you think is most appropriate for a qualitative approach designed to better define a marketing situation prior to conducting confirmatory research?

6. How might ethnography be used in concept testing?

7. What type of exploratory research would you suggest in the following situations?

   a. A product manager suggests development of a non-tobacco cigarette blended from wheat, cocoa, and citrus.

   b. A research project has the purpose of evaluating potential brand names for a new insecticide.

   c. A manager must determine the best site for a convenience store in an urban area.

   d. An advertiser wishes to identify the symbolism associated with cigar smoking.

8. What are the key differences between a focus group interview and a depth interview?

9. **'NET** Visit some Web sites for large companies like Honda, Qantas Airlines, Target, Tesco, and Marriot. Is there any evidence that they are using their Internet sites in some way to conduct a continuous online focus blog or intermittent online focus groups?

10. What is *laddering*? How might it be used in trying to understand which fast-food restaurant different segments of customers prefer?

11. How is a focus group outline used by an effective focus group moderator?

12. List at least four ways that recent technological advances have advanced the use of qualitative research. Explain your choices. Do you know any even newer ways that technological advancements could provide data in the form of text or picture messages? Can you think of a way that SMS text messages or MMS messages might provide qualitative input?

13. Comment on the following remark by a marketing consultant: "Qualitative exploration is a tool of marketing research and a stimulant to thinking. In and by itself, however, it does not constitute market research."

14. **ETHICS** A researcher tells a manager of a wine company that he has some "cool focus group results" suggesting that respondents like the idea of a screw-cap to top wine bottles. Even before the decision maker sees the report, the manager begins purchasing screw-caps and the new bottling equipment. Comment on this situation.

15. A packaged goods manufacturer receives many thousands of customer letters a year. Some are complaints, some are compliments. They cover a broad range of topics. Are these letters a possible source for exploratory research? Why or why not?

Research Activities

1. **'NET** How might the following organizations use an Internet social networking site for exploratory research? Can you find any such attempts on your favorite social networking site?
   a. A zoo
   b. A computer software manufacturer
   c. A video game manufacturer
2. Go back to the opening vignette. What if Vans approached you to do a focus group interview that explored the idea of offering casual attire (off-board) aimed at their primary segment (skateboarders) and offering casual attire for male retirees like Samuel Teel? How would you recommend the focus group(s) proceed? Prepare a focus group outline(s) to accomplish this task.
3. Interview two people about their exercise behavior. In one interview, try to use a semi-structured approach by preparing questions ahead of time and trying to have the respondent complete answers for these questions. With the other, try a conversational approach. What are the main themes that emerge in each? Which approach do you think was more insightful? Do you think there were any "sensitive" topics that a respondent was not completely forthcoming about?

Case 6.1 Disaster and Consumer Value

© GETTY IMAGES/
PHOTODISC GREEN

After September 11, 2001, U.S. consumers showed a desire to tone down their consumer activities. They ordered simpler foods in restaurants and spent more time at home. Therefore, a lot of marketing campaigns began emphasizing down-home themes.

At some point after a disaster, it is time to get back to business. But, major catastrophic events are likely to leave permanent changes on consumers and employees in those areas. Suppose you are approached by the owner of several delicatessens and full-service wine stores in the Gulf Coast area. It is January 2006, and they want to get back to business. But they are uncertain about whether they should simply maintain the same positioning they had previous to

Hurricane Katrina and Hurricane Rita. They would like to have a report from you within eighty days.

1. How could each classification of qualitative research be used here?
2. What qualitative research tool(s) would you recommend be used and why?
3. Where would you conduct any interviews and with whom would you conduct them?
4. **ETHICS** Are there ethical issues that you should be sensitive to in this process? Explain.
5. What issues would arise in conducting a focus group interview in this situation?
6. Prepare a focus group outline.

CHAPTER 7
SECONDARY DATA RESEARCH IN A DIGITAL AGE

After studying this chapter, you should be able to

1. Discuss the advantages and disadvantages of secondary data
2. Understand the types of objectives that can be achieved using secondary data
3. Identify various internal and proprietary sources of secondary data
4. Give examples of various external sources of secondary data
5. Describe the impact of single-source data and globalization on secondary data research

Chapter Vignette: Every (Virtual) Move You Make

So, do you like *Big Brother*? This television concept has been copied and altered many times since its advent in Europe a decade or so ago. Do people like to eavesdrop on others? Do people like to be eavesdropped upon? Considering the information conveyed via social networking sites like MySpace, Bebo, Facebook, and others, perhaps some do! But, nonetheless, a wealth of information is left behind. Many researchers would like to eavesdrop to address the research questions they face. Today, the fact that many of the "moves" that people make are done online means that these people are easier to watch than ever before.

Researchers with different motives are watching. All of these parties are very interested in the electronic records of behavior that are left behind when we do things online.

- A marketing research firm hired by a mobile phone service company is trying to find the appropriate target market for different types of products including pay as you go media devices.
- An online university is looking for target markets expressing dissatisfaction with their life situations. They want to test to see if these segments will be more receptive to marketing appeals to attend the online university than segments identified through more traditional methods.
- Employers hire a research firm to identify employees who have serious issues in their personal lives as evidenced by messages posted on their social networking sites or who are shirking on–the-job based on the amount of time they spend logged in to different Web sites.
- Security officials at the Pentagon and MI6 (British intelligence service) mine material posted on social networking sites looking for potential security theats.
- Political candidates have researchers mine data from blogs and social networks to identify potential targets for significant donations.

These efforts have led to successful marketing appeals, dismissal of employees, and security operations that may have prevented terrorist acts. One company in the U.K. identified an employee who spent 35 hours a week logged into a social networking site when he was supposed to be working. So, 35 out of 40 hours were spent logged in. The employee had no idea that the amount of time spent on the site could be monitored.

The information that we leave behind in our online behaviors can become stored as secondary data. Advances in technology, particularly something called Resource Description Framework or RDF, are enabling better communication across different Web-based interfaces so that once an individual is identified, information taken from different sources about different aspects of the individual's life can all be gathered together in a single record.

Obviously, the sheer volume of secondary data available reveals how important information that is collected and stored as a matter of routine or for some purpose other than a specific research purpose can be. But, perhaps questions about the morality or ethics of using this data are worth debating. Nonetheless, for marketing researchers who specialize in analyzing secondary data, this is a very good time to watch every virtual move consumers make.[1]

Introduction

Once research questions are stated, the research determines how concepts will be measured. Market researchers are always working under budget constraints. So, they are wise to ask if the data that will be needed to examine the research question already exist. If so, the analysis can proceed quickly and efficiently. If not, a much more laborious process lies ahead. This chapter focuses on instances where the data may indeed already exist in some usable format.

Using Secondary Data in Marketing Research

Research projects often begin with **secondary data**, which are gathered and recorded by someone else prior to (and for purposes other than) the current project. Secondary data usually are historical and already assembled. They require no additional access to research respondents or subjects. Secondary data is often thought of as quantitative, but many sources of qualitative secondary data also exist.

secondary data

Data that have been previously collected for some purpose other than the one at hand.

Advantages

The primary advantage of secondary data is their availability. Obtaining secondary data is almost always faster and less expensive than acquiring primary data. This is particularly true when researchers use electronic retrieval to access data stored digitally. In many situations, collecting secondary data is instantaneous.

Consider the money and time saved by researchers who obtained updated population estimates for a town during the interim between the 2000 and 2010 censuses. Instead of doing the fieldwork themselves, researchers could acquire estimates from a firm dealing in demographic information or from sources such as Claritas or PCensus. As in this example, the use of secondary data eliminates many of the activities normally associated with primary data collection, such as sampling and data processing.

Secondary data are essential in instances when data cannot be obtained using primary data collection procedures. For example, a manufacturer of farm implements could not duplicate the information in the *Census of Agriculture* because much of the information there (for example, amount of taxes paid) might not be accessible to a private firm.

TO THE POINT

If I have seen farther than others, it is because I have stood on the shoulders of giants.

—Isaac Newton

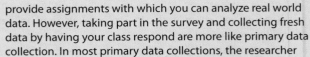

Secondary data are collected for a purpose other than the immediate research question at hand. When you participated in the survey as part of taking this course, you contributed to a database that your instructor can use to illustrate concepts with and provide assignments with which you can analyze real world data. However, taking part in the survey and collecting fresh data by having your class respond are more like primary data collection. In most primary data collections, the researcher could perhaps find secondary data that may not provide the precise information needed to address a research question, but it might at least be in the same general area as the research question. In our survey, the researcher had some interest in students' communication behaviors. Thus, quite a few questions address text messaging, e-mailing, and so on. Consider the accompanying screenshot from the survey.

Can you find secondary data, aside from the database that goes with this questionnaire, that address similar issues among consumers? If so, what do you find? Do you think the results reveal similar patterns of behavior to that exposed in the class survey? Discuss your results.

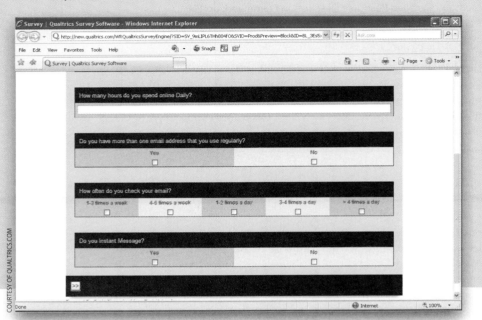

Disadvantages

An inherent disadvantage of secondary data is that they were not designed specifically to meet the researchers' needs. Thus, researchers must ask how pertinent are the data to their particular project. To evaluate secondary data, researchers should ask questions such as these:

- Do the data apply to the population of interest?
- Do the data apply to the time period of interest?
- Do the secondary data appear in the correct units of measurement?
- Do the data appear relevant to the research question?
- Do the data cover the subject of interest in adequate detail?
- Do the data show evidence of reliability and validity?

Researchers have to take care not to assume that secondary information is relevant, useful, and reliable simply because it is available. Consider the following typical situations:

- A researcher interested in forklift trucks finds that the secondary data on the subject are included in a broader, less pertinent category encompassing all industrial trucks and tractors. Furthermore, the data were collected twelve years earlier.
- An investigator who wishes to study individuals earning more than $100,000 per year finds the top category in a secondary study reported at $75,000 or more per year.
- A brewery that wishes to compare its per-barrel advertising expenditures with those of competitors finds that the units of measurement differ because some report point–of–purchase expenditures with advertising and others do not.
- Data from a previous warranty card study show where consumers prefer to purchase the product but provide no reasons why.

The most common reasons why secondary data do not adequately satisfy research needs are (1) outdated information, (2) variation in definition of terms, (3) different units of measurement, and (4) lack of information to verify the data's accuracy. Furthermore, in our rapidly changing environment, information quickly becomes outdated. Because the purpose of most studies is to predict the future, secondary data must be timely to be useful.

Every primary researcher has the right to define the terms or concepts under investigation to satisfy the purpose of his or her primary investigation. This practice provides little solace, however, to the investigator of the African-American market who finds secondary data reported as "percent nonwhite." Variances in terms or variable classifications should be scrutinized to determine whether differences are important. The populations of interest must be described in comparable terms. Researchers frequently encounter secondary data that report on a population of interest that is similar but not directly comparable to their population of interest. For example, Arbitron reports its television audience estimates by geographical areas known as ADIs (Areas of Dominant Influence). An ADI is a geographic area consisting of all counties in which the home market commercial television stations receive a preponderance of total viewing hours. This unique population of interest is used exclusively to report television audiences. The geographic areas used in the census of population, such as Metropolitan Statistical Areas, are not comparable to ADIs.

■ UNITS OF MEASUREMENT

Units of measurement may cause problems if they do not conform exactly to a researcher's needs. For example, student grades expressed on a 100 point scale are quite different than grades expressed in a letter format. Head-of-household income is not the same unit of measure as total family income. Often the objective of the original primary study may dictate that the data be summarized, rounded, or reported. When that happens, even if the original units of measurement were comparable, aggregated or adjusted units of measurement are not suitable in the secondary study.

When secondary data are reported in a format that does not exactly meet the researcher's needs, data conversion may be necessary. **Data conversion** (also called *data transformation*) is the process of changing the original form of data to a format more suitable for achieving a stated research objective. For example, sales for food products may be reported in pounds, cases, or dollars. An estimate of dollars per pound may be used to convert dollar volume data to pounds or another suitable format.

data conversion

The process of changing the original form of the data to a format suitable to achieve the research objective; also called data transformation.

■ RELIABILITY AND VALIDITY

Another disadvantage of secondary data is that the user has no control over their reliability and validity—topics we will discuss in more detail later but for now, think of these as representing data accuracy or trustworthiness. Although timely and pertinent secondary data may fit the researcher's requirements, the data could be inaccurate. Research conducted by other persons may be biased to support the vested interest of the source. For example, media often publish data from surveys to identify the characteristics of their subscribers or viewers, but they will most likely exclude derogatory data from their reports. If the possibility of bias exists, the secondary data should not be used.

Investigators are naturally more prone to accept data from reliable sources such as the U.S. government. Nevertheless, the researcher must assess the reputation of the organization that gathers the data and critically assess the research design to determine whether the research was correctly implemented. Researchers should try to find a detailed account of the research methods used to gather the data so that steps can be taken to evaluate reliability and validity. Unfortunately, such evaluation may be impossible because often full information that explains how the original research was conducted is not provided.

Researchers should verify data whenever possible. **Cross-checks** from multiple sources—that is, comparison of the data from one source with data from another—should be made to determine the similarity of independent projects. When the data are not consistent, researchers should attempt

cross-checks

The comparison of data from one source with data from another source to determine the similarity of independent projects.

to identify reasons for the differences or to determine which data are most likely to be correct. If the accuracy of the data cannot be established, the researcher must determine whether using the data is worth the risk. Exhibit 7.1 illustrates a series of questions that should be asked to evaluate secondary data before they are used.

EXHIBIT 7.1
Evaluating Secondary Data

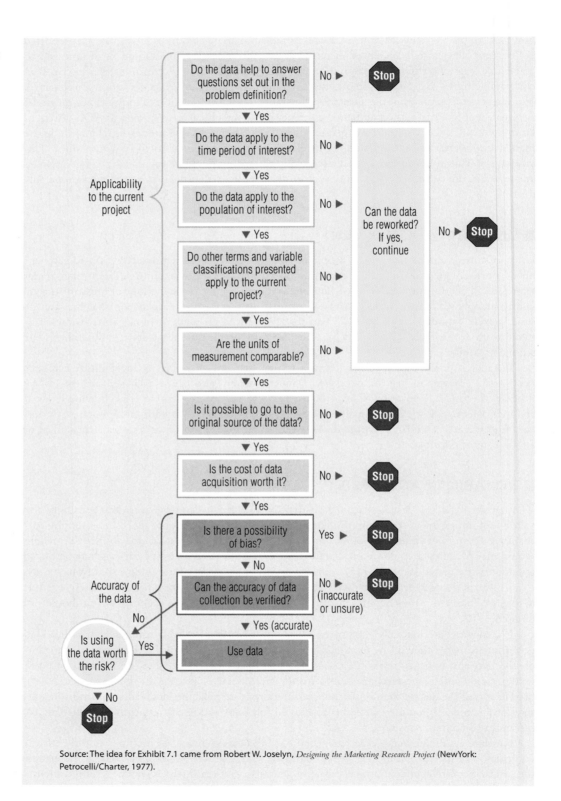

Source: The idea for Exhibit 7.1 came from Robert W. Joselyn, *Designing the Marketing Research Project* (New York: Petrocelli/Charter, 1977).

Typical Objectives for Secondary-Data Research Designs

All possible purposes of marketing research using secondary data cannot possibly be listed. However, some commonly occuring marketing problems can be addressed with secondary research designs. Exhibit 7.2 shows three general categories of research objectives: fact-finding, model building, and database marketing.

Broad Objective	Specific Research Example
Fact-finding	Identifying consumption patterns Tracking trends
Model building	Estimating market potential Forecasting sales Selecting trade areas and sites
Database marketing	Enhancing customer databases Developing prospect lists

EXHIBIT 7.2

Common Research Objectives for Secondary-Data Studies

Fact-Finding

The simplest form of secondary-data research is fact-finding. A restaurant serving breakfast might be interested in knowing what new products are likely to entice consumers. Secondary data available from National Eating Trends, a service of the NPD Group, show that the most potential may be in menu items customers can eat on the go.[2] According to data from the survey of eating trends, take-out breakfast sales have doubled since 1980 or so, and they have continued to surpass dine-in breakfast sales for over a decade. These trends make smoothies and breakfast sandwiches sound like a good bet for a breakfast menu. Also, NPD found that 41 percent of breakfast sandwiches are consumed by people in their cars and 24 percent of people polled take them to work. These findings suggest that the sandwiches should be easy to handle. But what to put on the biscuit or bun? Another research firm, Market Facts, says almost half of consumers say they would pay extra for cheese. These simple facts would interest a researcher who was investigating the market for take-out breakfasts. Fact-finding can serve more complex purposes as well.

Secondary-data research supports the fact that breakfast sandwiches are at the top of the menu.

■ IDENTIFICATION OF CONSUMER BEHAVIOR FOR A PRODUCT CATEGORY

A typical objective for a secondary research study might be to uncover all available information about consumption patterns for a

© DENNIS GOTTLIEB/JUPITER IMAGES

New Trends—Music for Mobile Phones

Until a few years ago, selling music involved recordings on CDs, but marketing researchers have lately been tracking the newer practice of selling tunes to serve as ringtones. According to Nielsen, consumers spent nearly $600 million dollars on ringtones in 2007. Strategy Analytics, a marketing research firm, forecasted that mobile music would generate $9 billion in sales by 2010 and much of that will be generated by ringtone sales. So far, the most popular song category is hip-hop, but videogame themes and movie themes also sell well.

Ringtones are profitable for music sellers. Today, almost all ringtones sold are song clips known as mastertones or true tones, and consumers are sometimes paying more for ringtones ($2.49) than for an entire song downloaded to an MP3 player. The music companies, such as Sony and EMI, get royalties of up to 50 percent for mastertones. In this environment, Sony BMG skipped the traditional approach of CD singles and MTV videos when Cassidy released an album in 2005; instead, the company made a

25-second sample of Cassidy's song "I'm a Hustla" and released it as a ringtone. Coldplay's song "Speed of Sound" was available as a ringtone from Cingular before the album went on sale.

Secondary data from Nielsen reveals that these are among the most purchased ringtones for 2007:

1. Shop Boyz, "Party Like a Rockstar"
2. Mims, "This Is Why I'm Hot"
3. Soulja Boy, "Crank That (Soulja Boy)"
4. Nickelback, "Rockstar"
5. Akon, "Don't Matter"
6. T-Pain, "Buy You A Drank (Shawty Snappin)"
7. Hurricane Chris, "A Bay Bay"
8. Sean Kingston, "Beautiful Girls"
9. Huey, "Pop, Lock & Drop It"
10. Fergie, "Big Girls Don't Cry"

Sources: Based on Matthew Maier, "Digital Entertainment: Can Cell Phones Save the Music Business?" *Business 2.0*, (September 2005), downloaded from InfoTrac at http://www.galenet.com; Sue Marek, "Ringing in the New Year," *Wireless Week*, (January 1, 2006), http://www.galenet.com; "Music Marketing Gets Digital Tune-Up," *Financial Express*, (January 28, 2006), http://www.galenet.com; "Nielsen Music 2007 Year-End Music Industry Report: Growth In Overall Music Purchases Exceeds 14%," *Wireless News*, (January 10, 2008), http://www.tmcnet.com/usubmit/2008/01/10/3203970.htm, accessed August 6, 2008.

---

particular product category or to identify demographic trends that affect an industry. For example, a company called Servigistics offers software that will scan a company's own parts inventory data and compare it with marketing objectives and competitors' prices to evaluate whether the company should adjust prices for its parts. Kia Motors tried using this service in place of the usual method of marking up cost by a set fraction. By considering secondary data including internal inventory data and external data about competitors' prices, it was able to make service parts a more profitable segment of its business.[3] This example illustrates the wealth of factual information about consumption and behavior patterns that can be obtained by carefully collecting and analyzing secondary data. The Research Snapshot above illustrates data about consumer preferences further.

■ TREND ANALYSIS

market tracking

The observation and analysis of trends in industry volume and brand share over time.

Marketers watch for trends in the marketplace and the environment. **Market tracking** is the observation and analysis of trends in industry volume and brand share over time. Scanner research services and other organizations provide facts about sales volume to support this work.

Almost every large consumer goods company routinely investigates brand and product category sales volume using secondary data. This type of analysis typically involves comparisons with competitors' sales or with the company's own sales in comparable time periods. It also involves industry comparisons among different geographic areas. Exhibit 7.3 shows the trend in cola market share relative to the total carbonated soft-drink industry.

■ ENVIRONMENTAL SCANNING

In many instances, the purpose of fact-finding is simply to study the environment to identify trends. Environmental scanning entails information gathering and fact-finding designed to detect indications of environmental changes in their initial stages of development. As mentioned in Chapter 2, the Internet can be used for environmental scanning; however, there are other means, such as periodic review of contemporary publications and reports. For example, environmental scanning has shown many marketers that consumer demand in China is skyrocketing. In the case of beauty products such as cosmetics, Chinese authorities in the early 1990s stopped discouraging the use

EXHIBIT 7.3
Cola's Share of the Carbonated Soft-Drink Market

Source: Theresa Howard, "Coca-Cola Hopes Taking New Path Leads to Success," *USA Today*, March 6, 2001, p. 6b. From USA Today a division of Gannett Co., Inc. Reprinted with Permission.

of makeup, and sales of these products took off—hitting $524 million in 2005 and expected to grow by over one-third, reaching $705 million by 2009. Marketers including Procter & Gamble, L'Oréal, and Shiseido have captured a sizable share of this market by realizing the potential and developing products to get into the market early.[4]

A number of online information services, such as Factiva and LexisNexis, routinely collect news stories about industries, product lines, and other topics of interest that have been specified by the researcher. As we mentioned in Chapter 2, push technology is an Internet information technology that automatically delivers content to the researcher's or manager's desktop. Push technology uses "electronic smart agents," custom software that filters, sorts, prioritizes, and stores information for later viewing.[5] This service frees the researcher from doing the searching. The true value of push technology is that the researcher who is scanning the environment can specify the kinds of news and information he or she wants, have it delivered to his or her computer quickly, and view it at leisure.

Model Building

The second general objective for secondary research, model building, is more complicated than simple fact-finding. **Model building** involves specifying relationships between two or more variables, perhaps extending to the development of descriptive or predictive equations. Models need not include complicated mathematics, though. In fact, decision makers often prefer simple models that everyone can readily understand over complex models that are difficult to comprehend. For example, market share is company sales divided by industry sales. Although some may not think of this simple calculation as a model, it represents a mathematical model of a basic relationship.

We will illustrate model building by discussing three common objectives that can be satisfied with secondary research: estimating market potential, forecasting sales, and selecting sites.

model building

The use of secondary data to help specify relationships between two or more variables; can involve the development of descriptive or predictive equations.

■ ESTIMATING MARKET POTENTIAL FOR GEOGRAPHIC AREAS

Marketers often estimate market potential using secondary data. In many cases exact figures may be published by a trade association or another source. However, when the desired information is unavailable, the researcher may estimate market potential by transforming secondary data from two or more sources. For example, managers may find secondary data about market potential for a country or other large geographic area, but this information may not be broken down into smaller geographical areas, such as by metropolitan area, or in terms unique to the company, such as sales territory. In this type of situation, researchers often need to make projections for the geographic area of interest.

A simple example will help explain how secondary data can be used to calculate market potential. Suppose a brewing company is looking for opportunities to expand sales by exporting or investing in other countries. Managers decide to begin by estimating market potential for four potential target markets, the Czech Republic, Germany, Japan, and Spain. Secondary research uncovered data for per capita beer consumption and population projections for the year 2010. The data for the four countries appear in Exhibit 7.4 on the next page.

EXHIBIT 7.4
**Market Potential for Four
Possible Beer Markets**

Country	Population Projection for 2010 (thousands)	Annual per Capita Beer Consumption (liters)	Market Potential Estimate (k liters)
Czech Republic	10,175	157	1,597,475
Germany	82,365	116	9,554,340
Japan	127,758	48	6,132,384
Spain	45,108	84	3,789,072

Source: Population data from Population Division of the Department of Economic and Social Affairs of the United Nations Secretariat, "World Population Prospects: The 2004 Revision and World Urbanization Prospects; The 2003 Revision," http:// esa.un.org/unpp, accessed February 9, 2006. Consumption data from "US Beer Consumption Reverses Decreases in 2007 - Research," http://www.just-drinks.com/article.aspx?id=95643, November 24, 2007, accessed December 10, 2008, http:// galenet.galegroup.com; and "Czechs Top World Cup Beer Consumption," http://www.worldcupblog.org/world-cup-2006/ czechs-top-world-beer-consumption.html, accessed December 10, 2008.

To calculate market potential for the Czech Republic in 2010, multiply that country's population in the year 2010 by its per capita beer consumption:

$$10,175,000 \ people \times 157 \ liters/person = 1,597,475,000 \ liters$$

In the Czech Republic, the market potential for beer is 1,597,475,000 liters. To get a sense of the expected sales volume, the marketer would have to multiply this amount by the price per liter at which beer typically sells in the Czech Republic. As Exhibit 7.4 reveals, Japan's population is much greater, so its market potential is greater, even though the average Czech drinks much more beer.

Of course, the calculated market potential for each country in Exhibit 7.4 is a rough estimate. One obvious problem is that not everyone in a country will be of beer-drinking age. If the marketer can get statistics for each country's projected *adult* population, the estimate will be closer. Also, the marketer will want to consider whether each country is experiencing growth or decline in the demand for beer to estimate whether consumption habits are likely to be different in 2010. For example, beer consumption is barely growing in Europe and Japan, but it is expanding in Latin America (at about 4 percent a year) and even faster in China (by at least 6 percent a year).[6] Additionally, the researcher can probably find information on competitive intensity (how many beer companies are marketing in the country) in each area to adjust the projections for the amount of competition. Perhaps this information will cause the marketer to investigate market potential in additional countries where more growth is expected.

■ FORECASTING SALES

Marketing managers need information about the future. They need to know what company sales will be next year and in future time periods. Sales forecasting is the process of predicting sales totals over a specific time period.

Accurate sales forecasts, especially for products in mature, stable markets, frequently come from secondary-data research that identifies trends and extrapolates past performance into the future. Marketing researchers often use internal company sales records to project sales. A rudimentary model would multiply past sales volume by an expected growth rate. A researcher might investigate a secondary source and find that industry sales are expected to grow by 10 percent; multiplying company sales volume by 10 percent would give a basic sales forecast.

Exhibit 7.5 illustrates trend projection using a moving average projection of growth rates. Average ticket prices for a major-league baseball game are secondary data from Team Marketing Report (http://www.teammarketing.com). The moving average is the sum of growth rates for the past three years divided by 3 (number of years). The resulting number is a forecast of the percentage increase in ticket price for the coming year. Using the three-year average growth rate of 6.4 percent for the 2008, 2007, and 2006 sales periods, we can forecast the average ticket price for 2009 as follows:

$$\$25.43 + (\$25.43 \times .064) = \$27.06$$

Year	Average Ticket Price ($)	Percentage Rate of Growth (Decline) from Previous Year	3-Year Moving Average Rate of Growth (Decline)
1996	11.20	5.2%	3.5%
1997	12.36	10.4%	5.8%
1998	13.59	10.0%	8.5%
1999	14.91	9.7%	10.0%
2000	16.67	11.8%	10.5%
2001	18.99	13.9%	11.8%
2002	18.30	−3.6%	7.4%
2003	19.01	3.9%	4.7%
2004	19.82	4.3%	1.5%
2005	21.17	6.8%	5.0%
2006	22.21	4.9%	5.3%
2007	22.70	2.2%	4.6%
2008	25.43	12.0%	6.4%

EXHIBIT 7.5

Sales Forecast Using Secondary Data and Moving Averages

Using the same information, the projected price of a beer at a ballgame in 2009 is $6.43. This lets the fan know how much to take out to the old ballgame. The prediction then means that attending a game will cost $33.48 if the fan has a beer!

Moving average forecasting is best suited to a static competitive environment. More dynamic situations make other sales forecasting techniques more appropriate.

Statistical trend analysis using secondary data can be much more advanced than this simple example. Many statistical techniques build forecasting models using secondary data. This chapter emphasizes secondary-data research rather than statistical analysis. Later chapters explain more sophisticated statistical model-building techniques for forecasting sales including multivariate approaches.

■ ANALYSIS OF TRADE AREAS AND SITES

Marketing managers examine trade areas and use **site analysis techniques** to select the best locations for retail or wholesale operations. Secondary-data research helps managers make these site selection decisions. Some organizations, especially franchisers, have developed special computer software based on analytical models to select sites for retail outlets. The researcher must obtain the appropriate secondary data for analysis with the computer software.

The **index of retail saturation** offers one way to investigate retail sites and to describe the relationship between retail demand and supply.[7] It is easy to calculate once the appropriate secondary data are obtained:

$$\text{Index of retail saturation} = \frac{\text{Local market potential (demand)}}{\text{Local market retailing space}}$$

For example, Exhibit 7.6 on the next page shows the relevant secondary data for shoe store sales in a five-mile radius surrounding a Florida shopping center. These types of data can be purchased from vendors of market information such as Urban Decision Systems. First, to estimate local market potential (demand), we multiply population by annual per capita shoe sales. This estimate, line 3 in Exhibit 7.6, goes in the numerator to calculate the index of retail saturation:

$$\text{Index of retail saturation} = \frac{\$14,249,000}{94,000} = 152$$

site analysis techniques

Techniques that use secondary data to select the best location for retail or wholesale operations.

index of retail saturation

A calculation that describes the relationship between retail demand and supply.

EXHIBIT 7.6
Secondary Data for Calculating an Index of Retail Saturation

1. Population	261,785
2. Annual per capita shoe sales	$54.43
3. Local market potential (line 1 x line 2)	$14,249,000
4. Square feet of retail space used to sell shoes	94,000 sq. ft.
5. Index of retail saturation (line 3/line 4)	152

The retailer can compare this index figure with those of other areas to determine which sites have the greatest market potential with the least amount of retail competition. An index value above 200 is considered to indicate exceptional opportunities.

■ DATA MINING

Large corporations' decision support systems often contain millions or even hundreds of millions of records of data. These complex data volumes are too large to be understood by managers. Consider, for example, Capital One, a consumer lending company with nearly 50 million customer accounts, including credit cards and auto loans. Suppose the company collects data on customer purchases, and each customer makes five transactions in a month, or sixty per year. With 50 million customers and decades of data (the company was founded in 1988), it's easy to see how record counts quickly grow beyond the comfort zone for most humans.[8]

Two points about data volume are important to keep in mind. First, relevant marketing data are often in independent and unrelated files. Second, the number of distinct pieces of information each data record contains is often large. When the number of distinct pieces of information contained in each data record and data volume grows too large, end users don't have the capacity to make sense of it all. Data mining helps clarify the underlying meaning of the data.

data mining

The use of powerful computers to dig through volumes of data to discover patterns about an organization's customers and products; applies to many different forms of analysis.

The term **data mining** refers to the use of powerful computers to dig through volumes of data to discover patterns about an organization's customers and products. It is a broad term that applies to many different forms of analysis. For example, **neural networks** are a form of artificial intelligence in which a computer is programmed to mimic the way that human brains process information. One computer expert put it this way:

neural network

A form of artificial intelligence in which a computer is programmed to mimic the way that human brains process information.

> A neural network learns pretty much the way a human being does. Suppose you say "big" and show a child an elephant, and then you say "small" and show her a poodle. You repeat this process with a house and a giraffe as examples of "big" and then a grain of sand and an ant as examples of "small." Pretty soon she will figure it out and tell you that a truck is "big" and a needle is "small." Neural networks can similarly generalize by looking at examples.[9]

market-basket analysis

A form of data mining that analyzes anonymous point-of-sale transaction databases to identify coinciding purchases or relationships between products purchased and other retail shopping information.

Market-basket analysis is a form of data mining that analyzes anonymous point-of-sale transaction databases to identify coinciding purchases or relationships between products purchased and other retail shopping information.[10] Consider this example about patterns in customer purchases: Osco Drugs mined its databases provided by checkout scanners and found that when men go to its drugstores to buy diapers in the evening between 6:00 p.m. and 8:00 p.m., they sometimes walk out with a six-pack of beer as well. Knowing this behavioral pattern, supermarket managers may consider laying out their stores so that these items are closer together.[11]

customer discovery

Involves mining data to look for patterns identifying who is likely to be a valuable customer.

A data-mining application of interest to marketers is known as **customer discovery**, which involves mining data to look for patterns identifying who is likely to be a valuable customer. For example, a larger provider of business services wanted to sell a new product to its existing customers, but it knew that only some of them would be interested. The company had to adapt each product offering to each customer's individual needs, so it wanted to save money by identifying the best prospects. It contracted with a research provider called DataMind to mine its data on sales, responses to marketing, and customer service to look for the customers most likely to be interested in the new product. DataMind assigned each of the company's customers an index number indicating their expected interest level, and the selling effort was much more efficient as a result.[12]

Mining Data from Blogs

One way to find out what people are thinking these days is to read what they are posting on their blogs. But with tens of millions of blogs available on the Internet, there is no way to read them all. One solution: data-mining software designed for the blogosphere.

Umbria Communications, based in Boulder, Colorado, offers a program called Buzz Report, which searches 13 million blogs, looking for messages related to particular products and trends. Marketers can buy the service to find out what people are saying about their new products, or they can explore unmet needs in areas they might consider serving. Not only does Buzz Report identify relevant blogs, but it also has a language processor that can identify positive and negative messages and analyze word choices and spelling to estimate the writer's age range and sex.

The company's CEO, Howard Kaushansky, says the program can even recognize sarcasm.

Most of Umbria's clients are large makers of consumer products, including Sprint and Electronic Arts. U.S. Cellular used Buzz Report to learn that teenage users of cell phones are particularly worried about using more than their allotted minutes, fearing that parents would take the extra amount from their allowance. Such knowledge is useful for developing new service plans and marketing messages.

Sources: Based on Bridget Finn, "Consumer Research: Mining Blogs for Marketing Insight," *Business 2.0*, (September 2005), downloaded from InfoTrac at http://www.galenet.com; Justin Martin, "Blogging for Dollars," *Fortune*, (December 12, 2005), http://www.galenet.com.

When a company knows the identity of the customer who makes repeated purchases from the same organization, an analysis can be made of sequences of purchases. The use of data mining to detect sequence patterns is a popular application among direct marketers, such as catalog retailers. A catalog merchant has information for each customer, revealing the sets of products that the customer buys in every purchase order. A sequence detection function can then be used to discover the set of purchases that frequently precedes the purchase of, say, a microwave oven. As another example, a sequence of insurance claims could lead to the identification of frequently occurring medical procedures performed on patients, which in turn could be used to detect cases of medical fraud.

Data mining requires sophisticated computer resources, and it is expensive. That's why companies like DataMind, IBM, Oracle, Information Builders, and Acxiom Corporation offer data-mining services. Customers send the databases they want analyzed and let the data-mining company do the "number crunching." The Research Snapshot above shows how one company mines data about the most recent "buzz."

■ DATABASE MARKETING AND CUSTOMER RELATIONSHIP MANAGEMENT

As we have already mentioned, a CRM (customer relationship management) system is a decision support system that manages the interactions between an organization and its customers. A CRM maintains customer databases containing customers' names, addresses, phone numbers, past purchases, responses to past promotional offers, and other relevant data such as demographic and financial data. **Database marketing** is the practice of using CRM databases to develop one-to-one relationships and precisely targeted promotional efforts with individual customers. For example, a fruit catalog company CRM contains a database of previous customers, including what purchases they made during the Christmas holidays. Each year the company sends last year's gift list to customers to help them send the same gifts to their friends and relatives.

database marketing
The use of customer databases to promote one-to-one relationships with customers and create precisely targeted promotions.

Because database marketing requires vast amounts of CRM data compiled from numerous sources, secondary data are often acquired for the exclusive purpose of developing or enhancing databases. The transaction record, which often lists the item purchased, its value, customer name, address, and zip code, is the building block for many databases. This may be supplemented with data customers provide directly, such as data on a warranty card, and by secondary data purchased from third parties. For example, credit services may sell databases about applications for loans, credit card payment history, and other financial data. Several companies, such as Donnelley Marketing (with its BusinessContentFile and ConsumerContentFile services) and Claritas (with PRIZM), collect primary data and then sell demographic data that can be related to small geographic areas, such as those with a certain zip code. (Remember that when the vendor collects the data, they are primary data, but when the database marketer incorporates the data into his or her database, they are secondary data.)

Now that some of the purposes of secondary-data analysis have been addressed, we turn to a discussion of the sources of secondary data.

Sources of Internal Secondary Data

Chapter 2 classified secondary data as either internal to the organization or external. Modern information technology makes this distinction seem somewhat simplistic. Some accounting documents are indisputably internal records of the organization. Researchers in another organization cannot have access to them. Clearly, a book published by the federal government and located at a public library is external to the company. However, in today's world of electronic data interchange, the data that appear in a book published by the federal government may also be purchased from an online information vendor for instantaneous access and subsequently stored in a company's decision support system.

Internal data should be defined as data that originated in the organization, or data created, recorded, or generated by the organization. **Internal and proprietary data** is perhaps a more descriptive term.

internal and proprietary data

Secondary data that originate inside the organization.

Internal and Proprietary Data

Most organizations routinely gather, record, and store internal data to help them solve future problems. An organization's accounting system can usually provide a wealth of information. Routine documents such as sales invoices allow external financial reporting, which in turn can be a source of data for further analysis. If the data are properly coded into a modular database in the accounting system, the researcher may be able to conduct more detailed analysis using the decision support system. Sales information can be broken down by account or by product and region; information related to orders received, back orders, and unfilled orders can be identified; sales can be forecast on the basis of past data. Other useful sources of internal data include salespeople's call reports, customer complaints, service records, warranty card returns, product returns, archived focus group recordings, and other records.

Researchers frequently aggregate or disaggregate internal data. For example, a computer service firm used internal secondary data to analyze sales over the previous three years, categorizing business by industry, product, purchase level, and so on. The company discovered that 60 percent of its customers represented only 2 percent of its business and that nearly all of these customers came through telephone directory advertising. This simple investigation of internal records showed that, in effect, the firm was paying to attract customers it did not want.

Internet technology is making it easier to research internal and proprietary data. Often companies set up Intranets so that employees can use Web tools to store and share data within the organization. And just as Google's search software lets people search the entire World Wide Web, Google is offering the enterprise search, which is essentially the same technology in a version that searches a corporate Intranet. The enterprise search considers not only how often a particular document has been viewed but also the history of the user's past search patterns, such as how often that user has looked at particular documents and for how long. In addition, other companies have purchased specialized software, such as Autonomy, which searches internal sources plus such external sources as news and government Web sites.[13]

External Secondary Data Sources

external data

Data created, recorded, or generated by an entity other than the researcher's organization.

External data are generated or recorded by an entity other than the researcher's organization. The government, newspapers and journals, trade associations, and other organizations create or produce information. Traditionally, this information has been in published form, perhaps available from a public library, trade association, or government agency. Today, however, computerized data archives and electronic data interchange make external data as accessible as internal data. Exhibit 7.7 illustrates some traditional and some modern ways of distributing information. The Research Snapshot on the next page illustrates a company that specializes in data archives.

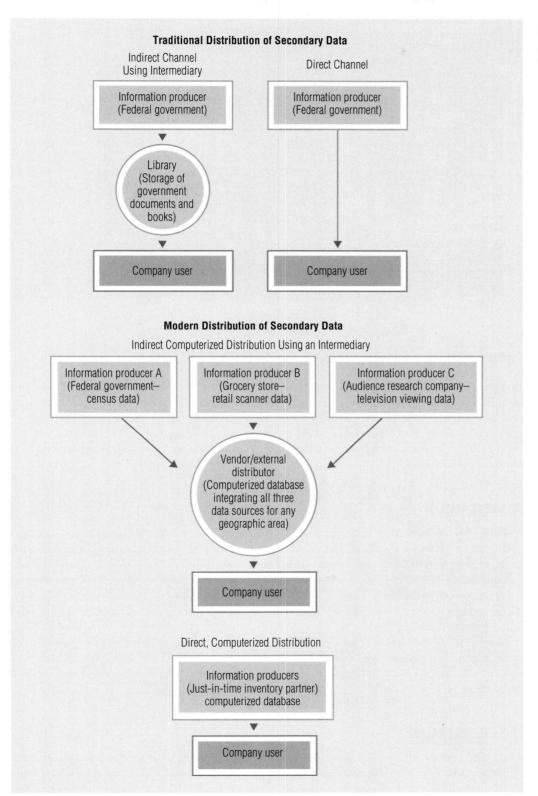

Traditional Distribution of Secondary Data

Indirect Channel Using Intermediary

Information producer (Federal government)

Library (Storage of government documents and books)

Company user

Direct Channel

Information producer (Federal government)

Company user

Modern Distribution of Secondary Data

Indirect Computerized Distribution Using an Intermediary

Information producer A (Federal government– census data)

Information producer B (Grocery store– retail scanner data)

Information producer C (Audience research company– television viewing data)

Vendor/external distributor (Computerized database integrating all three data sources for any geographic area)

Company user

Direct, Computerized Distribution

Information producers (Just-in-time inventory partner) computerized database

Company user

EXHIBIT 7.7

Information as a Product and Its Distribution Channels

UNCLE SAM FINDS YOU!

In a nation with an all-volunteer military, finding recruits is an ongoing need. The project is especially challenging in wartime, when more service members are necessary but the costs of serving are too daunting for many citizens. One way that the Department of Defense meets this challenge is by reviewing data that exist in a variety of sources. Its Joint Advertising, Market Research & Studies (JAMRS) project operates over a dozen research initiatives that make data available to military recruiters in all branches of the U.S. armed services. Some involve data collection, but many apply already-existing data (secondary data) to the task of recruitment.

JAMRS is partly a data warehouse storing all information gathered as potential recruits visit or contact recruiting stations. JAMRS also pays for data from third-party research firms. For example, it uses the PRIZM market segmentation data gathered and sold by Claritas, a marketing research firm. The PRIZM data describe the purchasing and media behavior of many market segments. Recruiters can use the data to identify the activities of potential recruits that live in their region—for example, to identify the magazines they read. This information can help local recruiters or branches of the military target messages likely to appeal to particular groups of young men and women. Research suggests that recruits are most likely to come from households with lower-middle incomes or below in rural areas and small towns. However, the PRIZM data go much deeper, showing, for example, that U.S. Army recruits often come from households that listen to Spanish-language radio and that prospective Marines tend to read *Outdoor Life* and enjoy fishing and hunting.

For the Defense Department, recruiting would no doubt be far more difficult and far less effective without access to secondary data, in this case, data gathered for purposes other than military recruitment. But the data are useful only with careful analysis and interpretation. In this way, Uncle Sam can communicate with receptive audiences in an efficient manner.

Sources: "Market Research and Studies," *Joint Advertising, Market Research & Studies*, JAMRS Web site, http://www.jamrs.org, accessed February 8, 2006; Arndorfer, James B., "Target Practice," *Advertising Age*, (November 28, 2005), 76, 1–41; Margolis, Emanuel, "Building a Database of Potential Soldiers," *Connecticut Law Tribune*, (October 24, 2005), http://www.ctlawtribune.com; Arndorfer, James B., "Army Looking for a Direct Hit," *Advertising Age*, (July 11, 2005), 76, 4–36.

©SONDA DAWES/THE IMAGE WORKS

©GEORGE DOYLE & CIARAN GRIFFIN

Information as a Product and Its Distribution Channels

Because secondary data have value, they can be bought and sold like other products. And just as bottles of perfume or plumbers' wrenches may be distributed in many ways, secondary data also flow through various channels of distribution. Many users, such as the Fortune 500 corporations, purchase documents and computerized census data directly from the government. However, many small companies get census data from a library or another intermediary or vendor of secondary information.

■ LIBRARIES

Traditionally, libraries' vast storehouses of information have served as a bridge between users and producers of secondary data. The library staff deals directly with the creators of information, such as the federal government, and intermediate distributors of information, such as abstracting and indexing services. The user need only locate the appropriate secondary data on the library shelves. Libraries provide collections of books, journals, newspapers, and so on for reading and reference. They also stock many bibliographies, abstracts, guides, directories, and indexes, as well as offer access to basic databases.

The word *library* typically connotes a public or university facility. However, many major corporations and government agencies also have libraries. A corporate librarian's advice on sources of industry information or the United Nations librarian's help in finding statistics about international markets can be invaluable.

■ THE INTERNET

Today, of course, much secondary data is conveniently available over the Internet. Its creation has added an international dimension to the acquisition of secondary data. For example, Library Spot, at http://www.libraryspot.com, provides links to online libraries, including law libraries, medical libraries, and music libraries. Its reference desk features links to calendars, dictionaries, encyclopedias, maps, and other sources typically found at a traditional library's reference desk. Exhibit 7.8 lists some of the more popular Internet addresses where secondary data may be found.

The chapter vignette discussed how Internet social networking sites and blogs can become repositories for secondary data. Consumers use information posted here as a form of secondary data to aid in their own purchases. This is a way of spreading word-of-mouth (WOM) or in this case word-of-mouse information. Interestingly, consumers are perceptive as to whose information is most valuable. Consider consumers seeking information from an Internet chat room. Consumers

EXHIBIT 7.8 **Selected Internet Sites for Secondary Data**

Name	Description	URL
Yahoo!	Portal that serves as a gateway to all kinds of sites on the Web.	http://www.yahoo.com
CEOexpress	The 80/20 rule applied to the Internet. A series of links designed by a busy executive for busy executives.	http://www.ceoexpress.com
The New York Public Library Home Page	Library resources and links available online.	http://www.nypl.org
Census Bureau	Demographic information from the U.S. Census Bureau.	http://www.census.gov
Statistical Abstract of the United States	Highlights from the primary reference book for government statistics.	http://www.census.gov/statab/www
STAT-USA/Internet	A comprehensive source of U.S. government information that focuses on economic, financial, and trade data.	http://www.stat-usa.gov/
Advertising Age magazine	Provides content on marketing media, advertising, and public relations.	http://www.adage.com
Inc.com	Inc. magazine's resources for growing a small business.	http://www.inc.com
The Wall Street Journal Online	Provides a continually updated view of business news around the world.	http://online.wsj.com
CNN Money	Provides business news, information on managing a business and managing money, and other business data.	http://money.cnn.com
NAICS—North American Industry Classification System	Describes the new classification system that replaced the SIC system.	http://www.census.gov/epcd/www/naics.html
MapQuest	Allows users to enter an address and zip code and see a map.	http://www.mapquest.com
Brint.com: The BizTech Network	Business and technology portal and global network for e-business, information, technology, and knowledge management.	http://www.brint.com

place more value on information provided by consumers who respond quickly to Internet queries for information, whose previous responses are positively evaluated by other consumers and who seem to show knowledge in their responses.[14] Marketing researchers may also begin to weight information posted based on some assessment of credibility. This consumer input provides insight into how this might be done.

■ VENDORS

The information age offers many channels besides libraries through which to access data. Many external producers make secondary data available directly from the organizations that produce the data or through intermediaries, which are often called *vendors*. Vendors such as Factiva now allow managers to access thousands of external databases via desktop computers and telecommunications systems. Hoovers (http://www.hoovers.com) specializes in providing information about thousands of companies' financial situations and operations.

■ PRODUCERS

Classifying external secondary data by the nature of the producer of information yields five basic sources: publishers of books and periodicals, government sources, media sources, trade association sources, and commercial sources. The following section discusses each type of secondary data source.

Books and Periodicals

Some researchers consider books and periodicals found in a library to be the quintessential secondary data source. A researcher who finds books on a topic of interest obviously is off to a good start.

Professional journals, such as the *Journal of the Academy of Marketing Science, Journal of Marketing, Journal of Marketing Research, The Journal of Business Research, Journal of Advertising Research, American Demographics,* and *The Public Opinion Quarterly,* as well as commercial business periodicals such as the *Wall Street Journal, Fortune,* and *BusinessWeek,* contain much useful material. *Sales and Marketing Management's Survey of Buying Power* is a particularly useful source of information about markets. To locate data in periodicals, indexing services such as the *ABI/INFORM and Business Periodicals Index* and the *Wall Street Journal Index* are very useful. Guides to data sources also are helpful. For example, *American Statistical Index and Business Information Sources* is a very valuable source. Most university libraries provide access to at least some of these databases.

Government Sources

Government agencies produce data prolifically. Most of the data published by the federal government can be counted on for accuracy and quality of investigation. Most students are familiar with the U.S. *Census of Population,* which provides a wealth of data.

The *Census of Population* is only one of many resources that the government provides. Banks and savings and loan companies rely heavily on the *Federal Reserve Bulletin* and the *Economic Report of the President* for data relating to research on financial and economic conditions. Builders and contractors use the information in the *Current Housing Report and Annual Housing Survey* for their research. The *Statistical Abstract of the United States* is an extremely valuable source of information about the social, political, and economic organizations of the United States. It abstracts data available in hundreds of other government publications and serves as a convenient reference to more specific statistical data.

The federal government is a leader in making secondary data available on the Internet. Visit FedWorld (http://www.fedworld.gov) for a central access point and links to many of these important documents. STAT-USA/Internet is another authoritative and comprehensive source of U.S. government information that focuses on economic, financial, and trade data. It contains the following types of information.

- More than 18,000 market research reports on individual countries and markets compiled by foreign experts at U.S. embassies
- Economic data series, current and historical, such as gross domestic product, balance of payment, and merchandise trade

- Standard reference works, such as the *Economic Report of the President,* the *Budget of the United States Federal Government,* and the *World Factbook*
- Worldwide listings of businesses interested in buying U.S. products

The STAT-USA/Internet Web address is http://www.stat-usa.gov. However, only subscribers who pay a fee have access to this service.

State, county, and local government agencies can also be useful sources of information. Many state governments publish state economic models and forecasts, and many cities have metropolitan planning agencies that provide data about the population, economy, transportation system, and so on. These are similar to federal government data but are more current and are structured to suit local needs.

Many cities and states publish information on the Internet. Many search engines have directory entries that allow easy navigation to a particular state's Web site. A researcher using Yahoo!, for example, needs only to click Regional Information to find numerous paths to information about states.

Media Sources

Information on a broad range of subjects is available from broadcast and print media. *CNN Financial News* and *BusinessWeek* are valuable sources for information on the economy and many industries. Media frequently commission research studies about various aspects of Americans' lives, such as financial affairs, and make reports of survey findings available to potential advertisers free of charge. Data about the readers of magazines and the audiences for broadcast media typically are profiled in media kits and advertisements.

Information about special-interest topics may also be available. *Hispanic Business* reports that the number of Hispanic-owned companies in the United States was expected to grow at a rate of 55 percent between 2004 and 2010, reaching 3.2 million firms, with revenue growth for the period of 70 percent. According to the magazine, most of these firms are located in twenty states, with over half in California and Florida. For researchers willing to pay a modest $85, *Hispanic Business* offers a more detailed report about Hispanic-owned businesses.[15]

Data such as these are plentiful because the media like to show that their vehicles are viewed or heard by advertisers' target markets. These types of data should be evaluated carefully, however, because often they cover only limited aspects of a topic. Nevertheless, they can be quite valuable for research, and they are generally available free of charge.

Trade Association Sources

Trade associations, such as the Food Marketing Institute or the American Petroleum Institute, serve the information needs of a particular industry. The trade association collects data on a number of topics of specific interest to firms, especially data on market size and market trends. Association members have a source of information that is particularly germane to their industry questions. For example, the Newspaper Advertising Bureau (NAB) has catalogued and listed in its computer the specialized sections that are currently popular in newspapers. The NAB has surveyed all daily, Sunday, and weekend newspapers in the United States and Canada on their editorial content and has stored this information, along with data on rates, circulation, and mechanical requirements, in its computer for advertisers' use.

Commercial Sources

Numerous firms specialize in selling and/or publishing information. For example, the Polk Company publishes information on the automotive field, such as average car values and new-car purchase rates by zip code. Dun and Bradstreet provide business soundness ratings for individual businesses across industries and regions while bankrate.com does much the same within the banking industry with a rating known as CAMEL. *Fortune* rates the most admired companies annually. Many of these organizations offer information in published formats and as CD-ROM or Internet databases. The following provides a sampling of the diverse data that are available.

Market-Share Data A number of syndicated services supply either wholesale or retail sales volume data based on product movement. Information Resources, Inc. collects market-share data using Universal Product Codes (UPC) and optical scanning at retail store checkouts. INFOS-CAN is a syndicated store tracking service that collects scanner data weekly from more than

32,000 supermarket, drug, and mass merchandiser outlets across the United States. Sales in France, Germany, Greece, Italy, the Netherlands, Spain, and the United Kingdom also are tracked by INFOSCAN. The *Market Share Reporter* is also available at the reference desk in many university libraries and available online to subscribers. It contains market share data on many, many industries and the firms that operate within these industries. The *Market Share Reporter* is produced each year and made available for sale.

Although it is best known for its television rating operations, ACNielsen also has a scanner-based marketing and sales information service called ScanTrack. This service gathers sales and marketing data from a sample of more than 4,800 stores representing more than 800 retailers in 50 major U.S. markets. As part of Nielsen's Retail Measurement Service, auditors visit the stores at regular intervals to track promotions to customers, retail inventories, displays, brand distribution, out-of-stock conditions, and other retail marketing activity. Scanner data allow researchers to monitor sales data before, during, and after changes in advertising frequency, price changes, distribution of free samples, and similar marketing tactics.

Wal-Mart operates its own in-store scanner system called RetailLink. Key suppliers can have online access to relevant data free of charge.[16]

Many primary data investigations use scanner data to measure the results of experimental manipulations such as altering advertising copy. For example, scanning systems combined with consumer panels are used to create electronic test-markets. Systems based on UPCs (bar codes) and similar technology have been implemented in factories, warehouses, and transportation companies to research inventory levels, shipments, and the like.

Demographic and Census Updates A number of firms, such as CACI Marketing Systems and Urban Information Systems, offer computerized U.S. census files and updates of these data broken down by small geographic areas, such as zip codes. Many of these research suppliers provide in-depth information on minority customers and other market segments.

Consumer Attitude and Public Opinion Research Many research firms offer specialized syndicated services that report findings from attitude research and opinion polls. For example, Yankelovich provides custom research, tailored for specific projects, and several syndicated services. Yankelovich's public opinion research studies, such as the voter and public attitude surveys that appear in *Time* and other news magazines, are a source of secondary data. One of the firm's services is the *Yankelovich MONITOR*, a syndicated annual census of changing social values and an analysis of how they can affect consumer marketing. The *MONITOR* charts the growth and spread of new social values, characterizes the types of customers who support the new values and those who continue to support traditional values, and outlines the ways in which people's values affect purchasing behavior.

Harris/Interactive is another public opinion research firm that provides syndicated and custom research for business. One of its services is its ABC News/Harris survey. This survey, released three times per week, monitors the pulse of the American public on topics such as inflation, unemployment, energy, attitudes toward the president, elections, and so on.

Consumption and Purchase Behavior Data NPD's *National Eating Trends* (NET) is the most detailed database available on consumption patterns and trends for more than 4,000 food and beverage products. This is a syndicated source of data about the types of meals people eat and when and how they eat them. The data, called *diary panel data,* are based on records of meals and diaries kept by a group of households that have agreed to record their consumption behavior over an extended period of time.

National Family Opinion (NFO), Marketing Research Corporation of America (MRCA), and many other syndicated sources sell diary panel data about consumption and purchase behavior. Since the advent of scanner data, diary panels are more commonly used to record purchases of apparel, hardware, home furnishings, jewelry, and other durable goods, rather than purchases of non-durable consumer packaged goods. More recently, services have been tracking consumer behavior online, collecting data about sites visited and purchases made over the Internet.

Advertising Research Advertisers can purchase readership and audience data from a number of firms. W. R. Simmons and Associates measures magazine audiences; Arbitron measures radio audiences; ACNielsen Media Measurement estimates television audience ratings. By specializing in collecting and selling audience information on a continuing basis, these commercial sources provide a valuable service to their subscribers.

Assistance in measuring advertising effectiveness is another syndicated service. For example, Roper Starch Worldwide measures the impact of advertising in magazines. Readership information can be obtained for competitors' ads or the client's own ads. Respondents are classified as noted readers, associated readers, or read-most readers.

Burke Marketing Research provides a service that measures the extent to which respondents recall television commercials aired the night before. It provides product category norms, or average DAR (Day-After Recall) scores, and DAR scores for other products.

An individual advertiser would be unable to monitor every minute of every television program before deciding on the appropriate ones in which to place advertising. However, numerous clients, agencies, television networks, and advertisers can purchase the Nielsen television ratings service.

Single-Source and Global Research Data

As business has become more global, so has the secondary data industry. Many private companies exist solely to provide secondary data and many marketing research firms provide this canned data as a big part of their business. Additionally, many government entities provide secondary information based on statistics that they must collect in administering programs in their own country. It's hard to think of a topic for which no secondary data would exist.

Single-Source Data-Integrated Information

ACNielsen Company offers data from both its television meters and scanner operations. The integration of these two types of data helps marketers investigate the impact of television advertising on retail sales. In other ways as well, users of data find that merging two or more diverse types of data into a single database offers many advantages.

PRIZM by Claritas Corporation, CACI, ClusterPlus by SMI, Mediamark Research Inc., and many other syndicated databases report product purchase behavior, media usage, demographic characteristics, lifestyle variables, and business activity by geographic area such as zip code. Although such data are often called *geodemographic,* they cover such a broad range of phenomena that no one name is a good description. These data use small geographic areas as the unit of analysis.

The marketing research industry uses the term **single-source data** for diverse types of data offered by a single company. Exhibit 7.9 on the next page identifies three major marketers of single-source data.

single-source data

Diverse types of data offered by a single company; usually integrated on the basis of a common variable such as geographic area or store.

Government Agencies

The Japan Management Association Research Institute, Japan's largest provider of secondary research data to government and industry, maintains an office in San Diego. The Institute's goal is to help U.S. firms access its enormous store of data about Japan to develop and plan their business there. The office in San Diego provides translators and acts as an intermediary between Japanese researchers and U.S. clients.

Secondary data compiled outside the United States have the same limitations as domestic secondary data. However, international researchers should watch for certain pitfalls that frequently are associated with foreign data and cross-cultural research. First, data may simply be unavailable in certain countries. Second, the accuracy of some data may be called into question. This is especially likely with official statistics that may be adjusted for the political purposes of foreign governments. Finally, although economic terminology may be standardized, various countries use different definitions and accounting and recording practices for many economic concepts. For example, different countries may measure disposable personal income in radically different ways.

EXHIBIT 7.9
Examples of Single-Source Databases

CACI Marketing Systems http://www.caci.com	Provides industry-specific marketing services, such as customer profiling and segmentation, custom target analysis, demographic data reports and maps, and site evaluation and selection. CACI offers demographics and data on businesses, lifestyles, consumer spending, purchase potential, shopping centers, traffic volumes, and other statistics.
PRIZM by Claritas Corporation http://www.claritas.com	PRIZM which stands for Potential Rating Index for Zip Markets, is based on the "birds-of-a-feather" assumption that people live near others who are like themselves. PRIZM combines census data, consumer surveys about shopping and lifestyle, and purchase data to identify market segments. Colorful names such as Young Suburbia, Shot Guns, and Pickups describe 40 segments that can be identified by zip code. Claritas also has a lifestyle census in the United Kingdom (http://www.claritas.co.uk).
MRI Cable Report—Mediamark Research Inc. http://www.mediamark.com.	Integrates information on cable television viewing with demographic and product com usage information.

International researchers should take extra care to investigate the comparability of data among countries. Exhibit 7.10 lists some potential sources for marketing information about various parts of the world.

The U.S. government and other organizations compile databases that may aid international marketers. For example, *The European Union in the US* (http://www.eurunion.org/) reports on historical and current activity in the European Union providing a comprehensive reference guide to information about laws and regulations. The *European Union in the U.S.* profiles in detail each European Union member state, investment opportunities, sources of grants and other funding, and other information about business resources.

The U.S. government offers a wealth of data about foreign countries. The CIA's World Factbook and the National Trade Data Bank are especially useful. Both can be accessed using the Internet. The National Trade Data Bank (NTDB), the U.S. government's most comprehensive source of world trade data, illustrates what is available.

The National Trade Data Bank was established by the Omnibus Trade and Competitiveness Act of 1988.[17] Its purpose was to provide "reasonable public access, including electronic access" to an export promotion data system that was centralized, inexpensive, and easy to use.

EXHIBIT 7.10
Some Example Sources of Global Marketing Information

- United States

  http://www.stat-usa.gov

- South Africa

  http://www.statssa.gov.za

- Australia

  http://www.nla.gov.au/oz/stats.html

- Japan

  http://www.stat.go.jp

- U.K.

  http://www.statistics.gov.uk

- France

  http://www.insee.fr

- South America

  http://www.internetworldstats.com/south.htm

- Norway

  http://www.ssb.no

- United Nations

  http://www.un.org/esa

- Global Information from the CIA Factbook

  http://www.cia.gov

© MICHAEL NEWMAN/PHOTOEDIT

The U.S. Department of Commerce has the responsibility for operating and maintaining the NTDB and works with federal agencies that collect and distribute trade information to keep the NTDB up-to-date. The NTDB has been published monthly on CD-ROM since 1990. Over one thousand public and university libraries offer access to the NTDB through the Federal Depository Library system.

The National Trade Data Bank consists of 133 separate trade- and business-related programs (databases). By using it, small- and medium-sized companies get immediate access to information that until now only Fortune 500 companies could afford.

Topics in the NTDB include export opportunities by industry, country, and product; foreign companies or importers looking for specific products; how-to market guides; demographic, political, and socioeconomic conditions in hundreds of countries; and much more. NTDB offers one-stop shopping for trade information from more than twenty federal sources. You do not need to know which federal agency produces the information: All you need to do is consult NTDB.

Some of the specific information that can be obtained from the NTDB is listed in Exhibit 7.11.

EXHIBIT 7.11

Examples of Information Contained in the NTDB

Agricultural commodity production and trade

Basic export information

Calendars of trade fairs and exhibitions

Capital markets and export financing

Country reports on economic and social policies and trade practices

Energy production, supply, and inventories

Exchange rates

Export licensing information

Guides to doing business in foreign countries

International trade terms directory

How-to guides

International trade regulations/agreements

International trade agreements

Labor, employment, and productivity

Maritime and shipping information

Market research reports

Overseas contacts

Overseas and domestic industry information

Price indexes

Small business information

State exports

State trade contacts

Trade opportunities

U.S. export regulations

U.S. import and export statistics by country and commodity

U.S. international transactions

World Fact Book

World minerals production

Summary

1. Discuss the advantages and disadvantages of secondary data. Secondary data are data that have been gathered and recorded previously by someone else for purposes other than those of the current researcher. The chief advantage of secondary data is that they are almost always less expensive to obtain than primary data. Generally they can be obtained rapidly and may provide information not otherwise available to the researcher. The disadvantage of secondary data is that they were not intended specifically to meet the researcher's needs. The researcher must examine secondary data for accuracy, bias, and soundness. One way to do this is to cross-check various available sources.

2. Understand the types of objectives that can be achieved using secondary data. Secondary research designs address many common marketing problems. There are three general categories of secondary research objectives: fact-finding, model building, and database marketing. A typical fact-finding study might seek to uncover all available information about consumption patterns for a particular product category or to identify business trends that affect an industry. Model building is more complicated; it involves specifying relationships between two or more variables. The practice of database marketing, which involves maintaining customer databases with customers' names, addresses, phone numbers, past purchases, responses to past promotional offers, and other relevant data such as demographic and financial data, is increasingly being supported by marketing research efforts.

3. Identify various internal and proprietary sources of secondary data. Managers often get data from internal proprietary sources such as accounting records. Data mining is the use of powerful computers to dig through volumes of data to discover patterns about an organization's customers and products. It is a broad term that applies to many different forms of analysis.

4. Give examples of various external sources of secondary data. External data are generated or recorded by another entity. The government, newspaper and journal publishers, trade associations, and other organizations create or produce information. Traditionally this information has been distributed in published form, either directly from producer to researcher, or indirectly through intermediaries such as public libraries. Modern computerized data archives, electronic data interchange, and the Internet have changed the distribution of external data, making them almost as accessible as internal data. *Push technology* is a term referring to an Internet information technology that automatically delivers content to the researcher's or manager's desktop. This service helps in environmental scanning. Consumers also use secondary data obtained from the Internet in their own research about products. In much the same way, researchers can use information provided from the Internet.

5. Describe the impact of single-source data and globalization on secondary data research. The marketing of multiple types of related data by single-source suppliers has radically changed the nature of secondary-data research. Businesses can measure promotional efforts and related buyer behavior by detailed customer characteristics. As business has become more global, so has the secondary-data industry. International researchers should watch for pitfalls that can be associated with foreign data and cross-cultural research, such as problems with the availability and reliability of data.

Key Terms and Concepts

Questions for Review and Critical Thinking

1. Secondary data have been called the first line of attack for marketing researchers. Discuss this description.
2. Suppose you wish to learn about the size of the soft-drink market, particularly root beer sales, growth patterns, and market shares. Indicate probable sources for these secondary data.
3. What is *push technology?*
4. Identify some typical research objectives for secondary-data studies.
5. How might a marketing researcher doing a job for a company such as Pulte Homes (http://www.pultehomes.com) or David Weekley Homes (http://www.davidweekley.com) use secondary data and data mining?
6. What would be a source for the following data?
   a. Population, average income, and employment rates for Oregon
   b. Maps of U.S. counties and cities
   c. Trends in automobile ownership
   d. Divorce trends in the United States
   e. Median weekly earnings of full-time, salaried workers for the previous five years
   f. Annual sales of the top ten fast-food companies
   g. Top ten Web sites ranked by number of unique visitors
   h. Attendance at professional sports events
7. Suppose you are a marketing research consultant and a client comes to your office and says, "I must have the latest information on the supply of and demand for Maine potatoes within the next 24 hours." What would you do?
8. Find the following data in the *Survey of Current Business:*
   a. U.S. gross domestic product for the first quarter of 2004
   b. Exports of goods and services for the fourth quarter of 2004
   c. Imports of goods and services for the fourth quarter of 2004
9. **ETHICS** A newspaper reporter finds data in a study that surveyed children that reports that a high percentage of children can match cartoon characters with the products they represent. For instance, they can match cereal with Captain Crunch and Ronald McDonald with a Big Mac. The reporter used this to write a story about the need to place limits on the use of cartoon characters. However, the study also provided data suggesting that matching the cartoon character and the product did not lead to significantly higher consumption. Would this be a proper use of secondary data?
10. **ETHICS** Go back to the opening chapter vignette. Do you believe it is ethical for an employer to mine social networking sites for personal information about employees? Does it matter if the information refers to behavior solely away from work or that is somehow tied to things done while at work? Address the same issue for a marketing research firm that distributes entertainment to mobile appliances (movies, music, games). Is it ethical for them to search for relationships and market segments using information people post about themselves on the Internet?

Research Activities

1. Use secondary data to learn the size of the U.S. golf market and to profile the typical golfer.
2. **'NET** Where could a researcher working for the U.S. Marine Corps (http://www.marines.com) find information that would identify the most productive areas of the United States in which to recruit? What would you recommend?
3. **'NET** POPClocks estimate the U.S. and world populations. Go to the Census Bureau home page (http://www.census.gov), navigate to the population section, and find today's estimate of the U.S. and world populations.
4. **'NET** Try to find the U.S. market share for the following companies within thirty minutes:
   a. Home Depot
   b. Burger King
   c. Marlboro
   d. Was this a difficult task? If so, why do you think it is this difficult?
5. **'NET** Use the Internet to learn what you can about Indonesia.
   a. Check the corruption index for Indonesia at http://www.transparency.org.
   b. What additional kinds of information are available from the following sources?
   - Go to http://freetheworld.com/member.html and view info for Indonesia.
   - Visit the CIA's World Factbook *at* https://www.cia.gov/library/publications/the-world-factbook.
   - Go to Google, Yahoo! Search, or another search engine, and use "Indonesia" as a search word.
6. **'NET** Go to Statistics Norway at http://www.ssb.no. What data, if any, can you obtain in English? What languages can be used to

search this Web site? What databases might be of interest to the business researcher?

7. **'NET** Go to Statistics Canada at http://www.statcan.ca. What languages can be used to search this Web site? What databases might be of interest to the business researcher?

8. **'NET** Suppose you were working for a company that wanted to start a business selling handmade acoustic guitars that are reproductions of classic vintage guitars. Pricing is a big part of the decision. Secondary information is available via the Internet. Use eBay (http://ebay.com) to identify four key brands of acoustic

guitars by studying the vintage acoustic guitars listed for sale. Since the company wishes to charge premium prices, they will model after the most expensive brand. What brand seems to be associated with the highest prices?

9. **'NET** Visit a social networking site (assuming you can log into a site). Search for information about Starbucks. Is there anything useful that turns up in your search that could be used by Starbucks to improve their sales and overall business operations? Explain.

Case 7.1 Demand for Gas Guzzlers

© GETTY IMAGES/
PHOTODISC GREEN

In fall 2005, Hurricanes Katrina and Rita churning in the Gulf of Mexico damaged oil rigs and refineries, contributing to a spike in oil prices. Many observers expressed confidence that those events were the long-expected trigger that would kill off demand for SUVs and other gas-guzzling vehicles.[18] They were only partly right.

In the months leading up to the hurricanes, sales of SUVs had already been falling, according to data from *Automotive News*. Automakers had been shifting ad dollars away from these products. CNW Market Research said that in August 2005, consumers had for the first time placed fuel economy ahead of performance when ranking factors for choosing a new vehicle. When gas prices approached three dollars a gallon in September 2005, marketers felt sure that fuel economy would remain a top concern. Advertisers began creating more ads featuring vehicles' gas mileage.

But by the end of the year, attitudes were shifting again. The National Automobile Dealers Association surveyed consumers

visiting its Web site for information about car purchases, and it learned they ranked price as most important, followed by make and model, then performance. Fuel economy ranked last, with 3 percent considering it most important and 11 percent considering it least important. What's a carmaker to do? General Motors gathers data from the shoppers who visit Web sites such as www.kbb.com to look up information, and it is analyzing the data to identify the price of fuel at which car buyers adjust their priorities.

Questions

1. From the standpoint of an automobile company, what sources of information in this article offer secondary data?

2. Suggest two or three other sources of data that might be of interest to auto companies interested in forecasting demand.

3. Online or at your library, look for information about recent trends in SUV purchases. Report what you learned, and forecast whether SUV sales are likely to recover or continue their decline. What role do gas prices play in your forecast?

Part 3
Research Designs for Collecting Primary Data

© JOHN LUND/THE IMAGE BANK/GETTY IMAGES

CHAPTER 8
SURVEY RESEARCH:
AN OVERVIEW

After studying this chapter, you should be able to

1. Define surveys and describe the type of information that may be gathered in a survey
2. Explain the advantages and disadvantages of surveys
3. Identify sources of error in survey research
4. Distinguish among the various categories of surveys
5. Discuss the importance of survey research to total quality management programs

Chapter Vignette: Intuit Gets Answers to Satisfy Customers

Intuit, maker of Quicken, QuickBooks, and Turbo Tax software for accounting and tax preparation, has enjoyed years of growth and profits, thanks in part to its efforts to learn what customers want.[1] One of its most important marketing research tools is called a "net promoter survey." That survey is extremely simple. Researchers simply ask customers, "On a scale of 0 to 10 [with 10 being most likely], how likely is it that you would recommend our product to your friends or colleagues?" Customers who respond with a 9 or 10 are called "promoters," and customers who respond with 0 through 6 are called "detractors." Subtracting the percentage of respondents who are detractors from the percentage who are promoters yields the net promoter score.

Intuit's CEO, Steve Bennett—who says he believes that "anything that can be measured can be improved"—encourages the ongoing collection of net promoter scores as a way to improve products and customer service and thereby build revenues and profits. Of course, making improvements requires that the company not only know *whether* customers are satisfied or dissatisfied but also know *why*. To learn more, the company asks survey respondents who are promoters to go online and provide more detailed opinions. For example, Intuit learned that claiming rebates was an annoying process (the company has simplified it) and that discount stores were offering some products for less than the prices offered online to frequent buyers (the company plans to adjust prices).

For even more in-depth information, Intuit supplements survey research with direct observation of customers. One year the company sent hundreds of employees, including CEO Bennett, to visit customers as they worked at their computers. The observers learned that a significant number of small-business owners were struggling with the accounting know-how they needed to use QuickBooks and were mystified by terms such as *accounts payable* and *accounts receivable*. In response, the company introduced QuickBooks: Simple Start Edition, which replaces the financial jargon with simple terms like *cash in* and *cash out*. In the first year after its launch, Simple Start Edition sold more copies than any other accounting software except the standard QuickBooks.

The purpose of survey research is to collect primary data—data gathered and assembled specifically for the project at hand. This chapter, the first of two on survey research, defines the subject. It also discusses typical research objectives that may be accomplished with surveys and various advantages of the survey method. The chapter explains many potential errors that researchers must be careful to avoid. Finally, it classifies the various survey research methods.

Introduction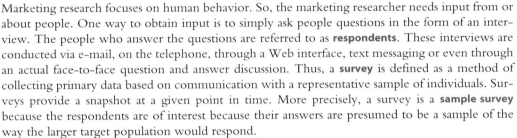

Marketing research focuses on human behavior. So, the marketing researcher needs input from or about people. One way to obtain input is to simply ask people questions in the form of an interview. The people who answer the questions are referred to as **respondents**. These interviews are conducted via e-mail, on the telephone, through a Web interface, text messaging or even through an actual face-to-face question and answer discussion. Thus, a **survey** is defined as a method of collecting primary data based on communication with a representative sample of individuals. Surveys provide a snapshot at a given point in time. More precisely, a survey is a **sample survey** because the respondents are of interest because their answers are presumed to be a sample of the way the larger target population would respond.

Surveys indicate that 40 percent of consumers select the electronics brand only after deciding on what store to shop in. As a result, Sony felt the need to redesign its brand image in a way that attracted more attention and made an emotional connection with consumers.[2] Sony followed up this key finding with a variety of research projects, both qualitative and quantitative, which helped them identify changes to their logo and packaging that not only enabled them to be more prominent in stores, but also helped sell the brand and not just the product.

respondents

People who verbally answer an interviewer's questions or provide answers to written questions.

survey

A method of collecting primary data based on communication (questions and answers) with a representative sample of respondents.

sample survey

A more formal term for a survey.

The Types of Information Gathered Using Surveys

The type of information gathered in a survey varies considerably depending on its objectives. Typically, surveys attempt to describe what is happening, what people believe, what they are like or to learn the reasons for a particular marketing activity. Marketers can make decisions about what products to sell, what the prices should be, where they should be sold, or other elements of the marketing mix. The Research Snapshot on page 191 illustrates how retailers can adjust merchandising with technological advances based on survey input.

More specifically, surveys gather information to assess consumer knowledge and awareness of products, brands, or issues and to measure consumer attitudes and feelings. Additionally, surveys describe consumer characteristics including purchasing patterns, brand usage, and descriptive characteristics including demographics and lifestyle. Thus, psychographic research involves surveys.

Most marketing surveys have multiple objectives; few gather only a single type of factual information. Questions about product use and desirable features help with product development and advertising messages. Demographic information and information on media exposure might also be collected in the survey to help plan a market segmentation strategy. A survey commissioned by eBay learned that almost 60 percent of respondents receive unwanted gifts, and 15 percent of them had sold an unwanted gift online, suggesting a possible source of demand for eBay's auction services.[3] In addition, the survey indicated that selling unwanted gifts online was twice as common among 25- to 34-year-olds. Although consumer surveys are a common form of

Take a look at the questions from the section of the student survey shown at left.

In particular, examine the results to the questions about how much time students spend blogging, how many social networking sites students subscribe to, and the question asking them to indicate which social networking sites they subscribe to. You can analyze the results just by taking frequencies (your instructor may do this for you).

Are these types of questions appropriate for survey research?

What sources of error might be present in these particular survey questions? Explain your response.

marketing research, not all survey research is conducted with the ultimate consumer. Frequently, studies focus on wholesalers, retailers, or industrial buyers.

Because most survey research is descriptive research, the term *survey* is most often associated with quantitative findings. Although most surveys are conducted to quantify certain factual information, some aspects of surveys may also be qualitative. In new-product development, a survey often has a qualitative objective of refining product concepts. Stylistic, aesthetic, or functional changes may be made on the basis of respondents' suggestions. Evaluating the qualitative nature of advertising may also be an objective of survey research, as in the following story told to advertiser Michael Arlen about testing a rough commercial for AT&T.

> We called it "Fishing Camp." The idea was this: These guys go off to a fishing camp in the north woods, somewhere far away, where they're going to have a terrific time together and do all this great fishing, only what happens is that it rains all the time and the fishing is a bust. Mind you, this was a humorous ad. The emphasis was on the humor. Anyway, the big moment occurs when the fishing guys are talking on the phone to their jealous friends back home—who naturally want to know how great the fishing is—and what you see are the fishing guys, huddled in this cabin, with the rain pouring down outside, and one of the guys is staring at a frying pan full of hamburgers sizzling on the stove while he says into the phone, "Boy, you should see the great trout we've got cooking here."[4]

However, much to the advertisers' astonishment, when they tested the advertisement and gave subjects a questionnaire, respondents recalled that what was cooking was trout. To counteract this misimpression, said the advertiser, "We ended up making it, but what we had to do was, when we came to that segment, we put the camera almost *inside* the frying pan, and in the frying pan we put huge, crude chunks of hamburger that were so raw they were almost red."

Advantages and Disadvantages of Surveys

No data source is perfect. All present opportunities for error from different sources. However, the sheer number of survey applications suggests that the advantages often outweigh the disadvantages of performing survey research.

Blu-rays are Best's Rays

LCD, HDTV, CD, DVD, and now Blu-ray. Truly, consumers just seem to get used to one technology when we are faced with another. HDTVs, which were novel ten years ago, are now mainstream and account for the majority of television purchases. Not all technologies succeed, however, and they are often produced and marketed without a sufficient understanding of whether consumers will indeed adopt the technology.

Blu-ray technology has now been around for several years. However, DVDs and even CDs have far from disappeared. Given the almost certain technological superiority of Blu-ray (associated with Sony), what seems to make Blu-ray discs so apparently slow to diffuse? Part of the problem lies in competition from HD DVD (associated with Panasonic) and part from the distribution channel. Survey research suggests that consumers prefer Blu-ray technology to HD DVD. A sample of over one thousand consumers suggests that 58 percent prefer Blu-ray Discs while only 16 percent preferred HD DVD technology. The surveys also asked what electronic format consumers would next purchase. Sixty-six percent of consumers expressed intentions to purchase Blu-ray as opposed to 15 percent who expressed intentions to purchase HD DVD. Nineteen percent reported being undecided. The surveys also suggested consumers saw Blu-ray as more flexible (able to be played in a wider range of appliances), better for gaming, having better company support, and able to store more.

As a result, Best Buy has bet that Blu-ray is the way to go and Wal-Mart has decided to stock Blu-ray products exclusively rather than HD DVD. A chain reaction has started as in-home movie companies such as Netflix switch from other HD formats to Blu-ray only. Certainly, the survey research eventually led to changes in the distribution channel that will speed the diffusion of Blu-ray technology through the marketplace. The Blu-ray is the best way, for now!

Sources: Lee, D., "Blu-ray Wins, So What?" *Marketing Magazine*, 113 (March 10, 2008), 12; LeClaire, J., "Survey Shows Consumers Favor Blu-ray Over HD DVD Format," TechNewsWorld, (July 14, 2005), http://www.technewsworld.com, accessed August 12, 2008.

Advantages of Survey Research

Survey research presents numerous advantages. Surveys provide a quick, often inexpensive, efficient, and accurate means of assessing information about a population. Researchers also can apply fairly straightforward statistical tools in analyzing sample survey results. The examples given earlier illustrate that surveys are quite flexible and, when properly conducted, extremely valuable to the manager.

As we discussed in Chapter 1, marketing research has proliferated among companies adopting the marketing concept. One simple way to understand what consumers think is to ask them questions. The consumer orientation that goes along with adopting the marketing concept forces companies to exchange ideas with customers and a survey is a primary tool for doing so.

Disadvantages of Survey Research

Over the last 50 years and particularly during the last two decades, survey research techniques and standards have become quite scientific and accurate. When properly conducted, surveys offer managers many advantages. However, they can also be ineffective or misleading when researchers do not follow basic research principles, such as taking care in designing both the survey instrument and the sampling frame. Sometimes even a well-designed and carefully executed survey is not helpful because the results are delivered too late or because they measure the wrong thing. Surveys are also an additional source of error when the researchers intend to study actual behavior because the respondent may error answering questions about what they have done or what they will do. Low response rates can also be a problem with many types of surveys.

Each survey tool also introduces some unique disadvantages. The disadvantages of specific survey tools—personal interview, telephone, e-mail, snail mail, Web-based, and other self-administered formats—are discussed in a later chapter. However, errors are common to all forms of surveys, so it is appropriate to describe them generally. Then, the researcher can hopefully better match a survey data collection approach with a given situation in the hope of mitigating ill effects due to error.

Sources of Error in Surveys

A manager who is evaluating the quality of a survey must estimate its accuracy. Exhibit 8.1 outlines the various forms of survey error. They have two major sources: random sampling error and systematic error.

random sampling error

A statistical fluctuation that occurs because of chance variation in the elements selected for a sample.

systematic error

Error resulting from some imperfect aspect of the research design that causes respondent error or from a mistake in the execution of the research.

sample bias

A persistent tendency for the results of a sample to deviate in one direction from the true value of the population parameter.

Random versus Systematic Sampling Error

Most surveys try to portray a representative cross-section of a particular target population. Even with technically proper random probability samples, however, statistical errors will occur because of chance variation in the elements selected for the sample. These statistical problems are unavoidable without very large samples (>400). However, the extent of **random sampling error** can be estimated. This topic is discussed in later chapters in more detail.

The other major source of survey error, **systematic error**, results from some imperfect aspect of the research design or from a mistake in the execution of the research. Because systematic errors include all sources of error other than those introduced by the random sampling procedure, these errors or biases are also called *nonsampling errors*. A **sample bias** exists when the results of a sample show a persistent tendency to deviate in one direction from the true value of the population parameter. The many sources of error that in some way systematically influence answers can be divided into two general categories: respondent error and administrative error.

EXHIBIT 8.1 **Categories of Survey Errors**

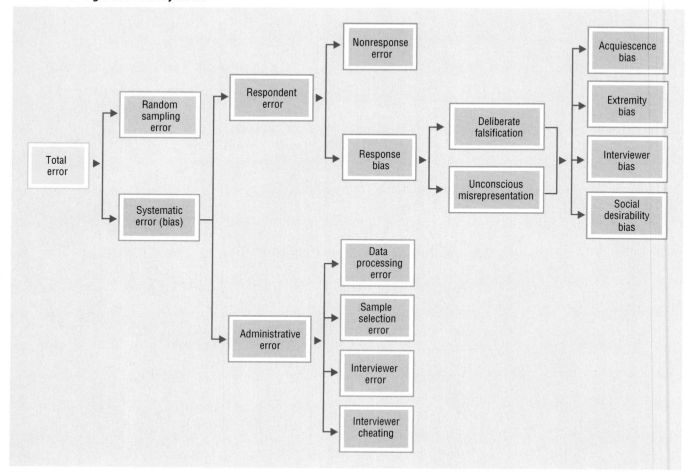

■ RESPONDENT ERROR

Surveys ask people for answers. If people cooperate and give truthful answers, a survey will likely accomplish its goal. If these conditions are not met, nonresponse error or response bias, the two major categories of **respondent error**, may cause sample bias.

Nonresponse Error

Few surveys have 100 percent response rates. But a researcher who obtains a 1 percent response to a five-page e-mail questionnaire concerning various brands of spark plugs may face a serious problem. To use the results, the researcher must believe that consumers who responded to the questionnaire are representative of consumers who did not respond. The statistical differences between a survey that includes only those who responded and a survey that also included those who failed to respond are referred to as **nonresponse error**. This problem is especially acute in mail and Internet surveys, but nonresponse also threatens telephone and face-to-face interviews. Of course, knowing exactly how big this error truly is becomes practically impossible because nonrespondents, by definition, have not provided input.

Survey approaches present researchers with the opportunity to ask consumers questions. However, getting consumers to respond can prove difficult. Those who do not respond can be placed into categories.

People who are not contacted or who refuse to cooperate are called **nonrespondents**. A nonresponse occurs if no one answers the phone at the time of both the initial call and a subsequent callback. The number of **no contacts** in survey research has been increasing because of the proliferation of answering machines, mobile phones, and the growing use of caller ID to screen telephone calls.[5] A parent who must juggle the telephone and a half-diapered child and refuses to participate in the survey because he or she is too busy also is a nonresponse. An e-mail request sent to a potential respondent via an old unused e-mail address likewise is a nonresponse.

Refusals occur when people are unwilling to participate in the research. A research team reviewed 50 mail surveys of pediatricians conducted by the American Academy of Pediatrics (AAP) and found that response rates declined through the first decade of the 21st century. In the early years of the study period, an average 70 percent of pediatricians returned completed surveys; the response rate fell to an average 63 percent in the second half of the period.[6] No contacts and refusals can seriously bias survey data. In the case of the pediatricians, the researchers found little difference in the response rates attributable to differences in such easy-to-measure variables as age, sex, and type of membership in the AAP, leaving them to wonder whether the cause of refusals was some unknown but important difference among these doctors.

Because of this problem, researchers investigate the causes of nonresponse. For example, a study analyzed a large database collected by AT&T and found that the effort required to participate in an ongoing study contributes to the problem.[7] People tend not to respond to questions that are difficult to answer. When they are asked to participate in a long-term panel, the rate of nonresponse to individual items grows over time, and eventually some people stop participating altogether. However, eventually it becomes easier to keep answering the same kinds of panel questions, and nonresponse rates level off.

Comparing the demographics of the sample with the demographics of the target population is one means of inspecting for possible biases in response patterns. If a particular group, such as older citizens, is underrepresented or if any potential biases appear in a response pattern, additional efforts should be made to obtain data from the underrepresented segments of the population. For example, personal interviews may be used instead of telephone interviews for the underrepresented segments.

respondent error

A category of sample bias resulting from some respondent action or inaction such as nonresponse or response bias.

nonresponse error

The statistical differences between a survey that includes only those who responded and a perfect survey that would also include those who failed to respond.

nonrespondents

People who are not contacted or who refuse to cooperate in the research.

no contacts

People who are not at home or who are otherwise inaccessible on the first and second contact.

refusals

People who are unwilling to participate in a research project.

Many e-mail addresses are actually inactive. Inactive e-mails contribute to low response rates.

© YURI ARCURS/SHUTTERSTOCK

After receiving a refusal from a potential respondent, an interviewer can do nothing other than be polite. The respondent who simply is not at home when called or visited can be scheduled to be interviewed at a different time of day or on a different day of the week.

With a mail survey, the researcher never really knows whether a nonrespondent has refused to participate or is just indifferent. Researchers know that those who are most involved in an issue are more likely to respond to a mail survey. **Self-selection bias** is a problem that frequently plagues self-administered questionnaires. In a restaurant, for example, a customer on whom a waiter spilled soup, a person who was treated to a surprise dinner, or others who feel strongly about the service are more likely to complete a self-administered questionnaire left at the table than individuals who are indifferent about the restaurant. Self-selection biases distort surveys because they overrepresent extreme positions while underrepresenting responses from those who are indifferent. Several techniques will be discussed later for encouraging respondents to reply to mail and Internet surveys.

self-selection bias

A bias that occurs because people who feel strongly about a subject are more likely to respond to survey questions than people who feel indifferent about it.

Response Bias

response bias

A bias that occurs when respondents either consciously or unconsciously tend to answer questions with a certain slant that misrepresents the truth.

A **response bias** occurs when respondents tend to answer questions with a certain slant. People may consciously or unconsciously misrepresent the truth. If a distortion of measurement occurs because respondents' answers are falsified or misrepresented, either intentionally or inadvertently, the resulting sample bias will be a response bias. When researchers identify response bias, they should include a corrective measure.

Deliberate Falsification. Occasionally people deliberately give false answers. It is difficult to assess why people knowingly misrepresent answers. A response bias may occur when people misrepresent answers to appear intelligent, conceal personal information, avoid embarrassment, and so on. For example, respondents may be able to remember the total amount of money spent grocery shopping, but they may forget the exact prices of individual items that they purchased. Rather than appear ignorant or unconcerned about prices, they may provide their best estimate and not tell the truth—namely, that they cannot remember. Sometimes respondents become bored with the interview and provide answers just to get rid of the interviewer. At other times respondents try to appear well informed by providing the answers they think are expected of them. On still other occasions, they give answers simply to please the interviewer.

One explanation for conscious and deliberate misrepresentation of facts is the so-called average-person hypothesis. Individuals may prefer to be viewed as average, so they alter their responses to conform more closely to their *perception* of the average person. Average-person effects have been found in response to questions about such topics as savings account balances, car prices, voting behavior, and hospital stays.

Unconscious Misrepresentation. Even when a respondent is consciously trying to be truthful and cooperative, response bias can arise from the question format, the question content, or some other stimulus. For example, bias can be introduced by the situation in which the survey is administered. The results of two in-flight surveys concerning aircraft preference illustrate this point. Passengers flying on B-747s preferred B-747s to L-1011s (74 percent versus 19 percent), while passengers flying on L-1011s preferred L-1011s to B-747s (56 percent versus 38 percent). The difference in preferences appears to have been largely a function of the aircraft the respondents were flying on when the survey was conducted. A likely influence was the respondent's satisfaction with the plane on which he or she was flying when surveyed. In other words, in the absence of any strong preference, the respondent may simply have identified the aircraft traveled on and indicated that as his or her preference.[8] The Research Snapshot on the next page illustrates how even small wording differences can lead to different results.

Respondents who misunderstand questions may unconsciously provide biased answers. Or, they may be willing to answer but unable to do so because they have forgotten the exact details. Asking "When was the last time you attended a concert?" may result in a best-guess estimate because the respondent has forgotten the exact date.

A bias may also occur when a respondent has not thought about an unexpected question. Many respondents will answer questions even though they have given them little thought. For example, in most investigations of consumers' buying intentions, the predictability of the intention scales depends on how close the subject is to making a purchase. The intentions of subjects who have little knowledge of the brand or the store alternatives being surveyed and the intentions of

My Opinion? It Depends on Your Words

It's hard to capture the nuances of a person's opinion with a simple survey question. Word choices seem to shape some respondents' answers. Carl Bialik, a columnist for the *Wall Street Journal,* observed this problem when he looked at responses to public-opinion polls exploring differences of opinion about activities of the National Security Agency. Bialik concluded that opinions varied based on the wording of the questions.

One pollster, Rasmussen Reports, asked, "Should the National Security Agency be allowed to intercept telephone conversations between terrorism suspects in other countries and people living in the United States?" Almost two-thirds of respondents said yes. But in a Gallup survey for *USA Today* and CNN, only 51 percent favored the NSA's wiretapping of "telephone conversations between U.S. citizens living in the United States and suspected terrorists living in other countries without getting a court order allowing it to do so."

One source of the difference might be the language "people" in the first poll and "U.S. citizens" in the second. A *Wall Street Journal*/NBC poll found 53 percent favoring the wiretapping program when it involved "American citizens in the United States," while more (56 percent) favored the program in a *Washington Post*/ABC poll asking about "some people in the United States." Scott Rasmussen, president of Rasmussen Reports, also hypothesizes that results of polls investigating this issue also may be swayed by whether the questions mention the lack of search warrants for the wiretaps. In these examples, the word choices shape which aspects of a complex issue the respondents focus on.

Source: *Wall Street Journal.* Online [Only Staff-Produced Materials May Be Used] by Carl Bialik. Copyright 2006 by Dow Jones & Co Inc. Reproduced with permission of Dow Jones & Co Inc in the format Textbook via Copyright Clearance Center.

---

subjects who have not yet made any purchase plans cannot be expected to predict purchase behavior accurately.

In many cases consumers cannot adequately express their feelings in words. The cause may be questions that are vague or ambiguous. Researchers may ask someone to describe his or her frustration when using a computer. The problem is, the researcher may be interested in software problems while the respondent is thinking of hardware issues. Language differences also may be a source of misunderstanding. A survey in the Philippines found that, despite seemingly high toothpaste usage, only a tiny percentage of people responded positively when asked, "Do you use toothpaste?" As it turned out, people in the Philippines tend to refer to toothpaste by using the brand name Colgate. When researchers returned and asked, "Do you use Colgate?" the positive response rate soared.

As the time following a purchase or a shopping event increases, people become more likely to underreport information about that event. Time lapse influences people's ability to precisely remember and communicate specific factors.

Unconscious misrepresentation bias may also occur because consumers unconsciously avoid facing the realities of a future buying situation. Housing surveys record that Americans overwhelmingly continue to aspire to own detached, single-family dwellings (preferably single-level, ranch-type structures that require two to five times the amount of land per unit required for attached homes). However, builders know that *attached* housing purchases by first buyers are more common than respondents expect.

Types of Response Bias

Response bias falls into four specific categories: acquiescence bias, extremity bias, interviewer bias, and social desirability bias. These categories overlap and are not mutually exclusive. A single biased answer may be distorted for many complex reasons, some distortions being deliberate and some being unconscious misrepresentations.

Acquiescence Bias. Some respondents are very agreeable. They seem to agree to practically every statement they are asked about. A tendency to agree with all or most questions is known as **acquiescence bias**. This bias is particularly prominent in new-product research. Questions about a new-product idea generally elicit some acquiescence bias because respondents give positive connotations to most new ideas. For example, consumers responded favorably to survey questions

acquiescence bias

A tendency for respondents to agree with all or most questions asked of them in a survey.

195

about pump baseball gloves (the pump inserts air into the pocket of the glove providing more cushioning). However, when these expensive gloves hit the market, they sat on the shelves. When conducting new-product research, researchers should recognize the high likelihood of acquiescence bias.

Another form of acquiescence is evident in some people's tendency to disagree with all questions. Thus, acquiescence bias is a response bias due to the respondents' tendency to concur with a particular position.

Extremity Bias. Some individuals tend to use extremes when responding to questions; others consistently avoid extreme positions and tend to respond more neutrally. Response styles vary from person to person, and extreme responses may cause an **extremity bias** in the data.[9]

Interviewer Bias. Response bias may arise from the interplay between interviewer and respondent. If the interviewer's presence influences respondents to give untrue or modified answers, the survey will be marred by **interviewer bias**. Sometimes, respondents may give answers they believe will please the interviewer rather than the truthful responses. Respondents may wish to appear intelligent and wealthy—of course they read *Scientific American* rather than *Playboy*.

Interviewer characteristics including age, sex, style of dress, tone of voice, facial expressions, or other nonverbal characteristics may have some influence on a respondent's answers. If an interviewer smiles and makes a positive statement after a respondent's answers, the respondent will be more likely to give similar responses. In a research study on sexual harassment against saleswomen, male interviewers might not obtain as candid responses from saleswomen as female interviewers would. Thus, interviewer techniques in which the interviewer remains unseen have an advantage of preventing this particular type of interviewer bias.

Many interviewers, contrary to instructions, shorten or rephrase questions to suit their needs. A researcher doing survey research for major U.S. newspapers asked a question about the Nazi holocaust in the following fashion:

"Do you believe it seems possible or does it seem impossible to you that the Nazi Extermination of the Jews never happened?"[10]

Obviously, this question is confusing and yielded a result that should be meaningless, but instead could be interpreted as suggesting that nearly 1 in 4 respondents doubted that the holocaust ever occurred.

This potential influence on responses can be avoided to some extent if interviewers receive training and supervision that emphasize the necessity of appearing neutral. Also, researchers with strong opinions may be steered toward other projects or be made aware that misleading results are unethical and likely do not further their cause in the long run.

The interviewer may also encourage error if a survey takes too long to complete. If interviews go on too long, respondents may feel that time is being wasted. They may answer as abruptly as possible with little forethought.

Social Desirability Bias. A **social desirability bias** may occur either consciously or unconsciously because the respondent wishes to create a favorable impression or save face in the presence of an

---

extremity bias

A category of response bias that results because some individuals tend to use extremes when responding to questions.

interviewer bias

A response bias that occurs because the presence of the interviewer influences respondents' answers.

social desirability bias

Bias in responses caused by respondents' desire, either conscious or unconscious, to gain prestige or appear in a different social role.

The more people are susceptible to interpersonal influence, the more likely a response bias will occur. One example of this can be found in adolescents' buying behavior.

© JEFF GREENBERG/PHOTOEDIT

interviewer. Incomes may be inflated, education overstated, or perceived respectable answers given to gain prestige. In contrast, answers to questions that seek factual information or responses about matters of public knowledge (zip code, number of children, and so on) usually are quite accurate. An interviewer's presence may increase a respondent's tendency to give inaccurate answers to sensitive questions such as "Did you vote in the last election?," "Do you have termites or roaches in your home?," or "Do you color your hair?"

The social desirability bias is especially significant in the case of research that addresses sensitive or personal topics, including respondents' sexual behavior. A group of researchers recently evaluated responses to questions about homosexual sexual activity, collected by NORC's long-running General Social Survey.[11] The researchers found that over time, as attitudes toward homosexual conduct have softened, the frequency of repeated female-female sexual contacts increased dramatically, suggesting the possibility that reporting levels have been subject to social desirability bias. However, the researchers noted that rates of male-male sexual contact were fairly steady over the period and that the rate of change for female-female sexual contact persisted even when adjusted for measures of greater tolerance. This evidence suggests that the data reflect more phenomena than mere social desirability bias.

■ ADMINISTRATIVE ERROR

The result of improper administration or execution of the research task is called an **administrative error**. Administrative errors are caused by carelessness, confusion, neglect, omission, or some other blunder. Four types of administrative error are data-processing error, sample selection error, interviewer error, and interviewer cheating.

Data-Processing Error

Processing data by computer, like any arithmetic or procedural process, is subject to error because data must be edited, coded, and entered into the computer by people. The accuracy of data processed by computer depends on correct data entry and programming. **Data-processing error** can be minimized by establishing careful procedures for verifying each step in the data-processing stage.

Sample Selection Error

Many kinds of error involve failure to select a representative sample. **Sample selection error** is systematic error that results in an unrepresentative sample because of an error in either the sample design or the execution of the sampling procedure. Executing a sampling plan free of procedural error is difficult. A firm that selects its sample from the phone book will have some systematic error, because unlisted numbers are not included. Stopping respondents during daytime hours in shopping centers excludes working people who shop by mail, Internet, or telephone. In other cases, researchers interview the wrong person. Consider a political pollster who uses random-digit dialing to select a sample, rather than a list of registered voters. Unregistered 17-year-olds may be willing to give their opinions, but they are the wrong people to ask because they cannot vote.

administrative error

An error caused by the improper administration or execution of the research task.

data-processing error

A category of administrative error that occurs because of incorrect data entry, incorrect computer programming, or other procedural errors during data analysis.

sample selection error

An administrative error caused by improper sample design or sampling procedure execution.

One problem with Web-based surveys is that there is no way of knowing who exactly responded to the questionnaire.

© BANANA STOCK/JUPITER IMAGES

The "Mere-Measurement" Effect

Will you eat high-fat food this week? Will you floss your teeth? Researchers have found that answering survey questions like these can actually shift your behavior. This influence, called the mere-measurement effect, means that simply answering a question about intentions will increase the likelihood of the underlying behavior—*if* the behavior is seen as socially desirable. If the behavior is considered undesirable, answering the question tends to decrease the likelihood of the behavior.

To test this, a group of business school professors conducted a series of surveys in which certain subjects were asked about their intentions to eat fatty food or to floss. In follow-up surveys, they found that subjects ate less fatty food and flossed more often if they were asked about those behaviors. However, the mere-measurement effect did not occur if the surveys indicated that they were sponsored by groups that would be likely to want to persuade the subjects (in this case, the American Fruit Growers Association and the Association of Dental Products Manufacturers). In fact, subjects *decreased* their frequency of flossing if they took the supposedly manipulative survey that asked about flossing. Follow-up experiments verified that changes to behavior were genuine, not merely a survey bias.

The researchers propose that the mere-measurement effect occurs because subjects of a survey generally do not think the questions are an attempt to persuade them. If they receive information that puts them on their guard against persuasion, the mere-measurement effect is lessened and sometimes even generates the opposite behavior. Their results suggest a need for caution when surveys attempt to predict future behavior.

Source: Williams, Patti, Gavan J. Fitzsimons, Lauren G. Block, "When Consumers Do Not Recognize 'Benign' Intention Questions as Persuasion Attempts," © 2004 by *Journal of Consumer Research*, Inc., 31, (December 2004). All rights reserved. Reprinted with permission by The University of Chicago Press.

Interviewer Error

interviewer error

Mistakes made by interviewers failing to record survey responses correctly.

Interviewers' abilities vary considerably. **Interviewer error** is introduced when interviewers record answers but check the wrong response or are unable to write fast enough to record answers verbatim. Also, selective perception may cause interviewers to misrecord data that do not support their own attitudes and opinions.

Interviewer Cheating

interviewer cheating

The practice of filling in fake answers or falsifying questionnaires while working as an interviewer.

Interviewer cheating occurs when an interviewer falsifies entire questionnaires or fills in answers to questions that have been intentionally skipped. Some interviewers cheat to finish an interview as quickly as possible or to avoid questions about sensitive topics.

If interviewers are suspected of faking questionnaires, they should be told that a small percentage of respondents will be called back to confirm whether the initial interview was actually conducted. This practice should discourage interviewers from cheating. The term *curb-stoning* is sometimes used to refer to interviewers filling in responses for respondents that do not really exist.

Rule-of-Thumb Estimates for Systematic Error

The techniques for estimating systematic, or nonsampling, error are less precise than many sample statistics. Researchers have established experience-based, conservative rules of thumb based on experience to estimate systematic error. In the case of consumer research, experienced researchers might determine that only a certain percentage of people who say they will definitely buy a new product actually do so. Evidence for a mere-measurement effect (see the Research Snapshot above) suggests that in some situations, researchers might conclude that respondents' own buying behavior will exaggerate overall sales. Thus, researchers often present actual survey findings *and* their interpretations of estimated purchase response based on estimates of nonsampling error. For example, one pay-per-view cable TV company surveys geographic areas it plans to enter and estimates the number of people who indicate they will subscribe to its service. The company knocks down the percentage by a "ballpark 10 percent" because experience in other geographic areas has indicated that there is a systematic upward bias of 10 percent on this intentions question.

What Can Be Done to Reduce Survey Error?

Now that we have examined the sources of error in surveys, you may have lost some of your optimism about survey research. Don't be discouraged! The discussion emphasized the bad news because it is important for marketing managers to realize that surveys are not a panacea. There are, however, ways to handle and reduce survey errors. For example, Chapter 15 on questionnaire design discusses the reduction of response bias; Chapters 16 and 17 discuss the reduction of sample selection and random sampling error. Indeed, much of the remainder of this book discusses various techniques for reducing bias in marketing research. The good news lies ahead!

Categorizing Survey Research Methods

Now that we have discussed some advantages and disadvantages of surveys in general, we turn to a discussion of classification of surveys according to several criteria. Surveys may be classified based on the method of communication, the degrees of structure and disguise in the questionnaire, and the time frame in which the data are gathered (temporal classification). Chapter 9 classifies surveys according to method of communicating with the respondent, covering topics such as personal interviews, telephone interviews, mail surveys, and Internet surveys. The classifications based on structure and disguise and on time frame will be discussed in the remainder of this chapter.

Structured and Disguised Questions

In designing a questionnaire (or an *interview schedule*), the researcher must decide how much structure or standardization is needed.[12] A **structured question** limits the number of allowable responses. For example, the respondent may be instructed to choose one alternative response such as "under 18," "18–35," or "over 35" to indicate his or her age. An **unstructured question** does not restrict the respondent's answers. An open-ended, unstructured question such as "Why do you shop at Wal-Mart?" allows the respondent considerable freedom in answering.

The researcher must also decide whether to use **undisguised questions** or **disguised questions**. A straightforward, or undisguised, question such as "Do you have dandruff problems?" assumes that the respondent is willing to reveal the information. However, researchers know that some questions are threatening to a person's ego, prestige, or self-concept. So, they have designed a number of indirect techniques of questioning to disguise the purpose of the study.

Questionnaires can be categorized by their degree of structure and degree of disguise. For example, interviews in exploratory research might use *unstructured-disguised* questionnaires. The projective techniques discussed in an earlier chapter fall into this category. Other classifications are *structured-undisguised, unstructured-undisguised,* and *structured-disguised*. These classifications have two limitations: First, the degree of structure and the degree of disguise vary; they are not clear-cut categories. Second, most surveys are hybrids, asking both structured and unstructured questions. Recognizing the degrees of structure and disguise necessary to meet survey objectives will help in the selection of the appropriate communication medium for conducting the survey.

structured question

A question that imposes a limit on the number of allowable responses.

unstructured question

A question that does not restrict the respondents' answers.

undisguised questions

Straightforward questions that assume the respondent is willing to answer.

disguised questions

Indirect questions that assume the purpose of the study must be hidden from the respondent.

Temporal Classification

Although most surveys are for individual research projects conducted only once over a short time period, other projects require multiple surveys over a long period. Thus, surveys can be classified on a temporal basis.

■ CROSS-SECTIONAL STUDIES

In 2006, the *Wall Street Journal* teamed up with Harris Interactive to ask people about their New Year's resolutions.[13] The survey asked people whether they had made resolutions the year before, which resolutions they had succeeded in keeping, and what they had resolved for the coming year. The results indicated that 43 percent of men and 52 percent of women made resolutions for 2006, even though less than half had kept their resolutions from the year before. This was a **cross-sectional study** because it collected the data at a single point in time. Such a study samples various segments of the population to investigate relationships among variables by cross-tabulation. Most marketing research surveys fall into this category, particularly those that deal with market segmentation.

cross-sectional study

A study in which various segments of a population are sampled and data are collected at a single moment in time.

The typical method of analyzing a cross-sectional survey is to divide the sample into appropriate subgroups. For example, if a winery expects income levels to influence attitudes toward wines, the data are broken down into subgroups based on income and analyzed to reveal similarities or differences among the income subgroups.

■ LONGITUDINAL STUDIES

longitudinal study

A survey of respondents at different times, thus allowing analysis of response continuity and changes over time.

In a **longitudinal study** respondents are questioned at multiple points in time. The purpose of longitudinal studies is to examine continuity of response and to observe changes that occur over time. Many syndicated polling services, such as Gallup, conduct regular polls. For example, the Bureau of Labor Statistics conducts the National Longitudinal Survey of Youth, interviewing the same sample of individuals repeatedly since 1979. (Respondents, who were "youth" at the beginning of the study, are now in their forties.) Research scientist Jay Zagorsky recently analyzed the longitudinal data from that study to determine that those who married and stayed with their spouse accumulated almost twice as much wealth as single and divorced people in the study.[14] The *Yankelovich MONITOR* has been tracking American values and attitudes for more than thirty years. This survey is an example of a longitudinal study that uses successive samples; its researchers survey several different samples at different times. Longitudinal studies of this type are sometimes called *cohort studies,* because similar groups of people who share a certain experience during the same time interval (cohorts) are expected to be included in each sample. Exhibit 8.2 illustrates the results of a longitudinal study by Harris Interactive, which since 1966 has been asking five questions related to powerlessness and isolation to create an "alienation index."

TOTHEPOINT

Time is but the stream I go a-fishing in.

—Henry David Thoreau

EXHIBIT 8.2
Longitudinal Research from a Harris Poll

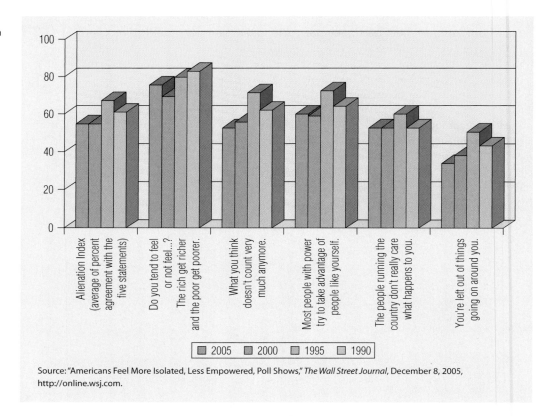

Source: "Americans Feel More Isolated, Less Empowered, Poll Shows," *The Wall Street Journal*, December 8, 2005, http://online.wsj.com.

In applied marketing research, a longitudinal study that uses successive samples is called a **tracking study** because successive waves are designed to compare trends and identify changes in variables such as consumer satisfaction, brand image, or advertising awareness. These studies are useful for assessing aggregate trends but do not allow for tracking changes in individuals over time.

Conducting surveys in waves with two or more sample groups avoids the problem of response bias resulting from a prior interview. A respondent who was interviewed in an earlier survey about a certain brand may become more aware of the brand or pay more attention to its advertising after being interviewed. Using different samples eliminates this problem. However, researchers can never be sure whether the changes in the variable being measured are due to a different sample or to an actual change in the variable over time.

Consumer Panel

A longitudinal study that gathers data from the same sample of individuals or households over time is called a **consumer panel**. Consider the packaged-goods marketer that wishes to learn about brand-switching behavior. A consumer panel that consists of a group of people who record their purchasing habits in a diary over time will provide the manager with a continuous stream of information about the brand and product class. Diary data that are recorded regularly over an extended period enable the researcher to track repeat-purchase behavior and changes in purchasing habits that occur in response to changes in price, special promotions, or other aspects of marketing strategy.

Panel members may be contacted by telephone, in a personal interview, by mail questionnaire, or by e-mail. Typically respondents complete media exposure or purchase diaries and mail them back to the survey organization. If the panel members have agreed to field test new products, face-to-face or telephone interviews may be required. The nature of the problem dictates which communication method to use.

Because establishing and maintaining a panel is expensive, panels often are managed by contractors who offer their services to many organizations. A number of commercial firms, such as National Family Opinion (NFO), Inc., Market Research Corporation of America, and Consumer Mail Panels, Inc., specialize in maintaining consumer panels. In recent years Internet panels have grown in popularity. Internet panel companies like Qualtrics and Zoomerang also have access to extensive consumer panels. Researchers can obtain a sample using one of these panels for a fee. The more specific and the longer time period needed, the more expensive the sample becomes. Clients can share expenses with other clients to acquire longitudinal data at a reasonable cost. When this occurs, panel members may be asked questions about a number of product classes.

The first questionnaire a panel member is asked to complete typically includes questions about product ownership, product usage, pets, family members, and demographic data. The purpose of such a questionnaire is to gather the behavioral and demographic data that will be used to identify heavy buyers, difficult-to-reach customers, and so on for future surveys. Individuals who serve as members of consumer panels usually are compensated with cash, attractive gifts, or the chance to win a sweepstakes.

Marketers whose products are purchased by few households find panels an economical means of reaching respondents who own their products. A two-stage process typically is used. A panel composed of around 15,000 households can be screened with a one-question statement attached to another project. For example, a question in an NFO questionnaire screens for ownership of certain uncommon products, such as snowmobiles and motorcycles. This information is stored in a database. Then households with the unusual item can be sampled again with a longer questionnaire.

Total Quality Management and Customer Satisfaction Surveys

Total quality management is a business strategy that emphasizes market-driven quality as a top priority. Total quality management involves implementing and adjusting the firm's business activities to assure customers' satisfaction with the quality of goods and services.

tracking study

A type of longitudinal study that uses successive samples to compare trends and identify changes in variables such as consumer satisfaction, brand image, or advertising awareness.

consumer panel

A longitudinal survey of the same sample of individuals or households to record their attitudes, behavior, or purchasing habits over time.

total quality management

A business philosophy that emphasizes market-driven quality as a top organizational priority.

Many U.S. organizations adopted total quality management in the 1980s when an increase in high-quality foreign competition challenged their former dominance. Today companies continue to recognize the need for total quality management programs. Executives and production workers are sometimes too far removed from the customer. Companies need a means to bridge this gap with feedback about quality of goods and services. This means marketing research. Of course, these programs are not the exclusive domain of marketing researchers. However, in an organization driven by the quality concept, marketing research plays an important role in the management of total product quality.

What Is Quality?

Organizations used to define quality by engineering standards. Most companies no longer see quality that way. Some managers say that having a quality product means that the good or service conforms to consumers' requirements, that the product is acceptable. Effective executives who subscribe to a total quality management philosophy, however, believe that the product's quality must go beyond acceptability for a given price range. Rather than merely being relieved that nothing went wrong, consumers should experience some delightful surprises or reap some unexpected benefits. In other words, quality assurance is more than just meeting minimum standards. The level of quality is the degree to which a good or service corresponds to buyers' expectations.

Obviously, an S-type Jaguar does not compete with a Nissan Altima. Buyers of these automobiles are in different market segments, and their expectations of quality differ widely. Nevertheless, managers at Jaguar and Nissan try to establish the quality levels their target markets expect and then to produce and market products that continually surpass expectations.

Internal and External Customers

Organizations that have adopted the total quality management philosophy believe that a focus on customers must include more than external customers. Like Arbor, Inc., they believe that everyone in the organization has customers.

> *Every person, in every department, and at every level, has a customer. The customer is anyone to whom an individual provides service, information, support, or product. The customer may be another employee or department (internal) or outside the company (external).*[15]

Total quality management programs work most effectively when every employee knows exactly who his or her customers are and what output internal and external customers expect. Also, it is important to know how customers perceive their needs are being met. All too often differences between perceptions and reality are not understood.

Implementing Total Quality Management

Implementing a total quality management program requires considerable survey research. A firm must routinely ask customers to rate it against its competitors. It must periodically measure employee knowledge, attitudes, and expectations. It must monitor company performance against benchmark standards. It must determine whether customers found any delightful surprises or major disappointments. In other words, a total quality management strategy expresses the conviction that to improve quality, an organization must regularly conduct surveys to evaluate quality improvement.

Exhibit 8.3 illustrates the total quality management process. The exhibit shows that overall tracking of quality improvement requires longitudinal research. The process begins with a *commitment and exploration stage,* during which management makes a commitment to total quality assurance and marketing researchers explore external and internal customers' needs and beliefs. The research must discover what product features customers value, what problems customers

EXHIBIT 8.3 Longitudinal Research for Total Quality Management

Time	Marketing Research Activity with External Consumers (Customers)	Marketing Management Activity	Marketing Research Activity with Internal Consumers (Employees)
Time 1 **Commitment and exploration stage**	Exploratory study to determine the quality the customer wants, discover customer problems, and identify the importance of specific product attributes.	Establish marketing objective that the customer should define quality.	Exploratory study to determine (1) whether internal customers, such as service employees, are aware of the need for service quality as a major means to achieve customer satisfaction and (2) whether they know the quality standards for their jobs. Establish whether employees are motivated and trained. Identify roadblocks that prevent employees from meeting customer needs.
Time 2 **Benchmarking stage**	Benchmarking study to measure overall satisfaction and quality ratings of specific attributes.	Identify brand's position relative to competitors' satisfaction and quality rating; establish standards for customer satisfaction.	Benchmarking to measure employees' actual performance and perceptions about performance.
Time 3 **Initial quality improvement stage**	Tracking wave 1 to measure trends in satisfaction and quality ratings.	Improve quality; reward performance.	Tracking wave 1 to measure and compare what is actually happening with what should be happening. Establish whether the company is conforming to its quality standards.
Time 4 **Continuous quality improvement**	Tracking wave 2 to measure trends in satisfaction and quality ratings.	Improve quality; reward performance.	Tracking wave 2 to measure trends in quality improvement.

are having with the product, what aspects of product operation or customer service have disappointed customers, what the company is doing right, and what the company may be doing wrong.

After internal and external customers' problems and desires have been identified, the *benchmarking stage* begins. Research must establish quantitative measures that can serve as benchmarks or points of comparison against which to evaluate future efforts. The surveys must establish initial measures of overall satisfaction, of the frequency of customer problems, and of quality ratings for specific attributes. Researchers must identify the company's or brand's position relative to competitors' quality positions. For example, when Anthony Balzarini became food-service manager at Empire Health Services in Spokane, Washington, he became responsible for serving meals to the patients of the company's two hospitals, plus retail food service (sales to visitors and employees who eat in the hospitals). He began tracking quality according to several measures, including satisfaction scores on patient surveys and sales volume and revenue on the retail side. Sales measurements include comparing the average sale with other locations, including restaurants, in the Spokane area.[16]

The *initial quality improvement* stage establishes a quality improvement process within the organization. Management and employees must translate quality issues into the internal vocabulary of the organization. The company must establish performance standards and expectations for improvement. For Balzarini, this stage included training food-service employees in providing patient service. He began holding meetings twice daily to identify any problems to be resolved. Managers were each assigned to one floor of the hospital and charged with building a close working relationship with the nursing staff there. They are expected to visit their floor every week and conduct fifteen interviews with patients to learn about what they like and dislike. On the retail side, the manager is expected to revise menus every twelve weeks to offer more variety. Waste is literally weighed and categorized to identify which types of food are rejected by patients and customers.

After managers and employees have set quality objectives and implemented procedures and standards, the firm continues to track satisfaction and quality ratings in successive waves. The purpose of tracking wave 1 is to measure trends in satisfaction and quality ratings. Marketing researchers determine whether the organization is meeting customer needs as specified by quantitative standards. At one of Empire's two hospitals, one of the food-service managers learned that a patient on a liquid diet disliked the broth he was being served. An investigation showed that the recipe had been changed, and a taste test confirmed that the original recipe was superior, so the hospital switched back to the original recipe.

The next stage, *continuous quality improvement,* consists of many consecutive waves with the same purpose—to improve over the previous period. Continuous quality improvement requires that management allow employees to initiate problem solving without a lot of red tape. Employees should be able to initiate proactive communications with consumers. In tracking wave 2, management compares results with those of earlier stages. Quality improvement management continues. At Empire, improvements have been reflected in rising patient satisfaction scores and growing sales in retail operations.

Management must also reward performance. At Empire, Balzarini set up a program called "You Rock." Any employee who observes an excellent action by another employee, beyond mere job requirements, acknowledges the good work with a card awarding points redeemable in the hospitals' retail areas. Balzarini also sends weekly thank-you cards to workers who showed outstanding performance.

Exhibit 8.3 shows that total quality management programs measure performance against *customers'* standards—not against standards determined by quality engineers within the company. All changes within the organization are oriented toward improvement of customers' perceptions of quality. The exhibit indicates the need for integration of establishing consumer requirements, quantifying benchmark measures, setting objectives, conducting marketing research studies, and making adjustments in the organization to improve quality. Continuous quality improvement is an ongoing process.

The activities outlined in Exhibit 8.3 apply to marketers of both goods and services. However, service products and customer services offered along with goods have some distinctive aspects. We will first discuss the quality of goods and then consider the quality of services.

In general, marketers of consumer and industrial goods track customer satisfaction to investigate customer perceptions of product quality by measuring perceptions of the product characteristics listed in Exhibit 8.4.[17] These studies measure whether a firm's perceptions about product characteristics conform to customers' expectations and how these perceptions change over time. For example, any customer satisfaction survey will investigate a good's performance by asking, "How well does the product perform its core function?" To determine the quality of a recycling lawn mower, a researcher might ask, "How well does the mower cut grass and eliminate the need for bagging clippings?" The researcher may ask questions to determine whether the product's quality of performance was a delightful surprise, something well beyond expected performance. Similar questions will cover the other major product characteristics.

Measuring service quality involves comparing expectations with performance. Consumers who perceive high service quality believe service providers matched their expectations. Time after time, studies have shown differences between what customers expected and what the service frontline, contact personnel delivered. Marketers who stress service quality strategies focus on the service encounter because service quality depends on what takes place during the service encounter.

EXHIBIT 8.4

Quality Dimensions for Goods and Services

Quality Dimension	Characteristic	Example
Goods		
Performance	The product performs its core function.	A razor gives a close shave.
Features	The product has auxiliary dimensions that provide secondary benefits.	A motor oil comes in a convenient package.
Conformance with specifications	There is a low incidence of defects. Product attributes are what they are supposed to be.	A wine labeled Napa Valley is made predominantly from grapes grown there (75% by law).
Reliability	The product performs dependably.	A lawn mower works properly each time it is used.
Durability	The economic life of the product is within an acceptable range.	A motorcycle runs fine for many years.
Serviceability	The system for servicing the product is efficient, competent, and convenient.	A computer software manufacturer maintains a toll-free phone number staffed by technical people who can answer questions quickly and accurately.
Aesthetic design	The product's design makes it look and feel like a quality product.	A snowmobile is aerodynamic.
Services		
Access	Contact with service personnel is easy.	A visit to the dentist does not involve a long wait.
Communication	The customer is informed and understands the service and how much it will cost.	A computer technician explains needed repairs without using overly technical terms.
Competence	The service providers have the required skills.	A tax accountant has a CPA certification.
Courtesy	Personnel are polite and friendly.	Bank tellers smile and wish the customer a "good day" at the close of each transaction.
Reliability	The service is performed consistently and personnel are dependable.	Employees of the office cleaning service arrive on schedule every Friday evening after working hours.
Credibility	Service providers have integrity and the necessary experience to serve.	The doctor who is performing a heart transplant is trustworthy and believable.

Source: Adapted from David A. Aaker, *Managing Brand Equity* (New York: Macmillan, 1991), pp. 90–95.

In organizations that wish to improve service quality, managers must identify and analyze customer service needs and then establish specifications for the level of service. They must then train frontline personnel and give them the responsibility for quality service. Frontline personnel need to be motivated and encouraged to deliver the service according to these specifications. Finally, regular surveys with both external customers and internal employees measure results against standards.

Marketers investigate service quality to measure customer satisfaction and perceived quality in terms of the service attributes listed in Exhibit 8.4. Considerations in the actual measurement of quality of goods and service delivery are further addressed in later chapters.

- Standard survey research works best for implementing a descriptive research design. In particular, survey research is very useful for describing:
  - Consumer beliefs
  - Consumer attitudes
  - Consumer opinions—particularly of a nonsensitive nature
  - Characteristics of respondents such as demographics and lifestyles
- Avoid studying sensitive topics with survey research approaches.

- The extent to which respondents will actually behave as they describe in survey research is often overstated. When measuring future behavior such as purchase intentions, some researchers routinely apply a rule of thumb that subtracts 10 percent from the stated probability.
- Quality can only be studied accurately by obtaining input from consumers. Ultimately, consumers determine quality.

© GEORGE DOYLE & CIARAN GRIFFIN

Summary

1. Define surveys and describe the type of information that may be gathered in a survey. A *survey* is defined as a method of collecting primary data based on communication with a representative sample of individuals. Members of the representative sample are known as respondents. The term *sample survey* is often used because a survey is expected to obtain a representative sample of the target population. The typical survey is part of a descriptive research design with the objective of measuring awareness, product knowledge, brand usage behavior, opinions, attitudes, purchasing behavior, and identifying characteristics of target markets.

2. Explain the advantages and disadvantages of surveys. The survey is a common tool for asking respondents questions. When executed properly, surveys provide quick, inexpensive, and accurate information for a variety of objectives. When executed improperly, surveys can provide misleading information that can precipitate poor decision making. Each survey data collection tool has unique disadvantages that lead to different types of error. However, surveys are particularly disadvantageous when the researcher is interested in actual behavior. While behavior can be observed directly with little error, the error introduced by respondents having to remember what they've done or being unwilling to report what they've done is a significant source of error.

3. Identify sources of error in survey research. Two major forms of error are common in survey research. The first, random sampling error, is caused by chance variation and results in a sample that is not absolutely representative of the target population. Such errors are inevitable, but they can be predicted using the statistical methods discussed in later chapters on sampling. The second major category of error, systematic error, takes several forms. Nonresponse error is caused by subjects' failing to respond to a survey. This type of error can be reduced by comparing the demographics of the sample population with those of the target population and making a special effort to contact underrepresented groups. In addition, response bias occurs when a response to a questionnaire is falsified or misrepresented, either intentionally or inadvertently. There are four specific categories of response bias: acquiescence bias, extremity bias, interviewer bias, and social desirability bias. An additional source of survey error comes from administrative problems such as inconsistencies in interviewers' abilities, cheating, coding mistakes, and so forth.

4. Distinguish among the various categories of surveys. Surveys may be classified according to methods of communication, by the degrees of structure and disguise in the questionnaires, and on a temporal basis. Questionnaires may be structured, with limited choices of responses, or unstructured, to allow open-ended responses. Disguised questions may be used to probe sensitive subjects. Surveys may consider the population at a given moment or follow trends over a period of time. The first approach, the cross-sectional study, usually is intended to separate the population into meaningful subgroups. The second type of study, the longitudinal study, can reveal important population changes over time. Longitudinal studies may involve contacting different sets of respondents or the same ones repeatedly. One form of longitudinal study is the consumer panel. Consumer panels are expensive to conduct, so firms often hire contractors who provide services to many companies, thus spreading costs over many clients.

5. Discuss the importance of survey research to total quality management programs. Total quality management is the process of implementing and adjusting a firm's business strategy to assure customers' satisfaction with the quality of goods or services. The level of quality is the degree to which a good or service corresponds to buyers' expectations. Marketing research provides companies with feedback about the quality of goods and services. Implementing a total quality management program requires considerable survey research, conducted routinely, to ask customers to rate a company against its competitors. It also measures employee attitudes and monitors company performance against benchmark standards. After identifying customer problems and desires, the firm tracks satisfaction and quality ratings in successive waves. Total quality management research is an ongoing process for continuous quality improvement that works for both marketers of goods and service providers.

Key Terms and Concepts

acquiescence bias, *195*	no contacts, *193*	self-selection bias, *194*
administrative error, *197*	nonrespondents, *193*	social desirability bias, *196*
consumer panel, *201*	nonresponse error, *193*	structured question, *199*
cross-sectional study, *200*	random sampling error, *192*	survey, *189*
data processing error, *197*	refusals, *193*	systematic error, *192*
disguised questions, *199*	respondent error, *193*	total quality management, *201*
extremity bias, *196*	respondents, *189*	tracking study, *201*
interviewer bias, *196*	response bias, *194*	undisguised questions, *199*
interviewer cheating, *198*	sample bias, *192*	unstructured question, *199*
interviewer error, *198*	sample selection error, *197*	
longitudinal study, *200*	sample survey, *189*	

Questions for Review and Critical Thinking

1. Name several nonbusiness applications of survey research.
2. What is *self-selection bias?*
3. Do surveys tend to gather qualitative or quantitative data? What types of information are commonly measured with surveys?
4. Give an example of each type of error listed in Exhibit 8.1.
5. In a survey, chief executive officers (CEOs) indicated that they would prefer to relocate their businesses to Atlanta (first choice), San Diego, Tampa, Los Angeles, or Boston. The CEOs who said they were going to build the required office space in the following year were asked where they were going to build. They indicated they were going to build in New York, Los Angeles, San Francisco, or Chicago. Explain the difference.
6. What potential sources of error might be associated with the following situations?
   a. In a survey of frequent fliers age 50 and older, researchers concluded that price does not play a significant role in airline travel because only 25 percent of the respondents check off price as the most important consideration in determining where and how they travel, while 35 percent rate price as being unimportant.
   b. A survey of voters finds that most respondents do not like negative political ads—that is, advertising by one political candidate that criticizes or exposes secrets about the opponent's "dirty laundry."
   c. Researchers who must conduct a 45-minute personal interview decide to offer $10 to each respondent because they

   believe that people who will sell their opinions are more typical than someone who will talk to a stranger for 45 minutes.
   d. A company's sales representatives are asked what percentage of the time they spend making presentations to prospects, traveling, talking on the telephone, participating in meetings, working on the computer, and engaging in other on-the-job activities.
   e. A survey comes with a water hardness packet to test the hardness of the water in a respondent's home. The packet includes a color chart and a plastic strip to dip into hot water. The respondent is given instructions in six steps on how to compare the color of the plastic strip with the color chart that indicates water hardness.
7. A sample of 14-year-old schoolchildren is asked if they have ever smoked a cigarette. The students are asked to respond orally in the presence of other students. What types of error might enter into this process?
8. A survey conducted by the National Endowment for the Arts asked, "Have you read a book within the last year?" What response bias might arise from this question?
9. Name some common objectives of cross-sectional surveys.
10. Give an example of a political situation in which longitudinal research might be useful. Name some common objectives for a longitudinal study in a business situation.
11. What are the advantages and disadvantages of using consumer panels?

12. Page through your local newspaper to find some stories derived from survey research results. Was the study's methodology appropriate? Could the research have been termed *advocacy research?*

13. Suppose you are the marketing research director for your state's tourism bureau. Assess the state's information needs, and identify the information you will collect in a survey of tourists who visit your state.

14. ETHICS A researcher sends out 2,000 questionnaires via e-mail. Fifty are returned because the addresses are inaccurate. Of the 1,950 delivered questionnaires, 100 are completed and e-mailed back. However, 40 of these respondents wrote that they did not want to participate in the survey. The researcher indicates the response rate was 5.0 percent. Is this the right thing to do?

15. 'NET Located at the University of Connecticut, the Roper Center is the largest library of public opinion data in the world. An online polling magazine and the methodology and findings of many surveys may be found at http://www.ropercenter.uconn.edu. Report on an article or study of your choice.

Research Activities

1. 'NET Go to Survey Monkey (http://www.surveymonkey.com). Then, visit http://www.mysurvey.com. What is the difference between the two Web sites in terms of the services they provide to users?

2. 'NET The National Longitudinal Surveys (NLS) conducted by the Bureau of Labor Statistics provide data on the labor force experience (current labor force and employment status, work history, and characteristics of current or last job) of five groups of the U.S. population. Go to http://www.bls.gov/opub/hom/ homtoc.htm to learn about the objectives and methodology for this study. How accurate do you believe the information reported here really is? What sources of error might be present in the data?

3. Ask a small sample of students at your local university to report their GPA. Then, try to find the average GPA of students at your school. If you have to, ask several professors to give their opinion. Does it seem that the student data are subject to error? Explain.

Case 8.1 SAT and ACT Writing Tests

© GETTY IMAGES/ PHOTODISC GREEN

The SAT and ACT college entrance exams once were completely multiple-choice, but both tests recently began including an essay portion (which is optional for the ACT). Some researchers have investigated how the essay tests are used by one group they serve: the admissions offices of the colleges that look at test results during the selection process.[18]

Early survey research suggests that some admissions officers harbor doubts about the essay tests. ACT, Inc. reported that among the schools it surveyed, only about one-fifth are requiring that applicants take the writing portion of the exam. Another one-fifth merely recommend (but don't require) the essay.

Kaplan, Inc., which markets test preparation services, conducted surveys as well. Kaplan asked 374 colleges whether they would be using the SAT writing test in screening candidates. Almost half (47 percent) said they would not use the essay at all. Another 22 percent said they would use it but give it less weight than the math and verbal SAT scores.

Kaplan also surveys students who take the exams for which it provides training. On its Web site, the company says, "More than 25 percent of students ran out of time on the essay!"

Questions

1. What survey objectives would ACT have in asking colleges how they use its essay test? What objectives would Kaplan have for its survey research?

2. If you were a marketer for the College Board (the SAT's company) or ACT, Inc., what further information would you want to gather after receiving the results described here?

3. What sources of error or response bias might be present in the surveys described here?

Case 8.2 Turner's Department Store

© GETTY IMAGES/ PHOTODISC GREEN

Turner's had been in business for 47 years. The first store was located downtown, but the organization had been expanding over the years. The local department store chain operated 10 department stores and junior department stores, ranging in size from 10,000 to 60,000 square feet. All stores were located in a single metropolitan area with a population of approximately 600,000 people. The firm's volume strength was in soft goods, although it also handled housewares and small appliances in all stores as well as major appliances in some stores. Price savings on name brands were the primary emphasis of Turner's merchandising strategy.

Turner's was considering its first major venture into survey research. Mr. Clay Turner, executive vice president, had indicated that "we want to find out what customers and noncustomers think about us and to learn what directions we may take to gain a bigger share of the market." He sent a list of research needs (see Case Exhibit 8.2–1) to several marketing research consultants.

Questions

1. Has the marketing research problem been adequately defined?
2. What type of survey would you recommend?
3. What sources of survey error are most likely in this project?
4. Prepare a brief research proposal for this project.

Note: Names are fictitious to ensure confidentiality.

CASE EXHIBIT 8.2–1 **Research Needs for Turner's Department Stores**

We're not looking for praise or compliments, but as honest an appraisal as possible. The questions contained here are merely suggestions and may be amplified, condensed, or changed as need be to arrive at a summary that can be acted on.

What Turner's wants to know is "How do people look upon Turner's, and what should we do to merit more of their patronage?" We will appreciate having from you

1. Your suggested questionnaire
2. Sampling size or sizes
3. Degree of expected accuracy
4. Cost or costs
5. Time frame in which the study may be completed
6. Type of summary or summaries to be presented on completion
7. Recommendations for action

Perhaps the study should encompass all or part of the following:

1. A sampling sufficient to give an overall picture
2. The sampling to be divided as equally as possible among people who shop frequently at Turner's and those who shop at Turner's occasionally, seldom, or never
3. The sampling to be done at various income levels, as equitably as possible in relationship of the specific income levels to the total, perhaps
   $8,000–$15,000
   $15,001–$35,000
   $35,001–$55,000
   $55,001–$75,000
   Over $75,000
4. The sampling to be done by age level breakdown: under 25, 25–35, 35–44, over 44
5. The sampling to include family composition: ages of children, if any, and number of boys and girls
6. To determine from those who shop often or occasionally at Turner's, what departments they depend on. (Examples: men's apparel; women's apparel, sportswear, hosiery, accessories; cosmetics and fragrances; men's, women's, and children's shoes; costume jewelry; fabrics, linens, sheets, towels, bedspreads, draperies; small appliances; major appliances; housewares;

giftware; china; glassware; lamps; radios and televisions; boys', girls', infants' wear.)

7. Some idea of readership of Turner's newspaper advertising, preferably among various income levels.
8. How people perceive us in relation to other local retail firms (Sears, Macy's, JC Penney's, Kmart, Bloomingdale's);
   Turner's merchandise is most like: _____
   Turner's fashions are most like: _____
   Turner's prices are most like: _____
   Turner's stores look most like: _____
   Turner's advertising is most like: _____
   Turner's prices are as low or lower than: _____
9. Turner's salespeople are: helpful _____ courteous _____ discourteous _____ not helpful _____
10. Of those who do not shop at Turner's: "I would shop more at Turner's if _____."
11. Turner's advertising is: informative _____ not informative _____ sometimes honest _____ not accurate _____
12. Do you think Turner's carries a large number of well-known brands?
13. Among those who shop often at Turner's: Do you shop most at the nearest Turner's store? Or do you go to another Turner's? Which one?
14. When you go to Turner's with a specific purchase in mind, do you usually find it in stock? (This applies particularly to everyday items such as hosiery, underwear, jeans, housewares, small appliances, etc.)
15. If the respondent has a Turner's charge account: Is charge authorization prompt?
16. When did you last shop at Turner's? (A week ago, a month ago, 3 months ago)
17. If the respondent has previously shopped at Turner's, but no longer does so, is it because of a bad experience? Credit? Exchange, refund, or adjustment of a merchandise purchase?
18. Turner's values are: _____ excellent _____ good _____ fair _____ poor
19. Turner's carries: some irregulars and seconds _____ many irregulars and seconds _____ all first quality
20. I believe seconds and irregulars offer excellent value: yes _____ no _____

CHAPTER 9
SURVEY RESEARCH:
BASIC METHODS OF COMMUNICATION WITH RESPONDENTS

LEARNING OUTCOMES

After studying this chapter, you should be able to

1. Summarize the different ways researchers implement surveys
2. Know the advantages and disadvantages of conducting surveys using personal interviews via door-to-door, mall intercept, landline telephone, or mobile-phone interviews
3. Choose an appropriate method of distributing a questionnaire from among mail, e-mail, Internet, fax, or mobile phone using SMS or MMS text
4. Appreciate the importance of pretesting questionnaires
5. Describe ethical issues that arise in survey research

Chapter Vignette: TLK 2 U L8TR

Sometimes it's not what you ask, but how you ask it that determines the quality of the answers you get. Researchers continue to have more options for asking questions. A researcher working for a 2008 Olympics advertiser wanted instant feedback on whether or not 30-second television spots during the Olympics were being viewed and understood. In this way, they could help their client understand if the investment in an Olympics commercial was worth the high price they paid. The firm eventually decided to send a text message to implement this survey. Wise decision?

In 2006, a British research firm used a text message survey to assess U.K. consumers' attitudes toward the World Cup. In contrast, research firms in the United States still rely heavily on day-after telephone surveys to assess consumer reactions to Super Bowl advertising. Does the method by which one asks a question affect the quality of responses? You betcha!

First, although text messaging has become commonplace among a wide cross section of consumers in many parts of the world, particularly in Japan and South Korea, text message usage is dominated by the youth culture in the United States and many parts of Europe. Additionally, each country has different rules and regulations that govern different media that can be used to implement a survey. Different cultures also respond differently to requests made through different technologies. For example, in the U.K., estimates suggest about 2 percent of consumers are generally receptive to surveys conducted through electronic media. However, in Japan and South Korea, consumers do not find such requests bothersome. So, if the manner of asking questions can be made interesting in some way, the odds of getting responses are improved. If the survey is intended to span different countries, then there are also issues of compatibility across countries. Not only might compatibility affect the likelihood of a questionnaire reaching a recipient in a useful manner, but it can also affect the researcher's ability to know just who responded.

Bottom line, know the population you want to represent. If your market resides in a place where sending text message survey requests is prohibited unless the consumer has opted in (as in the United States), or if your market is not in a demographic that is unreceptive to text messaging, and if your survey is sufficiently short and contains questions that can be answered in a text message format, then maybe a text message survey is for you. For example, contacting college students in Chongbuk, Korea to assess how much they have watched the Olympic games could be useful. Even better if the questions are asked in a form that contains some type of game involving flying gymnasts or divers doing impossible acrobatics.[1]

Introduction

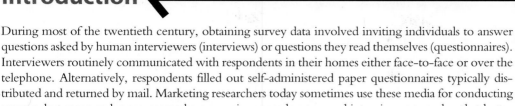

During most of the twentieth century, obtaining survey data involved inviting individuals to answer questions asked by human interviewers (interviews) or questions they read themselves (questionnaires). Interviewers routinely communicated with respondents in their homes either face-to-face or over the telephone. Alternatively, respondents filled out self-administered paper questionnaires typically distributed and returned by mail. Marketing researchers today sometimes use these media for conducting surveys, but more and more, researchers are using some less personal interview approaches that better leverage techological advances. Digital technology is having a profound impact on society in general and on marketing research in particular. Perhaps its greatest impact for research is in the creation of new forms of communications media. The increased technology may be needed. Response rates to all types of surveys continue to fall and perhaps by better matching a segment's preferred means of communication, researchers stand a better chance of getting someone to respond to their questions.[2] No matter how the researcher asks questions, the process of developing the survey instrument takes a great deal of time and effort.

interactive survey approaches

Communication that allows spontaneous two-way interaction between the interviewer and the respondent.

noninteractive survey approaches

Two-way communication by which respondents give answers to static questions.

Different Ways that Marketing Researchers Conduct Surveys

When two people engage in a conversation, human interaction takes place. Human interactive media are a personal form of communication. One human being directs a message to and interacts with another individual (or a small group). When most people think of interviewing, they envision two people engaged in a face-to-face dialogue or a conversation on the telephone. However, people don't always communicate in a two-way fashion. Sometimes, communication is one-way with little chance for spontaneous interaction. For example, traditional print advertisements are considered one-way communications because they are noninteractive in the sense that a consumer who views the ad has no immediate way of talking back to the ad designer. Likewise, we can summarize all the ways that marketing researchers communicate with survey respondents broadly into interactive and noninteractive media.

Electronic dating services have become a popular, successful example of electronic interactive media.

Interactive Survey Approaches

Interactive survey approaches are those that allow spontaneous two-way interaction between the interviewer and the respondent. These can be either personal or electronic. Either way, these approaches try to capture the dynamic exchange that is possible through face-to-face interviews. Survey respondents need not be passive audience members. Today's interactive approaches allow respondents to be involved in two-way communication using electronic media such as mobile phones or Web sites. More detail on various electronic options is provided later in this chapter.

Noninteractive Media

Noninteractive survey approaches are those that do not facilitate two-way communications and are thus largely a vehicle by which respondents give answers to static questions. The traditional

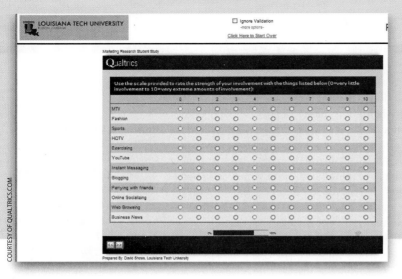

How would you classify the survey you participated in as part of this class? Which approach did it use? What media type was involved? What do you think the response rate for this survey is? E-mail the survey link to 10 of your friends and simply tell them it is a survey about everyday things and you would like for them to respond. Find out how many actually did respond. What is the click rate and response rate?

Take a look at the screenshot of this section. What other survey media could be used to effectively collect this specific information?

questionnaire received by mail, completed by a respondent, and mailed back to the researcher, does not allow a dialogue or an exchange of information providing immediate feedback. So, from this perspective, self-administered questionnaires printed on paper are noninteractive. This fact does not mean that they are without merit, just that this type of survey is less flexible than surveys using interactive communication media. In fact, noninteractive media can be the best approach in some situations. Simple opinion polls, awareness studies and even surveys assessing consumer attitudes can generally be collected adequately via one-way communication.

Each technique for conducting surveys has merits and shortcomings. The purpose of this chapter is to explain when researchers should use different types of surveys. We will begin with a discussion of surveys that use live interviews. Then we turn to noninteractive, self-administered questionnaires. Finally, we explain how the Internet and digital technology are dramatically changing survey research. The Research Snapshot on the next page provides an example of how survey research can provide market intelligence.

Conducting Personal Interviews

personal interview

Face-to-face communication in which an interviewer asks a respondent to answer questions.

A **personal interview** is a form of direct communication in which an interviewer asks respondents questions face-to-face. This versatile and flexible method is a two-way conversation between interviewer and respondent. Personal interviews are truly interactive. The researcher can communicate with individuals in person by going door-to-door or intercepting them in shopping malls, or interviews may take place over the phone. Traditionally, researchers have recorded interview results using paper and pencil, by reading questions and recording answers. Today, computers are increasingly supporting survey research by automatically recording responses. In this section, we examine the general characteristics of face-to-face personal interviews, then compare the characteristics of door-to-door personal interviews and personal interviews conducted in shopping malls. The next section examines telephone interviews.

Although the history of marketing research is sketchy, gathering information through face-to-face contact with individuals goes back many years. Periodic censuses were used to set tax rates and aid military conscription in the ancient empires of Egypt and Rome.[3] During the Middle Ages, the merchant families of Fugger and Rothschild prospered in part because their far-flung organizations enabled them to get information before their competitors could.[4] Today, survey researchers typically present themselves in shopping centers and train stations and announce, "Good afternoon, my name is _____. I am with _____ Marketing Research Company, and we are conducting a survey on _____."

iPod, uPod, FMPod?

Apple has revolutionized the way consumers listen to music by providing portability for personalized high-fidelity listening. The iPod is a fraction of the size of the old Sony Walkman and allows the user to store a virtually unlimited number of songs. Of course, the iPod owner can also store movies and even class lectures in the form of a podcast. Nothing is perfect, however, and Apple and other companies that offer MP3 players are constantly searching for ways to improve their products. So, what's the best method of survey to communicate with this market?

In 2007, a survey of iPod owners asked respondents what one thing they would most like added to their iPod. The number one choice was an FM radio tuner; 40 percent of respondents indicated that an FM tuner would be desirable. However, when an FM tuner was offered to iPod users as an accessory for about $50, the sell through rate proved far under 40 percent. Follow-up surveys studying the lack of success revealed several issues that may have made the 40 percent figure inflated.

- The survey was implemented through a noninteractive format that did not allow any elaboration on behalf of the respondent. Thus, Apple overlooked the fact that an integrated FM tuner would have produced far better results than an add-on accessory. As a result, Apple may have missed an opportunity to get consumers to upgrade to a newer iPod had the company simply introduced and emphasized new models with built-in FM tuners.
- The noninteractive survey also took advantage of a mailing list used by a group of FM radio stations that may have not represented the entire iPod population very well.
- The survey failed to ask questions about how the iPod was actually used. Follow-up Internet surveys suggest that the ability to easily use the iPod in the automobile was probably a more attractive improvement option that appealed to a large number of users.

Sources: Withers, S., "Do iPod Users Really Want FM Tuners?" *The Wire* (April 4, 2008), www.itwire.com, accessed June 16, 2008; Harris Interactive (2006), "Two-Thirds of Adult Automobile Owners Who Own MP3/iPod Players Use the Device in Their Vehicles," www.marketresearchworld.net, accessed June 15, 2008; Elliott, A.M., "iPod Use Sees Increase with under 10-year-olds," *Pocket-Lint* (2008), accessed at www.pocket-lint.co.uk on June 15, 2008.

© GEORGE DOYLE & CIARAN GRIFFIN

PR NEWSFOTO/©APPLE

Advantages of Personal Interviews

Marketing researchers find that personal interviews offer many unique advantages. One of the most important is the opportunity for feedback.

■ OPPORTUNITY FOR FEEDBACK

Personal interviews provide the opportunity for feedback and clarification. For example, if a consumer is reluctant to provide sensitive information, the interviewer may offer reassurance that his or her answers will be strictly confidential. Personal interviews offer the lowest chance that respondents will misinterpret questions, because an interviewer who senses confusion can clarify the instruction or questions. Circumstances may dictate that at the conclusion of the interview, the respondent be given additional information concerning the purpose of the study. This clarification is easily accomplished with a personal interview. If the feedback indicates that some question or set of questions is particularly confusing, the researcher can make changes that make the questionnaire easier to understand.

■ PROBING COMPLEX ANSWERS

Another important characteristic of personal interviews is the opportunity to follow up by probing. If a respondent's answer is too brief or unclear, the researcher may request a more comprehensive or clearer explanation. In probing, the interviewer asks for clarification with standardized questions such as "Can you tell me more about what you had in mind?" (See the chapter on qualitative research for an expanded discussion of probing.) Although interviewers are expected to ask questions exactly as they appear on the questionnaire, probing allows them some flexibility. Depending on the research purpose, personal interviews vary in the degree to which questions are structured and in the amount of probing required. The personal interview is especially useful for obtaining unstructured information. Skilled interviewers can handle complex questions that cannot easily be asked in telephone or mail surveys.

■ LENGTH OF INTERVIEW

If the research objective requires an extremely lengthy questionnaire, personal interviews may be the only option. A general rule of thumb on mail and e-mail surveys is that they should not take more than 12 minutes to complete and telephone interviews typically should take less than 10 minutes. In contrast, a personal interview can be much longer, perhaps an hour or even more. However, the longer the interview, no matter what the form, the more the respondent should be compensated for their time and participation. Researchers should also be clear about how long participation should take in the opening dialogue requesting participation. Online surveys should include a completion meter that shows the progress a respondent has made toward completing the task.

■ COMPLETENESS OF QUESTIONNAIRE

The social interaction between a well-trained interviewer and a respondent in a personal interview increases the likelihood that the respondent will answer all the items on the questionnaire. The respondent who grows bored with a telephone interview may terminate the interview at his or her discretion simply by hanging up the phone. Self-administration of a mail questionnaire requires even more effort by the respondent. Rather than write lengthy responses, the respondent may fail to complete some of the questions. **Item nonresponse**—failure to provide an answer to a question—is least likely to occur when an experienced interviewer asks questions directly.

item nonresponse

Failure of a respondent to provide an answer to a survey question.

■ PROPS AND VISUAL AIDS

Interviewing respondents face-to-face allows the investigator to show them new product samples, sketches of proposed advertising, or other visual aids. When Lego Group wanted to introduce new train model sets for its famous building bricks, the company targeted adults who build complex models with its product. The company invited adults who were swapping ideas at the Lego Web site to visit the New York office, where they viewed ideas and provided their opinions. The respondents wound up rejecting all the company's ideas, but they suggested something different: the Santa Fe Super Chief set, which sold out within two weeks, after being advertised only by enthusiastic word of mouth.[5] This research could not have been done in a telephone interview or mail survey.

Marketing research that uses visual aids has become increasingly popular with researchers who investigate film concepts, advertising problems, and moviegoers' awareness of performers. Research for movies often begins by showing respondents videotapes of the prospective cast. After the movie has been produced, film clips are shown and interviews conducted to evaluate the movie's appeal, especially which scenes to emphasize in advertisements. The Research Snapshot on the next page demonstrates how respondents can even taste new products—a real advantage for examining new products—at least until the virtual tongue takes over.

■ HIGH PARTICIPATION RATE

Although some people are reluctant to participate in a survey, the presence of an interviewer generally increases the percentage of people willing to complete the interview. People are often more hesitant to tell a person "no" face-to-face than they are over the phone, in a mail request, or through some other impersonal contact. Respondents typically are required to do no reading or writing—all they have to do is talk. A personable interviewer can also do much to improve response rates. Many people enjoy sharing information and insights with friendly and sympathetic interviewers.

Disadvantages of Personal Interviews

Personal interviews also have some disadvantages. Respondents are not anonymous and as a result may be reluctant to provide confidential information to another person. Suppose a survey asked top executives, "Do you see any major internal instabilities or threats (people, money, material, and so on) to the achievement of your marketing objectives?" Many managers may be reluctant to answer this sensitive question honestly in a personal interview in which their identities are known.

Matters of Taste

Asking an opinion is easy to do over the phone or online, but not if you want people's reactions to a new food, wine, or perfume. For those opinions, you probably want people to sample the new product first, so a face-to-face interview seems to be the only option. But, researchers have some creative options.

Sometimes researchers simply want to know whether consumers like the product, but in other situations they are trying to meet objectives such as maintaining the same taste after substituting a new ingredient. Sartori Foods uses a chart it calls the Italian Cheese Flavor Wheel to ask consumers to describe various cheeses. The chart matches consumer-friendly terms like *nutty, buttery,* and *creamy* with terms useful in the industry (for example, *aromatic amino acids* and *sulfur compounds*). Researchers can use an alternative to face-to-face interviews by sending both a sample of the product to potential respondents along with a color wheel. A phone interview can then have the respondent use the wheel to describe the taste.

Better yet, scientists have developed a virtual tongue. That's right! A synthetic surface absorbs foods and identifies certain tastes by feeding information into a computer. This may eliminate the need for a respondent altogether. For instance, the virtual tongue has quite a wine palate. It can tell Chardonnay from Malvasia and it can tell a 2005 vintage from a 2007 vintage. Well, this may be reliable, but many consumers are willing to stand in line to verify the wine's characteristics by tasting it for themselves!

Sources: Based on Claudia D. O'Donnell, "Tips for Sensory Tests," *Prepared Foods* (January 2005), downloaded from InfoTrac at http://www.galenet.com; Fran LaBell, "International Sensory Tests: When in Rome," *Prepared Foods* (February 2002), downloaded from Business & Company Resource Center, http://galenet. galegroup.com; Abend, L., "E-Tongue Passes Wine Taste Test," *Time* (August 12, 2008), http://www.time.com/time/ business/article/0,8599,1831413,00. html, accessed August 1, 2008.

■ INTERVIEWER INFLUENCE

Some evidence suggests that demographic characteristics of the interviewer influence respondents' answers. For example, one research study revealed that male interviewers produced larger amounts of interviewer variance than female interviewers in a survey in which 85 percent of the respondents were female. Older interviewers who interviewed older respondents produced more variance than other age combinations, whereas younger interviewers who interviewed younger respondents produced the least variance.

Differential interviewer techniques may be a source of bias. The rephrasing of a question, the interviewer's tone of voice, and the interviewer's appearance may influence the respondent's answer. Consider the interviewer who has conducted 100 personal interviews. During the next one, he or she may lose concentration and either selectively perceive or anticipate the respondent's answer. The interpretation of the response may differ somewhat from what the respondent intended. Typically, the public thinks of the person who does marketing research as a dedicated scientist. Unfortunately, some interviewers do not fit that ideal. Considerable interviewer variability exists. Cheating is possible; interviewers cut corners to save time and energy or fake parts of their reports by dummying up part or all of the questionnaire. Control over interviewers is important to ensure that difficult, embarrassing, or time-consuming questions are handled properly.

■ LACK OF ANONYMITY OF RESPONDENT

Because a respondent in a personal interview is not totally anonymous, he or she may be reluctant to provide confidential information to the interviewer. Researchers take care to phrase sensitive questions to avoid social desirability bias. For example, the interviewer may show the respondent a card that lists possible answers and ask the respondent to read a category number rather than be required to verbalize sensitive answers.

■ COST

Personal interviews are expensive, generally substantially more costly than mail, e-mail, Internet, or phone surveys. The geographic proximity of respondents, the length and complexity of the questionnaire, and the number of people who are nonrespondents because they could not be contacted (not-at-homes) will all influence the cost of the personal interview.

Door-to-Door Interviews and Shopping Mall Intercepts

Personal interviews can be conducted through several different media. The next sections provide an overview of the options for personal interviews.

Personal interviews may be conducted at the respondents' homes or offices or in many other places. Increasingly, personal interviews are being conducted in shopping malls. Mall intercept interviews allow many interviews to be conducted quickly. Respondents can be intercepted in public areas of shopping malls and then asked to come to a permanent research facility to taste new food items or to view advertisements. The locale for the interview generally influences the participation rate, and thus the degree to which the sample represents the general population.

■ DOOR-TO-DOOR INTERVIEWS

door-to-door interviews
Personal interviews conducted at respondents' doorsteps in an effort to increase the participation rate in the survey.

The presence of an interviewer at the door generally increases the likelihood that a person will be willing to complete an interview. Because **door-to-door interviews** increase the participation rate, they provide a more representative sample of the population than mail questionnaires. For example, response rates to mail surveys are substantially lower among Hispanics whether the questionnaire is printed in English or Spanish.[6] People who do not have telephones, who have unlisted telephone numbers, or who are otherwise difficult to contact may be reached using door-to-door interviews. However, door-to-door interviews may underrepresent some groups and overrepresent others based on the geographic areas covered.

Door-to-door interviews may exclude individuals who live in multiple-dwelling units with security systems, such as high-rise apartment dwellers, or executives who are too busy to grant personal interviews during business hours. Other people, for security reasons, simply will not open the door when a stranger knocks. Telephoning an individual in one of these subgroups to make an appointment may make the total sample more representative. However, obtaining a representative sample of this security-conscious subgroup based on a listing in the telephone directory may be difficult. For these reasons, door-to-door interviews are becoming a thing of the past.

■ CALLBACKS

callbacks
Attempts to recontact individuals selected for a sample who were not available initially.

When a person selected to be in the sample cannot be contacted on the first visit, a systematic procedure is normally initiated to call back at another time. **Callbacks**, or attempts to recontact individuals selected for the sample, are the major means of reducing nonresponse error. Calling back a sampling unit is more expensive than interviewing the person the first time around, because subjects who initially were not at home generally are more widely dispersed geographically than the original sample units. Callbacks in door-to-door interviews are important because not-at-home individuals (for example, working parents) may systematically vary from those who *are* at home (nonworking parents, retired people, and the like).

■ MALL INTERCEPT INTERVIEWS

mall intercept interviews
Personal interviews conducted in a shopping mall.

Personal interviews conducted in shopping malls are referred to as **mall intercept interviews**, or *shopping center sampling*. Interviewers typically intercept shoppers at a central point within the shopping center or at a main entrance. Mall intercept interviews are conducted because their costs are lower. No travel is required to the respondent's home; instead, the respondent comes to the interviewer, and many interviews can be conducted quickly in this way.

A major problem with mall intercept interviews is that individuals usually are in a hurry to shop, so the incidence of refusal is high—typically around 50 percent. Yet, the commercial marketing research industry conducts many more personal interviews in shopping malls or shoping centers than it conducts door-to-door.

In a mall interview, the researcher must recognize that he or she should not be looking for a representative sample of the total population. Each mall has its own target market's characteristics, and there is likely to be a larger bias than with careful household probability sampling. However, personal interviews in shopping malls are appropriate when the target group is a special market segment such as the parents of children of bike-riding age. If the respondent indicates that he or she has a child of this age, the parent can then be brought into a rented space and shown several bikes. The mall intercept interview allows the researcher to show large, heavy, or immobile visual materials, such as a television commercial. A mall interviewer can give an individual a product to take home to use and obtain a commitment that the respondent will cooperate when recontacted later by telephone. Mall intercept interviews are also valuable when activities such as cooking and tasting of food must be closely coordinated and timed to follow each other. They may also be appropriate when a consumer durable product must be demonstrated. For example, electronics manufacturers often do not want to test new appliances in consumers homes because they can be bulky or difficult to properly set up. Thus, bringing respondents to the appliances is a better option.

Global Considerations

Willingness to participate in a personal interview varies dramatically around the world. For example, in some Arab nations, women would never consent to be interviewed by a man. And in many countries the idea of discussing grooming behavior and personal-care products with a stranger would be highly offensive. Few people would consent to be interviewed on such topics.

The norms about appropriate business conduct also influence businesspeople's willingness to provide information to interviewers. For example, conducting business-to-business interviews in Japan during business hours is difficult because managers, strongly loyal to their firm, believe that they have an absolute responsibility to oversee their employees while on the job. In some cultures when a businessperson is reluctant to be interviewed, a reputable third party may be asked to intervene so that an interview may take place.

Telephone Interviews

In days past, a telephone was a telephone. Today however, phones can actually be any one of a number of appliances. The question to the researcher who wishes to do a phone interview returns to this: Do all types of phones produce identical survey results?

■ LANDLINE PHONES

For several decades, landline **telephone interviews** have been the mainstay of commercial survey research. The quality of data obtained by telephone is potentially comparable to the quality of data collected face-to-face. Respondents are more willing to provide detailed and reliable information on a variety of personal topics over the phone while in the privacy of their own homes than when answering questions face-to-face.

In-home phone surveys are still considered capable of providing fairly representative samples of the U.S. population. However, the "no-call" legislation dating back to the mid-2000s has limited this capability somewhat. Marketing researchers cannot solicit information via phone numbers listed on the do-not-call registry. Thus, to the extent that consumers who place their numbers on these lists share something in common, such as a greater desire for privacy, a representative sample of the general population cannot be obtained. Marketers and marketing researchers can obtain the do-not-call lists of phone numbers from the FTC for $62 per area code. The entire registry can be obtained for $17,050. This information can be obtained from the FTC do-not-call Web site at **http://www.ftc.gov/donotcall**. Although this may seem expensive, the FTC levies fines on the order of $10,000 per violation (per call), so obtaining the registry is a wise investment for those wishing to contact consumers via the telelphone. AT&T faced fines of over three-quarters of a million dollars for making 78 unwanted calls to 29 consumers listed on the do-not-call list. The Feds do take violations very seriously.

telephone interviews
Personal interviews conducted by telephone, the mainstay of commercial survey research.

The federal government provides information for both consumers and businesses about the National Do Not Call Registry through this Web site.

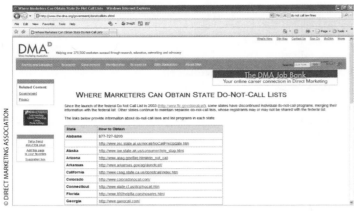

Information about do-not-call lists for each state can be found at the Direct Marketing Association's Web site at http:// www.the-dma.org/government/ donotcalllists.shtml.

Likewise, the Canadian government has instituted a nearly identical do-not-call program. The Canadian Radio-television and Telecommunications Commission imposes fines up to $11,000 per call for calls made to people on the Canadian do-not-call list. Other countries in Europe and elsewhere are also considering such legislation. The advantages of privacy simply make phones less capable of obtaining representative samples than they once were. Often however, a landline phone call is still the researcher's best option.

Inevitably though, even when calls do get through, an all too often outcome for the researcher is something like this:

Good evening, I'm with a nationwide marketing research company. Are you watching television tonight?
A: Yes.
Did you see 60 minutes on CBS?
A: "Click"

■ MOBILE PHONE INTERVIEWS

Mobile phone interviews differ from landline phones most obviously because they are directed toward a mobile (i.e., cell) phone number. However, there are other less obvious distinctions.

- In the United States, no telemarketing can be directed toward mobile phone numbers by law. The primary reason for enacting this law was because respondents would often have to pay to receive the call. A respondent would have to "opt in" before their phone number would be made available for such calls.
- The recipient of a mobile phone call is even more likely to be distracted than the recipient of a home or office call. In fact, the respondent may be driving a car, on a subway train, or walking down a noisy street. Factors such as this are not conducive to a high-quality interview.
- The area codes for mobile phones are not necessarily tied to geography. For instance, a person who moves from Georgia to Arizona can choose to keep his or her old phone number. Therefore, a researcher may be unable to determine whether or not a respondent fits into the desired geographic sampling population simply by taking note of the area code.
- The phones have varying abilities for automated responses and differing keypads. Some requests, such as "hit pound sign," may be more difficult to do on some keypads than on others.

We'll discuss the relative advantages and disadvantages of mobile phone interviews in the following sections. However, suffice it to say at this point, interviewing people via a landline phone is not the same as interviewing people via a mobile phone. Exhibit 9.1 provides a summary of potential differences in surveying by landline or mobile phones.

Phone Interview Characteristics

Phone interviews have several distinctive characteristics that set them apart from other survey techniques. These characteristics present significant advantages and disadvantages for the researcher.

■ REPRESENTATIVE SAMPLES

Practically every consumer over the age of 18 in developed nations around the world has a phone. In some of these countries, including the U.S. and countries throughout Europe, children often have their own mobile phone beginning around the age of 12 or 13. The widespread diffusion of phones through the population makes them attractive for trying to represent all different types of populations. Landline phone directories remain widely available and easy to access. Although a growing number of consumers are choosing not to have a landline phone, it's safe to say that about 90 percent

EXHIBIT 9.1

Landline and Mobile Phone Pros and Cons

Survey Characteristic	Landline Phones	Mobile Phones
Legal Issues (USA)	Calls limited due to do-not-call legislation. Times to call limited.	Calls to mobile phone numbers are prohibited unless user specifically allows calls.
Ability to Respond	Respond in the privacy of their home or office.	More likely to be distracted or involved in some other activity like driving.
Sampling Regionally	Region identified by area code.	Area code does not indicate region due to mobility.
Standardization	Landline appliances relatively standardized.	Mobile phone technologies vary from one appliance to another.
Response	About one in four calls is answered. Best time to get an answer is on weekend.	About one in three calls is answered. Best time to get an answer is during working hours on weekdays.
Refusals	Expect one-third of people who answer to refuse.	Expect half of people who answer to refuse.
Compensation	Answering does not usually cost respondent money.	Answering usually causes a charge so the respondent must be compensated.

of households in the U.S. can be reached via a traditional in-home telephone call. The less than 10 percent without a landline do cause some problems with obtaining a random sample. However, the desire for privacy causes many people to have an unlisted phone number and other consumers have recently moved and have a number that is too new to be in directories. The inaccuracy of directories is an even greater problem than the small percentage of people with no landline phone.

Individuals whose phone numbers are unlisted differ slightly from those with published numbers. Recent movers tend to be younger, more urban, and less likely to own their own home. Households that maintain unlisted phone numbers by choice tend to have higher incomes and live in the suburbs. In either case, the fact that these potential respondents are removed from the entire population means that they will be underrepresented in any sample that relies on landline phone directories. Researchers who wish to draw inferences about the entire U.S. population must be willing to accept the error due to this problem if they decide to sample in this way.

Random Digit Dialing

The problem of unlisted phone numbers can be partially resolved through the use of random digit dialing. **Random digit dialing** eliminates the counting of names in a list (for example, calling every fiftieth name in a column) and subjectively determining whether a directory listing is a business, institution, or legitimate household. In the simplest form of random digit dialing, telephone exchanges (prefixes) for the geographic areas in the sample are obtained. Using a table of random numbers, the last four digits of the telephone number are selected. Telephone directories can be ignored entirely or used in combination with the assignment of one or several random digits. By law, mobile phone numbers must be excluded as should numbers on the do-not-call list. Random digit dialing also helps overcome the problem due to new listings and recent changes in numbers. Unfortunately, the refusal rate in commercial random digit dialing studies is higher than the refusal rate for telephone surveys that use only listed telephone numbers.

Additionally, although most American households still have landline phones, some predictions suggest this is changing quickly. Some estimates suggest that within the next 5 years, the number of households that have only mobile phones may approach 40 percent.[7] Should this prediction be true, this will have a dramatic effect on polling and marketing research in the United States. The consumer movement toward solely mobile phones may have less effect on research in Europe and other nations where mobile phone numbers can be included in samples alongside landline phone numbers.

random digit dialing

Use of telephone exchanges and a table of random numbers to contact respondents with unlisted phone numbers.

Landline versus Mobile Phone Results

People do not use mobile phones the same way they use landline phones. Additionally, those with high mobile-phone usage are not entirely the same as those with low or no mobile-phone usage and perhaps high landline-phone usage. Researchers should not be surprised to observe differences in the characteristics of both sets of respondents. For example, the chances of getting someone to answer a phone vary across these two types. For instance, compared to mobile phone users:[8]

- Calls to mobile phone numbers are more likely to result in someone answering the phone on weekdays during working hours than are landline numbers. About one in three calls to mobile phones will be answered as opposed to about one in four calls to landline numbers.
- Calls to mobile phone numbers are less likely to result in someone answering the phone on weekends than are landline numbers. Less than one in three calls to mobile phones are answered on the weekends as opposed to nearly four in ten calls to landline numbers.
- Refusals are higher for calls to mobile phone numbers than for calls to landline numbers. About half of mobile phone calls result in refusals to participate in the survey whereas landline refusals average around 30 percent.
- Mobile phone users should be duly compensated for their responses given the potential costs involved and the calls should be kept to a short duration given that a mobile phone user is more likely in a situation involving attention to some other activity.

These factors all affect the equality of data and samples obtained from landline and mobile-phone sampling. Researchers should consider these factors before making a quick decision that any type of phone interviewing will satisfy the data needs at hand.

■ SPEED

One advantage of telephone interviewing is the relative speed of data collection. Data collection with mail or personal interviews can take weeks. In contrast, hundreds of telephone interviews can be conducted within a few hours. When an interviewer enters a respondent's answers directly into a computerized system, data processing speeds up even more relative to mail interviews or any other approach that would involve manual data coding and entry.

■ COST

As the cost of personal interviews continues to increase, phone interviews are becoming relatively inexpensive. The cost of telephone interviews is estimated to be less than 25 percent of the cost of door-to-door personal interviews. Travel time and costs are eliminated. However, the typical Internet survey is even less expensive than a phone-based survey.

■ ABSENCE OF FACE-TO-FACE CONTACT

Telephone interviews are more impersonal than face-to-face interviews. Respondents may answer embarrassing or confidential questions more willingly in a telephone interview than in a personal interview. However, mail and Internet surveys, although not perfect, are better media for gathering extremely sensitive information because they seem more anonymous. Some evidence suggests that people provide information on income and other financial matters only reluctantly, even in telephone interviews. Such questions may be personally threatening for a variety of reasons, and high refusal rates for this type of question occur with each form of survey research.

Although telephone calls may be less threatening because the interviewer is not physically present, the absence of face-to-face contact is more often a liability than an asset. When the interviewer isn't physically present, for instance, a respondent cannot see when the interviewer is still writing down the previous comment and may continue to elaborate on an answer. Thus, some important information may not get recorded. Likewise, the inability of the interviewer to see the respondent causes problems. If a respondent pauses to think about an answer, the interviewer may simply interpret the pause as "no response" and go on to the next question. Hence, there is a greater tendency for interviewers to record no answers and incomplete answers in telephone interviews than in personal interviews.

■ COOPERATION

One trend is very clear. In the last few decades, telephone response rates have fallen. Analysis of response rates for the long-running Survey of Consumer Attitudes conducted by the University of Michigan found that response rates fell from a high of 72 percent to 67 percent during the period from 1979 to 1996 and then even faster after 1996, dropping to 60 percent.[9] Lenny Murphy of the data collection firm Dialtek says he has observed a decline in survey response rates from a typical range of 30 to 40 percent in the past down to below 20 percent.[10] Fewer calls are answered because more households are using caller ID and answering machines to screen their calls, and many individuals do not pick up the phone when the display reads "out of area" or when an unfamiliar survey organization's name and number appear on the display. Also, more phone lines are dedicated to fax machines and computers. However, the University of Michigan study found that the rate of refusal actually grew faster in the more recent period than the rate of not answering research-ers' calls. Getting someone to answer the phone does not mean that the battle for a meaningful response is won.

One way researchers can try to improve response rates is to leave a message on the household's telephone answering machine or voice mail. However, many people will not return a call to help someone conduct a survey. Using a message explicitly stating that the purpose of the call is not sales related may improve responses. Other researchers simply hope to reach respondents when they call back, trying callbacks at different times and on different days.

Despite the restrictions in the United States, other countries may not adopt laws restricting calls to mobile phones. In addition, consumers in other countries are more open to responding to research delivered by voice or by text messaging. Thus, the mobile phone may be a better inter-view tool outside of the United States than in the United States.

Refusal to cooperate with interviews is directly related to interview length. A major study of survey research found that interviews of 5 minutes or less had a refusal rate of 21 percent; inter-views of between 6 and 12 minutes had 41 percent refusal rates; and interviews of 13 minutes or more had 47 percent rates. In unusual cases, a few highly interested respondents will put up with longer interviews. A good rule of thumb is to keep telephone interviews approximately 10 min-utes long. In general, 30 minutes is the maximum amount of time most respondents will spend unless they are highly interested in the survey subject.

Another way to encourage participation is to send households an invitation to participate in a survey. The invitation can describe the purpose and importance of the survey and the likely dura-tion of the survey. The invitation can also encourage subjects to be available and reassure them that the caller will not try to sell anything. In a recent study comparing response rates, the rates were highest among households that received an advance letter, somewhat lower when the notice came on a postcard, and lowest when no notice was sent.[11]

■ INCENTIVES TO RESPOND

Respondents should receive some incentive to respond. Research addresses different types of incen-tives. For telephone interviews, test-marketing involving different types of survey introduction suggests that not all introductions are equally effective. A financial incentive or some significant chance to win a desirable prize will produce a higher telephone response rate than a simple assur-ance that the research is not a sales pitch, a more detailed description of the survey, or an assurance of confidentiality.[12]

■ CALLBACKS

An unanswered call, a busy signal, or a respondent who is not at home requires a callback. Tele-phone callbacks are much easier to make than callbacks in personal interviews. However, as men-tioned, the ownership of telephone answering machines and the use of voice mail is widespread, and their effects on callbacks are not well understood. However, if a respondent decides not to answer a number the first time, one has to wonder why they would decide to answer it on a callback.

■ LIMITED DURATION

Respondents who run out of patience with the interview can merely hang up. To encourage participation, interviews should be relatively short. The length of the telephone interview is definitely limited. The shorter the better and seldom longer than 10 minutes. Interviewers should also inform the respondent at the start of the interview of the maximum time the interview will take.

■ LACK OF VISUAL MEDIUM

Because visual aids cannot be used in telephone interviews, this method is not appropriate for packaging research, copy testing of television and print advertising, and concept tests that require visual materials. Likewise, certain attitude scales and measuring instruments, such as the semantic differential (discussed more in a later chapter), require the respondent to see a graphic scale, so they are difficult to use over the phone.

Central Location Interviewing

central location interviewing

Telephone interviews conducted from a central location allowing firms to hire a staff of professional interviewers and to supervise and control the quality of interviewing more effectively.

Research agencies or interviewing services typically conduct all telephone interviews from a central location. Such **central location interviewing** allows firms to hire a staff of professional interviewers and to supervise and control the quality of interviewing more effectively. When telephone interviews are centralized and computerized, an agency or business can benefit from additional cost economies. Some of the cost economies are realized by outsourcing interviews to call centers where labor costs are low including centers in other countries.

Computer-Assisted Telephone Interviewing

computer-assisted telephone interviewing (CATI)

Technology that allows answers to telephone interviews to be entered directly into a computer for processing.

Advances in computer technology allow responses to telephone interviews to be entered directly into the computer in a process known as **computer-assisted telephone interviewing (CATI)**. Telephone interviewers are seated at computer terminals. Monitors display the questionnaires, one question at a time, along with precoded possible responses to each question. The interviewer reads each question as it appears on the screen. When the respondent answers, the interviewer enters the response directly into the computer, and it is automatically stored in the computer's memory. The computer then displays the next question on the screen. Computer-assisted telephone interviewing requires that answers to the questionnaire be highly structured. If a respondent gives an unacceptable answer (that is, one not precoded and programmed), the computer will reject it. The Research Snapshot on the next page further describes issues with CATI.

Computer-assisted telephone interviewing systems include telephone management systems that select phone numbers, dial the numbers automatically, and perform other labor-saving functions. These systems can automatically control sample selection by randomly generating names or fulfilling a sample quota. A computer can generate an automatic callback schedule. A typical call management system might schedule recontact attempts to recall unanswered calls after two hours and busy numbers after 10 minutes and allow the interviewer to enter a more favorable time slot (day and hour) when a respondent indicates that he or she is too busy to be interviewed. Software systems also allow researchers to request daily status reports on the number of completed interviews relative to quotas. CATI interviews can also be conducted by a pre-recorded voice with the respondent answering by punching buttons on the phone.

Computerized Voice-Activated Telephone Interview

Technological advances have combined computerized telephone dialing and voice-activated computer messages to allow researchers to conduct telephone interviews without human interviewers. However, researchers have found that computerized voice-activated telephone interviewing works best with very short, simple questionnaires. One system includes a voice-synthesized module controlled by a microprocessor. With it the sponsor is able to register a caller's single response

Automating Phone Surveys of Teens

Automatic telephone surveys are a good way to reach all members of the family, not just the head of the household. What if you wanted to ask questions about holiday shopping, what's for dinner, or what kind of vacation the family would like? A short telephone survey may be the answer. One advantage is that no "real person" has to hear the answers to potentially sensitive quesitons.

Computer-assisted telephone interviewing (CATI) and computerized self-interviewing, in which the subjects listened to pre-recorded questions and then responded by entering answers with the telephone's keypad, have been used to ask the "teen" in the house about smoking. The researchers predicted that the young people would be more likely to say they smoke in the self-administered survey than in response to a live interviewer, because pressing keys on the keypad would feel more confidential.

The interviewers were right. In the self-administered survey, the teens were more likely to say they had smoked in the past thirty days or, if they had not smoked, to lack a firm commitment not to smoke in the future. Many of them indicated a parent was present while they answered the questions, and when they did, their responses were less likely to indicate smoking desire or susceptibility. This pattern suggests that they might be underreporting their smoking behavior. These findings encourage researchers to be attentive to confidentiality when working with teenage subjects.

Sources: "Survey: Consumers Say 'Yes' To Holiday Shopping," *Stores*, (December 2001), 83 no. 12, 18; Moskowitz, Joel M., "Assessment of Cigarette Smoking and Smoking Susceptibility among Youth: Telephone Computer-Assisted Self-Interviews versus Computer-Assisted Telephone Interviews," *Public Opinion Quarterly*, 68 (Winter 2004), 565–587.

such as "true/false," "yes/no," "like/dislike," or "for/against." This type of system has been used by television and radio stations to register callers' responses to certain issues. One system, Telsol, begins with an announcement that the respondent is listening to a recorded message. The computer then asks questions, leaving blank tape in between to record the answers. If respondents do not answer the first two questions, the computer disconnects and goes to the next call. With this process, the entire data collection process can be automated because a recorded voice is used to ask the questions and responses are recorded automatically.

Global Considerations

Different cultures often have different norms about proper telephone behavior. For example, business-to-business researchers have learned that Latin American businesspeople will not open up to strangers on the telephone. So, researchers in Latin America usually find personal interviews more suitable than telephone surveys. In Japan, respondents consider it ill-mannered if telephone interviews last more than 20 minutes. Laws governing researchers ability to call via landline or mobile phones also vary based on factors such as do-not-call laws and the legality of calling mobile phone numbers. Calling mobile phones is generally prohibited in the United States but allowed in Europe, for instance.

Surveys Using Self-Administered Questionnaires

Many noninteractive surveys can be implemented without an interviewer. Marketing researchers distribute questionnaires to consumers through the mail and in many other ways (see Exhibit 9.2 on the next page). They insert questionnaires in packages and magazines. They may place questionnaires at points of purchase or in high-traffic locations in stores or malls. They may even fax questionnaires to individuals. Questionnaires can be printed on paper, but they may be posted on the Internet or sent via e-mail. No matter how the **self-administered questionnaires** are distributed, they are different from interviews because the respondent takes responsibility for reading and answering the questions.

self-administered questionnaires

Surveys in which the respondent takes the responsibility for reading and answering the questions.

EXHIBIT 9.2 **Self-Administered Questionnaires Can Be Either Printed or Electronic**

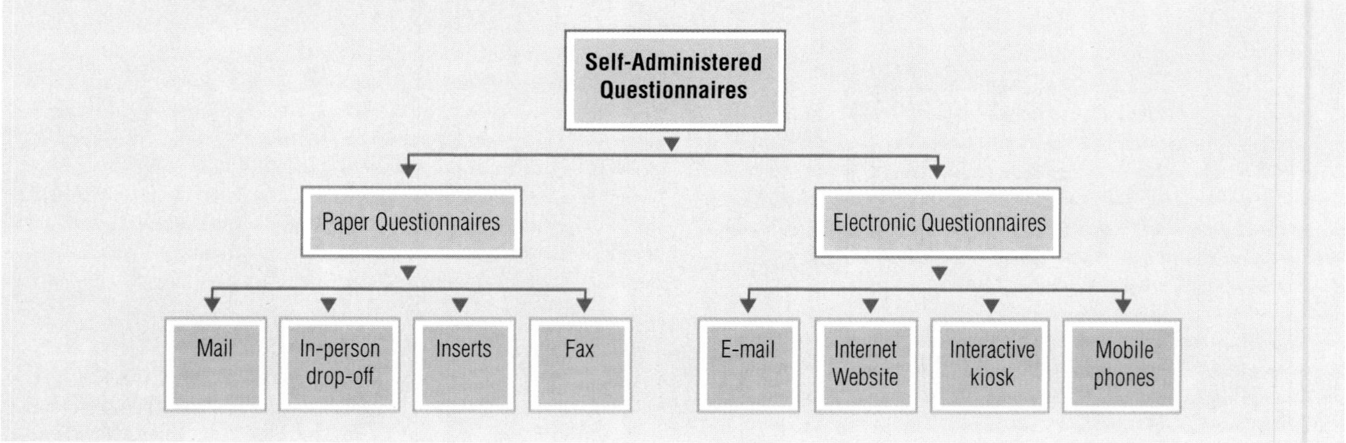

Self-administered questionnaires present a challenge to the marketing researcher because they rely on the clarity of the written word rather than on the skills of the interviewer. The nature of self-administered questionnaires is best illustrated by explaining mail questionnaires.

Mail Questionnaires

mail survey

A self-administered questionnaire sent to respondents through the mail.

A traditional **mail survey** is a self-administered questionnaire sent to respondents through a postal service, or as it is more frequently referred to today, snail mail. This paper-and-pencil method has several advantages and disadvantages.

■ GEOGRAPHIC FLEXIBILITY

Mail questionnaires can reach a geographically dispersed sample simultaneously because interviewers are not required. Respondents (such as farmers) who are located in isolated areas or those (such as executives) who are otherwise difficult to reach can easily be contacted by mail. For example, a pharmaceutical firm may find that doctors are not available for personal or telephone interviews. However, a mail survey can reach both rural and urban doctors who practice in widely dispersed geographic areas.

■ COST

Mail questionnaires are relatively inexpensive compared with personal interviews, though they are not cheap. Most include follow-up mailings, which require additional postage and printing costs. And it usually isn't cost-effective to try to cut costs on printing—questionnaires photocopied on low-grade paper have a greater likelihood of being thrown in the wastebasket than those prepared with more expensive, high-quality printing. The low response rates contribute to the high cost.

■ RESPONDENT CONVENIENCE

Mail surveys and other self-administered questionnaires can be filled out when the respondents have time, so respondents are more likely to take time to think about their replies. Many hard-to-reach respondents place a high value on convenience and thus are best contacted by mail. In some situations, particularly in business-to-business marketing research, mail questionnaires allow respondents to collect facts, such as sales statistics, that they may not be able to recall without checking. Being able to check information by verifying records or, in household surveys, by consulting with other family members should provide more valid, factual information than either personal or telephone interviews would allow. A catalog retailer may use mail surveys to estimate sales volume for catalog items by sending a mock catalog as part of the questionnaire. Respondents would be asked to indicate how likely they would be to order selected items. Using the mail allows respondents to consult other family members and to make their decisions within a reasonable timespan.

ANONYMITY OF RESPONDENT

In the cover letter that accompanies a mail or self-administered questionnaire, marketing researchers almost always state that the respondents' answers will be confidential. Respondents are more likely to provide sensitive or embarrassing information when they can remain anonymous. For example, personal interviews and a mail survey conducted simultaneously asked the question "Have you borrowed money at a regular bank?" Researchers noted a 17 percent response rate for the personal interviews and a 42 percent response rate for the mail survey. Although random sampling error may have accounted for part of this difference, the results suggest that for research on personal and sensitive financial issues, mail surveys are more confidential than personal interviews.

Anonymity can also reduce social desirability bias. People are more likely to agree with controversial issues, such as extreme political candidates, when completing self-administered questionnaires than when speaking to interviewers on the phone or at their doorsteps.

ABSENCE OF INTERVIEWER

Although the absence of an interviewer can induce respondents to reveal sensitive or socially undesirable information, this lack of personal contact can also be a disadvantage. Once the respondent receives the questionnaire, the questioning process is beyond the researcher's control. Although the printed stimulus is the same, each respondent will attach a different personal meaning to each question. Selective perception operates in research as well as in advertising. The respondent does not have the opportunity to question the interviewer. Problems that might be clarified in a personal or telephone interview can remain misunderstandings in a mail survey. There is no interviewer to probe for additional information or clarification of an answer, and the recorded answers must be assumed to be complete.

Respondents have the opportunity to read the entire questionnaire before they answer individual questions. Often the text of a later question will provide information that affects responses to earlier questions.

STANDARDIZED QUESTIONS

Mail questionnaires typically are highly standardized, and the questions are quite structured. Questions and instructions must be clear-cut and straightforward. Ambiguous questions only create additional error. Interviewing allows for feedback from the interviewer regarding the respondent's comprehension of the questionnaire. An interviewer who notices that the first 50 respondents are having some difficulty understanding a question can report this fact to the research analyst so that revisions can be made. With a mail survey, however, once the questionnaires are mailed, it is difficult to change the format or the questions.

TIME IS MONEY

If time is a factor in management's interest in the research results, or if attitudes are rapidly changing (for example, toward a political event), mail surveys may not be a good communication medium. A minimum of two or three weeks is necessary for receiving the majority of the responses. Follow-up mailings, which usually are sent when the returns begin to trickle in, require an additional two or three weeks. The time between the first mailing and the cut-off date (when questionnaires will no longer be accepted) normally is six to eight weeks. In a regional or local study, personal interviews may even be conducted more quickly.

LENGTH OF MAIL QUESTIONNAIRE

Mail questionnaires vary considerably in length, ranging from extremely short postcard questionnaires to multipage booklets that require respondents to fill in thousands of answers. A general rule of thumb is that a paper questionnaire should not exceed six pages in length. When a questionnaire requires a respondent to expend a great deal of effort, an incentive is generally required to induce the respondent to return the questionnaire. The following sections discuss several ways to pursue higher response rates even when questionnaires are relatively long.

Response Rates

All questionnaires that arrive via bulk mail are likely to get thrown away. Questionnaires that are boring, unclear, or too complex are even more likely to get thrown in the wastebasket. A poorly designed mail questionnaire often is returned by fewer than 5 percent of those sampled (that is, a 5 percent response rate). The basic calculation for obtaining a **response rate** is to count the number of questionnaires returned or completed, then divide the total by the number of eligible people who were contacted or requested to participate in the survey. Typically, the number in the denominator is adjusted for faulty addresses and similar problems that reduce the number of eligible participants.

The major limitations of mail questionnaires relate to response problems. Respondents who complete the questionnaire may not be typical of all people in the sample. Individuals with a special interest in the topic are more likely to respond to a mail survey than those who are indifferent.

A researcher has no assurance that the intended subject is the person who fills out the questionnaire. The wrong person answering the questions may be a problem when surveying corporate executives, physicians, and other professionals, who may pass questionnaires on to subordinates to complete. This probably is not unique to mail surveys since electronic surveying suffers similarly.

Evidence suggests that cooperation and response rates rise as home value increases. Conversely if the sample has a high proportion of retired households, response rates will be lower. Mail survey respondents tend to be better educated than nonrespondents. If they return the questionnaire at all, poorly educated respondents who cannot read and write well may skip open-ended questions to which they are required to write out their answers. Rarely will a mail survey have a 50 percent or greater response rate. However, the use of follow-up mailings and other techniques may increase the response rate to an acceptable percentage. The lower the response rate, the greater the concern that the resulting sample will not adequately represent the population.

response rate

The number of questionnaires returned or completed divided by the number of eligible people who were asked to participate in the survey.

Increasing Response Rates for Mail Surveys

Nonresponse error is always a potential problem with mail surveys. Individuals who are interested in the general subject of the survey are more likely to respond than those with less interest or little experience. Thus, people who hold extreme positions on an issue are more likely to respond than individuals who are largely indifferent to the topic. To minimize this bias, researchers have developed a number of techniques to increase the response rate to mail surveys. For example, almost all surveys include postage-paid return envelopes. Using a stamped return envelope instead of a business reply envelope increases response rates even more.[13] Designing and formatting attractive questionnaires and wording questions so that they are easy to understand also help ensure a good response rate. However, special efforts may be required even with a sound questionnaire. Several of these methods are discussed in the following subsections.

■ COVER LETTER

cover letter

Letter that accompanies a questionnaire to induce the reader to complete and return the questionnaire.

A **cover letter** that accompanies a questionnaire or is printed on the first page of the questionnaire booklet is an important means of inducing a reader to complete and return the questionnaire. Exhibit 9.3 illustrates a cover letter and some of the points considered by a marketing research professional to be important in gaining respondents' attention and cooperation. The first paragraph of the letter explains why the study is important. The basic appeal alludes to the social usefulness of responding. Two other frequently used appeals are asking for help ("Will you do us a favor?") and the egotistical appeal ("Your opinions are important!"). Most cover letters promise confidentiality, invite the recipient to use an enclosed postage-paid reply envelope, describe any incentive or

EXHIBIT 9.3
A Cover Letter Requesting Participation in a Survey

MKTR

Market Research Leaders

Component: → 111 Eustice Square,
Terroir, IL 39800-7600

Respondent's → Mr. Griff Mitchell
Address   821 Shrewsbury Ave
                 Hector Chase, LA 70809

Dear Mr. Mitchell:

Request/Time → We'd like your input as part of a study of family media habits. This study is not involved
involved   in any attempt to sell anything. Rather, the results will help provide better media options
               for families. The survey typically takes about 12 minutes to complete.

Selection → You were selected based on a random sample of home owners living in the 70809 zip
Method   code.

Reason to → We need your opinion about many important issues involving the way modern families
Respond   interact with various media including print, television, radio, and Internet sources.
            Companies need input to create the most appealing and useful options for consumers;
            and local, state, and federal agencies need input to know what types of regulations, if
            any, are most appropriate. Without the opinions of people like you, many of these key
            issues will likely not be resolved.

Confidentiality/ → The information you provide, just as with all the information collected within the
IRB Approval   scope of this project, will be entirely confidential. It will only be used for the purpose
                   of this research and no individuals will be identified within the data. Additionally, this
                   survey and the request for you to participate has been reviewed and approved by the
                   Institutional Review Board of MKTR which monitors all research conducted and assures
                   that procedures are consistent with ethical guidelines for federally funded research
                   (although this particular project is not funded federally). If you have any questions, the
                   MKTR IRB can be contacted at (888) 555-8888.

Incentive → Your response will improve the media choices that your family faces. In addition, a $10
            check that you can cash at your personal bank is included as a token of our appreciation.

Willingness → Additionally, you can direct any questions about this project directly to me. The contact
to answer   information is available at the top of this letter. Additionally, we will be happy to provide
questions   you a summary of the results. Simply complete the enclosed self-addressed postcard
               and drop it in the mail or include it with the completed questionnaire. A self-addressed,
               postage paid reply envelope is included for your return.

Thanks → Again, thank you so much for your time and for sharing your opinions.

Signature → *Laurie Thibodeaux*

reward for participation, explain that answering the questionnaire will not be difficult and will take only a short time, and describe how the person was scientifically selected for participation.

A personalized letter addressed to a specific individual shows the respondent that he or she is important. Including an individually typed cover letter on letterhead rather than a printed form is an important element in increasing the response rate in mail surveys.[14]

■ MONEY HELPS

The respondent's motivation for returning a questionnaire may be increased by offering monetary incentives or premiums. Although pens, lottery tickets, and a variety of premiums have been used, monetary incentives appear to be the most effective and least biasing incentive. Money attracts attention and creates a sense of obligation. Perhaps for this reason, monetary incentives work for all income categories. Often, cover letters try to boost response rates with messages such as "We know that the attached dollar cannot compensate you for your time but please accept it as a token of our appreciation." Response rates increase dramatically when a monetary incentive can be sent to a charity of the respondent's choice rather than directly to the respondent.

■ INTERESTING QUESTIONS

The topic of the research—and thus the point of the questions—cannot be manipulated without changing the definition of the marketing problem. However, certain interesting questions can be added to the questionnaire, perhaps at the beginning, to stimulate respondents' interest and to induce cooperation. By including questions that are of little concern to the researchers but that the respondents want to answer, the researchers may give respondents who are indifferent to the major questions a reason for responding.

■ FOLLOW-UPS

Most mail surveys generate responses in a pattern like that shown in Exhibit 9.4, which graphs the cumulative response rates for two mail surveys. The response rates are relatively high for the first two to three weeks (as indicated by the steepness of each curve), then the rates gradually taper off.

After responses from the first wave of mailings begin to trickle in, most studies use a follow-up letter or postcard reminder, which requests that the questionnaire be returned because a 100 percent return rate is important. A follow-up may include a duplicate questionnaire or may merely be a reminder to return the original questionnaire. Multiple contacts almost always increase response rates. The more attempts made to reach people, the greater the chances of their responding.[15]

Both of the studies in Exhibit 9.4 used follow-ups. The cumulative response rates picked up slightly around week four, about a week after the follow-up.

■ ADVANCE NOTIFICATION

Advance notification that a questionnaire will be arriving can increase response rates in some situations. ACNielsen has used this technique to ensure a high cooperation rate in filling out diaries of television watching. Advance notices that go out closer to the questionnaire mailing time produce better results than those sent too far in advance. The optimal lead time for advance notification is three days before the mail survey is to arrive. Advanced notification can come in the form of a postcard, a phone call, or even an e-mail.

■ SURVEY SPONSORSHIP

Sometimes, response quality is enhanced when the survey sponsor remains anonymous. Respondents may, perhaps unintentionally, provide biased results when the survey sponsor is known. One business-to-business marketer wished to conduct a survey of its wholesalers to learn their stocking

EXHIBIT 9.4
**Plots of Actual Response
Patterns for Two
Commercial Surveys**

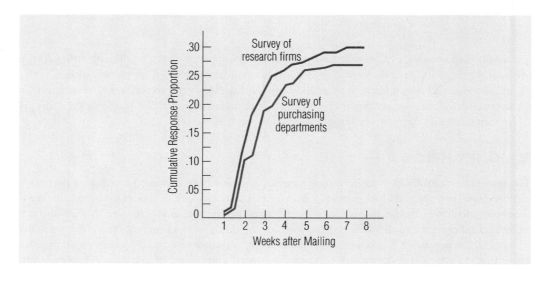

policies and their attitudes concerning competing manufacturers. A mail questionnaire sent on corporate letterhead very likely would have received a much lower response rate than the questionnaire actually sent, which used the letterhead of a commercial marketing research firm. So, whenever respondents may have some conflict of interest with the sponsor, or have some strong relational or emotional connection, response quality is likely highest when the sponsor is anonymous.

On the other hand, known sponsors can at times enhance response rates. Sponsorship by well-known and prestigious organizations such as universities or government agencies may significantly improve response rates. If a consumer belongs to a specific interest group or to a survey panel, identifying the group or panel as a sponsor of the research can be a good idea. A mail survey sent to members of a consumer panel will receive an exceptionally high response rate because panel members have already agreed to cooperate as part of membership.

■ OTHER TECHNIQUES

Numerous other devices have been used for increasing response rates. For example, the type of postage (commemorative versus regular stamp), envelope size, color of the questionnaire paper, and many other factors have been varied in efforts to increase response rates. Each has had at least limited success in certain situations; unfortunately, under other conditions each has failed to increase response rates significantly. The researcher should consider his or her particular situation. For example, the researcher who is investigating consumers faces one situation; the researcher who is surveying corporate executives faces quite another.

■ KEYING MAIL QUESTIONNAIRES WITH CODES

A marketing researcher planning a follow-up letter, postcard, or e-mail should not disturb respondents who already have completed and returned the questionnaire. The expense of mailing questionnaires to those who already have responded is usually avoidable. One device for eliminating those who have already responded from the follow-up mailing list is to mark the questionnaires so that they may be keyed to identify members of the sampling frame who are nonrespondents. Blind keying of questionnaires on a return envelope (systematically varying the job number or room number of the marketing research department, for example) or a visible code number on the questionnaire has been used for this purpose. Visible keying is indicated with statements such as "The sole purpose of the number on the last page is to avoid sending a second questionnaire to people who complete and return the first one." E-mail surveys will be discussed later. But, electronic questionnaires can sometimes allow identification using computer Internet protocols (IP addresses) or with other electronic identification methods as a way of noting which respondents have participated in a questionnaire. Ethical researchers key questionnaires only to increase response rates, thereby preserving respondents' anonymity.

Mail surveys can reach a geographically dispersed sample and are relatively inexpensive. One disadvantage is the length of time involved in getting responses back. Response rates themselves also offer a challenge to surveyors.

© AP PHOTO

Self-Administered Questionnaires Using Other Forms of Distribution

Many forms of self-administered, printed questionnaires are very similar to mail questionnaires. Airlines occasionally pass out questionnaires to passengers during flights. Restaurants, hotels, and other service establishments print short questionnaires on cards so that customers can evaluate the service. *Tennis Magazine, Advertising Age, Wired,* and many other publications have used inserted questionnaires to survey current readers inexpensively, and often the results provide material for a magazine article.

Many manufacturers use their warranty or owner registration cards to collect demographic information and data about where and why products were purchased. Using owner registration cards is an extremely economical technique for tracing trends in consumer habits. Again, problems may arise because people who fill out these self-administered questionnaires differ from those who do not.

Extremely long questionnaires may be dropped off by an interviewer and then picked up later. The **drop-off method** sacrifices some cost savings because it requires traveling to each respondent's location. However, the response rate is generally improved. In the U.S., drop-offs are more commonly applied when the sample involves businesspeople who can best be reached at their place of work.

drop-off method
A survey method that requires the interviewer to travel to the respondent's location to drop off questionnaires that will be picked up later.

Paper–and–Pencil Questionnaires: Global Considerations

Researchers conducting surveys in more than one country must recognize that postal services and cultural circumstances differ around the world. Some of the issues to consider are the reliability of mail delivery, literacy rates, and trust that researchers can and will provide confidentiality. In some cases, hand delivery of surveys or door-to-door interviewing may be necessary. In other cases, consumers (especially women or children) might be discouraged from talking to an interviewer who is not a family member, so mailed questionnaires would be superior to interviews.

Fax Surveys

With fax surveys, potential survey respondents receive and/or return questionnaires via fax machines.[16] A questionnaire inserted in a magazine may instruct the respondent to clip out the questionnaire and fax it to a certain phone number. In a mail survey, a prepaid-postage envelope places little burden on the respondent. But faxing a questionnaire to a long-distance number may require a respondent to pay for the transmission of the fax. Thus, a disadvantage of the **fax survey** is that only respondents with fax machines who are willing to exert the extra effort will return questionnaires. Again, people with extreme opinions will be more likely to respond.

fax survey
A survey that uses fax machines as a way for respondents to receive and return questionnaires.

To address this disadvantage, marketers may use faxing as one of several options for replying to a survey. The journal *American Family Physician* carried a reader survey that gave respondents the option of either returning the reply by fax or visiting the journal's Web site to answer the same questions online.[17] For busy physicians who likely have access to office equipment, this approach would improve the response rate.

Fax machines can also be used to distribute questionnaires. These fax surveys reduce the sender's printing and postage costs and can be delivered and returned faster than traditional mail surveys. Questionnaires distributed via fax can deal with timely issues. Although few households have fax machines, when the sample consists of organizations that are likely to have fax machines, the sample coverage may be adequate. The use of fax survey approaches though is largely being replaced by other electronic communication options.

E-Mail Surveys

E-mail surveys involve making the questionnaire available to a potential respondent via e-mail. Today, more questionnaires are distributed by e-mail in one way or another than by any other means. E-mail surveys can put a respondent together with a questionnaire in one of three ways.

e-mail surveys
Surveys distributed through electronic mail.

■ USING E-MAIL

Three ways to contact respondents via e-mail include the following.

- A questionnaire can be included in the body of an e-mail. In this case, the questionnaire should be very short (no more than 10 questions). These are likely to receive the highest response rate.

- Questionnaires can also be distributed as an attachment to an e-mail. The respondent may be asked to open the questionnaire and respond via radio boxes. **Radio boxes** (buttons) allow a respondent to enter a mark such as an "X" or a check mark as a way of making a response. As might be expected, response rates drop when a person is asked to open an attachment and perhaps save it to his or her computer or even print it before the response is complete. Researchers can use common software such as Microsoft Word or Adobe Acrobat to create these files. After completing the questionnaire, the respondent has

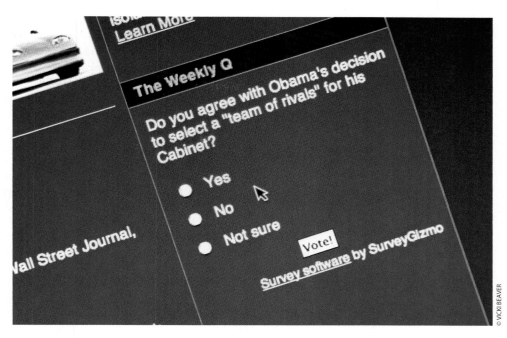

© VICKI BEAVER

radio boxes

A small box character (box or button) that can be inserted into a word-processing or JavaScript document that allows a respondent to indicate a choice with a check mark or X.

the burden of reattaching and returning by e-mail. Alternatively, the respondent may have the option of marking the questionnaire with a pen or pencil and returning via fax or mail. Obviously, the last approach should be avoided because of the burden placed on the respondent.

- A third option is to include a hyperlink within the body of an e-mail that will direct the respondent to a Web site that contains the questionnaire. The person can then complete the response directly on that Web site. This approach is fast becoming the most common way of soliciting responses via e-mail. In essence, the e-mail survey becomes an Internet survey at this point.

■ SAMPLING AND E-MAIL

Like phone surveys, most, but not all, people in developed countries have access to e-mail. Researchers must remember that some individuals cannot be reached this way. In particular, researchers targeting senior citizens may wish to avoid this approach if a true cross section of their opinion is desired. For many segments, researchers can reliably count on potential respondents having access to e-mail. Businesspeople are probably more reliably reached via e-mail than mail. Younger consumers between the ages of 15 and 45 almost certainly use e-mail on a regular basis. E-mail is now considered a viable alternative for contacting research respondents and soon will perhaps match or surpass the landline telephone as a vehicle useful for contacting a wide cross section of the population.

■ ADVANTAGES AND DISADVANTAGES OF E-MAIL

The benefits of incorporating a questionnaire in an e-mail include the speed of distribution, lower distribution and processing costs, faster turnaround time, more flexibility, and less handling of paper questionnaires. The speed of e-mail distribution and the quick response time can be major advantages for surveys dealing with time-sensitive issues.

Some researchers also believe that respondents are more candid in e-mail than in person or on the telephone. One caveat would exist when dealing with research directed at employers using company e-mail addresses. Employees often believe that their e-mails are not secure and "eavesdropping" by a supervisor could possibly occur. The belief that a response is not secure is particularly strong when the questionnaire is contained in the e-mail itself and a reply e-mail is needed to return a completed questionnaire. Researchers designing e-mail surveys in this way need to work especially hard to assure respondents that their answers will be confidential. Better yet, if any confidential subject matter is being exchanged, the respondent should be allowed to respond via a questionnaire accessed through a hyperlink rather than a reply e-mail. Thus, the ability to get candid responses remains an advantage.

One potential disadvantage is that not all e-mail systems have the same capacity. Some handle color and graphics well; others are limited to text. The extensive differences in the capabilities of respondents' computers and e-mail software limit the types of questions and the layout of the e-mail questionnaire. For example, the display settings for computer screens vary widely, and wrap-around of lines may put the questions and the answer choices into strange and difficult-to-read patterns.[18] Many novice e-mail users find it difficult to mark answers in brackets on an e-mail questionnaire and/or to send a completed questionnaire using the e-mail reply function. For very simple questionnaires, this is generally not a problem. Otherwise, the researcher can avoid these problems by using a hyperlinked survey approach.

In general, the guidelines for printed mail surveys apply to e-mail surveys. For example, delivering the material in the cover letter is more difficult because people generally do not like e-mails that are more than two or three lines. Thus, a traditional cover letter may need to be made as brief as possible if it is contained in the e-mail request itself. Another option is to move some of the cover letter material, such as the assurances of confidentiality and IRB approval, to the actual questionnaire introduction. Also, if the e-mail lists more than one address in the "to" or "CC" field, all recipients will see the entire list of names. This lack of anonymity has the potential to cause response bias and nonresponse error. When possible, the e-mail should be addressed to a single person. Alternatively, the blind carbon copy, or BCC, field can be used if the same message must be sent to an entire sample. A drawback to this approach is that some spam filters will identify any message addressed to a large number of respondents as junk e-mail. Bulk-mailing programs exist that attempt to work around this problem by e-mailing potential respondents a few at a time. As can be seen, the problems associated with successful delivery to respondents remain a disadvantage of e-mail surveys.

Internet Surveys

internet survey

A self-administered questionnaire posted on a Web site.

An **Internet survey** is a self-administered questionnaire posted on a Web site. Respondents provide answers to questions displayed onscreen by highlighting a phrase, clicking an icon, or actually typing in a response. Response rates remain an issue with Internet surveys. Typically, repondents are made aware of the existence of an Internet survey either by simply coming across it while browsing, through a pop-up notification, or via an e-mail containing a hyperlink as described above.

With Internet surveys, we can track both click rate, which assesses the portion of potential respondents who actually take a look at the questionnaire, and actual response rates. Of course, response rates will be no higher than the click rate. Generally, except for very long questionnaires, the vast majority of respondents who click through to view the questionnaire also respond to it. Like every other type of survey, Internet surveys have both advantages and disadvantages.

■ SPEED AND COST-EFFECTIVENESS

Internet surveys allow marketers to reach a large audience (possibly a global one), personalize individual messages, and secure confidential answers quickly and cost-effectively. These computer-to-computer self-administered questionnaires eliminate the costs of paper, postage, and data entry, as well as other administrative costs. Once an Internet questionnaire has been developed, the incremental cost of reaching additional respondents is minimal. So, samples can be larger than with interviews or other types of self-administered questionnaires. Even with large samples, surveys that used to take many weeks can be conducted in a week or less.

■ VISUAL APPEAL AND INTERACTIVITY

Surveys conducted on the Internet can have limted interactivity. The questionnaire can actually change based on the specific responses provided. The researcher can then use more sophisticated lines of questioning based on a respondent's prior answers. Many of these interactive surveys utilize color, sound, and animation, which may help to increase respondents' cooperation and willingness to spend time answering the questionnaires. The Internet is an excellent medium for the presentation of visual materials, such as photographs or drawings of product prototypes, advertisements, and movie trailers. Innovative measuring instruments that take advantage of the ability to adjust backgrounds, fonts, color, and other features have been designed and applied with considerable success.

RESPONDENT PARTICIPATION AND COOPERATION

Internet survey respondents can be highly involved in a particular issue when they intentionally click through to a particular questionnaire that they come across while browsing. For example, Ticketmaster quickly obtained more than 10,000 responses based on a survey invitation placed on their home page. The responses helped Ticketmaster better understand its customer purchase patterns and evaluate visitor satisfaction with the site. A response like this is possible only when consumers are involved and believe their cooperation will help make the experience better. Lacking involvement, and when participation is voluntary, Internet survey response rates can be very low.

Today, respondents are typically initially contacted via e-mail. Often they are members of consumer panels who have previously indicated their willingness to cooperate. When panel members receive an e-mail invitation to participate, they are given logon instructions and a password. This security feature prevents access by individuals who are not part of the scientifically selected sample. Requiring a login better enables the researcher to identify whether or not an invitee has already responded.

Panel members also need an incentive to respond. A study of German consumers showed that nothing beats financial incentives. In other words, the best way to get responses was to simply pay consumers for participating in surveys.[19] This may sound easy enough, although perhaps expensive, professional respondents could be an end result. Professional respondents may only be participating for the incentive and may even be giving bogus responses simply to finish each survey quickly. Such patterns are likely detectable as we discuss in a later chapter. Researchers using panel surveys need to be particularly vigilant in screening responses for authenticity.

ACCURATE REAL-TIME DATA CAPTURE

The computer-to-computer nature of Internet surveys means that each respondent's answers are entered directly into the researcher's computer as soon as the questionnaire is submitted. In addition, the questionnaire software may be programmed to reject improper data entry. For example, on a paper questionnaire a respondent might incorrectly check two responses even though the instructions call for a single answer. In an Internet survey, this mistake can be interactively corrected as the survey is taking place. Thus, the data capture is more accurate than when humans are involved.

Real-time data capture allows for real-time data analysis. A researcher can review up-to-the-minute sample size counts and tabulation data from an Internet survey in real time.

CALLBACKS

When the sample for an Internet survey is drawn from a consumer panel, those who have not completed the survey questionnaire can be easily recontacted. Computer software can simply automatically send e-mail reminders to panel members who did not visit the welcome page. Computer software can sometimes identify respondents who completed only a portion of the questionnaire and send those people customized messages. Sometimes such e-mails offer additional incentives to those individuals who terminated the questionnaire with only a few additional questions to answer, so that they are motivated to comply with the request to finish the questionnaire. On occasions when respondents are assured of complete anonymity and no individal tracking of computer identification takes place, the only callback option would be a reminder to the entire sample qualified by an "excuse me" message for those who may have already responded.

PERSONALIZED AND FLEXIBLE QUESTIONING

Computer-interactive Internet surveys are programmed in much the same way as computer-assisted telephone interviews. That is, the software that is used allows questioning to branch off into two or more different lines depending on a respondent's answer to a filtered question. The difference is that there is no interviewer. The respondent interacts directly with software on a Web site. In other words, the computer program asks questions in a sequence determined by the respondent's previous answers. The questions appear on the computer screen, and answers are recorded by simply pressing a key, clicking an icon, or typing a response, thus immediately entering the data into an electronic file. Of course, these methods avoid labor costs associated with data collection and processing of paper-and-pencil questionnaires.

This ability to sequence questions based on previous responses is a major advantage of computer-assisted surveys. The computer can be programmed to skip from question 6 to question 9 if the answer to question 6 is no. Furthermore, responses to previous questions can lead to questions that can be personalized for individual respondents (for example, "When you cannot buy your favorite brand, Revlon, what brand of lipstick do you prefer?"). Often the respondent's name appears in questions to personalize the questionnaire. Fewer and more relevant questions speed up the response process and increase the respondent's involvement with the survey.

A related advantage of using a Web survey is that it can prompt respondents when they skip over a question. In a test comparing telephone and Internet versions of the same survey, the rate of item nonresponse was less for the Internet version, which issued a prompt for each item that was left blank.[20] This was likely not a simple matter of motivation, because the rate of respondents who actually took the Web version was less than for the telephone version, even though the researchers offered a larger incentive to those who were asked to go online. (An earlier telephone screening had verified that everyone who was asked to participate had a computer.)

The ability to customize questions and the low cost per recipient also help researchers keep surveys short, an important consideration for boosting responses.[21] Jakob Nielsen, a consultant on Internet usability with the Nielsen Norman Group, emphasizes that "quick and painless" surveys generate the highest response and urges researchers to keep surveys as short as possible. He suggests that if the research objectives call for a long survey, the questions can be divided among several questionnaires, with each version sent to a different group of respondents.

■ RESPONDENT ANONYMITY

Respondents are more likely to provide sensitive or embarrassing information when they can remain anonymous. The anonymity of the Internet encourages respondents to provide honest answers to sensitive questions.

■ IMPROVING RESPONSE RATES

The methods for improving response rates for an Internet survey are similar to those for other kinds of survey research. A personalized invitation may be important. In many cases, the invitation is delivered via e-mail. The respondents may not recognize the sender's address, so the message's subject line is critical.[22] The subject line should refer to a topic likely to interest the audience, and legal as well as ethical standards dictate that it may not be deceptive. Thus, the line might be worded in a way similar to the following: "Please give your opinion on [subject matter of interest]." Researchers should avoid gimmicks like dollar signs and the word *free,* either of which is likely to alert the spam filters installed on most computers.

As mentioned earlier, with a password system, people who have not participated in a survey in a predetermined period of time can be sent a friendly e-mail reminder asking them to participate before the study ends. This type of follow-up, along with preliminary notification, interesting early questions, and variations of most other techniques for increasing response rates to mail questionnaires, is recommended for Internet surveys.

Unlike mail surveys, Internet surveys do not offer the opportunity to send a physical incentive, such as a dollar bill, to the respondent. Incentives to respond to a survey must be in the form of a coupon or a promise of a future reward. A coupon can be included that contains a discount code which can be applied at a retail Web site or even in a store. For example, a respondent might receive a $10 coupon good at www.target.com or in any Target store as a thanks for participating. Otherwise, a promise can be offered: "As a token of appreciation for completing this survey, the sponsor of the survey will make a sizable contribution to a national charity. You can vote for your preferred charity at the end of the survey." Although some researchers have had success with promising incentives, academic research about Internet surveys is sparse, and currently there are few definitive answers about the most effective ways to increase response rates.

A Web survey invitation or prenotification can also be sent via mail. The research firm can send postcards or letters informing potential respondents that an e-mail will be arriving in their inbox containing the hyperlink to the questionnaire. This is an alternative to sending a notification by e-mail only. For example, researchers studying why students enroll in the universities that they attend could be conducted by contacting recent college applicants. They might first receive a letter indicating that a survey invitation will arrive via e-mail. Alternatively, they may receive only the e-mail invitation. With a study like this, one might expect about 20 percent of potential respondents to click through to the questionnaire, and all but 1 or 2 percent of these would respond, for a final response rate of just under 20 percent. The response rate is relatively high when the respondent has shown some behavior indicative of involvement in the subject matter. In this case, applying to a university.

A mail notification has several potential advantages. Spammers do not send notifications via mail so the survey may end up having a little more legitimacy. Additionally, the prenotification establishes the potential for a relationship and can even include a request to put the sender on the receipient's safe sender list. However, research suggests that mail notifications offer little advantage in click and response rates. Response rates for respondents who were notified via mail respond in practically the same proportion as those receiving an e-mail prenotification.[23] Any advantage that the mail approach would have is likely countered by the additional costs of sending a mail notification. Thus, prenotifications do not appear very useful in increasing response rates.

Internet surveys, even those not associated with a panel, are often directed toward a finite population. For example, all members of the Atlanta area Sales and Marketing Executives Association might comprise a population of interest for researchers studying attitudes toward customer relationship management programs. What kind of response rate might be expected in this case? Recent research shows that a combination of pop-up notification on a software user forum's home page plus a single e-mail notification (to all members of the forum) yields a response rate of just about 14 percent.[24] While this does not seem very high, a response rate of this type is also common in mail surveys.

■ SECURITY CONCERNS

Many organizations worry that hackers or competitors may access Web sites to discover new product concepts, new advertising campaigns, and other top-secret ideas. Respondents may worry whether personal information will remain private. So may the organizations sponsoring the research. Recently, McDonald's conducted quality-control research in England and Scotland, automating the transmittal of data with a system in which consultants used handheld devices and sent the numbers to headquarters as e-mail messages. The system saved hours of work, but the company worried that confidential information could be compromised. McDonald's therefore purchased software that encrypted the data and allowed the handhelds to be remotely wiped clean of data if they were lost or stolen.[25]

As in the experience of McDonald's, no system can be 100 percent secure, but risks can be minimized. Many research service suppliers specializing in Internet surveying have developed password-protected systems that are very secure. One important feature of these systems restricts access and prevents individuals from filling out a questionnaire over and over again.

■ RESPONSE QUALITY

Internet surveys are still in their infancy in many ways. However, the prospects for a bright future are good. Surveys asking potential respondents questions that can be compared with known population demographics can be used to compare the response quality of different survey media. For instance, basic demographic information for each U.S. zip code is available through http://www.census.gov. Random samples taken from zip codes asking respondents to report these basic statistics should produce results that match the census data with allowance for a small amount of error. Thus far, indications are that Web-based survey approaches produce data that is as good as or better in quality than traditional phone surveys.[26]

Kiosk Surveys

A kiosk containing a computer with a touch screen may be used to administer a survey at a trade show, at a professional conference, in an airport, a retail store, or in any other high-traffic location to administer an interactive survey. Because the respondent chooses to interact with an on-site computer, self-selection often is a problem with this type of survey. Computer-literate individuals are most likely to complete these interactive questionnaires. At temporary locations such as conventions, these surveys often require a fieldworker to be at the location to explain how to use the computer system. This personal assistance is an obvious disadvantage.

Mixed-Mode Survey Research

mixed-mode survey
Study that employs any combination of survey methods.

For many surveys, research objectives dictate the use of some combination of telephone, mail, e-mail, Internet, and personal interview. For example, the researcher may conduct a short phone screening interview to determine whether respondents are eligible for recontact in a more extensive personal interview. Such a **mixed-mode survey** combines the advantages of the telephone survey (such as fast screening) and those of the personal interview. A mixed-mode survey can employ any combination of two or more survey methods. Conducting a research study in two or more waves, however, creates the possibility that some respondents will no longer cooperate or will be unavailable in the second wave of the survey.

Several variations of survey research use cable television channels. For example, a telephone interviewer calls a cable subscriber and asks him or her to tune in to a particular channel at a certain time. An appointment is made to interview the respondent shortly after the program or visual material is displayed. NBC uses this type of mixed-mode survey to test the concepts for many proposed new programs.

Text-Message Surveys

Yes, surveys are even being sent via text messages. These may use the SMS (short-message service) or MMS (Multi-Media Service). This technique is perhaps the newest survey approach. It has all the advantages of mobile-phone surveys in terms of reach and it also shares the disadvantages in terms of reaching respondents who have not opted in via a mobile phone. However, text-message surveys are catching on in other countries and are ideal for surveys involving only a few very short questions. Additionally, MMS messages can include graphic displays or even short videos. This technology is likely to see more applications in the near future.

Choosing an Appropriate Survey Approach

Earlier discussions of research design and problem definition emphasized that many research tasks may lead to similar decision-making information. There is no best form of survey; each has advantages and disadvantages. A researcher who must ask highly confidential questions may use a mail survey, thus sacrificing speed of data collection to avoid interviewer bias. If a researcher must have considerable control over question phrasing, central location telephone interviewing may be appropriate.

To determine the appropriate technique, the researcher must ask several questions: Is the assistance of an interviewer necessary? Are respondents interested in the issues being investigated? Will cooperation be easily attained? How quickly is the information needed? Will the study require a long and complex questionnaire? How large is the budget? The criteria—cost, speed, anonymity, and so forth—may differ for each project.

Exhibit 9.5 summarizes some major advantages and disadvantages of different survey approaches. It emphasizes typical types of surveys. For example, a creative researcher might be able to design highly versatile and flexible mail questionnaires, but most researchers use standardized questions. An elaborate mail survey may be far more expensive than a short personal interview, but generally this is not the case.

EXHIBIT 9.5 **Advantages and Disadvantages of Typical Survey Methods**

	Door-to-Door Personal Interview	**Mall Intercept Personal Interview**	**Telephone Interview**	**Mail Survey**	**Internet Survey**
Speed of data collection	Moderate to fast	Fast	Very fast	Slow; researcher has no control over return of questionnaire	Instantaneous; 24/7
Geographic flexibility	Limited to moderate	Confined, possible urban bias	High	High	High (worldwide)
Respondent cooperation	Excellent	Moderate to low	Good	Moderate; poorly designed questionnaire will have low response rate	Varies depending on website; high from consumer panels
Versatility of questioning	Quite versatile	Extremely versatile	Moderate	Not versatile; requires highly standardized format	Extremely versatile
Questionnaire length	Long	Moderate to long	Moderate	Varies depending on incentive	Moderate; length customized based on answers
Item non-response rate	Low	Medium	Medium	High	Software can assure none
Possibility for respondent misunderstanding	Low	Low	Average	High; no interviewer present for clarification	High
Degree of inter-viewer influence on answers	High	High	Moderate	None; interviewer absent	None
Supervision of interviewers	Moderate	Moderate to high	High, especially with central-location interviewing	Not applicable	Not applicable
Anonymity of respondent	Low	Low	Moderate	High	Respondent can be either anony-mous or known
Ease of callback or follow-up	Difficult	Difficult	Easy	Easy, but takes time	Difficult, unless e-mail address is known
Cost	Highest	Moderate to high	Low to moderate	Lowest	Low
Special features	Visual materials may be shown or demonstrated; extended probing possible	Taste tests, viewing of TV commercials possible	Fieldwork and supervision of data collection are simplified; quite adaptable to computer technology	Respondent may answer questions at own conven-ience; has time to reflect on answers	Streaming media software allows use of graphics and animation

Note: The emphasis is on *typical* surveys. For example, an elaborate mail survey may be far more expensive than a short personal interview, but this generally is not the case.

Pretesting Survey Instruments

A researcher who is surveying 3,000 consumers does not want to find out after the questionnaires have been completed or returned that most respondents misunderstood a particular question, skipped a series of questions, or misinterpreted the instructions for filling out the questionnaire. Problems such as these can be made less likely by various screening procedures, or *pretesting*. **Pretesting** involves a trial run with a group of colleagues or actual respondents to iron out fundamental problems in the instructions or design of a questionnaire. Researchers benefit by spotting problems in the pretest and rightly inferring that a problem with this very small sample will likely be a problem in the full sample once data collection actually begins.

Broadly speaking, researchers choose from three basic ways of pretesting. The first two involve screening the questionnaire with other research colleagues, and the third—the one most often called pretesting—is a trial run with an actual group of respondents. When screening the questionnaire with other research professionals, the investigator asks them to look for such problems as difficulties with question wording, leading questions, and bias due to question order. An alternative type of screening might involve a client or the research manager who ordered the research. Often, managers ask researchers to collect information, but when they see the questionnaire, they find that it does not really meet their needs. Only by checking with the individual who has requested the questionnaire does the researcher know for sure that the information needed will be provided. Additionally, other research experts may sometimes be asked to judge the content of survey items as a way of trying to verify that the items are measuring what the researcher intended. Later, we return to this idea under the heading of validity.

The third form is basically a trial run of the entire research project. Once the researcher has decided on the final questionnaire, data should be collected with a small number of respondents (perhaps as many as 100 but at least three dozen) to determine whether the questionnaire needs refinement. These particular respondents also may be asked to indicate specifically any items that are difficult to understand. The researcher can analyze these data for suspicious patterns that may indicate a problem. For example, in some cases the researcher may be surpised to find that all respondents have indicated the same answer to a specific question. Such a result is highly unlikely when more than a handful of respondents are included. Thus, a response like this probably indicates a problem.

Unfortunately, although the value of a pretest is readily apparent, this step is often skipped. The researcher may feel too much time pressure or pressure to produce the entire project within a certain budget. The risk of collecting some items that end up not being very helpful increases without a pretest. Needless to say, pretests are highly recommended in almost all types of primary data collection efforts.

pretesting
Screening procedure that involves a trial run with a group of respondents to iron out fundamental problems in the survey design.

TOTHEPOINT

Practice is the best of all instructors.

—Publius Syrus,
Circa 42 BC

Ethical Issues in Survey Research

Chapter 4 mentioned that codes of ethics express researchers' obligation to protect the public from misrepresentation and exploitation under the guise of marketing research. Thou shall not disguise selling as research! Many ethical issues apply to survey research, such as respondents' right to privacy, the use of deception, respondents' right to be informed about the purpose of the research, the need for confidentiality, the need for honesty in collecting data, and the need for objectivity in reporting data. You may wish to reexamine Chapter 4's coverage of these issues now that various survey research techniques have been discussed.[27]

At this time, a few points can be emphasized. Researchers should not ask for information in a misleading way. Also, researchers must be careful to guard the resulting data carefully. For instance, a researcher may end up with data that identifies children's responses to several different new products. The data may also contain demographics and other material. Once that data becomes stored on a laptop, it is vulnerable to theft or misplacement. The researcher should follow good security procedures in protecting the data stored on various storage mediums.

Additionally, technology brings new issues to the forefront. Although e-mail is an extremely useful tool, researchers should avoid needlessly contributing to spam volume by sending unsolicited e-mails seeking survey respondents. While at times, this may be the only way to reach a population, whenever possible, e-mail requests for responses should be sent to individuals who in some way

- Interpretative research involving a survey generally requires an interactive approach. On occasion, respondents may simply be asked to write a story without any elaboration, but generally, particularly with phenomenology, the researcher and the respondent are actively engaged.
- The longer the questionnaire, the lower the response rate.
  - When long questionnaires are absolutely necessary, the researcher should:
    - Look for respondents who are essentially a captive audience; like students in a class
    - Offer a nontrivial incentive to respond
    - Try to target the survey toward individuals who are highly involved in the topic

    - Use a survey research panel
- Mobile-phone survey calls are slightly more likely to be answered, particularly on weekdays, but mobile-phone users are more likely to refuse to participate than are landline phone users.
- E-mail surveys and Internet surveys are good approaches for most types of surveys.
  - When a panel or special interest group provides responses, the researcher should be extra vigilant for bogus response patterns.
  - Good response rates with no true special considerations such as a very high incentive or extreme levels of involvement can be expected to be between 10 and 15 percent.
- A short pretest is better than no pretest at all.

may have indicated that the e-mail may not be so unwanted. For example, members of consumer response panels have opted in and have given their explicit approval to receive such e-mails. Additionally, consumers who query about certain information may end up being good research respondents. Consider someone who has sought information about new hybrid cars from a Web site like Kelley Blue Book (www.kbb.com). A Web site like this may even include a place where a consumer can register and indicate whether they are open to being contacted in the future. If they appear to be open to responding to research that may be tied to new automobiles or environmentally sensitive products, sending a survey about attitudes toward new car features may not be an imposition. On the other hand, phoning someone during dinner or filling up a busy executive's in-box with requests to participate in irrelevant surveys pushes the boundaries of good ethics. Certainly, as technology continues to evolve, marketing researchers will be faced with even more challenges.

Summary

1. Summarize the different ways researchers implement surveys. Interviews can be categorized based on the medium used to communicate with respondents. A primary classification of survey approaches can be developed based on interactivity. An interactive approach facilitates two-way communication. Thus, the respondent and interviewer truly can have a dialogue. A face-to-face personal interview typifies this approach but other media including mobile phones and landline phones allow two-way communication. Noninteractive media primarily allow a way for respondents to give answers to predetermined questions with no opportunity for interactive two-way communication. Typical mail or e-mail questionnaires represent noninteractive media well. Both approaches have advantages and disadvantages.

2. Know the advantages and disadvantages of conducting surveys using personal interviews via door-to-door, mall intercept, landline telephone, or mobile-phone interviews. Door-to-door personal interviews can get high response rates, but they are more costly to administer than other types of surveys. Additionally, security issues make them increasingly rare today. Mall intercept interviews reduce costs and also provide the flexibility of a personal interview. The researcher has to be aware of the limitations of representing an entire consumer population from mall intercepts conducted in only one or a few locations. Phone interviewing has the advantage of providing data quickly and at a lower cost per personal interview. Phone interviews need to be shorter than other types of personal interviews. Although they are still considered fairly capable of producing a representative sample, they are not perfect. Do-not-call legislation also has provided challenges for traditional landline survey approaches. More and more consumers are choosing to own only a mobile phone. In the United States, mobile phones cannot be cold-called for research purposes. Thus, representativeness is limited because only consumers who opt in can be part of the sample.

Although landline and mobile phone calling share many characteristics, they also differ in several respects.

3. Choose an appropriate method of distributing a questionnaire from among mail, e-mail, Internet, fax, or mobile phone using SMS or MMS text. Traditionally, self-administered questionnaires have been distributed by mail, but self-administered questionnaires also may be dropped off to individual respondents, distributed from central locations, or administered via computer. Mail questionnaires generally are less expensive than telephone or personal interviews, but they also introduce a much larger chance of nonresponse error. E-mail and Internet survey approaches have become a more attractive and convenient way to conduct surveys. They are particularly a better option than mail surveys when budget is a major concern, when a quick response is needed, or when respondents need to see a video display before responding. Response rates are a major concern with e-mail and Internet surveys too. Early results indicate that steps can be taken to produce response rates similar to those observed in mail surveys.

4. Appreciate the importance of pretesting questionnaires. Pretesting a questionnaire on a small sample of respondents is a useful way to discover problems while they can still be corrected. Pretests may involve screening the questionnaire with other research professionals or conducting a trial run with a set of respondents.

5. Describe ethical issues that arise in survey research. Researchers must protect the public from misrepresentation and exploitation. This obligation includes honesty about the purpose of a research project and protection of subjects' right to refuse to participate or to answer particular questions. Researchers also should protect the confidentiality of participants and record responses honestly. Lastly, as technology evolves, researchers should be mindful of not needlessly contributing to unwanted electronic or personal communications. Thus, both the reason for and the method of contact should be carefully scrutinzed.

Key Terms and Concepts

callbacks, *216*
central location interviewing, *222*
computer-assisted telephone interviewing
   (CATI), *222*
cover letter, *226*
door-to-door interviews, *216*
drop-off method, *230*
e-mail surveys, *230*

fax survey, *230*
interactive survey approaches, *211*
internet survey, *232*
item nonresponse, *214*
mail survey, *224*
mall intercept interviews, *216*
mixed-mode survey, *236*
noninteractive survey approaches, *211*

personal interview, *212*
pretesting, *238*
radio boxes, *231*
random digit dialing, *219*
response rate, *226*
self-administered questionnaires, *223*
telephone interviews, *217*

Questions for Review and Critical Thinking

1. Why is it so important today for researchers to take advantage of new technologies in finding new ways to communicate with respondents?
2. Define interactive and noninteractive survey approaches. Why might a researcher choose an interactive survey approach over a noninteractive survey approach?
3. What type of survey approach would you use to conduct the following surveys? Why?
   a. Survey of the business-related buying motives of industrial engineers
   b. Survey of the satisfaction levels of rental car users
   c. Survey of television commercial advertising awareness
   d. Survey of the service quality offered at major tire retail stores
4. A publisher offers teenage boys (aged 14–17 years old) one of four best-selling famous rock posters as an incentive for filling out a 10-page mail questionnaire about guitars. What are the

pros and cons of offering this incentive? Yes or no, should the incentive be offered?
5. "Individuals are less willing to cooperate with surveys today than they were fifty years ago." Comment on this statement.
6. What do you think should be the maximum length of a self-administered e-mail questionnaire?
7. A survey researcher reports that "205 usable questionnaires out of 942 questionnaires delivered in our mail survey converts to a 21.7 percent response rate." What are the subtle implications of this statement?
8. What is do-not-call legislation? What effect has it had on survey research?
9. Agree or disagree with this statement: Landline and mobile-phone surveys are essentially the same and can be used in the same situations with the same results.

10. What are the advantages and disadvatanges of e-mail surveys? What are situations when they may not be appropriate?

11. Evaluate the following survey designs:

    a. A text message survey asking the potential respondent to indicate with yes or no responses whether they are driving or not, whether they are alone, whether they believe the roads in their area can adequately handle traffic, whether more money should be devoted to better roadways, whether or not traffic is adequately policed, and whether or not automatic cameras should be used to issue speeding tickets. The sample is drawn from people who have agreed to be contacted via mobile phone regarding their new Toyota.

    b. A shopping mall that wishes to evaluate its image places packets including a questionnaire, cover letter, and stamped return envelope in the mall where customers can pick them up if they wish.

    c. An e-mail message is sent asking respondents to complete a questionnaire on a Web site. Respondents answer the questions and then have the opportunity to play a slot-machine game on the Web site. Each respondent is guaranteed a monetary incentive but has the option to increase it by repeatedly playing the slot-machine game.

    d. A mall intercept interviewing service is located in a regional shopping center. The facility contains a small room for television and movie presentations. Shoppers are used as sampling units. However, mall intercept interviewers recruit additional subjects for television commercial experiments by offering them several complimentary tickets for special sneak previews. Individuals contacted at the mall are allowed to bring up to five guests. In some cases the complimentary tickets are offered through ads in a local newspaper.

    e. *Time* magazine opts to conduct a mobile-phone survey rather than mail survey for a study to determine the demographic characteristics and purchasing behavior of its subscribers in the U.K. and in France.

12. What type of survey approach is most likely to yield the highest reponse rate? What approach(es) will yield the lowest reponse rate? What can be done to improve response rates in e-mail and Internet surveys?

13. **ETHICS** Comment on the ethics of the following situations:

    a. A researcher plans to use invisible ink to code questionnaires to identify respondents in a mail survey designed to get honest opinions from people who have filed to run for political office. The code will allow their identities to be known by the researcher.

    b. A political action committee conducts a survey about its cause. At the end of the questionnaire, it includes a request for a donation.

    c. A telephone interviewer calls at 1 p.m. on Sunday and asks the person who answers the phone to take part in an interview.

    d. An industrial marketer wishes to survey its own distributors. It invents the name "Mountain States Marketing Research" and sends out an e-mail questionnaire under this name.

    e. A questionnaire is printed on the back of a warranty card included inside the package of a food processor. The questionnaire includes a number of questions about shopping behavior, demographics, and customer lifestyles. At the bottom of the warranty card is a short note in small print that says "Thank you for completing this questionnaire. Your answers will be used for marketing studies and to help us serve you better in the future. You will also benefit by receiving important mailings and special offers from a number of organizations whose products and services relate directly to the activities, interests, and hobbies in which you enjoy participating on a regular basis. Please indicate if there is some reason you would prefer not to receive this information."

14. **ETHICS** How might the marketing research industry take action to ensure that the public believes that landline phone surveys and door-to-door interviews are legitimate activities and that firms that misrepresent and deceive the public using marketing research as a sales ploy are not true marketing researchers?

15. **ETHICS** The American Testing Institute (also known as the U.S. Testing Authority) mails respondents what it calls a "television" survey. A questionnaire is sent to respondents, who are asked to complete it and mail it back along with a check for $14.80. In return for answering eight questions on viewing habits, the institute promises to send respondents one of twenty prizes ranging in value from $200 to $2,000—among which are video recorders, diamond watches, a lifetime supply of film, color televisions, and two nights of hotel accommodations at a land development resort community. The institute lists the odds of winning as 1 in 150,000 on all prizes except the hotel stay, for which the odds are 149,981 out of 150,000. During a three-month period, the institute sends out 200,000 questionnaires. What are the ethical issues in this situation?

16. **'NET** Go to the Pew Internet and American Life page at http://www.pewinternet.org. Several reports based on survey research will be listed. Select one of the reports. What were the research objectives? What were the first three questions on the survey?

17. **'NET** Go to the NPD Group Web site (http://www.npd.com) and click on the Retailers (click on "Products & Services" and then "For Retailers") link. What types of custom and syndicated survey research services does the company offer? Is information readily available describing how the information was gathered?

18. **'NET** Go to the CASRO (Council of American Survey Research Organizations) Web site (http://www.casro.org). Select "About CASRO" or other links to explore the organization. What are the key aspects of this research organization's mission?

Research Activities

1. **'NET** Visit this Web site: http://www.zoomerang.com. What unique service does this company offer? Then visit this site: http://www.qualtrics.com. How does this service differ from Zoomerang? Create a short survey and e-mail it to 10 of your friends without any advance notice. At the end of the survey, ask them if they would have responded had they not noticed the survey came from you. What is the response rate? What would it have been if the respondent did not know you?

Case 9.1 National Do Not Call Registry

Citizens' annoyance with phone calls from salespeople prompted Congress to pass a law setting up a National Do Not Call Registry. The registry was soon flooded with requests to have phone numbers removed from telemarketers' lists. By law, salespeople may not call numbers listed on this registry. The law makes exceptions for charities and researchers. However, a recent poll suggests that even though phone calls from researchers may be legal, they are not always well received.[28]

In late 2005, Harris Interactive conducted an Internet survey in which almost 2,000 adults answered questions about the National Do Not Call Registry. About three-quarters of the respondents said they had signed up for the registry, and a majority (61 percent) said they had since received "far less" contact from telemarketers. In addition, 70 percent said that since registering, they had been contacted by someone "who was doing a poll or survey" and wanted them to participate. But apparently respondents weren't sure whether this practice was acceptable. Only one-fourth (24 percent) of respondents said they knew that researchers "are allowed to call," and over half (63 percent) weren't sure about researchers' rights under the law.

Questions

1. Was an online survey the best medium for a poll on this subject? What were some pros and cons of conducting this poll online?
2. How might the results have differed if this poll had been conducted by telephone?
3. As a researcher, how would you address people's doubts about whether pollsters may contact households listed on the Do Not Call Registry?

Case 9.2 Royal Bee Electric Fishing Reel

Royal Barton started thinking about an electric fishing reel when his father had a stroke and lost the use of an arm. To see that happen to his dad, who had taught him the joys of fishing and hunting, made Barton realize what a chunk a physical handicap could take out of a sports enthusiast's life. Being able to cast and retrieve a lure and experience the thrill of a big bass trying to take your rig away from you were among the joys of life that would be denied Barton's father forever.

Barton was determined to do something about it, if not for his father, then at least for others who had suffered a similar fate. So, after tremendous personal expense and years of research and development, Barton perfected what is sure to be the standard bearer for all future freshwater electric reels. Forget those saltwater jobs, which Barton refers to as "winches." He has developed something that is small, compact, and has incredible applications.

He calls it the Royal Bee. The first word is obviously his first name. The second word refers to the low buzzing sound the reel makes when in use.

The Royal Bee system looks simple enough and probably is if you understand the mechanical workings of a reel. A system of gears ties into the gears of the spool, and a motor in the back drives the gears attached to the triggering system.

All gearing of the electrical system can be disengaged so that you can cast normally. But pushing the button for "Retrieve" engages two gears. After the gears are engaged, the trigger travels far enough to touch the switch that tightens the drive belt, and there is no slipping. You cannot hit the switch until the gears are properly engaged. This means that you cast manually, just as you would normally fish, then you reengage the reel for the levelwind to work. And you can do all that with one hand!

The system works on a 6-volt battery that you can attach to your belt or hang around your neck if you are wading. If you have a boat with a 6-volt battery, the reel can actually work off of the battery. There is a small connector that plugs into the reel, so you could easily use more than one reel with the battery. For instance, if you have two or three outfits equipped with different lures, you just switch the connector from reel to reel as you use it. A reel with the Royal Bee system can be used in a conventional manner. You do not have to use it as an electric reel unless you choose to do so.

Barton believes the Royal Bee may not be just for handicapped fishermen. Ken Cook, one of the leading professional anglers in the country, is sold on the Royal Bee. After he suffered a broken arm, he had to withdraw from some tournaments because fishing with one hand was difficult. By the time his arm healed, he was hooked on the Royal Bee because it increased bassing efficiency. As Cook explains, "The electric reel has increased my efficiency in two ways. One is in flipping, where I use it all the time. The other is for fishing topwater, when I have to make a long cast. When I'm flipping, the electric reel gives me instant control over slack line. I can keep both hands on the rod. I never have to remove them to take up slack. I flip, engage the reel, and then all I have to do is push the lever with my thumb to take up slack instantly."

Cook's reel (a Ryobi 4000) is one of several that can be converted to the electric retrieve. For flipping, Cook loads his reel with 20-pound test line. He uses a similar reel with lighter line when fishing a surface lure. "What you can do with the electric reel is eliminate unproductive reeling time," Cook says.

A few extra seconds may not mean much if you are out on a neighborhood pond just fishing on the weekend. But it can mean a lot if you are in tournament competition, where one extra cast might keep you from going home with $50,000 tucked in your pocket. "Look at it this way," Cook explains. "Let's suppose we're in clear water and it's necessary to make a long cast to the cover we want to fish with a topwater lure. There's a whole lot of unproductive water between us and the cover. With the electric reel, I make my long cast and fish the cover. Then, when I'm ready to reel in, I just press the retrieve lever so the battery engages the necessary gears, and I've got my lure back ready to make another cast while you're still cranking."

When Royal Barton retired from his veterinary supply business, he began enjoying his favorite pastimes: hunting, fishing, and developing the Royal Bee system. He realized he needed help in marketing his product, so he sought professional assistance to learn how to reach the broadest possible market for the Royal Bee system.

Questions

1. What marketing problem does Royal Barton face? What are his information needs? Outline some survey research objectives for a research project on the Royal Bee system.
2. What type of survey—personal interview, telephone interview, or mail survey—should be selected?
3. What sources of survey error are most likely to occur in a study of this type?
4. What means should be used to obtain a high response rate?

CHAPTER 10
OBSERVATION

After studying this chapter, you should be able to

1. Discuss the role of observation as a marketing research method
2. Describe the use of direct observation and contrived observation
3. Identify ethical issues particular to research using observation
4. Explain the observation of physical objects and message content
5. Describe major types of mechanical observation
6. Summarize techniques for measuring physiological reactions

Chapter Vignette: Neuroco Peers into the Consumer's Brain

When Hewlett-Packard was developing advertisements for its digital photography products, the firm wanted to ensure its ad images would evoke the desired response. For guidance, the company turned to Neuroco and its high-tech research method, known as neuromarketing.[1] Neuroco researchers showed subjects a pair of photos of the same woman, and about half of them preferred each picture. Then Neuroco measured the electrical activity in the brains of subjects looking at the same images, and the analysis showed a definite preference for one of the pictures in which the woman's smile was a little warmer.

Neuroco's approach uses a technology called *quantified electroencephalography (QEEG)*. Subjects wear light and portable EEG equipment that records brain activity; software presents the data in computer maps that display activity levels in areas of the brain. Researchers can then evaluate whether the person is attentive and whether brain activity signifies emotional involvement or analytical thinking. QEEG is more flexible than the better-known use of functional magnetic resonance imaging (fMRI), which has provided many advances in brain research but requires all subjects to lie still in a large, noisy machine. With QEEG, the measuring equipment can travel with subjects as they walk around a store or watch advertisements.

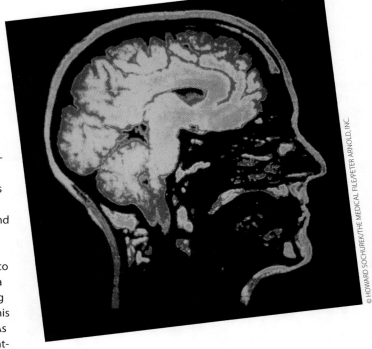

© HOWARD SOCHUREK/THE MEDICAL FILE/PETER ARNOLD, INC.

Consider a young woman demonstrating a Neuroco study by shopping with electrodes discreetly attached to her head. Neuroco chief scientist David Lewis observes a computer screen showing a map of her brain waves in red and green, with the colors signaling levels of alpha-wave activity. The zigzag pattern tells Lewis that this shopper is alert but not engaged in making purchase decisions. As the woman walks into a store's shoe department, however, the pattern changes when she picks up a pair of stiletto heels. An explosion of brain activity occurs, then the woman heads for the cash register, decision made.

As this example illustrates, observation can provide significant insights to marketers, and advances in observation technology are literally providing a view of what is happening in customers' brains. This chapter introduces the observation method of data gathering in marketing research.

Introduction

Scientists rely heavily on observation. This is true today, it will be true tomorrow, and it certainly was true in the past. Simple observation has played a key role in scientific discoveries for as long as people have pursued knowledge. Bernoulli developed the laws of buoyancy and fluid dynamics by observing what happened to his bath water when he entered the tub; it went up in proportion to his mass. What a simple observation! According to legend, Newton developed the laws of gravitation by observing (and feeling) the way an apple fell onto his head while he rested under the tree. Observation like this is how inductive learning begins. Researchers also deductively develop theories that require observation of some specific phenomena to empirically test them. This chapter focuses especially on observing marketing behavior directly. Like with surveys, modern technology has greatly enhanced marketing researchers ability to observe the actual behavior of consumers in the marketplace and marketing employees on their jobs.

Observation in Marketing Research

observation

The systematic process of recording the behavioral patterns of people, objects, and occurrences as they are witnessed.

In marketing research, **observation** is a systematic process of recording actual behavioral patterns of people, objects, and events as they happen. No questioning or communicating with people is needed. Researchers who use observation method data collection either witness and record information while watching events take place or take advantage of some tracking system such as checkout scanners or Internet activity records. These tracking systems can observe and provide data such as whether or not a specific consumer purchased more products on discount or at regular price or how much time a consumer spent viewing a particular Web page before either exiting or clicking through to the next page.

Observation can be a useful part of either qualitative or quantitative research. Additionally, actual observations of behavioral patterns can be part of an exploratory, descriptive, or even a causal design. For instance, researchers studying compliance with a diet program might manipulate different features of the program and then observe actual eating and exercise habits. These observations would play a key role as a dependent variable in a causal design. More often, however, observation is associated with qualitative research and with exploratory research designs. Observation is nearly synonymous with ethnographic research as researchers often try to blend into the environment and simply scrutinize the germane behavior. Callaway Golf may plant ethnographic researchers as caddies (who carry clubs for golfers) on nice golf courses to observe the actual behavior of golfers on the golf course. The caddies blend into the environment in a manner traditional to ethnographic research. Scientific observation is scarcely distinguished from simple observation. However, scientific observation is motivated by some research question aimed at discovering or testing market knowledge.

Retailers can learn a great deal about merchandising, store design, and promotion simply by watching their customers.

© ROBERT STAINFORTH/ALAMY

What Can Be Observed?

Observational studies gather a wide variety of information about behavior. Exhibit 10.1 lists eight kinds of observable phenomena: physical actions, such as shopping patterns (in-store or via a Web interface) or television viewing; verbal behavior, such as sales conversations; expressive behavior,

Perhaps you recall answering these questions about opinions and preferences for technological products. Take a look at the results from this section of the survey. In what way has behavioral observation been used to collect additional data—if at all? How might this information be useful to companies that sell small electronic appliances? Are there other places in the survey where behavioral observation has been combined with this traditional survey approach?

such as tone of voice or facial expressions; spatial relations and locations, such as traffic patterns; temporal patterns, such as amount of time spent shopping or driving; physical objects, such as the amount of newspapers recycled; verbal and pictorial records, such as the content of advertisements; and neurological activity such as brain activity in response to marketing stimuli.

The observation method may be used to describe a wide variety of behavior, but cognitive phenomena such as attitudes, motivations, and preferences cannot be observed. As a result, observation research cannot provide an explanation of why a behavior occurred or what actions were intended. Another limitation is that the observation period generally is short. Observing behavior patterns that occur over a period of several days or weeks generally is too costly or even impossible. The Research Snapshot on the next page illustrates a way that trends are tracked with observations.

TOTHEPOINT

Where observation is concerned, chance favors only the prepared mind.

—Louis Pasteur

The Nature of Observation Studies

Marketing researchers can observe people, objects, events, or other phenomena using either human observers or machines designed for specific observation tasks. Human observation best suits a

EXHIBIT 10.1 **What Are Things that People Do and Marketing Researchers Observe?**

Phenomenon	Example
Physical activities	The way a shopper moves through a store, patterns of motion and interaction with objects
Verbal behavior	Statements made by consumers at the Wal-Mart checkout either to each other or to a Wal-Mart employee
Expressive behavior and physiological reactions	Facial expressions of consumers in a restaurant or the body language of consumers visiting a day spa; measures of how much sweat a person is producing
Spatial relations and locations	How close shoppers stand to service providers while getting advice about fashion
Temporal patterns	How long patients in a doctor's office will wait before approaching the counter to inquire or complain
Physical objects	What brand of shoes, clothing, and skateboards teens at a skate park own and use
Verbal and pictorial records	Photographs or videos of early childhood Christmas experiences; comments left on Internet blogs
Neurological events	Brain activity in response to a consumer experiencing joy or disgust or perhaps while reading nutrition information

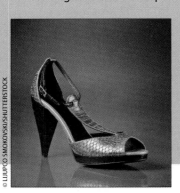

This Trend Brought to You by DDB SignBank

Extending the practice of observation beyond what can clearly be done scientifically, such as counting the number of tomato soup cans in a pantry or measuring the time spent watching television, some researchers have tried to catalog behaviors that may signal the beginning of important trends. This practice, called *trend spotting*, is controversial because the observations are subjective and unsystematic. In spite of the criticism, marketers are increasingly turning to trend spotters, so researchers have an incentive to develop this method's capabilities.

Starting in its office in Copenhagen, Denmark, giant ad agency DDB Worldwide has created a service called DDB SignBank, which invites all of DDB's staff throughout the world, plus other targeted groups such as members of youth organizations, to submit their observations to managers appointed as SignBankers. Staff members

are directed to identify consumer behaviors, rather than comments gathered from other research methods, that might signal a new trend in the society or culture. The Sign-Bankers classify the observations and enter them into a corporate database. The database is updated each day, and account teams at the agency can search it for signs related to their clients' advertising objectives.

The idea behind SignBank, developed by sociologist Eva Steensig, is that the size of the database (which contained thirty thousand signs at a recent count) will allow patterns to emerge in the sheer number of observations. The data may be most useful as a source of ideas to test more rigorously. Anthon Berg, a Scandinavian brand of chocolate, used SignBank data to identify new occasions for which to promote chocolate and new uses for chocolate in health and beauty treatments.

Source: Based on Matthew Creamer, "DDB Collects 'Signs' to Identify Trends," *Advertising Age* (December 5, 2005), downloaded from http://www.adage.com, June 16, 2006; Eric Pfanner, "On Advertising: Do I Spot a Trend?" *International Herald Tribune* (January 1, 2006), www.iht.com; and DDB Worldwide, "DDB Worldwide Introduces DDB SignBank, a New Consumer Knowledge Model," news release (November 29, 2005), http://www.ddbneedham.dk.

situation or behavior that is not easily predictable in advance of the research. Mechanical observation, as performed by supermarket scanners or traffic counters, can very accurately record situations or types of behavior that are routine, repetitive, or programmatic. Sophisticated machines that assess biological reactions such as a lie detector or neurological activities such as brain activation are also considered mechanical.

unobtrusive observation

No communication with the person being observed is necessary so that he or she is unaware that he or she is an object of research

visible observation

Observation in which the observer's presence is known to the subject.

hidden observation

Observation in which the subject is unaware that observation is taking place.

Human or mechanical observation is often **unobtrusive**, meaning no communication with a respondent takes place. For example, rather than asking customers how much time they spend shopping in the store, a supermarket manager might observe and record the intervals between when shoppers enter and leave the store. The unobtrusive nature of observational data collection often generates data without a subject's knowledge. A situation in which an observer's presence, or the mechanical device doing the recording, is easily known to the subject involves **visible observation**. A situation in which a subject is unaware that any observation is taking place is **hidden observation**. Hidden, unobtrusive observation minimizes respondent error. Asking subjects to participate in research is not generally required when they are unaware that they are being observed. A consumer who is asked to wash his or her hair in front of a video camera is visibly observed while a consumer observed by security cameras while shopping for shampoo is captured by hidden observation.

The major advantage of gathering data through unobtrusive observation over surveys, which obtain self-reported data from respondents, is that the data are free from distortions, inaccuracies, or other response biases due to memory error, social desirability bias, and so on. The data are recorded when and as the actual event takes place.

Observation of Human Behavior

Whereas surveys emphasize verbal responses, observation studies emphasize and allow for the systematic recording of nonverbal behavior. Toy manufacturers such as Fisher Price use the observation technique because children often cannot express their reactions to products. By observing children at play with a proposed toy, doll, or game, marketing researchers may be able to identify the elements of a potentially successful product. Toy marketing researchers might observe play to answer the following questions:

• How long does the child's attention stay with the product?

- Does the child put the toy down after two minutes or twenty minutes?
- Are the child's peers equally interested in the toy?

Behavioral scientists have recognized that nonverbal behavior can be a communication process by which meanings are exchanged among individuals. Head nods, smiles, raised eyebrows, and other facial expressions or body movements have been recognized as communication symbols. Observation of nonverbal communication may hold considerable promise for the marketing researcher. For example, a hypothesis about customer-salesperson interactions is that the salesperson would signal status based on the importance of each transaction. In low-importance transactions, in which potential customers are plentiful and easily replaced (say, a shoe store), the salesperson may show definite nonverbal signs of higher status than the customer. When customers are scarce, as in big-ticket purchase situations (real estate sales), the opposite should be true, with the salesperson showing many nonverbal indicators of deference. One way to test this hypothesis would be with an observation study using the nonverbal communication measures shown in Exhibit 10.2. Each row in the table indicates an aspect of nonverbal communication that might be observed in a common market situation.

Of course, researchers would not ignore verbal behavior. In fact, in certain observation studies, verbal expression is very important.

Complementary Evidence

The results of observation studies may amplify the results of other forms of research by providing *complementary evidence* concerning individuals' "true" feelings. Focus group interviews often are conducted behind two-way mirrors from which marketing executives observe as well as listen to what is occurring. This additional source allows for interpretation of nonverbal behavior such as facial expressions or head nods to supplement information from interviews.

For example, in one focus group session concerning women's use of hand lotion, researchers observed that all the women's hands were above the table while they were casually waiting for the session to begin. Seconds after the women were told that the topic was to be hand lotion, all their

EXHIBIT 10.2 **Observing and Interpreting Nonverbal Communication**

Behavior		Description	Example
Facial expressions		Expressions of emotion such as surprise (eyes wide open, mouth rounded and slightly open, brow furrowed)	A consumer reacts to the price quoted by a salesperson.
Body language		Posture, placement of arms and legs	A consumer crosses arms as salesperson speaks, possibly indicating a lack of trust.
Eye activity		Eye contact, staring, looking away, dilated pupils. In U.S. culture, not making eye contact is indicative of a deteriorating relationship. Dilated pupils can indicate emotion or degree of honesty.	A consumer avoids making eye contact with a salesperson knowing that he or she will not make a purchase.
Personal space		Physical distance between individuals; in the United States, people like to be about eight feet apart to have a discussion.	A consumer may back away from a salesperson who is viewed to be violating one's personal space.
Gestures		Responses to certain events with specific body reactions or gestures	A consumer who wins something (maybe at the casino or a sports contest) lifts arms, stands tall, and sticks out chest.
Manners		Accepted protocol for given situations	A salesperson may shake a customer's hand, but should not touch a customer otherwise.

hands were placed out of sight. This observation, along with the group discussion, revealed the women's anger, guilt, and shame about the condition of their hands. Although they felt they were expected to have soft, pretty hands, their housework required them to wash dishes, clean floors, and do other chores that were hard on their hands.

Some research studies combine visible observation with personal interviews. During or after in-depth observations, individuals are asked to explain their actions.[2] Direct observation of women applying hand and body lotion identified two kinds of users. Some women slapped on the lotion, rubbing it briskly into their skin. Others caressed their skin as they applied the lotion. When the women were interviewed about their behavior, the researchers were able to interpret this finding. Women who slapped the lotion on were using the lotion as a remedy for dry skin. Those who caressed their skin were more interested in making their skin smell nice and feel soft.

When focus group behavior is videotaped, observation of the nonverbal communication symbols can add even more to marketers' knowledge of the situation. Observations of customers in a shopping center may also be followed with survey research to follow up on some observed behavior. For example, if customers are observed looking into the window of a store for more than 30 seconds but then moving on without going in, researchers may intercept them with a few questions potentially revealing reasons for this behavior.

Recording the decision time necessary to make a choice is a relatively simple, unobtrusive task easily accomplished through direct observation; it is also an example of complementary evidence. Survey responses can be combined with information on how long the respondent took to make a choice. This recorded choice time is a measure of **response latency**. This measure is based on the hypothesis that the longer a decision maker takes, the more difficult that decision was and the more thought the respondent put into the choice. A quick decision presumably indicates an easy or obvious choice. Computer-administered surveys can incorporate an automatic measure of response latency and thereby offer a big advantage over paper and pencil approaches.

response latency

The amount of time it takes to make a choice between two alternatives; used as a measure of the strength of preference.

Direct and Contrived Observation

Researchers always are faced with a decision of how much they should interject themselves into the situation being studied. In a phenomenological approach, the researcher is often very much within the research situation. Consider the case where restaurant employees might be asked to talk about working in a restaurant and to explain how much emphasis is placed on hygiene and general concern for customer safety. The researcher has to ask questions and may even provide some prop or stimulus for the respondent to react to. On the other hand, hidden cameras might be placed within the restaurants so that data can be gathered with no researcher present. Alternatively, an ethnographer may actually take a job in the restaurant and perform certain acts to see how other employees react. This brings us to the difference between direct and contrived observation.

Direct Observation

direct observation

A straightforward attempt to observe and record what naturally occurs; the investigator does not create an artificial situation.

Direct observation can produce detailed records of what people actually do during an event. The observer plays a passive role, making no attempt to control or manipulate a situation, instead merely recording what occurs. Every effort is made for the interviewer not to interject him- or herself into the situation. For example, recording traffic counts and traffic flows within a supermarket can help managers design store layouts that maximize a typical customer's exposure to the merchandise offered while also facilitating search efforts. This data can be more accurately gathered simply by observing consumers rather than by asking consumers about their movement in the store. A manufacturer can then better determine shelf locations, the arrangement of departments and merchandise within those departments, the location of checkout facilities, and other characteristics that improve the shopping value consumers obtain from visiting a store. If directly questioned in a survey, most shoppers would be unable to accurately portray the time they spent in each department.

With the direct observation method, the data consist of records of events made as they occur. An observation form often helps keep researchers' observations consistent and ensures that they record all relevant information. A respondent is not required to recall—perhaps inaccurately—an event after it has occurred; instead, the observation is instantaneous. For instance, a response latency measure embedded in an online survey will "observe" how long a respondent took to answer a question without the respondent ever knowing the measure was taken. Will this provide more accurate information than if the respondent was asked to report how many seconds it took him or her to respond? Almost certainly the answer is yes!

■ WHY USE DIRECT OBSERVATION?

In many cases, direct observation is the most straightforward form of data collection—or the only form possible. A produce manager for Auchan (a France-based hypermart firm) may periodically gather competitive price information from Carrefour (also a France-based hypermart firm) stores within competing areas. Both Carrefour and Auchan can monitor each other's promotions by observing advertisements posted on the competitor's Web site (see http://www.auchan.fr and http://www.carrefour.fr), for example. In other situations, observation is the most economical technique. In a common type of observation study, a shopping center manager may observe the license plate (tag) numbers on cars in its parking lot. These data, along with automobile registration information, provide an inexpensive means of determining where customers live.

Certain data may be obtained more quickly or easily using direct observation than by other methods—gender, race, and other respondent characteristics can simply be observed. Researchers investigating a diet product may use observation when selecting respondents in a shopping mall. Overweight people may be prescreened by observing pedestrians, thus eliminating a number of screening interviews. Direct observation is used because it often is the simplest, quickest and most accurate way to gather data. On the other hand, direct observation has limited flexibility because not all phenomena are observable.

■ ERRORS ASSOCIATED WITH DIRECT OBSERVATION

Although direct observation involves no interaction with the subject, the method is not error-free; the observer may record events subjectively. The same visual cues that may influence the interplay between interviewer and respondent (e.g., the subject's age or sex) may come into play in some direct observation settings, such as when the observer subjectively attributes a particular economic status or educational background to a subject. A distortion of measurement resulting from the cognitive behavior or actions of the witnessing observer is called **observer bias**. For example, in a research project using observers to evaluate whether salesclerks are rude or courteous, fieldworkers may be required to rely on their own interpretations of people or situations during the observation process.

Also, accuracy may suffer if the observer does not record every detail that describes the persons, objects, and events in a given situation. Generally, the observer should record as much detail as possible. However, the pace of events, the observer's memory, the observer's writing speed, and other factors will limit the amount of detail that can be recorded.

Interpretation of observation data is another potential source of error. Facial expressions and other nonverbal communication may have several meanings. Does a smile always mean happiness? Does the fact that someone is standing or seated next to the president of a company necessarily indicate the person's status?

observer bias

A distortion of measurement resulting from the cognitive behavior or actions of a witnessing observer.

> **TOTHEPOINT**
>
> *What we see depends mainly on what we look for.*
>
> —Sir John Lubbock

Contrived Observation

Most observation takes place in a natural setting, but sometimes the investigator intervenes to create an artificial environment to test a hypothesis. This approach is called **contrived observation**. Contrived observation can increase the frequency of occurrence of certain behavior patterns, such as employee responses to complaints. An airline passenger complaining about a meal or service from the flight attendant may actually be a researcher recording that person's reactions. If situations were not contrived, the research time spent waiting and observing would expand considerably. A number of retailers use observers called *mystery shoppers* to visit a store and pretend to be interested in a particular product or service. After leaving the store, the "shopper" evaluates the salesperson's performance.

contrived observation

Observation in which the investigator creates an artificial environment in order to test a hypothesis.

Clean as We Say, or Clean as We Do?

People know that hand washing is a fundamental way to stay healthy, not to mention simple good manners. So, when you ask them, most people say they faithfully wash their hands. But according to observational research, what people say about this behavior is not what they necessarily do.

The American Society for Microbiology and the Soap and Detergent Association together arranged for a nationwide study of hand washing by U.S. adults. In an online survey by Harris Interactive, 91 percent of adults said they always wash their hands after using a public restroom. Men were somewhat less likely to make this claim—88 percent, versus 94 percent of women. The researchers followed up on the survey results by observing adults in public restrooms in Atlanta, Chicago, New York City, and San Francisco. A 2007 tally of the percentage who washed their hands found that only 77 percent did so. About 66 percent of men were observed washing their hands after going to the restroom while women washed their hands 88 percent of the time. The difference between reporting of hand washing and actual hand washing was greater for the men

(about a 22 percent difference) than for the women (6 percent). The numbers also vary geographically across the United States. Among major cities, Chicago has the cleanest hands as 81 percent of people can be observed washing after a toilet break while San Francisco scored lowest at 73 percent overall. Additionally, handwashing is down 6 percent since 2005.

This research showing a divide between what individuals believe they should be doing, what they say they do, and what they actually do could be useful in helping agencies craft messages aimed at improving citizens' health. In addition, soap marketers may want to learn more about what keeps individuals from washing their hands (is it inconvenient? are public sinks a turnoff?), even while being prepared for some response bias.

The study was conducted by having observers discreetly watch and record the frequency of the number of people using a public toilet facility and the number of people who washed their hands. Observers pretended to be grooming themselves while watching the visitors. Over 6,000 people were observed in four U.S. cities. Do you think a hidden camera would reveal different results?

Source: Based on "Hygiene Habits Stall: Public Handwashing Down," Cleaning 101, www.cleaning101.com/newsroom/09-17-07.cfm; Harris Interactive, "Many Adults Report Not Washing Their Hands When They Should, and More People Claim to Wash Their Hands than Who Actually Do," news release (December 14, 2005); "Hand Washing Survey Fact Sheet" (2005), http://www.cleaning101.com, accessed February 24, 2006; and Harris Interactive, "A Survey of Hand Washing Behavior (2005 Findings)" (September 2005), accessed at "2005 ASM/SDA Hand Hygiene Survey Results," http://www.cleaning101.com (SDA Web site), February 24, 2006.

The Research Snapshot above discusses direct observation of hand washing in public restrooms. Similarly, a study compared results from self-reported questionnaire data, focus group data, and observational data concerning hygiene among restaurant employees. The questionnaires suggested that 95 percent of employees washed their hands thoroughly after handling raw chicken, that number averaged about 82 percent in the face–to–face condition, but when observation was used, 75 percent of the restaurant employees did not wash their hands adequately after handling raw chicken.[3] This direct observation could be turned into a contrived situation if a participant observer, pretending to be a new employee, asked another employee to assist by in some way handling raw chicken, and then observed the other employee's behavior. In the latter case, the researcher has interjected him- or herself into a situation, but perhaps for a very good reason. This may allow a hypothesis stating that interruptions will be associated with less hand washing compared to a no interruption condition.

Ethical Issues in the Observation of Humans

Observation methods introduce a number of ethical issues. Hidden observation raises the issue of the respondent's right to privacy. Suppose a research firm is approached by a company interested in acquiring information about how women put on their bras by observing behavior in a spa dressing area. The researcher considers approaching spas in several key cities about placing small cameras inconspicuously to observe women getting dressed. Obviously, such a situation raises an ethical question. While to some extent the dressing room is an area where women often do dress where others can observe them, women do not expect to have their dressing behavior recorded. Therefore, unless a way can be found to have some women consent to such observation, this observational approach is unethical.

If the researcher obtains permission to observe someone, the subject may not act naturally. So, at times there is a strong temptation to observe without obtaining consent or gaining input from an IRB (Institutional Review Board). Many times, such as monitoring people walking through and waiting in an airport, obtaining consent from individual respondents is impractical if not impossible. Further, asking for consent just before the actual observation will likely change the behavior.

So, when should researchers feel comfortable collecting observational data? While exceptions exist to every rule, here are three questions that can help address this question:

1. Is the behavior being observed commonly performed in public where it is expected that others can observe the behavior?
2. Is the behavior performed in a setting in which the anonymity of the person being observed is assured (meaning there is no way to identify individuals)?
3. Has the person agreed to be observed?

If the answer to the first two questions is yes, then there is not likely a violation of privacy in collecting observational research data. If the answer to the third question is yes, then gathering the data also is likely to be ethical. Otherwise, the researcher should carefully consider input from an IRB or other authority before proceeding with the research.

Also, some might see contrived observation as unethical based on the notion of entrapment. To *entrap* means to deceive or trick into difficulty, which clearly is an abusive action. For instance, in the hand washing example above, when the experimenter interrupts the real employee, he/she may entrap the employee into a lower probability of washing hands thoroughly. In this instance, if the employee was caused or caused harm to others (by getting in trouble with a superior or making someone ill) then clearly the intrusion is unethical. However, if no possibility of harm exists, then the researcher can likely proceed although this particular instance should be done under the auspices of an IRB.

© PHOTODISC/GETTY IMAGES

Even if fashion companies could learn a lot about the types of problems consumers typically have when purchasing and wearing clothes, would observation through two-way mirrors (also referred to as one-way mirrors) be appropriate?

Observation of Physical Objects

Physical phenomena may be the subject of observation study. Physical-trace evidence is a visible mark of some past event or occurrence. For example, the wear on library books indirectly indicates which books are actually read (handled most) when checked out. A classic example of physical-trace evidence in a nonprofit setting was erosion on the floor tiles around the hatching-chick exhibit at Chicago's Museum of Science and Industry. These tiles had to be replaced every six weeks; tiles in other parts of the museum did not need to be replaced for years. The selective erosion of tiles, indexed by the replacement rate, was a measure of the relative popularity of exhibits.

TO THE POINT

What would you rather believe? What I say, or what you saw with your own eyes?

—Groucho Marx

Artifacts

Clearly, a creative marketing researcher has many options for determining the solution to a problem. The story about Charles Coolidge Parlin, generally recognized as one of the founders of commercial marketing research, examining garbage cans at the turn of the twentieth century illustrates another study of physical traces. Physical traces often involve artifacts. **Artifacts** are things that people made and consumed within a culture that signal something meaningful about

artifacts

The things that people made and consumed within a culture that signal something meaningful about the behavior taking place at the time of consumption

Picking through the garbage on the side of the road can reveal behaviors of fast-food customers.

the behavior taking place at the time of consumption. Ethnographers are particularly interested in examining artifacts and Parlin's garbage can escapades illustrate how a marketing researcher can apply an ethnographic approach involving observation of artifacts.

Parlin designed an observation study to persuade Campbell's Soup Company to advertise in the *Saturday Evening Post*. Campbell's was reluctant to advertise because it believed that the *Post* was read primarily by working people who would prefer to make soup from scratch, peeling the potatoes and scraping the carrots, rather than paying ten cents for a can of soup. To demonstrate that rich people weren't the target market, Parlin selected a sample of Philadelphia garbage routes. Garbage from each specific area of the city that was selected was dumped on the floor of a local National Guard Armory. Parlin had the number of Campbell's soup cans in each pile counted. The results indicated that the garbage from the rich people's homes didn't contain many cans of Campbell's soup. Although they may not have made soup from scratch themselves, their housekeepers may have. The garbage piles from the blue-collar area showed a larger number of Campbell's soup cans. This observation study was enough evidence for Campbell's. They advertised in the *Saturday Evening Post*.[4]

The method used in this study has since been used in a scientific project at the University of Arizona in which aspiring archaeologists have sifted through garbage for over thirty years. They examine soggy cigarette butts, empty milk cartons, and half-eaten Big Macs in an effort to understand modern life. Like other research involving observation, observations can be compared with the results of surveys about food consumption—and garbage does not lie. This type of observation can correct for potential overreporting of healthful item consumption and underreporting of, say, cigarettes or fast food.

Inventories

Another application of observing physical objects is to count and record physical inventories through retail or wholesale audits. This method allows researchers to investigate brand sales on regional and national levels, market shares, seasonal purchasing patterns, and so on. Marketing research suppliers offer audit data at both the retail and the wholesale levels.

An observer can record physical-trace data to discover information a respondent could not recall accurately. For example, measuring the number of ounces of liquid bleach used during a test provides precise physical-trace evidence without relying on the respondent's memory. The accuracy of respondents' memories is not a problem for the firm that conducts a pantry audit. The pantry audit requires an inventory of the brands, quantities, and package sizes in a consumer's home rather than responses from individuals. The problem of untruthfulness or some other form of response bias is avoided. For example, the pantry audit prevents the possible problem of respondents erroneously claiming to have purchased prestige brands. However, gaining permission to physically check consumers' pantries is not easy, and the fieldwork is expensive. In addition, the brand in the pantry may not reflect the brand purchased most often if consumers substituted it because they had a coupon, the usual brand was out of stock, or another reason.

Content Analysis

Besides observing people and physical objects, researchers may use **content analysis**, which obtains data by observing and analyzing the contents or messages of advertisements, newspaper articles, television programs, letters, and the like. This method involves systematic analysis as well as observation to identify the specific information content and other characteristics of the messages. Content analysis studies the message itself and involves the design of a systematic observation and recording procedure for quantitative description of the manifest content of communication. This technique measures the extent of emphasis or omission of a given analytical category. For example, content analysis of advertisements might evaluate their use of words, themes, characters, or space and time relationships. Content analysis often counts the frequency of themes or occurences within the hermeneutic unit being studied. For instance, the frequency with which women, African-Americans, Hispanics, or Asians appear in advertising displayed on a cable network can be studied with content analysis.

Content analysis might be used to investigate questions such as whether some advertisers use certain themes, appeals, claims, or deceptive practices more than others or whether recent consumer-oriented actions by the Federal Trade Commission have influenced the contents of advertising. A cable television programmer might do a content analysis of network programming to evaluate its competition. Every year researchers analyze the Super Bowl telecast to see how much of the visual material is live-action play and how much is replay, or how many shots focus on the cheerleaders and how many on spectators. Content analysis also can explore the information content of television commercials directed at children, the company images portrayed in ads, and numerous other aspects of advertising.

Study of the content of communications is more sophisticated than simply counting the items; it requires a system of analysis to secure relevant data. After one employee role-playing session involving leaders and subordinates, researchers analyzed videotapes to identify categories of verbal behaviors (e.g., positive reward statements, positive comparison statements, and self-evaluation requests). Trained coders, using a set of specific instructions, then recorded and coded the leaders' behavior into specific verbal categories.

content analysis

The systematic observation and quantitative description of the manifest content of communication.

Mechanical Observation

In many situations, the primary—and sometimes the only—means of observation is mechanical rather than human. Video cameras, traffic counters, and other machines help observe and record behavior. Some unusual observation studies have used motion-picture cameras and time-lapse photography. An early application of this observation technique photographed train passengers and determined their levels of comfort by observing how they sat and moved in their seats. Another time-lapse study filmed traffic flows in an urban square and resulted in a redesign of the streets. Similar techniques may help managers design store layouts and resolve problems in moving people or objects through spaces over time.

Television and Radio Monitoring

Perhaps the best-known marketing research project involving mechanical observation and computerized data collection is ACNielsen's **television monitoring** system for estimating national television audiences. Nielsen Media Research uses a consumer panel and a monitoring device called a PeopleMeter to obtain ratings for television programs nationwide.[5] The Nielsen PeopleMeter gathers data on what each television in a household is playing and who is watching it at the time. Researchers attach electronic boxes to television sets and remote controls to capture information on program choices and the length of viewing time. Nielsen matches the signals captured through these devices with its database of network broadcast and cable program schedules so that it can identify the specific programs being viewed.

television monitoring

Computerized mechanical observation used to obtain television ratings.

Traffic cameras that monitor speeding on major highways are becoming commonplace in Europe, Australia, and even in some parts of the United States. Would car companies learn anything from the observed behavior?

When a television in the panel household is turned on, a red light on the PeopleMeter periodically flashes to remind viewers to indicate who is watching. The viewer then uses a remote control to record who is watching. One button on the control is assigned to each member of the household and a separate visitor button is used for potential guests. The household member presses his or her button to indicate the sex and age of the person who is watching. Knowing who in the family is watching allows executives to match television programs with demographic profiles.

Each night, Nielsen's computers automatically retrieve the data stored in the PeopleMeter's recording box. In this way, Nielsen gathers daily estimates of when televisions are in use, which channels are used, and who is viewing each program. The panel includes more than five thousand households, selected to be representative of the U.S. population. For local programming, Nielsen uses additional panels equipped with recording devices but not PeopleMeters to record viewer demographics. (Nielsen uses surveys to record demographic data for local programming.)

Critics of the PeopleMeter argue that subjects in Nielsen's panel grow bored over time and do not always record when they begin or stop watching television. Arbitron, best known for measuring radio audiences, has attempted to answer this objection with its own measuring system, which it calls the Portable People Meter.[6] The Portable People Meter, which occupies about 4 cubic inches and weighs less than 3 ounces, reads inaudible codes embedded in audio signals to identify their source. Study participants wear or carry the meter throughout the day, and it automatically picks up codes embedded in whatever radio and television signals they encounter. At the end of the day, the participant inserts the meter into a "base station," which extracts the data collected, sends it to a household hub, and recharges the battery. The household hub then sends the data to Arbitron's computer over phone lines. To encourage cooperation, the meter has a motion sensor connected to a green light signaling that the meter senses it is being carried. Each participant is awarded points for the amount of time the meter is on. Total points are displayed in the base station and used to determine the size of the incentive paid to each participant. Arbitron's meter simplifies the participants' role and collects data on exposure to radio and television programming outside the home. However, the device records only signals that the radio or television system embeds using Arbitron's equipment.

Other devices gather data about the viewing of advertisements. The TiVo digital television recorder collects detailed viewing data, such as what commercials people skip by using fast-forward. The PreTesting Company sets up contrived observational studies in which viewers equipped with a remote control are invited to watch any of three prerecorded channels playing different programs and advertisements, including the client's ads to be tested.[7] The system records the precise points at which the viewer changes the channel. By combining the results from many participants, the company arrives at a Cumulative Zapping Score, that is, the percentage of viewers who had exited the client's advertisement by each point in the ad. So that viewing behavior will be more natural, subjects are told they are evaluating the programming, not the ads.

Mobiltrak, a research firm based in Herndon, Virginia, uses a device that can observe what is playing on cars' stereos. The company installs observation equipment the size of a shoebox on towers located at heavily traveled intersections. Sensors on the equipment measure the level of electronic radiation emitted by the radio of each car as it passes by. The data describe the volume of traffic listening to each station, not the stations being played by individual vehicles or any demographic data about the vehicles' drivers or passengers.[8] By paying a subscription fee to Mobiltrak, radio stations in the company's service areas can obtain data about their listeners. They can use the data to sell advertising time to businesses located where the most listeners are driving. In addition, advertisers can pay for data collected at particular locations. For example, Home Depot, which has used Mobiltrak, can find out which stations people are listening to as they travel on roads leading past one of the company's stores.

Monitoring Web Site Traffic

Computer technology makes gathering detailed data about online behavior easy and inexpensive. The greater challenges are to identify which measures are meaningful and to interpret the data correctly. For instance, most organizations record the level of activity at their Web sites. They may count the number of *hits*—mouse clicks on a single page of a Web site. If the visitor clicks on many links, that page receives multiple hits. Similarly, they can track *page views,* or single, discrete clicks to load individual pages of a Web site. Page views more conservatively indicate how many users visit each individual page on the Web site and may also be used to track the path or sequence of pages that each visitor follows. The Research Snapshot on the next page provides a brief illustration.

■ CLICK-THROUGH RATES

A **click-through rate** (CTR) is the percentage of people who are exposed to an advertisement who actually click on the corresponding hyperlink which takes them to the company's Web site. Counting hits or page views can suggest the amount of interest or attention a Web site is receiving, but these measures are flawed. First, hits do not differentiate between a lot of activity by a few visitors and a little activity by many visitors. In addition, the researcher lacks information about the meaning behind the numbers. If a user clicks on a site many times, is the person finding a lot of useful or enjoyable material, or is the user trying unsuccessfully to find something by looking in several places? Additionally, some hits are likely made by mistake. The consumers may have had no intention of clicking through the ad or may not have known what they were doing when they clicked on the ad.

A more refined count is the number of *unique visitors* to a Web site. This measurement counts the initial access to the site but not multiple hits on the site by the same visitor during the same day or week. Operators of Web sites can collect the data by attaching small files, called *cookies*, to the computers of visitors to their sites and then tracking those cookies to see whether the same visitors return. Some marketing research companies, notably Jupiter Research and Nielsen// NetRatings, specialize in monitoring this type of Internet activity. A typical approach is to install a special tracking program on the personal computers of a sample of Internet users who agree to participate in the research effort. Nielsen//NetRatings has its software installed in thirty thousand computers in homes and workplaces. Internet monitoring enables these companies to identify the popularity of Web sites. The information that remains stored in cookies and other system files can also help researchers know about the habits of Internet usage for consumers. In recent years, accurate measurement of unique visitors and Web surfing behavior is becoming more difficult because over half of computer users routinely delete cookies and many users keep cookies turned off to help them remain *virtually* anonymous.[9] Computer security systems are also limiting the extent to which this information is transferred from the user's machine to the server.

■ CTR AND ONLINE ADVERTISING

As online advertising has become more widespread, marketing research has refined methods for measuring the effectiveness of the advertisements. The companies that place these ads can keep count of the click-through rate (CTR). Applying the CTR to the amount spent on the advertisement gives the advertiser a *cost per click*. These measures have been hailed as a practical way to

click-through rate

Proportion of people who are exposed to an Internet ad who actually click on it's hyperlink to enter the Web site; click-through rates are generally very low.

Klipmart Watches Ad Viewership Online

As bandwidth widens, more and more computer users are going online to download audio and video content. Providers of that content are earning revenues through a combination of user fees and advertising. This situation is creating demand for information about how many people are seeing Internet ads and whether they are paying attention. Klipmart not only provides video content online but also is finding ways to measure the behavior of computer users—in particular, their viewership of ads using video.

Klipmart sets up tests in which computer users are presented with 30-second video ads as they perform other tasks. The company's equipment then measures how long the users spend watching each advertisement.

The assumption is that a 30-second ad is too long for a computer user, so the company can get an upper limit of viewers' interest in the ads by seeing how many seconds out of the 30 the viewers keep watching. Early results suggest that the length of time spent viewing an online video ad averages 21 seconds but varies according to what the user is trying to accomplish. Users stayed with an ad the longest—an average of 22.5 seconds—when they were waiting for the download of a home video. They were least patient, clicking away from the ad after 19 seconds, if they were downloading a finance video. The results surprised some people, who expected that computer users would exit advertisements within a few seconds.

Klipmart also can measure the user's interaction with an advertisement. Data from Klipmart indicate that users interact more with ads that contain more interactive elements.

Source: Based on Zachary Rodgers, "What's the Optimal Length for Video Ads?" *ClickZ Internet Advertising News* (October 4, 2005), http://www.clickz.com; Klipmart, "About Us" and "Research," http://www.klipmart.com, accessed February 6, 2006.

evaluate advertising effectiveness. However, marketers have to consider that getting consumers to click on an ad is rarely the ad's objective. Companies are more often advertising to meet short- or long-term sales goals.

Google has benefited from CTR research indicating that the highest click-through rates tend to occur on pages displaying search results. (Not surprisingly, someone who searches for the term *kayaks* is more likely to be interested in an advertisement offering a good deal on kayaks.) The company showed Vanguard, for example, that its banner ads cost the financial firm less than fifty cents per click and generated a 14 percent click-through rate. That CTR is far above typical response rates for direct-mail advertising, but it does not indicate whether online clicks are as valuable in terms of sales.[10]

Scanner-Based Research

Lasers performing optical character recognition and bar code technology like the universal product code (UPC) have accelerated the use of mechanical observation in marketing research. Chapter 7 noted that a number of syndicated services offer secondary data about product category movement generated from retail stores using scanner technology.

This technology allows researchers to investigate questions that are demographically or promotionally specific. Scanner research has investigated the different ways consumers respond to price promotions and the effects of those differences on a promotion's profitability. One of the primary means of implementing this type of research is through the establishment of a **scanner-based consumer panel** to replace consumer purchase diaries. In a typical scanner panel, each household is assigned a bar-coded card, like a frequent-shopper card, which members present to the clerk at the register. The household's code number is coupled with the purchase information recorded by the scanner. In addition, as with other consumer panels, background information about the household obtained through answers to a battery of demographic and psychographic survey questions can also be coupled with the household code number.

scanner-based consumer panel

A type of consumer panel in which participants' purchasing habits are recorded with a laser scanner rather than a purchase diary.

Aggregate data, such as actual store sales as measured by scanners, are available to clients and industry groups. Data may also be aggregated by product category. To interpret the aggregated data, researchers can combine them with secondary research and panel demographics. For instance, data from Information Resources Inc. (IRI) have indicated a downward trend in sales of hair-coloring products. Demographic data suggest that an important reason is the aging of the population; many consumers who dye their hair reach an age at which they no longer wish to cover their gray hair. A smaller segment of the population is at an age where consumers typically begin using hair coloring.[11]

Data from scanner research parallel data provided by a standard mail diary panel, with some important improvements:

1. The data measure observed (actual) purchase behavior rather than reported behavior (recorded later in a diary).
2. Substituting mechanical for human record-keeping improves accuracy.
3. Measures are unobtrusive, eliminating interviewing and the possibility of social desirability or other bias on the part of respondents.
4. More extensive purchase data can be collected, because all UPC categories are measured. In a mail diary, respondents could not possibly reliably record all items they purchased. Because all UPC-coded items are measured in the panel, users can investigate many product categories to determine loyalty, switching rates, and so on for their own brands as well as for other companies' products and locate product categories for possible market entry.
5. The data collected from computerized checkout scanners can be combined with data about advertising, price changes, displays, and special sales promotions. Researchers can scrutinize them with powerful analytical software provided by the scanner data providers.

Scanner data can show a marketer week by week how a product is doing, even in a single store, and track sales in response to local ads or promotions. Also, several organizations have developed scanner panels, such as Information Resources Inc. Behavior Scan System, and expanded them into electronic test-market systems. These issues are discussed in greater detail in Chapter 12.

Advances in bar-code technology have led to **at-home scanning systems** that use handheld wands to read UPC symbols. Consumer panelists perform their own scanning *after* they have taken home the products. This advance makes it possible to investigate purchases made at stores that lack in-store scanning equipment.

at-home scanning systems
Systems that allow consumer panelists to perform their own scanning after taking home products, using handheld wands that read UPC symbols.

Camera Surveillance

Cameras are increasingly used in modern society to keep tabs on all sorts of behaviors. In 2005, London's famous tube (subway) system was rocked by multiple terrorist attacks. Within just a few hours of the attacks, London's video surveillance recordings were analyzed and potential suspects had begun to be identified. On a typical day, a Londoner's behavior is recorded automatically hundreds of times. Likewise, cameras planted inconspicuously in places can be useful in marketing research. Shopping center security video can help identify problems with merchandising and the types of things that attract consumers to come into and remain in an environment. However, cameras have many more applications.

Researchers sometimes ask and get permission to place cameras inconspicuously in consumers' homes, offices, or even cars.[12] If Microsoft Vista fails, it is not because of a lack of research. Microsoft commissioned research involving the observation of 50 homes via inconspicuous, in-home cameras. As consumers encountered problems using the operating system in their homes, Microsoft was able to study the consumer behavior involved and try to find a way to avoid the problems in the future. Other companies including Kimberly-Clark, Sony, and Old Spice have also successfully applied observational research using cameras. The Old Spice research involved videos of guys taking showers in their homes (with permission and swimsuits) and the Kimberly-Clark research involved young parents wearing small hat cams while changing a baby's diaper. This type of research allows close inspection of activities in places and at times when having an actual observer present would not work.

Marketing researchers are also using something dubbed a Mindcam to understand various aspects of consumer activity, such as shopping.[13] A small camera and microphone combination is placed on the consumer's person. All of their sights and sounds are recorded. Typically, this is followed up with an interview where the consumer tries to explain his or her behavior and any purchases made. Small cameras and other recording devices make these types of developments possible.

Neurological Devices

The chapter's opening vignette described a technology that observed brain activity as a person went about everyday behaviors. More and more, we are able to observe what goes on in the consumer's mind. Neurological activity can reveal how much thought takes place and what types of feelings a person is probably experiencing. Similar processes involve things such as magnetic resonance imaging or transcranial magnetic simulation.[14] If these things sound complicated, it's because they are. These have the potential of allowing researchers to actually directly observe what is going on in the mind of a respondent as they perform an activity. Thus, these techniques may revolutionize research on information processing. We may still be several years away from widespread marketing applications of these approaches; researchers also will have to be concerned about the ethical implications of looking into someone's mind.

Measuring Physiological Reactions

Marketing researchers have used a number of other mechanical devices to evaluate consumers' physical and physiological reactions to advertising copy, packaging, and other stimuli. Researchers use such means when they believe consumers are unaware of their own reactions to stimuli such as advertising or that consumers will not provide honest responses. Four major categories of mechanical devices are used to measure physiological reactions: (1) eye-tracking monitors, (2) pupilometers, (3) psychogalvanometers, and (4) voice-pitch analyzers.

A magazine or newspaper advertiser may wish to grab readers' attention with a visual scene and then direct it to a package or coupon. Or a television advertiser may wish to identify which selling points to emphasize. Eye-tracking equipment records how the subject reads a print ad or views a television commercial and how much time is spent looking at various parts of the stimulus.

eye-tracking monitor

A mechanical device used to observe eye movements; some eye monitors use infrared light beams to measure unconscious eye movements.

Physiological responses to advertising can be recorded with a device like this one.

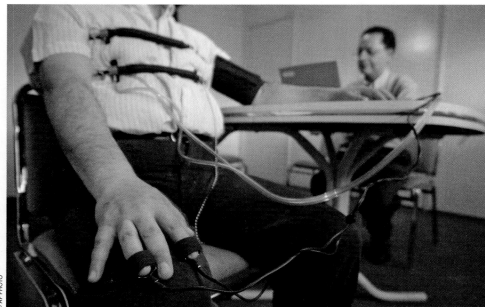

© AP PHOTO

In physiological terms, the gaze movement of a viewer's eye is measured with an **eye-tracking monitor**, which measures unconscious eye movements. Originally developed to measure astronauts' eye fatigue, modern eye-tracking systems need not keep a viewer's head in a stationary position. The devices track eye movements with invisible infrared light beams that lock onto a subject's eyes. The light reflects off the eye, and eye-movement data are recorded while another tiny video camera monitors which magazine page is being perused. The data are analyzed by computer to determine which components in an ad (or other stimuli) were seen and which were overlooked. Eye-tracking monitors have recently been used to measure the way subjects view e-mail and Web marketing messages. OgilvyOne has used this technology to learn that people often skip over more than half of the words in e-mail advertising, especially words on the right side of the message. Interestingly, consumers generally ignore the word *free*.[15]

Other physiological observation techniques are based on a common principle: that adrenaline is released when the body is aroused. This hormone causes the heart to enlarge and to beat harder and faster. These changes increase the flow of blood to the fingers and toes. The blood vessels dilate, and perspiration increases, affecting the skin's electrical conductivity. Other physical changes following the release of adrenaline include dilation of the pupils, more frequent brain wave activity, higher skin temperature, and faster breathing. Methods that measure these and other changes associated with arousal can apply to a variety of marketing questions, such as subjects' reactions to advertising messages or product concepts.

A **pupilometer** observes and records changes in the diameter of a subject's pupils. A subject is instructed to look at a screen on which an advertisement or other stimulus is projected. When the brightness and distance of the stimulus from the subject's eyes are held constant, changes in pupil size may be interpreted as changes in cognitive activity that result from the stimulus, rather than from eye dilation and constriction in response to light intensity, distance from the object, or other physiological reactions to the conditions of observation. This method of research is based on the assumption that increased pupil size reflects positive attitudes toward and interest in advertisements.

A **psychogalvanometer** measures galvanic skin response (GSR), a measure of involuntary changes in the electrical resistance of the skin. This device is based on the assumption that physiological changes, such as increased perspiration, accompany emotional reactions to advertisements, packages, and slogans. Excitement increases the body's perspiration rate, which increases the electrical resistance of the skin. The test is an indicator of emotional arousal or tension and can be used to help detect dishonest responses as a lie detector.

Voice-pitch analysis is a relatively new physiological measurement technique that gauges emotional reactions as reflected in physiological changes in a person's voice. Abnormal frequencies in the voice caused by changes in the autonomic nervous system are measured with sophisticated, audio-adapted computer equipment. Computerized analysis compares the respondent's voice pitch during warm-up conversations (normal range) with verbal responses to questions about his or her evaluative reaction to television commercials or other stimuli. This technique, unlike other physiological devices, does not require the researcher to surround subjects with mazes of wires or equipment.

All of these devices assume that physiological reactions are associated with persuasiveness or predict some cognitive response. This assumption has not yet been clearly demonstrated. No strong theoretical evidence supports the argument that such a physiological change is a valid measure of future sales, attitude change, or emotional response. Another major problem with physiological research is the *calibration,* or sensitivity, of measuring devices. Identifying arousal is one thing, but precisely measuring *levels* of arousal is another. In addition, most of these devices are expensive. However, as a prominent researcher points out, physiological measurement is coincidental: "Physiological measurement isn't an exit interview. It's not dependent on what was remembered later on. It's a live blood, sweat, and tears, moment-by-moment response, synchronous with the stimulus."[16]

Each of these mechanical devices has another limitation: The subjects are usually placed in artificial settings, such as watching television in a laboratory rather than at home, and they know they are being observed.

pupilometer

A mechanical device used to observe and record changes in the diameter of a subject's pupils.

psychogalvanometer

A device that measures galvanic skin response, a measure of involuntary changes in the electrical resistance of the skin.

voice-pitch analysis

A physiological measurement technique that records abnormal frequencies in the voice that are supposed to reflect emotional reactions to various stimuli.

Companies like Visiontrack specialize in research that tracks how the eye moves during an activity. Think about how useful this might be to companies considering product placements within video games or in designing more efficient instrument panels for airplanes.

PHOTO COURTESY OF VICKI BEAVER

- Generally, observations have the most validity when the actual observations are performed unobtrusively. The big reason for this is that social influences such as may occur from an interviewer's presence or the knowledge that one is being observed are eliminated.
- Marketing research often involves information processing. Researchers should strongly consider using measures of response latency when studying information processing. Computer-aided survey technology makes observing response latency easy and accurate.

- Artifacts are great ways to put together a physical trace of human activities and to understand the value of those objects to the individuals involved.
- To avoid ethical issues, the anonymity of people whose behavior is captured using observational data collection should be protected at all times unless consent has been obtained to identify the person.

© GEORGE DOYLE & CIARAN GRIFFIN

Summary

1. Discuss the role of observation as a marketing research method. Observation is a powerful tool for the marketing researcher. Scientific observation is the systematic process of recording the behavioral patterns of people, objects, and occurrences as they are witnessed. Questioning or otherwise communicating with subjects does not occur. A wide variety of information about the behavior of people and objects can be observed. Seven kinds of phenomena are observable: physical actions, verbal behavior, expressive behavior, spatial relations and locations, temporal patterns, physical objects, and verbal and pictorial records. Thus, both verbal and nonverbal behavior may be observed. Observation may not, however, be used for cognitive phenomena. Attitudes, motivations, expectations, intentions, and preferences are not observable; only overt behavior of short duration can be observed.

2. Describe the use of direct observation and contrived observation. Human observation, whether direct or contrived, is commonly used when the situation or behavior to be recorded is not easily predictable in advance of the research. The most advantageous observational data techniques are unobtrusive, meaning the observation is done without the knowledge of the person being watched. It may be unobtrusive, and many types of data can be obtained more accurately through direct observation than by questioning respondents. Direct observation involves watching and recording what naturally occurs, without creating an artificial situation. For some data, observation is the most direct or the only method of collection. For example, researchers can measure response latency, the time it takes individuals to choose between alternatives. Observer bias may be a problem in correctly perceiving the behaviors being observed. Observation can also be contrived by creating the situations to be observed. This can reduce the time and expense of obtaining reactions to certain circumstances.

3. Identify ethical issues particular to research using observation. Contrived observation, hidden observation, and other observation research designs have the potential to involve deception. For this reason, these methods often raise ethical concerns about subjects' right to privacy and right to be informed. The chapter includes a short checklist that can be useful in determining the morality of an observational data gathering approach.

4. Explain the observation of physical objects and message content. Physical-trace evidence serves as a visible record of past events. Researchers may examine whatever evidence provides such a record, including inventory levels, the contents of garbage cans, or the items in a consumer's pantry. Researchers can take advantage of artifacts that are left behind to try and explain the behavior associated with that particular object. Content analysis obtains data by observing and analyzing the contents of the messages in written or spoken communications.

5. Describe major types of mechanical observation. Mechanical observation uses a variety of devices to record behavior directly. It may be an efficient and accurate choice when the situation or behavior to be recorded is routine, repetitive, or programmatic. National television audience ratings are based on mechanical observation (for example, PeopleMeters) and computerized data collection. Web site traffic may be measured electronically. Scanner-based research provides product category sales data recorded by laser scanners in retail stores. Many syndicated services offer secondary data collected through scanner systems. Additionally, cameras can be used to study consumers in their homes and employees at their workplace. Small cameras can even be placed on people as they go about their daily activities. These cameras record the sights and sounds they experience. Additionally, new approaches exist to perform neural imaging which provide a more direct insight into the mind of the consumers or employees being studied.

6. Summarize techniques for measuring physiological reactions. Physiological reactions, such as arousal or eye movement patterns, may be observed using a number of mechanical devices. Eye-tracking monitors identify the direction of a person's gaze, and a pupilometer observes and records changes in the diameter of the pupils of subjects' eyes, based on the assumption that a larger pupil signifies a positive attitude. A psychogalvanometer measures galvanic skin response as a signal of a person's emotional reactions. Voice-pitch analysis measures changes in a person's voice and associates the changes with emotional response.

Key Terms and Concepts

artifacts, 251
at-home scanning systems, *257*
click-through rate, *255*
content analysis, *253*
contrived observation, *249*
direct observation, *248*

eye-tracking monitor, *258*
hidden observation, *246*
observation, *244*
observer bias, *249*
psychogalvanometer, *259*
pupilometer, *259*

response latency, *248*
scanner-based consumer panel, *256*
television monitoring, *253*
unobtrusive observation, *246*
visible observation, *246*
voice-pitch analysis, *259*

Questions for Review and Critical Thinking

1. Yogi Berra, former New York Yankee catcher, said, "You can observe a lot just by watching." How does this fit in with the definition of scientific observation?

2. What are the major advantages of unobtrusive observation over other types of data collection?

3. Under what conditions are observation studies most appropriate and what situations may make them inappropriate?

4. **ETHICS** The chapter showed a photograph of a traffic monitoring camera. Do you think the use of these cameras to issue speeding tickets is ethical? What types of behavior might cameras like these capture that would help automobile designers produce products that better match our needs as drivers?

5. A multinational fast-food corporation plans to locate a restaurant in La Paz, Bolivia. Secondary data for this city are sketchy and outdated. How might you determine the best location using observational data collection?

6. Discuss how an observation study might be combined with a personal interview.

7. **'NET** Click-through rates for advertisements placed in Web sites are usually very, very low (1 percent or less). What types of error might exist in using click-through rate data as a measure of an advertisement's success?

8. Outline a research design using observation for each of the following situations:

   a. A bank wishes to collect data on the number of customer services and the frequency of customer use of these services.

   b. A state government wishes to determine the driving public's use of seat belts.

   c. A researcher wishes to know how many women have been featured on *Time* covers over the years.

   d. A fast-food franchise wishes to determine how long a customer entering a store has to wait for his or her order.

   e. A magazine publisher wishes to determine exactly what people look at and what they pass over while reading one of its magazines.

   f. A food manufacturer wishes to determine how people use diet foods in their homes.

   g. An overnight package delivery service wishes to observe delivery workers beginning at the moment when they stop the truck, continuing through the delivery of the package, and ending when they return to the truck.

   h. A political consulting agency would like to study the thought patterns of consumers as they view national candidates' political commercials on television.

9. What is an artifact to a marketing researcher? How might one use artifacts to study the types of things that fans at major sporting events might be willing to purchase when attending an event? Can artifacts also be used to study ergonomics in the office? If so, how?

10. What is a scanner-based consumer panel?

11. What are the major types of mechanical observation? What types of observations might eBay potentially have access to that would be of interest to basic marketing researchers?

12. How can a marketing researcher determine if an observational data collection involving hidden cameras is ethical?

13. **ETHICS** Comment on the ethics of the following situations:

   a. During the course of telephone calls to investors, a stockbroker records respondents' voices when they are answering sensitive investment questions and then conducts a voice-pitch analysis. The respondents do not know that their voices are being recorded.

b. A researcher plans to invite consumers to be test users in a simulated kitchen located in a shopping mall and then to videotape their reactions to a new microwave dinner from behind a two-way mirror (one that an observer behind the mirror can see through but the person looking into the mirror sees only the reflection).

c. A marketing researcher arranges to purchase the trash from the headquarters of a major competitor. The purpose is to sift through discarded documents to determine the company's strategic plans.

14. What is a psychogalvanometer?

15. **'NET** William Rathje, a researcher at the University of Arizona, Department of Anthropology, has become well-known for the "Garbage Project." The project involves observational research.

Use http://www.ask.com to find information about the garbage project at the University of Arizona. What is the name of the book that describes some of the key findings of the Garbage Project? How do you think it involves observational research?

16. **'NET** The Internet is filled with webcams. For example, Pebble Beach Golf Club has several webcams (http://www.pebblebeach.com). How could a researcher use webcams like these to collect behavioral data?

17. Look back to Chapter 6 and find the definition for ethnography. Why is observation such a big part of this important qualitative research approach?

18. What is a contrived observational approach? Are contrived observational approaches ethical? Would they be considered unobtrusive?

Case 10.1 Mazda and Syzygy

© GETTY IMAGES/
PHOTODISC GREEN

When Mazda Motor Europe set out to improve its Web site, the company wanted details about how consumers were using the site and whether finding information was easy. Mazda hired a research firm called Syzygy to answer those questions with observational research.[17] Syzygy's methods include the use of an eye-tracking device that uses infrared light rays to record what areas of a computer screen a user is viewing. For instance, the device measured the process computer users followed in order to look for a local dealer or arrange a test drive. Whenever a process seemed confusing or difficult, the company looked for ways to make the Web site easier to navigate.

To conduct this observational study, Syzygy arranged for sixteen subjects in Germany and the United Kingdom to be observed as they used the Web site. The subjects in Germany were observed with

the eye-tracking equipment. As the equipment measured each subject's gaze, software recorded the location on the screen and graphed the data. Syzygy's results included three-dimensional contour maps highlighting the "peak" areas where most of the computer users' attention was directed.

Questions

1. What could Mazda learn from eye-tracking software that would be difficult to learn from other observational methods?

2. What are the shortcomings of this method?

3. Along with the eye-tracking research, what other research methods could help Mazda assess the usability of its Web site? Summarize your advice for how Mazda could use complementary methods to obtain a complete understanding of its Web site usability.

Case 10.2 Texas Instruments and E-Lab

© GETTY IMAGES/
PHOTODISC GREEN

E-Lab, LLC is a business research and design firm in Chicago that specializes in observing people, identifying patterns in behavior, and developing an understanding of why these patterns exist.[18] The company then uses the knowledge that it gains as a framework in the product development process. Texas Instruments (TI) used E-Lab to investigate the mobility, connectivity, and communications needs of law enforcement officers, which led to ideas for a set of computing and communications products. As part of its product development research, TI's Advanced Integrated Systems Department and E-Lab researchers spent 320 hours shadowing police officers in three Texas police departments. Shadowing involves asking questions while observing. Researchers walked foot patrols, rode in patrol cars, and pedaled with bike patrols. They spent time with crowd control, narcotics, homicide, dispatch, and juvenile teams. They recorded their observations and interviews on paper, digital camera, and video.

A number of interesting findings emerged from all this research. First, police officers are very social, so it was important that any

product TI developed should enhance socialization rather than detract from it. For example, an in-car computing and communications device should be able to access a database that lists names and numbers of experts on the force so officers can call or e-mail the experts directly. Second, police officers are not driven by procedure. That told TI that the procedures for an investigation should reside in the device and that the device should prompt the officer at each step in the process. And third, officers rely on informal information about people and activities on their beats. This information may be kept on scraps of paper, on a spreadsheet back in the office, or in the police officer's head. Business researchers concluded that any device that TI develops should have a place to compile and share informal information.

Questions

1. Identify the research design used by E-Lab.

2. Compare this research design with a survey research design. What advantages, if any, did this research design have over a survey?

Case 10.3 Tulsa's Central Business District

The metropolitan Tulsa Chamber of Commerce recognized that there was a critical gap between the availability of timely information about the central business district (CBD) and the need for this information for investment decision making, commercial marketing efforts, and the continued pursuit of the goal of downtown revitalization. The Chamber of Commerce undertook four separate research projects to gather information about the CBD. One project was a physical inventory of the existing downtown commercial base. The objectives of the study were to determine what types of establishments were operating in the CBD and the number of vacancies there and to generally profile the commercial geography of the CBD. The researchers found that the central business district was based on the U.S. Bureau of the Census classification scheme. The CBD was identified as the area encompassed by the inner dispersal loop (a system of expressways),

which corresponded identically with census tract 25 (see Case Exhibit 10.3–1).

A team of ten pedestrian fieldworkers covered each block in the inner dispersal loop. The fieldworkers used the observation form in Case Exhibit 10.3–2 to record the company name, address, primary business activity, estimated frontage, and other relevant information about each building site or office. Fieldworkers recorded Standard Industrial Classification (SIC) codes for retailers. SIC codes for all other establishments were recorded by research assistants after the data were collected. All the data were identified by census block.

Questions

1. Evaluate this research design.
2. What changes, if any, would you make in the observation form?
3. What problems would you expect in the data collection stage?
4. What techniques would you use to analyze the data?

CASE EXHIBIT 10.3–1 **Census Blocks in Census Tract 25**

Source: U.S. Bureau of the Census.

CASE EXHIBIT 10.3–2 **Observation Study Recording Form**

Company Name _____

_____

Address: _____

       Tulsa, Oklahoma

Activities: ___ 1 Vacant   ___ 2 Retail   ___ 3 Wholesale   ___ 4 Manufacturing

       ___ 5 Service ___ 6 Other (Specify) _____

Retail SIC: ___ 52   ___ 53   ___ 54   ___ 55   ___ 56   ___ 57   ___ 58   ___ 59   ___ 60

Other Activities (describe): _____

_____

Is the Building: ___ 1 For Sale?   ___ 2 For Rent?

  Leasable Space: _____

  Realtor's Name: _____

  Realtor's Phone: _____

  Rent (per sq. foot)

Is the Building Being: ___ 1 Restored?   ___ 2 Remodeled?

  Estimated Frontage (Feet): _____

  Estimated Number of Stories: _____

Comments: _____

_____

_____

CHAPTER 11
EXPERIMENTAL RESEARCH:
AN OVERVIEW

After studying this chapter, you should be able to

1. Know the basic characteristics of research experiments
2. Minimize experimental error by effective experimental design
3. Know ways of minimizing experimental demand characteristics
4. Avoid unethical experimental practices
5. Understand the advantages of a between-subjects experimental design
6. Weigh the trade-off between internal and external validity

Chapter Vignette: Warning! This Product May Cause . . .

"What cigarette do you smoke, Doctor?" This was the question posed in a 1949 ad for Camel cigarettes. Not surprisingly, the result stated in the ad was that more doctors smoked Camels than any other cigarette. The intended inference here is obvious—if doctors choose Camels, then they must not cause as many harmful effects as those of other cigarettes! The whole question of smoking has advanced a great deal since that time. Inevitably, debates about smoking involve questions of cause.

- Does smoking cause cancer?
- Does smoking cause death?
- Does advertising cause people to smoke?

Warning labels say things like "Smoking causes lung cancer, heart disease, and emphysema." In U.S. courts, plaintiffs' attorneys and in some cases state governments have successfully argued that cigarette companies are responsible for the health problems and even deaths associated with long-term smoking.[1] As a result, tobacco companies have paid huge settlements. However, a U.K.-based tobacco company, Imperial Tobacco, faced with a £500,000 law suit filed on behalf of a cancer patient who had smoked Player Cigarettes for 40 years, is basing a legal defense on the notion that a lack of certainty remains over whether or not cigarettes cause cancer. They claim that the only evidence for this is statistical association and that many other factors are also statistically associated with the occurrence of cancer including a patient's socioeconomic status, childhood experiences (orientation toward healthy behaviors like exercise and diet), ethnicity, personality, and diet.

The defense is based on Imperial Tobacco's claim that no experimental evidence isolates the extent to which smoking truly causes cancer.[2] Further, they argued that advertising could not have caused the plaintiff to begin smoking. The Imperial defense was successful as the court ruled in their favor stating that the causal evidence was insufficient to hold the company responsible.

Nonetheless, many lawsuits in U.S. courts name the brand that a smoker first started smoking even if the person smoked many brands of cigarettes in the years and decades that followed. This tactic is based on the assumption that the branding and advertising efforts initially caused a person to smoke. The research evidence on this point is mixed, but researchers now are turning their attention toward experiments testing hypotheses related to the effectiveness of anti-smoking advertisements—particularly those aimed at adolescents. Typically, these experiments involve multiple groups of individuals, each subjected to a different set of conditions, and then each measured on variables related to their actual smoking behavior or favorableness toward smoking.[3] For instance, a set of four groups are given magazines with different types of ads.

- Group 1 views a magazine with several actual ads for cigarettes.
- Group 2 views a magazine with several anti-smoking ads which emphasize negative effects on health.
- Group 3 views a magazine with several anti-smoking ads which emphasize negative effects on one's social life.
- Group 4, a control group, views a magazine with no cigarette or anti-smoking ads.

The differences in responses across groups can then be analyzed to examine the effectiveness of the ads. In this case, groups 2 and 3 should be less favorably inclined toward smoking than either group 1 or group 4 if anti-smoking ads are effective. Then, the results from groups 2 and 3 can be compared to each other to see whether teens are more affected by fear of becoming ill or becoming less popular! The extent to which the researchers can truly establish causal evidence eventually will boil down to control.

Introduction

Most students are familiar with scientific experiments from studying physical sciences like physics and chemistry. The term *experiment* typically conjures up an image of a chemist surrounded by bubbling test tubes and Bunsen burners. Behavioral and physical scientists have used experimentation far longer than have marketing researchers. Nevertheless, both social scientists and physical scientists use experiments for much the same purpose.

As described in Chapter 3, experiments are widely used in causal research designs. Experimental research allows a researcher to control the research situation so that *causal* relationships among variables may be evaluated. The marketing experimenter manipulates one or more independent variables and holds constant all other possible independent variables while observing effects on dependent variables. Events may be controlled in an experiment to a degree not possible in a survey.

Independent variables are expected to determine the outcomes of interest. In an experiment, they are controlled by the researcher through manipulations. Dependent variables are the outcomes of interest to the researcher and the decision makers. A simple example would be thinking about how changes in price would influence sales. Price would be an independent variable and sales would be a dependent variable. In our opening vignette, the type of appeal used in an anti-smoking ad (health or social implications) would be an experimental independent variable and a ratings scale indicating likelihood of smoking would be an important dependent variable.

If researchers can isolate a situation where adolescents view these different appeals, and everything else is held constant (time of day, age, social status, etc.), then any differences in this dependent variable must have been caused by the type of appeal. Only then can a causal inference be supported (recall the conditions of causality from Chapter 3).

A famous marketing experiment investigated the influence of brand name on consumers' taste perceptions. An experimenter manipulated whether consumers preferred the taste of beer in labeled or unlabeled bottles. One week respondents were given a six-pack containing bottles labeled only with letters (A, B, C). The following week, respondents received another six-pack with brand labels (like Budweiser, Coors, Miller, and so forth). The experimenter measured reactions to the beers after each tasting. In every case, the beer itself was the same. So, every person involved in the experiment drank the very same beer. Therefore, the differences observed in taste, the key dependent variable, could only be attributable to the difference in labeling. When the consumers participating in the experiment expressed a preference for the branded beer, the conclusion is that brand name does influence consumers' taste perceptions.

The Characteristics of Experiments

The next two chapters deal with marketing experiments. Marketing experiments often can best be illustrated through examples. Here, we illustrate the characteristics of experiments by describing a study aimed at testing hypotheses inferring the potential causal effects of color. We will refer back to this example through the next two chapters. Key characteristics of experiments are described in the sections that follow.

By now, perhaps you've had an opportunity to explore the editing features of the Qualtrics survey platform. As the name implies, the tool edits a "survey." Typically, surveys are thought of in association with descriptive research designs. Consider the following points in trying to understand the role such tools may play in causal designs.

1. What types of variables can be measured using survey items created with Qualtrics?
2. Would it be possible to implement an experimental manipulation within or in conjunction with a Qualtrics survey application?
3. Is it possible to create a manipulation check with a Qualtrics survey item?
4. How might computer technology assist in randomly assigning subjects to experimental conditions?

© GEORGE DOYLE & CIARAN GRIFFIN

COURTESY OF QUALTRICS.COM

Subjects

Here, let's take a look at an experiment investigating how color and lights might influence shoppers. This particular research is highly relevant for those involved in retail management and design. The key decisions center around ways color and lighting can be changed to produce favorable consumer reactions. A corresponding research question is, "What is the effect of color and lighting on shopper patronage (meaning how much someone would shop in the store)?"[4]

Over two hundred female consumers were recruited to participate in the experiment. Participants in experimental research are referred to as **subjects** rather than respondents. This is because the experimenter subjects them to some experimental treatment. Each subject in this experiment was simply asked to provide responses to a "new fashion store" concept. The store would sell women's clothing and accessories to the fashion–minded professional woman.

subjects

The sampling units for an experiment, usually human respondents who provide measures based on the experimental manipulation.

Experimental Conditions

Perhaps the characteristic that most differentiates experimental research from survey research is the manner in which independent variables are created rather than simply measured. The illustration experiment involves two relevant independent variables. Fictitious store environments were created for the experiment. Four different hypothetical store environments were created corresponding to

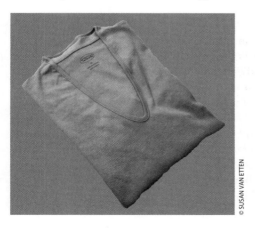

© SUSAN VAN ETTEN

© SUSAN VAN ETTEN

An experiment can capture whether or not color can cause differences in consumer preference for products.

different combinations of the independent variable values. Thus, the only thing differing between the four is combination of the predominant store color and the type of lighting.

The color independent variable was created by variously describing the new store as either predominantly blue or predominantly orange. Similarly, the lighting independent variable was created by describing the store as either having bright or soft lights. Exhibit 11.1 illustrates the four different experimental conditions created by combining the two possible values for each independent variable. An **experimental condition** refers to one of the possible levels of an experimental variable manipulation.

experimental condition

One of the possible levels of an experimental variable manipulation.

EXHIBIT 11.1

Experimental Conditions in Color and Lighting Experiment

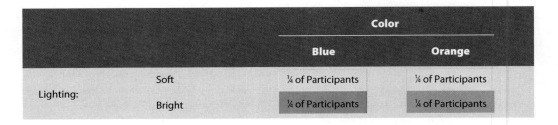

		Color	
		Blue	**Orange**
Lighting:	Soft	¼ of Participants	¼ of Participants
	Bright	¼ of Participants	¼ of Participants

Subjects were assigned to one of these four condition groups. Each group was assigned a store with one of the four color and lighting combinations as shown in the exhibit. Thus, all participants within a group received the same description. Subjects in different groups received different descriptions. By analyzing differences between the groups, the researcher can see what effects occur due to the two experimentally controlled independent variables.

Independent variables that are not experimental conditions can also be included as a means of statistical control in the analysis of experiments. Researchers refer to these as either blocking variables or covariates. **Blocking variables** are categorical variables like a subject's gender or ethnicity. For example, researchers may group results based on whether respondents are male or female. On the other hand, a continuous variable that is expected to show a statistical relationship with the dependent variables is known as a **covariate**. Once statistical analysis begins, blocking variables are treated in much the same way as experimental variables and covariates are treated like a regression variable. We'll cover the statistical analysis of experiments later in the text.

blocking variables

Categorical variables included in the statistical analysis of experimental data as a way of statistically controlling or accounting for variance due to that variable.

covariate

A continuous variable included in the statistical analysis as a way of statistically controlling for variance due to that variable.

Effects

The key outcome, or dependent variable, in this example is a subject's perception of how much he or she would patronize the store. In this case, a rating scale asking how much each participant thought they would actually visit and buy things at the store was created. The possible scores ranged from 0 to 300. A higher score means higher patronage. Effects are the characteristics of experiments that allow hypotheses to be tested. They can be classified several ways. Here, we will focus on the difference between main effects and interaction effects.

■ MAIN EFFECTS

main effect

The experimental difference in dependent variable means between the different levels of any single experimental variable.

A **main effect** refers to the experimental difference in means between the different levels of any single experimental variable. In this case, there are potential main effects for color and for lighting. Main effects are examined by taking a look at the differences between the experimental variable levels for each experimental variable.

Exhibit 11.2 shows the average patronage score for each experimental condition. The results show that among experimental subjects who rated a blue store, an average patronage score of 153.8 was reported, which is considerably higher than the average of 131.8 reported by subjects who rated an orange store. The lighting experimental variable, however, doesn't seem to make much difference. Subjects in the soft lighting condition reported an average of 144.7 and subjects in the bright lighting condition reported only a slightly lower average of 140.4.

Thus, the conclusion at this point seems to be that changing a store's color can change consumer patronage. A blue store is better than an orange store! On the other hand, lighting doesn't seem to make much difference. Or does it?

EXHIBIT 11.2

Consumer Average Patronage Scores in Each Condition

		Color		
		Blue	**Orange**	
Lighting:	Soft	148.5	140.1	144.7
	Bright	159.1	122.6	**140.4**
		153.8	131.8	

■ INTERACTIONS

An **interaction effect** is due to a specific combination of independent variables. In this case, it's possible that the combination of color and lighting creates effects that are not clearly represented in the two main effects.

Experimental results are often shown with a line graph as shown in Exhibit 11.3. Main effects are illustrated when the lines are at different heights as is the case here. Notice the blue line is higher than the orange line. The midpoints of the lines correspond to the means of 153.8 and 131.8 for the blue and orange condition, respectively. A lighting main effect is less obvious because the difference between the midpoint between the two soft points (144.7) is not too different than the corresponding height of the two bright points (140.4). When the lines have very different slopes, an interaction is likely present. In this case, the combination of lights and color is presenting an interaction leading to the following interpretation.

interaction effect

Differences in dependant variable means due to a specific combination of independent variables.

EXHIBIT 11.3

Experimental Graph Showing Results within Each Condition

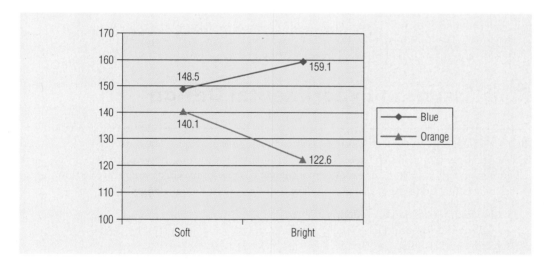

The best possible reaction occurs when the store has a blue color with bright lights and the worst combination occurs when the store is orange with bright lights. In contrast, the means are essentially the same for either color when the lights are soft. So, lights may indeed matter. When the lights are soft, there is little difference in patronage between a blue and orange store. But, when the lights are bright, there is quite a difference between blue and orange.

The pattern of results depicted in Exhibit 11.3 can be contrasted with those from another experiment shown in Exhibit 11.4 on the next page. Here, researchers conducted an experiment to see how different promotions offered by a nightclub might affect the amount of drinks a college student would have during the promotion.[5] The researchers were also interested in potential differences between men and women—a blocking variable. Notice that the line for men is higher than the line for women, suggesting a main effect of sex; men have more drinks than women. Also, the mean number of drinks is higher for the fifty-cent drink promotion than for either of the other two. But, in contrast to our illustration above, the lines are parallel to each other, suggesting that no interaction effect has occurred. In other words, men and women respond to the promotions in the same way.

EXHIBIT 11.4
**Results from Nightclub
Promotion Experiment**

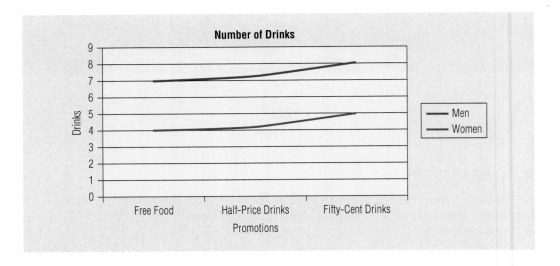

EXHIBIT 11.4
**Results from Nightclub
Promotion Experiment**

Summary of Experimental Characteristics

Experiments differ from ordinary survey research. The differences can be understood by identifying characteristics of experiments. These characteristics include the following:

- Experiments use subjects instead of respondents.
- Experimental variables become the key independent variables. The researcher creates the experimental variables rather than simply measuring them. Measured variables are called blocking variables or covariates in experiments.
- Experimental effects are determined by differences between groups formed in the experiment. Main effects are differences in the means based on a single variable. Interaction effects are differences in means based on combinations of two or more variables.

Basic Issues in Experimental Design

Experimental design is a major research topic. In fact, there are courses and books devoted only to that topic.[6] Here, an introduction into experimental design is provided. The terminology introduced in describing experimental characteristics will be helpful in learning how to implement a simple experimental design. Fortunately, most experimental designs in marketing are relatively simple.

Experimental designs involve no less than four important design elements:

1. manipulation of the independent variable
2. selection and measurement of the dependent variable
3. selection and assignment of experimental subjects
4. control over extraneous variables

Manipulation of the Independent Variable

Recall from Chapter 3, the thing that makes independent variables special in experimentation is that the researcher can actually create its values. This is how the researcher manipulates, and therefore controls, independent variables. In our color experiment, the researcher manipulated the values of the color independent variable by assigning it a value of either blue or orange. Experimental independent variables are hypothesized to be causal influences. Therefore, experiments are very appropriate in causal designs.

experimental treatment

The term referring to the way an experimental variable is manipulated.

An **experimental treatment** is the term referring to the way an experimental variable is manipulated. For example, the illustration manipulates the store environment experimental treatment by assigning consumers to evaluate either a blue or orange store. Thus, there were two levels (or values) of the color variable. A medical researcher may manipulate an experimental variable by treating some subjects with one drug and the other subjects with a separate drug. Experimental variables often involve treatments with more than two levels. For instance, prices of $229, $269, and $299 might represent treatments in a pricing experiment examining how price causes sales for a small under-counter LCD television.

Experimental variables like these can not only be described as independent variables, but they also can be described as a *categorical variable* because they take on a value to represent some classifiable or qualitative aspect. Color, for example, is either orange or blue. Advertising copy style is another example of a categorical or classificatory variable that might be manipulated in an experiment. In other situations, an independent variable may truly exist as a *continuous variable*.

Marketing research sometimes involves experiments that manipulate different elements of physical environments.

When this is the case, the researcher must select appropriate levels of that variable as experimental treatments. For example, lighting can actually be varied over any level from no brightness onward. Price can take on any value but the researcher will only include levels representing relevant distinctions in price in an experiment. Before conducting the experiment, the researcher decides on levels that would be relevant to study. The levels should be noticeably different and realistic.

■ EXPERIMENTAL AND CONTROL GROUPS

In perhaps the simplest experiment, an independent variable is manipulated over two treatment levels resulting in two groups, an experimental group and a control group. An **experimental group** is one in which an experimental treatment is administered. A **control group** is one in which no experimental treatment is administered. For example, consider an experiment studying how advertising affects sales. In the experimental group, the advertising budget may be set at $200,000. In the control condition, advertising may remain at zero or may not change from its current level. By holding conditions constant in the control group, the researcher controls potential sources of error in the experiment. Sales (the dependent variable) in the two treatment groups are compared at the end of the experiment to determine whether the level of advertising (the independent variable) had any effect. Note that this simple experiment can only produce a main effect. Multiple independent variables are necessary for an interaction to occur.

experimental group

A group of subjects to whom an experimental treatment is administered.

control group

A group of subjects to whom no experimental treatment is administered.

■ SEVERAL EXPERIMENTAL TREATMENT LEVELS

The advertising/sales experiment with one experimental and one control group may not tell the advertiser everything he or she wishes to know. If the advertiser wished to understand the functional nature of the relationship between sales and advertising at several treatment levels, additional experimental groups with advertising expenditures of $250,000, $500,000, and $1 million might be studied. This experiment may still involve a control variable. By analyzing more groups, each with a different treatment level, a more precise result may be obtained than in the simple experimental group–control group experiment described above. This design also can produce only a main effect.

■ MORE THAN ONE INDEPENDENT VARIABLE

An experiment can also be made more complicated by including the effect of another experimental variable. Our extended example involving retail atmosphere would typify a still relatively simple

TO THE POINT

You never know what is enough unless you know what is more than enough.

—William Blake

We are never deceived; we deceive ourselves.

—Johann Wolfgang Von Goethe

cell

Refers to a specific treatment combination associated with an experimental group.

two-variable experiment. Since there are two variables, each with two different levels, four experimental groups are obtained. Often, the term **cell** is used to refer to a treatment combination within an experiment. The number of cells involved in any experiment can be easily computed as follows:

$$K = (T_1)(T_2)..(T_m)$$

where K = the number of cells, T_1 = the number of treatment levels for experimental group number one, T_2 = the number of treatment levels for experimental group number two, and so forth through the mth experimental group (T_m). In the illustration experiment, there are two variables each with two levels so the computation is quite simple:

$$K = 2 \text{ (color levels)} \times 2 \text{ (lighting levels)} = 4 \text{ cells}$$

Including multiple variables allows a comparison of experimental treatments on the dependent variable. Since there are more than two experimental variables, this design involves both main effects and interactions. We will return to the topic of multiple variable experiments in the next chapter.

Selection and Measurement of the Dependent Variable

Selecting dependent variables is crucial in experimental design. Unless the dependent variables are relevant and truly represent an outcome of interest, the experiment will not be useful. Sometimes, the logical dependent variable is fairly obvious. If researchers introduce a new cinnamon, pink grapefruit tea mix in a test-market, sales volume is most likely to be a key dependent variable. However, if researchers are experimenting with different forms of advertising copy appeals, defining the dependent variable may be more difficult. For example, measures of advertising awareness, recall, changes in brand preference, or sales might be possible dependent variables. In the retail atmosphere example, retail patronage was the key dependent variable. However, other potential dependent variables might include perceived product quality, excitement, or price perceptions.

Choosing the right dependent variable is part of the problem definition process. Like the problem definition process in general, it sometimes is considered less carefully than it should be. The experimenter's choice of a dependent variable determines what type of answer is given to assist managers in decision making.

Consider how difficult it can be to select the right dependent variable in a test-market. While sales are almost certainly important, when should sales be measured? The amount of time needed for effects to become evident should be considered in choosing the dependent variable. Sales may be measured several months after the experiment to determine if there were any carryover effects. Changes that are relatively permanent or longer lasting than changes generated only during the period of the experiment should be considered. Repeat purchase behavior may be important too since some consumers may try a product once but then never choose that product again. Consumers often try a "loser" once, but they do not buy a "loser" again and again.

The introduction of the original Crystal Pepsi illustrates the need to think beyond consumers' initial reactions. When Crystal Pepsi, a clear cola, was introduced, the initial trial rate was high, but only a small percentage of customers made repeat purchases. The brand never achieved high repeat sales within a sufficiently large market segment. Brand awareness, trial purchase, and repeat purchase are all possible dependent variables in an experiment. The dependent variable therefore should be considered carefully and more than one can be included in an experiment. Thorough problem definition will help the researcher select the most important dependent variable(s).

Selection and Assignment of Test Units

test units

The subjects or entities whose responses to the experimental treatment are measured or observed.

Test units are the subjects or entities whose responses to the experimental treatment are measured or observed. Individual consumers, employees, organizational units, sales territories, market segments, brands, stores, or other entities may be the test units. People are the most common test units in most marketing and consumer behavior experiments. In our unit retail atmospherics example, individual consumers are the test units as in the Research Snapshot on the next page.

Goldfishing or Bluefishing?

Food marketers are often claiming that their brand tastes better than the competitors. When a claim like this is made, it has to be supported somehow or else the company making the claim is liable and risks being sued for making a false or unsubstantiated claim. Thus, research is often needed to produce evidence supporting such claims. Marketers need to be very careful, however, that this type of research is conducted in a rigorous fashion.

Sea Snapper brand gourmet frozen fish products claimed in advertising that their fish sticks are preferred more than two to one over the most popular brand, Captain John's.[7] The advertisements all included a definitive statement indicating that research existed that substantiated this claim. Captain John's sued Sea Snapper over the claim and based the suit on the fact that the research was faulty. Sea Snapper managers conducted taste tests involving four hundred consumers who indicated that they regularly ate frozen food products. Two hundred tasted Sea Snapper premium fish sticks and the other two hundred tasted Captain John's premium fish sticks. Results showed a main effect with an average preference score for Sea Snapper of 78.2 compared to 39.0 for Captain John's. Case closed? Not hardly. Captain John's attorney hired a marketing research firm to assist in the lawsuit.

The research firm was unable to duplicate the result. After intense questioning of subjects involved in the original research, it turned out that Sea Snapper fish sticks were always presented to consumers on a blue plate while Captain John's were always presented to consumers on a goldfish-colored (a sort of orangish gold) plate. Therefore, the Sea Snapper results could be attributable to a variable other than taste and Captain John's came out as the winner of this legal action—with the help of marketing research.

■ SAMPLE SELECTION AND RANDOM SAMPLING ERRORS

As in other forms of marketing research, random sampling errors and sample selection errors may occur in experimentation. For example, experiments sometimes go awry even when a geographic area is specially chosen for a particular investigation. A case in point is an experiment testing a new lubricant for outboard motors by Dow Chemical Company. The lubricant was tested in Florida. Florida was chosen because researchers thought the hot, muggy climate would provide the most demanding test. In Florida the lubricant was a success. However, the story was quite different when the product was sold in Michigan. Although the lubricant sold well and worked well during the summer, the following spring Dow discovered the oil had congealed, allowing the outboard motors, idle all winter, to rust. The rusting problem never came to light in Florida, where the motors were in year-round use. Thus, sample selection error occurs because of flaws in procedures used to assign experimental test units. Here, testing units in Florida created error if the goal was understanding how the product worked in Michigan.

Systematic or nonsampling error may occur if the sampling units in an experimental cell are somehow different than the units in another cell, and this difference affects the dependent variable. For example, suppose some professors are interested in testing the effect of providing snacks during exams on students' scores. The experimental variable is snacks, manipulated over three levels: (1) fruit, (2) cookies, and (3) chocolate. The test units in this case are individual students. When the professors conduct the experiment, for convenience, they decide to give all of the 8 a.m. classes chocolate for a snack, all of the 1 p.m. classes get fruit, and all of the 7 p.m. classes get cookies. While this type of procedure is often followed, if our tastes and digestive systems react differently to different foods at different times of the day, systematic error is introduced into the experiment. Furthermore, because the night classes contain students who are older on average, the professors may reach the conclusion that students perform better when they eat cookies, when it may really be due to the fact that students who are older perform better no matter what they are fed.

systematic or nonsampling error

Occurs if the sampling units in an experimental cell are somehow different than the units in another cell, and this difference affects the dependent variable.

Although experiments are often administered in groups, if all groups are not the same, then systematic error is introduced.

■ RANDOMIZATION

Randomization—the random assignment of subject and treatments to groups—is one device for equally distributing the effects of extraneous variables to all conditions. The presence of nuisance variables will not be eliminated, but they will be controlled because they are likely to exist to the same degree in every experimental cell. Thus, all cells would be expected to yield similar average scores on the dependent variables if it were not for the experimental treatments administered in a particular cell. In other words, the researcher would like to set up a situation where everything in every cell is the same except for the experimental treatment. Random assignment of subjects allows the researcher to make this assumption, thereby reducing the chance of systematic error.

■ MATCHING

Random assignment of subjects to the various experimental groups is the most common technique used to prevent test units from differing from each other on key variables; it assumes that all characteristics of the subjects have been likewise randomized. Matching the respondents on the basis of pertinent background information is another technique for controlling systematic error by assigning subjects in a way that their characteristics are the same in each group. This is best thought of in terms of demographic characteristics. If a subject's sex is expected to influence dependent variable responses, as in a taste test, then the researcher may make sure that there are equal numbers of men and women in each experimental cell. In general, if a researcher believes that certain extraneous variables may affect the dependent variable, he or she can make sure that the subjects in each group are the same on these characteristics.

For example, in a taste test experiment for a dog food, it might be important to match the dogs in various experimental groups on the basis of age or breed. That way, the same number of basset hounds and Dobermans will test formula A, formula B, and formula C. While matching can be a useful approach, the researcher can never be sure that sampling units are matched on all characteristics. Here, for example, even though breeds can be matched, it is difficult to know if all dogs live in the same type of environment (indoors, outdoors, spacious, cramped, with table scraps or without, and so on).

■ REPEATED MEASURES

Experiments in which an individual subject is exposed to more than one level of an experimental treatment are referred to as **repeated measures** designs. Although this approach has advantages, including being more economical since the same subject provides more data than otherwise, it has several drawbacks that can limit its usefulness. We will discuss these in more detail later.

Time series designs inherently involve repeated measures. Researchers that are addressing the way learning affects employee performance over time may have no choice but to employ a repeated measures design. For, example, if two variations of a two-year continuous improvement program is being applied in some plant facilities for a manufacturing firm, the researcher may need to make periodic measures over the two-year period on the same sampling units.

■ EXTRANEOUS VARIABLES

The fourth decision about the basic elements of an experiment concerns control over extraneous variables. This is related to the various types of experimental error. In Chapter 8 we classified total survey error into two basic categories: random sampling error and systematic error. The same dichotomy applies to all research designs, but the terms *random (sampling) error* and *systematic error* are more frequently used when discussing experiments.

Experimental Confounds

We have already discussed how systematic error can occur when the extraneous variables or the conditions of administering the experiment are allowed to influence the dependent variables. When this occurs, the results will be confounded because the extraneous variables have not been controlled or eliminated. The results can be confounded by an extraneous cause. A **confound** in an experiment means that there is an alternative explanation beyond the experimental variables for any observed differences in the dependent variable. Once a potential confound is identified, the validity of the experiment is severely questioned.

Recall from the Research Snapshot on page 273 that the experimental procedures involved a taste test. The Research Snapshot illustrates how a confound can ruin an experiment. Sea Snapper fish sticks were always presented on a blue plate and Captain John's fish sticks were always presented on a goldish-colored plate. The plate's color is confounding the explanation that the difference in brands is responsible for the difference in liking. Is the difference in liking due to the color or the product quality?

In a simple experimental group–control group experiment aimed at employee task efficiency, if subjects in the experimental group are always administered a treatment (an energy drink) in the morning and then have their efficiency measured also in the morning, and the control group always has their efficiency measured in the afternoon, a constant error has been introduced. In other words, the results will show a difference not only due to the treatment, but also due to the added efficiency that naturally occurs in the morning. In such a situation, time of day represents a confound. On the other hand, other types of error are random and not constant. For example, the natural fluctuations in efficiency that occur from day to day. Random errors are less of a problem for experiments than are contant errors because they do not cause systematic changes in outcomes.

Identifying Extraneous Variables

Most students of marketing realize that the marketing mix variables—price, product, promotion, and distribution—interact with uncontrollable forces in the market, such as competitors' activities and consumer trends. Thus, marketing experiments are subject to the effect of extraneous variables. Since extraneous variables can produce confounded results, they must be identified before the experiment if at all possible.

Cigarette smoking has been a topic of much debate and research. The chapter vignette illustrates how important isolating causes can be in developing theoretical explanations. Does cigarette advertising cause young people to smoke? One of the primary reasons for the inconclusiveness of this debate is the failure for most of the research to control for extraneous variables.[8] For instance, consider a study in which two groups of U.S. high school students are studied over the course of a year. One is exposed to a greater percentage of foreign television media in which American cigarettes are more often shown in a flattering and glamorous light. In fact, the programming includes cigarette commercials. The other group is a control group in which their exposure to media is not controlled. At the end of the year, the experimental group reports a greater frequency and incidence of cigarette smoking. Did the increased media exposure involving cigarettes cause smoking behavior?

While the result seems plausible at first, the careful researcher may ask the following questions:

- Was the demographic makeup of the two groups the same? While it is clear that the ages of the two groups are likely the same, it is well known that different ethnic groups have different smoking rates. Approximately 28 percent of all high school students report smoking, but the rate is higher among Hispanic teens, for example.[9] Therefore, if one group contained more Hispanics or Asians, we might expect it to report different smoking rates than otherwise. Similarly, smoking varies with social class.
- How did the control group fill the time consumed by the experimental group in being exposed to the experimental treatment? Could it be that it somehow dissuaded them from smoking? Perhaps they were exposed to media with more anti-smoking messages?
- Were the two groups of the same general achievement profiles? Those who are high in the need for achievement may be less prone to smoke than are other students.
- Although it is a difficult task to list all possible extraneous factors, some that even sound unusual can sometimes have an effect. For example, did the students have equally dispersed birthdays? Researchers have even shown that smoking rates correspond to one's birthday, meaning that different astrological groups have different smoking rates.[10]

Because an experimenter does not want extraneous variables to affect the results, he or she must control or eliminate such variables. It is always better to spend time thinking about how to control for possible extraneous variables before the experiment since often there is nothing that can be done to salvage results after a confounding effect is identified.

Demand Characteristics

What are Demand Characteristics?

demand characteristic

Experimental design element or procedure that unintentionally provides subjects with hints about the research hypothesis.

The term **demand characteristic** refers to an experimental design element that unintentionally provides subjects with hints about the research hypothesis. Researchers cannot reveal the research hypotheses to subjects before the experiment or else they can create a confounding effect. Think about the retail atmospherics experiment. If the subjects were told before they participated that they were going to be involved in an experiment to see if they liked stores that were predominantly orange or predominantly blue, the researcher would never be sure if their responses to the dependent variable were really due to the differences in the experimental stimuli or due to the fact that the subjects were trying to provide a "correct" response. In addition, once subjects know the hypotheses, there is little hope that they will respond naturally.

So, knowledge of the experimental hypothesis creates a confound. This particular type of confound is known as a **demand effect**. Demand characteristics make demand effects very likely.

demand effect

Occurs when demand characteristics actually affect the dependent variable.

Experimenter Bias and Demand Effects

The experimenter unintentionally can create a demand effect by smiling, nodding, or frowning at the wrong time.

Demand characteristics are aspects of an experiment that *demand* (encourage) that the subjects respond in a particular way. Hence, they are a source of systematic error. If participants recognize the experimenter's expectation or demand, they are likely to act in a manner consistent with the experimental treatment. Even slight nonverbal cues may influence their reactions.

Prominent demand characteristics are often presented by the person administering experimental procedures. If an experimenter's presence, actions, or comments influence the subjects' behavior or sway the subjects to slant their answers to cooperate with the experimenter, the experiment has introduced *experimenter bias*. When subjects slant their answers to cooperate with the experimenter, they are exhibiting behaviors that might not represent their behavior in the marketplace. For example, if subjects in an advertising experiment understand that the experimenter is interested in whether they changed their attitudes in accord with a given advertisement, they may answer in the desired direction. Acting in this manner reflects a demand effect rather than a true experimental treatment effect.

Hawthorne Effect

A famous management experiment illustrates a common demand characteristic. Researchers were attempting to study the effects on productivity of various working conditions, such as hours of work, rest periods, lighting, and methods of pay, at the Western Electric Hawthorne plant in Cicero, Illinois. The researchers found that workers' productivity increased whether the work hours were lengthened or shortened, whether lighting was very bright or very dim, and so on. The surprised investigators realized that the workers' morale was higher because they were aware of being part of a special experimental group. This totally unintended effect is now known as the **Hawthorne effect** because researchers realize that people will perform differently when they know they are experimental subjects.[11]

If subjects in a laboratory experiment interact (i.e., are not relatively isolated), their conversations may produce joint decisions rather than a desired individual decision. For this reason, social interaction generally is restricted in laboratory experiments.

Hawthorne effect

People will perform differently from normal when they know they are experimental subjects.

Reducing Demand Characteristics

Although it is practically impossible to eliminate demand characteristics from experiments, there are steps that can be taken to reduce them (see Exhibit 11.5). Many of these steps make it difficult for subjects to know what the researcher is trying to find out. Some or all of these may be appropriate in a given experiment.

1. Use an experimental disguise.
2. Isolate experimental subjects.
3. Use a "blind" experimental administrator.
4. Administer only one experimental treatment level to each subject.

■ EXPERIMENTAL DISGUISE

Subjects participating in the experiment can be told that the purpose of the experiment is somewhat different than the actual purpose. Most often, they are simply told less than the complete "truth" about what is going to happen. For instance, in the retail atmosphere study above, subjects were told that they would be asked to react to a new retail store concept. This really is true, but they were not told anything about color, lighting, or any other potential experimental effect.

In other cases, more deceit may be needed. Psychologists studying how much pain one person may be willing to inflict on another might use a ruse telling the subject that they are actually interested in the effect of pain on human performance. The researcher tells the actual subject to administer a series of questions to another person (who is actually a research assistant) and to provide the person with an increasingly strong electric shock each time an incorrect answer is given. In reality, the real dependent variable has something to do with how long the actual subject will continue to administer shocks before stopping.

A **placebo** is an experimental deception involving a false treatment. A **placebo effect** refers to the corresponding effect in a dependent variable that is due to the psychological impact that goes along with knowledge that a treatment has been administered. A placebo is particularly important when the experimental variable involves physical consumption of some product. The placebo should not be different in any manner that is actually noticeable by the research subject. If someone is told that a special food additive will suppress appetite, and they are supposed to sprinkle it

placebo

A false experimental treatment disguising the fact that no real treatment is administered.

placebo effect

The effect in a dependent variable associated with the psychological impact that goes along with knowledge of some treatment being administered.

EXHIBIT 11.5
Reducing Demand Effects

One treatment/subject · Use a disguise · Use a blind administrator · Isolate subjects on their dinner before eating as part of an experiment, another group should receive a placebo that looks exactly like the actual food additive but actually is some type of inert compound. Both groups are likely to show some difference in consumption compared to someone undergoing no effect. The difference in the actual experimental group and the placebo group would represent the true effect of the additive.

Placebo effects exist in marketing research. For example, when subjects are told that an energy drink is sold at a discount price, they believe it is significantly less effective than when it is sold at the regular, non-discounted price.[12] Later, we will return to the ethical issues involved in experimental deception.

■ ISOLATE EXPERIMENTAL SUBJECTS

Researchers should minimize the extent to which subjects are able to talk about the experimental procedures with each other. Although it may be unintentional, discussion among subjects may lead them to guess the experimental hypotheses. For instance, it could be that different subjects received different treatments. The experimental integrity will be higher when each only knows enough to participate in the experiment.

■ USE A "BLIND" EXPERIMENTAL ADMINISTRATOR

When possible, the people actually administering the experiment may not be told the experimental hypotheses. The advantage is that if they do not know what exactly is being studied, then they are less likely to give off clues that result in demand effects. Like the subjects, when there is some reason to expect that their knowledge may constitute a demand characteristic, administrators best know only enough to do their job.

■ ADMINISTER ONLY ONE EXPERIMENTAL CONDITION PER SUBJECT

When subjects know more than one experimental treatment condition, they are much more likely to guess the experimental hypothesis. So, even though there are cost advantages to administering multiple treatment levels to the same subject, it should be avoided when possible. For example, in the retail atmospherics example, if subjects responded first to a blue retail store concept, and then saw the same store that was exactly the same except the walls had become orange, then he or she is very likely to know that the researcher is interested in color.

Establishing Control

The major difference between experimental research and descriptive research is an experimenter's ability to control variables by either holding conditions constant or manipulating the experimental variable. If the color of beer causes preference, a brewery experimenting with a new clear beer must determine the possible extraneous variables other than color that may affect an experiment's results and attempt to eliminate or control those variables. Marketing theory tells us that brand image and packaging design are important factors in beer drinkers' reactions. Therefore, the researcher may wish to control the influence of these variables. He or she may eliminate these two extraneous variables by packaging the test beers in plain brown packages without any brand identification.

constancy of conditions

Means that subjects in all experimental groups are exposed to identical conditions except for the differing experimental treatments.

When extraneous variables cannot be eliminated, experimenters may strive for **constancy of conditions**. This means that subjects in all experimental groups are exposed to identical conditions except for the differing experimental treatments. The principle of matching discussed earlier helps make sure that constancy is achieved.

A supermarket experiment involving four test products shows the care that must be taken to hold all factors constant. The experiment required that all factors other than shelf space be kept constant throughout the testing period. In all stores the shelf level that had existed before the tests began was to be maintained throughout the test period. Only the *amount* of shelf space (the treatment) was changed. One problem involved store personnel accidentally changing shelf level when stocking the test products. This deviation from the constancy of conditions was minimized by auditing each store four times a week. In this way, any change could be detected in a minimum amount of time. The experimenter personally stocked as many of the products as possible, and the cooperation of stock clerks also helped reduce treatment deviations.

If an experimental method requires that the same subjects be exposed to two or more experimental treatments, an error may occur due to the *order of presentation*. For instance, if subjects are examining the effects of different levels of graphical interface on video game enjoyment, and they are asked to view each of four different levels, the order in which they are presented may influence enjoyment. Subjects might perform one level simply because it follows a very poor level. **Counterbalancing** attempts to eliminate the confounding effects of order of presentation by requiring that one fourth of the subjects be exposed to treatment A first, one fourth to treatment B first, one fourth to treatment C first, and finally one fourth to treatment D first. Likewise, the other levels are counterbalanced so that the order of presentation is rotated among subjects.

Problems Controlling Extraneous Variables

In marketing experiments it is not always possible to control every possible extraneous variable. For example, competitors may bring out a product during the course of a test-market. This form of competitive interference occurred in a Boston test-market for Anheuser-Busch's import beer, Wurzburger Hofbrau. During the test, Miller Brewing Company introduced its own brand, Munich Oktoberfest, and sent eight salespeople out to blitz the Boston market. A competitor who learns of a test-market experiment may knowingly change its prices or increase advertising to confound the test results. This brings us to ethical issues in experimentation.

Fundamental Questions in Experimentation ←

Basic versus Factorial Experimental Designs

In *basic experimental designs* a single independent variable is manipulated to observe its effect on a single dependent variable. However, we know that complex marketing dependent variables such as sales, product usage, and preference are influenced by several factors. The simultaneous change in independent variables such as price and advertising may have a greater influence on sales than if either variable is changed alone. *Factorial experimental designs* are more sophisticated than basic experimental designs and allow for an investigation of the interaction of two or more independent variables. Factorial experiments are discussed further in a section on complex experimental designs in Chapter 12.

Laboratory Experiments

A marketing experiment can be conducted in a natural setting (a field experiment) or in an artificial or laboratory setting. In social sciences, the actual laboratory may be a behavioral lab, which is somewhat like a focus group facility. However, it may simply be a room or classroom dedicated to collecting data, or it can even take place in one's home.

In a **laboratory experiment** the researcher has more complete control over the research setting and extraneous variables. For example, subjects are recruited and brought to an advertising agency's office, a research agency's office, or perhaps a mobile unit designed for research purposes. They are exposed to a television commercial within the context of a program that includes competitors' ads among the commercials shown. They are then allowed to purchase either the advertised product or one of several competing products in a simulated store environment. Trial purchase measures are thus obtained. A few weeks later,

counterbalancing

Attempts to eliminate the confounding effects of order of presentation by requiring that one fourth of the subjects be exposed to treatment A first, one fourth to treatment B first, one fourth to treatment C first, and finally one fourth to treatment D first.

Facilities like this one can break down the food that companies sell and tell them exactly what it should taste like. Is this a good way to test the taste of new products?

PHOTO COURTESY OF VICKI BEAVER

laboratory experiment

The researcher has more complete control over the research setting and extraneous variables.

Celling Experiments

We all know cell phones sell! But what kinds of effects can cell phones cause? Many people are calling for experiments examing the potential health effects of heavy cell phone usage. Additionally, ancillary technologies such as Bluetooth devices, which many people hook to their ear for hours on end each day, constantly bombard us with radio waves. While most people do not believe these to be serious threats to our health, others aren't so sure. One of the challenges in studying this issue is the difficulty in implementing an experimental design on human subjects—much as in the case of smoking.

One thing is certain though, more and more marketing researchers are finding ways to conduct experiments with mobile phone technology. For instance, advertising appeals can be delivered via text message or voice mail. Advertisers can manipulate the size of a discount offered for a brief period of time and then track to see whether the subject takes advantage of the discount. For instance, advertisers in Hong Kong, where consumers are more receptive to advertising via mobile phones, can send a short text blast to all consumers near a Starbucks. They can then have the consumer send back a reply to activate a discount at that store. In this way, they might be able to test whether a free cookie or a half-price latte is a better incentive and results in more patronage.

However, conducting experiments in this manner threatens internal validity in several ways. Although the large number of mobile phones in use has made them more practical for doing research, and their increased flexibility in delivering messages has provided more capability for doing research, it is nearly impossible to control for extraneous variables. Is the subject in a car, on a train, in a meeting, alone, or with others? Many factors like these might interfere with experimental results. Despite the weaknesses, the convenience and technological advantages will likely lead to more rather than less "celling" experiments.

Sources: Committee on Identification of Research Needs Relating to Potential Biological or Adverse Health Effects of Wireless Communication Devices, National Research Council, "Identification of Research Needs Relating to Potential Biological or Adverse Health Effects of Wireless Communication Devices," The National Academies Press (2008); Long, J., K. Tomak, and A. B. Whinston, "Calling All Customers," Marketing News, (January 20, 2003), p. 18; Grapentine, T., "Don't Cell Yourself Short," Marketing Research, 17 (Fall 2005), 5.

© PHOTODISC/GETTY IMAGES

© GEORGE DOYLE & CIARAN GRIFFIN

subjects are contacted again to measure their satisfaction and determine repeat purchasing intention. This laboratory experiment gives the consumer an opportunity to "buy" and "invest." In a short timespan, the marketer is able to collect information on decision making. Our retail atmospheric experiment also illustrates a laboratory experiment.

tachistoscope

Device that controls the amount of time a subject is exposed to a visual image.

Other laboratory experiments may be more controlled or artificial. For example, a **tachistoscope** allows a researcher to experiment with the visual impact of advertising, packaging, and so on by controlling the amount of time a subject is exposed to a visual image. Each stimulus (for example, package design) is projected from a slide to the tachistoscope at varying exposure lengths (1/10 of a second, 2/10, 3/10, and so on). The tachistoscope simulates the split-second duration of a customer's attention to a package in a mass display.

Field Experiments

field experiments

Research projects involving experimental manipulations that are implemented in a natural environment.

Field experiments are research projects involving experimental manipulations that are implemented in a natural environment. They can be useful in fine-tuning marketing strategies and determining sales forecasts for different marketing mix designs. Test-markets are field experiments. Betty Crocker's Squeezit (a 10 percent fruit juice drink in a squeeze bottle) was so successful in a test-market that production could not keep up with demand. As a result, the product's national introduction was postponed until production capacity could be increased. The Research Snapshot above illustrates how technological developments can be leveraged for new ways to conduct field experiments.

McDonald's conducted a field experiment testing the Triple Ripple, a three-flavor ice cream product. The product was dropped because the experiment revealed that distribution problems reduced product quality and limited customer acceptance. In the distribution system the product would freeze, defrost, and refreeze. Solving the problem would have required each McDonald's city to have a local ice cream plant with special equipment to roll the three flavors into one. A naturalistic setting for the experiment helped McDonald's executives realize the product was impractical.

Experiments vary in their degree of artificiality and control. Exhibit 11.6 shows that as experiments increase in naturalism, they begin to approach a pure field experiment. As they become more artificial, they approach a pure laboratory experiment.

In field experiments, a researcher manipulates experimental variables but cannot possibly control all the extraneous variables. An example is NBC's research on new television programs. Viewers who subscribe to a cable television service are asked to watch a cable preview on their home television sets at a certain time on a certain cable channel. While the program is being aired, telephone calls from the viewers' friends cannot be controlled. In

The naturally occurring noise that exists in the field can interfere with experimental manipulations.

contrast, an advertising professor may test some advertising effect by showing subjects advertising in a classroom setting. Here, there are no phone calls and little to distract the subject. Which produces a better experiment?

Generally, subjects know when they are participating in a laboratory experiment. Performance of certain tasks, responses to questions, or some other form of active involvement is characteristic of laboratory experiments. In field experiments, as in test-markets, subjects do not even know they have taken part in an experiment. Ethically, consent should be sought before having someone participate in an experiment. However, with field experiments the consent is implied since subjects are not asked to do anything departing from their normal behavior to participate in the experiment. All precautions with respect to safety and confidentiality should be maintained.

Field experiments involving new products or promotions are often conducted in a retail store. These are known as controlled store tests. The products are put into stores in a number of small cities or into selected supermarket chains. Product deliveries are made not through the traditional warehouse but by the research agency, so product information remains confidential. While they can be less expensive than a full-blown market test, they also have drawbacks because of the relatively small sample of stores and the limitations on the type of outlet where the product is tested. Thus, their results may not generalize to all consumers in a population.

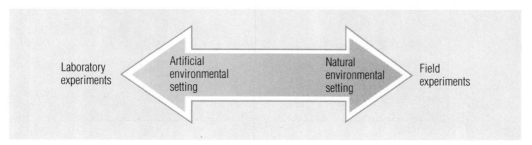

Laboratory experiments ← Artificial environmental setting — Natural environmental setting → Field experiments

EXHIBIT 11.6
The Artificiality of Laboratory versus Field Experiments

Advantages of Between-Subjects Designs

A basic question faced by the researchers involves how many treatments a subject should receive. For economical reasons, the researcher may wish to apply multiple treatments to the same subject. For instance, in the retail atmosphere experiment, each subject could rate each combination of colors and lighting. Thus, four observations on the dependent variable can be obtained from a single subject. Such a design is called a **within-subjects design**. Within-subjects designs involve repeated measures because with each treatment the same subject is measured.

In contrast, the researcher could decide that each person will receive only one treatment combination. This is referred to as a **between-subjects design**. Each dependent variable is measured only once for every subject. Exhibit 11.7 illustrates this point. In the between subjects condition a different person is measured for each different lighting/color combination.

Between-subjects designs are usually advantageous although they are usually more costly. The validity of between-subjects designs is usually higher because by applying only one treatment combination to one subject, demand characteristics are greatly reduced. When a subject sees multiple conditions, he or she is more likely to guess what the study is about. In addition, as we will see later, statistical analyses of between subjects designs are simpler than within-subjects designs. This also means the results are easier to report and explain to management.

within-subjects design

Involves repeated measures because with each treatment the same subject is measured.

between-subjects design

Each subject receives only one treatment combination.

EXHIBIT 11.7
Within- and Between-Subjects Designs

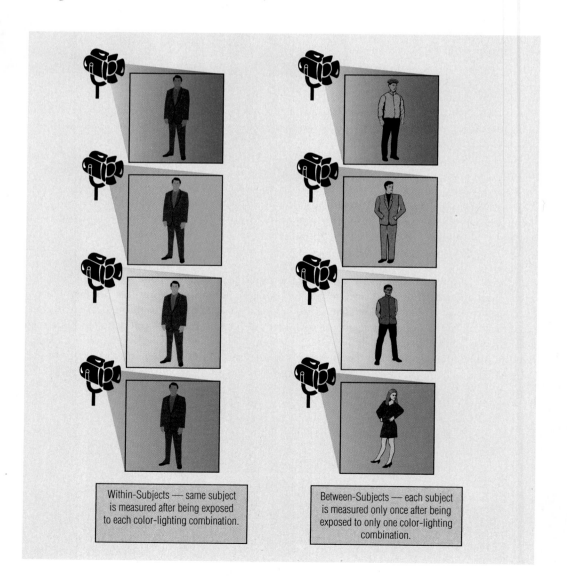

Within-Subjects — same subject is measured after being exposed to each color-lighting combination.

Between-Subjects — each subject is measured only once after being exposed to only one color-lighting combination.

A Lethal Interaction

In pharmacology, the interaction effect is usually called a *synergistic effect*.[13] An example is the lethal combination of barbiturate sleeping pills and alcohol. Each of these is a drug, and each reduces the number of heartbeats per minute. Their combined effect, however, is a much more severe reduction than one would expect knowing their individual effects. These two treatments together are not merely additive—their combined effect is much more than the sum of their individual effects. Another way of phrasing the synergistic effect is the following: The effect of one treatment differs depending on the level of the other treatment; that is, the reduction in pulse due to alcohol differs depending on whether or not barbiturates are in a person's system.

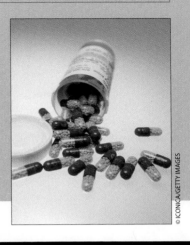

Issues of Experimental Validity

An experiment's quality is judged by two types of validity. These are known as internal and external validity.

Internal Validity

Internal validity exists to the extent that an experimental variable is truly responsible for any variance in the dependent variable. In other words, does the experimental manipulation truly cause changes in the specific outcome of interest? If the observed results were influenced or confounded by extraneous factors, the researcher will have problems making valid conclusions about the relationship between the experimental treatment and the dependent variable.

Thus, a lab experiment enhances internal validity because it maximizes control of outside forces. If we wish to know whether a certain odor causes increased productivity among service workers, we may set up a task in a room with a tightly controlled airflow so we can be sure that the specific odor exists in the air in the amount and intensity desired. We can also control temperature, lighting, density, sounds, and many other factors that would be difficult or impossible to control outside of a lab environment. If the only thing that varies from subject to subject is the odor, then we can safely say that any differences in performance must be attributable to human reactions to the scent. Medical researchers wanting to isolate synergestic effects like those discussed in the Research Snapshot above may use a lab experiment to isolate the chemicals that are placed into a subject's body as closely as possible.

internal validity

Exists to the extent that an experimental variable is truly responsible for any variance in the dependent variable.

■ MANIPULATION CHECKS

Internal validity depends in large part on successful manipulations. Manipulations should be carried out in a way that varies the experimental variable over meaningfully different levels. If the levels are too close together, the experiment may lack the power necessary to observe differences in the dependent variable. In a pricing experiment, it may be that manipulating the price of an automobile over two levels, $24,800 and $24,600, would not be successful in creating truly different price categories.

The validity of manipulations can often be checked with a **manipulation check**. If a drug is administered in different dosages that should affect blood sugar levels, the researcher could actually measure blood sugar level after administering the drug to make sure that the dosages were different enough to produce a change in blood sugar. In marketing, the manipulation check is often conducted by asking a survey question or two. In the pricing example above, subjects may be asked a question about how low they believe the price of the car to be. A valid manipulation would produce substantially different average responses to that question in a "high" and "low" price group. Manipulation checks should always be administered after dependent variables

manipulation check

A validity test of an experimental manipulation to make sure that the manipulation does produce differences in the independent variable.

in self-response format experiments. This keeps the manipulation check item from becoming a troublesome demand characteristic.

Extraneous variables can jeopardize internal validity. The six major ones are *history, maturation, testing, instrumentation, selection,* and *mortality.*

■ HISTORY

history effect

Occurs when some change other than the experimental treatment occurs during the course of an experiment that affects the dependent variable.

A **history effect** occurs when some change other than the experimental treatment occurs during the course of an experiment that affects the dependent variable. A common history effect occurs when competitors change their marketing strategies during a test marketing experiment. History effects are particularly prevalent in repeated measures experiments that take place over an extended time. If we wanted to assess how much a change in recipe improves individual subjects' consumption of a food product, we would first measure their consumption and then compare it with consumption after the change. Since several weeks may pass between the first and second measurement, there are many things that could occur that would also influence subjects' diets.

Although it may sound extreme, examining the effect of some dietary supplement on various health-related outcomes may require that a subject be confined during the experiment's course. This may take several weeks. Without confining the subject in something like a hospital setting, there would be little way of controlling food and drink consumption, exercise activities, and other factors that may also affect the dependent variables.

cohort effect

Refers to a change in the dependent variable that occurs because members of one experimental group experienced different historical situations than members of other experimental groups.

A special case of the history effect is the **cohort effect**, which refers to a change in the dependent variable that occurs because members of one experimental group experienced different historical situations than members of other experimental groups. For example, two groups of managers used as subjects may be in different cohorts because one group encountered different experiences over the course of an experiment. If the experimental manipulation involves different levels of financial incentives and performance is the dependent variable, one group may be affected by an informative article appearing in a trade magazine during the experiment. Since the other group participated prior to this group, members of that group could not benefit from the article. Therefore, the possibility exists that the article rather than the change in incentive is truly causing differences in performance.

■ MATURATION

maturation effect

A function of time and the naturally occurring events that coincide with growth and experience.

A **maturation effect** is a function of time and the naturally occurring events that coincide with growth and experience. Experiments taking place over longer timespans may see lower internal validity as subjects simply grow older or more experienced. Suppose an experiment were designed to test the impact of a new compensation program on sales productivity. If this program were tested over a year's time, some of the salespeople probably would mature as a result of more selling experience or perhaps gain increased knowledge. Their sales productivity might improve because of their knowledge and experience rather than the compensation program.

■ TESTING

testing effects

A nuisance effect occurring when the initial measurement or test alerts or primes subjects in a way that affects their response to the experimental treatments.

Testing effects are also called *pretesting effects* because the initial measurement or test alerts or primes subjects in a way that affects their response to the experimental treatments. Testing effects only occur in a before-and-after study. A before-and-after study is one requiring an initial baseline measure be taken before an experimental treatment is administered. So, before-and-after experiments are a special case of a repeated measures design. For example, students taking standardized achievement and intelligence tests for the second time usually do better than those taking the tests for the first time. The effect of testing may increase awareness of socially approved answers, increase attention to experimental conditions (that is, the subject may watch more closely), or make the subject more conscious than usual of the dimensions of a problem.

■ INSTRUMENTATION

instrumentation effect

A nuisance that occurs when a change in the wording of questions, a change in interviewers, or a change in other procedures causes a change in the dependent variable.

A change in the wording of questions, a change in interviewers, or a change in other procedures used to measure the dependent variable causes an **instrumentation effect**, which may jeopardize internal validity. If the same interviewers are used to ask questions for both before and after measurement, some problems may arise. With practice, interviewers may acquire increased skill in interviewing, or they may become bored and decide to reword the questionnaire in their own terms. To avoid this problem, new interviewers are hired, but different individuals are also a source of extraneous variation due to instrumentation variation. There are numerous other sources of instrument decay or variation. Again, instrumentation effects are problematic with any type of repeated measures design.

■ SELECTION

The selection effect is a sample bias that results from differential selection of respondents for the comparison groups, or sample selection error, discussed earlier.

■ MORTALITY

If an experiment is conducted over a period of a few weeks or more, some sample bias may occur due to the **mortality effect (sample attrition)**. Sample attrition occurs when some subjects withdraw from the experiment before it is completed. Mortality effects may occur if subjects drop from one experimental treatment group disproportionately from other groups. Consider a sales training experiment investigating the effects of close supervision of salespeople (high pressure) versus low supervision (low pressure). The high-pressure condition may misleadingly appear superior if those subjects who completed the experiment did very well. If, however, the high-pressure condition caused more subjects to drop out than the other conditions, this apparent superiority may be due to the fact that only very determined and/or talented salespeople stuck with the program.

mortality effect (sample attrition)
Occurs when some subjects withdraw from the experiment before it is completed.

External Validity

External validity is the accuracy with which experimental results can be generalized beyond the experimental subjects. External validity is increased when the subjects comprising the sample truly represent some population and when the results extend to market segments or other groups of people. The higher the external validity, the more researchers and managers can count on the fact that any results observed in an experiment will also be seen in the "real world" (marketplace, workplace, sales floor, and so on).

external validity
Is the accuracy with which experimental results can be generalized beyond the experimental subjects.

For instance, to what extent would results from our retail atmosphere experiment, which represents a simulated shopping experiment, transfer to a real-world retail store in a shopping mall, downtown mall, or lifestyle center? Can one extrapolate the results from a tachistoscope to an in-store shopping situation? Lab experiments are associated with low external validity because the limited set of experimental conditions, holding all else constant, do not adequately represent all the influences existing in the real world. In other words, the experimental situation may be too artificial. When a study lacks external validity, the researcher will have difficulty repeating the experiment with any change in subjects, settings, or time.

■ STUDENT SURROGATES

Basic researchers often use college students as experimental subjects.[14] Convenience, time, money, and a host of other practical considerations often lead to using students as research subjects. This practice is widespread in academic studies. Some evidence shows that students are quite similar to household consumers, but other evidence indicates that they do not provide sufficient external validity to represent most consumer or employee groups. This is particularly true when students are used as substitutes or surrogates for businesspeople.

The issue of external validity should be seriously considered because the student population is likely to be atypical. Students are easily accessible, but they often are not representative of the total population. This is not always the case, however, and when behaviors are studied for which students have some particular expertise, then they are certainly appropriate. For instance, when researchers are only interested in whether or not some effect might exist at all under any situation, students are as good as any other human subjects. This places the emphasis predominantly on internal validity with no consideration of generalizability. Additionally, students sometimes are very relevant. For example, research directed at understanding how young adults react to mobile phone promotions or how different studying techniques affect test performance can have a great deal of internal and external validity using students. This is because students fit within the population of interest. However, researchers wishing to conduct an experiment addressing a research question aimed at understanding how renovating church facilities affects clergy members' job satisfaction would probably not benefit much from using typical undergraduate business students as subjects. Why would anyone expect these students to behave like clergy?

Trade-Offs Between Internal and External Validity

Naturalistic field experiments tend to have greater external validity than artificial laboratory experiments. Marketing researchers often must trade internal validity for external validity. A researcher who wishes to test advertising effectiveness by manipulating treatments via a split-cable experiment has the assurance that the advertisement will be viewed in an externally valid situation, the subjects' homes. However, the researcher has no assurance that some interruption (for example, a telephone call) will not have some influence that will reduce the internal validity of the experiment. Laboratory experiments with many controlled factors usually are high in internal validity, while field experiments generally have less internal validity, but greater external validity. Ideally, results from lab experiments would be followed up with some type of field test.

Ethical Issues in Experimentation

Ethical issues with experimentation were discussed in Chapter 4 so we touch on them lightly here. The question of deception was raised as a key ethical dilemma in experimentation. Although deception is necessary in most experiments, when subjects can be returned to their prior condition through debriefing, then the experiment is probably consistent with high moral standards. When subjects have been injured significantly or truly psychologically harmed, debriefing will not return them to their formal condition and the experiment should not proceed. Therefore, some additional commentary on debriefing is presented.

Researchers should debrief experimental subjects following an experimental procedure. In fact, many academic researchers, such as those conducting basic marketing research, are required to debrief subjects by their university IRB procedures. Debriefing experimental subjects by communicating the purpose of the experiment and the researcher's hypotheses about the nature of consumer behavior is expected to counteract negative effects of deception, relieve stress, and provide an educational experience for the subject.

> Proper debriefing allows the subject to save face by uncovering the truth for himself. The experimenter should begin by asking the subject if he has any questions or if he found any part of the experiment odd, confusing, or disturbing. This question provides a check on the subject's suspiciousness and effectiveness of manipulations. The experimenter continues to provide the subject cues to the deception until the subject states that he believes there was more to the experiment than met the eye. At this time the purpose and procedure of the experiment [are] revealed.[15]

Debriefing therefore is critical because it allows us to return subjects to normal. If this cannot be done through a simple procedure like debriefing, the experiment is likely to be unethical. If an experimenter, for example, took 100 nonsmokers, divided them into 4 groups of 25, and had them smoke 20 or 40 cigarettes a day for 5 years (one experimental variable) that were either called Nicky's or BeFrees (another experimental variable), no debriefing could restore them to normal and therfore, this experiment would likely never be conducted.

Additionally, there is the issue of test-markets and efforts extended toward interfering with a competitor's test-market. When a company puts a product out for public consumption, they should be aware that competitors may also now freely consume the product. When attempts to interfere with a test-market are aimed solely at invalidating test results or they are aimed at infringing on some copyright protection, those acts are ethically questionable. This topic is illustrated in the next chapter which focuses specifically on test markets.

- Experiments are used to establish causal evidence and represent the primary tool for causal research designs.
- Experimental manipulations in marketing research should have the following characteristics:
  - Distinct categories or magnitudes of effects
  - Two, three or, at most, four treatment levels per experimental variable. This is particularly true when multiple experimental variables are used in a single study.
  - Randomly applied across the experimental subjects
- Experimental graphs are useful in displaying results, particularly when interactions are involved.
- Laboratory experiments maximize internal validity.
- Field experiments increase external validity at the cost of internal validity.

Summary

1. Know the basic characteristics of research experiments. Independent variables are created through manipulation in experiments rather than through measurement. The researcher creates unique experimental conditions that represent unique levels of an independent variable. Experiments are also distinguished from other research in that human sampling units are referred to as subjects rather than respondents. This is because they are subjected to the experimental manipulations. Experimental manipulations are examined for the extent to which they affect outcomes. Main effects are due to differences in observed outcomes based on any single experimental variable. Interaction effects are due to combinations of independent variables.

2. Minimize experimental error by effective experimental design. Systematic experimental error occurs because sampling units (research subjects) in one experimental cell are different from those in another cell in a way that affects the dependent variable. In an experiment involving how people respond to color, the researcher would not want to have all males in one color group and all females in another. Randomization is an important way of minimizing systematic experimental error. If research subjects are randomly assigned to different treatment combinations, then the differences among people that exist naturally within a population should also exist within each experimental cell. Additionally, the researcher must try to control for all possible extraneous variables. Extraneous variables can render any causal inference as spurious. Control is possible by holding nonexperimental variables constant across experimental conditions. In this way, the researcher can also help prevent confounds.

3. Know ways of minimizing experimental demand characteristics. Demand characteristics are experimental procedures that somehow inform the subject about the actual research purpose. Demand effects can result from demand characteristics. When this happens, the results are confounded. Demand characteristics can be minimized by following these simple rules: using an experimental disguise, isolating experimental subjects, using a "blind" experimental administrator, and administering only one experimental treatment combination to each subject.

4. Avoid unethical experimental practices. Experiments involve deception. Additionally, research subjects are sometimes exposed to stressful or possibly dangerous manipulations. Every precaution should be made to ensure that subjects are not harmed. Debriefing subjects about the true purpose of the experiment following its conclusion is important for the ethical treatment of subjects. If debriefing can restore subjects to their preexperimental condition, the experimental procedures are likely consistent with ethical practice. If subjects are affected in some way that makes it difficult to return them to their prior condition, then the experimental procedures probably go beyond what is considered ethical.

5. Understand the advantages of a between-subjects experimental design. A between-subjects design means that every subject receives only one experimental treatment combination. The main advantages of between-subjects designs are the reduced likelihood of demand effects and simpler analysis and presentation. The main disadvantage is that they are less economical because subjects are measured only one time. Generally, between-subjects designs reduce the likelihood of contamination due to extraneous variables.

6. Weigh the trade-off between internal and external validity. Lab experiments offer higher internal validity because they maximize control of extraneous variables. High internal validity is a good thing because we can be more certain that the experimental variable is truly the cause of any variance in the dependent variable. Field experiments maximize external validity because they are conducted in a more natural setting meaning that the results are more likely to generalize to the actual business situation. The increased external validity comes at the expense of internal validity.

Key Terms and Concepts

between-subjects design, *282*
blocking variables, *268*
cell, *272*
cohort effect, *284*
confound, *274*
constancy of conditions, *278*
control group, *271*
counterbalancing, *279*
covariate, *268*
demand characteristic, *276*
demand effect, *276*
experimental condition, *268*

experimental group, *271*
experimental treatment, *270*
external validity, *285*
field experiments, *280*
Hawthorne effect, *277*
history effect, *284*
instrumentation effect, *284*
interaction effect, *269*
internal validity, *283*
laboratory experiment, *279*
main effect, *268*
manipulation check, *283*

maturation effects, *284*
mortality effect (sample attrition), *285*
placebo, *277*
placebo effect, *277*
randomization, *274*
repeated measures, *274*
subjects, *267*
systematic or nonsampling error, *273*
tachistoscope, *280*
test units, *272*
testing effects, *284*
within-subjects design, *282*

Questions for Review and Critical Thinking

1. Define *experimental condition, experimental treatment,* and *experimental group.* How are these related to the implementation of a valid manipulation?
2. A tissue manufacturer that has the fourth-largest market share plans to experiment with a 50¢ off coupon during November and a buy one, get one free coupon during December. The experiment will take place at Target stores in St. Louis and Kansas City. Sales will be recorded by scanners from which mean tissue sales for each store for each month can be computed and interpreted.
   a. What are the experimental variable and the dependent variable?
   b. Prepare a "dummy" table (covered in Chapter 5) that would describe what the results of the experiment would look like.
3. What is the difference between a *main effect* and an *interaction* in an experiment? In question 2, what will create a main effect? Is an interaction possible?
4. In what ways might the design in question 2 yield systematic or nonsampling error?
5. How can experimental graphs be used to show main effects and interactions?
6. What purpose does the random assignment of subjects serve?
7. Why is an experimental confound so damaging to the conclusions drawn from an experiment?
8. What are demand characteristics? How can they be minimized?
9. **ETHICS** Suppose researchers were experimenting with how much more satisfied consumers are with a "new and improved"

version of some existing product. How might the researchers design a placebo within an experiment testing this research question? Is using such a placebo ethical or not?
10. If a company wanted to know whether to implement a new management training program based on how much it would improve ROI in its southwest division, would you recommend a field or lab experiment?
11. **'NET** Suppose you wanted to test the effect of three different e-mail requests inviting people to participate in a survey posted on the Internet. One simply contained a hyperlink with no explanation, the other said if someone participated $10 would be donated to charity, and the other said if someone participated he or she would have a chance to win $1,000. How would this experiment be conducted differently based on whether it was a between-subjects or within-subjects design? What are the advantages of a between-subjects design?
12. What is a manipulation check? How does it relate to internal validity?
13. **ETHICS** What role does debriefing play in ensuring that experimental procedures are consistent with good ethical practice?
14. Define internal validity and external validity. It's been said that external validity decreases when internal validity is high. Do you believe that is so? Explain your answer.
15. The idea of nonspurious association was introduced in Chapter 3. How does a confounding variable affect whether an association is spurious or nonspurious?

Research Activities

1. Consider the situation of a researcher approached by Captain John's in the Research Snapshot on page 273.
   a. Provide a critique of the procedures used to support the claim that Sea Snapper's product is superior. Prepare it in a way that it could be presented as evidence in court.
   b. Design an experiment that would provide a more valid test of the research question, "Do consumers prefer Sea Snapper fish sticks compared to Captain John's fish sticks?"

2. Conduct a taste test involving some soft drinks with a group of friends. Pour them several ounces of three popular soft drinks and simply label the cups A, B, and C. Make sure they are blind to the actual brands. Then, let them drink as much as they want and record how much of each they drink. You may also ask them some questions about the drinks. Then, allow other subjects to participate in the same test, but this time, let them know what the three brands are. Record the same data and draw conclusions. Does brand knowledge affect behavior and attitudes about soft drinks?

Case 11.1 Examining Product Failure at No-Charge Electronics

© GETTY IMAGES/ PHOTODISC GREEN

No-Charge Electronics owner Buzz Auphf needs to know how much product failure affects customer loyalty. Buzz contacts David Handy, a local market researcher, and they ultimately decide on examining a research question asking, "How do current customers react to different levels of product failure?" David designs the following experiment to examine the causal effect of product failure on customer purchase intentions, satisfaction, and loyalty.

The experiment is implemented via e-mail using a sample of current and prospective customers. Three free MP3 movies are provided as an incentive to participate. Subjects are asked to click through to an Internet site to download a product that will enhance their computer's graphics capability. In the low-failure condition, after the subjects click to the site, there is no change in the graphics of their computers. In the high-failure condition, once they click through to the site, the subjects' computers go into an infinite loop of obscene graphical images until a message arrives indicating that a severe virus has infected their computer and some files may be permanently damaged. This goes on for forty-five minutes with no remedy. At that time, a debriefing message pops up telling subjects that it was all part of an experiment and that their computer should now function properly. Prepare a position statement either agreeing or disagreeing that the experiment is consistent with good ethical practice.

Case 11.2 Tooheys

© GETTY IMAGES/ PHOTODISC GREEN

Sixty-six willing Australian drinkers helped a Federal Court judge decide that Tooheys didn't engage in misleading or deceptive advertising for its 2.2 beer. The beer contains 2.2 percent alcohol, compared to 6 percent for other beers leading to a claim that could be interpreted as implying it was non-alcoholic.

Volunteers were invited to a marathon drinking session after the Aboriginal Legal Service claimed Tooheys' advertising implied beer drinkers could imbibe as much 2.2 as desired without becoming legally intoxicated. Drunken driving laws prohibit anyone with a blood–alcohol level above 0.05 from getting behind the wheel in Australia.

So, an experiment was conducted to see what happens when a lot of 2.2 is consumed. But the task wasn't easy or that much fun. Some subjects couldn't manage to drink the required 10 "middies," an Aussie term for a beer glass of 10 fluid ounces, over the course of an hour.

Thirty-six participants could manage only nine glasses. Four threw up and were excluded. Two more couldn't manage the "minimum" nine glasses and had to be replaced.

Justice J. Beaumont observed that consuming enough 2.2 in an hour to reach the 0.05 level was "uncomfortable and therefore an unlikely process." Because none of the ads mentioned such extreme quantities, he ruled they couldn't be found misleading or deceptive.[16]

Questions

1. Would a lab experiment or a field experiment be more "valid" in determining whether Tooheys could cause a normal beer consumer to become intoxicated? Explain.
2. Describe an alternate research design that would have higher validity.
3. Is the experiment described in this story consistent with good ethical practice? Likewise, comment on how the design described in part 2 would be made consistent with good ethical practices.
4. Is validity or ethics more important?

APPENDIX 11A
CLASSIFICATION
OF EXPERIMENTAL
DESIGNS

An experimental design may be compared to an architect's plans for a building. The basic requirements for the structure are given to the architect by the prospective owner. Several different plans may be drawn up as options for meeting the basic requirements. Some may be more costly than others. One may offer potential advantages that another does not.

basic experimental design

An experimental design in which only one variable is manipulated.

There are various types of experimental designs. If only one variable is manipulated, the experiment has a **basic experimental design**. If the experimenter wishes to investigate several levels of the independent variable (for example, four price levels) or to investigate the interaction effects of two or more independent variables, the experiment requires a *complex,* or *statistical,* experimental design.

Symbolism for Diagramming Experimental Designs

Previous researchers developed a notation that helps some students master the subject of basic experimental designs.[17] The following symbols will be used in describing the various experimental designs:

X = *exposure of a group to an experimental treatment*
O = *observation or measurement of the dependent variable; if more than one observation or measurement is taken, subscripts (that is, O_1, O_2, etc.) indicate temporal order*
$\boxed{R}$ = *random assignment of test units; $\boxed{R}$ symbolizes that individuals selected as subjects for the experiment are randomly assigned to the experimental groups*

The diagrams of experimental designs that follow assume a time flow from left to right. Our first example will make this clearer.

Three Examples of Quasi-Experimental Designs

quasi-experimental designs

Experimental designs that do not involve random allocation of subjects to treatment combinations. Used for an experiment investigating long-term structural changes.

Quasi-experimental designs do not involve random allocation of subjects to treatment combinations. In this sense, they do not qualify as true experimental designs because they do not adequately control for the problems associated with loss of internal validity. However, they are used particularly when it is the only way to implement a study.

◼ ONE-SHOT DESIGN

The one-shot design, or *after-only design,* is diagrammed as follows:

$$X \qquad O_1$$

Suppose that during a very cold winter an automobile dealer finds herself with a large inventory of cars. She decides to experiment for the month of January with a promotional scheme. She offers a free trip to New Orleans with every car sold. She experiments with the promotion (X = experimental treatment) and measures sales (O_1 = measurement of sales after the treatment is administered).

This one-shot design is a case study of a research project fraught with problems. Subjects or test units participate because of voluntary self-selection or arbitrary assignment, not because of random assignment. The study lacks any kind of comparison or any means of controlling extraneous influences. There should be a measure of what will happen when the test units have not been exposed to X to compare with the measures of when subjects have been exposed to X. Nevertheless, under certain circumstances, even though this design lacks internal validity, it is the only viable choice.

◼ ONE-GROUP PRETEST–POSTTEST DESIGN

Suppose a real estate franchiser wishes to provide a training program for franchisees. If the franchiser measures subjects' knowledge of real estate selling before (O_1) they are exposed to the experimental treatment (X) and then measures real estate selling knowledge after (O_2) they are exposed to the treatment, the design will be as follows:

$$O_1 \qquad X \qquad O_2$$

In this example the trainer is likely to conclude that the difference between O_2 and O_1 ($O_2 - O_1$) is the measure of the influence of the experimental treatment. This one-group pretest–posttest design offers a comparison of the same individuals before and after training. Although this is an improvement over the one-shot design, this research still has several weaknesses that may jeopardize internal validity. For example, if the time lapse between O_1 and O_2 was a period of several months, the trainees may have matured as a result of experience on the job (maturation effect). History effects may also influence this design. Perhaps some subjects dropped out of the training program (mortality effect). The effect of testing may also have confounded the experiment.

Although this design has a number of weaknesses, it is used in marketing research. Remember, the cost of the research is a consideration in most business situations. While there will be some problems of internal validity, the researcher must always take into account questions of time and cost.

◼ STATIC GROUP DESIGN

In a static group design each subject is identified as a member of either an experimental group or a control group (for example, exposed or not exposed to a commercial). The experimental group is measured after being exposed to an experimental treatment, and the control group is measured without having been exposed to this experimental treatment:

Experimental group: $X \qquad O_1$
Control group: $\qquad\quad O_2$

The results of the static group design are computed by subtracting the observed results in the control group from those in the experimental group ($O_1 - O_2$). A major weakness of this design is its lack of assurance that the groups were equal on variables of interest before the experimental group received the treatment. If the groups were selected arbitrarily by the investigator, or if entry into either group was voluntary, systematic differences between the groups could invalidate the conclusions about the effect of the treatment. Random assignment of subjects may eliminate problems with group differences. If groups are established by the experimenter rather than existing as a function of some other causation, the static group design is referred to as an *after-only design with control group*.

On many occasions, an after-only design is the only possible option. This is particularly true when conducting use tests for new products or brands. Cautious interpretation and recognition of the design's shortcomings may make this design valuable.

Three Alternative Experimental Designs

In a formal scientific sense, the three designs just discussed are not pure experimental designs. Subjects for the experiments were not selected from a common pool of subjects and randomly assigned to one group or another. In the following discussion of three basic experimental designs, the $\boxed{R}$ symbol to the left of the diagram indicates that the first step in a true experimental design is the randomization of subject assignment.

◼ PRETEST–POSTTEST CONTROL GROUP DESIGN (BEFORE–AFTER WITH CONTROL)

A pretest–posttest control group design, or *before–after with control group design,* is the classic experimental design:

Experimental group: $\boxed{R} \qquad O_1 \qquad X \qquad O_2$
Control group: $\boxed{R} \qquad O_3 \qquad\qquad O_4$

As the diagram indicates, the subjects in the experimental group are tested before and after being exposed to the treatment. The control group is tested at the same two times as the experimental group, but subjects are not exposed to the experimental treatment. This design has the advantages of the before–after design with the additional advantages gained by its having a control group. The effect of the experimental treatment equals

$$(O_2 - O_1) - (O_4 - O_3)$$

If there is brand awareness among 20 percent of the subjects ($O_1 = 20$ percent, $O_3 = 20$ percent) before an advertising treatment and then 35 percent awareness in the experimental group ($O_2 = 35$ percent) and 22 percent awareness in the control group ($O_4 = 22$ percent) after exposure to the treatment, the treatment effect equals 13 percent:

$$(0.35 - 0.20) - (0.22 - 0.20) = (0.15) - (0.02) = 0.13 \ or \ 13\%$$

The effect of all extraneous variables is assumed to be the same on both the experimental and the control groups. For instance, since both groups receive the pretest, no difference between them is expected for the pretest effect. This assumption is also made for effects of other events between the before and after measurements (history), changes within the subjects that occur with the passage of time (maturation), testing effects, and instrumentation effects. In reality there will be some differences in the sources of extraneous variation. Nevertheless, in most cases assuming that the effect is approximately equal for both groups is reasonable.

However, a testing effect is possible when subjects are sensitized to the subject of the research. This is analogous to what occurs when people learn a new vocabulary word. Soon they discover that they notice it much more frequently in their reading. In an experiment the combination of being interviewed on a subject and receiving the experimental treatment might be a potential source of error. For example, a subject exposed to a certain advertising message in a split-cable experiment might say, "Ah, there is an ad about the product I was interviewed about yesterday!" The subject may pay more attention than normal to the advertisement and be more prone to change his or her attitude than in a situation with no interactive testing effects. This weakness in the before–after with control group design can be corrected (see the next two designs).

Testing the effectiveness of television commercials in movie theaters provides an example of the before–after with control group design. Subjects are selected for the experiments by being told that they are going to preview several new television shows. When they enter the theater, they learn that a drawing for several types of products will be held, and they are asked to complete a product preference questionnaire (see Exhibit 11.8). Then a first drawing is held. Next, the television pilots and commercials are shown. Then the emcee announces additional prizes and a second drawing. Finally, subjects fill out the same questionnaire about prizes. The information from the first questionnaire is the before measurement, and that from the second questionnaire is the after measurement. The control group receives similar treatment except that on the day they view the pilot television shows, different (or no) television commercials are substituted for the experimental commercials.

■ POSTTEST-ONLY CONTROL GROUP DESIGN (AFTER-ONLY WITH CONTROL)

In some situations pretest measurements are impossible. In other situations selection error is not anticipated to be a problem because the groups are known to be equal. The posttest-only control group design, or *after-only with control group design,* is diagrammed as follows:

Experimental group: R   X O_1
Control group: R O_2

The effect of the experimental treatment is equal to $O_2 - O_1$.

Suppose the manufacturer of an athlete's-foot remedy wishes to demonstrate by experimentation that its product is better than a competing brand. No pretest measure about the effectiveness of the remedy is possible. The design is to randomly select subjects, perhaps students, who have contracted athlete's foot and randomly assign them to the experimental or the control group. With only the posttest measurement, the effects of testing and instrument variation are eliminated.

EXHIBIT 11.8 **Product Preference Measure in an Experiment**

We are going to give away a series of prizes. If you are selected as one of the winners, which brand from each of the groups listed below would you truly want to win?

Special arrangements will be made for any product for which bulk, or one-time, delivery is not appropriate.

Indicate your answers by filling in the box like this: ■

Do not "X," check, or circle the boxes please.

Cookies			**Allergy Relief Products**		
(A 3-month supply, pick ONE.)			(A year's supply, pick ONE.)		
NABISCO OREO	☐	(1)	ALLEREST	☐	(1)
NABISCO OREO DOUBLE STUFF	☐	(2)	BENADRYL	☐	(2)
NABISCO NUTTER BUTTER	☐	(3)	CONTAC	☐	(3)
NABISCO VANILLA CREMES	☐	(4)	TAVIST-D	☐	(4)
HYDROX CHOCOLATE	☐	(5)	DRISTAN	☐	(5)
HYDROX DOUBLES	☐	(6)	SUDAFED	☐	(6)
NABISCO COOKIE BREAK	☐	(7)	CHLOR–TRIMETON	☐	(7)
NABISCO CHIPS AHOY	☐	(8)			
KEEBLER E. L. FUDGE	☐	(9)			
KEEBLER FUDGE CREMES	☐	(10)			
KEEBLER FRENCH VANILLA CREMES	☐	(11)			

Furthermore, researchers make the same assumptions about extraneous variables described above—that is, that they operate equally on both groups, as in the before–after with control group design.

■ COMPROMISE DESIGNS

True experimentation is often simply not possible. The researcher may compromise by approximating an experimental design. A compromise design is one that falls short of assigning subjects or treatments randomly to experimental groups.

Consider a situation in which a researcher would ideally implement a pretest–posttest control group design to study the effect of training on employee performance. In this case, subjects may not be able to be assigned randomly to the experimental and control group because the researcher cannot take workers away from their work groups. Thus, one entire work group is used as the experimental group and a separate work group is used as a control group. The researcher has no assurance that the groups are equivalent. The situation has forced a compromise to experimental integrity.

The alternative to the compromise design when random assignment of subjects is not possible is to conduct the experiment *without* a control group. Generally this is considered a greater weakness than using groups that have already been established. When the experiment involves a longitudinal study, circumstances usually dictate a compromise with true experimentation.

Time Series Designs

Many marketing experiments may be conducted in a short period of time (a few hours, a week, or a month). However, a marketing experiment investigating long-term structural changes may require a time series design. Time series designs are quasi-experimental because they generally do not allow the researcher full control over the treatment exposure or influence of extraneous variables. When experiments are conducted over long periods of time, they are most vulnerable to history effects due to changes in population, attitudes, economic patterns, and the like. Although seasonal patterns and other exogenous influences may be noted, the experimenter can do little about them when time is a major factor in the design.

Political tracking polls provide an example. A pollster normally uses a series of surveys to track candidates' popularity. Consider the candidate who plans a major speech (the experimental treatment) to refocus the political campaign. The simple time series design can be diagrammed as follows:

$$O_1 \qquad O_2 \qquad O_3 \qquad X \qquad O_4 \qquad O_5 \qquad O_6$$

Several observations have been taken to identify trends before the treatment (X) is administered. After the treatment has been administered, several observations are made to determine if the patterns *after* the treatment are similar to those *before*. If the longitudinal pattern shifts after the political speech, the researcher may conclude that the treatment had a positive impact on the pattern. Of course, this time series design cannot give the researcher complete assurance that the treatment caused the change in the trend. Problems of internal validity are greater than in more tightly controlled before-and-after designs for experiments of shorter duration.

One unique advantage of the time series design is its ability to distinguish temporary from permanent changes. Exhibit 11.9 shows some possible outcomes in a time series experiment.

EXHIBIT 11.9
Selected Time Series Outcomes

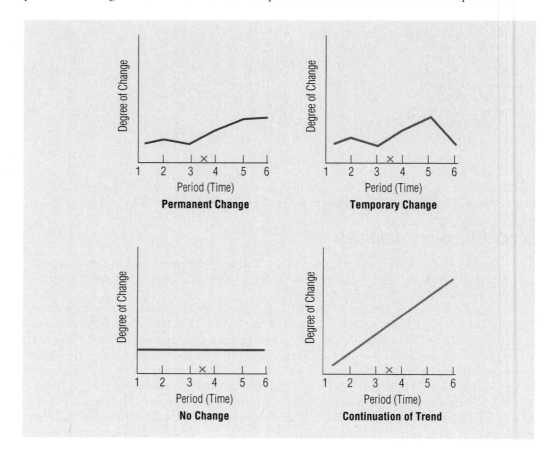

Complex Experimental Designs

Complex experimental designs are statistical designs that isolate the effects of confounding extraneous variables or allow for manipulation of more than one independent variable in the experiment. *Factorial designs, Latin square designs, completely randomized designs,* and *randomized block designs,* as well as statistical discussions of these techniques, are covered in later chapters under the headings of complex experimental designs tests of differences.

Appendix Key Terms and Concepts

After studying this chapter, you should be able to

1. Recognize the appropriate uses of test-marketing
2. Know the basics of test-marketing, including how experimental manipulations can be used to test marketing strategies in a real world setting
3. List the advantages and disadvantages of test-marketing
4. Select an appropriate test-market city for a specific test
5. Use manipulations to implement a completely randomized experimental design, a randomized-block design, and a factorial experimental design
6. Display experimental results using graphical charts

Chapter Vignette: Imported Lights!

Heineken, the Dutch beer that many Americans mistake as German, is the leading selling European import beer in the United States. Whereas Anheuser-Busch and Miller Brewing Company have long been differentiated marketers, offering a portfolio of beer products each for a slightly different taste, Heineken has won its position almost entirely with the product in the familiar green can.

In more recent years, Heineken has enjoyed some success with a second label, Amstel Light, but they continue to struggle with the decision of whether or not to offer a premium light beer under the Heineken label itself. Finally, after noticing a trend among American consumers to trade up to brands perceived as higher in quality, Heineken commissioned a test-market of Heineken Premium Light in 2005.[1] The test-market addressed research questions related not only to whether or not Heineken Premium Light (HPL) would sell, but also where potential sales would come from. If HPL simply cannibalizes traditional Heineken sales, then it may not be wise to introduce the product. The test-market also addressed issues related to promotion. What promotional appeal would do the most to create favorable attitudes about HPL?

Researchers for Heineken selected four locations for the experiment. Consumers in Providence, Rhode Island; Tampa, Florida; Dallas, Texas; and Phoenix, Arizona, would be included in the test-market. The light beer would be sold in all the traditional retail outlets alongside traditional Heineken. Key dependent variables include sales of Heineken Light, sales of Heineken, sales of Amstel Light, and sales of domestic light beers such as Bud Light and Miller Lite.

Heineken researchers revealed several key findings in a presentation to company executives:

1. HPL did cannibalize Amstel Light, but not as much as expected. A slight repositioning of Amstel can minimize cannibalization.
2. The introduction of HPL lowered Heineken sales in only one test-market city. So, fears of cannibalization are reduced.
3. HPL sales were associated with slightly lower sales among domestic light beers.
4. HPL sales were overall equal or above expectations in three of four cities. HPL sales were higher than expected among ethnic market segments.

The presentation and report led Heineken to introduce the beer throughout the United States in 2006. An advertising budget of $40 million was allocated to spread the word about Heineken Light. The ad theme that tested best appeared to be consistent with their current advertising theme. Thus, the test-market proved vital to the decision to launch Heineken Light.

During this same time period, competitors introduced their own light rivals. Anheuser-Busch introduced a premium Dutch light import to the U.S. market. Grolsch Light was originally introduced in five states but is now distributed throughout the United States by Miller Brewing Company. Corona Light was introduced with a $10 million ad campaign of its own.

Introduction

Test-marketing combines scientific testing with controlled field experimentation. As such, test-marketing goes well beyond merely "trying something out in the marketplace." Just because a product is introduced in a small marketing area before deciding whether to do a national launch does not mean a test-market has been conducted. Those who underestimate the need for a rigorous approach to test-marketing often "succeed" in their test-market but fail in their product launch. Test-marketing is the most prominent type of field experiment.

Chapter 3 briefly introduced test-marketing. Recall that a *test-market* is a market experiment conducted in an actual product market, meaning under real-world conditions. While we most often think of test-markets in conjunction with a decision about the viability of some newly developed product, they are equally useful in examining other elements of marketing strategy. Even though test-markets are not "small scale" research projects, they do test-marketing questions under a smaller scale than the entire market. So, before implementing a marketing strategy throughout the United States or Europe, test cities such as Tampa, Florida, and Frankfurt, Germany, may be used to represent the way consumers in other cities might react.

Using Test-Marketing

Test-marketing has three broad primary uses in marketing research. Each use can be broken down more specifically to look at some issue in close detail. The three broad uses are as follows:

1. Forecasting the success of a newly developed product.
2. Testing hypotheses about different options for marketing mix elements.
3. Identifying weaknesses in product designs or marketing strategies.

Forecasting New Product Success

Test-markets have long been used as a pilot test for a new product introduction. While test-markets can be complicated to implement, the basic idea is simple. A product can be marketed on a small scale under actual market conditions and the results used to forecast the success or failure once the product is introduced on a large scale. The opening vignette described how Heineken used a test-market to forecast the success of Heineken Premium Light (HPL) beer. Not to be outdone, Miller is test-marketing very low calorie, amber beer to appeal to health-conscious segments of the population.[2]

Companies using test-markets should realize that a new product concept also involves issues like advertising, pricing, supply chains, and retail placement. These issues may also be manipulated within a test-market. Estimates can then be made about the optimal advertising level, the need for product sampling, retail channel fit, or perhaps even advertising and retail channel selection interaction. Test-marketing permits evaluation of the entire new product concept, not just the physical good itself.

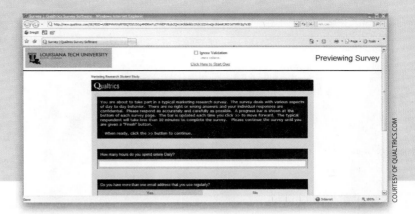
A marketing manager for Life Savers candies vividly portrays this function of experimentation in the marketplace:

> *A market test may be likened to an orchestra rehearsal. The violinists have adjusted their strings, the trumpeters have tested their keys, and the drummer has tightened his drums. Everything is ready to go. But all these instruments have not worked in unison. So a test-market is like an orchestra rehearsal where you can practice with everything together before the big public performance.*[3]

A researcher conducting a test-market may evaluate not only new products' sales as a dependent variable, but also existing products' sales as relevant dependent variables, as seen in the HPL vignette. In this way, test-marketing allows a firm to determine whether a new offering will **cannibalize** sales from existing products, meaning that consumers are choosing the new offering as a replacement for another product offered by the same company.

For example, Nabisco's cracker business is mature. The company has many brands, and to add positively to overall sales, a new product must tap just the right market segment. Concept testing may suggest that a new cheese flavored saltine is a great concept. But a test-market may show that the consumers who are actually buying the new product are already Nabisco Cheese Nips fans. Rather than buying more Nabisco products, they are actually substituting the lower priced cheese saltines for the old product. Thus, Nabisco may decide not to proceed with the new product. Test-marketing provides the most effective examination of cannibalization prior to full-scale production.

cannibalize

When consumers choose a new offering as a replacement for another product offered by the same company.

TOTHEPOINT

You cannot create experience. You must undergo it.

—Albert Camus

Testing the Marketing Mix

Test-markets are not confined to studying new products or product modifications. They also are equally useful as a field experiment manipulating different marketing plans for existing products. Any element of the marketing mix can be examined with a test-market.

As we all know, retailers rely heavily on weekly flyers distributed through newspapers or through direct mail. This is particularly true in France, where retail advertising is restricted by law in many ways, including the ability to advertise on television. In France, the average French household receives over 12 kg (26.4 lbs) of retail flyers annually![4] Yet, many have little idea about the effectiveness of different approaches. Should the flyers simply promote low price, or should they emphasize products related to a specific theme? In fact, different flyer styles can significantly affect not only sales, but retailer image too.[5]

Test-marketing can provide an effective way of estimating the effect of a different flyer approach. Interestingly, Staples recently tested the effect of several different flyer approaches

© SUSAN VAN ETTEN

Test-marketing can be used to determine the impact of different promotional approaches on sales and brand image.

on sales. Different flyers were tested in different market areas. Prior to the test, top managers at Staples were given a chance to guess which flyer would produce the most positive effect. Results of the test showed how valid "expert" opinion can sometimes be. The consensus pick for the best flyer came in dead last in the market test![6] Thus, although a test-market can be timely and expensive, even for an existing offering, the advantages of a field test can prevent mistakes in decision making.

The most effective distribution channel may also be indicated in a test-market. DVDs are facing increased competition from other technologies that allow consumers to access movies. Paramount recently test-marketed a different channel for the distribution of a motion picture.[7] In December of 2007, Paramount released *Jackass 2.5*, actually the third in the *Jackass* series of films, for online distribution at the same time the movie was released to theaters. The online version was free, but contained embedded advertisements. Paramount was testing to see how consumers would warm up to this novel method of distribution.

Identifying Product Weaknesses

Test-market experimentation also allows identification of previously undetected product or marketing plan weaknesses. The weaknesses can then be dealt with before the company commits to the actual sales launch. Although often this use of test-markets is accidental, in the sense that it isn't the reason for conducting the test-markets, huge sums of resources can be saved by spotting problems before the full-scale marketing effort begins. Often, this use of test-marketing occurs when a product underperforms in at least one location. Researchers can then follow up with other research approaches to try and reveal the reason for the lack of performance. Once identified, product modifications can be made that address these reasons specifically.

McDonald's test-marketed pizza periodically for years. The first test-market provided lower than expected sales results. The reasons for the underperformance included a failure to consider competitors' reactions and problems associated with the small, single portion pizza, which was the only way McPizza was sold. Additionally, McPizza didn't seem to bring any new customers to McDonald's. In the next round of test-marketing, the marketing strategy repositioned the pizza, shifting to a 14-inch pizza that was only sold from about 4 p.m. until closing. With still underwhelming results, McDonald's test-marketed "Pizza Shoppes" within the test McDonald's where employees could be seen assembling ingredients on ready-made pizza dough. Although the concept is still alive, McDonald's has shied away from pizza for the U.S. adult market. A McPizza Happy Meal remains as a sole pizza concept with promise for American stores. Pizza-like products, however, exist and succeed at many McDonald's locations in other nations.

Note that just because a product fails its market test, the test-market can't be considered a failure. In most cases, this represents an important *research success*. Encountering problems in a test-market either properly leads the company to introduce the new product or to make the planned change in marketing strategy. Thus, a huge mistake is likely avoided. In addition, test-market results may lead management to make adjustments that will turn the poor test-market results into a market success. The managerial experience gained in test-marketing can be extremely valuable, even when the performance results are disappointing.

Projecting Test-Market Results

Notice that in all of the uses of test-marketing there is an emphasis on generalizing the results. In other words, researchers do a trial test on a small scale with the hope that the results conducted on that small scale will be equally true when a product is introduced on a larger scale. Therfore, external validity is a key consideration in designing a test-market. Test-markets are not appropriate for research questions that require very rigorous control of internal validity. These latter tests are better done in a lab experiment. However, the fundamental reason that test-markets are conducted is the hope that results can be accurately projected from the sample to the entire market or population of customers. Researchers take several steps to try to make these projections as accurate as they possibly can.

■ STRAIGHT TREND PROJECTIONS

Sales can be identified and the market share for the test area calculated. The simplest method of projecting test-market results involves straight trend projections. Suppose the market share is 3.5 percent in a test-market region. A straight-line projection assumes that the true actual market share after launch will be 3.5 percent. Researchers using straight-line projections assume that the test-market is representative of the larger target market. Often, this assumption is based on the fact that there is no good reason to provide a different projection. After all, the test-market is supposed to be representative of the entire market.

■ RATIO OF TEST PRODUCT SALES TO TOTAL COMPANY SALES

A measure of the company's competitive strength in the test-market region might be used as a basis for adjusting test-market results. Calculating a ratio of test product sales to total company sales in the area may provide a benchmark for modifying projections into other markets. In other words, if a new product accounts for 5 percent of the total company sales in a test-market area(s), then the projection is that the new product will account for 5 percent of total company sales in all markets.

■ MARKET PENETRATION × REPEAT-PURCHASE RATE

A third way that sales projections can be taken into account is the likelihood of repeat purchases. To calculate market share for products that are subject to repeat purchases, the following formula is used:

market penetration (trial buyers) × repeat purchase rate = market share

For example, suppose a product is tried by 30 percent of the population and the repeat purchase rate is 25 percent. Market share will then be 7.5 percent (30 percent × 25 percent = 7.5 percent).

The repeat-purchase rate must be obtained from longitudinal research that establishes some form of historical record. Traditionally, a consumer panel has been necessary for recording purchases over time. Thus, panel data may indicate a cumulative product class buying rate, or **market penetration**, in the early weeks of the test-market. One way to look at market penetration is as the percentage of target market customers who purchased the product. As the test-market continues, repeat purchases from these buyers can be recorded until the number of trial purchases has leveled off. Exhibit 12.1 on the next page indicates typical purchase and repurchase patterns for a new product in a test-market.

market penetration

The percentage of target market customers who purchased the product—often measured early in a test-market.

EXHIBIT 12.1
**New-Product Trial Purchase
Curve and Repeat-Purchase
Curve**

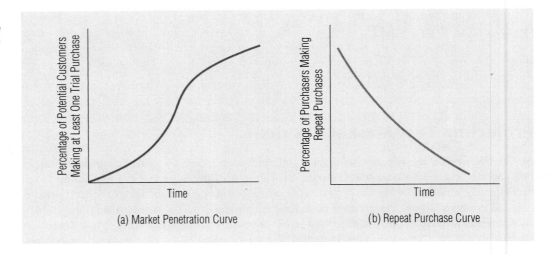

CONSUMER SURVEYS

Most researchers support sales data with consumer survey data during test-markets. These help monitor consumer awareness and attitudes toward the test-marketed product as well as the repeat-purchase likelihood. Frequently this information is acquired via consumer panels.

Estimating Sales Volume: Some Problems

Test-marketing is all about estimating how well some product will do in the marketplace. This means that sales projections must be made based on how well a product performs in a test-market. Numerous methodological factors cause problems in estimating national sales results based on regional tests. Often, these problems result from mistakes in the design or execution of the test-market itself.

OVERATTENTION

If too much attention is paid to testing a new product, the product may be more successful than it would be under more normal marketing conditions. In the test-market, the firm's advertising agency may make sure that the test-markets have excellent television coverage (which may or may not be representative of the national television coverage). If salespeople are aware that a test is being conducted in their territory, they may spend unusual amounts of time making sure the new product is available or displayed better. This also means that managers should avoid any added incentives that would encourage extra sales efforts to sell the test-marketed product.

UNREALISTIC STORE CONDITIONS

Store conditions may be set at the level of the market leader rather than at the national level. For example, extra shelf facings, eye-level stocking, and other conditions resulting from artificial distribution may be obtained in the test-market.

This situation may result from research design problems or overattention, as previously described. For example, if retailers are made aware that someone is paying more attention to their efforts with a given product, they may give it artificially high distribution and extra retail support.

READING THE COMPETITIVE ENVIRONMENT INCORRECTLY

test-market sabotage

Intentional attempts to disrupt
the results of a test-market being
conducted by another firm.

Another common mistake is to assume that the competitive environment will be the same nationally as in the test-market. If competitors are unaware of a test-market, the results will not measure competitors' reactions to company strategy. Competitors' responses after a national introduction may differ substantially from the way they reacted in the test-market. On the other hand, competitors may react to a test-market by attempting to undermine it. If they know that a firm is testing, they may attempt to disrupt test-market results with increased promotions and lower prices for their own products, among other potential acts of **test-market sabotage**.

When Starbucks test-marketed its supermarket brand coffee in Chicago, Procter & Gamble broadcast television commercials touting Millstone coffee's victory over Starbucks in taste tests. The commercials lampooned Starbucks for being more interested in selling T-shirts and novelties than coffee. P&G also offered free samples of Millstone to disrupt the result of Starbucks' test-market.[8] Similarly, Heineken competitors may have launched heavy price cutting or other acts, which, whether they are intentionally meant to or not, may disrupt the test-market and make the results a less valid representation of what would happen under actual market conditions.

■ INCORRECT VOLUME FORECASTS

In the typical test-market, unit sales volume or market share is a focus of attention. Shipments, warehouse withdrawals, or store scanner data may be the major basis for projecting sales. Forecasted volume for test-markets should be adjusted to reflect test distribution levels, measurement problems with store data, and other differences between test-markets and national markets.

Smooth and Easy Sauce ("the gravy stick with all the gravy basics in one refrigerated bar") had a short product life. Test-market sales volume projections were inaccurate because the sauce was initially sold in what turned out to be an eight-month supply. At one point in the test-market, more bars were returned and discarded due to spoilage (372,000) than were sold (207,000).

Initial penetration, if projected directly, may overstate the situation. Many consumers who make a trial purchase may not repurchase the product. Researchers must be concerned with repurchase rates as well as with initial trial purchases. Supplementing retail store scanner data with purchase diaries and panel data will help indicate what sales volume will be over time.

■ TIME LAPSE

One relatively uncontrolled problem results from the time lapse between the test-market experiment and the national introduction of the product. Often, the time period between the test-market and national introduction is a year or more. Given the time needed to build production capacity, develop channels of distribution, and gain initial sales acceptance, this may be unavoidable. However, the longer the time between the test-market and the actual selling market, the less accurate one should expect the results to be.

Advantages and Disadvantages of Test-Marketing

Advantages of Test-Marketing

This discussion of test-marketing should make it clear that test-markets are advantageous in ways that are very difficult to match with other research approaches. The key advantage of test-marketing is the real-world setting in which the experiment is performed. Although focus groups and surveys also can be useful in describing what people may like in a new product, the actual behavior of consumers in a real test-market location is far more likely to lead to accurate projections.

A second advantage of test-marketing is that the results are usually easily communicated to management. Although the experiment itself can be difficult to implement for a host of reasons, most of which are related to small-scale or temporary marketing, the data analysis is usually very simple. Very often, the same procedures used in any simple experiment can be used with test-markets. As we will see, this relies heavily on comparing means in some way. Researchers find marketing managers much more receptive to these types of results than they may be to results drawn from complicated mathematical models or qualitative approaches relying on deep subjective

All Fed Up!

Are consumers all fed up? Fast-food companies are among the leaders in test-marketing. Wendy's has had some of the most successful new sandwich launches ever, including the Big Bacon Classic. However, many fast-food restaurants have tried so many variations of food products, that they end up simply recycling old ideas. Marketing managers at these fast-food restaurants are more and more turning toward beverage items as a way of boosting sales and popularity. After all, Starbucks grew from one to over 10,000 locations in just over two decades—and they did it with drinks!

Which fast-food restaurant has the most locations? Well, it turns out the Subway in the subway station is just one of about 30,000 Subway stores making it the most prolific of fast-food franchises. Subway is eyeing the coffee market. So how should they enter this market? Should they offer Starbucks-style coffee drinks in their current locations? Or, should they open stand-alone coffee shops? Subway turned to marketing research to answer this question and

test-marketed five Subway Café coffee shops, all in the Washington D.C. area. Many of the fast-food players offer coffee, but the long run strategy is to take advantage of convenient locations in topping the others.

Test-marketing is dynamic in part because of competitve pressures. McDonald's is also trying to capitalize on coffee and other drinks. They too are trying out McCafé stores that are aimed at directly competing with Starbucks. Additionally though, they are test-marketing different types of beverages for their normal menus. Ideally, they would steer people toward fountain beverages that don't conflict with their current soft drink contracts, but they also are test-marketing green tea and diet green tea as well as different soft drinks like Diet Mountain Dew. Considering the relatively high profit margin on drinks relative to food products, Subway, McDonald's, and others focusing on beverages may be glad to have consumers drink up whether they are fed up or not!

Sources: Zmuda, N., "McD's Tries to Slake Consumer Thirst for Wider Choice of Drinks," *Advertising Age*, 79 (June 9, 2008), 1–45; Young, E. B., "Drink Fresh? Subway Tests Out Coffee Concept," *Advertising Age*, 79 (July 14, 2008), 4–26.

interpretation. Many consumer industries depend heavily on test market results for help in decision making. The Research Snapshot above illustrates how marketing managers in the fast-food industry can use test marketing.

Disadvantages of Test-Marketing

Test-markets also have disadvantages. While the power of test-markets in providing accurate predictions are apparently such that companies would use test-markets for all major marketing changes, this is hardly the case. The disadvantages are such that test-markets are used less frequently than one might think.

■ COST

Test-marketing is very expensive. Consider that for most new products, companies have to actually create production facilities on a small scale, develop distribution within selected test-market cities, arrange media coverage specific to those locations, and then have systems and people in place to carefully monitor market results. All of this leads to high cost overall and very high unit costs. Heineken was faced with all these issues in test-marketing HPL. As a result, each six-pack could cost several times over the actual selling price. However, when HPL was introduced throughout the United States, the economies of scale that come with full-scale marketing left unit costs below the selling price.

Test-marketing a packaged-goods product typically costs millions. As with other forms of marketing research, the value of the information must be compared with the research costs. The expense of test-marketing certainly is a primary reason why marketing managers refuse to use the approach. Although they do reduce error in decision making, they are not perfect and certainly some risk remains in basing decisions on test-market results. If they were risk-free, managers would use them far more frequently. Because they are not risk-free and are so expensive, managers may decide to make go or no-go decisions based on less expensive techniques that are often less accurate.

Exhibit 12.2 illustrates the magnitude of costs typically associated with getting a single new product through the new product pipeline and into the marketplace,[9] where success is still not

EXHIBIT 12.2 **The Risks and Costs Associated with Product Development Research**

Testing Procedure	Number of Ideas Considered	Number That Survive	Approximate Cost of Testing	Total Expense
Initial Idea Screening	80	8	$50	$4,000
Concept Testing	8	4	$4,000	$32,000
Product Development	4	2	$250,000	$1,000,000
Test-marketing	2	1	$2,500,000	$5,000,000
Initial Full Launch	1	1	$10,000,000	$10,000,000
				$16,036,000

Sources: Ding, M. and J. Eliashberg (2002), "Structuring the New Product Development Principle," *Management Science,* 48 (March) 343–363; P. Kotler (1997), *Marketing Management: Analysis, Planning and Control* (Upper Saddle River, NJ: Prentice Hall), p. 310.

guaranteed. As can be seen from the chart, the research approaches used for early product testing are relatively inexpensive per idea tested. Once the test-marketing stage is reached however, testing an idea can cost millions. Thus, managers like to be somewhat certain that a new product idea is good before they commit to a test-market. Therefore, products that are test-marketed are usually expected to succeed. In this sense, the test-market can be thought of as the last line of defense against a marketing blunder.

■ TIME

Test-markets cost more than just money. Test-markets cannot be put together overnight. Simply planning a test-market usually takes months. Actually implementing one takes much longer. On top of the time for planning and implementation, researchers also must decide how long is long enough. In other words, when is the amount of data collected sufficient to have confidence in drawing valid conclusions?

The appropriate time period for a test-market varies depending on the research objectives. Sometimes, as in Procter & Gamble's testing of its unique new products Febreze, Dryel, and Fit Fruit & Vegetable Wash, the research takes several years. In other situations, as in P&G's testing of Encaprin pain reliever (a product that ultimately failed in national distribution), the time period may be shorter. HPL's test-markets lasted less than a year, relatively short by most standards.

Thus, even a quickly planned and implemented test-market can cost the firm a year or more in time. During this time, competitors are also trying to gain competitive advantage. The fear that competitors may make a big move first puts added pressure on marketing managers to move quickly. For this reason, the time costs associated with test-markets are a primary reason for forgoing them.

How long should a test-market be? Test-markets should be long enough for consumers to become aware of the product, have a chance to purchase it, consume it, and repurchase it at least one more time. Thus, it must be longer than the average purchase cycle for that particular product. A test-market that is too short may overestimate sales, because typically the early adopters are heavy users of the product. Thus, projections are based on consumers who are far from average.

Time must be allowed for sales to settle down from their initial honeymoon level. In addition, the share and sales levels must be allowed to stabilize. After the introduction of a product, peaks and troughs will inevitably stem from initial customer interest and curiosity as well as from competitive product retaliation.[10]

Thus, the time required for test-marketing depends on the product. The purchase cycle for chewing gum is much shorter than a bottle of shampoo. After high initial penetration and when the novelty of the product has stabilized, the researcher may make an estimate of market share. The average test-market requires about twelve months.

The Hidden in Hidden Valley Ranch

A few years ago, Hidden Valley Ranch (HVR) conducted a field market experiment to examine how effective three new flavors of salad dressings would be in the marketplace. Thus, there were three levels of the experimental variable, each representing a different flavor. HVR had to produce small batches of each flavor, get them bottled, and ship them to their sales representatives, who then had to stock the dressings in the participating retail stores. All of this was very expensive and the costs to produce each bottle used in a test-market were almost $20.

So, the first day of the test was consumed with sales reps placing the products in the salad dressing sections of retail stores. The second day, each rep went back to each store to record the number of sales for each flavor. By the third day, all of the bottles of all flavors had sold!! Amazing! Was every flavor a huge success?? Actually, one of HVR's competitors had sent their sales reps around beginning on the second day of the test to buy every bottle of the new HVR dressings in every store it had been placed in. Thus, HVR was unable to produce any sales data (the dependent variable) and the competitor was able to break down the dressing in their labs and determine the recipe.

This illustrates one risk that comes along with field tests. Once a product is available for sale, there are no secrets. Also, you risk espionage of this type that can render the experiment invalid.

© SUSAN VAN ETTEN

© GEORGE DOYLE & CIARAN GRIFFIN

■ LOSS OF SECRECY

As pointed out in the Research Snapshot above, one drawback to actual field experimentation is that the marketplace is a public forum. Therefore, secrets no longer exist. In the case of a new product, not only does the competition know about the new product, but a competitor can sometimes benefit from the test-market by monitoring the same dependent variables as is the sponsoring firms. This may cause them to launch a competing product. In some cases, the competitor can even beat the originating company to the national marketplace.

While Clorox Super Detergent with Bleach remained in the test-market stage, P&G introduced Tide with Bleach across the country. Fab 1 Shot, a pouch laundry from Colgate-Palmolive, preempted Cheer Power Pouches by Procter & Gamble, but P&G wasn't sorry. Fab 1 Shot was not a commercial success. Perhaps Colgate-Palmolive should have observed the test-market results more closely. Food companies also are notorious for buying new food products and breaking down the recipe.

During the 1980s, soft, "homestyle" cookies were a market success. However, only one company perfected the recipe. The rest simply purchased the cookies and had their chemists determine how to make them. This resulted in legal actions that lasted for years.

When Not to Test-Market

Not all product introductions are test-marketed. Expensive durables, such as refrigerators, automobiles, or heavy equipment, are rarely test-marketed because of the prohibitive cost of producing test units. Products that involve very little investment to get to market also are not appropriate for test-marketing. This may be the case with small modifications to existing products. In other cases, test-marketing is used as a last resort because a new concept might be easily imitated by competitors. Secrecy is more important than research in these cases.

Bacardi recently decided not to test-market a line of low calorie spirits. One important reason was the loss of secrecy and the fear that competitors would hasten a similar product to market.[11] Also, Bacardi believes it is riding the crest of a strong consumer trend toward lower calorie options. Thus, the calorie-conscious segment may be growing as consumers turn away from beer toward something less damaging to the waistline.

Many times, the decision whether to test-market or not is difficult. If a company chooses to forgo test-marketing, millions may be saved, but perhaps even more millions are lost when a product fails.

Anheuser-Busch's Catalina Blonde beer (a "super light" beer targeted at women), Frito-Lay's Max Snax, and P&G's Pampers Rash Guard all failed in test-markets. However, the mistakes would have been even more costly had the brands immediately been introduced nationally. Like all research, test-marketing should only be conducted when the potential benefit exceeds the likely costs.

Selecting a Test-Market Site

Selecting test-markets is, for the most part, a sampling problem. The researcher seeks a sample of test-market cities that is representative of the population comprised of all consumers in the relevant marketing area. If a new product is being launched throughout Australia, for example, the researcher must choose cities that are typical of all Australians.

Thus, test-market cities should represent the entire competitive marketplace. For companies wishing to market a product through the United States, there is no single ideal test-market city. Nevertheless, the researcher must usually avoid cities that are not representative of the nation. Regional or urban differences, atypical climates, unusual ethnic compositions, or different life-styles may dramatically affect a marketing program. Sometimes, although the researchers may wish to sell a product throughout the entire region of the United States, they may have a certain benefit segment in mind. Food companies may introduce a product that is intended for segments that enjoy spicy food, for example. In this case, they may choose cities known to favor spicier, more flavor-filled foods, such as New Orleans and San Antonio. In this case, those test-market cites have populations that fit the benefit segment to which the product is aimed.

U.S. Test-Market Cities

Researchers who wish to select representative U.S. test-markets have a more complex problem because it is usually necessary to use three or four cities. Cities are selected as experimental units, and one or more additional cities may be used as control markets. The experimental and control markets should be similar in population size, income, ethnic composition, and so on. Differences in these demographic factors and other characteristics among the experimental or control markets affect the test results. Using the terminology introduced in the last chapter, these factors represent extraneous variables that can produce potential confounds.

Because of the importance of having representative markets for comparisons, certain cities are used repeatedly for test-market operations. Whereas some larger cities like Tampa; Peoria, Illinois; and San Antonio are attractive test-markets, many test-markets are conducted in smaller cities. Exhibit 12.3 lists several of the most popular U.S. test-markets.[12] Their popularity lies in how close they come to duplicating the average U.S. demographic profile. Researchers may find that some cities, like Wichita,

City	2000 Population	Median Age	Percent of Households w/Children	Hispanic Proportion (Percent)
Cedar Rapids, IA	191,701	35.2	31.8	1.4
Eau Claire, WI	148,337	34.7	31.4	0.8
Grand Junction, CO	116,255	38.1	31.4	10.0
Odessa-Midland, TX	237,132	33.0	38.4	35.8
Pittsfield, MA	84,699	40.6	27.6	1.7
Wichita Falls, TX	140,518	33.6	33.8	11.8
Entire U.S.	281,000,000	35.3	32.8	12.5
Wichita, KS	344,284	34.1	34.6	7.4

EXHIBIT 12.3
Popular test-markets and Selected Demographic Characteristics

Kansas and Cedar Rapids, Iowa, are particularly representative of the United States based on median age and households with children. On the other hand, they have very small percentages of Hispanic population. This may not pose a problem if the product is not thought to have any strong ethnic identification. Conversely, if a product is expected to have appeal based on ethnicity, then the test-market may be better conducted in Grand Junction, Colorado, and Wichita Falls, Texas. Because of this, Wichita Falls, Texas is considered by many to be the most typical U.S. city.[13]

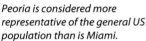

Peoria is considered more representative of the general US population than is Miami.

International Test-Markets

More and more companies become international companies every day. As a result, they may be test-marketing in foreign lands. The principles are still the same: "What cities best represent the larger market?"

Americans and Canadians are similar in many respects. However, one shouldn't assume that a product that is successful in the United States will be successful in Canada. Thus, even after a successful American launch, a company may wish to conduct a test-market in Canada. In addition, even if a new product is liked by the Canadian market, a unique marketing approach may be in order. Generally, Calgary, Alberta, is considered a prime test-market location for the Canadian market. When Italy's Podere Castorani Winery wished to expand to Canada, the product was tested in Calgary. Likewise, when Shell introduced a fast-pay charge system, Calgary again proved a suitable test-market. Edmonton also is frequently used to test-market products. Imperial Tobacco selected Edmonton for a test market of SNUS, a smokeless, spitless tobacco product, positioned as a safe alternative relative to smoking cigarettes.[14]

Like the United States, Canada is comprised of many different ethnic segments. Companies should also be aware that French Canada is quite different from the rest of the country. Edmonton may represent Canadians well enough but not French Canadians. Thus, companies may consider a test-market in Quebec City, Quebec, to see how French Canadian consumers will react.

Test-marketing in Europe can be particularly difficult. While companies can test their products country by country, the sheer costs involved with test-marketing motivate firms to look for cities more representative of large parts of Europe. Copenhagen, Denmark, is one such city. While the population is somewhat homogenous demographically, it is also multilingual and receptive to new ideas.[15] Copenhagen is particularly representative of northern Europe. Other cities to be considered include Frankfurt, Germany, Birmingham, England, and Madrid, Spain.

One benefit of test-marketing in the United States is the large ethnic population base. For instance, some companies considering expansion to Brazil have test-marketed the ideas in Provo, Utah. Provo, better known for the Church of the Latter-Day Saints and Brigham Young University, contains a large percentage of Brazilians and Americans who have spent time in Brazil. Students at Brigham Young are required to do missionary work, and many do so in Brazil.[16] Therefore, the way a product performs in Provo may indicate to some degree the way a product would perform in San Paulo.

Companies may sometimes test-market a product in one country with plans of introducing it in another. Singapore has been used to test products made for the U.S. market. While Singapore consumers may not be as representative of the United States as is Wichita Falls, Texas, competitors are less likely to spot the new product and take some kind of action aimed at spoiling the test-market results or piggy-backing on these results and launching their own product. As Singapore is sometimes used for products intended for the United States, European cities are sometimes used to project how well a product will do in China.

Factors to Consider in Test-Market Selection

Obtaining a representative test-market requires considering many factors that may not be obvious to the inexperienced researcher. Consider the observation of a vice president of ITT Continental Banking:

> When I started in the business, I thought people picked cities like Columbus, Ohio, because their populations were typical. But I found the main reasons were that they were isolated media markets and the distribution patterns were such that they didn't have to worry about the chain warehouse shipping outside of Columbus. It's difficult to translate information from a city which represents 0.1 percent of the United States and multiply that to get 99.9 percent. I think it is much more important to get control of the distribution and the advertising message.[17]

As with all decisions, the objectives of the decision makers will influence the choice of alternative. The following factors should be considered in the selection of a test-market.

■ POPULATION SIZE

No one size represents the best population for a test-market city. Practically all metropolitan areas in the United States are large enough. The population simply should be large enough to provide meaningful results with respect to the larger population, yet small enough to ensure that costs are not prohibitive. New York City is far too large to be a popular test-market, as are Chicago and Los Angeles in the United States. Likewise, Tokyo and Mexico City are considered too large for practical test-markets. Conversely, notice that the attractive test-market cities shown in Exhibit 12.3 are all well under 1 million in population. This allows far greater control at a far lower price than using the largest U.S. cities.

■ DEMOGRAPHIC COMPOSITION AND LIFESTYLE CONSIDERATIONS

Ethnic backgrounds, incomes, age distributions, lifestyles, and so on within the market should be representative of the market segment to which an offering is targeted. If a product is intended to be equally targeted toward the entire U.S. market, the product should then be test-marketed in cities that most closely match the entire U.S. population, like Wichita Falls, Texas. test-marketing on the West Coast may not be representative because people residing in metropolitan areas along the Pacific tend to be unique in some ways. For instance, West Coast consumers are quick to accept innovations that might not ever be adopted on a large scale elsewhere. Additionally, most of these cities have large percentages of either Hispanic and/or Asian populations, making them less appropriate for representing the entire country.

In contrast, if an offering is targeted only toward a specific geographic segment, then the test-markets should have profiles that reflect that particular segment. Many products have demand patterns that vary regionally. In the United States, alcoholic beverage consumption varies by region. While spirit sales (i.e., whiskey) dominate in the Northeast, Southerners consume the most beer per capita. Thus, beer companies may favor the South whereas whiskey companies would do better to emphasize New England in their test-marketing.

Products geared toward ethnic markets should likewise emphasize cities with high proportions of the respective consumer group. Mobile phone companies realize that Hispanics have different usage habits on average than many other consumer groups.[18] Thus, test-market cities may include Miami, Florida, or Midland, Texas, where very large numbers of Hispanic consumers reside.

■ COMPETITIVE SITUATION

Competitive market shares, competitive advertising, and distribution patterns should be typical so that test-markets will represent other geographic regions. If they are not representative, it will be difficult to project the test-market results to other markets.

Consider a firm that test-markets a new product in a specific geographical area in which the company has a dominant market share. Here, the sales force may have a much easier time getting shelf space than in an area where market share is low. The result is a higher acceptance level among retailers, lower cost of sell-in (obtaining initial distribution), and a greater upside potential for test-market results. Hence, projecting the results of this particular test-market into those where the same level of past success is not enjoyed proves difficult.

■ MEDIA COVERAGE AND EFFICIENCY

Local media (television spots, newspapers) will never exactly replicate national media. However, duplicating the national media plan or using one similar to it is important. Sunday newspaper supplements are sometimes used as a substitute for national magazine advertising. This does not duplicate a national plan, but may provide a rough estimate of the plan's impact. Ideally, a market should be represented by the major television networks, typical cable television programming, and newspaper coverage. Some magazines have regional editions or advertising inserts.

■ MEDIA ISOLATION

Advertising in communities outside of the test-market may contaminate the test-market. Furthermore, advertising money is wasted when it reaches consumers who cannot buy the advertised product because they live outside the test area. Markets such as Tulsa, Oklahoma, and Green Bay, Wisconsin, are highly desirable because advertising does not spill over into other areas. Notice how the cities in Exhibit 12.3 would also seem to share this characteristic.

■ SELF-CONTAINED TRADING AREA

Distributors should sell primarily or exclusively in the test-market area. Shipments in and out of markets from chain warehouses can produce confusing shipping figures. Frito-Lay test-marketed Olean-based versions of Ruffles, Lay's, Doritos, and Tostitos under the Max name in Cedar Rapids, Iowa. However, large amounts of the chips were purchased by droves of consumers in markets far from the test site.[19] Publicity about the no-fat chips had retailers fielding telephone orders from as far away as California, Texas, and New Jersey. Had the company relied solely on shipment information, the plants it built for what became WOW! Chips would have been much larger than needed.

■ OVERUSED TEST-MARKETS

If consumers or retailers become aware of the tests, they will react in a manner different from their norm. Thus, it is not a good idea to establish one great test-market and use it time and time again. Tucson, Arizona, is one area now used less frequently than in the past because Tuscsonian consumers now display atypical reactions to new-product introductions. Perhaps they are so accustomed to in-store promotion and advertising of new products that the reaction to innovative marketing is now below average.

Alternative Test-Market Methods

Standard and Control Methods

The discussion so far has focused on the *standard method* of test-marketing. This means that the firm chooses test-markets and then obtains distribution within those markets using members of its own sales force. External validity is very high with this approach. Everything is just as it would be in a full-scale introduction.

In recent years, researchers have reduced test-market costs and the probability of competitive interference by using controlled store tests that simulate actual retail conditions. The **control method of test-marketing** involves a "minimarket test" in a small city, using *control store distribution,* or forced distribution. A marketing research company that specializes in test-marketing performs the entire test-marketing task, including the initial sale to retailers (referred to as *sell-in*), warehousing, distribution, and shelving of the test product. The research company pays retailers for shelf space and therefore can guarantee distribution to stores that represent a predetermined percentage of the market's all-commodity volume (the total dollar sales for that product in a defined market). Thus, the firm is guaranteed distribution in stores that represent a predetermined percentage of the market.

The warehousing function and portions of the retailer's stocking function are performed by the research agency. Therefore, the retailer may be more willing to cooperate with the research because selling the product will be effortless. However, this raises the question of whether the retailer would react to the product in the same fashion if the product were going through its normal distribution channels. With controlled store testing, out-of-stocks—a potential problem in the traditional channel of distribution—rarely occur. The research agency monitors the sales results without the use of an outside auditing firm.

For example, Market Facts, which conducts controlled store tests in metropolitan areas including Orlando, Florida; Erie, Pennsylvania; and Fort Wayne, Indiana, has auditors in test cities visit cooperating stores a minimum of two times each week during controlled store tests, minimizing out-of-stock conditions and ensuring maintenance of desired shelf conditions, location, facings, price, and so on. Thus, the experimental error that often interferes with sales tests is controlled.

Using the control method of test-marketing has several advantages:

1. Reduced costs
2. Shorter time period needed for reading test-market results
3. Increased secrecy from competitors
4. No distraction of company salespeople from regular product lines

Lower costs result from the smaller market tests. Distribution is guaranteed. Secrecy is increased and monitoring the test product's movement is increasingly difficult for competitors. One potential problem with a controlled store test is that distribution may be abnormally high. Also, retailers' complete cooperation with promotions, such as ensuring that the product is never out of stock, may result in higher-than-normal sales. This type of study becomes more like a laboratory study, in which factors are increasingly controlled. Thus, if a firm's objective is to test distribution for a product, a standard test-market will be much more appropriate. However, when the problem is to test a specific set of alternatives and determine which is best for a particular segment, controlled store testing may be superior.

High-Technology Systems Using Scanner Data

Several research suppliers offer test-marketing systems that combine scanner-based consumer panels with high-technology broadcasting systems. This allows experimentation with different advertising messages via split-cable broadcasts or other technology. These systems, sometimes called **electronic test-markets**, enable researchers to measure the immediate impact of commercial television viewing of specific programs on unit sales volume.

A household's barcoded identification number is entered into a store's computer when a household member makes a purchase. The computer links the household's item-by-item purchases with television viewing data during extensive test-marketing programs. For example, Information Resources Incorporated (IRI) has selected certain medium-sized cities, such as Pittsfield, Massachusetts, to serve as scanner-based test-markets. The company installs an electronic device on every television in selected households that become scanner-based panel members. In these electronically wired households, the device measures television viewing habits in five-second increments to determine whether a particular television commercial was viewed.

However, IRI's system also allows the researcher to manipulate what advertising the panel households see. The electronic device on the television set allows the researcher to cut into the

control method of test-marketing

A "minimarket test" using forced distribution in a small city; retailers are paid for shelf space so that the test-marketer can be guaranteed distribution.

electronic test-markets

A system of test-marketing that measures dependent variables with scanner-based consumer panels and manipulates advertising based on a special delivery system that can swap out one television commercial or advertisement for another.

regularly scheduled broadcasts and substitute a test commercial (introducing a new product, for example) for the commercial that is transmitted nationally over the television network. Furthermore, IRI has arranged with local newspapers and national magazines to print special editions for the test households. One household may find a cents-off coupon for a test product in the morning paper, whereas the house next door receives a regular newspaper without even a mention of the product. In this way experimental and control groups may be established and scanner-based sales data used as the dependent variable.

Needless to say, the high-tech electronic test-marketing systems increase the speed and accuracy of test-marketing. But they also can be expensive. A full IRI test costs several million dollars per year.

Simulated Test-Markets

simulated test-market

A research laboratory in which the traditional shopping process is compressed into a short timespan.

Marketing research program strategies often include plans for simulated test-markets because managers wish to minimize the number of products that go through the lengthy and costly process of full-scale marketing. A **simulated test-market** is a research laboratory in which the traditional shopping process is compressed into a short timespan. Consumers visit a research facility, where they are exposed to advertisements (usually as part of a television program shown in a theater setting). They then shop in a room that resembles a supermarket aisle. Researchers estimate trial purchase rates and how frequently consumers will repurchase the product based on their simulated purchases in the experimental store.

Simulated test-markets almost always use a computer model of sales to produce estimates of sales volume. For example, M/A/R/C Inc. offers the ASSESSOR modeling system. Simulated test-markets cannot replace full-scale test-marketing, but they allow researchers to make early predictions about the likelihood of success of a go/no-go decision. These results become significant information for determining which products ultimately will be introduced into real test-markets.

A major problem with simulated test-marketing occurs when the marketer does not execute the marketing plan that was tested during the simulated test. If the marketer changes the advertising copy, price, or another variable, the model used to measure product acceptance will no longer be accurate.

virtual-reality simulated test-market

An experiment that attempts to reproduce the atmosphere of an actual retail store with visually compelling images appearing on a computer.

Companies like this one specialize in simulated test-markets that they call virtual test-markets.

Virtual-Reality Simulations

The Research Snapshot on the next page illustrates how computer-based simulations can be used to mimic actual consumer behavior. In some cases, virtual consumers can be programmed using complex mathematical derivations. The math is intended to represent consumer decisions. Virtual consumers can then react to virtual markets with virtual new stores and virtual new products. Although high-tech, this can be a less expensive method of testing than an actual test-market.

Other virtual test-markets have consumers actually logging on to simulated shopping environments and selecting different products for different situations. At **http://www.threadless.com**, consumers can choose their favorite T-shirt design from among several concepts. The designs that are selected most often are then taken from the virtual market to the real market.[20] Consumers can even participate in the design process and then dress their personal avatar in the new designs. If the consumers like the clothes for their avatars, then the presumption is that the consumers will be favorable toward purchasing these products.

Retailers can also test-market the way consumers may react in a new retail store environment. A **virtual-reality simulated test-market** attempts to reproduce the atmosphere of an actual retail store with visually compelling images appearing on a computer screen.[21] Real consumers

Testing in a Virtual World

Modern technologies are offering alternatives to conventional test-markets. These come in several different forms. High-tech firms have developed Web-based software that allows consumers to enter virtual worlds where they can select, among other things, what types of clothes to wear to certain events, or what kind of shoes to wear to get there. Companies like Levi's can provide a virtual world through their Web site and include some new jean designs for consumers to try out virtually. Certainly much cheaper than a conventional test-market, the company can get a sense for what types of consumers are turned on by which types of jeans.

Video-game-type test-markets can also be conducted. These work much like the popular simulation games in which consumers control the daily lives of virtual families. However, these simulated people are programmed to act like real consumers. Among other things, a soft-drink company can use these to estimate how vending machine usage is affected by different arrangements of pop machines within a given building. Pepsi and Coke have both taken advantage of virtual test-markets of this type. The

simulated test-market has even been a basis for pricing and promotion budgets in North Africa. The simulated consumers were programmed based on brand and media preferences for several thousand actual Moroccan consumers.

Only time will tell whether these virtual test-markets have accuracy approaching actual test-markets or not. Certainly, the cost advantages will make them attractive to many companies. In fact, technology is advancing so that Ferrari soon will be able to virtually test-market new models. Consumers should virtually stand in line for a shot at test drive!

Sources: Elkin, Tobi, "Virtual test-markets," *Advertising Age*, 74, no. 43 (October 27, 2003), 6; Fass, Allison, "Game Theory," *Forbes*, 176 (November 14, 2005), 93–99; "Moog Selected to Provide Driving Simulator for Ferrari," *Computer Worstations*, 21 (July 2008), 4–5.

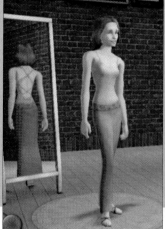

© GEORGE DOYLE & CIARAN GRIFFIN

© VICKI BEAVER

can virtually shop by moving through the store using a computer mouse. They can even click on things to place them in a virtual shopping cart. In this way, retailers can estimate how long consumers spend in certain parts of the store and where it is that their attention may be attracted.

Virtual-reality simulated test-markets have many potential uses. For example, managers for a chain of fast-food restaurants noticed that customers would stand at registers, staring at the menu board, and take a long time to place an order. Often this created long lines and customers waiting in these lines became frustrated and walked away. Managers speculated that the menu boards were too extensive and confusing. A virtual-reality simulated test-market with multiple virtual menu boards was easily designed on a computer. The research findings revealed that grouping products together into meals with a small discount increased ordering speed and total order size for most research subjects. This issue would have been very difficult to study with another research design. Manipulations can be implemented much more easily in virtual environments compared to actual retail environments.

Complex Experimental Designs

The previous chapter focused on simple experimental designs. Most discussion centered on experiments manipulating a single variable. Here, the focus shifts to more complex experimental designs involving multiple experimental variables. Most laboratory marketing experiments involve complex experimental designs and even test-markets can involve multiple experimental manipulations. A popular magazine recently conducted a test-market that combined manipulations of term of subscription (12 or 18 months), unit price ($20 or $13) and the method of listing expiration date (by number of days or a specific date).[22] This allowed them not only to analyze each of those variables' effects on subscriptions, but also the combinations of those variables. As a result, the research suggested that a $13 unit price yielded about the same number of subscribers no matter what the subscription term was, but that a $20 price yielded far fewer subscriptions for an 18-month term than for a 12. A $20 price with a 12-month subscription may yield the most revenue. These types of results can be analyzed with multivariate techniques such as analysis of variance, which is discussed at length later.

Completely Randomized Design

A **completely randomized design** is an experimental design that uses a random process to assign subjects to treatment levels of an experimental variable. Randomization of experimental units is the researcher's attempt to control extraneous variables while manipulating potential causes. A one-variable experimental design can be completely randomized, so long as subjects are assigned in a random way to a particular experimental treatment level.

Consider an experiment to examine the effects of various incentives on response rate in a mail survey. Thus, the experimental variable is the incentive. This can be manipulated over three treatment levels:

1. no incentive to the control group
2. a one-dollar personal incentive
3. a one-dollar charity incentive

Suppose the sample frame is divided into three groups of 15 each ($n_1 + n_2 + n_3 = 45$). Assigning treatments to groups is a simple random process. Exhibit 12.4 illustrates the experiment and provides a dummy table of hypothetical results.

A random number process could be used to assign subjects to one of the three groups. Suppose each of the 45 subjects is assigned a number ranging from 1 to 45. If a random number is selected between 1 and 45 (i.e., 12), that person can be assigned to the first group, with every third person afterward and before also assigned to the first group (12, 15, 18, . . . 45 and 9, 6, 3). The process can be repeated with the remaining 30 subjects by selecting a random number between 1 and 30, and then selecting every other subject. At this point, only 15 subjects remain and will comprise the third group. All 45 subjects are now assigned to one of three groups. Each group corresponds to one of the three levels of incentive. A variable representing which group a subject belongs to becomes the independent variable. The dependent variable is measured for each of the three treatment groups to determine which method of increasing response was the best. In this example, if the results turn out as indicated in the dummy table, the conclusion would be that the one-dollar incentive to charity would cause the highest response rate.

EXHIBIT 12.4
Experiment Examining Effect of Incentive on Response Rate

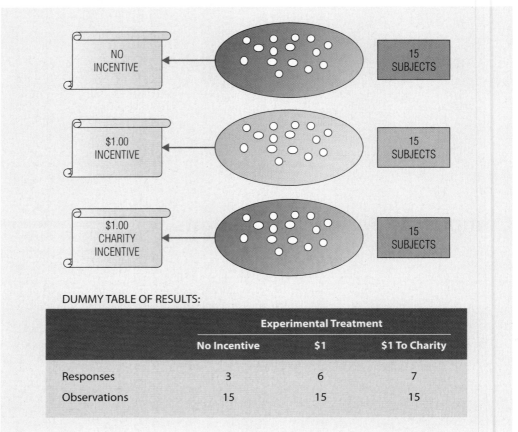

DUMMY TABLE OF RESULTS:

	Experimental Treatment		
	No Incentive	**$1**	**$1 To Charity**
Responses	3	6	7
Observations	15	15	15

Randomized-Block Design

The **randomized-block design** is an extension of the completely randomized design. A form of randomization is used to control for *most* extraneous variation; however, the researcher has identified a single extraneous variable that might affect subjects' responses systematically. The researcher will attempt to isolate the effects of this single variable by blocking out its effects.

Blocking variables (defined in the last chapter) provide for statistical control. For instance, gender is a common blocking variable. Many potential dependent variables are expected to be different for men and women. For instance, women are more price-conscious than men. So, if a researcher is studying the effect of price and package design on purchase, they may want to also record a person's gender and include it as an extra explanatory variable over and above the experimental variable's price and packaging.

The term *randomized block* originated in agricultural research that applied several levels of a treatment variable to each of several blocks of land. Systematic differences in agricultural yields due to the quality of the blocks of land may be controlled in the randomized-block design. In marketing research the researcher may wish to isolate block effects such as store size, territory location, market shares of the test brand or its major competition, per capita consumption levels for a product class, city size, and so on. Suppose that a manufacturer of Mexican food is considering two packaging alternatives. Marketers suspect that geographic region might confound the experiment. They have identified three regions where attitudes toward Mexican food may differ (Midland, Texas; Normal, Illinois; and Naples, Florida). In a randomized-block design, each block must receive every treatment level. Assigning treatments to each block is a random process. In this example the two treatments will be randomly assigned to different cities within each region.

Sales results such as those in Exhibit 12.5 might be observed. The logic behind the randomized-block design is similar to that underlying the selection of a stratified sample rather than a simple random one. By isolating the block effects, one type of extraneous variation is partitioned out and a more efficient experimental design therefore results. This is because experimental error is reduced with a given sample size.

> **randomized-block design**
>
> An extension of the completely randomized design in which a single, categorical extraneous variable that might affect test units' responses to the treatment is identified and the effects of this variable are isolated by being blocked out.

EXHIBIT 12.5 **Randomized-Block Design**

Treatment	Mountain	Percentage Who Purchase Product		Mean for Treatments
		North Central West	North Central East	
Package A	14.0% (Phoenix)	12.0% (St. Louis)	7.0% (Milwaukee)	11.0%
Package B	16.0% (Albuquerque)	15.0% (Kansas City)	10.0% (Indianapolis)	13.6%
Mean for cities	15.0%	13.5%	8.5%	

Graphing Results of Factorial Designs ⬅

Suppose a brand manager believes that an experiment that only manipulates a price factor is too limited because price changes have to be communicated with increased promotional support. The brand manager suggests that more than one independent variable must be incorporated into the research design. Even though the single-factor experiments considered so far may have one specific variable blocked and other confounding sources controlled, they are still limited. A **factorial design** allows for the testing of the effects of two or more treatments (factors) at various levels.

Recall from the last chapter that experiments produce main effects and interactions. Main effects are differences (in the dependent variable) between treatment levels. Interactions produce differences (in the dependent variable) between experimental cells based on combinations of variables.

> **factorial design**
>
> An experiment that investigates the interaction of two or more independent variables on a single dependent variable.

To further explain the terminology of experimental designs, let us use the example of a manufacturer of toy robots that wishes to measure the effect of different prices and packaging designs on consumers' perceptions of product quality. Exhibit 12.6 indicates three experimental treatment levels of price ($25, $30, and $35) and two levels of packaging design (red and gold). The table shows that every combination of treatment levels requires a separate experimental group. In this experiment, with three levels of price and two levels of packaging design, we have a 3 × 2 (read "three by two") factorial design because the first factor (variable) is varied in three ways and the second factor is varied in two ways. A 3 × 2 design requires six cells, or six experimental groups (3 × 2 = 6). If the subjects each receive only one combination of experimental variables, then we use the term 3 × 2 between-subjects design to describe the experiment.

EXHIBIT 12.6

Factorial Design—Toy Robots

Price	Package Design	
	Red	**Gold**
$25	Cell 1	Cell 4
$30	Cell 2	Cell 5
$35	Cell 3	Cell 6

The number of treatments (factors) and the number of levels of each treatment identify the factorial design. A 3 × 3 design incorporates two factors, each having three levels; a 2 × 2 × 2 design has three factors, each having two levels. The treatments need not have the same number of levels; for example, a 3 × 2 × 4 factorial design is possible. The important idea is that in a factorial experiment, each treatment level is combined with every other treatment level.

In addition to the advantage of investigating two or more independent variables simultaneously, factorial designs allow researchers to measure interaction effects. In a 2 × 2 experiment the interaction is the effect produced by treatments A and B combined. If the effect of one treatment differs at various levels of the other treatment, interaction occurs.

To illustrate the value of a factorial design, suppose a researcher is comparing two magazine ads. The researcher is investigating the believability of ads on a scale from 0 to 100 and wishes to consider the gender of the reader as a blocking factor. The experiment has two independent variables: gender and ads. This 2 × 2 factorial experiment permits the experimenter to test three hypotheses. Two hypotheses yield main effects:

- Ad A is more believable than ad B.
- Men believe ads more than women.

However, the primary research question may deal with the interaction hypothesis:

- Ad A is more believable than ad B among women, but ad B is more believable than ad A among men.

A high score indicates a more believable ad. Exhibit 12.7 shows that the mean believability score for both genders is 65. This suggests that there is no main sex effect. Men and women

EXHIBIT 12.7

A 2 × 2 Factorial Design That Illustrates the Effects of Gender and Ad Content on Believability

	Ad A	Ad B	
Men	60	70	65 ⎫
Women	80	50	65 ⎬ Main effects of gender
	70	60	
	Main effects of ad		

evaluate believability of the advertisements equally. The main effect for ads indicates that ad A is more believable than ad B (70 versus 60), supporting the first hypothesis. However, if we inspect the data and look within the levels of the factors, we find that men find ad B more believable and women find ad A more believable. This is an interaction effect because the believability score of the advertising factor differs at different values of the other independent variable, sex. Thus, the interaction hypothesis is supported.

Exhibit 12.8 graphs the results of the believability experiment. The line for men represents the two mean believability scores for ads A and B. The other line represents the same relationship for women. Notice the difference between the slopes of the two lines. This also illustrates support for the interaction of the ad copy with biological sex. The difference in the slopes means that the believability of the advertising copy depends on whether a man or a woman is reading the advertisement. Later, we'll see how tests of statistical significance can be added to this analysis.

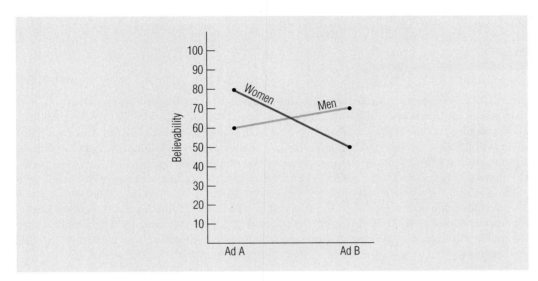

EXHIBIT 12.8

Graphic Illustration of Interaction between Gender and Advertising Copy

Latin Square Design

The **Latin square design** attempts to control or block out the effect of two or more confounding extraneous factors. This design is so named because of the layout of the table that represents the design. A Latin square is a balanced, two-way classification scheme.[23] In the following 3 × 3 matrix, each letter occurs only once in each row and in each column:

Latin square design

A balanced, two-way classification scheme that attempts to control or block out the effect of two or more extraneous factors by restricting randomization with respect to the row and column effects.

		Order of Usage		
		1	**2**	**3**
	1	A	B	C
Subject	2	B	C	A
	3	C	A	B

The letters A, B, and C identify the three treatments; the rows and columns of the table identify the confounding factors. For example, a taste test might be confounded by the order of tasting; the first taste may seem better than the last. The taste test might also be confounded by individual taste preferences. To control for these factors, each subject is exposed to every treatment. If all the subjects receive three tastes and the order in which they taste is randomized, neither individual

- Test-markets clearly illustrate the trade-off of internal validity for external validity.
  - They remain one of the best tools for forecasting marketing success prior to implementing an idea full scale.
  - Test-markets remain expensive. Technology offers some virtual alternatives.
- Two big disadvantages of test-markets involve the time they take and the loss of secrecy.
  - When a product can easily be duplicated by competitors simply because they can obtain an actual product, then a test-market may not be wise.
  - Once a competitor knows a test-market is occurring, the risk of sabotage becomes real.
- Choosing a test-market city is a critical decision. Remember, the relevant population is defined by the market characteristics for a product, not by the entire profile of a nation. Cold weather products are not appropriate for test-marketing in Florida because Floridians are not likely consistent with the expected consumer market characteristics.
- Reinforce test-market sales data with survey data to assess attitudinal or knowledge-related variables.

preference nor order effects can confound the experiment; thus, the order of treatment may be randomized under the restriction of balance required for the Latin square. The same type of balance is required for the second confounding factor. The end result of this design is that each treatment will be administered under conditions that involve all levels of both confounding factors. In summary, the Latin square design manipulates one independent variable and controls for two additional sources of extraneous variation by restricting randomization with respect to the row and column effects.

A major assumption of the Latin square design is that interaction effects are expected to be minimal or nonexistent. Thus, it is assumed that the first subject does not have a strong preference for the first product tasted, and the third subject does not have a strong preference for the last product tasted.

A Latin square may have any number of treatments; for example, the matrix for a five-treatment experiment is as follows:

	1	2	3	4	5
1	A	B	C	D	E
2	B	C	D	E	A
3	C	D	E	A	B
4	D	E	A	B	C
5	E	A	B	C	D

Note that this 5 × 5 matrix requires 25 cells. It also indicates that the number of treatment levels for confounding both factor 1 and factor 2 must be equal. This may present certain problems. For example, suppose a retail grocery chain wishes to control for shelf space and city where the product is sold. The chain may be limited in its experiment because it markets in only three cities, but wishes to experiment with four levels of shelf height.

Having an unequal number of levels for each factor may be one drawback that will eliminate the Latin square design as a possibility. A second limitation is the assumption that there is no interaction effect. However, making this assumption allows the experiment to be conducted with fewer subjects than would be required for a comparable factorial design. Like most other forms of marketing research, the Latin square design has its drawbacks, but in certain situations it has advantages.

Summary

1. Recognize the appropriate uses of test-marketing. Major uses of test-marketing include forecasting the success of a newly developed product, testing hypotheses about different options for marketing mix elements, and identifying weaknesses in product designs or marketing strategies. Whereas the first two reasons are usually intentional results in that they are the reason a test-market is implemented in the first place, the last reason often occurs when results from a test-market are less favorable than expected. Test-marketing is concerned with projecting results. This is seldom as simple as it sounds and various approaches to performing this projection exist.

2. Know the basics of test-marketing, including how experimental manipulations can be used to test marketing strategies in a real world setting. Test-marketing is an experimental procedure providing an opportunity to test a new product or marketing plan under realistic conditions. Test-markets maximize external validity because the conditions closely approximate reality. Test-marketing provides the opportunity to estimate the outcomes of alternative courses of action by implementing experimental manipulations within the test-market study. Researchers can even examine combinations of marketing mix variable effects by examining interactions.

3. List the advantages and disadvantages of test-marketing. The two major advantages of test-markets discussed in the chapter are the real-world setting and the ease in interpretation and communication of results. These advantages have to be weighed against several key disadvantages. These include the great amount of money that it costs to conduct a test-market, the length of time it takes to design, implement, and analyze a test-market, and the loss of secrecy that comes when the product is marketed publicly. A full test-market can cost millions of dollars and take well over a year, and the competitors will know most of your strategic thinking.

4. Select an appropriate test-market city for a specific test. Test-market cities are selected based on how well they represent the consumer market of interest. Also, medium-sized cities are often used for test-markets because it is less expensive than using a big city. However, test-markets should also be selected by considering the nature of the product. Products should not be test-marketed in areas where consumers are known to have a negative predisposition toward that type of product or where the product might be culturally unacceptable.

5. Use manipulations to implement a completely randomized experimental design, a randomized-block design, and a factorial experimental design. The key to randomization is to assign subjects to experimental cells in a way that spreads extraneous variables out evenly across every condition. Blocking variables can be added to simple randomized experimental designs to control for categorical variables that are expected to be related to the dependent variable. Finally, a factorial design results when multiple experimental and/or blocking variables are included in a single model. Both main effects and interactions result.

6. Display experimental results using graphical charts. The graphical charts show main effects when there are differences in the height of the lines connecting points that indicate an experimental treatment condition. Interactions are indicated when lines have different slopes.

Key Terms and Concepts

cannibalize, *297*	factorial design, *313*	simulated test-market, *310*
completely randomized design, *312*	Latin square design, *315*	test-market sabotage, *300*
control method of test-marketing, *309*	market penetration, *299*	virtual-reality simulated test-market, *310*
electronic test-markets, *309*	randomized-block design, *313*	

Questions for Review and Critical Thinking

1. Why is a test-market usually considered an experiment?
2. When is test-marketing likely to be conducted? When is it not as appropriate? Which type of validity is most relevant to test-marketing?
3. List three typical uses of test-markets.
4. What is market-penetration rate? How is it relevant to test-marketing?
5. What are the advantages and disadvantages of test-marketing?

6. Which of the following products or marketing strategies are likely to be test-marketed? Why or why not?
   a. A computerized robot lawn mower
   b. A line of 8-ounce servings of vegetarian dishes for senior citizens
   c. A forklift truck
   d. A new brand of eyedrops especially for brown-eyed people
   e. A new, heavy-duty KitchenAid mixer
   f. An advertising campaign to get people to drink a cola drink in the morning

7. Suppose a new golf ball is introduced by a major manufacturer. It is called "Hi-Ball." The company introduces the product in four cities: Tampa, Florida; Baton Rouge, Louisiana; Fort Worth, Texas; and Minneapolis, Minnesota. They test four different prices using a different price in each city. They also use coupons in Minneapolis and Fort Worth but not in Tampa and Baton Rouge. The plan is for the test-market to start in September 2009 and run through December 2010.
   a. Critique this test-market design.
   b. How can the design be improved?

c. If this design has problems, why might a company sometimes use some design very much like this one?
d. **ETHICS** In what ways could a competitor sabotage this test-market?
e. How long should the test-market periods last for golf balls?

8. What are six popular U.S. test-market cities? What makes them popular? Is there such a thing as a bad test-market city? Explain.

9. What is test-market sabotage?

10. What is the difference between standard test-marketing, controlled test-marketing, and simulated test-marketing?

11. How are the results of a test-market projected to a national level? What problems arise in making such projections? What factors are important in selecting test-markets?

12. What advantages does simulated test-marketing have over traditional test-marketing? What limitations does it have?

13. What is a completely randomized design? Provide an example in the context of a test-market examining three product variations (X, Y, and Z) and two different price levels (low and high).

Research Activities

1. **'NET** Use the *Wilson Business Index* or a library search engine to search for stories about "test-markets." Read a couple and write a brief report.

2. In a 2 × 2 factorial design, there are eight possible patterns of effects. Assume that independent variable A and independent variable B have significant main effects, but there is no interaction between them. Another combination might be no effects of variable A, but a significant effect of variable B with a significant interaction effect between them. Diagram each of these eight possible effects.

3. **ETHICS** A mouthwash manufacturer learns that a competitor is test-marketing a new lemon-flavored mouthwash in an Arizona city. The marketing research department of the competing firm is told to read the results of the test-market, and the marketing manager is told to lower the price of the company's brand to disrupt the test-market. Is this ethical?

Case 12.1 Bueno, Chiles Rellenos

Mike Gavagan and Kathy Parker were discussing their test-market plans for a new item, frozen chiles rellenos for the microwave oven. Chiles rellenos, a traditional Mexican dish, are roasted poblano chile peppers filled with Monterey Jack cheese and encrusted in a cornmeal batter.

The idea to develop a microwavable chiles rellenos meal had struck Parker, manager of new product development, the day after she dined in a Mexican restaurant and enjoyed her first chiles rellenos. She thought that Mexican food was a lot of fun and that adults should have it more often. Of course, working for a large grocery product firm had helped direct her thinking toward the frozen meal. The product had passed the concept stages and was now ready for the big step. Parker wanted a test either in Cedar Rapids, Iowa, or in Eau Claire, Wisconsin.

Gavagan said, "Let's go to Texas. They love Mexican food there. If it goes over well there, it will go over anywhere. If we were testing a new soup, Eau Claire would be fine. The nation's eating habits change ever so slowly. A conservative market like that would be great for soup, but not for our new Mexican meal. We should test in Wichita Falls, Texas."

Questions

1. What factors should be considered when selecting a test-market? Are there any special demographic considerations for this product?

2. Where could you find demographic and retail sales information about the three locations being considered as test-markets? Find some information about these markets that would help to determine which area should be used as a test-market.

3. Which test-market should the company select?

Part 4
Measurement Concepts

© BRAND X PICTURES/JUPITER IMAGES

After studying this chapter, you should be able to

1. Determine what needs to be measured based on a research question or hypothesis
2. Distinguish levels of scale measurement
3. Know how to form an index or composite measure
4. List the three criteria for good measurement
5. Perform a basic assessment of scale reliability and validity

Chapter Vignette: Money Matters?

Griff Mitchell is the Vice President of Customer Relationship Management (CRM) for one of the world's largest suppliers of industrial heavy equipment. In this role, he oversees all sales and service operations. This year, for the first time, the company has decided to perform a CRM employee evaluation process that will allow an overall ranking of all CRM employees. Griff knows this will be a difficult task for many reasons, not the least of which is that he oversees over a thousand employees worldwide.

The ranking will be used to single out the best performers. These employees will be recognized at the company's annual CRM conference. The rankings will also be used to identify the lowest 20 percent of performers. These employees will be put on a probationary list with specific targeted improvement goals that will have to be met within 12 months or they will be fired. Griff becomes really stressed out trying to define the performance ranking process.

Griff's key question is, *What is performance*? Although these employees are now often referred to as CRM employees, they have traditionally performed the sales function. Griff calls a meeting of senior CRM managers to discuss how ranking decisions should be made.

One manager simply argues that sales volume should be the sole criteria. She believes that "sales figures provide an objective performance measure that will make the task easy and difficult to refute." Another counters that for the past 22 years, he has simply used his opinion of each employee's performance to place each of them into one of three groups: top performers, good performers, and underperformers. "I think about who is easy to work with and doesn't cause much trouble. It has worked for twenty-two years, why won't it work now?" Another responds curtly, "It's margin! It's margin! I don't care about sales volume; I want my guys selling things that improve my division's profit!" One of the newer managers sits silently through most of the meeting and finally summons up the courage to speak. "Aren't we CRM? That means performance should not be tied to sales, profits, or convenience, it should be based on how well a salesperson

© AP PHOTO/FAIRMONT SENTINEL, CHIP PEARSON

builds and maintains relationships with customers. So, we should see how satisfied the customers assigned to the employee are and use this in the evaluation process!" After this, the meeting disintegrates into a shouting match with each manager believing the others' ideas are flawed.

Griff feels like he is back to square one. "How do I make sure I have a valid performance measure so that all of our people are treated fairly?" He decides to seek out an opinion from a long-time friend in the research business, Robin Donald. Robin suggests that a research project may be needed to define a reliable and valid measure. She also brings up the fact that because employees from all over the world will be considered, the measure will have to maintain its reliability and validity anywhere it is used! Griff agrees to the project. He also feels good about letting someone outside the company develop the measure.

Introduction ⬅

Not every cook or chef needs to follow a recipe to create a great dish, but most amateur chefs find one very useful. Look at Exhibit 13.1. The recipe shows ingredients that can produce a tasty chicken dish. However, many readers, even those with some cooking ability, may have a difficult time following this recipe. Why? First, many may have difficulty translating all the French terms. Second, even when this is done, many will have difficulty knowing just what amounts of what ingredients should be included. How many could easily deal with the different measures listed by the ingredients? "How much is 50 ml?" "What is 454 g?" "How much is a pinch?" "Can I use my normal measuring utensils (scales)?"

If one tries to follow the recipe, one will certainly realize that even common things like weights and amounts can be measured multiple ways. If a mistake is made in measuring something, the dish

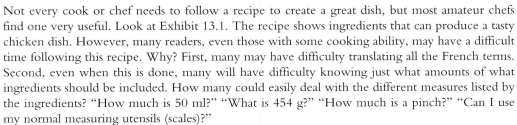

(a) Recette de la Jour	(b) Dogtes de Poulet Faibles avec Crackers

454 g	Poitrine de Poulet
50 ml	Farine Tout Usage
2 ml	De Poudre D'ail
2 ml	De Poudre D'oignon
1 ml	De Sel
2	Blancs d'oeuf
50 ml	De Lait Écrémé
Pincée	De le Poivre Rouge
36	Crackers (Tout Crounche)

© FOOD PIX/JUPITER IMAGES

EXHIBIT 13.1
More Ways Than 1 to Measure Ingredients

Take a look at the section of the student survey shown in the screenshot. Suppose someone thought the items made a composite scale and you are asked to analyze its quality. Answer the following questions:

Please read the following statements. After reading click the square that best describes how much you agree with each statement.

	Strongly Agree	Agree	Neutral	Disagree	Strongly Disagree
I make time to study every day.	○	○	○	○	○
I know the material better after I study.	○	○	○	○	○
I can't study when it's quiet.	○	○	○	○	○
I prefer to not be around others when I study.	○	○	○	○	○
I can study the night before and be ready for a test.	○	○	○	○	○
I like to study with others.	○	○	○	○	○
I arrange time to study with others.	○	○	○	○	○

COURTESY OF QUALTRICS.COM

1. Is the level of measurement nominal, ordinal, interval, or ratio?
2. Assuming the scale items represent studying concentration, do you think any of the items need to be reverse-coded before a summated scale could be formed? If so, which ones?
3. Using the data for these items, compute the coefficient α and draw some conclusion about the scale's reliability.
4. At this point, how much can be said about the scale's validity? Are there any items that do not belong on the scale?

© GEORGE DOYLE

may be completely ruined. Just as in the culinary arts, business and marketing concepts can often be measured in more than one way. Also, researchers often may have to use imperfect measurement devices. When a concept is measured poorly, the "recipe" is a likely disaster. Only in this case, the "recipe" is usually an important business decision poorly made instead of a ruined dish.

What to Measure

The chapter vignette describes a situation in which Griff must develop a "recipe" for distinguishing employees based on job performance. Before the measurement process can be defined, he will have to decide exactly what needs to be produced. In this case, the outcome should be a valid job performance measure.

The decision statement, corresponding research questions, and research hypotheses can be used to decide what concepts need to be measured in a given project. **Measurement** is the process of describing some property of a phenomenon, usually by assigning numbers, in a reliable and valid way. The numbers convey information about the property being measured. When numbers are used, the researcher must have a rule for assigning a number to an observation in a way that provides an accurate description.

Measurement can be illustrated by thinking about the way instructors assign students' grades. A grade represents a student's performance in a class. Students with higher performance should receive a different grade than do students with lower performance. Even the apparently simple concept of student performance is measured in many different ways. Consider the following options:

measurement

The process of describing some property of a phenomenon of interest, usually by assigning numbers in a reliable and valid way.

1. A student can be assigned a letter corresponding to his/her performance as is typical of U.S.-based grading systems.
   a. A — Represents excellent performance
   b. B — Represents good performance
   c. C — Represents average performance
   d. D — Represents poor performance
   e. F — Represents failing performance
2. A student can be assigned a number from 1 to 20, which is the system more typically used in France.
   a. 20 — Represents outstanding performance
   b. 11–20 — Represent differing degrees of passing performance
   c. Below 11 — Represent failing performance
3. A student can be assigned a number corresponding to a percentage performance scale.
   a. 100 percent — Represents a perfect score. All assignments are performed correctly.

b. 60–99 percent — Represents differing degrees of passing performance, each number representing the proportion of correct work.

c. 0–59 percent — Represents failing performance but still captures proportion of correct work.

4. A student can be assigned one of two letters corresponding to performance.

a. P — Represents a passing mark

b. F — Represents a failing mark

Actually, this is not terribly different than a manager who must assign performance scores to employees. In each case, students with different marks are distinguished in some way. However, some scales may better distinguish students. Each scale also has the potential of producing error or some lack of validity. Exhibit 13.2 illustrates a common student performance measurement application.

Often, instructors may use a percentage scale all semester long and then at the end, have to assign a letter grade for a student's overall performance. Does this produce any measurement problems? Consider two students who have percentage scores of 79.4 and 70.0, respectively. The most likely outcome when these scores are translated into "letter grades" is that each receives a C (the common ten-point spread would yield a 70–80 percent range for a C). Consider a third student who finishes with a 69.0 percent average and a fourth student who finishes with a 79.9 percent average.

Which students are happiest with this arrangement? The first two students receive the same grade, even though their scores are 9.4 percent apart. The third student gets a grade lower (D) performance than the second student, even though their percentage scores are only 1.0 percentage point different. The fourth student, who has a score only 0.5 percent higher than the first student, would receive a B. Thus, the measuring system (final grade) suggests that the fourth student outperformed the first (assuming that 79.9 is rounded up to 80) student (B versus C), but the first student did not outperform the second (each gets a C), even though the first and second students have the greatest difference in percentage scores.

A strong case can be made that error exists in this measurement system. All measurement, particularly in the social sciences, contains error. Researchers, if we are to represent concepts truthfully, must make sure that the measures used, if not perfect, are accurate enough to yield correct

EXHIBIT 13.2
Are There Any Validity Issues with This Measurement?

Student	Percentage Grade	Difference from Next Highest Student	Letter Grade
1	79.4%	0.5%	C
2	70.0%	9.4%	C
3	69.0%	1.0%	D
4	79.9%	NA	B

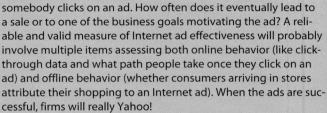

Measuring Yahoo! Impact

Earlier in the book, the concept of marketing metrics was introduced. The whole idea behind marketing metrics is measurement of key characteristics that indicate business performance in some way. Billions of dollars are being spent on Internet advertising in the United States, and those numbers are rising every year. In 2007, over $15 billion was spent. Does this make sense? Even though Internet advertising and promotion is just over a decade old, most firms struggle with ways to measure the effectiveness of an ad placed on a Web page.

The key question is, "What is the impact of an Internet ad?" Companies seem fixated with sales as a measure of impact. However, this overlooks other potential ways an ad can have impact, such as changing attitudes or creating awareness. Companies like Yahoo!, Google, and Ask try

to base advertising rates on "impact." Marketing Management Analytics is a research company in Wilton, Connecticut, that will soon offer research to advertisers (for a fee) to measure the impact of Internet ads. This research will examine what happens when somebody clicks on an ad. How often does it eventually lead to a sale or to one of the business goals motivating the ad? A reliable and valid measure of Internet ad effectiveness will probably involve multiple items assessing both online behavior (like click-through data and what path people take once they click on an ad) and offline behavior (whether consumers arriving in stores attribute their shopping to an Internet ad). When the ads are successful, firms will really Yahoo!

Sources: Aaron, Patrick O., "Yahoo to Track Impact of Internet Ads," *Wall Street Journal* (December 15, 2005), B4; Marketing Management Analytics, Inc., "Yahoo! and MMA to Offer Measurement Service to Enable Marketers to Optimize Advertising Spending Across Media," press release (December 16, 2005), http://biz.yahoo.com/prnews

conclusions. Making use of measures requires that the flaws in measures are at least somewhat understood. When this is the case, researchers can sometimes account for the error statistically. Ultimately, research would be impossible without measurement. The Research Snapshot above illustrates how Yahoo uses marketing research to measure its impact.

Concepts

concept

A generalized idea that represents something of meaning.

A researcher has to know what to measure before knowing how to measure something. The problem definition process should suggest the concepts that must be measured. A **concept** can be thought of as a generalized idea that represents something of meaning. Concepts such as *age, sex, education,* and *number of children* are relatively concrete having relatively unambiguous meanings. They present few problems in either definition or measurement. Other concepts are more abstract. Concepts such as *loyalty, personality, channel power, trust, corporate culture, customer satisfaction, value,* and so on are more difficult to both define and measure. For example, *loyalty* has been measured as a combination of customer share, the relative proportion of a person's purchases going to one competing brand/store and commitment, or the degree to which a customer will sacrifice to do business with a brand/store.[1] The first component is a behavioral measure and the second is attitudinal.

Operational Definitions

operationalization

The process of identifying scale devices that correspond to properties of a concept involved in a research process.

scale

A device providing a range of values that correspond to different characteristics or amounts of a characteristic exhibited in observing a concept.

correspondence rules

Indicate the way that a certain value on a scale corresponds to some true value of a concept.

Researchers measure concepts through a process known as **operationalization**. This process involves identifying scales that correspond to properties of the concept. **Scales**, just as a scale you may use to check your weight, provide a range of values that correspond to different characteristics in the concept being measured. In other words, scales provide **correspondence rules** that indicate that a certain value on a scale corresponds to some true value of a concept. Hopefully, they do this in a truthful way.

Here is an example of a correspondence rule: "Assign numerals 1 through 7 according to how much individual customers trust a sales representative. If a customer judges a sales representative as completely trustworthy, assign a 7. If the sales rep is perceived as completely untrustworthy, assign the numeral 1. Numbers in between represent varying degrees of trust." Most likely, these numbers would require an interview with the customers. In either case, accurate measurement would result if the numbers truly corresponded to each customer's amount of trust.

■ VARIABLES

Researchers use the variance in concepts to make meaningful diagnoses. Therefore, when we defined *variables* in an earlier chapter, we really were suggesting that variables capture different values of a concept. Scales capture a concept's variance and, as such, the scales provide the researcher's variables. Thus, for practical purposes, once a research project is under way, a *concept* and a *variable* represent essentially the same thing. Consider the following hypothesis:

> H1: *Experience* is positively related to *job performance*.

The hypothesis implies a relationship between two variables, experience and job performance. The variables capture variance in the experience and performance concepts. One employee may have fifteen years of experience and be a top performer. A second may have ten years experience and be a good performer. The scale used to measure experience is quite simple in this case and would involve simply providing the number of years an employee has been with the company. Job performance is captured by a scale in which a supervisor places the employee into a category as described in the vignette.

■ CONSTRUCTS

Sometimes, a single variable cannot capture a concept alone. Using multiple variables to measure one concept can often provide a more complete account of some concept than could any single variable. Even in the physical sciences, multiple measurements are often used to make sure an accurate representation is obtained. In social science, many concepts are measured with multiple measurements.

A **construct** is a term used for concepts that are measured with multiple variables. For instance, when a marketing researcher wishes to measure a salesperson's customer orientation, several variables like these may be used, each captured on a 1–5 scale of some type:

1. I offer the product that is best suited to a customer's problem.
2. A good employee has to have the customer's best interests in mind.
3. I try to find out what kind of products will be most helpful to a customer.[2]

Operational definitions translate conceptual definitions into measurement scales. An operational definition is like a manual of instructions or a recipe: even the truth of a statement like "Gaston likes seafood gumbo" depends on the recipe and the ingredients. Different instructions lead to different results.[3]

An operational definition tells the investigator, "Do such-and-such in so-and-so manner."[4] Exhibit 13.3 presents a concept definition and an operational definition from a study on a construct called *media skepticism*.

TO THE POINT

Not everything that can be counted counts, and not everything that counts can be counted.

—Albert Einstein

construct

A term used to refer to concepts measured with multiple variables.

EXHIBIT 13.3 **Media Skepticism: An Operational Definition**

Concept	Conceptual Definition	Operational Definition
Media skepticism	*Media skepticism* is the degree to which individuals are skeptical of the reality presented in the mass media. Media skepticism varies across individuals, from those who are mildly skeptical and accept most of what they see and hear in the media to those who completely discount and disbelieve the facts, values, and portrayal of reality in the media.	Please tell me how true each statement is about the media. Is it very true, not very true, or not at all true? 1. The program was *not* very accurate in its portrayal of the problem. 2. Most of the story was staged for entertainment purposes. 3. The presentation was slanted and unfair. 4. I think the story was fair and unbiased. 5. I think important facts were purposely left out of the story. Individual items were scored on a 4-point scale with values from 1 to 4; higher scores represented greater skepticism. Media skepticism is defined as the sum of these five scores.

Source: Michael D. Cozzens and Noshir S. Contractor, "The Effects of Conflicting Information on Media Skepticism," *Communications Research*, August 1987, pp. 437–451.

Levels of Scale Measurement

Marketing researchers use many scales or numbering systems. Not all scales capture the same richness in a measure. Not all concepts require a rich measure. But, all measures can be classified based on the way they represent distinctions between observations of the variable being captured. The four levels or types of scale measurement are *nominal, ordinal, interval,* and *ratio level scales.* Traditionally, the level of scale measurement is seen as important because it determines the mathematical comparisons that are allowable. Each of the four scale levels offers the researcher progressively more power in analyzing and testing the validity of a scale.

Nominal Scale

nominal scales

Represent the most elementary level of measurement in which values are assigned to an object for identification or classification purposes only.

Nominal scales represent the most elementary level of measurement. A nominal scale assigns a value to an object for identification or classification purposes. The value can be a number, but does not have to be a number, because no quantities are being represented. In this sense, a nominal scale is truly a qualitative scale. Nominal scales are extremely useful even though some may consider them elementary.

Marketing researchers use nominal scales quite often. For instance, suppose Barq's Root Beer was experimenting with three different types of sweeteners (cane sugar, corn syrup, or fruit extract) in an effort to see which created the best tasting soft drink. Basically, Barq's researchers designed a taste test experiment. Experimental subjects taste one of the three recipes and then rate how much they like it and how likely they would be to buy that particular drink. The researchers would like the experiment to be blind so that subjects' perceptions are not biased by their beliefs about different sweeteners. Thus, when subjects are actually asked to taste one of the three root beers, the drinks are labeled A, B, or C, not cane sugar, corn syrup, or fruit extract. The A, B and C becomes the measuring system that represents the variance in sweeteners.

Nominal scaling is arbitrary in the sense that each label can be assigned to any of the categories without introducing error; for instance, in the root beer example above, the researcher can assign the letter C to any of the three options without damaging scale validity. Cane sugar could just as properly be labeled C as A, or B. The researcher might use numbers instead of letters without any change in the validity of the measuring system. If so, cane sugar, corn syrup, and fruit extract might be identified with the numbers 1, 2, and 3, respectively, or even 543, −26, and 8080, respectively.

Athletes wear nominal numbers on their jerseys.

© AP PHOTO/RUSTY KENEDY

Either set of numbers is equally valid since the numbers are not representing different quantities. They are simply identifying the type of sweetener.

We encounter nominal numbering systems all the time. Uniform numbers are nominal numbers. Tom Brady is identified on the football field by his jersey number. What is his number? Airport terminals are identified with a nominal numbering system. In the Atlanta airport, a departing traveler has to go through terminals T, A, B, C, and D before reaching an international departure gate at terminal E. School bus numbers are nominal in that they simply identify a bus. Elementary school buses sometimes use both a number and an animal designation to help small children get on the right bus. So, bus number "8" may also be the "tiger" bus.

The first drawing in Exhibit 13.4 depicts the number 7 on a horse's colors. This is merely a label to allow bettors and racing enthusiasts to identify the horse. The assignment of a 7 to this horse does not mean that it is the seventh fastest horse or that it is the seventh biggest, or anything else meaningful. But, the 7 does let you know when you have won or lost your bet!

Exhibit 13.5 lists some nominal scales commonly used by marketing researchers. Nominal scale properties mean the numbering system simply identifies things.

EXHIBIT 13.4

Nominal, Ordinal, Interval, and Ratio Scales Provide Different Information

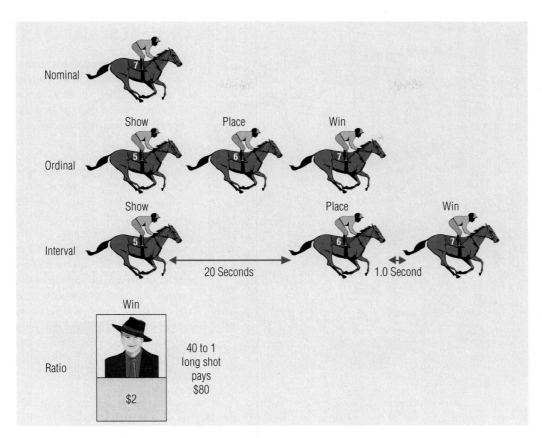

EXHIBIT 13.5

Facts About the Four Levels of Scales

Level	Examples	Numerical Operations	Descriptive Statistics
Nominal	Yes – No Female – Male Buy – Did Not Buy Postal Code: _____	Counting	• Frequencies • Mode
Ordinal	Rankings Choose from the Following: • Dissatisfied • Satisfied • Very Satisfied • Delighted Indicate Your Level of Education: • HS Diploma • Some College • Bachelor's Degree • Graduate Degree	Counting and Ordering	• Frequencies • Mode • Median • Range
Interval	100-Point Job Performance Ratings Assigned by Supervisors: 0% = Worst Performers 100% = Best Performers Temperature-Type Attitude Scales: Low Temperature = Bad Attitude High Temperature = Good Attitude	Common Arithmetic Operations	• Mean • Median • Variance • Standard Deviation
Ratio	Amount Purchased Salesperson Sales Volume Likelihood of performing some act: • 0%=No Likelihood to • 100%=Certainty Number of stores visited Time spent viewing a particular web page Number of web pages viewed	All Arithmetic Operations	• Mean • Median • Variance • Standard Deviation

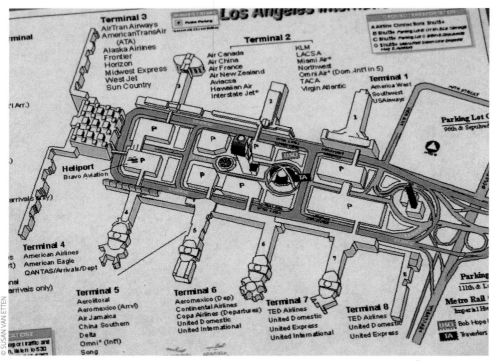

Without nominal scales, how would you know which terminal to go to at this airport?

ordinal scales

Ranking scales allowing things to be arranged based on how much of some concept they possess.

Ordinal Scale

Ordinal scales have nominal properties, but they also allow things to be arranged based on how much of some concept they possess. In other words, an ordinal scale is a ranking scale. When a professor assigns an A, B, C, D, or F to a student at the end of the semester, he or she is using an ordinal scale.

Research participants often are asked to *rank order* things based on preference. So, preference is the concept, and the ordinal scale lists the options from most to least preferred, or vice versa. In this sense, ordinal scales are somewhat arbitrary, but not nearly as arbitrary as a nominal scale. Five objects can be ranked from 1–5 (least preferred to most preferred) or 1–5 (most preferred to least preferred) with no loss of meaning.

When business professors take some time off and go to the race track, even they know that a horse finishing in the "show" position has finished after the "win" and "place" horses (see the second drawing in Exhibit 13.4). The order of finish can be accurately represented by an ordinal scale using an ordered number rule:

- Assign 1 to the "win" position
- Assign 2 to the "place" position
- Assign 3 to the "show" position

Sometimes, the winning horse defeats the place horse by only a nose, but other times, the place horse defeats the show horse by 20 seconds or more. An ordinal scale does not tell by how much a horse won, but is good enough to separate winning bets from losing bets. Typical ordinal scales in marketing research ask respondents to rate brands, companies, and the like as excellent, good, fair, or poor. Researchers know excellent is higher than good, but they do not know by how much.

Interval Scale

interval scales

Scales that have both nominal and ordinal properties, but that also capture information about differences in quantities of a concept from one observation to the next.

Interval scales have both nominal and ordinal properties, but they also capture information about differences in quantities of a concept. So, not only would a sales manager know that a particular salesperson outperformed a colleague, but the manager would know by how much. If a professor assigns grades to term papers using a numbering system ranging from 1.0–20.0, not only does the scale represent the fact that a student with a 16.0 outperformed a student with a 12.0, but the scale would show by how much (4.0).

The third drawing in Exhibit 13.4 depicts a horse race in which the win horse is one second ahead of the place horse, which is 20 seconds ahead of the show horse. Not only are the horses identified by the order of finish, but the difference between each horse's performance is known. So, using an interval scale we know horse number 7 and horse number 6 performed similarly, but horse number 5 performed not nearly as well.

A classic example of an interval scale is a Fahrenheit temperature scale. Consider the following weather:

- June 6 was 80° F
- December 7 was 40° F

The interval Fahrenheit scale lets us know that December 7 was 40° F colder than June 6. But, we cannot conclude that December 7 was twice as cold as June 6. Although the actual numeral 80 is indeed twice as great as 40, remember that this is a scaling system. In this case, the scale is not iconic, meaning that it does not exactly represent some phenomenon. In fact, these temperatures can be converted to the more common Celsius scale. Then, the following would result:

- June 6 was 26.7° C
- December 7 was 4.4° C

Obviously, now we can see that December 7 was not twice as cold as June 6. December 7 was 40° F or 22.3° C cooler, depending upon your thermometer. Interval scales are very useful because they capture relative quantities in the form of distances between observations. No matter what thermometer is used, December 7 was colder than June 6.

Ratio Scale

Ratio scales represent the highest form of measurement in that they have all the properties of interval scales with the additional attribute of representing absolute quantities. Interval scales represent only relative meaning whereas ratio scales represent absolute meaning. In other words, ratio scales provide iconic measurement. Zero, therefore, has meaning in that it represents an absence of some concept.

An absolute zero is a defining characteristic in determining between ratio and interval scales. For example, money is a way to measure economic value. Consider the following items offered for sale in an online auction:

- Antique railroad pocket watch circa 1910—sold for $50
- Authentic Black Forest cuckoo clock—sold for $75
- Antique gold-filled Elgin wristwatch circa 1950—sold for $100
- "Antique" 1970s digital watch—did not sell and there were no takers for free

We can make the ordinal conclusions that the cuckoo clock was worth more than the pocket watch and that the wristwatch was worth more than the cuckoo, all of which were worth more than the 1970s digital watch. We can make interval conclusions such as that the cuckoo was worth $25 more than the pocket watch. We can also conclude that the wristwatch was worth twice as much as the pocket watch and that the 1970s watch was worthless (selling price = $0.00). The latter two conclusions are possible because money price represents a ratio scale.

Temperature can also be captured by a ratio scale. The Kelvin scale begins at 0 K, corresponding to −273.2° on the Celsius scale (an interval scale). This temperature is known as absolute zero. Zero K is the point at which the kinetic energy of atoms in a water molecule approaches 0, meaning that they are moving as slowly as possible. This is as cold as water can get since there is no way of slowing the molecules further (they never completely stop). Thus, 0 K indeed has absolute meaning.

When a manager assigns a performance commission based directly on the amount of sales produced, the bonus is based on a ratio scale. Zero has an absolute meaning, particularly if you are the one without a bonus! Griff could decide to use a ratio sales measure to rank performance for the CRM division. This would be valid only if performance was truly equal to sales.

ratio scales

Represent the highest form of measurement in that they have all the properties of interval scales with the additional attribute of representing absolute quantities; characterized by a meaningful absolute zero.

Mathematical and Statistical Analysis of Scales

While it is true that mathematical operations can be performed with numbers from nominal scales, the result may not have a great deal of meaning. For instance, a school district may perform mathematical operations on the nominal school bus numbers. With this, they may find that the average school bus number is 77.7 with a standard deviation of 20.5. Will this help them use the buses

Football Follies

The subject of whether or not certain mathematical properties can be conducted with certain types of scales has been debated in the social science literature for decades. One famous statistician used a funny parable about a football folly to make a point about this very well. The story goes something like this:

A football coach purchased a vending machine that would assign numbers (0 to 99) to the school's football players randomly. Over the years, then, all numbers should be equally used. By randomly assigning the numbers in this way, no players were treated unequally because no one could choose one of their favorite numbers. Everybody simply got the number the machine spit out.

Professor Aaron Urd, naturally curious about anything having to do with numbers, became suspicious that the football players had secretly been breaking into the machine to select more preferred numbers. Professor Urd believed that football had no place in college and would have loved to show how unscrupulous the football players really were—stealing numbers no less! However, Professor Urd had a problem. Football numbers are nominal numbers; all they do is identify! Therefore, as all good statisticians know, you cannot compute averages with nominal numbers. In fact, all you can do is count nominal numbers. This problem tormented Professor Urd for years. He desperately wanted to test his hypothesis about the football number theft. Many times he entered the football numbers into a spreadsheet but could not bring himself to add, multiply, or divide them. It just wouldn't be right!

One fall, Aleck Smart, a star defensive tackle on the football team, wrote a term paper for Professor Aaron Urd entitled "A Statistical Treatment of the Football Team Numbering System." Aleck, not being the brightest student, missed the day when Professor Urd taught students that you could not do arithmetic with nominal numbers. So, Aleck Smart computed all manner of statistics with data consisting of the last ten years of football numbers worn by the team. Among these, he showed that the average football number over those years was 40.1. Professor Aaron Urd was conflicted with this result. How can this be? If the numbers were assigned randomly, then shouldn't the average be 50? This must confirm his suspicion about the football number theft. But even to think this troubled him because it meant his brain was unintentionally computing the average of nominal numbers!

A few days later, Aleck dropped by Professor Aaron Urd's office to pick up his paper (after office hours of course). Professor Urd lit into Aleck: "I have given you a failing grade, Mr. Smart. Numbers from football jerseys are nominal numbers! Don't you know that you cannot take the average of nominal numbers?"

Aleck thought about that a while and answered, "Professor Urd, the numbers don't know where they came from."

Professor Urd decided to change Aleck's grade to a B–. He then used Aleck's calculations to try and show the faculty senate that the football team was indeed breaking into the machine.

Sources: Lord, F. M., "On the Statistical Treatment of Football Numbers," *American Psychologist*, 8 (1953), 750–751; Cohen, Jacob, "Things I Have Learned (So Far),"
American Psychologist, 45 (December 1990), 1304–1312.

© DAVE KAUP/CORBIS

© GEORGE DOYLE & CIARAN GRIFFIN

discrete measures

Measures that take on only one of a finite number of values.

more efficiently or better assign bus routes? Probably not. Thus, although you can put numbers into formulas and perform calculations with almost any numbers, the researcher has to know the meaning behind the numbers before useful conclusions can be drawn.[5] The Research Snapshot just above illustrates this point further.

■ DISCRETE MEASURES

Discrete measures are those that take on only one of a finite number of values. A discrete scale is most often used to represent a classificatory variable. Therefore, discrete scales do not represent intensity of measures, only membership. Common discrete scales include any yes-or-no response, matching, color choices, or practically any scale that involves selecting from among a small number of categories. Thus, when someone is asked to choose from the following responses

- Disagree
- Neutral
- Agree

the result is a discrete value that can be coded 1, 2, or 3, respectively. This is also an ordinal scale to the extent that it represents an ordered arrangement of agreement. Nominal and ordinal scales are discrete measures.

Certain statistics are most appropriate for discrete measures. Exhibit 13.5 shows statistics for each scale level. The largest distinction is between statistics used for discrete versus continuous measures. For instance, the central tendency of discrete measures is best captured by the mode.

When a student wants to know what the most likely grade is for MKTG4311, the mode will be very useful. Observe the results below from the previous semester:

A	5 Students	D	6 Students
B	20 Students	F	6 Students
C	12 Students		

The mode is a "B" since more students obtained that value than any other value. Therefore, the "average" student would expect a B in MKTG4311.

■ CONTINUOUS MEASURES

Continuous measures are those assigning values anywhere along some scale range in a place that corresponds to the intensity of some concept. Ratio measures are continuous measures. Thus, when we measure sales for each salesperson using the dollar amount sold, we are assigning continuous measures. A number line could be constructed ranging from the least amount sold to the most and a spot on the line would correspond exactly to a salesperson's performance.

Strictly speaking, interval scales are not necessarily continuous. Consider the following common type of survey question:

continuous measures

Measures that reflect the intensity of a concept by assigning values that can take on any value along some scale range.

	Strongly Disagree	Disagree	Neutral	Agree	Strongly Agree
I enjoy participating in online auctions	1	2	3	4	5

This is a discrete scale because only the values 1, 2, 3, 4, or 5 can be assigned. Furthermore, it is an ordinal scale because it only orders based on agreement. We really have no way of knowing that the difference in agreement somebody marking a 5 and somebody marking a 4 is the same as the difference in agreement between somebody marking a 2 and somebody marking 1. The scale difference is 1 in either case but is the difference in true agreement the same? There is no way to know. Therefore, the mean is not an appropriate way of stating central tendency, and we really shouldn't use many common statistics on these responses.

However, as a scaled response of this type takes on more values, the error introduced by assuming that the differences between the discrete points are equal becomes smaller. This may be seen by imagining a *Likert scale* with a thousand levels of agreement rather than three or four. The differences between the different levels become so small with a thousand levels that only tiny errors could be introduced by assuming each interval is the same. Therefore, marketing researchers generally treat interval scales containing five or more categories of response as interval. When fewer than five categories are used, this assumption is inappropriate. So, interval scales are treated as continuous when five or more categories are used.

The researcher should keep in mind, however, the distinction between ratio and interval measures. Errors in judgment can be made when interval measures are treated as ratio. For example, attitude is usually measured with an interval scale. An attitude of zero means nothing. In fact, attitude would only have meaning in a relative sense. Therefore, attitude takes on meaning when one person's response is compared to another or through some other comparison.

The mean and standard deviation may be calculated from continuous data. Using the actual quantities for arithmetic operations is permissible with ratio scales. Thus, the ratios of scale values are meaningful. A ratio scale has all the properties of nominal, ordinal, and interval scales. However, the same cannot be said in reverse. An ordinal scale, for example, has nominal properties, but it does not have interval or ratio properties (see Exhibit 13.5).

Chapters 19 through 23 further explore the limitations scales impose on the mathematical analysis of data.

Index Measures

Earlier, we distinguished constructs as concepts that require multiple variables to measure them adequately. Looking back to the chapter vignette, could it be that multiple items will be required to adequately represent job performance? Likewise, a consumer's attitude toward some product is usually a function of multiple attributes. An **attribute** is a single characteristic or fundamental feature of an object, person, situation, or issue.

attribute
A single characteristic or fundamental feature of an object, person, situation, or issue.

Indexes and Composites

Multi-item instruments for measuring a construct are either called *index measures* or *composite measures*. An **index measure** assigns a value based on how characteristic an observation is of the thing being measured. Indexes often are formed by putting several variables together. For example, a social class index is based on three weighted variables: income, occupation, and education. Usually, occupation is seen as the single best indicator and would be weighted highest. Someone with a highly prestigious occupation and a graduate degree but without a great income would be more characteristic of high social class than someone with a high income but lacking formal education and a prestigious occupation.

index measure
An index assigns a value based on how much of the concept being measured is associated with an observation. Indexes often are formed by putting several variables together.

With an index, the different attributes may not be strongly correlated with each other. A person's income does not always relate strongly to their education. The American Consumer Satisfaction Index shows how satisfied American consumers are based on an index of satisfaction scores. Readers are likely not surprised to know that Americans appear more satisfied with soft drinks than they are with cable TV companies based on this index.[6]

composite measures
Assign a value to an observation based on a mathematical derivation of multiple variables.

Composite measures also assign a value based on a mathematical derivation of multiple variables. For example, restaurant satisfaction may be measured by combining questions such as "How satisfied are you with your restaurant experience today? How pleased are you with your visit to our restaurant? How satisfied are you with the overall service quality provided today?" For most practical applications, composite measures and indexes are computed in the same way.[7] However, composite measures are distinguished from index measures in that the composite's indicators should be both theoretically and statistically related to each other. In the customer satisfaction items listed above, one can hardly imagine that respondents would say they were highly satisfied and then provide a low score for how pleased they felt. That simply wouldn't make a lot of sense. Likewise, they should show correlation.

Computing Scale Values

Exhibit 13.6 demonstrates how a composite measure can be created from common rating scales. This particular scale can be used to assess how much a consumer trusts a Web site.[8] This particular composite represents a **summated scale**. A summated scale is created by simply summing the response to each item making up the composite measure. In this case, the consumer would have a trust score of 13 based on responses to five items. A researcher may sometimes choose to average the scores rather than summing them. The advantage to this is that the composite measure is expressed on the same scale as are the items that make it up. So, instead of a 13, the consumer would have a score of 2.6. The information content is the same.

summated scale
A scale created by simply summing (adding together) the response to each item making up the composite measure. The scores can be but do not have to be averaged by the number of items making up the composite scale.

Sometimes, a response may need to be reverse-coded before computing a summated or averaged scale value. **Reverse coding** means that the value assigned for a response is treated oppositely from the other items. If a sixth item was included on the trust scale that said, "I do not trust this Web site," reverse coding would be necessary to make sure the composite made sense. The content of this item is the reverse of trust (distrust), so the scale itself should be reversed. Thus, on a 5-point scale, the values are reversed as follows:

reverse coding
Means that the value assigned for a response is treated oppositely from the other items.

- 5 becomes 1
- 4 becomes 2
- 3 stays 3

Recoding Made Easy

Most computer statistical software makes scale recoding easy. The screenshot shown here is from SPSS, perhaps the most widely used statistical software in business-related research. All that needs to be done to reverse-code a scale is to go through the right click-through sequence. In this case, the following steps would be followed:

1. Click on transform.
2. Click on recode.
3. Choose to recode into the same variable.
4. Select the variable(s) to be recoded.
5. Click on old and new values.
6. Use the menu that appears to enter the old values and the matching new values. Click add after entering each pair.
7. Click continue.

This would successfully recode variable X13 in this case.

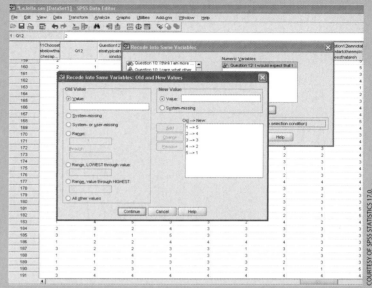

- 2 becomes 4
- 1 becomes 5

Therefore, if the same consumer described in Exhibit 13.6 responded to this new item with a 5, it would be reverse coded as a 1 before computing the summated scale. Thus, the summated scale value would become 14. The Research Snapshot above shows how a recode can be carried out using SPSS.

EXHIBIT 13.6

Computing a Composite Scale

Item	Strongly Disagree (SD) → Strongly Agree (SA)				
This site appears to be more trustworthy than other sites I have visited.	SD	(D)	N	A	SA
My overall trust in this site is very high.	SD	D	(N)	A	SA
My overall impression of the believability of the information on this site is very high.	SD	(D)	N	A	SA
My overall confidence in the recommendations on this site is very high.	SD	(D)	N	A	SA
The company represented in this site delivers on its promises.	SD	D	N	(A)	SA

Computation:
Scale Values: SD = 1, D = 2, N = 3, A = 4, SA = 5

Thus, the Trust score for this consumer is
2 + 3 + 2 + 2 + 4 = 13

333

Three Criteria for Good Measurement

The three major criteria for evaluating measurements are reliability, validity, and sensitivity.

Reliability

Reliability is an indicator of a measure's internal consistency. Consistency is the key to understanding reliability. A measure is reliable when different attempts at measuring something converge on the same result. If a professor's marketing research tests are reliable, a student should tend toward consistent scores on all tests. In other words, a student that makes an 80 on the first test should make scores close to 80 on all subsequent tests. Another way to look at this is that the student who makes the best score on one test will exhibit scores close to the best score in the class on the other tests. If it is difficult to predict what students would make on a test by examining their previous test scores, the tests probably lack reliability. When a measuring process provides reproducible results, the measuring instrument is reliable.

■ INTERNAL CONSISTENCY

Internal consistency is a term used by researchers to represent a measure's homogeneity. An attempt to measure trust may require asking several similar but not identical questions, as shown above. The set of items that make up a measure are referred to as a *battery* of scale items. *Internal consistency* of a multiple-item measure can be measured by correlating scores on subsets of items making up a scale.

The **split-half method** of checking reliability is performed by taking half the items from a scale (for example, odd-numbered items) and checking them against the results from the other half (even-numbered items). The two scale *halves* should correlate highly. They should also produce similar scores. However, multiple techniques exist for estimating scale reliability.

Coefficient alpha (α) is the most commonly applied estimate of a composite scale's reliability.[9] Coefficient α estimates internal consistency by computing the average of all possible split-half reliabilities for a multiple-item scale. The coefficient demonstrates whether or not the different items converge. Although coefficient α does not address validity, many researchers use α as the sole indicator of a scale's quality largely because it is simply and readily computed by statistical programs like SPSS. Coefficient α can only take on values ranging from 0, meaning no consistency among items (they are all statistically independent), to 1, meaning complete consistency (all items yield perfect correlation with each other).

Generally speaking, scales exhibiting a coefficient α between 0.80 and 0.96 are considered to have very good reliability. Scales with a coefficient α between 0.70 and 0.80 are considered to have good reliability, and an α value between 0.60 and 0.70 indicates fair reliability. When the coefficient α is below 0.60, the scale has poor reliability.[10] Researchers generally report coefficient α for each composite measure involved in a study.

■ TEST-RETEST RELIABILITY

The **test-retest method** of determining reliability involves administering the same scale or measure to the same respondents at two separate times to test for stability. If the measure is stable over time, the test, administered under the same conditions each time, should obtain similar results. Test-retest reliability represents a measure's repeatability.

Suppose a researcher at one time attempts to measure buying intentions and finds that 12 percent of the population is willing to purchase a product. If the study is repeated a few weeks later under similar conditions, and the researcher again finds that 12 percent of the population is willing to purchase the product, the measure appears to be reliable. High stability correlation or consistency between two measures at time 1 and time 2 indicates high reliability.

Assume that a person does not change his or her attitude about dark beer. Attitude might be measured with an item like the one shown below:

I prefer dark beer to all other types of beer.

If repeated measurements of that individual's attitude toward dark beer are taken with the same scale, a reliable instrument will produce the same results each time the scale is measured. Thus one's attitude in March 2009 should tend to be the same as one's attitude in October 2009 or May 2010. When a measuring instrument produces unpredictable results from one testing to the next, the results are said to be unreliable because of error in measurement.

As another example, consider these remarks by a Gillette executive made about the reliability problems in measuring reactions to razor blades:

> There is a high degree of noise in our data, a considerable variability in results. It's a big mish-mash, what we call the night sky in August. There are points all over the place. A man will give a blade a high score one day, but the next day he'll cut himself a lot and give the blade a terrible score. But on the third day, he'll give the same blade a good score. What you have to do is try to see some pattern in all this. There are some gaps in our knowledge.[11]

Measures of test-retest reliability pose two problems that are common to all longitudinal studies. First, the pre-measure, or first measure, may sensitize the respondents to their participation in a research project and subsequently influence the results of the second measure. Furthermore, if the time between measures is long, there may be an attitude change or other maturation of the subjects. Thus, a reliable measure can indicate a low or a moderate correlation between the first and second administration, but this low correlation may be due to an attitude change over time rather than to a lack of reliability.

Reliability is a necessary but not sufficient condition for validity. A reliable scale may not be valid. For example, a purchase intention measurement technique may consistently indicate that 20 percent of those sampled are willing to purchase a new product. Whether the measure is valid depends on whether 20 percent of the population indeed purchases the product. A reliable but invalid instrument will yield consistently inaccurate results. Perhaps you've come across results from polls or other research in the media that appear reliable but inaccurate in this manner?

Reliability

Scale: Positive Feelings

Case Processing Summary

		N	%
Cases	Valid	457	100.0
	Excluded[a]	0	.0
	Total	457	100.0

a. Listwise deletion based on all variables in the procedure.

Reliability Statistics

Cronbach's Alpha	N of Items
.960	5

Item-Total Statistics

	Scale Mean if Item Deleted	Scale Variance if Item Deleted	Corrected Item-Total Correlation	Cronbach's Alpha if Item Deleted
Excited...	14.58	51.459	.859	.955
Happy	14.16	51.611	.886	.950
Interested	14.04	50.138	.891	.949
Pleased	14.29	51.352	.910	.946
Satisfied	14.30	51.603	.886	.950

Here are some results from using a software package to estimate coefficient α for a 5-item scale measuring the positive feelings shoppers had during a shopping trip. The results show a value of 0.96 for the scale. Also, the item-total statistics indicate that all the items correlate highly with the scale. Overall, these are positive results.

Validity ⬅

Good measures should be both precise and accurate. Reliability represents how precise a measure is in that the different attempts at measuring the same thing converge on the same point. Accuracy deals more with how a measure assesses the intended concept. **Validity** is the accuracy of a measure or the extent to which a score truthfully represents a concept.

Achieving validity is not a simple matter. The opening vignette describes this point. The job performance measure should truly reflect job performance. If a supervisor's friendship affects the performance measure, then the scale's validity is diminished. Likewise, if the performance scale is defined as effort, the result may well be a reliable scale but not one that maximizes validity. Effort may well lead to performance but effort probably does not equal performance.

Another example of a validity question might involve a media researcher who wonders what it means when respondents indicate they have been *exposed* to a magazine. The researcher wants to know if the measure is valid. The question of validity expresses the researcher's concern with accurate measurement. Validity addresses the problem of whether a measure (for example, an attitude measure used in marketing) indeed measures what it is supposed to measure. When a measure lacks validity, any conclusions based on that measure are also likely to be faulty.

Students should be able to empathize with the following validity problem. Consider the controversy about highway patrol officers using radar guns to clock speeders. A driver is clocked

validity

The accuracy of a measure or the extent to which a score truthfully represents a concept.

© BRAND X PICTURES/JUPITER IMAGES

at 75 mph in a 55 mph zone, but the same radar gun aimed at a house registers 28 mph. The error occurred because the radar gun had picked up impulses from the electrical system of the squad car's idling engine. The house was probably not speeding—and the radar gun was probably not completely valid.

■ ESTABLISHING VALIDITY

Researchers have attempted to assess validity in many ways. They attempt to provide some evidence of a measure's degree of validity by answering a variety of questions. Is there a consensus among my colleagues that my attitude scale measures what it is supposed to measure? Does my measure correlate with other measures of the same concept? Does the behavior expected from my measure predict actual observed behavior? The three basic approaches to establishing validity are *face* or *content validity, criterion validity,* and *construct validity.*

A golfer may hit reliable but not valid putts and thus tend to miss them in some repeated fashion. This golfer's putts tend to converge to the left of—rather than in—the hole!

face (content) validity
A scale's content logically appears to reflect what was intended to be measured.

criterion validity
The ability of a measure to correlate with other standard measures of similar constructs or established criteria.

Face (content) validity refers to the subjective agreement among professionals that a scale logically reflects the concept being measured. Simply, do the test items make sense given a concept's definition? When an inspection of the test items convinces experts that the items match the definition, the scale is said to have face validity.

Clear, understandable questions such as "How many children do you have?" generally are agreed to have face validity. In scientific studies, however, researchers generally prefer stronger evidence because of the elusive nature of attitudes and other marketing phenomena. For example, the ACNielsen television rating system is based on the PeopleMeter system, which mechanically records whether a sample household's television is turned on and records the channel selection. If one of the viewers leaves the room or falls asleep, the measure is not a valid measure of audience.

Criterion validity addresses the question, "Does my measure correlate with measures of the similar concepts or known quantities?" Criterion validity may be classified as either *concurrent validity* or *predictive validity* depending on the time sequence in which the new measurement scale and the criterion measure are correlated. If the new measure is taken at the same time as the criterion measure and is shown to be valid, then it has concurrent validity. Predictive validity is established when a new measure predicts a future event. The two measures differ only on the basis of a time dimension—that is, the criterion measure is separated in time from the predictor measure.

A practical example of predictive validity is illustrated by a commercial research firm's test of the relationship between a rough commercial's effectiveness (as determined, for example, by recall scores) and a finished commercial's effectiveness (also by recall scores). Ad agencies often test animatic rough, photomatic rough, or live-action rough commercials before developing actual finished commercials. One marketing research consulting firm suggests that this testing has high predictive validity. Rough commercial recall scores provide correct estimates of the final finished commercial recall scores more than 80 percent of the time.[12] While face (content) validity is a subjective evaluation, criterion validity provides a more rigorous empirical test.

Construct validity exists when a measure reliably measures and truthfully represents a unique concept. Construct validity consists of several components, including:

- Face or content validity
- Convergent validity
- Criterion or validity
- Discriminant validity

Convergent validity is another way of expressing internal consistency. Highly reliable scales contain convergent validity. Criterion validity and face validity were discussed in the preceding paragraphs. **Discriminant validity** represents how unique or distinct is a measure. A scale should not correlate too highly with a measure of a different construct. For example, a customer satisfaction measure should not correlate too highly with a cognitive dissonance scale if the two concepts are truly different. As a rough rule of thumb, when two scales are correlated above 0.75, discriminant validity may be an issue. Multivariate procedures like factor analysis can be useful in establishing construct validity. The reader is referred to other sources for a more detailed discussion.[13]

Reliability versus Validity

The differences between reliability and validity can be illustrated by the rifle targets in Exhibit 13.7. Suppose someone fires an equal number of rounds with a century-old rifle and a modern rifle.[14] The shots from the older gun are considerably scattered, but those from the newer gun are closely clustered. The variability of the old rifle compared with that of the new one indicates it is less reliable. The target on the right illustrates the concept of a systematic bias influencing validity. The shots fired with the new rifle are reliable because they show little variance. However, because the person firing the gun is not very good at it, they all miss the target in much the same way. The shots are reliable, but not valid. Only if they were reliable and valid would it be a good idea to test by having him shoot an apple off your head!

Sensitivity

The sensitivity of a scale is an important measurement concept, particularly when *changes* in attitudes or other hypothetical constructs are under investigation. **Sensitivity** refers to an instrument's ability to accurately measure variability in a concept. A dichotomous response category, such as "agree or disagree," does not allow the recording of subtle attitude changes. A more sensitive measure with numerous categories on the scale may be needed. For example, adding "strongly agree," "mildly agree," "neither agree nor disagree," "mildly disagree," and "strongly disagree" will increase the scale's sensitivity.

The sensitivity of a scale based on a single question or single item can also be increased by adding questions or items. In other words, because composite measures allow for a greater range of possible scores, they are more sensitive than single-item scales. Thus, sensitivity is generally increased by adding more response points or adding scale items.

construct validity

Exists when a measure reliably measures and truthfully represents a unique concept; consists of several components including face validity, convergent validity, criterion validity, and discriminant validity.

convergent validity

Another way of expressing internal consistency; highly reliable scales contain convergent validity.

discriminant validity

Represents how unique or distinct is a measure; a scale should not correlate too highly with a measure of a different construct.

sensitivity

A measurement instrument's ability to accurately measure variability in stimuli or responses.

EXHIBIT 13.7
Reliability and Validity on Target

Old Rifle
Low Reliability
(Target A)

New Rifle
High Reliability
(Target B)

New Rifle—Bad Shot
Reliable but not Valid
(Target C)

- Good research cannot be done without good measurement. This means the measures must be valid. Take extra care in selecting and designing measures. Double- and triple-check face validity to make sure the scale items match the concept definition. An invalid scale is useless at best and dangerous at worst.
- Well-stated hypotheses are extremely useful in designing a research project. Each hypothesis reveals the concepts that have to be measured during the research project.
- In some ways that will be covered later, nominal and ordinal measures are easier to deal with as independent rather than dependent variables. Put another way, continuous variables are easier to deal with as dependent variables than are non-continuous measures.

- Coefficient α provides an estimate of scale reliability. It is only applicable to multiple item scales—particularly those with three or more items to be formed into a composite. The following guide can be used in judging the results from estimating coefficient α.
  - Above 0.8, very good reliability
    - Scale can be used as is from a reliability standpoint.
  - From 0.7 to 0.79, good reliability
    - Scale can be used as is from a reliability standpoint.
  - From 0.6 to 0.69, fair reliability
    - Scale can be used as is with caution.
    - Below 0.6, further refinement or modifications to the scale must be made before using.

Summary

1. Determine what needs to be measured based on a research question or hypothesis. Researchers can determine what concepts must be measured by examining research questions and hypotheses. A hypothesis often states that one concept is related to another or that differences in some outcome concept will be observed across different groups. Therefore, the concepts listed in the hypotheses must have operational measures if the research testing them is to be performed.

2. Distinguish levels of scale measurement. Four levels of scale measurement can be identified. Each level is associated with increasingly more complex properties. Nominal scales assign numbers or letters to objects for identification or classification. Ordinal scales arrange objects based on relative magnitude of a concept. Thus, ordinal scales represent rankings. Interval scales also represent an ordering based on relative amounts of a concept, but they also capture the differences between scale values. Thus, interval scales allow stimuli to be compared to each other based on the difference in their scale scores. Ratio scales are absolute scales, starting with absolute zeros at which there is a total absence of the attribute. Nominal and ordinal scales are discrete. The mode is the best way to represent central tendency for discrete measures. Ratio measures are continuous and interval scales are generally treated as continuous. For continuous measures, the mean represents a valid representation of central tendency.

3. Know how to form an index or composite measure. Indexes and composite measures are formed by combining scores from multiple items. For instance, a composite score can be formed by adding the scores to multiple scale items, each intended to represent the same concept. Index scores and composite measures scores are often obtained in much the same way. However, they differ theoretically in that index scores do not have to be theoretically or statistically related to one another.

4. List the three criteria for good measurement. Good measurement exists when a measure is reliable, valid, and sensitive. Thus, reliability, validity, and sensitivity are characteristics of good measurement. Reliability represents the consistency and repeatability of a measure. Validity refers to the degree to which the instrument measures the concept the researcher wants to measure. Sensitivity is the instrument's ability to accurately measure variability in stimuli or responses.

5. Perform a basic assessment of scale reliability and validity. Reliability is most often assessed using coefficient α. Coefficient α should be at least above 0.6 for a scale to be considered as acceptably reliable. Validity is assessed in components. A measure that has adequate construct validity is one that is likely to be well measured. Construct validity consists of face or content validity, convergent validity (internal consistency), discriminant validity, and criterion validity. Statistical procedures like factor analysis can be helpful in providing evidence of construct validity.

Key Terms and Concepts

Questions for Review and Critical Thinking

1. Define *measurement*. How is your performance in a marketing research class being measured?
2. What is the difference between a *concept* and a *construct*? In what ways is the definition of the term *variable* similar or different?
3. Suppose a researcher takes over a project only after a proposal has been written by another researcher. The project needs to be implemented very quickly. Where will the researcher quickly find the things that need to be measured during the study?
4. Consider the following research questions or hypotheses. What variables need to be measured in each?
   a. What are the characteristics of consumers who belong to the frequent shopper segment of GameStop (video games and accessories) stores?
   b. The temperature inside the market will determine how much time that shoppers spend in the store such that when the store is cold they will spend less time shopping than when the store is warm.
   c. The more times a consumer is exposed to an advertisement the more product features they will be able to recall.
   d. Product price is positively related to product quality.
5. An official in the financial office is considering an applicant for financial aid. The officer uses the following process. If the student has a GPA in the 90th percentile among the admission group, 5 points are added. If the student has an ACT or SAT score in the 90th percentile among the admission group, 5 points are added. If the student comes from a family whose cumulative household income was less than $70,000/year for the last 3 years, 8 points are added. If the student is from out of state, 5 points are added. What variables are being used to determine eligibility for this financial aid? What would your approximate score be on this scale? Is it best described as an index or a composite scale? Explain your response.
6. Describe the four different levels of scale measurement.
7. Consider the different grading measuring scales described at the beginning of the chapter. Describe what level of measurement is represented by each. Which method do you think contains the least opportunity for error?
8. Look at the responses to the following survey items that describe how stressful consumers believed a Christmas shopping trip was using a ten-point scale ranging from 1 (= no stress at all) to 10 (= extremely stressful):
   a. How stressful was finding a place to park? _9_
   b. How stressful was the checkout procedure? _5_
   c. How stressful was trying to find exactly the right product? _4_
   d. How stressful was finding a store employee? _6_
      i. What would be the stress score for this respondent based on a summated scale score?
      ii. What would be the stress score for this respondent based on an average composite scale score?
      iii. Do any items need to be reverse-coded? Why or why not?
      iv. How could the concept of split-half reliability be applied using a sample of 100 respondents who gave answers to these four questions?
9. How is it that marketing researchers can justify treating a seven-point Likert scale as interval?
10. What are the components of construct validity? Describe each.
11. Why might a researcher wish to use more than one question to measure satisfaction with a particular aspect of retail shopping?
12. How can a researcher assess the reliability and validity of a multi-item composite scale?
13. Comment on the validity and reliability of the following:
   a. A respondent's report of an intention to subscribe to *Consumer Reports* is highly reliable. A researcher believes this constitutes a valid measurement of dissatisfaction with the economic system and alienation from big business.
   b. A general-interest magazine claimed that it was a better advertising medium than television programs with similar content. Research had indicated that for a soft drink and other test products, recall scores were higher for the magazine ads than for thirty-second commercials.
   c. A respondent's report of frequency of magazine reading consistently indicates that she regularly reads *Good Housekeeping* and *Gourmet* and never reads *Cosmopolitan*.
14. Indicate whether the following measures use a nominal, ordinal, interval, or ratio scale:
   a. Prices on the stock market
   b. Marital status, classified as "married" or "never married"
   c. Whether a respondent has ever been unemployed
   d. Professorial rank: assistant professor, associate professor, or professor
   e. Course grades: A, B, C, D, or F
   f. Blood-alcohol content
   g. The color of one's eyes
   h. The size of one's pupils

Research Activities

1. **'NET** As well as possible, find out and describe how *Sales and Marketing Management* magazine constructs its buying-power index.

2. Define each of the following concepts, and then operationally define each one by providing correspondence rules between the definition and the scale:
   a. A good bowler
   b. The television audience for *The Tonight Show*
   c. Purchasing intention for a palm-sized computer
   d. Consumer involvement with cars
   e. A workaholic
   f. Fast-food restaurant
   g. The American Dream

3. **'NET** Use the ACSI scores found at http://www.theacsi.org to respond to this question. Using the most recent two years of data, test the following two hypotheses:

   a. American consumers are more satisfied with breweries than they are with wireless telephone services.
   b. **'NET** American consumers are more satisfied with discount and department stores than they are with automobile companies.

4. Refer back to the opening vignette. Use library/Internet sources to search for news stories or research papers dealing with job performance. In particular, pay attention to stories that may be related to CRM. Make a recommendation to Griff concerning a way that job performance should be measured. Would your scale be nominal, ordinal, interval, or ratio?

5. **'NET/ETHICS** Go to http://www.queendom.com/tests. Click on the lists of personality tests. Take the hostility test. Do you think this is a reliable and valid measure of how prone someone is to generally act in a hostile manner? Would it be ethical to assign prospective employees a hostility score to be used in a hiring index based on results from this or a similar test?

Case 13.1 FlyAway Airways

© GETTY IMAGES/
PHOTODISC GREEN

Wesley Shocker, research analyst for FlyAway Airways, was asked by the director of research to make recommendations regarding the best approach for monitoring the quality of service provided by the airline.[15] FlyAway Airways is a national air carrier that has a comprehensive route structure consisting of long-haul, coast-to-coast routes and direct, nonstop routes between short-haul metropolitan areas. Current competitors include Midway and Alaska Airlines. FlyAway Airlines is poised to surpass the billion-dollar revenue level required to be designated as a major airline. This change in status brings a new set of competitors. To prepare for this move up in competitive status, Shocker was asked to review the options available for monitoring the quality of FlyAway Airways service and the service of its competitors. Such monitoring would involve better understanding the nature of service quality and the ways in which quality can be tracked for airlines.

After some investigation, Shocker discovered two basic approaches to measuring quality of airline service that can produce similar ranking results. His report must outline the important aspects to consider in measuring quality as well as the critical points of difference and similarity between the two approaches to measuring quality.

Some Background on Quality

In today's competitive airline industry, it's crucial that an airline do all it can do to attract and retain customers. One of the best ways to do this is by offering quality service to consumers. Perceptions of service quality vary from person to person, but an enduring element of service quality is the consistent achievement of customer satisfaction. For customers to perceive an airline as offering quality service, they must be satisfied, and that usually means receiving a service outcome that is equal to or greater than what they expected.

An airline consumer usually is concerned most with issues of schedule, destination, and price when choosing an airline. Given that most airlines have competition in each of these areas, other factors that relate to quality become important to the customer when making a choice between airlines. Both subjective aspects of quality (that is, food, pleasant employees, and so forth) and objective aspects

(that is, on-time performance, safety, lost baggage, and so forth) have real meaning to consumers. These secondary factors may not be as critical as schedule, destination, and price, but they do affect quality judgments of the customer.

There are many possible combinations of subjective and objective aspects that could influence a customer's perception of quality at different times. Fortunately, since 1988, consumers of airline services have had access to objective information from the Department of Transportation regarding service performance in some basic categories. Unfortunately, the average consumer is most likely unaware of or uninterested in these data on performance; instead, consumers rely on personal experience and subjective opinion to judge quality of service. Periodic surveys of subjective consumer opinion regarding airline service experience are available through several sources. These efforts rely on contact with a sample of consumers who may or may not have informed opinions regarding the quality of airline service for all airlines being compared.

A Consumer Survey Approach

In his research, Shocker discovered a recent study conducted to identify favorite airlines of frequent fliers. This study is typical of the survey-based, infrequent (usually only annually), subjective efforts conducted to assess airline quality. A New York firm, Research & Forecasts, Inc., published results of a consumer survey of frequent fliers that used several criteria to rate domestic and international airlines. Criteria included comfort, service, reliability, food quality, cost, delays, routes served, safety, and frequent-flier plans. The questionnaire was sent to 25,000 frequent fliers.

The 4,462 people who responded were characterized as predominantly male (59 percent) professional managers (66 percent) whose average age was 45 and who traveled an average of at least 43 nights a year for both business and pleasure. This group indicated that the most important factors in choosing an airline were 1) route structure (46 percent), 2) price (42 percent), 3) reliability (41 percent), 4) service (33 percent), 5) safety (33 percent), 6) frequent-flier plans (33 percent), and 7) food (12 percent). When asked to rate twenty different airlines, respondents provided the rankings in Case Exhibit 13.1–1.

CASE EXHIBIT 13.1–1 Ranking of Major Airlines: Consumer Survey Approach

1. American	11. Lufthansa
2. United	12. USAir
3. Delta	13. KLM
4. TWA	14. America West
5. SwissAir	15. JAL
6. Singapore	16. Alaska
7. British Airways	17. Qantas
8. Continental	18. Midway
9. Air France	19. Southwest
10. Pan Am	20. SAS

A Weighted Average Approach

Shocker also discovered a newer, more objective approach to measuring airline quality in a study recently published by the National Institute for Aviation Research at the Wichita State University in Wichita, Kansas. The Airline Quality Rating (AQR) is a weighted average of nineteen factors that have relevance when judging the quality of airline services (see Case Exhibit 13.1–2). The AQR is based on data that are readily obtainable (most of the data are updated monthly) from published sources for each major airline operating in the United States. Regularly published data on such factors as consumer complaints, on-time performance, accidents, number of aircraft, and financial performance are available from the

CASE EXHIBIT 13.1–2 Factors Included in the Airline Quality Rating (AQR)[a]

Factor	Weight
1. Average age of fleet	−5.85
2. Number of aircraft	+4.54
3. On-time performance	+8.63
4. Load factor	−6.98
5. Pilot deviations	−8.03
6. Number of accidents	−8.38
7. Frequent-flier awards	−7.35
8. Flight problems[b]	−8.05
9. Denied boardings[b]	−8.03
10. Mishandled baggage[b]	−7.92
11. Fares[b]	−7.60
12. Customer service[b]	−7.20
13. Refunds	−7.32
14. Ticketing/boarding[b]	−7.08
15. Advertising[b]	−6.82
16. Credit[b]	−5.94
17. Other[b]	−7.34
18. Financial stability	−6.52
19. Average seat-mile cost	−4.49

$$AQR = \frac{w_1F_1 - w_2F_2 + w_3F_3 + \cdots - w_{19}F_{19}}{w_1 + w_2 + w_3 + \cdots + w_{19}}$$

a. The 19-item rating has a reliability coefficient (Cronbach's Alpha) of 0.87.
b. Data for these factors come from consumer complaints registered with the Department of Transportation.

Department of Transportation, the National Transportation Safety Board, Moody's Bond Record, industry trade publications, and annual reports of individual airlines.

To establish the nineteen weighted factors, an opinion survey was conducted with a group of 65 experts in the aviation field. These experts included representatives of most major airlines, air travel experts, Federal Aviation Administration (FAA) representatives, academic researchers, airline manufacturing and support firms, and individual consumers. Each expert was asked to rate the importance that each individual factor might have to a consumer of airline services using a scale of 0 (no importance) to 10 (great importance). The average importance ratings for each of the nineteen factors were then used as the weights for those factors in the AQR. Case Exhibit 13.1-2 shows the factors included in the Airline Quality Rating, the weight associated with each factor, and whether the factor has a positive or negative impact on quality from the consumer's perspective.

Using the Airline Quality Rating formula and recent data, produce AQR scores and rankings for the 10 major U.S. airlines shown in Case Exhibit 13.1–3.

CASE EXHIBIT 13.1–3 Airline Rankings

Rank	Airline	AQR Score
1	American	+0.328
2	Southwest	+0.254
3	Delta	+0.209
4	United	+0.119
5	USAir	+0.054
6	Pan Am	+0.003
7	Northwest	−0.063
8	Continental	−0.346
9	America West	−0.377
10	TWA	−0.439

What Course to Chart?

Shocker has discovered what appear to be two different approaches to measuring quality of airlines. One relies on direct consumer opinion and is mostly subjective in its approach to quality and the elements considered. The other relies on performance data that are available through public sources and appear to be more objective. Both approaches incorporate pertinent elements that could be used by consumers to judge the quality of an airline. Shocker's recommendation must consider the comprehensiveness and usefulness of these approaches for FlyAway Airways as it moves into a more competitive environment. What course of action should he recommend?

Questions

1. How comparable are the two different methods? In what ways are they similar? In what ways are they different?
2. What are the positive and negative aspects of each approach that Shocker should consider before recommending a course of action for FlyAway Airways?
3. What aspects of service quality does each approach address well and not so well?
4. Considering the two methods outlined, what types of validity would you consider to be demonstrated by the two approaches to measuring quality? Defend your position.
5. Which of the methods should Shocker recommend? Why?

CHAPTER 14
ATTITUDE MEASUREMENT

LEARNING OUTCOMES

After studying this chapter, you should be able to

1. Define attitude and understand why it is so important in business research
2. Produce a Likert rating scale that measures an attitudinal concept
3. Discuss the use of other types of scales that assess attitudinal concepts
4. Understand factors important to selecting an appropriate measurement scale
5. Implement a multi-attribute model

Chapter Vignette: Do You Know How to Score?

What if you could predict a firm's profitability by asking consumers a single survey question? Obviously, such a breakthrough would be extremely beneficial in diagnosing problems with company performance and trying to take corrective action. This is the idea behind the net promoter score (NPS). It represents how favorable a customer is toward a business by asking them a single survey item scored on a 0 to 10 scale:

On the 0 to 10 point scale shown below, how likely is it that you would recommend Blackberry to a friend or colleague?										
0	1	2	3	4	5	6	7	8	9	10

Consumers are labeled based on their scale response. A score of 6 or below is associated with a label of detractor, a score of 7 or 8 is labeled passively satisfied, and a score of 9 or 10 signifies a promoter. Companies with a high proportion of promoters are said by some to significantly outperform competitors.

Obviously, the simplicity of this approach is attractive to many businesses. However, the method is not without controversy. Questions about the usefulness and the validity of this approach have surfaced. Some question exactly what this item measures. The content does not match well with satisfaction, nor does it perfectly match loyalty or patronage intention. Each is undoubtedly important. The NPS best represents an intent to spread positive word of mouth. Others question the one-size-fits-all approach or suggest that although the item may predict, the prediction

accuracy is far from perfect and leaves room for other concepts to explain variance in performance. Still others question just how well this single item predicts performance by conducting survey research and tying the result to firm performance.

Some question how valuable this single rating item really is. They claim that without controlling for other factors, any correlation that is found could be misleading. Alternatively, some firms have broken their organizations down into functions (service, sales, etc.) and developed an NPS for each area, claiming the information obtained is richer and more useful. However, despite the shortcomings, it is doubtful that competitive firms would trade even a single promoter for dozens of detractors or even a handful of passively satisfied customers. So, this single item certainly helps managers know the score![1]

Introduction

Ultimately, the vast majority of marketing research is motivated by a need to better understand behavior. While respondents can accurately tell a researcher about their past behavior, effective business decisions are facilitated by an ability to predict future behavior. Thus, the **net promoter score**, determined by the "ultimate" question as described in the vignette, is aimed at forecasting the future based on the valence and strength of someone's current attitude. If a customer is willing to promote the business to others, then their attitude is both positive and strong, and management can count on this customer continuing on as a customer and even seeding business with other customers. Researchers have many choices in what types and forms of questions they should ask. A single question seldom brings all the answers. This chapter describes some of the decisions researchers face in trying to ask questions that will accurately predict the future.

net promoter score

The score based on customer responses to a question asking how likely he or she would be to recommend the company to a friend or colleague.

What Is an Attitude?

"You've got a bad attitude!" Perhaps many of us have heard this phrase before. The idea is that one's disposition about the relevant matter is not positive and the result is less than productive behavior. Formally, an **attitude** is a social-psychological concept that can be defined as a relatively enduring predisposition to respond consistently to various things including people, activities, events, and objects. Attitudes are predispositions toward behavior and as such represent rules that inform a person of the appropriate reaction in a given situation. If someone's attitude toward broccoli is best described as a dislike, then that person is likely to avoid eating, smelling or even approaching any dish with the obvious presence of broccoli. If a fan "loves the Bulldogs," he or she is more likely to buy tickets to their games and to attend them. Additionally, attitudes are latent constructs and because of this, they are not directly observable.

Attitudes are thought to have three components:

attitude

An enduring disposition to consistently respond in a given manner to various aspects of the world; composed of affective, cognitive, and behavioral components.

- An affective component that expresses how much affinity someone has toward the relevant matter. More simply, this is the feeling of liking or not liking something. For example, a consumer might say "I love Wendy's." This would express very high liking.
- A cognitive component that represents a person's awareness and knowledge of the relevant matter. In other words, what a person believes about the subject matter. When someone says, "Wendy's has a wide selection," they are expressing knowledge or a belief about this particular consumer alternative.
- A behavioral component that represents the action that corresponds to a certain type of attitude. If the attitude is positive, the person will display approach responses. If the attitude is negative, the person will display avoidance reactions. "I'll never eat at Wendy's again" expresses a behavioral component of a negative attitude. Often, the behavioral component is expressed as intentions of future behavior.

As you went through the student survey, you responded to many different types of scale approaches. Many of these involved attitudinal type scales. For example, you responded to the screenshot shown.

What type of scale is this? In this case, does this scale format work well to provide a respondent's feelings about exercise? Could another scale approach have been used that would have been at least equally as valid?

Also, you may notice that some of the Likert scales are five-item scales and some are seven. Compare the results for a couple of the items for each number of scale response points. In other words, compare a couple of five-point scales with a couple of seven-point scales. Is there any evidence that suggests one is preferable or more valid than the other? Explain your choice.

© GEORGE DOYLE

Lucozade was transformed from a product for children with stomach problems into a sports, fitness, and energy product for adults. Attitudinal research helped track this brand transformation.

Sometimes researchers need to study overall attitude. Other times, they may focus on one of these components more than others. Whenever overall attitude or any of these components are measured through survey research, the researcher is conducting attitudinal research.

Marketing managers place a great deal of importance on attitudes because they have been shown to predict behavior with some accuracy. If consumers' aggregate attitude about some product can be changed, sales volume will increase accordingly. If employees' aggregate attitude about their job improves, their work output is likely to increase in proportion. Further, if the knowledge about a product can be changed, the product can be repositioned to capture some new market. For example, Lucozade was transformed from a liquid nutritional supplement for pediatric digestive illness patients into a sports and fitness drink for adults.[2]

This brand transformation required careful coordination of communications with consumers that involved advertising and merchandising. Additionally, a great deal of survey research tracked consumers' attitudes along the way.

Attitudinal Rating Scales

Researchers face a wide variety of choices in measuring attitudinal concepts. One reason for the variety is that no complete consensus exists over just what constitutes an attitude or an attitudinal variable. Researchers generally argue that the affective, cognitive, and behavioral components of an attitude can be measured by different means. For example, sympathetic nervous system responses may be recorded using physiological measures to quantify affect, but they are not good measures of behavioral intentions. Direct verbal statements concerning affect, belief, or behavior are used to measure behavioral intent. However, attitudes may also be interpreted using qualitative techniques like those discussed in Chapter 6.

Research may assess the affective (emotional) components of attitudes through physiological measures like galvanic skin response (GSR), blood pressure, and pupil dilation (see Chapter 10). These measures provide a means of assessing attitudes without verbally questioning the respondent. In general, they can provide a gross measure of likes or dislikes, but they are not extremely sensitive to the different gradients of an attitude.

Obtaining verbal statements from respondents generally requires that the respondents perform a task such as ranking, rating, sorting, or making choices. A **ranking** task requires the respondent to rank order a small number of stores, brands, feelings, or objects on the basis of overall preference or some characteristic of the stimulus. **Rating** asks the respondent to estimate the magnitude or the extent to which some characteristic exists. A quantitative score results. The rating task involves marking a response indicating one's position using one or more attitudinal or cognitive scales. A **sorting** task might present the respondent with several product concepts printed on cards and require the respondent to classify the concepts by placing the cards into groups (stacks of cards). Another type of attitude measurement is **choice** between two or more alternatives. If a respondent chooses one object over another, the researcher assumes that the respondent prefers the chosen object, at least in this setting.

© DON MASON/CORBIS

Generally, consumers act in a way consistent with their attitudes. Therefore, attitudes are a popular marketing research topic.

Marketing researchers commonly use rating scales to measure attitudes. This section discusses many rating scales designed to enable respondents to report the intensity of their attitudes. In its most basic form, attitude scaling requires that an individual agree or disagree with a statement or indicate how much some term describes his or her feeling. For example, respondents in a political poll may be asked whether they agree or disagree with a statement like, "Politicians are likable." Or, an individual might indicate whether he or she likes or dislikes jalapeño bean dip. This type of self-rating scale merely classifies respondents into one of two categories, thus having only the properties of a nominal scale, and the types of mathematical analysis that may be used with this basic scale are limited.

Simple attitude scaling can be a practical way of implementing a survey when questionnaires are extremely long, when respondents have little education, or for other specific reasons. In fact, a number of simplified scales are merely checklists where a respondent indicates past experience, preference or likes and dislikes simply by checking an item. A recent checklist survey showed that 77 percent of small business owners believe small and medium size businesses "have less bureaucracy," 76 percent said smaller companies "have more flexibility" than large ones, and 73 percent were optimistic heading into 2008 as opposed to 75 percent indicating optimism at the end of 2006.[3] Answers like these can be obtained very quickly through simple questioning techniques.

Most attitude theorists believe that attitudes vary along a continuum. Thus, the purpose of an attitude scale is to find an individual's position on the continuum. However, simple nominal scales do not allow for fine distinctions between attitudes. Several other scales have been developed for making more precise measurements. The following sections describe the most popular techniques for measuring attitudes.

Category Scales

The simplest rating scale contains only two response categories: agree/disagree. For instance, a researcher might include a simple question like this:

I like the idea of attending Southpaw State University.

☐ *Yes*   ☐ *No*

Expanding the response categories provides the respondent with more flexibility in the rating task. Even more information is provided if the categories are ordered according to a particular descriptive or evaluative dimension. Consider the following question:

How often do you think favorably about attending Southpaw State University?

☐ *Never*   ☐ *Rarely*   ☐ *Sometimes*   ☐ *Often*   ☐ *Very often*

This **category scale** measures attitude with greater sensitivity than a two-point response scale. By having more choices, the potential exists to provide more information. However, a researcher will

ranking

A measurement task that requires respondents to rank order a small number of stores, brands, or objects on the basis of overall preference or some characteristic of the stimulus.

rating

A measurement task that requires respondents to estimate the magnitude of a characteristic or quality that a brand, store, or object possesses.

sorting

A measurement task that presents a respondent with several objects or product concepts and requires the respondent to arrange the objects into piles or classify the product concepts.

choice

A measurement task that identifies preferences by requiring respondents to choose between two or more alternatives

category scale

A rating scale that consists of several response categories, often providing respondents with alternatives to indicate positions on a continuum.

create measurement error if he/she uses a category scale for something that is truly bipolar (yes/ no, female/male, member/non-member, and so on).

Response category wording is an extremely important factor. Exhibit 14.1 shows some common wordings used in category scales measuring common marketing research variables. As you can see, the more categories, the more difficulty a researcher has in coming up with precise and readily understandable category labels.

EXHIBIT 14.1 Selected Category Scales

Quality				
Excellent	Good	Fair	Poor	
Very good	Fairly good	Neither good nor bad	Not very good	Not good at all
Well above average	Above average	Average	Below average	Well below average
Importance				
Very important	Fairly important	Neutral	Not so important	Not at all important
Interest				
Very interested		Somewhat interested		Not very interested
Satisfaction				
Completely satisfied	Somewhat satisfied	Neither satisfied nor dissatisfied	Somewhat dissatisfied	Completely dissatisfied
Very satisfied	Quite satisfied	Somewhat satisfied	Not at all satisfied	
Frequency				
All of the time	Very often	Often	Sometimes	Hardly ever
Very often	Often	Sometimes	Rarely	Never
All of the time	Most of the time	Some of the time	Just now and then	
Truth				
Very true	Somewhat true	Not very true	Not at all true	
Definitely yes	Probably yes	Probably no	Definitely no	
Uniqueness				
Very different	Somewhat different	Slightly different	Not at all different	
Extremely unique	Very unique	Somewhat unique	Slightly unique	Not at all unique

The Likert Scale

Likert scale

A measure of attitudes designed to allow respondents to rate how strongly they agree or disagree with carefully constructed statements, ranging from very positive to very negative attitudes toward some object.

The Likert scale may well be the most commonly applied scale format in marketing research. Likert scales are simple to administer and understand. Likert scales were developed by and named after Rensis Likert, a 20th century social scientist. With a **Likert scale**, respondents indicate their attitudes by checking how strongly they agree or disagree with carefully constructed statements. The scale results reveal the respondent's attitude ranging from very positive to very negative. The Research Snapshot on the next page illustrates results from a Likert scaling approach. Individuals generally choose from multiple response alternatives such as, strongly agree, agree, neutral, disagree, and strongly disagree. Researchers commonly employ five choices although as discussed later, they

RESEARCH SNAPSHOT

Attitudes of the Rich

Testing that old saying about the rich being "different from you and me," the Harrison Group, a marketing research firm, conducted a survey of five hundred rich households—those with at least $5 million in liquid assets, placing them in the top 0.5 percent of the United States in terms of their economic status. The interviews asked members of these households about their habits and attitudes. What they learned about attitudes might surprise you, at least if your ideas about wealth come from the fabulous misbehavior displayed in soap operas and supermarket tabloids.

The survey asked respondents to agree or disagree with statements on a variety of topics. It found that a sizable share of this group does not care to show off with a lavish lifestyle. Only 11 percent said they want others to "know they are wealthy," and almost half said luxury items like fancy watches, jewelry, and cars are a

"waste of money." Many stand firm on ethical grounds. Less than 10 percent admitted they had more than once "compromised their values" to make money, and only half expressed concern that living in comfort may interfere with their children's work ethic.

If some of these responses surprise you, you have company, including people who should know better. The Harrison Group also teamed up with advertising firm AgencySacks to ask marketers specializing in luxury products to predict how wealthy people would answer the same questions. The marketers expected that few rich people would see luxury goods as a waste and that most would worry about their children's work ethic.

Source: Based on Sandra O'Loughlin, "Luxe Marketing: Perception vs. Reality," *Brandweek*, 46 (September 19, 2005), 22–28; Harrison Group, "About Us" and "Wealth Study Methodology," http://www.harrisongroup.com, accessed March 6, 2006.

---

also often use six, seven or even more response points. In the following example, from a study of food-shopping behavior, there are five alternatives:

I like to go to Wal-Mart when buying food for my family.				
Strongly disagree	Disagree	Neutral	Agree	Strongly agree
☐	☐	☐	☐	☐
(1)	*(2)*	*(3)*	*(4)*	*(5)*

Researchers assign scores to each possible response. In this example, numerical scores of 1, 2, 3, 4, and 5 are assigned to each level of agreement, respectively. The numerical scores, shown in parentheses, may not be printed on the questionnaire. Typically, with paper and pencil questionnaires, the numbers are displayed primarily because they facilitate data coding. The numbers are much less likely to be displayed as researchers increasingly adopt electronic questionnaires. Here, strong agreement indicates the most favorable attitude on the statement, and a numerical score of 5 is assigned to this response.

Realize that if the statement were worded in a way that indicated dislike for shopping for food at Wal-Mart, a 5 would mean a less favorable attitude about this activity. For example, responses to the item above could even be combined with those from an item like this:

Wal-Mart is a bad place to shop for fresh foods.				
Strongly disagree	Disagree	Neutral	Agree	Strongly agree
☐	☐	☐	☐	☐
(1)	*(2)*	*(3)*	*(4)*	*(5)*

However, before a composite scale could be created, the responses to this item would have to be reverse coded as shown in the previous chapter. An attitude score is arbitrary and has little cardinal meaning—in other words, attitude scores are at best interval and not ratio. They could also just as easily be scored so that a higher score indicated less favorable attitudes. However, the convention is to score attitude scales so that a higher score means a more favorable attitude.

Exhibit 14.2 provides another example, this time the 5-point scale items capture attitudinal items describing beliefs about a physician's service staff. The total score is the summation of the numerical scores assigned to an individual's responses. Item 3 is negatively worded and therefore it is reverse coded. Thus, the maximum possible score for the composite would be 20 for a respondent marking the most positive responses and a 4 for a respondent marking the most negative responses.

EXHIBIT 14.2
Likert Scale Items for Measuring Attitudes toward Patients' Interaction with a Physician's Service Staff

1. My doctor's office staff takes a warm and personal interest in me.
2. My doctor's office staff is friendly and courteous.
3. My doctor's office staff is more interested in serving the doctor's needs than in serving my needs.
4. My doctor's office staff always acts in a professional manner.

Source: Brown, S. W., Swartz, T. A. (1989), "A gap analysis of professional services quality", *Journal of Marketing*, Vol. 54, pp. 92–8. Copyright 1989 by Am. Marketing Assn (AMA (Chic). Reproduced with permission of Am. Marketing Assn (AMA (Chic) in the format Textbook via Copyright Clearance Center.

■ SELECTING ITEMS FOR A LIKERT SCALE

Typically, a researcher will use multiple items to represent a single attitudinal concept. The researcher may generate a large number of statements before putting together the final question-naire. A pretest may be conducted using these items allowing for an *item analysis* to be performed. The item analysis helps select items that evoke a wide response (meaning all respondents are not selecting the same response point such as all strongly agree) allowing the item to discriminate among those with positive and negative attitudes. Items are also analyzed for clarity or unusual response patterns. Thus, the final Likert items should be clearly understood and elicit an accurate range of responses corresponding to respondents' true attitudes.

Assessing Item and Scale Quality

Another big advantage of using multiple items is that reliability and validity can be estimated using a wide range of statistical approaches. For instance, coefficient α for reliability can only be assessed with multiple items. Later chapters will discuss multivariate procedures for assessing validity in more detail. These are also facilitated by using multiple items. In the end, only a set of items that show acceptable reliability and validity should be summed or averaged for scores representing hypothetical constructs. Unfortunately, not all researchers are willing or able to thoroughly assess reliability and validity. Without this assessment, the researcher has no way of knowing exactly what the items represent or how well they represent anything of interest.

Other Scale Types

Researchers rely heavily on Likert scales. However, many other scale approaches exist. Each has unique characteristics that may make them more or less applicable in certain situations. Additionally, researchers sometimes develop personal preferences that influence the types of scales they use. The following sections discuss several other scale types.

Semantic Differential

semantic differential

A measure of attitudes that consists of a series of seven-point rating scales that use bipolar adjectives to anchor the beginning and end of each scale.

A **semantic differential** is a scale type that has respondents describe their attitude using a series of bipolar rating scales. Bipolar rating scales involve respondents choosing between opposing adjectives—such as "good" and "bad," "modern" and "old-fashioned," or "clean" and "dirty." One adjective anchors the beginning and the other the end (or poles) of the scale. The subject makes repeated judgments about the concept under investigation on each of the scales. Exhibit 14.3 shows an example semantic differential approach for assessing consumer attitudes toward hypermarts.

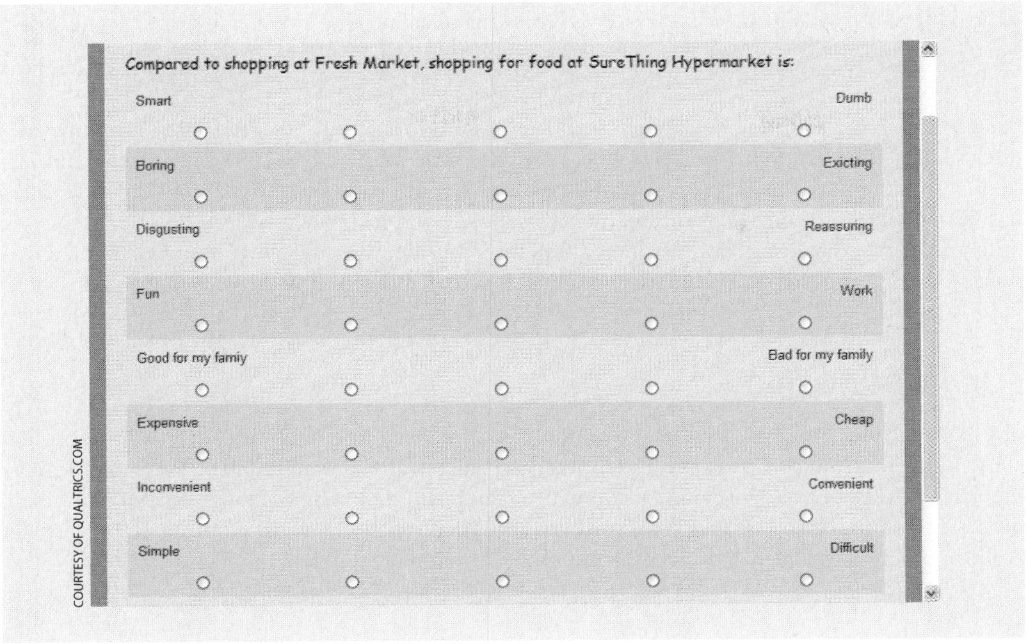

EXHIBIT 14.3

An Example Semantic Differential Scale

The scoring of the semantic differential can be illustrated using the scale bounded by the anchors "modern" and "old-fashioned." Respondents are instructed to check the place that indicates the nearest appropriate adjective. From left to right, the scale intervals are interpreted as "extremely modern," "very modern," "slightly modern," "neither modern nor old-fashioned," "slightly old-fashioned," "very old-fashioned," and "extremely old-fashioned":

Extremely modern	Very modern	Slightly modern	Neither modern nor old-fashioned	Slightly old-fashioned	Very old-fashioned	Extremely old-fashioned
☐	☐	☐	☐	☐	☐	☐

■ SEMANTIC DIFFERENTIALS AND MEANING

The semantic differential technique originally was developed as a method for measuring the meanings of objects or the "semantic space" of interpersonal experience.[4] Researchers see the semantic differential as versatile and useful in a wide variety of business situations.

When opposites are available, the semantic differential is a good scale choice. In typical attitude or image studies, simple anchors such as very unfavorable and very favorable work well. However, the validity of the semantic differential depends on finding scale anchors that are semantic opposites and this can sometimes prove difficult. For example, consider the following scale in which the respondent is asked to place a check on the line closest to the way they feel about the phrase:

Shopping at Bebe makes me:

Happy __ __ __ __ __ __ **Sad**

Few would question that sad is the opposite of happy. However, what if this were to be combined with an item capturing how angry shopping at Bebe makes a respondent feel? Then, what would the opposite of angry be? Clearly, using happy as the opposite of angry would present a problem because the items above suggests happy is the opposite of sad. Thus, a semantic differential may not be best for capturing anger unless some distinctive and unambiguous opposite can be found.

■ SCORING SEMANTIC DIFFERENTIALS

Like Likert scales, a numerical score can be assigned to each position on a semantic differential scale. For a seven-point semantic differential the scores could be 1, 2, 3, 4, 5, 6, 7 or –3, –2, –1, 0, +1, +2, +3. Marketing researchers generally assume that the semantic differential provides interval data. This assumption does have critics who argue that the data have only ordinal properties because the numerical scores are arbitrary and there is no way of knowing that the differences between choices are equal. Practically, the vast majority of social science researchers treat semantic differential scales as metric (at least interval). This is justified because the amount of error introduced by assuming the intervals between choices are equal (even though this is uncertain at best) is fairly small.

■ IMAGE PROFILE

image profile

A graphic representation of semantic differential data for competing brands, products, or stores to highlight comparisons.

Exhibit 14.4 illustrates a typical **image profile** based on semantic differential data. Image profiles allow a side–by–side comparison on each image characteristic measured. The arithmetic mean or median across all respondents rating a competitor can be used to compare the profile of competing products, brands, or stores. Here, we can see that Rue 21 has an advantage on price image over Anthropologie. However, the reverse is true for pleasant atmosphere.

EXHIBIT 14.4
Image Profiles for Two Competing Fashion Retailers

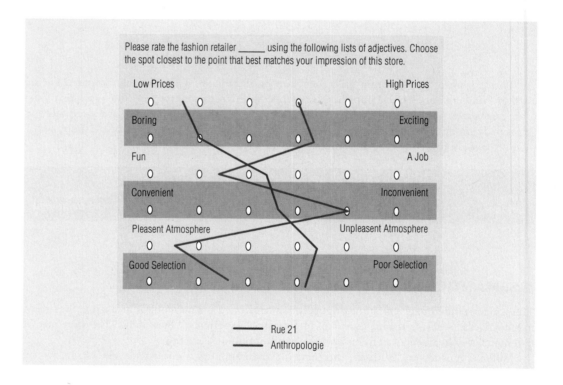

Stapel Scale

Stapel scale

A measure of attitudes that consists of a single adjective in the center of an even number of numerical values.

The **Stapel scale** was originally developed in the 1950s to measure simultaneously the direction and intensity of an attitude. Modern versions of the scale, with a single adjective, are used as a substitute for the semantic differential when it is difficult to create pairs of bipolar adjectives. The modified Stapel scale places a single adjective in the center of an even number of numerical values (ranging, perhaps, from +3 to –3). The scale measures how close to or distant from the adjective a given stimulus is perceived to be. Exhibit 14.5 illustrates a Stapel scale item used in measurement of a retailer's store image.

The advantages and disadvantages of the Stapel scale are very similar to those of the semantic differential. However, the Stapel scale is easier to administer over the telephone. The Stapel

EXHIBIT 14.5
A Stapel Scale for Measuring a Store's Image

Bloomingdale's

+3

+2

+1

Wide Selection

−1

−2

−3

Select a *plus* number for words that you think describe the store accurately. The more accurately you think the word describes the store, the larger the plus number you should choose. Select a *minus* number for words you think do not describe the store accurately. The less accurately you think the word describes the store, the larger the minus number you should choose. Therefore, you can select any number from +3 for words that you think are very accurate all the way to −3 for words that you think are very inaccurate.

Source: Dennis Menezes and Norbert F. Elbert, "Alternative Semantic Scaling Formats for Measuring Store Image: An Evaluation," *Journal of Marketing Research*, February 1979, pp. 80–87. Reprinted by permission of the American Marketing Association.

scale is easier to construct than a semantic differential because bipolar adjectives are not necessary. Research comparing the semantic differential with the Stapel scale indicates that results from the two techniques are largely the same.[5]

Constant-Sum Scale

A **constant-sum scale** demands that respondents divide points among several attributes to indicate their relative importance. Suppose United Parcel Service (UPS) wishes to determine the importance of delivery attributes such as accurate invoicing, delivery as promised, and price to organizations that use its service in business-to-business marketing. Respondents might be asked to divide a constant sum of 100 points to indicate the relative importance of those attributes:

> *Divide 100 points among the following characteristics of a delivery service according to how important each characteristic is to you when selecting a delivery company.*
> _____ *Accurate invoicing*
> _____ *Delivery as promised*
> _____ *Lower price*

constant-sum scale

A measure of attitudes in which respondents are asked to divide a constant sum to indicate the relative importance of attributes; respondents often sort cards, but the task may also be a rating task.

The constant-sum scale requires respondents to understand that their responses should total to the number of points being allocated. In the case above, that number is 100. As the number of stimuli increases, this technique becomes increasingly complex. Fortunately, with electronic questionnaires math errors can be eliminated by having the software trigger an error notice whenever the responses provided do not match the total. The respondent could adjust the responses until the sums do indeed match the total. If respondents follow the instructions correctly, the results will approximate interval measures.

This technique may be used for measuring brand preference. The approach, which is similar to the paired-comparison method, is as follows:

> *Divide 100 points among the following brands according to your preference for each brand:*
> _____ *Brand A*
> _____ *Brand B*
> _____ *Brand C*

Although the constant sum scale is widely used, strictly speaking, the scale is flawed because the last response is completely determined by the way the respondent has scored the other choices. Although this is probably somewhat complex to understand, the fact is that practical reasons often outweigh this concern. The Research Snapshot on the next page provides an illustration.

A Measuring Stick for Web Site Usability

Two technology experts looking for a standard way to measure Web sites' usability developed metrics emphasizing attitudes. Rather than, say, measuring how long it took users to accomplish a particular task, they asked users to rate their experiences using each site. Each rater evaluated the site's content (information and transactions), ease of use, promotion (advertising on the site), "made for the medium" (features that make the site fit the user's particular needs), and emotions (sense of accomplishment, interest in the site's content, credibility, and control over the flow of content).

Of course, what is very important on one site may be minor on another. A prospective investor looking for information about an airline would likely seek a different online experience than a consumer visiting the same site to plan a vacation, and they both would have still different expectations for an online bookstore. As a result, the usability assessment begins by asking respondents to rate each category being evaluated in terms of how important it is for a particular kind of company, assuming the rater is either a consumer or an investor. For example, a user might rate an airline Web site's content, ease of use, and so on for a consumer. These ratings use a 100-point constant-sum scale. Each rater divides 100 points among the five categories. The rater then evaluates, on a scale of 1 to 10, how well the site performs in each category. The importance ratings weight those scores. So, if a rater assigns 5 points to the emotion category and thinks the site performs at a 6 on the 1-to-10 scale, the weighted score is 30. By combining all the ratings for a Web site, a site can earn between 0 and 1,000 points. In the researchers' test of this rating system, it delivered helpful insights.

Source: Based on Ritu Agarwal and Viswanath Venkatesh, "Assessing a Firm's Web Presence: A Heuristic Evaluation Procedure for the Measurement of Usability," *Information Systems Research* (June 2002), downloaded from Business & Company Resource Center at http://galenet.galegroup.com; and G. A. Buchholz, "Losability vs. Usability," *Digital Web* (2005), http://www.digital-web.com, accessed July 11, 2005.

Graphic Rating Scales

graphic rating scale

A measure of attitude that allows respondents to rate an object by choosing any point along a graphic continuum.

A **graphic rating scale** presents respondents with a graphic continuum. The respondents are allowed to choose any point on the continuum to indicate their attitude. Exhibit 14.6 shows a traditional graphic scale, ranging from one extreme position to the opposite position. Typically a respondent's score is determined by measuring the length (in millimeters) from one end of the graphic continuum to the point marked by the respondent. Many researchers believe that scoring in this manner strengthens the assumption that graphic rating scales of this type are interval scales. Alternatively, the researcher may divide the line into predetermined scoring categories (lengths) and record respondents' marks accordingly. In other words, the graphic rating scale has the advantage of allowing the researcher to choose any interval desired for scoring purposes. The disadvantage of the graphic rating scale is that there are no standard answers.

EXHIBIT 14.6
Graphic Rating Scale

Please evaluate each attribute in terms of how important it is to you by placing an X at the position on the horizontal line that most reflects your feelings.

Seating comfort   Not important _____ Very important

In-flight meals   Not important _____ Very important

Airfare   Not important _____ Very important

Graphic rating scales are not limited to straight lines as sources of visual communication. Picture response options or another type of graphic continuum may be used to enhance communication with respondents. A variation of the graphic ratings scale is the ladder scale. This scale also includes numerical options:

Exhibit 14.7 shows a ladder scale. It represents the "ladder of life." As you see, it is a ladder with eleven rungs numbered 0 to 10. Let's suppose the top of the ladder represents the best possible life for you as you describe it, and the bottom rung represents the worst possible life for you as you describe it.

On which rung of the ladder do you feel your life is today?

0   1   2   3   4   5   6   7   8   9   10

EXHIBIT 14.7
A Ladder Scale

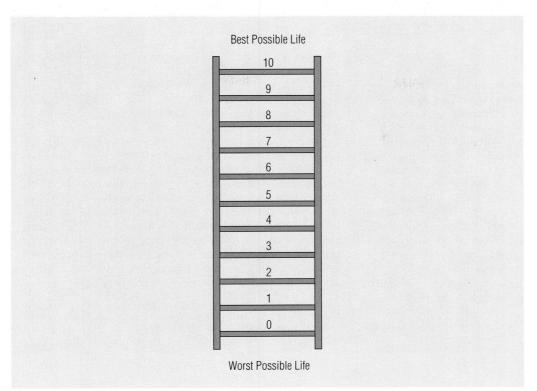

Research to investigate children's attitudes has used happy-sad face scales. Exhibit 14.8 illustrates one such approach. Here, the respondent chooses an attitude by sliding the scale up and down using the tab to the right of the face. As the respondent moves the tab up or down, the face smiles or frowns, correspondingly. The first respondent is fairly pleased with the idea of hot breakfast items at Starbucks. However, the second respondent has a very negative attitude toward the idea. Notice the position of the tab corresponding to each face.

EXHIBIT 14.8
Choose the Face that Matches Your Attitude: A Happy/Sad Face Scale

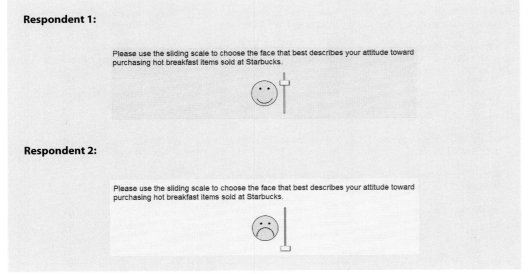

Exhibit 14.9 on the next page summarizes the attitude-rating techniques discussed thus far. The advantages and disadvantages of each approach are discussed. Among these approaches, Likert scales and semantic differentials account for the majority of applications. The Research Snapshot on the next page suggests that attitudes can help make a story complete.

Click, Click, Click

Marketing metrics, as discussed earlier, are clearly increasingly being applied. The quantitative results can be extremely useful in helping determine how much some marketing tactic is really worth. For example, when marketers use a banner ad on a Web site, the ad agency can monitor the way click-through rates change with varying ad placements and characteristics. For example, do click-throughs become more likely when the ad is placed in a content consistent site such as an ad for an airline in an island resort's Web site? Using metrics like this, the ad agency might be able to inform clients how much an ad placement is worth.

However, recent research suggests these numbers do not tell the whole story because they ignore consumer attitudes. A banner ad, for instance, may affect consumer awareness and attitudes even if a consumer does not click through to view the contents of the actual Web page. For example, when British Airways introduced its Club World perks for good customers, the click-through rate on banner ads may have been low, but a test showed that respondents who were exposed to the ads were approximately 20 percent more likely to be aware of Club World than respondents who were not exposed to these ads. Thus, the click metrics did not tell the whole story. Similarly, leading financial institutions supplement their marketing metrics with attitudinal research to better understand which consumers are likely to become loyal. The attitudinal research helps firms better understand the customer-based brand equity. In the end, behavioral metrics have not replaced attitudinal research. The two approaches complement each other quite well.

Sources: Howell, N., "Looking Deeper," *New Media Age* (December 1, 2005), 24–25; Taylor, S. A. and G. L. Hunter, "Understanding Brand Equity in Financial Services," *Journal of Services Marketing*, 21, no. 4 (2007), 241–252.

EXHIBIT 14.9 **Summary of Advantages and Disadvantages of Rating Scales**

Rating Measure	Subject Must	Advantages	Disadvantages
Category scale	Indicate a response category	Flexible, easy to respond to	Items may be ambiguous; with few categories, only gross distinctions can be made
Likert scale	Evaluate statements on a scale of agreement	Easiest scale to construct; respondent familiarity	Hard to judge what a single score means
Semantic differential and numerical scales	Choose points between bipolar adjectives on relevant dimensions	Easy to construct; norms exist for comparison, such as profile analysis	Bipolar adjectives must be found; data may be ordinal, not interval
Stapel scale	Choose points on a scale with a single adjective in the center	Easier to construct than semantic differential, easy to administer	Endpoints are numerical, not verbal, labels
Constant-sum scale	Divide a constant sum among response alternatives	Approximates an interval measure	Difficult for respondents with low education levels
Graphic scale	Choose a point on a continuum	Visual impact, unlimited scale points	No standard answers
Graphic scale with picture response categories	Choose a visual picture	Visual impact, easy for poor readers	Hard to attach a verbal explanation to a response

Ranking

A ranking is different than a rating scale in that respondents simply order alternatives on some characteristic. Consumers often *rank order* their preferences so, in this sense, ranking scales have considerable validity. An ordinal scale may be developed by asking respondents to rank order (from most preferred to least preferred) a set of objects or attributes. Respondents easily understand the task of rank ordering product attributes or arranging a set of brand names according to preference. Like the constant-sum scale however, the ranking scale suffers from inflexibility in that if we know how someone ranked five out of six alternatives, we know the answer to the sixth. Thus, the characteristics are not independently rated as in most types of ratings scales. Additionally, ordinal scaling only allows us to know that one option is preferred over another—not how much one option is preferred over another.

TOTHEPOINT

My tastes are very simple. I only want the best.

—Oscar Wilde

Paired Comparisons

Consider a situation in which a chain saw manufacturer learned that a competitor had introduced a new lightweight (6-pound) chain saw. The manufacturer's lightest chain saw weighed 9 pounds. Executives wondered if they needed to introduce a 6-pound chain saw into the product line. The research design chosen was a **paired comparison**. A 6-pound chain saw was designed, and a prototype built. To control for color preferences, the competitor's chain saw was painted the same color as the 9- and 6-pound chain saws. Respondents were presented with two chain saws at a time and asked to pick which of the two they preferred. Three pairs of comparisons were required to determine the most preferred chain saw.

paired comparison

A measurement technique that involves presenting the respondent with two objects and asking the respondent to pick the preferred object; more than two objects may be presented, but comparisons are made in pairs.

The following question illustrates the typical format for asking about paired comparisons.

I would like to know your overall opinion of two brands of adhesive bandages. They are Curad and Band-Aid. Overall, which of these two brands—Curad or Band-Aid—do you think is the better one? Or are both the same?

Curad is better. _____
Band-Aid is better. _____
They are the same. _____

If researchers wish to compare four brands of pens on the basis of attractiveness or writing quality, six comparisons $[(n)(n-1)/2]$ will be necessary. Paired comparisons are sometimes used to assess similarity instead of preference by asking which of the two choices is more similar to some third choice.

When comparing only a few items, such as products or advertisements, ranking objects with respect to one attribute is not difficult. As the number of items increases, the number of comparisons increases geometrically. If the number of comparisons is too large, respondents may become fatigued and no longer carefully discriminate among them.

Sorting

Sorting tasks requires that respondents indicate their attitudes or beliefs by arranging items on the basis of perceived similarity or some other attribute. One advertising agency has had consumers sort photographs of people to measure their perceptions of a brand's typical user. Another agency used a sorting technique in which consumers used a deck of fifty-two cards illustrating elements from advertising for the brand name being studied. The study participants created a stack of cards showing elements they recalled seeing or hearing, and the interviewer then asked the respondent to identify the item on each of those cards. National City Corporation, a banking company, has used sorting as part of its research into the design of its Web site. Consumers participating in the research were given a set of cards describing various parts of processes that they might engage in when they are banking online. The participants were asked to arrange the cards to show their idea of a logical way to complete these processes. This research method showed the Web site designers how consumers go about doing something—sometimes very differently from the way the bankers expected.[6]

A variant of the constant-sum technique uses physical counters (for example, poker chips or coins), to be divided among the items being tested. In an airline study of customer preferences, the following sorting technique could be used:

Here is a sheet that lists several airlines. Next to the name of each airline is a pocket. Here are 10 cards. I would like you to put these cards in the pockets next to the airlines you would prefer to fly on your next trip. Assume that all of the airlines fly to wherever you would choose to travel. You can put as many cards as you want next to an airline, or you can put no cards next to an airline.

Cards

American Airlines
Delta Airlines
United Airlines
Southwest Airlines
Northwest Airlines

Direct Assessment of Consumer Attitudes

Attitudes, as hypothetical constructs, cannot be observed directly. We can, however, infer one's attitude by the way he or she responds to multiple attitude indicators. A summated rating scale can be made up of three indicators of attitude. Consider the following three semantic differential items that may capture a consumer's attitude toward Microsoft Word:

very good ___ ___ ___ ___ ___ ___ ___*very bad*

very unfavorable ___ ___ ___ ___ ___ ___ ___*very favorable*

very positive ___ ___ ___ ___ ___ ___ ___ *very negative*

The terminology is such that now attitude would be represented as a latent (unobservable) construct indicated by a consumer's response to these items. How do you feel about Microsoft Word?

Selecting a Measurement Scale: Some Practical Decisions

Now that we have looked at a number of attitude measurement scales, a natural question arises: "Which is most appropriate?" As in the selection of a basic research design, there is no single best answer for all research projects. The answer to this question is relative, and the choice of scale will depend on the nature of the attitudinal object to be measured, the manager's problem definition, and the backward and forward linkages to choices already made (for example, telephone survey versus mail survey). However, several questions will help focus the choice of a measurement scale:

1. Is a ranking, sorting, rating, or choice technique best?
2. Should a monadic or a comparative scale be used?
3. What type of category labels, if any, will be used for the rating scale?
4. How many scale categories or response positions are needed to accurately measure an attitude?
5. Should a balanced or unbalanced rating scale be chosen?
6. Should a scale that forces a choice among predetermined options be used?
7. Should a single measure or an index measure be used?

We will discuss each of these issues.

Ranking, Sorting, Rating, or Choice Technique?

The decision whether to use ranking, sorting, rating, or a choice technique is determined largely by the problem definition and especially by the type of statistical analysis desired. For example, ranking provides only ordinal data, limiting the statistical techniques that may be used.

Monadic or Comparative Scale?

If the scale to be used is not a ratio scale, the researcher must decide whether to include a standard of comparison in the verbal portion of the scale. Consider the following rating scale:

Now that you've had your automobile for about one year, please tell us how satisfied you are with its engine power and pickup.

Completely Dissatisfied	Dissatisfied	Somewhat Satisfied	Satisfied	Completely Satisfied
☐	☐	☐	☐	☐

This is a **monadic rating scale**, because it asks about a single concept (the brand of automobile the individual actually purchased) in isolation. The respondent is not given a specific frame of reference. A **comparative rating scale** asks a respondent to rate a concept, such as a specific brand, in comparison with a benchmark—perhaps another similar concept, such as a competing brand—explicitly used as a frame of reference. In many cases, the comparative rating scale presents an ideal situation as a reference point for comparison with the actual situation.

Please indicate how the amount of authority in your present position compares with the amount of authority that would be ideal for this position.

Too much ☐   About right ☐   Too little ☐

monadic rating scale

Any measure of attitudes that asks respondents about a single concept in isolation.

comparative rating scale

Any measure of attitudes that asks respondents to rate a concept in comparison with a benchmark explicitly used as a frame of reference.

What Type of Category Labels, If Any?

We have discussed verbal labels, numerical labels, and unlisted choices. Many rating scales have verbal labels for response categories because researchers believe they help respondents better understand the response positions. The maturity and educational levels of the respondents will influence this decision. The semantic differential, with unlabeled response categories between two bipolar adjectives, and the numerical scale, with numbers to indicate scale positions, often are selected because the researcher wishes to assume interval-scale data.

How Many Scale Categories or Response Positions?

Should a category scale have four, five, or seven response positions or categories? Or should the researcher use a graphic scale with an infinite number of positions? The original developmental research on the semantic differential indicated that five to eight points is optimal. However, the researcher must determine the number of meaningful positions that is best for the specific project. This issue of identifying how many meaningful distinctions respondents can practically make is basically a matter of sensitivity. For example, how sensitively can students discriminate the difficulty of college courses? The answer to the question may help determine the number of response categories.

The number of response categories can influence research conclusions. Think about a service employee asked to respond to an item asking about job satisfaction using a two-point response scale of either "no" or "yes." Can the two-point scale adequately capture the range of responses that employees might actually feel? Would we really expect that all people who respond "yes" have the same amount of satisfaction? Typically, a yes or no satisfaction question will yield about 80 percent yes responses. In other words, the data are typically skewed with a small number of scale points. If the scale is expanded to the typical five-point Likert format, the "yes" responses are likely to be spread across multiple categories. Similarly, a scale with too few points may suppress variance that truly exists. Thus, a scale should be adequately sensitive to actually capture a respondent's opinion or feelings.

What happens if the same question is asked with scales of varying numbers of response categories? Some research suggests that skewness is reduced by including more scale points, particularly for attitudinal and satisfaction type items. Additionally, including more scale points produces less extreme patterns of results with typical responses closer to the midpoint of the scale. Thus, as long as adding category responses does not become taxing to respondents, more categories are better than fewer. However, scales with five to ten scale points typically display results suggesting they are appropriate for use in statistical procedures like regression.[7]

Balanced or Unbalanced Rating Scale?

balanced rating scale

A fixed-alternative rating scale with an equal number of positive and negative categories; a neutral point or point of indifference is at the center of the scale.

The fixed-alternative format may be balanced or unbalanced. For example, the following question, which asks about parent-child decisions relating to television program watching, is a **balanced rating scale**:

Who decides which television programs your children watch?

_____ *Child decides all of the time.*
_____ *Child decides most of the time.*
_____ *Child and parent decide together.*
_____ *Parent decides most of the time.*
_____ *Parent decides all of the time.*

unbalanced rating scale

A fixed-alternative rating scale that has more response categories at one end than the other resulting in an unequal number of positive and negative categories.

This scale is balanced because a neutral point, or point of indifference, is at the center of the scale.

Unbalanced rating scales may be used when responses are expected to be distributed at one end of the scale, producing a skewed distribution. The skewed distribution may indicate error and can also interfere with the ability to draw meaningful statistical inferences. Marketing researchers often face situations where "end-piling" will occur. One reason for this is that researchers often ask questions for which respondents are fully expected to give more positive than negative responses. For instance, satisfaction scales (job or customer) generally show this pattern. After all, if an employee has stayed in one job for some years or a customer has already selected a place to do business, we should expect that they would provide a positive response. Unbalanced scales, such as the following one, may mitigate this type of "end piling":

Completely Dissatisfied	Dissatisfied	Somewhat Satisfied	Satisfied	Completely Satisfied
☐	☐	☐	☐	☐

Notice that there are three "satisfied" responses and only two "dissatisfied" responses above. The choice of a balanced or unbalanced scale generally depends on the nature of the concept or the researcher's knowledge about attitudes toward the stimulus to be measured. When respondents are expected to be predisposed toward one end of a concept or the other, unbalanced scales are appropriate. Otherwise, researchers are better off with balanced scales.

Forced-Choice Scales?

forced-choice rating scale

A fixed-alternative rating scale that requires respondents to choose one of the fixed alternatives.

non-forced-choice scale

A fixed-alternative rating scale that provides a "no opinion" category or that allows respondents to indicate that they cannot say which alternative is their choice.

In many situations, a respondent has not formed an attitude toward the concept being studied and simply cannot provide an answer. If a **forced-choice rating scale** compels the respondent to answer, the response is merely a function of the question. If answers are not forced, the midpoint of the scale may be used by the respondent to indicate unawareness as well as indifference. If many respondents in the sample are expected to be unaware of the attitudinal object under investigation, this problem may be eliminated by using a **non-forced-choice scale** that provides a "no opinion" category, as in the following example:

How does the Bank of Commerce compare with the First National Bank?

☐ *Bank of Commerce is better than First National Bank.*
☐ *Bank of Commerce is about the same as First National Bank.*

☐ *Bank of Commerce is worse than First National Bank.*

☐ *Can't say.*

Asking this type of question allows the investigator to separate respondents who cannot make an honest comparison from respondents who have had experience with both banks. The argument for forced choice is that people really do have attitudes, even if they are unfamiliar with the banks, and should be able to answer the question. Respondents are not provided with an easy out by simply selecting "neutral." The use of forced-choice questions is associated with higher incidences of "no answer." Perhaps when respondents really can't make up their mind, they will leave an item blank if they are given that choice. Internet surveys make forced-choice questions easy to implement because the delivery can be set up so that a respondent cannot go to the next question until the previous question is answered. Realize, however, if a respondent truly has no opinion, and the no opinion option is not included, he or she may give a bogus response or simply quit responding to the questionnaire. Thus, if the researcher believes the respondent may have trouble making up his or her mind, a "no answer" option may be provided for respondents. This is usually done out to the side of the valid scale items.

Single or Multiple Items?

Whether to use a single measure or an index measure depends on the complexity of the issue to be investigated, the number of dimensions the issue contains, and whether individual attributes of the stimulus are part of a holistic attitude or are seen as separate items. The researcher's conceptual definition will be helpful in making this choice. Some very simple or concrete concepts can be assessed with a single item. "Did you visit the dealership?" "Do you like pistachio ice cream?" Other indices such as social class require multiple items. Latent constructs also generally require multiple items. Again, problem definition becomes a determining factor influencing the research design.

Attitudes and Intentions

Behavioral researchers often model behavior as a function of intention, which in turn, is considered a function of attitudes. Attitudes are considered a function of a person's beliefs about some activity weighted by their evaluations of those characteristics. This type of research is sometimes referred to as a **multi-attribute model** or reasoned action approach. For example, a consumer's attitude to opt in to SMS advertising can be modeled by their intention to do so, which in turn, is a function of their attitude.[8] Likewise, a researcher may first measure attitude as a way of knowing how likely a consumer would be to purchase apparel made of American alligator skin.

multi-attribute model

A model that constructs an attitude score based on the multiplicative sum of beliefs about an option times the evaluation of those belief characteristics

Multi-attribute Attitude Score

Attitudes are modeled with a multi-attribute approach by taking belief scores assessed with some type of rating scale like those described in this chapter and multiplying each belief score by an evaluation also supplied using some type of rating scale, and then summing each resulting product. For instance, a series of Likert statements might assess a respondent's beliefs about the reliability, price, service, and styling of a Honda Fit.

The Honda Fit is the most reliable car in its class.	*SD*	*D*	*N*	*A*	*SA*
The Honda Fit has a low price for a car of its type.	*SD*	*D*	*N*	*A*	*SA*
I know that my Honda dealer will provide great service if I buy a Honda Fit.	*SD*	*D*	*N*	*A*	*SA*
The Honda Fit is one of the most stylish cars you can buy.	*SD*	*D*	*N*	*A*	*SA*

Then, respondents may use a simple rating scale to assess how good or bad each charcteristic is. For example, the scale may appear something like this with instructions for the respondent to indicate the relative evaluation of each characteristic.

All things considered ...							
			Buying a car that is reliable is				
Very bad	☐	☐	☐	☐	☐	☐	Very good
			Buying a car with a low price is				
Very bad	☐	☐	☐	☐	☐	☐	Very good
			Buying a car from a dealer with excellent service is				
Very bad	☐	☐	☐	☐	☐	☐	Very good
			Buying a car with the latest styling is				
Very bad	☐	☐	☐	☐	☐	☐	Very good

The respondent's attitude toward buying a Honda Fit would be found by multiplying beliefs by evaluations. If a respondent provided the following belief scores using Likert scales for each belief item

Honda Fit reliability	*5*
Honda Fit pricing	*3*
Honda Fit dealer service	*2*
Honda Fit styling	*1*

and the following evaluation scores using the rating scale shown in the preceding

Reliability	*6*
Low pricing	*3*
Dealer service	*4*
Styling	*2*

then her attitude score could be computed as

Beliefs	×	Evaluations	=	(B)(E)
5		*6*		*30*
3		*3*		*9*
2		*4*		*8*
1		*2*		*2*
	Total			*49*

The multi-attribute attitude score for this consumer would be 49. A researcher may also ask respondents to rate a competitor's product. In this case, the product might be a Ford Focus. Using the same four characteristics, a score for the competitor can be obtained. The scores can then be compared to see which brand has a competitive advantage in terms of consumer attitudes.

This type of approach is frequently employed. The key advantages lie in how diagnostic the results can be. Not only can a researcher provide management with feedback on the relative attitude scores, but he or she can also identify characteristics that are most in need of being improved. In particular, poor belief scores on characteristics that respondents rate very favorably (or as highly important) indicate the characteristics that most need to be changed to improve competitive positioning. In this case, the Fit does well on reliability, and the strong belief score on this characteristic is largely responsible for shaping this consumer's attitude. If the Ford Focus scored only a 2 on reliability, the result would diagnose a problem that should be addressed. The focus has a relatively low score on a very meaningful characteristic.

Behavioral Intention

According to reasoned action theory, people form intentions consistent with the multi-attribute attitude score. Intentions represent the behavioral expectations of an individual toward an attitudinal object. Typically, the component of interest to marketers is a buying intention, a tendency to seek additional information, or plans to visit a showroom. Category scales for measuring the behavioral component of an attitude ask about a respondent's likelihood of purchase or intention to perform some future action, using questions such as the following:

How likely is it that you will purchase a Honda Fit?

- *I definitely will buy.*
- *I probably will buy.*
- *I might buy.*
- *I probably will not buy.*
- *I definitely will not buy.*

I would write a letter to my representative in Congress or other government official in support of this company if it were in a dispute with government.

- *Extremely likely*
- *Very likely*
- *Somewhat likely*
- *Likely, about a 50–50 chance*
- *Somewhat unlikely*
- *Very unlikely*
- *Absolutely unlikely*

The wording of statements used in these scales often includes phrases such as "I would recommend," "I would write," or "I would buy" to indicate action tendencies.

Expectations also may be measured using a scale of subjective probabilities, ranging from 100 for "absolutely certain" to 0 for "absolutely no chance." Researchers have used the following subjective probability scale to estimate the chance that a job candidate will accept a sales position:

100%	*(Absolutely certain) I will accept.*
90%	*(Almost sure) I will accept.*
80%	*(Very big chance) I will accept.*
70%	*(Big chance) I will accept.*
60%	*(Not so big a chance) I will accept.*
50%	*(About even) I will accept.*
40%	*(Smaller chance) I will accept.*
30%	*(Small chance) I will accept.*
20%	*(Very small chance) I will accept.*
10%	*(Almost certainly not) I will accept.*
0%	*(Certainly not) I will accept.*

Alternatively, respondents may simply be asked to fill in a blank indicating the percentage likelihood of performing the relevant behavior. The attitude scores obtained above should correlate positively with the behavioral intent scores.

Behavioral Differential

A general instrument, the **behavioral differential**, is used to measure the behavioral intentions of subjects toward an object or category of objects. As in the semantic differential, a description of the object to be judged is followed by a series of scales on which subjects indicate their behavioral intentions toward this object. For example, one item might be something like the following:

A 25-year-old female sales representative

would ___ ___ ___ ___ ___ ___ ___ *would not*

ask this person for advice.

behavioral differential

A rating scale instrument similar to a semantic differential, developed to measure the behavioral intentions of subjects toward future actions.

- Attitudinal research can involve numerous types of rating or ranking scales.
  - Rating scales are generally preferable to ranking scales because they offer more flexibility in application and analysis.
  - Ranking scales become useful when respondents might rate all or most of the alternative responses equally if they are not forced to discriminate choices from one another.
- Semantic differentials are easy to apply and are very useful. However, they are applicable only when scale items can be formed using truly unambiguous opposites.
- Likert scales are very widely applied. All things considered, attitudinal scale items such as Likert scales typically involve between five and ten scale points. On some occasions fewer than five are used and sometimes more than ten.
  - Whenever there is a question about the number of scale points to use, it is better to use more rather than fewer scale points to produce valid results with a more normal distribution.
  - Typically, an even number of response points results in a forced-choice scale because no place for a neutral response in the middle of the scale can be included. When using an even number of scale points, researchers should consider providing an option outside of the scale for respondents who simply cannot reach a decision on

which response to choose (i.e., "no response" or "cannot decide").
- Unbalanced scales have a place when skewed results would be fully expected.
  - Such is the case with most types of satisfaction studies or any attitudinal variable for which respondents have displayed behavior that would predispose them toward one end of a concept or another. For example, someone who has used the same hairdresser for several years is most likely to indicate some level of positive attitude. If the attitude was truly negative, chances are a new hairdresser would have been sought out!
- Basic multi-attribute attitude studies are very useful in diagnosing competitive positions.
  - Different competitors' relative strengths and weaknesses can be identified by the combinations of beliefs and evaluations.
  - Attitude scores have no absolute meaning so results for more than one company are needed to provide reference.
  - Remember, when conducting these studies belief scores must be collected for every alternative that a respondent is evaluating. However, the evaluation scores need only be collected once.

Summary

1. Define attitude and understand why it is so important in business research. Attitudes are a relatively enduring predisposition to respond consistently to various things including people, activities, events and objects. Attitudes are predispositions toward behavior and as such represent rules that inform a person as to the appropriate reaction in a given situation. Attitudes consist of three components: the affective, or the emotions or feelings involved; the cognitive, or awareness or knowledge; and the behavioral, or the predisposition to action. Attitudes are so important because when an attitude is known, behavior can be predicted with some degree of confidence.

2. Produce a Likert rating scale that measures an attitudinal concept. With a Likert scale, respondents indicate their attitudes by checking how strongly they agree or disagree with carefully constructed statements. An attitude can be represented with a series of Likert scale items. Typically, Likert scales contain between five and seven response points. A five-item Likert scale states a phrase with which a respondent expresses agreement. The response points would be "strongly disagree," "disagree," "neutral," "agree," "strongly agree."

3. Discuss the use of other types of scales that assess attitudinal concepts. Although the Likert scale is perhaps the most widely applied attitudinal scale format, many others exist. A semantic differential uses a series of attitude scales anchored by bipolar adjectives. The respondent indicates where his or her attitude falls between the polar attitudes. Variations on this method, such as numerical scales and the Stapel scale, are also used. The Stapel scale puts a single adjective in the center of a range of numerical values from +3 to −3. Constant-sum scales require the respondent to divide a constant sum into parts, indicating the weights to be given to various attributes of the item being studied.

4. Understand factors important to selecting an appropriate measurement scale. The researcher can choose among a number of attitude scales. Choosing among the alternatives requires considering several questions, each of which is generally answered by comparing the advantages of each alternative to the problem definition. A monadic rating scale asks about a single concept. A comparative rating scale asks a respondent to rate a concept in comparison with a benchmark used as a frame of reference. Scales may be balanced or unbalanced. Unbalanced scales may prevent responses from piling up at one end. Forced-choice scales require the respondent to select an alternative; non-forced-choice scales allow the respondent to indicate an inability to select an alternative.

5. Implement a multi-attribute model. A multiattribute model represents a respondent's attitude about some activity, object, event, or idea by taking belief scores assessed with some type of rating scale and multiplying each belief score by an evaluation of the matching characteristic, also supplied using some type of rating scale, and then summing those products together. These attitude scores are expected to predict behavioral intentions with some degree of confidence. Multi-attribute models provide highly diagnostic information to competitive businesses and thus, they are widely applied.

Key Terms and Concepts

attitude, *343*
balanced rating scale, *358*
behavioral differential, *361*
category scale, *345*
choice, *345*
comparative rating scale, *357*
constant-sum scale, *351*
forced-choice rating scale, *358*

graphic rating scale, *352*
image profile, *350*
Likert scale, *346*
monadic rating scale, *357*
multi-attribute model, *359*
net promoter score, *343*
non-forced-choice scale, *358*
paired comparison, *355*

ranking, *345*
rating, *345*
semantic differential, *348*
sorting, *345*
Stapel scale, *350*
unbalanced rating scale, *358*

Questions for Review and Critical Thinking

1. What is a net promoter score?
2. What is an *attitude*? Why do businesses place so much emphasis on measuring attitudinal concepts?
3. Attitudes are sometimes called tri-partite, meaning they have three components. What are the three components of an attitude?
4. Distinguish between *rating* and *ranking*. Which is a better attitude measurement technique? Why?
5. Construct a Likert scale that would measure student attitudes toward constructing a new business building on campus.

6. What is the difference between a five-item and a six-item Likert scale?
7. Assume the researcher wanted to create a summated scale indicating a respondent's attitude toward the trucking industry. What would the result be for the respondent whose response is as indicated below?
8. Describe the way a semantic differential scale could be constructed to measure the behavioral component of attitudes.
9. What is a fundamental weakness of a constant sum or ranking scale?

	Strongly Disagree	Disagree	Somewhat Disagree	Somewhat Agree	Agree	Strongly Agree
6. I feel the trucking industry in Canada is very important to our economy.	☐	☐	☐	☒	☐	☐
7. Truck drivers go out of their way to help make the roads safer.	☐	☐	☐	☐	☒	☐
8. The trucking industry is harmful to Canadians in more ways than one.	☐	☒	☐	☐	☐	☐
9. Without the trucking industry, our communities would be much better off.	☐	☐	☒	☐	☐	☐
10. Truck drivers are among the most courteous drivers.	☐	☐	☐	☐	☐	☒

10. Identify issues a researcher should consider when choosing a measurement scale.
11. Name some situations in which a graphics rating scale could be useful.
12. Should a Likert scale ever be treated as though it has interval properties?
13. In each of the following, identify the type of scale and evaluate it:
    a. A U.S. representative's questionnaire sent to constituents:

    Do you favor or oppose the Fair Tax Proposal?

In Favor	*Opposed*	*No Opinion*
☐	☐	☐

    b. How favorable are you toward the Fair Tax Proposal?

    Very unfavorable ☐ ☐ ☐ ☐ ☐ *Very favorable*

    c. A psychographic statement asking the respondent to circle the appropriate response:

    I shop a lot for specials.

Strongly disagree	*Disagree*	*Neutral*	*Agree*	*Strongly agree*
1	2	3	4	5

14. What is a multi-attribute model of consumer attitudes?
15. Look at the table below. The b columns represent belief scores for two competing products. The e column represents the evaluations of those characteristics. Compute the attitude score for each competitor and comment on the competitive positioning of each.

Characteristic	b—Brand A	b—Brand B	e
Price	5	3	6
Quality	6	2	3
Convenience	1	2	4
Ease of use	3	5	1
Looks	1	7	5

16. If a Likert summated scale has 10 scale items, do all 10 items have to be phrased as either positive or negative statements, or can the scale contain a mix of positive and negative statements? Explain.
17. If a semantic differential has 10 scale items, should all the positive adjectives be on the right and all the negative adjectives on the left? Explain.
18. Design a brief section of a survey instrument that could be used to conduct a multi-attribute model study of portable computers. The research question involves searching for competitive advantages and disadvantages of a basic Dell PC against an Apple MacBook. The relevant beliefs include what a respondent would think about the processing speed, ease of use, compatibility with other systems, weight, and price. (Hint: you will have to collect the beliefs for both the Dell PC and the Apple ThinkPad separately. If possible, use the Qualtrics Survey tool to design the survey instrument.)
19. ETHICS A researcher thinks many respondents will answer "don't know" or "can't say" if these options are printed on an attitude scale along with categories indicating level of agreement. The researcher does not print either "don't know" or "can't say" on the questionnaire because the resulting data would be more complicated to analyze and report. Is this proper?
20. 'NET SRI International investigates U.S. consumers by asking questions about their attitudes and values. It has a Web site so people can VALS-type themselves. To find out your VALS type, go to **http://www.sric-bi.com/VALS/presurvey.shtml**.

Research Activities

1. A researcher wishes to compare two hotels on the following attributes:
   Convenience of location
   Friendly personnel
   Value for money
   a. Design a Likert scale to accomplish this task.
   b. Design a semantic differential scale to accomplish this task.
   c. Design a graphic rating scale to accomplish this task.

Case 14.1 Roeder-Johnson Corporation

A decade ago, the talk in business circles was all about the central role of technology, especially the Internet, in the success of new businesses. Some investors seemed eager to back almost any start-up with "dot-com" in its name or its business plan. Although the go-go investment climate of the 1990s seems far away, entrepreneurs still start companies every year, and they are still making their case to the investment community. What business ideas do investors like? Is high-tech still important? Public relations firm Roeder-Johnson Corporation, which specializes in start-up companies and those involved in technology innovation, conducted an online survey into the attitudes of 70 subjects, including venture capitalists, entrepreneurs, journalists, and company analysts.[9] The central question was this:

Do you believe that unique technology is crucial to the success of startup companies today?

1. Rarely
2. Occasionally
3. Frequently
4. Usually
5. Always

The remainder of the survey asked for reasons why technology is important to start-ups and invited comments from the respondents.

In its news release, Roeder-Johnson reported that 91 percent of respondents consider technology to be important at least frequently. The breakdown was 39 percent frequently, 39 percent usually, and 13 percent always. The remaining 9 percent of respondents cited technology as important only occasionally, and none said it is rarely important.

Questions

1. Evaluate the rating scale used for the question in this survey. Is it balanced? Are the category labels clear? Is the number of categories appropriate?
2. Suggest three ways that Roeder-Johnson could improve this survey without a major cost increase.
3. Based on the information given here, what do you think the research objectives for this survey might have been? Do you think the survey met its objectives? Explain.

Case 14.2 Ha-Pah-Shu-Tse

Raymond RedCorn is an Osage Indian. The Ha-Pah-Shu-Tse (Osage for "red corn") restaurant in Pawhuska, Oklahoma, is the only authentic Native American restaurant in the state and one of few in the country.

The Ha-Pah-Shu-Tse restaurant opened in 1972 with a seating capacity of eight; today, after expansion, crowds of up to 90 keep RedCorn and his wife busy. They are currently marketing an Indian fry bread mix, and they are planning on increased sales for their only packaged good. Indian fry bread mix has long been a staple of the Native American diet. The bread is sweet and contains basic ingredients such as flour, shortening, and sugar.

The Restaurant

Waltina RedCorn married into the Osage tribe 47 years ago and learned how to cook from two women named Grandma Baconrind and Grandma Lookout. They must have taught her well, because customers of the Ha-Pah-Shu-Tse are not content just to eat there—they often have the RedCorns mail them fry bread mix. Raymond RedCorn finds that people who eat the unusual native dish usually request the recipe. He says, "I have not found anyone who does not like the bread." Customers aren't limited to local fans of Indian food. Because the fry bread is sold or served in restaurants and stores in Oklahoma as well as at a museum, people from as far away as Europe have tried it.

According to RedCorn, "About once a week, someone from England comes in." He serves these British customers fry bread or the restaurant's "best-sellers," Indian Meat Pie or Navaho Taco, and tells them the story of fry bread and how it got him an invitation to Buckingham Palace. When he was 18 years old, he was in London for a Boy Scout Jamboree. One evening he was frying the Indian bread when the British Boy Scout organizer approached with two young men. It was only after everyone had tasted RedCorn's culinary effort that the Prince of Wales was introduced. "The Indian delegation from Oklahoma was invited to set up their tents on the ground at the palace and spend the weekend being entertained by the young royalty," RedCorn says.

The Product

The product as it is today took several years to perfect. The Red-Corns wanted a mix that would need only the addition of water. Each batch was sent to relatives and friends for judgment on the taste until everyone was convinced it was the best it could be.

The mix, consisting of Indian flour, is already distributed in Tulsa, Bartlesville, and surrounding towns under the Ha-Pah-Shu-Tse brand name. It is packaged in 2- and 5-pound silver bags with Raymond RedCorn in Osage tribal costume pictured on the front. Directions for making the fry bread are listed on the back of the package.

The Research Problem

When planning the marketing for the Indian fry bread mix, student consultants working with the Small Business Administration suggested some attitude research. They felt that successfully marketing the Ha-Pah-Shu-Tse product depended on knowing what consumer reactions to Indian foods would be. They believed that if the image of Indian foods and consumers' awareness of them were measured, RedCorn would have a better chance of marketing his product. In addition, the student consultants felt that the name Ha-Pah-Shu-Tse violated many of the requirements for a good brand name—it was not short, simple, or easy to recall, and was difficult to pronounce and spell.

Questions

1. What marketing questions must be answered as Ha-Pah-Shu-Tse plans for expansion? How can marketing research help answer those questions?
2. What type of attitude scale would you recommend? How would you generate a set of items (attributes) to be measured?
3. Does an image profile seem appropriate in this case?

Case 14.3 Attitudes toward Technology and Lifestyle

A marketing research company sent the attitude scales in Case Exhibit 14.3–1 to members of its consumer panel. Other questions on the questionnaire were about ownership and/or use of computers, consumer electronic devices, satellite TV ownership, cellular phones, and Internet activity.

Questions

1. What type of attitude scale appears in the case study?
2. Evaluate the list of statements. Do the statements appear to measure a single concept?
3. What do they appear to be measuring?

CASE EXHIBIT 14.3–1 **Attitude Scale**

Below is a list of statements that may or may not be used to describe your attitudes toward technology and your lifestyle. Please indicate to what extent each statement describes your attitudes by placing an X in a box from 1 to 10, where 10 means that statement "Describes your attitudes completely" and a 1 means that statement "Does not describe your attitudes at all." (X ONE BOX ACROSS FOR EACH STATEMENT.)

	Does Not Describe Your Attitudes At All									Describes Your Attitudes Completely
	1	2	3	4	5	6	7	8	9	10
I like to impress people with my lifestyle.	☐	☐	☐	☐	☐	☐	☐	☐	☐	☐
Technology is important to me.	☐	☐	☐	☐	☐	☐	☐	☐	☐	☐
I am very competitive when it comes to my career.	☐	☐	☐	☐	☐	☐	☐	☐	☐	☐
Having fun is the whole point of life.	☐	☐	☐	☐	☐	☐	☐	☐	☐	☐
Family is important, but I have other interests that are just as important to me.	☐	☐	☐	☐	☐	☐	☐	☐	☐	☐
I am constantly looking for new ways to entertain myself.	☐	☐	☐	☐	☐	☐	☐	☐	☐	☐
Making a lot of money is important to me.	☐	☐	☐	☐	☐	☐	☐	☐	☐	☐
I spend most of my free time doing fun stuff with my friends.	☐	☐	☐	☐	☐	☐	☐	☐	☐	☐
I like to spend time learning about new technology products.	☐	☐	☐	☐	☐	☐	☐	☐	☐	☐
I like to show off my taste and style.	☐	☐	☐	☐	☐	☐	☐	☐	☐	☐
I like technology.	☐	☐	☐	☐	☐	☐	☐	☐	☐	☐
My family is by far the most important thing in my life.	☐	☐	☐	☐	☐	☐	☐	☐	☐	☐
I put a lot of time and energy into my career.	☐	☐	☐	☐	☐	☐	☐	☐	☐	☐
I am very likely to purchase new technology products or services.	☐	☐	☐	☐	☐	☐	☐	☐	☐	☐
I spend most of my free time working on improving myself.	☐	☐	☐	☐	☐	☐	☐	☐	☐	☐

After studying this chapter, you should be able to

1. Know the key decisions in questionnaire design
2. Choose between open-ended and fixed-alternative questions
3. Summarize guidelines for questions that avoid mistakes in questionnaire design
4. Describe how the proper sequence of questions may improve a questionnaire
5. Discuss how to design a questionnaire layout
6. Describe criteria for pretesting and revising a questionnaire and for adapting it to global markets

Chapter Vignette: J.D. Power Asks Consumers to Get Real

Are you driving your dream car? Most of us can't, because we bump up against the practical reality that we can't pay for every great new feature. As carmakers consider adding new features, they have to evaluate not only which ones appeal to consumers but also which ones will actually sell, considering their likely cost. J.D. Power and Associates recently addressed this issue in a survey of about seventeen thousand consumers.[1]

In the J.D. Power survey, consumers were asked whether they were familiar with 22 different emerging technologies. Then they were asked about their interest in each technology, rating their interest using a scale ("definitely interested," "probably interested," and so on). Next, the study indicated the likely price of each technology, and consumers were asked their interest, given the price. The results ranked the features according to interest level, based on the percentage who indicated they were either definitely or probably interested in the feature.

Learning price information often changed consumers' interest levels. Night vision systems appealed to 72 percent of consumers, placing it in second place in the rankings. But when consumers learned the systems would likely add $1,500 to the price of a car, this technology dropped to a rank of 17, near the bottom. In contrast, HD radio ranked in sixteenth place until consumers saw a price tag of just $150. That price pushed the feature up to third place. Still, two features remained in the top five even with pricing information: run-flat tires and stability control. And three of the bottom-five features—a reconfigurable cabin, lane departure warning system, and smart sensing power-swing front doors—stayed in the bottom rankings. Automakers can use findings such as these to determine which features are price-sensitive and which might be appealing even at a higher price.

In the J.D. Power survey, answers changed when respondents were given more information. This chapter outlines a procedure for questionnaire design, which addresses concerns such as the wording and order of questions and the layout of the questionnaire.

© RF/CORBIS

By now, you are probably quite familiar with the online course questionnaire. As you went through the questionnaire, did you spot any problem questions? You should be able to describe the problems better after finishing this chapter. Here are some questions to consider:

- What are problem items, if any?
- Are there any topics covered in the survey that would result in more valid responses through a) a phone interview or b) a personal interview?
- Look at the section of the questionnaire shown. Describe any potential problems with these particular items using terminology from the chapter. In other words, do the items display characteristics that should be avoided?

Please read the following statements. After reading click the square that best describes whether you agree or disagree with the statement.

	Strongly Agree	Agree	Neutral	Disagree	Strongly Disagree
I visit a website from another country at least once a week.	○	○	○	○	○
I feel that keeping up with the opinions of other nations is important.	○	○	○	○	○
I think it's important to go to the library and read a newspaper every week.	○	○	○	○	○
It is important to understand the opinions of other countries.	○	○	○	○	○
I think it's important to engage my friends from other countries as to what it's like where they are from.	○	○	○	○	○
I don't have enough time to read a newspaper.	○	○	○	○	○
I get my opinions on other countries from television.	○	○	○	○	○

Introduction

Survey researchers use a questionnaire like a carpenter uses a hammer. The questionnaire is the primary tool for building responses to research questions. Many people may believe asking a question is really very simple. But, the quality of response can't be expected to be good when the question itself was bad.

The importance of question wording is easily overlooked, but questionnaire design is one of the most critical stages in the survey research process. Businesspeople and managers who are inexperienced at marketing research frequently believe that constructing a questionnaire is a simple task that they can do without the assistance of a professional researcher. Amateur researchers like these think a short questionnaire can be written in minutes. Unfortunately, newcomers who naively believe a good printer is all a person needs to construct a questionnaire generally end up with useless results. Ask a bad question, get bad results.

Basic Considerations in Questionnaire Design

Good questionnaire design requires far more than correct grammar. People don't understand questions just because they are grammatically correct. Respondents simply may not know what is being asked. They may be unaware of the product or topic of interest. They may confuse the subject with something else. The question may not mean the same thing to everyone interviewed. Finally, people may refuse to answer personal questions. Most of these problems can be minimized, however, if a skilled researcher composes the questionnaire.

Even though we discuss questionnaire items as questions, often they are not questions at all but simply words, statements, phrases, or images that are used to evoke a response. We saw examples of different approaches in the previous chapter.

For a questionnaire to fulfill a researcher's purposes, the questions must meet the basic criteria of *relevance* and *accuracy*. To achieve these ends, a researcher who is systematically planning a questionnaire's design must make several decisions—typically, but not always, the decisions take place in the following sequence:

1. What should be asked?
2. How should questions be phrased?

TO THE POINT

How often misused words generate misleading thoughts.

—Herbert Spencer

3. In what sequence should the questions be arranged?
4. What questionnaire layout will best serve the research objectives?
5. How should the questionnaire be pretested? Does the questionnaire need to be revised?

What Should Be Asked?

Certain decisions made during the early stages of the research process will influence the questionnaire design. The preceding chapters stressed good problem definition and clear research questions. This leads to specific research hypotheses that in turn, clearly indicate what must be measured. Different types of questions may be better at measuring certain things than are others. In addition, the communication medium used for data collection—that is, telephone interview, personal interview, snail mail, or Web-based questionnaire—must be determined. This decision is another forward linkage that influences the structure and content of the questionnaire. The specific questions to be asked will be a function of the previous decisions.

The latter stages of the research process will have an important impact on questionnaire wording. The questions that should be asked will, of course, take the form of data analysis into account. When designing the questionnaire, the researcher should consider the types of statistical analysis that will be conducted.

Questionnaire Relevancy

A questionnaire is *relevant* to the extent that all information collected addresses a research question that will help the decision maker address the current marketing problem. Asking a wrong question or an irrelevant question is a common pitfall. If the marketing task is to pinpoint store image problems, questions asking for political opinions may be irrelevant. The researcher should be specific about data needs and have a rationale for each item requesting information. Irrelevant questions are more than a nuisance because they make the survey needlessly long. In a study where two samples of the same group of businesses received either a one-page or a three-page questionnaire, the response rate was nearly twice as high for the one-page survey.[2]

Conversely, many researchers, after conducting surveys, find that they omitted some important questions. Therefore, when planning the questionnaire design, researchers must think about possible omissions. Is information on the relevant demographic and psychographic variables being collected? Would certain questions help clarify the answers to other questions? Will the results of the study provide the answer to the marketing manager's problem?

Questionnaire Accuracy

Once a researcher decides what should be asked, the criterion of accuracy becomes the primary concern. *Accuracy* means that the information is valid. While experienced researchers generally believe that questionnaires should use simple, understandable, unbiased, unambiguous, and non-irritating words, no step-by-step procedure for ensuring accuracy in question writing can be generalized across projects. Obtaining accurate answers from respondents depends strongly on the researcher's ability to design a questionnaire that will facilitate recall and motivate respondents to cooperate. Respondents tend to be more cooperative when the subject of the research interests them. When questions are not lengthy, difficult to answer, or ego threatening, there is a higher probability of obtaining unbiased answers.

Question wording and sequence also substantially influence accuracy, which can be particularly challenging when designing a survey for technical audiences. The Department of Treasury commissioned a survey of insurance companies to evaluate their offering of terrorism insurance as required by the government's terrorism reinsurance program. But industry members complained that the survey misused terms such as "contract" and "high risk," which have precise meanings for insurers, and asked for policy information "to date," without specifying which date. These questions caused confusion and left room for interpretation, calling the survey results into question.[3]

Question Phrasing: Open- or Close-Ended Statements?

Questions can be phrased in any one of many ways. The research may choose from many standard question formats developed over time in previous research studies. This section presents a classification of question types and provides some helpful guidelines for writing questions.

Open-Ended Response versus Fixed-Alternative Questions

Two basic types of questions can be identified based on the amount of freedom respondents have in answering. Thus, they call for responses that are either open-ended or closed (from a fixed set of choices).

open-ended response questions

Questions that pose some problem and ask respondents to answer in their own words.

Open-ended response questions pose some problem or topic and ask respondents to answer in their own words. If the question is asked in a personal interview, the interviewer may probe for more information, as in the following examples:

- *What names of local banks can you think of offhand?*
- *What comes to mind when you look at this advertisement?*
- *In what way, if any, could this product be changed or improved? I'd like you to tell me anything you can think of, no matter how minor it seems.*
- *What things do you like most about Federal Express's service?*
- *Why do you buy more of your clothing in Nordstrom than in other stores?*
- *How can our stores better serve your needs?*
- *Please tell me anything at all that you remember about the BMW commercial you saw last night.*

fixed-alternative questions

Questions in which respondents are given specific, limited-alternative responses and asked to choose the one closest to their own viewpoint.

Open-ended response questions are free-answer questions. They may be contrasted with **fixed-alternative questions**—sometimes called *closed questions*—which give respondents specific limited-alternative responses and ask them to choose the one closest to their own viewpoints. For example:

Did you use any commercial feed or supplement for livestock or poultry in 2006?

☐ *Yes*　　　☐ *No*

Compared with ten years ago, would you say that the quality of most products made in Japan today is higher, about the same, or not as good?

☐ *Higher*
☐ *About the same*
☐ *Not as good*

Do you think the Renewable Energy Partnership Program has affected your business?

☐ *Yes, for the better*
☐ *Yes, for the worse*
☐ *Not especially*

In which type of bookstore is it easier for you to shop—a regular bookstore or a Web-based bookstore?

☐ *Regular "brick and mortar" bookstore*
☐ *Web bookstore*

How much of your shopping for clothes and household items do you do in wholesale club stores?

☐ *All of it*
☐ *Most of it*
☐ *About one-half of it*
☐ *About one-quarter of it*
☐ *Less than one-quarter of it*

Corporate Reputations: Consumers Put Johnson & Johnson on Top

To report the reputations of well-known companies, the *Wall Street Journal* sponsors an annual research project, the Corporate Reputation Survey. The idea is to see what U.S. adults think about corporations, not to rate a predetermined set of companies, so the study has two phases.

In the first phase, the researchers identified the companies that were most "visible," meaning companies that people were most likely to think about—and therefore have an attitude toward. This phase avoided the problem of asking individuals to rate the qualities of a company they have never heard of. This research used open-ended questions asking respondents to name two companies they felt had the best reputation and two that had the worst. Because of the open-ended format, some respondents mistakenly gave names that were subsidiaries or brands of the same company. The researchers counted those responses as mentions of the parent company so that all responses would be included. The researchers determined the number of times each company was mentioned and selected the sixty named most often for the second phase of the study.

The second phase was aimed at generating rankings of the corporations, so questions and answer choices needed to be more specific. The researchers identified six dimensions of a corporate reputation: products and services, financial performance, workplace environment, social responsibility, vision and leadership, and emotional appeal. Within these categories, they identified twenty attributes, such as whether respondents would trust the company if they had a problem with its goods or services and how sincere its corporate communications were. In an online survey, each respondent was asked to rate one company on all twenty attributes. Then the respondent was invited (not required) to rate a second company. More than 250 ratings were generated for each company. These responses were combined to create an overall rating for the company.

The top-ranked company for two years running was Johnson & Johnson, followed by Coca-Cola and Google. On the six dimensions of reputation, J&J was tops in emotional appeal and its goods and services, and it made the top five on the other dimensions. This honor is more than just good publicity; J&J also was the firm from which the largest share of people said they would "definitely purchase" products.

Source: Based on Ronald Alsop, "Ranking Corporation Reputations," *Wall Street Journal* (December 6, 2005), http://online.wsj.com; "Corporate Reputation Survey Methodology," *Wall Street Journal* (December 5, 2005), http://online.wsj.com; "2005 Reputation Quotient Rankings," *Wall Street Journal* (December 6, 2005), http://online.wsj.com; "Corporate Reputation Survey," *Wall Street Journal* (December 6, 2005), http://online.wsj.com.

© GEORGE DOYLE & CIARAN GRIFFIN

© AP PHOTO

■ USING OPEN-ENDED RESPONSE QUESTIONS

Open-ended response questions are most beneficial when the researcher is conducting exploratory research, especially when the range of responses is not known. Such questions can be used to learn which words and phrases people spontaneously give to the free-response question. Respondents are free to answer with whatever is uppermost in their minds. By obtaining free and uninhibited responses, the researcher may find some unanticipated reaction toward the product. Such responses will reflect the flavor of the language that people use in talking about goods or services and thus may provide a source of new ideas for advertising copywriting or a good way of wording structured scale items. Also, open-ended response questions are valuable at the beginning of an interview. They are good first questions because they allow respondents to warm up to the questioning process.

The cost of administering open-ended response questions is substantially higher than that of administering fixed-alternative questions because the job of editing, coding, and analyzing the data is quite extensive. As each respondent's answer is somewhat unique, there is some difficulty in categorizing and summarizing the answers. The process requires that an editor go over a sample of questions to develop a classification scheme. This scheme is then used to code all answers according to the classification scheme.

Another potential disadvantage of the open-ended response question is the possibility that interviewer bias will influence the answer. While most interviewer instructions state that answers are to be recorded verbatim, rarely does even the best interviewer get every word spoken by the respondent. Interviewers have a tendency to take shortcuts. When this occurs, the interviewer may well introduce error because the final answer may reflect a combination of the respondent's and interviewer's ideas.

Also, articulate individuals tend to give longer answers to open-ended response questions. Such respondents often are better educated and from higher income groups and therefore may not be representative of the entire population, and yet they may give a large share of the responses. The Research Snapshot above describes how Johnson & Johnson takes advantage of open-ended responses.

■ USING FIXED-ALTERNATIVE QUESTIONS

In contrast, fixed-alternative questions require less interviewer skill, take less time, and are easier for the respondent to answer. This is because answers to closed questions are classified into standardized groupings prior to data collection. Standardizing alternative responses to a question provides comparability of answers, which facilitates coding, tabulating, and ultimately interpreting the data.

However, when a researcher is unaware of the potential responses to a question, fixed-alternative questions obviously cannot be used. If the researcher assumes what the responses will be but is in fact wrong, he or she will have no way of knowing the extent to which the assumption was incorrect. Sometimes this type of error comes to light after the questionnaire has been used. Researchers found cross-cultural misunderstandings in a survey of mothers called the Preschooler Feeding Questionnaire. By talking to a group of African-American mothers, a researcher at the University of Chicago determined that they had experiences with encouraging children to eat more and using food to calm children, but they used different language for these situations than the questionnaire used, so they misinterpreted some questions.[4]

Unanticipated alternatives emerge when respondents believe that closed answers do not adequately reflect their feelings. They may make comments to the interviewer or write additional answers on the questionnaire indicating that the exploratory research did not yield a complete array of responses. After the fact, little can be done to correct a closed question that does not provide enough alternatives. Therefore, a researcher may find exploratory research with open-ended responses valuable before writing a descriptive questionnaire. The researcher should strive to ensure that there are sufficient response choices to include almost all possible answers.

Respondents may check off obvious alternatives, such as price or durability, if they do not see the choice they would prefer. Also, a fixed-alternative question may tempt respondents to check an answer that is more prestigious or socially acceptable than the true answer. Rather than stating that they do not know why they chose a given product, they may select an alternative among those presented, or as a matter of convenience, they may select a given alternative rather than think of the most correct response.

Most questionnaires mix open-ended and closed questions. As we have discussed, each form has unique benefits. In addition, a change of pace can eliminate respondent boredom and fatigue.

Types of Fixed-Alternative Questions

Earlier in the chapter a variety of fixed-alternative questions were presented. We will now identify and categorize the various types.

simple-dichotomy (dichotomous-alternative) question

A fixed-alternative question that requires the respondent to choose one of two alternatives.

The **simple-dichotomy (dichotomous-alternative) question** requires the respondent to choose one of two alternatives. The answer can be a simple "yes" or "no" or a choice between "this" and "that." For example:

Did you make any long-distance calls last week?

☐   *Yes*   ☐   *No*

determinant-choice question

A fixed-alternative question that requires the respondent to choose one response from among multiple alternatives.

Several types of questions provide the respondent with *multiple-choice alternatives*. The **determinant-choice question** requires the respondent to choose one—and only one—response from among several possible alternatives. For example:

Please give us some information about your flight. In which section of the aircraft did you sit?

☐   *First class*
☐   *Business class*
☐   *Coach class*

frequency-determination question

A fixed-alternative question that asks for an answer about general frequency of occurrence.

The **frequency-determination question** is a determinant-choice question that asks for an answer about the general frequency of occurrence. For example:

How frequently do you watch the MTV television channel?

☐   *Every day*

☐ *5–6 times a week*
☐ *2–4 times a week*
☐ *Once a week*
☐ *Less than once a week*
☐ *Never*

Attitude rating scales, such as the Likert scale, semantic differential, Stapel scale, and so on, are fixed-alternative questions too. These scales were discussed in Chapter 14.

The **checklist question** allows the respondent to provide multiple answers to a single question. The respondent indicates past experience, preference, and the like merely by checking off items. In many cases the choices are adjectives that describe a particular object. A typical checklist question might ask the following:

Please check which of the following sources of information about investments you regularly use, if any.

☐ *Personal advice of your broker(s)*
☐ *Brokerage newsletters*
☐ *Brokerage research reports*
☐ *Investment advisory service(s)*
☐ *Conversations with other investors*
☐ *Web page(s)*
☐ *None of these*
☐ *Other (please specify)* _____

checklist question

A fixed-alternative question that allows the respondent to provide multiple answers to a single question by checking off items.

A major problem in developing dichotomous or multiple-choice alternatives is the framing of the response alternatives. There should be no overlap among categories. Alternatives should be *mutually exclusive,* meaning only one dimension of an issue should be related to each alternative. The following listing of income groups illustrates a common error:

- *Under $15,000*
- *$15,000–$30,000*
- *$30,000–$55,000*
- *$55,000–$70,000*
- *Over $70,000*

How many people with incomes of $30,000 will be in the second group, and how many will be in the third group? A respondent who actually had a $30,000 income could equally as likely choose either. Researchers have no way of knowing how a true $30,000–per-year respondent responded. Grouping alternatives without forethought about analysis is likely to diminish accuracy.

Also, few people relish being in the lowest category. To negate the potential bias caused by respondents' tendency to avoid an extreme category, researchers often include a category lower than the lowest expected answers.

Phrasing Questions for Self-Administered, Telephone, and Personal Interview Surveys

The means of data collection—telephone interview, personal interview, self-administered questionnaire—will influence the question format and question phrasing. In general, questions for mail, Internet, and telephone surveys must be less complex than those used in personal interviews. Questionnaires for telephone and personal interviews should be written in a conversational style. Exhibit 15.1 on the next page illustrates how a question may be revised for a different medium.

In a telephone survey about attitudes toward police services, the questionnaire not only asked about general attitudes such as how much respondents trust their local police officers and whether the police are "approachable," "dedicated," and so on, but also provided basic scenarios to help respondents put their expectations into words. For example, the interviewer asked respondents to imagine that someone had broken into their home and stolen items, and that the respondent called the police to report the crime. The interviewer asked how quickly or slowly the respondent expected the police to arrive.[5]

EXHIBIT 15.1
Reducing Question Complexity by Providing Fewer Responses for Telephone Interviews

Mail Form:

How satisfied are you with your community?

1 Very satisfied
2 Quite satisfied
3 Somewhat satisfied
4 Slightly satisfied
5 Neither satisfied nor dissatisfied
6 Slightly dissatisfied
7 Somewhat dissatisfied
8 Quite dissatisfied
9 Very dissatisfied

Revised for Telephone:

How satisfied are you with your community? Would you say you are very satisfied, somewhat satisfied, neither satisfied nor dissatisfied, somewhat dissatisfied, or very dissatisfied?

Very satisfied	1
Somewhat satisfied	2
Neither satisfied nor dissatisfied	3
Somewhat dissatisfied	4
Very dissatisfied	5

Source: Don A. Dillman, *Mail and Telephone Surveys: The Total Design Method* (New York: John Wiley & Sons, 1978), p. 209. Reprinted with permission of John Wiley & Sons, Inc.

When a question is read aloud, remembering the alternative choices can be difficult. Consider the following question from a personal interview:

There has been a lot of discussion about the potential health risks to nonsmokers from tobacco smoke in public buildings, restaurants, and business offices. How serious a health threat to you personally is the inhaling of this secondhand smoke, often called passive smoking: Is it a very serious health threat, somewhat serious, not too serious, or not serious at all?

1. *Very serious*
2. *Somewhat serious*
3. *Not too serious*
4. *Not serious at all*
5. *(Don't know)*

The last portion of the question was a listing of the four alternatives that serve as answers. This listing at the end is often used in interviews to remind the respondent of the alternatives, since they are not presented visually. The fifth alternative, "Don't know," is in parentheses because, although the interviewer knows it is an acceptable answer, it is not read. The researcher only uses this response when the respondent truly cannot provide an answer.

The data collection technique also influences the layout of the questionnaire. Layout will be discussed later in the chapter.

Avoiding Mistakes

No hard-and-fast rules determine how to develop a questionnaire. Fortunately, research experience has yielded some guidelines that help prevent the most common mistakes.

Avoid Complexity: Simpler Language is Better

Words used in questionnaires should be readily understandable to all respondents. The researcher usually has the difficult task of adopting the conversational language of people at the lower education levels without talking down to better-educated respondents. Remember, not all people have the vocabulary of a college graduate. Many consumers, for instance, have never gone beyond a high school education.

Respondents can probably tell an interviewer whether they are married, single, divorced, separated, or widowed, but providing their *marital status* may present a problem. The technical jargon of top corporate executives should be avoided when surveying retailers or industrial users. "Brand image," "positioning," "marginal analysis," and other corporate language may not have the same meaning for or even be understood by a store owner-operator in a retail survey. The vocabulary used in the following question from an attitude survey on social problems probably would confuse many respondents:

> *When effluents from a paper mill can be drunk and exhaust from factory smokestacks can be breathed, then humankind will have done a good job in saving the environment. . . . Don't you agree that what we want is zero toxicity: no effluents?*

Besides being too long and confusing, this question is leading.

Avoid Leading and Loaded Questions

Leading and loaded questions are a major source of bias in question wording. A **leading question** suggests or implies certain answers. A media study of environmental consciousness asked consumers this question:

> *Many people are washing their clothes less often because of concerns for the environment. How has your concern for the environment affected the way you wash and wear clothes?*
>
> ☐ *Wash less*   ☐ *No change*   ☐ *Wash more*

The potential "bandwagon effect" implied in this question threatens the study's validity. *Partial mention of alternatives* is a variation of this phenomenon:

> *Do small imported cars, such as a Smart Car, get better gas mileage than small U.S. made cars?*
> *How do you generally spend your free time, watching television or what?*

A **loaded question** suggests a socially desirable answer or is emotionally charged. Consider the following question from a survey about media influence on cooking and home-decorating behavior:[6]

> *What most influences you to buy food equipment?*
>
> ☐ *My own need for equipment at the time*
> ☐ *Salesperson at store*
> ☐ *Food magazines*
> ☐ *Food shows on TV*
> ☐ *Internet food sites*
> ☐ *Family or friends*
> ☐ *Food/dining section of newspaper*
> ☐ *Other*
> ☐ *I rarely/never buy food preparation equipment*

Over half the respondents chose the first alternative. Although this question is not emotionally loaded, many people could be reluctant to say they are swayed by the media rather than making purchases out of their own, independently experienced need.

A television station produced the following 10-second spot asking for viewer feedback:

> *We are happy when you like programs on Channel 7. We are sad when you dislike programs on Channel 7. Write us and let us know what you think of our programming.*

Few people wish to make others sad. This question may elicit positive comments disproportionate to negative comments.

Certain answers to questions are more socially desirable than others. For example, a truthful answer to the following classification question might be painful:

> *Where did you rank academically in your high school graduating class?*
>
> ☐ *Top quarter*
> ☐ *2nd quarter*
> ☐ *3rd quarter*
> ☐ *4th quarter*

TO THE POINT

I don't know the rules of grammar. . . . If you're trying to persuade people to do something, or buy something, it seems to me you should use their language, the language they use every day, the language in which they think. We try to write in the vernacular.

—David Ogilvy

leading question
A question that suggests or implies certain answers.

loaded question
A question that suggests a socially desirable answer or is emotionally charged.

When taking personality or psychographic tests, respondents frequently can interpret which answers are most socially acceptable even if those answers do not portray their true feelings. For example, which are the socially desirable answers to the following questions on a self-confidence scale?

I feel capable of handling myself in most social situations.

☐   *Agree*   ☐   *Disagree*

I seldom fear my actions will cause others to have low opinions of me.

☐   *Agree*   ☐   *Disagree*

An experiment conducted in the early days of polling illustrates the unpopularity of change.[7] Comparable samples of respondents were simultaneously asked two questions about the presidential succession. One sample was asked, **"Would you favor or oppose adding a law to the Constitution preventing a president from succeeding himself more than once?"** The other sample was asked, **"Would you favor or oppose changing the Constitution in order to prevent a president from succeeding himself more than once?"** Fifty percent of respondents answered negatively to the first question. For the second question, 65 percent of respondents answered negatively. Thus, the public would rather add to than change the Constitution.

Asking respondents "how often" they use a product or visit a store leads them to generalize about their habits, because there usually is some variance in their behavior. In generalizing, a person is likely to portray an *ideal* behavior rather than an *average* behavior. For instance, brushing your teeth after each meal may be ideal, but busy people may skip a brushing or two. An introductory **counterbiasing statement** or preamble to a question that reassures respondents that their "embarrassing" behavior is not abnormal may yield truthful responses:

Some people have the time to brush three times daily but others do not. How often did you brush your teeth yesterday?

If a question embarrasses the respondent, it may elicit no answer or a biased response. This is particularly true with respect to personal or classification data such as income or education. The problem may be mitigated by introducing the section of the questionnaire with a statement such as this:

To help classify your answers, we'd like to ask you a few questions. Again, your answers will be kept in strict confidence.

A question statement may be leading because it is phrased to reflect either the negative or the positive aspects of an issue. To control for this bias, the wording of attitudinal questions may be reversed for 50 percent of the sample. This **split-ballot technique** is used with the expectation that two alternative phrasings of the same question will yield a more accurate total response than will a single phrasing. For example, in a study on small-car buying behavior, one-half of a sample of imported-car purchasers received a questionnaire in which they were asked to agree or disagree with the statement **"Small U.S. cars are cheaper to maintain than small imported cars."** The other half of the import-car owners received a questionnaire in which the statement read **"Small imported cars are cheaper to maintain than small U.S. cars."**

> **counterbiasing statement**
>
> An introductory statement or preamble to a potentially embarrassing question that reduces a respondent's reluctance to answer by suggesting that certain behavior is not unusual.

> **split-ballot technique**
>
> Using two alternative phrasings of the same question for respective halves of a sample to elicit a more accurate total response than would a single phrasing.

Avoid Ambiguity: Be as Specific as Possible

Items on questionnaires often are ambiguous because they are too general. Consider such indefinite words as *often, occasionally, regularly, frequently, many, good,* and *poor.* Each of these words has many different meanings. For one consumer *frequent* reading of *Fortune* magazine may be reading six or seven issues a year. Another consumer may think reading two issues a year is frequent.

Questions such as the following one, used in a study measuring the reactions of consumers to a television boycott, should be interpreted with care:

Please indicate the statement that best describes your family's television viewing during the boycott of Channel 7.

☐   *We did not watch any television programs on Channel 7.*

☐ *We watched hardly any television programs on Channel 7.*
☐ *We occasionally watched television programs on Channel 7.*
☐ *We frequently watched television programs on Channel 7.*

Some marketing scholars have suggested that the rate of diffusion of an innovation is related to the perception of product attributes such as *divisibility,* which refers to the extent to which the innovation may be tried or tested on a limited scale.[8] An empirical attempt to test this theory using semantic differentials was a disaster. Pretesting found that the bipolar adjectives *divisible–not divisible* were impossible for consumers to understand because they did not have the theory in mind as a frame of reference. A revision of the scale used these bipolar adjectives:

Testable ____ ____ ____ ____ ____ ____ *Not testable*
(sample use possible)   *(sample use not possible)*

However, the question remained ambiguous because the meaning was still unclear.

A brewing industry study on point-of-purchase advertising (store displays) asked:

What degree of durability do you prefer in your point-of-purchase advertising?

☐ *Permanent (lasting more than 6 months)*
☐ *Semipermanent (lasting from 1 to 6 months)*
☐ *Temporary (lasting less than 1 month)*

Here the researchers clarified the terms *permanent, semipermanent,* and *temporary* by defining them for the respondent. However, the question remained somewhat ambiguous. Beer marketers often use a variety of point-of-purchase devices to serve different purposes—in this case, what is the purpose? In addition, analysis was difficult because respondents were merely asked to indicate a preference rather than a *degree* of preference. Thus, the meaning of a question may not be clear because the frame of reference is inadequate for interpreting the context of the question.

A student research group asked this question:

What media do you rely on most?

☐ *Television*
☐ *Radio*
☐ *Internet*
☐ *Newspapers*

This question is ambiguous because it does not ask about the content of the media. "Rely on most" for what—news, sports, entertainment?

Avoid Double-Barreled Items

A question covering several issues at once is referred to as a **double-barreled question** and should always be avoided. Making the mistake of asking two questions rather than one is easy—for example, **"Please indicate how much you agree with the following statement: 'Labor unions and management are responsible for the auto crisis.'"** Which intermediaries are responsible, the wholesalers or the retailers?

When multiple questions are asked in one question, the results may be exceedingly difficult to interpret. Consider the following question from a magazine's survey entitled "How Do You Feel about Being a Woman?":

Between you and your husband, who does the housework (cleaning, cooking, dishwashing, laundry) over and above that done by any hired help?

☐ *I do all of it.*
☐ *I do almost all of it.*
☐ *I do over half of it.*
☐ *We split the work fifty-fifty.*
☐ *My husband does over half of it.*

double-barreled question

A question that may induce bias because it covers two issues at once.

Who's *Really* Doing the Housework?

Married women have been a large part of the workforce for decades, but wives continue to complain that when both spouses hold jobs, women bear the heavier responsibility for housework. Researchers have recently considered whether the problem is one of fairness or misperception.

Some evidence suggests that the difference in estimates depends partly on data gathering. First, it matters whom the researchers question and when they ask. If the study asks men and women to recall how they used their time at home, both groups tend to overestimate the time they devote to housework. Also, defining time spent on housework turns out to be more complex than you might guess. Why? People often combine activities. For example, someone might grab an armload of dirty clothes to shove into the washing machine on the way to the den to use the computer. Is that housework?

Detailed data from the long-term Sloan 500 Family

Study provide some insights. This study used the Experience Sampling Method (ESM) to overcome problems associated with asking people to remember how they used their time. With ESM, participants wear programmed wristwatches that beep at randomly chosen times. Whenever the watch beeps, participants are supposed to answer a short questionnaire indicating what their primary and secondary activities are and what they are thinking about at that time. With regard to housework, researchers found that if they count time spent on housework as either a primary or secondary activity, the overreporting of housework time shrinks. If the definition of housework is further expanded to include time spent thinking about it—not necessarily procrastinating, but maybe planning or managing household tasks—the overreporting shrinks again. The way housework is defined also affects the size of the gap between husbands' and wives' contributions.

Source: Based on Yun-Suk Lee and Linda J. Waite, "Husbands' and Wives' Time Spent on Housework: A Comparison of Measures," *Journal of Marriage and Family* 67, no. 2 (2005): 328–36, abstract downloaded from OCLC First Search, http://firstsearch.oclc.org; Barbara Schneider and Linda Waite, "Timely and Timeless: Working Parents and Their Children," Conference on Work, Family, Health and Well-Being, Washington, DC (June 16–18, 2003), downloaded from Maryland Population Research Center Web site, http://www.popcenter.umd.edu; Alfred P. Sloan Center on Parents, Children and Work, "Overview of Center Research," http://www.sloanworkingfamilies.org, accessed March 8, 2006.

© RF CORBIS

© GEORGE DOYLE & CIARAN GRIFFIN

The answers to this question do not tell us if the wife cooks and the husband washes the dishes. The Research Snapshot above provides additional insight into this question.

A survey by a consumer-oriented library asked,

Are you satisfied with the present system of handling "closed-reserve" and "open-reserve" readings? (Are enough copies available? Are the required materials ordered promptly? Are the borrowing regulations adequate for students' use of materials?)

    ☐ *Yes*   ☐ *No*

A respondent may feel torn between a "yes" to one part of the question and a "no" to another part. The answer to this question does not tell the researcher which problem or combination of problems concerns the library user. Further, a Likert statement from a study dealing with student perceptions of managerial ethics:

National Sales Managers buy liquor and prostitutes for   *SD*   *D*   *N*   *A*   *SA*
important customers

The item intends to discover students' attitudes about selling as a career.[9] However, perhaps this would be better as two separate questions rather than one to learn respondents' specific beliefs. Then no ambiguity would exist about what sales managers might buy for customers. A sales manager who takes a customer out for dinner may buy drinks but might never think of buying prostitutes. So, as is, what would a strongly agree or strongly disagree response really mean?

The following comment offers good advice regarding double-barreled questions:

Generally speaking, it is hard enough to get answers to one idea at a time without complicating the problem by asking what amounts to two questions at once. If two ideas are to be explored, they deserve at least two questions. Since question marks are not rationed, there is little excuse for the needless confusion that results [from] the double-barreled question.[10]

Avoid Making Assumptions

Consider the following question:

Should Macy's continue its excellent gift-wrapping program?

☐ *Yes*   ☐ *No*

This question has a built-in assumption: that people believe the gift-wrapping program is excellent. By answering "yes," the respondent implies that the program is, in fact, excellent and that things are fine just as they are. When a respondent answers "no," the opinion is to discontinue the program implying that it isn't excellent. But, perhaps the respondent simply doesn't think gift wrapping offers any value whether the service is excellent or not.

Another frequent mistake is assuming that the respondent had previously thought about an issue. For example, the following question appeared in a survey concerning Jack-in-the-Box: **"Do you think Jack-in-the-Box restaurants should consider changing their name?"** Respondents have not likely thought about this question beforehand. Most respondents answered the question even though they had no prior opinion concerning the name change. Researchers that desire an informed opinion will end up with responses based on too low a level of involvement in a case like this.

Avoid Burdensome Questions That May Tax the Respondent's Memory

A simple fact of human life is that people forget. Researchers writing questions about past behavior or events should recognize that certain questions may make serious demands on the respondent's memory. Writing questions about prior events requires a conscientious attempt to minimize the problems associated with forgetting.

In many situations, respondents cannot recall answers. For example, a telephone survey conducted during the 24-hour period following the airing of the Super Bowl might establish whether the respondent watched the Super Bowl and then ask, "Do you recall any commercials on that program?" If the answer is positive, the interviewer might ask, "What brands were advertised?" These two questions measure **unaided recall**, because they give the respondent no clue as to the brand of interest.

If the researcher suspects that the respondent may have forgotten the answer to a question, he or she may rewrite the question in an **aided-recall** format—that is, in a format that provides a clue to help jog the respondent's memory. For instance, the question about an advertised beer in an aided-recall format might be "Do you recall whether there was a brand of beer advertised on that program?" or "I am going to read you a list of beer brand names. Can you pick out the name of the beer that was advertised on the program?" While aided recall is not as strong a test of attention or memory as unaided recall, it is less taxing to the respondent's memory.

Telescoping and squishing are two additional consequences of respondents' forgetting the exact details of their behavior. *Telescoping* occurs when respondents believe that past events happened more recently than they actually did. The opposite effect, *squishing,* occurs when respondents think that recent events took place longer ago than they really did. A solution to this problem may be to refer to a specific event that is memorable—for example, "How often have you gone to a sporting event since the World Series?" Because forgetting tends to increase over time, the question may concern a recent period: "How often did you watch HBO on cable television last week?" (During the editing stage, the results can be transposed to the appropriate time period.)

In situations in which "I don't know" or "I can't recall" is a meaningful answer, simply including a "don't know" response category may solve the question writer's problem.

unaided recall

Asking respondents to remember something without providing any clue.

aided-recall

Asking the respondent to remember something and giving them a clue to help.

What Is the Best Question Sequence?

The order of questions, or the question sequence, may serve several functions for the researcher. If the opening questions are interesting, simple to comprehend, and easy to answer, respondents' cooperation and involvement can be maintained throughout the questionnaire. Asking easy-to-answer questions teaches respondents their role and builds their confidence.

A mail survey among department store buyers drew an extremely poor return rate. A substantial improvement in response rate occurred, however, when researchers added some introductory questions seeking opinions on pending legislation of great importance to these buyers. Respondents completed all the questions, not only those in the opening section.

In their attempt to "warm up" respondents toward the questionnaire, student researchers frequently ask demographic or classificatory questions at the beginning. This generally is not advisable, because asking for personal information such as income level or education may embarrass or threaten respondents. Asking potentially embarrassing questions at the middle or end of the questionnaire usually is better, after rapport has been established between respondent and interviewer.

order bias

Bias caused by the influence of earlier questions in a question-naire or by an answer's position in a set of answers.

Order bias can result from a particular answer's position in a set of answers or from the sequencing of questions. In political elections in which candidates lack high visibility, such as elections for county commissioners and judges, the first name listed on the ballot often receives the highest percentage of votes. For this reason, many election boards print several ballots so that each candidate's name appears in every possible position on the ballot.

Order bias can also distort survey results. For example, suppose a questionnaire's purpose is to measure levels of awareness of several charitable organizations. If Big Brothers and Big Sisters is always mentioned first, the American Red Cross second, and the American Cancer Society third, Big Brothers and Big Sisters may receive an artificially high awareness rating because respondents are prone to yea-saying (by indicating awareness of the first item in the list).

Asking specific questions before asking about broader issues is a common cause of order bias. For example, bias may arise if questions about a specific clothing store are asked prior to those concerning the general criteria for selecting a clothing store. Suppose a respondent indicates in the first portion of a questionnaire that she shops at a store where parking needs to be improved. Later in the questionnaire, to avoid appearing inconsistent, she may state that parking is less important than she really believes it is. Specific questions may thus influence the more general ones. As a result, it is advisable to ask general questions before specific questions to obtain the freest of open-ended responses. This procedure, known as the **funnel technique**, allows the researcher to understand the respondent's frame of reference before asking more specific questions about the level of the respondent's information and the intensity of his or her opinions.

funnel technique

Asking general questions before specific questions in order to obtain unbiased responses.

Consider how later answers might be biased by previous questions in this questionnaire on environmental pollution:

Circle the number on the following table that best expresses your feelings about the severity of each environmental problem:

Problem	Not Severe				Extremely Severe
Air pollution from automobile exhausts	1	2	3	4	5
Air pollution from open burning	1	2	3	4	5
Air pollution from industrial smoke	1	2	3	4	5
Air pollution from foul odors	1	2	3	4	5
Noise pollution from airplanes	1	2	3	4	5
Noise pollution from cars, trucks, motorcycles	1	2	3	4	5
Noise pollution from industry	1	2	3	4	5

Not surprisingly, researchers found that the responses to the air pollution questions were highly correlated—in fact, almost identical.

With attitude scales, there also may be an *anchoring effect*. The first concept measured tends to become a comparison point from which subsequent evaluations are made. Randomization of items on a questionnaire susceptible to the anchoring effect helps minimize order bias.

A related problem is bias caused by the order of alternatives on closed questions. To avoid this problem, the order of these choices should be rotated if producing alternative forms of the questionnaire is possible. However, marketing researchers rarely print alternative questionnaires to eliminate problems resulting from order bias. A more common practice is to pencil in Xs or check marks on printed questionnaires to indicate where the interviewer should start a series of repetitive questions. For example, the capitalized phrases in the following question provide instructions to the interviewer to "rotate" brands, starting with the one checked:

> *I would like to determine how likely you would be to buy certain brands of candy in the future. Let's start with (X'ED BRAND). (RECORD BELOW UNDER APPROPRIATE BRAND. REPEAT QUESTIONS FOR ALL REMAINING BRANDS.)*

Start Here:	( ) Mounds	(X) Almond Joy	( ) Snickers
Definitely would buy	−1	−1	−1
Probably would buy	−2	−2	−2
Might or might not buy	−3	−3	−3
Probably would not buy	−4	−4	−4
Definitely would not buy	−5	−5	−5

One advantage of Internet surveys is the ability to reduce order bias by having the computer randomly order questions and/or response alternatives. With complete randomization, question order is random and respondents see response alternatives in different random positions.

Asking a question that does not apply to the respondent or that the respondent is not qualified to answer may be irritating or cause a biased response because the respondent wishes to please the interviewer or to avoid embarrassment. Including a **filter question** minimizes the chance of asking questions that are inapplicable. Asking **"Where do you generally have check–cashing problems in Springfield?"** may elicit a response even though the respondent has had no check-cashing problems. He or she may wish to please the interviewer with an answer. A filter question such as **"Do you ever have a problem cashing a check in Springfield? — Yes — No"** would screen out the people who are not qualified to answer.

Another form of filter question, the **pivot question,** can be used to obtain income information and other data that respondents may be reluctant to provide. For example,

> *"Is your total family income over or under $50,000?" IF UNDER, ASK, "Is it over or under $25,000?" IF OVER, ASK, "Is it over or under $75,000?"*

> Under $25,000 $50,001–$75,000
> $25,001–$50,000   Over $75,000

filter question

A question that screens out respondents who are not qualified to answer a second question.

pivot question

A filter question used to determine which version of a second question will be asked.

Exhibit 15.2 on the next page gives an example of a flowchart plan for a questionnaire. Structuring the order of the questions so that they are logical will help to ensure the respondent's cooperation and eliminate confusion or indecision. The researcher maintains legitimacy by making sure that the respondent can comprehend the relationship between a given question (or section of the questionnaire) and the overall purpose of the study. Furthermore, a logical order may aid the individual's memory. Transitional comments explaining the logic of the questionnaire may ensure that the respondent continues. Here are two examples:

> *We have been talking so far about general shopping habits in this city. Now I'd like you to compare two types of grocery stores—regular supermarkets and grocery departments in wholesale club stores.*
>
> *So that I can combine your answers with those of other farmers who are similar to you, I need some personal information about you. Your answers to these questions—as to all of the others you've answered—are confidential, and you will never be identified to anyone without your permission. Thanks for your help so far. If you'll answer the remaining questions, it will help me analyze all your answers.*

What Is the Best Layout?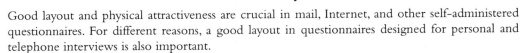

Good layout and physical attractiveness are crucial in mail, Internet, and other self-administered questionnaires. For different reasons, a good layout in questionnaires designed for personal and telephone interviews is also important.

EXHIBIT 15.2 Flow of Questions to Determine the Level of Prompting Required to Stimulate Recall

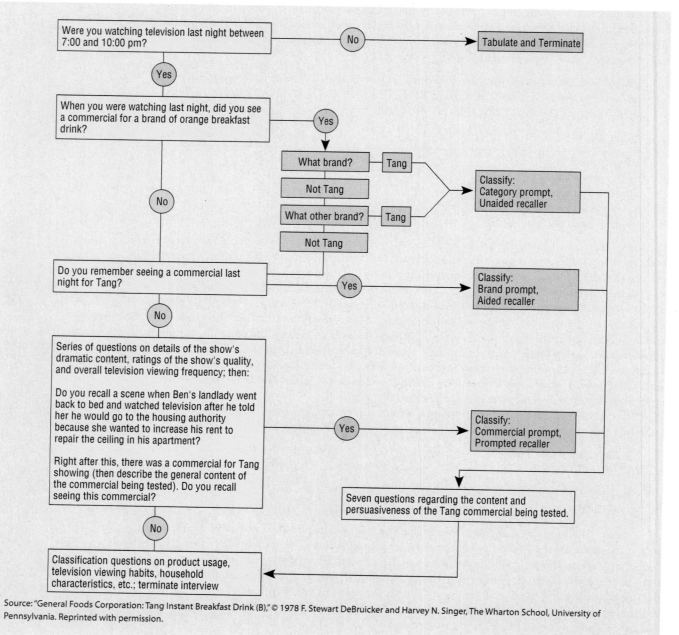

Source: "General Foods Corporation: Tang Instant Breakfast Drink (B)," © 1978 F. Stewart DeBruicker and Harvey N. Singer, The Wharton School, University of Pennsylvania. Reprinted with permission.

Traditional Questionnaires

Exhibit 15.3 shows a page from a telephone questionnaire. The layout is neat and attractive, and the instructions for the interviewer (all boldface capital letters) are easy to follow. The responses "It Depends," "Refused," and "Don't Know" are enclosed in a box to indicate that these answers are acceptable but responses from the five-point scale are preferred.

Often rate of return can be increased by using money that might have been spent on an incentive to improve the attractiveness and quality of the questionnaire. Mail questionnaires should never be overcrowded. Margins should be of decent size, white space should be used to separate blocks of print, and the unavoidable columns of multiple boxes should be kept to a minimum. A question should not begin on one page and end on another page. Splitting questions may cause a respondent to read only part of a question, to pay less attention to answers on one of the pages, or to become confused.

EXHIBIT 15.3 Layout of a Page from a Telephone Questionnaire

5. Now I'm going to read you some types of professions. For each one, please tell me whether you think the work that profession does, on balance, has a very positive impact on society, a somewhat positive impact, a somewhat negative impact, a very negative impact, or not much impact either way on society. First . . . **(START AT X'D ITEM. CONTINUE DOWN AND UP THE LIST UNTIL ALL ITEMS HAVE BEEN READ AND RATED.)**

START HERE:	Very Positive Impact	Some-what Positive Impact	Some-what Negative Impact	Very Negative Impact	Not Much Impact	It Depends	Refused	Don't Know
						(DO NOT READ)		
[ ] Members of Congress	1	2	3	4	5	0	X	Y (24)
[X] Business executives	1	2	3	4	5	0	X	Y (25)
[ ] Physicians	1	2	3	4	5	0	X	Y (26)
[ ] Political pollsters—that is, people who conduct surveys for public officials or political political candidates	1	2	3	4	5	0	X	Y (27)
[ ] Researchers in the media—that is, people in media such as television, newspapers, magazines and radio, who conduct surveys about issues later reported in the media	1	2	3	4	5	0	X	Y (28)
[ ] Telemarketers—that is, people who sell products or services over the phone	1	2	3	4	5	0	X	Y (29)
[ ] Used car salesmen	1	2	3	4	5	0	X	Y (30)
[ ] Market researchers—that is, people who work for commercial research firms who conduct surveys to see what the public thinks about certain kinds of consumer products or services	1	2	3	4	5	0	X	Y (31)
[ ] Biomedical researchers	1	2	3	4	5	0	X	Y (32)
[ ] Public-opinion researchers—that is, people who work for commercial research firms who conduct surveys to see what the public thinks about important social issues	1	2	3	4	5	0	X	Y (33)
[ ] College and university professors	1	2	3	4	5	0	X	Y (34)
[ ] Attorneys	1	2	3	4	5	0	X	Y (35)
[ ] Members of the clergy	1	2	3	4	5	0	X	Y (36)
[ ] Journalists	1	2	3	4	5	0	X	Y (37)

Questionnaires should be designed to appear as short as possible. A booklet form of questionnaire is preferable to stapling a large number of pages together. Also, do not try to put too many questions on a page or on a single computer screen. In situations in which it is necessary to conserve space on the questionnaire or to facilitate data entry or tabulation of the data, a multiple-grid layout may be used. The **multiple-grid question** presents several similar questions and corresponding response alternatives arranged in a grid format. For example:

Airlines often offer special fare promotions. On a vacation trip would you take a connecting flight instead of a nonstop flight if the connecting flight were longer?

	Yes	No	Not sure
One hour longer?	☐	☐	☐
Two hours longer?	☐	☐	☐
Three hours longer?	☐	☐	☐

Experienced researchers have found that the title of a questionnaire should be phrased carefully. In self-administered and mail questionnaires, a carefully constructed title may capture the respondent's interest, underline the importance of the research ("Nationwide Study of Blood Donors"), emphasize the interesting nature of the study ("Study of Internet Usage"), appeal to the respondent's ego ("Survey among Top Executives"), or emphasize the confidential nature of the study ("A Confidential Survey among . . ."). The researcher should take steps to ensure that the wording of the title will not bias the respondent in the same way that a leading question might.

By using several forms, special instructions, and other tricks of the trade, the researcher can design the questionnaire to facilitate the interviewer's job of following interconnected questions. Exhibits 15.4 and 15.5 on pages 385–387 illustrate portions of telephone and personal interview questionnaires. Note how the layout and easy-to-follow instructions for interviewers in Questions 1, 2, and 3 of Exhibit 15.4 help the interviewer follow the question sequence.

Instructions are often capitalized or printed in bold to alert the interviewer that it may be necessary to proceed in a certain way. For example, if a particular answer is given, the interviewer or respondent may be instructed to skip certain questions or go to a special sequence of questions. To facilitate coding, question responses should be precoded when possible, as in Exhibit 15.4.

Exhibit 15.5 illustrates some other useful techniques that are possible with personal interviews. Questions 3 and 6 instruct the interviewer to hand the respondent a card bearing a list of alternatives. Cards may help respondents grasp the intended meaning of the question and remember all the brand name or other items they are being asked about. Also, Questions 2, 3, and 6 instruct the interviewer that rating of the banks will start with the bank that has been checked in red pencil on the printed questionnaire. The name of the red-checked bank is not the same on every questionnaire. By rotating the order of the check marks, the researchers attempted to reduce order bias caused by respondents' tendency to react more favorably to the first set of questions.

Exhibit 15.6 on page 387 illustrates a series of questions that includes a *skip question*. Either skip instructions or an arrow drawn pointing to the next question informs the respondent which question comes next.

Layout is extremely important when questionnaires are long or require the respondent to fill in a large amount of information. In many circumstances, using headings or subtitles to indicate groups of questions will help the respondent grasp the scope or nature of the questions to be asked. Thus, at a glance, the respondent can follow the logic of the questionnaire.

Internet Questionnaires

Layout is also an important issue for questionnaires appearing on the Internet. A questionnaire on a Web site should be easy to use, flow logically, and have a graphic look and overall feel that motivate the respondent to cooperate from start to finish. Many of the guidelines for layout of paper questionnaires apply to Internet questionnaires. There are, however, some important differences.

With *graphical user interface (GUI) software,* the researcher can exercise control over the background, colors, fonts, and other visual features displayed on the computer screen so as to create an attractive and easy-to-use interface between the computer user and the Internet survey. GUI

EXHIBIT 15.4 Telephone Questionnaire with Skip Questions

1. Did you take the car you had checked to the Standard Auto Repair Center for repairs?

   —1 Yes **(SKIP TO Q. 3)**   —2 No

2. **(IF NO, ASK:)** Did you have the repair work done?

   —1 Yes   —2 No

   ⬇   ⬇

1. Where was the repair work done? _____   1. Why didn't you have the car repaired?
   _____   _____
                                                              _____
2. Why didn't you have the repair work done   _____
   at the Standard Auto Repair Center? _____
   _____
   _____
   _____

3. **(IF YES TO Q. 1, ASK:)** How satisfied were you with the repair work? Were you . . .

   —1 Very satisfied

   —2 Somewhat satisfied

   —3 Somewhat dissatisfied

   —4 Very dissatisfied

   (IF SOMEWHAT OR VERY DISSATISFIED:) In what way were you dissatisfied?
   _____
   _____
   _____

4. **(ASK EVERYONE:)** Do you ever buy gas at the 95th Street Standard Center?

   —1 Yes   —2 No   **(SKIP TO Q. 6)**

5. **(IF YES, ASK:)** How often do you buy gas there?

   —1 Always

   —2 Almost always

   —3 Most of the time

   —4 Part of the time

   —5 Hardly ever

6. Have you ever had your car washed there?

   —1 Yes   —2 No

7. Have you ever had an oil change or lubrication done there?

   —1 Yes   —2 No

software allows the researcher to design questionnaires in which respondents click on the appropriate answer rather than having to type answers or codes.

Researchers often use specialized Web publishing services such as Qualtrics, Survey Monkey, or Zoomerang to build online questionnaires. However, several features of a respondent's computer may influence the appearance of an Internet questionnaire. For example, discrepancies between the designer's and the respondent's computer settings for screen configuration (e.g., 640 × 480 pixels versus 800 × 600 pixels) may result in questions not being fully visible on the respondent's screen, misaligned text, or other visual problems. The possibility that the questionnaire the researcher/designer constructs on his or her computer may look different from the questionnaire that appears

EXHIBIT 15.5 **Personal Interview Questionnaire**

"Hello, my name is _____. I'm a Public Opinion Interviewer with Research Services, Inc. We're making an opinion survey about banks and banking, and I'd like to ask you . . ."

1. What are the names of local banks you can think of offhand? (INTERVIEWER: List names in order mentioned.)
   a. _____
   b. _____
   c. _____
   d. _____
   e. _____
   f. _____
   g. _____

2. Thinking now about the experiences you have had with the different banks here in Boulder, have you ever talked to or done business with . . . (INTERVIEWER: Insert name of bank checked in red below.)
   a. Are you personally acquainted with any of the employees or officers at _____?
   b. (If YES) Who is that? _____
   c. How long has it been since you have been inside _____?
             (INTERVIEWER: Now go back and repeat 2–2c for all other banks listed.)

	(2) Talked		(2a and 2b) Know Employee Or Officer		(2c) Been in Bank in:				
	Yes	No	No	Name	Last Year	1–5	5-Plus	No	DK
Arapahoe National Bank	1	2	1	_____	1	2	3	4	5
First National Bank	1	2	1	_____	1	2	3	4	5
Boulder National Bank	1	2	1	_____	1	2	3	4	5
Security Bank	1	2	1	_____	1	2	3	4	5
United Bank of Boulder	1	2	1	_____	1	2	3	4	5
National State Bank	1	2	1	_____	1	2	3	4	5

3. (HAND BANK RATING CARD) On this card there are a number of contrasting phrases or statements—for example, "Large" and "Small." We'd like to know how you rate (NAME OF BANK CHECKED IN RED BELOW) in terms of these statements or phrases. Just for example, let's use the terms "fast service" and "slow service." If you were to rate a bank #1 on this scale, it would mean you find their service "very fast." On the other hand, a 7 rating would indicate you feel their service is "very slow," whereas a 4 rating means you don't think of them as being either "very fast" or "very slow." Are you ready to go ahead? Good! Tell me then how you would rate (NAME OF BANK CHECKED IN RED) in terms of each of the phrases or statements on that card. How about (READ NEXT BANK NAME)? . . . (INTERVIEWER: Continue on until respondent has evaluated all six banks.)

	Arapahoe National	First National	Boulder National	Security Bank	United Bank	National State
a. Service	_____	_____	_____	_____	_____	_____
b. Size	_____	_____	_____	_____	_____	_____
c. Business vs. Family	_____	_____	_____	_____	_____	_____
d. Friendliness	_____	_____	_____	_____	_____	_____
e. Big/Small Business	_____	_____	_____	_____	_____	_____
f. Rate of Growth	_____	_____	_____	_____	_____	_____
g. Modernness	_____	_____	_____	_____	_____	_____
h. Leadership	_____	_____	_____	_____	_____	_____
i. Loan Ease	_____	_____	_____	_____	_____	_____
j. Location	_____	_____	_____	_____	_____	_____
k. Hours	_____	_____	_____	_____	_____	_____
l. Ownership	_____	_____	_____	_____	_____	_____
m. Community Involvement	_____	_____	_____	_____	_____	_____

4. Suppose a friend of yours who has just moved to Boulder asked you to recommend a bank. Which local bank would you recommend? Why would you recommend that particular bank?

    Arapahoe National   1
    First National   2
    Boulder National   3
    Security Bank   4
    United Bank of Boulder   5

(continued)

EXHIBIT 15.5 **Personal Interview Questionnaire** *(continued)*

National State Bank   6
Other (Specify) _____
DK/Wouldn't   9

5. Which of the local banks do you think of as: (INTERVIEWER: Read red-checked item first, then read each of the other five.)

   the newcomer's bank? _____

   the student's bank? _____

   the Personal Banker bank? _____

   the bank where most C.U. faculty and staff bank? _____

   the bank most interested in this community? _____

   the most progressive bank? _____

6. Which of these financial institutions, if any, (HAND CARD 2) are you or any member of your immediate family who lives here in this home doing business with now?

   Bank   1
   Credit Union   2
   Finance Company   3
   Savings and Loan   4
   Industrial Bank   5
   None of these   6
   DK/Not sure   7

   (IF NONE, Skip to 19.)

7. If a friend asked you to recommend a place where he or she could get a loan with which to buy a home, which financial institution would you probably recommend? (INTERVIEWER: Probe for specific name.) Why would you recommend (INSTITUTION NAMED)?
   Would Recommend: _____

   _____

   Wouldn't   0
   DK/Not Sure   9

   Source: Reprinted with permission from the Council of American Survey Research, http://www.casro.org.

EXHIBIT 15.6
Example of a Skip Question

1. If you had to buy a computer tomorrow, which of the following three types of computers do you think you would buy?

   1 Desktop—Go to Q. 3
   2 Laptop—Go to Q. 3
   3 Palm-sized (PDA)

2. (If "Palm-sized" on Q. 1, ask): What brand of computer do you think you would buy?

3. What is your age?

on the respondent's computer should always be considered when designing Internet surveys. The researchers should preview the questionnaire with different browsers and different computers to make sure the appearance is not altered in a way that affects the meaning of the items.

■ LAYOUT ISSUES

Even if the questionnaire designer's computer and the respondents' computers are compatible, a Web questionnaire designer should consider several layout issues. The first decision is whether the questionnaire will appear page by page, with individual questions on separate screens (Web pages), or on a scrolling basis, with the entire questionnaire appearing on a single Web page that the respondent scrolls from top to bottom. The *paging layout* (going from screen to screen) greatly facilitates skip patterns. Based on a respondent's answers to filter questions, the computer can automatically insert relevant questions on subsequent pages. If the entire questionnaire appears on one page (the *scrolling layout*), the display should advance smoothly, as if it were a piece of paper being moved up or down. The scrolling layout gives the respondent the ability to read any portion of the questionnaire at any time, but the absence of page boundaries can cause problems. For example, suppose a Likert scale consists of fifteen statements in a grid-format layout, with the response categories **Strongly Agree, Agree, Neutral, Disagree**, and **Strongly Disagree** at the beginning of the questionnaire. Once the respondent has scrolled down beyond the first few statements, he or she may not be able to see both the statements at the end of the list and the response categories at the top of the grid simultaneously. Thus, avoiding the problems associated with splitting questions and response categories may be difficult with scrolling questionnaires.

When a scrolling questionnaire is long, category or section headings are helpful to respondents. It is also a good idea to provide links to the top and bottom parts of each section, so that users can navigate through the questionnaire without having to scroll through the entire document.[11]

Whether a Web survey is page-by-page or scrolling format a **push button** with a label should clearly describe the actions to be taken. For example, if the respondent is to go to the next page, a large arrow labeled "NEXT" might appear in color at the bottom of the screen.

Decisions must be made about the use of color, graphics, animation, sound, and other special features that the Internet makes possible. One point to remember is that, although sophisticated graphics are not a problem for people with very powerful computers, many respondents' computers are not powerful enough to deliver complex graphics at a satisfactory speed, if at all. A textured background, colored headings, and small graphics can make a questionnaire more interesting and appealing, but they may present problems for respondents with older computers and/or low-bandwidth Internet connections.

With a paper questionnaire, the respondent knows how many questions he or she must answer. Because many Internet surveys offer no visual clues about the number of questions to be asked, it is important to provide a **status bar** or some other visual indicator of questionnaire length. For example, including a partially filled rectangular box as a visual symbol and a statement such as "The status bar at top right indicates approximately what portion of the survey you have completed" increases the likelihood that the respondent will finish the entire sequence of questions. Exhibit 15.7 shows a question from an online survey that uses a simple and motivating design. The survey presents one question at a time for simplicity. So that respondents can see their progress toward the end of the questionnaire, a gauge in the upper right corner fills from left to right as the respondent proceeds from Start to Finish.

An Internet questionnaire uses windows known as dialog boxes to display questions and record answers. Exhibit 15.8 portrays four common ways of displaying questions on a computer screen. Many Internet questionnaires require the respondent to activate his or her answer by clicking on the **radio button** for a response. Radio buttons work like push buttons on automobile radios: clicking on an alternative response deactivates the first choice and replaces it with the new response. A **drop-down box** (sometimes called a drill down question), such as the one shown in Exhibit 15.8, is a space-saving device that allows the researcher to provide a list of responses that are hidden from view until they are needed. These are sometimes called drill-down questions as well. A general statement, such as "Please select" or "Click here," is shown initially. Clicking on the downward-facing arrow makes the full range of choices appear. If the first choice in a list, such as "Strongly Agree," is shown while the other responses are kept hidden, the chance that response bias will occur is increased. Drop-down boxes may present a problem for individuals with minimal computer skills, as they may not know how to reveal hidden responses behind a drop-down menu or how to move from one option to another in a moving-bar menu.

Checklist questions may be followed by **check boxes**, several, none, or all of which may be checked by the respondent. **Open-ended boxes** are boxes in which respondents type their answers

---

push button

In a dialog box on an Internet questionnaire, a small outlined area, such as a rectangle or an arrow, that the respondent clicks on to select an option or perform a function, such as submit.

status bar

In an Internet questionnaire, a visual indicator that tells the respondent what portion of the survey he or she has completed.

radio button

In an Internet questionnaire, a circular icon, resembling a button, that activates one response choice and deactivates others when a respondent clicks on it.

drop-down box

In an Internet questionnaire, a space-saving device that reveals responses when they are needed but otherwise hides them from view.

check boxes

In an Internet questionnaire, small graphic boxes, next to answers, that a respondent clicks on to choose an answer; typically, a check mark or an **X** appears in the box when the respondent clicks on it.

open-ended boxes

In an Internet questionnaire, boxes where respondents can type in their own answers to open-ended questions.

EXHIBIT 15.7

Question in an Online Screening Survey for Joining a Consumer Panel

Start ▮▭▭▭ Finish

Though your plans may change, approximately when do you plan to purchase or lease your next automobile? Please indicate both the year and month.

[Select Year ▾]   [Select Month ▾]

[Next page]

©2006 J.D. Power and Associates, The McGraw-Hill Companies, Inc. All Rights Reserved.

Source: J.D. Power and Associates, "JDPowerPanel," https://ia.jdpa.com/20/survey/onsurvey.phtml, accessed March 9, 2006.

EXHIBIT 15.8
Alternative Ways of Displaying Internet Questions

Radio button

Last month, did you purchase products or services over the Internet?

○ Yes

○ No

How familiar are you with Microsoft's Xbox video game player?

Know Extremely Well	Know Fairly Well	Know a Little	Know Just Name	Never Heard of
○	○	○	○	○

Drop-down box, closed position

In which country or region do you currently reside?

| Click Here | ▼ |

Drop-down box, open position

In which country or region do you currently reside?

| Click Here | ▼ |

Click Here
United States
Asia/Pacific (excluding Hawaii)
Africa
Australia or New Zealand
Canada
Europe
Latin America, South America, or Mexico
Middle East
Other

Check box

From which location(s) do you access the Internet? Select all that apply.
☐ Home
☐ Work
☐ Other Location

Please indicate which of the following Web sites you have ever visited or used. (CHOOSE ALL THAT APPLY.)
☐ E*Trade's Web site
☐ Waterhouse's Web site
☐ Merrill Lynch's Web site
☐ Fidelity's Web site
☐ Schwab's Web site
☐ Powerstreet
☐ Yahoo! Finance
☐ Quicken.com
☐ Lycos Investing
☐ AOL's Personal Finance
☐ None of the above

Open-ended, one-line box

What company do you think is the most visible sponsor of sports?

Open-ended, scrolling text box

What can we do to improve our textbook?

▲

▼

to open-ended questions. Open-ended boxes may be designed as *one-line text boxes* or *scrolling text boxes*, depending on the breadth of the expected answer. Of course, open-ended questions require that respondents have both the skill and the willingness to keyboard lengthy answers on the computer. Some open-ended boxes are designed so that respondents can enter numbers for frequency response, ranking, or rating questions. For example:

> *Below you will see a series of statements that might or might not describe how you feel about your career. Please rate each statement using a scale from 1 to 4, where 4 means "Totally Agree," 3 means "Somewhat Agree," 2 means "Somewhat Disagree," and 1 means "Totally Disagree." Please enter your numeric answer in the box provided next to each statement. Would you say that . . .*
>
> ☐ *A lack of business knowledge relevant to my field/career could hurt my career advancement.*
> ☐ *My career life is an important part of how I define myself.*

In some cases, respondents can learn more about how to use a particular scale or get a definition of a term by clicking on a link, which generates a pop-up box. One of the most common reasons for using pop-up boxes is *error trapping*, a topic discussed in the next section.

Chapter 14 described graphic rating scales, which present respondents with a graphic continuum. On the Internet, researchers can take advantage of scroll bars or other GUI software features to make these scales easy to use. For example, the graphic continuum may be drawn as a measuring rod with a plus sign on one end and a minus sign on the other. The respondent then moves a small rectangle back and forth between the two ends of the scale to scroll to any point on the continuum. Scoring, as discussed in Chapter 14, is in terms of some measure of the length (millimeters) from one end of the graphic continuum to the point marked by the respondent.

Finally, researchers often include a customized thank-you page at the end of an Internet questionnaire, so that a brief thank-you note pops onto respondents' screens when they click on the Submit push button.[12]

■ SOFTWARE THAT MAKES QUESTIONNAIRES INTERACTIVE

Computer code can be written to make Internet questionnaires interactive and less prone to errors. The writing of software programs is beyond the scope of this discussion. However, several of the interactive functions that software makes possible should be mentioned here.

As discussed in Chapter 9, Internet software allows the branching off of questioning into two or more different lines, depending on a particular respondent's answer, and the skipping or filtering of questions. Questionnaire-writing software with Boolean skip and branching logic is readily available. Most of these programs have *hidden skip logic* so that respondents never see any evidence of skips. It is best if the questions the respondent sees flow in numerical sequence. However, some programs number all potential questions in numerical order, and the respondent sees only the numbers on the questions he or she answers. Thus, a respondent may answer questions 1 through 11 and then next see a question numbered 15 because of the skip logic.

Software can systematically or randomly manipulate the questions a respondent sees. **Variable piping software** allows variables, such as answers from previous questions, to be inserted into unfolding questions. Other software can randomly rotate the order of questions, blocks of questions, and response alternatives from respondent to respondent.

Researchers can use software to control the flow of a questionnaire. Respondents can be blocked from backing up, or they can be allowed to stop in mid-questionnaire and come back later to finish. A questionnaire can be designed so that if the respondent fails to answer a question or answers it with an incorrect type of response, an immediate error message appears. This is called **error trapping**. With **forced answering software**, respondents cannot skip over questions as they do in mail surveys. The program will not let them continue if they fail to answer a question. The software may insert a boldfaced error message on the question screen or insert a pop-up box instructing the respondent how to continue. For example, if a respondent does not answer a question and tries to proceed to another screen, a pop-up box might present the following message:

> *You cannot leave a question blank. On questions without a "Not sure" or "Decline to answer" option, please choose the response that best represents your opinions or experiences.*

variable piping software
Software that allows variables to be inserted into an Internet questionnaire as a respondent is completing it.

error trapping
Using software to control the flow of an Internet questionnaire—for example, to prevent respondents from backing up or failing to answer a question.

forced answering software
Software that prevents respondents from continuing with an Internet questionnaire if they fail to answer a question.

The respondent must close the pop-up box and answer the question in order to proceed to the next screen.

Some designers include an **interactive help desk** in their Web questionnaire so that respondents can solve problems they encounter in completing a questionnaire. A respondent might e-mail questions to the survey help desk or get live, interactive, real-time support via an online help desk.

Some respondents will leave the questionnaire Web site, prematurely terminating the survey. In many cases sending an e-mail message to these respondents at a later date, encouraging them to revisit the Web site, will persuade them to complete the questionnaire. Through the use of software and cookies, researchers can make sure that the respondent who revisits the Web site will be able to pick up at the point where he or she left off.

Once an Internet questionnaire has been designed, it is important to pretest it to ensure that it works with Internet Explorer, Netscape, AOL, WebTV, and other browsers. Some general-purpose programming languages, such as Java, do not always work with all browsers. Because different browsers have different peculiarities, a survey that works perfectly well with one may not function at all with another.[13]

interactive help desk

In an Internet questionnaire, a live, real-time support feature that solves problems or answers questions respondents may encounter in completing the questionnaire.

Pretesting and Revising Questionnaires

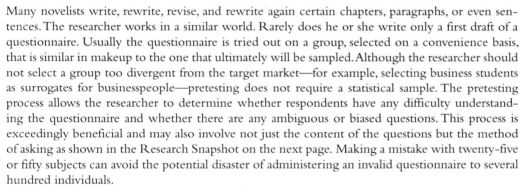

Many novelists write, rewrite, revise, and rewrite again certain chapters, paragraphs, or even sentences. The researcher works in a similar world. Rarely does he or she write only a first draft of a questionnaire. Usually the questionnaire is tried out on a group, selected on a convenience basis, that is similar in makeup to the one that ultimately will be sampled. Although the researcher should not select a group too divergent from the target market—for example, selecting business students as surrogates for businesspeople—pretesting does not require a statistical sample. The pretesting process allows the researcher to determine whether respondents have any difficulty understanding the questionnaire and whether there are any ambiguous or biased questions. This process is exceedingly beneficial and may also involve not just the content of the questions but the method of asking as shown in the Research Snapshot on the next page. Making a mistake with twenty-five or fifty subjects can avoid the potential disaster of administering an invalid questionnaire to several hundred individuals.

For a questionnaire investigating teaching students' experience with Web-based instruction, the researcher had the questionnaire reviewed first by university faculty members to ensure the questions were valid, then asked 20 teaching students to try answering the questions and indicate any ambiguities they noticed. Their feedback prompted changes in the format and wording. Pretesting was especially helpful because the English-language questionnaire was used in a school in the United Arab Emirates, where English is spoken but is not the primary language.[14]

Tabulating the results of a pretest helps determine whether the questionnaire will meet the objectives of the research. A **preliminary tabulation** often illustrates that, although respondents can easily comprehend and answer a given question, that question is inappropriate because it does not provide relevant information to help solve the marketing problem. Consider the following example from a survey among distributors of power-actuated tools such as stud drivers concerning the percentage of sales to given industries:

preliminary tabulation

A tabulation of the results of a pretest to help determine whether the questionnaire will meet the objectives of the research.

Please estimate what percentage of your fastener and load sales go to the following industries:

_____ *% heating, plumbing, and air conditioning*
_____ *% carpentry*
_____ *% electrical*
_____ *% maintenance*
_____ *% other (please specify)*

The researchers were fortunate to learn that asking the question in this manner made it virtually impossible to obtain the information actually desired. Most respondents' answers did not total 100 percent, and the question had to be revised. In general, getting respondents to add everything correctly is a problem. Pretesting difficult questions such as these is essential.

It's Not Always What You Ask, but How You Ask It!

Are there certain types of things that are best discussed face to face? Or, are there some things you'd rather ask a friend by email? Just as in everyday life, survey responses can vary based on the medium used. For instance, can you expect people to be 100 percent honest when you ask them sensitive questions that may even sometimes have moral content? Or, if you are phoned and asked to list your favorite brand, would you give the same response as if you were asked that question on a comprehensive Web survey? Well, the evidence suggests that in either case differences in responses should be expected based on the question medium.

- "Do you give financial support to charitable causes on a regular basis?"
- "Do you go to church on a regular basis?"
- "Have you had an alcoholic drink in the last week?"

Are these sensitive questions? Results of asking people these questions varies based on how they are asked. Specifically, people who are asked these questions on the telephone

give responses that are more protective of their image than do people asked the very same questions via a typical Internet-type questionnaire. Phone survey results suggest a 10 percent difference in the response to the charitable giving question with phone respondents displaying a greater inclination to give to charities than people answering the question via the electronic questionnaire. On the phone, almost 6 in 10 respondents report going to church almost weekly but via the computer, that number drops to 1 in 4. Less than half of all phone respondents had a drink in one week but over half of the computer questionnaire respondents reported that they had a drink.

Brand ratings also vary based on the way questions are asked. That's partly why in the same period you might see a poll showing T.J. Maxx as the leading brand and another may have Google. Some of the companies that conduct these polls rely on telephone interviews and others rely on comprehensive questionnaires delivered by mail or on the Internet. In any case, these results make the case that the way a question is asked is equally as important as how the question is asked!

Sources: Boyle, M., "Microsoft and GE: Not Old and In the Way," *Fortune* (October 31, 2007), http://money.cnn.com/2007/10/31/magazines/fortune/microsoft_ge.fortune/index.htm, accessed September 12, 2008; Gamerman, E., "When Voters Lie," *Wall Street Journal* (August 2, 2008), W1; Seattle Times, "Microsoft Brand Sinks in this Survey," (March 23, 2008), http://seattletimes.nwsource.com/html/microsoft/2004301551_btdownload24.html, accessed September 12, 2008.

What administrative procedures should be implemented to maximize the value of a pretest? Administering a questionnaire exactly as planned in the actual study often is not possible. For example, mailing out a questionnaire might require several weeks that simply cannot be spared. Pretesting a questionnaire in this manner would provide important information on response rate but may not point out why questions were skipped or what questions are ambiguous or confusing. Personal interviewers can record requests for additional explanation or comments that indicate respondents' difficulty with question sequence or other factors. This is the primary reason why interviewers are often used for pretest work. Self-administered questionnaires are not reworded to be personal interviews, but interviewers are instructed to observe respondents and ask for their comments after they complete the questionnaire. When pretesting personal or telephone interviews, interviewers may test alternative wordings and question sequences to determine which format best suits the intended respondents.

No matter how the pretest is conducted, the researcher should remember that its purpose is to uncover any problems that the questionnaire may cause. Thus, pretests typically are conducted to answer questions about the questionnaire such as the following:

- Can the questionnaire format be followed by the interviewer?
- Does the questionnaire flow naturally and conversationally?
- Are the questions clear and easy to understand?
- Can respondents answer the questions easily?
- Which alternative forms of questions work best?

Pretests also provide means for testing the sampling procedure—to determine, for example, whether interviewers are following the sampling instructions properly and whether the procedure is efficient. Pretests also provide estimates of the response rates for mail surveys and the completion rates for telephone surveys.

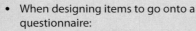
- When designing items to go onto a questionnaire:
  - Simpler wording is better than complex wording.
  - Phrase items as if they were being asked to the person in the sample that will have the most difficulty understanding them.
    - Break complicated ideas into multiple questions.
- A researcher with a strong opinion toward the decision issues is prone to construct leading and loaded questions. Often, this is unintentional.
  - When possible, have an objective person involved in wording questionnaire items.
- Questionnaires should be short. But, for any length questionnaire, the respondent should know about how long it will take to complete at the beginning.

- Include a status bar whenever possible.
- Expect response quality to drop as questionnaires take five minutes or longer.
- Long questionnaires should include some check questions to make sure respondents are still paying attention. These should be questions such as an instruction to mark 4 for an item or sequential questions that contain opposite responses.
- Dependent variables should usually be measured before independent variables.
- Sensitive items are generally best collected through impersonal media like mail or Internet questionnaires.
  - But, when asking questions that a respondent believes can be verified easily (i.e., a bank asking typical credit card balance), more accurate answers result when respondents are not anonymous.

©GEORGE DOYLE & CIARAN GRIFFIN

Usually a questionnaire goes through several revisions. The exact number of revisions depends on the researcher's and client's judgment. The revision process usually ends when both agree that the desired information is being collected in an unbiased manner.

Designing Questionnaires for Global Markets

Now that marketing research is being conducted around the globe, researchers must take cultural factors into account when designing questionnaires. The most common problem involves translating a questionnaire into other languages. A questionnaire developed in one country may be difficult to translate because equivalent language concepts do not exist or because of differences in idiom and vernacular. Although Spanish is spoken in both Mexico and Venezuela, one researcher found out that the Spanish translation of the English term *retail outlet* works in Mexico but not in Venezuela. Venezuelans interpreted the translation to refer to an electrical outlet, an outlet of a river into an ocean, or the passageway onto a patio.

Counting on an international audience to speak a common language such as English does not necessarily bridge these gaps, even when the respondents actually do speak more than one language. Cultural differences incorporate many shades of meaning that may not be captured by a survey delivered in a language used primarily for, say, business transactions. In a test of this idea, undergraduate students in 24 countries completed questionnaires about attitudes toward school and career. Half received the questionnaire in English, and half in their native language. The results varied, with country-to-country differences being smaller when students completed the questionnaire in English.[15]

International marketing researchers often have questionnaires back translated. **Back translation** is the process of taking a questionnaire that has previously been translated from one language to another and having it translated back again by a second, independent translator. The back translator is often a person whose native tongue is the language that will be used for the questionnaire. This process can reveal inconsistencies between the English version and the translation. For example, when a soft-drink company translated its slogan "Baby, it's cold inside" into Cantonese for research in Hong Kong, the result read "Small Mosquito, on the inside, it is very cold." In Hong Kong, *small mosquito* is a colloquial expression for a small child. Obviously the intended meaning of the advertising message had been lost in the translated questionnaire.[16]

As indicated in Chapter 8, literacy influences the designs of self-administered questionnaires and interviews. Knowledge of the literacy rates in foreign countries, especially those that are just developing modern economies, is vital.

back translation

Taking a questionnaire that has previously been translated into another language and having a second, independent translator translate it back to the original language.

Summary

1. Know the key decisions in questionnaire design. The data gathered via a questionnaire must be both relevant and accurate to be of value. A researcher who is systematically planning a questionnaire's design must face several decisions that will shape the value of the questionnaire. What should be asked? How should questions be phrased? In what sequence should the questions be arranged? What questionnaire layout will best serve the research objectives? How should the questionnaire be pretested? Does the questionnaire need to be revised?

2. Choose between open-ended and fixed-alternative questions. Knowing how each question should be phrased requires some knowledge of the different types of questions possible. Open-ended response questions pose some problem or question and ask the respondent to answer in his or her own words. Fixed-alternative questions require less interviewer skill, take less time, and are easier to answer. In fixed-alternative questions the respondent is given specific limited alternative responses and asked to choose the one closest to his or her own viewpoint. Standardized responses are easier to code, tabulate, and interpret. Care must be taken to formulate the responses so that they do not overlap. Respondents whose answers do not fit any of the fixed alternatives may be forced to select alternatives that do not communicate what they really mean. Open-ended response questions are especially useful in exploratory research or at the beginning of a questionnaire. They make a questionnaire more expensive to analyze because of the uniqueness of the answers. Also, interviewer bias can influence the responses to such questions.

3. Summarize guidelines for questions that avoid mistakes in questionnaire design. Some guidelines for questionnaire construction have emerged from research experience. The language should be simple to allow for variations in educational level. Researchers should avoid leading or loaded questions, which suggest answers to the respondents, as well as questions that induce them to give socially desirable answers. Respondents have a bias against questions that suggest changes in the status quo. Their reluctance to answer personal questions can be reduced by explaining the need for the questions and by assuring respondents of the confidentiality of their replies. The researcher should carefully avoid ambiguity in questions. Another common problem is the double-barreled question, which asks two questions at once.

4. Describe how the proper sequence of questions may improve a questionnaire. Question sequence can be very important to the success of a survey. The opening questions should be designed to capture respondents' interest and keep them involved. Personal questions should be postponed to the middle or end of the questionnaire. General questions should precede specific ones. In a series of attitude scales the first response may be used as an anchor for comparison with the other responses. The order of alternatives on closed questions can affect the results. Filter questions are useful for avoiding unnecessary questions that do not apply to a particular respondent. Such questions may be put into a flowchart for personal or telephone interviewing.

5. Discuss how to design a questionnaire layout. The layout of a mail or other self-administered questionnaire can affect its response rate. An attractive questionnaire encourages a response, as does a carefully phrased title. Internet questionnaires present unique design issues. Decisions must be made about the use of color, graphics, animation, sound, and other special layout effects that the Internet makes possible.

6. Describe criteria for pretesting and revising a questionnaire and for adapting it to global markets. Pretesting helps reveal errors while they can still be corrected easily. A preliminary tabulation may show that, even if respondents understand questions, the responses are not relevant to the marketing problem. Often, the most efficient way to conduct a pretest is with interviewers to generate quick feedback. International marketing researchers must take cultural factors into account when designing questionnaires. The most widespread problem involves translation into another language. International questionnaires are often back translated.

Key Terms and Concepts

aided-recall, *379*

back translation, *393*

check boxes, *388*

checklist question, *373*

counterbiasing statement, *376*

determinant-choice question, *372*

double-barreled question, *377*

drop-down box, *388*

error trapping, *390*

filter question, *381*

fixed-alternative questions, *370*

forced answering software, *390*

frequency-determination question, *372*

funnel technique, *380*

interactive help desk, *391*

leading question, *375*

loaded question, *375*

multiple-grid question, *384*

Questions for Review and Critical Thinking

1. Evaluate and comment on the following questions, taken from several questionnaires:

   a. A university computer center survey on SPSS usage:

   How often do you use SPSS statistical software? Please check one.

   - *Infrequently (once a semester)*
   - *Occasionally (once a month)*
   - *Frequently (once a week)*
   - *All the time (daily)*

   b. A survey of advertising agencies:

   Do you understand and like the Federal Trade Commission's new corrective advertising policy?

   ——Yes   ——No

   c. A survey on a new, small electric car:

   Assuming 90 percent of your driving is in town, would you buy this type of car?

   ——Yes   ——No

   If this type of electric car had the same initial cost as a current "Big 3" full-size, fully equipped car, but operated at one-half the cost over a five-year period, would you buy one?

   ——Yes   ——No

   d. A student survey:

   Since the beginning of this semester, approximately what percentage of the time do you get to campus using each of the forms of transportation available to you per week?

   Walk —— Bicycle ——
   Public transportation —— Motor vehicle ——

   e. A survey of motorcycle dealers:

   Should the company continue its generous cooperative advertising program?

   f. A survey of media use by farmers:

   Thinking about yesterday, put an X in the box below for each quarter-hour time period during which, so far as you can recall, you personally listened to radio. Do the same for television.

6:00 to 10:00 A.M. by quarter-hours	6:00–6:15	6:15–6:30	6:30–6:45	6:45–7:00		7:00–7:15	7:15–7:30	7:30–7:45	7:45–8:00
Radio →									
TV →									

	8:00–8:15	8:15–8:30	8:30–8:45	8:45–9:00		9:00–9:15	9:15–9:30	9:30–9:45	9:45–10:00
Radio →									
TV →									

   If you did not watch TV any time yesterday, X here ☐
   If you did not listen to radio any time yesterday, X here ☐

   g. A government survey of gasoline retailers:

   Suppose the full-service pump selling price for regular gasoline is 232.8 cents per gallon on the first day of the month. Suppose on the 10th of the month the price is raised to 234.9 cents per gallon, and on the 25th of the month it is reduced to 230.9 cents per gallon. In order to provide the required data you should list the accumulator reading on the full-service regular gasoline pump when the station opens on the 1st day, the 10th day, and the 25th day of the month and when the station closes on the last day of the month.

   h. An anti-gun-control group's survey:

   Do you believe that private citizens have the right to own firearms to defend themselves, their families, and their property from violent criminal attack?

   ——Yes   ——No

   i. A survey of the general public:

   In the next year, after accounting for inflation, do you think your real personal income will go up or down?

   1. Up
   2. (Stay the same)
   3. Down
   4. (Don't know)

   j. **ETHICS** A survey of the general public:

   Some people say that companies should be required by law to label all chemicals and substances that the government states are potentially harmful. The label would tell what the chemical or substance is, what dangers it might pose, and what safety procedures should be used in handling the substance. Other people say that such laws would be too strict. They say the law should require labels on only those chemicals and substances that the companies themselves decide are potentially harmful. Such a law, they say, would be less costly for the companies and would permit them to exclude those chemicals and substances they consider to be trade secrets. Which of these views is closest to your own?

   1. Require labels on all chemicals and substances that the government states are potentially harmful.
   2. (Don't know)
   3. Require labels on only those chemicals and substances that companies decide are potentially harmful.

   k. A survey of voters:

   Since agriculture is vital to our state's economy, how do you feel about the administration's farm policies?

   Strongly favor
   Somewhat favor
   Somewhat oppose
   Strongly oppose
   Unsure

2. The following question was asked of a sample of television viewers:

We are going to ask you to classify the type of fan you consider yourself to be for different sports and sports programs.

- **Diehard Fan: Watch games, follow up on scores and sports news multiple times a day**
- **Avid Fan: Watch games, follow up on scores and sports news once a day**
- **Casual Fan: Watch games, follow up on scores and sports news occasionally**
- **Championship Fan: Watch games, follow up on scores and sports news only during championships or playoffs**
- **Non-Fan: Never watch games or follow up on scores**
- **Anti-Fan: Dislike, oppose, or object to a certain sport**

Does this question do a good job of avoiding ambiguity?

3. How might the wording of a question about income influence respondents' answers?

4. What is the difference between a *leading question* and a *loaded question*?

5. Design one or more open-ended response questions to measure reactions to a magazine ad for a Xerox photocopier.

6. Design one or more questions to measure how a person who has just been shown a television commercial might describe the commercial.

7. Evaluate the layout of the filter question that follows:

> Are you employed either full time or part time?
>
> | *Mark (x) one.*   ☐ Yes   ☐ No
>
> If yes: How many hours per week are you usually employed? *Mark (x) one.*
>
> ☐ Less than 35   ☐ 35 or more
>
> What is the zip code at your usual place of work?
>
> ------------------

8. It has been said that surveys show that consumers hate advertising, but like specific ads. Comment.

9. Design a complete questionnaire to evaluate a new fast-food fried chicken restaurant.

10. Design a short but complete questionnaire to measure consumer satisfaction with an airline.

11. Develop a checklist of things to consider in questionnaire construction.

12. Design a complete personal interview questionnaire for a zoo that wishes to determine who visits the zoo and how they evaluate it.

13. Design a complete self-administered questionnaire for a bank to give to customers immediately after they open new accounts.

14. Design a questionnaire for your local Big Brothers and Big Sisters organization to investigate awareness of and willingness to volunteer time to this organization.

15. Design a questionnaire for a bank located in a college town to investigate the potential for attracting college students as checking account customers.

16. The Apple Assistance Center is a hotline to solve problems for users of Macintosh computers and other Apple products. Design a short (postcard-size) consumer satisfaction/service quality questionnaire for the Apple Assistance Center.

17. 'NET Visit the following Web site: http://www.history.org. What type of questions might be asked in a survey to evaluate the effectiveness of this Web site in terms of being informative and in terms of being an effective sales medium?

18. A client tells a researcher that she wants a questionnaire that evaluates the importance of 30 product characteristics and rates her brand and 10 competing brands on these characteristics. The researcher believes that this questionnaire will induce respondent fatigue because it will be far too long. Should the researcher do exactly what the client says or risk losing the business by suggesting a different approach?

19. ETHICS A lobbying organization designs a short questionnaire about its political position. It also includes a membership solicitation with the questionnaire. Is this approach ethical?

20. 'NET Visit Mister Poll at http://www.misterpoll.com, where you will find thousands of user-contributed polls on every imaginable topic from the controversial to the downright zany. What you find will depend on when you visit the site. However, you might find something such as a Movie Poll, where you pick your favorite film of the season. Evaluate the questions in the poll.

21. 'NET Try to find two friends that know the same foreign language. Write 10 Likert questions that measure how exciting a retail store environment is to shop in. Have one of your friends interpret the question into the foreign language. Have the other take the translation and state each question in English. How similar is the translated English to the original English? Comment.

22. List the decisions that researchers face in trying to construct a valid and reliable questionnaire. At what stage do you think most questionnaires directed at students are most likely to go wrong?

Research Activity

1. Design eight questions that assess how effective an undergraduate college business course has been.

Case 15.1 Frontier Golf Simulators

It's "Virtually" the Same Game?!

Prepared by Kevin James, Louisiana Tech University

The business of sports is growing tremendously and it is fueled in part by athletes that take on celebrity status. None typifies this better than Tiger Woods. Tiger is a brand representing a multimillion dollar entity unto itself. Traditionally, golf had a stigma of being for wealthy, stodgy, old businessmen who hardly knew how to have a good time. That image is common in many countries outside of the United States to this day. Companies like Nike and Callaway have invested large sums of money and effort to draw a different and more diverse demographic to the game of golf.

With the changing demographic of the actual players comes a marketing challenge of just how to best meet the needs of these segments that are quite new to the game. For instance, indoor golf simulators have started to increase in popularity and offer a chance to play some golf even in an urban setting. These simulators have the distinct advantage of being able to accurately show the player's ball flight and ball spin, as well as the actual yardage the ball travels. A further advantage is that with these simulators, a foursome can finish an entire round of golf in just under an hour instead of four hours or more! Additionally, this round of golf can be played at St. Andrews or Pebble Beach without the expense and hassle of traveling to these mystical sites.

Brian Scheffler is the Director of Marketing for Frontier Golf Simulators, a San Antonio, Texas-based company which operates five state-of-the-art golf simulators. The pricing structure is either $30 per hour for "walk-ins" or a player can take a membership much like he or she might at a real golf club. In addition to the simulators, the facility has a restaurant and bar so that patrons can eat and drink while they tee it up. Brian has the unique challenge of marketing and ultimately selling time on these simulators.

Unfortunately, Mr. Scheffler is unsure how to best spend his very limited marketing budget. Mr. Scheffler understands that the traditional golfer has different wants and needs than does the entertainment-seeking golfer. Does virtual golf offer value in the same way as real golf? If not, the simulators may not appeal to real or traditional golfers at all.

Faced with not knowing exactly what people like most about the simulators, Brian decides to create a survey to determine what people like most about their simulator experience and how to most effectively market his product to maximize the customer's experience and ultimately create returning customers.

1. What are some of the issues Brian should consider when designing the survey?
2. What types of issues can be addressed with open-ended questions and what type of issues can be addressed with fixed-alternative questions?
3. How would the structure of the survey change if Brian decides to administer the survey via the telephone versus face-to-face mall intercept interviews?
4. Develop a survey that will address Brian's need to better understand his customers.

Case 15.2 Canterbury Travels

Hometown, located in the northcentral United States, had a population of about fifty thousand. There were two travel agencies in Hometown before Canterbury Travels opened its doors.

Canterbury Travels was in its second month of operations. Owner Roxanne Freeman had expected to have more business than she actually had. She decided that she needed to conduct a survey to determine how much business Hometown offered. She also wanted to learn whether people were aware of Canterbury Travels. She thought that this survey would determine the effectiveness of her advertising.

The questionnaire that Roxanne Freeman designed is shown in Case Exhibit 15.2–1.

Questions

1. Critically evaluate the questionnaire.
2. Will Canterbury Travels gain the information it needs from this survey?
3. Design a questionnaire to satisfy Roxanne Freeman's information needs.

CASE EXHIBIT 15.2–1 **Travel Questionnaire**

The following questionnaire pertains to a project being conducted by a local travel agency. The intent of the study is to better understand the needs and attitudes of Hometown residents toward travel agencies. The questionnaire will take only 10 to 15 minutes to fill out at your convenience. Your name will in no way be connected with the questionnaire.

1. Have you traveled out of state? _____Yes _____No
2. If yes, do you travel for:
   Business   Both
   Pleasure
3. How often do you travel for the above?
   0–1 times per month   0–1 times per year
   2–3 times per month   2–3 times per year
   4–5 times per month   4–5 times per year
   6 or more times per month   6 or more times per year
4. How do you make your travel arrangements?
   Airline   Travel agency
   Other (please specify) _____
5. Did you know that travel agencies do not charge the customer for their services?
   _____Yes _____No

(continued)

CASE EXHIBIT 15.2–1 **Travel Questionnaire** (continued)

6. Please rate the following qualities that would be most important to you in the selection of a travel agency:

	Good				**Bad**
Free services (reservations, advice, and delivery of tickets and literature)	___	___	___	___	___
Convenient location	___	___	___	___	___
Knowledgeable personnel	___	___	___	___	___
Friendly personnel	___	___	___	___	___
Casual atmosphere	___	___	___	___	___
Revolving charge account	___	___	___	___	___
Reputation	___	___	___	___	___
Personal sales calls	___	___	___	___	___

7. Are you satisfied with your present travel agency?

	Very satisfied				**Very dissatisfied**
Holiday Travel	___	___	___	___	___
Leisure Tours	___	___	___	___	___
Canterbury Travels	___	___	___	___	___
Other _____	___	___	___	___	___

8. If not, what are you dissatisfied with about your travel agency?

	Good				**Bad**
Free services (reservations, advice, and delivery of tickets and literature)	___	___	___	___	___
Convenient location	___	___	___	___	___
Knowledgeable personnel	___	___	___	___	___
Friendly personnel	___	___	___	___	___
Casual atmosphere	___	___	___	___	___
Revolving charge account	___	___	___	___	___
Reputation	___	___	___	___	___
Personal sales calls	___	___	___	___	___

9. Did you know that there is a new travel agency in Hometown?
   _____Yes   _____No

10. Can you list the travel agencies in Hometown and their locations?
    _____
    _____
    _____

11. Do you use the same travel agency repeatedly?

	0–1 times per month	2–3 times per month	4–5 times per month	6 or more times per month	0–1 times per year	2–3 times per year	4–5 times per year	6 or more times per year
Holiday Travel								
Leisure Tours								
Canterbury Travels								
Other (please specify)								

12. Have you visited the new travel agency in Hometown?
    _____Yes   _____No

13. If yes, what is its name? _____

14. How do you pay for your travel expenses?
    Cash   Company charge
    Check   Personal charge
    Credit card   Other _____

15. Which of these have you seen advertising for?
    Holiday Travel
    Canterbury Travels
    Other _____

16. Where have you seen or heard the advertisement you describe above?

17. Would you consider changing travel agencies?
    _____Yes   _____No

(continued)

CASE EXHIBIT 15.2–1 **Travel Questionnaire** *(continued)*

The following are some personal questions about you that will be used for statistical purposes only. Your answers will be held in the strictest confidence.

18. What is your age?

19–25	46–55
26–35	56–65
36–45	Over 65

19. What is your sex?

Male	Female

20. What is your marital status?

Single	Divorced
Married	Widowed

21. How long have you lived in Hometown?

0–6 months	5–10 years
7–12 months	11–15 years
1–4 years	Over 15 years

22. What is your present occupation?

Business and professional	Laborer
Salaried and semiprofessional	Student
Skilled worker	

23. What is the highest level of education you have completed?

Elementary school	1–2 years of college
Junior high school	3–4 years of college
Senior high school	More than 4 years of college
Trade or vocational school	

24. What is your yearly household income?

$0–$5,000	$25,001–$40,000
$5,001–$10,000	$40,001–$60,000
$10,001–$15,000	$60,000 and above
$15,001–$25,000	

Case 15.3 McDonald's Spanish Language Questionnaire

The questions in Case Exhibit 15.3–1, about a visit to McDonald's, originally appeared in Spanish and were translated into English.

Questions

1. What is the typical process for developing questionnaires for markets where consumers speak a language other than English?

2. Find someone who speaks Spanish and have him or her back translate the questions that appear in Case Exhibit 15.3–1. Are these Spanish-language questions adequate?

CASE EXHIBIT 15.3–1 **McDonald's Questionnaire**

AQUI SE EMPIEZA ➡

1. En general, ¿qué tan satisfecho/a quedó con su visita a este McDonald's hoy?
   ☹ NADA SATISFECHO/A ⓵ ⓶ ⓷ ⓸ MUY SATISFECHO/A ☺ ⓹

2. Su visita fue....... Adentro (**A**) o en el Drive-thru (**DT**)
   Ⓐ Adentro ⒹⓉ Drive-thru

3. Su visita fue....... Durante el Desayuno (**D**), Almuerzo (**A**), Cena (**C**)
   Ⓓ Desayuno Ⓐ Almuerzo Ⓐ Cena

4. Su visita fue....... Entre semana (**E**) o Fin de semana (**F**)
   Ⓔ Entre semana Ⓕ Fin de semana

COMIDA

5. ¿Quedó satisfecho/a con la comida que recibió hoy? Ⓢ Sí Ⓝ No
   Si NO, ¿cuál fue el problema?
   Favor de rellenar el(los) círculo(s) apropiado(s).
   - Sandwich / platillo frío
   - Apariencia desagradable
   - Mal sabor de la comida
   - Pocas papas en la bolsa / caja
   - Papas / tortitas de papa frías
   - Papas no bien saladas
   - Bebida aguada / de mal sabor

Case 15.4 Schönbrunn Palace in Vienna

The Schönbrunn Palace in Vienna was constructed in the eighteenth century during the reign of the Hapsburgs. Today this former summer residence of the imperial family is one of Austria's top tourist attractions.

The questions in Case Exhibit 15.4–1, about a visit to the Schönbrunn Palace, originally appeared in German and were translated into English.

© GETTY IMAGES/ PHOTODISC GREEN

Questions

1. What is the typical process for developing questionnaires for markets where consumers speak a different language?
2. Find someone who speaks German and have him or her back translate the questions that appear in Case Exhibit 15.4–1. Do the questions make sense? Do they exhibit any problematic wording?

CASE EXHIBIT 15.4–1 **Schönbrunn Palace Questionnaire**

Befragung der Besucher   **Schloß Schönbrunn**

Land/Staat _____   Bundesland (nur für Ö) _____

Alter _____ Jahre   Geschlecht □ männlich □ weiblich

Heutiges Datum ___ . ___ . 199__   Uhrzeit _____

- **Waren Sie heute zum ersten Mal im Schloß Schönbrunn?**
  □ ja   □ nein, zum ___. Mal

- **Welche Tour haben Sie gemacht?**
  □ *Grand Tour* (40 Räume)
  □ *Imperial Tour* (22 Räume)

- **Welche Art von Führung haben Sie gewählt?**
  □ *Schönbrunn Führung (Angebot des Schlosses)*
  □ *eigener Reiseführer (Reisegruppe, Fremdenführer)*
  □ *Tonbandführer (Audioguide) in* _____ *Sprache*
  □ *keinerlei Führung*

- **Falls Sie an einer Führung teilgenommen haben:**
  Wie finden Sie Ihren Führer bzw. Ihre Führerin?
  □ sehr freundlich   □ eher freundlich   □ eher unfreundlich   □ sehr unfreundlich
  weil ... _____

- **Bei Verwendung eines Tonbandführers (Audioguide):**
  Wie finden Sie die angebotenen Audioguides?
  □ sehr gut   □ eher gut   □ eher schlecht   □ sehr schlecht
  weil ... _____

- **Wie ist Ihr Gesamteindruck vom Schloß Schönbrunn alles in allem?**
  □ sehr gut   □ eher gut   □ eher schlecht   □ sehr schlecht
  weil ... _____

- **Wie ist Ihr Eindruck vom Personal im Schloß?**
  □ sehr gut   □ eher gut   □ eher schlecht   □ sehr schlecht
  weil ... _____

- **Wie gut finden Sie sich im Schloß Schönbrunn/Park zurecht (Hinweisschilder, kennt man sich gut aus, findet man die Kassen, Toiletten, den Ausgang, etc.)?**
  □ sehr gut   □ eher gut   □ eher schlecht   □ sehr schlecht
  weil ... _____

- **Fühlten Sie sich nach dem Besuch gut informiert über das Schloß und seine Geschichte?**
  □ sehr gut   □ eher gut   □ eher schlecht   □ sehr schlecht

- **Wurden Sie bei der Besichtigung gestört?**
  durch (andere) Gruppen:
  □ sehr stark   □ etwas   □ kaum   □ gar nicht
  durch Einzelbesucher:
  □ sehr stark   □ etwas   □ kaum   □ gar nicht

- **Wie finden Sie die Art, wie die Räume dargestellt werden (Einrichtung, Möblierung, Beleuchtung, Dekoration, etc.)?**
  □ sehr gut   □ eher gut   □ eher schlecht   □ sehr schlecht
  weil ... _____

- **Haben Sie nach dem Besuch im Schloß Schönbrunn eine lebendige Vorstellung vom einstigen Leben bei Hof?**
  □ ja   □ etwas   □ kaum   □ nein
  weil ... _____

- **Was würden Sie noch gerne über das Schloß erfahren?**
  _____

- **Wie finden Sie die Eintrittspreise?**
  □ viel zu teuer   □ etwas zu teuer   □ angemessen   □ günstig

- **Wie finden Sie das Angebot im Museumshop?**
  □ sehr gut   □ eher gut   □ eher schlecht   □ sehr schlecht
  weil ... _____

- **Was könnte Ihrer Meinung nach noch verbessert werden?**
  _____
  _____
  _____
  _____

Vielen Dank für Ihren Besuch und Ihre Anregungen!

As Chapters 13, 14, and 15 explain, problem definitions and research objectives determine the nature of the questions to be asked. In most cases researchers construct custom questions for their specific projects. However, in many instances different research projects have some common research objectives. This appendix compiles question wordings and measurement scales frequently used by marketing researchers. It is by no means exhaustive. It does not repeat every question already discussed in the text. For example, it does not include the hundreds of possible semantic differential items or Likert scale items discussed in Chapter 14.

The purpose of this appendix is to provide a bank of questions and scales for easy reference. It can be used when marketing research objectives dictate investigation of commonly researched issues.

Questions About Advertising

Awareness

Have you ever seen any advertising for (brand name)?

☐ Yes ☐ No

Are you aware of (brand name)?

☐ Yes ☐ No

If yes, how did you first become aware of (brand name)?

- *In-flight airline magazine*
- *Poster or billboard at airport*
- *Television at airport*
- *Card in the seatback pocket*
- *Other (please specify)* _____

Unaided Recall/Top of the Mind Recall

Can you tell me the names of any brands of (product category) for which you have seen or heard any advertising recently?

_____
_____
_____

(After reading a magazine or viewing a TV program with commercials) Please try to recall all the brands you saw advertised on/in (name of program or magazine). (DO NOT PROBE. WRITE BRAND NAMES IN ORDER MENTIONED BY RESPONDENT.)

(After establishing that the respondent watched a certain television program) Do you recall seeing a commercial for any (product category)? (IF YES) What brand of (product category) was advertised?

Aided Recall

(After establishing that the respondent watched a certain television program or read a certain magazine) Now, I'm going to read you a list of brands. Some of them were advertised on/in (name of program or magazine); others were not. Please tell me which ones you remember seeing, even if you mentioned them before.

Brand A (Advertised)
Brand B (Not advertised)
Brand C (Advertised)

Do you remember seeing a commercial for (specific brand name)?

☐ *Yes*   ☐ *No*

Recognition

(Show advertisement to respondent) Did you see or read any part of this advertisement?

☐ *Yes*   ☐ *No*

Message Communication/Playback (Sales Point Playback)

These questions require that the researcher first qualify awareness with a question such as **"Have you ever seen any advertising for (brand name)?"** The interviewer then asks message playback questions.

(If yes) What did the advertising tell you about (brand name or product category)?

_____

_____

Other than trying to sell you the product, what do you think was the main idea in the description you just read (commercial you just saw)?

_____

_____

What was the main thing it was trying to communicate about the product?
What did the advertising for (brand name) say about the product?

_____

_____

What did you learn about (brand name) from this advertisement?

_____

_____

Attitude Toward the Advertisement

Please choose the statement below that best describes your feelings about the commercial you just saw.

☐ *I liked it very much.*
☐ *I liked it.*
☐ *I neither liked nor disliked it.*
☐ *I disliked it.*
☐ *I disliked it very much.*

Was there anything in the commercial you just saw that you found hard to believe?

☐ *Yes*   ☐ *No*

What thoughts or feelings went through your mind as you watched the advertisement?

_____

Attitude Toward Advertised Brand (Persuasion)

Based on what you've seen in this commercial, how interested would you be in trying the product?

☐ *Extremely interested*
☐ *Very interested*
☐ *Somewhat interested*
☐ *Not very interested*
☐ *Not at all interested*

The advertisement tried to increase your interest in (brand). How was your buying interest affected?

☐ *Increased considerably*
☐ *Increased somewhat*
☐ *Not affected*
☐ *Decreased somewhat*
☐ *Decreased considerably*

Based on what you've just seen in this commercial, how do you think (brand name) might compare to other brands you've seen or heard about?

☐ *Better*
☐ *As good as*
☐ *Not as good as*

_____

Readership/Viewership

Have you ever read (seen) a copy of (advertising medium)?

☐ *Yes*   ☐ *No*

How frequently do you (watch the evening news on channel X)?

☐ *Every day*
☐ *5–6 times a week*
☐ *2–4 times a week*
☐ *Once a week*
☐ *Less than once a week*
☐ *Never*

Several of the questions about products or brands in the following section are also used to assess attitudes toward advertised brands.

Questions About Ownership and Product Usage ◀━━━━━━━━

_____

Ownership

Do you own a (product category)?

☐ *Yes*   ☐ *No*

Purchase Behavior

Have you ever purchased a (product category or brand name)?

☐ *Yes*   ☐ *No*

Regular Usage

Which brands of (product category) do you regularly use?

___ *Brand A*
___ *Brand B*
___ *Brand C*
___ *None, I use _____*

Which brands of (product category) have you used in the past month?

____ *Brand A*
____ *Brand B*
____ *Brand C*
____ *None, but I have used _____*

In an average month, how often do you buy (product category or brand name)?

Record Number of Times per Month _____

How frequently do you buy (product category or brand name)?

☐ *Every day*
☐ *5–6 times a week*
☐ *2–4 times a week*
☐ *Once a week*
☐ *Less than once a week*
☐ *Never*

Would you say you purchase (product category or brand name) more often than you did a year ago, about the same as a year ago, or less than a year ago?

☐ *More often than a year ago*
☐ *About the same as a year ago*
☐ *Less than a year ago*

Questions About Goods and Services

Ease of Use

How easy do you find using (brand name)?

☐ *Very easy*
☐ *Easy*
☐ *Neither easy nor difficult*
☐ *Difficult*
☐ *Very difficult*

Uniqueness

How different is this brand from other brands of (product category)?

☐ *Very different*
☐ *Somewhat different*

☐ *Slightly different*
☐ *Not at all different*

How would you rate this product (brand name) on uniqueness?

☐ *Extremely unique*
☐ *Very unique*
☐ *Somewhat unique*
☐ *Slightly unique*
☐ *Not at all unique*

Please form several piles of cards so that statements that are similar to each other or say similar things are in the same pile. You may form as many piles as you like, and you may put as many or as few cards as you want in a pile. You can set aside any statements that you feel are unique or different and are not similar to any of the other statements.

Attribute Ratings/Importance of Characteristics

Measurement scales such as the semantic differential and Likert scales are frequently used to assess product attributes, especially when measuring brand image or store image. See Chapter 15.

How important is (specific attribute), as far as you are concerned?

☐ *Very important*
☐ *Of some importance*
☐ *Of little importance*
☐ *Of absolutely no importance*

We would like you to rate (brand name or product category) on several different characteristics. (For concept tests, add: Since you may not have used this product before, please base your answers on your impressions from what you've just read.)

Characteristic A

☐ *Excellent*   ☐ *Good*   ☐ *Fair*   ☐ *Poor*   ☐ *Terrible*

Interest

In general, how interested are you in trying a new brand of (product category)?

☐ *Very interested*
☐ *Somewhat interested*
☐ *Not too interested*
☐ *Not at all interested*

Like/Dislike

What do you like about (brand name)?

_____

_____

What do you dislike about (brand name)?

_____

_____

How do you like the taste of (brand name)?

☐ *Like it very much*
☐ *Like it*
☐ *Neither like nor dislike it*
☐ *Dislike it*
☐ *Strongly dislike it*

Preference

Which credit card do you prefer to use?

- ☐ *American Express*
- ☐ *MasterCard*
- ☐ *Visa*
- ☐ *No preference*

Expectations

How would you compare the way (company's) service was actually delivered with the way you had anticipated that (company) would provide the service?

- ☐ *Much better than expected*
- ☐ *Somewhat better than expected*
- ☐ *About the same as expected*
- ☐ *Somewhat worse than expected*
- ☐ *Much worse than expected*

Satisfaction

How satisfied were you with (brand name)?

- ☐ *Very satisfied*
- ☐ *Satisfied*
- ☐ *Somewhat satisfied*
- ☐ *Dissatisfied*
- ☐ *Very dissatisfied*

How satisfied were you with (brand name)? Please respond with a score ranging from 0 (no satisfaction at all) to 100 (complete satisfaction)?

_____ %

Now that you have owned (brand name) for 6 months, please tell us how satisfied you are with it.

- • *Completely satisfied*
- • *Very satisfied*
- • *Fairly well satisfied*
- • *Somewhat dissatisfied*
- • *Very dissatisfied*

Quality

How would you rate the quality of (brand name)?

- ☐ *Excellent*
- ☐ *Good*
- ☐ *Average*
- ☐ *Fair*
- ☐ *Poor*

Please indicate how the quality of (Brand A) compares with the quality of (Brand B).

- ☐ *Better*
- ☐ *About the same*
- ☐ *Worse*

Problems

Have you experienced problems with (company's) service?

☐ *Yes* ☐ *No*

When attempting to contact (company's) representative, how much of a problem, if any, was each of the following:

Phones busy

☐ *No problem at all* ☐ *Slight problem* ☐ *Somewhat of a problem* ☐ *Major problem*

Put on hold too long or too often

☐ *No problem at all* ☐ *Slight problem* ☐ *Somewhat of a problem* ☐ *Major problem*

What are the major shortcomings of (brand name)? (PROBE: What other shortcomings are there?)

Benefits

Do you think (product concept) would have major benefits, minor benefits, or no benefits at all?

☐ *Major benefits*
☐ *Minor benefits*
☐ *No benefits at all*

Improvements

In what ways, if any, could (brand name) be changed or improved? We would like you to tell us anything you can think of, no matter how minor it seems.

Buying Intentions for Existing Products

Do you intend to buy a (brand name or product category) in the next month (3 months, year, etc.)?

☐ *Yes* ☐ *No*

If a free (product category) were offered to you, which would you select?

☐ *Brand A*
☐ *Brand B*
☐ *Brand C*
☐ *Do not use*

Buying Intentions Based on Product Concept

(Respondent is shown a prototype or asked to read a concept statement.) Now that you have read about (product concept), if this product were available at your local store, how likely would you be to buy it?

☐ *Would definitely buy it*
☐ *Would probably buy it*
☐ *Might or might not buy it*
☐ *Would probably not buy it*
☐ *Would definitely not buy it*

(Hand response card to respondent.) Which phrase on this card indicates how likely you would be to buy this product the next time you go shopping for a product of this type?

☐ *Would definitely buy it*

☐ *Would probably buy it*
☐ *Might or might not buy it*
☐ *Would probably not buy it*
☐ *Would definitely not buy it*

Now that you have read about (product concept), if this product were available at your local store for (price), how likely would you be to buy it?

☐ *Would definitely buy it*
☐ *Would probably buy it*
☐ *Might or might not buy it*
☐ *Would probably not buy it*
☐ *Would definitely not buy it*

How often, if ever, would you buy (product concept)?

☐ *Once a week or more*
☐ *Once every 2 to 3 weeks*
☐ *Once a month/every 4 weeks*
☐ *Once every 2 to 3 months*
☐ *Once every 4 to 6 months*
☐ *Less than once a year*
☐ *Never*

Based on your experience, would you recommend (company) to a friend who wanted to purchase (product concept)?

☐ *Recommend that the friend buy from (company)*
☐ *Recommend that the friend not buy from (company)*
☐ *Offer no opinion either way*

Reason for Buying Intention

Why do you say that you would (would not) buy (brand name)? (PROBE: What other reason do you have for feeling this way?)

Questions About Demographics

Age

What is your age, please?

What year were you born?

Education

What is your level of education?

☐ *Some high school or less*
☐ *Completed high school*
☐ *Some college*
☐ *Completed college*
☐ *Some graduate school*
☐ *Completed graduate school*

What is the highest level of education you have obtained?

☐ *Some high school or less*
☐ *High school graduate*

☐ *Some college*
☐ *College graduate*
☐ *Postgraduate school*
☐ *Completed graduate school*

Marital Status

What is your marital status?

☐ *Married*
☐ *Divorced/separated*
☐ *Widowed*
☐ *Never married/single*

Children

Are there any children under the age of 6 living in your household?

☐ *Yes*   ☐ *No*

If yes, how many?

Income

Which group describes your annual family income (before taxes)?

☐ *0 to $19,999*
☐ *$20,000–$39,999*
☐ *$40,000–$59,999*
☐ *$60,000–$79,999*
☐ *$80,000–$99,999*
☐ *$100,000–$149,999*
☐ *$150,000–$199,999*
☐ *$200,000 or more*

Disposable Income

After taxes and paying bills each month, about how much spending cash or savings do you have left over? _____

Occupation

What is your occupation?

- *Professional*
- *Executive*
- *Managerial*
- *Administrative*
- *Sales*
- *Technical*
- *Labor*
- *Secretarial*
- *Clerical*
- *Other*

What is your occupation?

- *Homemaker*
- *Professional/technical*
- *Upper management/executive*
- *Middle management*
- *Sales/marketing*
- *Clerical or service worker*
- *Tradesperson/machine operator*
- *Laborer*
- *Retired*
- *Student*

Part 5
Sampling and Fieldwork

© MATTHIAS CLAMER/STONE+/GETTY IMAGES

After studying this chapter, you should be able to

1. Explain reasons for taking a sample rather than a complete census
2. Describe the process of identifying a target population and selecting a sampling frame
3. Compare random sampling and systematic (nonsampling) errors with an emphasis on how the Internet is intertwined with this issue
4. Identify the types of nonprobability sampling, including their advantages and disadvantages
5. Summarize various types of probability samples
6. Discuss how to choose an appropriate sample design

Chapter Vignette: At Cadbury, Gum Chewing Takes Expertise

After Cadbury Schweppes acquired Pfizer's candy brands, including Bubbaloo, Dentyne, and Trident, new technology and marketing research pointed the company to a new product idea.[1] From a consumer survey, Cadbury knew that most Americans chew gum, and more than two-thirds of those gum chewers said one reason was to avoid snacking. Looking for a product that would serve as a junk-food alternative, company researchers identified gum pellets with liquid centers as a possible new product. Pfizer's sale to Cadbury had included a manufacturing technology that used different flavors for the candy coating and liquid filling. By delivering two flavors and three textures (crunchy, chewy, and liquid), Cadbury hoped the new gum would satisfy customers' cravings for more substantial snacks. And the small pellets of gum seemed more adult-friendly than other liquid-center gums, which were sold under the Freshen Up and Bubbaloo brands.

The developers' next step was to come up with appealing flavor combinations. Peppermint was one obvious choice since most gum has a mint flavor, which tends to maintain a good taste in the chewer's mouth. Another idea came from consumer testing showing that the most popular fruit flavor is strawberry. Cadbury worked with food scientists to select a strawberry flavoring that was less like the jam-sweet flavor popular with children and more like the taste of a fresh strawberry. Then company marketers selected vanilla centers for the mint gum and lime centers for the strawberry gum.

Finally, the new products were ready for consumer testing. Here, Cadbury faced a problem typically associated with testing foods: Most consumers don't pay enough attention to tastes and smells to give helpful feedback. Their comments are vague, so a truly random sample of the consumer population would not give the company the information it needed. Instead, Cadbury recruited a sample from a sensory panel. Panel members passed tests rating their sense of smell and even the rate at which they salivate. Cadbury trained the panelists for the gum-chewing job, teaching them to chew steadily along with the beats of a metronome.

Testers chewed samples of the gum for precisely three minutes, timing themselves with electronic clocks. At the end of each chewing period, a panel leader asked for comments. Panelists cleared their palates with crackers and water before trying the next sample. Eventually, the panelists provided enough feedback for the company to pinpoint winning flavor combinations and move on to engineering the production process.

Just as Cadbury needed a sample of gum chewers to make judgments about its products, sampling is a familiar part of daily life. A customer in a bookstore picks up a book, looks at the cover, and skims a few pages to get a sense of the writing style and content before deciding whether to buy. A high school student visits a college Web site to listen to a classroom lecture and view the notes. Selecting a university on the basis of one Web site visit may not be scientific sampling, but in a personal situation, it may be a meaningful and practical sampling experience. When measuring every item in a population is impossible, inconvenient, or too expensive, we intuitively take a sample.

Although sampling is commonplace in daily activities, these familiar samples are seldom scientific. For researchers, the process of sampling can be quite complex. Sampling is a central aspect of marketing research, requiring in-depth examination. Sampling does much to determine how realistic marketing results will be. This chapter explains the nature of sampling and ways to determine the appropriate sample design.

Introduction

The sampling process involves drawing conclusions about an entire population by taking measurements from only a portion of all population elements. Sampling makes research possible in cases where taking measurements from everyone or on everything is impossible. A **sample** can be defined as a subset, or some part, of a larger population, from which population characteristics are estimated.

sample

A subset, or some part, of a larger population.

Sampling is defined in terms of the population being studied. A **population (universe)** is any complete group—for example, of people, sales territories, stores, products, or college students—whose members share some common set of characteristics. Each individual member is referred to as a **population element**.

population (universe)

Any complete group of entities that share some common set of characteristics.

Researchers could study every element of a population to draw some conclusion. A **census** is an investigation of all the individual elements that make up the population—a total enumeration rather than a sample. Thus, if we wished to know whether more adult Texans drive pickup trucks than sedans, we could contact every adult Texan and find out whether or not they drive a pickup truck or a sedan. We would then know the answer to this question definitively.

population element

An individual member of a population.

Why Sample?

At a wine-tasting, guests sample wine by having a small taste from multiple bottles of wine. From this, the consumer decides if he or she likes a particular wine. If each guest consumed the entire bottle before making a decision, he or she would be far too inebriated to have any idea about the other bottles. In addition, if the goal is to decide whether or not the wines taste good, giving each person a bottle of wine would soon get very expensive. Similarly, and for some of the same reasons, scientific studies try to draw conclusions about populations by measuring a small portion (sample) rather than taking a census.

census

An investigation of all the individual elements that make up a population.

Pragmatic Reasons

Applied marketing research projects usually have budget and time constraints. If Ford Motor Corporation wished to take a census of past purchasers' reactions to the company's recalls of defective models, the researchers would have to contact millions of automobile buyers. Some of them

This survey asks a variety of questions of college students. Suppose you were an online university interested in studying the habits of college students in general. Consider the following questions:

1. How well do the results collected from this survey represent the market for undergraduate college students?
2. How well do the results represent American undergraduate college students? [Hint: Compare the profile on the questions shown below with data showing typical characteristics of American undergraduate students.]
3. How well do the results represent American business students?
4. Can the data be stratified in a way that would allow it to represent more specific populations? Explain your answer.

would be inaccessible (for example, out of the country), and it would be impossible to contact all these people within a short time period.

A researcher who wants to investigate a population with an extremely small number of population elements may elect to conduct a census rather than a sample because the cost, labor, and time drawbacks would be relatively insignificant. For a company that wants to assess salespersons' satisfaction with its computer networking system, circulating a questionnaire to all 25 of its employees is practical. In most situations, however, many practical reasons favor sampling. Sampling cuts costs, reduces labor requirements, and gathers vital information quickly. These advantages may be sufficient in themselves for using a sample rather than a census, but there are other reasons. The Research Snapshot on page 417 describing the origins of the Gallup poll describe its very practical origins. Ultimately, sampling is a practical matter.

Accurate and Reliable Results

Another major reason for sampling is that most properly selected samples give results that are reasonably accurate. If the elements of a population are quite similar, only a small sample is necessary to accurately portray the characteristic of interest. Thus, a population consisting of 10,000 eleventh grade students in all-boys Catholic high schools will require a smaller sample than a broader population consisting of 10,000 high school students from coeducational, public, secondary schools.

A visual example of how different-sized samples allow one to draw conclusions is provided in Exhibit 16.1 on the next page. A sample is similar to a jigsaw puzzle that isn't solved yet. Even without looking at the box cover, the puzzler probably doesn't have to wait until every piece is in place to draw a conclusion of what the picture will be. However, as more pieces are put in place, which is analogous to more units being sampled, conclusions can be made with greater confidence. Thus, larger samples allow conclusions to be drawn with more confidence that they truly represent the population.

A sample may even on occasion be more accurate than a census. Interviewer mistakes, tabulation errors, and other nonsampling errors may increase during a census as workers suffer from burnout, fatigue, incompetence, or dishonesty. In a sample, increased accuracy may sometimes be possible because the fieldwork and tabulation of data can be more closely supervised. In a field survey, a small, well-trained, closely supervised group may do a more careful and accurate

EXHIBIT 16.1

A Puzzle Is a Sample Until It Is Done! The Sample Allows One to Guess at the Picture.

job of collecting information than a large group of nonprofessional interviewers who try to contact everyone. The U.S. Census Bureau conducts surveys on samples of populations as a way of checking the accuracy of the actual census of those populations. If the conclusions drawn from the sample disagree with the census results, the census is deemed inaccurate and becomes a candidate to be redone because an accurate census is required by law every 10 years.

Destruction of Test Units

Many research projects, especially those in quality-control testing, require the destruction of the items being tested. If a manufacturer of firecrackers wished to find out whether each unit met a specific production standard, no product would be left after the testing. This is the exact situation in many marketing strategy experiments. For example, if an experimental sales presentation were presented to every potential customer, no prospects would remain to be contacted after the experiment. In other words, if there is a finite population and everyone in the population participates in the research and cannot be replaced, no population elements remain to be selected as sampling units. The test units have been destroyed or ruined for the purpose of the research project. Obviously, taking a census in these cases would not be too wise!

Identifying a Relevant Population and Sampling Frame

Before taking a sample, researchers must make several decisions. Exhibit 16.2 presents these decisions as a series of sequential stages, but the order of the decisions does not always follow this sequence. These decisions are highly interrelated. The steps listed in this exhibit are discussed here and in the next two chapters.

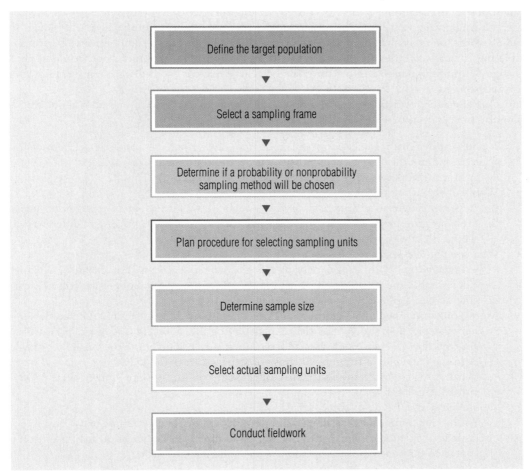

EXHIBIT 16.2

Stages in the Selection of a Sample

Defining the Target Population

The first question in sampling is "What population are we trying to project?" In other words, what larger group is intended to be represented by using a sample? This question is rarely as easy as it may seem and often the matter isn't given much thought.

Polling agencies conduct research to predict election results. What is the relevant sample? Registered voters seems to be a reasonable choice and fortunately, a list of registered voters is generally available in public records. However, the actual election results will be determined by who actually votes, not who is registered to vote. If a study is supposed to represent those who actually will vote, registered voters no longer form the most relevant population. Identifying a sample that represents likely voters is much more difficult because no such list exists.

The population must be defined accurately for the research to produce good results. One survey concerning organizational buyer behavior had purchasing agents whom sales representatives regularly contacted rate preferred product characteristics. After the research proved less than helpful, investigators discovered that industrial engineers were actually making the purchasing decisions. For consumer research, the appropriate population element frequently is the household rather than an individual member of the household. This presents some problems if household lists are not available or if input cannot be obtained from the entire household.

Consider how difficult identifying a relevant population is for a company like Anthropologie or Bebe. What is the population of "fashion consumers?" However, the entire population of fashion consumers is likely not relevant for either of these companies. Clearly, no precise list of population members exists in this case. Even if they are directing a study at "loyal customers," questions such as defining a loyal or a disloyal consumer remain. Companies that use loyalty cards can maintain a list, but the presumption is that only these consumers are truly loyal. In other words, no consumers that do not have a card are loyal. This assumption may be reasonable but is clearly not perfect. Thus, a sample drawn from this list is more precisely described as representing the population of customers who have a loyalty card than as representing truly loyal customers.

One approach for defining the target population is to ask and answer questions about crucial population characteristics. This list illustrates the process:

- Is a list available that matches our population? If so, can we use it? Is valid contact information available and can they be reached with an appropriate communication method?
  - A firm studying its own employees probably has a good list.
- Who are we not interested in?
  - A North American pharmaceutical firm studying how HMOs adopt prescription lists is probably not interested in respondents from Mexico or Canada because of differences in the health care systems.
- What are the relevant market segment characteristics?
  - Companies generally appeal only to specific market segments. For example, consider Abercrombie and Fitch's (A&F) Brand Image. Certainly, A&F shoppers belong to a specific market segment with specific characteristics.
- Are we only interested in a regional population? If so, how do we determine the borders?
  - For example, does the "U.K. market" include England, Scotland, and Wales (Great Britain)? Or does it include only England, or does it also include Northern Ireland, or maybe even the Republic of Ireland, which is not actually part of the U.K?
  - What states comprise the southern United States or the western United States? Does either include Hawaii?
- Should the study include multiple populations?
  - When launching a new product in multiple countries, each country may constitute a distinct population rather than the entire population. Each population may need to be contacted through a different medium with a different approach.

Obviously, A&F caters to a specific market segment with specific demographic and lifestyle characteristics. A researcher studying A&F customers would err by studying the "clothing market."

Answers to these questions help researchers and decision makers focus on the right populations of potential respondents. The sample is implemented using the tangible, identifiable characteristics that also define the population. A baby food manufacturer might define the population as women of childbearing age. However, a more specific *operational definition* would be women between the ages of 18 and 50. While this definition by age may exclude a few women who are capable of childbearing and include some who are not, it is still more explicit and provides a manageable basis for the sample design. Perhaps there are other reasons why this isn't a perfect population description? One important thing to remember is that if the population members cannot be reached by an appropriate communication method, they cannot be part of a sample.

George Gallup's Nation of Numbers

George H. Gallup ... born in 1901 ... left [his] hometown, Jefferson, [Iowa,] as soon as he could find his way in a bigger world. The first step was Iowa City and the State University of Iowa. Then in 1922, between his junior and senior years, George answered an advertisement for summer employment in St. Louis. The Post-Dispatch *hired fifty students to "survey" the city, questioning readers about what they liked and didn't like in the newspaper.*

Each and every reader was to be interviewed – in effect resulting in a census. The students were hired to go to every door in St. Louis—there were 55,000 homes in the city then—and ask the same questions. Gallup, one hot day, knocked on one door too many, got the same answers one time too many, and decided, there's got to be a better way.

"A New Technique for Objective Methods for Measuring Reader Interest in Newspapers" was the way, and the title of Gallup's doctoral thesis at Iowa. Working with the Des Moines *Register* and *Tribune* and 200-year-old statistical theory probabilities, Gallup developed "sampling" techniques. You didn't have to talk to everybody, he said, as long as you randomly selected interviews according to a sampling plan that took into account whatever diversity was present in the relevant population— geographic, ethnic, economic, and so on.

Well, it seemed to work for newspapers, and George Gallup, instructor and later professor, was in great demand around the country. He was a hot commodity, and in that summer of 1932, a new advertising agency, Young & Rubicam, invited him to New York to create a research department. He did that and one of his first Y&R surveys indicated that the number of readers of advertisements was proportional to the length of the paragraphs in a piece of copy. Therefore, Y&R should judiciously add to the length of copy if the desire was to expose a large portion of the sample to the message.

Most of Gallup's work was based on the idea of random sampling. Today, truly random sampling has become increasingly difficult based on changes in the methods of communication. Door–to-door sampling is almost unheard of and even random digit dialing will likely lead to systematic variation from the characteristics of most populations. Although most polling agencies stick to telephone interviews to predict things like election outcomes, with varying success, major companies have turned to the Web to generate samples. The results are not perfect, but companies like Proctor & Gamble, General Mills, and McDonald's, are discovering ways that the shortcomings of online samples can be corrected using many of the same techniques that phone interviewers have used for years. The ease and convenience of online surveying offers a tremendous advantage just as Gallup found that sampling offered an advantage over canvassing an entire population. Thus, online surveys, just like sampling, are here to stay.

Source: Excerpted from "George Gallup's Nation of Numbers," *Esquire* (December 1983), pp. 91–92. Helm, B., "Online Polls: How Good Are They?" *Business Week* 4088 (June 16, 2008), 86.

© GEORGE DOYLE & CIARAN GRIFFIN

© BETTMANN/CORBIS

The Sampling Frame

In practice, the sample will be drawn from a list of population elements that often differ somewhat from the defined target population. A list of elements from which the sample may be drawn is called a **sampling frame**. The sampling frame is also called the *working population* because these units will eventually provide units involved in analysis. A simple example of a sampling frame would be a list of all members of the American Medical Association.

A **sampling frame error** occurs when certain sample elements are excluded or when the entire population is not accurately represented in the sampling frame. An election poll relying on a telephone directory as a sampling frame uses households with listed phone numbers, not households who are likely to vote. Phone directories also underrepresent people with disabilities. Some disabilities, such as hearing and speech impairments, might make telephone use impossible. However, when researchers in Washington State tested for this possible sampling frame error by comparing Census Bureau data on the prevalence of disability with the responses to a telephone survey, they found the opposite effect. The reported prevalence of a disability was actually higher in the phone survey.[2] How could this be? Perhaps it has something to do with the likelihood that a member of the sample would be available to take a call. The Research Snapshot on page 431 describes this issue in more detail.

In practice, almost every list excludes some members of the population. For example, would a university e-mail directory provide an accurate sampling frame for a given university's student population? Perhaps the sampling frame excludes students who registered late and includes students who have resigned from the university. The e-mail directory also will likely list only the

sampling frame

A list of elements from which a sample may be drawn; also called working population.

sampling frame error

An error that occurs when certain sample elements are not listed or are not accurately represented in a sampling frame.

student's official university e-mail address. However, many students may not ever use this address, opting to use a private e-mail account instead. Thus, the university e-mail directory could not be expected to perfectly represent the student population. However, a perfect representation isn't always possible or needed.

■ SAMPLING SERVICES

Some firms, called *sampling services* or *list brokers,* specialize in providing lists or databases that include the names, addresses, phone numbers, and e-mail addresses of specific populations. Exhibit 16.3 shows a page from a mailing list company's offerings. Lists offered by companies such as this are compiled from subscriptions to professional journals, credit card applications, warranty card registrations, and a variety of other sources. One sampling service obtained its listing of households with children from an ice cream retailer who gave away free ice cream cones on children's birthdays. The children filled out cards with their names, addresses, and birthdays, which the retailer then sold to the mailing list company.

A valuable source of names is Equifax's series of city directories. Equifax City Directory provides complete, comprehensive, and accurate business and residential information. The city directory records the name of each resident over eighteen years of age and lists pertinent information about each household. The reverse directory pages offer a unique benefit. A **reverse directory** provides, in

reverse directory

A directory similar to a telephone directory except that listings are by city and street address or by phone number rather than alphabetical by last name.

EXHIBIT 16.3 Mailing List Directory Page

Lists Available - *Alphabetical*

S.I.C. Code	List Title	United States Total Count	United States State Count Page	Canadian Count
A				
5122-02	Abdominal Supports	201	‡	28
8399-03	Abortion Alternatives Organizations	946	‡	*
8093-04	Abortion Information & Services	551	‡	*
5085-23	Abrasives	1811	‡	277
5169-04	Absorbents	145	‡	*
6541-03	Abstracters	4057	58	*
6411-06	Accident & Health Insurance	2113	‡	9
8748-52	Accident Reconstruction Service	125	‡	*
8721-01	Accountants	127392	64	6933
8721-02	Accounting & Bookkeeping General Svc	27996	64	2072
5044-08	Accounting & Bookkeeping Machines/Supls	889	‡	50
5044-01	Accounting & Bookkeeping Systems	624	‡	1230
8711-02	Acoustical Consultants	381	‡	91
1742-02	Acoustical Contractors	3063	47	433
1742-01	Acoustical Materials	878	‡	210
8999-10	Actuaries	1185	‡	*
8049-13	Acupuncture (Acupuncturists)	2921	62	493
5044-02	Adding & Calculating Machines/Supplies	5524	49	648
5044-09	Addressing Machines & Supplies	345	‡	29
5169-12	Adhesives & Glues	1187	‡	4
3579-02	Adhesives & Gluing Equipment	170	‡	204
6411-02	Adjusters	6164	57	8357
6411-01	Adjusters-Public	161	‡	*
8322-07	Adoption Agencies	1621	‡	32
8059-01	Adult Care Facilities	596	‡	*
8361-08	Adult Congregate Living Facilities	170	‡	*
7319-03	Advertising-Aerial	337	‡	26
7311-01	Advertising-Agencies & Counselors	27753	59	2552
7336-05	Advertising-Art Layout & Production Svc	457	‡	101
7331-05	Advertising-Direct Mail	6347	59	540
7311-03	Advertising-Directory & Guide	2465	‡	124
7319-01	Advertising-Displays	3441	59	571
7319-11	Advertising-Indoor	209	‡	63
7311-05	Advertising-Motion Picture	143	‡	11
7311-06	Advertising-Newspaper	4274	59	404
7312-01	Advertising-Outdoor	3052	59	297
7311-08	Advertising-Periodical	817	‡	78

S.I.C. Code	List Title	United States Total Count	United States State Count Page	Canadian Count
7313-03	Advertising-Radio	2866	59	247
7311-07	Advertising-Shoppers' Guides	392	‡	4
5199-17	Advertising-Specialties	12827	52	1648
7389-12	Advertising-Telephone	120	‡	*
7313-05	Advertising-Television	1746	‡	102
7319-02	Advertising-Transit & Transportation	179	‡	38
0721-03	Aerial Applicators (Service)	1479	‡	61
3999-01	Aerosols	158	‡	*
3812-01	Aerospace Industries	426	‡	*
	Affluent Americans		73	
5191-04	Agricultural Chemicals	549	‡	210
8748-20	Agricultural Consultants	1047	‡	474
9999-32	Air Balancing	353	‡	*
5084-64	Air Brushes	219	‡	*
4512-02	Air Cargo Service	6005	48	*
5075-01	Air Cleaning & Purifying Equipment	2055	‡	342
5084-02	Air Compressors (See Compressors Air & Gas)	4358	50	717
1711-17	Air Conditioning Contractors & Systems	50951	47	2667
	Available By Brands Sold			
	Airtemp (A)	187		
	Amana (B)	1450		
	Arco Aire (2)	673		
	Armstrong/Magic Chef (C)	395		
	Arvin (4)	106		
	Bryant (D)	2223		
	Carrier (E)	5927		
	Coleman (5)	1176		
	Comfortmaker/Singer (O)	989		
	Day & Night (Z)	749		
	Fedders (H)	318		
	Heli/Quaker (3)	1977		
	Janitrol (7)	587		
	Kero-Sun (W)	2		
	Lennox (K)	4390		
	Luxaire (L)	510		
	Payne (M)	553		

a different format, the same information contained in a telephone directory. Listings may be by city and street address or by phone number, rather than alphabetical by last name. Such a directory is particularly useful when a retailer wishes to survey only a certain geographical area of a city or when census tracts are to be selected on the basis of income or another demographic criterion.

■ ONLINE PANELS

Online survey services routinely make **online panels** available. Generally, for a modest fee, a list of e-mail addresses can be obtained with each address identifying an individual who has agreed to participate in research surveys. Qualtrics, the company that hosts the survey involved in the Survey This! Features, provides such services. These panels generally contain millions of potential respondents, which enables a panel to be obtained that matches practically any demographic profile imaginable. The more specific the profile requested, the more expensive the panel. Online panels are increasingly used to provide sampling frames in marketing research. Later, the advantages and disadvantages of using an online panel as a sampling frame will be discussed.

online panels

Lists of respondents who have agreed to participate in marketing research along with the e-mail contact information for these individuals.

■ SAMPLING FRAMES FOR INTERNATIONAL MARKETING RESEARCH

The availability of sampling frames varies dramatically around the world. Not every country's government conducts a census of population. In some countries telephone directories are incomplete, no voter registration lists exist, and accurate maps of urban areas are unobtainable. However, in Taiwan, Japan, and other Asian countries, a researcher can build a sampling frame relatively easily because those governments release some census information. If a family changes households, updated census information must be reported to a centralized government agency before communal services (water, gas, electricity, education, and so on) are made available.[3] This information is then easily accessible in the local *Inhabitants' Register*. Fortunately, many of the online panels include members in nations around the world. The panels can be stratified by country or by region within a country just as they can in the United States. For example, if a company wishes to survey part-time fast-food employees in Canada and Japan, a panel can probably provide potential respondents.

Sampling Units

The elements of a population must be selected according to a specified procedure when sampling. The **sampling unit** is a single element or group of elements that is eligible for selection via the sampling process. For example, an airline may sample passengers by taking every 25th name on a complete list of passengers flying on a specified day. In this case the sampling unit would be the same as the element. Alternatively, the airline could first select certain flights as the sampling unit and then select certain passengers on each flight. In this case the sampling unit would contain many elements.

If the target population has first been divided into units, such as airline flights, additional terminology must be used. A unit selected in the first stage of sampling is called a **primary sampling unit (PSU)**. A unit selected in a successive stage of sampling is called a **secondary sampling unit** or (if three stages are necessary) **tertiary sampling unit**. When there is no list of population elements, the sampling unit generally is something other than the population element. In a random-digit dialing study, the sampling unit will be telephone numbers.

sampling unit

A single element or group of elements subject to selection in the sample.

primary sampling unit (PSU)

A term used to designate a unit selected in the first stage of sampling.

secondary sampling unit

A term used to designate a unit selected in the second stage of sampling.

tertiary sampling unit

A term used to designate a unit selected in the third stage of sampling.

Random Sampling and Nonsampling Errors

An advertising agency sampled a small number of shoppers in grocery stores that used Shopper's Video, an in-store advertising network. The agency hoped to measure brand awareness and purchase intentions. Investigators expected this sample to be representative of the grocery-shopping population. However, if a difference exists between the value of a sample statistic of interest (for example, the sample group's average willingness to buy the advertised brand) and the value of the corresponding population parameter (the population's average willingness to buy), a *statistical error* has occurred. Chapter 8 classified two basic causes of differences between statistics and parameters:

1. random sampling errors
2. systematic (nonsampling) error

random sampling error

The difference between the sample result and the result of a census conducted using identical procedures.

An estimation made from a sample is not the same as a census count. **Random sampling error** is the difference between the sample result and the result of an accurate census. Of course, the result of a census is unknown unless one is taken, which is rarely done. Random sampling error occurs because of chance variation in the selection of sampling units. The sampling units, even if properly selected according to sampling theory, may not perfectly represent the population because of chance variation.

Picture 50 students in a typical undergraduate research class. If the class is the population and a random sample of 10 students is used to estimate the average height of a student in the class, a random selection process should make sure that the 10 tallest students are not selected for the sample. Although this is theoretically possible, the odds that this would occur are astronomical. The difference between the average of the 10 students and the actual average of the 50 represent random sampling error.

Random Sampling Error

Random sampling error will come back into play later when the issue of hypothesis testing surfaces. At this point, simply recognize that *random sampling error* is a technical term that refers *only* to statistical fluctuations that occur because of chance variations in the elements selected for the sample. Random sampling error is a function of sample size. As sample size increases, random sampling error decreases.

Let's return to the classroom of 50 students. If the researcher is very lazy, a sample of 1 can be used to estimate student height. The chance of randomly selecting the tallest student is 1 in 50, the same as the odds of selecting the student that matched the median. Either way, the confidence that the sample is matching the true population value should not be very high. A strong likelihood exists that by doubling the sample size to two observations, the estimated value could change a great deal. Conversely, if the researcher is very cautious, a sample of 49 might be taken. Now, even if the tallest person in the class is in the sample, there are 48 other observations that are also considered. The estimate of the average height now is much more confident. Also, the value should not change very much when one more observation is added to the calculation. When someone releases poll results and describes them with a margin of error of 3, 5, or 10 percent, that margin of error is determined by the sample size.

Systematic Sampling Error

Systematic (nonsampling) errors result from nonsampling factors, primarily the nature of a study's design and the correctness of execution. These errors are systematic in some way and *not* due to chance fluctuations. For example, in our classroom example, if some chose a sampling frame consisting of all students sitting in the first two rows, a strong likelihood exists that systematic error would be introduced because shorter students tend to sit up front in an effort to see what is going on instead of the back of another student's head. Sample biases such as these account for a large portion of errors in marketing research. Nonsampling errors were discussed in an earlier chapter. Errors due to sample selection problems are nonsampling errors and should not be classified as random sampling errors.

■ SYSTEMATIC BUT NOT OBVIOUS SAMPLING ERROR

Many of these topics have already been mentioned. For example, the telephone samples are biased in terms of representing the entire population because the types of people without an in-home phone usually share something in common with each other. Researchers have many years of experience with face-to-face and telephone interviewing, however, the Internet presents some unique challenges. A random sample of Internet users would be representative only of Internet users, who tend to be younger, better educated, and more affluent than the general population. However, a truly random sample of all Internet users would be practically impossible or unfeasible to obtain. Sampling on the Internet involves finding the right subset of users.

Internet surveys allow researchers to reach a large sample rapidly—both an advantage and a disadvantage. Sample size requirements can be met overnight or in some cases almost instantaneously. A researcher can, for instance, release a survey during the morning in the Eastern Standard Time zone and have all sample size requirements met before anyone on the West Coast wakes up. If rapid response rates are expected, and a national sample is desired, steps must be taken to distribute the questionnaire evenly across all time zones. In addition, a survey released during the middle of the day, just like a phone sample conducted in the middle of the day, is likely to exclude people with full-time jobs in a systematic way because they are at work. Thus, the survey should probably remain active for a minimum of 12 hours or so.

The ease and low cost of an Internet survey also has contributed to a flood of online questionnaires, some more formal than others. As a result, frequent Internet users may be more selective about which surveys they bother answering. Researchers investigating college students' attitudes toward environmental issues found that those who responded to an e-mail request that had been sent to all students tended to be more concerned about the environment than students who were contacted individually through systematic sampling. The researchers concluded that students who cared about the issues were more likely to respond to the online survey.[4]

Web Site Visitors

As noted earlier, many Internet surveys are conducted with volunteer respondents who visit an organization's Web site intentionally or by happenstance. These *unrestricted samples* are clearly not random samples. They may not even represent people with an interest in that particular Web site because of the haphazard manner by which many respondents arrived at a particular site.

A better technique for sampling Web site visitors is to randomly select sampling units. Survey software can be used to trigger a pop-up survey to each 100th (or whatever number) visitor. Or, the software can even adjust the triggering of the survey based on information gathered on the respondent's Web behavior. For example, the opportunity to become a respondent might be timed so that at least 30 seconds have to be spent on the home page before the respondent becomes part of the sampling frame. This may prevent random page visitors from becoming a large part of the sample. Respondents who are selected to participate are first prompted to see if they would like to participate. If the person clicks "Yes," the electronic questionnaire is presented to them as a pop-up or as a new browser window. The person can then browse the site at his or her own pace and switch to the survey at any time to express an opinion.[5] More and more, the questionnaire should be presented in a new browser window as today's security features make using pop-ups very unreliable.

Randomly selecting Web site visitors can cause a problem by overrepresenting frequent visitors. Several programming techniques and technologies (using cookies, registration data, or prescreening) are available to help accomplish more representative sampling based on site traffic.[6] These cookies contain information that reveals the frequency of visits.

Panel Samples

Consumer panels provide a practical sampling frame in many situations. They are particularly useful in screening out panel members who do not fit the characteristics of a relevant population. If the relevant population is men, it is an easy matter to exclude the e-mail addresses of women. However, they are not perfect.

Often panel members are compensated for their time with a sweepstakes, a small cash incentive, or redeemable points. The panel members may also contain a high proportion of respondents who simply like to fill out questionnaires or give their opinion. In either case, the opportunity for sample bias is presented. Fortunately, research suggests that personality variables and demographic variables are not strongly related to panel membership.[7] However, attempts to validate survey results using different panels or different communication methods often show variance.[8] Thus, as the concern for representativeness increases, the more steps the researcher must take to ensure that the sampling units do indeed represent the population.

Consider Harris Interactive Inc., an Internet survey research organization, which maintains a panel of more than 6 million individuals in over 125 countries.[9] A database this large allows the company to draw simple random samples, stratified samples, and quota samples from its panel members. Harris Interactive finds that two demographic groups are not fully accessible via Internet sampling: people ages 65 and older—a group that is rapidly growing—and those from very low social classes. In contrast, 18- to 25-year-olds—a group that historically has been very hard to reach by traditional research methods—are now extremely easy to reach over the Internet.[10]

To ensure that survey results are representative, Harris Interactive uses a *propensity-weighting* scheme. The research company does parallel studies—by phone as well as over the Internet—to test the accuracy of its Internet data-gathering capabilities. Researchers look at the results of the telephone surveys and match those against the Internet-only survey results. Next, they use propensity weighting to adjust the results, taking into account the motivational and behavioral differences between the online and offline populations. (How propensity weighting adjusts for the difference between the Internet population and the general population is beyond the scope of this discussion.)

In addition to these steps, panel members may be asked screening questions to make sure that the screening characteristics are accurately working. For example, a researcher interested in coffee shop drinkers in the Midwest may want respondents to compare other shops to Starbucks. Thus, the population may be limited to consumers who frequent Starbucks. Although the online panel may be screened to include only communities where Starbucks has coffee shops, the researcher would be well advised to include screening questions that check on the familiarity of respondents with Starbucks.

Opting In

opt in

To give permission to receive selected e-mail, such as questionnaires, from a company with an Internet presence.

Survey Sampling International concentrates its efforts on providing valid sampling frames. Notice how they place emphasis on profiling questions to help maintain the match between the sample and the population.

Survey Sampling International specializes in providing sampling frames and scientifically drawn samples. The company offers more than 3,500 lists of high-quality, targeted e-mail addresses of individuals who have given permission to receive e-mail messages related to a particular topic of interest. Survey Sampling International's database contains millions of Internet users who **opt in** for limited participation. An important feature of Survey Sampling International's database is that the company has each individual confirm and reconfirm interest in communicating about a topic before the person's e-mail address is added to the company's database.[11]

By whatever technique the sampling frame is compiled, it is important *not* to send unauthorized e-mail to respondents. If individuals do not *opt in* to receive e-mail from a particular organization, they may consider unsolicited survey requests to be spam. A researcher cannot expect high response rates from individuals who have not agreed to be surveyed. Spamming is not tolerated by experienced Internet users and can easily backfire, creating a host of problems—the most extreme being complaints to the Internet service provider (ISP), which may shut down the survey site.

Less than Perfectly Representative Samples

Random sampling errors and systematic errors associated with the sampling process may combine to yield a sample that is less than perfectly representative of the population. Exhibit 16.4 illustrates two nonsampling errors (sampling frame error and nonresponse error) related to sample design. The total population is represented by the area of the largest square. Sampling frame errors eliminate some potential respondents. Random sampling error (due exclusively to random, chance fluctuation) may cause an imbalance in the representativeness of the group. Additional errors will occur if individuals refuse to be interviewed or cannot be contacted. Such nonresponse error

EXHIBIT 16.4 **Errors Associated with Sampling**

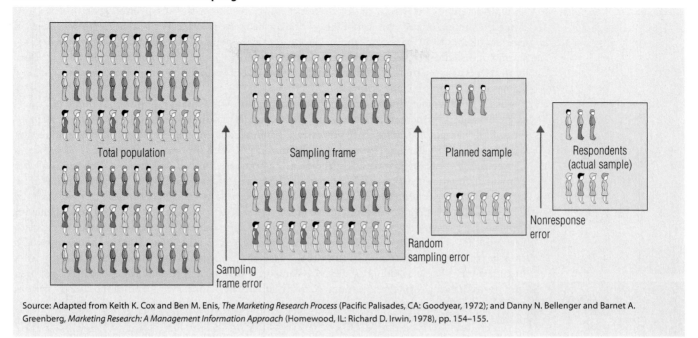

Source: Adapted from Keith K. Cox and Ben M. Enis, *The Marketing Research Process* (Pacific Palisades, CA: Goodyear, 1972); and Danny N. Bellenger and Barnet A. Greenberg, *Marketing Research: A Management Information Approach* (Homewood, IL: Richard D. Irwin, 1978), pp. 154–155.

may also cause the sample to be less than perfectly representative. Notice that if the top half of the total population comes from one part of town, and the bottom half comes from another part of town, by the time the planned sample is reached, the portion from the lower part of the exhibit is overrepresented and this continues to the actual sample where 25 percent more of the sample (represented by 4 people as opposed to 3) comes from the lower portion of town. The actual sample overrepresents this portion of town.

Probability versus Nonprobability Sampling

Several alternative ways to take a sample are available. The main alternative sampling plans may be grouped into two categories: probability techniques and nonprobability techniques.

In **probability sampling**, every element in the population has a *known, nonzero probability* of selection. The simple random sample, in which each member of the population has an equal probability of being selected, is the best-known probability sample.

In **nonprobability sampling**, the probability of any particular member of the population being chosen is unknown. The selection of sampling units in nonprobability sampling is quite arbitrary, as researchers rely heavily on personal judgment. Technically, no appropriate statistical techniques exist for measuring random sampling error from a nonprobability sample. Therefore, projecting the data beyond the sample is, technically speaking, statistically inappropriate. Nevertheless, researchers sometimes find nonprobability samples best suited for a specific researcher purpose. As a result, nonprobability samples are pragmatic and are used in market research.

Although probability sampling is preferred, this section on nonprobability sampling illustrates some potential sources of error and other weaknesses in sampling.

Convenience Sampling

As the name suggests, **convenience sampling** refers to sampling by obtaining people or units that are conveniently available. A research team may determine that the most convenient and

probability sampling

A sampling technique in which every member of the population has a known, nonzero probability of selection.

nonprobability sampling

A sampling technique in which units of the sample are selected on the basis of personal judgment or convenience; the probability of any particular member of the population being chosen is unknown.

convenience sampling

The sampling procedure of obtaining those people or units that are most conveniently available.

economical method is to set up an interviewing booth from which to intercept consumers at a shopping center. Television stations often present person-on-the-street interviews that are presumed to reflect public opinion. Thus, whoever happens to walk by the reporter is surveyed on matters of the day. (Of course, the television station generally warns that the survey was "unscientific and random" [*sic*].) Comedians do these interviews and commonly demonstrate that the typical "person–on–the–street" can't answer basic questions like who the vice-president is or the names of two supreme court justices.

Researchers generally use convenience samples to obtain a large number of completed questionnaires quickly and economically, or when obtaining a sample through other means is impractical. For example, many Internet surveys are conducted with volunteer respondents who, either intentionally or by happenstance, visit an organization's Web site. Although this method produces a large number of responses quickly and at a low cost, selecting all visitors to a Web site is clearly convenience sampling. Respondents may not be representative because of the haphazard manner by which many of them arrived at the Web site or because of self-selection bias.

Similarly, research looking for cross-cultural differences in organizational or consumer behavior typically uses convenience samples. Rather than selecting cultures with characteristics relevant to the hypothesis being tested, the researchers conducting these studies often choose cultures to which they have access (for example, because they speak the language or have contacts in that culture's organizations). Further adding to the convenience, cross-cultural research often defines "culture" in terms of nations, which are easier to identify and obtain statistics for, even though many nations include several cultures and some people in a given nation may be more involved with the international business or academic community than with a particular ethnic culture.[12] Here again, the use of convenience sampling limits how well the research represents the intended population.

The user of research based on a convenience sample should remember that projecting the results beyond the specific sample is inappropriate. Convenience samples are best used for exploratory research when additional research will subsequently be conducted with a probability sample. University professors conducting marketing research will frequently use a student sample out of convenience. This can be appropriate if the emphasis in the research design is largely on internal validity. In other words, to see if the effect put forth in a hypothesis holds under circumstances allowing maximum control of outside effects. The use of student sample is inappropriate when the results are intended to generalize to a larger population.

Judgment Sampling

**judgment (purposive)
sampling**

A nonprobability sampling technique in which an experienced individual selects the sample based on personal judgment about some appropriate characteristic of the sample member.

Judgment (purposive) sampling is a nonprobability sampling technique in which an experienced individual selects the sample based on his or her judgment about some appropriate characteristics required of the sample member. Researchers select samples that satisfy their specific purposes, even if they are not fully representative. The consumer price index (CPI) is based on a judgment sample of market-basket items, housing costs, and other selected goods and services expected to reflect a representative sample of items consumed by most Americans. Test-market cities often are selected because they are viewed as typical cities whose demographic profiles closely match the national profile. A fashion manufacturer regularly selects a sample of key accounts that it believes are capable of providing information needed to predict what may sell in the fall. Thus, the sample is selected to achieve this specific objective.

Judgment sampling often is used in attempts to forecast election results. People frequently wonder how a television network can predict the results of an election with only 2 percent of the votes reported. Political and sampling experts judge which small voting districts approximate overall state returns from previous election years; then these *bellwether precincts* are selected as the sampling units. Of course, the assumption is that the past voting records of these districts are still representative of the political behavior of the state's population.

Quota Sampling

Suppose a firm wishes to investigate consumers who currently subscribe to an HDTV (high definition television) service. The researchers may wish to ensure that each brand of HDTV televisions is included proportionately in the sample. Strict probability sampling procedures would likely underrepresent certain brands and overrepresent other brands. If the selection process were left strictly to chance, some variation would be expected.

The purpose of **quota sampling** is to ensure that the various subgroups in a population are represented on pertinent sample characteristics to the exact extent that the investigators desire. Stratified sampling, a probability sampling procedure described in the next section, also has this objective, but it should not be confused with quota sampling. In quota sampling, the interviewer has a quota to achieve. For example, an interviewer in a particular city may be assigned 100 interviews, 35 with owners of Sony TVs, 30 with owners of Samsung TVs, 18 with owners of LG TVs, and the rest with owners of other brands. The interviewer is responsible for finding enough people to meet the quota. Aggregating the various interview quotas yields a sample that represents the desired proportion of each subgroup.

quota sampling

A nonprobability sampling procedure that ensures that various subgroups of a population will be represented on pertinent characteristics to the exact extent that the investigator desires.

■ POSSIBLE SOURCES OF BIAS

The logic of classifying the population by pertinent subgroups is essentially sound. However, because respondents are selected according to a convenience sampling procedure rather than on a probability basis (as in stratified sampling), the haphazard selection of subjects may introduce bias. For example, a college professor hired some of his students to conduct a quota sample based on age. When analyzing the data, the professor discovered that almost all the people in the "under 25 years" category were college-educated. Interviewers, being human, tend to prefer to interview people who are similar to themselves.

Quota samples tend to include people who are easily found, willing to be interviewed, and middle class. Fieldworkers are given considerable leeway to exercise their judgment concerning selection of actual respondents. Interviewers often concentrate their interviewing in areas with heavy pedestrian traffic such as downtowns, shopping malls, and college campuses. Those who interview door-to-door learn quickly that quota requirements are difficult to meet by interviewing whoever happens to appear at the door. People who are more likely to stay at home generally share a less active lifestyle and are less likely to be meaningfully employed. One interviewer related a story of working in an upper-middle-class neighborhood. After a few blocks, he arrived in a neighborhood of mansions. Feeling that most of the would-be respondents were above his station, the interviewer skipped these houses because he felt uncomfortable knocking on doors that would be answered by these people or their hired help.

■ ADVANTAGES OF QUOTA SAMPLING

The major advantages of quota sampling over probability sampling are speed of data collection, lower costs, and convenience. Although quota sampling has many problems, carefully supervised data collection may provide a representative sample of the various subgroups within a population. Quota sampling may be appropriate when the researcher knows that a certain demographic group is more likely to refuse to cooperate with a survey. For instance, if older men are more likely to refuse, a higher quota can be set for this group so that the proportion of each demographic category will be similar to the proportions in the population. A number of laboratory experiments also rely on quota sampling because it is difficult to find a sample of the general population willing to visit a laboratory to participate in an experiment.

■ SNOWBALL SAMPLING

A variety of procedures known as **snowball sampling** involve using probability methods for an initial selection of respondents and then obtaining additional respondents through information provided by the initial respondents. This technique is used to locate members of rare populations by referrals. Suppose a manufacturer of sports equipment is considering marketing a mahogany croquet set for serious adult players. This market is certainly small. An extremely large sample would be necessary to find 100 serious adult croquet players. It would be much more economical to survey, say, 300 people, find 15 croquet players, and ask them for the names of other players.

snowball sampling

A sampling procedure in which initial respondents are selected by probability methods and additional respondents are obtained from information provided by the initial respondents.

Reduced sample sizes and costs are clear-cut advantages of snowball sampling. However, bias is likely to enter into the study because a person suggested by someone also in the sample has a higher probability of being similar to the first person. If there are major differences between those who are widely known by others and those who are not, this technique may present some serious problems. However, snowball sampling may be used to locate and recruit heavy users, such as consumers who buy more than 50 compact disks per year, for focus groups. As the focus group is not expected to be a generalized sample, snowball sampling may be appropriate.

Probability Sampling

All probability sampling techniques are based on chance selection procedures. Because the probability sampling process is random, the bias inherent in nonprobability sampling procedures is eliminated. Note that the term *random* refers to the procedure for selecting the sample; it does not describe the data in the sample. *Randomness* characterizes a procedure whose outcome cannot be predicted because it depends on chance. Randomness should not be thought of as unplanned or unscientific—it is the basis of all probability sampling techniques. This section will examine the various probability sampling methods.

Simple Random Sampling

simple random sampling

A sampling procedure that assures each element in the population of an equal chance of being included in the sample.

A sampling procedure ensuring that each element in the population will have an equal chance of being included in the sample is called **simple random sampling**. Examples include drawing names from a hat and selecting the winning raffle ticket from a large drum. If the names or raffle tickets are thoroughly stirred, each person or ticket should have an equal chance of being selected. In contrast to other, more complex types of probability sampling, this process is simple in that only one stage of sample selection is required.

Although drawing names or numbers out of a fishbowl, rolling dice, or turning a roulette wheel may be an appropriate way to draw a sample from a small population, when populations consist of large numbers of elements, sample selection can be based on tabled random numbers or computer-generated random numbers (see http://www.samurajdata.se/~cj/rnd.html for a simple random number generator).

TOTHEPOINT

Make everything as simple as possible, but not simpler.

—Albert Einstein

Random number tables are also found on the Internet. This is just one example.

Suppose a researcher is interested in selecting a simple random sample of all the Honda dealers in California, New Mexico, Arizona, and Nevada. Each dealer's name is assigned a number from 1 to 105. The numbers can be written on paper slips, and all the slips can be placed in a bowl. If a researcher desires a sample of 25, he or she can use a random number generator to randomly select a number between 1 and 105. For example, if 60 is the random number generated, then the dealer assigned that number is selected for the sample. This procedure can then be repeated until the sample of 25 is obtained.

To use a table of random numbers, a serial number is first assigned to each element of the population. Assuming the population is 99,999 or fewer, five-digit numbers may be selected from the table of random numbers merely by reading the numbers in any column or row, moving up, down, left, or right. A random starting point should be selected at the outset. For convenience, we will assume that we have randomly selected as our starting point the first five digits in columns 1 through 5, row 1, of Table A1 in the Appendix. The first number in our sample would be 37751; moving down, the next numbers would be 50915, 99142, and so on.

The random-digit dialing technique of sample selection requires that the researcher identify the exchange or exchanges of interest (the first three numbers) and then use a table of numbers to select the next four numbers. In practice, the exchanges are not always selected randomly. Researchers who wanted to find out whether black Americans with African ancestry prefer being called "black" or "African-American" narrowed their sampling frame by selecting exchanges associated with geographic areas where the proportion of this population was at least 30 percent. The reasoning was that this made the survey procedure far more efficient, considering that the researchers were trying to contact a group representing less than 15 percent of U.S. households. This initial judgment sampling raises the same issues we discussed regarding nonprobability sampling. In this study, the researchers found that respondents were most likely to prefer the term *black* if they had attended schools that were about half black and half white.[13] If such experiences influence the answers to the question of interest to the researchers, the fact that blacks who live in predominantly white communities are underrepresented may introduce bias into the results.

Systematic Sampling

Suppose a researcher wants to take a sample of 1,000 from a list of 200,000 names. With **systematic sampling**, every 200th name from the list would be drawn. This simple process illustrates how to find the interval between selected observations:

$$\frac{Population}{Sample} = Interval$$

$$\frac{200,000}{1,000} = 200$$

A starting point is selected by a random process such as taking a random number; then every nth number on the list is selected. In this case, every 200th name would be selected. Because the starting point may well not be at the beginning, this may actually yield only 199 names. A random number can be used to select one more if the sample needs to be exactly 1,000.

Exhibit 16.5 on the next page illustrates this process. Here, suppose someone wished to take a sample of the average monthly temperature in Colombia over a 100-month period. Thus, the exhibit shows the first in what will be a total of 104 total observations. If a sample of 20 is to be obtained, every 5th observation is taken. A die is rolled to find what the first observation will be. Thus, the sequence of selected observations is show in the rows highlighted in green.

While systematic sampling is not actually a random selection procedure, it does yield random results if the arrangement of the items is not in some sequence corresponding to the interval in some way. The problem of *periodicity* can occur otherwise. Returning to Exhibit 16.5, what would happen if the average temperature in this time period were compared with a historical average of 17 degrees and a sample was formed with a sampling interval of 12 and a random starting point of August? Obviously, the comparison would be biased because all of the readings would be summertime readings. This could hardly be considered random.

systematic sampling
A sampling procedure in which a starting point is selected by a random process and then every nth number on the list is selected.

Stratified Sampling

The usefulness of dividing the population into subgroups, or *strata,* whose members are more or less equal with respect to some characteristic, was illustrated in our discussion of quota sampling. The first step is the same for both stratified and quota sampling: choosing strata on the basis of existing information—for example, classifying retail outlets based on annual sales volume. However, the process of selecting sampling units within the strata differs substantially. In **stratified sampling**, a subsample is drawn using simple random sampling within each stratum. This is not true of quota sampling.

The reason for taking a stratified sample is to obtain a more efficient sample than would be possible with simple random sampling. Suppose, for example, that urban and rural groups have

stratified sampling
A probability sampling procedure in which simple random subsamples that are more or less equal on some characteristic are drawn from within each stratum of the population.

EXHIBIT 16.5
Systematically Sampling from a List

	Observation	Month	Year	Average Temperature (C°)
	1	January	2008	4
Random Starting Point	2	February	2008	6
	3	March	2008	10
	4	April	2008	15
	5	May	2008	16
	6	June	2008	22
Select	7	July	2008	26
	8	August	2008	22
	9	September	2008	27
	10	October	2008	19
	11	November	2008	10
Select	12	December	2008	6
	13	January	2009	−2
	14	February	2009	9
	15	March	2009	9
	16	April	2009	12
Select	17	May	2009	18
	18	June	2009	26
	19	July	2009	30
	20	August	2009	31
	21	September	2009	24
Select	22	October	2009	14
	23	November	2009	12
	24	December	2009	7
	25	January	2010	5
	26	February	2010	4
Select	27	March	2010	9
	28	April	2010	14
	29	May	2010	18
	30	June	2010	24
	31	July	2010	24
Select	32	August	2010	25

widely different attitudes toward energy conservation, but members within each group hold very similar attitudes. Random sampling error will be reduced with the use of stratified sampling, because each group is internally homogeneous but there are comparative differences between groups. More technically, a smaller standard error may result from this stratified sampling because the groups will be adequately represented when strata are combined.

Another reason for selecting a stratified sample is to ensure that the sample will accurately reflect the population on the basis of the criterion or criteria used for stratification. This is a concern because occasionally simple random sampling yields a disproportionate number of one group or another and the sample ends up being less representative than it could be.

A researcher can select a stratified sample as follows. First, a variable (sometimes several variables) is identified as an efficient basis for stratification. A stratification variable must be a characteristic of the population elements known to be related to the dependent variable or other variables of interest. The variable chosen should increase homogeneity within each stratum and increase heterogeneity between strata. The stratification variable usually is a categorical variable or one easily converted into categories (that is, subgroups). For example, a pharmaceutical company interested in measuring how often physicians prescribe a certain drug might choose physicians' training as a basis for stratification. In this example the mutually exclusive strata are MDs (medical doctors) and ODs (osteopathic doctors).

Next, for each separate subgroup or stratum, a list of population elements must be obtained. (If such lists are not available, they can be costly to prepare, and if a complete listing is not available, a true stratified probability sample cannot be selected.) Using a table of random numbers or some other device, a *separate* simple random sample is then taken within each stratum. Of course, the researcher must determine how large a sample to draw for each stratum. This issue is discussed in the following section.

Proportional versus Disproportional Sampling

If the number of sampling units drawn from each stratum is in proportion to the relative population size of the stratum, the sample is a **proportional stratified sample**. Sometimes, however, a disproportional stratified sample will be selected to ensure an adequate number of sampling units in every stratum. Sampling more heavily in a given stratum than its relative population size warrants is not a problem if the primary purpose of the research is to estimate some characteristic separately for each stratum and if researchers are concerned about assessing the differences among strata. Consider, however, the percentages of retail outlets presented in Exhibit 16.6. A proportional sample would have the same percentages as in the population. Although there is a small percentage of warehouse club stores, the average store size, in dollar volume, for the warehouse club store stratum is quite large and varies substantially from the average store size for the smaller independent stores. To avoid overrepresenting the chain

proportional stratified sample

A stratified sample in which the number of sampling units drawn from each stratum is in proportion to the population size of that stratum.

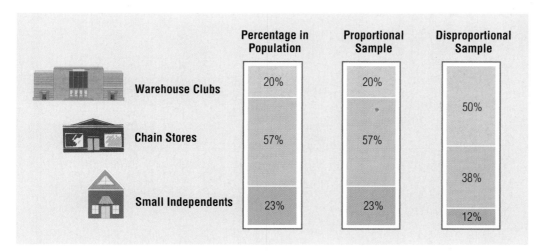

EXHIBIT 16.6
Disproportional Sampling: Hypothetical Example

stores and independent stores (with smaller sales volume) in the sample, a disproportional sample is taken.

In a **disproportional stratified sample** the sample size for each stratum is not allocated in proportion to the population size but is dictated by analytical considerations, such as variability in store sales volume. The logic behind this procedure relates to the general argument for sample size: As variability increases, sample size must increase to provide accurate estimates. Thus, the strata that exhibit the greatest variability are sampled more heavily to increase sample efficiency—that is, produce smaller random sampling error. Complex formulas (beyond the scope of an introductory course in marketing research) have been developed to determine sample size for each stratum. A simplified rule of thumb for understanding the concept of optimal allocation is that the stratum sample size increases for strata of larger sizes with the greatest relative variability. Other complexities arise in determining population estimates. For example, when disproportional stratified sampling is used, the estimated mean for each stratum has to be weighed according to the number of elements in each stratum in order to calculate the total population mean.

disproportional stratified sample

A stratified sample in which the sample size for each stratum is allocated according to analytical considerations.

Cluster Sampling

Cluster sampling is an economical sampling approach that retains the characteristics of a probability sample. Consider a researcher who must conduct five hundred personal interviews with consumers scattered throughout the United States. Travel costs are likely to be enormous because the amount of time spent traveling will be substantially greater than the time spent in the interviewing process. If an aspirin marketer can assume the product will be equally successful in Phoenix and Baltimore, or if a frozen pizza manufacturer assumes its product will suit the tastes of Texans equally as well as Oregonians, cluster sampling may be used to represent the United States.

In a **cluster sample**, the primary sampling unit is no longer the individual element in the population (for example, grocery stores) but a larger cluster of elements located in proximity to one another (for example, cities). The *area sample* is the most popular type of cluster sample. A grocery store researcher, for example, may randomly choose several geographic areas as primary sampling units and then interview all or a sample of grocery stores within the geographic clusters. Interviews are confined to these clusters only. No interviews occur in other clusters. Cluster sampling is classified as a probability sampling technique because of either the random selection of clusters or the random selection of elements within each cluster. Some examples of clusters appear in Exhibit 16.7.

cluster sampling

An economically efficient sampling technique in which the primary sampling unit is not the individual element in the population but a large cluster of elements; clusters are selected randomly.

EXHIBIT 16.7
Examples of Clusters

Population Element	Possible Clusters in the United States
U.S. adult population	States Counties Metropolitan Statistical Areas Census Tracts Blocks Households
College seniors	Colleges
Manufacturing firms	Counties Metropolitan Statistical Areas Localities Plants
Airline travelers	Airports Planes
Sports fans	Football Stadiums Basketball Arenas Baseball Parks

Who's at Home? Different Ways to Select Respondents

A carefully planned telephone survey often involves multistage sampling. First the researchers select a sample of households to call, and then they select someone within each household to interview—not necessarily whoever answers the phone. Cecilie Gaziano, a researcher with Research Solutions in Minneapolis, conducted an analysis of various selection procedures used in prior research, looking for the methods that performed best in terms of generating a representative sample, achieving respondent cooperation, and minimizing costs.

Gaziano found several methods worth further consideration. One of these was full enumeration, in which the interviewer requests a list of all the adults living in the household, generates a random number, uses the number to select a name from that list, and asks to speak with that person. In a variation of this approach, called the *Kish method,* the interviewer requests the number of males by age and the number of females by age, and then uses some form of randomization to select either a male or a female and a number—say, the oldest male or the third oldest female. A third method is to interview the person who last had a birthday.

In the studies Gaziano examined, the Kish method did not seem to discourage respondents by being too intrusive. That method was popular because it came close to being random. The last-birthday method generated somewhat better cooperation rates, which may have made that method more efficient in terms of costs. However, some question whether the person on the phone accurately knows the birthdays of every household member, especially in households with several adults. Methods that request the gender of household members also address a challenge of getting a representative phone survey sample: females tend to answer the phone more often than males.

Source: Cecilie Gaziano, "Comparative Analysis of Within-Household Respondent Selection Techniques," *Public Opinion Quarterly* 69 (Spring 2005), 124–157; "Communication Researchers and Policy-Making," *Journal of Broadcasting & Electronic Media* (March 2004), accessed at http://www.allbusiness.com, accessed September 20, 2008.

Cluster samples frequently are used when lists of the sample population are not available. For example, when researchers investigating employees and self-employed workers for a downtown revitalization project found that a comprehensive list of these people was not available, they decided to take a cluster sample, selecting organizations (business and government) as the clusters. A sample of firms within the central business district was developed, using stratified probability sampling to identify clusters. Next, individual workers within the firms (clusters) were randomly selected and interviewed concerning the central business district.

Ideally a cluster should be as heterogeneous as the population itself—a mirror image of the population. A problem may arise with cluster sampling if the characteristics and attitudes of the elements within the cluster are too similar. For example, geographic neighborhoods tend to have residents of the same socioeconomic status. Students at a university tend to share similar beliefs. This problem may be mitigated by constructing clusters composed of diverse elements and by selecting a large number of sampled clusters.

Multistage Area Sampling

Multistage area sampling is a cluster sampling approach involving multiple steps that combine some of the probability techniques already described. Typically, geographic areas are randomly selected in progressively smaller (lower-population) units. For example, a political pollster investigating an election in Arizona might first choose counties within the state to ensure that the different areas are represented in the sample. In the second step, precincts within the selected counties may be chosen. As a final step, the pollster may select blocks (or households) within the precincts, then interview all the blocks (or households) within the geographic area. Researchers may take as many steps as necessary to achieve a representative sample.

The Bureau of the Census provides maps, population information, demographic characteristics for population statistics, and so on, by several small geographical areas; these may be useful in sampling. Census classifications of small geographic areas vary, depending on the extent of urbanization within Metropolitan Statistical Areas (MSAs) or counties. Exhibit 16.8 on the next page illustrates the geographic hierarchy inside urbanized areas.

multistage area sampling

Sampling that involves using a combination of two or more probability sampling techniques.

EXHIBIT 16.8
Geographic Hierarchy inside Urbanized Areas

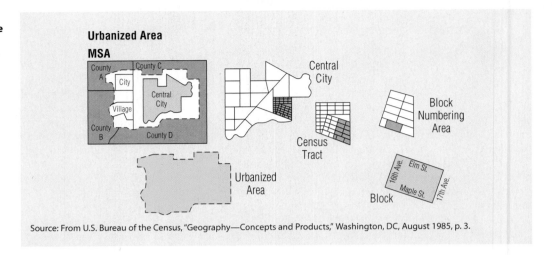

Source: From U.S. Bureau of the Census, "Geography—Concepts and Products," Washington, DC, August 1985, p. 3.

What Is the Appropriate Sample Design?

A researcher who must decide on the most appropriate sample design for a specific project will identify a number of sampling criteria and evaluate the relative importance of each criterion before selecting a sampling design. This section outlines and briefly discusses the most common criteria. Exhibit 16.9 summarizes the advantages and disadvantages of each nonprobability sampling technique, and Exhibit 16.10 does the same for the probability sampling techniques. The Research Snapshot on the next page also illustrates that there is a role for convenience samples.

EXHIBIT 16.9 **Comparison of Sampling Techniques: Nonprobability Samples**

Nonprobability Samples			
Description	**Cost and Degree of Use**	**Advantages**	**Disadvantages**
1. *Convenience:* The researcher uses the most convenient sample or economical sample units.	Very low cost, extensively used	No need for list of population	Unrepresentative samples likely; random sampling error estimates cannot be made; projecting data beyond sample is relatively risky
2. *Judgment:* An expert or experienced researcher selects the sample to fulfill a purpose, such as ensuring that all members have a certain characteristic.	Moderate cost, average use	Useful for certain types of forecasting; sample guaranteed to meet a specific objective	Bias due to expert's beliefs may make sample unrepresentative; projecting data beyond sample is risky
3. *Quota:* The researcher classifies the population by pertinent properties, determines the desired proportion to sample from each class, and fixes quotas for each interviewer.	Moderate cost, very extensively used	Introduces some stratification of population; requires no list of population	Introduces bias in researcher's classification of subjects; nonrandom selection within classes means error from population cannot be estimated; projecting data beyond sample is risky
4. *Snowball:* Initial respondents are selected by probability samples; additional respondents are obtained by referral from initial respondents.	Low cost, used in special situations	Useful in locating members of rare populations	High bias because sample units are not independent; projecting data beyond sample is risky

Reactions to Handbills in Hong Kong

On busy city sidewalks, pedestrians often encounter a form of advertising called *handbills,* leaflets handed to passersby, informing them of a new store, a theater event, or some other nearby product or service. In highly populated urban centers, handbills are a common and successful method of direct marketing promotion—reaching tens of thousands of potential customers. Two marketing researchers in Hong Kong recently decided that this form of advertising had received little research attention, so they conducted exploratory research into consumer attitudes about handbills.

The selection of a sample design started with advance knowledge of the researchers' population. They decided to interview people in Hong Kong because the city has an extremely dense population—6 million people within 419 square miles. As a result, pedestrian traffic is heavy, and handbill distribution is a common sight on Hong Kong streets. A sample drawn from the Hong Kong population would be likely to include many people who have experiences with and attitudes toward handbills. The Hong Kong population provided another advantage. The researchers wished to use a telephone questionnaire,

and the majority of households in Hong Kong have a telephone line with a registered number. Finally, language was unlikely to be a problem; the survey was conducted in Chinese, spoken by all but a small percentage of Hong Kong's population.

In a sense, this survey involved a convenience sample, drawn from a population where the researchers live and work, rather than other parts of the world, where perhaps opinions would have been more diverse. Nevertheless, for an exploratory study into a formerly unexplored topic, the greater resources required for a more complex sampling method might not have been justified. The researchers were able to find response patterns for further investigation: People who accepted handbills were more likely to be female, relatively young, and have the equivalent of a high school education. Most of them took the handbills to help the distributor finish his or her work, and most read the handbills.

Source: Gerard Prendergast and Yuen Sze Man, "Perceptions of Handbills as a Promotional Medium: An Exploratory Study," *Journal of Advertising Research* 45 (March 2005), 124–131; "Direct Delivery," Direct Marketing of Asia, Limited, http://www.dm-asia.com, accessed September 20, 2008.

EXHIBIT 16.10 **Comparison of Sampling Techniques: Probability Samples**

Probability Samples			
Description	**Cost and Degree of Use**	**Advantages**	**Disadvantages**
1. *Simple random:* The researcher assigns each member of the sampling frame a number, then selects sample units by random method.	High cost, moderately used in practice (most common in random digit dialing and with computerized sampling frames)	Only minimal advance knowledge of population needed; easy to analyze data and compute error	Requires sampling frame to work from; does not use knowledge of population that researcher may have; larger errors for same sampling size than in stratified sampling; respondents may be widely dispersed, hence cost may be higher
2. *Systematic:* The researcher uses natural ordering or the order of the sampling frame, selects an arbitrary starting point, then selects items at a preselected interval.	Moderate cost, moderately used	Simple to draw sample; easy to check	If sampling interval is related to periodic ordering of the population, may introduce increased variability
3. *Stratified:* The researcher divides the population into groups and randomly selects subsamples from each group. Variations include proportional, disproportional, and optimal allocation of subsample sizes.	High cost, moderately used	Ensures representation of all groups in sample; characteristics of each stratum can be estimated and comparisons made; reduces variability for same sample size	Requires accurate information on proportion in each stratum; if stratified lists are not already available, they can be costly to prepare
4. *Cluster:* The researcher selects sampling units at random, then does a complete observation of all units or draws a probability sample in the group.	Low cost, frequently used	If clusters geographically defined, yields lowest field cost; requires listing of all clusters, but of individuals only within clusters; can estimate characteristics of clusters as well as of population	Larger error for comparable size than with other probability samples; researcher must be able to assign population members to unique cluster or else duplication or omission of individuals will result
5. *Multistage:* Progressively smaller areas are selected in each stage by some combination of the first four techniques.	High cost, frequently used, especially in nationwide surveys	Depends on techniques combined	Depends on techniques combined

Degree of Accuracy

Selecting a representative sample can be crucial for a researcher desiring to make accurate predictions or forecasts. However, the degree of accuracy required or the researcher's tolerance for sampling and nonsampling error may vary from project to project, especially when cost savings or another benefit may be a trade-off for a reduction in accuracy.

For example, when the sample is being selected for an exploratory research project, a high priority may not be placed on accuracy. For other, more conclusive projects, the sample result must precisely represent a population's characteristics, and the researcher must be willing to spend the time and money needed to achieve accuracy. When researchers use a convenience sample, they may sometimes even think backwards and only describe what population the results extend to based on the sample that can be obtained. Typically, a market research report will qualify results based on sampling characteristics.

Resources

The cost associated with the different sampling techniques varies tremendously. If the researcher's financial and human resources are restricted, certain options will have to be eliminated. For a typical graduate student working on a thesis or dissertation, conducting a national survey is often out of the question because of limited resources. Managers concerned with the cost of the research versus the value of the information often will opt to save money by using a nonprobability sampling design rather than make the decision to conduct no research at all.

Time

A researcher who needs to meet a deadline or complete a project quickly will be more likely to select a simple, less time-consuming sample design. A telephone survey that uses a sample based on random-digit dialing takes considerably less time than a survey that uses an elaborate disproportional stratified sample.

Advance Knowledge of the Population

Advance knowledge of population characteristics, such as the availability of lists of population members, is an important criterion. In many cases, however, no list of population elements will be available to the researcher. This is especially true when the population element is defined by ownership of a particular product or brand, by experience in performing a specific job task, or on a qualitative dimension. A lack of adequate lists may automatically rule out systematic sampling, stratified sampling, or other sampling designs, or it may dictate that a preliminary study, such as a short telephone survey using random digit dialing, be conducted to generate information to build a sampling frame for the primary study. In many developing countries, things like reverse directories are rare. Thus, researchers planning sample designs have to work around this limitation.

National versus Local Project

Geographic proximity of population elements will influence sample design. When population elements are unequally distributed geographically, a cluster sample may become much more attractive. A sample that represents all households in the United States and Canada becomes the goal for the few household products that show no regional, demographic, or lifestyle bias. Few products exhibit this characteristic. For instance, market research investigating opinions of North Americans about the Smart Car would be served better by sampling from large urban areas rather than giving rural residents an equal chance of being included in the research.

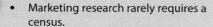

TIPS OF THE TRADE

- Marketing research rarely requires a census.
- Accurately defining the target population is critical in research involving forecasts of how that population will react to some event. Consider the following in defining the population:
  - Who are we not interested in?
  - What are the relevant market segment characteristics involved?
  - Is region important in defining the target population?
  - Is the issue being studied relevant to multiple populations?
  - Is a list available that contains all members of the population?
- Online panels are a practical reality in marketing research. A sample can be quickly measured that matches the demographic profiles of the target population.
  - As with all panels, the researcher faces a risk that systematic error is introduced in some way. For example, this

  sample may be higher in willingness to give opinions or may be responding only for an incentive.
  - The researcher should take extra steps such as including more screening questions to make sure the responses are representative of the target population.
- Convenience samples do have appropriate uses in marketing research. Convenience samples are particularly appropriate when:
  - Exploratory research is conducted.
  - The researcher is primarily interested in internal validity (testing a hypothesis under any condition) rather than external validity (understanding how much the sample results project to a target population).
  - When cost and time constraints only allow a convenience sample:
    - Researchers can think backwards and project the population for whom the results apply to based on the nature of the convenience sample.
- The research report should address the adequacy of the sample. Researchers seldom have a perfectly representative sample. Thus, the report should qualify the generalizability of the results based on sample limitations.

Summary

1. Explain reasons for taking a sample rather than a complete census. Sampling involves drawing conclusions about an entire population by taking measurements from only a portion of that population. The practical nature of research is clearly illustrated in sampling. Sampling is used because of the practical impossibility of measuring every population member. Seldom would a researcher have the time or budget to do so. Also, a researcher would rarely need to measure every unit, as a well-designed and executed sampling plan can yield results that may even be more accurate than an actual census. Samples also are needed in cases where measurement involves destruction of the measured unit.

2. Describe the process of identifying a target population and selecting a sampling frame. The first problem in sampling is to define the target population. Incorrect or vague definition of this population is likely to produce misleading results. The chapter contains an example list of questions that illustrate considerations needed in making a decision about the relevant population. A sampling frame is a list of elements, or individual members, of the overall population from which the sample is drawn. A sampling unit is a single element or group of elements subject to selection in the sample. Sometimes, a list of actual population members exists and can serve as a sampling frame. More often, the researcher will need the assistance of a directory, panel, or mailing list in forming the sampling frame.

3. Compare random sampling and systematic (nonsampling) errors with emphasis on how the Internet is interwined with this issue. Two sources of discrepancy between the sample results and the population parameters exist. One, random sampling error, arises from chance variations of the sample from the population. Random sampling error is a function of sample size and may be estimated using the central-limit theorem (discussed in a later chapter). Systematic, or nonsampling, error comes from sources such as sampling frame error, mistakes in recording responses, or nonresponses from persons who are not contacted or who refuse to participate. When researchers do not have an accurate list of population members, some type of systematic error becomes very likely. Internet surveys and consumer panels are very convenient but make truly random selection difficult. Thus, when these methods are chosen, extra care needs to be taken to make sure that the sample has characteristics that indeed allows it to represent the target population.

4. Identify the types of nonprobability sampling, including their advantages and disadvantages. The two major classes of sampling methods are probability and nonprobability techniques. Nonprobability techniques include convenience sampling, judgment sampling, quota sampling, and snowball sampling. They are convenient to use, but more subject to systematic sampling error. Sorting out the systematic sampling error from the random sampling error also proves problematic.

5. Summarize various types of probability samples. Probability samples are based on chance selection procedures. These include simple random sampling, systematic sampling, stratified sampling, and cluster sampling. With these techniques, random sampling error can be accurately predicted. The process for selecting sample units from a population is described in the chapter. A true probability sample can be costly both in terms of money and time.

6. Discuss how to choose an appropriate sample design. A researcher who must determine the most appropriate sampling design for a specific project will identify a number of sampling criteria and evaluate the relative importance of each criterion before selecting a design. The most common criteria concern accuracy requirements, available resources, time constraints, knowledge availability, and analytical requirements. Internet sampling presents some unique issues. Researchers must be aware that samples may be unrepresentative because not everyone has a computer or access to the Internet. Convenience samples drawn from Web site visitors can create problems. Drawing a probability sample from an established consumer panel whose members opt in can be effective.

Key Terms and Concepts

census, *412*
cluster sampling, *430*
convenience sampling, *423*
disproportional stratified sample, *430*
judgment (purposive) sampling, *424*
multistage area sampling, *431*
nonprobability sampling, *423*
online panels, *419*
opt in, *422*

population (universe), *412*
population element, *412*
primary sampling unit (PSU), *419*
probability sampling, *423*
proportional stratified sample, *429*
quota sampling, *425*
random sampling error, *420*
reverse directory, *418*
sample, *412*

sampling frame, *417*
sampling frame error, *417*
sampling unit, *419*
secondary sampling unit, *419*
simple random sampling, *426*
snowball sampling, *425*
stratified sampling, *427*
systematic sampling, *427*
tertiary sampling unit, *419*

Questions for Review and Critical Thinking

1. If you decide whether you want to see a new movie or television program on the basis of the "coming attractions" or television commercial previews, are you using a sampling technique? Could this be described as a scientific sampling technique?
2. What is the difference between a population and a sample? What are the reasons why a sampling process is so often used in place of a census? Why is it that a population can sometimes be as accurate as, or more accurate than, a census?
3. How can a market researcher try to be confident that the target population involved in some research situation is defined properly?
4. How might the target population differ for a researcher doing separate projects for two retailing companies—one for A&F and one for Nordstrom?
5. Name some possible sampling frames for the following:
   a. An online travel agency like Orbitz.com
   b. Golf course greenskeepers (responsible for the condition of the golf course)
   c. Dog owners
   d. Harley Davidson owners
   e. Tattoo wearers
   f. Minority-owned businesses
   g. Women over six feet tall
   h. Children who may consider engineering as a career
   i. Fast-food consumers in California

6. Describe the difference between a random and systematic sampling error.
7. Consider the following research situations and sample frames and indicate how they influence systematic error due to sampling procedures:
   a. The city of Houston phone book in a study of Houston Astros potential season ticket customers
   b. An online national panel such as the Harris Interactive Panel in a study of PC computer users conducted by Apple
   c. A list of customers who have stayed in a Starwood hotel property over the past 12 months in a study aimed at consumer attitudes toward visiting Europe for vacation.
8. What is a nonprobability sample? What are some examples?
9. Is a convenience sample ever appropriate? Explain.
10. Comment on the following sampling designs:
   a. A citizen's group interested in generating public and financial support for a new university basketball arena prints a questionnaire in area newspapers. Readers return the questionnaires by mail.
   b. A department store that wishes to examine whether it is losing or gaining customers draws a sample from its list of credit card holders by selecting every tenth name.
   c. A motorcycle manufacturer decides to research consumer characteristics by sending one hundred questionnaires to

each of its dealers. The dealers will then use their sales records to track down buyers of this brand of motorcycle and distribute the questionnaires.

d. An advertising executive suggests that advertising effectiveness be tested in the real world. A one-page ad is placed in a magazine. One-half of the space is used for the ad itself. On the other half, a short questionnaire requests that readers comment on the ad. An incentive will be given for the first thousand responses.

e. A research company obtains a sample for a focus group through organized groups such as church groups, clubs, and schools. The organizations are paid for securing respondents; no individual is directly compensated.

f. A researcher suggests replacing an online consumer panel with a sample of customers intercepted at Wal-Mart stores in Atlanta, Jacksonville, St. Louis, and Seattle. The goal is to understand basic consumer opinions on products sold by General Mills and Procter & Gamble.

g. A banner ad on a business-oriented Web site reads, "Are you a large company Sr. Executive? Qualified execs receive $50 for under 10 minutes of time. Take the survey now!" Is this an appropriate way to select a sample of business executives?

11. When would a researcher use a judgment, or purposive, sample?

12. A telephone interviewer asks, "I would like to ask you about race. Are you Native American, Hispanic, African-American, Asian, or white?" After the respondent replies, the interviewer says, "We have conducted a large number of surveys with people of your background, and we do not need to question you further. Thank you for your cooperation." What type of sampling is likely being used?

13. What role can screening questions play in trying to understand and control systematic variance from sources such as Internet surveys, online panels or other types of directories?

14. What are the benefits of stratified sampling?

15. What geographic units within a metropolitan area are useful for sampling?

16. Marketers often are particularly interested in the subset of a market that contributes most to sales (for example, heavy beer drinkers or large-volume retailers). What type of sampling might be best to use with such a subset? Why?

17. Outline the step-by-step procedure you would use to select the following:

a. A simple random sample of 150 students from the student list at your university

b. A quota sample of 50 light users and 50 heavy users of beer in a shopping mall intercept study

c. A stratified sample of 50 mechanical engineers, 40 electrical engineers, and 40 civil engineers from the subscriber list of an engineering journal

18. Selection for jury duty is supposed to be a totally random process. Comment on the following computer selection procedures, and determine if they are indeed random:

a. A program instructs the computer to scan the list of names and pick names that were next to those from the last scan.

b. Three-digit numbers are randomly generated to select jurors from a list of licensed drivers. If the weight information listed on the license matches the random number, the person is selected.

c. The juror source list is obtained by merging a list of registered voters with a list of licensed drivers.

19. Provide an example of marketing research in which a sample that is truly representative of all of North America is needed. When would the relevant target population for marketing research be all U.S. consumers? How often would such a target population be needed?

20. ETHICS To ensure a good session, a company selects focus group members from a list of articulate participants instead of conducting random sampling. The client did not inquire about sample selection when it accepted the proposal. Is this ethical?

21. 'NET Go to http://www.reversephonedirectory.com and put in your phone number. How accurate is this database?

22. 'NET Go to the U.S. Census Bureau's home page at http://www.census.gov, click on M in Subjects A to Z, and then click on Metropolitan Area and State Data Book. You can find profiles of every state from this Web site. Suppose a representative sample of the state of Louisiana is used to represent the current U.S. population. How well does Louisiana represent the United States overall? How well does Louisiana represent California or Maine? Use the profiles of the states and of the country to form your opinion.

Research Activity

1. Develop a sampling plan to study the lunch habits of undergraduate and graduate students of your university. Research questions involve who has the most market share and what are the preferred food types and price points for this particular school. Explain your choices.

Case 16.1 Who's Fishing?

Washington Times columnist Gene Mueller writes about fishing and other outdoor sporting activities.[14] Mueller commented recently that although interest groups express concerns about the impact of saltwater fishers on the fish population, no one really knows how many people fish for recreation or how many fish they catch. This situation would challenge marketers interested in the population of anglers.

How could a marketer get an accurate sample? One idea would be to contact residents of coastal counties using random-digit dialing. This sampling frame would include many, if not all, of the people who fish in the ocean, but it would also include many people who do not fish—or who fish for business rather than recreation. A regional agency seeking to gather statistics on anglers, the Atlantic Coastal Cooperative Statistics Program, prefers to develop a sampling frame more related to people who fish.

Another idea would be to use state fishing license records. Privacy would be a drawback, however. Some people might not want their records shared, and they might withhold phone numbers. Further complicating this issue for Atlantic fishing is that most states in the Northeast do not require a license for saltwater fishing. Also exempt in some states are people who fish from the shore and from piers.

A political action group called the Recreational Fishing Alliance suggests that charter fishing businesses collect data.

Questions

1. Imagine that an agency or business has asked for help in gathering data about the number of sports anglers who fish off the coast of Georgia. What advice would you give about sampling? What method or combination of methods would generate the best results?
2. What other criteria besides accuracy would you expect to consider? What sampling methods could help you meet those criteria?

Case 16.2 Scientific Telephone Samples

Scientific Telephone Samples (STS), located in Santa Ana, California, specializes in selling sampling frames for marketing research.[15] The STS sampling frame is based on a database of all working residential telephone exchanges in the United States. Thus, STS can draw from any part of the country—no matter how large or how small. The information is updated several times per year and cross-checked against area code and assigned exchange lists furnished by telephone companies. Exchange and/or working blocks designated for business or governmental telephones, mobile phones, and other commercial services are screened out.

STS can furnish almost any type of random digit sample desired, including

- National samples (continental United States only, or with Alaska and Hawaii)
- Stratified national samples (by census region or division)
- Census region or division samples
- State samples
- Samples by MSA
- County samples
- Samples by zip code
- City samples by zip code
- Exchange samples generated from lists of three-digit exchanges
- Targeted random-digit dialing samples (including over 40 variables and special databases for high-income areas, Hispanics, African-Americans, and Asians)

STS offers two different methods for pulling working blocks. Either method can be used regardless of the geographic sampling unit (for example, state, county, zip). The two versions are Type A (unweighted) and Type B (weighted/efficient).

Type A samples are pulled using a strict definition of randomness. They are called "unweighted" samples because each working block has an equal chance of being selected to generate a random digit number. Completed interviews from a Type A sample that has been dialed to exhaustion should be highly representative of the population under study.

Type B, or "efficient," samples are preweighted, so random digit dialing numbers are created from telephone working blocks in proportion to the number of estimated household listings in each working block. Working blocks that are more filled with numbers will be more prevalent in a sample. For example, a working block that had fifty known numbers in existence would have twice the probability of being included as one that had just twenty-five numbers.

Type B samples are most useful when a researcher is willing to overlook a strict definition of randomness in favor of slightly more calling efficiency because of fewer "disconnects." In theory, completed interviews from Type B samples may tend to overrepresent certain types of working blocks, but many researchers feel there is not much difference in representativeness.

Questions

1. Evaluate the geographic options offered by STS. Do they seem to cover all the bases?
2. Evaluate the STS method of random-digit dialing.

Case 16.3 Action Federal Savings and Loan Corporation

Steve Miles made a big move six months ago. He quit his job as director of retail marketing at the largest bank in the state to become marketing manager for Action Federal Savings and Loan. It had been only three-and-a-half years since he received his bachelor's degree in marketing at the largest university in the state, but he was bright, personable, and ambitious. Now, after several months of orientation at Action Federal (Steve called it "Mickey Mouse"), he was beginning his own marketing operations, hiring Roberta Nimoy from City University as his marketing research assistant.

Steve wanted to do an image study of each of the thirteen branches of Action Federal located throughout the state. The main branch and three others were located in tall office buildings in the capital city and nearby suburbs. The other branches were located in

rural areas, and their architecture was designed to fit into the surroundings. One was located in a restored colonial home. Another, the Old Mill branch, located next to a park with a historic windmill, was designed to be compatible with the nearby river and mill.

Steve asked Roberta to develop the sampling plan for the study. After some investigation, she learned that all the accounts were listed alphabetically in the main branch's computer. She thought that a list of names and addresses could be generated by taking a sample of 1,300. The computer would be programmed to randomly select every nth name. Since the savings and loan had approximately 112,000 customers, every 86th name would be selected.

Questions

1. Evaluate Action Federal's sampling plan.
2. What alternative sampling plans might be used?

After studying this chapter, you should be able to

1. Use descriptive statistics indicating central tendency and dispersion to make inferences about a population
2. Distinguish among population, sample, and sampling distributions
3. Explain the central-limit theorem
4. Use confidence intervals to express population estimates
5. Understand the major issues in specifying sample size

Chapter Vignette: Bigger Is Better—Right?

Product innovation is always a risky business. Marketing efforts for technologically oriented products like video game consoles and games have to be highly innovative. What kinds of games *should* be created? How racy should they be, particularly when aimed for a less-than-mature audience?

One study indicates that 60 percent of American consumers believe that there is too much violence in video games. In fact, the same study reports that 55 percent of gamers believe more regulation is needed to curb violence in new video games. Another study conducted by a gaming company provides different data. It suggests that 75 percent of parents with adolescent children do not believe that violence in video games harms their children. Still another provides *top box* statistics showing that 40 percent of Nintendo GameCube owners are highly likely to buy a new game that has been concept tested. Several decisions have to be made:

© PYMCA/JUPITER IMAGES

- Should the federal government implement law that further restricts the amount of violence and material with adult content in video games?
- Should gaming companies continue to push the envelope on gratuitous violence and sex in video games?
- Should a video game be developed and marketed based on a 40 percent top box result?

How good are the descriptive statistics discussed previously in helping make decisions like these? Before jumping to conclusions, consider some details seldom reported in media accounts of opinion results. The 60 and 55 percent figures come from a national consumer panel of 1,100 consumers. The 75 percent figure from parents is taken from a focus group of

12 consumers. The 40 percent top box result is based on input from 150 GameCube owners in Texas aged 12 to 17 years old.

Knowing the size of the sample certainly helps us know how valuable the information is. In the first case, a sample of 1,100 means that sample result is likely within 2 to 3 percent of the actual population values. Thus, a majority of consumers and even gamers appear concerned. In the second case, a sample of 12 means that the true population value could actually be 100 percent, meaning all parents are not concerned about the effect of violence on their own children, or it could be practically 0 percent! Finally, in the third case, the sample of 150 consumers means the actual population value can be confidently projected to be between 32 and 48 percent.

Is there enough confidence to act? Not all decisions are the same. Enacting federal legislation is no small matter and steps that restrict market freedom should be considered only with very solid data. Thus, the sample of 1,100 provides a relatively high degree of confidence, but perhaps this alone isn't quite enough. The political and financial risks associated with a bad regulatory decision require very great precision. On the other hand, introducing a new video game, particularly if it is a variant of one that already exists, is not so risky and less precision is needed. If 40 percent is the benchmark upon which to make the go—no go decision for the firm, the 32 to 48 percent range may provide enough confidence to move forward. While the firm might like more specific evidence, a larger sample will be costly in both money and time. Further, the longer the introduction is put off, the greater the risk that a competitor will be able to upstage the new introduction. So, at least in this case, bigger may not be better![1]

Introduction

The first portion of the chapter summarizes key statistical concepts necessary for understanding the theory that underlies the derivation of sample size. Students who need to review the basic aspects of statistics theory should pay particular attention to this material. Even those students who received good grades in elementary statistics classes probably will benefit from a quick review of these basic statistical concepts. The chapter then turns to issues related to sample size and the degree with which this affects the confidence with which population estimates can be made.

Raw data alone are seldom useful. They have to be organized and summarized to become useful and have the possibility of becoming actual market intelligence. The most basic ways for doing this include frequency distributions, proportions, and measures of central tendency and dispersion. Beyond these results, information about the sample helps decision makers know how much confidence can be placed in a given number.

Basic Descriptive and Inferential Statistics

The *Statistical Abstract of the United States* presents table after table of figures associated with numbers of births, number of employees in each county of the United States, and other data that the average person calls "statistics." They are descriptive statistics. Another type of statistics, inferential statistics, is used to make inferences about a whole population from a sample. For example, when a firm test-markets a new product in Sacramento and Birmingham, it wishes to make an inference from these sample markets to predict what will happen throughout the United States. So, two applications of statistics exist: (1) to describe characteristics of the population or sample and (2) to generalize from a sample to a population.

What are Sample Statistics and Population Parameters?

The primary purpose of inferential statistics is to make a judgment about a population, or the total collection of all elements about which a researcher seeks information. A sample is a subset or relatively small portion of the total number of elements in a given population. Data from a sample are always uncertain but when data come from all elements of a population, certainty is possible.

SURVEY THIS!

You probably recall responding to the part of the student survey shown in the screenshot. Using data obtained from the students responding to this survey and the assumptions provided, reply to the questions that follow.

1. Suppose a marketing manager was trying to determine how many students had only one e-mail account that they used regularly. Their intention is to market additional Internet services to students who have only one or no e-mail account.

   a. What is the proportion of students in the sample that have more than one e-mail account?

   b. What is the 95% confidence interval for this proportion?

   c. What is the 99% confidence interval for this proportion?

   d. If the student population is several million students, what sample size is needed to estimate the actual proportion of students with less than 2 e-mail accounts within +/−1%?

   e. What sample size is needed to estimate the actual proportion of students with less than 2 e-mail accounts within +/−5%?

   f. If the decision to launch this marketing activity involves an investment of approximately $75,000 for this company (with median annual revenues of $3M), what level of precision would you recommend?

   g. Approximately what level of precision exists given the total sample size available to you to make the computation in part a?

Sample statistics are measures computed from sample data. **Population parameters** are measured characteristics of a specific population. Sample statistics are used to make inferences (guesses) about population parameters.[2] In our notation, we will generally represent population parameters with Greek lowercase letters—for example, μ or α—and sample statistics with English letters, such as X or S.

■ FREQUENCY DISTRIBUTIONS

One of the most common ways to summarize a set of data is to construct a *frequency table,* or **frequency distribution**. The process begins with recording the number of times a particular value of a variable occurs. This is the frequency of that value. Continuing the example of a telephone survey for a savings and loan association, Exhibit 17.1 represents a frequency distribution of respondents' answers to a question that asked how much money customers had in their bank account.

sample statistics

Variables in a sample or measures computed from sample data.

population parameters

Variables in a population or measured characteristics of the population.

frequency distribution

A set of data organized by summarizing the number of times a particular value of a variable occurs.

EXHIBIT 17.1
Frequency Distribution of Deposits

Amount	Frequency (Number of People Who Hold Deposits in Each Range)
Under $3,000	499
$3,000 — $4,999	530
$5,000 — $9,999	562
$10,000 — $14,999	718
$15,000 or more	811
	3,120

percentage distribution

A frequency distribution organized into a table (or graph) that summarizes percentage values associated with particular values of a variable.

A similar method is a distribution of relative frequency, or a **percentage distribution**. To develop a frequency distribution of percentages, divide the frequency of each value by the total number of observations, and multiply the result by 100. Based on the data in Exhibit 17.1, Exhibit 17.2 shows the percentage distribution of deposits; that is, the percentage of people holding deposits within each range of values.

EXHIBIT 17.2

Percentage Distribution of Deposits

Amount	Percent (Percentage of People Who Hold Deposits in Each Range)
Under $3,000	16
$3,000—$4,999	17
$5,000—$9,999	18
$10,000—$14,999	23
$15,000 or more	26
	100

probability

The long-run relative frequency with which an event will occur.

Probability is the long-run relative frequency with which an event will occur. Inferential statistics uses the concept of a probability distribution, which is conceptually the same as a percentage distribution except that the data are converted into probabilities. Exhibit 17.3 shows the probability distribution of the savings and loan deposits.

EXHIBIT 17.3

Probability Distribution of Deposits

Amount	Probability
Under $3,000	.16
$3,000—$4,999	.17
$5,000—$9,999	.18
$10,000—$14,999	.23
$15,000 or more	.26
	1.00

■ PROPORTIONS

proportion

The percentage of elements that meet some criterion.

Frequencies can also be expressed in terms of percentages. When a frequency distribution portrays only a single characteristic in terms of a percentage of the total, it defines the **proportion** of occurrence. A proportion, such as the proportion of tenured professors at a university, indicates the percentage of population elements that successfully meet some standard concerning the particular characteristic. A proportion may be expressed as a percentage, a fraction, or a decimal value. In the example used here and illustrated in Exhibit 17.3, the probabilities are equal to the proportion of consumers in each deposit category. For example, 23 percent have a bank balance between $10,000 and $14,999.

■ TOP BOX SCORES

top-box score

Proportion of respondents who chose the most positive choice in a multiple choice question.

Managers are often very interested in the proportion of consumers choosing extreme responses. A **top box score** generally refers to the portion of respondents who choose the most favorable response toward a company. Typically, this means the portion that would highly recommend a business to a friend or, if the scale item simply addresses buying intentions, the portion expressing the highest likelihood of doing business again. The logic is that respondents who choose the most extreme response are really quite unique compared to the others. Managers are often asking what the top box score or number is.[3]

Measures of Central Tendency

On a typical day, a sales manager counts the number of sales calls each sales representative makes. He or she wishes to inspect the data to find the center, or middle area, of the frequency distribution. Put another way, what is the most typical number of sales calls? Central tendency can be measured with the mean, median, or mode. Each is determined in a slightly different way.

■ THE MEAN

We all have been exposed to the average known as the **mean**. The mean is simply the arithmetic average, and it is a common measure of central tendency. To express this mathematically, we use the summation symbol, the capital Greek letter *sigma* (Σ). A typical use might look like this:

$$\sum_{i=1}^{n} X_i$$

which is a shorthand way to write the sum

$$X_1 + X_2 + X_3 + X_4 + X_5 + \cdots + X_n$$

Below the Σ is the initial value of an index, usually, i, j, or k, and above it is the final value, in this case n, the number of observations. The shorthand expression says to replace i in the formula with the values from 1 to 8 and total the observations obtained. Without changing the basic formula, the initial and final index values may be replaced by other values to indicate different starting and stopping points.

Suppose a sales manager supervises the eight salespeople listed in Exhibit 17.4. To express the sum of the salespeople's calls in Σ notation, we just number the salespeople (this number becomes the index number) and associate subscripted variables with their numbers of calls:

Index		Salesperson	Variable		Number of Calls
1	=	Mike	X_1	=	4
2	=	Patty	X_2	=	3
3	=	Billie	X_3	=	2
4	=	Bob	X_4	=	5
5	=	John	X_5	=	3
6	=	Frank	X_6	=	3
7	=	Chuck	X_7	=	1
8	=	Samantha	X_8	=	5

mean

A measure of central tendency; the arithmetic average.

Salesperson	Number of Sales Calls
Mike	4
Patty	3
Billie	2
Bob	5
John	3
Frank	3
Chuck	1
Samantha	5
Total	26

EXHIBIT 17.4

Number of Sales Calls per Day by Salesperson

We then write an appropriate Σ formula and evaluate it:

$$\sum_{i=1}^{8} X_i = X_1 + X_2 + X_3 + X_4 + X_5 + X_6 + X_7 + X_8$$
$$= 4 + 3 + 2 + 5 + 3 + 3 + 1 + 5$$
$$= 26$$

This notation is the numerator in the formula for the arithmetic mean:

$$\text{Mean} = \frac{\sum_{i=1}^{n} X_i}{n} = \frac{26}{8} = 3.25$$

The notation $\sum_{i=1}^{n} X_i$ means add together all the Xs whose subscripts are between 1 and n inclusive, where n equals the number of observations. Here there are eight observations so i varies between 1 and 8. The formula shows that the mean number of sales calls in this example is 3.25.

Researchers generally wish to know the population mean, μ (lowercase Greek letter mu), which is calculated as follows:

$$\mu = \frac{\sum_{i=1}^{N} X_i}{N}$$

where

N = number of members in the population

Often we will not have enough data to calculate the population mean, μ, so we will calculate a sample mean, $\overline{X}$ (read "X bar"), with the following formula:

$$\overline{X} = \frac{\sum_{i=1}^{N} X_i}{n}$$

where

n = number of observations made in the sample

More likely than not, you already know how to calculate a mean. However, knowing how to distinguish among the symbols Σ, μ, and X is helpful to understand statistics.

In this introductory discussion of the summation sign (Σ), we have used very detailed notation that includes the subscript for the initial index value (i) and the final index value (n). However, from this point on, references to Σ will sometimes omit the subscript for the initial index value (i) and the final index value (n). The mean is the most widely applied measure of central tendency. However, the mean can sometimes be misleading, particularly when extreme values or outliers are present as in the Research Snapshot on the next page.

■ THE MEDIAN

median

A measure of central tendency that is the midpoint; the value below which half the values in a distribution fall.

The next measure of central tendency, the **median**, is the midpoint of the distribution, or the 50th percentile. In other words, the median is the value below which half the values in the sample fall. In the sales manager example, 3 is the median because half the observations are greater than 3 and half are less than 3. The median is a better indicator of central tendency in the presence of extreme values or outliers. For instance, a professor gives a marketing research test and one student makes a 99, another makes a 98, but the next highest grade is 51 with the remaining 17 grades ranging from 30 to 50. In this case, if the professor curves the grades so that everyone who scores "above average" will pass, the result could be only 5 or 6 students passing as the mean would be on the order of 46. Perhaps the students would prefer a curve based around the median which would mean that half of the students would pass by definition.

The Well-Chosen Average

When you read an announcement by a corporate executive or a business proprietor that the average pay of the people who work in his or her establishment is so much, the figure may mean something or it may not. If the average is a median, you can learn something significant from it: half of the employees make more than that; half make less. But if it is a mean (and believe me, it may be, if its nature is unspecified), you may be getting nothing more revealing than the average of one $450,000 income—the proprietor's—and the salaries of a crew of lower wage workers. "Average annual pay of $57,000" may conceal both the $20,000 salaries and the owner's profits taken in the form of a whopping salary.

Let's take a longer look at this scenario. This table shows how many people get how much. The boss might like to express the situation as "average wage $57,000," using that deceptive mean. The mode, however, is more revealing: The most common rate of pay in this business is $20,000 a year. As usual, the median tells more about the situation than any other single figure. Half of the people get more than $30,000 and half get less.

Number of People	Title	Salary	
1	Controller	57,000	◆ Mean (arithmetical average)
3	Directors	50,000	
4	Managers	37,000	
1	Supervisor	30,000	◆ Median *(the one in the middle; 12 above, 12 below)*
12	Workers	20,000	◆ Mode *(occurs most frequently)*
1	Proprietor	$450,000	
1	President	150,000	
2	Vice presidents	100,000	

Imagine what would happen to your hometown's average income if Ross Perot and Bill Gates moved into town.

Do politicians use statistics to lie or do the statistics lie? Politicians sometimes try to play one class of people against another in trying to get elected. One political claim is that the "rich do not pay taxes" or the "rich do not pay their fair share of taxes." If you are curious about this, some facts are available at http://www.taxfoundation.org or http://www.american.com/archive/2007/november-december-magazine-contents/guess-who-really-pays-the-taxes. Do the top 5 percent of wage earners pay taxes?

Sources: Darrell Huff and Irving Geis, *How to Lie with Statistics* (New York: W.W. Norton, 1954), p. 33; Jackson, Brooks and Kathleen H. Jamieson, "Finding Fact in Political Debate," *American Behavioral Scientist* 48 (October 1, 2004), 233–247.

■ THE MODE

In the apparel industry, *mode* refers to the most popular fashion. In statistics the **mode** is the measure of central tendency that identifies the value that occurs most often. In our example of sales calls, Patty, John, and Frank each made three sales calls. The value 3 occurs most often, so 3 is the mode. The mode is determined by listing each possible value and noting the number of times each value occurs. The mode is the best measure of central tendency for data that is less than interval and for data that are distributed unimodally with one large peak (many observations have the same response).

mode
A measure of central tendency; the value that occurs most often.

Measures of Dispersion

The mean, median, and mode summarize the central tendency of frequency distributions. Accurate analysis of data also requires knowing the tendency of observations to depart from the central tendency. Thus, another way to summarize the data is to calculate the dispersion of the data, or how the observations vary from the mean. Consider, for instance, the twelve-month sales patterns of the two products shown in Exhibit 17.5 on the next page. Both have a mean monthly sales volume of 200 units, but the dispersion of observations for product B is much greater than that for product A. There are several measures of dispersion.

■ THE RANGE

The simplest measure of dispersion is the range. It is the distance between the smallest and the largest values of a frequency distribution. In Exhibit 17.5, the range for product A is between 196 units and 202 units (6 units), whereas for product B the range is between 150 units and 261 units (111 units). The range does not take into account all the observations; it merely tells us about the extreme values of the distribution.

Just as people may be fat or skinny, distributions may be fat or skinny. While we do not expect all observations to be exactly like the mean, in a skinny distribution they will lie a short distance

EXHIBIT 17.5
**Sales Levels for Two
Products with Identical
Average Sales**

	Units Product A	Units Product B
January	196	150
February	198	160
March	199	176
April	200	181
May	200	192
June	200	200
July	200	201
August	201	202
September	201	213
October	201	224
November	202	240
December	202	261
Average	**200**	**200**

from the mean. Product A is an example; the observations are close together and reasonably close to the mean. In a fat distribution, such as the one for Product B, they will be spread out. Exhibit 17.6 illustrates this concept graphically with two frequency distributions that have identical modes, medians, and means but different degrees of dispersion.

The interquartile range is the range that encompasses the middle 50 percent of the observations—in other words, the range between the bottom quartile (lowest 25 percent) and the top quartile (highest 25 percent).

EXHIBIT 17.6
**Low Dispersion versus High
Dispersion**

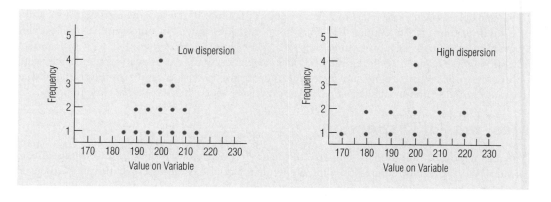

■ DEVIATION SCORES

A method of calculating how far any observation is from the mean is to calculate individual deviation scores. To calculate a deviation from the mean, use the following formula:

$$d_{i_i} = X_i - \overline{X}$$

For the value of 150 units for product B for the month of January, the deviation score is -50; that is, $150 - 200 = -50$. If the deviation scores are large, we will have a fat distribution because the distribution exhibits a broad spread.

■ WHY USE THE STANDARD DEVIATION?

Statisticians have derived several quantitative indexes to reflect a distribution's spread, or variability. The *standard deviation* is perhaps the most valuable index of spread, or dispersion. Students often have difficulty understanding it. Learning about the standard deviation will be easier if we first look at several other measures of dispersion that may be used. Each of these has certain limitations that the standard deviation does not.

First is the average deviation. We compute the average deviation by calculating the deviation score of each observation value (that is, its difference from the mean), summing these scores, and then dividing by the sample size (n):

$$\text{Average deviation} = \frac{\Sigma\,(X_i - \overline{X})}{n}$$

While this measure of spread seems interesting, it is never used. Positive deviation scores are canceled out by negative scores with this formula, leaving an average deviation value of zero no matter how wide the spread may be. Hence, the average deviation is a useless spread measure.

One might correct for the disadvantage of the average deviation by computing the absolute values of the deviations. In other words, we ignore all the positive and negative signs and use only the absolute value of each deviation. The formula for the mean absolute deviation is

$$\text{Mean absolute deviation} = \frac{\Sigma\,|X_i - \overline{X}|}{n}$$

While this procedure eliminates the problem of always having a zero score for the deviation measure, it becomes even more useful to express deviations in terms of variance.

Variance

Another means of eliminating the sign problem caused by the negative deviations canceling out the positive deviations is to square the deviation scores. The following formula gives the mean squared deviation:

$$\text{Mean squared deviation} = \frac{\Sigma\,(X_i - \overline{X})^2}{n}$$

This measure is useful for describing the sample variability. However, we typically wish to make an inference about a population from a sample, and so the divisor $n - 1$ is used rather than n in most pragmatic marketing research problems.[4] The divisor changes from n to $n - 1$ to provide an unbiased estimator. This new measure of spread, called **variance**, has the following formula:

$$\text{Variance} = S^2 = \frac{\Sigma\,(X_i - \overline{X})^2}{n - 1}$$

variance

A measure of variability or dispersion. Its square root is the standard deviation.

Variance is a very good index of dispersion. The variance, S^2, will equal zero if and only if each and every observation in the distribution is the same as the mean. The variance will grow larger as the observations tend to differ increasingly from one another and from the mean.

Standard Deviation

While the variance is frequently used in statistics, it has one major drawback. The variance reflects a unit of measurement that has been squared. For instance, if measures of sales in a territory are made in dollars, the mean number will be reflected in dollars, but the variance will be in squared dollars. Because of this, statisticians often take the square root of the variance. Using the square root of the variance for a distribution, called the **standard deviation**, eliminates the drawback of having the measure of dispersion in squared units rather than in the original measurement units. The formula for the standard deviation is

standard deviation

A quantitative index of a distribution's spread, or variability; the square root of the variance for a distribution.

$$S = \sqrt{S^2} = \sqrt{\frac{\Sigma\,(X_i - \overline{X})^2}{n - 1}}$$

Exhibit 17.7 on the next page illustrates that the calculation of a standard deviation requires the researcher to first calculate the sample mean. In the example with eight salespeople's sales calls (Exhibit 17.4), we calculated the sample mean as 3.25. Exhibit 17.7 illustrates how to calculate the standard deviation for these data.

At this point we can return to thinking about the original purpose for measures of dispersion. We want to summarize the data from survey research and other forms of marketing research. Indexes of central tendency, such as the mean, help us interpret the data. In addition, we wish to calculate a measure of variability that will give us a quantitative index of the dispersion of the distribution. We have looked at several measures of dispersion to arrive at two very adequate means of measuring dispersion: the variance and the standard deviation. The formula given is for the sample standard deviation, S.

EXHIBIT 17.7
Calculating a Standard Deviation: Number of Sales Calls per Day for Eight Salespeople

X	$(X - \bar{X})$	$(X - \bar{X})^2$
4	$(4 - 3.25) = \quad .75$	.5625
3	$(3 - 3.25) = \quad -.25$	.0625
2	$(2 - 3.25) = -1.25$	1.5625
5	$(5 - 3.25) = \quad 1.75$	3.0625
3	$(3 - 3.25) = \quad -.25$	.0625
3	$(3 - 3.25) = \quad -.25$	.0625
1	$(1 - 3.25) = -2.25$	5.0625
$\underline{5}$	$(5 - 3.25) = \quad 1.75$	$\underline{3.0625}$
Σ^a	a^0	13.5000

$$n = 8 \quad \bar{X} = 3.25$$

$$S = \sqrt{\frac{\Sigma(X - \bar{X})^2}{n - 1}} = \sqrt{\frac{13.5}{8 - 1}} = \sqrt{\frac{13.5}{7}} = \sqrt{1.9286} = 1.3887$$

[a]The summation of this column is not used in the calculation of the standard deviation.

The formula for the population standard deviation, σ, which is conceptually very similar, has not been given. Nevertheless, you should understand that σ measures the dispersion in the population and S measures the dispersion in the sample. These concepts are crucial to understanding statistics. Remember, the student must learn the language of statistics to use it in a research project. If you do not understand the language at this point, review this material now.

Distinguish Between Sample and Sample Distribution

By recording the results of spins of the roulette wheel, one could find a pattern or distribution of the results.

Roulette is a common casino game and a casino may contain many roulette wheels. If someone wanted to know whether the roulette wheels were fair, they may make many observations of which number the ball lands on as the result of a spin. The results would follow some pattern. While it might not be possible to record the results of all spins of the roulette wheel, someone could probably record results over a several-hour period on one or more wheels. This basic image provides the idea behind statistical distributions.

The Normal Distribution

One of the most common probability distributions in statistics is the **normal distribution**, commonly represented by the *normal curve*. This mathematical and theoretical distribution describes the expected distribution of sample means and many other chance occurrences. The normal curve is bell shaped, and almost all (99.7 percent) of its values are within ±3 standard deviations from its mean. An example of a normal curve, the distribution of IQ scores, appears in Exhibit 17.8. The IQ score is normed to 100 meaning that 100 is an average IQ score. In this example, 1 standard deviation for IQ equals 15. Someone with an IQ score of 70 is 2 standard deviations below average and scores better than 2.14 percent of others. A person scoring 145 is 3 standard deviations above average and better than 99.8 percent of others.

normal distribution

A symmetrical, bell-shaped distribution that describes the expected probability distribution of many chance occurrences.

EXHIBIT 17.8

Normal Distribution: Distribution of Intelligence Quotient (IQ) Scores

The **standardized normal distribution** is a specific normal curve that has several characteristics:

1. It is symmetrical about its mean.
2. The mean identifies the normal curve's highest point (the mode) and the vertical line about which this normal curve is symmetrical.
3. The normal curve has an infinite number of cases (it is a continuous distribution), and the area under the curve has a probability density equal to 1.0.
4. The standardized normal distribution has a mean of 0 and a standard deviation of 1.

Exhibit 17.9 illustrates these properties. Exhibit 17.10 on the next page is a summary version of the typical standardized normal table found at the end of most statistics textbooks. A more complex table of areas under the standardized normal distribution appears in Table A.1 in the appendix.

The standardized normal distribution is a purely theoretical probability distribution, but it is the most useful distribution in inferential statistics. Statisticians have spent a great deal of time

standardized normal distribution

A purely theoretical probability distribution that reflects a specific normal curve for the standardized value, z.

> ## TOTHEPOINT
>
> *Order is heaven's law.*
>
> —Alexander Pope

EXHIBIT 17.9

Standardized Normal Distribution

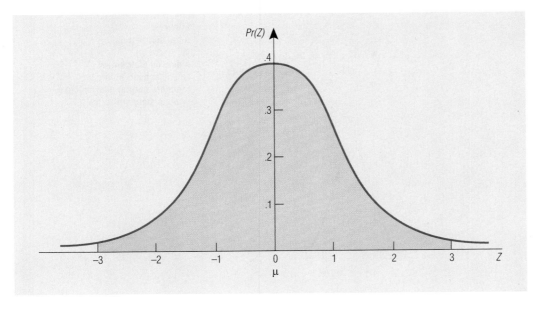

EXHIBIT 17.10 **Standardized Normal Table: Area Under Half of the Normal Curve[a]**

Z Standard Deviations from the Mean (Units)	Z Standard Deviations from the Mean (Tenths of Units)[a]									
	.0	.1	.2	.3	.4	.5	.6	.7	.8	.9
0.0	.000	.040	.080	.118	.155	.192	.226	.258	.288	.315
1.0	.341	.364	.385	.403	.419	.433	.445	.455	.464	.471
2.0	.477	.482	.486	.489	.492	.494	.495	.496	.497	.498
3.0	.499	.499	.499	.499	.499	.499	.499	.499	.499	.499

[a]Area under the segment of the normal curve extending (in one direction) from the mean to the point indicated by each row-column combination. For example, about 68 percent of normally distributed events can be expected to fall within 1.0 standard deviation on either side of the mean (0.341 × 2). An interval of almost 2.0 standard deviations around the mean will include 95 percent of all cases (.477 + .477).

and effort making it convenient for researchers to find the probability of any portion of the area under the standardized normal distribution. All we have to do is transform, or convert, the data from other observed normal distributions to the standardized normal curve. In other words, the standardized normal distribution is extremely valuable because we can translate, or transform, any normal variable, X, into the standardized value, Z. Exhibit 17.11 illustrates how either a skinny distribution or a fat distribution can be converted into the standardized normal distribution. This ability to transform normal variables has many pragmatic implications for the marketing researcher. The standardized normal table in the back of most statistics and marketing research books allows us to evaluate the probability of the occurrence of many events without any difficulty.

EXHIBIT 17.11

Standardized Values can be Computed from Flat or Peaked Distributions Resulting in a Standardized Normal Curve

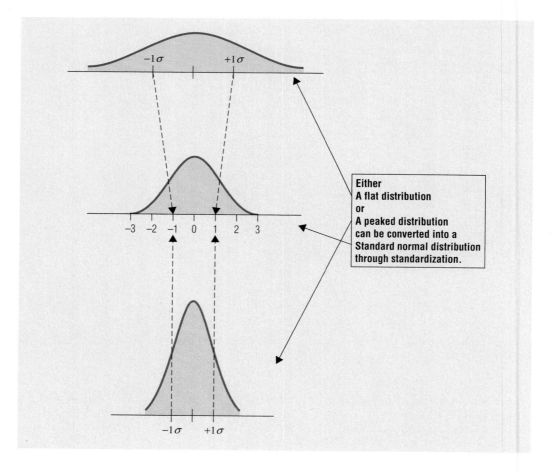

Computing the standardized value, Z, of any measurement expressed in original units is simple: Subtract the mean from the value to be transformed, and divide by the standard deviation (all expressed in original units). The formula for this procedure and its verbal statement follow. In the formula, note that σ, the population standard deviation, is used for calculation.[5]

$$\text{Standardized value} = \frac{\text{Value to be transformed} - \text{Mean}}{\text{Standard deviation}}$$

$$Z = \frac{X - \mu}{\sigma}$$

where

μ = hypothesized or expected value of the mean

Suppose that in the past a toy manufacturer has experienced mean sales, μ, of 9,000 units and a standard deviation, σ, of 500 units during September. The production manager wishes to know whether wholesalers will demand between 7,500 and 9,625 units during September of the upcoming year. Because no tables are available showing the distribution for a mean of 9,000 and a standard deviation of 500, we must transform our distribution of toy sales, X, into the standardized form using our simple formula. The following computation shows that the probability (Pr) of obtaining sales in this range is equal to .893:

$$Z = \frac{X - \mu}{\sigma} = \frac{7,500 - 9,000}{500} = -3.00$$

$$Z = \frac{X - \mu}{\sigma} = \frac{9,625 - 9,000}{500} = 1.25$$

Using Exhibit 17.10, we find that

When $Z = -3.00$, the area under the curve (probability) equals 0.499.

When $Z = 1.25$, the area under the curve (probability) equals 0.394.

Thus, the total area under the curve is .499 + .394 = .893. (The area under the curve corresponding to this computation is the shaded areas in Exhibit 17.12.) The sales manager, therefore, knows there is a .893 probability that sales will be between 7,500 and 9,625.

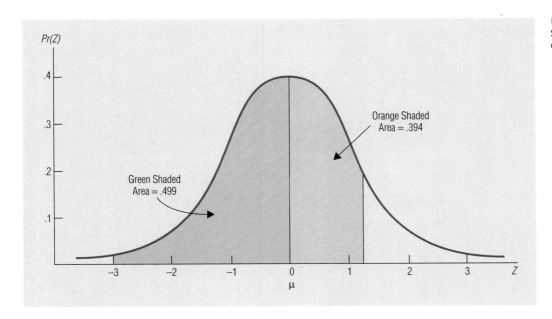

EXHIBIT 17.12
Standardized Distribution Curve

Population Distribution and Sample Distribution

Before we outline the technique of statistical inference, three additional types of distributions must be defined: population distribution, sample distribution, and sampling distribution. When conducting a research project or survey, the researcher's purpose is not to describe the sample of respondents, but to make an inference about the population. As defined previously, a population, or universe, is the total set, or collection, of potential units for observation. The sample is a smaller subset of this population.

A frequency distribution of the population elements is called a **population distribution**. The mean and standard deviation of the population distribution are represented by the Greek letters μ and σ. A frequency distribution of a sample is called a **sample distribution**. The sample mean is designated $\overline{X}$, and the sample standard deviation is designated S.

population distribution

A frequency distribution of the elements of a population.

sample distribution

A frequency distribution of a sample.

Sampling Distribution

The concepts of population distribution and sample distribution are relatively simple. However, we must now introduce another distribution, which is the crux of understanding statistics: the *sampling distribution of the sample mean*. The sampling distribution is a theoretical probability distribution that in actual practice would never be calculated. Hence, practical, business-oriented students have difficulty understanding why the notion of the sampling distribution is important. Statisticians, with their mathematical curiosity, have asked themselves, "What would happen if we were to draw a large number of samples (say, 50,000), each having n elements, from a specified population?" Assuming that the samples were randomly selected, the sample means, $\overline{X}$s, could be arranged in a frequency distribution. Because different people or sample units would be selected in the different samples, the sample means would not be exactly equal. The shape of the sampling distribution is of considerable importance to statisticians. If the sample size is sufficiently large and if the samples are randomly drawn, we know from the central-limit theorem that the sampling distribution of the mean will be approximately normally distributed.

A formal definition of the sampling distribution is as follows:

*A **sampling distribution** is a theoretical probability distribution that shows the functional relation between the possible values of some summary characteristic of n cases drawn at random and the probability (density) associated with each value over all possible samples of size n from a particular population.*[6]

The sampling distribution's mean is called the *expected value* of the statistic. The expected value of the mean of the sampling distribution is equal to μ. The standard deviation of a sampling distribution of $\overline{X}$ is called **standard error of the mean** ($S_{\overline{X}}$) and is approximately equal to

sampling distribution

A theoretical probability distribution of sample means for all possible samples of a certain size drawn from a particular population.

standard error of the mean

The standard deviation of the sampling distribution.

$$S_{\overline{X}} = \frac{\sigma}{\sqrt{n}}$$

To review, for us to make an inference about a population from a sample, we must know about three important distributions: the population distribution, the sample distribution, and the sampling distribution. They have the following characteristics:

	Mean	Standard Deviation
Population distribution	μ	σ
Sample distribution	X	S
Sampling distribution	$\mu_x = \mu$	$S_{\overline{x}}$

We now have much of the information we need to understand the concept of statistical inference. To clarify why the sampling distribution has the characteristic just described, we will elaborate on two concepts: the standard error of the mean and the central-limit theorem. You may be wondering why the standard error of the mean, $S_{\overline{X}}$, is defined as $S_{\overline{X}} = \sigma/\sqrt{n}$. The reason is based on the notion that the variance within the sampling distribution of the mean will be less if we have a larger sample size for independent samples. We can see intuitively that a larger sample size allows the researcher to be more confident that the sample mean is closer to the population mean. In actual practice, the standard error of the mean is estimated using the sample's standard deviation. Thus, $S_{\bar{x}}$ is estimated using $S/\sqrt{n}$.

Exhibit 17.13 shows the relationship among a population distribution, the sample distribution, and three sampling distributions for varying sample sizes. In part (a) the population distribution is not a normal distribution. In part (b) the sample distribution resembles the distribution of the population; however, there may be some differences. In part (c) each sampling distribution is normally distributed and has the same mean. Note that as sample size increases, the spread of the sample means around μ decreases. Thus, with a larger sample size we will have a skinnier sampling distribution.

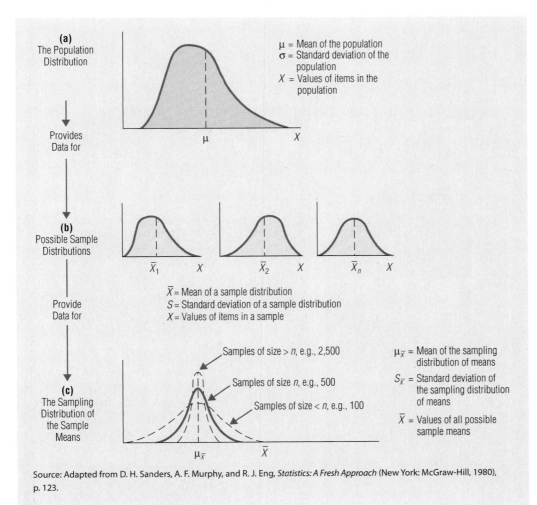

Source: Adapted from D. H. Sanders, A. F. Murphy, and R. J. Eng, *Statistics: A Fresh Approach* (New York: McGraw-Hill, 1980), p. 123.

EXHIBIT 17.13

Fundamental Types of Distributions

Central-Limit Theorem

Finding that the means of random samples of a sufficiently large size will be approximately normal in form and that the mean of the sampling distribution will approach the population mean is very useful. Mathematically, this is the assertion of the **central-limit theorem**, which states, as the sample size, n, increases, the distribution of the mean, $\bar{X}$, of a random sample taken from practically any population approaches a normal distribution (with a mean μ and a standard deviation $\sigma/\sqrt{n}$).[7] The central-limit theorem works regardless of the shape of the original population distribution.

central-limit theorem

The theory that, as sample size increases, the distribution of sample means of size n, randomly selected, approaches a normal distribution.

In other words, the distribution of averages quickly approaches normal as sample size increases. Exhibit 17.14 illustrates how the distribution of means of bimodal observations will increasingly approach normal.

A simple example will demonstrate the central-limit theorem. Assume that a consumer researcher is interested in the number of dollars children spend on toys each month. Assume further that the population the consumer researcher is investigating consists of eight-year-old children in a certain school. In this elementary example, the population consists of only six individuals. Exhibit 17.15 shows the population distribution of toy expenditures. Alice, a relatively deprived child, has only \$1 per month, whereas Freddy, the rich kid, has \$6 to spend. The average expenditure on toys each month is \$3.50, so the population mean, μ, equals 3.5 (see Exhibit 17.16).

Now assume that we do not know everything about the population, and we wish to take a sample size of two, to be drawn randomly from the population of the six individuals. How many possible samples are there?

EXHIBIT 17.14

The Mean Distribution of Any Distribution Approaches Normal as *n* Increases

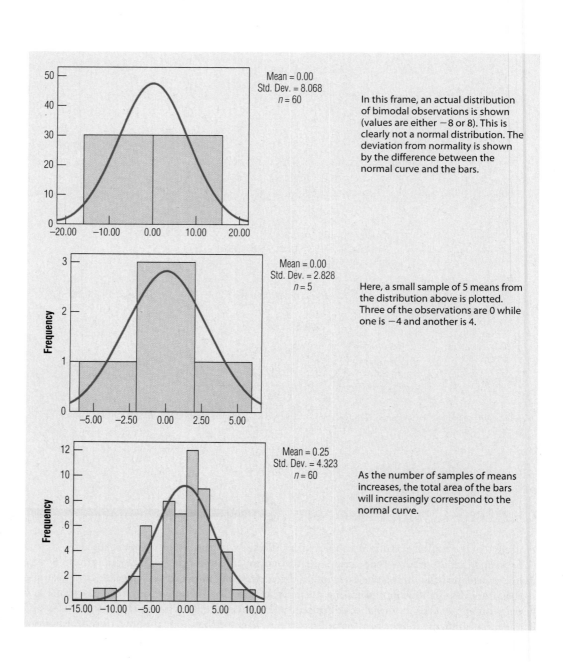

Mean = 0.00
Std. Dev. = 8.068
n = 60

In this frame, an actual distribution of bimodal observations is shown (values are either −8 or 8). This is clearly not a normal distribution. The deviation from normality is shown by the difference between the normal curve and the bars.

Mean = 0.00
Std. Dev. = 2.828
n = 5

Here, a small sample of 5 means from the distribution above is plotted. Three of the observations are 0 while one is −4 and another is 4.

Mean = 0.25
Std. Dev. = 4.323
n = 60

As the number of samples of means increases, the total area of the bars will increasingly correspond to the normal curve.

Child	Toy Expenditures
Alice	$1.00
Becky	2.00
Noah	3.00
Tobin	4.00
George	5.00
Freddy	6.00

EXHIBIT 17.15
Population Distribution: Hypothetical Toy Expenditures

X
$1.00
2.00
3.00
4.00
5.00
6.00
Σ $21.00

Calculations: $\mu = \frac{\Sigma X}{n} = \frac{21}{6} = 3.5 = \mu_{\bar{x}}$

EXHIBIT 17.16
Calculation of Population Mean

The answer is 15, as follows (these are the possible combinations):

1, 2
1, 3   2, 3
1, 4   2, 4   3, 4
1, 5   2, 5   3, 5   4, 5
1, 6   2, 6   3, 6   4, 6   5, 6

Exhibit 17.17 on the next page lists the sample mean for each of the possible fifteen samples and the frequency distribution of these sample means with their appropriate probabilities. These sample means comprise a sampling distribution of the mean, and the distribution is *approximately* normal. If we increased the sample size to three, four, or more, the distribution of sample means would more closely approximate a normal distribution. While this simple example is not a proof of the central-limit theorem, it should give you a better understanding of the nature of the sampling distribution of the mean.

This theoretical knowledge about distributions can be used to solve two practical marketing research problems: estimating parameters and determining sample size.

Estimation of Parameters and Confidence Intervals

A catalog retailer, such as Land's End, may rely on sampling and statistical estimation to prepare for Christmas orders. The company can expect that 28 days after mailing a catalog, it will have received X percent of the orders it will get. With this information, the company can tell within 5 percent how many ties it will sell by Christmas. Making a proper inference about population parameters is highly practical for a marketer that must have the inventory appropriate for a short selling season.

EXHIBIT 17.17
Arithmetic Means of Samples and Frequency Distribution of Sample Means

Sample Means			
Sample	**ΣX**	**X̄**	**Probability**
$1, $2	$3.00	$1.50	1/15
1, 3	4.00	2.00	1/15
1, 4	5.00	2.50	1/15
1, 5	6.00	3.00	1/15
1, 6	7.00	3.50	1/15
2, 3	5.00	2.50	1/15
2, 4	6.00	3.00	1/15
2, 5	7.00	3.50	1/15
2, 6	8.00	4.00	1/15
3, 4	7.00	3.50	1/15
3, 5	8.00	4.00	1/15
3, 6	9.00	4.50	1/15
4, 5	9.00	4.50	1/15
4, 6	10.00	5.00	1/15
5, 6	11.00	5.50	1/15

Frequency Distribution		
Sample Mean	**Frequency**	**Probability**
$1.50	1	1/15
2.00	1	1/15
2.50	2	2/15
3.00	2	2/15
3.50	3	3/15
4.00	2	2/15
4.50	2	2/15
5.00	1	1/15
5.50	1	1/15

Suppose you are a product manager for Beatrice Foods and you recently conducted a taste test to measure intention to buy a reformulated Swiss Miss Lite Cocoa Mix. The results of the research indicate that when the product was placed in eight hundred homes and a callback was made two weeks later, 80 percent of the respondents said they would buy it: 76 percent of those who had not previously used low-calorie cocoa and 84 percent of those who had. How can you be sure there were no statistical errors in this estimate? How confident can you be of these figures?

Students often wonder whether statistics are really used in the business world. The two situations just described provide contemporary examples of the need for statistical estimation of parameters and the value of statistical techniques as managerial tools.

Measuring Viewership ... with Confidence

Media research firms like Arbitron and Nielsen provide data on audience sizes after programs have aired, but can advertisers predict audiences ahead of time? One way to get an estimate is to ask people about their intended media behavior. For example, Harris Interactive used an online poll to ask people whether they intended to watch the Winter Olympics held in Turin, Italy, and if so, which events they planned to watch.

The Harris poll obtained responses from 1,002 adults. The data represented percentages who planned to watch any of the television coverage of the Olympics and percentages who planned to watch specific events. Results were segmented by age, sex, and other demographics. According to the researchers, the confidence level was 95 percent that the sampling error was not greater than ±3 percentage points.

The poll found that 61 percent of men and 69 percent of women planned to watch the Winter Olympics. Given the confidence interval, we can say with 95 percent confidence that more women than men planned to watch, because the true value for men would be within the range of 58 percent to 64 percent and the true value for women would be between 66 percent and 72 percent. However, we cannot say from this poll whether more men or women actually watched the games. For that, advertisers had to wait for the after-the-fact data from the media researchers. Finding data on actual ratings can be difficult because selling this data is a large part of Nielsen's business. However, in 2008, just over 20 million Americans tuned in to the Olympics on one of the first two nights. Thus, over the entire two-week period, chances are that the 2006 confidence interval expectations were exceeded.

Source: Based on "Two-Thirds of U.S. Adults Plan to Watch the Winter Olympics," *Wall Street Journal* (February 10, 2006), http://online.wsj.com; Liz Clarke, "2006 Winter Olympic Games," *Washington Post* (February 21, 2006), http://www.washingtonpost.com; Futterman, M. and S. Schechner, "NBC's Olympic Ratings Get a Web-Based Boost," *Wall Street Journal* 252 (August 11, 2008), B7.

Point Estimates

Our goal in using statistics is to make an estimate about population parameters. A population mean, μ, and standard deviation, σ, are constants, but in most instances of marketing research, they are unknown. To estimate population values, we are required to sample. As we have discussed, $\overline{X}$ and S are random variables that will vary from sample to sample with a certain probability (sampling) distribution. The Research Snapshot above discusses estimates of Olympic game viewership.

Our previous example of statistical inference was somewhat unrealistic because the population had only six individuals. Consider a practical example of a prospective racquetball entrepreneur who wishes to estimate the average number of days players participate in this sport each week. When statistical inference is needed, the population mean, μ, is a constant but unknown parameter. To estimate the average number of playing days, we could take a sample of three hundred racquetball players throughout the area where our entrepreneur is thinking of building club facilities. If the sample mean, $\overline{X}$, equals 2.6 days per week, we might use this figure as a **point estimate**. This single value, 2.6, would be the best estimate of the population mean. However, we would be extremely lucky if the sample estimate were exactly the same as the population value. A less risky alternative would be to calculate a confidence interval.

point estimate

An estimate of the population mean in the form of a single value, usually the sample mean.

Confidence Intervals

If we specify a range of numbers, or interval, within which the population mean should lie, we can be more confident that our inference is correct. A **confidence interval estimate** is based on the knowledge that $\mu = \overline{X} \pm$ a small sampling error. After calculating an interval estimate, we can determine how probable it is that the population mean will fall within this range of statistical values. In the racquetball project, the researcher, after setting up a confidence interval, would be able to make a statement such as "With 95 percent confidence, I think that the average number of days played per week is between 2.3 and 2.9." This information can be used to estimate market demand because the researcher has a certain confidence that the interval contains the value of the true population mean.

The crux of the problem for a researcher is to determine how much random sampling error to tolerate. In other words, what should the confidence interval be? How much of a gamble should be taken that μ will be included in the range? Do we need to be 80 percent, 90 percent,

confidence interval estimate

A specified range of numbers within which a population mean is expected to lie; an estimate of the population mean based on the knowledge that it will be equal to the sample mean plus or minus a small sampling error.

or 99 percent sure? The **confidence level** is a percentage or decimal that indicates the long-run probability that the results will be correct. Traditionally, researchers have used the 95 percent confidence level. While there is nothing magical about the 95 percent confidence level, it is useful to select this confidence level in our examples.

As mentioned, the point estimate gives no information about the possible magnitude of random sampling error. The confidence interval gives the estimated value of the population parameter, plus or minus an estimate of the error. We can express the idea of the confidence interval as follows:

$$\mu = \overline{X} \pm \text{a small sampling error}$$

More formally, assuming that the researchers select a large sample (more than thirty observations), the small sampling error is given by

$$\text{Small sampling error} = Z_{c.l.}\, S_{\overline{X}}$$

where

$Z_{c.l.}$ = value of Z, or standardized normal variable, at a specified confidence level ($c.l.$)

$S_{\overline{X}}$ = standard error of the mean

The precision of our estimate is indicated by the value of $Z_{c.l.}\, S_{\overline{X}}$. It is useful to define the range of possible error, E, as follows:

$$E = Z_{c.l.}\, S_{\overline{X}}$$

Thus,

$$\mu = \overline{X} \pm E$$

where

$\overline{X}$ = sample mean (commonly pronounced X-bar)

E = range of sampling error

or

$$\mu = \overline{X} \pm Z_{c.l.}S_{\overline{X}}$$

The expression of "confidence" using $\pm E$ is stated as one–half of the total confidence interval. One half of the interval is less than the mean and the other half is greater than the mean.

The following step-by-step procedure can be used to calculate confidence intervals:

1. Calculate $\overline{X}$ from the sample.
2. Assuming σ is unknown, estimate the population standard deviation by finding S, the sample standard deviation.
3. Estimate the standard error of the mean, using the following formula:

$$S_{\overline{X}} = \frac{S}{\sqrt{n}}$$

4. Determine the Z-value associated with the desired confidence level. The confidence level should be divided by 2 to determine what percentage of the area under the curve to include on each side of the mean.
5. Calculate the confidence interval.

The following example shows how calculation of a confidence interval can be used in preparing a demographic profile, a useful tool for market segmentation. Suppose you plan to open a sporting goods store to cater to working women who play golf. In a survey of 100 women in your market area, you find that the mean age ($\overline{X}$) is 37.5 years, with a standard deviation (S) of 12.0 years. Even though 37.5 years is the "expected value" and the best guess for the true mean age in the population (μ), the likelihood is that the mean is not exactly 37.5. Thus, a confidence interval around the sample mean computed using the steps just given will be useful:

1. $\overline{X} = 37.5$ years

2. $S = 12.0$ years

3. $S_{\overline{X}} = \dfrac{12.0}{\sqrt{100}} = 1.2$

4. Suppose you wish to be 95 percent confident—that is, assured that 95 times out of 100, the estimates from your sample will include the population parameter. Including 95 percent of the area requires that 47.5 percent (one-half of 95 percent) of the distribution on each side be included. From the Z-table (Table A.1 in the appendix), you find that 0.475 corresponds to the Z-value 1.96.

5. Substitute the values for $Z_{c.l.}$ and $S_{\overline{X}}$ into the confidence interval formula:

$$\mu = 37.5 \pm (1.96)(1.2)$$
$$= 37.5 \pm 2.352$$

You can thus expect that μ is contained in the range from 35.15 to 39.85 years. Intervals constructed in this manner will contain the true value of μ 95 percent of the time.

Step 3 can be eliminated by entering S and n directly in the confidence interval formula:

$$\mu = \overline{X} \pm Z_{c.l.} \frac{S}{\sqrt{n}}$$

Remember that $S/\sqrt{n}$ represents the standard error of the mean, $S_{\overline{X}}$. Its use is based on the central-limit theorem.

If you wanted to increase the probability that the population mean will lie within the confidence interval, you could use the 99 percent confidence level, with a Z-value of 2.57. You may want to calculate the 99 percent confidence interval for the preceding example; you can expect that μ will be in the range between 34.416 and 40.584 years.

We have now examined the basic concepts of inferential statistics. You should understand that sample statistics such as the sample means, $\overline{X}$s, can provide good estimates of population parameters such as μ. You should also realize that there is a certain probability of being in error when you estimate a population parameter from sample statistics. In other words, there will be a random sampling error, which is the difference between the survey results and the results of surveying the entire population. If you have a firm understanding of these basic terms and ideas, which are the essence of statistics, the remaining statistics concepts will be relatively simple for you. Several ramifications of the simple ideas presented so far will permit you to make better decisions about populations based on surveys or experiments. The Research Snapshot on the next page shows how simple descriptive statistics can be used to contrast Wal-Mart and Target shoppers.

Sample Size ⬅

Random Error and Sample Size

When asked to evaluate a marketing research project, most people, even those with little marketing research training, begin by asking, "How big was the sample?" Intuitively we know that the larger the sample, the more accurate the research. This is in fact a statistical truth; random sampling error varies with samples of different sizes. In statistical terms, increasing the sample size decreases the width of the confidence interval at a given confidence level. When the standard deviation of the population is unknown, a confidence interval is calculated using the following formula:

$$\text{Confidence interval} = \overline{X} \pm Z\frac{S}{\sqrt{n}}$$

Observe that the equation for the plus or minus error factor in the confidence interval includes n, the sample size:

$$E = Z\frac{S}{\sqrt{n}}$$

Target and Wal-Mart Shoppers Really Are Different

Scarborough Research conducts ongoing consumer research that combines a telephone interview on media behavior with mail and Internet surveys about shopping habits and lifestyle to provide detailed data about television viewing and other consumer habits. They measure continuously and present reports periodically. Scarborough recognizes the importance of sample size for minimizing errors. The result is a sample including over 220,000 adults in 81 designated market areas used to estimate characteristics of the U.S. population.

An example is a comparison of consumers who shop exclusively at either Target or Wal-Mart. When respondents were asked to identify the stores at which they had shopped during the preceding three months, the largest share (40 percent) named both Target and Wal-Mart. However, 31 percent shopped at Wal-Mart but not Target, and 12 percent shopped at Target but not Wal-Mart. Scarborough compared the consumer behavior of the latter two groups.

Target shoppers who shunned Wal-Mart were more likely to shop at more upscale stores, including Macy's and Nordstrom. They also were more likely than the average shopper to visit many different stores. To a Target-only shopper, value is defined by quality and choice. Wal-Mart shoppers who stayed away from Target were more likely to shop at discounters such as Dollar General and Kmart, and they were more likely to be at least 50 years old. Wal-Mart shoppers define value in a utilitarian way by emphasizing price and convenience. Target-only shoppers tended to be younger and were more likely to have a high household income.

Given a U.S. adult population of approximately 240 million, do you think the sample size is adequate to make these comparisons?

Source: Based on Scarborough Research, "In the Battle for Discount Shoppers, Target and Wal-Mart Find Brand Loyalty in Different Customer Groups," news release (September 19, 2005), http://www.scarborough.com, accessed September 24, 2008; Scarborough Research, "About Scarborough: Methodology," http://www.scarborough.com, accessed September 24, 2008.

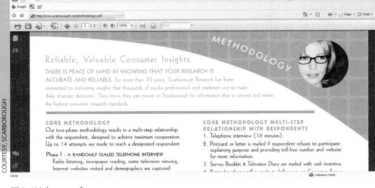

This Web page from Scarborough defines its survey methodology in some detail. Information about the sample size is included.

If n increases, E is reduced. Exhibit 17.18 illustrates that the confidence interval (or magnitude of error) decreases as the sample size, n, increases.

We already noted that it is not necessary to take a census of all elements of the population to conduct an accurate study. The laws of probability give investigators sufficient confidence

EXHIBIT 17.18

Relationship between Sample Size and Error

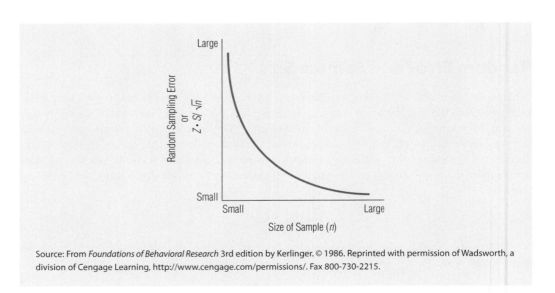

Source: From *Foundations of Behavioral Research* 3rd edition by Kerlinger. © 1986. Reprinted with permission of Wadsworth, a division of Cengage Learning, http://www.cengage.com/permissions/. Fax 800-730-2215.

regarding the accuracy of data collected from a sample. Knowledge of the characteristics of the sampling distribution helps researchers make reasonably precise estimates.

Students familiar with the law of diminishing returns in economics will easily grasp the concept that increases in sample size reduce sampling error at a *decreasing rate*. For example, doubling a sample of 1,000 will reduce random sampling error by 1 percentage point, but doubling the sample from 2,000 to 4,000 will reduce random sampling error by only another half percentage point. More technically, random sampling error is inversely proportional to the square root of *n*. (Exhibit 17.18 gives an approximation of the relationship between sample size and error.) Thus, the main issue becomes one of determining the optimal sample size.

Factors in Determining Sample Size for Questions Involving Means

Three factors are required to specify sample size: (1) the variance, or heterogeneity, of the population; (2) the magnitude of acceptable error; and (3) the confidence level. Suppose a researcher wishes to find out whether nine-year-old boys are taller than four-year-old boys. Intuitively we know that even with a very small sample size, the correct information probably will be obtained. This is based on the fact that the determination of sample size depends on the research question and the variability within the sample.

The *variance*, or *heterogeneity*, of the population is the first necessary bit of information. In statistical terms, this refers to the *standard deviation* of the population. Only a small sample is required if the population is homogeneous. For example, predicting the average age of graduate students requires a smaller sample than predicting the average age of people who visit the zoo. As *heterogeneity* increases, so must sample size. A pharmaceutical company testing the effectiveness of an acne medicine, for instance, should require a sample large enough to account for the varying range of skin types.

The *magnitude of error*, or the confidence interval, is the second necessary bit of information. Defined in statistical terms as *E,* the magnitude of error indicates how precise the estimate must be. It indicates a certain precision level. From a managerial perspective, the importance of the decision in terms of profitability will influence the researcher's specifications of the range of error. If, for example, favorable results from a test-market sample will result in the construction of a new plant and unfavorable results will dictate not marketing the product, the acceptable range of error probably will be small; the cost of an error would be too great to allow much room for random sampling errors. In other cases, the estimate need not be extremely precise. Allowing an error of $\pm\$1,000$ in total family income instead of $E = \pm50$ may be acceptable in most market segmentation studies.

The third factor of concern is the *confidence level*. In our examples, we will typically use the 95 percent confidence level. This, however, is an arbitrary decision based on convention; there is nothing sacred about the 0.05 chance level (that is, the probability of 0.05 of the true population parameter being incorrectly estimated). Exhibit 17.19 summarizes the information required to determine sample size.

EXHIBIT 17.19 **Statistical Information Needed to Determine Sample Size for Questions Involving Means**

Variable	Symbol	Typical Source of Information
Standard deviation	S	Pilot study or rule of thumb
Magnitude of error	E	Managerial judgment or calculation ($Z S_{\bar{x}}$)
Confidence level	$Z_{c.l.}$	Managerial judgment

Estimating Sample Size for Questions Involving Means

Once the preceding concepts are understood, determining the actual size for a simple random sample is quite easy. The researcher must follow three steps:

1. Estimate the standard deviation of the population.
2. Make a judgment about the allowable magnitude of error.
3. Determine a confidence level.

The only problem is estimating the standard deviation of the population. Ideally, similar studies conducted in the past will give a basis for judging the standard deviation. In practice, researchers who lack prior information conduct a pilot study to estimate the population parameters so that another, larger sample of the appropriate sample size may be drawn. This procedure is called *sequential sampling* because researchers take an initial look at the pilot study results before deciding on a larger sample to provide more precise information.

A rule of thumb for estimating the value of the standard deviation is to expect it to be one-sixth of the range. If researchers conducting a study on television purchases expected the price paid to range from $100 to $700, a rule-of-thumb estimate for the standard deviation would be $100.

For the moment, assume that the standard deviation has been estimated in some preliminary work. If our concern is to estimate the mean of a particular population, the formula for sample size is

$$n = \left(\frac{ZS}{E}\right)^2$$

where

Z = standardized value that corresponds to the confidence level

S = sample standard deviation or estimate of the population standard deviation

E = acceptable error amount, plus or minus error factor (recall the range is one-half of the total confidence interval)[8]

Suppose a survey researcher studying annual expenditures on lipstick wishes to have a 95 percent confidence level ($Z = 1.96$) and a range of error (E) of less than $2. If the estimate of the standard deviation is $29, the sample size can be calculated as follows:

$$n = \left(\frac{ZS}{E}\right)^2 = \left(\frac{(1.96)(29)}{2}\right)^2 = \left(\frac{56.84}{2}\right)^2 = 28.42^2 = 808$$

If a range of error (E) of $4 is acceptable, sample size can be reduced:

$$n = \left(\frac{ZS}{E}\right)^2 = \left(\frac{(1.96)(29)}{4}\right)^2 = \left(\frac{56.84}{4}\right)^2 = 14.21^2 = 202$$

Thus, doubling the range of acceptable error reduces sample size requirements dramatically. Stated conversely in a general sense, doubling sample size will reduce error by only approximately one-quarter. Thus, the added precision may often not be worth the added costs.

Population Size and Sample Size

The ACNielsen Company estimates television ratings. Throughout the years, it has been plagued with questions about how it is possible to rate 100 million plus television homes with a sample of approximately 5,000 households. The answer to that question is that in most cases the size of the population does not have a major effect on the sample size. As we have indicated, the variance of the population has the largest effect on sample size. However, a finite correction factor may be needed to adjust a sample size that is more than 5 percent of a finite population. If the sample is large relative to the population, the foregoing procedures may overestimate sample size, and the researcher may need to adjust sample size. The finite correction factor is:

$$\sqrt{\frac{(N-n)}{(N-1)}}$$

where

N = population size

n = sample size.

Determining Sample Size for Proportions

Researchers frequently are concerned with determining sample size for problems that involve estimating population proportions or percentages. When the question involves the estimation of a proportion, the researcher requires some knowledge of the logic for determining a confidence interval around a sample proportion estimation (p) of the population proportion (π). For a confidence interval to be constructed around the sample proportion (p), an estimate of the standard error of the proportion (S_p) must be calculated and a confidence level specified.

The precision of the estimate is indicated by the value $Z_{c.l.}S_p$. Thus, the plus-or-minus estimate of the population proportion is

$$\text{Confidence interval} = p \pm Z_{c.l.}S_p$$

If the researcher selects a 95 percent probability for the confidence interval, $Z_{c.l.}$ will equal 1.96 (see Table A.1 in the appendix). The formula for S_p is

$$S_p = \sqrt{\frac{pq}{n}} \text{ or } S_p = \sqrt{\frac{p(1-p)}{n}}$$

where

S_p = estimate of the standard error of the proportion

p = proportion of successes

$q = 1 - p$, or proportion of failures

Suppose that 20 percent of a sample of 1,200 television viewers recall seeing an advertisement. The proportion of successes (p) equals 0.2, and the proportion of failures (q) equals 0.8. We estimate the 95 percent confidence interval as follows:

$$\text{Confidence Interval} = p \pm Z_{c.l.}S_p$$

$$= 0.2 \pm 1.96 S_p$$

$$= 0.2 \pm 1.96\sqrt{\frac{p(1-p)}{n}}$$

$$= 0.2 \pm 1.96\sqrt{\frac{0.2(1-0.2)}{1,200}}$$

$$= 0.2 \pm 1.96\sqrt{\frac{0.16}{1,200}}$$

$$= 0.2 \pm 1.96(0.0115)$$

$$= 0.2 \pm 0.023$$

Thus, the population proportion who see an advertisement is estimated to be included in the interval between 0.177 (0.2 − 0.023) and 0.223 (0.2 + 0.023), or roughly between 18 and 22 percent, with 95 percent confidence (95 out of 100 times).

Sample size for a proportion requires the researcher to make a judgment about confidence level and the maximum allowance for random sampling error. Furthermore, the size of the proportion influences random sampling error, so an estimate of the expected proportion of successes must be made, based on intuition or prior information. The formula is

$$n = \frac{Z_{c.l.}^2 \, pq}{E^2}$$

where

n = number of items in sample

$Z_{c.l.}^2$ = square of the confidence level in standard error units

p = estimated proportion of successes

$q = 1 - p$, or estimated proportion of failures

E^2 = square of the maximum allowance for error between the true proportion and the sample proportion, or $Z_{c.l.}S_p$ squared

Suppose a researcher believes that a simple random sample will show that 60 percent of the population (p) recognizes the name of an automobile dealership. The researcher wishes to estimate with 95 percent confidence ($Z_{c.l.} = 1.96$) that the allowance for sampling error is not greater than 3.5 percentage points (E). Substituting these values into the formula gives

$$n = \frac{(1.96)^2(0.6)(0.4)}{0.035^2}$$

$$= \frac{(3.8416)(0.24)}{0.001225}$$

$$= \frac{0.922}{0.001225}$$

$$= 753$$

Calculating Sample Size for Sample Proportions

In practice, a number of tables have been constructed for determining sample size. Exhibit 17.20 illustrates a sample size table for problems that involve sample proportions (p).

The theoretical principles underlying calculation of sample sizes of proportions are similar to the concepts discussed in this chapter. Suppose we wish to take samples in two large cities, New Orleans and Miami. We wish no more than 2 percentage points of error, and we will be satisfied with a 95 percent confidence level (see Exhibit 17.20). If we assume all other things are equal, then in the New Orleans market, where 15 percent of the consumers favor our product and 85 percent prefer competitors' brands, we need a sample of 1,222 to get results with only 2 percentage points of error. In the Miami market, however, where 30 percent of the consumers favor our brand and 70 percent prefer other brands (a less heterogeneous market), we need a sample size of 2,009 to get the same sample reliability.

Exhibit 17.21 on page 466 shows a sampling error table typical of those that accompany research proposals or reports. Most studies will estimate more than one parameter. Thus, in a survey of 100 people in which 50 percent agree with one statement and 10 percent with another, the sampling error is expected to be 10 and 6 percentage points of error, respectively.

Determining Sample Size on the Basis of Judgment

Just as sample units may be selected to suit the convenience or judgment of the researcher, sample size may also be determined on the basis of managerial judgments. Using a sample size similar to those used in previous studies provides the inexperienced researcher with a comparison with other researchers' judgments.

Another judgmental factor that affects the determination of sample size is the selection of the appropriate item, question, or characteristic to be used for the sample size calculations. Several different characteristics affect most studies, and the desired degree of precision may vary for these items. The researcher must exercise some judgment to determine which item will be used. Often

EXHIBIT 17.20 **Selected Tables for Determining Sample Size When the Characteristic of Interest Is a Proportion**

| Size of Population | Sample Size for a 95 Percent Confidence Level when Parameter in Population Is Assumed to Be over 70 Percent or under 30 Percent | | | |
| | Reliability | | | |
	±1% Point	±2% Points	±3% Points	±5% Points
1,000	a	a	473	244
2,000	a	a	619	278
3,000	a	1,206	690	291
4,000	a	1,341	732	299
5,000	a	1,437	760	303
10,000	4,465	1,678	823	313
20,000	5,749	1,832	858	318
50,000	6,946	1,939	881	321
100,000	7,465	1,977	888	321
500,000 to ∞	7,939	2,009	895	322

| Size of Population | Sample Size for a 95 Percent Confidence Level when Parameter in Population Is Assumed to Be over 85 Percent or under 15 Percent | | | |
| | Reliability | | | |
	±1% Point	±2% Points	±3% Points	±5% Points
1,000	a	a	353	235
2,000	a	760	428	266
3,000	a	890	461	278
4,000	a	938	479	284
5,000	a	984	491	289
10,000	3,288	1,091	516	297
20,000	3,935	1,154	530	302
50,000	4,461	1,195	538	304
100,000	4,669	1,210	541	305
500,000 to ∞	4,850	1,222	544	306

[a]In these cases, more than 50 percent of the population is required in the sample. Since the normal approximation of the hypergeometric distribution is a poor approximation in such instances, no sample value is given.

Source: Nan Lin, *Foundations of Social Research* (New York: McGraw-Hill, 1976), p. 447. Copyright © 1976 by Nan Lin. Used with permission.

the item that will produce the largest sample size will be used to determine the ultimate sample size. However, the cost of data collection becomes a major consideration, and judgment must be exercised regarding the importance of such information.

Another consideration stems from most researchers' need to analyze various subgroups within the sample. For example, suppose an analyst wishes to look at differences in retailers' attitudes by geographic region. The analyst will want to make sure to sample an adequate number of retailers in the New England, Mid-Atlantic, and South Atlantic regions to ensure that subgroup

- Measures of central tendency are often used.
  - The mean is the most commonly used measure of central tendency.
  - The median is more appropriate than the mean as a measure of central tendency when the data display extreme values or outliers.
  - The mode is most appropriate as a measure of central tendency when the data are less than interval.
- Sample size estimates often require some estimate of the standard deviation that will exist in the sample.
  - A rule of thumb for estimating the standard deviation is that it will be about one-sixth of the expected range.
- Larger samples allow predictions with greater precision that can be expressed over a smaller range.

- Increases in precision usually require disproportionately large increases in sample size.
  - Larger samples require more resources.
- The amount of risk involved in a decision should be strongly considered in making decisions about the sample.
  - Only the riskiest of decisions require very large samples (i.e., thousands of respondents).
  - Samples of 300–500 respondents can provide adequate results for many marketing decisions that do not involve extremely high risk.

© GEORGE DOYLE & CIARAN GRIFFIN

EXHIBIT 17.21 **Allowance for Random Sampling Error (Plus and Minus Percentage Points) at 95 Percent Confidence Level**

Response	Sample Size						
	2,500	1,500	1,000	500	250	100	50
10 (90)	1.2	1.5	2.0	3.0	4.0	6.0	8.0
20 (80)	1.6	2.0	2.5	4.0	5.0	8.0	11.0
30 (70)	1.8	2.5	3.0	4.0	6.0	9.0	13.0
40 (60)	2.0	2.5	3.0	4.0	6.0	10.0	14.0
50 (50)	2.0	2.5	3.0	4.0	6.0	10.0	14.0

Source: Nan Lin, *Foundations of Social Research* (New York: McGraw-Hill, 1976).

comparisons are reliable. There is a judgmental rule of thumb for selecting minimum subgroup sample size: Each subgroup to be separately analyzed should have a minimum of 100 units in each category of the major breakdowns. With this procedure, the total sample size is computed by totaling the sample sizes necessary for these subgroups.

Determining Sample Size for Stratified and Other Probability Samples

Stratified sampling involves drawing separate probability samples within the subgroups to make the sample more efficient. With a stratified sample, the sample variances are expected to differ by strata. This makes the determination of sample size more complex. Increased complexity may also characterize the determination of sample size for cluster sampling and other probability sampling methods. The formulas are beyond the scope of this book. Students interested in these advanced sampling techniques should investigate advanced sampling textbooks.

Summary

1. Use descriptive statistics indicating central tendency and dispersion to make inferences about a population. Calculating a mean and a standard deviation to "describe" or profile a sample is a commonly applied descriptive statistical approach. Inferential statistics investigate samples to draw conclusions about entire populations. If a mean is computed and then compared to some preconceived standard, then inferential statistics are being implemented. A frequency distribution shows how frequently each response or classification occurs. A simple tally count illustrates a frequency distribution. A proportion indicates the percentage of group members that have a particular characteristic. Three measures of central tendency are commonly used: the mean, the median, and the mode. These three values may differ, and care must be taken to understand distortions that may arise from using the wrong measure of central tendency. Measures of dispersion further describe a distribution. The range is the difference between the largest and smallest values observed. The most useful measures of dispersion are the variance and standard deviation.

2. Distinguish among population, sample, and sampling distributions. The techniques of statistical inference are based on the relationship among the population distribution, the sample distribution, and the sampling distribution. The population distribution is a frequency distribution of the elements of a population. The sample distribution is a frequency distribution of a sample. A sampling distribution is a theoretical probability distribution of sample means for all possible samples of a certain size drawn from a particular population. The sampling distribution's mean is the expected value of the mean, which equals the population's mean. The standard deviation of the sampling distribution is the standard error of the mean, approximately equal to the standard deviation of the population, divided by the square root of the sample size.

3. Explain the central-limit theorem. The central-limit theorem states that as sample size increases, the distribution of sample means of size n, randomly selected, approaches a normal distribution. This means that even if some distribution has some non-normal distribution, the distribution of averages taken from samples of these numbers is normally distributed. This allows inferential statistics to be used. This theoretical knowledge can be used to estimate parameters and determine sample size.

4. Use confidence intervals to express population estimates. Estimating a population mean with a single value gives a point estimate. The confidence interval estimate is a range of numbers within which the researcher is confident that the population mean will lie. The confidence level is a percentage that indicates the long-run probability that the confidence interval estimate will be correct. Many research problems involve the estimation of proportions. Statistical techniques may be used to determine a confidence interval around a sample proportion.

5. Understand the major issues in specifying sample size. The statistical determination of sample size requires knowledge of (1) the variance of the population, (2) the magnitude of acceptable error, and (3) the confidence level. Several computational formulas are available for determining sample size. Furthermore, a number of easy-to-use tables have been compiled to help researchers calculate sample size. The main reason a large sample size is desirable is that sample size is related to random sampling error. A smaller sample makes a larger error in estimates more likely. Calculation of sample size for a sample proportion is not difficult. However, most researchers use tables that indicate predetermined sample sizes.

Key Terms and Concepts

central-limit theorem, *453*
confidence interval estimate, *457*
confidence level, *458*
frequency distribution, *441*
mean, *443*
median, *444*
mode, *445*
normal distribution, *448–449*

percentage distribution, *442*
point estimate, *457*
population distribution, *452*
population parameters, *441*
probability, *442*
proportion, *442*
sample distribution, *452*
sample statistics, *441*

sampling distribution, *452*
standard deviation, *447*
standard error of the mean, *452*
standardized normal distribution, *449*
top-box score, *442*
variance, *447*

Questions for Review and Critical Thinking

1. What is the difference between descriptive and inferential statistics?
2. Suppose the speed limits in thirteen countries in miles per hour are as follows:

Country	Highway Miles per Hour
Italy	87
France	82
Hungary	75
Belgium	75
Portugal	75
Great Britain	70
Spain	62
Denmark	62
Netherlands	62
Greece	62
Japan	62
Norway	56
Turkey	56

What is the mean, median, and mode for these data? Feel free to use your computer (statistical software or spreadsheet) to get the answer. Which is the best measure of central tendency for this data?

3. Prepare a frequency distribution for the data in question 2.
4. Why is the standard deviation rather than the average deviation typically used?
5. Calculate the standard deviation for the data in question 2.
6. Draw three distributions that have the same mean value but different standard deviation values. Draw three distributions that have the same standard deviation value but different mean values.
7. A manufacturer of MP3 players surveyed one hundred retail stores in each of the firm's sales regions. An analyst noticed that in the South Atlantic region the average retail price was $165 (mean) and the standard deviation was $30. However, in the Mid-Atlantic region the mean price was $170, with a standard deviation of $15. What do these statistics tell us about these two sales regions?
8. What is the sampling distribution? How does it differ from the sample distribution?
9. What would happen to the sampling distribution of the mean if we increased sample size from 5 to 25?
10. Suppose a fast-food restaurant wishes to estimate average sales volume for a new menu item. The restaurant has analyzed the sales of the item at a similar outlet and observed the following results:

$$\overline{X} = 500 \text{ (mean daily sales)}$$
$$S = 100 \text{ (standard deviation of sample)}$$
$$n = 25 \text{ (sample size)}$$

The restaurant manager wants to know into what range the mean daily sales should fall 95 percent of the time. Perform this calculation.

11. In the example on page 452 of research on lipstick, where $E = \$2$ and $S = \$29$, what sample size would we require if we desired a 99 percent confidence level?
12. Suppose you are planning to sample cat owners to determine the average number of cans of cat food they purchase monthly. The following standards have been set: a confidence level of 99 percent and an error of less than 5 units. Past research has indicated that the standard deviation should be 6 units. What is the required sample size?
13. In a survey of 500 people, 60 percent responded positively to an attitude question. Calculate a confidence interval at 95 percent to get an interval estimate for a proportion.
14. What is a standardized normal curve?
15. A researcher expects the population proportion of Cubs fans in Chicago to be 80 percent. The researcher wishes to have an error of less than 5 percent and to be 95 percent confident of an estimate to be made from a mail survey. What sample size is required?
16. ETHICS Using the formula in this chapter, a researcher determines that at the 95 percent confidence level, a sample of 2,500 is required to satisfy a client's requirements. The researcher actually uses a sample of 1,200, however, because the client has specified a budget cap for the survey. What are the ethical considerations in this situation?
17. 'NET Go to http://www.dartmouth.edu/~chance/ to visit the Chance course. The Chance course is an innovative program to creatively teach introductory materials about probability and statistics. The Chance course is designed to enhance quantitative literacy. Numerous videos can be played online.
18. 'NET Go to http://www.researchinfo.com. Click on "Market Research Calculators." Which of the calculators can be used to help find the sample size required? How big of a sample is needed to make an inference about the U.S. population +/−5 percent? How large a sample is needed to make an inference about the population of Norway +/−5 percent? Remember, population statistics can be found in the CIA World Factbook online. Comment.
19. 'NET A random number generator and other statistical information can be found at http://www.random.org. Flip some virtual coins. Perform 20 flips with an Aurelian coin. Perform 20 flips with a Constatius coin. Perform frequency tables for each result. What conclusion might you draw? Would the result change if you flipped the coins 200 times or 2,000 times?

Research Activities

1. 'NET Go to http://www.surveypro.com. Click on pricing. Write a brief report that describes how prices are charged to someone wishing to use this service to host a survey. What happens as the desired sample size increases? Why is this?
2. 'NET Use an online library service to find basic business research studies that report a "response rate" or number of respondents compared to number of contacts. You may wish to consult journals such as the *Journal of Business Research*, the *Journal of Marketing*, the *Journal of the Academy of Marketing Science* or the *Journal of Personal Selling and Sales Management*. Find at least 25 such studies. What is the average response rate across all of these studies? Do there appear to be any trends or factors that are associated with lower response rates? Write a brief report on your findings.

Case 17.1 Pointsec Mobile Technologies

When salespeople, construction supervisors, managers, and other employees are away from the workplace, many of them carry mobile devices such as laptop computers and PDAs, often containing valuable, private data related to their jobs. Pointsec provides security systems to protect such data. To bring home the vulnerability of mobile devices, Pointsec decided to share information about the number of such devices left behind in taxis.[9]

The research involved conducting a survey of taxi drivers. Staff members at Pointsec's public relations firm called major taxi companies in nine cities in Australia, Denmark, Finland, France, Germany, Norway, Sweden, Great Britain, and the United States. Each of the cooperating companies put these interviewers in touch with about one hundred drivers. Drivers were asked how many devices of each type—cell phones, PDAs, computers, and so on—had been left in their cab over the preceding six months. From these numbers, they came up with the rate of items left behind. Multiplying by the size of taxi fleets in each city, the researchers came up with city-by-city numbers: 3.42 cell phones per cab yielded 85,619 cell phones left behind in Chicago, for example. In London, the researchers concluded 63,135 cell phones were left in cabs, a startling increase of 71 percent compared to four years earlier.

Questions

1. Discuss why the sampling method and sample size make these results questionable, even though the numbers were reported as if they were precise.
2. The simple survey method described in the case may have been sufficient as a way to draw attention to the issue of data security. However, if the company were using data on lost mobile devices to predict demand for a product, accuracy might be more significant. Imagine that you have been asked to collect data on mobile devices left in cabs, and you wish to be able to report results with a 95 percent confidence level. How can you improve the sample design and select an appropriate sample size?

Case 17.2 Coastal Star Sales Corporation

Download the data sets for this case from www .cengage.com/marketing/zikmund *or request them from your instructor.*

Coastal Star Sales Corporation is a West Coast wholesaler that markets leisure products from several manufacturers. Coastal Star has an 80-person sales force that sells to wholesalers in a six-state area, which is divided into two sales regions. Case Exhibit 17.2−1 shows the names of a sample of eleven salespeople, some descriptive information about each person, and sales performance for each of the last two years.

Questions

1. Calculate a mean and a standard deviation for each variable.
2. Set a 95 percent confidence interval around the mean for each variable.
3. Calculate the median, mode, and range for each variable.
4. Organize the data for current sales into a frequency distribution with three classes: (a) under $500,000, (b) $500,000 to $999,999, and (c) $1,000,000 and over.
5. Organize the data for years of selling experience into a frequency distribution with two classes: (a) less than five years and (b) five or more years.
6. Convert the frequency distributions from question 5 to percentage distributions.

CASE EXHIBIT 17.2–1 **Salesperson Data: Coastal Star Sales Corporation**

Region	Salesperson	Age	Years of Experience	Sales Previous Year	Sales Current Year
Northern	Jackson	40	7	$ 412,744	$ 411,007
Northern	Gentry	60	12	1,491,024	1,726,630
Northern	La Forge	26	2	301,421	700,112
Northern	Miller	39	1	401,241	471,001
Northern	Mowen	64	5	448,160	449,261
Southern	Young	51	2	518,897	519,412
Southern	Fisk	34	1	846,222	713,333
Southern	Kincaid	62	10	1,527,124	2,009,041
Southern	Krieger	42	3	921,174	1,030,000
Southern	Manzer	64	5	463,399	422,798
Southern	Weiner	27	2	548,011	422,001

CHAPTER 18
FIELDWORK

LEARNING OUTCOMES

After studying this chapter, you should be able to

1. Describe the role and job requirements of fieldworkers
2. Summarize the skills to cover when training inexperienced interviewers
3. List principles of good interviewing
4. Describe the activities involved in the management of fieldworkers
5. Discuss how supervisors should minimize errors in the field

Chapter Vignette: Game's the Same, but the "Field" Is Changing!

Recent economic times are putting more and more pressure on all areas of business to lower costs, including marketing research. Fieldwork is needed to gather information. But more and more, companies are considering the techniques of fieldwork and whether or not information that is comparable in quality can be obtained from some less expensive technique. One result is that less and less fieldwork actually involves in-person interviews. New technologies enable call centers, often outsourced in places where labor is cheap, to conduct phone interviews in an economical fashion.

Even better, the Internet represents a technology that brings the cost per interview down to a small fraction of that of a face-to-face interview. As recently as 1990, no research was conducted online. By 2005, 11 percent of market research data was obtained online. By 2008, that number had reached 20 percent and shows no sign of decreasing. This trend is, at least in part, driven by companies freezing or cutting their marketing research budget, and in part by researchers who have learned how to obtain valid responses through this medium.[1]

These trends have a number of implications for the fieldworker and for marketing research firms. The implication for the research firm is the need to identify relationships with new partners who help with the fieldwork. While many research firms commonly outsourced their fieldwork to specialty research companies, even more are now outsourcing their online survey hosting to specialty companies like Qualtrix, Zoomerang, or Survey Monkey. In some instances, fieldwork that used to take hundreds of hours of personal interviews costing thousands of dollars can now be practically automated using online survey hosting and electronic distribution lists.

The implications for the fieldworker are also critical. Obviously, fewer fieldworkers are needed for any given number of interviews. The emphasis becomes more on validating online responses or following up when a problem occurs. A fieldworker will need to be able to understand the control mechanisms available to online research, such as checking surveys for accuracy by examining the time a respondent spent filling out the survey or checking to ensure a respondent didn't simply click down the right side on every question.

Of course, the drive to cut down costs via automation can yield unwanted results. The move toward online research can hamstring value-added research methods. For example, probing techniques such as the silent probe and asking a neutral question to ensure that a respondent understands the question are increasingly difficult or impossible using structured online research methods. Follow-up must come through some other form or the structured responses need to be enhanced with qualitative data collection which also is increasingly done via the Internet.

The lack of ability to visually size up a respondent has inevitable drawbacks. One fieldworker lamented what he perceived to be the poor quality of online research querying physicians about prescribing behavior. He recalls this situation: During a fast-paced personal interview, a physician said that "Each of us has a computer on his desk and we use these for literature searches and to check for dosing, side effects, and possible drug interactions before writing a prescription." On the way out of the office, the fieldworker notices that an obviously often-used, dog-eared copy of *Drug Facts and Comparisons* (a prescription drug encyclopedia of sorts) was among the stack of materials taken to the examining room station—where no computer was located. Clearly, if left to a simple one-shot face-to-face interview, the data would show that this physician always checks his computer before prescribing medication when in fact, this is not the case. If left to an Internet survey, this valuable piece of information would have remained a secret! So, this is one fieldworker who really wants back on the old field!

Introduction

When primary data collection is undertaken, somebody eventually has to record answers to questions. This could come in the form of a telephone interview, a Web survey or by observing the actions of a consumer. In any event, work must be done in the field. Thus, fieldwork is a big part of marketing research.

A recent survey sponsored by Dell addressed an issue related to information security—lost laptop computers. Imagine the researcher who has to determine the best way to estimate the number of laptops lost or stolen and the particular characteristics associated with losing a laptop. Eventually, Dell worked with Ponemon Institute (**http://www.ponemon.org**), an organization interested in information security, in implementing a laptop study.[2] The study involved traditional field research interviewing employees and customers at 106 airports in practically every part of the United States. Estimates suggest that of over 12,000 laptop computers lost or stolen each week in the United States, less than half are recovered. Surprisingly, only one-third that are simply left behind at airport security, in flight lounges, or in planes accidentally, are ever recovered by their forgetful owners. This fieldwork is vital when one considers the enormous amounts of information, some of it potentially sensitive, contained on all those lost or stolen laptops. Further, a comprehensive study of this type still eventually requires putting people on the ground, or in the field, to measure market phenomena.

The Research Snapshot on page 473 provides a brief overview of a firm specializing in designing, implementing and supervising marketing research work in the field.

Who Conducts the Fieldwork? Fieldworkers Do!

A personal interviewer administering a questionnaire door to door, a telephone interviewer calling from a central location, an observer counting pedestrians in a shopping mall, a census worker or enumerator who goes door to door to count people, and others involved in the collection of data and the supervision of that process—each of these people is a **fieldworker**. Fieldworkers gather research information and data in the field. The activities they perform vary substantially. The supervision of data collection for a mail survey differs from that for an observation study as much as the factory production process for cereal differs from that for a pair of ski boots. Yet, just as quality control is basic to each production operation, the same basic issues arise in the various types of fieldwork. For ease of presentation, this chapter focuses on the interviewing process conducted by personal interviewers. However, many of the issues apply to all fieldworkers, no matter what their specific settings.

fieldworker
An individual who is responsible for gathering data in the field.

SURVEYTHIS!

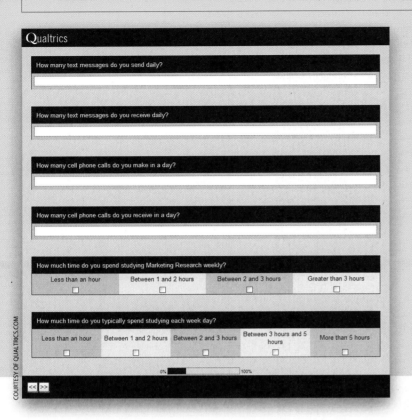

Qualtrics

How many text messages do you send daily?

How many text messages do you receive daily?

How many cell phone calls do you make in a day?

How many cell phone calls do you receive in a day?

How much time do you spend studying Marketing Research weekly?

Less than an hour	Between 1 and 2 hours	Between 2 and 3 hours	Greater than 3 hours
☐	☐	☐	☐

How much time do you typically spend studying each week day?

Less than an hour	Between 1 and 2 hours	Between 2 and 3 hours	Between 3 hours and 5 hours	More than 5 hours
☐	☐	☐	☐	☐

0% █████ 100%

<< >>

COURTESY OF QUALTRICS.COM

Examine the results from the portion of the Qualtrics survey shown in the screenshot. Researchers often try to validate responses found in one medium with results found from another. In this case, the question becomes whether or not responses to these same questions can be validated using a telephone interview or a personal interview.

1. Conduct a survey with three friends via the telephone trying to acquire responses to these questions. Record the responses.
2. Conduct a matching survey with three different friends in a face-to-face setting.
3. After conducting the interview, are there any particular instructions that would be helpful to others trying to conduct these surveys?
4. Try to put your results together with those of other students in your class. Do the results seem consistent with those obtained using the online survey? Comment.

© GEORGE DOYLE

The actual data collection process is rarely carried out by the person who designs the research. However, the data–collecting stage is crucial, because the marketing research project is no better than the data collected in the field. So, the marketing research administrator must select capable people and trust them to gather the data. An irony of marketing research is that highly educated and trained individuals design the research, but when typical surveys are conducted, the people who gather the data usually have little research training or experience. Knowing that research is no better than the data collected in the field, research administrators must concentrate on carefully selecting fieldworkers.

Much fieldwork is conducted by research suppliers that specialize in data collection. When a second party is subcontracted, the job of the study designer at the parent firm is not only to hire a research supplier but also to build in supervisory controls over the field service. In some cases a third-party firm is employed. For example, a company may contact a marketing research firm that in turn subcontracts the fieldwork to a **field interviewing service**.

Various field interviewing services and full-service marketing research agencies perform all manner of personal surveys including central location telephone interviewing, mall intercepts, and other forms of fieldwork for a fee. These agencies typically employ field supervisors who supervise and train interviewers, edit completed questionnaires in the field, and telephone or recontact respondents to confirm that interviews have been conducted.

Whether the research administrator hires an **in-house interviewer** or selects a field interviewing service, fieldworkers should ideally meet certain job requirements. Although the job requirements for different types of surveys vary, normally interviewers should be healthy, outgoing, and of pleasing appearance—that is, well groomed and tailored. People who enjoy talking with strangers usually make better interviewers. An essential part of the interviewing process is establishing rapport with the respondent. An outgoing nature may help interviewers ensure respondents' full cooperation. Interviewer bias may occur if the fieldworker's clothing or physical appearance is unattractive or unusual. One exception to this would be ethnographic research. In ethnographic research, the interviewer should dress to blend in with the group being studied. So, if holey jeans and a dirty T-shirt are the dress *du jour*, then the interviewer should dress likewise.

field interviewing service

A research supplier that specializes in gathering data.

in-house interviewer

A fieldworker who is employed by the company conducting the research.

TOTHEPOINT

The knowledge of the world is only to be acquired in the world and not in the closet.

—Lord Chesterfield

472

Interviewing for Horizon Research Services

Along with the big-name national and international research firms like Yankelovich, Nielsen, and Gallup, many smaller research companies offer interviewing and other services to clients in their city or region. An example is Horizon Research Services (http://www.horizonresearch.com), located in Columbia, Missouri. Founded by Kathleen Anger, a psychologist with a deep sense of curiosity, Horizon has served local organizations including Columbia's banks and hospitals. The company conducts focus groups, telephone surveys, and other research projects.

Horizon uses part-time employees to staff its dozen computer workstations whenever a client requests a telephone survey. Lauren Brengarth, who is pursuing a doctorate at University of Missouri–Columbia, supervises this staff. When Horizon needs calls to be made, she supervisors fieldworkers who put in a six- to nine-o'clock shift in the evening.

One of the most significant challenges of the interviewer's job is simply to keep the respondent from hanging up. In the first few seconds of the phone call, fieldworkers quickly reassure the person that the call is for research, not to sell them something. After that, retaining respondents becomes a matter of reinforcing that they are "doing a good service [because] it's for research."

Horizon's telephone interviewers also recruit people to participate in focus groups. Typically, the company needs four interviewers to spend about three hours just to fill a twelve-person focus group. The reason is that finding willing individuals who meet the project's specifications may require up to six hundred phone calls!

Horizon has recently formed partnerships with World Marketing and Fusion Marketing & Design. As a result, a researcher can get both consulting services and creative design to go along with the field research. In the end, they can get the total package by using all three partners together.

Source: Based on Kevin Coleman, "Research Firm Reflects Consumer Trends," *Columbia (Missouri) Daily Tribune* (May 21, 2005), downloaded at http://www.columbiatribune.com; and Horizon Research Services Web site, http://www.horizonresearch.com, accessed October 1, 2008.

Survey interviewers generally are paid hourly rates or per-interview fees. Often interviewers are part-time workers from a variety of backgrounds—homemakers, graduate students, schoolteachers, and others. Some research projects require special knowledge or skills, such as familiarity with the topic they are asking about. In a survey investigating whether health education improves the likelihood that people who have suffered a stroke will quit smoking, the researchers used trained nurses to administer questionnaires that included each patient's medical history.[3] Taking an accurate medical history is a skill that requires more training than most interviewers would likely have.

Training Inexperienced Interviewers

After personnel are recruited and selected, they must be trained.[4] Suppose a woman who has just sent her youngest child off to first grade is hired by a marketing research interviewing firm. She has decided to become a professional interviewer. The training she will receive after being hired may vary from virtually no training to an extensive, three-day program if she is selected by one of the larger marketing research agencies. Almost always, trainees will receive a **briefing session** on the particular project.

The objective of training is to ensure that the data collection instrument will be administered in a uniform fashion by all fieldworkers. The goal of training sessions is to ensure that each respondent is provided with common information. If the data are collected in a uniform manner from all respondents, the training session will have succeeded.

More extensive training programs are likely to cover the following topics:

- How to make initial contact with the respondent and secure the interview
- How to ask survey questions
- How to probe
- How to record responses
- How to terminate the interview

Each of these points is discussed briefly.

briefing session

A training session to ensure that each interviewer is provided with common information.

Fieldworkers need training both in the basics and required practices of good interviewing principles.

Making Initial Contact and Securing the Interview

The method by which the fieldwork will take place is an important consideration in deciding what type of information can be obtained. The Research Snapshot on the next page illustrates how certain techniques are more appropriate for gathering qualitative data.

■ PERSONAL INTERVIEWS

A field researcher can't conduct an interview unless the respondent participates. Interviewers are trained to make appropriate opening remarks that will convince the respondent that his or her cooperation is important, as in this example:

> *Good afternoon, my name is _____, and I'm with [insert name of firm], an international marketing research company. We are simply conducting a survey concerning _____. I would like to get a few of your ideas, and I will not try to sell you anything. It will take [insert accurate time estimate] minutes and there are no right or wrong answers.*

■ TELEPHONE INTERVIEWS

For the initial contact in a telephone interview, the introduction might be something like this:

> *Good evening, my name is _____. I am not trying to sell anything. I'm calling from [insert name of firm] in Mason, Ohio. We are seeking your opinions on some important matters and it will only take [insert accurate time estimate] minutes of your time.*

Giving the interviewer's name personalizes the call. Personal interviewers may carry a letter of identification or an ID card to indicate that the study is a *bona fide* research project and not a sales call. The name of the research agency is used to imply that the caller is trustworthy. The respondent must be given an accurate estimate of the amount of time participating in the interview will take. If someone is told that only three minutes will be required for participation, and the questioning proceeds to five minutes or more, the respondent will tend to quit before completing the interview. Providing an accurate estimate of the time not only helps gain cooperation, but it is also the ethically correct thing to do.

■ INTERNET SURVEYS

A similar approach may be used to an Internet survey. The potential respondent may receive an e-mail requesting assistance, as in the following example:

> *We are contacting you because of your interest in [subject matter inserted here]. We would like to invite you to participate in a survey that asks your opinion on matters related to [subject matter inserted here]. In return for your participation, we will [insert incentive here]. To participate, click on this URL:* http://www.clickhere.com.

■ GAINING PARTICIPATION

The Interviewer's Manual from the Survey Research Center at the University of Michigan recommends avoiding questions that ask permission for the interview, such as "May I come in?" and "Would you mind answering some questions?" Some people will refuse to participate or object to being interviewed. Interviewers should be instructed on handling objections. For example, if the respondent says, "I'm too busy right now," the interviewer might be instructed to respond, "Will

Questioning and Probing on an Electronic Bulletin Board

Online research often involves self-administered questionnaires with little role for an interviewer. An exception is interviewing with electronic bulletin boards, in which the interviewer posts comments and participants submit their responses for all the participants to read. Generally, the research firm screens and invites a sample of participants via e-mail, and those who accept receive a password to access the bulletin board for several days. The resulting small-group discussion takes place online, rather than in a meeting room.

Typically, the interviewer, or moderator, works from a discussion guide that specifies the questions to cover each day. The guide may indicate when each question is to be posted in order to spread the questions out and give participants time to visit the bulletin board and reply. Because the online format allows some time for reading and reflection, questions can be complex. The following question, for example, encourages participants to ponder several dimensions of a company's reputation:

"Could you now do the same for Dell: What are your perceptions of the company? What adjectives would you use to describe your image of the company? Why? How would you describe Dell's advertising?" Such a complex question would be difficult to answer in a phone interview. But in the context of a bulletin board, one respondent

might address one aspect of Dell's reputation, while another thinks of a different aspect, and the moderator then probes for more reaction to each line of thought as responses are posted to the bulletin board.

Because the moderator cannot see or hear participants, word choice is critical. The moderator should encourage participation. Often the moderator must seek clarification because messages are harder to interpret without clues from body language and vocal tones. Occasionally, someone makes inappropriate remarks, and bulletin boards allow this situation to be handled with private messages. Those messages should not only indicate the kind of information that is needed from the respondent, but also mention that his or her continued participation is valuable.

Source: Based on "GfK Qualitative and Ethnography," accessed at http://www.gfkamerica.com, October 1, 2008; and "Frequently Asked Questions: Participation in Surveys," Harris Poll Online, http://www.harrispollonline.com, accessed September 30, 2008.

PHOTO COURTESY OF VICKI BEAVER

© GEORGE DOYLE & CIARAN GRIFFIN

---

you be in at four o'clock this afternoon? I would be happy to schedule a time with you." In other cases, client companies will not wish to offend any individual. In this case, the interviewer will be instructed to merely say, "Thank you for your time."

The **foot-in-the-door compliance technique** and the **door-in-the-face compliance technique** are useful in securing interviews. Foot-in-the-door theory attempts to explain compliance with a large or difficult task on the basis of respondents' earlier compliance with a smaller initial request. One experiment has shown that compliance with a minor telephone interview (that is, a small request that few people refuse) will lead to greater compliance with a second, larger request to fill out a long mail questionnaire. An interviewer employing door-in-the-face technique begins by making an initial request so large that nearly everyone will react negatively (that is, slam the door in his or her face). When this happens, the interviewer can then request a smaller favor, such as asking a respondent to participate in a "short" survey. However, this technique presents an ethical issue if the respondent is deceived. Thus, the initial request should also be a legitimate request.

foot-in-the-door compliance technique

A technique for obtaining a high response rate, in which compliance with a large or difficult task is induced by first obtaining the respondent's compliance with a smaller request.

door-in-the-face compliance technique

A two-step process for securing a high response rate. In step 1 an initial request, so large that nearly everyone refuses it, is made. Next, a second request is made for a smaller favor; respondents are expected to comply with this more reasonable request.

Asking the Questions

The purpose of an interview is, of course, to record a respondent's answers. An interview can involve ethnography or phenomenology. In those cases, a specialist is needed to conduct an interview. However, even basic surveys conducted via a personal interview can be difficult to conduct properly. Training in the art of asking questions via a typical survey interview can be extremely beneficial. Otherwise, interviewer bias can become a source error in survey research.

There are five major rules for asking questions:

1. Ask questions exactly as they are worded in the questionnaire.
2. Read each question very carefully and clearly.
3. Ask the questions in the specified order.
4. Ask every question specified in the questionnaire.
5. Repeat questions that are misunderstood or misinterpreted.[5]

Interviewers are generally trained to know these rules, but when working in the field, many do not follow these procedures exactly. Inexperienced interviewers may not understand the importance of strict adherence to the instructions. Also, interviewers may be tempted to rely on memory rather than reading questions. However, the interviewer becomes likely to shorten the question or rephrase it slightly when working from memory instead of paper. This can become problematic as even the slightest change in wording may inject some bias into a study. Even when reading the question word for word, the interviewer may be reminded to concentrate on avoiding slight variations in tone of voice on particular words or phrases. Each respondent should hear exactly the same question.

If respondents do not understand a question, they usually will ask for some clarification. The recommended procedure is to repeat the question. If the person does not understand a word such as LDL cholesterol (low-density lipoprotein) in the question "Do you feel concerned about LDL cholesterol?" the interviewer should respond with the full name of the acronym and perhaps a standard colloquialism such as "bad cholesterol." If the respondent still doesn't understand, then the interviewer may say, "Just whatever it means to you." However, interviewers often supply their own personal definitions or simply ad lib some clarification. While this may be simple enough in some situations, the fact that other interviewers may provide different definitions creates the potential for error. One reason interviewers may stray from the instructions is that field supervisors reward an interviewer based on how many completed questionnaires he or she produces. The interviewer also may be penalized based on how many questions are unanswered. Field research firms should carefully consider how such a policy is implemented or risk encouraging interviewers to stray from good practices.

Respondents sometimes offer information before it is even asked. In other words, the respondent provides an answer to a question that is supposed to be asked at a later point in time. In this situation the response should be recorded under the question that deals specifically with that subject. Then, rather than skip the question that was answered out of sequence, the interviewer should be trained to say something like "We have briefly discussed this, but let me ask you . . . ." By asking every question, the interviewer can be sure that complete answers are recorded. If the partial answer to a question answered out of sequence is recorded on the space reserved for the earlier question and the subsequent question is skipped, an omission error will occur when the data are tabulated.

Probing When No Response Is Given

Similar to the approach discussed for qualitative interviews, interviewers should be provided instructions on when and how to probe when respondents give no answer, incomplete answers, or provide an answer that needs clarification. First, probing is necessary when a respondent must be motivated to expand on, clarify, explain, or complete his or her answer. Interviewers must encourage respondents to clarify or expand on answers by providing a stimulus that will not suggest their own ideas or attitudes. An ability to probe with neutral stimuli is a mark of an experienced and effective interviewer. Second, probing may be necessary when a respondent begins to ramble or lose track. In such cases, a respondent must be led to focus on the specific content of the interview and to avoid irrelevant and unnecessary information.

Interviewers have several possible probing tactics to choose from, depending on the situation:

- *Repeating the question.* When the respondent remains completely silent, he or she may not have understood the question or decided how to answer it. Mere repetition may encourage the respondent to answer in such cases. For example, if the question is "What do you not like about Guinness?" and the respondent does not answer, the interviewer may probe: "Just to check, is there anything that you do not like about Guinness?"
- *Using a silent probe.* If the interviewer believes that the respondent has more to say, a silent probe—that is, an expectant pause or look—may motivate the respondent to gather his or her thoughts and give a complete response.
- *Repeating the respondent's reply.* As the interviewer records the response, he or she may repeat the respondent's reply verbatim. This may stimulate the respondent to expand on the answer.
- *Asking a neutral question.* Asking a neutral question may specifically indicate the type of information that the interviewer is seeking. For example, if the interviewer believes that the

respondent's motives should be clarified, he or she might ask, "Tell me about this feeling." If the interviewer feels that there is a need to clarify a word or phrase, he or she might say, "What do you mean by _____?"

- *Triangulation*. This approach is useful when a less structured interview process such as laddering is applied. Triangulation is a typical qualitative interview tool. The respondent will be asked to compare and contrast a response with alternatives. For example, if a respondent provides Google in response to "What is your favorite search engine?" then the interviewer may ask the respondent to list another search engine that is similar (i.e., Yahoo) and a third that is different from these two (i.e., Ask.com). The interviewer can then probe by having the respondent elaborate on the differences.

Exhibit 18.1 summarizes some key probes. Some probes are simply trying to be clear on the respondent's true answer. Such probes should be neutral and not leading. As the interview becomes more qualitatively sophisticated, probes are intended to evoke deeper meaning. The more sophisticated the probe, the more training the interviewer needs.

EXHIBIT 18.1

Probing Respondents for Accuracy or Elaboration

Interviewer's Intention	Probe	Effectiveness
Evoking an answer	Repeat the question word for word.	Effective if the person did not hear the question well or needed a moment to think of a response.
Evoking an answer	Silence	When respondent shows visual cues of wanting to respond or hesitation, simply being silent may encourage the respondent to fill the time with a response. This approach also can be effective in a depth interview.
Seeking clarification or elaboration	Repeat the respondent's answer. Interviewer: "What is your favorite place to have coffee away from home?" Respondent: McDonald's. Interviewer: McDonald's?	Often encourages respondent to provide a simple clarification. This may evoke some attributes associated with a given response.
Probing for elaboration or a deeper response	Ask a neutral question such as "Tell me about _____," or "What do you mean by _____?" Respondent: "I prefer a coffee shop with character." Interviewer: "Tell me, what do you mean by character?"	An effective way of getting the respondent to express their thought in a more tangible way or to express deeper feelings and meanings associated with some opinion.
Triangulation (laddering)	Ask a respondent to compare and contrast alternative responses. Respondent: McDonald's is my favorite place to have coffee. Interviewer: What other place is similar to McDonald's? Respondent: Wendy's Interviewer: What place is different? Respondent: Starbucks Interviewer: Tell me how it is different.	A very effective way of identifying a means-end chain (discussed in an earlier chapter). Respondent will describe differences in terms of attributes and benefits and how these tap key personal values.

Recording the Responses

An analyst who fails to instruct fieldworkers in the techniques of properly recording survey answers rarely forgets to do so a second time. Although recording an answer seems extremely simple, mistakes can occur in this phase of the research. Each fieldworker should use the same recording process.

Rules for recording responses to fixed-alternative questions vary with the specific questionnaire. A general rule, however, is to place a check mark in the box that correctly reflects the respondent's answer. All too often interviewers don't bother recording the answer to a filter question because they believe the subsequent answer will make the answer to the filter question obvious. However, editors and coders do not know how the respondent actually answered a question.

The general instruction for recording open-ended questions is to record the response verbatim, a task that is difficult for most people. Inexperienced interviewers should be given an opportunity to practice verbatim recording of answers before being sent into the field. Some suggestions for recording open-ended answers include

- Record responses during the interview.
- Use the respondent's own words.
- Do not summarize or paraphrase the respondent's answer.
- Include everything that pertains to the question objectives.
- Include all of your probes.[6]

Especially for sensitive topics, decisions about how to record responses may be more difficult than these guidelines suggest. For a survey that included open-ended questions about sexual behavior, researchers found that some decisions about how to record answers affected the way responses were later interpreted. For example, they defined notation that would indicate pauses and vocal emphasis, which helped researchers identify answers that involved confusion or strong emotions. However, recording every nonverbal behavior led researchers to speculate about whether one respondent was crying or using drugs (he had a cold). Likewise, when transcriptions recorded the respondent's exact words and pronunciation, including dialects and mistakes in grammar and word usage, researchers were tempted to speculate about demographic characteristics, such as a speaker's race or educational level. As the researchers evaluated the effects of these decisions about how to record answers, they concluded that such decisions should be made carefully in light of the research objectives.[7]

Exhibit 18.2 shows an example of a completed questionnaire page. Note how the interviewer adds supplementary comments to the fixed-alternative questions and indicates probing questions by placing them in parentheses. Answers have been recorded without paraphrasing. In this case,

EXHIBIT 18.2

A Completed Portion of a Response Form with Notes

What is the last time you filled your automobile with gas?

about 10 days ago

How much did you pay for that gas?

about $5
NOTE: RQ

How much do you typically drive each week?

I commute about 40 miles each way to downtown Cincinnati and back home.

How often do you fill your automobile with gas?

about once every 2 weeks or so
NOTE: Response does not seem to make sense.

How much have gas price increases changed your entertainment behaviors?

not at all

the interviewer has resisted the temptation to conserve time and space by filtering comments. The *RQ* indicates that the interviewer repeated the question to evoke a response. Also note that the interviewer expresses concern over the validity of the responses because the answers do not seem consistent. These notes will be helpful later when the data are coded.

Terminating the Interview

The final aspect is training interviewers about closing an interview. Although it may seem obvious, fieldworkers should be trained not to close an interview until all pertinent items have been discussed by the respondent. Also, respondents should be offered an opportunity to provide closing comments following the interview. An interviewer that is in too much of a hurry may be unable to record the spontaneous comments respondents offer after all formal questions have been asked. Merely recording one of these comments may result in a new product idea or creative marketing campaign. Avoiding hasty departures is also a matter of courtesy. The fieldworker also should provide the respondent with an opportunity to ask questions concerning the nature and purpose of the study. Fieldworkers should answer these questions when possible and offer to follow up with answers that cannot be answered immediately.

Finally, it is extremely important to thank the respondent for his or her time and cooperation. If some incentive is being provided, this is the time to hand it over. The fieldworker may be required to reinterview the respondent at some future time. So, the respondent should be left with a positive feeling about having cooperated in a worthwhile operation.

Principles of Good Interviewing

Yankelovich Partners is one of the nation's top marketing research organizations.[8] One reason for its success is its careful attention to fieldwork. This section presents this organization's principles of good interviewing. These principles apply no matter what the nature of the specific assignment; they are universal and represent the essence of sound data collection for marketing research purposes. For clarity, they have been divided into two categories: *the basics* (the interviewing point of view) and *required practices* (standard inquiry premises and procedures). The Research Snapshot on the next page illustrates benefits of focusing on the questions in hand.

The Basics

Basic interviewing is a skilled occupation so not everyone can do it, and even fewer can do it extremely well. Exhibit 18.3 on the next page displays traits and practices of good interviewing as a checklist or tear sheet. Good practice begins with these basic principles:

1. *Have integrity, and be honest.* This is the cornerstone of all professional inquiry, regardless of its purpose.
2. *Have patience and tact.* Interviewers ask for information from people they do not know. Thus, all the rules of human relations that apply to inquiry situations—patience, tact, and courtesy—apply even more to interviewing. You should at all times follow the standard business conventions that control communications and contact.
3. *Pay attention to accuracy and detail.* Among the greatest interviewing "sins" are inaccuracy and superficiality, for the professional analyst can misunderstand, and in turn mislead, a client. A good rule to follow is not to record a response unless you fully understand it yourself. Probe for clarification and rich, full answers. Record responses verbatim: Never assume you know what a respondent is thinking or jump to conclusions as to what he or she might have said but did not.
4. *Exhibit a real interest in the inquiry at hand, but keep your own opinions to yourself.* Impartiality is imperative—if your opinions were wanted, you would be asked, not your respondent. You are an asker and a recorder of other people's opinions, not a contributor to the study data.
5. *Be a good listener.* Too many interviewers talk too much, wasting time when respondents could be supplying more pertinent facts or opinions on the study topic.

Don't Blush: Just Move On!

Many principles of good interviewing are universal. Sticking to these principals and systematically moving from one question to another is a good way to stay out of trouble too. Eventually, just about every field interviewer finds him or herself in an interesting, irritating, or potentially embarrassing situation.

Interesting: Susan Cholette does field interviews used in wine marketing research. In one project, she interviewed wine makers in an effort to compare and contrast the wine business in California with the wine business in France. Along the way, friendly wine makers just might insist on her sampling the wares. As long as the field interviewer sticks to the questions and provides valid responses, this is a fringe benefit. During a long day of interviews, an interviewer in this situation would have to carefully monitor his or her dexterity!

Irritating: In Jerusalem, a research firm called Dialog conducts political polls. Interviewer Oded Blech says he encounters a variety of challenges, not the least of which is gaining cooperation. Some respondents claim they will be out shopping for the entire night so calling back will be futile. Some simply tell outright lies. For instance, a father can be heard hissing at a child who answered the phone and telling the child to say that he isn't at home. Blech and his colleagues know they must continue to be polite anyway. One coworker, Inbal Bracha, an engineering student, says refusals are less likely when she smiles as she talks, which makes her voice more pleasant. Her other technique for

obtaining compliance is to speak rapidly but politely, telling the person that the survey will be brief and giving him or her "the feeling that he [or she] is very important."

Embarrassing: Researchers often study sensitive topics. Researchers may ask questions about a person's charitable giving, true hair color, or even sex life. Although respondents monitor their responses in an effort to mitigate their own embarrassment, the interviewer's only buffer is sticking to the procedure. In Canberra, field interviewer Genevieve Power was doing personal interviews for the Australian Bureau of Statistics. She intercepts respondents at their home to ask demographic questions and inquire about topics such as literacy and spending. Power needs strong interpersonal skills to speak with people from a variety of backgrounds. Once Power was working near the city of Darwin, traveling to a home with a forbidding gate at the end of a long, narrow driveway bordered by closely planted trees. Power entered the gate, closed it carefully behind her, and drove to the house. There she found a man seated in a bathtub in the front yard, enjoying a quiet bath. Though he was naked, he rose and shook Power's hand politely. She conducted the interview as he replied from the bathtub. When she finished, her nude subject rose again to say good-bye. In this case, it was a really good idea to *focus* on the questions!

Source: Based on Hilary Leila Krieger, "Even the Pollsters Take Some of Their Surveys with a Grain of Salt," *Jerusalem Post* (December 30, 2005), p. 1; and "Fielding Answers All in a Day's Work for Interviewers," *Canberra Times* (December 8, 2005), http://web1.infotrac.galegroup.com, accessed March 1, 2006; Tourangeau, T. Y., "Sensitive Questions in Surveys," *Psychological Bulletin* 133 (2007), 859; Cholette, S., "A Tale of Two Wine Regions: Similarities, Differences and Trends in the French and Californian Wine Industries," *International Journal of Wine Marketing* 16 (2004), 24–48.

6. *Keep the inquiry and respondents' responses confidential.* Do not discuss the studies you are doing with relatives, friends, or associates; it is unacceptable to both the research agency and its clients. Above all, *never* quote one respondent's opinion to another—that is the greatest violation of privacy.

EXHIBIT 18.3

Check-sheet for Effective Interviewing

The Basics	Required Practices
Integrity	Obtain the required number of responses.
Patience	Follow the directions.
Attention	Stay on schedule.
Show interest	Keep control of interview.
Listen well	Finish each question.
Confidential	Check over each question.
Respect	Compare assigned quota with total number of finished questionnaires.
	Make sure instructions are understood and clear up any ambiguities in assignment.

7. *Respect others' rights.* Marketing research depends on people's willingness to provide information. In obtaining this information, you must follow a happy medium path. Between the undesirable extremes of failure to get it all and unnecessary coercion, this middle road is one of clear explanation, friendliness, and courtesy, offered in an interested and persuasive tone. Impress upon prospective respondents that their cooperation is important and valuable.

Required Practices

The list below contains practical rules of marketing research inquiry that should be followed and used without exception:

1. *Complete the number of interviews according to the sampling plan assigned to you.* Both are calculated with the utmost precision so that when assignments are returned, the study will benefit from having available the amount and type of information originally specified.

2. *Follow the directions provided.* Remember that many other interviewers are working on the same study in other places. Lack of uniformity in procedure can only spell disaster for later analysis. Each direction has a purpose, even though it may not be completely evident to you.

3. *Make every effort to keep schedules.* Schedules range from "hurry up" to "there should be plenty of time," but there is always a good reason, and you should be as responsive as possible. If you foresee problems, call and explain.

4. *Keep control of each interview you do.* It is up to you to determine the pace of a particular interview, keeping several points in mind:
   a. There is an established *average* length of an interview from the time you start to talk to the respondent to the time you finish. It represents a *guideline,* but some interviews will be shorter and some longer.
   b. Always get the whole story from the respondent, and write it all down in the respondent's own words. Also, remember to keep the interview focused on the subject at hand and prevent it from wandering off into unnecessary small talk.
   c. Avoid offending the respondent by being too talkative yourself.

5. *Complete the questionnaires meticulously.*
   a. Follow exactly all instructions that appear directly on the questionnaire. Before you start interviewing, learn what these instructions direct you to do.
   b. Ask the questions from the first to the last in the exact numerical order (unless directed to do otherwise in some particular instances). Much thought and effort go into determining the order of the questioning to avoid bias or to set the stage for subsequent questions.
   c. Ask each question exactly as it is written. There is never a justifiable reason for rephrasing a question. The cost of doing so is lack of uniformity; the research agency would never know whether all respondents were replying to the same question or replying to 50 different interviewers' interpretations of the question.
   d. Never leave a question blank. It will be difficult to tell whether you failed to ask it, whether the respondent could not answer it because of lack of knowledge or certainty, or whether the respondent refused to answer it for personal reasons. If none of the answer categories provided prove suitable, write in what the respondent said, in his or her own words.

EuroInterview is a company that specializes in conducting marketing fieldwork in Europe. They offer standard services including personal interviews and ethnography, including mystery shopping.

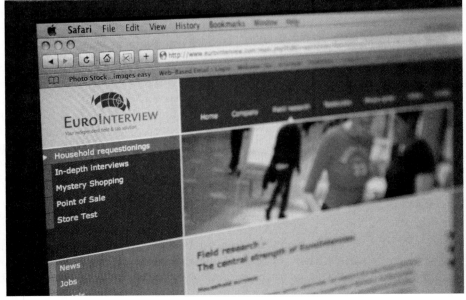

   e. Use all the props provided to aid both interviewers and respondents: show cards, pictures, descriptions, sheets of questions for the respondents to answer themselves, and so on. All have a specific interview purpose. Keys to when and how to use them appear on the questionnaire at the point at which they are to be used.

6. *Check over each questionnaire you have completed.* This is best done directly after it has been completed. If you find something you did wrong or omitted, correct it. Often you can call a respondent back, admit you missed something (or are unclear about a particular response), and then straighten out the difficulty.

7. *Compare your sample execution and assigned quota with the total number of questionnaires you have completed.* Do not consider your assignment finished until you have done this.

8. *Clear up any questions with the research agency.* At the start of an assignment or after you have begun, if you have questions for which you can find no explanatory instructions, call the agency to get the matter clarified. (Many agencies provide toll-free numbers so that there will be no expense to you.)

Qualitative Interviews

The rules above apply to traditional structured and straightforward unstructured interviews. Many of these hold in all types of interviews; however, qualitative research often involves different types of interviews with additional procedures. Earlier chapters focused more specifically on qualitative research and provided guides for conducting focus group and in-depth interviews. However, an interviewer taking a phenomenological approach may need to pay special attention to making a respondent feel comfortable. In this case, a few minutes of small talk prior to beginning the interview may provide a natural segue into matters of primary interest.

Additionally, ethnographers need to work hard to blend in so that they become a natural part of the environment. Ethnographers observe more than interview. The observations include comments made by people in the environment—but the comments are elicited as a natural part of conversation. Many research firms that specialize in fieldwork also will offer various types of ethnographical interviews. Mystery shoppers even fall into this category to the extent that the interviewer now is simply playing the role of a customer and observing what happens. In these cases, it's important to take copiously detailed field notes. A number of computer programs exist which assist ethnographers and other qualitative researchers in organizing field notes. One such program is AnSWR, which is free to the public and available through the Centers for Disease Control and Prevention (http://www.cdc.gov/hiv/topics/surveillance/resources/software/answr/index.htm).

Phenomenologists and ethnographers need to be particularly careful that they are indeed getting information that is what it purports to be from a source that is who it purports to be. This is particularly relevant because the focus is no longer on a quantity of responses that will be statistically analyzed but on the quality and richness of responses from only a few observations. Researchers applying ethnographic or phenomenological approaches in the field should keep these three additional considerations in mind:[9]

1. Act natural. Fit in and don't do anything that would call attention to the fact that you are a fieldworker. Thus, small talk that strays from the actual topic, which might be inappropriate in a structured format, can be very appropriate.

2. Don't rush. Time is on your side. The longer the fieldworker is in the field, the more he or she becomes part of the environment. Also, the greater the likelihood for rich or unusual findings.

3. Be flexible. While in traditional fieldwork, all the questions should be asked the same way, with ethnography and phenomenology, the fieldworker should adjust to the individual situation and respondent. The fieldworker must possess adequate people skills to know the best way of getting valid information.

Ethnographic research also is now conducted via online panels. Here, follow-up is often needed to be certain that what is sometimes an anonymous source (identified only by a moniker) is providing true information. If someone in a chat room indicates that they drink a dozen cups of coffee a day, one may want to follow up with questions about when all this coffee is consumed or where it is acquired as a way of checking its validity. Follow-ups and cross-checks of this type become important. Are there multiple responses all consistent with this reported behavior? When online communities are used for actual in-depth interviews, follow-up of this type can become more formal. Quester Corporation has developed a program called Socrates that automatically generates follow-up questions aimed at verifying or increasing validity.[10]

Management

Marketing managers preparing for the fieldwork stage should consider the meaning of the following stanza from Robert Burns's poem "To a Mouse":

> *The best laid schemes o' mice and men*
> *Gang aft a—gley;*
> *An' lea'e us nought but grief and pain,*
> *For promis'd joy.*

The best plans of mice, men, and marketing researchers may go astray. An excellent research plan may go astray if the field operations are performed incorrectly. A proper research design will eliminate numerous sources of error, but careful execution of the fieldwork is necessary to produce results without substantial error. For these reasons fieldwork management is an essential part of the marketing research process.

Briefing Session for Experienced Interviewers

Whether interviewers have just completed their training in fundamentals or are already experienced, they always need to be informed about the individual project. Both experienced and inexperienced fieldworkers must be briefed on the background of the sponsoring organization, sampling techniques, asking of questions, callback procedures, and other matters specific to the particular project.

If there are any special instructions—for example, about using show cards or video equipment or restricted interviewing times—they should also be covered during the training session. Instructions for handling certain key questions are always important. For example, the following fieldworker instructions appeared in a survey of institutional investors who make buy-and-sell decisions about stocks for banks, pension funds, and so on:

> *Questions 13a, 13b*
> *These questions will provide verbatim comments for the report to the client. Probe for more than one- or two-word answers and record verbatim. Particularly, probe for more information when respondent gives a general answer—e.g., "Poor management," "It's in a good industry." Ask, In what ways is management poor? What's good about the industry? And so on.*

A training session for experienced interviewers might go something like this: All interviewers report to the central office, where they receive a brief explanation of the firm's background and the general aims of the study. Interviewers are provided with minimal information about the purpose of the study to ensure that they will not transmit any preconceived notions to respondents. For example, in a survey about the banks in a community, the interviewers would be told that the research is a banking study but not the name of the sponsoring bank. To train the interviewers about the questionnaire, a field supervisor conducts an interview with another field supervisor who acts as a respondent. The trainees observe the interviewing process, after which they each interview and record the responses of another field supervisor who acts as a respondent. After the practice interview, the trainees receive additional instructions.

Training to Avoid Procedural Errors in Sample Selection

The briefing session also covers the sampling procedure. A number of research projects allow the interviewer to be at least partially responsible for selecting the sample. These sampling methods offer the potential for selection bias. This potential for bias is obvious in the case of quota sampling but less obvious in other cases. For example, in probability sampling in which every nth house is selected, the fieldworker uses his or her discretion in identifying housing units. Avoiding selection bias may be more difficult than it sounds. For example, in an old, exclusive neighborhood, a mansion's coach house or servants' quarters may have been converted into an apartment that should be identified as a housing unit. This type of dwelling and other unusual housing units (apartments with alley entrances only, lake cottages, or rooming houses) may be overlooked, giving rise to selection error. Errors may also occur in the selection of random-digit dialing samples. Considerable effort should be expended in training and supervisory control to minimize these errors.

Another selection problem is the practice of contacting a respondent when and where it is convenient for both parties. Consider the following anecdote from an industrial marketing research interviewer:

> *Occasionally getting to the interview is half the challenge and tests the interviewer's ingenuity. Finding your way around a huge steel mill is not easy. Even worse is trying to find a correct turn-off to gravel pit D when it's snowing so hard that most direction signs are obliterated. In arranging an appointment with an executive at a rock quarry outside Kansas City, he told me his office was in "Cave Number 3." It was no joke. To my surprise, I found a luxurious executive office in a cave, which had long ago been hollowed by digging for raw material.*[11]

In that case, finding the sample unit was half the battle.

Supervision to Minimize Errors

Although briefing and training interviewers will minimize the probability of their interviewing the wrong households or asking biased questions, there is still considerable potential for errors in the field. Direct supervision of personal interviewers, telephone interviewers, and other fieldworkers is necessary to ensure that the techniques communicated in the training sessions are implemented in the field.

Supervision of interviewers, like other forms of supervision, refers to controlling the efforts of workers. Field supervision of interviewers requires checking to see that field procedures are being properly followed. A supervisor checks field operations to ensure that the interviewing schedule is being met. Supervisors collect the questionnaires or other instruments daily and edit them for completeness and legibility. If problems arise, supervisors discuss them with the fieldworkers, providing training when necessary.

In addition to quality control, continual training may be provided. For example, if a telephone supervisor notices that interviewers are allowing the phone to ring more than eight times before considering the call a "no answer," the supervisor can instruct interviewers not to do so, as the person who eventually answers is likely to be annoyed.

Sampling Verification

Another important job of a supervisor is to verify that interviews are being conducted according to the sampling plan rather than with the sampling units most accessible to the interviewer. An interviewer might be tempted to go to the household next door for an interview rather than record the sampling unit as not at home, which would require a callback. Carefully recording the number of completed interviews will help ensure that the sampling procedure is being properly conducted. Supervisors are responsible for motivating interviewers to follow the sampling plan carefully.

Closer supervision of the interviewing procedure can occur in central-location telephone interviewing. Supervisors may be able to listen to the actual interview by switching onto the interviewer's line. Of course, this is harder to do when interviewers call from their own homes.

Supervisors must also make sure that the right people within the household or sampling unit are being contacted. One research project for a children's cereal required that several products be placed in the home and that children record their daily consumption and reactions to each cereal in a diary. Although the interviewers were supposed to contact the children to remind them to fill out the diaries, a field supervisor observed that in almost half the cases the mothers were filling out the diaries after the children left for school because their children had not done so. The novelty of the research project had worn off after a few days; eating a specific cereal each day was no longer fun after the first few times, and the children had stopped keeping the diaries. Similar situations may occur with physicians, executives, and other busy people. The interviewer may find it easier to interview a nurse, secretary, or other assistant rather than wait to speak with the right person.

Interviewer Cheating

The most blatant form of **interviewer cheating** occurs when an interviewer falsifies interviews, merely filling in fake answers rather than contacting respondents. This is sometimes referred to as **curb-stoning**. Although this situation does occur, it is not common if the job of selection has been properly accomplished. However, less obvious forms of interviewer cheating occur with greater frequency. Interviewers often consider quota sampling to be time consuming, so an interviewer may stretch the requirements a bit to obtain seemingly qualified respondents. In the interviewer's eyes, a young-looking 36-year-old may be the same as a 30-year-old who fits the quota requirement; checking off the under-30 category thus isn't really cheating. Consider the fieldworker who must select only heavy users of a certain brand of hand lotion that the client says is used by 15 percent of the population. If the fieldworker finds that only 3 percent qualify as heavy users, he or she may be tempted to interview an occasional user to stretch the quota somewhat. All of these approaches are unethical.

An interviewer may fake part of a questionnaire to make it acceptable to the field supervisor. In a survey on automobile satellite radio systems, suppose an interviewer is requested to ask for five reasons why consumers have purchased this product. If he or she finds that people typically give two or perhaps three reasons and even with extensive probing cannot think of five reasons, the interviewer might be tempted to cheat. Rather than have the supervisor think he or she was goofing off on the probing, the interviewer may fill in five reasons based on past interviews. In other cases, the interviewer may cut corners to save time and energy.

Interviewers may fake answers when they find questions embarrassing or troublesome to ask because of sensitive subjects. Thus, the interviewer may complete most of the questionnaire but leave out a question or two because he or she found it troublesome or time-consuming. For example, in a survey among physicians, an interviewer might find questions about artificial-insemination donor programs embarrassing, skip these questions, and fill in the gaps later.

What appears to be interviewer cheating often is caused by improper training or fieldworkers' inexperience. A fieldworker who does not understand the instructions may skip or miss a portion of the questionnaire.

Interviewers may be reluctant to interview sampling units who they feel may be difficult or undesirable to interview. Sometimes fieldworkers are instructed to say at the conclusion of each interview, "Thank you for your time—and by the way, my supervisor may call you to ask about my work. Please say whatever you wish." This or a similar statement not only increases the number of respondents willing to cooperate with the verification process but also improves the quality of fieldwork.

Verification by Reinterviewing

Supervision for quality control attempts to ensure that interviewers are following the sampling procedure and to detect falsification of interviews. Supervisors verify approximately 15 percent of the interviews by reinterviewing. Normally the interview is not repeated; rather, supervisors recontact respondents and ask about the length of the interview and their reactions to the interviewer; then they collect basic demographic data to check for interviewer cheating. Such **verification** does not detect the more subtle form of cheating in which only portions of the interview have been falsified. A validation check may simply point out that an interviewer contacted the proper household but interviewed the wrong individual in that household—which, of course, can be a serious error.

interviewer cheating
The practice by fieldworkers of filling in fake answers or falsifying interviews.

curb-stoning
A form of interviewer cheating in which an interviewer makes up the responses instead of conducting an actual interview.

verification
Quality-control procedures in fieldwork intended to ensure that interviewers are following the sampling procedures and to determine whether interviewers are cheating.

- Fieldworkers are a potential source of error in gathering information. Investing resources into making sure fieldworkers are competent in carrying out their assigned task is money and time well spent.
- Fieldworkers should wear name badges and/or clearly introduce themselves and their employer (the research firm) to the potential respondent.
- Triangulation (a form of laddering) is an effective means of linking tangible differences in product, brand, and store alternatives to the personal values of consumers.

- Avoid incentives that strongly encourage (coerce) fieldworkers to submit a large amount of completed interviews. This motivates the fieldworkers to be sloppy or dishonest.
- Unusual responses need to be followed up with probing questions that attempt to verify the initial response.
- Respondents in online panels or chat rooms should routinely be asked follow-up questions for the purpose of validating the reported behavior.

© GEORGE DOYLE & CIARAN GRIFFIN

Fieldworkers should be aware of supervisory verification practices. Knowing that there may be a telephone or postcard validation check often reminds interviewers to be conscientious in their work. The interviewer who is conducting quota sampling and needs an upper-income Hispanic male will be less tempted to interview a middle-income Hispanic man and falsify the income data in this situation.

Certain information may allow for partial verification without recontacting the respondent. Computer-assisted telephone interviewers often do not know the phone number dialed by the computer or other basic information about the respondent. Thus, answers to questions added to the end of the telephone interview to identify a respondent's area code, phone number, city, zip code, and so on may be used to verify the interview. The computer can also record every attempted call, the time intervals between calls, and the time required to conduct each completed interview—data that may help in identifying patterns related to cheating by interviewers.

Summary

1. Describe the role and job requirements of fieldworkers. Fieldworkers are responsible for gathering data in the field. These activities may be performed by the organization that needs the information, by research suppliers, or by third-party field service organizations. Proper execution of fieldwork is essential to produce research results without substantial error. Proper control of fieldwork begins with interviewer selection. Fieldworkers generally should be healthy, outgoing, and well groomed.

2. Summarize the skills to cover when training inexperienced interviewers. New fieldworkers must be trained in opening the interview, asking the questions, probing for additional information, recording the responses, and terminating the interview.

3. List principles of good interviewing. Exhibit 18.3 summarizes these characteristics. Good interviewers have integrity, patience, and tact. They are attentive to detail and interested in the inquiry at hand. They behave impartially, listen carefully, and maintain confidentiality. They respect the rights of others. Interviewing should adhere to several required practices. Interviewers should complete all interviews according to the sample plan and follow the directions provided. They should try to meet schedules and maintain control of the interview. They should fill in answers meticulously and then check over the questionnaire to make sure it is complete. Before finishing an assignment, they should verify that the number of completed questionnaires matches the sampling plan and assigned quotas. If they have questions, they should check with the agency conducting the research.

Additionally, ethnographic researchers need special skills to blend in to the environment. Phenomenologists need skills that allow them to establish a comfortable rapport with respondents.

4. Describe the activities involved in the management of fieldworkers. Experienced fieldworkers are briefed for each new project to familiarize them with its specific requirements. A particular concern of the briefing session is reminding fieldworkers to adhere closely to the prescribed sampling procedures.

5. Discuss how supervisors should minimize errors in the field. Careful supervision of fieldworkers also is necessary. Supervisors gather and edit questionnaires each day. They check to see that field procedures are being properly followed and that interviews are on schedule. They also check to ensure that the correct sampling units are being used and that the proper people are responding in the study. Finally, supervisors check for interviewer cheating and verify portions of the interviews by reinterviewing a certain percentage of each fieldworker's respondents.

Key Terms and Concepts

briefing session, *473*	field interviewing service, *472*	in-house interviewer, *472*
curb-stoning, *485*	fieldworker, *471*	interviewer cheating, *485*
door-in-the-face compliance technique, *475*	foot-in-the-door compliance technique, *475*	verification, *485*

Questions for Review and Critical Thinking

1. What qualities should fieldworkers possess?
2. **ETHICS** An interviewer has a rather long telephone interview. The estimate suggests that fully completing the survey will take 30 minutes. However, what do you think the response rate will be if people are told ahead of time that it will take 30 minutes to finish participating in the survey? Should the interviewer fudge a little and state that the survey will take only 15 minutes? Explain.
3. What are the five topics that require extensive training before an interviewer can actually participate in fieldwork administering surveys?
4. Suppose an interview involves a potentially embarrassing situation. Which of the five topics is likely to come into play most in obtaining valid responses?
5. What should the interviewer do if a question is misunderstood? If a respondent answers a question before encountering it in the questionnaire?
6. When should interviewers probe? Give some examples of how probing should be done.
7. How should the fieldworker terminate the interview?
8. What special considerations are needed for interviews involving ethnography or phenomenology?
9. How does mystery shopping qualify as a type of ethnography?
10. Why is it important to ensure that fieldworkers adhere to the sampling procedure specified for a project?
11. **ETHICS** What forms does interviewer cheating take? How can such cheating be prevented or detected?
12. **ETHICS** Two interviewers are accused of curb-stoning. What have they done?
13. Comment on the following field situations.
    a. After conducting a survey with ten people, an interviewer noticed that many of the respondents were saying "Was I right?" after a particular question.
    b. A questionnaire asking about a new easy-opening can has the following instructions to interviewers:

1. *(Hand respondent can and matching instruction card.)*
2. "Would you please read the instructions on this card and then open this can for me?" *(Interviewer: Note any comments respondent makes. Do not under any circumstances help him or her to open the can or offer any explanation as to how to open it. If respondent asks for help, tell him that the instructions are on the card. Do not discuss the can or its contents.)*
    c. A researcher gives balloons to children of respondents to keep the children occupied during the interview.
    d. An interviewer tells the supervisor, "With the price of gas, this job isn't paying as well as before!"
    e. When a respondent asks how much time the survey will take, the interviewer responds, "15 to 20 minutes." The respondent says, "I'm sorry, I have to refuse. I can't give you that much time right now."
14. Write some interviewer instructions for an interview involving a chat-room interview with a member of an online video game community.
15. **ETHICS** A fieldworker conducting a political poll is instructed to interview registered voters. The fieldworker interviews all willing participants who are eligible to vote (those who may register in the future) because allowing their opinions to be recorded is part of her patriotic duty. Is she doing the right thing?
16. **ETHICS** An interviewer finds that when potential respondents ask how much time the survey will take, most refuse if they are told 15 minutes. The interviewer now says 10 minutes and finds that most respondents enjoy answering the questions. Is this the right thing to do?
17. **ETHICS** A fieldworker asks respondents whether they will answer a few questions about the shopping center and neighboring community. However, the interviewer also records the respondent's race and approximate age as well as a few other visible characteristics including manner of dress. Is this ethical?

Research Activities

1. **'NET** Go to http://www.greenbook.org/. What does GreenBook do? Using this service, find at least two firms that specialize in or provide the following types of fieldwork:
   a. Mystery shopping in the United States
   b. Personal interviews in Japan
   c. CATI telephone interviews
   d. Fieldwork in Australia
   e. Ethnography

2. **NET** Find a link to AnSWR at the Centers for Disease Control and Prevention (http://www.cdc.gov/hiv/topics/surveillance/resources/software/answr/index.htm). Write a paragraph description of the program. How do you think a program like this might assist in fieldwork?

Case 18.1 Thomas and Dorothy Leavey Library

© GETTY IMAGES/PHOTODISC GREEN

The Thomas and Dorothy Leavey Library serves the students and faculty of the University of Southern California. Staff at the busy library wanted to know more about its patrons, what library resources they find helpful, and whether they are satisfied with the library's services. However, like many libraries, this organization had a tiny budget for marketing research. As a result, the goal was to conduct exploratory research while spending less than $250.[12]

Staff members studied surveys conducted by other libraries to get ideas for a one-page printed questionnaire. Colleagues on the library staff provided suggestions, and a few undergraduates tested the survey for clarity. Next, the survey schedule was chosen: 36 continuous hours that did not conflict with any holidays or exams.

The fieldwork involved setting up and staffing a table offering the survey and then inviting library patrons to stop and fill out a questionnaire. Possible locations included space near an elevator, stairs, or computers, but the lobby area offered the greatest opportunity, because everyone passed through the lobby when using the facility's only entrance. The survey's planners divided the time into 60 slots and recruited students with jobs at the library to serve as the fieldworkers. Other members of the library staff also volunteered to fill time slots. The students in particular were enthusiastic about inviting library patrons to complete questionnaires. A bowl of candy for participants was a small incentive, combined with a raffle for donated prizes.

Questions

1. Imagine that you were asked to help prepare for this survey. What fieldwork challenges would you expect to arise in a survey such as this, to be carried out by inexperienced fieldworkers?
2. What training would you recommend for the students and other library staffers conducting this survey? Suggest topics to cover and advice to give these fieldworkers.

Case 18.2 Margaret Murphy O'Hara

© GETTY IMAGES/PHOTODISC GREEN

Margaret Murphy O'Hara was fatigued. As she wiped the perspiration from her brow, she felt that the Massachusetts summer sun was playing a trick on her. It was her first day at work, and the weather was hot. She had no idea that being a field interviewer required so much stamina. Even though she was tired, she was happy with her new job. She didn't yet have the knack of holding her purse, questionnaires, and clipboard while administering the show cards, but she knew she'd get the hang of it. The balancing act can be learned, she thought.

When she met her supervisor, Mary Zagorski, at the end of her first day, Margaret described her day. Margaret said she thought the questionnaire was a bit too long. She laughed, saying that an elderly lady had fallen asleep after about 20 minutes of interviewing.

Margaret mentioned that a number of people had asked why they were selected. Margaret said she did not know exactly what to say when somebody asked, "Why did you pick me?"

She said that the nicest person she had interviewed was a man whose wife wasn't home to be surveyed. He was very friendly and didn't balk at being asked about his income and age like some of the other people she had interviewed.

She said she had one problem that she needed some help with resolving. Four or five people refused to grant the interview. Margaret explained that one woman answered the door and said she was too busy because her son, an army private, was leaving the country. The woman was throwing a little party for him before he went off to the airport. Margaret didn't want to spoil their fun with the survey. Another lady said that she was too busy and really didn't know anything about the subject anyway. However, she did suggest her next-door neighbor, who was very interested in the subject. Margaret was able to interview this person to make up for the lost interview. It actually went quite well.

Margaret said another woman wouldn't be interviewed because she didn't know anything about the Zagorski interviewing service, and Margaret didn't know quite what to tell her. Finally, she couldn't make one interview because she didn't understand the address: 9615 South Francisco Rear. Margaret told Mary it was quite a day, and she looked forward to tomorrow.

Questions

1. Is Margaret going to be a good professional interviewer?
2. What should Mary Zagorski tell Margaret?

Part 6
Data Analysis and Presentation

© NONSTOCK/JUPITER IMAGES

CHAPTER 19
EDITING AND CODING:
TRANSFORMING RAW DATA INTO INFORMATION

LEARNING OUTCOMES

After studying this chapter, you should be able to

1. Edit responses to maintain data integrity
2. Know the basics of coding qualitative responses
3. Understand when and how to code using a dummy variable approach
4. Appreciate the ways that technological advances have simplified the coding process
5. Understand the way data are represented in a data file

Chapter Vignette: I Hate My Boss!

Elizabeth Aimee, a private research consultant, has been pouring through employee "suggestions" all day. Her firm has been hired to try and improve company performance and morale at Chop-Mart, a local mega-store. Employees can fill out a form that contains a few open-ended questions, including

1. How do you feel about your job?
2. Is the company meeting expectations?
3. What feelings do you experience when you are at work?

The form also contains a few closed-ended questions, including

1. How clear are your job responsibilities?
   - Always clear _____
   - Sometimes clear _____
   - Completely unclear _____
2. Do you like your job?
   - Yes _____
   - No _____

Among the responses to the first question she finds the following:

- I hate my boss!
- Miserable, just like my coworkers.
- My boss is an ogre!!
- The job's fine, my supervisors are jerks.
- I love my boss—not!
- I like coming to work.
- I have mixed feelings about my job.
- Terrified
- Ashamed

Also, among the closed-ended questions, she finds that many people failed to answer the question about job responsibilities and that about 75 percent of employees say they like their jobs. A few employees checked both "sometimes clear" and "always clear" in responding to their job responsibilities.

"How can I possibly make sense of this?" Ms. Aimee knows she must code the open-ended responses. Since this is difficult, she asks an assistant to help with the task. What does it mean when someone says, "I hate my boss"? How should the response be coded when someone says, "The job's fine, my supervisors are jerks"? She recalls reading a paper indicating that emotions are important drivers of performance.[1] Perhaps employees are experiencing too much fear in the workplace and this is tied to managerial behavior? However, more detailed analysis of these responses is needed. The results from this analysis will only be as good as the coding.

This chapter deals with coding and editing raw data. Researchers must pay careful attention to their coding because poor coding leads directly to nonresponse error.[2]

Introduction

Once the fieldwork is completed, the researcher will be anxious to begin data analysis. This will complete the transformation from data into intelligence. However, the **raw data** may not be in a form that lends itself well to data analysis. Raw data are recorded just as the respondent indicated. For an oral response, the raw data are in the words of the respondent, whereas for a questionnaire response, the actual number checked is the number stored. Raw data will often also contain errors both in the form of respondent errors and nonrespondent errors. Whereas a respondent error, as discussed in a previous chapter, is a mistake made by the respondent, a **nonrespondent error** is a mistake made by an interviewer or by a person responsible for creating an electronic data file representing the responses.

Exhibit 19.1 provides an overview of data analysis. The first two stages result in an electronic file suitable for data analysis. This file can then be used in the application of various statistical routines including those associated with descriptive, univariate, bivariate, or multivariate analysis. Each of these data analysis approaches will be discussed in the subsequent chapters. An important part of the editing, coding, and filing stages is checking for errors. As long as error remains in the data, the process of transformation from raw data to intelligence will be made more risky and more difficult. Editing and coding are the first two stages in the data analysis process.

raw data

The unedited responses from a respondent exactly as indicated by that respondent.

nonrespondent error

Error that the respondent is not responsible for creating, such as when the interviewer marks a response incorrectly.

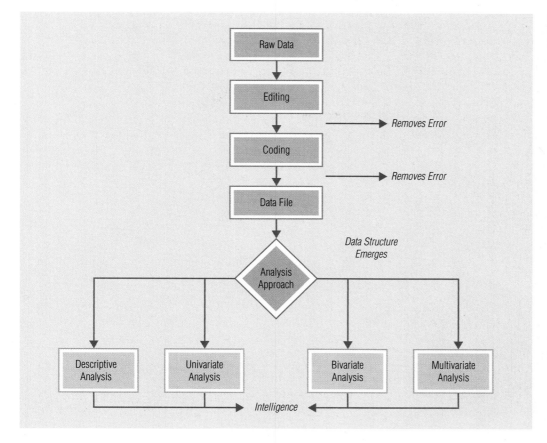

EXHIBIT 19.1

Edit Gets Removed by Editing and Coding

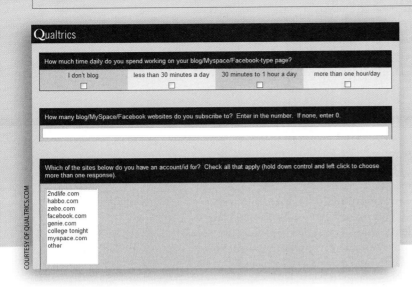

How are data entry, editing, and coding made easier by using a Qualtrics-type survey approach relative to a paper and pencil survey approach? Do any of the questions in the survey present any particular coding problems? Are there questions that can be coded using dummy coding? If so, what are they? Have you noticed any inconsistent responses in the data? If so, how should they be addressed?

Edit Responses to Maintain Data Integrity

Field edits allow supervisors to spot errors before the data file is created.

In an ideal world, all responses could be trusted to represent exactly what the researcher wants them to represent. However, error creeps in from all sorts of sources. Some mistakes can be spotted and corrected during data editing. Although researchers often are motivated to rush through this portion of the research process, proper editing is one way to maintain high integrity in the data.

Data integrity refers to the notion that the data file actually contains the information that the researcher is trying to obtain to adequately address research questions. Otherwise, the research can't fulfill the responsibility of providing valid input to decision making. Additionally, data integrity extends to the fact that the data have been edited and properly coded so that they are useful to the decision maker. Any errors in this process, just as with errors or shortcuts in the interview process itself, harm the integrity of the data. The Research Snapshot on the next page deals with integrity.

Editing

Fieldwork often produces data containing mistakes. Respondents make mistakes, interviewers make mistakes, and even marketing professors make mistakes! Thus, raw data need to be carefully checked for mistakes. For example, consider the following simple questionnaire item and response:

How long have you lived at your current address? __48__

The researcher had intended the response to be in years. Perhaps the respondent has indicated the number of months rather than years he or she has lived at this address? Alternatively, if this was an interviewer's form, he or she may have marked the response in months without

Do You Have Integrity?

Data integrity is essential to successful research and decision making. Sometimes, this is a question of ethics. Whereas data integrity can suffer when an interviewer or coder simply makes up data, other things can occur that limit data integrity. For instance, data with a large portion of nonresponse has lower integrity than data without so much missing data. However, if respondents have truly left questions blank, the editor should not feel compelled to just "make up" responses.

Data integrity can also suffer simply because the data are edited or coded poorly. For example, the data coder should be aware that data may be used by other downstream users. Therefore, consistent coding should exist. For example, if a coder sometimes uses a 1 for women and a 2 for men, while in another data set uses a 1 for men and 0 for women, the possibility exists that analyses using these categories will be confused. What happens if the data sets are combined? Who exactly are the men and who are the women? Confusion like this is particularly likely if the coder does not enter value labels for nominal variables.

Consider how important consistent coding is for companies that share or sell secondary data. Occupations need a common coding just as do product classes, industries, and numerous other potential data values. Fortunately, industries have standard codes such as NAICS (North American Industrial Classification System) and SIC (Standardized Industrial Classification) codes. Some professional coders have adopted postal service guidelines for coding things like states and addresses. A search of the U.S. Post Office Web site should come to a page with these guidelines (http://pe.usps.gov). Without a standardized approach, analysts may never be quite sure what they are looking at from one data set to another. Thus, research firms need to carefully maintain information coding systems that help maximize data integrity.

Sources: Dubberly, Hugh, "The Information Loop," *CIO Insight* 43 (September 2004), 55–61; Shonerd, René, "Data Integrity Rules," *Association Management* 55, no. 9 (2003), 14.

© GEORGE DOYLE & CIARAN GRIFFIN

© ROYALTY FREE/CORBIS

---

indicating this on the form. How should this be treated? Sometimes, responses may be contradictory. What if the same respondent above gives this response?

What is your age? __32__

This answer contradicts the earlier response. If the respondent is 32 years of age, then how could he or she have lived at the same address for 48 years? Certainly, the responded isn't 32 months old! Therefore, an adjustment should be made to accommodate this information. The most likely case is that this respondent has lived at the current address for four years.

This example illustrates data **editing**. Editing is the process of checking and adjusting data for omissions, consistency, and legibility. In this way, the data become ready for analysis by a computer. So, the editor's task is to check for errors and omissions on questionnaires or other data collection forms. When the editor discovers a problem, he or she adjusts the data to make them more complete, consistent, or readable.

At times, the editor may need to reconstruct data. In the example above, the researcher can guess with some certainty that the respondent entered the original questions in months instead of years. Therefore, the probable true answer can be reconstructed. While the editor should try to make adjustments in an effort to represent as much information from a respondent as possible, reconstructing responses in this fashion should be done only when the probable true response is obvious. Had the respondent's age been 55 years, filling in the response with years would not have been advisable barring other information. Perhaps the respondent has lived in the house since childhood? That possibility would seem real enough to prevent changing the response.

Field Editing

Field supervisors often are responsible for conducting preliminary **field editing**. Field editing often takes place immediately after an interview is completed. The field supervisor is looking for three things in particular:

1. Technical omissions such as a blank page on an interview form

data integrity

The notion that the data file actually contains the information that the researcher promised the decision maker he or she would obtain, meaning in part that the data have been edited and properly coded so that they are useful to the decision maker.

editing

The process of checking the completeness, consistency, and legibility of data and making the data ready for coding and transfer to storage.

field editing

Preliminary editing by a field supervisor on the same day as the interview to catch technical omissions, check legibility of handwriting, and clarify responses that are logically or conceptually inconsistent.

2. The legibility and lucidness of any handwritten responses or responses entered into an open-ended response box in an electronic questionnaire
3. Responses that are logically or conceptually inconsistent.

Field editing is particularly useful when personal interviews have been used to gather data. In these cases, a daily field edit allows supervisors to deal with some questions while the interviewer may still remember what took place. Pertinent facts may allow errors to be identified and perhaps corrected. In addition, the number of unanswered questions or incomplete responses can occasionally be reduced with rapid follow-up. Of course, this is only possible when the respondent can be personally identified.

The supervisor may also use field edits to spot the need for further interviewer training or to correct faulty procedures. For example, if an interviewer did not correctly follow skip patterns, training may be indicated. The supervisor may also notice that an interviewer is not properly probing some open-ended responses.

In-House Editing

in-house editing
A rigorous editing job performed by a centralized office staff.

Although simultaneous field editing is highly desirable, in many situations (particularly with mail questionnaires) early reviewing of the data is not always possible. **In-house editing** rigorously investigates the results of data collection. The research supplier or research department normally has a centralized office staff perform the editing and coding function.

For example, Arbitron measures radio audiences by having respondents record their listening behavior—time, station, and place (home or car)—in diaries. After the diaries are returned by mail, in-house editors perform usability edits in which they check that the postmark is after the last day of the survey week, verify the legibility of station call letters (station WKXY could look like KWXY), look for completeness of entries on each day of the week, and perform other editing activities. If the respondent's age or sex is not indicated, the respondent is called to ensure that this information is included.

Editing for Consistency

The chapter vignette describes some research responses that appear contradictory at first glance. For instance, can employees hate their bosses but still like their jobs? Ms. Aimee (from the opening vignette) is performing an in-house editing task and may need to adjust for inconsistent or contradictory responses. Did the respondent make a mistake or can someone really experience these two opposing reactions?

■ ILLUSTRATING INCONSISTENCY—FACT OR FICTION?

Consider another situation in which a telephone interviewer has been instructed to interview only registered voters in a state that requires voters to be at least eighteen years old. If the editor's review of a questionnaire indicates that the respondent was only seventeen years old, the editor's task is to correct this mistake by deleting this response because this respondent should never have been considered as a sampling unit. The sampling units (respondents) should all be consistent with the defined population.

The editor also should check for consistency within the data collection framework. For example, a survey on out-shopping behavior (shopping in towns other than the one in which the person resides) might have a question such as the following:

In which of the following cities have you shopped for clothing during the last year?(Check all that apply.)

☐ *San Francisco*
☐ *Sacramento*
☐ *San José*
☐ *Los Angeles*
☐ *Other* _____

Please list the clothing stores where you have shopped during the last two months.

_____

_____

_____

_____

Suppose a respondent checks Sacramento and San Francisco to the first question. If the same respondent lists a store that has a location only in Los Angeles in the second question, an error is indicated. Either the respondent failed to list Los Angeles in the first question or listed an erroneous store in the second question. These answers are obviously inconsistent.

■ TAKING ACTION WHEN RESPONSE IS OBVIOUSLY AN ERROR

What should the editor do? If solid evidence exists that points to the fact that the respondent simply failed to check Los Angeles, then the response to the first question can be changed to indicate that the person shopped in that city as well. Since Los Angeles is not listed next to Sacramento or San Francisco, it is unlikely that the respondent checked the wrong city inadvertently. Perhaps the question about the stores triggered a memory that did not come to the respondent when checking off the cities. This seems quite possible, and if another question can also point strongly to the fact that the respondent actually shopped at the store in Los Angeles, then the change should be made.

However, perhaps the respondent placed a mail order with the store in Los Angeles and simply did not physically shop in the store. If other evidence suggests this possibility, then the researcher should not make an adjustment to the first question. For example, a later question may have the respondent list any clothing orders placed via mail order (or by telephone or Internet order).

Responses should be logically consistent, but the researcher should not jump to the conclusion that a change should be made at the first sign of an inconsistency. In all but the most obvious situations, a change should only be made when multiple pieces of evidence exist that some response is in error and when the likely true response is obvious.

Many surveys use filter or "skip" questions that direct a respondent to a specific set of questions depending on how the filter question is answered according to the respondent's answers. Common filter questions involve age, sex, home ownership, or product usage. A survey might involve different questions for a home owner than for someone who does not own a home. A data record may sometimes contain data on variables that the respondent should never have been asked. For example, if someone indicated that he or she did not own a home, yet responses for the home maintenance questions are provided, a problem is indicated. The editor may check other responses to make sure that the screening question was answered accurately. For instance, if the respondent also left the question about home value unanswered, then the editor will be confident that the person truly does not own a home. In cases like this, the editor should adjust these answers by considering all answers to the irrelevant questions as "no response" or "not applicable."

■ EDITING TECHNOLOGY

Today, computer routines can check for inconsistencies automatically. Thus, for electronic questionnaires, rules can be entered which prevent inconsistent responses from ever being stored in the file used for data analysis. These rules should represent the conservative judgment of a trained data analyst. Some online survey services can assist in providing this service. In fact, the rules can even be pre-programmed to prevent many inconsistent responses. Thus, if a person who is 25 indicates that he or she has lived in the same house for 48 years, a pop-up window can inform the respondent that answers are inconsistent and instruct the respondent to review and fix incorrect responses. Electronic questionnaires can also prevent a respondent from being directed to the wrong set of questions based on a screening question response. Thus, no possibility of answering questions that should be skipped is present.

Editing for Completeness

In some cases the respondent may have answered only the second portion of a two-part question. The following question creates a situation in which an in-house editor may have to adjust answers for completeness:

Does your organization have more than one computer network server?

☐ *Yes*
☐ *No*

If yes, how many? _____

If the respondent checked neither yes nor no but indicated three servers, the editor should change the first response to a "yes" as long as other information doesn't indicate otherwise. Here again, a computerized questionnaire may either not allow a response to the "how many" question if someone checked yes or require the respondent to go back to the previous question once he or she tries to enter a number for the "how many" question.

■ ITEM NONRESPONSE

item nonresponse

The technical term for an unanswered question on an otherwise complete questionnaire resulting in missing data.

plug value

An answer that an editor "plugs in" to replace blanks or missing values to permit data analysis; choice of value is based on a predetermined decision rule.

Item nonresponse is the technical term for items left blank. Missing data results from item nonresponse. Specific decision rules for handling this problem should be meticulously outlined in the editor's instructions. In many situations the decision rule is to do nothing with the missing data and simply leave the item blank. However, when the relationship between two questions is important, such as that between a question about job satisfaction and one's pay, the editor may be tempted to insert a **plug value**. If so, several choices are available:

1. Leave the response blank. Because the question is so important, the risk of creating error by plugging a value is too great.
2. Plug in a neutral response (i.e., 3 on a 5-point Likert scale).
3. Plug in alternate choices for missing data ("yes" the first time, "no" the second time, "yes" the third time, and so forth).
4. Randomly select an answer. The editor may flip a coin with heads for "yes" and tails for "no."
5. Insert the mean value of a variable for the missing response (i.e., take the mean of all responses not missing across all respondents for that question and insert the value).

impute

To fill in a missing data point through the use of a statistical process providing an educated guess for the missing response based on available information

6. The editor can **impute** a missing value based on the respondent's choices to other questions. Many different techniques exist for imputing values. Some involve complex statistical estimation approaches that use the available information to forecast a best guess for the missing response.[3]

■ DELETIONS FOR MISSING DATA

list-wise deletion

A method of handling missing data in which the entire record for a respondent that has left a response missing is excluded from use in statistical analyses.

pair-wise deletion

A method of handling missing data in which only the actual variables for a respondent that do not contain information are eliminated from use in statistical analyses.

This issue used to be a bigger deal years ago when some statistical software programs required complete data for statistical computations analysis to take place. Other routines required that an entire sampling unit be eliminated from analysis if even a single response was missing (**list-wise deletion**). Today, most statistical programs can accommodate an occasional missing response through the use of **pair-wise deletion**. Pair-wise deletion means the data that the respondent did provide can still be used in statistical analysis. The statistical routine will only show nonresponse on the particular variable a respondent left blank. As a result, pair-wise deletion produces a larger effective sample size than list-wise deletion.

Option one above is not a bad option unless a response for that particular respondent is crucial, which would rarely be the case. Option six could also be a good option if the response is important or if the effective sample size would be too small if all missing responses are deleted. As long as the researcher is confident that the imputation methods are providing good guesses, this method may allow a response to this item to be salvaged.

The editor must decide whether an entire questionnaire is usable. When a questionnaire has too many missing answers, it may not be suitable for the planned data analysis. While no exact answer exists for this question, a questionnaire with a quarter of the responses or more missing is suspect. In such a situation the editor can record that a particular incomplete questionnaire has been dropped from the sample. Technology is also making the data editor's job easier, since with electronic questionnaires the respondent can be prompted or even required to respond to items that were overlooked or skipped on purpose. Similarly, they can prevent a respondent from indicating multiple responses to a single response question.

This section covers the basics of missing data. However, this topic can become very complex as more sophisticated statistics are applied. Two things to keep in mind with regard to missing data:

- A small amount of missing data (less than 5 percent) is normal and to be expected.
- Missing data that follow a random pattern are less problematic than missing values that display some systematic pattern.

Editing Questions Answered Out of Order

Another task an editor may face is rearranging the answers given to open-ended questions such as may occur in a focus group interview. The respondent may have provided the answer to a subsequent question in his or her comments to an earlier open-ended question. Because the respondent already had clearly identified the answer, the interviewer may not have asked the subsequent question, wishing to avoid hearing "I already answered that earlier" and to maintain interview rapport. If the editor is asked to list answers to all questions in a specific order, the editor may move certain answers to the section related to the skipped question.

Facilitating the Coding Process

Several editing procedures are designed specifically to simplify the coding process for paper and pencil questionnaires. For example, the editor should check written responses for any stray marks. Respondents are often asked to circle responses. Sometimes, a respondent may accidentally draw a circle that overlaps two numbers. For example, the circle may include both 3 and 4. The editor may be able to decide which is the most accurate response and indicate that on the form. Occasionally, a respondent may do this to indicate indecision between the 3 and the 4. Again, if the editor sees that the circle is carefully drawn to include both responses, he or she may indicate a 3.5 on the form. Such ambiguity is impossible with an electronic questionnaire. Computer questionnaires can prohibit a respondent from making two choices on a single item.

■ EDITING AND TABULATING "DON'T KNOW" ANSWERS

In many situations, respondents answer "don't know." On the surface, this response seems to indicate unfamiliarity with the subject matter at question. A *legitimate* "don't know" response is the same as "no opinion." However, there may be reasons for this response other than the legitimate "don't know." A *reluctant* "don't know" is given when the respondent simply does not want to answer a question. For example, asking an individual who is not the head of the household about family income may elicit a "don't know" answer meaning, "This is personal, and I really do not want to answer the question." If the individual does not understand the question, he or she may give a *confused* "I don't know" answer.

In some situations the editor can separate the legitimate "don't knows" ("no opinion") from the other "don't knows." The editor may try to identify the meaning of the "don't know" answer from other data provided on the questionnaire. For instance, the value of a home could be derived from knowledge of the zip code and the average value of homes within that area.

In structured questionnaires, the researcher has to decide whether to provide the respondent with a "don't know" or "no opinion" option. If neither of these is offered, the respondents may simply choose not to answer when they honestly don't know how or don't want to respond to a question. A computerized questionnaire can be set up to require a response to every question. Here, if a "no opinion" or "don't know" opinion is not made available, the result is a forced choice design. The advantages and disadvantages of forced choice questioning were discussed in Chapter 14.

Pitfalls of Editing

Subjectivity can enter into the editing process. Data editors should be intelligent, experienced, and *objective*. A *systematic procedure* for assessing the questionnaires should be developed by the research analyst so that the editor has clearly defined decision rules to follow. Any inferences such as imputing missing values should be done in a manner that limits the chance for the data editor's subjectivity to influence the response.

Pretesting Edit

Editing questionnaires during the pretest stage can prove very valuable. For example, if respondents' answers to open-ended questions were longer than anticipated, the fieldworkers, respondents, and analysts would benefit from a change to larger spaces for the answers. Answers will be more legible because the writers have enough space, answers will be more complete, and answers will be verbatim rather than summarized. Examining answers to pretests may identify poor instructions or inappropriate question wording on the questionnaire.

Error Checking

The final stage in the coding process is error checking and verification, or *data cleaning,* to ensure that all codes are legitimate. For example, computer software can examine the entered data and identify coded values that lie outside the range of acceptable answers. For example, if *sex* is coded 1 for "male" and 2 for "female" and a 3 is found as a value for *sex*, a mistake obviously has occurred and an adjustment must be made.

Coding Qualitative Responses

Qualitative coding was introduced in Chapter 6. The interpretation of these responses may be aided by some type of computer analysis. Sometimes they will even be combined with quantitative responses to address some research question. Either way, some coding is necessary. The coding of qualitative responses is especially important when a truly interpretive approach is taken. Any mistakes in coding can dramatically change the conclusions.

coding

The process of assigning a numerical score or other character symbol to previously edited data.

codes

Rules for interpreting, classifying, and recording data in the coding process; also, the actual numerical or other character symbols assigned to raw data.

Coding represents the way a specific meaning is assigned to a response within previously edited data. Careful editing makes the coding job easier. Codes are meant to represent the meaning in the data by assigning some measurement symbol to the data. This may be a number, letter, or word. The proper form of coding can be tied back to the level of measurement present. Nominal measurement can be represented by a word, letter, or any identifying mark. On the other hand, numbers typically are most appropriate for ordinal, interval, or ratio measures. Thus, **codes** often, but not always, are numerical symbols. However, they are more broadly defined as rules for interpreting, classifying, and recording data. In interpretive research, numbers are seldom used for codes.

In qualitative research, the codes are usually words or phrases that represent themes. Exhibit 19.2 shows a hermeneutic unit in which a qualitative researcher is applying a code to a text describing in detail a respondent's reactions to several different glasses of wine. The researcher is trying to understand in detail what defines the wine drinking experience. In this case, coding is facilitated by the use of qualitative software.

After reading through the text several times, and applying a word-counting routine, the researcher realizes that appearance, the nose (aroma), and guessing (trying to guess what the wine will be like or what type of wine is in the glass) are important themes. A code is assigned to these categories. Similarly, other codes are assigned as shown in the *code manager window.* The density column shows how often a code is applied. After considerable thought and questioning of the experience, the researcher builds a network, or grounded theory, that suggests how a wine may come to be associated with feelings of romance. This theory is shown in the network view. The reader interested in learning more about using software to help with qualitative coding should refer to the software sources provided in Chapter 6.

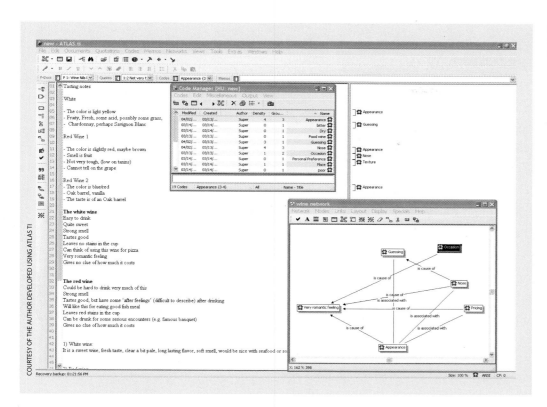

COURTESY OF THE AUTHOR DEVELOPED USING ATLAS TI

EXHIBIT 19.2
Coding Qualitative Data with Words

Structured Qualitative Responses and Dummy Variables

Dummy coding is a simple (dummy-proof) way to represent classification variables.

Qualitative responses to structured questions such as "yes" or "no" can be stored in a data file with letters such as "Y" or "N." Alternatively, they can be represented with numbers, one each to represent the respective category. So, the number 1 can be used to represent "yes" and 2 can be used to represent "no." Since this represents a nominal numbering system, the actual numbers used are arbitrary. Even though the codes are numeric, the variable is classificatory, simply separating the positive from the negative responses.

For reasons that should become increasingly apparent in later chapters, the research may consider adopting **dummy coding** for dichotomous responses like yes or no. Dummy coding assigns a 0 to one category and a 1 to the other. So, for yes/no responses, a 0 could be "no" and a 1 would be "yes." Similarly, a "1" could represent a female respondent and a "0" would be a male respondent. Dummy coding provides the researcher with more flexibility in how structured, qualitative responses are analyzed statistically.

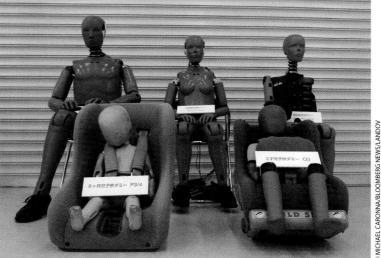

Dummy coding can be used when more than two categories exist, but because a dummy variable can only represent two categories, multiple dummy variables are needed to represent a single qualitative response that can take on more than two categories. In fact, the rule is that if k is the number of categories for a qualitative variable, $k-1$ dummy variables are needed to represent the variable.

dummy coding
Numeric "1" or "0" coding where each number represents an alternate response such as "female" or "male."

effects coding

An alternative to dummy coding using the values of −1 and +1 to represent two categories of responses.

An alternative to dummy coding is **effects coding**. Effects coding is performed by assigning a +1 to one value of a dichotomous variable and a −1 to the other. Dummy coding is more widely used in general, although effects coding has some advantages in the way experimental results are presented. Either way is an acceptable technique for coding structured qualitative data.

Technological Advances and Computerized Data Entry

data entry

The activity of transferring data from a research project to computers.

optical scanning system

A data processing input device that reads material directly from mark-sensed questionnaires.

The process of transferring data from a research project, such as answers to a survey questionnaire, to computers is referred to as **data entry**. Several alternative means exist for entering data into a computer. In studies involving highly structured paper and pencil questionnaires, an **optical scanning system** may be used to read material directly into the computer's memory from *mark-sensed questionnaires*. The form may look similar to the type a student uses to take a multiple-choice test.

In a research study using computer-assisted telephone interviewing (CATI) or a self-administered Internet questionnaire, responses are automatically stored and tabulated as they are collected. Direct data capture substantially reduces clerical errors that occur during the editing and coding process. If researchers have security concerns, the data collected in an Internet survey should be encrypted and protected behind a firewall.

When data are not optically scanned or directly entered into the computer the moment they are collected, data processing begins with keyboarding. A data entry process transfers coded data from the questionnaires or coding sheets onto a hard drive or floppy disk. As in every stage of the research process, there is some concern about whether the data entry job has been done correctly. Data entry workers, like anyone else, may make errors. When 100 percent accuracy is necessary, the data entry results should be *verified* by a second data entry worker. If an error has been made, the verifier corrects the data entry. This process of verifying the data is never performed by the same person who entered the original data. A person who misread the coded questionnaire during the keyboarding operation might make the same mistake during the verifying process, and the mistake might go undetected.

Today, this process is being greatly aided by technology. Web-based surveys eliminate any manual data entry as a respondent's choices are automatically recorded in real time. Thus, the chances for manual keypunching errors are eliminated. The only possible source for such a mistake is with the respondent. However, errors like multiple responses to a single choice response, responding to skipped questions (they simply do not show up to someone who shouldn't answer them) or even order effects can be eliminated as questions can be presented in randomized order from respondent to respondent. Voice recognition software is also providing a way that telephone interviews can have simple results automatically entered into a data file. Technology may eliminate the job for data entry in some situations; however, data coding is still necessary to better prepare the data for the analyst.

Creating Data Files

Once structured, qualitative responses are coded and stored in an electronic data file. Here, both the qualitative responses and quantitative responses are likely stored for every respondent involved in a survey or interview. A terminology exists that helps describe this process and the file that results.

Some of the terminology seems strange these days. For instance, what does a "card" have to do with a simple computer file? Most of the terminology describing files goes back to the early days of computers. In those days, data and the computer programs that produced results were stored on actual computer cards. Hopefully, readers will no longer have to use physical cards to store data. Much easier and more economical ways exist.

Researchers organize coded data into cards, fields, records, and files. Cards are the collection of records that make up a file. A **field** is a collection of characters (a *character* is a single number, letter, or special symbol such as a question mark) that represents a single piece of data, usually a variable. Some variables may require a large field, particularly for text data; other variables may require a field of only one character. Text variables are represented by **string characters**, which is computer terminology for a series of alphabetic characters (non-numeric characters) that may form a word. String characters often contain long fields of eight or more characters. In contrast, a dummy variable is a numeric variable that needs only one character to form a field.

A **record** is a collection of related fields. A record was the way a single, complete computer card was represented. Researchers may use the term *record* to refer to one respondent's data. A **data file** is a collection of related records that make up a data set.

Exhibit 19.3 shows the SPSS variable view used to describe an SPSS file storing a data set that will be used later in the text. Most of the headings are straightforward, beginning with the name of the variable, the type of variable (numeric or string), the size, the label, and so forth. Notice that the variable *car* is a string variable. The values for this variable are words that correspond to whether the car is an "import" or "domestic."

The coder will sometimes like to associate a label with specific values of a numeric variable. Exhibit 19.3 shows the value labels dialog box that opens when the "Values" column is clicked. **Value labels** are extremely useful and allow a word or short phrase to be associated with a numeric value. In this case, the value label helps describe a respondent's home country. A "0" is assigned to respondents from Germany while a "1" is assigned to respondents from the United States.

field

A collection of characters that represents a single type of data—usually a variable.

string characters

Computer terminology to represent formatting a variable using a series of alphabetic characters (nonnumeric characters) that may form a word

record

A collection of related fields that represents the responses from one sampling unit.

data file

The way a data set is stored electronically in spreadsheet-like form in which the rows represent sampling units and the columns represent variables.

value labels

Unique labels assigned to each possible numeric code for a response.

EXHIBIT 19.3 **Variable Values Can Be Labeled**

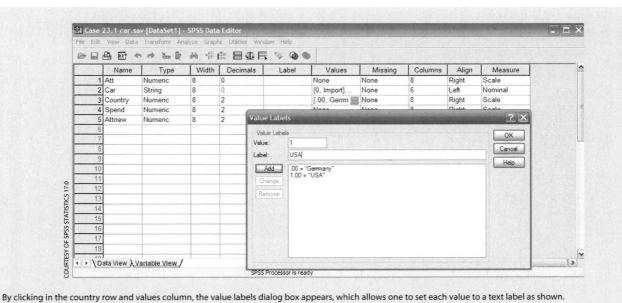

By clicking in the country row and values column, the value labels dialog box appears, which allows one to set each value to a text label as shown.

The analysts will no doubt appreciate the coder's value labeling. Now, when frequencies or other statistical output is created for this variable, the value label will appear instead of simply a number. The advantage is that the analyst will not have to remember what coding was used. In other words, he or she won't have to remember that a "1" meant United States. Other statistical programs accommodate value labels in similarly easy fashions. With SAS, the coder could create a format statement as follows:

```
proc format;
value labels
    0 = 'Germany'
    1 = 'USA';
```

```
data chap19;
input att car country speed attnew;
format country labels.;
```

Just as in the SPSS example, the sequence assigns the label "Germany" to a value of 0 for *country* and a label of "USA" to a value of 1 for this dummy variable.

What Is a Data File?

Data are generally stored in a matrix that resembles a common spreadsheet file. A data file stores the data from a research project and is typically represented in a rectangular arrangement (matrix) of data in rows and columns. Typically, each row represents a respondent's scores on each variable and each row represents a variable for which there is a value for every respondent. Exhibit 19.4 illustrates a data matrix corresponding to the variable view in Exhibit 19.3. In this case, data exist for 40 respondents. No doubt, the data file appears to be a spreadsheet. A spreadsheet program like Excel is an acceptable way to store a data file, and increasingly, statistical programs like SPSS, SAS, and others can work easily with an Excel spreadsheet.

Each column in Exhibit 19.4 represents a particular variable. The first column is an interval variable representing a respondent's attitude toward his or her car. The next two columns are nominal variables indicating the origins of the respondent's car and country (USA/Europe). Finally, the last two variables, Spend and Attnew, represent a ratio variable indicating how much one typically spends keeping their car in good order and an interval variable indicating their attitude toward a new type of car called the Cycle. All the data were obtained through a survey approach.

EXHIBIT 19.4 **Car Data File Stored in SPSS**

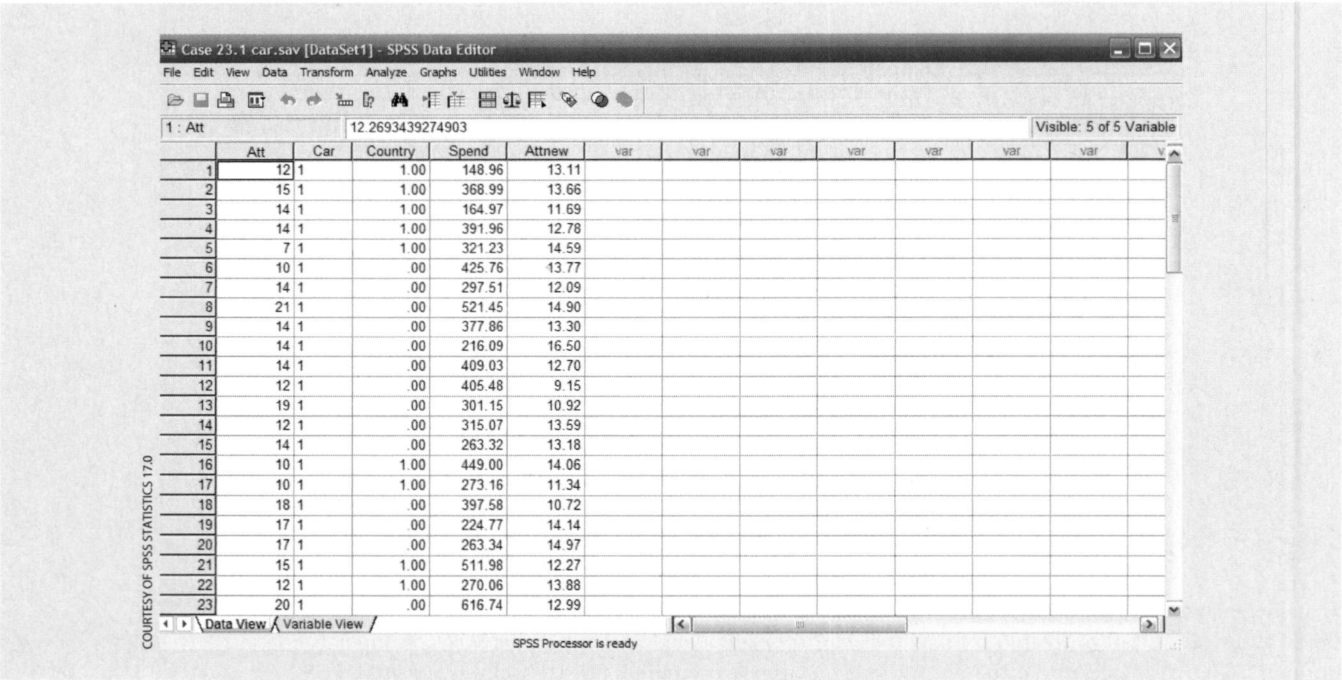

	Att	Car	Country	Spend	Attnew
1	12	1	1.00	148.96	13.11
2	15	1	1.00	368.99	13.66
3	14	1	1.00	164.97	11.69
4	14	1	1.00	391.96	12.78
5	7	1	1.00	321.23	14.59
6	10	1	.00	425.76	13.77
7	14	1	.00	297.51	12.09
8	21	1	.00	521.45	14.90
9	14	1	.00	377.86	13.30
10	14	1	.00	216.09	16.50
11	14	1	.00	409.03	12.70
12	12	1	.00	405.48	9.15
13	19	1	.00	301.15	10.92
14	12	1	.00	315.07	13.59
15	14	1	.00	263.32	13.18
16	10	1	1.00	449.00	14.06
17	10	1	1.00	273.16	11.34
18	18	1	.00	397.58	10.72
19	17	1	.00	224.77	14.14
20	17	1	.00	263.34	14.97
21	15	1	1.00	511.98	12.27
22	12	1	1.00	270.06	13.88
23	20	1	.00	616.74	12.99

COURTESY OF SPSS STATISTICS 17.0

Code Construction

There are two basic rules for code construction. First, the coding categories should be *exhaustive,* meaning that a coding category should exist for all possible responses. With a categorical variable such as sex, making categories exhaustive is not a problem. However, trouble may arise when a response represents only a few respondents or when responses might be out of the ordinary. For example, when questioned about automobile ownership, an antique car collector might mention that he drives a Packard Clipper. This may present a problem if separate categories have been developed for all possible makes of cars. Solving this problem frequently requires inclusion of an "other" code category to ensure that the categories are all-inclusive. For example, household size might be coded 1, 2, 3, 4, and 5 or more. The "5 or more" category assures a category for all respondents.

Second, the coding categories should be *mutually exclusive* and *independent*. This means that there should be no overlap among the categories to ensure that a subject or response can be placed in only one category.

Missing Data Codes

Missing data is also recognized with a code. In the "good old days" of computer cards, a numeric value such as 9 or 99 was used to represent missing data. Today, most software will understand that either a period or a blank response represents missing data. Occasionally however, researchers still use the convention of representing missing data with a "9" value of some sort.

Precoding

When a questionnaire is highly structured, the categories may be precoded before the data are collected. Exhibit 19.5 on the next page presents a questionnaire for which the precoded response categories were determined before the start of data collection. The codes in the data file will correspond to the small numbers beside each choice option. In most instances, the codes will not actually appear on the questionnaire.

The questionnaire in Exhibit 19.5 shows several demographic questions classifying individuals' scores. Question 29 has three possible answers, and they are precoded 1, 2, 3. Question 30 asks a person to respond "yes" (1) or "no" (2) to the question "Are you the male or female head of the household?" Once again, technology is making things easier and much of this type of coding is automated. For users of Web-based survey services, all that one need do is submit a questionnaire and in return he or she will receive a coded data file in the software of his or her choice.

Telephone interviews are still widely used. The partial questionnaire in Exhibit 19.6 on the next page shows a precoded format for a telephone interview. In this situation the interviewer circles the coded numerical score as the answer to the question.

Precoding can be used if the researcher knows what answer categories exist before data collection occurs. Once the questionnaire has been designed and the structured (or closed-form) answers identified, coding then becomes routine. In some cases, predetermined responses are based on standardized classification schemes. A coding framework that standardizes occupation follows:

What is your occupation? (PROBE: *What kind of work is that?*)

01	Professional, technical, and kindred workers	08	Service workers
02	Farmers	09	Laborers, except farm and mine
03	Managers, officials, and proprietors	10	Retired, widow, widower
		11	Student
04	Clerical	12	Unemployed, on relief, laid off
05	Sales workers	13	Homemaker
06	Craftsmen, foremen, and kindred workers	14	Other (specify)
07	Operatives and kindred workers	99	No occupation given

Computer-assisted telephone interviewing (CATI) requires precoding. Changing the coding framework after the interviewing process has begun is extremely difficult because it requires changes in the computer programs. In any event, coding closed-ended structured responses is a straightforward process of entering the code into the data file.

EXHIBIT 19.5 **Precoding Fixed-Alternative Responses**

29. **Do you—or does anyone else in your immediate household—belong to a labor union?**

    ¹☐ <u>Yes</u>, I personally belong to a labor union.
    ²☐ <u>Yes</u>, another member of my household belongs to a labor union.
    ³☐ <u>No</u>, no one in my household belongs to a labor union.

30. **Are you the male or female head of the household—that is, <u>the person whose income is the chief source of support of the household?</u>**

    ¹☐ Yes   ²☐ No

31. **Would you please check the appropriate combined yearly income *(before income taxes and any other payroll deductions)* from <u>all sources of all those</u> in your immediate household? *(Please include income from salaries, investments, dividends, rents, royalties, bonuses, commissions, etc.)* <u>Please remember that your individual answers will not be divulged.</u>**

¹☐ Less than $4,000	⁷☐ $8,000–$8,999	¹³☐ $25,000–$29,999
²☐ $4,000–$4,999	⁸☐ $9,000–$9,999	¹⁴☐ $30,000–$39,999
³☐ $5,000–$5,999	⁹☐ $10,000–$12,499	¹⁵☐ $40,000–$49,999
⁴☐ $6,000–$6,999	¹⁰☐ $12,500–$14,999	¹⁶☐ $50,000–$74,999
⁵☐ $7,000–$7,499	¹¹☐ $15,000–$19,999	¹⁷☐ $75,000–$99,999
⁶☐ $7,500–$7,999	¹²☐ $20,000–$24,999	¹⁸☐ $100,000 or more

32 a. **Do you personally own corporate stocks?**   ¹☐ Yes   ²☐ No

    b. **Do you own stocks in the corporation for which you work?**
       Do you own them in a corporation for which you do <u>not</u> work?
       (Please check as many as apply.)

       Own <u>STOCK</u> in:

       ¹☐ Company for which I work   ²☐ Other company

       <u>THANK YOU VERY MUCH FOR YOUR COOPERATION</u>

       If you would like to make any comments on any of the subjects covered in this study, please use the space below:

       _____
       _____

EXHIBIT 19.6 **Precoded Format for Telephone Interview**

Study #45641   For office use only
Travel (Telephone Screening)   Respondent #_____
City:
Chicago
Gary
Ft. Wayne
Bloomington

Hello, I'm _____ from_____, a national survey research company. We are conducting a study and would like to ask you a few questions.

A. Before we begin, do you—or any member of your family—work for . . .
   1 A travel agency   2 An advertising agency   3 A marketing research company
   (If "yes" to any of the above, terminate and tally on contact sheet)

B. By the way, have you been interviewed as part of a survey research study within the past month?
   1 Yes—(Terminate and tally on contact sheet)
   2 No—(Continue)
   1. Have you yourself made any trips of over 100 miles within the continental 48 states in the past 3 months?
      1 Yes
      2 No—(Skip to Question 10)
   2. Was the trip for business reasons (paid for by your firm), vacation, or personal reasons?

	Last Trip	Second Last Trip	Other Trips
Business	1	1	1
Vacation	2	2	2
Personal (excluding a vacation)	3	3	3

Naturally Negative

Data coders often extract meaning from short open-ended comments written by research respondents. Coders may code these at different levels beginning by grouping responses based on whether they are positive or negative. One thing that might surprise someone new to coding is how many of the responses are negative. Respondents seem very anxious to complain.

Many workplaces have a suggestion box for employees. Research suggests that dissatisfied employees are much more likely to express comments anonymously than are satisfied employees. The open-ended comments tend to look far more negative than the average employee satisfaction ratings. The length of comments also increases as employees are more dissatisfied.

Americans are not the only respondent group that focuses on the negative. A recent study compared the business ethics of several countries with a particular focus on Japan. The study asked Japanese consumers:

"What particular ethical or unethical behavior did you personally experience or hear from others or the media?"

The sample of Japanese consumers produced 201 ethical comments and 462 comments about unethical treatment from businesses. Are businesses in Japan really that unethical or do respondents focus on the negative? What would happen when the same question is asked of American, Canadian, or Mexican consumers? In either case, the coder's job is not to draw a conclusion on the overall results but simply to enter the appropriate response into a data file for each and every respondent—without complaining!

Sources: Tsalikas, J. and B. Seaton, "The International Business Ethics Index: Japan," *Journal of Business Ethics* 80 (2008), 379–385; Poncheri, R. M., J. T. Lindberg, L. F. Thompson and E. A. Surface, "A Comment on Employee Surveys: Negativity Bias in Open-Ended Responses," *Organizational Research Methods* 11 (July 2008), 614.

More on Coding Open-Ended Questions

Surveys sometimes contain some semi-structured open-ended questions. These questions may be exploratory or they may be potential follow-ups to structured questions. The purpose of coding such questions is to reduce the large number of individual responses to a few general categories of answers that can be assigned numerical codes.

Similar answers should be placed in a general category and assigned the same code much as the codes are assigned in the qualitative sample involving wine consumption above. Except in this case, a small amount of data may be obtained from a large number of respondents, whereas in the hermeneutic unit above, a large amount of data is obtained from one or a small number of respondents. For example, a consumer survey about frozen food also asked why a new microwaveable product would or would not be purchased:

- We don't buy frozen food very often.
- I like to prepare fresh food and to me, frozen isn't fresh.
- Frozen foods are not as tasty as fresh foods.
- I don't like the freezer taste that the product would have.

All of these answers could be categorized under "dislike frozen foods" and assigned the code 1. Code construction in these situations reflects the judgment of the researcher. The Research Snapshot above describes how coders can expect negative responses on such questions.

A major objective in the code-building process is to accurately transfer the meanings from written responses to numeric codes. Experienced researchers recognize that the key idea in this process is that code building is based on thoughts, not just words. The end result of code building should be a list, in an abbreviated and orderly form, of all comments and thoughts given in answers to the questions.

Developing an appropriate code from the respondent's exact comments is somewhat of an art. Researchers generally perform a test tabulation to identify verbatim responses from approximately 20 percent of the completed questionnaires and then establish coding categories reflecting the judgment of the person constructing the codes. **Test tabulation** is the tallying of a small sample of the total number of replies to a particular question. The purpose is to preliminarily identify the stability and distribution of answers that will determine a coding scheme. Exhibit 19.7 on the next page illustrates open-ended responses and preliminary open-ended codes generated for the question "Why does the chili you just tasted taste closer to homemade?" During the coding procedure, the

test tabulation

Tallying of a small sample of the total number of replies to a particular question in order to construct coding categories.

EXHIBIT 19.7 Coding Open-Ended Questions about Chili

You don't get that much meat in a can.
The beans are cooked just right.
It just (doesn't look) like any canned chili I've had. I can see spices;
    I've never seen it in any canned chili.
It is not too spicy,
but it is tasty—savory.
It's not (loaded with beans)—just enough beans.
It's moist—not too chewy.

Tastes (fresh).
The canned stuff is too (soft). Too overcooked usually.
It doesn't have a lot of filler and not too many beans.

It's not too spicy. It's not too hot, it's mild.
Has enough spice to make it tastier.
It seems to have a pretty good gravy. Some are watery.

1. Don't get that much meat in a can
2. Beans are cooked just right

3. I can see spices
4. Not too spicy
5. It is tasty
6. Has just enough beans
7. Moist
8. Not too chewy
9. Fresh taste
10. Canned is usually overcooked
11. Not a lot of filler
12. Not too many beans
13. Not too hot, it's mild
14. Has enough spice
15. Gravy not watery

Walker Research, "Coding Open Ends Based on Thoughts," *The Marketing Researcher*, December 1979, pp. 1–3.

The coder will try to classify all of the comments from the interviewer in a code that facilitates analysis.

respondent's opinions are divided into mutually exclusive thought patterns. These separate divisions may consist of a single word, a phrase, or a number of phrases, but in each case represent only one thought. Each separate thought is coded once. When a thought is composed of more than one word or phrase, only the most specific word or phrase is coded.

After tabulating the basic responses, the researcher must determine how many answer categories will be acceptable. This will be influenced by the purpose of the study and the limitations of the computer program or plan for data entry. For example, if only one single-digit field is assigned to a particular survey question, the number of possible categories is limited. If an "other" or "miscellaneous" code category appears along with a "don't know/no answer" category, the code construction will be further limited.

Devising the Coding Scheme

A coding scheme should not be too elaborate. The coder's task is only to summarize the data. Exhibit 19.8 shows a test tabulation of airport visitors' responses to a question that asked for comments about the Honolulu Airport. After the first pass at devising the coding scheme, the researcher must decide whether to revise it and whether the codes are appropriate for answering management's questions. A preliminary scheme with too many categories can always be collapsed or reduced later in the analysis. If initial coding is too abstract and only a few categories are established, revising the codes to more concrete statements will be difficult unless the raw data are recorded.

In the Honolulu Airport example, the preliminary tabulation contained too many codes, but it could be reduced to a smaller number of categories. For example, the heading "Friendly/Attractive Personnel" could include the responses "Friendly staff/people," "Polite VIP/friendly/helpful," and "Cute VIP." Experienced coders group answers under generalized headings that are pertinent to

EXHIBIT 19.8
Open-Ended Responses to a Survey about the Honolulu Airport

	Number
Prices high: restaurant/coffee shop/snack bar	90
Dirty—filthy—smelly restrooms/airport	65
Very good/good/excellent/great	59
Need air-conditioning	52
Nice/beautiful	45
Gift shops expensive	32
Too warm/too hot	31
Friendly staff/people	25
Airport is awful/bad	23
Long walk between terminal/gates	21
Clean airport	17
Employees rude/unfriendly/poor attitude	16
More signs/maps in lobby/streets	16
Like it	15
Love gardens	11
Need video games/arcade	10
More change machines/different locations	8
More padded benches/comfortable waiting area	8
More security personnel including HPD	8
Replace shuttle with moving walkways	8
Complaint: flight delay	7
Cool place	7
Crowded	7
Provide free carts for carry-on bags	7
Baggage storage inconvenient/need in different locations	6
Floor plan confusing	6
Mailbox locations not clear/more needed	6
More restaurants and coffee shops/more variety	6
Need a place to nap	6
Polite VIP/friendly/helpful	6
Poor help in gift shops/rude/unfriendly	6
Slow baggage delivery/service	6
Very efficient/organized	6
Excellent food	5
Install chilled water drinking fountains	5
Love Hawaii	5
More TV sets	5
Noisy	5
People at sundries/camera rude	5
Shuttle drivers rude	5
Something to do for passengers with long waits	5
Airport too spread out	4
Better information for departing/arriving flights	4
Better parking for employees	4
Better shuttle service needed	4
Cute VIP	4

the research question. Individual coders should give the same code to similar responses. The categories should be sufficiently unambiguous that coders will not classify items in different ways.

Coding open-ended questions is a very complex issue. Certainly, this task cannot be mastered simply from reading this chapter. However, the reader should have a feel for the art of coding responses into similar categories. With practice, and by using multiple coders so that consistency can be examined, one can become skilled at this task.

Coding Sheet

A **coding sheet** documents the location of each variable in a data matrix. In essence, a coding sheet provides a quick summary for the analyst that is very useful when a data file becomes quite large or when data are entered into a plain text file in a fixed format. For instance, the first entry in a data matrix is usually the respondent's ID. If the IDs range from 1 to 1,000, a minimum of four spaces would need to be used for this data entry. In an experiment, the second entry would

coding sheet

A book that identifies each variable in a study and gives the variable's description, code name, and position in the data matrix.

often be the value of an experimental variable. The coding sheet would indicate this information as follows:

Variable	Field (columns)	Description	Value Labels
ID	1–4	Respondent Identification Number	None
Treat1	5	Package Color Experimental Treatment	0 = Blue 1 = Red

This type of data entry is increasingly rare as most statistical packages can handle comma separated values (CSV) or read data directly from a spreadsheet. Even then, a data sheet describing the variables and the data value labels often is contained as a separate sheet in a workbook or file. Recent versions of SPSS contain a separate worksheet called a data view that provides a description of the data matrix. This is also where the data coder can enter or change things like value labels. Exhibit 19.9 shows an example.

EXHIBIT 19.9 Data View in SPSS Serves Much the Same Purpose of a Coding Sheet

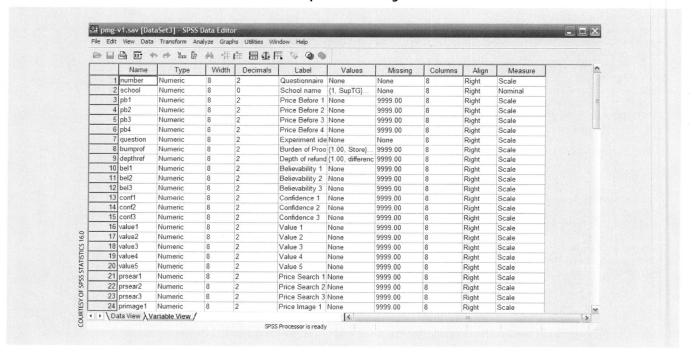

Editing and Coding Combined

Frequently the person coding the questionnaire performs certain editing functions, such as translating an occupational title provided by the respondent into a code for socioeconomic status. A question that asks for a description of the job or business often is used to ensure that there will be no problem in classifying the responses. For example, respondents who indicate "salesperson" as their occupation might write their job description as "selling shoes in a shoe store" or "selling IBM supercomputers to the Defense Department." Generally, coders are instructed to perform this type of editing function, seeking the help of a tabulation supervisor if questions arise. In all cases, the coder's job is to make the data analyst's job easier by making the data set intuitively easy to understand.

- Check responses for inconsistent answers.
  - Remove the data (becomes missing) when contradiction cannot be resolved.
  - Replace the data with correct value when proper answer is clear
  - Include check questions on questionnaires that are lengthy or for which respondents may have low involvement or may provide misleading responses.
- Missing values can be a problem in statistical analysis, particularly when there is more than a trivial amount (5 percent) and especially when the missing values are not randomly dispersed throughout the data.
  - Best options for missing data:
    - Replace missing values with an actual entry with caution and using the most appropriate imputation method.
    - Pair-wise deletion is a good way to handle missing data in most applications as it preserves information

and is very amenable to even advanced statistical procedures.

- Dummy variables should be used to represent categorical variables, particularly dichotomous (only two values possible) data, whenever possible. Dummy variables provide greater flexibility for dichotomous responses in later statistical analysis.
- Take advantage of technology. If a computerized interface can be used to collect data, strongly consider using it. Data entry errors (nonrespondent errors) are greatly reduced or eliminated and respondent errors can also be mitigated.
- Use value labels for categorical responses. This greatly reduces the chance for later confusion in interpreting statistical results for these variables.
- Spreadsheets provide a good way to store data today because not only can basic analyses be conducted with a spreadsheet program, but statistical packages like SAS and SPSS can easily use data in spreadsheet or CSV format.

Summary

1. Edit responses to maintain data integrity. Data editing is necessary before coding and storing the data file. The data editor sometimes alters a respondent's answer to avoid an error. Often, this situation arises because a respondent has provided inconsistent answers; that is, responses to different questions that contradict each other. The editor should be cautious in altering a respondent's answer. Only when a certain response is obviously wrong and the true response is easily determined should the coder substitute a new value for the original response. Ideally, multiple pieces of evidence would suggest the original response as inaccurate and also suggest the accurate response before the respondent takes such a step. Missing data should generally be left as missing although imputation methods exist to provide an educated guess for missing values. These imputation methods can be used when the sample size is small and the researcher needs to retain as many responses as possible.

2. Know the basics of coding qualitative responses. Qualitative research, such as typified by depth interviews, conversations, or other responses, is coded by identifying the themes underlying some interview. The codes become a key component of a hermeneutic unit that ultimately can be linked to one another to form a grounded theory. The frequency with which some thought is expressed helps to identify appropriate coding for unstructured qualitative data.

3. Understand when and how to code using a dummy variable approach. Quantitative structured responses are generally coded simply by marking the number corresponding to the choice selected by the respondent. Qualitative structured responses must also be coded. Dichotomous variables lend themselves well to dummy coding. With dummy coding, the two possible choices to a question are coded with a "1" for one response and a "0" for the other. Short-answer or list questions are coded by assigning a value to all responses that seem to suggest the same theme even if different words are used.

4. Appreciate the ways that technological advances have simplified the coding process. Throughout the chapter, technological advances in data collection were mentioned. These advances have automated a great deal of data entry and reduced the chances for nonresponse error due to incorrect data entry. These techniques also reduce response error in the form of multiple responses to a single-response question or giving out of range responses. Inconsistent or contradictory responses can be automatically flagged and the respondent can be prompted to go back and correct the potential errors. Also, if a respondent fails to answer a question, a pop-up window can take that respondent back to the question and force him or her to respond in order to continue through the rest of the questionnaire. In addition, optical scanners can read responses from paper and pencil questionnaires automatically. All of these are greatly simplifying data entry and doing some of the job of the data editor.

5. Understand the way data are represented in a data file. A survey provides an overview of respondents based on their answers to questions. These answers are edited, coded, and then stored in a data file. The data file is generally structured as a data matrix in which the rows represent respondents and the columns represent variables. More and more, data can be analyzed directly from a spreadsheet format. Value labels can make a data file much easier to work with. Value labels indicate a verbal description associated with specific values for a given variable.

Key Terms and Concepts

codes, *498*
coding, *498*
coding sheet, *507*
data entry, *500*
data file, *501*
data integrity, *492, 493*
dummy coding, *499*
editing, *493*

effects coding, *500*
field, *501*
field editing, *493*
impute, *496*
in-house editing, *494*
item nonresponse, *496*
list-wise deletion, *496*
nonrespondent error, *491*

optical scanning system, *500*
pair-wise deletion, *496*
plug value, *496*
raw data, *491*
record, *501*
string characters, *501*
test tabulation, *505*
value labels, *501*

Questions for Review and Critical Thinking

1. What is the purpose of editing? Provide some examples of questions that might need editing.

2. When should the raw data from a respondent be altered by a data editor?

3. Ms. Aimee, the data editor from the opening vignette, is going through responses. After reviewing the first eight responses each indicating the respondent has very negative feelings about his or her supervisors, she comes across a response that suggests the employee believes his or her boss is the best possible boss in the world. Ms. Aimee is tempted to dismiss this as a potentially misleading response. What evidence might she look to in making the decision to alter or delete this response?

4. How is data coding different from data editing?

5. What are the options for handling missing data? What is the difference between list-wise and pair-wise deletion?

6. A 25-year-old respondent indicates that she owns her own house in Springfield, Illinois, and it is valued at $990 million. Later in the interview, she indicates that she didn't finish high school and that she drives a 1993 Buick Century. Should the editor consider altering any of these responses? If so, how?

7. What role might a word counter play in coding qualitative research results?

8. A survey respondent from Florida has been asked to respond about whether or not he or she owns a boat, and if so, whether he or she stores the boat at a marina. Over two hundred respondents are included in this sample. What suggestions do you have for coding the information provided?

9. How would a dummy variable be used to represent whether or not a respondent in a restaurant ordered dessert after their meal?

10. List at least three ways in which recent technological advances have changed the way data are coded.

11. How do you think the large portion of online surveys has changed data entry and data editing? Do you think it has reduced overall error? Explain.

12. **ETHICS** A large retail company implements an employee survey that ostensibly is aimed at customer satisfaction. The survey includes a yes or no question that asks whether or not the employee has ever stolen something from the workplace. How could this data be coded? What steps could be attempted to try and ensure that the employee's response is honest? Do you believe it is fair to ask this question? Should the employer take action against employees who have indicated that they have stolen something?

13. A researcher asks, "What do you remember about advertising for Gillette Turbo razors?" A box with enough room for 100 words is provided in which the respondent can answer the question. The survey involves responses from 250 consumers. How should the code book for this question be structured? What problems might it present?

14. **'NET** Use http://www.naicscode.com to help with this response. What is the NAICS code for golf (country) clubs? What is the NAICS code for health clubs? How can these codes be useful in creating data files?

15. **'NET** Explore the advantages of computerized software such as ATLAS.ti. The Web site is at http://www.atlasti.com. How do you think it might assist in coding something like a depth interview or a collage created by a respondent?

Research Activities

1. Design a short questionnaire with fewer than five fixed-alternative questions to measure student satisfaction with your college bookstore. Interview five classmates and then arrange the database into a data matrix.

2. **'NET** The Web page of the Research Triangle Institute (http://www.rti.org) describes its research tools and methods in some detail. Click on *Survey Research and Services, for instance,* and explore the surveys and survey tools described there. How might these methods assist in coding?

Case 19.1 U.S. Department of the Interior Heritage Conservation and Recreation Service

© GETTY IMAGES/PHOTODISC GREEN

Some years ago the U.S. Department of the Interior conducted a telephone survey to help plan for future outdoor recreation. A nine-page questionnaire concerning participation in outdoor recreational activities and satisfaction with local facilities was administered by the Opinion Research Corporation of Princeton, New Jersey, to 4,029 respondents. The last two pages of the questionnaire appear in Case Exhibit 19.1–1. Assume the data will be entered into a data file in which each data entry should include the following information:

- Respondent number
- State code (all 50 states)

Question

Design the coding for this portion of the questionnaire. Assume that the data from previous pages of the questionnaire will follow these data.

CASE EXHIBIT 19.1–1 **Sample Page from Questionnaire**

The following questions are for background purposes.

32. Do you live in an . . .
   ☐ Urban location
   ☐ Suburban location
   ☐ Rural location

33. Counting yourself, how many members of your family live here? (If "1" on Q.33, go to Q.35) _____

34. How many family members are . . .
   Over 65 years _____
   40 to 65 years _____
   21 to 39 years _____
   12 to 20 years _____
   5 to 11 years _____
   Under 5 years _____

35. What is your age? (Years) _____

36. In school, what is the highest grade (or year) you have completed? (Circle response)

Elementary school	01	02	03	04	05 06
Junior high school	07	08			
High school	09	10	11	12	
College	13	14	15	16	
Graduate school	17	18	19	20	21

37. What is your occupation? What kind of work is that?
   ☐ Professional, technical, and kindred workers
   ☐ Farmers
   ☐ Managers, officials, and proprietors
   ☐ Clerical and kindred workers
   ☐ Sales workers
   ☐ Craftspersons, forepersons, and kindred workers
   ☐ Operatives and kindred workers

☐ Service workers
☐ Laborers, except farm and mine

☐ Retired, widow, widower
☐ Student
☐ Unemployed, on relief, laid off → Go to Q.40
☐ Housewife

☐ Other (specify) _____

38. How many hours a week do you work at your place of employment? _____ (hours)

39. How many days of vacation do you get in a year? _____ (days)

40. Please tell me which of the following income categories most closely describe the total family income for the year before taxes, including wages and all other income. Is it . . .
   ☐ Under $12,000
   ☐ $12,000–$20,000
   ☐ $20,001–$30,000
   ☐ $30,001–$50,000
   ☐ $50,001–$100,000
   ☐ Over $100,001

41. Sex of respondent . . .
   ☐ Male
   ☐ Female

42. What is the zip code at your place of employment?
This concludes the interview; thank you very much for your cooperation and time.

Case 19.2 Shampoo 9–10

A shampoo, code named "9–10," was given to women for trial use.[4] The respondents were asked what they liked and disliked about the product. Some sample codes are given in Case Exhibits 19.2–1 and 19.2–2.

There were two separate sets of codes: The codes in Case Exhibit 19.2–1 were for coding the respondents' likes, and the codes in Case Exhibit 19.2–2 were for coding their dislikes. The headings identify fields in the data matrix and the different attributes of shampoo. The specific codes are listed under each attribute. The coding instructions were first to look for the correct heading, and then to locate the correct comment under that heading and use that number as the code.

For example, if, in response to a "like" question, a respondent had said, "The shampoo was gentle and mild," a coder would look in field 10, the "gentleness" field, and find the comment "Gentle/mild/not harsh"; then the coder would write "11" next to the comment. If, under "dislikes," someone had said, "I would rather have a shampoo with a crème rinse," the coder would look in field 16 for comparison to other shampoos and write "74" ("Prefer one with a crème rinse") beside that response.

The sample questionnaires appear in Case Exhibit 19.2–3.

Questions

1. Code each of the three questionnaires.
2. Evaluate this coding scheme.

CASE EXHIBIT 19.2–1 **Sample Codes for "Like" Questions**

Test No. Shampoo
Question: Likes

Field 10 Gentleness	Field 11 Result on Hair
11 Gentle/mild/not harsh	21 Good for hair/helps hair
12 Wouldn't strip hair of natural oils	22 Leaves hair manageable/no tangles/no need for crème rinse
13 Doesn't cause/helps flyaway hair	23 Gives hair body
14 Wouldn't dry out hair	24 Mends split ends
15 Wouldn't make skin/scalp break out	25 Leaves hair not flyaway
16 Organic/natural	26 Leaves hair silky/smooth
17	27 Leaves hair soft
18	28 Leaves hair shiny
19	29 Hair looks/feels/good/clean
20	30
1–	2–
1+ Other gentleness	2+ Other results on hair

Field 12 Cleaning	Field 13 Miscellaneous
31 Leaves no oil/keeps hair dry	41 Cheaper/economical/good price
32 It cleans well	42 Smells good/nice/clean
33 Lifts out oil/dirt/artificial conditioners	43 Hairdresser recommended
34 Don't have to scrub as much	44 Comes in different formulas
35 No need to wash as often/keeps hair cleaner longer	45 Concentrated/use only a small amount
36 Doesn't leave a residue on scalp	46 Good for whole family (unspecified)
37 Good lather	47
38 Good for oily hair	48
39	49
40	50
3–	4– Other miscellaneous
3+ Other cleaning	4+ Don't know/nothing

CASE EXHIBIT 19.2-2 **Sample Codes for "Dislike" Questions**

Test No. <u>Shampoo</u>
Question: Dislikes

Field 14 Harshness

51	Too strong
52	Strips hair/takes too much oil out
53	Dries hair out
54	Skin reacts badly to it
55	
56	
57	
58	
59	
60	
5−	
5+	Other harshness

Field 15 Cleaning

61	Doesn't clean well
62	Leaves a residue on scalp
63	Poor lather
64	Not good for oily hair
65	
66	
67	
68	
69	
70	
6−	
6+	Other cleaning

Field 16 Comparison to Others

71	Prefer herbal/organic shampoo
72	Prefer medicated/dandruff shampoo
73	Same as other shampoos—doesn't work any differently
74	Prefer one with a crême rinse
75	Prefer another brand (unspecified)
76	
77	
78	
79	
80	
7−	
7+	Other comparison to others

Field 17 Miscellaneous

81	Don't like the name
82	Too expensive
83	Not economical for long hair
84	Use what hairdresser recommends
85	
86	
87	
88	
89	
90	
8−	Other miscellaneous
8+	Don't know what/disliked/nothing

1. What, if anything, did you particularly like about this shampoo?

    My hairdresser recommends it, so it must be good for your hair. It smells good too.

2. What, if anything, did you particularly dislike about this shampoo?

    It's too expensive. It doesn't have a cream rinse, so you still have to buy that too. It really doesn't work any better than other shampoos for the amount of money you pay for it.

---

1. What, if anything, did you particularly like about this shampoo?

    There are different kinds for different types of hair. I use the one for dry hair. It doesn't dry out my hair. It leaves it soft & shiny. It works so well I only have to use a little bit for each shampoo.

2. What, if anything, did you particularly dislike about this shampoo?

    Nothing. I liked it.

---

1. What, if anything, did you particularly like about this shampoo?

    I have limp, oily hair and have to wash it real often. With this shampoo I found it stayed cleaner longer, so I don't have to shampoo as often and my hair has more body.

2. What, if anything, did you particularly dislike about this shampoo?

    I like the shampoo but I don't think the name is very appealing.

CHAPTER 20
BASIC DATA ANALYSIS:
DESCRIPTIVE STATISTICS

Chapter Vignette: Choose Your "Poison"

Most Americans enjoy an adult beverage occasionally. But not all Americans like the same drink. Many decision makers are interested in what Americans like to drink. Retailers need to have the correct product mix for their particular customers if profits are to be increased and customers made more satisfied. Restaurants need to know what their customers like to have with the types of food they serve. Policy makers need to know what types of restrictions should be placed on what types of products to prevent underage drinking and alcohol abuse. Researchers could apply sophisticated statistics to address questions related to Americans' drinking preferences, but a lot can be learned from just counting what people are buying.

A grocery store built in 1975 in Chicago allocates 15 percent of floor space to adult beverage products. Out of this 15 percent, 60 percent is allocated to beer, 25 percent to spirits, and 15 percent to wine. Since the products are not merchandised the same way (different types of shelving, aisles, and racking are needed), adjusting the floor space to change these percentages is not an easy task. Over the three-decade history of the store, the customer base has changed. Originally, stay-at-home moms buying groceries for the family best characterized the customer base. During the 1990s, empty nesters, including retirees with high disposable incomes, characterized the customer base. More recently, younger singles just starting careers have moved into the nearby neighborhoods. Should the store reconsider its adult beverage merchandising?

© STEPHEN OLIVER/DORLING KINDERSLEY/GETTY IMAGES

In 1992, American consumers showed a heavy preference toward beer. Among American adults who drank adult beverages,[1]

- 47 percent drank beer
- 21 percent drank spirits
- 27 percent drank wine

By 2005, Americans had changed their drinking preferences.

- 36 percent drank beer
- 21 percent drank spirits
- 39 percent drank wine

But, by 2008, beer appeared to regain the lead.[2] Now,

- 42 percent prefer beer
- 23 percent prefer spirits
- 31 percent prefer wine

A couple of other facts have become clear. A count of the preferred beverages among American adult consumers twenty-nine and younger shows that they drink almost three times as much beer as wine.[3] Conversely, consumers born before 1960 drink far more wine than beer.[4] Thus, age groups appear to relate to drink preference.

Across America, grocers account for 35 percent of all beer sales, but convenience stores, where younger consumers tend to shop, account for 45 percent.[5] If the grocery store is converting more to a convenience store, maybe a continued emphasis on beer is wise. This is particularly true if the customer demographics suggest a young consumer. However, wine consumers are more *attractive* from several perspectives. Wine now ranks among the top 10 food categories in America, based on grocery store dollar sales volume. Grocery stores account for 45 percent of all wine sold. The consumer who buys wine is also more likely to buy products like prime or choice beef and imported cheeses, instead of lower quality and lower priced meat and cheese products. As a result, the average $14 spent on wine in a grocery store (as opposed to $12 on beer) is only part of the story in explaining why wine customers may be *grape* customers![6]

What should the grocer emphasize in marketing adult beverages? Perhaps the research based on counting can address this decision.

Introduction

The next few chapters introduce some basic statistical tools. The tools discussed here allow inferences to be made. These inferences often involve testing some hypothesis that states a condition thought to exist in a population. As researchers, we infer whether or not that condition exists based on what we observe in a sample. Alternatively, the research could be more exploratory and the statistics could be directed simply at a search for some pattern within the data. On rare occasions, the data may represent a census of a population, in which case no statistical inferences are necessary because parameters are known. Descriptive statistical tools like these provide a straightforward way of succinctly describing the information content within a data set.

The Nature of Descriptive Analysis

descriptive analysis

The elementary transformation of raw data in a way that describes the basic characteristics such as central tendency, distribution, and variability.

Perhaps the most basic statistical analysis is descriptive analysis. **Descriptive analysis** is the elementary transformation of data in a way that describes the basic characteristics such as central tendency, distribution, and variability. A researcher takes responses from 1,000 American consumers and tabulates their favorite soft drink brand and the price they expect to pay for a six-pack of that product. The mode for favorite soft drink and the average price across all 1,000 consumers would be descriptive statistics that describe central tendency in two different ways. Averages, medians, modes, variance, range, and standard deviation typify widely applied descriptive statistics.

Descriptive statistics can summarize responses from large numbers of respondents in a few simple statistics. When a sample is used, the sample descriptive statistics are used to make inferences about characteristics of the entire population of interest. The researcher examining descriptive statistics for any particular variable is using univariate statistics. Descriptive statistics are simple but powerful. Because they are so simple, descriptive statistics are used very widely.

In an earlier chapter, we learned that the level of scale measurement can help the researcher choose the most appropriate statistical tool. Exhibit 20.1 shows the specific descriptive statistic appropriate for each level of measurement. Also, remember that all statistics appropriate for lower-order scales (nominal is the lowest) are suitable for higher-order scales (ratio is the highest). So, a frequency table could also be used for interval or ratio data. Frequencies can be represented graphically as shown and are a good way of visually depicting typical survey results.

Consider the following data. Sample consumers were asked where they most often purchased beer. The result is a nominal variable which can be described with a frequency distribution (see the bar chart in Exhibit 20.1). Ten percent indicated they most often purchased beer in a drug store, 45 percent indicated a convenience store, 35 percent indicated a grocery store, and 7 percent

SURVEY THIS!

Take a look at the section of the student survey shown.

Compute the appropriate descriptive statistic for each question using the data from the results for your class or school (across all sections of marketing research classes taking the survey). What conclusions would you draw from these results?

Qualtrics

How much time to you watch television daily?

| Less than an hour | Between 1 and 2 hours | Between 2 and 3 hours | More than 3 hours |

How many Text Message "buddies" do you have in your cell phone?

How many text messages do you send daily?

How many text messages do you receive daily?

How many cell phone calls do you make in a day?

How many cell phone calls do you receive in a day?

How much time do you spend studying Marketing Research weekly?

| Less than an hour | Between 1 and 2 hours | Between 2 and 3 hours | Greater than 3 hours |

indicated a specialty store. Three percent listed "other" (not shown in the bar chart). The mode is convenience store since more respondents chose this than any other category. A similar distribution may have been obtained if the chart plotted the number of respondents ranking each store as their favorite type of place to purchase beer.

The bottom part of Exhibit 20.1 displays example descriptive statistics for interval and ratio variables. In this case, the chart displays results of a question asking respondents how much they typically spend on a bottle of wine purchased in a store. The mean and standard deviation are displayed beside the chart as 11.7 and 4.5, respectively. Additionally, the frequency distribution is

EXHIBIT 20.1

Levels of Scale Measurement and Suggested Descriptive Statistics

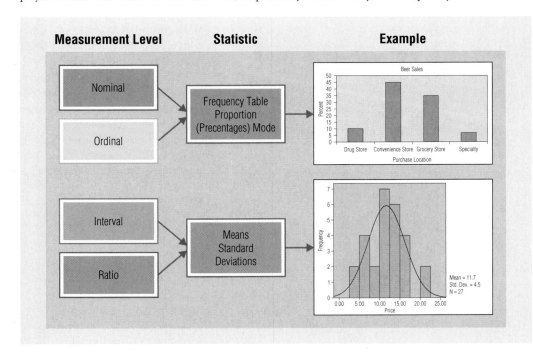

PHOTO COURTESY OF VICKI BEAVER

histogram

A graphical way of showing a frequency distribution in which the height of a bar corresponds to the observed frequency of the category.

shown with a histogram. A **histogram** is a graphical way of showing the frequency distribution in which the height of a bar corresponds to the frequency of a category. Histograms are useful for any type of data, but with continuous variables (interval or ratio) the histogram is useful for providing a quick assessment of the distribution of the data. A normal distribution line is superimposed over the histogram providing an easy comparison to see if the data are skewed or multi-modal.

Creating and Interpreting Tabulation

tabulation

The orderly arrangement of data in a table or other summary format showing the number of responses to each response category; tallying.

frequency table

A table showing the different ways respondents answered a question.

Tabulation refers to the orderly arrangement of data in a table or other summary format. When this tabulation process is done by hand the term *tallying* is used. Counting the different ways respondents answered a question and arranging them in a simple tabular form yields a **frequency table**. The actual number of responses to each category is a variable's frequency distribution. A simple tabulation of this type is sometimes called a *marginal tabulation*.

Simple tabulation tells the researcher how frequently each response occurs. This starting point for analysis requires the researcher to count responses or observations for each category or code assigned to a variable. A frequency table showing where consumers generally purchase beer can be computed easily. The tabular results that correspond to the chart would appear as follows:

Response	Frequency	Percent	Cumulative Percentage
Drug store	50	10	10
Convenience store	225	45	55
Grocery store	175	35	90
Specialty	35	7	97
Other	15	3	100

Web sites like this one provide a secondary data source in the form of descriptive statistics or details that can easily be used to compute tabulations, means, cross-tabulations, and so on.

The frequency column shows the tally result or the number of respondents listing each store, respectively. The percent column shows the total percentage in each category. The cumulative percentage shows the percentage indicating either a particular category or any preceding category as their preferred place to purchase beer. From this chart, the mode indicates that the typical consumer buys beer at the convenience store since more people indicated this as their top response.

Similarly, a recent tabulation of Americans' responses to the simple question of "Who is your favorite TV personality?" revealed the response varied by generation. For respondents aged 18–30 (Echo Boomers), Stephen Colbert was listed first. For respondents aged 31–42 (Gen X), Jay Leno and Jon Stewart tied as the preferred TV personalities, Oprah Winfrey was the top TV celebrity for Boomers (43–61), and she is tied with Bill O'Reilly among Matures (62+).[7] The idea that generation may influence choice of favorite celebrity brings us to cross-tabulation. The Research Snapshot on the next page provides more information on favorite celebrities.

Contingent Personalities

Who is the world's favorite celebrity? This is an important question because the answer helps to determine how much a celebrity endorsement is worth. Sports stars like Tiger Woods are effective in shaping consumers' product preferences worldwide. Pop stars like the Spice Girls have been effectively used to increase soft drink sales in the United Kingdom. In other parts of the world, perhaps Filipino "Megastar" Sharon Cuneta (www.sharoncuneta.com) could do the same. Perhaps some celebrities are effective nearly everywhere, but others may only be effective in a given country. Their effectiveness is contingent upon region.

Television personalities also influence the public's opinion by giving their own. But, all opinions may not be equal. Polling agencies like the Harris interactive poll (http://www.harrisinteractive.com) monitor the popularity of celebrities. Who is America's favorite television personality? The 2008 results put Ellen DeGeneres on top. But, does everybody feel the same way? Or, do relationships exist among person variables and favorite celebrity? Cross-tabulations can help answer this question. Consider the following 2-by-2 contingency table showing hypothetical results of 1,000 respondents asked to choose whether they prefer Ellen or Jay:

	Ellen DeGeneres	Jay Leno	Totals
Men	150	350	500
Women	380	120	500
	530	470	1,000

Or, consider the 3-by-3 contingency table:

	Ellen DeGeneres	Bill O'Reilly	Jay Leno	Totals
Independents	40	100	200	340
Republicans	20	240	60	320
Democrats	310	10	20	340
	370	350	280	1,000

Here again, a relationship is apparent. This time, one's political orientation is associated with choice of celebrity. In either cross-tabulation table, opinions about the preferred celebrity are contingent, or depend on some characteristic. Thus, marketing managers should consider the contingencies when trying to identify preferred celebrities.

Sources: Erdogan, B. Zater, Michael J. Baker and Stephen Tagg, "Selecting Celebrity Endorsers: The Practitioner's Perspective," *Journal of Advertising Research* 41 (May/June 2001), 39–48; Goetzl, David and Wayne Friedman, "What We're Talking About," *Advertising Age* 73 (December 2, 2002), 51–57; Corso, R. A. "The Harris Poll #6," (January 14, 2008), www.harrisinteractive.com, accessed October 6, 2008.

© GEORGE DOYLE & CIARAN GRIFFIN

© D VAN/UPI/LANDOV

Cross-Tabulation

A frequency distribution or tabulation can address many research questions. As long as a question deals with only one categorical variable, tabulation is probably the best approach. Although frequency counts, percentage distributions, and averages summarize considerable information, simple tabulation may not yield the full value of the research. **Cross-tabulation** is the appropriate technique for addressing research questions involving relationships among multiple less-than interval variables. A cross-tabulation is a combined frequency table. Cross-tabulation allows the inspection and comparison of differences among groups based on nominal or ordinal categories. One key to interpreting a cross-tabulation table is comparing the observed table values with hypothetical values that would result from pure chance.

Exhibit 20.2 on the next page summarizes several cross-tabulations from consumers' responses to a questionnaire on ethical behavior in the United States.[8] Panel A suggests how two questionable behaviors (variables—taking home supplies, calling in sick) may vary with basic demographic variables. A researcher interested in the relative ethical perspectives of business executives and the general public can inspect panel B and compare the two groups. If business executives and the general public have the same ethical attitudes, the observed percentages should be equal for each question. This does not appear to be the case. The data lead to the conclusion that business executives participate in these behaviors more than the general public. However, before reaching the conclusion that business executives are less ethical than the general public, one must carefully scrutinize this finding for possible extraneous variables.

cross-tabulation

The appropriate technique for addressing research questions involving relationships among multiple less-than interval variables; results in a combined frequency table displaying one variable in rows and another in columns.

EXHIBIT 20.2 **Cross-Tabulation Tables from a Survey on Ethics in America**

(A) Reported Behavior (Percentage of General Public Who Have Ever Done Each Activity)						
	Age		Gender		Education	
Activity	Under 50 Years Old	Over 50 Years Old	Men	Women	College Graduate	High School Graduate
Taken home work supplies	50	26	47	33	58	21
Called in sick to work when not ill	40	18	Not reported		36	21

(B) Reported Behavior (Percentage Who Have Ever Done Each Activity)		
Activity	Business Executives	General Public
Taken home work supplies	74	40
Called in sick to work when not ill	14	31
Used company telephone for personal long-distance calls	78	15
Overstated deductions somewhat on tax forms	35	13
Driven while drunk	80	33
Saw a fellow employee steal something at work and did not report it	7	26

From Roger Ricklefs, "Ethics in America," *The Wall Street Journal*, October 31, 1983, pp. 33, 42; November 1, 1983, p. 33; November 2, 1983, p. 33; and November 3, 1983, pp. 33, 37.

Contingency Tables

contingency table

A data matrix that displays the frequency of some combination of possible responses to multiple variables; cross-tabulation results.

Exhibit 20.3 shows example cross-tabulation results using contingency tables. A **contingency table** is a data matrix that displays the frequency of some combination of possible responses to multiple variables. Two-way contingency tables, meaning they involve two less–than interval variables, are used most often. A three-way contingency table involves three less–than interval variables. Beyond three variables, contingency tables become difficult to analyze and explain easily.

Two variables are depicted in the contingency table shown in panel A:

- Row Variable: Biological Sex _____M _____F
- Column Variable: "Do you shop at Target? YES or NO"

Several conclusions can be drawn initially by examining the row and column totals:

1. 225 men and 225 women responded as can be seen in the row totals column. This means that altogether 450 consumers responded.
2. Out of this 450 total consumers, 330 consumers indicated that "yes" they do shop at Target and 120 indicated "no," they do not shop at Target. This can be observed in the column totals at the bottom of the table. These row and column totals often are called **marginals** because they appear in the table's margins.

marginals

Row and column totals in a contingency table, which are shown in its margins.

Researchers usually are more interested in the inner cells of a contingency table. The inner cells display conditional frequencies (combinations). Using these values, we can draw some more specific conclusions:

3. Out of 330 consumers who shop at Target, 150 are male and 180 are female.
4. Alternatively, out of the 120 respondents not shopping at Target, 75 are male and 45 are female.

This finding helps us know whether the two variables are related. If men and women equally patronize Target, we would expect that hypothetically 165 of the 330 shoppers would be male and 165 would be female. Clearly, these hypothetical expectations (165m/165f) are not observed. What

EXHIBIT 20.3

Different Ways of Depicting the Cross-Tabulation of Biological Sex and Target Patronage

(A) Cross-Tabulation of Question "Do you shop at Target?" by Sex of Respondent			
	Yes	No	Total
Men	150	75	225
Women	180	45	225
Total	330	120	450

(B) Percentage Cross-Tabulation of Question "Do you shop at Target?" by Sex of Respondent, Row Percentage			
	Yes	No	Total (Base)
Men	66.7%	33.3%	100% (225)
Women	80.0%	20.0%	100% (225)

(C) Percentage Cross-Tabulation of Question "Do you shop at Target?" by Sex of Respondent, Column Percentage		
	Yes	No
Men	45.5%	62.5%
Women	54.5%	37.5%
Total	100%	100%
(Base)	(330)	(120)

is the implication? A relationship exists between respondent sex and shopping choice. Specifically, Target shoppers are more likely to be female than male. Notice that the same meaning could be drawn by analyzing non-Target shoppers.

A two-way contingency table like the one shown in part A is referred to as a *2 × 2 table* because it has two rows (Men and Women) and two columns (Yes and No). Each variable has two levels. A two-way contingency table displaying two variables one (the row variable) with three levels and the other with four levels would be referred to as a *3 × 4 table*. Any cross-tabulation table may be classified according to the number of rows by the number of columns (*R* by *C*).

Percentage Cross-Tabulations

When data from a survey are cross-tabulated, percentages help the researcher understand the nature of the relationship by making relative comparisons simpler. The total number of respondents or observations may be used as a **statistical base** for computing the percentage in each cell. When the objective of the research is to identify a relationship between answers to two questions (or two variables), one of the questions is commonly chosen to be the source of the base for determining percentages. For example, look at the data in parts A, B, and C of Exhibit 20.3. Compare part B with part C. Selecting either the row percentages or the column percentages will emphasize a particular comparison or distribution. The nature of the problem the researcher wishes to answer will determine which marginal total will serve as a base for computing percentages.

Fortunately, a conventional rule determines the direction of percentages. The rule depends on which variable is identified as an independent variable and which is a dependent variable. Simply put, independent variables should form the rows in a contingency table. The marginal total of the independent variable should be used as the base for computing the percentages. Although survey research does not establish cause-and-effect evidence, one might argue that it would be logical to assume that a variable such as biological sex might predict beverage preference. This makes more sense than thinking that beverage preference would determine biological sex.

statistical base

The number of respondents or observations (in a row or column) used as a basis for computing percentages.

Elaboration and Refinement

elaboration analysis

An analysis of the basic cross-
tabulation for each level of a variable not previously considered,
such as subgroups of the sample.

The *Oxford Universal Dictionary* defines *analysis* as "the resolution of anything complex into its simplest elements." Once a researcher has examined the basic relationship between two variables, he or
she may wish to investigate this relationship under a variety of different conditions. Typically, a third
variable is introduced into the analysis to elaborate and refine the researcher's understanding by
specifying the conditions under which the relationship between the first two variables is strongest
and weakest. In other words, a more elaborate analysis asks, "Will interpretation of the relationship
be modified if other variables are simultaneously considered?"

Elaboration analysis involves the basic cross-tabulation within various subgroups of the sample. The
researcher breaks down the analysis for each level of another variable. If the researcher has cross-
tabulated shopping preference by sex (see Exhibit 20.3) and wishes to investigate another variable (say,
marital status), a more elaborate analysis may be conducted. Exhibit 20.4 breaks down the responses to
the question "Do you shop at Target?" by sex and marital status. The data show women display the same
preference whether married or single. However, married men are much more likely to shop at Target
than are single men. The analysis suggests that the original conclusion about the relationship between
sex and shopping behavior for women be retained. However, a relationship that was not discernible in
the two-variable case is evident. Married men more frequently shop at Target than do single men.

EXHIBIT 20.4
**Cross-Tabulation of Marital
Status, Sex, and Responses
to the Question "Do You
Shop at Target?"**

	Single		Married	
	Men	Women	Men	Women
"Do you shop at Target?"				
Yes	55%	80%	86%	80%
No	45%	20%	14%	20%

The finding is consistent with an interaction effect. The combination of the two variables, sex
and marital status, is associated with differences in the dependent variable. Interactions between
variables examine moderating variables. A **moderator variable** is a third variable that changes the
nature of a relationship between the original independent and dependent variables. Marital status
is a moderator variable in this case. The interaction effect suggests that marriage changes the relationship between sex and shopping preference.

moderator variable

A third variable that changes the
nature of a relationship between
the original independent and
dependent variables.

In other situations the addition of a third variable to the analysis may lead us to reject the
original conclusion about the relationship. When this occurs, the elaboration analysis suggests the
relationship between the original variables is spurious.

The chapter vignette described data suggesting a relationship between the type of store in
which a consumer shops and beverage preference. Convenience store shoppers seem to choose
beer over wine while grocery store shoppers choose wine over beer. Does store-type drive drinking preference? Perhaps age determines both the type of store consumers choose to buy in and
their preference for adult beverages. Younger consumers both disproportionately shop in convenience stores and drink beer.

How Many Cross-Tabulations?

Surveys may ask dozens of questions and hundreds of categorical variables can be stored in a data
warehouse. Computer-assisted marketing researchers can "fish" for relationships by cross-tabulat-
ing every categorical variable with every other categorical variable. Thus, every possible response
becomes a possible explanatory variable. A researcher addressing an exploratory research question
may find some benefit in such a fishing expedition. Software exists that can automatically search
through volumes of cross-tabulations. These may even provide some insight into the market segment
structure for some product. Alternatively, the program may flag the cross-tabulations suggesting the
strongest relationship. CHAID (chi-square automatic interaction detection) software exemplifies
software that makes searches through large numbers of variables possible.[9] Data-mining can be conducted in a similar fashion and may suggest relationships that are worth considering further.

Outside of exploratory research, researchers should conduct cross-tabulations that address specific research questions or hypotheses. When hypotheses involve relationships among two categorical variables, cross-tabulations are the right tool for the job.

Quadrant Analysis

Quadrant analysis is a variation of cross-tabulation in which responses to two rating scale questions are plotted in four quadrants of a two-dimensional table. Most quadrant analysis in marketing research portrays or plots relationships between average responses about a product attribute's importance and average ratings of a company's (or brand's) performance on that product feature. The term **importance-performance analysis** is sometimes used because consumers rate perceived importance of several attributes and rate how well the company's brand performs on that attribute. Generally speaking, the marketer would like to end up in the quadrant indicating high performance on an important attribute.

Exhibit 20.5 illustrates a quadrant analysis for an international, mid-priced hotel chain.[10] The chart shows the importance and the performance ratings provided by business travelers. After plotting the scores for each of eight attributes, the analysis suggests areas for improvement. The arrows indicate attributes that the hotel firm should concentrate on to move from quadrant three, which means the performance on those attributes is low but business consumers rate those attributes as important, to quadrant four, where attributes are both important and rated highly for performance. Hotel management may also consider reallocating resources used to provide 24 hour room service toward things that customers rate as more important. Even though they perform well on this characteristic, consumers do not view it as important.

quadrant analysis

An extension of cross-tabulation in which responses to two rating-scale questions are plotted in four quadrants of a two-dimensional table.

importance-performance analysis

Another name for quadrant analysis.

EXHIBIT 20.5

An Imortance-Performance or Quadrant Analysis of Hotels

Data Transformation

Simple Transformations

Data transformation (also called *data conversion*) is the process of changing the data from their original form to a format suitable for performing a data analysis that will achieve research objectives. Researchers often modify the values of scalar data or create new variables. For example, many researchers believe that less response bias will result if interviewers ask respondents for their year of birth rather than their age. This presents no problem for the research analyst, because a simple data transformation is possible. The raw data coded as birth year can easily be transformed to age by subtracting the birth year from the current year.

In earlier chapters, we discussed recoding and creating summated scales. These also are common data transformations.

data transformation

Process of changing the data from their original form to a format suitable for performing a data analysis addressing research objectives.

Collapsing or combining adjacent categories of a variable is a common form of data transformation used to reduce the number of categories. A Likert scale may sometimes be collapsed into a smaller number of categories. For instance, consider the following Likert item administered to a sample of state university seniors:

	Strongly Disagree	Disagree	Neutral	Agree	Strongly Agree
I am satisfied with my college experience at this university	☐	☐	☐	☐	☐

The following frequency table describes results for this survey item:

Strongly Disagree	Disagree	Neutral	Agree	Strongly Agree
110	30	15	35	210

The distribution is bimodal because two peaks exist in the distribution, one at either end of the scale. Since the vast majority of respondents (80 percent = (110 + 210)/400) indicated either strongly disagree or strongly agree, the variable closely resembles a categorical variable. Customers either strongly disagreed or strongly agreed with the statement. So, the research may wish to collapse the responses into two categories. While multiple ways exist to accomplish this, the researcher may assign the value zero to all respondents who either strongly disagreed or disagreed and the value one to all respondents who either agreed or strongly agreed. Respondents marking neutral would be excluded from analysis.

Perhaps the 110 dissatisfied students differ in some important way from the 210. Perhaps their exam scores are also bimodal. Exhibit 20.6 shows an example of a bimodal distribution.

EXHIBIT 20.6
Bimodal Distributions Are Consistent with Transformations into Categorical Values

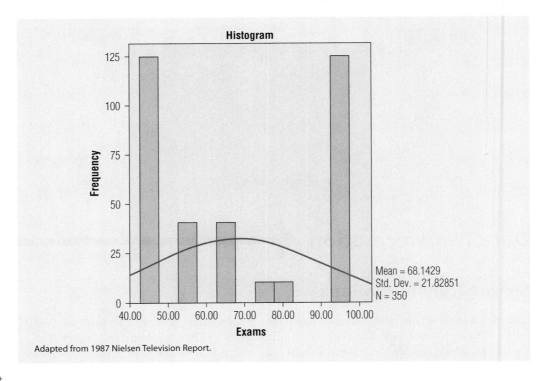

Mean = 68.1429
Std. Dev. = 21.82851
N = 350

Adapted from 1987 Nielsen Television Report.

median split

Dividing a data set into two categories by placing respondents below the median in one category and respondents above the median in another.

Problems with Data Transformations

Researchers often perform a median split to collapse a scale with multiple response points into two categories. The **median split** means respondents below the observed median go into one category and respondents above the median go into another. Although this is common, the approach is best applied only when the data do indeed exhibit bimodal characteristics. When the data are unimodal, such as would be the case with normally distributed data, a median split will lead to error.

Exhibit 20.7 illustrates this problem. Clearly, most respondents either slightly agree or slightly disagree with this statement. The central tendency could be represented by the median of 3.5, a mean of 3.5, or the mode of 3.5 (3 and 4 each have the same number of responses so the mode is set between the two). The "outliers," if any, appear to be those not indicating something other than slight agreement or slight disagreement. A case can be made that the respondents indicating slight disagreement are more similar to those indicating slight agreement than they are to those respondents indicating strong disagreement. Yet, the recode places values 1 and 3 in the same new category, but places values 3 and 4 in a different category (see the recoding scheme in Exhibit 20.7). The data distribution does not support a median split into two categories and so a transformation collapsing these values into agreement and disagreement is inappropriate.

EXHIBIT 20.7 **The Problem with Median Splits with Unimodal Data**

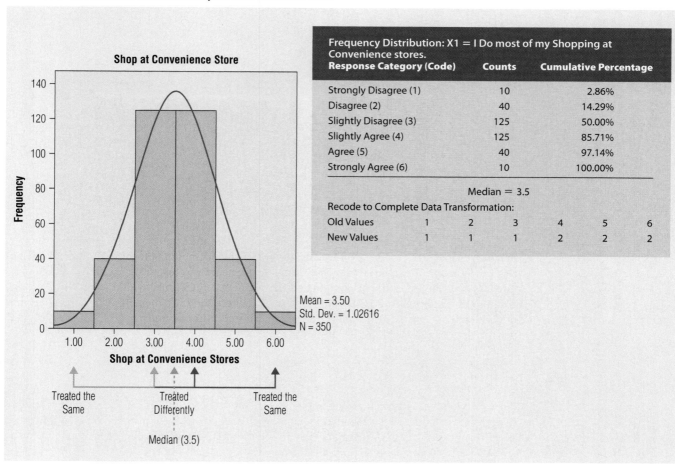

Frequency Distribution: X1 = I Do most of my Shopping at Convenience stores.		
Response Category (Code)	**Counts**	**Cumulative Percentage**
Strongly Disagree (1)	10	2.86%
Disagree (2)	40	14.29%
Slightly Disagree (3)	125	50.00%
Slightly Agree (4)	125	85.71%
Agree (5)	40	97.14%
Strongly Agree (6)	10	100.00%

Median = 3.5

Recode to Complete Data Transformation:

Old Values	1	2	3	4	5	6
New Values	1	1	1	2	2	2

Mean = 3.50
Std. Dev. = 1.02616
N = 350

When a sufficient number of responses exist and a variable is ratio, the researcher may choose to delete one-fourth to one-third of the responses around the median to effectively ensure a bimodal distribution. This helps to mitigate the logical inconsistency illustrated in Exhibit 20.7. Median splits should always be performed only with great care, though, as the inappropriate collapsing of continuous variables into categorical variables ignores the information contained within the untransformed values.

Index Numbers

The consumer price index and wholesale price index are secondary data sources that are frequently used by marketing researchers. Price indexes, like other **index numbers**, represent simple data transformations that allow researchers to track a variable's value over time and compare a variable(s)

index numbers

Scores or observations recalibrated to indicate how they relate to a base number.

with other variables. Recalibration allows scores or observations to be related to a certain base period or base number.

Consider the information in Exhibit 20.8. Weekly television viewing statistics are shown grouped by household size. Index numbers can be computed for these observations in the following manner:

1. A base number is selected. The U.S. household (hh) average of 52 hours and 36 minutes represents the central tendency and will be used.
2. Index numbers are computed by dividing the score for each category by the base number and multiplying by 100. The index reflects percentage changes from the base:

$$1 \text{ person hh:} \qquad \frac{41:01}{52:36} = 0.7832 \times 100 = 78.32$$

$$2 \text{ person hh:} \qquad \frac{47:58}{52:36} = 0.9087 \times 100 = 90.87$$

$$3+ \text{ person hh:} \qquad \frac{60:49}{52:36} = 1.1553 \times 100 = 115.53$$

$$\text{Total U.S. average:} \qquad \frac{52:36}{52:36} = 1.0000 \times 100 = 100.00$$

EXHIBIT 20.8
Hours of Television Usage per Week

Household Size	Hours:Minutes
1	41:01
2	47:58
3+	60:49
Total U.S. average	52:36

Adapted from 2007 Nielsen Television Report.

If the data are time-related, a base year is chosen. The index numbers are then computed by dividing each year's activity by the base-year activity and multiplying by 100. Index numbers require ratio measurement scales. Marketing managers may often chart consumption in some category over time. Relating back to the chapter vignette, grocers may wish to chart the U.S. wine consumption index. Using 1968 as a base year (4.05 liters per year), the 2007 U.S. wine consumption index is just over 2.3, meaning that the typical American consumer drinks 9.35 liters of wine per year (see the Research Snapshot on the next page).[11]

Calculating Rank Order

Survey respondents are often asked to rank order brand or store preferences. Employee respondents may provide rankings of several different employee benefit plans. Ranking data can be summarized by performing a data transformation. The transformation involves multiplying the frequency by the ranking score for each choice to result in a new scale.

For example, suppose a manager of a frequent-flier program had ten executives rank their preferences for locations in which to hold the company's annual conference. Exhibit 20.9 shows how executives ranked each of four locations: Hawaii, Paris, Greece, and Hong Kong. Exhibit 20.10 tabulates frequencies for these rankings. A ranking summary can be computed by assigning the destination with the highest preference the lowest number (1) and the least preferred destination the highest consecutive number (4). The summarized rank orderings were obtained with the following calculations:

Hawaii:	$(3 \times 1) + (5 \times 2) + (1 \times 3) + (1 \times 4) = 20$
Paris:	$(3 \times 1) + (1 \times 2) + (3 \times 3) + (3 \times 4) = 26$
Greece:	$(2 \times 1) + (2 \times 2) + (4 \times 3) + (2 \times 4) = 26$
Hong Kong:	$(2 \times 1) + (2 \times 2) + (2 \times 3) + (4 \times 4) = 28$

Wine Index Can Help Retailers

Indexes can be very useful, and researchers are sometimes asked to create index values from secondary data. The chapter vignette described a situation where a retailer was making decisions about merchandising based on the consumption habits of store customers. If a U.S. grocer is considering wine merchandising in another country, he or she may be interested to know wine indexes of other countries.

Using 1968 U.S. wine consumption as a base, the current wine consumption index for the United Kingdom is 4.7, South Africa's index value is 2.2, Israel's index is 0.3, Luxembourg's wine index is 13.0 (52.7 liters/person/year) but the top of the list is Vatican City where the just under 1,000 residents have a wine index of 15.3! This information would be helpful in making decisions about the amount of space and attention given to wine in different countries. Similarly, U.S. retailers could compute wine or beer indices by state. Policy agencies could also chart indices on alcohol consumption that may be helpful in regulating underage consumption.

Sources: Per capita consumption figures derived from The Wine Institute, http://www.wineinstitute.org/ as accessed October 7, 2008.

Executive	Hawaii	Paris	Greece	Hong Kong
1	1	2	4	3
2	1	3	4	2
3	2	1	3	4
4	2	4	3	1
5	2	1	3	4
6	3	4	1	2
7	2	3	1	4
8	1	4	2	3
9	4	3	2	1
10	2	1	3	4

EXHIBIT 20.9
Executive Rankings of Potential Conference Destinations

Destination	Preference Rankings			
	1st	2nd	3rd	4th
Hawaii	3	5	1	1
Paris	3	1	3	3
Greece	2	2	4	2
Hong Kong	2	2	2	4

EXHIBIT 20.10
Frequencies of Conference Destination Rankings

Three executives chose Hawaii as the best destination (ranked "1"), five executives selected Hawaii as the second best destination, and so forth. The lowest total score indicates the first (highest) preference ranking. The results show the following rank ordering: (1) Hawaii, (2) Paris, (3) Greece, and (4) Hong Kong. Company employees may be glad to hear their conference will be in Hawaii.

Tabular and Graphic Methods of Displaying Data

Tables, graphs, and charts may simplify and clarify data. Graphical representations of data may take a number of forms, ranging from a computer printout to an elaborate pictograph. Tables, graphs,

527

and charts, however, all facilitate summarization and communication. For example, see how the simple frequency table and histogram shown in Exhibit 20.7 provide a summary that quickly and easily communicates meaning that would be more difficult to see if all 350 responses were viewed separately.

Today's researcher has many convenient tools to quickly produce charts, graphs, or tables. Even basic word processing programs like Word include chart functions that can construct the chart within the text document. Bar charts (histograms), pie charts, curve/line diagrams, and scatter plots are among the most widely used tools. Some choices match well with certain types of data and analyses.

Bar charts and pie charts are very effective in communicating frequency tabulations and simple cross-tabulations. Exhibit 20.11 displays frequency data from the chapter vignette with pie charts. Each pie summarizes preference in the respective year. The size of each pie slice corresponds to a frequency value associated with that choice. When the two pie charts are compared, the result communicates a cross-tabulation. Here, the comparison clearly communicates that wine preference has increased at the expense of beer preference. In other words, the relative slice of pie for wine has become larger.

EXHIBIT 20.11
Pie Charts Work Well with Tabulations and Cross-Tabulations

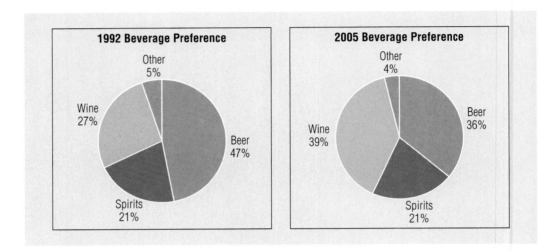

Chapter 25 discusses how these and other graphic aids may improve the communication value of a written report or oral presentation.

Computer Programs for Analysis

Statistical Packages

Just 50 years ago, the thought of a typical U.S. company performing even basic statistical analyses like cross-tabulations on a thousand or more observations was unrealistic. The personal computer brought this capability not just to average companies, but even to small companies with limited resources. Today, computing power is seldom a barrier to completing a research project.

In the 1980s and early 1990s, when the PC was still a relatively novel innovation, specialized statistical software formerly used on mainframe computers made its way into the personal computing market. Today, most spreadsheet packages can perform a wide variety of basic statistical options. Excel's basic data analysis tool will allow descriptive statistics including frequencies and measures of central tendency to be easily computed.[12] Most of the basic statistical features are now menu driven, reducing the need to memorize function labels. Spreadsheet packages like Excel continue to evolve and become more viable for performing many basic statistical analyses (see Exhibit 20.12).

EXHIBIT 20.12

Using Excel for Basic Data Analysis

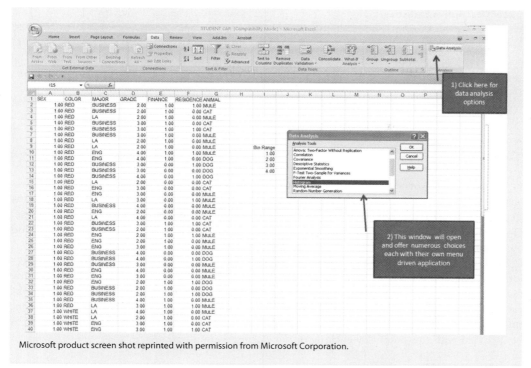

Microsoft product screen shot reprinted with permission from Microsoft Corporation.

Despite the advances in spreadsheet applications, commercialized statistical software packages remain extremely popular among researchers. They continue to become easier to use and more compatible with other data interface tools including spreadsheets and word processors. Like any specialized tool, statistical packages are more tailored to the types of analyses performed by statistical analysts, including marketing researchers. Thus, any serious business or social science researcher should still become familiar with at least one general computer software package.

Two of the most popular general statistical packages are SAS (http://www.sas.com) and SPSS (http://www.spss.com). SAS revenues exceed $1.5 billion and its software can be found on computers worldwide. SAS was founded in 1976, and its statistical software historically has been widely used in engineering and other technical fields. SPSS was founded in 1968 and its sales exceed $224 million. SPSS stands for *Statistical Package for the Social Sciences.* SPSS is commonly used by university business and social science students. Marketing researchers have traditionally used SPSS more than any other statistical software tool. SPSS has been viewed as more user-friendly in the past. However, today's versions of both SPSS and SAS are very user friendly and give the user the option of using drop-down menus to conduct analysis rather than writing computer code.

Excel, SAS, and SPSS account for most of the statistical analysis conducted in marketing research. University students are sometimes exposed to MINITAB. MINITAB's revenues are approximately $10 million per year. Economists sometimes favor MINITAB; however, it has traditionally been viewed as less user-friendly than other choices such as SPSS.

In the past, data entry was an issue as specific software required different types of data input. Today, however, all the major software packages including SAS and SPSS can work from data entered into a spreadsheet. The spreadsheets can be imported into the data windows or simply read by the program. Most conventional online survey tools will return data to the user in the form of either an SPSS data file, an Excel spreadsheet, or a plain text document.

Exhibit 20.13 on the next page shows a printout of descriptive statistics generated by SAS for two variables: EMP (number of employees working in an MSA, or Metropolitan Statistical Area) and SALES (sales volume in dollars in an MSA) for 10 MSAs. The number of data elements (*N*), mean, standard deviation, and other descriptive statistics are displayed. SAS output is generally simple and easy to read.

EXHIBIT 20.13 SAS Computer Output of Descriptive Statistics

State = NY Variable	N	Mean	Standard Deviation	Minimum Value	Maximum Value	Std Error of Mean	Sum	Variance	C.V.
EMP	10	142.930	232.665	12.800	788.800	73.575	1429.300	54133.0	162.782
SALES	10	5807.800	11905.127	307.000	39401.000	3764.732	58078.000	141732049.1	204.985

Key: EMP = number of employees (000)   SALES = Sales (000)

As an example of SPSS output, each histogram shown in the exhibits on pages 524–525 was created by SPSS. By clicking on "charts" in the SPSS tool menu, one can see the variety of charts that can be created. The key place to click to generate statistical results in tabular form is "analyze." Here, one can see the many types of analysis that can be created. In this chapter, the choices found by clicking on "analyze" and then "descriptive statistics" are particularly relevant.

Exhibit 20.14 shows an SPSS cross-tabulation of two variables, class status and smoking behavior. The data come from a sample intercepted on an urban university campus. It addresses the research question, "Does smoking on campus vary across groups?" More non-smokers than smokers are found. However, the results show that graduate students, and to a lesser extent instructors, smoke more than the norm. The SPSS user can ask for any number of statistics and percentages to be included with this output by clicking on the corresponding options.

EXHIBIT 20.14
Examples of SPSS Output for Cross-Tabulation

CLASS * SMOKING Cross-Tabulation				
		Smoking		
Count		Smoker	Non-smoker	Total
Class	instructors	7	9	16
	undergraduate	9	22	31
	graduate	15	10	25
	career	6	6	12
Total		37	47	84

Computer Graphics and Computer Mapping

Graphic aids prepared by computers have practically replaced graphic presentation aids drawn by artists. Computer graphics are extremely useful for descriptive analysis. As mentioned in Chapter 2, decision support systems can generate two- or three-dimensional computer maps to portray data about sales, demographics, lifestyles, retail stores, and other features. Exhibit 20.15 shows a computer graphic depicting how fast-food consumption varies from state to state. The chart shows the relative frequencies of eating fast-food burgers, chicken, tacos, or other types of fast-food across several states. Computer graphics like these have become more common as software applications have introduced easy ways of generating 3-D graphics. Researchers need to realize that not every audience may like 3-D displays. Thus, a simpler, albeit less impressive looking, chart may often be preferable. Many computer maps are used by marketers to show locations of high-quality customer segments. Competitors' locations are often overlaid for additional quick and easy visual reference. Scales that show miles, population densities, and other characteristics can be highlighted in color, with shading, and with symbols.

box and whisker plots

Graphic representations of central tendencies, percentiles, variabilities, and the shapes of frequency distributions.

interquartile range

A measure of variability.

Many computer programs can draw **box and whisker plots**, which provide graphic representations of central tendencies, percentiles, variabilities, and the shapes of frequency distributions. Exhibit 20.16 shows a computer-drawn box and whisker plot for 100 responses to a question measured on a 10-point scale. The response categories are shown on the vertical axis. The small box inside the plot represents responses for half of all respondents. Thus, half of respondents marked 4, 5, or 6. This gives a measure of variability called the **interquartile range**, but the term *midspread* is less complex and more descriptive. The location of the line within the box indicates the median.

The dashed lines that extend from the top and bottom of the box are the whiskers. Each whisker extends either the length of the box (the midspread in our example is 2 scale points) or to the most extreme observation in that direction.

An **outlier** is a value that lies outside the normal range of the data. In Exhibit 20.16 outliers are indicated by either a 0 or an asterisk. Box and whisker plots are particularly useful for spotting outliers or comparing group categories (e.g., men versus women).

outlier

A value that lies outside the normal range of the data.

EXHIBIT 20.15
A 3-D Graph Showing Fast-Food Consumption Patterns around the United States

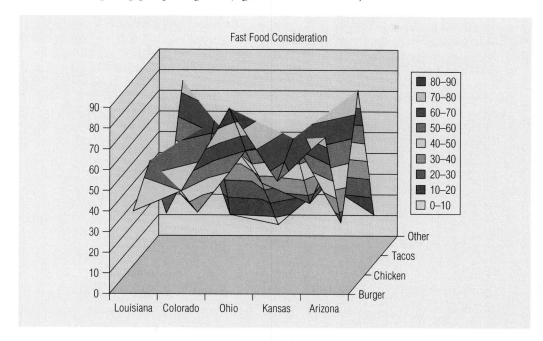

EXHIBIT 20.16
Computer Drawn Box and Whisker Plot

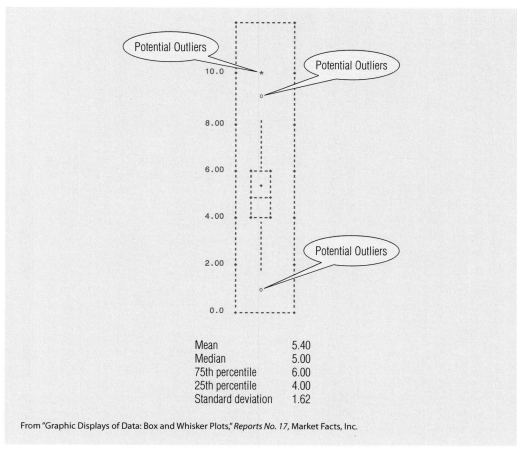

Mean	5.40
Median	5.00
75th percentile	6.00
25th percentile	4.00
Standard deviation	1.62

From "Graphic Displays of Data: Box and Whisker Plots," *Reports No. 17*, Market Facts, Inc.

- A frequency table can be a very useful way to depict basic tabulations.
- Cross-tabulation and contingency tables are a simple and effective way to examine relationships among less than interval variables.
  - When a distinction can be made between independent and dependent variables (that are nominal or ordinal), the convention is that rows are independent variables and columns are dependent variables.
- Importance-performance charts are a good way to illustrate market positioning by showing where brands are strong or weak on important variables. A weakness on an important variable is a call to action.

- A continuous variable that displays a bimodal distribution is appropriate for a median split.
  - Median splits should be performed on variables that display a normal distribution only with caution.
  - Importantly, median splits on continuous variables should be performed only after deleting one-fourth to one-third of the responses around the median to help prevent logically inconsistent classifications.
- Box and whisker plots can reveal outliers.
  - Outliers can distort statistical analysis. Therefore, they become candidates for deletion.

© GEORGE DOYLE & CIARAN GRIFFIN

Interpretation

An interpreter at the United Nations translates a foreign language into another language to explain the meaning of a foreign diplomat's speech. In marketing research, the interpretation process explains the meaning of the data. After the statistical analysis of the data, inferences and conclusions about their meaning are developed.

interpretation

The process of drawing inferences from the analysis results.

A distinction can be made between *analysis* and *interpretation*. **Interpretation** is drawing inferences from the analysis results. Inferences drawn from interpretations lead to managerial implications. In other words, each statistical analysis produces results that are interpreted with respect to insight into a particular decision. The logical interpretation of the data and statistical analysis are closely intertwined. When a researcher calculates a cross-tabulation of a demographic variable with brand choice, an interpretation is drawn suggesting that one segment may be more or less likely to choose a given brand. This interpretation of the statistical analysis may lead to a suggestion that a brand be withdrawn from certain demographic markets.

From a management perspective, however, the qualitative meaning of the data and their managerial implications are an important aspect of the interpretation. Consider the crucial role played by interpretation of research results in investigating one new product, a lip stain that could color the lips a desired shade semi-permanently and last for about a month at a time:

> *The lip stain idea, among lipstick wearers, received very high scores on a rating scale ranging from "excellent" to "poor," presumably because it would not wear off. However, it appeared that even among routine wearers of lipstick the idea was being rated highly more for its interesting, even ingenious, nature than for its practical appeal to the consumer's personality. They liked the idea, but for someone else, not themselves. . . . [Careful interpretation of the data] revealed that not being able to remove the stain for that length of time caused most women to consider the idea irrelevant in relation to their own personal needs and desires. Use of the product seems to represent more of a "permanent commitment" than is usually associated with the use of a particular cosmetic. In fact, women attached overtly negative meaning to the product concept, often comparing it with hair dyes instead of a long-lasting lipstick.*[13]

TOTHEPOINT

The thing to do is to supply light.

—Woodrow Wilson

This example shows that interpretation is crucial. However, the process is difficult to explain in a textbook because there is no one best way to interpret data. Many possible interpretations of data may be derived from a number of thought processes. Experience with selected cases will help you develop your own interpretative ability.

Data are sometimes merely reported and not interpreted. Research firms may provide reams of computer output that do not state what the data mean. At the other extreme, some researchers tend to analyze every possible relationship between each and every variable in the study. Such an approach is a sign that the research problem was not adequately defined prior to beginning the research and the researcher really doesn't know what business decision the research is addressing. Researchers who have a clear sense of the purpose of the research do not request statistical analysis of data that have little or nothing to do with the primary purpose of the research.

Summary

1. Know what descriptive statistics are and why they are used. Descriptive analyses provide descriptive statistics. These include measures of central tendency and variation. Statistics such as the mean, mode, median, range, variance, and standard deviation are all descriptive statistics. These statistics provide a basic summary describing the basic properties of a variable.

2. Create and interpret tabulation tables. Statistical tabulation is another way of saying that we count the number of observations in each possible response category. In other words, tabulation is the same as tallying. Tabulation is an appropriate descriptive analysis for less-than interval variables. Frequency tables and histograms are used to display tabulation results.

3. Use cross-tabulations to test for relationships. Cross-tabulation is the appropriate technique for assessing relationships among multiple less-than interval variables. The key to interpreting a cross-tabulation result is to compare actual observed values with hypothetical values that would result from pure chance. When observed results vary from these values, a relationship is indicated.

4. Perform basic data transformations. Data transformations are often needed to assist in data analysis and involve changing the mathematical form of data in some systematic way. Basic data transformations include reverse coding, summating scales, creating index numbers, and collapsing a variable based on a median split.

5. List different computer software products designed for descriptive statistical analysis. While spreadsheets like Excel have improved with respect to their ability to conduct basic statistical analyses, marketing researchers still rely heavily on specialized statistical software. SAS and SPSS are two of the best-known statistical packages. Each is available for even the most basic modern PC and can be used with a drop-down window interface, practically eliminating the need for writing computer code.

Key Terms and Concepts

box and whisker plots, *530*
contingency table, *520*
cross-tabulation, *519*
data transformation, *523*
descriptive analysis, *516*
elaboration analysis, *522*
frequency table, *518*

histogram, *518*
importance-performance analysis, *523*
index numbers, *525*
interpretation, *532*
interquartile range, *530*
marginals, *520*
median split, *524*

moderator variable, *522*
outlier, *531*
quadrant analysis, *523*
statistical base, *521*
tabulation, *518*

Questions for Review and Critical Thinking

1. What are five descriptive statistics used to describe the basic properties of variables?
2. What is a *histogram?* What is the advantage of overlaying a normal distribution over a histogram?
3. A survey asks respondents to respond to the statement "My work is interesting." Interpret the frequency distribution shown here (taken from an SPSS output):

Category Label	Code	Abs. Freq.	Rel. Freq. (Pct.)	Adj. Freq. (Pct.)	Cum. Freq. (Pct.)
Very true	1	650	23.9	62.4	62.4
Somewhat true	2	303	11.2	29.1	91.5
Not very true	3	61	2.2	5.9	97.3
Not at all true	4	28	1.0	2.7	100.0
	•	1,673	61.6	Missing	
	Total	2,715	100.0	100.0	
Valid cases	1,042		Missing cases	1,673	

4. Use the data in the following table to
   a. prepare a frequency distribution of the respondents' ages

b. cross-tabulate the respondents' genders with cola preference
c. identify any outliers

Individual	Gender	Age	Cola Preference	Weekly Unit Purchases
John	M	19	Coke	2
Al	M	17	Pepsi	5
Bill	M	20	Pepsi	7
Mary	F	20	Coke	2
Jim	M	18	Coke	4
Karen	F	16	Coke	4
Tom	M	17	Pepsi	12
Sassi	F	22	Pepsi	6
Amie	F	20	Pepsi	2
Dawn	F	19	Pepsi	3

5. Data on the average size of a soda (in ounces) at all thirty major league baseball parks are as follows: 14, 18, 20, 16, 16, 12, 14, 16, 14, 16, 16, 16, 14, 32, 16, 20, 12, 16, 20, 12, 16, 16, 24, 16, 16, 14, 14, 12, 14, 20. Compute descriptive statistics for this variable including a box and whisker plot. Comment on the results.

6. The following computer output shows a cross-tabulation of frequencies and provides frequency number (N) and row (R) percentages.
   a. Interpret this output including an impression about whether or not the row and column variables are related.
   b. Critique the way the analysis is presented.
   c. Draw a pie chart indicating percentages for having read a book in the past three months for those with and those without high school diplomas.

Have You Read a Book in Past 3 Months?	Have High School Diploma?		
	Yes	No	Total
Yes	489 73.8	174 26.2	663
No	473 55.6	378 44.4	851
	......	......	......
TOTAL	962	552	1514

7. List and describe at least three basic data transformations.
8. What conditions suggest that a ratio variable should be transformed into a dichotomous (two group) variable represented with dummy coding?
9. **ETHICS** A data processing analyst for a research supplier finds that preliminary computer runs of survey results show that consumers love a client's new product. The employee buys a large block of the client's stock. Is this ethical?`
10. **'NET** Use a Web site such as http://www.styledrops.com to find some prices for 4 Prada handbags, 4 Gucci handbags, 4 Yves Saint Laurent handbags, 4 Burberry handbags, and 4 Ferragamo handbags. Enter these into a spreadsheet. Using the lowest priced Prada handbag as a base, compute an index displaying the price of all other handbags. Which brand offers the best value in your opinion? Compute the appropriate statistic for central tendency using the spreadsheet and one other method (which could be SPSS or SAS). Use the chart feature (in Excel or another package) to depict the prices as a frequency distribution.
11. Investigate to see which of the software packages discussed in the chapter are available to you either through your university or via the use of this book. Explore the programs. Which seems most user friendly at this point?

Research Activities

1. **'NET** Go the Web site for the Chicago Cubs baseball team (http://chicago.cubs.mlb.com). Use either the schedule listing or the stats information to find their record in the most recent season. Create a data file with a variable indicating whether each game was won or lost and a variable indicating whether the game was played at home in Wrigley Field or away from home. Using computerized software like SPSS or SAS,
   a. Compute a frequency table and histogram for each variable.

   b. Use cross-tabulations to examine whether a relationship exists between where the game is played (home or away) and winning.
   c. Extra Analysis: Repeat the analyses for the Houston Astros baseball team (http://www.astros.com). What does this suggest for the relationship between playing at home and winning?
2. **'NET** Go to http://www.spss.com and click on a few tabs such as "Solutions," "Software," and "Customers." What kinds of business problems can SPSS products help address?

Case 20.1 Body on Tap

A few years ago Vidal Sassoon, Inc., took legal action against Bristol-Myers over a series of TV commercials and print ads for a shampoo that had been named Body on Tap because of its beer content.[14] The prototype commercial featured a well-known high fashion model saying, "In shampoo tests with over 900 women like me, Body on Tap got higher ratings than Prell for body. Higher than Flex for conditioning. Higher than Sassoon for strong, healthy-looking hair."

The evidence showed that several groups of approximately 200 women each tested just one shampoo. They rated it on a six-step qualitative scale, from "outstanding" to "poor," for 27 separate attributes, such as body and conditioning. It became clear that 900 women did not, after trying both shampoos, make product-to-product comparisons between Body on Tap and Sassoon or between Body on Tap and any of the other brands mentioned. In fact, no woman in the tests tried more than one shampoo.

The claim that the women preferred Body on Tap to Sassoon for "strong, healthy-looking hair" was based on combining the data for the "outstanding" and "excellent" ratings and discarding the lower four ratings on the scale. The figures then were 36 percent for Body

on Tap and 24 percent (of a separate group of women) for Sassoon. When the "very good" and "good" ratings were combined with the "outstanding" and "excellent" ratings, however, there was only a difference of 1 percent between the two products in the category of "strong, healthy-looking hair."

The research was conducted for Bristol-Myers by Marketing Information Systems, Inc. (MISI), using a technique known as blind monadic testing. The president of MISI testified that this method typically is employed when what is wanted is an absolute response to a product "without reference to another specific product." Although he testified that blind monadic testing was used in connection with comparative advertising, that was not the purpose for which Bristol-Myers retained MISI. Rather, Bristol-Myers wished to determine consumer reaction to the introduction of Body on Tap. And Sassoon's in-house research expert stated flatly that blind monadic testing cannot support comparative advertising claims.

Question

Comment on the professionalism of the procedures used to make the advertising claim. Why do you believe the researchers performed the data transformations described?

Case 20.2 Downy-Q Quilt

The research for Downy-Q is an example of a commercial test that was conducted when an advertising campaign for an established brand had run its course.[15] The revised campaign, "Fighting the Cold," emphasized that Downy-Q was an "extra-warm quilt"; previous research had demonstrated that extra warmth was an important and deliverable product quality. The commercial test was requested to measure the campaign's ability to generate purchase interest.

The marketing department had recommended this revised advertising campaign and was now anxious to know how effectively this commercial would perform. The test concluded that "Fighting the Cold" was a persuasive commercial. It also demonstrated that the new campaign would have greater appeal to specific market segments.

Method

Brand choices for the same individuals were obtained before and after viewing the commercial. The commercial was tested in 30-second, color-moving, storyboard form in a theater test. Invited viewers were shown programming with commercial inserts. Qualified respondents were women who had bought quilts in outlets that carried Downy-Q. The results are shown in Case Exhibits 20.2–1 through 20.2–4.

Question

Interpret the data in these tables. What recommendations and conclusions would you offer to Downy-Q management?

CASE EXHIBIT 20.2–1 **Shifts in Brand Choice Before and After Showing of Downy-Q Quilt Commercial**

Question: We are going to give away a sample of fabric softener. You can select the brand you most prefer. Which brand would you chose?

Brand Choice before Commercial	Brand Choice after Commercial (%)	
	Downy-Q (n = 23)	Other Brand (n = 237)
Downy-Q	78	19
Other brand	22	81

CASE EXHIBIT 20.2–2 **Pre/Post Increment in Choice of Downy-Q**

Improvement in score based on exposure to commercial.

Demographic Group	"Fighting the Cold"		Norm: All Quilt Commercials	
	Base	Score	Average	Range
Total audience	(260)	+15	+10	6–19
By marital status				
Married	(130)	+17		
Not married	(130)	+12		
By age				
Under 35	(130)	+14		
35 and over	(130)	+15		
By employment status				
Not employed	(90)	+13		
Employed	(170)	+18		

CASE EXHIBIT 20.2–3 **Adjective Checklist for Downy-Q Quilt Commercial**

Question: Which of these words do you feel come closest to describing the commercial you've just seen? (Check all the apply.)

Adjective	"Fighting the Cold" (%)	Norm: All Quilt Commercials (%)
Positive		
Appealing	18	24
Clever	11	40
Convincing	20	14
Effective	19	23
Entertaining	5	24
Fast moving	12	21
Genuine	7	4
Imaginative	7	21
Informative	24	18
Interesting	13	17
Original	7	20
Realistic	8	3
Unusual	3	8
Negative		
Amateurish	9	11
Bad Taste	4	4
Dull	33	20
Repetitious	17	16
Silly	8	19
Slow	8	7
Unbelievable	3	5
Unclear	3	2
Unimportant	14	14
Uninteresting	32	19

CASE EXHIBIT 20.2–4 **Product Attribute Checklist for Downy-Q**

Question: Which of the following statements do you feel apply to Downy-Q? (Mark as many or as few as you feel apply.)

Attributes	"Fighting the Cold" (%)
Extra warm	56
Lightweight	48
Pretty designs	45
Durable fabrics	28
Nice fabrics	27
Good construction	27

CHAPTER 21
UNIVARIATE STATISTICAL ANALYSIS

After studying this chapter, you should be able to

1. Conduct a hypothesis-test following a step–by-step procedure
2. Use p-values to assess statistical significance
3. Choose the right statistical test for a given hypothesis
4. Test a hypothesis about an observed mean compared to some standard
5. Know the difference between Type I and Type II errors
6. Know when a univariate χ^2 test is appropriate and how to conduct one

Chapter Vignette: Pizza Targets

We all sometimes have trouble deciding where to eat or shop. Consumers have some idea in mind about the type of food they wish to eat, the atmosphere they want to experience, and the price they wish to pay. They use these *benchmarks* in the decision-making process.

Consider the other side of the coin. Companies like Domino's, Papa John's, and Pizza Hut each operate thousands of stores and have to decide which locations will remain open and where new locations are needed. Domino's operates over 8,300 stores across the United States and in over 55 countries internationally.[1] However, recent trends show approximately a 6 percent drop in same-store U.S. sales while international same-store sales have increased by over 5 percent. In recent years, Domino's has closed over 400 stores and is considering closing more stores around the United States in a reponse to poor store-unit sales.[2]

Location decisions are very important in retailing, and an important part of the marketing strategy for firms like Domino's involves rules that help make these decisions. Restaurants and retailers with thousands of locations can establish benchmarks based on historical performance trends. Pizza Hut, Domino's, and their major competitors can use demographic data to help identify potentially good restaurant locations, and they can use demographics along with profitability and sales growth statistics to help make store closure decisions.

© VICKI BEAVER

Fortunately for Domino's, families and college students eat a lot of pizza. Researchers may be asked to perform research to determine if enough families live within a 10-minute drive to support a restaurant. Location rules may involve comparing a sample's demographic characteristics to demographic benchmarks. For instance, if historical data indicated that a successful restaurant generally was surrounded by families with an average of 1.5 children or more, the research may sample prospective locations and compare the observed average family size to this benchmark. Similarly, the company may have benchmarks for household income or the proportion of specific ethnic groups within a market. Benchmarks like these can help make difficult decisions like these manageable.

Introduction

Students learn the scientific method during their childhood and although they may not remember the details, most will associate the scientific method with experimentation, at least in the colloquial sense. Researchers conduct tests and observe the results carefully and eventually compare them to prestudy conjecture. In the chapter vignette, the restaurant may wish to test hypotheses about a single variable—family size. A sample will be drawn from the relevant population and tested against a benchmark of 1.5.

Hypothesis Testing

Descriptive research and causal research designs often climax with hypotheses tests. Hypotheses were defined in Chapter 3 as formal statements of explanations stated in a testable form. Generally, hypotheses should be stated in concrete fashion so that the method of empirical testing seems almost obvious. Types of hypotheses tested commonly in marketing research include the following:

1. Hypotheses about differences from some standard examine how some variable differs from some preconceived standard. The preconceived standard sometimes represents the true value of the variable in a population. These tests can involve either a test of a mean for better-than-ordinal variables or a test of frequencies if the variable is ordinal or nominal. These tests typify univariate statistical tests.
2. Hypotheses about differences between groups examine how some variable varies from one group to another. These tests are very common in causal designs, which very often involve a comparison of means between groups.
3. Relational hypotheses examine how changes in one variable vary with changes in another. This often is tested by assessing covariance in some way, very often with regression analysis.

Empirical testing typically involves inferential statistics. This means that an inference will be drawn about some population based on observations of a sample representing that population. Statistical analysis can be divided into several groups based on how many variables are involved:

univariate statistical analysis

Tests of hypotheses involving only one variable.

bivariate statistical analysis

Tests of hypotheses involving two variables.

multivariate statistical analysis

Statistical analysis involving three or more variables or sets of variables.

- **Univariate statistical analysis** tests hypotheses involving only one variable.
- **Bivariate statistical analysis** tests hypotheses involving two variables.
- **Multivariate statistical analysis** tests hypotheses and models involving multiple (three or more) variables or sets of variables.

The focus in this chapter is on univariate statistics. Thus, we examine statistical tests appropriate for drawing inferences about a single variable.

Hypothesis Testing Procedure

Hypotheses are tested by comparing an educated guess with empirical reality. The process can be described as follows:

- First, the hypothesis is derived from the research objectives. The hypothesis should be stated as specifically as possible and should be theoretically sound.
- Next, a sample is obtained and the relevant variables are measured. In univariate tests, only one variable is of interest.
- The measured value obtained in the sample is compared to the value either stated explicitly or implied in the hypothesis. If the value is consistent with the hypothesis, the hypothesis is supported. If the value is not consistent with the hypothesis, the hypothesis is not supported.

A univariate hypothesis consistent with the chapter vignette would be:

H_1: *The average number of children per family in zip code 70360 is greater than 1.5.*

If a sample is drawn from this zip code and the average number of children per family is 0.075, the hypothesis is not supported. If the average number of children is 3.3, the hypothesis is supported. As the mean becomes smaller and approaches the theoretical expected value of 1.5, the chance becomes smaller that the hypothesis can indeed be supported. The exact point where

The section below asks students some questions about everyday behavior. Let's examine some of this behavior and see what students spend their time doing. Test the following univariate hypotheses using the students from your university and/or from the entire sample.

- H_1: The typical student sends more than 25 text messages per day.
- H_2: The typical student makes more than 15 cell phone calls each day.
- H_3: Students are evenly distributed in the time they spend watching television. That is, one-fourth watch less than 1 hour a week, one-fourth watch 1–2 hours per day, one-fourth watch 2–3 hours per day, and one-fourth watch more than 3 hours per day.
- H_4: Students average studying 2–3 hours per week.

© GEORGE DOYLE & CIARAN GRIFFIN

COURTESY OF QUALTRICS.COM

the hypothesis changes from not being supported to being supported depends on how much risk the researcher is willing to accept and on the variability of the measure.

Univariate hypotheses are typified by tests comparing some observed sample mean against a benchmark value. The test addresses the question, is the sample mean truly different from the benchmark? But, how different is really different? If the observed sample mean is 1.55 and the benchmark is 1.50, would the hypothesis still be supported? Probably not! When the observed mean is so close to the benchmark, we do not have sufficient confidence that a second set of data using a new sample taken from the same population might not produce a finding conflicting with the benchmark. In contrast, when the mean turns out well above 1.50, perhaps 3.3, then we could more easily trust that another sample would not produce a mean equal to or less than 1.50. The Research Snapshot on the next page provides an illustration.

In statistics classes, students are exposed to hypothesis testing as a contrast between a *null* and an *alternative* hypothesis. A "null" hypothesis can be thought of as the expectation of findings as if no hypothesis existed (i.e., "no" or "null" hypothesis) or put another way, if nothing is really happening. In other words, the state implied by the statistical null hypothesis is generally the opposite of the state represented by the actual hypothesis. A null to the hypothesis listed above is

H_n: *The average number of children per family in zip code 70360 is equal to 1.5 (not greater than).*

The alternative hypothesis states the opposite of the null, which normally conforms to one of the common types of relationships above. So, the researcher's hypothesis is generally stated in the form of an "alternative" hypothesis. Are you confused? Well, if so, don't worry so much about the null hypothesis and simply think about the hypothesis you would like to test and what kind of evidence will be needed to corroborate it or show it isn't true.

While the terminology is common in statistical theory, the idea of a null hypothesis indeed can be confusing. Therefore, we'll avoid using the term *null hypothesis* when at all possible. The reader should instead focus on what the findings should look like if the proposed hypothesis is true. If the hypothesis above is true, an observed sample's mean should be noticeably greater than 1.50. We test to see if this idea can be supported by the empirical evidence.

Empirical evidence is provided by test results comparing the observed mean against some sampling distribution. The variance in observations also plays a role because with greater variance, there is more of a chance that the range of values includes 1.50. A statistical test's significance level or p-value becomes a key indicator of whether or not a hypothesis can be supported.

F-22 Target Tests

In January 2006, the F-22 Raptor fighter plane, jointly produced by Boeing and Lockheed-Martin, flew its first operational missions in support of operation Noble Eagle. In 2007, the U.S. Air Force allocated over $100 billion to purchase more F-22 Raptors as it became the fifth generation U.S. fighter plane. Imagine all the tests that must be conducted before a fighter plane with a price tag somewhere in the neighborhood of $160–$350 million each ever goes into service.

Many of the tests involve statistical analyses comparing actual performance against benchmarks. In this sense, they are not entirely different than traditional business research tests comparing sample performance against some target. These tests involve how much stress some component can take before failing, how much acceleration the jet can achieve, how much maintenance is required, how accurate the plane's weapons systems are in hitting air-to-air targets, and the accuracy of the plane's air-to-ground weapons systems. Many tests like these can be analyzed with univariate statistical tests.

Imagine a test involving the accuracy of the plane's air-to-air defense systems. An F-22 pilot is asked to practice evasive maneuvers while trying to hit multiple moving targets playing the role of an enemy aircraft. Designers of the plane claim that with equally qualified pilots, an F-22 could defend itself in combat against six F-15 fighters, the plane it is making obsolete. After considering these claims, suppose the Air Force performed a test requiring that the F-22 would be able to shoot down more than five targets per flight during this test. The diagram that follows depicts the hypothesized case and the contrasting case (statistically, this would be the null). The test is conducted 50 times with the results shown below:

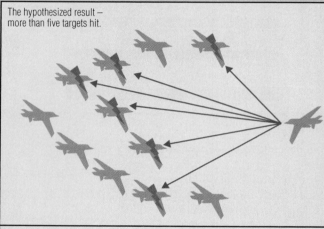

The hypothesized result – more than five targets hit.

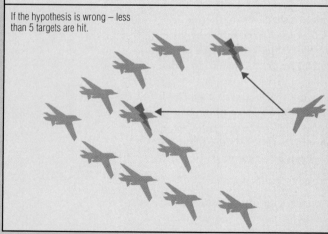

If the hypothesis is wrong – less than 5 targets are hit.

	N	Mean	Std. Deviation	Std. Error Mean
targets	50	7.1000	2.35822	.33350

The F-22 averaged 7.1 targets hit per test flight. The fewest targets hit was 2 and the most hit was 12. Is this performance good enough to support the hypothesis? The univariate statistic testing this result suggests the answer to this question is yes. The p-value for this test is less than .001 which supports the premise that the mean number of hits will be greater than 5.

					Test Value = 5		
						95% Confidence Interval of the Difference	
	T	d.f.	p-value (2-tailed)	Mean Difference		Lower	Upper
targets	6.297	49	.000	2.10000		1.4298	2.7702

Sources: Scott, William B., "F-22 Flight Tests Paced by Aircraft Availability," *Aviation Week and Space Technology* 153 (October 16, 2000), 53; Scott, William B., "F-22 Raptor Scores First Air-to-Air Kill During Test," *Aviation Week and Space Technology* 155 (October 1, 2001), 5; http://www.f-22raptor.com; Nelson, Melissa, "Pilot Says U.S. Stealth Fighter Has No Equal," HeraldToday.com, (December 21, 2005), accessed Feb. 7, 2006.

An Example Hypothesis to Be Tested

The example described here illustrates the conventional statistical approach to testing a univariate hypothesis with an interval or ratio variable. Suppose the Pizza-In restaurant is concerned about store image before deciding whether to expand. Pizza-In managers are most interested in how friendly customers perceive the service to be. A sample of 225 customers was obtained and asked to indicate their perceptions of service on a five-point scale, where 1 indicates "very unfriendly" service and 5 indicates "very friendly" service. The scale is assumed to be an interval scale, and experience has shown that the previous distribution of this attitudinal measurement assessing the service dimension was approximately normal.

Now, suppose Pizza-In believes the service has to be different from 3.0 before a decision about expansion can be made. In conventional statistical terminology, the null hypothesis for this test is that the mean is equal to 3.0:

$$H_0: \mu = 3.0$$

The alternative hypothesis is that the mean does not equal 3.0:

$$H_1: \mu \neq 3.0$$

More practically, the researcher is likely to write the substantive hypotheses (as it would be stated in a research report or proposal) something like this:

H_1: Customer perceptions of friendly service are significantly greater than three.

Note that the substantive hypothesis matches the "alternative" phrasing. In practical terms, researchers do not state null and alternative hypotheses. Only the substantive (i.e., alternative) hypothesis implying what is expected to be observed in the sample is formally stated.

significance level

A critical probability associated with a statistical hypothesis test that indicates how likely an inference supporting a difference between an observed value and some statistical expectation is true. The acceptable level of Type I error.

Significance Levels and p-values ◀

A **significance level** is a critical probability associated with a statistical hypothesis test that indicates how likely it is that an inference supporting a difference between an observed value and some statistical expectation is true. The term **p-value** stands for probability-value and is essentially another name for an *observed* or *computed* significance level. Exhibit 21.1 discusses interpretations

p-value

Probability value, or the observed or computed significance level; p-values are compared to significance levels to test hypotheses.

EXHIBIT 21.1
p-Values and Statistical Tests

Test Description	Test Statistic	
Compare an Observed Mean with Some Predetermined Value	Z or t-test—Low p-values Indicate the Observed Mean Is Different than Some Predetermined Value (Often 0)	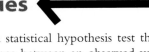 $\alpha = .025$ $\alpha = .025$ $m = 3.0$ X
Compare an Observed Frequency with a Predetermined Value	X^2—Low p-values Indicate that Observed Frequency Is Different than Predetermined Value	df = 1 $\quad$ 1
Compare an Observed Proportion with Some Predetermined Value	Z or t-test for Proportions—Low p-values Indicate that the Observed Proportion Is Different than the Predetermined Value	50%
Bivariate Tests:		
Compare Whether Two Observed Means Are Different from One Another.	Z or t-test—Low p-values Indicate the Means Are Different	$\mu = 0$
Compare Whether Two Less-than Interval Variables Are Related Using Cross-tabs	X^2—Low p-values Indicate the Variables Are Related to One Another	df = 3 $\quad$ 3
Compare Whether Two Interval or Ratio Variables Are Correlated to One Another	t-test for Correlation—Low p-values Indicate the Variables Are Related to One Another	$r = 0$

of p-values for different kinds of statistical tests. The probability in a p-value is that the statistical expectation (null) for a given test is true. So, low p-values mean there is little likelihood that the statistical expectation is true. This means the researcher's hypothesis positing (suggesting) a difference between an observed mean and a population mean, or between an observed frequency and a population frequency, or for a relationship between two variables, is likely supported.

Traditionally, researchers have specified an acceptable significance level for a test prior to the analysis. Later, we will discuss this as an acceptable amount of Type I error. For most applications, the acceptable amount of error, and therefore the acceptable significance level, is 0.1, 0.05, or 0.01. If the p-value resulting from a statistical test is less than the pre-specified significance level, then a hypothesis about differences is supported.

p-values as a Comparison Standard

Exhibit 21.2 illustrates an important property of p-values. In this case, the comparison standard of 1.5 is shown as a red line. The sample result is shown as a blue line (3.1). The blue normal curve illustrates what other sample results drawn from the population would likely be. What is most important to realize is that as the observed value gets further from 1.5, the p-value gets smaller, meaning that the chance of the mean actually equaling 1.5 also is smaller. With the observed mean of 3.1 and the observed standard deviation of 1.02, there is very little chance that the researcher would be wrong in concluding the actual number of children per family is greater than 1.5. In fact, that chance appears to be 0.0001.

Consider the test in the Research Snapshot box on page 540. The statistical test is whether or not the mean computed from the 50 observations is different from 5. Given the risk associated with being wrong, the researcher uses a most conservative acceptable significance level of 0.01. After computing the appropriate test, the researcher observes a computed significance level or p-value that is less than 0.001. Therefore, the hypothesis is supported.

In discussing confidence intervals, statisticians use the term *confidence level,* or *confidence coefficient,* to refer to the level of probability associated with an interval estimate. However, when

EXHIBIT 21.2

As the observed mean gets further from the standard (proposed population mean), the p-value decreases. The lower the p-value, the more confidence you have that the sample mean is different.

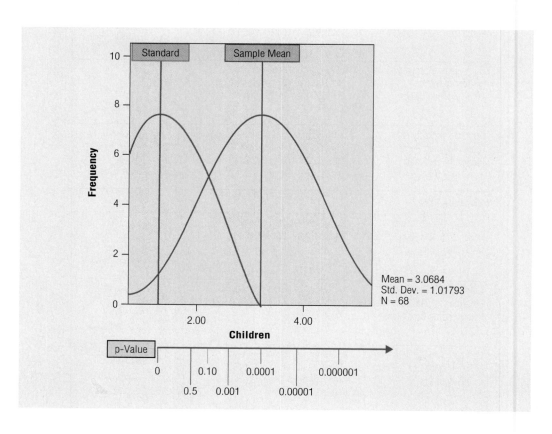

discussing hypothesis testing, statisticians change their terminology and call this a *significance level*, α (the Greek letter *alpha*).

The researcher must decide on an acceptable significance level value. This level corresponds to a region of rejection on a normal sampling distribution (see the top of Exhibit 21.1). The peak of the distribution is the theoretical expected value for the population mean. In this case it would be 3. If the acceptable significance level is 0.05, then the 0.025 on either side of the mean that is furthest away from the mean forms the rejection zone (shaded blue in Exhibit 21.1). The values within the unshaded area are considered *acceptable at the 95 percent confidence level* (or 0.05 alpha level), and if we find that our sample mean lies within this region we conclude that the means are not different from the expected value, 3 in this case. More precisely, we fail to reject the conclusion that the mean is equal to 3.0. In other words, the range of acceptance (1) identifies those values that reflect random variation from the mean that would be predicted by a null (i.e., no difference) hypothesis, and (2) shows the range within which any difference is small enough that the difference is due to random sampling error rather than to a false null hypothesis. Simply put, H_1 would not be supported when the observed mean falls in the unshaded area around the mean.

In our example, the Pizza-In restaurant hired research consultants who collected a sample of 225 interviews. The mean friendliness score on a five-point scale equaled 3.78. If the *population* standard deviation, σ, is known, it is used in the analysis; however, this is rarely true and is not true in this case.[3] The *sample* standard deviation can be computed and is $S = 1.5$. Now we have enough information to test the hypothesis.

The researcher has decided that the acceptable significance level will be set at 0.05. This means that the researcher wishes to draw conclusions that will be erroneous no more than 5 times in 100 (0.05). From the table of the standardized normal distribution, the researcher finds that the Z score of 1.96 represents a probability of 0.025 that a sample mean will be above 1.96 standard errors from μ. Likewise, the table shows that 0.025 of all sample means will fall below −1.96 standard errors from μ. Adding these two "tails" together, we get 0.05.

The values that lie exactly on the boundary of the region of rejection are called **critical values** of μ. Theoretically, the critical values are $Z = -1.96$ and $+1.96$. Now we must transform these critical Z-values to the sampling distribution of the mean for this image study. The critical values are

critical values
The values that lie exactly on the boundary of the region of rejection.

$$\text{Critical value} - \text{lower limit} = \mu - ZS_{\overline{X}} \quad \text{or} \quad \mu - Z\frac{S}{\sqrt{n}}$$
$$= 3.0 - 1.96\left(\frac{1.5}{\sqrt{225}}\right)$$
$$= 3.0 - 1.96(.1)$$
$$= 3.0 - 0.196$$
$$= 2.804$$

$$\text{Critical value} - \text{upper limit} = \mu + ZS_{\overline{X}} \quad \text{or} \quad \mu + Z\frac{S}{\sqrt{n}}$$
$$= 3.0 + 1.96\left(\frac{1.5}{\sqrt{225}}\right)$$
$$= 3.0 + 1.96(.1)$$
$$= 3.0 + 0.196$$
$$= 3.196$$

Based on survey results, the sample mean ($\overline{X}$) is 3.78. The sample mean is contained in the region of rejection (see the grayish shaded areas of Exhibit 21.3 on the next page). Since the sample mean is greater than the critical value of 3.196, falling in one of the tails (regions of rejection), the researcher concludes that the sample result is statistically significant beyond the 0.05 level. A region of rejection means that the thought that the observed sample mean equals the predetermined value of 3.0 will be rejected when the computed value takes a value within the range. Here is another way to express this result: If we took 100 samples from a population where the mean was actually 3.0, fewer than 5 will show results that deviate this much.

What does this mean to the management of the Pizza-In? The results indicate that customers believe the service is pretty friendly. The probability is less than 5 in 100 that this result ($\overline{X} = 3.78$) would occur because of random sampling error. This suggests that friendliness of the

EXHIBIT 21.3
**A Hypothesis Test Using
the Sampling Distribution
of $\overline{X}$ under the Hypothesis
$\mu = 3.0$**

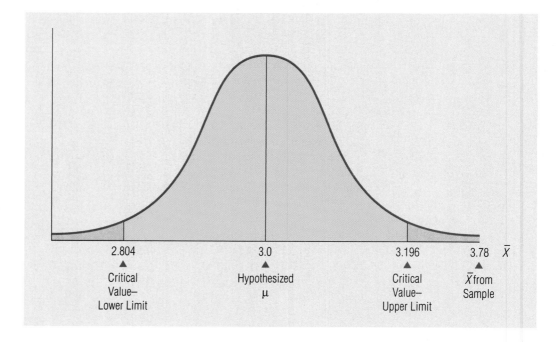

service personnel may not be a problem. However, perhaps Pizza-In should compare its friendliness rating with the friendliness rating of a key competitor. That analysis will have to wait until
we cover bivariate tests.

An alternative way to test the hypothesis is to formulate the decision rule in terms of the
Z-statistic. Using the following formula, we can calculate the observed value of the Z-statistic
given a certain sample mean, $(\overline{X})$:

$$Z_{obs} = \frac{\overline{X} - \mu}{S_{\overline{X}}}$$

$$= \frac{3.78 - \mu}{S_{\overline{X}}}$$

$$= \frac{3.78 - 3.0}{.1}$$

$$= \frac{.78}{.1}$$

$$= 7.8$$

In this case, the Z-value is 7.8 and we find that we have met the criterion of statistical significance
at the 0.05 level. This result produces a p-value of 0.000001. Once again, since the p-value is less than
the acceptable significance level, the hypothesis is supported. The service rating is significantly higher
than 3.0. This example used the conventional statistical terminology involving critical values and a
statistical null hypothesis. As mentioned earlier, rarely do researchers have to look up tabled values for
critical values anymore since the statistical packages will usually return a p-value for a given test. Thus,
the p-value, or a confidence interval associated with the p-value, is the key to interpretation.

Type I and Type II Errors

Hypothesis testing using sample observations is based on probability theory. We make an observation of a sample and use it to infer the probability that some observation is true within the population the sample represents. Because we cannot make any statement about a sample with complete
certainty, there is always the chance that an error will be made. When a researcher makes the
observation using a census, meaning that every unit (person or object) in a population is measured,
then conclusions are certain. Researchers very rarely use a census.

The researcher using sampling runs the risk of committing two types of errors. Exhibit 21.4
summarizes the state of affairs in the population and the nature of Type I and Type II errors. The
four possible situations in the exhibit result because the null hypothesis (using the example above,

The Law and Type I and Type II Errors

Although most attorneys and judges do not concern themselves with the statistical terminology of Type I and Type II errors, they do follow this logic. For example, our legal system is based on the concept that a person is innocent until proven guilty. Assume that the null hypothesis is that the individual is innocent. If we make a Type I error, we will send an innocent person to prison. Our legal system takes many precautions to avoid Type I errors. A Type II error would occur if a guilty party were set free (the null hypothesis would have been accepted). Our society places such a high value on avoiding Type I errors that Type II errors are more likely to occur.

© GEORGE DOYLE & CIARAN GRIFFIN

© CORBIS RF

$\mu = 3.0$) is actually either true or false and the observed statistics ($\overline{X} = 3.78$) will result in acceptance or rejection of this null hypothesis. The Research Snapshot above puts these alternative outcomes in a different light.

EXHIBIT 21.4
Type I and Type II Errors in Hypothesis Testing

	Decision	
Actual State in the Population	**Accept H_0**	**Reject H_0**
H_0 is true	Correct—no error	Type I error
H_0 is false	Type II error	Correct—no error

Type I Error

Suppose the observed sample mean described above leads to the conclusion that the mean is greater than 3.0 when in fact the true population mean is equal to 3.0. A **Type I error** has occurred. A Type I error occurs when a condition that is true in the population is rejected based on statistical observations. When a researcher sets an acceptable significance level a priori (α), he or she is determining how much tolerance he or she has for a Type I error. Simply put, a Type I error occurs when the researcher concludes that there is a statistical difference based on a sample result when in reality one does not exist in the population. When testing for relationships, a Type I error occurs when the researcher concludes a relationship exists when in fact one does not exist.

Type II Error

If the alternative condition is in fact true (in this case the mean is not equal to 3.0) but we conclude that we should not reject the belief that the mean equals 3.0, we make what is called a **Type II error**. A type II error is the probability of failing to reject a false null hypothesis. Alternatively, one can think of this as failing to identify a hypothesized difference using a sample result when one really does exist in the population. This incorrect decision is called beta (β). In practical terms, a Type II error means that we fail to reach the conclusion that some difference between an observed mean and a benchmark exists when in fact the difference is very real. In terms of a bivarate correlation, a Type II error would mean the idea that a relationship exists between two variables is rejected when in fact the relationship does indeed exist.

Unfortunately, without increasing sample size the researcher cannot simultaneously reduce Type I and Type II errors. They are inversely related. Thus, reducing the probability of a Type II error increases the probability of a Type I error. In marketing problems, Type I errors generally are considered more serious than Type II errors. Thus more emphasis is placed on determining the significance level, α, than in determining β.[4]

TO THE POINT

It is terrible to speak well and be wrong.

—Sophocles

Type I error

An error caused by rejecting the null hypothesis when it is true; has a probability of alpha. Practically, a Type I error occurs when the researcher concludes that a relationship or difference exits in the population when in reality it does not exist.

Type II error

An error caused by failing to reject the null hypothesis when the alternative hypothesis is true; has a probability of beta. Practically, a Type II error occurs when a researcher concludes that no relationship or difference exists when in fact one does exist.

Statistical Power

Marketing researchers may not be the most powerful people in a large firm, but they need to know just how much power they have. In this case, power refers to statistical power. **Statistical power** is how much ability exists to find a significant effect using a specific statistical tool. Mathematically, power is a direct function of Type II error rate:

$$Power = 1 - \beta$$

So, for a Type II error rate of 0.2, power is 0.8. Type II error rates vary with sample size. A larger sample reduces the chance of a Type II error and increases statistical power. A sample that is too small makes finding an effect that might really exist in the population difficult, particularly if that effect is small. Conversely, a very large sample yields very high power. Although this may seem like a good thing, a very large sample presents a problem in the sense that even very small and perhaps trivial effects will show up as statistically significant. Small effect-sizes require greater power than larger ones. At times, particularly in consumer research, researchers are dealing with hypothesized effects that may be expected to be relatively small. Thus, from a statistical inference standpoint, the researcher would like a sample that has appropriate power to find an effect if it truly exists. One complicating factor is that the researcher doesn't know how big is the effect size he or she is looking for before the research is conducted. Given the complexity of power calculations, researchers conventionally rely on a rule of thumb that statistical power should be 0.80.

A complete treatment of statistical power is beyond the scope of this text. However, some general guidelines can be given that will assist in assessing the appropriate sample size requirements for a given situation. The recommendations shown in Exhibit 21.5 apply to medium effect-sizes for given types of statistics.[5] Not all of the statistical tools have been covered yet, but the reader will become familiar with each over the remaining chapters. Exhibit 21.5 can provide a handy reference when using these common procedures.

EXHIBIT 21.5
Statistical Power Guidelines for 1 − β = .80

Statistical Tool Used	Type I Error	Sample Size Required
Comparison of Means	0.05	64
Frequencies /Cross-Tabulations	0.05	
(Frequency table)		87
(2 rows × 2 columns)		87
(3 rows × 2 columns)		107
(3 rows × 3 columns)		133
Larger		150
Pearson Correlation (r)	0.05	85
Regression Analysis	0.05	
2 independent variables		67
3 independent variables		76
4 independent variables		84
5 independent variables		91
More		100
Analysis of Variance	0.05	
2 treatment cells		64
4 treatment cells		45
6 treatment cells		39
More		35

The entire field of statistics is very broad and even experts in statistics are not typically experts on all statistical approaches and details. Typical users of statistics, like marketing researchers, need to know the types of statistical tests that they commonly perform and sometimes they need ready

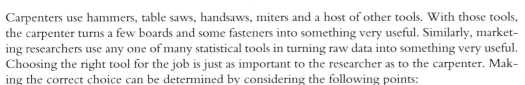

Living in a Statistical Web

Having trouble learning statistical concepts? Do a little surfing and the concepts may become clear. Many sources exist that illustrate statistical problems and provide data for practice. Here are just a few:

STATLIB

http://lib.stat.cmu.edu/

StatLib is a system for distributing statistical software, data-sets, and information by electronic mail, FTP, and the World Wide Web.

STAT-HELP

http://www.stat-help.com/

Stat-Help.com provides help with statistics via the Internet and contains spreadsheets for performing many basic calculations.

SURFSTAT.AUSTRALIA

http://surfstat.anu.edu.au/surfstat-home/surfstat-main.html

SurfStat.australia is an online text in introductory statistics from the University of Newcastle and the Australian government.

ELECTRONIC ENCYCLOPEDIA OF STATISTICAL EXAMPLES AND EXERCISES

http://www.stat.ohio-state.edu/~eesee/

The Electronic Encyclopedia of Statistical Examples and Exercises is a resource for the study of statistics that includes real-world examples of the uses and abuses of statistics and statistical inference.

THE RICE VIRTUAL LAB IN STATISTICS

http://onlinestatbook.com/rvls.html

http://davidmlane.com/hyperstat/

The Rice Virtual Lab in Statistics provides hypertext materials such as HyperStat Online.

STATCRUNCH

http://www.statcrunch.com/

Stat-Crunch is a statistical software package via the World Wide Web.

GRAPHPAD

http://www.graphpad.com/quickcalcs/Statratio1.cfm

GraphPad software is a p-value calculator.

reference sources to help out in situations that stray from the typical applications they face. The Research Snapshot above provides some sources that can be found on the Internet.

Choosing the Appropriate Statistical Technique

Carpenters use hammers, table saws, handsaws, miters and a host of other tools. With those tools, the carpenter turns a few boards and some fasteners into something very useful. Similarly, marketing researchers use any one of many statistical tools in turning raw data into something very useful. Choosing the right tool for the job is just as important to the researcher as to the carpenter. Making the correct choice can be determined by considering the following points:

1. The type of question to be addressed
2. The number of variables involved
3. The level of scale measurement involved in each variable

Today, the researcher rarely has to perform a paper and pencil calculation. Hypotheses are more often tested by using a correct click-through sequence in a statistical software package. The mathematics of these packages is highly reliable. Therefore, if the researcher can choose the right statistic, know the right click-through sequence, and read the output that results, the right statistical conclusion should be easy to reach.

Type of Question to Be Answered

Knowing the type of question the researcher is attempting to answer is an important consideration in choosing the right statistical technique. For example, a researcher may be concerned simply with the central tendency of a variable or with the distribution of a variable. Comparison of different business divisions' sales results with some target level will require a univariate (one-sample) *t*-test. Comparison of two salespeople's average monthly sales will require a *t*-test of two means, but a comparison of quarterly sales distributions across regions will probably require a cross-tabulation with a chi-square test.

The researcher should consider the method of statistical analysis before choosing the research design and before determining the type of data to collect. Once the data have been collected, the initial orientation toward analysis of the problem will be reflected in the research design.

Number of Variables

The number of variables that will be simultaneously investigated is a primary consideration in the choice of statistical technique. A researcher who is interested only in the average number of times a prospective home buyer visits financial institutions to shop for interest rates can concentrate on investigating only one variable at a time. In that case, the researcher should select a univariate tool. However, a researcher trying to measure multiple complex organizational variables cannot do the same and may very well need a multivariate tool. Simply put, univariate, bivariate, and multivariate statistical procedures are distinguished based on the number of variables involved in an analysis.

Additionally, knowing whether the research questions involve a distinction between independent and dependent variables is important. Beyond this, the researcher eventually can choose a technique based on how many variables are independent and/or dependent. This chapter, however, focuses only on univariate analysis so the distinction between independent and dependent variables is not in play here.

Level of Scale of Measurement

The scale measurement level helps choose the most appropriate statistical techniques and appropriate empirical operations. Testing a hypothesis about a mean, as we have just illustrated, is appropriate for interval-scaled or ratio-scaled data. Suppose a researcher is working with a nominal scale that identifies users versus nonusers of bank credit cards. Because of the type of scale, the researcher may use only the mode as a measure of central tendency. In other situations, where data are measured on an ordinal scale, the median may be used as the average or a percentile may be used as a measure of dispersion. For example, ranking brand preferences generally employs an ordinal scale. Nominal and ordinal data are often analyzed using frequencies or cross-tabulation.

parametric statistics

Involve numbers with known, continuous distributions; when the data are interval- or ratio-scaled and the sample size is large, parametric statistical procedures are appropriate.

nonparametric statistics

Appropriate when the variables being analyzed do not conform to any known or continuous distribution.

The terms **parametric statistics** and **nonparametric statistics** refer to the two major groupings of statistical procedures. The major distinction between them lies in the underlying assumptions about the data to be analyzed. Parametric statistics involve numbers with known, continuous distributions. When the data are interval or ratio scaled and the sample size is large, parametric statistical procedures are appropriate. Nonparametric statistics are appropriate when the numbers do not conform to a known distribution.

Parametric statistics are based on the assumption that the data in the study are drawn from a population with a normal (bell-shaped) distribution and/or normal sampling distribution. For example, if an investigator has two interval-scaled measures, such as gross national product (GNP) and industry sales volume, parametric tests are appropriate. Possible statistical tests might include product-moment correlation analysis, analysis of variance, regression, or a *t*-test for a hypothesis about a mean.

Nonparametric methods are used when the researcher does not know how the data are distributed. Making the assumption that the population distribution or sampling distribution is normal generally is inappropriate when data are either ordinal or nominal. Thus, nonparametric statistics are referred to as distribution free.[6] Data analysis of both nominal and ordinal scales typically uses nonparametric statistical tests.

Exhibit 21.6 illustrates how an appropriate univariate statistical method can be selected. The exhibit demonstrates how statistical techniques vary according to scale properties and the type of question being asked. Although more univariate statistical tests exist than shown, these basic options are the most frequently applied. A complete discussion of all univariate techniques is beyond the scope of this text.

EXHIBIT 21.6 **Univariate Statistical Choice Made Easy**

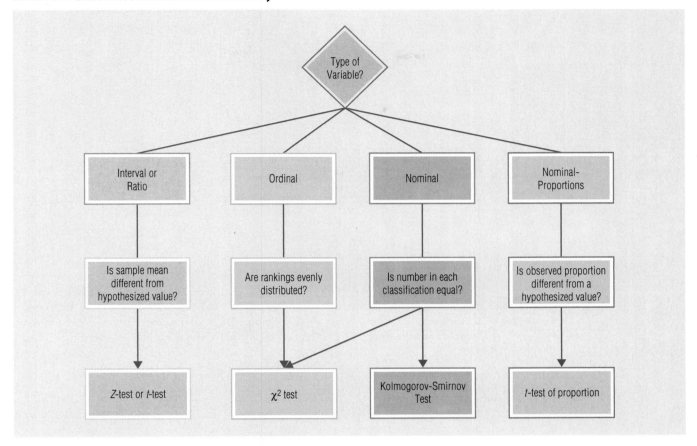

The *t*-Distribution

A univariate **t-test** is appropriate for testing hypotheses involving some observed mean against some specified value. The **t-distribution**, like the standardized normal curve, is a symmetrical, bell-shaped distribution with a mean of 0 and a standard deviation of 1.0. When sample size (n) is larger than 30, the *t*-distribution and *Z*-distribution are almost identical. Therefore, while the *t*-test is strictly appropriate for tests involving small sample sizes with unknown standard deviations, researchers commonly apply the *t*-test for comparisons involving the mean of an interval or ratio measure.

t-test

A hypothesis test that uses the *t*-distribution. A univariate *t*-test is appropriate when the variable being analyzed is interval or ratio.

t-distribution

A symmetrical, bell-shaped distribution that is contingent on sample size; has a mean of 0 and a standard deviation equal to 1.

Degrees of Freedom

The precise height and shape of the *t*-distribution vary with sample size. More specifically, the shape of the *t*-distribution is influenced by its **degrees of freedom (d.f.)**. The degrees of freedom are determined by the number of distinct calculations that are possible given a set of information. In the case of a univariate *t*-test, the degrees of freedom are equal to the sample size (n) minus one.

degrees of freedom (d.f.)

The number of observations minus the number of constraints or assumptions needed to calculate a statistical term.

Exhibit 21.7 on the next page illustrates *t*-distributions for 1, 2, 5, and an infinite number of degrees of freedom. Notice that the *t*-distribution approaches a normal distribution rapidly with increasing sample size. This is why, in practice, marketing researchers usually apply a *t*-test even with large samples. The practical effect is that the conclusion will be the same since the distributions are so similar with large samples and the correspondingly larger numbers of degrees of freedom.

Another way to look at degrees of freedom is to think of adding four numbers together when you know their sum—for example,

$$
\begin{array}{r}
4 \\
2 \\
1 \\
+X \\
\hline
12
\end{array}
$$

The value of the fourth number has to be 5. The values of the first three digits could change to any value (freely vary), but the fourth value would have to be determined for the mean to still equal to 12. In this example there are three degrees of freedom. Degrees of freedom can be a difficult concept to understand fully. For most basic statistical analyses, the user only needs to

Ultra-luxury car makers have sales goals that may involve selling 1,000 cars or fewer a year worldwide. What questions are asked in marketing a car like this that might involve a univariate analysis?[7]

remember the rule for determining the number of degrees of freedom for a given test. Today, with computerized software packages, even that number is provided automatically for most tests.

The calculation of t closely resembles the calculation of the Z-value. To calculate t, use the formula

$$
t = \frac{\overline{X} - \mu}{S_{\overline{X}}}
$$

with $n - 1$ degrees of freedom.

The Z-distribution and the t-distribution are very similar, and thus the Z-test and t-test will provide much the same result in most situations. However, when the population standard deviation (σ) is known, the Z-test is most appropriate. When σ is unknown (the situation in most marketing research studies), and the sample size greater than 30, the Z-test also can be used. When σ is unknown and the sample size is small, the t-test is most appropriate. Since the two distributions are similar with larger sample sizes, the two tests often yield the same conclusion.

EXHIBIT 21.7
The *t*-Distribution for Various Degrees of Freedom

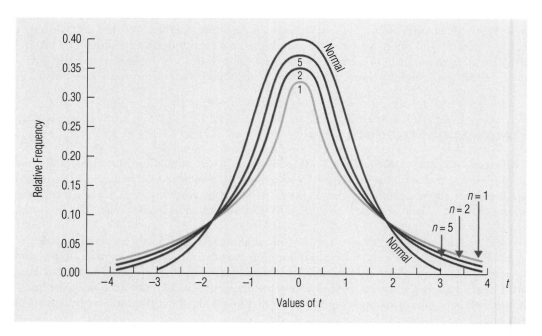

One and Two-Tailed *t*-Tests

Univariate Z-tests and *t*-tests can be one or two-tailed. A two-tailed test is one that tests for differences from the population mean that are either greater or less. Thus, the extreme values of the normal curve (or tails) on both the right and the left are considered. In practical terms, when a research question does not specify whether a difference should be greater than or less than, a two-tailed test is most appropriate. For instance, the following research question could be examined using a two-tailed test:

The number of take-out pizza restaurants within a postal-code in Germany is not equal to 5.

A one-tailed univariate test is appropriate when a research hypothesis implies that an observed mean can only be greater than or less than a hypothesized value. Thus, only one of the "tails" of the bell-shaped normal curve is relevant. For instance, the following hypothesis could be appropriately examined with a one-tailed test:

H₁:The number of pizza restaurants with a postal code in Florida is greater than five.

In this case, if the observed value is significantly less than five, the hypothesis is still not supported. Practically, a one-tailed test can be determined from a two-tailed test result by taking half of the observed p-value. When the researcher has any doubt about whether a one- or two-tailed test is appropriate, he or she should opt for the less conservative two-tailed test. Most computer software will assume a two-tailed test unless otherwise specified.

Univariate Hypothesis Test Using the *t*-Distribution

The step-by-step procedure for a *t*-test is conceptually similar to that for hypothesis testing with the Z-distribution. Suppose a Pizza-In store manager believes that the average number of customers who return a pizza or ask for a refund is 20 per day. The store records the number of returns and exchanges for each of the 25 days it was open during a given month. Are the return/complaint observations different than 20 per day? The substantive hypothesis is

$$H_1: \mu \neq 20$$

1. The researcher calculates a sample mean and standard deviation. In this case, $\overline{X} = 22$ and S (sample standard deviation) $= 5$.
2. The standard error is computed ($S_{\overline{X}}$):

$$S_{\overline{X}} = \frac{S}{\sqrt{n}}$$
$$= \frac{5}{\sqrt{25}}$$
$$= 1$$

3. The researcher then finds the *t*-value associated with the desired level of confidence level or statistical significance. If a 95 percent confidence level is desired, the significance level is 0.05.
4. The critical values for the *t*-test are found by locating the upper and lower limits of the confidence interval. The result defines the regions of rejection. This requires determining the critical value of *t*. For 24 degrees of freedom ($n = 25$, $d.f. = n - 1$), the critical *t*-value is 2.064. Tabled critical values of the *t*-distribution are provided in the Appendix at the end of this book (Table A-2).
5. The formula below is then used to compute the *t*-statistic for this set of observations.

$$t_{obs} = \frac{\overline{X} - \mu}{S_{\overline{X}}}$$
$$t_{obs} = \frac{22 - 20}{1} = \frac{2}{1} = 2$$

The observed mean of 22 is inserted for the sample mean ($\overline{X}$) and the hypothesized value of 20 is inserted for the population mean (μ). We can see that the observed *t*-value of 2.00 is less than the critical *t*-value of 2.064 at the 0.05 level when there are $25 - 1 = 24$ degrees of freedom. As a result, the p-value is greater than .05 and the hypothesis is not supported. We cannot conclude with 95 percent confidence that the mean is not 20.

Calculating a Confidence Interval Estimate Using the *t*-Distribution

The *t*-test can also be expressed using confidence intervals. Suppose a business organization is interested in finding out how long newly hired MBA graduates remain on their first jobs. The researcher wishes to estimate the population mean time on first job with 95 percent confidence. The data from the sample are presented below.

Number of years on first job:
3 5 7 1 12 1 2 2 5
4 2 3 1 3 4 2 6 7

To find the confidence interval estimate of the population mean for this sample, we use the formula

$$\mu = \overline{X} \pm t_{c.l.} S_{\overline{X}}$$

or

$$\text{Upper limit} = \overline{X} + t_{c.l.} \left(\frac{S}{\sqrt{n}} \right)$$

$$\text{Lower limit} = \overline{X} - t_{c.l.} \left(\frac{S}{\sqrt{n}} \right)$$

where

μ = population mean
$(\overline{X})$ = sample mean
$t_{c.l.}$ = critical value of *t* at a specified confidence level
$S_{\overline{X}}$ = standard error of the mean
S = sample standard deviation
n = sample size

More specifically, the step-by-step procedure for calculating the confidence interval is as follows:

1. We calculate $(\overline{X})$ from the sample. Summing our data values yields $\Sigma X = 70$, and $(\overline{X}) = \Sigma X/n = 70/18 = 3.89$.
2. Since σ is unknown, we estimate the population standard deviation by finding S, the sample standard deviation. For our example, $S =$

$$S = \sqrt{\frac{\sum_{i=1}^{18} (X_i - \overline{X})}{(n-1)}} = \sqrt{\frac{133.8}{17}} = 2.81$$

3. We next estimate the standard error of the mean $(S_{\overline{X}} = S/\sqrt{n})$:

$$S_{\overline{X}} = \frac{S}{\sqrt{n}} = \frac{2.81}{\sqrt{18}} = 0.66$$

4. We next determine the critical *t*-values associated with the desired confidence level. To do this, we go to Table A-2 in the appendix or use a table at an Internet statistics site. Although the *t*-table provides information similar to that in the Z-table, it is somewhat different. The *t*-table format emphasizes the chance of error, or significance level (α). Our example is a two-tailed test. Since a 95 percent confidence level has been selected, α equals 0.05 $(1.00 - 0.95 = 0.05)$. Now all we have to do to find the critical *t*-value is look under the 0.05 column for *two-tailed tests* in the row in which degrees of freedom $(d.f.)$ equal the appropriate value, in this case 17 $(n - 1 = 18 - 1)$. $(n - 1 = 17 - 1 = 16)$, the *t*-value at the 95 percent confidence level (two-tailed 0.05 level of significance) is $t = 2.11$.
5. We calculate the lower and upper limits of the confidence interval as:

$$\text{Lower Limit} = \overline{X} - t_{crit} \left(\frac{S}{\sqrt{n}} \right) = 3.89 - 2.11 \left(\frac{2.81}{\sqrt{18}} \right) = 2.49$$

$$\text{Upper Limit} = \overline{X} + t_{crit} \left(\frac{S}{\sqrt{n}} \right) = 3.89 + 2.11 \left(\frac{2.81}{\sqrt{18}} \right) = 5.28$$

6. The appropriate conclusion is that the mean number of years spent on the first job is between 2.49 and 5.28 years with 95 percent confidence.

7. The confidence interval can be used as another way to test a hypothesis as well. If the researcher had hypothesized that the mean number of years spent on the first job is 2.0 years, that hypothesis would be rejected because 2.0 does not fall within the confidence interval. Some researchers find the confidence interval approach an intuitive way of testing a hypothesis.

The Chi-Square Test for Goodness-of-Fit

A **chi-square (χ^2) test** is one of the most basic tests for statistical significance and is particularly appropriate for testing hypotheses about frequencies arranged in a frequency or contingency table. Univariate tests involving nominal or ordinal variables are examined with a χ^2. More generally, the χ^2 test is associated with **goodness-of-fit (GOF)**. GOF can be thought of as how well some matrix (table) of numbers matches or *fits* another matrix of the same size. Most often, the test is between a table of observed frequency counts and another table of expected values (central tendency) for those counts.

A chi-square test is the appropriate way for testing whether the values in a one-way frequency table are different than would be expected by chance. The values in a frequency table are very often just tallies of a nominal or ordinal variable such as store location in this case (stand-alone or shopping center) or perhaps grade distributions (A, B, C, D, or F).

Consider the following hypothesis that relates back to the chapter vignette:

H_1: *Papa John's Pizza stores are more likely to be located in a stand-alone location than in a shopping center.*

A competitor may be interested in this hypothesis as part of the competitor analysis in a marketing plan. A researcher for the competitor gathers a random sample of 100 Papa John's locations in California (where the competitor is located). The sample is selected from phone directories and the locations are checked by having an assistant drive to each location. The following observations are recorded in a frequency table.

Location	One-Way Frequency Table
Stand-alone	60 stores
Shopping center	40 stores
Total	100 stores

These observed values (O_i) can be compared to the expected values for this distribution (Ei) to complete a χ^2 test. The χ^2 value will reflect the likelihood that the observed values come from a distribution reflected by the expected values. The higher the value of the χ^2 test, the less likely it is that the expected and observed values are the same.

In statistical terms, a χ^2 test determines whether the difference between an observed frequency distribution and the corresponding expected frequency distribution is due to sampling variation. Computing a χ^2 test is fairly straightforward and easy. Students who master this calculation should have little trouble understanding future significance tests since the basic logic of the χ^2 test underlies these tests as well.

The steps in computing a χ^2 test are as follows:

1. Gather data and tally the observed frequencies for the categorical variable.
2. Compute the expected values for each value of the categorical variable.
3. Calculate the χ^2 value, using the observed frequencies from the sample and the expected frequencies.
4. Find the degrees of freedom for the test.

chi-square (χ^2) test

One of the most basic tests for statistical significance that is particularly appropriate for testing hypotheses about frequencies arranged in a frequency or contingency table.

goodness-of-fit (GOF)

A general term representing how well some computed table or matrix of values matches some population or predetermined table or matrix of the same size.

5. Make the statistical decision by comparing p-value associated with the calculated χ^2 against the predetermined significance level (acceptable Type I error rate).

    These steps can be illustrated with the pizza store location example.

- The data for the location variable (stand-alone or shopping center) are provided in the frequency table on previous page.

- The next step asks, What are the expected frequencies for the location variable? This is another way of asking the central tendency for each category. Since the sample size is 100, finding the expected values is easy. If no pattern exists in the locations, they should be distributed randomly across the two categories. We would expect that half (50) of the locations would be stand-alone and half (50) would be in a shopping center. This is another way of saying that the expected probability of being one type of location is 50 percent. The expected values also can be placed in a frequency table:

Location	Expected Frequencies
Stand-alone	100/2 = 50 stores
Shopping center	100/2 = 50 stores
Total	100 stores

- The actual χ^2 value is computed using the following formula:

$$\chi^2 = \sum_{i=1}^{k} \frac{(O_i - E_i)^2}{E_i}$$

where,

χ^2 = chi-square statistic
O_i = observed frequency in the ith cell
E_i = expected frequency in the ith cell

Sum the squared differences:

$$\chi^2 = \frac{(O_1 - E_1)}{E_1} + \frac{(O_2 - E_2)}{E_2}$$

Thus, we determine that the chi-square value equals 4:

$$\chi^2 = \frac{(60 - 50)^2}{50} + \frac{(40 - 50)^2}{50}$$

$$= 4$$

Alternatively, the calculation can be followed in tabular form:

Location:	O_i	E_i	$(O_i - E_i)$	$\frac{(O_i - E_i)^2}{E_i}$
Stand-alone	60	50	10	100/50 = 2.0
Shopping center	40	50	-10	100/50 = 2.0
Total	100	100	0	χ^2 = 4.0

- Like many other probability distributions, the χ^2 distribution is not a single probability curve, but a family of curves. These curves vary slightly with the degrees of freedom. In this case, the degrees of freedom can be computed as

$$d.f. = k - 1$$

where

k = number of cells associated with column or row data.

Thus, the degrees of freedom equal 1 ($d.f. = 2 - 1 = 1$).

Art for Girls and Boys

Chi-square tests are used often in marketing research. Consider a private art museum that sponsors a program of summer art classes for children. They need to plan the number and types of activities and exhibits that should be included in the museum. One question is whether or not an equal number of boys and girls will come to the museum. A random sample from its list of students shows more girls than boys. They decide to observe the relative frequencies of boys and girls for the first 1,000 visitors under the age of 16. The results are shown in the bar charts below:

Therefore, the acceptable level of Type I error is set at 0.01. Rather than referring to a critical value table, the p-value associated with a χ^2 value and the associated degrees of freedom can be found on any one of several statistical calculators found on the Internet. In this case, the researcher uses the calculator found at http://faculty.vassar.edu/lowry/tabs.html#csq. By simply plugging in the observed value of 38.4 and the number of degrees of freedom as indicated, 1 in this case, the calculator returns a p-value. In this case, the p-value returned is less than 0.0001. Therefore, since the p-value is less than the acceptable level of risk, the researcher reaches the conclusion that the children visiting the museum are

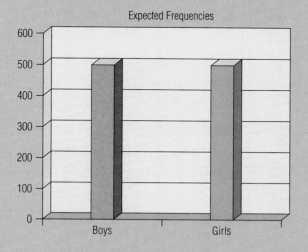

Expected Frequencies

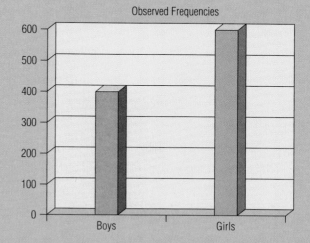

Observed Frequencies

The χ^2 value can be computed as shown below:

	Expected	Observed	O − E	(O − E)²	(O − E)²/E
Boys	500	402	−98	9604	19.208
Girls	500	598	98	9604	19.208
	1000	1000			38.416

The museum managers want to be sure a difference exists before investing resources into activities designed for girls or boys only.

not equally distributed between boys and girls. Clearly, more girls visit than boys.

Thus, the museum can go about designing features that appeal to boys and girls proportionately to the observed frequency distribution.

- Now the computed χ^2 value needs to be compared with the critical chi–square values associated with the 0.05 probability level with 1 degree of freedom. In Table A.3 of the appendix the critical χ^2 value is 3.84. Since the calculated χ^2 is larger than the tabular chi–square, the conclusion is that the observed values do not equal the expected values. Therefore, the hypothesis is supported. More Papa John's restaurants are located in stand–alone locations.

We discuss the chi–square test further in Chapter 22, as it is also frequently used to analyze contingency tables. The Research Snapshot above provides another illustration.

Hypothesis Test of a Proportion

Researchers often test univariate statistical hypotheses about population proportions. The population proportion (π) can be estimated on the basis of an observed sample proportion (p). Conducting a **hypothesis test of a proportion** is conceptually similar to hypothesis testing when the mean is the characteristic of interest. Mathematically the formulation of the standard error of the proportion differs somewhat, though.

hypothesis test of a proportion

A test that is conceptually similar to the one used when the mean is the characteristic of interest but that differs in the mathematical formulation of the standard error of the proportion.

Consider the following example. A state legislature is considering a proposed right-to-work law. One legislator has hypothesized that more than 50 percent of the state's labor force is unionized. In other words, the hypothesis to be tested is that the proportion of union workers in the state is greater than 0.5.

The researcher formulates the hypothesis that the population proportion (π) exceeds 50 percent (0.5):

$$H_1: = \pi > 0.5$$

Suppose the researcher conducts a survey with a sample of 100 workers and calculates $p = 0.6$. Even though the population proportion is unknown, a large sample allows use of a Z-test (rather than the t-test). If the researcher decides that the decision rule will be set at the 0.01 level of significance, the critical Z-value of 2.57 is used for the hypothesis test. Using the following formula, we can calculate the observed value of Z given a certain sample proportion:

$$Z_{obs} = \frac{p - \pi}{S_p}$$

where

> p = sample proportion
> π = hypothesized population proportion
> S_p = estimate of the standard error of the proportion

The formula for S_p is

$$S_p = \sqrt{\frac{pq}{n}} \text{ or } S_p = \sqrt{\frac{p(1 - p)}{n}}$$

where

> Sp = estimate of the standard error of the proportion
> p = proportion of successes
> $q = 1 - p$, = proportion of failures

In our example,

$$S_p = \sqrt{\frac{(0.6)(0.4)}{100}}$$

$$= \sqrt{\frac{0.24}{100}}$$

$$= \sqrt{0.0024}$$

$$= 0.04899$$

Z_{obs} can now be calculated:

$$Z_{obs} = \frac{p - \pi}{S_p}$$

$$= \frac{0.6 - 0.5}{0.04899}$$

$$= \frac{0.1}{0.04899}$$

$$= 2.04$$

The Z_{obs} value of 2.04 is less than the critical value of 2.57, so the hypothesis is not supported.

Additional Applications of Hypothesis Testing

The discussion of statistical inference in this chapter has been restricted to examining the difference between an observed sample mean and a population or pre-specified mean, a χ^2 test examining the difference between an observed frequency and the expected frequency for a given distribution, and Z-tests to test hypotheses about sample proportions when sample sizes are large. Other hypothesis tests for population parameters estimated from sample statistics exist but are not mentioned here. Many of these tests are no different conceptually in their methods of hypothesis testing. However, the formulas are mathematically different. The purpose of this chapter has been to discuss basic statistical concepts. Once you have learned the basic terminology in this chapter, you should have no problem generalizing to other statistical problems.

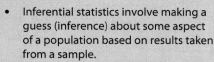
- Inferential statistics involve making a guess (inference) about some aspect of a population based on results taken from a sample.
  - Do not use inferential statistics when a census is available. When the entire population is measured, any observed difference is a real difference.
- P-values are probability values and the lower they get, generally, the more likely a researcher's substantive hypothesis is supported. This is because hypotheses usually are proposing that a difference exists or that a relationship exists.
  - Low p-values of 0.05 or less generally support hypotheses about differences or relationships.

- In almost all practical marketing research situations, a Z-test and t-test will yield the same result. Because of this and the fact that t-tests are more readily available in statistics packages, t-tests are more commonly used.
- As a rule of thumb, statistical power should be about 0.80.
  - Samples of 100 or more provide adequate power (0.80) to identify significant relationships using regression analysis at the 0.05 level.
  - A sample of 150 or more is generally sufficient for cross-tabulations.
  - A sample of 45 or more is sufficient for a 2 × 2 experiment.
- Internet sites provide easy ways to find statistical tables and p-values for various statistical tests. They can be faster than using tabled values in books.

As we emphasized in Chapter 17, the key to understanding statistics is learning the basics of the language. This chapter has presented verbs, nouns, and some of the rules of the grammar of statistics. Here, we begin to adopt a more practical perspective by focusing on the p-values to determine whether a hypothesis is supported rather than discussing null and alternative hypotheses. In more cases than not, low p-values (below the specified α) support researchers' hypotheses.[8] It is hoped that some of the myths about statistics have been shattered and that they are becoming easier to use.

Summary

1. Conduct a hypothesis-test following a step-by-step procedure. Hypothesis testing can involve univariate, bivariate, or multivariate statistics. In this chapter, the focus is on univariate statistics. These are tests that involve one variable. Usually, this means that the observed value for one variable will be compared to some benchmark or standard. Statistical analysis is needed to test hypotheses when sample observations are used to draw an inference about some corresponding population. The basic procedure for testing a univariate hypothesis involves (a) hypothesizing a difference between the observed values and some standard, (b) obtaining a sample, and (c) comparing the sample result with the hypothesized standard.

2. Use p-values to assess statistical significance. A p-value is the probability value associated with a statistical test. The probability in a p-value is the probability that the expected value for some test distribution is true. In other words, for a t-test, the expected value of the t-distribution is 0. If a researcher is testing whether or not a variable is significantly different from 0, then the p-value that results from the corresponding computed t-value represents the probability that the true population mean is actually 0. For most marketing research hypotheses, a low p-value supports the hypothesis. If a p-value is lower than the researcher's acceptable significance level (α), then the hypothesis is usually supported.

3. Choose the right statistical test for a given hypothesis. A large part of getting good answers from statistics is choosing the right tool. The selection of the right tool depends on (1) the type of question being asked, (2) the number of variables involved, and (3) the level of measurement involved in these variables. Univariate tests that involve an interval or ratio variable are often tested with a Z-test or t-test. Univariate tests that involve a nominal or ordinal variable are often examined using a frequency tabulation together with a χ^2 test.

4. Test a hypothesis about an observed mean compared to some standard. Researchers often have to compare an observed sample mean with some specified value. The appropriate statistical test to compare an interval or ratio level variable's mean with some value is either the Z- or t-test. The Z-test is most appropriate when the sample size is large or the population standard deviation is known. The t-test is most appropriate when the sample size is small or the population standard deviation is not known. In most practical applications the t-test and Z-test will result in the same conclusion. The t-test is used more often in practice.

5. Know the difference between Type I and Type II errors. A Type I error occurs when a researcher reaches the conclusion that some difference or relationship exists within a population when in fact none exists. In the context of a univariate *t*-test, the researcher may conclude that some mean value for a variable is greater than 0 when in fact the true value for that variable in the population being considered is 0. A Type II error is the opposite situation. When the researcher reaches the conclusion that no difference exists when one truly does exist in the population, the researcher has committed a Type II error. Type II errors are made less likely by increasing statistical power. Larger samples provide more statistical power but also increase the chance of finding a very small difference to be statistically significant.

6. Know when a univariate χ^2 test is appropriate and how to conduct one. A χ^2 test is one of the most basic tests for statistical significance. The test is particularly appropriate for testing hypotheses about frequencies arranged in a frequency or contingency table. The χ^2 test value is a function of the observed value for a given entry in a frequency table minus the statistical expected value for that cell. The observed statistical value can be compared to critical values to determine the p-value with any test. The χ^2 test is often considered a goodness-of-fit test because it can test how well an observed matrix represents some theoretical standard.

Key Terms and Concepts

bivariate statistical analysis, *538*	multivariate statistical analysis, *538*	*t*-distribution, *549*
chi-square (χ^2) test, *553*	nonparametric statistics, *548*	*t*-test, *549*
critical values, *543*	parametric statistics, *548*	Type I error, *545*
degrees of freedom (d.f.), *549*	p-value, *541*	Type II error, *545*
goodness-of-fit (GOF), *553*	significance level, *541*	univariate statistical analysis, *538*
hypothesis test of a proportion, *555*	statistical power, *546*	

Questions for Review and Critical Thinking

1. What is the purpose of a statistical hypothesis?
2. What are the three general steps in testing a hypothesis?
3. What is a *significance level*? How does a researcher choose a significance level?
4. What is the difference between a *significance level* and a *p-value*?
5. How is a p-value used to test a hypothesis?
6. Distinguish between a *Type I* and *Type II error*.
7. Define the concept of statistical power and provide an indication of how it relates to sample size. Suppose one were using a χ^2 test with a frequency table illustrating the number of Best Buy consumers purchasing a computer who purchase either a 3-year extended service plan, a 1-year extended service plan, or no extended service plan. What sample size would you recommend based on your knowledge of statistical power?
8. What are the factors that determine the choice of the appropriate statistical technique?
9. A researcher is asked to determine whether or not a sales objective of better than $75,000 per salesperson is possible. A market test is done involving 20 salespeople. What conclusion would you reach? The sales results are as follows:

28,000	105,000	58,000	93,000	96,000
67,000	82,500	75,000	81,000	59,000
101,000	60,500	77,000	72,500	48,000
99,000	78,000	71,000	80,500	78,000

10. Assume you have the following data: $H_1: \mu \neq 200$, $S = 30$, $n = 64$, and $\overline{X} = 218$. Conduct a two-tailed hypothesis test at the 0.05 significance level.
11. If the data in question 10 had been generated with a sample of 9 ($n = 9$), and everything else remained the same, what would the result be? Comment on the comparison of results.

12. A professor would like to have evenly distributed distributions of grades such that the same number of As, Bs, Cs, Ds, and Fs are given in each class. What statistical test is appropriate for comparing a sample of grade distributions taken from his class with this hypothesized population condition?
13. A researcher plans to ask employees whether they favor, oppose, or are indifferent about a change in the company retirement program. Formulate a hypothesis for a chi-square test and the way the variable would be created.
14. Why might one believe that Type I errors are more serious than Type II errors? Give an example in which a Type I error may be more serious than a Type II error.
15. Refer to the pizza store location χ^2 data on pages 553–555. What statistical decisions could be made if the 0.01 significance level were selected rather than the 0.05 level?
16. Determine a hypothesis that the following data may address and perform a χ^2 test on the survey data.
    a. *American Idol* should be broadcast before 9 p.m.

Agree	40
Neutral	35
Disagree	25
	100

    b. What is your political affiliation?

Republican	102
Democrat	98
	200

17. A researcher hypothesizes that 15 percent of the people in a test-market will recall seeing a particular advertisement. In a sample of 1,200 people, 20 percent say they recall the ad. Perform a hypothesis test.

Research Activities

1. **'NET** What is the ideal climate? Fill in the following blanks: The lowest temperature in January should be no lower than _____ degrees. At least _____ days should be sunny in January.
   a. List at least 15 places where you would like to live. Using the Internet, find the average low temperature in January for each place. This information is available through various weather related Web sites such as http://www.weather.com or through each community's local news Web site. Record the data in a spreadsheet or statistical package file such as SPSS. Using the benchmark (preferred population low temperature) you filled in above, test whether the sample places that you would like to live have an ideal January minimum temperature.
   b. Using the same Web site, record how many days in January are typically sunny. Test whether or not the number of sunny days meets your standard.
   c. For each location, record whether or not there was measurable precipitation yesterday. Test the following hypothesis: H_1: Among places you would like to live, there is less than a 33.3 percent chance of rain/snow on a given day (five days out of fifteen).

2. **ETHICS** Examine the statistical choices under "analyze" in SPSS. Click on "compare means." To compare an observed mean to some benchmark or hypothesized population mean, the available choice is a one-sample t-test. A researcher is preparing a report and finds the following result testing a hypothesis that suggested the sample mean did not equal 14:
   a. What is the p-value? Is the hypothesis supported?
   b. Write the 95% confidence interval which corresponds to an α of 0.05.
   c. Technically, since the sample size is greater than 30, a Z-test might be more appropriate. However, since the t-test result is readily available with SPSS, the research presents this result. Is there an ethical problem in using the one-sample t-test?

One-Sample Statistics

	N	Mean	Std. Deviation	Std. Error Mean
2007–2010	67	14.5337	16.02663	1.95796

Test Value = 14

	t	d.f.	Sig. (two-tailed)	Mean Difference	95% Confidence Interval of the Difference	
					Lower	Upper
2007–2010	0.273	66	0.786	0.53373	−3.3755	4.4429

Case 21.1 Quality Motors

Download the data sets for this case from www.cengage.com/marketing/zikmund *or request them from your instructor.*

Quality Motors is an automobile dealership that regularly advertises in its local market area. It claims that a certain make and model of car averages 30 miles to a gallon of gas and mentions that this figure may vary with driving conditions. A local consumer group wishes to verify the advertising claim. To do so, it selects a sample of recent purchasers of this make and model of automobile. It asks them to drive their cars until two tanks of gasoline have been used up and to record the mileage. The group then calculates and records the miles per gallon for each year. The data in Case Exhibit 21.1–1 portray the results of the tests.

Questions

1. Formulate a statistical hypothesis appropriate for the consumer group's purpose.
2. Calculate the mean average miles per gallon. Compute the sample variance and sample standard deviation.
3. Construct the appropriate statistical test for your hypothesis, using a 0.05 significance level.

CASE EXHIBIT 21.1–1 **Miles per Gallon Information**

Purchaser	Miles per Gallon	Purchaser	Miles per Gallon
1	30.9	14	27.0
2	24.5	15	26.7
3	31.2	16	31.0
4	28.7	17	23.5
5	35.1	18	29.4
6	29.0	19	26.3
7	28.8	20	27.5
8	23.1	21	28.2
9	31.0	22	28.4
10	30.2	23	29.1
11	28.4	24	21.9
12	29.3	25	30.9
13	24.2		

Case 21.2 Coastal Star Sales Corporation (B)

Download the data sets for this case from www.cengage.com/marketing/zikmund *or request them from your instructor.*

See Coastal Star Sales Corporation (A), Case17.1, for a description of the data.

Questions

1. Develop a hypothesis concerning the average age of the sales force at Coastal Star and test the hypothesis.
2. Calculate the mean for the previous year's sales, and use it as the basis for forming a hypothesis concerning the current year's sales. Test the hypothesis concerning the current year's sales.

CHAPTER 22
BIVARIATE STATISTICAL ANALYSIS:
DIFFERENCES BETWEEN TWO VARIABLES

After studying this chapter, you should be able to

1. Construct a cross-tabulation table and the corresponding χ^2 statistic.
2. Use a *t*-test to compare a difference between two means.
3. Know how a *Z*-test can be used to compare two proportions.
4. Conduct a one-way analysis of variance test (ANOVA).
5. Appreciate the practicality of modern statistical software packages.

Chapter Vignette: Is the Price Right?

The objective in most of the pricing games on *The Price is Right* is knowing the right price. When consumers know the right price, they save money, and saving money can be very exciting. Perhaps *The Price is Right* is ready for a new pricing game called "Bricks or Clicks"? The game would involve examining several products and then letting the host know whether or not a specific product is priced lower on the Internet (clicks) or at a traditional retailer (bricks).

© AP PHOTO/DEVORK DJANSEZIAN

Are prices lower on the Internet? This has been a subject of much debate over the last decade. In the early days of Internet retailing, so-called experts made many grand predictions about how e-tailing would evolve. A few predictions may have been correct, but most have proved wrong. For instance, some predicted that e-tailing would make traditional retailers obsolete. Almost all predictions involving price forecasted that the wide availability of price information on the Internet would force prices to their lowest level. Smart software systems called *bots* would quickly search the Internet and inform the consumer where an item could be purchased at the lowest price. However, consumers who think the Internet is always the avenue to the lowest price may not be right.[1]

Are prices offered by e-tailers really lower? Are the price discounts greater on the Internet? The answers depend on what a consumer is trying to buy. A 2001 study of the prices of DVDs showed the following average prices:[2]

Retail Type	DVD Average Price	DVD Percentage-Price
E-tailers	$19.92	72.0%
Traditional (multi-channel retailers)	$23.19	83.9%

A comparison of the prices suggests that dot-com retailers offer better prices.

Case closed? Not so fast! If consumers need a DVD player instead of a DVD, they may have better luck with a more traditional retailer, or at least one that offers both real and virtual retail shopping opportunities (multi-channel). In consumer electronics, the following results are seen:

Retail Type	DVD Player Average Price	Percentage-Price
E-tailers	$371.95	75.6%
Multi-channel retailers	$360.30	74.8%

A comparison of these prices suggests that the multi-channel retailers offer better prices. Even though they may never appear on a television game show, consumers and businesses alike find many occasions to compare prices.

Introduction

The vignette describes some comparisons involving prices over two groups. The groups represent the type of retailer. If we look at the type of retailer as a categorical variable and prices as an interval variable, these comparisons really involve drawing inferences about how one variable, type of retailer, influences another, prices. A surprising number of inferences involve two variables. In fact, sometimes even a more complex analysis may be reduced to a two-variable comparison because presenting the results becomes very simple. This chapter illustrates some common ways that such statistical tests can be performed.

What Is the Appropriate Test of Difference?

In marketing research, differences in behavior, characteristics, beliefs, opinions, emotions, or attitudes are commonly examined. For example, in the most basic experimental design, the researcher tests differences between subjects assigned to an experimental group and subjects assigned to the control group. A survey researcher may be interested in whether male and female consumers purchase a product in the same amount. Business researchers may also test whether or not business units in Europe are as profitable as business units in the United States. Such tests are bivariate **tests of differences** when they involve only two variables: a variable that acts like a dependent variable and a variable that acts as a classification variable.

Exhibit 22.1 on next page illustrates that the type of measurement, the nature of the comparison, and the number of groups to be compared influence the statistical choice. Often researchers are interested in testing differences in mean scores between groups or in comparing how two groups' scores are distributed across possible response categories. We will focus our attention on these issues.[3] The rest of the chapter focuses on how to choose the right statistic for two-group comparisons and perform the corresponding test. Exhibit 22.1 provides a frame of reference for the rest of the chapter by illustrating various possible comparisons involving a few golfers.

Construction of contingency tables for χ^2 analysis gives a procedure for comparing observed frequencies of one group with the frequencies of another group. This is a good starting point from which to discuss testing of differences.

test of differences
An investigation of a hypothesis stating that two (or more) groups differ with respect to measures on a variable.

Cross-Tabulation Tables: The χ^2 Test for Goodness-of-Fit

Cross-tabulation is among the most widely used statistical techniques among marketing researchers. Cross-tabulations are intuitive and easily understood. They also lend themselves well to graphical analysis using tools like bar charts.

A cross-tabulation, or contingency table, is a joint frequency distribution of observations on two or more nominal or ordinal variables. Researchers use two-variable cross-tabulations the most because the results can be very easily communicated. Cross-tabulations are much like tallying. When two variables exist, each with two categories, four cells result. Each cell contains the count of observations matching a particular combination of characteristics. The χ^2 distribution provides a means for testing the statistical significance of a contingency table. In other words, the bivariate χ^2 test examines the statistical significance of relationships among two less-than interval variables.

The χ^2 test for a contingency table involves comparing the observed frequencies (O_i) with the expected frequencies (E_i) in each cell of the table. The goodness- (or closeness-) of-fit of the observed distribution with the expected distribution is captured by this statistic. Remember that

How many hours do you spend online Daily?

Do you have more than one email address that you use regularly?

Yes ☐   No ☐

How often do you check your email?

1-3 times a week ☐   4-6 times a week ☐   1-2 times a day ☐   3-4 times a day ☐   > 4 times a day ☐

Do you Instant Message?

Yes ☐   No ☐

0%   100%

Are men or women more preoccupied with their mobile phones and Internet networking opportunities? You may be able to answer this question by looking at the data from the student survey. Test the following hypotheses using data obtained from the survey either from your class only or using data obtained from all users (either from the Web site or from your instructor):

H_1: Women are more likely to instant message than men.

H_2: Men are more likely to have more than one e-mail address.

H_3: Women check their e-mail more often than do men.

H_4: Men spend more time online daily than do women.

EXHIBIT 22.1 Some Bivariate Hypotheses

Information	Golfer Dolly	Lori	Mel	Hypothesis or Research Question	Level of Measurement Involved	Statistic Used	Comment	Result
Average Driver Distance (meters) σ	135 30	150 25	185 30	Lori hits her drives further than Dolly	Golfer = Nominal; Drive Distance = Ratio	Independent Samples t-test to compare mean distance	The data for Lori and Dolly are used.	Supported (t = 2.07, df = 56, p < .05)
Average 7-Wood Distance (meters) σ	140 30	145 30	150 30	Mel hits her driver further than her 7-wood	Club = Nominal (7-wood or driver); 7-Wood Distance = Ratio	Paired-Samples t-test to compare mean distances for Mel	Only the data for Mel are used (std of diff = 30)	Supported (t = 6.39, df = 29, p < .05)
Sample size (number of balls hit)	28 drives 28 7-woods	30 drives 28 7-woods	29 drives 28 7-woods	A relationship exists between golfers and 7-wood distance	Golfer = Nominal; Distance = Ratio	One-Way ANOVA to compare means for the three groups	All data for 7-wood distance are used (MSE = 30)	Not supported (F = 0.83, ns)
Number of Drives in Fairway	4	22	11	Mel drives the ball more accurately than Dolly	Golfer = Nominal; Accuracy = Nominal (Right, Fairway, Left)	Cross-Tabulation with χ^2 Statistic	Resulting cross tabulation table is 2 rows × 3 columns (rows = golfer and columns = accuracy (fairway, right left)	Supported (χ^2 = 10.3, df = 3, p < .05)
Drives missing right of fairway	16	7	9	A relationship exist between golfers and accuracy	Golfer = Nominal; Accuracy = Nominal (Right, Fairway, Left)	Cross-Tabulation with χ^2 Statistic	Cross-tabulation is now 3 rows × 3 columns	Supported (χ^2 = 23.7, df = 4, p < .05)
Drives missing left of fairway	8	1	9					

the convention is that the row variable is considered the independent variable and the column variable is considered the dependent variable. Cross-tabulation is appropriate when both variables are categorical. For instance, if both the independent and dependent variable are nominal or ordinal, a cross-tabulation is appropriate. Interval variables may sometimes be used in a cross-tabulation if the range is very small meaning the variable only takes on values of 1, 2, or 3, for example. Once a variable has more than four categories, a cross-tabulation table can be difficult to interpret.

Recall that in Chapter 21 we used a x^2 test to examine whether or not Papa John's restaurants in California were more likely to be located in a stand-alone location or in a shopping center. The univariate (one-dimensional) analysis suggests that the majority of the locations (60 percent) are stand-alone units:

Location	One-Way Frequency Table
Stand-alone	60 stores
Shopping Center	40 stores
Total	100 stores

Recall that the $x^2 = 4.0$ with 1 degree of freedom ($p < 0.01$).

Is there any effect of location of Papa John's restaurants? Suppose the researcher wishes to examine the following hypothesis:

Stand-alone locations are more likely to be profitable than are shopping center locations.

While the researcher is unable to obtain the dollar figures for profitability of each unit, a press release indicates which Papa John's units were profitable and which were not. Cross-tabulation using a x^2 test is appropriate because

- The independent variable (location) is less-than interval.
- The dependent variable (profitable/not profitable) is less-than interval.

The data can be recorded in the following 2 × 2 contingency table:

Location	Profitable	Not Profitable	Total
Stand-alone	50	10	60
Shopping Center	15	25	40
Totals	65	35	100

Several conclusions appear evident. One, it seems that more stores are profitable than not profitable (65 versus 35, respectively). Secondly, more of the profitable restaurants seem to be in stand-alone locations (50 out of 65). However, is the difference strong enough to be statistically significant?

Is the observed difference between stand-alone and shopping center locations the result of chance variation due to random sampling? Is the discrepancy more than sampling variation? The x^2 test allows us to conduct tests for significance in the analysis of the $R \times C$ contingency table (where R = row and C = column). The formula for the x^2 statistic is the same as that for one-way frequency tables (see Chapter 21):

$$x^2 = \sum \frac{(O_i - E_i)^2}{E_i}$$

where

x^2 = chi-square statistic

O_i = observed frequency in the ith cell

E_i = expected frequency in the ith cell

Again, as in the univariate x^2 test, a frequency count of data that nominally identify or categorically rank groups is acceptable.

If the researcher's hypothesis is true, the frequencies shown in the contingency table should not resemble a random distribution. In other words, if location has no effect on profitability, the profitable and unprofitable stores would be spread evenly across the two location categories. This is really the logic of the test in that it compares the observed frequencies with the theoretical expected values for each cell.

After obtaining the observations for each cell, the expected values for each cell must be obtained. The expected values for each cell can be computed easily using this formula:

$$E_{ij} = \frac{R_i C_j}{n}$$

where

R_i = total observed frequency count in the ith row

C_j = total observed frequency count in the jth column

n = sample size

Only the total column and total row values are needed for this calculation. Thus, the calculation could be performed before the data are even tabulated. The following values represent the expected values for each cell:

Location	Profitable	Not Profitable	Total
Stand-alone	(60 × 65)/100 = 39	(60 × 35)/100 = 21	60
Shopping Center	(40 × 65)/100 = 26	(40 × 35)/100 = 14	40
Totals	65	35	100

Notice that the row and column totals are the same for both the observed and expected contingency matrices. These values also become useful in providing the substantive interpretation of the relationship. Variance from the expected value indicates a relationship.

The actual bivariate χ^2 test value can be calculated in the same manner as for the univariate test. The one difference is that the degrees of freedom are now obtained by multiplying the number of rows minus one $(R - 1)$ times the number of columns minus one $(C - 1)$:

$$\chi^2 = \sum \frac{(O_i - E_i)^2}{E_i}$$

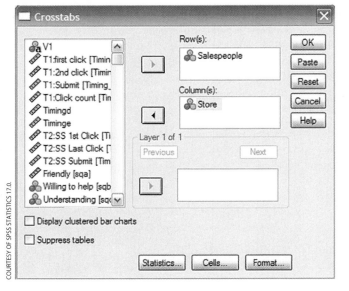

The cross-tab window in SPSS. In this case, a cross-tab between the variables salespeople and store would be conducted.

COURTESY OF SPSS STATISTICS 17.0.

with $(R - 1)(C - 1)$ degrees of freedom. The observed and expected values can be plugged into the formula as follows:

$$\chi^2 = \frac{(50 - 39)^2}{39} + \frac{(10 - 21)^2}{21} + \frac{(15 - 26)^2}{26} + \frac{(25 - 14)^2}{14}$$

$$= 3.102 + 5.762 + 4.654 + 8.643$$

$$= 22.16$$

The number of degrees of freedom equals 1:

$$(R - 1)(C - 1) = (2 - 1)(2 - 1) = 1$$

From Table A.3 in the appendix at the back of the book, we see that the critical value at the 0.05 probability level with 1 d.f. is 3.84. Thus, we are 95 percent confident that the observed values do not equal the expected values. Before the hypothesis can be supported, however, the researcher must check and see that the deviations from the expected values are in the hypothesized direction. Since the difference between the stand-alone locations' observed profitability and the expected values for that cell are positive, the hypothesis is supported. Location is associated with profitability. Thus, testing the hypothesis involves two key steps:

1. Examine the statistical significance of the observed contingency table.
2. Examine whether the differences between the observed and expected values are consistent with the hypothesized prediction.

The Research Snapshot on the next page provides a further illustration of when cross-tabulation and the χ^2 test are appropriate.

Proper use of the χ^2 test requires that each expected cell frequency (E) have a value of at least 5. If this sample size requirement is not met, the researcher should take a larger sample as a way of increasing the frequency.

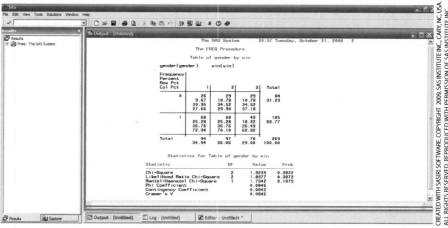

A cross-tabulation result from SAS showing an insignificant difference between men and women on a dependent variable "win."

The SAS screenshot shown on this page shows a cross-tabulation result depicting whether or not men or women are more successful at winning a hand of blackjack (a card game). Each person played three games and the "win" variable indicates whether they won 1, 2, or 3 of the games. The results show no difference between men and women as the chi-square test is not significant (p = .38). Thus, the cell values show approximately the same proportion of people in each cell although more women than men took part in the contest (84 men and 185 women).

The *t*-Test for Comparing Two Means

Independent Samples *t*-Test

When a researcher needs to compare means for a variable grouped into two categories based on some less-than interval variable, a *t*-test is appropriate. One way to think about this is as testing the way a dichotomous (two-level) independent variable is associated with changes in a continuous dependent variable. Several variations of the *t*-test exist.

Most typically, the researcher will apply the **independent samples *t*-test**, which tests the differences between means taken from two independent samples or groups. So, for example, if we measure the price for some designer jeans at 30 different retail stores, of which 15 are Internet-only stores (pure clicks) and 15 are traditional stores, we can test whether or not the prices are different based on store type with an independent samples *t*-test. The *t*-test for difference of means assumes the two samples (one Internet and one traditional store) are drawn from normal distributions and that the variances of the two populations are approximately equal (homoscedasticity).

independent samples *t*-test

A test for hypotheses stating that the mean scores for some interval- or ratio-scaled variable grouped based on some less-than interval classificatory variable are not the same.

Independent Samples *t*-test Calculation

The *t*-test actually tests whether or not the differences between two means is zero. Not surprisingly, this idea can be expressed as the difference between two population means:

$$\mu_1 = \mu_2, \text{ which is equivalent to, } \mu_1 - \mu_2 = 0$$

However, since this is inferential statistics, we test the idea by comparing two sample means $(\overline{X}_1 - \overline{X}_2)$.

A verbal expression of the formula for *t* is

$$t = \frac{\text{Sample Mean 1} - \text{Sample Mean 2}}{\text{Variability of random means}}$$

Chi-Training

When is a cross-tabulation with a χ^2 test appropriate? The answer to this question can be determined by answering these questions:

- Are multiple variables expected to be related to one another?
- Is the independent variable nominal or ordinal?
- Is the dependent variable nominal or ordinal?

When the answer to all of these questions is yes, cross-tabulation with a χ^2 test will address the research question. One common application involves the effect of some workplace change. For instance, this might involve the adoption of a new technology or the effect of training. For instance, consider the following contingency data represented in bar charts to the left.

The data show whether or not the adoption of a new information system produced accurate or inaccurate information. The 2-by-2 contingency table underlying this bar chart produces a χ^2 value of 5.97 with 1 degree of freedom. The p-value is less than 0.05; thus, the new technology does seem to have changed accuracy. However, we must examine the actual cell counts to see exactly what this effect has been. In this case, the bar chart indicates that the new technology is associated with more incidences of accurate rather than inaccurate information.

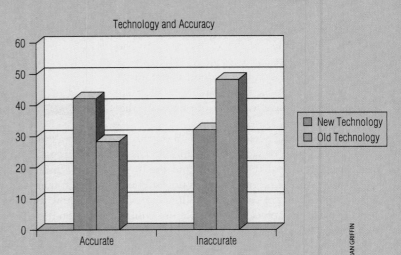

Sources: For examples of research involving this type of analysis, see Gohmann, S. E., R. M. Barker, D. J. Faulds and J. Guan, "Salesforce Automation, Perceived Information Accuracy and User Satisfaction," *Journal of Business and Industrial Marketing* 20 (2005), 23–32; Makela, C. J. and S. Peters, "Consumer Education: Creating Consumer Awareness Among Adolescents in Botswana," *International Journal of Consumer Studies* 28 (September 2004), 379–387.

Thus, the *t*-value is a ratio with information about the difference between means (provided by the sample) in the numerator and the standard error in the denominator. The question is whether the observed differences have occurred by chance alone. To calculate *t*, we use the following formula:

$$t = \frac{\overline{X}_1 - \overline{X}_2}{S_{\overline{X}_1 - \overline{X}_2}}$$

where

$\overline{X}_1$ = mean for group 1

$\overline{X}_2$ = mean for group 2

$S_{\overline{X}_1 - \overline{X}_2}$ = pooled, or combined, standard error of difference between means

pooled estimate of the standard error

An estimate of the standard error for a *t*-test of independent means that assumes the variances of both groups are equal.

A **pooled estimate of the standard error** is a better estimate of the standard error than one based on the variance from either sample. The pooled standard error of the difference between means of independent samples can be calculated using the following formula:

$$S_{\overline{X}_1 - \overline{X}_2} = \sqrt{\left(\frac{(n_1 - 1)S_1^2 + (n_2 - 1)S_2^2}{n_1 + n_2 - 2}\right)\left(\frac{1}{n_1} + \frac{1}{n_2}\right)}$$

where

S_1^2 = variance of group 1

S_2^2 = variance of group 2

n_1 = sample size of group 1

n_2 = sample size of group 2

Are business majors or sociology majors more positive about a career in business? A *t*-test can be used to test the difference between sociology majors and business majors on scores on a scale measuring attitudes toward business. We will assume that the attitude scale is an interval scale. The result of the simple random sample of these two groups of college students is shown below:

Business Students	Sociology Students
$\bar{X}_1 = 16.5$	$\bar{X}_2 = 12.2$
$S_1 = 2.1$	$S_2 = 2.6$
$n_1 = 21$	$n_2 = 14$

A high score indicates a favorable attitude toward business. This particular *t*-test tests whether the difference in attitudes between sociology and business students is significant. A higher *t*-value is associated with a lower p-value. As the *t* gets higher and the p-value gets lower, the researcher has more confidence that the means are truly different. The relevant data computation is

$$S_{\bar{X}_1 - \bar{X}_2} = \sqrt{\left(\frac{(n_1 - 1)S_1^2 + (n_2 - 1)S_2^2}{n_1 + n_2 - 2}\right)\left(\frac{1}{n_1} + \frac{1}{n_2}\right)}$$

$$= \sqrt{\left(\frac{(20)(2.1)^2 + (13)(2.6)^2}{33}\right)\left(\frac{1}{21} + \frac{1}{14}\right)}$$

$$= 0.797$$

The calculation of the *t*-statistic is:

$$t = \frac{\bar{X}_1 - \bar{X}_2}{S_{\bar{X}_1 - \bar{X}_2}}$$

$$t = \frac{16.5 - 12.2}{0.797}$$

$$= \frac{4.3}{0.797}$$

$$= 5.395$$

In a test of two means, degrees of freedom are calculated as follows:

$$d.f. = n - k$$

where

$n = n_1 + n_2$

k = number of groups

In our example d.f. equals 33 (21 + 14 − 2). If the 0.01 level of significance is selected, reference to Table A.2 in the appendix yields the critical *t*-value. The critical *t*-value of 2.75 must be surpassed by the observed *t*-value if the hypothesis test is to be statistically significant at the 0.01 level. The calculated value of *t*, 5.39, far exceeds the critical value of *t* for statistical significance, so it is significant at $\alpha = 0.01$. The p-value is less than 0.01. In other words, this research shows that business students have significantly more positive attitudes toward business than do sociology students. The Research Snapshot on the next page provides an overview of situations calling for an independent samples *t*-test.

RESEARCH SNAPSHOT

Expert "T-eeze"

When is an independent samples *t*-test appropriate? Once again, we can find out by answering some simple questions:

- Is the dependent variable interval or ratio?
- Can the dependent variable scores be grouped based upon some categorical variable?
- Does the grouping result in scores drawn from independent samples?
- Are two groups involved in the research question?

When the answer to all questions is yes, an independent samples *t*-test is appropriate. Often, business researchers may wish to examine how some process varies between novices and experts. Consider the following example.

Researchers looked at the difference in decision speed for expert and novice salespeople faced with the same situation. Decision speed is a ratio dependent variable and the scores are grouped based on whether or not the salesperson is an expert or a novice. Thus, this categorical variable produces two groups. The results across 40 respondents, 20 experts and 20 novices, are shown at the top right.

The average difference in decision time is 38 seconds. Is this significantly different

from 0? The calculated *t*-test is 2.76 with 38 d.f. The one-tailed p-value is 0.0045; thus the conclusion is reached that experts do take less time to make a decision than do novices.

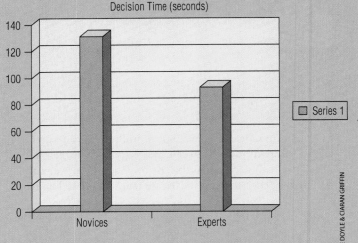

Source: Shepherd, D. G., S. F. Gardial, M. G. Johnson and J. O. Rentz, "Cognitive Insights into the Highly Skilled or Expert Salesperson," *Psychology and Marketing* 23 (February 2006), 115–138. Reprinted with permission of John Wiley & Sons, Inc.

Practically Speaking

In practice, computer software is used to compute the *t*-test results. Exhibit 22.2 displays a typical *t*-test printout. These particular results examine the following research question:

> *RQ: Does religion relate to price sensitivity?*

This question was addressed in the context of restaurant and wine consumption by allowing 100 consumers to sample a specific wine and then tell the researcher how much they would be willing to pay for a bottle of the wine. The sample included 57 Catholics and 43 Protestants. Because no direction of the relationship is stated (no hypothesis is offered), a two–tailed test is appropriate. Although instructors still find some value in having students learn to perform the *t*-test calculations, computer generated *t*-test results are almost always generated and interpreted in practice today.

The interpretation of the *t*-test is made simple by focusing on either the p-value or the confidence interval and the group means. Here are the basic steps:

1. Examine the difference in means to find the "direction" of any difference. In this case, Catholics are willing to pay nearly $11 more than Protestants.
2. Compute or locate the computed *t*-test value. In this case, $t = 0.998$.
3. Find the p-value associated with this *t* and the corresponding degrees of freedom. Here, the p-value (two-tailed significance level) is 0.321. This suggests a 32 percent chance that the means are actually equal given the observed sample means. Assuming a 0.05 acceptable Type I error rate (α), the appropriate conclusion is that the means are not significantly different.

EXHIBIT 22.2 **Independent Samples *t*-Test Results**

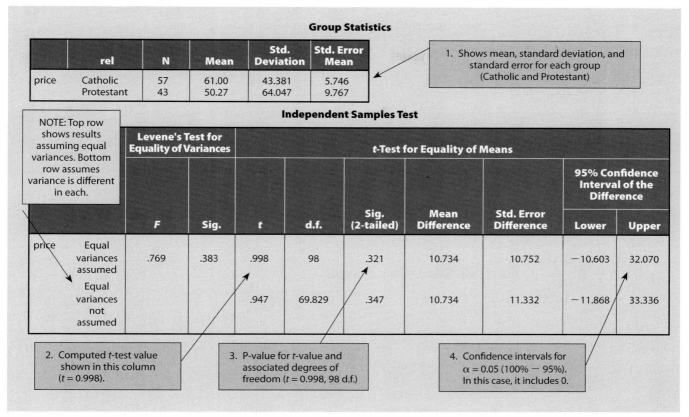

Group Statistics

	rel	N	Mean	Std. Deviation	Std. Error Mean
price	Catholic	57	61.00	43.381	5.746
	Protestant	43	50.27	64.047	9.767

1. Shows mean, standard deviation, and standard error for each group (Catholic and Protestant)

NOTE: Top row shows results assuming equal variances. Bottom row assumes variance is different in each.

Independent Samples Test

		Levene's Test for Equality of Variances		t-Test for Equality of Means						95% Confidence Interval of the Difference	
		F	Sig.	t	d.f.	Sig. (2-tailed)	Mean Difference	Std. Error Difference		Lower	Upper
price	Equal variances assumed	.769	.383	.998	98	.321	10.734	10.752		−10.603	32.070
	Equal variances not assumed			.947	69.829	.347	10.734	11.332		−11.868	33.336

2. Computed *t*-test value shown in this column (*t* = 0.998).

3. P-value for *t*-value and associated degrees of freedom (*t* = 0.998, 98 d.f.)

4. Confidence intervals for $\alpha = 0.05$ (100% − 95%). In this case, it includes 0.

4. The difference can also be examined using the 95 percent confidence interval ($-10.603 < \overline{X}_1 - \overline{X}_2 < 32.070$). Since the confidence interval includes 0, we lack sufficient confidence that the true difference between the population means is not really 0. The result suggests that it may well be 0.

A few points are worth noting about this particular result. First, strictly speaking, the *t*-test assumes that the two population variances are equal. A slightly more complicated formula exists which will compute the *t*-statistic assuming the variances are not equal.[4] SPSS provides both results when an independent samples *t*-test is performed. The sample variances appear considerably different in this case as evidenced by the standard deviations for each group (43.4, 64.0). Nonetheless, the conclusions are the same using either assumption. In marketing research, we often deal with values that have variances close enough to assume equal variance. This isn't always the case in the physical sciences where variables may take on values of drastically different magnitude. Thus, the rule of thumb in marketing research is to use the equal variance assumption. In the vast majority of cases, the same conclusion will be drawn using either assumption.

Second, notice that even though the means appear to be not so close to each other, the statistical conclusion is that they are the same. The substantive conclusion is that Catholics and Protestants would not be expected to pay different prices. Why is it that means do not appear to be similar, yet that is the conclusion? The answer lies in the variance. Respondents tended to provide very wide ranges of acceptable prices. Notice how large the standard deviations are compared to the mean for each group. Since the *t*-statistic is a function of the standard error, which is a function of the standard deviation, a lot of variance means a smaller *t*-value for any given observed difference. When this occurs, the researcher may wish to double-check for outliers. A small number of wild price estimates could be inflating the variance for one or both groups. An additional consideration would be to increase the sample size and test again.

Third, a *t*-test is used even though the sample size is greater than 30. Strictly speaking, a *Z*-test could be used to test this difference. Researchers often employ a *t*-test even with large samples. As samples get larger, the *t*-test and *Z*-test will tend to yield the same result. Although a *t*-test can be used with large samples, a *Z*-test should not be used with small samples. Also, a *Z*-test can be used in instances where the population variance is known ahead of time.

As another example, consider 11 sales representatives categorized as either young (1) or old (2) on the basis of their ages in years, as shown in Exhibit 22.3. The exhibit presents a SAS computer output that compares the mean sales volume for these two groups.

EXHIBIT 22.3 SAS *t*-Test Output

indicator					*t*-Test Procedure Variable: CR Sales						
Age	*n*	Mean	Standard Deviation	Standard Error	Minimum	Maximum	Variances	*t*	DF	Prob > |T|
1	6	61879.33333	22356.20845	9126.88388	41152.00000	103059.0000	Unequal	−0.9758	5.2	0.3729
2	5	86961.80000	53734.45098	24030.77702	42775.00000	172530.0000	Equal	−1.0484	9.0	0.3218

For H_0: Variances are equal, $F = 5.78$ with 4 and 5 DF, Prob. $> F = 0.0815$.

Paired-Samples *t*-Test

What happens when means need to be compared that are not from independent samples? Such might be the case when the same respondent is measured twice; for instance, when the respondent is asked to rate both how much he or she likes shopping on the Internet and how much he or she likes shopping in traditional stores. Since the liking scores are both provided by the same person, the assumption that they are independent is not realistic. Additionally, if one compares the prices the same retailers charge in their stores with the prices they charge on their Web sites, the samples cannot be considered independent because each pair of observations is from the same sampling unit.

paired-samples *t*-test

An appropriate test for comparing the scores of two interval variables drawn from related populations.

A **paired-samples *t*-test** is appropriate in this situation. The idea behind the paired-samples *t*-test can be seen in the following computation:

$$t = \frac{\bar{d}}{s_d / \sqrt{n}}$$

where $\bar{d}$ is the average difference between means, s_d is the standard deviation of the observed differences between means; and *n* is the number of observed differences between means. The test has degrees of freedom equal to one minus the total number of paired differences. Researchers also can compute the paired-samples *t*-test using statistical software. For example, using SPSS, the click-through sequence would be:

Analyze → *Compare Means* → *Paired-Samples* t-test

A dialog box then appears in which the "paired variables" should be entered. When a paired-samples *t*-test is appropriate, the two numbers being compared are usually scored as separate variables.

Exhibit 22.4 displays a paired samples *t*-test result. A sample of 143 young adult consumers was asked to rate how likely they would be to consider purchasing an engagement ring (or want their ring purchased) via (a) an Internet retailer and (b) a well-known jewelry store. Each respondent provided two responses much as in a within-subjects experimental design. The bar chart depicts the means for each variable (Internet purchase likelihood and store purchase likelihood). The *t*-test results suggest that average difference of −42.4 is associated with a *t*-value of −16.0. As can be seen using either the p-value (0.000 rounded to 3 decimals) or the confidence interval ($-47.6 < \bar{d} < -37.1$), which does not include 0, the difference is significantly different from 0. Therefore, the results suggest a higher likelihood to buy a wedding ring in a well-known real retail store than via an Internet merchant. Maybe that is a good idea!

Management researchers have used paired-samples *t*-tests to examine the effect of downsizing on employee morale. For instance, job satisfaction for a sample of employees can be measured immediately after the downsizing. Some months later, employee satisfaction can be measured again. The difference between the satisfaction scores can be compared using a paired-samples *t*-test. Results suggest that the employee satisfaction scores increase within a few months of the downsizing as evidenced by statistically significant paired-samples *t*-values.[5]

EXHIBIT 22.4 **Example Results for a Paired-Samples *t*-Test**

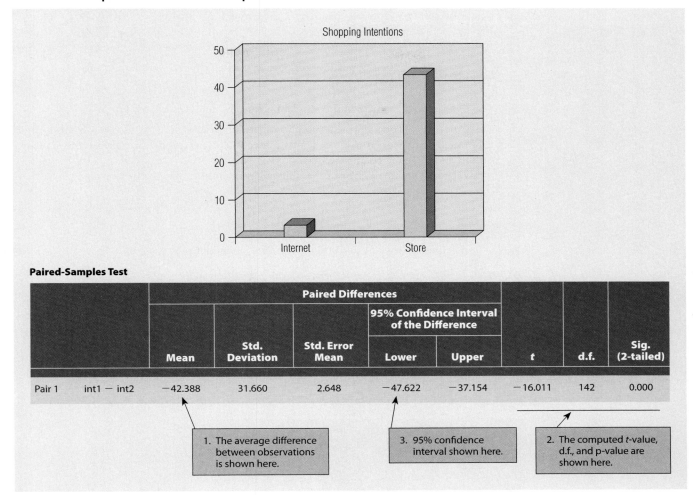

Paired-Samples Test

| | | **Paired Differences** | | | | | | | |
| | | Mean | Std. Deviation | Std. Error Mean | 95% Confidence Interval of the Difference | | *t* | d.f. | Sig. (2-tailed) |
					Lower	Upper			
Pair 1	int1 − int2	−42.388	31.660	2.648	−47.622	−37.154	−16.011	142	0.000

1. The average difference between observations is shown here.

3. 95% confidence interval shown here.

2. The computed *t*-value, d.f., and p-value are shown here.

The *Z*-Test for Comparing Two Proportions

What type of statistical comparison can be made when the observed statistics are proportions? Suppose a researcher wishes to test the hypothesis that wholesalers in the northern and southern United States differ in the proportion of sales they make to discount retailers. Testing whether the population proportion for group 1 (p_1) equals the population proportion for group 2 (p_2) is conceptually the same as the *t*-test of two means. This section illustrates a **Z-test for differences of proportions**, which requires a sample size greater than 30.

The test is appropriate for a hypothesis of this form:

$$H_0: \pi_1 = \pi_2$$

which may be restated as

$$H_0: \pi_1 - \pi_2 = 0$$

Comparison of the observed sample proportions p_1 and p_2 allows the researcher to ask whether the difference between two *large* random samples occurred due to chance alone. The *Z*-test statistic can be computed using the following formula:

$$Z = \frac{(p_1 - p_2) - (\pi_1 - \pi_2)}{S_{p_1 - p_2}}$$

Z-test for differences of proportions

A technique used to test the hypothesis that proportions are significantly different for two independent samples or groups.

where

p_1 = sample proportion of successes in group 1

p_2 = sample proportion of successes in group 2

$\pi_1 - \pi_2$ = hypothesized population proportion 1 minus hypothesized population proportion 2

$S_{P_1-P_2}$ = pooled estimate of the standard error of differences in proportions

The statistic normally works on the assumption that the value of $\pi_1 - \pi_2$ is zero, so this formula is actually much simpler than it looks at first inspection. Readers also may notice the similarity between this and the paired-samples t-test.

To calculate the standard error of the differences in proportions, use the formula

$$S_{P_1-P_2} = \sqrt{\bar{p}\,\bar{q}\left(\frac{1}{n_1} + \frac{1}{n_2}\right)}$$

where

$\bar{p}$ = pooled estimate of proportion of successes in a sample

$\bar{q} = 1 - \bar{p}$, or pooled estimate of proportion of failures in a sample

n_1 = sample size for group 1

n_2 = sample size for group 2

To calculate the pooled estimator, $\bar{p}$, use the formula

$$\bar{p} = \frac{n_1 p_1 + n_2 p_2}{n_1 + p_2}$$

Suppose the survey data are as follows:

Northern Wholesalers	Southern Wholesalers
$p_1 = 0.35$	$p_2 = 0.40$
$n_1 = 100$	$n_2 = 100$

First, the standard error of the difference in proportions is

$$S_{P_1-P_2} = \sqrt{\bar{p}\,\bar{q}\left(\frac{1}{n_1} + \frac{1}{n_2}\right)}$$

$$= \sqrt{(0.375)(0.625)\left(\frac{1}{100} + \frac{1}{100}\right)} = 0.068$$

where

$$\bar{p} = \frac{(100)(0.35) + (100)(0.40)}{100 + 100} = 0.375$$

If we wish to test the two-tailed question of no difference, we must calculate an observed Z-value. Thus,

$$Z = \frac{(p_1 - p_2) - (\pi_1 - \pi_2)}{S_{P_1-P_2}}$$

$$= \frac{(0.35 - 0.40) - (0)}{0.068}$$

$$= -0.73$$

In this example the idea that the proportion of sales differs by region is not supported. The calculated Z-value is less than the critical Z-value of 1.96. Therefore, the p-value associated with the test is greater than 0.05.

One-Way Analysis of Variance (ANOVA) ⬅

When the means of more than two groups or populations are to be compared, one-way **analysis of variance (ANOVA)** is the appropriate statistical tool. ANOVA involving only one grouping variable is often referred to as *one-way* ANOVA because only one independent variable is involved. Another way to define ANOVA is as the appropriate statistical technique to examine the effect of a less-than interval independent variable on an at-least interval dependent variable. Thus, a categorical independent variable and a continuous dependent variable are involved. An independent samples *t*-test can be thought of as a special case of ANOVA in which the independent variable has only two levels. When more levels exist, the *t*-test alone cannot handle the problem.

The statistical null hypothesis for ANOVA is stated as follows:

$$\mu_1 = \mu_2 = \mu_3 = \cdots = \mu_k$$

The symbol k is the number of groups or categories for an independent variable. In other words, all group means are equal. The substantive hypothesis tested in ANOVA is[6]

At least one group mean is not equal to another group mean.

As the term *analysis of variance* suggests, the problem requires comparing variances to make inferences about the means.

The chapter vignette discussed how a sample of prices taken from the Internet could be explained by the source of the price. Specifically, the independent variable could be thought of as "source," meaning either Internet or multi-channel retailer. The dependent variable is price. Since only two groups exist for the independent variable, either an independent samples *t*-test or one-way ANOVA could be used. The results would be identical.

However, assume that source involved three group levels. Prices would now be compared based on whether the retailer was a bricks-and-clicks retailer (multi-channel, meaning real and virtual stores), a bricks-only store (only physical stores) or a clicks-only retailer (virtual or Internet stores only). One-way ANOVA would be the choice for this analysis.

> **analysis of variance (ANOVA)**
>
> Analysis involving the investigation of the effects of one treatment variable on an interval-scaled dependent variable—a hypothesis-testing technique to determine whether statistically significant differences in means occur between two or more groups.

Simple Illustration of ANOVA

ANOVA's logic is fairly simple. Look at the data table below that describes how much coffee respondents report drinking each day based on which shift they work (GY stands for Graveyard shift, which is typically from about 5:00 p.m. until about 1:00 a.m.).

Day	1
Day	3
Day	4
Day	0
Day	2
GY	7
GY	2
GY	1
GY	6
Night	6
Night	8
Night	3
Night	7
Night	6

The following table displays the means for each group and the overall mean:

Shift	Mean	Std. Deviation	N
Day	2.00	1.58	5
GY	4.00	2.94	4
Night	6.00	1.87	5
Total	4.00	2.63	14

Exhibit 22.5 plots each observation with a bar. The long blue vertical line illustrates the total range of observations. The lowest is 0 cups and the highest is 8 cups of coffee for a range of 8. The overall mean is 4 cups. Each group mean is shown with a different colored line that matches the bars corresponding to the group. The day shift averages 2 cups of coffee a day, the graveyard shift 4 cups, and the night shift 6 cups of coffee per day.

EXHIBIT 22.5 Illustration of ANOVA Logic

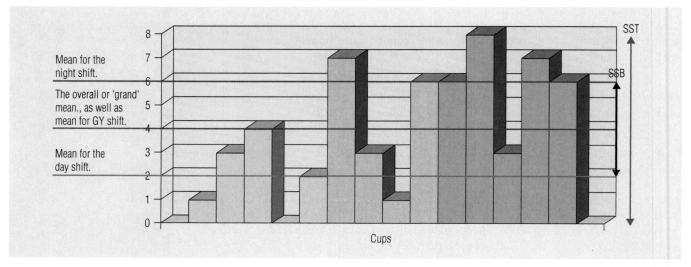

Here is the basic idea of ANOVA. Look at the dark double-headed arrow in Exhibit 22.5. This line represents the range of the differences between group means. In this case, the lowest mean is 2 cups and the highest mean is 6 cups. Thus, the blue vertical line corresponds to the total variation (range) in the data and the thick double-headed black vertical line corresponds to the variance accounted for by the group differences. As the thick black line accounts for more of the total variance, then the ANOVA model suggests that the group means are not all the same, and in particular, not all the same as the overall mean. This also means that the independent variable, in this case work shift, explains the dependent variable. Here, the results suggest that knowing when someone works explains how much coffee they drink. Night-shift workers drink the most coffee.

Partitioning Variance in ANOVA

■ TOTAL VARIABILITY

An implicit question with the use of ANOVA is, "How can the dependent variable best be predicted?" Absent any additional information, the error in predicting an observation is minimized by choosing the central tendency, or mean for an interval variable. For the coffee example, if no information was available about the work shift of each respondent, the best guess for coffee drinking consumption would be four cups. The total error (or variability) that would result from using the **grand mean**, meaning the mean over all observations, can be thought of as

grand mean

The mean of a variable over all observations.

$$SST = \text{Total of (observed value} - \text{grand mean)}^2$$

Although the term error is used, this really represents how much total variation exists among the measures.

Using the first observation, the error of observation would be

$$(1 \text{ cup} - 4 \text{ cups})^2 = 9$$

The same squared error could be computed for each observation and these squared errors totaled to give SST.

■ BETWEEN-GROUPS VARIANCE

ANOVA tests whether "grouping" observations explains variance in the dependent variable. In Exhibit 22.5, the three colors reflect three levels of the independent variable, work shift. Given this additional information about which shift a respondent works, the prediction changes. Now, instead of guessing the grand mean, the group mean would be used. So, once we know that someone works the day shift, the prediction would be that he or she consumes 2 cups of coffee per day. Similarly, the graveyard and night-shift predictions would be 4 and 6 cups, respectively. Thus, the **between-groups variance** can be found by taking the total sum of the weighted difference between group means and the overall mean as shown:

$$SSB = \text{Total of } n_{\text{group}}(\text{Group Mean} - \text{Grand Mean})^2$$

The weighting factor (n_{group}) is the specific group sample size. Let's consider the first observation once again. Since this observation is in the day shift, we predict 2 cups of coffee will be consumed. Looking at the day shift group observations in Exhibit 22.5, the new error in prediction would be

$$(2 \text{ cups} - 4 \text{ cups})^2 = (2)^2 = 4$$

The error in prediction has been reduced from 3 using the grand mean to 2 using the group mean. This squared difference would be weighted by the group sample size of 5, to yield a contribution to SSB of 20.

Next, the same process could be followed for the other groups yielding two more contributions to SSB. Because the graveyard shift group mean is the same as the grand mean, that group's contribution to SSB is 0. Notice that the night-shift group mean is also 2 different than the grand mean, like the day shift, so this group's contribution to SSB is likewise 20. The total SSB then represents the variation explained by the experimental or independent variable. In this case, total SSB is 40. The reader may look at the statistical results shown in Exhibit 22.6 to find this value in the sums of squares column.

between-groups variance

The sum of differences between the group mean and the grand mean summed over all groups for a given set of observations.

EXHIBIT 22.6 Interpreting ANOVA

Tests of Between-Subjects Effects (Dependent Variable: Coffee)

Source	Type III Sum of Squares	d.f.	Mean Square	F	Sig.
Corrected Model	40.000[a]	2	20.000	4.400	.039
Intercept	221.538	1	221.538	48.738	.000
Shift	40.000	2	20.000	4.400	.039
Error	50.000	11	4.545		
Total	314.000	14			

[a]R Squared = .444 (Adjusted R Squared = .343)

1. This row shows overall *F*-value testing whether all group means are equal. The sums of squares column calculates the SST, SSE, and SSB (shift row).

Shift	Mean	Std. Error	95% Confidence Interval	
			Lower Bound	Upper Bound
Day	2.000	.953	−.099	4.099
GY	4.000	1.066	1.654	6.346
Night	6.000	.953	3.901	8.099

2. This column shows the group means for each level of the independent variable.

■ WITHIN-GROUP ERROR

within-group error or variance

The sum of the differences between observed values and the group mean for a given set of observations; also known as total error variance.

Finally, error within each group would remain. Whereas the group means explain the variation between the total mean and the group mean, the distance from the group mean and each individual observation remains unexplained. This distance is called **within-group error or variance**. The values for each observation can be found by

$$SSE = \text{Total of (Observed Mean} - \text{Group Mean})^2$$

Again, looking at the first observation, the SSE component would be

$$SSE = (1 \text{ cup} - 2 \text{ cups})^2 = 1 \text{ cup}$$

This process could be computed for all observations and then totaled. The result would be the total error variance—a name sometimes used to refer to SSE since it is variability not accounted for by the group means. These three components are used in determining how well an ANOVA model explains a dependent variable.

The *F*-Test

F-test

A procedure used to determine whether there is more variability in the scores of one sample than in the scores of another sample.

The **F-test** is the key statistical test for an ANOVA model. The *F*-test determines whether there is more variability in the scores of one sample than in the scores of another sample. The key question is whether the two sample variances are different from each other or whether they are from the same population. Thus, the test breaks down the variance in a total sample and illustrates why ANOVA is *analysis of variance*.

The *F*-statistic (or *F*-ratio) can be obtained by taking the larger sample variance and dividing by the smaller sample variance. Using Table A.5 or A.6 in the appendix is much like using the tables of the *Z*- and *t*-distributions that we have previously examined. These tables portray the *F*-distribution, which is a probability distribution of the ratios of sample variances. These tables indicate that the distribution of *F* is actually a family of distributions that change quite drastically with changes in sample sizes. Thus, degrees of freedom must be specified. Inspection of an *F*-table allows the researcher to determine the probability of finding an *F* as large as a calculated *F*.

■ USING VARIANCE COMPONENTS TO COMPUTE *F*-RATIOS

In ANOVA, the basic consideration for the *F*-test is identifying the relative size of variance components. The three forms of variation described briefly above are:

1. SSE—variation of scores due to random error or within-group variance due to individual differences from the group mean. This is the error of prediction.
2. SSB—systematic variation of scores between groups due to manipulation of an experimental variable or group classifications of a measured independent variable or between-group variance.
3. SST—the total observed variation across all groups and individual observations.

The Research Snapshot on the next page provides additional insight into the mechanics of ANOVA. In addition, the Web resources provided with the text provide some illustrations of how to perform an analysis like this using SPSS, SAS, or EXCEL.

Thus, we can partition total variability into *within-group variance* and *between-group variance*. The *F*-distribution is a function of the ratio of these two sources of variances:

$$F = f\left(\frac{SSB}{SSE}\right)$$

A larger ratio of variance between groups to variance within groups implies a greater value of *F*. If the *F*-value is large, the results are likely to be statistically significant.

More than One-Way

An independent samples *t*-test is a special case of one-way ANOVA. When the independent variable in ANOVA has only two groups, the results for an independent samples *t*-test and ANOVA will be the same.

The two sets of statistical results below demonstrate this fact. Both outputs are taken from the same data. The test considers whether men or women are more excited about a new Italian restaurant in their town. Sex2 is dummy coded so that 0 = men and 1 = women. Excitement was measured on a scale ranging from 0 to 6.

Independent Samples *t*-test Results:

Group Statistics

	Sex2	N	Mean	Std. Deviation	Std. Error Mean
Excitement	0.00	69	2.64	2.262	0.272
	1.00	73	2.32	2.140	0.250

Independent Samples Test

		Levene's Test for Equality of Variances		t-Test for Equality of Means						
									95% Confidence Interval of the Difference	
		F	Sig.	t	d.f.	Sig. (two-tailed)	Mean Difference	Std. Error Difference	Lower	Upper
Excitement	Equal variances assumed	1.768	.186	.873	140	.384	.323	.369	−.408	1.053
	Equal variances not assumed			.872	138.265	.385	.323	.370	−.409	1.054

In this case, we would conclude that men and women are equally excited—or unexcited as the case may be. The *t* of 0.873 with 140 d.f. is not significant (p = 0.384).

ANOVA Results:

Descriptives

		N	Mean	Std. Deviation	Std. Error	95% Confidence Interval for Mean		Minimum	Maximum
						Lower Bound	Upper Bound		
Excitement	0.00	69	2.64	2.262	0.272	2.09	3.18	0	7
	1.00	73	2.32	2.140	0.250	1.82	2.81	0	7
	Total	142	2.47	2.198	0.184	2.11	2.84	0	7

ANOVA

		Sum of Squares	d.f.	Mean Square	F	Sig.
Excitement	Between Groups	3.692	1	3.692	0.763	0.384
	Within Groups	677.695	140	4.841		
	Total	681.387	141			

Notice that the *F*-ratio shown in the ANOVA table is associated with the same p-value as is the *t*-value above. This is no accident since the *F* and *t* are mathematical functions of one another. So, when two groups are involved, the researcher can skin the cat either way!

- Cross-tabulations are widely applied in market research reports and presentations.
  - Take advantage of graphical tools like bar charts to present cross-tabulation results in presentations and reports.
  - Cross-tabulations are appropriate for research questions involving predictions of categorical dependent variables using categorical independent variables. These are usually nominal or ordinal.
    - When more than four categories exist, cross-tabulation tables can become difficult to present clearly.
    - Independent variables are placed in rows and dependent variables are placed in columns.
- A *t*-test is used to compare means between two groups.
  - An independent samples *t*-test predicts a continuous (interval or ratio) dependent variable with a categorical (nominal or ordinal) independent variable.

- A paired samples *t*-test compares means from two different responses from the same sampling unit. Therefore, the sampling is dependent.
- A one-way ANOVA extends the concept of an independent samples *t*-test to more than two groups.
  - Don't be fooled by the fact that it involves an *F*-test instead of a *t*-test. They are mathematically related and, in fact, an *F*-value is the square of a *t*-value that would result from the same analysis.
  - Stat packages usually have an ANOVA package or a one-way ANOVA package. However, general linear model procedures can also conduct these tests and offer more flexibility as we will see in later chapters.
- Simple hand calculations can be useful in learning what statistical procedures actually do. However, in conducting actual tests, take advantage of computer software whenever permissible.

Two of the most popular software packages, SAS and SPSS, display ANOVA results for the coffee drinking problem.

■ A DIFFERENT BUT EQUIVALENT REPRESENTATION

F also can be thought of as a function of the between–group variance and total variance.

$$F = f\left(\frac{SSB}{SST - SSB}\right)$$

In this sense, the ratio of the thick black line to the blue line representing the total range of data presents the basic idea of the *F*-value. Appendix 22A explains the calculations in more detail with an illustration.

Practically Speaking

Exhibit 22.6 displays the ANOVA result for the coffee-drinking example. Again, one advantage of living in modern times is that even a simple problem like this one need not be hand computed. Even though this example presents a small problem, one-way ANOVA models with more observations or levels would be interpreted similarly.

The first thing to check is whether or not the overall model *F* is significant. In this case, the computed $F = 4.40$ with 2 and 11 degrees of freedom. The p-value associated with this value is 0.039. Thus, we have high confidence in concluding that the group means are not all the same. Second, the researcher must remember to examine the actual means for each group to properly interpret the result. Doing so, the conclusion reached is that the night-shift people drink the most coffee, followed by the graveyard-shift workers, and then lastly, the day-shift workers.

As there are three groups, we may wish to know whether or not group 1 is significantly different than group 3 or group 2, and so on. In a later chapter, we will describe ways of examining specifically which group means are different from one another. In this particular example, the answer is fairly obvious.

SAS:

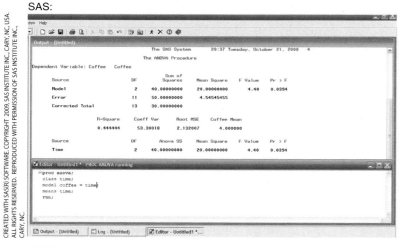

SPSS:

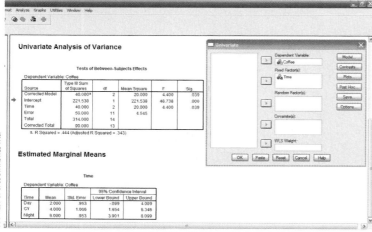

Summary

1. Construct a cross-tabulation table and the corresponding χ^2 statistic. Bivariate statistical techniques analyze scores on two variables at a time. A cross-tabulation is a useful way of depicting and analyzing the way two categorical variables are related to one another. For instance, a nominal independent variable may be used to predict a nominal dependent variable. Cross-tabulations are very useful and lend themselves well to depicting results in charts. The χ^2 statistic is the test statistic appropriate for testing relationships among variables used in a cross-tabulation table. Higher χ^2 values are generally associated with lower p-values and therefore greater probability of a relationship between the row and column variable. The process of testing a hypothesis using a χ^2 statistic is similar in concept to practically all the hypotheses testing procedures that follow.

2. Use a t-test to compare a difference between two means. When a researcher needs to compare means for a variable grouped into two categories based on some less-than interval variable, a t-test is appropriate. An independent samples t-test examines whether a dependent variable like price differs based on a grouping variable like biological sex. Statistically, the test examines whether the difference between the mean for men and women is different from 0. Larger t-values are associated with smaller p-values and statistical significance. A paired-samples t-test examines whether or not the means from two variables that are not independent are different. A common situation calling for this test is when the two observations are from the same respondent. A simple before-and-after test calls for a paired-sample t-test so long as the dependent variable is continuous.

3. Know how a Z-test can be used to compare two proportions. A bivariate Z-test can be applied when a researcher wants to test the difference between two proportions. The idea is examining whether the population proportion for one group (or sample) is the same as that from another group (or sample).

4. Conduct a one-way analysis of variance test (ANOVA). ANOVA is the appropriate statistical technique to examine the effect of a less-than interval independent variable on an at-least interval dependent variable. Conceptually, ANOVA partitions the total variability into three types: total variation, between-group variation, and within-group variation. As the explained variance represented by SSB becomes larger relative to SSE or SST, the ANOVA model is more likely to be significant, indicating that at least one group mean is different from another group mean.

5. Appreciate the practicality of modern statistical software packages. Hand calculations using a simple calculator can sometimes be a good way for getting the feel of exactly what some statistic is doing; however, even small applications are usually better performed with the help of some statistical software whether it be Excel, SPSS, SAS or some other package. This saves time and helps reduce mathematical errors.

Key Terms and Concepts

analysis of variance (ANOVA), *573*
between-groups variance, *575*
F-test, *576*
grand mean, *574*

independent samples t-test, *565*
paired-samples t-test, *570*
pooled estimate of the standard error, *566*
test of differences, *561*

within-group error or variance, *576*
Z-test for differences of proportions, *571*

Questions for Review and Critical Thinking

1. What tests of difference are appropriate in the following situations?
   a. Average campaign contributions (in $) of Democrats, Republicans, and Independents are to be compared.
   b. Advertising managers and brand managers have responded "yes," "no," or "not sure" to an attitude question. The advertising and brand managers' responses are to be compared.
   c. One-half of a sample received an incentive in a mail survey while the other half did not. A comparison of response rates is desired.
   d. A researcher believes that married men will push the grocery cart when grocery shopping with their wives. How would the hypothesis be tested?
   e. A manager wishes to compare the job performance of a salesperson before ethics training with the performance of that same salesperson after ethics training.

2. Perform a χ^2 test on the following data (hint: set up a spreadsheet to perform the calculations):
   a. Increased regulation is the best way to ensure safe products.

	Agree	Disagree	No Opinion
Managers	58	66	8
Line Employees	34	24	10
Totals	92	90	18

b. Ownership of residence

	Yes	No
Male	25	20
Female	16	14

3. Interpret the following computer cross-tab output including a χ^2 test. Variable EDUCATION is a response to "What is your highest level of educational achievement?" HS means a high school diploma, SC means some college, BS means a bachelor's degree, and MBA means a master of business administration. Variable WIN is how well the respondent did on a set of casino games of chance. A 1 means they would have lost more than $100, a 2 means they approximately broke even, and a 3 means they won more than $100. What is the result of exploring a research question that education influences performance on casino gambling? Comment on your conclusion and any issues in interpreting the result.

The SAS System
The FREQ Procedure
Table of education by win

EDUCATION Frequency Percent Row Pct Col Pct	WIN			
	1	2	3	Total
MBA	3	10	4	17
	1.12	3.72	1.49	6.32
	17.65	58.82	23.53	
	3.19	10.31	5.13	
BS	11	19	12	42
	4.09	7.06	4.46	15.61
	26.19	45.24	28.57	
	11.70	19.59	15.38	
SC	33	30	27	90
	12.27	11.15	10.04	33.45
	35.67	33.33	30.00	
	35.11	30.93	34.62	
HS	47	38	35	120
	17.47	14.13	13.01	44.61
	29.17	31.67	29.17	
	50.00	39.18	44.57	
Total	94	97	78	269
	34.94	36.06	29.00	100.00

Statistics for Table of education by win

Statistic	DF	Value	Prob
Chi-Square	6	7.5275	0.2748

Sample Size = 269

4. A store manager's computer-generated list of all retail sales employees indicates that 70 percent are full-time employees, 20 percent are part-time employees, and 10 percent are furloughed or laid-off employees. A sample of 50 employees from the list indicates that there are 40 full-time employees, 6 part-time employees, and 4 furloughed/laid-off employees. Conduct a statistical test to determine whether the sample is representative of the population.

5. Test the following hypothesis using the data summarized in the table below. Interpret your result:

H1: Internet retailers offer lower prices for DVD players than do traditional in-store retailers.

Retail Type	DVD Player Average Price	Standard Deviation	n
E-tailers	$371.95	$50.00	25
Multi-channel retailers	$360.30	$45.00	25

6. Selected territories in a company's eastern and western regions were rated for sales potential based on the company's evaluation system. A sales manager wishes to conduct a *t*-test of means to determine whether there is a difference between the two regions. Conduct this test, preferably using a statistical software package, and draw the appropriate conclusion:

Region	Territory	Rating	Region	Territory	Rating
West	1	74	East	8	81
West	2	88	East	9	63
West	3	78	East	10	56
West	4	85	East	11	68
West	5	100	East	12	80
West	6	114	East	13	79
West	7	98	East	14	69

How would this result change if the company only had seven territories in the West and seven in the East?

7. How does an independent samples *t*-test differ from the following?
   a. one-way ANOVA   b. paired-samples *t*-test
   c. a χ^2 test   d. a *Z*-test for differences

8. Are *t*-tests or *Z*-tests used more often in marketing research? Why?

9. A sales force received some management-by-objectives training. Are the before/after mean scores for salespeople's job performance statistically significant at the 0.05 level? The results from a sample of employees are as follows (use your computer and statistical software to solve this problem):

Skill	Before	After	Skill	Before	After
Carlos	4.84	5.43	Tommy	4.00	5.00
Sammy	5.24	5.51	Laurie	4.67	4.50
Melanie	5.37	5.42	Ronald	4.95	4.40
Philippe	3.69	4.50	Amanda	4.00	5.95
Cargill	5.95	5.90	Brittany	3.75	3.50
Dwight	4.75	5.25	Mathew	3.85	4.00
Amy	3.90	4.50	Alice	5.00	4.10
Kallua	3.20	3.75	Jake	4.00	5.15

10. Using the "CAR" data that accompanies the text (see Web site), consider the following problem. The data describe attitudes of car owners from Germany and the United States toward their automobiles. The variable "ATT" is how much respondents like their current car (attitude), "ATTNEW" is their attitude toward a new car called the Cycle. The "COUNTRY" variable is self-explanatory. The "SPEND" variable is how much the respondents spend on average on products to keep their cars clean (in Euros). Using SPSS or other statistical software, test the following hypotheses:

The owners' attitudes toward the Cycle are more favorable than attitudes toward their current cars.
Germans like their cars more than Americans.

11. Conduct a Z-test to determine whether the following two samples indicate that the population proportions are significantly different at the 0.05 level:

	Sample 1	Sample 2
Sample proportion	0.77	0.68
Sample size	55	46

12. In an experiment with wholesalers, a researcher manipulated perception of task difficulty and measured level of aspiration for performing the task a second time. Group 1 was told the task was very difficult, group 2 was told the task was somewhat difficult but attainable, and group 3 was told the task was easy. Perform an ANOVA on the resulting data:

Level of Aspiration (10-Point Scale)

Subjects	Group 1	Group 2	Group 3
1	6	5	5
2	7	4	6
3	5	7	5
4	8	6	4
5	8	7	2
6	6	7	3
Cases	6	6	6

13. Interpret the following output examining group differences for purchase intentions. The three groups refer to consumers from three states: Florida, Minnesota, and Hawaii.

Tests of Between-Subjects Effects
Dependent Variable: int2

Source	Type III Sum of Squares	d.f.	Mean Square	F	Sig.
Corrected Model	681.746[a]	2	3340.873	3.227	.043
Intercept	308897.012	1	308897.012	298.323	.000
State	6681.746	2	3340.873	3.227	.043
Error	148068.543	143	1035.444		
Total	459697.250	146			
Corrected Total	154750.289	145			

[a]R Squared = 0.043 (Adjusted R Squared = 0.030)

Law
Dependent Variable: int2

State	Mean	Std. Error	95% Confidence Interval	
			Lower Bound	Upper Bound
F	37.018	4.339	28.441	45.595
M	50.357	4.965	40.542	60.172
H	51.459	4.597	42.373	60.546

Research Activities

1. **ETHICS/'NET** How ethical is it to do business in different countries around the world? An international organization, Transparency International, keeps track of the perception of ethical practices in different countries. Visit the Web site and search for the latest corruption indices (http://www.transparency.org/policy_and_research/surveys_indices/cpi/2008). Using the data found here, test the following research questions.
   a. Are nations from Europe and North America perceived to be more ethical than nations from Asia, Africa, and South America? Include Australia and New Zealand with Europe.

   b. Are there differences among the corruption indices between 2004 and 2008?

2. **'NET** The Federal Reserve Bank of St. Louis maintains a database called FRED (Federal Reserve Economic Data). Navigate to the FRED database at http://research.stlouisfed.org/fred. Randomly select a five-year period between 1970 and today and then compare average figures for U.S. employment in retail trade with those for U.S. employment in wholesale trade. What statistical tests are appropriate?

Case 22.1 Old School versus New School Sports Fans

Download the data sets for this case from www.cengage.
com/marketing/zikmund *or request them from your
instructor.*

Three academic researchers investigated
the idea that, in American sports, there are two
segments with opposing views about the goal
of competition (i.e., winning versus self-actualization) and the
acceptable/desirable way of achieving this goal.[7] Persons who believe
in "winning at any cost" are proponents of sports success as a product
and can be labeled new school (NS) individuals. The new school is
founded on notions of the player before the team, loyalty to the highest bidder, and high-tech production and consumption of professional
sports. On the other hand, persons who value the process of sports
and believe that "how you play the game matters" can be labeled old
school (OS) individuals. The old school emerges from old-fashioned
American notions of the team before the player, sportsmanship, and
loyalty above all else, and competition simply for "love of the game."

New School/Old School was measured by asking agreement with
10 attitude statements. The scores on these statements were combined.
Higher scores represent an orientation toward old school values. For
purposes of this case study, individuals who did not answer every
question were eliminated from the analysis. Based on their summated
scores, respondents were grouped into low score, middle score, and high
score groups. Case Exhibit 22.1–1 shows the SPSS computer output of a
cross-tabulation to relate the gender of the respondent (GENDER) with
the New School/Old School grouping (OLDSKOOL).

Questions

Is this form of analysis appropriate?

Interpret the computer output and critique the analysis.

Explore the GLM (General Linear Model) procedure in SAS or
SPSS by testing a model using show_off as the dependent variable
and gender as the independent variable (a fixed effect in the SPSS
GLM window and a class variable in SAS Proc GLM).

CASE EXHIBIT 22.1–1 SPSS Output

OLDSKOOL * GENDER Crosstabulation

			GENDER women	GENDER men	Total
OLDSKOOL	high	Count	9	17	26
		% within OLDSKOOL	34.6%	65.4%	100.0%
		% within GENDER	10.6%	9.2%	9.6%
		% of Total	3.3%	6.3%	9.6%
	low	Count	45	70	115
		% within OLDSKOOL	39.1%	60.9%	100.0%
		% within GENDER	52.9%	37.8%	42.6%
		% of Total	16.7%	25.9%	42.6%
	middle	Count	31	98	129
		% within OLDSKOOL	24.0%	76.0%	100.0%
		% within GENDER	36.5%	53.0%	47.8%
		% of Total	11.5%	36.3%	47.8%
Total		Count	85	185	270
		% within OLDSKOOL	31.5%	68.5%	100.0%
		% within GENDER	100.0%	100.0%	100.0%
		% of Total	31.5%	68.5%	100.0%

Chi-Square Tests

	Value	df	Asymp. Sig. (2-sided)
Pearson Chi-Square	6.557[a]	2	.038
Likelihood Ratio	6.608	2	.037
N of Valid Cases	270		

[a] 0 cells (.0%) have expected count less than 5. The minimum expected count is 8.19.

Manual calculations are almost unheard of these days. However, understanding the calculations can be very useful in gaining a thorough understanding of ANOVA. The data in Exhibit 22A.1 are from a hypothetical packaged-goods company's test-market experiment on pricing. Three pricing treatments were administered in four separate areas (12 test areas, A–L, were required). These data will be used to illustrate ANOVA.

Terminology for the variance estimates is derived from the calculation procedures, so an explanation of the terms used to calculate the *F*-ratio should clarify the meaning of the analysis of variance technique. The calculation of the *F*-ratio requires that we partition the total variation into two parts:

$$\text{Total sum of squares} \atop (SST) \quad = \quad {\text{Within-group} \atop \text{sum of squares} \atop (SSE)} \quad + \quad {\text{Between-group} \atop \text{sum of squares} \atop (SSB)}$$

or

$$SST = SSE + SSB$$

SST is computed by squaring the deviation of each score from the grand mean and summing these squares:

$$SST = \sum_{i=1}^{n} \sum_{j=1}^{c} \left(X_{ij} - \overline{\overline{X}} \right)^2$$

where

X = individual score—that is, the ith observation or test unit in the jth group

$\overline{\overline{X}}$ = grand mean

n = number of all observations or test units in a group

c = number of jth groups (or columns)

	Sales in Units (thousands)		
	Regular Price, $.99	Reduced Price, $.89	Cents-Off Coupon, Regular Price
Test-Market A, B, or C	130	145	153
Test-Market D, E, or F	118	143	129
Test-Market G, H, or I	87	120	96
Test-Market J, K, or L	84	131	99
Mean	$\overline{X}_1 = 104.75$	$\overline{X}_2 = 134.75$	$\overline{X}_3 = 119.25$
Grand mean	$\overline{\overline{X}} = 119.58$		

In our example,

$$SST = (130 - 119.58)^2 + (118 - 119.58)^2 + (87 - 119.58)^2$$
$$+ (84 - 119.58)^2 + (145 - 119.58)^2 + (143 - 119.58)^2$$
$$+ (120 - 119.58)^2 + (131 - 119.58)^2 + (153 - 119.58)^2$$
$$+ (129 - 119.58)^2 + (96 - 119.58)^2 + (99 - 119.58)^2$$
$$= 5,948.93$$

SSE, the variability that we observe within each group, or the error remaining after using the groups to predict observations, is calculated by squaring the deviation of each score from its group mean and summing these scores:

$$SSE = \sum_{i=1}^{n} \sum_{j=1}^{c} (X_{ij} - \overline{X}_j)^2$$

where

X = individual score

$\overline{X}_j$ = group mean for the *j*th group

n = number of observations in a group

c = number of *j*th groups

In our example,

$$SSE = (130 - 104.75)^2 + (118 - 104.75)^2 + (87 - 104.75)^2$$
$$+ (84 - 104.75)^2 + (145 - 134.75)^2 + (143 - 134.75)^2$$
$$+ (120 - 134.75)^2 + (131 - 134.75)^2 + (153 - 119.25)^2$$
$$+ (129 - 119.25)^2 + (96 - 119.25)^2 + (99 - 119.25)^2$$
$$= 4,148.25$$

SSB, the variability of the group means about a grand mean, is calculated by squaring the deviation of each group mean from the grand mean, multiplying by the number of items in the group, and summing these scores:

$$SSB = \sum_{j=1}^{c} n_j (\overline{X}_j - \overline{\overline{X}})^2$$

where

$\overline{X}_j$ = group mean for the *j*th group

$\overline{\overline{X}}$ = grand mean

n_j = number of items in the *j*th group

In our example,

$$SSB = 4(104.75 - 119.58)^2 + 4(134.75 - 119.58)^2$$
$$+ 4(119.25 - 119.58)^2$$
$$= 1,800.68$$

The next calculation requires dividing the various sums of squares by their appropriate degrees of freedom. These divisions produce the variances, or *mean squares*. To obtain the mean square between groups, we divide *SSB* by $c - 1$ degrees of freedom:

$$MSB = \frac{SSB}{c - 1}$$

In our example,

$$MSB = \frac{1,800.68}{3 - 1} = \frac{1,800.68}{2} = 900.34$$

To obtain the mean square within groups, we divide SSE by $cn - c$ degrees of freedom:

$$MSE = \frac{SSE}{cn - c}$$

In our example,

$$MSE = \frac{4,148.25}{12 - 3} = \frac{4,148.25}{9} = 460.91$$

Finally, the F-ratio is calculated by taking the ratio of the mean square between groups to the mean square within groups. The between-groups mean square is the numerator and the within-groups mean square is the denominator:

$$F = \frac{MSB}{MSE}$$

In our example,

$$F = \frac{900.34}{460.91} = 1.95$$

There will be $c - 1$ degrees of freedom in the numerator and $cn - c$ degrees of freedom in the denominator:

$$\frac{c - 1}{cn - c} = \frac{3 - 1}{3(4) - 3} = \frac{2}{9}$$

In Table A.5 in the text appendix, the critical value of F at the 0.05 level for 2 and 9 degrees of freedom indicates that an F of 4.26 would be required to reject the null hypothesis.

In our example we conclude that we cannot reject the null hypothesis. It appears that all the price treatments produce approximately the same sales volume.

The information produced from an analysis of variance is traditionally summarized in table form. Exhibits 22A.2 and 22A.3 summarize the formulas and data from our example.

Source of Variation	Sum of Squares	Degrees of Freedom	Mean Square	F-Ratio
Between groups	$SSB = \sum_{j=1}^{c} n_j (\bar{X}_j - \bar{\bar{X}})^2$	$c - 1$	$MSB = \frac{SSB}{c - 1}$	—
Within groups	$SSE = \sum_{i=1}^{n} \sum_{j=1}^{c} (X_{ij} - \bar{X}_j)^2$	$cn - c$	$MSE = \frac{SSE}{cn - c}$	$F = \frac{MSB}{MSE}$
Total	$SST = \sum_{i=1}^{n} \sum_{j=1}^{c} (X_{ij} - \bar{\bar{X}})^2$	$cn - 1$	—	—

where c = number of groups
n = number of observations in a group
cn = total number of observations

EXHIBIT 22A.2
ANOVA Summary Table

Source of Variation	Sum of Squares	Degrees of Freedom	Mean Square	F-Ratio
Between groups	1,800.68	2	900.34	—
Within groups	4,148.25	9	460.91	1.953
Total	5,948.93	11	—	—

EXHIBIT 22A.3
Pricing Experiment ANOVA Table

APPENDIX 22B
ANOVA FOR COMPLEX EXPERIMENTAL DESIGNS

To test for statistical significance in a randomized block design, or RBD (see Chapter 12), another version of analysis of variance is utilized. The linear model for the RBD for an individual observation is*

$$Y_{ij} = \mu + \alpha_j + \beta_i + \varepsilon_{ij}$$

where

Y_{ij} = individual observation on the dependent variable

μ = grand mean

α_j = jth treatment effect

β_i = ith block effect

ε_{ij} = random error or residual

The statistical objective is to determine whether significant differences exist among treatment means and block means. This is done by calculating an F-ratio for each source of effects.

The same logic that applies in single-factor ANOVA—using variance estimates to test for differences among means—applies in ANOVA for randomized block designs. Thus, to conduct the ANOVA, we partition the total sum of squares (SS_{total}) into non-overlapping components.

$$SS_{\text{total}} = SS_{\text{treatments}} + SS_{\text{blocks}} + SS_{\text{error}}$$

The sources of variance are defined as follows.

Total sum of squares:

$$SS_{\text{total}} = \sum_{i=1}^{r} \sum_{j=1}^{c} (Y_{ij} - \overline{\overline{Y}})^2$$

where

Y_{ij} = individual observation

$\overline{\overline{Y}}$ = grand mean

r = number of blocks (rows)

c = number of treatments (columns)

Treatment sum of squares:

$$SS_{\text{treatments}} = \sum_{i=1}^{r} \sum_{j=1}^{c} (\overline{Y}_j - \overline{\overline{Y}})^2$$

where

$\overline{Y}_j$ = jth treatment mean

$\overline{\overline{Y}}$ = grand mean

Block sum of squares:

$$SS_{\text{blocks}} = \sum_{i=1}^{r} \sum_{j=1}^{c} (\overline{Y}_i - \overline{\overline{Y}})^2$$

---

*We assume no interaction effect between treatments and blocks.

where

$$\overline{Y}_i = i\text{th block mean}$$

$$\overline{\overline{Y}} = \text{grand mean}$$

Sum of squares error:

$$SS_{\text{error}} = \sum_{i=1}^{r}\sum_{j=1}^{c} (Y_{ij} - \overline{Y}_i - \overline{Y}_j - \overline{\overline{Y}})^2$$

The SS_{error} may also be calculated in the following manner:

$$SS_{\text{error}} = SS_{\text{total}} - SS_{\text{treatments}} - SS_{\text{blocks}}$$

The degrees of freedom for $SS_{\text{treatments}}$ are equal to $c - 1$ because $SS_{\text{treatments}}$ reflects the dispersion of treatment means from the grand mean, which is fixed. Degrees of freedom for blocks are $r - 1$ for similar reasons. SS_{error} reflects variations from both treatment and block means. Thus, *d.f.* $= (r - 1)(c - 1)$.

Mean squares are calculated by dividing the appropriate sum of squares by the corresponding degrees of freedom.

Exhibit 22B.1 is an ANOVA table for the randomized block design. It summarizes what has been discussed and illustrates the calculation of mean squares.

EXHIBIT 22B.1
ANOVA Table for
Randomized Block Designs

Source of Variation	Sum of Squares	Degrees of Freedom	Mean Squares
Between blocks	SS_{blocks}	$r - 1$	$\dfrac{SS_{\text{blocks}}}{r - 1}$
Between treatments	$SS_{\text{treatments}}$	$c - 1$	$\dfrac{SS_{\text{treatments}}}{c - 1}$
Error	SS_{error}	$(r - 1)(c - 1)$	$\dfrac{SS_{\text{error}}}{(r - 1)(c - 1)}$
Total	SS_{total}	$rc - 1$	—

F-ratios for treatment and block effects are calculated as follows:

$$F_{\text{treatment}} = \frac{\text{Mean square treatment}}{\text{Mean square error}}$$

$$F_{\text{blocks}} = \frac{\text{Mean square blocks}}{\text{Mean square error}}$$

Factorial Designs

There is considerable similarity between the factorial design (see Chapter 12) and the one-way analysis of variance. The sum of squares for each of the treatment factors (rows and columns) is similar to the between-groups sum of squares in the single-factor ANOVA model. Each treatment sum of squares is calculated by taking the deviation of the treatment means from the grand mean. Determining the sum of squares for the interaction is a new calculation because this source of variance is not attributable to the treatment sum of squares or the error sum of squares.

ANOVA for a Factorial Experiment

In a two-factor experimental design the linear model for an individual observation is

$$Y_{ijk} = \mu + \beta_i + \alpha_j + I_{ij} + \varepsilon_{ijk}$$

where

Y_{ijk} = individual observation on the dependent variable

μ = grand mean

β_i = ith effect of factor B—row treatment

α_j = jth effect of factor A—column treatment

I_{ij} = interaction effect of factors A and B

ε_{ijk} = random error or residual

Partitioning the Sum of Squares for a Two-Way ANOVA

Again, the total sum of squares can be allocated into distinct and overlapping portions:

Sum of squares total	=	Sum of squares rows (treatment B)	+	Sum of squares columns (treatment A)	+	Sum of squares interaction	+	Sum of squares error

or

$$SS_{total} = SSR_{treatment\ B} + SSC_{treatment\ A} + SS_{interaction} + SS_{error}$$

Sum of squares total:

$$SS_{total} = \sum_{i=1}^{r}\sum_{j=1}^{c}\sum_{k=1}^{n} (Y_{ijk} - \overline{\overline{Y}})^2$$

where

Y_{ijk} = individual observation on the dependent variable

$\overline{\overline{Y}}$ = grand mean

j = level of factor A

i = level of factor B

k = number of an observation in a particular cell

r = total number of levels of factor B (rows)

c = total number of levels of factor A (columns)

n = total number of observations in the sample

Sum of squares rows (treatment B):

$$SSR_{treatment\ B} = \sum_{i=1}^{r} (\overline{Y}_i - \overline{\overline{Y}})^2$$

where

$\overline{Y}_j$ = mean of ith treatment—factor B

Sum of squares columns (treatment A):

$$SSC_{treatment\ A} = \sum_{j=1}^{c} (Y_j - \overline{\overline{Y}})^2$$

where

$\overline{Y}_j$ = mean of jth treatment—factor A

Sum of squares interaction:

$$SS_{interaction} = \sum_{i=1}^{r}\sum_{j=1}^{c}\sum_{k=1}^{n} (Y_{ij} - \overline{Y}_i - \overline{Y}_j - \overline{\overline{Y}})^2$$

The above is one form of calculation. However, $SS_{\text{interaction}}$ generally is indirectly computed in the following manner:

$$SS_{\text{interaction}} = SS_{\text{total}} - SSR_{\text{treatment B}} - SSC_{\text{treatment A}} - SS_{\text{error}}$$

Sum of squares error:

$$SS_{\text{error}} = \sum_{i=1}^{r}\sum_{j=1}^{c}\sum_{k=1}^{n} (Y_{ijk} - \overline{Y}_{ij})^2$$

where

$\overline{Y}_{ij}$ = mean of the interaction effect

These sums of squares, along with their respective degrees of freedom and mean squares, are summarized in Exhibit 22B.2.

EXHIBIT 22B.2
ANOVA Table for Two-Factor Design

Source of Variation	Sum of Squares	Degrees of Freedom	Mean Square	F-Ratio
Treatment B	$SSR_{\text{treatment B}}$	$r - 1$	$MSR_{\text{treatment B}} = \dfrac{SSR_{\text{treatment B}}}{r - 1}$	$\dfrac{MSR_{\text{treatment B}}}{MS_{\text{error}}}$
Treatment A	$SSC_{\text{treatment A}}$	$c - 1$	$MSC_{\text{treatment A}} = \dfrac{SSC_{\text{treatment A}}}{c - 1}$	$\dfrac{MSC_{\text{treatment A}}}{MS_{\text{error}}}$
Interaction	$SS_{\text{interaction}}$	$(r - 1)(c - 1)$	$MS_{\text{interaction}} = \dfrac{SS_{\text{interaction}}}{(r - 1)(c - 1)}$	$\dfrac{MS_{\text{interaction}}}{MS_{\text{error}}}$
Error	SS_{error}	$rc(n - 1)$	$MS_{\text{error}} = \dfrac{SS_{\text{error}}}{rc(n - 1)}$	
Total	SS_{total}	$rcn - 1$		

CHAPTER 23
BIVARIATE
STATISTICAL
ANALYSIS:
MEASURES OF
ASSOCIATION

After studying this chapter, you should be able to

1. Compute and use bivariate correlations
2. Interpret a correlation matrix
3. Understand simple (bivariate) regression analysis
4. Know the basics of ordinary least-squares estimation
5. Know how to test a hypothesis using regression analysis output

Chapter Vignette: What's for Lunch?

Why do some people eat more than others? What an interesting question! In fact, many, many people have an interest in explaining what we eat and how much of it we eat. Policy makers are concerned with public obesity. Nutritionists are concerned with the extent to which

our diets provide necessary nutrients without unnecessary or harmful ingredients. Restaurants are concerned with providing attractive menu choices that satisfy consumers. While some companies benefit when we eat more, others benefit when we eat less.

What makes someone eat more? The list of factors that correlate with food intake is wide-ranging and includes personality variables, cultural variables, and demographics. Some more basic findings suggest food intake actually can be easily controlled. For instance, guess what happens when less food is placed on a plate? Surprise (or no surprise)! Consumers eat less! Put more food on the plate and a consumer tends to eat more![1] This affects nutrition two ways. For overweight consumers, the finding suggests that putting less on your plate or ordering smaller size portions in restaurants is a way to control calorie intake. However, other results suggest that consumers who place too little on their plate can end up showing signs of malnutrition.[2]

Who benefits when people eat more? Well, consumers need a certain minimum number of calories each day for a healthy lifestyle. Interestingly, as fast-food companies have moved into third world nations, the dietary health of some of these communities has actually improved. So, consumers sometimes benefit. Fast-food companies can benefit. Fast-food employees highly encourage customers to "super-size" their meals because, frankly, the more consumers eat, the more profit the restaurants make. However, as tastes change, so do the types of foods that are successful. While McDonald's has had success with salads, a typical Burger King restaurant offering salads sells about three a day.[3]

This short story about our eating habits illustrates how important measures of association can be. The story shows how researchers would be asked to demonstrate the strength of association for each of the following:

- Menu choice and customer satisfaction
- Food portion size and consumption

- Food consumption and health
- Portion size and restaurant profitability
- Personal taste and restaurant patronage

Knowing the relationships among these factors can mean the difference between winning and losing for many business decision makers and between effective and ineffective dietary guidelines for health organizations.

Introduction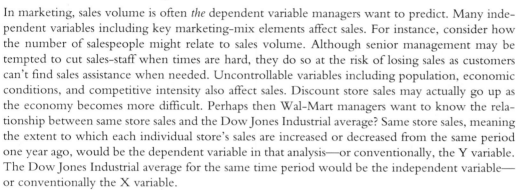

In marketing, sales volume is often *the* dependent variable managers want to predict. Many independent variables including key marketing-mix elements affect sales. For instance, consider how the number of salespeople might relate to sales volume. Although senior management may be tempted to cut sales-staff when times are hard, they do so at the risk of losing sales as customers can't find sales assistance when needed. Uncontrollable variables including population, economic conditions, and competitive intensity also affect sales. Discount store sales may actually go up as the economy becomes more difficult. Perhaps then Wal-Mart managers want to know the relationship between same store sales and the Dow Jones Industrial average? Same store sales, meaning the extent to which each individual store's sales are increased or decreased from the same period one year ago, would be the dependent variable in that analysis—or conventionally, the Y variable. The Dow Jones Industrial average for the same time period would be the independent variable— or conventionally the X variable.

In Chapter 21, we introduced the chi-square (χ^2) test. Together with a cross-tabulation, this test provides information about whether two or more less-than interval variables are related. For example, a χ^2 test between a measure of package color and product choice provides information about the independence or interrelationship of the two variables. Over the years, psychological statisticians have developed several other techniques that demonstrate empirical association, particularly for situations involving interval or better measures.

Simple Correlation Coefficient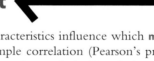

Exhibit 23.1 on the next page shows how measurement characteristics influence which **measure of association** is most appropriate. This chapter describes simple correlation (Pearson's product-moment correlation coefficient, *r*) and bivariate or simple regression analysis. Correlation analysis is most appropriate for interval or ratio variables. Regression can accommodate either less-than interval or interval independent variables, but the dependent variable must be continuous. Other techniques mentioned are for advanced students who have specific needs.[4]

One simple technique that indicates how much one variable is related to another is statistical correlation. A **correlation coefficient** is a statistical measure of association or covariation between two variables. **Covariance** is the extent to which a change in one variable corresponds systematically to a change in another. Statistically speaking, correlation is a standardized representation of covariance.

Several different correlation statistics exist based on the measurement level of the variables. Relationships between continuous variables are represented by the Pearson product-moment correlation. A Spearman correlation is more appropriate for ordinal level data. The researcher should be familiar with these terms as software packages often will provide options. Here, we focus on the Pearson product-moment correlation coefficient when a correlation statistic is used unless specified otherwise.

A statistical correlation coefficient, *r*, can only take on values between −1.0 and +1.0. If the value of *r* equals +1.0, a perfect positive relationship exists. Perhaps the two variables are one and the same! If the value of *r* equals −1.0, a perfect negative relationship exists. The implication is that one variable is a mirror image of the other. As one goes up, the other goes down in proportion and vice versa. No correlation is indicated if *r* equals 0. This means as one variable goes up, the other is as likely to go up as it is down or it may even remain unchanged. Knowing the value of one

measure of association

A general term that refers to a number of bivariate statistical techniques used to measure the strength of a relationship between two variables.

correlation coefficient

A statistical measure of the covariation, or association, between two at-least interval variables.

covariance

Extent to which two variables are associated systematically with each other.

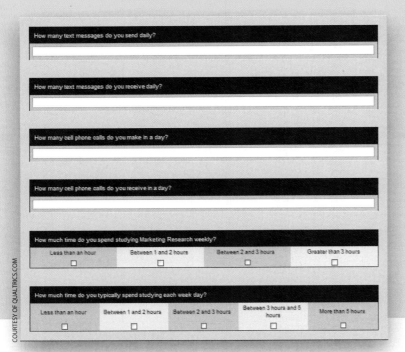

How many text messages does a typical student send? This is a question that can be addressed with correlation or simple regression analysis. Use number of text messages sent and one other variable of your choice to explore this issue. Use a variable that is better than ordinal. Conduct both a correlation analysis and a simple regression analysis. Interpret the results and draw an appropriate conclusion.

© GEORGE DOYLE

COURTESY OF QUALTRICS.COM

EXHIBIT 23.1

Bivariate Analysis— Common Procedures for Testing Association

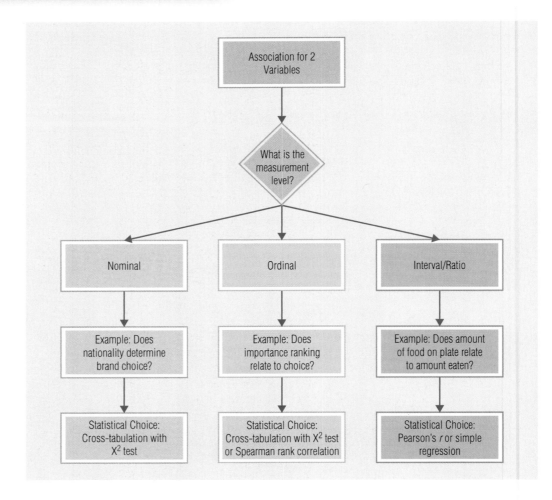

variable says nothing reliable about the value of another. A correlation coefficient indicates both the magnitude of the linear relationship and the direction of that relationship. For example, if we find that $r = -0.85$, we know we have a very strong inverse relationship—that is, the greater the value measured by variable X, the lower the value measured by variable Y.

The formula for calculating the correlation coefficient for two variables X and Y is as follows:

$$r_{xy} = r_{yx} = \frac{\sum_{i=1}^{n}(X_i - \overline{X})(Y_i - \overline{Y})}{\sqrt{\sum_{i=1}^{n}(X_i - \overline{X})^2 \sum_{i=1}^{n}(Y_i - \overline{Y})^2}}$$

where the symbols $\overline{X}$ and $\overline{Y}$ represent the sample averages of X and Y, respectively. An alternative way to express the correlation formula is:

$$r_{xy} = r_{yx} = \frac{\sigma_{xy}}{\sqrt{\sigma_x^2 \sigma_y^2}}$$

where

σ_x^2 = variance of X

σ_y^2 = variance of Y

σ_{xy} = covariance of X and Y

with

$$\sigma_{xy} = \frac{\sum_{i=1}^{n}(X_i - \overline{X})(Y_i - \overline{Y})}{n}$$

If associated values of X_i and Y_i differ from their means in the same direction, their covariance will be positive. If the values of X_i and Y_i tend to deviate in opposite directions, their covariance will be negative.

As mentioned above, a correlation coefficient is a standardized measure of covariance. Covariance coefficients retain information about the absolute scale ranges. Thus, large values tend to produce larger numbers and in this sense, more information is available. A covariance representing distance in millimeters will be much larger than a covariance representing the same distance in kilometers. In this sense, covariance coefficients are advantageous compared with correlation coefficients. However, this same characteristic means that covariance coefficients only can be compared to one another when all measures use the same numeric scale. Thus, researchers find the correlation coefficient typically more useful because they can compare two correlations without regard for the amount of variance exhibited by each variable separately.

Exhibit 23.2 on the next page illustrates the degree of correlation associated with various scatter diagrams each representing a different set of data. Each diagram shows a second set of axes that reorient the data around the mean of X and the mean of Y. So, each observation is represented not only by its raw values but also by the deviations from each mean. We can easily see from the equations above that the sum of the deviations from the variable means is an important determinant in calculating covariance and correlation:

$$\sum_{i=1}^{n}(X_i - \overline{X})(Y_i - \overline{Y})$$

Notice that in the no correlation condition the observations are scattered rather evenly about the space. A correlation of zero happens when positive cross-products of deviations are canceled out by an approximately equal number of negative cross-products of deviations. Sum these deviations up and something around 0 results. In contrast, when correlations are strong and positive, the observations are scattered mostly in quadrants II and IV where the cross-products of the deviations are positive. So, the sum of the cross-products of the deviations adds up to some positive total. If correlation was strong and negative, the observations would lie mostly in quadrants I and III where the sum of the cross-products of the deviations would add up to some negative total. These plots provide an intuitive and accurate way of understanding exactly what underlies statistics like covariance, correlation, and regression coefficients.

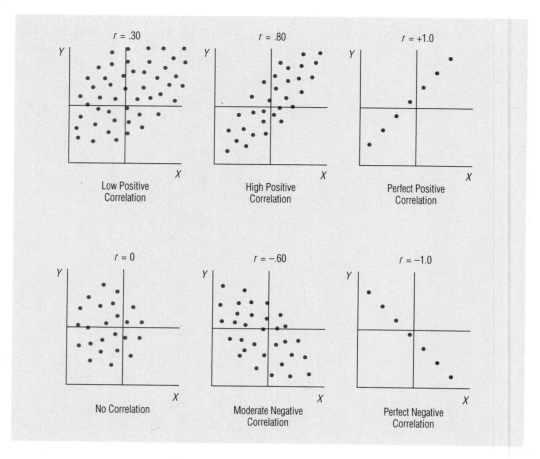

An Example Correlation

The correlation coefficient can be illustrated with a simple example. Today, researchers do not need to calculate correlation manually. However, the calculation process helps illustrate exactly what is meant by correlation and covariance. Consider an investigation made to determine whether the average number of hours worked in manufacturing industries is related to unemployment. A correlation analysis of the data is carried out in Exhibit 23.3.

The correlation between the two variables is −0.635, indicating a **negative (inverse) relationship**. When number of hours goes up, unemployment comes down. This makes intuitive sense. If factories are increasing output, regular workers will typically work more overtime and new employees will be hired (reducing the unemployment rate). Both variables are probably related to overall economic conditions.

**negative (inverse)
relationship**

Covariation in which the association between variables is in the opposite direction. As one goes up, the other goes down.

Correlation, Covariance, and Causation

TO THE POINT

Statistics are like a bikini. What they reveal is suggestive, but what they conceal is vital.

—Aaron Levenstein

Recall from Chapter 3 that concomitant variation is one condition needed to establish a causal relationship between two variables. When two variables covary, they display concomitant variation. This systematic covariation does not in and of itself establish causality. Remember that the relationship would also need to be nonspurious and that any hypothesized "cause" would have to occur before any subsequent effect. Work experience typically displays a significant correlation with job performance.[5] However, in a retail context, workers with more experience often get assigned to newer stores. Thus, the researcher would need to sort out to what extent age of the store may also be responsible for *causing* store performance.

EXHIBIT 23.3 **Correlation Analysis of Number of Hours Worked in Manufacturing Industries with Unemployment Rate**

Unemployment Rate (X_i)	Number of Hours Worked (Y_i)	$X_i - \bar{X}$	$(X_i - \bar{X})^2$	$Y_i - \bar{Y}$	$(Y_i - \bar{Y})^2$	$(X_i - \bar{X})(Y_i - \bar{Y})$
5.5	39.6	.51	.2601	−.71	.5041	−.3621
4.4	40.7	−.59	.3481	.39	.1521	−.2301
4.1	40.4	−.89	.7921	.09	.0081	−.0801
4.3	39.8	−.69	.4761	−.51	.2601	.3519
6.8	39.2	1.81	3.2761	−1.11	1.2321	−2.0091
5.5	40.3	.51	.2601	−.01	.0001	−.0051
5.5	39.7	.51	.2601	−.61	.3721	−.3111
6.7	39.8	1.71	2.9241	−.51	.2601	−.8721
5.5	40.4	.51	.2601	.09	.0081	.0459
5.7	40.5	.71	.5041	.19	.0361	.1349
5.2	40.7	.21	.0441	.39	.1521	.0819
4.5	41.2	−.49	.2401	.89	.7921	−.4361
3.8	41.3	−1.19	1.4161	.99	.9801	−1.1781
3.8	40.6	−1.19	1.4161	.29	.0841	−.3451
3.6	40.7	−1.39	1.9321	.39	.1521	−.5421
3.5	40.6	−1.49	2.2201	.29	.0841	−.4321
4.9	39.8	−.09	.0081	−.51	.2601	.0459
5.9	39.9	.91	.8281	−.41	.1681	−.3731
5.6	40.6	.61	.3721	.29	.0841	.1769

$$\bar{X} = 4.99$$

$$\bar{Y} = 40.31$$

$$\sum (X_i - \bar{X})^2 = 17.8379$$

$$\sum (Y_i - \bar{Y})^2 = 5.5899$$

$$\sum (X_i - \bar{X})(Y_i - \bar{Y}) = -6.3389$$

$$r = \frac{\sum (X_i - \bar{X})(Y_i - \bar{Y})}{\sqrt{\sum (X_i - \bar{X})^2 \sum (Y_i - \bar{Y})^2}} = \frac{-6.3389}{\sqrt{(17.8379)(5.5899)}} = \frac{-6.3389}{\sqrt{99.712}} = -.635$$

Coefficient of Determination

If we wish to know the proportion of *variance* in Y that is explained by X (or vice versa), we can calculate the **coefficient of determination (R^2)** by squaring the correlation coefficient:

$$R^2 = \frac{\text{Explained variance}}{\text{Total variance}}$$

coefficient of determination (R^2)

A measure obtained by squaring the correlation coefficient; the proportion of the total variance of a variable accounted for by another value of another variable.

The coefficient of determination, R^2, measures that part of the total variance of Y that is accounted for by knowing the value of X. In the example about unemployment and hours worked, $r = -0.635$; therefore, $R^2 = 0.403$. About 40 percent of the variance in unemployment can be explained by the variance in hours worked, and vice versa. As can be seen, R-*squared* really is just r squared!

Correlation Matrix

correlation matrix

The standard form for reporting correlation coefficients for more than two variables.

A **correlation matrix** is the standard form for reporting observed correlations among multiple variables. Although any number of variables can be displayed in a correlation matrix, each entry represents the bivariate relationship between a pair of variables. Exhibit 23.4 shows a correlation matrix that relates some measures of salesperson job performance to characteristics of the sales force.[6]

EXHIBIT 23.4 Pearson Product-Moment Correlation Matrix for Salesperson Example[a]

Variables	S	JS	GE	SE	OD	VI	JT	RA	TP	WL
Performance (S)	1.00									
Job satisfaction (JS)	.45[b]	1.00								
Generalized self-esteem (GE)	.31[b]	.10	1.00							
Specific self-esteem (SE)	.61[b]	.28[b]	.36[b]	1.00						
Other-directedness (OD)	.05	−.03	−.44[b]	−.24[c]	1.00					
Verbal intelligence (VI)	−.36[b]	−.13	−.14	−.11	−.18[d]	1.00				
Job-related tension (JT)	−.48[b]	−.56[b]	−.32[b]	−.34[b]	.26[b]	−.02	1.00			
Role ambiguity (RA)	−.26[c]	−.24[c]	−.32[b]	−.39[b]	.38[b]	−.05	−.44[b]	1.00		
Territory potential (TP)	.49[b]	.31[b]	.04	.29[b]	.09	−.09	−.38[b]	−.26[b]	1.00	
Workload (WL)	.45[b]	.11	.29[c]	.29[c]	−.04	−.12	−.27[c]	−.22[d]	.49[b]	1.00

[a]Numbers below the diagonal are for the sample; those above the diagonal are omitted.
[b]$p < .001$.
[c]$p < .01$.
[d]$p < .05$.

Note that the main diagonal consists of correlations of 1.00. Why is this? Simply put, any variable is correlated with itself perfectly. Had this been a covariance matrix, the diagonal would display the variance for any given variable.

Performance (S) was measured by identifying the salesperson's actual annual sales volume in dollars. Notice that the performance variable has a 0.45 correlation with the workload variable (WL), which was measured by recording the number of accounts in a sales territory. Notice also that the salesperson's perception of job-related tension (JT) as measured by an attitude scale has a −0.48 correlation with performance (S). Thus, when perceived job tension is high, performance is low.

Researchers are also concerned with statistical significance. The procedure for determining statistical significance is the t-test of the significance of a correlation coefficient. Typically it is hypothesized that $r = 0$, and then a t-test is performed. The logic behind the test is similar to that for the significance tests already considered. Statistical programs usually indicate the p-value associated with each correlation and/or star significant correlations using asterisks. The Research Snapshot on the next page displays the way correlation matrices are often reported.

What Makes Someone Attractive?

What are the things that make someone attractive? Many people are interested in this question. Among these are companies that hire people to sell fashion. The correlation matrix below was computed with SPSS. The correlations show how different characteristics relate to each other. Variables include a measure of fit, meaning how well the person matches a fashion retail concept, attractiveness, weight (how overweight someone appears), age, manner of dress (how modern), and personality (warm–cold). Thus, a sample of consumers rated a model shown in a photograph on those characteristics. The results reveal the following:

Correlations

		Fit	Attract	Weight	Age	Modern	Cold
Fit	Pearson Correlation	1	0.831**	−0.267*	0.108	−0.447**	−0.583**
	Sig. (2-tailed)		0.000	0.036	0.404	0.000	0.000
	N	62	62	62	62	62	62
Attract	Pearson Correlation	0.831**	1	−0.275*	0.039	−0.428**	−0.610**
	Sig. (2-tailed)	0.000		0.030	0.766	0.001	0.000
	N	62	62	62	62	62	62
Weight	Pearson Correlation	−0.267*	−0.275*	1	0.082	0.262*	0.058
	Sig. (2-tailed)	0.036	0.030		0.528	0.040	0.653
	N	62	62	62	62	62	62
Age	Pearson Correlation	0.108	0.039	0.082	1	−0.019	0.104
	Sig. (2-tailed)	0.404	0.766	0.528		0.882	0.423
	N	62	62	62	62	62	62
Modern	Pearson Correlation	−0.447**	−0.428**	0.262*	−0.019	1	0.603**
	Sig. (2-tailed)	0.000	0.001	0.040	0.882		0.000
	N	62	62	62	62	62	62
Cold	Pearson Correlation	−0.583**	−0.610**	0.058	0.104	0.603**	1
	Sig. (2-tailed)	0.000	0.000	0.653	0.423	0.000	
	N	62	62	62	62	62	62

*Correlation is significant at the 0.05 level (2-tailed).

**Correlation is significant at the 0.01 level (2-tailed)

Thus, if the model seems to "fit" the store concept, she seems attractive. If she is too big, she is seen as less attractive. Age is unrelated to attractiveness or fit. Modern dress style and coldness of personality also are associated with lower attractiveness. Using these correlations, a retailer can help determine what employees should look like!

Correlations can be found using SPSS by navigating as shown:

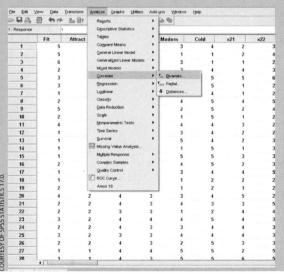

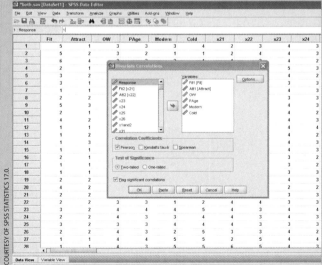

Simple (Bivariate) Regression Analysis

Regression analysis is another technique for measuring the linear association between a dependent and an independent variable. Although simple regression and correlation are mathematically equivalent in most respects, regression is a dependence technique where correlation is an interdependence technique. We'll discuss these terms at more length in the next chapter; however, at this point recognize that a dependence technique draws a distinction between dependent and independent variables. An interdependence technique does not make this distinction and simply is concerned with how variables relate to one another. So, dependence techniques imply causality whether or not all conditions for causality are met.

Thus, with simple regression, a dependent (or criterion) variable, Y, is linked to an independent (or predictor) variable, X. Regression analysis attempts to predict the values of a continuous, interval-scaled dependent variable from specific values of the independent variable.

The Regression Equation

simple (bivariate) linear regression

A measure of linear association that investigates straight-line relationships between a continuous dependent variable and an independent variable that is usually continuous, but can be a categorical dummy variable.

The discussion here concerns **simple (bivariate) linear regression**. Simple regression investigates a *straight-line relationship* of the type

$$Y = \alpha + \beta X,$$

where Y is a continuous dependent variable and X is an independent variable that is usually continuous, although dichotomous nominal or ordinal variables can be included in the form of a dummy variable. Alpha (α) and beta (β) are two parameters that must be estimated so that the equation best represents a given set of data. These two parameters determine the height of the regression line and the angle of the line relative to horizontal. When these parameters change, the line changes. Regression techniques have the job of estimating values for these parameters that make the line *fit* the observations the best.

The result is simply a linear equation, or the equation for a line, just as in basic algebra! α represents the Y intercept (where the line crosses the y-axis) and β is the slope coefficient. The slope is the change in Y associated with a change of one unit in X. Slope may also be thought of as rise over run. That is, how much Y rises (or falls if negative) for every one unit change in the X-axis.

Parameter Estimate Choices

The estimates for α and β are the key to regression analysis. In most business research, the estimate of β is most important. The explanatory power of regression rests with β because this is where the direction and strength of the relationship between the independent and dependent variable is explained.

A Y-intercept term is sometimes referred to as a constant because α represents a fixed point. An estimated slope coefficient is sometimes referred to as a regression weight, regression coefficient, parameter estimate, or sometimes even as a *path* estimate. The term path estimate is a descriptive term adapted because of the way hypothesized causal relationships are often represented in diagrams:

$$\boxed{X} \xrightarrow{\beta_1} \boxed{Y}$$

For all practical purposes, these terms are used interchangeably.

Parameter estimates can be presented in either raw or standardized form. One potential problem with raw parameter estimates is due to the fact that, like covariance values, they reflect the measurement scale range. So, if a simple regression involved distance measured with miles, very small parameter estimates may indicate a strong relationship. In contrast, if the very same distance is measured with centimeters, a very large parameter estimate would be needed to indicate a strong relationship.

Exhibit 23.5 provides an illustration. Suppose a researcher was interested in how much space was allocated to a specific snack food on a shelf and how it related to sales. Fifteen observations are taken from 15 different stores. The blue line represents a typical distance showing shelf space measured in cm. The green line is the same distance shown in miles. The top frame shows hypothetical regression results if the independent variable is measured in centimeters. The bottom frame shows

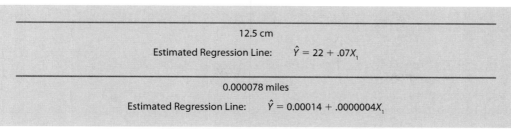

EXHIBIT 23.5
The Disadvantage of Unstandardized Regression Weights

the very same regression results if the independent variable is measured in miles. Even though these two regression lines are the same, the parameter coefficients do not seem comparable. Actually though, both equations are equivalent ways of expressing the exact same information.

Researchers often explain regression results by referring to a **standardized regression coefficient** (β). A standardized regression coefficient, like a correlation coefficient, provides a common metric allowing regression results to be compared to one another no matter what the original scale range may have been. Due to the mathematics involved in standardization, the standardized Y-intercept term is always 0.[7] The estimated regression line for the shelf space example would then become:

$$\hat{Y} = 0 + 0.16X_1$$

Even if the distance measures for the 15 observations were converted to some other metric (feet, meters, and so on), the standardized regression weight would still be 0.16.

Researchers use shorthand to label regression coefficients as either "raw" or "standardized." The most common shorthand is as follows:

- $\mathbf{B}_0$ or $\mathbf{b}_0$ = raw (unstandardized) Y-intercept term; what was referred to as α above.
- $\mathbf{B}_1$ or $\mathbf{b}_1$ = raw regression coefficient or estimate.
- $\boldsymbol{\beta}_1$ = standardized regression coefficients.

■ RAW REGRESSION ESTIMATES (b_1)

Raw regression weights have the advantage of retaining the scale metric—which is also their key disadvantage. Where should the researcher focus then? Should the standardized or unstandardized coefficients be interpreted? The answer to this question is fairly simple.

- If the purpose of the regression analysis is forecasting, then raw parameter estimates must be used. This is another way of saying that the researcher's primary interest is in prediction.

Thus, when the researcher above wants to predict how much product will be sold based on the amount of shelf space, raw regression coefficients must be used. The forecast for 14 cm of shelf space can be found as follows:

$$\hat{Y} = 22 + 0.07(14) = 23.0$$

The same result can be found by using the equation representing the distance in miles. Regression is often used for forecasting but regression forecast that involve values of the independent variable that are quite different from those included in the analysis can be unreliable. Here, if no values for X above 30 cm were involved, the researcher would only forecast values for $X = 75$ with great caution.

■ STANDARDIZED REGRESSION ESTIMATES

Standardized regression estimates have the advantage of a constant scale. No matter what range of values the independent variables take on, β will not be affected. When should standardized regression estimates be used?

- Standardized regression estimates should be used when the researcher is testing explanatory hypotheses; in other words, when the purpose of the research is more explanation than prediction.

In this case, the researcher can use the regression result indicating a β of 0.16 to support a positive relationship between shelf-space and sales. The 0.16 might later be compared to other relationships in building an explanation of product sales. Like the correlation coefficient, β's plausible range is from -1.00 to $+1.00$. Occasionally, a user will find a result indicating a β lying outside

standardized regression coefficient (β)

The estimated coefficient indicating the strength of relationship between an independent variable and dependent variable expressed on a standardized scale where higher absolute values indicate stronger relationships (range is from -1 to 1).

these values. Such a finding should serve as a red flag indicating other potential problems with the data (more on this next chapter).

Visual Estimation of a Simple Regression Model

As mentioned above, simple regression involves finding a best-fit line given a set of observations plotted in two-dimensional space. Many ways exist to estimate where this line should go. Estimation techniques involve terms such as instrumental variables, maximum likelihood, visual estimation, and ordinary least squares (OLS). We focus on the latter two in this text.

Suppose a researcher is interested in forecasting sales for a construction distributor (wholesaler) in Florida. The distributor believes a reasonable association exists between sales and building permits issued by counties. Using bivariate linear regression on the data in Exhibit 23.6, the researcher will be able to explain sales potential (Y) in various counties based on the number of building permits (X).

EXHIBIT 23.6

Relationship of Sales Potential to Building Permits Issued

Dealer	Y Dealer's Sales Volume (Thousands)	X Building Permits
1	77	86
2	79	93
3	80	95
4	83	104
5	101	139
6	117	180
7	129	165
8	120	147
9	97	119
10	106	132
11	99	126
12	121	156
13	103	129
14	86	96
15	99	108

The data are plotted in a scatter diagram in Exhibit 23.7. In the diagram the vertical axis indicates the value of the dependent variable, Y, and the horizontal axis indicates the value of the independent variable, X. Each single point in the diagram represents an observation of X and Y at a given point in time. The values are simply points in a Cartesian plane.

One way to determine the relationship between X and Y is to simply visually draw the best-fit straight line through the points in the figure. That is, try to draw a line that goes through the center of the plot of points. If the points are thought of as bowling pins, the best-fit line can be thought of as the path that would on average knock over the most bowling pins. For any given value of the independent variable, a prediction can be made by selecting the dependent variable that goes along with that value. For example, if we want to forecast sales if building permits are 150, we simply follow the dotted green lines shown in the exhibit to yield a prediction of about 112. The better one can estimate where the best-fit line should be, the less will be the error in prediction.

■ ERRORS IN PREDICTION

Any method of drawing a line can be used to perform regression. However, some methods will obviously have more error than others. Consider our bowling ball line above. One person may be better at guessing where the best-fit line, meaning the one that would knock over the most pins, should go. We would know who was better by determining the total error of prediction.

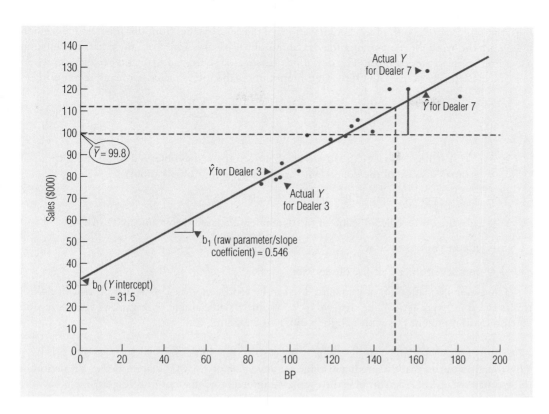

EXHIBIT 23.7
The Best-Fit Line or Knocking Out the Pins

Let's consider error by first thinking about what value of sales would be the best guess if we had no information about any other variable. In that case, our univariate best guess would be the mean sales of 99.8. If the green spot corresponding to 156 building permits ($X = 156$) were predicted with the mean, the resulting error in prediction would be represented by the distance of the blue and red vertical line.

Once information about the independent variable is provided, we can then use the prediction provided by the best-fit line. In this case, our best-fit line is the "bowling ball" line shown in the exhibit. The error in prediction using this line would be indicated by the red vertical line extending from the regression line to the actual observation. Thus, it appears that at least for this observation, our prediction using the regression line has reduced the error in prediction that would result from guessing with the mean. Statistically, this is the goal of regression analysis. We would like an estimation technique that would place our line so that the total sum of all errors over all observations is minimized. In other words, no line fits better. Although with good guess work, visual estimation may prove somewhat accurate, perhaps there is a more certain way.

Ordinary Least-Squares Method of Regression Analysis (OLS)

The researcher's task is to find the best means for fitting a straight line to the data. OLS is a relatively straightforward mathematical technique that guarantees that the resulting straight line will produce the least possible total error in using X to predict Y. The logic is based on how much better a regression line can predict values of Y compared to simply using the mean as a prediction for all observations no matter what the value of X may be.

Using Squared Deviations

Unless the dependent and independent variables are perfectly related, no straight line can connect all observations. More technically, the procedure used in the least-squares method generates a straight line that minimizes the sum of squared deviations of the actual values from this predicted regression line. With the symbol e representing the deviations of the observations from the regression line, no other line can produce less error. The deviations are squared so that positive and negative misses do not cancel each other out. The OLS criterion minimizes the total squared error of prediction:

$$sum\ of\ squared\ errors = SSE = \sum_{i=1}^{n} e_i^2$$

where

$e_i = Y_i - \hat{Y}_i$ (the residual = the difference between the actual observed value and the estimated value of the dependent variable for any of i observations)

Y_i = actual observed value of the dependent variable

$\hat{Y}_i$ = estimated or predicted value of the dependent variable (pronounced "Y-hat")

n = number of observations

i = number of the particular observation

The general equation for any straight line can be represented as $Y = b_0 + b_1 X$. If we think of this as the true hypothetical line that we try to estimate with sample observations, the regression equation will represent this with a slightly different equation:

$$Y_i = b_0 + b_1 X_1 + e_i$$

The equation means that the predicted value for any value of X (X_i) is determined as a function of the estimated slope coefficient, plus the estimated intercept coefficient + some error.

The raw parameter estimates can be found using the following formulas:

$$b_1 = \frac{n(\Sigma X_i Y_i) - (\Sigma X_i)(\Sigma Y_i)}{n(\Sigma X_i^2)(\Sigma X_i)^2}$$

and

$$b_0 = \overline{Y} - b_1 \overline{X}$$

where

Y_i = ith observed value of the dependent variable

X_i = ith observed value of the independent variable

$\overline{Y}$ = mean of the dependent variable

X = independent variable

$\overline{X}$ = mean of the independent variable

n = number of observations

b_0 = intercept estimate

b_1 = slope estimate (regression weight)

The careful reader may notice some similarity between the correlation calculation and the equation for b_1. In fact, the standardized regression coefficient from a simple regression equals the Pearson correlation coefficient for the two variables. Once the estimates are obtained, a predicted value for the dependent variable can be found for any value of X_i with this equation:

$$\hat{Y}_i = b_0 + b_i X_i$$

Appendix 23A demonstrates the arithmetic necessary to calculate the parameter estimates.

■ STATISTICAL SIGNIFICANCE OF REGRESSION MODEL

As with ANOVA, the researcher needs a way of testing the statistical significance of the regression model. Also like ANOVA, an F-test provides the answer to this question.

The overall F-test for regression can be illustrated with Exhibit 23.7. Once again examine the multicolored line showing the predicted value for $X = 156$.

1. The total line including the blue and red line represents the *total deviation* of the observation from the mean:

$$Y_i - \overline{Y}$$

2. The blue portion represents how much of the total deviation is *explained* by the *regression* line:

$$\hat{Y}_i - \overline{Y}$$

3. The red portion represents how much of the total deviation is not explained by the regression line (also equal to e_i):

$$Y_i - \hat{Y}_i$$

These three components are mathematically related because the total deviation is a sum of what is explained by the regression line and what is not explained by the regression line. This can be expressed mathematically as

$$(Y_i - \overline{Y}) = (\hat{Y}_i - \overline{Y}) + (Y_i - \hat{Y}_i)$$

	Deviation	Deviation
Total	explained by	unexplained by
deviation =	the regression +	the regression
(SST)	(SSR)	(SSE)

Just as in ANOVA, the total deviation represents the total variation to be explained. Thus, the partitioning of the variation into components allows us to form a ratio of the explained variation versus the unexplained variation. The corresponding abbreviation for this partitioning is

$$SST = SSR + SSE$$

An **F-test (regression)**, or an *analysis of variance,* can be applied to a regression to test the relative magnitudes of the SSR (Sums of Squares—Regression) and SSE (Sums of Squared Errors) with their appropriate degrees of freedom. The equation for the F-test is

$$F_{(k-1)(n-k)} = \frac{SSR/(k-1)}{SSE/(n-k)} = \frac{MSR}{MSE}$$

where,

MSR is an abbreviation for Mean Squared Regression

MSE is an abbreviation for Mean Squared Error

k is the number of independent variables (always 1 for simple regression)

n is the sample size

Once again, researchers today don't need to and do not calculate this statistic by hand. Regression programs will produce an "ANOVA" table, which will provide the F-value and a p-value (significance level), and will generally show the partitioned variation in some form. For the sales example, the following table is obtained:

F-test (regression)

A procedure to determine whether more variability is explained by the regression or unexplained by the regression.

ANOVA

	df	SS	MS	F	p-value
Regression (SSR)	1	3398.48911	3398.489	91.29854	0.0000003
Residual (SSE)	13	483.910892	37.22391		
Total	14	3882.4			

Thus, building permits explains a significant portion of the variation in sales as evidenced by the very low p-value.

■ R^2

The *coefficient of determination*, R^2, reflects the proportion of variance explained by the regression line. In this example, R^2 can be found with this formula:

$$R^2 = \frac{SSR}{SST} = \frac{3398.5}{3882.4} = 0.875$$

The coefficient of determination may be interpreted to mean that 87.5 percent of the variation in sales is explained by the independent variable building permits.

What is an "acceptable" R^2 value? This question is asked frequently. However, guidelines for R^2 values are neither simple nor straightforward. Indeed, good and bad values for the coefficient of determination depend on so many factors that a single precise guideline is considered inappropriate. The focus should be on the F-test. However, in practice, do not expect to often see a simple regression result with an R^2 anywhere near 0.875. They will normally be considerably lower.[8]

Testing Hypotheses Using Regression Output

Researchers use regression output to test hypotheses. In particular, relational hypotheses lend themselves well to regression analysis. Exhibit 23.8 displays output for the building permit problem. Most computerized software provides similar output for regression analysis. Interpreting simple regression output is a simple two-step process.

1. Interpret the overall significance of the model.
    a. The output will include the "model F" and a significance value. When the model F is significant (low p-value), the independent variable explains a significant portion of the variation in the dependent variable. In this case, the model F of 91.3 with 1 and 13 degrees of freedom is significant as shown by the significance level (p-value) of 0.000 (which means the actual value is less than 0.001). If the model F were not significant, no hypothesis stating a relationship could be supported and no further interpretation is needed.
    b. The coefficient of determination or R^2 can be interpreted. As mentioned earlier, this is the percentage of total variation in the dependent variable accounted for by the independent variable. Another way to think of this is as the extent to which the variances of the independent and dependent variable overlap. Here, the model R^2 of 0.875 indicates a substantial portion of variance is explained.

EXHIBIT 23.8
Simple Regression Results for Building Permit Example

R	R Square	Adjusted R Square	Std. Error of the Estimate
.936[a]	.875	.866	6.10114

a Predictors: (Constant), Permits

ANOVA[b]

	Sum of Squares	df	MeanSquare	F	Sig.
Regression	3398.489	1	3398.489	91.299	.000[a]
Residual	483.911	13	37.224		
Total	3882.400	14			

a Predictors: (Constant), Permits
b Dependent Variable: Sales

1. Is model significant?

2. Interpret parameter estimates?

Coefficients[a]

Model	Unstandardized Coefficients: B	Std. Error	Standardized Coefficient: Beta (β)	t	Sig.
1.000 (Constant)	31.502	7.319		4.304	0.001
Permits	0.546	0.057	0.936	9.555	0.000

a Dependent Variable: Sales

2. The individual parameter coefficient is interpreted.

a. The *t*-value associated with the slope coefficient can be interpreted. In this case, the *t* of 9.555 is associated with a very low p-value (0.000 to 3 decimal places). Therefore, the slope coefficient is significant. For simple regression, the p-value for the model *F* and for the *t*-test of the individual regression weight will be the same. This result would support a hypothesis stating that permits are positively related to sales.

b. A *t*-test for the intercept term (constant) is also provided. However, this is seldom of interest since the explanatory power rests in the slope coefficient.

c. If a need to forecast sales exists, the estimated regression equation is needed. Using the raw coefficients, the estimated regression line is

$$\hat{Y} = 31.502 + 0.546X$$

d. The regression coefficient (slope) indicates that for every building permit issued, sales increase 0.546. Moreover, the standardized regression coefficient of 0.936 would allow the researcher to compare the explanatory power of building permits versus some other potential independent variable. For simple regression, β_1 equals *r*.

Once these steps are completed, the basic simple regression analysis is complete and any hypothesis stating a linear relationship has been tested.

Plotting the OLS Regression Line

To draw a regression line on the scatter diagram, only two predicted values of *Y* need to be plotted. The data for two dealers is used to illustrate how this is done:

$$\text{Dealer 7 (actual Y value = 129): } \hat{Y}_7 = 31.5 + 0.546(165)$$
$$= 121.6$$

$$\text{Dealer 3 (actual Y value = 80): } \hat{Y}_3 = 31.5 + 0.546(95)$$
$$= 83.4$$

Using the data for dealer 7 and dealer 3, we can draw a straight line connecting the points 121.6 and 83.4. Exhibit 23.9 shows the regression line.

EXHIBIT 23.9
OLS Regression Line

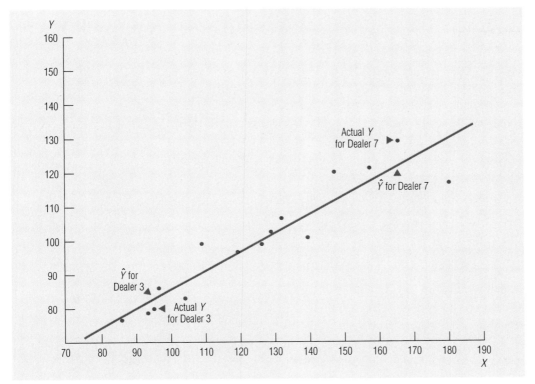

Size and Weight

America seems obsessed with weight control. Thin seems to stay in and the fight to get thin is a multibillion dollar business. Recall in an earlier Research Snapshot correlations between factors related to attractiveness were discussed. What if the following hypothesis were tested?

H1: Perceptions that a female model is over-weight are related negatively to perceptions of attractiveness.

Using the scales from the earlier Snapshot, this can be tested with a simple regression. The results can be summarized as shown here:

Model		Sum of Squares	d.f.	Mean Square	F	Sig.
1	Regression	9.228	1	9.227	4.914	0.030
	Residual	112.660	60	1.877		
	Total	121.8870968	61			

Model		Unstandardized Coefficients B	Std. Error	Standardized Coefficients β	t	Sig.
1	(Constant)	4.413	0.952		4.636	0.00002
	x113	−0.582	0.262	−0.275	−2.216	0.030

The results support the hypothesis. The $\beta = -0.275$ is both in the expected direction (negative) and significant (p < 0.05). Therefore, if respondents perceived someone as "too big," they likewise saw the person as less attractive.

To determine the error (residual) of any observation, the predicted value of Y is first calculated. The predicted value is then subtracted from the actual value. For example, the actual observation for dealer 9 is 97, and the predicted value is 96.5; thus only a small margin of error, $e = 0.5$, is involved in this regression line:

$$e_9 = Y_9 - \hat{Y}_9$$
$$= 97 - 96.5$$
$$= 0.5$$

where

$$\hat{Y}_9 = 31.5 + 0.546(119)$$

■ STATING HYPOTHESES FOR SIMPLE REGRESSION

The explanatory power of regression lies in hypothesis testing. Regression is often used to test relational hypotheses. For example, from the chapter vignette, simple regression could be used to test the hypothesis relating food quantity to food consumption.

H1: The amount of food eaten during a meal is related positively to the amount of food placed on a plate.

In the sales example, the regression addresses a hypothesis linking permits to sales.

H1: Sales are positively related to the number of building permits.

In the sales example, this particular hypothesis is supported if the following results are found:

1. The regression weight must be in the hypothesized direction. Positive relationships require a positive coefficient and negative relationships require a negative coefficient.
2. The *t*-test associated with the regression weight must be significant.

A word of caution can be offered. Users just learning regression analysis often remember to check the second step and forget to verify step 1. When this happens, the researcher may falsely support

- A correlation coefficient is the most basic way of depicting the extent of a bivariate relationship between two continuous (better than ordinal) variables.
- A correlation matrix is a good way of quickly summarizing the individual bivariate relationships that exist between a set of variables.
- Simple regression also depicts a bivariate relationship but distinguishes an independent variable from a dependent variable.
  - The relationship implies causality.
  - Regression analysis can at best establish evidence only of concomitant variation between the two variables.
- Regression coefficients can either be the actual slope coefficient scaled consistent with the measures used or standardized.
  - Raw slope coefficients (b_1) are most appropriate when:
    - All variables use the same numeric scale, particularly when the dependent variable is a monetary unit and the independent variable is the same monetary unit such as would be the case when predicting the selling price of a product in auction with the initial bid price (\$/\$).
    - The researcher is interested in prediction only, meaning obtaining values of $\overline{Y}_i$.
- Standardized regression coefficients (β_1) are most appropriate when:
  - The researcher needs to compare coefficients with each other.
  - The researcher's emphasis is on explanation as opposed to prediction.
- When a regression returns a β coefficient less than -1.0 or greater than $+1.0$ the researcher should examine the data for some problem.
  - When testing a hypothesis using regression analysis:
    - Check the statistical significance of the t-test for a parameter estimate.
    - Check the sign of the parameter estimate.

a hypothesis as significant based on a p-value below 0.05, but the reality is that the hypothesis is not supported because while the hypothesis stated a positive relationship, the actual result is negative (or vice versa). The Research Snapshot on the previous page illustrates how a hypothesis is tested with simple regression.

Summary

1. Compute and use bivariate correlations. A bivariate correlation is an index that displays how much two variables covary. Another way to think of correlation is as a standardized measure of covariance. When two variables display a correlation of 1.0, they are perfectly correlated. That means that they have no unique variance. In most ways, they are one and the same. When two variables are correlated -1.0 they are perfectly negatively correlated. In this sense, they are mirror images of one another. Thus, correlations can range between -1.0 and 1.0. Correlations near 0 indicate a lack of relationship between two variables.

2. Interpret a correlation matrix. A correlation matrix presents all possible bivariate correlations among a set of variables. The statistical significance of each variable can be tested with a t-test. Low p-values for this test indicate significant correlations. Patterns of strong correlations among variables indicate variables that share variance in common. Correlation matrices can be easily computed using statistical software.

3. Understand simple (bivariate) regression analysis. Simple linear regression investigates a straight-line relationship between one dependent variable and one independent variable. The simple regression results allow a regression equation to be estimated. Key results include parameter estimates for both the slope coefficient of the line and the y-intercept. Additionally, the results also will display how much of the dependent variable's variance is shared in common with this single independent variable.

4. Know the basics of ordinary least-squares estimation. OLS estimation mathematically determines the best-fitting regression line for the observed data. The idea of OLS is to find a line which minimizes the squared distance between the regression line comprising all estimated values of Y and the actual observed values (Y_i). The line determined by this method may be used to forecast values of the dependent variable, given any value for the independent variable. The regression analysis also involves an ANOVA (analysis of variance) table which contains values used in calculating the coefficient of determination (R^2).

5. Know how to test a hypothesis using regression analysis output. Hypotheses stating that a positive or negative relationship exists between an independent and dependent variable can be tested using regression analysis. The researcher should first check for the significance of the overall model using the model F statistic. Next, the researcher should check the estimated results for the parameter coefficient. A t-test is provided for the parameter estimate. In the case of simple regression, the t-test result and overall model F will be the same. However, users should get in the habit of verifying the result using the t-test. When the results are significant, the researcher also needs to be certain that the relationship is in the hypothesized direction before reaching the conclusion that a hypothesis is supported.

Key Terms and Concepts

coefficient of determination (R^2), *595*
correlation coefficient, *591*
correlation matrix, *596*

covariance, *591*
F-test (regression), *603*
negative (inverse) relationship, *594*

measure of association, *591*
simple (bivariate) linear regression, *598*
standardized regression coefficient (β), *599*

Questions for Review and Critical Thinking

1. What is *covariance?*
2. How are covariance and correlation different?
3. What types of variables are involved in correlation analyses?
4. How does a researcher determine if a correlation coefficient is significant?
5. The data below represent two variables. X5 is a respondent's agreement with a statement that says "A college degree is essential to succeed in today's society" and X7 is the same respondent's agreement with a statement that says "Compared to my peers, I have more academic ability."
   a. Compute the correlation between these two variables.
      i. Use at least two different ways of obtaining the correlation (i.e., in SPSS using the click-through sequence shown in the chapter, in SAS using the appropriate program statements (proc corr; var X5 and X7), in Excel using the Data Analysis feature, or some other way including manual calculations).
      ii. What t-value is associated with this correlation? Is the correlation significant? Why or why not?
      iii. Based on the two different ways of computing the correlations, can you say that one is preferable to another? Explain.

X5	X7
1	1
6	3
1	4
3	4
3	6
4	3
1	1
1	2
3	2
4	2
4	1
3	4
4	1
5	2
2	4
2	5
3	5
1	4
1	6
3	6

6. Why can't a correlation be greater than $|1.0|$?
7. What is the difference between a correlation and a covariance coefficient? What is the difference between a raw parameter coefficient and a standardized parameter coefficient?
8. When one thinks about what covariance, correlation, and simple regression really do, one is helped by thinking of the "sum of the deviations from the mean." What patterns are evident among a pair of variables that may help understand the nature of any relationship?
9. Interpret the following data with respect to the nature of the relationships (not the statistical significance):
   a. $\hat{Y} = 5.0 + .30X_1$
      i. Where the dependent variable equals turnover intentions for line managers and the independent variable equals number of employees supervised.
   b. $\hat{Y} = 250 - 4.0X_1$
      i. **'NET** Where the dependent variable is the number of hits on a new banner ad and the independent variable is the number of weeks the ad has run.
10. The following ANOVA summary table is the result of a regression of sales on year of sales. Is the relationship statistically significant at the 0.95 significance level? Fill in the value for Sums of Squares in the SST row. Comment.

Source of Variation	Sum of Squares	d.f.	Mean Square	F-Value	p-value
SSR	605,370,750	1	605,370,750	3.12	0.115
SSE	1,551,381,712	8	193,922,714		
SST		9			

11. Address the following questions about regression analysis:
   a. Define *simple linear regression.*
   b. When is it most appropriate to rely on raw parameter coefficients and when is it most appropriate to rely on standardized parameter coefficients?
   c. Why is the Y-intercept estimate equal to 0 for standardized estimates?
   d. What are the steps in interpreting a regression model?

12. The following table gives a football team's season-ticket sales, percentage of games won, and number of active alumni for the years 1998–2007.

Year	Season-Ticket Sales	Percentage of Games Won	Number of Active Alumni
1998	4,995	40	NA
1999	8,599	54	3,450
2000	8,479	55	3,801
2001	8,419	58	4,000
2002	10,253	63	4,098
2003	12,457	75	6,315
2004	13,285	36	6,860
2005	14,177	27	8,423
2006	15,730	63	9,000
2007	15,805	70	9,500

a. Produce a correlation matrix for the variables. Interpret the correlation between each pair of variables.

b. Estimate a regression model for sales = Percentage of games won.

c. Estimate a regression model for sales = Number of active alumni.

d. If *sales* is the dependent variable, which of the two independent variables do you think explains sales better? Explain.

13. Interpret the correlations among the different forms of consumer installment credit shown in the following table. Each record shows the debt remaining at year end for each credit type for each year.

Debt Outstanding (millions of dollars)

Year	Gas Cards	Travel and Entertainment Cards	Bank Credit Cards	Retail Cards	Total Credit Cards	Total Installment Credit
1	$ 939	$ 61	$ 828	$ 9,400	$ 11,228	$ 79,428
2	1,119	76	1,312	10,200	12,707	87,745
3	1,298	110	2,639	10,900	14,947	98,105
4	1,650	122	3,792	11,500	17,064	102,064
5	1,804	132	4,490	13,925	20,351	111,295
6	1,762	164	5,408	14,763	22,097	127,332
7	1,832	191	6,838	16,395	25,256	147,437
8	1,823	238	8,281	17,933	28,275	156,124
9	1,893	273	9,501	18,002	29,669	164,955
10	1,981	238	11,351	19,052	32,622	185,489
11	2,074	284	14,262	21,082	37,702	216,572

14. A manufacturer of disposable washcloths/wipes told a retailer that sales for this product category closely correlated with sales of disposable diapers. The retailer thought he would check this out for his own sales-forecasting purposes. The researcher says, "Disposable washcloths/wipes sales can go up as sales of disposable diapers also go up. In fact, the diaper sales cause purchases of disposable wipes." What type of evidence is needed in this case? Is the executive's statement worded appropriately?

15. Explain how OLS determines where a regression line should be placed among a plot of observations?

Research Activities

1. **'NET** The Federal Reserve Bank of St. Louis maintains a database called FRED (Federal Reserve Economic Data). Navigate to the FRED database at http://www.stls.frb.org/fred/index.html. Randomly select a five-year period between 1970 and 2000 and then find the correlation between average U.S. employment in retail trade and U.S. employment in wholesale trade. Which statistical test is appropriate?

2. **'NET/ETHICS** Go to http://www.transparency.org. Find the corruption perception indices for 2005. Go to http://www.geert-hofstede.com/hofstede_dimensions.php. Create a data set that includes the corruption perception indices for at least 15 countries and the score for one of the Hofstede cultural value dimensions. Conduct a regression and interpret the relationship between cultural values and corruption perceptions.

Case 23.1 International Operations at CarCare Inc.

CarCare is considering expanding its operations beyond the United States. The company wants to know whether it should target countries with consumers who tend to have a positive attitude toward their current cars. It has gathered data on U.S. and German car owners. The data are included in the "car" data set that can be viewed on the Web site at www.cengage.com/marketing/zikmund (car.sav or car.xls) or available

from your instructor. Using the data, conduct a correlation and simple regression analysis using spending as the dependent variable and attitude toward the current car as the independent variable.

1. Test the hypothesis: Attitude toward one's car is related positively to spending for car-care products.

2. Would you recommend they do more research to identify nations with relatively favorable attitudes toward the cars they own? [Note: This data set was referred to for the first time in Chapter 22.]

APPENDIX 23A
ARITHMETIC
BEHIND OLS

With simple arithmetic we can solve for the parameter estimates using the OLS equations. Here, the data from Exhibit 23.6 are used. The different pieces of the equations are calculated and shown in Exhibit 23A.1. To estimate the relationship between the distributor's sales to a dealer and the number of building permits, we insert values from the table as shown below:

$$b_1 = \frac{n(\Sigma X_i Y_i) - (\Sigma X_i)(\Sigma Y_i)}{n(\Sigma X_i^2) \ (\Sigma X_i)^2}$$

$$b_1 = \frac{15(193,345) - 2,806,875}{15(245,759) - 3,515,625}$$

$$= 0.546$$

$$b_0 = \overline{Y} - b_1 \overline{X}$$

$$= 99.8 - 0.546(125)$$

$$= 31.5$$

EXHIBIT 23A.1 **Least-Squares Computation**

	Y	Y²	X	X²	XY
1	77	5,929	86	7,396	6,622
2	79	6,241	93	8,649	7,347
3	80	6,400	95	9,025	7,600
4	83	6,889	104	10,816	8,632
5	101	10,201	139	19,321	14,039
6	117	13,689	180	32,400	21,060
7	129	16,641	165	27,225	21,285
8	120	14,400	147	21,609	17,640
9	97	9,409	119	14,161	11,543
10	106	11,236	132	17,424	13,992
11	99	9,801	126	15,876	12,474
12	121	14,641	156	24,336	18,876
13	103	10,609	129	16,641	13,287
14	86	7,396	96	9,216	8,256
15	99	9,801	108	11,664	10,692
	$\Sigma Y = 1,497$ $\overline{Y} = 99.8$	$\Sigma Y^2 = 153,283$	$\Sigma X = 1,875$ $\overline{X} = 125$	$\Sigma X^2 = 245,759$	$\Sigma XY = 193,345$

The formula $\hat{Y}_1 = 31.5 + 0.546X_1$ is the regression equation used for the prediction of the dependent variable. Suppose the wholesaler is considering opening a new dealership in an area where the number of building permits equals 89. We would need to compute a predicted value for $X = 89$. Sales in this area may be forecasted as

$$\hat{Y} = 31.5 + 0.546(X)$$
$$= 31.5 + 0.546(89)$$
$$= 31.5 + 48.6$$
$$= 80.1$$

Thus, the distributor may expect sales of 80.1 (or $80,100) in this new area.

Calculation of the correlation coefficient gives an indication of how accurate the predictions are. In this example the correlation coefficient is $r = 0.94$ and the coefficient of determination is $R^2 = 0.88$.

CHAPTER 24
INTRODUCING MULTIVARIATE DATA ANALYSIS

After studying this chapter, you should be able to

1. Understand what multivariate data analysis involves and know the two basic types of multivariate analysis
2. Interpret results from multiple regression analysis
3. Interpret results from multivariate analysis of variance (MANOVA)
4. Know what multiple discriminant analysis can be used to do
5. Interpret basic exploratory factor analysis results
6. Understand how cluster analysis can identify market segments

Chapter Vignette: Bringing 'em Back!

Marketing managers in practically every industry everywhere in the world are interested in bringing 'em back! What does that mean? Well, they want to bring customers back. Managers recognize that getting a current customer to return for more business is almost always far cheaper than getting that same business from a new customer. However, how to bring customers back is a complex question involving many possible variables.

Imagine all the possible factors that could possibly influence how likely a customer is to return and do business with the same hotel chain or the same resort property. Researchers are interested in the answers to many different questions:

- What role does service play in affecting whether a customer returns?
- How does the customer define service quality?
- Is personalization a key component of service quality?
- What are the key attributes that lead to high customer satisfaction?
- Are the emotions that a customer experiences during a stay important value drivers?
- What are the key emotions?
- How does the customer define value? Is value driven more by tangible characteristics like the availability of breakfast or more experiential characteristics like comfortable beds and ambiance?
- What are the market segments in the industry and which segments are most likely to repeat their purchase behavior over again?

Questions like these can be addressed with multivariate statistical procedures. Although the term may sound complicated, one advantage of multivariate procedures is that they often can simplify information and thus allow for a more focused decision. For example, researchers studying resort consumers were able to reduce the information from a large number of scale items down to a handful of determinants of repeat purchases. Using a combination of factor analysis and multiple regression, they determined that the key drivers behind repeat purchase behavior are the positive feelings and the negative feelings that customers experience during a stay. Among these factors, negative feelings have a greater impact and thus discourage repeated stays more than the like amount of positive feelings encourage them to return.[1]

© MICHAEL G. SMITH/SHUTTERSTOCK

Retailing research also uses customers' survey responses as input to cluster analysis to identify segments with labels such as basic shoppers, apathetic shoppers, destination shoppers, and enthusiastic shoppers. Each customer responds best to a certain retail design and thus, each is more likely to come back when a shopping environment matches these characteristics.[2] Multivariate research can even help researchers know about love by identifying eleven dimensions of the love experience.[3] Certainly, when the customer loves you, he or she is probably coming back!

Introduction

If only business problems were really as simple as most textbook examples. Most coursework involves solving problems that have a definite answer. They are relatively well-defined problems in which the information provided in the problem can be used to produce *one* solution.

Unfortunately, in the real world, most business problems are ill defined. Not only do they not have a definite answer, but generally information needs to be massaged and generated before any solution can be obtained. Therefore, most business research studies involve many variables that must be organized for meaning. As researchers become increasingly aware of the multidimensional nature of business problems, they gain a greater appreciation for multivariate data analysis.

What Is Multivariate Data Analysis?

The preceding chapters have addressed univariate and bivariate analyses. Research that involves three or more variables, or that is concerned with underlying dimensions among multiple variables, will involve multivariate data analysis. Multivariate statistical methods analyze multiple variables or even multiple sets of variables simultaneously.

Marketers increasingly see nostalgia as something that will create value for consumers and help make them loyal customers. How do we know when someone has experienced nostalgia and whether or not the experience has altered behavior? Nostalgia itself is a latent factor that involves multiple indicators that together represent nostalgia. As such, the measurement and outcomes of nostalgia lend themselves well to multivariate analysis.[4] Likewise, many other marketing problems involve multivariate data analysis including most psychographic research and most research that seeks to identify viable market segments.

The "Variate" in Multivariate

Another distinguishing characteristic of multivariate analysis is the **variate**. The variate is a mathematical way in which a set of variables can be represented with one equation. Variates are formed as a linear combination of variables, each contributing to the overall meaning of the variate based upon an empirically derived weight. Mathematically, the variate is a function of the measured variables involved in an analysis:

$$V_k = f(X_1, X_2, \ldots, X_m)$$

V_k is the kth variate. Every analysis could involve multiple sets of variables, each represented by a variate. X_1 to X_m represent the measured variables.

Here is a simple illustration. Recall that constructs are distinguished from variables by the fact that multiple variables are needed to measure a construct. If we measured nostalgia with five variables, a variate of the following form could be created:

$$V_k = L_1X_1 + L_2X_2 + L_3X_3 + L_4X_4 + L_5X_5$$

V_k represents the score for nostalgia, X_1 to X_5 represent the observed scores on the five scale items that are expected to indicate nostalgia, and L_1 to L_5 are parameter estimates much like regression weights that suggest how highly related each variable is to the overall nostalgia score.

variate

A mathematical way in which a set of variables can be represented with one equation.

As you approach the end of this course, you may be interested in understanding what factors are associated with success in the course. While we may not be able to get at that question specifically, particularly because your grades are not in yet, we can try to understand factors that are associated with studying. Notice that at least two questions deal with how much people study and one in particular deals with how much time students spend studying for marketing research. Take a look at the portion of the questionnaire shown.

Let's examine this research question:

Student involvement with different social behaviors is related to their study habits.

Use the responses to the items shown in the screenshot or from other portions of the questionnaire as you see fit to explore this research question.

- This could be done by using each item as an individual predictor in a multiple regression model. However, there is a risk of multicollinearity and the results will be more complex than if data reduction is applied first.
  - So, an alternative is to first identify underlying factors among the variables above by applying exploratory factor analysis with a varimax rotation. Then, create the small number of independent variables using the multi-item composites indicated by the factor analysis. The regression model becomes simpler to test and understand.
  - Can you come up with a better model? Try adding 2–3 independent variables of your own using other variables to the model. Is your model better? Explain.

Qualtrics

Use the scale provided to rate the strength of your involvement with the things listed below (0=very little involvement to 10= very extreme amounts of involvement):

	0	1	2	3	4	5	6	7	8	9	10
MTV	○	○	○	○	○	○	○	○	○	○	○
Fashion	○	○	○	○	○	○	○	○	○	○	○
Sports	○	○	○	○	○	○	○	○	○	○	○
HDTV	○	○	○	○	○	○	○	○	○	○	○
Exercising	○	○	○	○	○	○	○	○	○	○	○
YouTube	○	○	○	○	○	○	○	○	○	○	○
Instant Messaging	○	○	○	○	○	○	○	○	○	○	○
Blogging	○	○	○	○	○	○	○	○	○	○	○
Partying with friends	○	○	○	○	○	○	○	○	○	○	○
Online Socializing	○	○	○	○	○	○	○	○	○	○	○
Web Browsing	○	○	○	○	○	○	○	○	○	○	○
Business News	○	○	○	○	○	○	○	○	○	○	○

Don't worry! We do not have to manually calculate these scores anymore. We'll rely on the computer to do the heavy lifting. However, this type of relationship is common to multivariate procedures.

Classifying Multivariate Techniques

Exhibit 24.1 presents a very basic classification of multivariate data analysis procedures. Two basic groups of multivariate techniques are *dependence methods* and *interdependence methods*.

EXHIBIT 24.1
Which Multivariate Approach Is Appropriate?

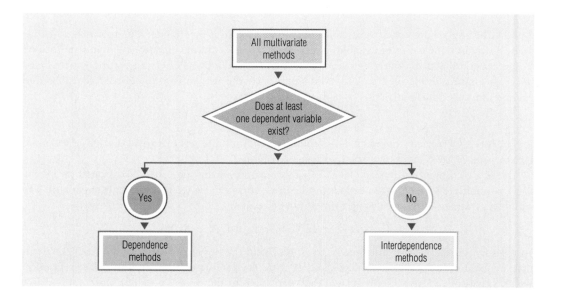

Dependence Techniques

When hypotheses involve distinction between independent and dependent variables, **dependence techniques** are needed. For instance, when we hypothesize that nostalgia is related positively to purchase intentions, nostalgia takes on the character of an independent variable and purchase intentions take on the character of a dependent variable. Predicting the dependent variable "sales" on the basis of numerous independent variables is a problem frequently investigated with dependence techniques. *Multiple regression analysis, multiple discriminant analysis, multivariate analysis of variance,* and *structural equations modeling* are all dependence methods.

dependence techniques

Multivariate statistical techniques that explain or predict one or more dependent variables.

Interdependence Techniques

When researchers examine questions that do not distinguish between independent and dependent variables, **interdependence techniques** are used. No one variable or variable subset is to be predicted from or explained by the others. The most common interdependence methods are *factor analysis, cluster analysis,* and *multidimensional scaling.* A marketing manager might utilize these techniques to identify profitable market segments or clusters or to classify cities on the basis of population size, income distribution, race and ethnic distribution, and consumption of a manufacturer's product to select comparable test-markets. Interdependence techniques can also be useful in examining the validity of multiple item measures.

interdependence techniques

Multivariate statistical techniques that give meaning to a set of variables or seek to group things together; no distinction is made between dependent and independent variables.

Influence of Measurement Scales

As in other forms of data analysis, the nature of the measurement scales will determine which multivariate technique is appropriate for the data. Exhibit 24.2 and Exhibit 24.3 on the next page show that selection of a multivariate technique requires consideration of the types of measures used for both independent and dependent sets of variables. These exhibits refer to nominal and ordinal scales as *nonmetric* and interval and ratio scales as *metric.*

EXHIBIT 24.2
Which Multivariate Dependence Technique Should I Use?

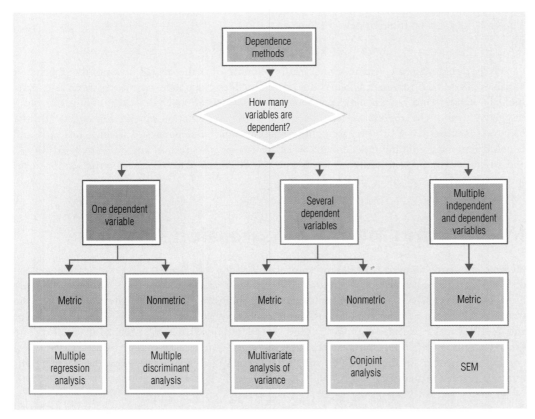

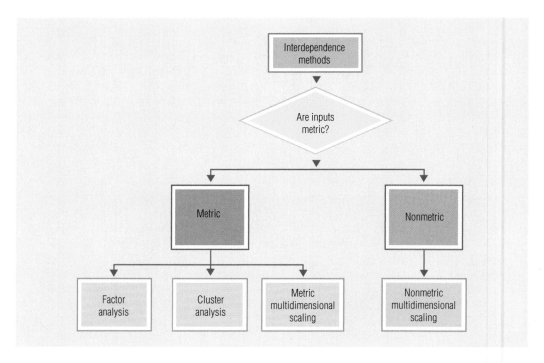

Analysis of Dependence

general linear model (GLM)

A way of explaining and predicting a dependent variable based on fluctuations (variation) from its mean. The fluctuations are due to changes in independent variables.

Multivariate dependence techniques are variants of the **general linear model (GLM)**. Simply, the GLM is a way of modeling some process based on how different variables cause fluctuations from the average dependent variable. Fluctuations can come in the form of group means that differ from the overall mean as is in ANOVA or in the form of a significant slope coefficient as in regression. The basic idea can be thought of as follows:

$$\hat{Y}_i = \mu + \Delta X + \Delta F + \Delta XF$$

Here, μ represents a constant, which can be thought of as the overall mean of the dependent variable, ΔX and ΔF represent changes due to main effect independent variables (such as experimental variables) and blocking independent variables (such as covariates or grouping variables), respectively, and ΔXF represents the change due to the combination (interaction effect) of those variables. Realize that Y_i in this case could represent multiple dependent variables, just as X and B could represent multiple independent variables. Multiple regression analysis, n-way ANOVA, and MANOVA represent common forms that the GLM can take. The following section turns specifically toward multiple regression analysis.

Interpreting Multiple Regression Analysis

multiple regression analysis

An analysis of association in which the effects of two or more independent variables on a single, interval-scaled dependent variable are investigated simultaneously.

Multiple regression analysis is an extension of simple regression analysis allowing a metric dependent variable to be predicted by multiple independent variables. Chapter 23 illustrated simple linear regression analysis with an example explaining a construction dealer's sales volume with the number of building permits issued. Thus, one dependent variable is explained by one independent variable. Yet reality is more complicated and several additional factors probably affect sales. The other plausible independent variables include prices, economic factors, advertising intensity, and consumers' incomes in the area. The simple regression equation can be expanded to represent multiple regression analysis:

$$Y_i = b_0 + b_1 X_1 + b_2 X_2 + b_3 X_3 + \cdots + b_n X_n + e_i$$

Thus, as a form of the GLM, dependent variable predictions ($\hat{Y}$) are made by adjusting the constant (b_0, which would be equal to the mean if all slope coefficients are 0) based on the slope coefficients associated with each independent variable.[5]

Less-than interval (nonmetric) independent variables can be used in multiple regression. This can be done by implementing dummy variable coding. Recall that a **dummy variable** uses 0 and 1 to code the different levels of dichotomous variable. Multiple dummy variables can be included in a regression model. Dummy coding is appropriate when data from two countries are being compared. Suppose the average labor rate for automobile production is included in a sample taken from respondents in Mexico and in South Korea. A response from Mexico could be assigned a 0 and responses from South Korea could be assigned 1 to create a country variable appropriate for use with multiple regression.

dummy variable

The way a dichotomous (two group) independent variable is represented in regression analysis by assigning a 0 to one group and a 1 to the other.

A Simple Example

Assume that a toy manufacturer wishes to explain store sales (dependent variable) using a sample of stores from Canada and Europe. Several hypotheses are offered:

- H1: *Competitor's sales* are related negatively to sales.
- H2: Sales are higher in communities with a *sales office* than in communities where no sales office is present.
- H3: *Grammar school enrollment* in a community is related positively to sales.

Competitor's sales is how much the primary competitor sold in the same stores over the same time period. Both the dependent variable and the competitors' sales (X_1) is a ratio variable measured in Euros (Canadian sales were converted to Euros). The presence of a sales office is a categorical variable (X_2) that can be represented with dummy coding (0 = no office in this particular region, 1 = office in this region). Grammar school enrollment is also a ratio variable (X_3) simply represented by the number of students enrolled in elementary schools in each community (in thousands).[6] A sample of 24 communities is gathered and the data are entered into a regression program to produce the following results:

$$Regression\ equation:\ \hat{Y} = 102.18 + 0.387X_1 + 115.2X_2 + 6.73X_3$$
$$Coefficient\ of\ multiple\ determination\ (R^2) = 0.845$$
$$F\text{-value} = 14.6;\ p < 0.05$$

The regression equation indicates that sales are positively related to X_1, X_2, and X_3. The coefficients show the effect on the dependent variable of a 1-unit increase in any of the independent variables. The value $b_2 = 115.2$ indicates that an increase of \$115,200 (115.2 thousands) in toy sales is expected with each additional unit of X_2. Thus, it appears that having a company sales office in a community is associated with a very positive effect on sales. Grammar school enrollments also may help predict sales. An increase of 1 unit of enrollment (1,000 students) indicates a sales increase of \$6,730. A one-unit increase in competitors' sales volume (X_1) in the territory adds little to the toy manufacturer's sales (\$387).

Because the effect associated with X_1 is positive, H1 is not supported because the sign of the regression coefficient is opposite the prediction. Instead of losing sales to the competition, as competitors' sales go up, so do the sales of this. The effects associated with H2 and H3 are in the hypothesized direction. Thus, if the coefficients are statistically significant, each will be supported.

Regression Coefficients in Multiple Regression

Recall that in simple regression, the coefficient $\mathbf{b}_1$ represents the slope of X on Y. Multiple regression involves multiple slope estimates, or regression weights. One challenge in regression models is to understand how one independent variable affects the dependent variable considering the effect of other independent variables. As long as the independent variables are related to each other, the regression weight associated with one independent variable is affected by the regression weight of another. Regression coefficients are unaffected by each other only when independent variables are independent.

Conventional regression programs can provide standardized parameter estimates, β_1, β_2, and so on, that can be thought of as *partial* regression coefficients. The correlation between Y and X_1, controlling for the correlation that X_2 has with the Y, is called **partial correlation**. Consider a standardized regression model with only two independent variables:[7]

partial correlation

The correlation between two variables after taking into account the fact that they are correlated with other variables too.

$$Y = \beta_1 X_1 + \beta_2 X_2 + e_i$$

The coefficients β_1 and β_2 are partial regression coefficients, which express the relationship between the independent variable and dependent variable taking into consideration that the other variable also is related to the dependent variable. As long as the correlation between independent variables is modest, partial regression coefficients adequately represent the relationships. When the correlation between two independent variables becomes high, the regression coefficients may not be reliable. We return to this issue later in the chapter.

When researchers want to know which independent variable is most predictive of the dependent variable, the standardized regression coefficient (β) is used. One huge advantage of β is that it provides a constant scale. Therefore, the greater the absolute value of the standardized regression coefficient, the more that particular independent variable is responsible for explaining the dependent variable. For example, suppose in the toy example above, the following standardized regression coefficients were found:

$$\beta_1 = 0.10$$
$$\beta_2 = 0.30$$
$$\beta_3 = 0.10$$

The resulting standardized regression equation would be

$$Y = 0.10X_1 + 0.30X_2 + 0.10X_3 + e_i$$

Using standardized coefficients, the researcher concludes that the relationship between competitor's sales (X_1) and company sales (Y) is the same strength as is the relationship between grammar school enrollment (X_3) and company sales. Perhaps more importantly, though, the conclusion can also be reached that the relationship between having a sales office in the area (X_2) and sales is three times as strong as the other two relationships. Thus, management may wish to place more emphasis on locating sales offices in major markets.

R^2 in Multiple Regression

The coefficient of multiple determination in multiple regression indicates the percentage of variation in Y explained by *all* independent variables. A value of $R^2 = 0.845$ means that 84.5 percent of the variance in the dependent variable is explained by the independent variables. If two independent variables are truly independent (uncorrelated with each other), the R^2 for a multiple regression model is equal to the separate R^2 values that would result from two separate simple regression models. More typically, the independent variables are related to one another, meaning that the model R^2 from a multiple regression model will be less than the separate R^2 values resulting from individual simple regression models. This reduction in R^2 is proportionate to the extent to which the independent variables are interrelated or *collinear.*

Statistical Significance in Multiple Regression

Following from simple regression, an F-test is used to test statistical significance by comparing the variation explained by the regression equation to the residual error variation. The F-test allows for testing of the relative magnitudes of the sum of squares due to the regression (SSR) and the error sum of squares (SSE).

$$F = \frac{(SSR)/k}{(SSE)/(n-k-1)} = \frac{MSR}{MSE}$$

where
$\quad k$ = number of independent variables

n = number of observations
MSR = Mean Squares Regression
MSE = Mean Squares Error

Degrees of freedom for the F-test $(d.f.)$ are:

$$d.f.\text{ for the numerator} = k$$
$$d.f.\text{ for the denominator} = n - k - 1$$

For the example above,

$$d.f.\text{ (numerator)} = 3$$
$$d.f.\text{ (denominator)} = 12 - 3 - 1 = 8$$

A table of critical F-values shows that for 3 and 8 d.f., and a 0.05 Type I error rate, a value of 4.07 or more is necessary for the regression model to be considered significant, meaning that it explains a significant portion of the total variation in the dependent variable. In practice, statistical programs will report the p-value associated with the F-test directly. Similarly, the programs report the statistical test for each individual independent variable. Independent variables with p-values below the acceptable Type I error rate are considered significant predictors of the dependent variable.

Running multiple regression using SPSS.

Steps in Interpreting a Multiple Regression Model

Multiple regression models often are used to test some proposed theoretical model. For instance, a researcher may be asked to develop and test a model explaining business unit performance. Why do some business units outperform others? Multiple regression models can be interpreted using these steps:

1. Examine the model F-test. If the test result is not significant, the model should be dismissed and there is no need to proceed to further steps.
2. Examine the individual statistical tests for each parameter estimate. Independent variables with significant results can be considered a significant explanatory variable.
3. Examine the model R^2. No cutoff values exist that can distinguish an acceptable amount of explained variation across all regression models. However, the absolute value of R^2 is more important when the researcher is more interested in prediction than explanation. In other words, the regression is run for pure forecasting purposes. When the model is more oriented toward explaining which variables are most important in explaining the dependent variable, cutoff values for the model R^2 are inappropriate.
4. Examine collinearity diagnostics. **Multicollinearity** in regression analysis refers to how strongly interrelated the independent variables in a model are. When multicollinearity is too high, the individual parameter estimates become difficult to interpret. One simple way to think about this is to consider the most extreme case. Imagine a regression model predicting Y with two independent variables, X1 and X2, that are correlated perfectly (1.0) with each other. Therefore, each has the same variance and will share exactly the same amount of variance with Y. Each variable would predict exactly the same simple regression model including an identical R^2. Since X1 and X2 contain the same information, a multiple regression with both independent variables predicting Y would produce the same R^2 as does either simple regression. But, how can the multiple regression determine which variable is responsible for explaining this variance? The answer is that it cannot and will likely produce unreliable results. Most regression programs can compute variance inflation factors (VIF) for each variable. VIFs provide an indication of how much multicollinearity exists among a set of independent variables. As a rule of thumb, any VIF above 5.0 suggests problems with multicollinearity.[8] Additionally, if multiple VIFs exceed 3.0 or so, the researcher should be very careful about potential problems due to multicollinearity. The Research Snapshot on the next page illustrates the type of problems caused by multicollinearity.

multicollinearity

The extent to which independent variables in a multiple regression analysis are correlated with each other; high multicollinearity can make interpreting parameter estimates difficult or impossible.

Too Much of a Good Thing!

Researchers often test hypotheses by examining regression coefficients. Thus, we are often looking for correlations, sometimes in all the wrong places. Financial data can be problematic to analyze. Consider the case of a financial manager trying to analyze gross margin (dependent variable = margin per employee) using the following independent variables:

- Average sales per square foot per quarter
- Average labor costs per week
- Years of experience for the manager
- Job performance rating for the previous year (100-point scale)

Regression results can be obtained using SAS by using a "proc reg;" statement followed by a model statement like "margin = sales labor experience performance." Regression can be conducted in SPSS by clicking on ANALYZE, REGRESSION, and then LINEAR. The VIF (variance inflation factors) column must be requested by clicking on STATISTICS and then checking COLINEARITY DIAGNOSTICS. After doing so, the following results are obtained. For the overall model,

ANOVA(b)

Model		Sum of Squares	d.f.	Mean Square	F	Sig.
1	Regression	142566.5332	4	35641.6333	13.57	.0000008
	Residual	91934.43848	35	2626.698242		
	Total	234500.9717	39			

A   Predictors: (constant), performance, experience, labor, sales
B   Dependent Variable: margin

The F of 13.57 is highly significant (<0.001), so the variables explain a large portion of the variance in the dependent variable.

The model R^2 is 0.61 also supporting this conclusion. The results for the independent variable tests show the following:

Coefficients(a)

Model		Unstandardized Coefficients B	Std. Error	Standardized Coefficients Beta	t	Sig.	VIF
1	(Constant)	171.242614	235.9374392		0.725797	0.47279	
	Sales	0.090784631	0.030835442	2.339759409	2.944165	0.00572	56.3836
	Labor	−0.070267446	0.035014493	−1.587938574	−2.00681	0.05254	55.8971
	Experience	−0.488078747	0.955764142	−0.054331204	−0.51067	0.61279	1.0105
	Performance	−1.856084354	3.034080822	−0.068978263	−0.61175	0.54466	1.1351

a   Dependent Variable: margin

Even though the model results appear strong, only one independent variable is significant at a Type I error rate of 0.050 — sales. However, the β coefficients do not make sense. The β coefficients for both sales and labor are beyond the range that β should theoretically take (-1.0 to 1.0). Nothing can be correlated with something more than perfectly (which would be a correlation of 1.0 or -1.0). Notice also that the two VIF factors for sales and labor are in the 50s. Generally, when multiple VIF factors approach 5 or greater, problems with multicollinearity can be expected. The high correlation between sales and labor is a problem.

As often occurs with financial data, they can be difficult to use as independent variables. In this case, the researcher may wish to rerun the model after dropping one of the offending variables.

Exhibit 24.4 illustrates these steps. The regression model explains business unit profitability for a sample of 28 business units for a Fortune 500 company. The independent variables are hours (average hours spent in training for the workforce), budget (the percentage of the promotional budget used), and state (a dummy variable indicating whether the business unit is in Arizona and coded 0, or in Ohio and coded 1). In this case, the researcher is using a maximum acceptable Type I error rate of 0.05. The conclusion reached from this analysis is that hours spent in training seem to pay off in increased business unit profitability as evidenced by the significant, positive regression coefficient ($\beta = 0.55$, p < 0.05).

EXHIBIT 24.4 **Interpreting Multiple Regression Results**

The SAS System

The REG Procedure
Model: MODEL1
Dependent Variable: Paid

Number of Observations Read   28
Number of Observations Used   28

Analysis of Variance

Source	DF	Sum of Squares	Mean Square	F Value	Pr > F
Model	3	1770668	590223	19.38	<.0001
Error	24	731035	30460		
Corrected Total	27	2501703			

Root MSE	174.52738	R-Square	0.7078
Dependent Mean	654.03571	Adj R-Sq	0.6713
Coeff Var	26.68469		

> 1. Interpret model *F*-test. Test is significant (p < .05).

Parameter Estimates

Variable	DF	Parameter Estimate	Standard Error	t Value	Pr > |t|	Standardized Estimate	VIF
Intercept	1	−109.90538	217.46253	−0.51	0.6179	0	
Hours	1	0.99438	0.27688	3.59	0.0015	0.55433	1.96
Budget	1	6.60121	3.54784	1.86	0.0751	0.28210	1.89
State	1	−66.36397	84.82434	−0.78	0.4416	−0.11073	1.65

> 3. The model R^2 is interpreted. The IVs explain over 70% of variation in the dependent variable.

> 2. Interpret individual parameter estimates. In this case, only hours is significant based on a p-value below .05 (0.0015).

> 4. VIFs are checked for multicollinearity problems. None are indicated here.

ANOVA (*n*-way) and MANOVA

An ANOVA or MANOVA model also represents a form of the GLM. ANOVA can be extended beyond one-way ANOVA to predict a dependent variable with multiple categorical independent variables. **Multivariate analysis of variance (MANOVA)**, is a multivariate technique that predicts multiple continuous dependent variables with multiple independent variables. The independent variables are categorical, although a continuous control variable can be included in the form of a covariate. MANOVA stands for multivariate analysis of variance. Statistical programs usually refer to any ANOVA with only one dependent variable as univariate analysis of variance or simply by ANOVA.

multivariate analysis of variance (MANOVA)

a multivariate technique that predicts multiple continuous dependent variables with multiple categorical independent variables.

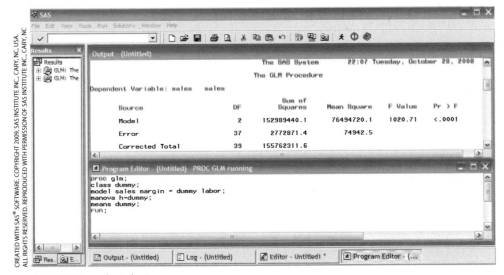

A MANOVA conducted using SAS. This model predicts two related dependent variables, sales and margin, using a dummy variable indicating region of firm (north or south) and amount of labor expended as a ratio level covariate.

N-way (Univariate) ANOVA

The interpretation of an *n*-way ANOVA model follows closely from the regression results described above. The steps involved are essentially the same with the addition of interpreting differences between means:

1. Examine the overall model *F*-test result. If significant, proceed.
2. Examine individual *F*-tests for individual independent variables.
3. For each significant categorical independent variable, interpret the effect by examining the group means (see Chapter 11).
4. For each significant, continuous covariate, interpret the parameter estimate (**b**).
5. For each significant interaction, interpret the means for each combination. A graphical representation as illustrated in Chapter 11 can greatly assist in this interpretation.

■ INTERPRETING MANOVA RESULTS

MANOVA models produce an additional layer of testing. The first layer of testing involves the multivariate *F*-test, which is based on a statistic called Wilke's Lambda ($\wedge$). This test examines whether or not an independent variable explains significant variation among the dependent variables within the model. If this test is significant, then the *F*-test results from individual univariate regression models nested within the MANOVA model are interpreted. The rest of the interpretation results follow from the one-way ANOVA or multiple regression model results above. See the Research Snapshot on the next page for a specific guide to interpretation.

Discriminant Analysis

Researchers often need to produce a classification of sampling units. This process may involve using a set of independent variables to decide if a sampling unit belongs in one group or another. A physician might record a person's blood pressure, weight, and blood cholesterol level and then categorize that person as having a high or low probability of a heart attack. A researcher interested in retailing failures might be able to group firms as to whether they eventually failed or did not fail on the basis of independent variables such as location, financial ratios, or management changes. A bank might want to discriminate between potentially successful and unsuccessful sites for electronic fund transfer system machines. A sales manager might want to distinguish between applicants to hire and those not to hire. The challenge is to find the discriminating variables to use in a predictive equation that will produce better than chance assignment of the individuals to the two groups.

discriminant analysis

A statistical technique for predicting the probability that an object will belong in one of two or more mutually exclusive categories (dependent variable), based on several independent variables.

Discriminant analysis is a multivariate technique that predicts a categorical dependent variable (rather than a continuous, interval-scaled variable, as in multiple regression) based on a linear combination of independent variables. In each problem above, the researcher determines which variables explain why an observation falls into one of two or more groups. A linear combination of independent variables that explains group memberships is known as a discriminant function. Discriminant analysis is a statistical tool for determining such linear combinations. The researcher's task is to derive the coefficients of the discriminant function (a straight line).

How to Get MANOVA Results

A department store developer gathered data looking at the effect of nostalgia on customer impressions. A field experiment was set up in which a key department was either given a modern design or a retro design. The retro design was hoped to create feelings of nostalgia. Several hundred consumers were interviewed.

Since two related dependent variables are involved (y1 = interest and y2 = excitement), MANOVA is the appropriate technique.

MANOVA can be conducted using SPSS by clicking on ANALYZE, then GENERAL LINEAR MODEL, and then MULTIVARIATE (if only one dependent variable was involved, the choice would be UNIVARIATE). This opens a dialog box as shown here:

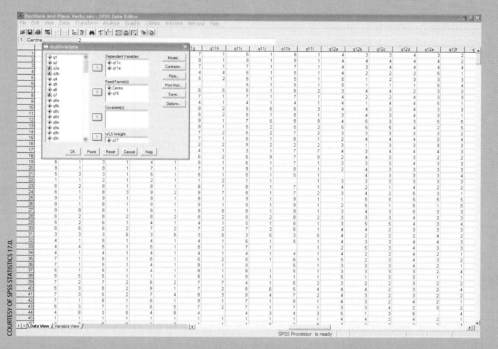

COURTESY OF SPSS STATISTICS 17.0.

The dialog box includes places to enter dependent variables, fixed factors (between-subjects categorical independent variables), and covariates. In this case, the fixed factors are

1. Experimental variable (0 = modern, 1 = retro)
2. Respondent sex (0 = male, 1 = female)

Respondent age is included as a covariate or control variable (years).

SPSS provided output that can be summarized briefly:

1. Multivariate Results:
    a. Wilke's Lambda = 0.964
    b. Overall multivariate F = 9.6 with 2 and 510 d.f.
    c. The p-value associated with this result is less than 0.001. Thus, the multivariate results are significant so the research proceeds to interpret the individual univariate ANOVA results for each dependent variable (SPSS provides these results automatically).
2. The univariate model F statistics for each dependent variable are both significant (p < 0.001) so the researcher moves on to the next step.
3. The individual effects associated with y1 (interest) are interpreted. For example, for the experimental variable, the result is,
    a. F = 0.4, with 1 and 511 d.f. for interest (p = 0.531).

b. Age is not significant.
c. The interaction is not significant.
4. The individual effects associated with y2 (excitement) are interpreted. For example, for the experimental variable, the result is,
    a. F = 13.4, with 1 and 511 d.f. for excitement (p < 0.001).
    b. Sex and age are both significant predictors too (p < 0.001).
    c. The interaction of sex and the retro/modern experimental variable is also significant.
5. After carefully reviewing the means for each experimental cell as well as the covariate results, the researcher reaches the following conclusions:
    a. The retro look produced more excitement but not necessarily more interest.
    b. Women are more interested and more excited about shopping.
    c. The effect of the retro condition was stronger for men than women. That is, the difference in means between the retro and modern condition is larger for men than for women.
    d. Younger consumers are more excited about shopping.

© GEORGE DOYLE & CIARAN GRIFFIN

© EDDI BOEHNKE/ZEFA/CORBIS

We will consider an example of the two-group discriminant analysis problem where the dependent variable, Y, is measured on a nominal scale. (Although n-way discriminant analysis is possible, it is beyond the scope of this discussion.) Suppose a personnel manager for an electrical wholesaler has been keeping records on successful versus unsuccessful sales employees. The personnel manager believes it is possible to predict whether an applicant will succeed on the basis of age, sales aptitude test scores, and mechanical ability scores. As stated at the outset, the problem is to find a linear function of the independent variables that shows large differences in group means. The first task is to estimate the coefficients of the applicant's discriminant function. To calculate the individuals' discriminant scores, the following linear function is used:

$$Z_i = b_1 X_{1i} + b_2 X_{2i} + \cdots + b_n X_{ni}$$

where

Z_i = ith applicant's discriminant score
b_n = discriminant coefficient for the nth variable
X_{ni} = ith applicant's value on the nth independent variable

Using scores for all the individuals in the sample, a discriminant function is determined based on the criterion that the groups be maximally differentiated on the set of independent variables.

Returning to the example with three independent variables, suppose the personnel manager finds the standardized weights in the equation to be

$$Z = b_1 X_1 + b_2 X_2 + b_3 X_3$$
$$= 0.069 X_1 + 0.013 X_2 + 0.0007 X_3$$

This means that age (X_1) is much more important than sales aptitude test scores (X_2). Mechanical ability (X_3) has relatively minor discriminating power.

In the computation of the linear discriminant function, weights are assigned to the variables to maximize the ratio of the difference between the means of the two groups to the standard deviation within groups. The standardized discriminant coefficients, or weights, provide information about the relative importance of each of these variables in discriminating between the two groups.

A major goal of discriminant analysis is to perform a classification function. The purpose of classification in our example is to predict which applicants will be successful and which will be unsuccessful and to group them accordingly. To determine whether the discriminant analysis can be used as a good predictor of applicant success, information provided in the "confusion matrix" is used. Suppose the personnel manager has 40 successful and 45 unsuccessful employees in the sample. The confusion matrix shows that the number of correctly classified employees (72 out of 85) is much higher than would be expected by chance:

Confusion Matrix			
	Predicted Group		
Actual Group	**Successful**	**Unsuccessful**	
Successful	34	6	40
Unsuccessful	7	38	45

Tests can be performed to determine whether the rate of correct classification is statistically significant.

Exhibit 24.5 summarizes multivariate dependence techniques.

Factor Analysis

Suppose we wished to identify the factors that are associated with pleasant shopping experiences,[9] identify factors that would allow better flexibility and control of logistics programs,[10] or identify groups of students each associated with a unique learning style.[11] All of these are problems that

EXHIBIT 24.5 **Multivariate Dependence Techniques Summary**

Technique	Purpose	Number of Dependent Variables	Number of Independent Variables	Type of Measurement	
				Dependent	**Independent**
Multiple regression	To investigate simultaneously the effects of several independent variables on a dependent variable	1	2 or more	Interval	Interval
Discriminant analysis	To predict the probability that an object or individual will belong in one of two or more mutually exclusive categories, based on several independent variables	1	2 or more	Nominal	Interval
MANOVA	To determine simultaneously whether statistically significant mean differences occur between groups on several variables	2 or more	1 or more	Interval	Nominal

have been addressed through the use of a multivariate interdependence technique. Rather than attempting to predict a variable or set of variables from a set of independent variables, we use techniques like *factor analysis, cluster analysis,* and *multidimensional scaling* to better understand the structure of a set of variables or objects.

Factor analysis is a prototypical multivariate, interdependence technique. Factor analysis is a technique of statistically identifying a reduced number of factors from a larger number of measured variables. The factors themselves are not measured, but instead, they are identified by forming a variate using the measured variables. Factors are usually latent constructs like attitude or satisfaction or an index like social class. A researcher need not distinguish between independent and dependent variables to conduct factor analysis. Factor analysis can be divided into two types:

factor analysis

A prototypical multivariate, interdependence technique that statistically identifies a reduced number of factors from a larger number of measured variables.

1. Exploratory factor analysis (EFA)—performed when the researcher is uncertain about how many factors may exist among a set of variables. The discussion here concentrates primarily on EFA.
2. Confirmatory factor analysis (CFA)—performed when the researcher has strong theoretical expectations about the factor structure before performing the analysis. CFA is the best single tool for assessing construct validity. One big advantage is that CFA provides a test of how well the researcher's "theory" about the factor structure fits the actual observations. Several more advanced sources cover CFA in detail and the reader is referred to any of those sources for more on CFA.[12]

Exhibit 24.6 on the next page illustrates factor analysis graphically. Suppose a researcher is asked to examine the effectiveness of creating feelings of nostalgia on restaurant customer loyalty. Three hundred fifty customers at themed restaurants around the country are interviewed and asked to respond to the following Likert scales (1 = Strongly Disagree to 7 = Strongly Agree):

X_1—I feel a strong connection to the past when I am in this place.
X_2—This place evokes memories of the past.
X_3—I feel a yearning to relive past experiences when I dine here.
X_4—This place looks like a page out of the past.
X_5—I am willing to pay more to dine in this restaurant.
X_6—I feel very loyal to this establishment.
X_7—I enjoy recommending this place to others.
X_8—I will go out of my way to dine here.

Factor analysis can summarize the information in the eight variables in a smaller number of variables, perhaps two in this case. More than one technique exists for estimating the variates that

EXHIBIT 24.6
A Simple Illustration of Factor Analysis

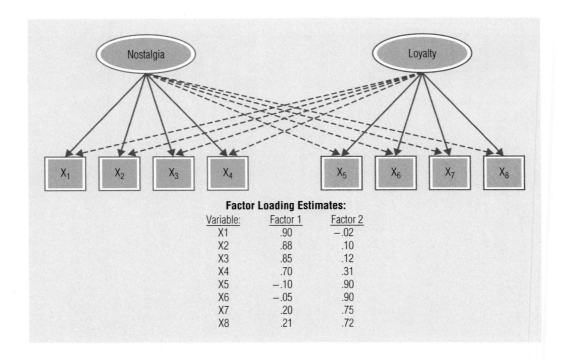

Factor Loading Estimates:

Variable:	Factor 1	Factor 2
X1	.90	−.02
X2	.88	.10
X3	.85	.12
X4	.70	.31
X5	−.10	.90
X6	−.05	.90
X7	.20	.75
X8	.21	.72

form the factors. However, the general idea is to mathematically produce variates that explain the most total variance among the set of variables being analyzed. If the factor results suggested two factors, Exhibit 24.6 would represent the results. Thus, EFA provides two important pieces of information:

1. How many factors exist among a set of variables?
2. What variables match up or "load on" which factors?

Factor Loadings

factor loading

Indicates how strongly a measured variable is correlated with a factor.

Each arrow connecting a factor (represented by an oval in the Exhibit) to a variable (represented by a box in the Exhibit) is associated with a **factor loading**. A factor loading indicates how strongly correlated a factor is with a measured variable. In other words, to what extent does a variable "load" on a factor? EFA depends on the loadings for proper interpretation. A latent construct can be interpreted based on the pattern of loadings and the content of the variables. In this way, the latent construct is measured indirectly by the variables.

Loading estimates are provided by factor analysis programs. In Exhibit 24.6, the factor loading estimates are shown beneath the factor diagram. The thick arrows indicate high loading estimates and the thin dashed lines correspond to weak loading estimates. Factors are interpreted by examining any patterns that emerge from the factor results. Here, a clear pattern emerges. The first four variables produce high loadings on factor 1 and the last four variables produce high loadings on factor 2.

When a clear pattern of factor loadings emerges, interpretation is easy. Because the first four variables all have content consistent with nostalgia and the second four variables all have content consistent with customer loyalty, the two factors can easily be labeled. Factor 1 represents the latent construct nostalgia and factor 2 represents the latent construct customer loyalty.

Data Reduction Technique

data reduction technique

Multivariate statistical approaches that summarize the information from many variables into a reduced set of variates formed as linear combinations of measured variables.

Factor analysis is considered a **data reduction technique.** Data reduction techniques allow a researcher to summarize information from many variables into a reduced set of variates or composite variables. Data reduction is advantageous for many reasons. In general, the rule of parsimony suggests an explanation involving fewer components is better than one involving many more. Factor analysis accomplishes data reduction by capturing variance from many variables with a single variate. Data reduction is also a way of identifying which variables among a large set might be important in some analysis. Thus, data reduction simplifies decision making.

In our example, the researcher can now form two composite factors representing the latent constructs nostalgia and customer loyalty. These can be formed using factor equations of this form:

$$F_k = L_1 X_1 + L_2 X_2 + L_3 X_3 + L_4 X_4 + L_5 X_5 + L_6 X_6 + L_7 X_7 + L_8 X_8$$

where

F_k is the factor score for the kth factor—in this case there are two factors

L represents factor loadings (ith) 1 through 8 for the corresponding factor

X represents the value of the corresponding measured variable

Using this type of equation, the scores for variables $X_1 - X_8$ can be summarized by two scores, one for factor 1 and one for factor 2. If the researcher wanted to analyze the correlation among these variables, now all that needs to be done is to analyze the bivariate correlation between factor 1 (nostalgia) and factor 2 (loyalty). This should prove much easier than analyzing an 8 × 8 correlation matrix. Statistical programs like SPSS and SAS will produce factor scores automatically if requested (see Appendix 24A).

We can see that because F_1 is associated with high values for L_1 through L_4 (and low values for L_5, L_6, L_7, and L_8) and F_2 is associated with high values for L_5 through L_8 (and low for L_1, L_2, L_3, and L_4), F_1 is determined almost entirely by the nostalgia items and F_2 is determined almost entirely by the customer loyalty items. The factor pattern of high and low loadings can be used to match measured variables to factors in this way.

Creating Composite Scales with Factor Results

When a clear pattern of loadings exists as in this case, the researcher may take a simpler approach. F_1 could be created simply by summing the four variables with high loadings and creating a summated scale representing nostalgia. F_2 could be created by summing the second four variables (those loading highly on F_2) and creating a second summated variable. This would introduce very little error given the pattern of loadings. In other words, very low loadings suggest a variable does not contribute much to the factor. The researcher could test the reliability of each summated scale by computing a coefficient alpha estimate. Then, the research could conduct a regression analysis that would test how much nostalgia contributed to loyalty.

Factor analysis is commonly used to reduce the number of variables that need to be included in a regression analysis. For instance, a set of 24 variables may be factor analyzed and the results used to create 4 independent variables. The variables could each be represented by a summated or averaged scale for each modeled variable.

■ COMMUNALITY

A researcher may wish to know how much a single variable has in common with all factors. Communality is a measure of the percentage of a variable's variation that is explained by the factors. A relatively high communality indicates that a variable has much in common with the other variables taken as a group. Communality for any variable is equal to the sum of the squared loadings for that variable across all factors extracted. The communality for X1 is:

$$0.90^2 - 0.02^2 = 0.8104$$

These values are shown on factor analysis printouts.

■ AVERAGE VARIANCE EXPLAINED

Along with the factor loadings and communalities, the percentage of variance explained (or extracted) among the original variables by the factors can be useful. Recall that variance is correlation squared. Thus, if each loading is squared, the result represents how much variance that particular factor and that particular variable have in common. If these summed factor loadings are averaged, we can estimate how much variance a factor has in common with the entire set of variables. This explanation of variance is much the same as R^2 in multiple regression. In this case, though, the variance accounted for among the eight variables by the nostalgia factor is 0.36 and the variance among the eight variables explained by the loyalty factor is 0.35. This can be illustrated using the loadings from factor 1:

$$AVE = \frac{(0.90^2 + 0.88^2 + 0.85^2 + 0.70^2 - 0.10^2 - 0.05^2 + 0.20^2 + 0.21^2)}{8} = 0.36$$

Thus, the two factors explain 71 percent of the variance in the eight variables:

$$0.36 + 0.35 = 0.71$$

An extension of this idea is often used to help validate composite factors. Simply put, if only four items are used to create a summated scale, then the average variance explained for each of the four items can be used to indicate convergent validity for a factor. This is one statistic that is sometimes necessary to compute manually. If four items are used to form a composite scale and they have loadings of 0.7, −0.7, 0.8, and 0.9, respectively, the variance explained for the scale is

$$\frac{0.7^2 + (-0.7)^2 + 0.8^2 + 0.9^2}{4} = 0.61$$

In the example shown in Exhibit 24.6, a nostalgia construct made up of X1 − X4 would produce an average variance explained of:

$$AVE_{Nostalgia} = \frac{(0.90^2 + 0.88^2 + 0.85^2 + 0.70^2)}{4} = 0.70$$

Ideally, the researcher would like scales to explain at least half of the total variation among the measured variables. Thus, the nostalgia measure passes this guideline.

■ HOW MANY FACTORS?

Oftentimes, the researcher asks the question, "How many factors will exist among a large number of variables?" While a detailed discussion is beyond the scope of this text, the question is usually addressed based on the eigenvalues for a factor solution. Eigenvalues are a measure of how much variance is explained by each factor. The most common rule is to base the number of factors on the number of eigenvalues greater than 1.0. This is the default rule for most statistical programs. So, unless some other rule is specified, the number of factors shown in a factor solution is based on this rule.

■ FACTOR ROTATION

factor rotation

A mathematical way of simplifying factor analysis results to better identify which variables "load on" which factors; the most common procedure is varimax.

Factor rotation is a mathematical way of simplifying factor results. The most common type of factor rotation is a process called varimax. A discussion of the technical aspects of the concept of factor rotation is far beyond the scope of this book. However, it involves creating new reference axes for a given set of variables. An initial factor solution is often difficult to interpret. Rotation clears things up by producing more obvious patterns of loadings. Users should experiment with this by looking at unrotated and rotated solutions. Unless a user has some reason not to, a rotation should be applied in conducting factor analysis.

Cluster Analysis

cluster analysis

A multivariate approach for grouping observations based on similarity among measured variables.

Cluster analysis is a multivariate approach for identifying objects or individuals that are similar to one another in some respect. Thus, cluster analysis is an important tool for identifying market segments. Cluster analysis classifies individuals or objects into a small number of mutually exclusive and exhaustive groups. Objects or individuals are assigned to groups so that there is great similarity within groups and much less similarity between groups. The cluster should have high internal (within-cluster) homogeneity and external (between-cluster) heterogeneity.

Cluster analysis facilitates market segmentation by identifying subjects or individuals who have similar needs, lifestyles, or responses to marketing promotions. Clusters, or subgroups, of recreational vehicle owners may be identified on the basis of their similarity with respect to recreational vehicle usage and the benefits they want from recreational vehicles. Alternatively, the researcher might use demographic or lifestyle variables to group individuals into clusters identified as market segments.

We will illustrate cluster analysis with a hypothetical example relating to the types of vacations taken by 12 individuals. Vacation behavior is represented on two dimensions: number of vacation days and dollar expenditures on vacations during a given year. Exhibit 24.7 is a scatter diagram that represents the geometric distance between each individual in two-dimensional space. The diagram portrays three clear-cut clusters. The first subgroup, consisting of individuals L, H, and B, suggests a group of individuals who have many vacation days but do not spend much money on their vacations. The second cluster, represented by individuals A, I, K, G, and F, represents intermediate values on both variables—average amounts of vacation days and average dollar expenditures on vacations. The third group, individuals C, J, E, and D, consists of individuals who have relatively few vacation days but spend large amounts on vacations.

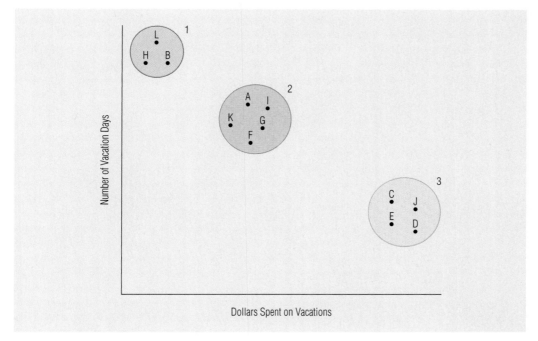

EXHIBIT 24.7
Clusters of Individuals on Two Dimensions

In this example, individuals are grouped on the basis of their similarity or proximity to one another. The logic of cluster analysis is to group individuals or objects by their similarity to or distance from each other. The mathematical procedures for deriving clusters will not be dealt with here, as our purpose is only to introduce the technique.

A classic study provides a very pragmatic example of the use of cluster analysis.[13] Marketing managers frequently are interested in finding test-market cities that are very similar so that no extraneous variation will cause differences between the experimental and control markets. In this study the objects to be clustered were cities. The characteristics of the cities, such as population, retail sales, number of retail outlets, and percentage of nonwhites, were used to identify the groups. Cities such as Omaha, Oklahoma City, Dayton, Columbus, and Fort Worth were similar and cities such as Newark, Cleveland, Pittsburgh, Buffalo, and Baltimore were similar, but individual cities within each group were dissimilar to those within other groups or clusters. (See Exhibit 24.8 on the next page for additional details.)

This example should help to clarify the difference between factor analysis and cluster analysis. In factor analysis the researcher might search for constructs that underlie the variables (population, retail sales, number of retail outlets); in cluster analysis the researcher would seek constructs that underlie the objects (cities).

Cluster analysis differs from multiple discriminant analysis in that the groups are not predefined. The purpose of cluster analysis is to determine how many groups really exist and to define their composition. Cluster analysis has seen increasing application with the advance of data mining

EXHIBIT 24.8 **Cluster Analysis of Test-Market Cities**

Cluster Number	City	Cluster Number	City	Cluster Number	City
1	Omaha Oklahoma City Dayton Columbus Fort Worth	7	Sacramento San Bernardino San Jose Phoenix Tucson	13	Allentown Providence Jersey City York Louisville
2	Peoria Davenport Binghamton Harrisburg Worcester	8	Gary Nashville Jacksonville San Antonio Knoxville	14	Paterson Milwaukee Cincinnati Miami Seattle
3	Canton Youngstown Toledo Springfield Albany	9	Indianapolis Kansas City Dallas Atlanta Houston	15	San Diego Tacoma Norfolk Charleston Fort Lauderdale
4	Bridgeport Rochester Hartford New Haven Syracuse	10	Mobile Shreveport Birmingham Memphis Chattanooga	16	New Orleans Richmond Tampa Lancaster Minneapolis
5	Wilmington Orlando Tulsa Wichita Grand Rapids	11	Newark Cleveland Pittsburgh Buffalo Baltimore	17	San Francisco Detroit Boston Philadelphia
6	Bakersfield Fresno Flint El Paso Beaumont	12	Albuquerque Salt Lake City Denver Charlotte Portland	18	Washington St. Louis

Note: Points not in a cluster—Honolulu, Wilkes-Barre.

Source: Reprinted by permission, Paul E. Green, Ronald E. Frank, and Patrick J. Robinson, "Cluster Analysis in Test-Market Selection," *Management Science*, Vol. 13, P.B393 (Table 2), April 1967. Copyright © 1967, the Institute for Operations Research and the Management Sciences (INFORMS), 7240 Parkway Drive, Suite 310, Hanover, MD 21076 USA

and predictive analytics. Cluster analysis routines help identify patterns of similarity in consumers based on all data available about that particular consumer. Clustering routines may even be useful in identifying groups of consumers who are more or less susceptible to various diseases based on the records that accumulate through each consumer's health care experiences. The consumer's HMO card can help provide the data that may make this possible.

Other Multivariate Techniques

multidimensional scaling

A statistical technique that measures objects in multidimensional space on the basis of respondents' judgments of the similarity of objects.

Another interdependence technique is multidimensional scaling. **Multidimensional scaling** provides a means for measuring objects in a multidimensional space based on respondents' judgments of how similar different objects are. Like factor analysis, multidimensional scaling can be useful in identifying the dimensions among which consumers differentiate products. The data are typically collected by having consumers rate how similar product or brand alternatives are to each other. For example, consumers may be asked to rate the similarity of the top auto brands. Here, we may find that Acura and Lexus are very similar but that each is very different from Chrysler and GM. The researcher may be able to use results to interpret reliability and comfort as key dimensions that distinguish the brands. Exhibit 24.9 summarizes the multivariate techniques for analysis of interdependence.

structural equations modeling (SEM)

A multivariate tool that combines an interdependence and dependence technique to allow a researcher to test theory by providing an omnibus assessment of fit centered around a χ^2 goodness of fit test.

Additionally, a few newer techniques combine elements of interdependence and dependence techniques into one. **Structural equations modeling (SEM)** allows a researcher to build and test a

- Dependence techniques are useful for predicting specific outcomes like performance, profit, sales, or value.
  - Interdependence techniques are useful for understanding the structure or dimensionality of data.
    - Researchers can use the measurement scale level along with the purpose of the research (prediction or understanding the structure of the data) to help identify the appropriate multivariate data analysis tool for a given situation.
- Multiple regression results should use independent variables that are not highly correlated with each other.
  - VIFs greater than 5 signify problems with multicollinearity.
  - Multiple VIFs greater 3 signifies potential multicollinearity problems
- Factor analysis can be useful in reducing data prior to conducting a multiple regression analysis. The factor results can help identify and create factors that are not highly related.

- Varimax rotation is the most frequently applied factor rotation technique.
  - When varimax rotation is used, the researcher can use factor scores to form composite measures for independent variables (constructs) and the resulting measures will be unrelated – meaning no multicollinearity.
- Factor analysis is useful in providing evidence of measurement validity.
  - The average variance extracted should be 0.5 or greater to provide evidence of convergent validity.
    - Varimax loadings should be 0.7 or greater.
  - Confirmatory factor analysis is a premier tool for assessing measurement quality and construct validity.
- Cluster analysis is a great tool for identifying market segments.
- Statistical results from any technique (regression, SEM, PLS, etc.), must be interpreted in light of the overall concern for internal and external validity—including generalizability.

EXHIBIT 24.9
Summary of Multivariate Techniques for Analysis of Interdependence

Technique	Purpose	Type of Measurement
Factor analysis	To summarize into a reduced number of factors the information contained in a large number of variables	Interval
Cluster analysis	To classify individuals or objects into a small number of mutually exclusive and exhaustive groups, ensuring that there will be as much likeness within groups and as much difference among groups as possible	Interval
Multidimensional scaling	To measure objects in multidimensional space on the basis of respondents' judgments of their similarity	Varies depending on technique

theory represented by a series of regression equations, each involving multiple item measures, that are solved simultaneously. SEM tests both the measurement structure (with CFA) and the structural model (explaining the key outcomes) by providing an omnibus assessment of fit. This test of fit is centered around a χ^2 goodness-of-fit test. In this case, fit represents how well the researcher's model matches reality as represented by the data. Several software programs are devoted especially to solving structural equations models including LISREL, AMOS (which is available with SPSS), and M-Plus, among others.

Marketing researchers have also sometimes adopted a tool that originated in the physical sciences and is capable of providing statistical results even when only a small amount of data exists or when the measurement quality is not particular strong. **Partial least squares (PLS)** also combines a factor analytic approach with a regression approach to produce path estimates between multiple item independent variables and dependent variables (constructs). PLS is particularly useful when the data are messy and the measurement quality is not strong enough for use in SEM. PLS is also very easy to use. However, the researcher needs to use caution because although PLS can produce results when other tools may fail, problems such as a lack of generalizability due to a small sample don't go away just because statistical results can be obtained. SAS provides a PLS module as do more recent versions of SPSS. Specialized software also exists such as SmartPLS. The reader is referred to other sources for more information on these more complex techniques. However, they are defined here because they are used widely enough so that they are part of the marketing researcher's vocabulary.

partial least squares (PLS)

A multivariate tool that combines a factor analytic and regression approach to provide path estimates to a proposed model but falls short of providing an assessment of fit. PLS is appropriate when the data are insufficient for use in SEM.

Summary

1. Understand what multivariate data analysis involves and know the two basic types of multivariate analysis. Multivariate statistical methods analyze multiple variables or even multiple sets of variables simultaneously. They are particularly useful for identifying latent constructs using multiple individual measures. Multivariate techniques represent data through the use of variates. Variates are mathematical combinations of variables. The two major types of multivariate procedures are interdependence and dependence techniques. Interdependence techniques do not distinguish dependent and interdependent variables, whereas dependence techniques do make this distinction.

2. Interpret results from multiple regression analysis. Multiple regression analysis predicts a continuous dependent variable with multiple independent variables. The independent variables can be either continuous or categorical. Categorical variables must be coded as dummy variables. Multiple regression results are analyzed by examining the significance of the overall model using the F-test results, the individual parameter estimates, the overall model R^2, and the model collinearity diagnostics. Standardized regression coefficients have the advantage of a common scale making them comparable from model to model and variable to variable.

3. Interpret results from multivariate analysis of variance (MANOVA). MANOVA is an extension of ANOVA involving multiple related dependent variables. Thus, MANOVA represents a form of the GLM predicting that multiple categorical independent variables affect multiple, related dependent variables. Interpretation of a MANOVA model is similar to interpretation of a regression model. However, the multivariate F-test results associated with Wilke's Lambda (Λ) are interpreted first, followed by interpretation of the individual ANOVA results.

4. Know what multiple discriminant analysis can be used to do. Another dependence technique is discriminant analysis. Discriminant analysis uses multiple independent variables to classify observations into one of a set of mutually exclusive categories. In other words, discriminant analysis predicts a categorical dependent variable with multiple independent variables.

5. Interpret basic exploratory factor analysis results. EFA is a data reduction technique in which the variance in multiple variables is represented by a smaller number of factors. The factors generally represent latent factors or indexes. Factor loadings resulting from rotated factor solutions are important in properly interpreting factor analysis results. The pattern of loadings that results both suggests the number of latent factors that may exist and helps validate scales that may be used in other statistical analysis. EFA results often are used to help identify factors that can be used to create composite scales all of which may be entered into a multiple regression analysis.

6. Understand how cluster analysis can identify market segments. Cluster analysis classifies multiple observations into a smaller number of mutually exclusive and exhaustive groups. These should have as much similarity within groups and as much difference between groups as possible. In cluster analysis the groups are not predefined. However, clusters can be used to represent market segments because market segments also represent consumers that are similar to each other within a segment, but who are different from consumers in other segments.

Key Terms and Concepts

cluster analysis, *628*
data reduction technique, *626*
dependence techniques, *615*
discriminant analysis, *622*
dummy variable, *617*
factor analysis, *625*
factor loading, *626*

factor rotation, *628*
general linear model (GLM), *616*
interdependence techniques, *615*
multicollinearity, *619*
multidimensional scaling, *630*
multiple regression analysis, *616*

multivariate analysis of variance
 (MANOVA), *621*
partial correlation, *618*
partial least squares (PLS), *631*
structural equations modeling (SEM), *630*
variate, *613*

Questions for Review and Critical Thinking

1. Define *multivariate data analysis*.
2. What is the *variate* in multivariate? What is an example of a variate in multiple regression and in factor analysis?

3. What is the distinction between *dependence techniques* and *interdependence techniques?* Provide examples of each.

4. What is *GLM*? How can multiple regression and *n*-way ANOVA be described as GLM approaches?

5. What are the steps in interpreting a multiple regression analysis result? Can the same steps be used to interpret a univariate ANOVA model?

6. A researcher dismisses a regression result because the model R^2 was under 0.70. Do you think this was necessarily wise? Explain.

7. Consider a simple regression result for a toy company like that presented in the chapter. The result suggests that grammar school enrollment relates to toy company sales. However, if the data come equally from Europe and Canada, does this represent a potential source of variation that is not accounted for in the researcher's model? How could the researcher examine whether or not sales may be dependent upon country?

8. What multivariate data analysis technique is appropriate for a researcher analyzing results from an experiment manipulating package color and price on three independent variables: attitude toward the product, intention to purchase the product, and intention to recommend the product to others?

9. What multivariate data analysis technique is appropriate for an analysis predicting whether students choose to live on campus or off campus based on their family's income, how far away from the university the family home is, the student's SAT or ACT score, and the student's gender? Explain your answer.

10. What is a *factor loading*?

11. How does factor analysis allow for data reduction?

12. How is the number of factors decided in most EFA programs?

13. Give an example of a situation in which each of the techniques mentioned in question 5 might be used.

14. What is *multidimensional scaling*? When might a researcher use this technique?

15. What is *cluster analysis*? When might a researcher use this technique?

16. Name at least two multivariate techniques that can be useful in constructing perceptual maps.

17. A researcher uses multiple regression to predict a client's sales volume based on gross domestic product, personal income, disposable personal income, unemployment, and the consumer price index. What problems might be anticipated with this multiple regression model?

Research Activities

1. Use the multistep process to interpret the regression results below. This model has been run by a researcher trying to explain customer loyalty to a restaurant. The independent variables are customer perceptions of value, atmosphere, quality, and a location variable labeled center. This is a dummy variable that takes the value of 1 if the restaurant is in a shopping center and 0 if it is a stand-alone location. What substantive conclusions would you recommend to the restaurant company?

Model Summary

Model	R	R Square	Adjusted R Square	Std. Error of the Estimate
1	0.176	0.031	0.027	0.996

DV = Loyalty

ANOVA(b)

Model		Sum of Squares	df	Mean Square	F	Sig.
1	Regression	27.9731	4	6.9933	7.049	0.0000138
	Residual	876.0469	883	0.9921		
	Total	904.0200	887			

Coefficients(a)

Model		Unstandardized Coefficients B	Std. Error	Standardized Coefficients Beta	t	Sig.	VIF
1	(Constant)	−0.306	0.229		−1.338	0.181	
	Value	0.104	0.036	0.099	2.877	0.004	1.087
	Atmosphere	0.048	0.026	0.067	1.883	0.060	1.144
	Quality	0.044	0.028	0.054	1.590	0.112	1.038
	Center	−0.250	0.071	−0.124	−3.508	0.000	1.132

2. Interpret the following GLM results. Following from an example in the chapter, *performance* is the performance rating for a business unit manager. *Sales* is a measure of the average sales for that unit. *Experience* is the number of years the manager has been in the industry. The variable *dummy* has been added. This variable is a 0 if the manager has no advanced college degree and a 1 if the manager has an MBA. Do you have any recommendations?

```
                          The SAS System
                          The GLM Procedure
                   Dependent Variable: performance
```

| | | | Sum of | | | |
Source		DF	Squares	Mean Square	F Value	Pr > F
Model		3	173.6381430	57.8793810	13.87	<.0001
Error		36	150.2341040	4.1731696		
Corrected Total		39	323.8722470			

R-Square	Coeff Var	Root MSE	performance Mean
0.536132	2.514731	2.042834	81.23468

Source	DF	Type III SS	Mean Square	F Value	Pr > F
dummy	1	136.9511200	136.9511200	32.82	<.0001
sales	1	22.4950649	22.4950649	5.39	0.0260
Experience	1	2.2356995	2.2356995	0.54	0.4689

| Level of | | -------performance------- | | -----------sales---------- | | ----Experience-------- | |
dummy	N	Mean	Std Dev	Mean	Std Dev	Mean	Std Dev
0	22	79.4848842	1.78987031	15979.7723	2008.32604	23.8984087	8.27327485
1	18	83.3733171	2.50773844	16432.0080	2015.18863	20.6788050	8.96324112

3. Interpret the following regression results. All of the variables are the same as in number 2. These results are produced with a regression program instead of the GLM–univariate ANOVA program.
   a. What do you notice when the results are compared to those in number 2? Comment.
   b. List the independent variables in order from greatest to least in terms of how strong the relationship is with performance.
   c. When might one prefer to use an ANOVA program instead of a multiple regression program?

```
                          The SAS System
                          The REG Procedure
                          Model: MODEL1
                   Dependent Variable: performance

                   Number of observations Read 40
                   Number of observations Used 40
```

```
                        Analysis of Variance
```

| | | | Sum of | Mean | | |
Source		DF	Squares	Square	F Value	Pr > F
Model		3	173.63814	57.87938	13.87	<.0001
Error		36	150.23410	4.17317		
Corrected Total		39	323.87225			

Root MSE	2.04283	R-Square	0.5361
Dependent Mean	81.23468	Adj R-Sq	0.4975
Coeff Var	2.51473		

```
                        Parameter Estimates
```

| | | | Parameter | Standard | | | Standardized |
Variable	Label	DF	Estimate	Error	t Value	Pr > |t|	Estimate
Intercept	Intercept	1	72.68459	2.88092	25.23	<.0001	0
dummy	dummy	1	3.80621	0.66442	5.73	<.0001	0.66546
sales	sales	1	0.00038324	0.00016507	2.32	0.0260	0.26578
Experience	Experience	1	0.02829	0.03866	0.73	0.4689	0.08475

4. Interpret the following factor analysis results. The variables represent sample results of self-reported emotions while viewing a film. What two summated scales might be produced based on these results?

Total Variance Explained

Component	Initial Eigenvalues Total	% of Variance	Cumulative %	Extraction Sums of Squared Loadings Total	% of Variance	Cumulative %
1	2.94	36.74	36.74	2.94	36.74	36.74
2	2.51	31.34	68.08	2.51	31.34	68.08
3	0.71	8.84	76.92			
4	0.60	7.53	84.45			
5	0.42	5.20	89.65			
6	0.29	3.67	93.32			
7	0.29	3.64	96.96			
8	0.24	3.04	100.00			

Extraction Method: Principal Component Analysis.

Component Matrix(a)

	Factor 1	Factor 2
Interesting	0.664	−0.327
Anxious	0.444	0.511
Enthusiastic	0.842	−0.332
Worried	0.295	0.828
Exciting	0.812	−0.206
Tired	0.269	0.835
Happy	0.784	−0.383
Guilty	0.398	0.675

Extraction Method: Principal Component Analysis.
A   2 components extracted.

Rotated Component Matrix(a)

	Component Factor 1	Factor 2
Interesting	0.739	−0.024
Anxious	0.194	0.648
Enthusiastic	0.904	0.044
Worried	−0.073	0.876
Exciting	0.825	0.147
Tired	−0.100	0.872
Happy	0.872	−0.025
Guilty	0.084	0.779

Extraction Method: Principal Component Analysis.
Rotation Method: Varimax with Kaiser Normalization.
A   Rotation converged in 3 iterations.

5. **'NET** Go to http://www.census.gov and examine some of the tables for your area. Cut and paste the table into a spreadsheet or statistical program. Run one dependence and one interdependence technique on the data. Interpret the results.

6. **'NET** Use http://www.ask.com to find an F-ratio calculator that will return a p-value given a calculated F-ratio and the degrees of freedom associated with the test.

7. **'NET** The Federal Reserve Bank of St. Louis maintains a database called FRED (Federal Reserve Economic Data). Navigate to the FRED database at http://www.stls.frb.org/fred/index.html. Use the consumer price index, exchange rates, interest rates, and one other variable to predict the consumer price index for the same time period. The data can either be downloaded or cut and pasted into another file.

Case 24.1 The Utah Jazz

The Utah Jazz are interested in understanding the market for the National Basketball Association. A study is conducted as described here.

Data Collection

Data came from a survey of adult residents of a large western metropolitan area. Respondents were selected in accordance with a quota sample of the area that was based on the age and sex characteristics reported in the most recent census. Six age categories for both males and females were used to gain representation of these characteristics in the market. In addition, interviewers were assigned to various parts of the area to ensure representation of the market with respect to socioeconomic characteristics. A total of 225 respondents age 18 and over provided data for the study.

Interviews were conducted by trained interviewers using a self-completion questionnaire. The presence of the interviewers served to answer any questions that might arise as well as to ensure compliance with the instructions.

Measures for the variables in the three categories of AIO (attitudes, interest, and opinions) were obtained using six-point rating scales. For example, the item for price proneness asked, "When you are buying a product such as food, clothing, and personal care items, how important is it to get the lowest price?" This item was anchored with "Not at all important" and "Extremely important."

The broadly defined category of demographics included standard socioeconomic characteristics as well as media preferences and attendance at professional hockey matches and university basketball games. Demographics were obtained using a variety of forced-choice and free-response measures, the natures of which are indicated in the variable information presented in Case Exhibit 24.1−1. The categorical measures of type of dwelling and preferred type of radio programming were coded as dummy variables for analysis. The criterion measure of patronage came from an open-ended question asking how many NBA games the respondent had attended during the past season.

CASE EXHIBIT 24.1−1 **Characteristics of the Market for Professional Basketball**

Variables	Means			F-Ratio	P	Loading	
	None (n = 129)	Low (n = 47)	High (n = 49)			I	II
Market Orientation[a]							
Price proneness	3.99	4.04	3.63	1.31	.271		
Quality proneness	4.95	4.74	4.82	.74	.480		
Product awareness	4.45	4.02	4.00	3.71	.026		
Product involvement	4.34	4.43	4.14	.66	.517		
Prepurchase planning	4.21	3.85	3.82	2.03	.134		
Brand loyalty	3.95	4.39	3.92	.96	.384		
Information search	3.83	3.55	3.96	1.06	.347		
Interests in Leisure Pursuits[b]							
Need for change from work routine	4.11	4.34	4.55	1.92	.150	.34	
Need for independence in leisure choice	4.88	4.94	4.96	.09	.911	.08	
Need for companionship during leisure	4.85	5.13	4.88	1.16	.317	.10	
Preference for passive versus active pursuits	3.64	4.15	4.57	7.28	.001	.70	
Self-image as athletic	3.67	4.38	4.47	5.89	.003	.60	
Childhood attendance at sporting events	3.38	3.89	4.18	5.41	.005	.60	
Pleasure from sporting events	3.14	3.66	4.27	10.62	.000	.84	
Opinions about Professional Sports[c]							
Athletes as a reference group	3.51	3.64	4.18	3.90	.022	.30	−.19
Excitement from enthusiastic crowd	4.27	4.72	4.73	2.70	.069	.24	.20
Excitement from animosity between teams	3.29	3.28	4.27	6.94	.001	.36	−.41
Acceptance of alcoholic beverages at games	2.60	3.64	3.39	6.88	.001	.34	.46
Enjoyment from large crowds	3.91	3.85	4.49	3.22	.042	.23	−.32
Enjoyment when standing at games	3.37	3.44	3.90	2.25	.108	.22	−.17
Excitement of professional basketball	4.09	3.91	4.67	5.34	.005	.27	−.49
Satisfaction from professional basketball	3.17	3.70	4.80	24.98	.000	.78	−.26
Importance of a winning team	4.26	4.69	5.07	6.12	.003	.39	.02
Demographics[d]							
Years in local area (number of years)	24.47	23.51	19.04	2.02	.135	−.24	
Sex (0 = female, 1 = male)	.40	.55	.65	5.45	.006	.39	
Marital status (0 = single, 1 = married)	.60	.62	.45	2.00	.138	−.21	
Household size (number of persons)	3.13	3.27	3.14	.11	.896	.01	
Rents apartment (0 = no, 1 = yes)	.18	.32	.35	3.70	.026	.30	
Rents a house (0/1)	.09	.09	.08	.03	.967	−.03	
Owns a house (0/1)	.60	.49	.41	3.08	.048	−.29	
Owns a condominium (0/1)	.05	.02	.06	.50	.607	.01	
Head of household (0/1)	.52	.64	.67	2.19	.115	.24	

(Continued)

CASE EXHIBIT 24.1–1 **Characteristics of the Market for Professional Basketball** (*Continued*)

Variables	Means			F-Ratio	P	Loading	
	None (n = 129)	Low (n = 47)	High (n = 49)			I	II
Demographics[d]							
Occupational prestige of self (NORC scale)	68.05	69.36	70.63	1.27	.284	.19	
Job leaves evenings free for entertainment (0/1)	.87	.85	.92	.57	.567	.10	
Prefers easy-listening music radio programming (0/1)	.39	.34	.29	.83	.438	−.15	
Prefers contemporary popular music radio (0/1)	.16	.28	.27	1.96	.143	.20	
Prefers rock music radio (0/1)	.14	.11	.27	2.76	.066	.23	
Prefers country-western music radio (0/1)	.15	.19	.08	1.22	.299	−.12	
Prefers talk and news radio programming (0/1)	.09	.04	.06	.52	.597	−.08	
Education (years of schooling)	13.08	13.66	13.56	5.11	.007	.38	
Age (years)	41.51	39.79	33.59	4.21	.016	−.34	
Annual household income (7-point scale)	4.88	5.11	5.16	.65	.523	.13	
Monthly personal expenditures on entertainment for household (dollars)	85.10	112.45	101.29	1.38	.254	.13	
Attendance at university basketball (games last year)	.92	1.89	4.14	15.29	.000	.66	
Attendance at professional hockey (matches last year)	.69	2.28	2.78	5.33	.006	.37	

[a]Canonical discriminant analysis not significant at $p = .189$; therefore, no loadings are given.

[b]Canonical discriminant analysis significant at $p = .004$, first function significant. Centroids for the market segment groups are as follows: none, −.29; low, .19; high, .59.

[c]Canonical discriminant analysis significant at $p = .000$, both functions significant. Centroids for the market segment groups on the first function are as follows: none, −.47; low, .26; high, 1.00. Centroids on the second function are as follows: none, −.10; low, .57; high, −.27.

[d]Canonical discriminant analysis significant at $p = .004$, first function significant. Centroids for the market segment groups are as follows: none, −.41; low, .14; high, .97.

Data Analysis

The distribution of responses to the attendance item was skewed, as might be expected. Thus, 57.3 percent of the respondents reported having attended none of the 41 possible games. Those who attended at least one game were recorded in accordance with specification of the light half and the heavy half of the market. This category of patrons was split as nearly as possible at the median, *giving 20.9 percent who attended one or two games and 21.8 percent who attended three or more.* The three patronage categories thus used for analysis were subsequently termed the *none, low,* and *high* segments.

Given the categorical nature of the criterion measure and the continuous nature of the predictor variables, both univariate analysis of variance and discriminant analysis were employed for the survey. Each of the four categories of predictor variables was subjected to a *separate discriminant* analysis to test the multivariate hypothesis of relationship between patronage and the predictor set in question. The univariate ANOVAs were used to provide complementary information about the nature of the segments.

Results

Case Exhibit 24.1−1 gives the results of the analyses conducted on the four sets of predictor variables. Each set produced at least one variable that was significant in univariate analysis. Three of the four discriminant analyses were significant.

The first predictor set involving AIOs, "marketing orientation," provided only a single variable that ANOVA showed to differentiate among the members of the three patronage segments. The discriminant analysis was nonsignificant.

"Interests in leisure pursuits" emerged as more predictive. By univariate ANOVA, four variables were found significant at the 0.05 level. The discriminant analysis was significant at $p = 0.004$.

"Opinions about professional sports" provided significant prediction of patronage. Seven of the nine variables reached significance at the 0.05 level in univariate analysis. The discriminant analysis was significant beyond $p = 0.001$, and it produced two significant functions. The first significant function provided 79.8 percent of the explained variance, and the second function provided 20.2 percent.

Finally, the set "demographics" was also found to be related to patronage. Counting the four dummy-coded measures of dwelling type and the five similar preferences for radio programming as separate variables, 7 of the 22 demographics reached significance in univariate analysis. The discriminant analysis was significant at $p = 0.004$.

Question

Interpret the managerial significance of the ANOVA and multiple discriminant analysis results.

Source: Courtesy of the American Marketing Association. Adapted from paper presented at AMA conference, 1984.

APPENDIX 24A
GETTING FACTOR RESULTS WITH SAS OR SPSS

Although researchers may choose to use a spreadsheet to produce simple or even multiple regression results, they will almost always turn to a specialized program for procedures like factor analysis. As a way of familiarizing readers with the mechanics involved, here are some instructions for getting factor results in each program.

SAS is most typically interfaced by writing short computer programs. SAS can read EXCEL spreadsheets quite easily. The data simply need to be "imported" into SAS by using the File dialog box (click on File to begin this process—see SAS documentation contained in the help files for more on how to do this). Once the data are set up, a factor program can be easily produced. Suppose we wished to run a factor program including a varimax rotation on 12 variables labeled X1−X12. The program would be

proc factor rotate = v;
var X1−X12;

After clicking "run," the results appear in the output window.

In SPSS, the click-through sequence is as follows:

- ANALYZE
- DATA REDUCTION
- FACTOR ANALYSIS

This produces a dialog box. Now follow the following steps to get results that would match those above:

- Highlight variables X1 to X12 (either individually or in multiples).
- Click the ▶ to move them into the "Variables" window.
- Click "ROTATION."
  ○ Select VARIMAX.
- Optional: Click "OPTIONS."
  ○ Select "SORT BY SIZE."
  ○ Select "SUPPRESS ABSOLUTE VALUES LESS THAN."
    ■ These two options make the output easier to read by organizing the output around the size of the loadings on each factor and by not showing loadings below some specified absolute value (0.1 by default). For factor analyses involving many variables, this is particularly helpful.
- Click "CONTINUE."
- Click "OK."

The results will appear in the output window.

CHAPTER 25
COMMUNICATING RESEARCH RESULTS:
RESEARCH REPORT, ORAL PRESENTATION, AND RESEARCH FOLLOW-UP

After studying this chapter, you should be able to

1. Define the parts of a research report following a standard format
2. Explain how to use tables for presenting numerical information
3. Summarize how to select and use the types of research charts
4. Know how to give an effective oral presentation
5. Discuss the importance of Internet reporting and research follow-up

Chapter Vignette: Effective Research Is a Stone's Throw Away

The Rosetta Stone represents one of the greatest findings in the history of communication. The stone dates back to several centuries before Christ but was discovered near the ancient city of Rosetta, Egypt at the end of the eighteenth century. What made this discovery so special? The etchings on the stone represented a decree to the peoples of that time that was not only written in hieroglyphics but also in ancient Greek. French and British researchers worked for decades and eventually produced a translation between the ancient Greek and the hieroglyphic script. They learned that hieroglyphics were not just pictures but that over time, hieroglyphics had developed into a language with symbols that took on phonetic characteristics including sound. This breakthrough meant that scores of ancient etchings could now communicate effectively because of the translation code made possible by the Rosetta Stone.[1]

© SUSAN VAN ETTEN

Fortunately, marketing researchers don't have to write research reports on stones, but effective communication can still be pretty hard! The research report is the tool that translates what most people could not possibly understand into a useful report that communicates important information for business managers, marketing executives, policy makers, or other marketing researchers. Marketing practitioners are not generally schooled in multivariate data analysis, ethnography, phenomenology or most other technical aspects of marketing research. So, even if the marketing research is properly conducted, the research can still be a complete failure if the researcher is unable to produce a user-friendly, concise, and actionable research report. In fact, science itself is of little use unless one can effectively communicate its meaning.[2]

In fact, employers often view excellent writing skills as a necessary requisite when evaluating marketing research candidates. Unfortunately, these same employers are often disappointed with technical employees' communication skills. These employees are expected not only to write formal research reports, but also to make effective oral presentations and increasingly, to deliver effective and accurate communication via Internet media including online meetings, blogs, and even tweets. (A tweet is an electronic micromessage of 140 characters or less that can be posted and distributed through http://twitter.com.) Imagine the chore of translating results of a months-long research project into a 140-character tweet! Sounds like a job for another Rosetta Stone![3]

Introduction

Researchers can easily be tempted into rushing through the research report. By the time the report is written, the researchers may well feel exhausted or burned out and ready to move on to something new. All the "real" work has been done; it just has to be put on paper. This feeling can be disastrous, however. If people who need to use the research results have to wade through a disorganized presentation, are confused by technical jargon, or find sloppiness of language or thought, they will probably discount the report and make decisions without it, just as if the project had never been done. So, the research report is a crucial means for communicating the whole project. This chapter explains the communication of research results using written reports, presentations, and follow-up conversations.[4]

Communication Process

Some insights from the theory of communications help to clarify the importance of the research report. Exhibit 25.1 illustrates one view of the **communication process**. Several elements influence successful communication.

- The *communicator*—the source or sender of the message (the writer of the report)
- The *message*—the set of meanings being sent to or received by the audience (the *findings* of the research project)
- The *medium*—the way in which the message is delivered to the audience (the oral or written report itself)
- The *audience*—the receiver or destination of the message (the manager who will make a decision based—we hope—on the report findings)
- *Feedback*—a communication, also involving a message and channel, that flows in the reverse direction (from the audience to the original communicator) and that may be used to modify subsequent communications (the manager's response to the report)

The Research Snapshot on page 642 illustrates how simple words can lead to incorrect meanings.

This model may make communication seem simple. Perhaps communication is simple when the message flows smoothly from writer to reader, and then in return, from reader to writer to provide feedback. Actually, communication is more complex. Exhibit 25.2 illustrates one key difficulty. The communicator and the audience each have individual fields of experience. These overlap to some extent; otherwise no communication would be possible. Still, a great deal of experience is not common to both parties. As communicators send a message, they encode it in terms that make sense to them based on their fields of experience. As the individuals in the audience receive the message, they decode it based on their own fields of experience. The message is successfully communicated only if the parties share enough common experience for it to be encoded, transmitted, and decoded with roughly the same meaning.

communication process

The process by which one person or source sends a message to an audience or receiver and then receives feedback about the message.

TOTHEPOINT

It is a luxury to be understood.

—Ralph Waldo Emerson

EXHIBIT 25.1
The Communication Process

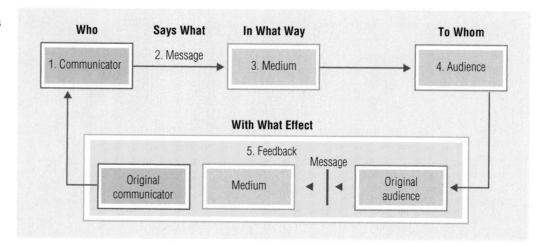

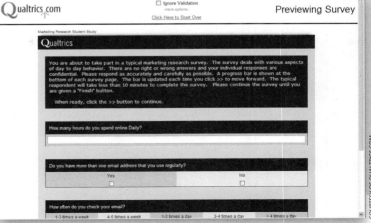

Now, the end is near. The Survey This! feature has covered quite a bit of ground about marketing research students' preferences and behaviors. The topics include how students interact with technology, preferences for communicating, studying, and how they spend their time, among other things. Additionally, you may be interested in comparing how different groups of respondents are similar or alike. Perhaps you are curious about some of these issues. Develop at least three research questions. Examine these questions using the data from the survey. Prepare a written report and slide show presentation that could be used to brief an interested audience of businesspeople who wish to better serve this particular market. Try to pick issues that you are truly curious about and you'll find yourself anxious to get to the answer!

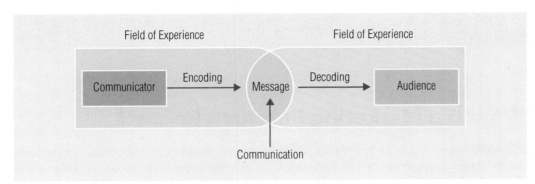

EXHIBIT 25.2

Communication Occurs in a Common Field of Experience

Communication in Practice

In the research setting, the communicator (the researcher) has spent a great deal of time studying a problem. He or she has looked at secondary sources, gathered primary data, used statistical techniques to analyze the data, and reached conclusions. When the report on the project is written, all this baggage will affect its contents. On the assumption that the reader has a lot of background information on the project, the researcher may produce pages and pages of unexplained tables, expecting the reader to unearth from them the same patterns that the researcher has observed. The report may contain technical terms such as *parameter estimate*, F–*distribution*, *statistical significance*, *correlations*, and *eigenvalue*, on the assumption that the reader will understand them. Another researcher may assume that the reader does not have a lot of background information and may go overboard explaining everything in the report in sixth-grade terms. Although the researcher's intent is to ensure that the reader will not get lost, this effort may insult the reader.

Usually when readers receive a report, they have not thought much about the project. They may not know anything about statistics and may have many other responsibilities. If they cannot understand the report quickly, they may put it on a stack of things to do someday.

Simply delivering a report to its audience is not sufficient to ensure that it gets attention. The report needs to be written so as to draw on the common experience of the researcher and the reader. And the person responsible for making sure that it does so is the writer—not the reader. Unless a report is really crucial, a busy reader will not spend time and effort struggling through an inadequate or difficult-to-read document.

Sloppy Numbers in the Crosshairs of Dow Jones Newspaper Fund's Director

As executive director of the Dow Jones Newspaper Fund, former *Wall Street Journal* editor Richard Holden has a mission to improve the quality of journalism education. His formal role emphasizes high school and college students, but Holden finds that even the professionals can use some education in reporting data. He has gathered examples of newspaper reports that present numbers in ways that are confusing, misleading, or even incorrect.

Consider the following examples, taken from a seminar Holden presented to journalists. See if you can identify the problem with each statement:

"Visa announced that its new credit card will carry an adjustable rate set monthly at four percent above the prime rate, in line with other variable-rate cards."

This is a common mistake: confusing *percentage* and *percentage points*. A rate set so slightly above the prime rate would be an unusually good bargain. For example, at the time of this writing, the U.S. federal prime rate is 4.0 percent; prime plus 4 percent would be just 4.16 percent, far below the rates charged by most credit cards. The writer probably meant Visa would charge prime rate plus four percentage points, which in this example would be 8 percent.

"Battling Hunger, a food pantry, said it delivered 110,000 tons of food to Detroit last Thanksgiving. The food was delivered to help residents there overcome the effects of a severe economic slump, particularly in the automobile industry."

This example shows that it is important to check whether numbers themselves, including the units of measure, are logical. In this case, 110,000 tons equals 220 million pounds of food. Can that be reasonable? Even if the food pantry served a million people—all of Detroit plus some suburbanites—it would have distributed 220 pounds of food to each individual. Not likely. When numbers are this unrealistic, the writer should check the calculations, including the decimal point's location, and the units. Perhaps this writer meant 110,000 pounds or 110 tons.

Source: Based on Carl Bialik, "Monitoring the Numbers in the News," *Wall Street Journal*, January 20, 2006, http://online.wsj.com/article/SB113764595134250640.html, accessed November 2, 2008; Carl Bialik, "The Results Are In," *Wall Street Journal*, January 27, 2006, http://online.wsj.com/mdc/public/page/2_3020-moneyrate.html, accessed November 2, 2008.

What Is a Marketing Research Report?

research report

An oral presentation or written statement of research results, strategic recommendations, and/ or other conclusions to a specific audience.

A **research report** is a formal presentation and/or written statement that communicates research results and draws appropriate conclusions following from the research. A market research report is directed to the client or management team who initiated the research. If the proposal's deliverables include specific managerial recommendations, they are included and highlighted in the report. In fact, they should be a logical conclusion of the report contents. A basic marketing researcher writes a very similar report but it often takes the form of a white paper or scholarly research paper targeted for publication in a research journal such as the *Journal of Marketing* or the *Journal of the Academy of Marketing Science*. More often than not, a written research report will also be supported by a formal presentation delivered in person or via the Internet.

More and more research companies are finding a ready research market for marketing research reports sold online for a fee. Several Web sites serve as brokers or warehouses for reports on virtually any business topic. For example, Research and Markets (http://www.researchandmarkets.com) offers hundreds of thousands of research reports through its Web site. These reports are compiled from some of the top consulting firms and leading publishers around the world.[5] Potential customers can preview these reports by examining a summary of each. At an average price of about $4,000 per piece, one can see that they had best be very well done and communicate clearly or the customer is not likely to use this service again.

Report Format

report format

The makeup or arrangement of parts necessary to a good research report.

Although every research report is custom-made for the project it represents, some conventions of **report format** are universal. They represent a consensus about the parts necessary for a good research report and how they should be ordered. This consensus is not a law, however. Every book on report writing suggests the use of its own unique format, and every report writer has to pick and choose the section and order that will work best for the project at hand. Many companies and universities also have in-house report formats or writing guides for writers to follow. The format described in this section serves as a starting point from which a writer can shape his or her own appropriate format. It includes seven major elements:

1. Title page (sometimes preceded by a title fly page)
2. Letter of transmittal
3. Letter of authorization
4. Table of contents (and lists of figures and tables)
5. Executive summary
   a. Objectives
   b. Results
   c. Conclusions
   d. Recommendations
6. Body
   a. Introduction
      1. Background
      2. Objectives
   b. Methodology
   c. Results
   d. Limitations
   e. Conclusions and recommendations
7. Appendix
   a. Data collection forms
   b. Detailed calculations
   c. General tables
   d. Bibliography
   e. Other support material

This format is illustrated graphically in Exhibit 25.3.

EXHIBIT 25.3 **Report Format**

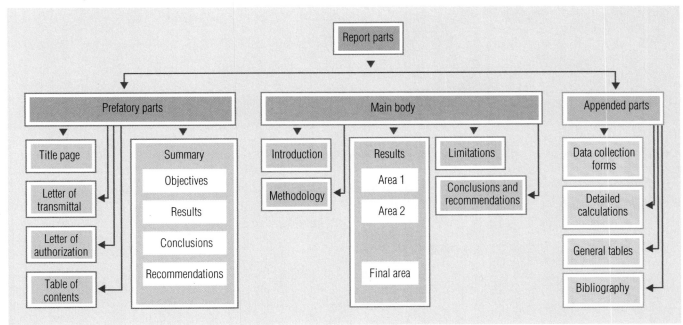

Tailoring the Format to the Project

The format of a research report may need to be adjusted for two reasons: (1) to obtain the proper level of formality and (2) to decrease the complexity of the report. The format given here is for the most formal type of report, such as one for a large project done within an organization or one done by a research agency for a client company. This type of report is usually bound in a permanent cover and may be hundreds of pages long.

In less formal reports, each part is shorter, and some parts are omitted. Exhibit 25.4 illustrates how the format is adapted to shorter, less formal reports. The situation may be compared to the way people's clothing varies according to the formality of the occasion. The most formal report is dressed, so to speak, in a tuxedo or long evening gown. It includes the full assortment of prefatory parts—title fly page, title page, letters of transmittal and authorization, and table of contents. Like changing into an everyday business suit, dropping down to the next level of formality involves eliminating parts of the prefatory material that are not needed in this situation and reducing the complexity of the report body. In general, as the report moves down through the sport coat and slacks and then blue jeans stages, more prefatory parts are dropped, and the complexity and length of the report body are reduced.

How does the researcher decide on the appropriate level of formality? The general rule is to include all the parts needed for effective communication in the particular circumstances—and no more. This depends on how far up in management the report is expected to go and how routine the matter is. A researcher's immediate supervisor does not need a 100-page, "black-tie" report on a routine project. However, the board of directors does not want a one-page "blue jeans" report on a big project that backs a major expansion program. The formal report to top management may later be stripped of some of the prefatory parts (and thus reduced in formality) for wider circulation within the company.

EXHIBIT 25.4 Adapting Report Format to Required Formality

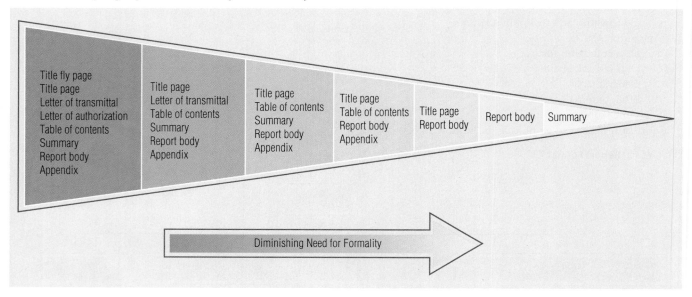

The Parts of the Report

Typically, research reports follow the same general outline. Research reports are a form of technical writing and as such, readers may well expect the paper to follow this format. Here, the old adage, "If it ain't broke, don't fix it," truly applies.

■ TITLE PAGE

The *title page* should state the title of the report, for whom the report was prepared, by whom it was prepared, and the date of release or presentation. The title should give a brief but complete indication of the purpose of the research project. Addresses and titles of the preparer and recipient may also be included. On confidential reports, the title page may list the people to whom the report should be circulated. For the most formal reports, the title page is preceded by a title fly page, which contains only the report's title.

■ LETTER OF TRANSMITTAL

Relatively formal and very formal reports include a *letter of transmittal*. Its purpose is to release or deliver the report to the recipient. It also serves to establish some rapport between the reader and the writer. This is the one part of the formal report in which a personal or even slightly informal tone should be used. The transmittal should not dive into the report findings except in the broadest terms.

Exhibit 25.5 presents a sample letter of transmittal. Note that the opening paragraph releases the report and briefly identifies the factors of authorization. The letter comments generally on findings and matters of interest regarding the research. The closing section expresses the writer's personal interest in the project just completed and in doing additional, related work.

EXHIBIT 25.5
Example Transmittal Letter

EMR ResearchGroup
Moving you forward!

August 30, 2009

Mr. Mario Lagasto
President, Leading Edge Food Group
Columbia, IA 50057

Re: Presentation of Research Identifying Customer Loyalty

Dear Mr. Lagasto:

The report outlined in the research proposal of March 15, 2009 is complete. I have personally supervised the project, conducted the statistical analyses, and prepared this report along with my two senior research associates, Natalia James and David Parker.

The report addresses the key decision statement: In what ways can your restaurants build customer loyalty so that revenues increase through more frequent patronage? The key research questions involve identifying controllable characteristics that end up relating to greater share of wallet. As agreed upon in the proposal, the report offers no specific recommendations for managerial action, but rather, it presents conclusions which should enable you to make informed decisions. Thus, the conclusions conform to the deliverables described in the proposal letter.

We successfully accomplished the research project as described in the outline. We were able to meet our goals for interviewing groups of customers and non-customers in a timely fashion. We are grateful for your business and look forward to working with you as you develop strategic plans of action based on this report. Once you have taken a look at the report, please contact me and we will schedule a formal presentation and question and answer period for your management team.

Sincerely,

Barry J. Babin
President

EMR Research Group
114 Railroad Ave
Choudrant, LA71272

COURTESY OF THE AUTHOR

■ LETTER OF AUTHORIZATION

The *letter of authorization* is a letter to the researcher that approves the project, details who has responsibility for it, and describes the resources available to support it. Because the researcher would not write this letter personally, writing guidelines will not be discussed here. In many situations, simply referring to the authorization in the letter of transmittal is sufficient. If so, the letter of authorization need not be included in the report. In some cases, though, the reader may be unfamiliar with the authorization or may need detailed information about it. In such cases, the report should include this letter, preferably an exact copy of the original.

■ THE TABLE OF CONTENTS

A *table of contents* is essential to any report more than a few pages long. It should list the divisions and subdivisions of the report with page references. The table of contents is based on the final outline of the report, but it should include only the first-level subdivisions. For short reports it is sufficient to include only the main divisions. If the report includes many figures or tables, a list of these should immediately follow the table of contents.

■ THE EXECUTIVE SUMMARY

The *summary*, or executive summary as it is called more often, briefly explains why the research project was conducted, what aspects of the problem were considered, what the outcome was, and what should be done. It is a vital part of the report. Studies have indicated that nearly all managers read a report's summary, while only a minority read the rest of the report. Thus, the writer's only chance to produce an impact may be in the summary.

The summary should be written only after the rest of the report has been completed. It represents the essence of the report. It should be one page long (or, at most, two pages), so the writer must carefully sort out what is important enough to be included in it. Several pages of the full report may have to be condensed into one summarizing sentence. Some parts of the report may be condensed more than others; the number of words in the summary need not be in proportion to the length of the section being discussed. The summary should be written to be self-sufficient. In fact, the summary is often detached from the report and circulated by itself.

The summary contains four elements. First, it states the objectives of the report, including the most important background information and the specific purposes of the project. Second, it presents the methodology and the major results. Next come the conclusions. These are opinions based on the results and constitute an interpretation of the results. Finally come recommendations, or suggestions for action, based on the conclusions. In many cases, managers prefer not to have recommendations included in the report or summary. Whether or not recommendations are to be included should be clear from the particular context of the report.

■ THE BODY

introduction section

The part of the body of a research report that discusses background information and the specific objectives of the research.

The *body* constitutes the bulk of the report. It begins with an **introduction section** setting out the background factors that made the project necessary as well as the objectives of the report. It continues with discussions of the methodology, results, and limitations of the study and finishes with conclusions and recommendations based on the results.

The introduction explains why the project was done and what it aimed to discover. It should include the basic authorization and submittal data. The relevant background comes next. Enough background should be included to explain why the project was worth doing, but unessential historical factors should be omitted. The question of how much is enough should be answered by referring to the needs of the audience. A government report that will be widely circulated requires more background than a company's internal report on customer satisfaction. The last part of the introduction explains exactly what the project tried to discover. It discusses the statement of the problem and research questions as they were stated in the research proposal. Each purpose presented here should have a corresponding entry in the results section later in the report.

research methodology section

The part of the body of a report that presents the findings of the project. It includes tables, charts, and an organized narrative.

The second part of the body is the **research methodology section**. This part is a challenge to write because it must explain technical procedures in a manner appropriate for the audience. The material in this section may be supplemented with more detailed explanations in the appendix or a glossary of technical terms. This part of the report should address four topics:

1. *Research design.* Was the study exploratory, descriptive, or causal? Did the data come from primary or secondary sources? Were results collected by survey, observation, or experiment?

A copy of the survey questionnaire or observation form should be included in the appendix. Why was this particular design suited to the study?

2. *Sample design*. What was the target population? What sampling frame was used? What sample units were used? How were they selected? How large was the sample? What was the response rate? Detailed computations to support these explanations should be saved for the appendix.

3. *Data collection and fieldwork*. How many and what types of fieldworkers were used? What training and supervision did they receive? Was the work verified? This section is important for establishing the degree of accuracy of the results.

4. *Analysis*. This section should outline the general statistical methods used in the study, but the information presented here should not overlap with what is presented in the results section.

The **results section** should make up the bulk of the report and should present, in some logical order, those findings of the project that bear on the objectives. The results should be organized as a continuous narrative, designed to be convincing but not to oversell the project. Summary tables and charts should be used to aid the discussion. These may serve as points of reference to the data being discussed and free the prose from excessive facts and figures. Comprehensive or detailed charts, however, should be saved for the appendix.

results section

The part of the body of a report that presents the findings of the project. It includes tables, charts, and an organized narrative.

Because no research is perfect, its limitations should be indicated. If problems arose with nonresponse error or sampling procedures, these should be discussed. However, the discussion of limitations should avoid overemphasizing the weaknesses; its aim should be to provide a realistic basis for assessing the results.

The last part of the body is the **conclusions and recommendations section**. As mentioned earlier, conclusions are opinions based on the results, and recommendations are suggestions for action. The conclusions and recommendations should be presented in this section in more detail than in the summary, and the text should include justification as needed.

conclusions and recommendations section

The part of the body of a report that provides opinions based on the results and suggestions for action.

■ THE APPENDIX

The *appendix* presents the "too . . . " material. Any material that is too technical or too detailed to go in the body should appear in the appendix. This includes materials of interest only to some readers or subsidiary materials not directly related to the objectives. Some examples of appendix materials are data collection forms, detailed calculations, discussions of highly technical questions, detailed or comprehensive tables of results, and a bibliography (if appropriate). Since the advent of company intranets, much appendix material is posted on internal Web pages.

Basic Marketing Research Report

The outline described applies especially to applied market research projects. When basic research reports are written, such as might be submitted and potentially published in an academic business journal, the outline changes slightly since some components become irrelevant. A common outline used in basic marketing research proceeds as follows:

1. Abstract
2. Introduction
3. Background
   a. Literature Review
   b. Hypotheses
4. Research Methods
5. Results
6. Discussion
   a. Implications
   b. Limitations
   c. Future Research
7. Conclusions
8. References
9. Appendixes

The material in the sections does not change very much between market and marketing research. So, the elements within each section are the same with only the noted exceptions. The basic research report will place a greater emphasis on how the current research is integrated into the previous literature dealing with the research topic. This section finishes with a specific set of theoretical hypotheses. The research methodology and results section may contain more statistical detail and jargon since the reader is expected to be knowledgeable in basic research methodology. A quick look at an academic business journal like the *Journal of Business Research*, the *Journal of Marketing*, the *Journal of the Academy of Marketing Science*, or the *Journal of Management* will give a reader a feel for this type of writing. Overall, though, both basic and applied marketing research reports involve technical writing and the principles of good technical writing apply.

Using Tables Effectively

graphic aids

Pictures or diagrams used to clarify complex points or emphasize a message.

Used properly, **graphic aids** can clarify complex points or emphasize a message. Used improperly or sloppily, they can distract or even mislead a reader. Graphical aids work best when they are an integral part of the text. The graphics should always be interpreted in the text. This does not mean that the writer should exhaustively explain an obvious chart or table, but it *does* mean that the text should point out the key elements of any graphic aid and relate them to the discussion in progress.

Several types of graphic aids may be useful in research reports including tables, charts, maps, and diagrams. The following discussion briefly covers the most common ones, tables and charts. The reader interested in other types of graphic material should consult more specialized sources.

Creating Tables

Tables are most useful for presenting numerical information, especially when several pieces of information have been gathered about each item discussed. For example, consider how hard following the information in Exhibit 25.6 might be with only narrative text and no graphical aids. Using tables allows a writer to point out significant features without getting bogged down in

EXHIBIT 25.6 Parts of a Table

Table number → Title →
Table 1024. Retail Sales—New Passenger Cars: 1990 to 2003
[In thousands 9,300 represents 9,300, 000, except as indicated. Retail new car sales include both sales to individuals and to corporate fleets. It also includes leased cars.]

Item	1990	1995	1997	1998	1999	2000	2001	2002	2003
Total retail new passenger car sales	9,300	8,635	8,272	8,142	8,698	8,847	8,423	8,103	7,510
Domestic[1]	6,897	7,129	6,917	6,762	6,979	6,831	6,325	5,676	5,527
Imports	2,403	1,506	1,355	1,380	1,719	2,016	2,098	2,226	2,083
Japan	1,719	982	726	691	758	863	837	923	817
Germany	265	207	297	367	467	517	523	547	544
Other	419	317	332	322	494	637	798	756	722

Stubheads →   Bannerheads →

[1] Includes cars produced in Canada and Mexico.
Source: U.S. Bureau of Transportation Statistics, *National Transportation Statistics 2004*. Data supplied by following source: *Motor Vehicle Facts & Figures, 1997*. Southfield, MI: *Ward's Motor Vehicle Facts & Figures, 2002*. Southfield, MI: 2002. See also <http://www.bts.gov>.

Footnote →   ┌── Source

— Represents zero.   [1]Change from prior year.
Source: U.S. Census Bureau, *Statistical Abstract of the United States*, 2006, table 1024, p. 678.

detail. The body of the report should include only relatively short summary tables, with comprehensive tables reserved for an appendix.

Each table should include the following elements:

- *Table number.* This allows for simple reference from the text to the table. If the text includes many tables, a list of tables should be included just after the table of contents.
- *Title.* The title should indicate the contents of the table and be complete enough to be intelligible without referring to the text.
- *Stubheads and bannerheads.* The stubheads contain the captions for the rows of the table, and the bannerheads (or boxheads) contain those for the columns.
- *Footnotes.* Any explanations or qualifications for particular table entries or sections should be given in footnotes.
- *Source notes.* If a table is based on material from one or more secondary sources rather than on new data generated by the project, the sources should be acknowledged, usually below the table.

Tables in a survey research report typically follow the format shown in Exhibit 25.7. This example cross-tabulates demographics with survey responses. Data from a statistical test also might be reported in table form, as shown in Exhibit 25.8.

EXHIBIT 25.7 Reporting Format for a Typical Cross-Tabulation

Online Activity	Age Group						
	12–17	18–28	29–40	41–50	51–59	60–69	70+
E-mail	89%	88%	92%	90%	94%	90%	89%
Online games	81%	54%	37%	29%	25%	25%	32%
Instant messaging	75%	66%	52%	38%	42%	33%	14%
Downloading music	51%	45%	28%	16%	14%	8%	5%
Job hunting	30%	62%	51%	40%	36%	17%	2%
Job research	—	44%	59%	59%	54%	31%	13%

Source: Excerpted from Susannah Fox and Mary Madden, "Generations Online," Pew Internet and American Life Project, December 2005, p. 3, http://www.pewinternet.org.

EXHIBIT 25.8 Reporting Format for a Typical Statistical Test

Will investors be more cautious about buying stock in companies with questionable advertising?

	Business	Advertising Management
Yes	57%	46%
No	27	35
Not sure	16	19
	$n = 177$	$n = 154$
	$x^2 = 4.933$ $d.f. = 2$ $p < .08$	

Source: *Report to the Federal Trade Commission on the Effects of the STP "Public Notice" Advertising Campaign*, June 1979.

Suppose an airline asks a question about customers' satisfaction with its baggage-handling service. In addition to showing the simple frequency for each category, most research analysts would cross-tabulate answers to the baggage-handling questions with several demographic variables such as gender, income, education, and age. To present multiple cross-tabulations individually in separate tables requires considerable space. Thus, many research reports use a space-saving format, with either stubheads for rows or bannerheads for columns, to allow the reader to view several cross-tabulations at the same time. Exhibit 25.9 presents several cross-tabulations in a single table with stubheads.

EXHIBIT 25.9 Using a Stubhead Format to Include Several Cross-Tabulations in One Table

Characteristic	Total Persons	Level of Highest Degree							
		Not a High School Graduate	High School Graduate Only	Some College, No Degree	Associate's	Bachelor's	Master's	Professional	Doctorate
All persons*	$37,046	$18,734	$27,915	$29,533	$35,958	$51,206	$62,514	$115,212	$88,471
Age:									
25 to 34 years old	33,212	18,920	26,073	28,954	32,276	43,794	51,040	74,120	62,109
35 to 44 years old	42,475	22,123	31,479	36,038	38,442	57,438	66,264	126,165	101,382
45 to 54 years old	45,908	23,185	32,978	40,291	41,511	59,208	68,344	132,180	92,229
55 to 64 years old	45,154	23,602	31,742	38,131	39,147	57,423	66,760	138,845	98,433
65 years old and over	28,918	17,123	20,618	28,017	23,080	41,323	42,194	77,312	56,724
Sex:									
Male	44,726	21,447	33,286	36,419	43,462	63,084	76,896	136,128	95,894
Female	28,367	14,214	21,659	22,615	29,537	38,447	48,205	72,445	73,516

*For persons 18 years old and over with earnings.
Source: Excerpted from U.S. Census Bureau, *Statistical Abstract of the United States,* 2006, table 217, p. 148.

Using Charts Effectively

Charts translate numerical information into visual form so that relationships may be easily grasped. The accuracy of the numbers is reduced to gain this advantage. Each chart should include the following elements:

- *Figure number.* Charts (and other illustrative material) should be numbered in a separate series from tables. The numbers allow for easy reference from the text. If there are many charts, a list of them should be included after the table of contents.
- *Title.* The title should describe the contents of the chart and be independent of the text explanation. The number and title may be placed at the top or bottom of the chart.
- *Explanatory legends.* Enough explanation should be put on the chart to spare the reader a need to look at the accompanying text. Such explanations should include labels for axes, scale numbers, and a key to the various quantities being graphed.
- *Source and footnotes.* Any secondary sources for the data should be acknowledged. Footnotes may be used to explain items, although they are less common for charts than for tables.

Charts are subject to distortion, whether unintentional or deliberate. Researchers must use special care to faithfully represent true scale values in all graphical aids. In fact, scale values can be intentionally altered in an effort to skew the interpretation of the data. Intentionally altering scales for this purpose is clearly unethical and unintentionally doing so is sloppy.

A particularly severe kind of distortion comes from treating unequal intervals as if they were equal; this generally results from a deliberate attempt to distort data. Exhibit 25.10 shows this type of distortion. Here, both charts show average quarterly gas prices for regular gas in the Gulf South region of the United States over a three-year period. The top frame makes the case that gas prices have really been quite stable during this period. However, the bottom frame shows a fairly sharp spike in prices during 2008. The two charts supposedly showing the same data tell quite a different story. On close inspection, however, the two charts are not using the same intervals. The data from the top chart omit observations for three-quarters of 2008 allowing the reader

EXHIBIT 25.10

Using Unequal Intervals

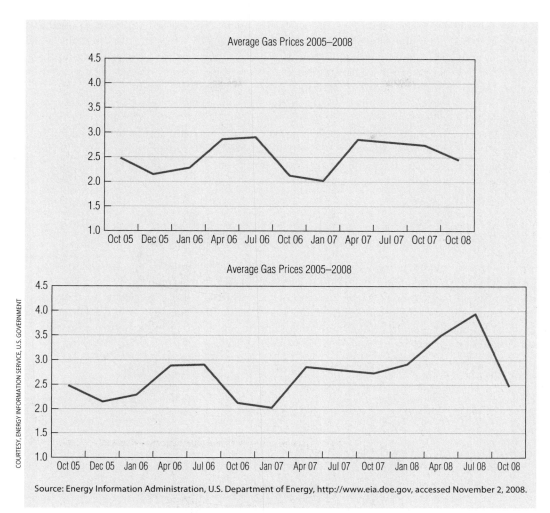

COURTESY, ENERGY INFORMATION SERVICE, U.S. GOVERNMENT

Source: Energy Information Administration, U.S. Department of Energy, http://www.eia.doe.gov, accessed November 2, 2008.

to draw the conclusion that gas prices have been stable. When those observations are added to the chart so that equal quarterly intervals are used between observations, the picture becomes much clearer.

Researchers sometimes are tempted to choose the scale values for axes on charts in a way that may make a small finding seem much larger than it really is. This also can occur by accident as statistical tools that generate such graphs may automatically insert inappropriate minimum and maximum values. Consider Exhibit 25.11. Here the results of an experiment testing the difference between two alternative advertising designs on purchase intention are displayed in both frames. Subjects recorded their purchase intentions after viewing one of the ads using a 10-point scale scored from 1 (Extremely Unlikely to Buy) to 10 (Very Likely to Buy). Both frames display exactly the same data. However, would the conclusion be the same? Frame A makes ad 2 seem much more advantageous relative to ad 1. In contrast, frame B leads to the conclusion that there

EXHIBIT 25.11

Axes Values Can Influence Interpretation

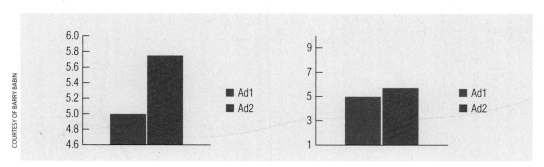

COURTESY OF BARRY BABIN

is very little difference between the two. In this case, frame A is misleading because notice that the y-axis uses a minimum value of 4.6 and a maximum value of 6.0 while frame B uses the actual scale minimum and maximum values of 1 and 10. Similar distortions can occur when using charts to interaction effects. Again, great caution should be taken in making sure that the chart can be used to help support the old adage, "Statistics don't lie, but liars use statistics."

Marketing researchers should always try to present results as faithfully as possible. In this case, using the entire scale range would lead to a more accurate conclusion. In other instances where a larger range of values may be in play, perhaps in plotting the price someone actually paid for their last car, the minimum axes value need not be 0, but it should reflect the minimum plausible price that someone would pay. For example, one may set the scale range in this instance by the actual minimum and maximum prices reported across all respondents.

Pie Charts

One of the most useful kinds of charts is the pie chart, which shows the composition of some total quantity at a particular time. As shown in the example in Exhibit 25.12, each angle, or "slice," is proportional to its percentage of the whole. Companies often use pie charts to show how revenues were used or the composition of their sales. Each of the segments should be labeled with its description and percentage. The writer should not try to include too many small slices; about six slices is a typical maximum.

A Simple Pie Chart with Slices Representing the Frequency of Sales at Each Price Level

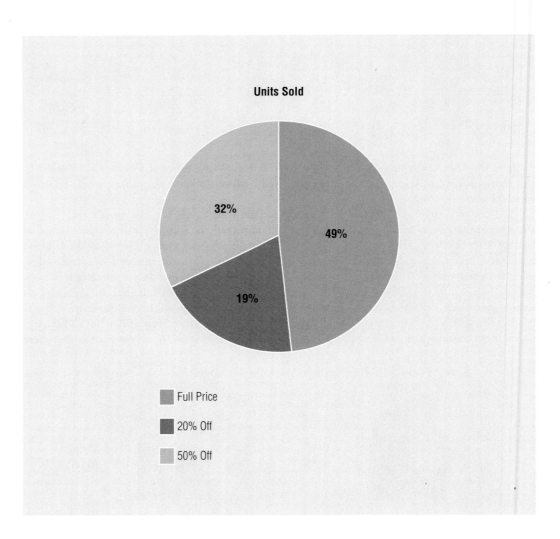

Line Graphs

Line graphs are useful for showing the relationship of one variable to another. The dependent variable generally is shown on the vertical axis, and the independent variable on the horizontal axis. The most common independent variable for such charts is time, but it is by no means the only one. Exhibit 25.13 depicts a *simple line graph*.

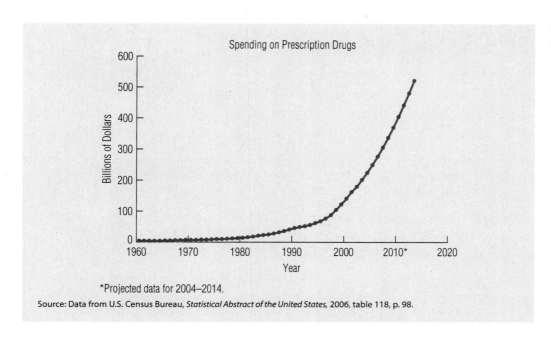

*Projected data for 2004–2014.

Source: Data from U.S. Census Bureau, *Statistical Abstract of the United States,* 2006, table 118, p. 98.

EXHIBIT 25.13
Simple Line Graph

Bar Charts

A bar chart shows changes in the value of a dependent variable (plotted on the vertical axis) at discrete intervals of the independent variable (on the horizontal axis). A simple bar chart is shown in Exhibit 25.14.

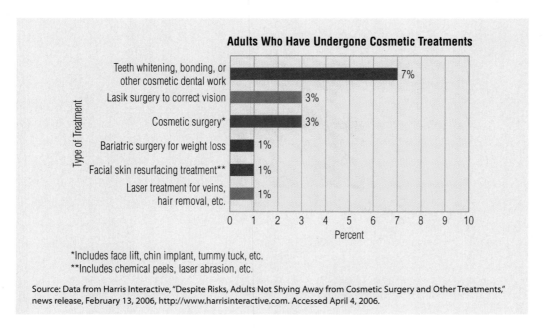

*Includes face lift, chin implant, tummy tuck, etc.
**Includes chemical peels, laser abrasion, etc.

Source: Data from Harris Interactive, "Despite Risks, Adults Not Shying Away from Cosmetic Surgery and Other Treatments," news release, February 13, 2006, http://www.harrisinteractive.com. Accessed April 4, 2006.

EXHIBIT 25.14
Simple Bar Chart

Like the line graph, the bar chart format has variations. A common variant is the *subdivided-bar chart* (see Exhibit 25.15). It is much like a stratum chart, showing the composition of the whole quantity. The *multiple-bar chart* (see Exhibit 25.16) shows how multiple variables are related to the primary variable. In each of these cases, each bar or segment of the bar needs to be clearly identified with a different color or pattern. The writer should not use too many divisions or dependent variables. Too much detail obscures the essential advantage of charts, which is to make relationships easy to grasp.

EXHIBIT 25.15
Subdivided Bar Chart

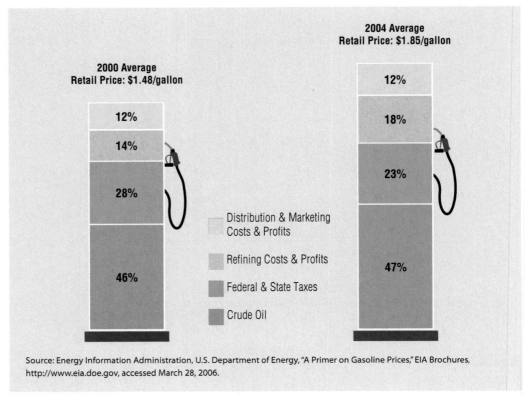

Source: Energy Information Administration, U.S. Department of Energy, "A Primer on Gasoline Prices," EIA Brochures, http://www.eia.doe.gov, accessed March 28, 2006.

EXHIBIT 25.16
Multiple-Bar Chart

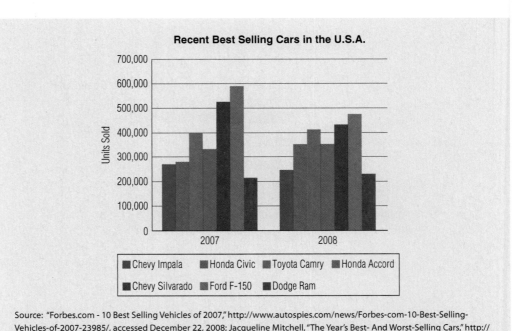

Source: "Forbes.com - 10 Best Selling Vehicles of 2007," http://www.autospies.com/news/Forbes-com-10-Best-Selling-Vehicles-of-2007-23985/, accessed December 22, 2008; Jacqueline Mitchell, "The Year's Best- And Worst-Selling Cars," http://www.forbes.com/2008/12/03/2008-car-sales-forbeslife-cx_jm_1203cars.html, accessed December 22, 2008.

Noah's Law of Slide Presentations

During oral presentations of research reports, many presenters use slides that viewers in the back row cannot read. In fact, some presenters use slides that viewers in the front row cannot read.

All viewers would be much happier if all presenters were to follow Noah's Law of Slide Presentations. Noah's Law says, Never, ever, under any circumstances whatsoever, put more than 40 words on a single slide. A number counts as a word. Noah's Law is called Noah's Law because when God made it rain for 40 days and 40 nights, He flooded the whole world, and no presenter should attempt that with one overhead.

Note that, in Noah's Law, 40 is the absolute upper limit. Twenty is a good average. Seven is even better. If seven words look lonely, presenters can always MAKE THE LETTERS BIGGER.

Advertising legendary David Ogilvy was a devout follower of Noah's Law. He thought so highly of it that he invented and enforced Ogilvy's Corollary. Ogilvy's Corollary says, Never put anything on a slide that you don't intend to read out loud to your audience word for word. He reasoned that when one message comes in on the visual channel while another comes in on the auditory channel, the audience will probably neglect one message or the other.

Source: Adapted with permission from William D. Wells, University of Minnesota, "Noah's Law of Overhead Transparencies," *ACR Newsletter* June 1993, p. 10. Published by the Association for Consumer Research, Provo, UT

The Oral Presentation

The conclusions and recommendations of most research reports are presented orally as well as in writing. The purpose of an **oral presentation** is to highlight the most important findings of a research project and provide clients or line managers with an opportunity to ask questions. The oral presentation may be as simple as a short video conference with a manager at the client organization's location or as formal as a report to the company board of directors. One rule stands above all when preparing a presentation—be as simple as possible. The Research Snapshot above illustrates one way to be simple and to be understood.

In either situation, the key to effective presentation is preparation. Communication specialists often suggest that a person preparing an oral presentation begin at the end.[6] In other words, while preparing a presentation, a researcher should think about what he or she wants the client to know when it has been completed. The researcher should select the three or four most important findings for emphasis and rely on the written report for a full summary. The researcher also needs to be ready to defend the results of the research. This is not the same as being defensive; instead, the researcher should be prepared to deal in a confident, competent manner with the questions that arise. Remember that even the most reliable and valid research project is worthless if the managers who must act on its results are not convinced of its importance.

As with written reports, a key to effective oral presentation is adapting to the audience. Delivering an hour-long formal speech when a 10-minute discussion is called for (or vice versa) will reflect poorly on both the presenter and the report.

Lecturing or reading to the audience is sure to impede communication at any level of formality. The presenter should refrain from reading prepared text word for word. By relying on brief notes, familiarity with the subject, and as much rehearsal as the occasion calls for, the presenter will foster better communication. He or she should avoid research jargon and use short, familiar words. The presenter should maintain eye contact with the audience and repeat the main points. Because the audience cannot go back and replay what the speaker has said, an oral presentation often is organized around a standard format: "Tell them what you are going to tell them, tell them, and tell them what you just told them."

Graphic and other visual aids can be as useful in an oral presentation as in a written one. Presenters can choose from a variety of media. Slides, overhead-projector acetates, and on-screen computer-generated graphics are useful for larger audiences. For smaller audiences, the researcher may put the visual aids on posters or flip charts. Another possibility is to make copies of the charts for each participant, possibly as a supplement to one of the other forms of presentation.

oral presentation

A spoken summary of the major findings, conclusions, and recommendations, given to clients or line managers to provide them with the opportunity to clarify any ambiguous issues by asking questions.

Online Reports: Easy to Get, Easy to Ignore

A variety of commercially available computer programs provide detailed data on Web site usage. Among these titles are ClickTracks Analytics, Fireclick, Sane Solutions, Urchin, WebSideStore, WebtrafficIQ, and WebTrends. These programs can gather details and generate reports about the behavior of various customer

segments who visit a Web site (for example, new visitors, returning visitors, and subscribers to the company's e-mail newsletter). Behaviors that can be tracked include the links that visitors click on, the purchases they make, the amount of time they spend at the Web site and the number of customers abandoning their electronic cart without making a purchase.

With reports so easy to obtain whenever they are needed or as frequently as every day, marketers can quickly accumulate mounds of data. But what do they do with the reports? Ideally, someone should be analyzing the reports and acting on the information. However, when reporters for *Network Computing* recently asked two hundred Web administrators about their use of Web analytics software, the responses indicated a widespread lack of follow-up. Almost all the administrators used the software, but not a single one could think of a change they had made to their Web sites in response to information they obtained from the resulting reports. Some of the lack of response is due to the fact that the results from these efforts are not reported effectively.

Source: Based on Jeffrey Rubin and Ravind Budhiraja, "Intelligence Services," *Network Computing* (July 7, 2005); Joshua Kaufman, "Practical Usability Testing," *Digital Web* (February 13, 2006), http://www.digital-web.com, accessed April 2, 2006.

Whatever medium is chosen, each visual aid should be designed to convey a simple, attention-getting message that supports a point on which the audience should focus its thinking. As they do in written presentations, presenters should interpret graphics for the audience. The best slides are easy to read and interpret. Large typeface, multiple colors, bullets that highlight, and other artistic devices can enhance the readability of charts.

Using gestures during presentations also can help convey the message and make presentations more interesting. Also, invite participation from the audience. Here are some tips on actually making the presentation:[7]

Software like Fireclicks can provide useful information to present in reports.

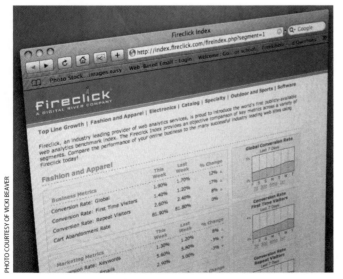

- Generally, introduce yourself while displaying the title of the presentation. Acknowledge any others who materially assisted in the project.
  - Tell the audience if you are comfortable entertaining questions as the presentation proceeds. This is a highly recommended approach.
  - Open up your arms to embrace your audience. Keep your arms between your waist and shoulders.
  - Drop your arms to your sides when not using them.
  - Avoid quick and jerky gestures, which make you appear nervous. Hold gestures longer than you would in normal conversation.
  - Vary gestures. Switch from hand to hand and at other times use both hands or no hands.
  - Don't overuse gestures.

Some gestures are used to draw attention to points illustrated by visual aids. For these, gesturing with an open hand can seem more friendly and can even release tension related to nervousness. In contrast, a nervous speaker who uses a laser pointer may distract the audience as the pointer jumps around in the speaker's shaky hand.[8]

- Research reports, like all communications, are interpreted by the receiver. Try to be clear and unambiguous in preparing the research report.
  - Research reports should generally follow the principles of good technical writing.
  - Whenever possible, have someone else proof the report and slides before submitting them to the client or editor.
  - Whenever possible, stick to the standard outline for the paper.
- The executive summary is critically important because on occasion it is the only part read in detail by the client.
  - Keep it short—about 400 words maximum except for the longest reports.
  - Highlight the key findings with bullet points.
  - Write it last—after finishing the rest of the report and presentation.
- Consider the audience in preparing the report and presentation.
  - Make the communication understandable.
  - Avoid jargon and put any complex statistical output in a technical appendix.

- Use charts and tables to illustrate findings.
  - Graphics are to aid understanding, not to mislead the reader. When preparing charts and tables, make sure that any scale used is not chosen in a way that makes a big effect seem small or a small effect seem big.
  - When possible, use the same scale for all charts. For example, if quality and satisfaction are each measured with 10-item scales, use a 10-item scale to display results for each.
  - When using ratio data such as sales, prices, or salaries, use the minimum and maximum values reported (after omitting outliers) to form the axes of a chart
- Presentation slides should be clear and legible.
  - Err toward larger font, not smaller. Assume the screen will be small and people will sit far away.
  - Err toward fewer words, not more. No more than 40 words on any one slide!
  - Use contrasting background and foreground so that slides are easy to read. Avoid any complex or artistic background that interferes with the readability of the presentation.
- When slides are posted to be viewed via the Internet, annotate complex issues with pop-ups or balloon inserts.

Reports on the Internet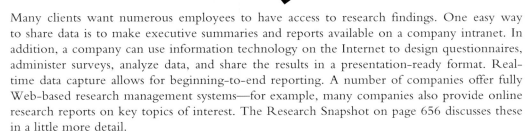

Many clients want numerous employees to have access to research findings. One easy way to share data is to make executive summaries and reports available on a company intranet. In addition, a company can use information technology on the Internet to design questionnaires, administer surveys, analyze data, and share the results in a presentation-ready format. Real-time data capture allows for beginning-to-end reporting. A number of companies offer fully Web-based research management systems—for example, many companies also provide online research reports on key topics of interest. The Research Snapshot on page 656 discusses these in a little more detail.

The Research Follow-Up

Research reports and oral presentations should communicate research findings so that managers can make business decisions. In many cases, the manager who receives the research report is unable to interpret the information and draw conclusions relevant to managerial decisions. For this reason, effective researchers do not treat the report as the end of the research process. They conduct a **research follow-up**, in which they recontact decision makers and/or clients after the latter have had a chance to read over the report. The purpose is to determine whether the researchers need to provide additional information or clarify issues of concern to management. Just as marketing research may help an organization learn about its customers' satisfaction, the research follow-up can help marketing research staffers ensure the satisfaction of their customers, marketing managers.

research follow-up

Recontacting decision makers and/or clients after they have had a chance to read over a research report in order to determine whether additional information or clarification is necessary.

Summary

1. **Define the parts of a research report following a standard format.** A research report is an oral or written presentation of research findings directed to a specific audience to accomplish a particular purpose. Report preparation is the final stage of the research project. The consensus is that the format for a research report should include certain prefatory parts, the body of the report, and appended parts. The report format should be varied to suit the level of formality of the particular situation. The prefatory parts of a formal report include a title page, letters of transmittal and authorization, a table of contents, and a summary. The summary is the part of a report most often read and should include a brief statement of the objectives, results, conclusions, and (depending on the research situation) recommendations. The report body includes an introduction that gives the background and objectives, a statement of methodology, and a discussion of the results, their limitations, and appropriate conclusions and recommendations. The appendix includes various materials too specialized to appear in the body of the report.

2. **Explain how to use tables for presenting numerical information.** Tables present large amounts of numerical information in a concise manner. They are especially useful for presenting several pieces of information about each item discussed. Short tables are helpful in the body of the report; long tables are better suited for an appendix. Each table should include a number, title, stubheads and bannerheads, footnotes for any explanations or qualifications of entries, and source notes for data from secondary sources.

3. **Summarize how to select and use the types of research charts.** Charts present numerical data in a way that highlights their relationships. Each chart should include a figure number, title, explanatory legends, and a source note for secondary sources. Pie charts show the composition of a total (the parts that make up a whole). Line graphs show the relationship of a dependent variable (on the vertical axis) to an independent variable (horizontal axis). Most commonly, the independent variable is time. Bar charts show changes in a dependent variable at discrete intervals of the independent variable—for example, comparing one year with another or one subset of the population with another. Variants of these charts are useful for more complex situations. Researchers need to pay careful attention to avoid distorted interpretations of graphics based on manipulations of the scale values used on axes or some other intentional or careless inaccuracy.

4. **Know how to give an effective oral presentation.** Most research projects are reported on orally as well as in writing, so the researcher needs to prepare an oral presentation. The presentation should defend the results without being defensive. The presentation must be tailored to the situation and the audience. The presenter should practice delivering the presentation in a natural way, without reading to the audience. Graphic aids are useful supplements when they are simple and easy to read. Gestures also add interest and emphasis.

5. **Discuss the importance of Internet reporting and research follow-up.** Posting a summary of results online gives clients ready access to that information. Some online survey software processes the data and displays results in a presentation-ready format. In the follow-up stage of a research project, the researchers recontact decision makers after submitting the report. This helps the researchers determine whether they need to provide further information or clarify any issues of concern to management.

Key Terms and Concepts

communication process, *640*
conclusions and recommendations
    section, *647*
graphic aids, *648*

introduction section, *646*
oral presentation, *655*
report format, *642*
research follow-up, *657*

research methodology section, *646*
research report, *642*
results section, *647*

Questions for Review and Critical Thinking

1. Why is it important to think of the research report from a communications perspective?
2. What are the parts of a market research report?
3. How does an applied market research report differ from a basic or marketing research report?
4. What types of tables might be used to describe some of the various statistical tests discussed in previous chapters?
5. What is the difference between a *basic marketing research paper* and *an applied market research report?*
6. What is a *pie chart?* What is a *bar chart?* When might one be preferable over the other?
7. How might a marketing research unintentionally distort results of an independent t-test examining brand A's customer satisfaction against brand B's customer satisfaction where customer satisfaction is measured on a 0 to 100 point satisfaction scale (0 = no satisfaction to 100 = complete satisfaction)? How might the researcher intentionally distort the interpretation of these results?
8. What are some basic business research journals? Find some published research reports in these journals. How do they meet the standards set forth in this chapter?
9. What rules should be followed when preparing slides for computer-generated presentations?
10. **ETHICS** What ethical concerns arise when you prepare (or read) a report?
11. **ETHICS** A researcher working for Hi Time prepares a bar chart comparing the number of customers visiting two competing booths at a fashion trade show. One booth is the Hi Time booth, the other is for a competing company, So Cool. First, the chart is prepared as shown here:

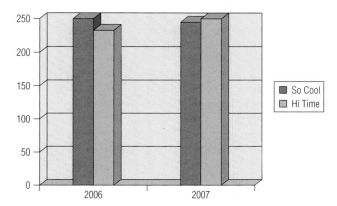

In preparing for a presentation to the Hi Time Board, the client tells the researcher that the chart doesn't seem to reflect the improvements made since 2008. Therefore, the researcher prepares the chart as shown here:

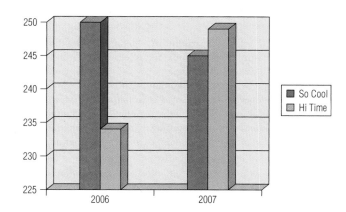

a. What has reformatting the bar chart accomplished?
b. Was it ethical for the client to ask for the bar chart to be redrawn?
c. Would it be ethical for the researcher to use the new chart in the presentation?

Research Activity

1. **'NET** Input "Starbucks" or "McDonald's" in an Internet search engine available through your library's reference service or even a general search engine such as Google News. Look at the articles for that company. Limit the search by using the word "report." Find one of the articles that actually presents some research reports, such as consumer reactions to a new product. Prepare PowerPoint slides that contain appropriate charts to present the results.

Case 25.1 Annenberg Public Policy Center

A recent study by the Annenberg Public Policy Center investigated one major area of marketing decisions: pricing practices.[9] Specifically, the study addressed consumer knowledge and attitudes about the practice of online retailers adjusting their prices according to customer characteristics, such as how frequently they buy from the retailer. For example, a Web site selling cameras charged different prices for the same model depending on whether the visitor to the site had previously visited sites that supply price comparisons. In general, charging different prices is called price discrimination and is legal unless it discriminates by race or sex or involves antitrust or price-fixing laws (such as two competitors agreeing to charge certain prices).

The Annenberg study consisted of telephone interviews conducted with a sample of 1,500 adults, screened to find persons who had used the Internet in the preceding 30 days. The questionnaire gathered demographic data and data about Internet usage. In addition, the interviewer read 17 statements about basic laws and practices related to price discrimination and the targeting of consumers according to their shopping behaviors. Respondents were asked whether each of these statements was true or false. Case Exhibits 25.1–1 through 25.1–4 summarize some of the results from this study.

Questions

1. The information provided here is not detailed enough for a formal report, but assume that you are making an informal report in a preliminary stage of the reporting process. Which of these findings do you want to emphasize as your main points? Why?

2. Prepare a written summary of the findings, using at least two tables or charts.

3. Prepare two tables or charts that would be suitable to accompany an oral presentation of these results. Are they different from the visual aids you prepared for question 2? Why or why not?

CASE EXHIBIT 25.1–1 **Selected Information about the Sample**

Sex	
Male	48%
Female	52%
Online Connection at Home	
Dial-up connection only	31%
Cable modem (with/without dial-up)	18%
DSL (with/without dial-up)	25%
Cable or DSL with another method	13%
Don't know	4%
No connection at home	9%
Self-Ranked Expertise Navigating the Internet	
Beginner	14%
Intermediate	40%
Advanced	34%
Expert	12%

Source: Joseph Turow, Lauren Feldman, and Kimberly Meltzer, "Open to Exploitation: American Shoppers Online and Offline," APPC report, June 2005, p. 15, downloaded at http://www.annenbergpublicpolicycenter.org.

CASE EXHIBIT 25.1–2 **Responses to Selected Knowledge Questions**

	Response*		
Statement	**True**	**False**	**Don't Know**
Companies today have the ability to follow my activity across many sites on the web.	**80%**	8%	12%
It is legal for an *online* store to charge different people different prices at the same time of day.	**38%**	29%	33%
By law, a site such as Expedia or Orbitz that compares prices on different airlines must include the lowest airline prices.	37%	**32%**	31%
It is legal for an *offline* store to charge different people different prices at the same time of day.	**29%**	42%	29%
When a website has a privacy policy, it means the site will not share my information with other websites or companies.	59%	**25%**	16%

*When the numbers do not add up to 100%, it is because of a rounding error. **Boldface** type indicates the correct answer.

Source: Joseph Turow, Lauren Feldman, and Kimberly Meltzer, "Open to Exploitation: American Shoppers Online and Offline," APPC report, June 2005, p. 20, downloaded at http://www.annenbergpublicpolicycenter.org. Accessed April 5, 2006.

CASE EXHIBIT 25.1-3 **Responses to Selected Attitude Questions**

Statement	Response*			
	Agree	Disagree	Neutral	Don't Know
It's okay if a store charges me a price based on what it knows about me.	8%	91%	—	1%
It's okay if an *online* store I use charges different people different prices for the same products during the same hour.	11%	87%	1%	1%
It would bother me to learn that other people pay less than I do for the same products.	76%	22%	1%	1%
It would bother me if websites I shop at keep detailed records of my buying behavior.	57%	41%	2%	1%
It's okay if a store I shop at frequently uses information it has about me to create a picture of me that improves the services it provides for me.	50%	47%	2%	1%

*When the numbers do not add up to 100%, it is because of a rounding error.

Source: Joseph Turow, Lauren Feldman, and Kimberly Meltzer, "Open to Exploitation: American Shoppers Online and Offline," APPC report, June 2005, p. 22, downloaded at http://www.annenbergpublicpolicycenter.org. Accessed April 7, 2006.

CASE EXHIBIT 25.1-4 **Predicting Knowledge Score from Selected Demographics**

	Unstandardized Regression Coefficient (B)	Standardized Regression Coefficient (β)
Education	0.630*	0.200
Income	0.383*	0.150
Self-perceived ability to navigate Internet	0.616*	0.149
Constant	2.687	
R^2	0.148	

*Significance <0.001 level.

Source: Joseph Turow, Lauren Feldman, and Kimberly Meltzer, "Open to Exploitation: American Shoppers Online and Offline," APPC report, June 2005, p. 29, downloaded at http://www.annenbergpublicpolicycenter.org. Accessed April 6, 2006.

A Final Note on Marketing Research

We began by drawing an analogy between research and a needle in a haystack. Hopefully, after reading and studying the material in this book, you can now understand and apply basic processes that help identify key information needs and turn raw data into intelligence. Thus, after sifting through a vast sea of information, this intelligence helps someone make a better decision, which, in turn, helps make someone's life better. The consumer who gets something of greater value is better off and the people who produced and marketed the product also are better off. Marketing research is a very important and useful area of knowledge that can lead to meaningful skills. The set of cases that follows provides the reader with one last chance to gain experience through real-world applications of marketing research. If you are still hungry for more about marketing research, there are many more advanced topics that can increase your skills in one of the specialized areas of research!

Part 7
Comprehensive Cases with Computerized Databases

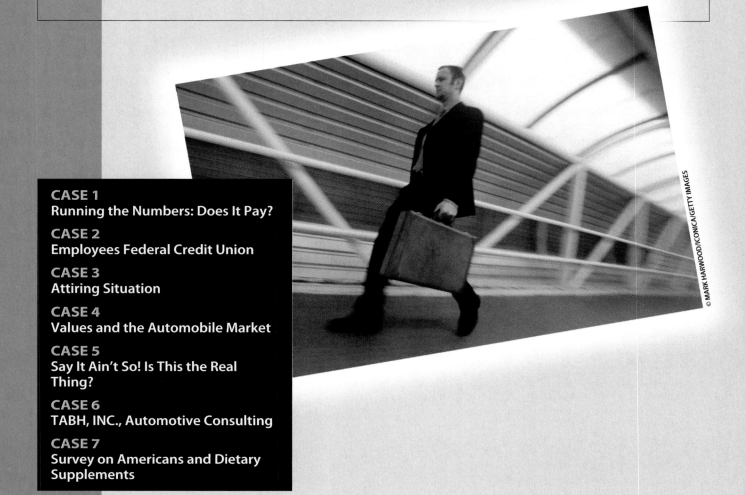

© MARK HARWOOD/ICONICA/GETTY IMAGES

Case 1 Running the Numbers: Does It Pay?

(Download the data sets for this case from www.cengage.
com/marketing/zikmund or request them from your instructor.)
Dr. William Ray, a research consultant, has received a government grant of $75,000 to fund research examining how aspects of a student's college experiences relate to his or her job performance. Senator B. G. Shot is being lobbied by his constituents that employers are discriminating against people who do not like math by giving them lower salaries. Senator Shot has obtained $50,000 of the $75,000 grant from these constituents. The Senator was also instrumental in the selection of Dr. Ray as the recipient and hopes the research supported by the grant will help provide a basis to support the proposed legislation making discrimination against those people who do not like math illegal.

The research questions listed in this particular grant proposal include:

RQ1: Does a student's liking of quantitative coursework in college affect his or her future earnings?

RQ2: Do people with an affinity for quantitative courses get promoted more quickly than those who do not?

Dr. Ray has gained the cooperation of a Fortune 500 service firm that employs over 20,000 employees across eight locations. The company allows Dr. Ray to survey employees who have been out of college for three years. Three hundred responses were obtained by sending an e-mail invitation to approximately 1,000 employees who fit this profile. The invitation explained that the research was about various employee attitudes and indicated that employees would not be required to identify themselves during the survey. Respondents were informed that all responses would be strictly confidential. The e-mail provided a click-through questionnaire which directed respondents to a Web site where the survey was conducted using an online survey provider. Each invitation was coded so that the actual respondents could be identified by both e-mail address and name. Dr. Ray, however, kept this information confidential so the company could not identify any particular employee's response.

The following table describes the variables that were collected.

Variables Available from Company Records

Variable Name	Variable Type	Coding
PROM	Nominal indicating whether the employee has been promoted	1 = "Promoted" 0 = "Not Promoted"
GPA	Self-Reported GPA in Last Year of College	0 (lowest) to 4 (highest)
Sex	Nominal	1 = "Female" 0 = "Male"
School	Nominal	School Initials
Salary	Ratio	Actual annual salary from last year

Questions from Survey

	Coding	Strongly Disagree (1)	Disagree (2)	Neutral (3)	Agree (4)	Strongly Agree (5)
X_1	The quantitative courses I took in school were the most useful courses.	☐	☐	☐	☐	☐
X_2	Very few topics can be understood if you do not understand the arithmetic.	☐	☐	☐	☐	☐
X_3	I hated going to math classes in college.	☐	☐	☐	☐	☐
X_4	I learned a great deal from the quantitative projects assigned to me in college.	☐	☐	☐	☐	☐
X_5	Students do not need to study quantitative topics in college to succeed in their careers.	☐	☐	☐	☐	☐

Please use the following items to describe your undergraduate college experience. For each pair of items, choose the check box closest to the adjective that best describes your experience.

Coding		(–3)	(–2)	(–1)	(0)	(1)	(2)	(3)	
S_1	Dull	☐	☐	☐	☐	☐	☐	☐	Exciting
S_2	Laborious	☐	☐	☐	☐	☐	☐	☐	Playful
S_3	Stressful	☐	☐	☐	☐	☐	☐	☐	Relaxing
S_4	Boring	☐	☐	☐	☐	☐	☐	☐	Fun
S_5	Carefree	☐	☐	☐	☐	☐	☐	☐	Responsible

Questions:

1. Does this grant present Dr. Ray with an ethical dilemma(s) in any way?
2. Derive at least one hypothesis for each research question listed above. Provide a sound rationale or theoretical explanation that leads to the hypothesis.
3. Use the data that corresponds to this case to perform an adequate test of each hypothesis. Interpret the results.
4. Is there evidence supporting the discrimination claim? Explain.
5. List another hypothesis (unrelated to the research questions in the grant) that could be tested with this data.
6. Test that hypothesis.
7. Considering employees' attitudes about their college experience, does the amount of fun that students had in college or the degree to which they thought quantitative classes were a positive experience relate more strongly to salary?
8. Would the "problem" that led to the grant be a better candidate for ethnographic research? Explain.

Case 2 Employees Federal Credit Union

(Download the data sets for this case from www.cengage.com/marketing/zikmund or request them from your instructor.) Employees Federal Credit Union (EFCU) is the credit union for a Fortune 500 firm. Any employee of the organization is eligible for membership in the employees' credit union.

Over the past few years, the Employees Federal Credit Union has accumulated a large amount of surplus funds, which have been invested in certificates of deposit. It has also experienced a lower loan/share ratio than other credit unions of similar size. Because of these factors, the credit union's average earnings on its investments have slowly declined and its profit margins are being squeezed. The EFCU Board of Directors decided that a research project should be conducted to determine why its members are not borrowing money from the credit union. More specifically, the research project was mandated to answer the question of why members are borrowing money from other alternative sources instead of from the credit union.

In addition to the above, the EFCU Board of Directors expressed its desire to determine what the members' attitudes were toward the overall management and operations of the credit union. It was determined that the following questions should be addressed, as well:

- How informed is the membership about the services provided by the credit union?
- Are there any differences between members who live in the area of the firm's headquarters and members who live outside of the area in opinion toward borrowing funds and the services provided by the credit union?

RESEARCH OBJECTIVES

To respond to the questions raised by the board, the following objectives were developed. The research design was formulated to address each of the objectives stated below:

- To determine the reasons why people join the credit union

- To determine the reasons why members use other financial institutions when they need to borrow funds
- To measure member attitudes and beliefs about the proficiencies of credit union employees
- To determine whether there are any perceived differences between members who live in the area of the firm's headquarters and members who live elsewhere
- To determine member awareness of the services offered by the credit union
- To measure member attitudes and beliefs about how effectively the credit union is operated

RESEARCH DESIGN AND DATA COLLECTION METHOD

The research data were collected using a mail questionnaire survey. This technique was determined to be the best method for collecting the research data for the following reasons:

- The credit union members were widely dispersed geographically.
- The board wanted to minimize the cost of conducting the research.
- Several of the questions asked in the questionnaire were of a sensitive nature.
- The board had the flexibility of being able to wait for the survey results before taking any action.

A copy of the questionnaire used to gather the research data is provided in Case Exhibit 2.1. Most of the questions were designed as structured questions because of the variation in the educational backgrounds, job functions, and interests of the members surveyed. However, the respondents were given the flexibility to answer several key questions in an unstructured format. The Likert scale was principally used where attitude measurements were requested.

CASE EXHIBIT 2.1 **EFCU Member Opinion Survey**

1. Are you currently a member of the Employees Federal Credit Union (EFCU)?
Yes ( )   No ( )

If no, please have the member of your household who is a member of the EFCU complete the questionnaire. If no one in your household is a member, please return the questionnaire in the enclosed prepaid envelope.

2. Why did you join the credit union? (Check as many answers as are applicable.)
___ Convenience
___ Higher interest rates on my savings than other financial institutions pay
___ More personal than other facilities
___ Wanted a readily available source for borrowing money
___ Advertisements prompted me to join
___ Other—please explain: _____
_____

Statements 3 through 6 ask for your opinion of the credit union employees. Check the response that best describes your rating of the credit union employees in each category. Please check only one response for each statement.

3. The credit union employees are courteous.

Strongly disagree	Disagree	Uncertain	Agree	Strongly agree
( )	( )	( )	( )	( )

4. The credit union employees are helpful.

Strongly disagree	Disagree	Uncertain	Agree	Strongly agree
( )	( )	( )	( )	( )

5. The credit union employees are professional.

Strongly disagree	Disagree	Uncertain	Agree	Strongly agree
( )	( )	( )	( )	( )

6. The credit union employees are always available.

Strongly disagree	Disagree	Uncertain	Agree	Strongly agree
( )	( )	( )	( )	( )

7. What is your opinion about the rates the credit union is paying on its share (members/savings) accounts?
A. Very high _____   B. High _____   C. Average _____
D. Low _____   E. Very low _____   F. No opinion _____

8. What is your opinion about the rates the credit union is charging its members to borrow funds?
A. Very high _____   B. High _____   C. Average _____
D. Low _____   E. Very low _____   F. No opinion _____

9. How often do you receive a financial statement of your account activity?

Too often	Very often	About right	Not often enough	Never
( )	( )	( )	( )	( )

10. How would you rate the accuracy of your statements?

Excellent	Good	Fair	Poor
( )	( )	( )	( )

11. Are they easy to understand?
Yes ( )   No ( )

12. Do you feel that the credit union maintains your account information in a confidential manner?
Yes ( )   No ( )

The questions in the next set are important in determining how effective the credit union has been in communicating its different services to the members. Please answer each question honestly—remember, there are no right or wrong answers.
Circle the response that best describes your awareness of the services offered by the credit union.

Circle 1—If you were aware of the service and have used it.
Circle 2—If you were aware of the service but have not used it.
Circle 3—If you did not know this service was offered by the credit union.

(Continued)

CASE EXHIBIT 2.1 **EFCU Member Opinion Survey** (*Continued*)

	Aware and Have Used	Aware but Have Not Used	Unaware of Service
13. Regular share accounts	1	2	3
14. Special subaccounts	1	2	3
15. Christmas club accounts	1	2	3
16. Individual retirement accounts	1	2	3
17. MasterCard credit cards	1	2	3
18. Signature loans	1	2	3
19. New car loans	1	2	3
20. Late model car loans	1	2	3
21. Older model car loans	1	2	3
22. Household goods/appliance loans	1	2	3
23. Recreational loans	1	2	3
24. Share collateralized loans	1	2	3
25. IRA loans	1	2	3
26. Line of credit loans	1	2	3

27. Do you currently have a loan with the credit union?
Yes ( )   No ( )

28. During the past year, have you borrowed money from a bank or other lending source other than the credit union?
Yes ( )   No ( )
If no, go to question 30.

29. Why did you go to a source other than the credit union?
___ My loan application at the credit union was not approved.
___ The credit union did not offer this type of credit.
___ I found better loan rates elsewhere.
___ I have an established credit line elsewhere.
___ I prefer to use a local financial institution.
___ Other: _____
_____

For statements 30 through 34, check the response that best describes your feelings about the statements. Check only one response for each statement given.

30. The credit union's loan rates are lower than those offered by other institutions.

Strongly disagree	Disagree	Uncertain	Agree	Strongly agree
( )	( )	( )	( )	( )

31. The credit union personnel will keep my personal financial information confidential.

Strongly disagree	Disagree	Uncertain	Agree	Strongly agree
( )	( )	( )	( )	( )

32. The credit union is prompt in processing loan applications.

Strongly disagree	Disagree	Uncertain	Agree	Strongly agree
( )	( )	( )	( )	( )

33. The current financial services provided by the credit union meet the needs of its members.

Strongly disagree	Disagree	Uncertain	Agree	Strongly agree
( )	( )	( )	( )	( )

34. The loan applications used by the credit union are simple and easy to complete.

Strongly disagree	Disagree	Uncertain	Agree	Strongly agree
( )	( )	( )	( )	( )

35. Which of the services provided by the credit union do you like best?
_____

36. Which of the services provided by the credit union do you like least?
_____

37. Overall, how do you feel the credit union is being managed and operated?
A. Excellent _____   B. Good _____   C. Average _____
D. Poor _____   E. Very poor _____   F. No opinion _____

(*Continued*)

CASE EXHIBIT 2.1 **EFCU Member Opinion Survey** (Continued)

38. Do you live in the headquarters area?
    Yes ( )   No ( )
    If yes, go to question 40.

39. Do you feel the credit union meets your needs as well as those of members who live in the headquarters area?
    Yes ( )   No ( )
    If no, please explain:_____
    _____

40. If you were managing the credit union, what changes would you make and what additional services, if any, would you provide?
    _____
    _____
    _____
    _____
    _____
    _____

We sincerely appreciate the time and effort you made in completing this questionnaire. Thank you for your help.

SAMPLING PROCEDURES

The population of the EFCU is well-defined; consequently, a simple random sample of the membership was selected. A sample size of 300 was calculated using the estimated population standard deviation based on the responses from 15 members to question 37 of the questionnaire. Question 37 was used because it capsulized the essence of the research project.

The random numbers used in making the selection of the sampling units were generated with the help of a personal computer. The sampling frame used was the January 31 trial balance listing of the EFCU membership. According to the sampling frame, EFCU had 3,531 members on that date. As a result, the 300 random numbers were generated within the range of 1 to 3,531. Each random number was matched to a corresponding number in the sampling frame, and those individuals were selected to receive copies of the survey questionnaire.

FIELDWORK

Most of the fieldwork for the research project, including all of the editing and coding of the survey data, was performed by the Supervisory Committee Chairperson. The following is a list of the (much-appreciated) assistance received during the field procedures:

- Bob Perkins obtained a copy of the most currently available listing of the membership of the EFCU.
- The payroll department prepared mailing labels for all the members in the sample who were having withholding for the credit union taken out of their payroll checks.
- The credit union clerks obtained the addresses and prepared mailing labels for all the remaining individuals selected in the sample.
- Administrative assistants helped copy and collate the survey questionnaires and prepare them for mailing.
- Ron Walker mailed all of the survey questionnaires.

The survey data from the structured questions were coded based on classifications established by the researcher. The codes were input into a series of databases using an IBM personal computer and a statistical software package.

Of the 125 returned questionnaires, two were not included in the survey results. One of the questionnaires was returned without the first two pages attached, and the other questionnaire appeared to be deliberately falsified; not only were all the responses on this questionnaire at the extremes, but a number of contradictions were noted as well.

ADDITIONAL INFORMATION

Several of the questions will require the use of a computerized database. Each variable name is represented by its question number. Q1 is the variable name for question 1, "Are you a member of the Employees Federal Credit Union?" Q2 is the variable name for question 2, etc. Case Exhibit 2.2 presents the coding. Your instructor will provide information about obtaining the EFCU's data set if this material is part of the case assignment. (The data are available in SPSS or Excel format.)

CASE EXHIBIT 2.2 **Codes for Questionnaire**

strongly disagree = 1, strongly agree = 5
very high = 1, very low = 5, no opinion = 6
too often = 1, never = 5
excellent = 1, poor = 4
excellent = 1, very poor = 5, no answer = 6
yes = 1, no = 2, no answer = 3
aware and have used = 1, unaware = 3

Questions

1. Evaluate the research objectives.
2. Evaluate the research design in light of the stated research objectives.
3. Using the computerized database, obtain simple frequencies for the answers to each question (the answers to the open-ended questions are not included in the database).
4. Perform the appropriate cross-tabulations.
5. Perform the appropriate univariate and bivariate statistical tests after you develop hypotheses for these particular tests.

This case was prepared by John H. Walkup, senior project manager, Mapco, Inc.

Case 3 Attiring Situation

RESERV is a national level placement firm specializing in putting retailers and service providers together with potential employees who fill positions at all levels of the organization. This includes entry-level positions and senior management positions. One international specialty clothing store chain has approached them with issues involving key characteristics of retail employees. The two key characteristics of primary interest involve the appearance of potential employees and problems with customer integrity.

Over the last five years, store management has adopted a very flexible dress code that allowed employees some flexibility in the way they dressed for work. Casual attire was permitted with the idea that younger customers could better identify with store employees, most of whom are younger than average. However, senior management had just become aware of how some very successful companies tightly control the appearance of their sales force. The Walt Disney Company, for example, has strict grooming policies for all employees, provides uniforms (or costumes) for most *cast members*, and does not permit any employee to work if they have a visible tattoo. Disney executives discuss many positive benefits from this policy and one is that customers are more responsive to the employees. Thus, it just may be that the appearance of employees can influence the behavior of customers. This influence can be from the greater identity that employees display—meaning, they stand out better and may encourage acquiescence through friendliness.

Senior research associate, Michael Neil, decides to conduct an experiment to examine relevant research questions including:

RQ1: How does employee appearance affect customer purchasing behavior?

RQ2: How does employee appearance affect customer ethics?

Mr. Neil decides the problem can best be attacked by conducting a laboratory experiment. In the experiment, two variables are manipulated in a between-subjects design. The experiment includes two experimental variables which are controlled by the researcher and subjects' biological sex which was recorded and included as a blocking variable. The experimental variables (and blocking variable) are:

Name	Description	Values
X_1	A manipulation of the attire of the service-providing employee	0 = Professional Attire (Neatly groomed w/ business attire) 1 = Unprofessional Attire (Unkempt hair w/ jeans and t-shirt)
X_2	The manner with which the service-providing employee tries to gain extra sales—or simply, the close approach	0 = Soft Close 1 = Hard Close
Gender	Subject's biological sex	0 = Male 1 = Female

Four dependent variables are included:

Name	Description	Range
Time	How much time the subject spent with the employee beyond what was necessary to choose the slacks and shirt.	0–10 minutes
Spend	How much of the $25 the subject spent on extra products offered for sale by the retail service provider	$0–$25
Keep	How much of the $25 the subject kept rather than returning to the researcher	$0–$25

Additionally, several variables were collected following the experiment that tried to capture how the subject felt during the exercise. All of these items were gathered using a 7-item semantic differential scale.

Name	Description
SD1	Low Quality–High Quality
SD2	Dislike–Like
SD3	Unfavorable–Favorable
SD4	Negative–Positive
SD5	Easy–Difficult
SD6	Restful–Tiring
SD7	Comfortable–Uncomfortable
SD8	Calm–Tense

The experiment was conducted in a university union. Subjects were recruited from the food court area. RESERV employees approached potential subjects and requested their participation in a study that examined how customers really bought things. Subjects would each receive vouchers that could be exchanged for merchandise in return for their participation. Each potential subject was informed that the participation could take between 20 and 40 minutes to complete. Upon agreeing to participate, subjects were escorted to a waiting area where they were provided with further instructions and mingled with other participants before entering a small room that was set up to resemble an actual retail clothing counter.

Each subject was told to play the role of a customer who had just purchased some dress slacks and a shirt. The employee was to complete the transaction. Once the subject entered the mock retail environment, a research assistant who was playing the role of the retail employee entered the room. As a retail sales associate, one important role was to suggest add-on sales. Several dozen accessory items ranging from socks and handkerchiefs to small jewelry items were displayed at the counter.

As a result of this experimental procedure, each subject was randomly assigned to one of four conditions, each corresponding to a unique combination of the experimental variables described above. In other words, the employee was either:

1. Dressed professionally and used a soft close (i.e., "Perhaps you would like to see some additional accessories") in trying to sell merchandise beyond the slacks and shirt.
2. Dressed unprofessionally and used a soft close.
3. Dressed professionally and used a hard close (i.e., "You really need to match this up with some coordinated accessories which happen to be on sale today only") in trying to sell merchandise beyond the slacks and shirt.
4. Dressed unprofessionally and used a hard close.

Thus, RESERV wishes to use this information to explain how employee appearance encourages shoppers to continue shopping (TIME) and spend money (SPEND). Rather than simply ask purchase intentions, each subject was given $25 (in one-dollar bills) which they were allowed to *spend* on accessories. This allowed each subject to participate in an actual transaction. In addition, the experiment did not provide explicit instructions on what was to be done with the money that was left over. Once the simulated shopping trip was complete, subjects were taken to another small room where they completed a questionnaire containing the semantic differential scales and demographic information alone and at their own pace. Because the instructions did not specifically tell subjects what to do with the money they possessed following the experiment, this allowed the researchers to operationalize a behavioral dependent variable (KEEP) that simulated questionable consumer behavior based on the implied assumption that the money was to be either handed to the research assistant when complete or turned in along with the questionnaire. In other words, subjects who kept money were considered as behaving less ethically than those who left the money behind or turned it in to a member of the research team.

1. Develop at least three hypotheses that correspond to the research questions.
2. Test the hypotheses using an appropriate statistical approach.
3. Suppose the researcher is curious about how the feelings captured with the semantic differentials influence the dependent variables SPEND and KEEP. Conduct an analysis to explore this possibility. Are any problems present in testing this?
4. Is there a role for factor analysis in any of this analysis?
5. Critique the experiment from an internal and external validity viewpoint.
6. What conclusions would be justified by management regarding their employee appearance policy?

Case 4 Values and the Automobile Market

(Download the data sets for this case from www.cengage.com/marketing/zikmund **or request them from your instructor.)** In the last decade, the luxury car segment became one of the most competitive in the automobile market. Many American consumers who purchase luxury cars prefer imports from Germany and Japan.

A marketing vice president with General Motors once commented, "Import-committed buyers have been frustrating to us." This type of thinking has led industry analysts to argue that to successfully compete in the luxury car segment, U.S. carmakers need to develop a better understanding of the consumers so that they can better segment the market and better position their products via more effective advertising. Insight into the foreign-domestic luxury car choice may result from examining owners' personal values in addition to their evaluations of car attributes, because luxury cars, like many other conspicuously consumed luxury products, may be purchased mainly for value-expressive reasons.

Industry analysts believe it would be important to assess whether personal values of consumers could be used to explain ownership of American, German, and Japanese luxury cars. Further, they believe they should also assess whether knowledge of owners' personal values provides any additional information useful in explaining ownership of American, German, and Japanese luxury cars beyond that obtained from their evaluations of the cars' attributes.

Personal values are likely to provide insights into reasons for ownership of luxury cars for at least two reasons. First, Americans have always had a very personal relationship with their cars and have used them as symbols of their self-concept. For instance, people who value a *sense of accomplishment* are quite likely to desire a luxury car that they feel is an appropriate symbol of their achievement, whereas people who value *fun, enjoyment, and excitement* are likely to desire a luxury car that they perceive as fun and exciting to drive. An advertiser trying to persuade the former segment to purchase a luxury car should position the car as a status symbol that will help its owners demonstrate their accomplishments to others. Similarly, an advertiser trying to persuade the latter segment to purchase a luxury car should position the car as a fun and exciting car to drive. In other words, effective advertising shows consumers how purchasing a given product will help them achieve their valued state, because brands tied to values will be perceived more favorably than brands that deliver more mundane benefits.

Second, when a market is overcrowded with competing brands offering very similar options—as is the case with the luxury car market—consumers are quite likely to choose between brands on the basis of value-expressive considerations.

METHOD

Data were collected via a mail survey sent to 498 consumers chosen at random from a list obtained from a syndicated research company located in an affluent county in a southern state. The list contained names of people who had purchased either a luxury American car (Cadillac or Lincoln Mercury), a luxury German car (Mercedes or BMW), or a luxury Japanese car (Infiniti or Lexus) within the last year. A cover letter explained that the survey was part of an academic research project. People were asked to return the questionnaires anonymously to a university address (a postage-paid envelope was provided with each survey). Beyond an appeal to help the researchers, respondents were not offered any other incentive to complete the surveys. Of the 498 questionnaires originally sent, 17 were returned by the post office as undeliverable. One hundred fifty-five completed surveys were received, for a response rate of 32.2 percent.

The Survey Instrument

The survey included questions on (1) various issues that people consider when purchasing new cars, (2) importance of car attributes, (3) importance of different values, and (4) demographics (sex, age,

education, and family income). Questions relating to the issues that people consider when purchasing new cars were developed through initial interviews with consumers and were measured with a 7-point Likert scale with end anchors of "strongly agree" and "strongly disagree." (See Case Exhibit 4.1.) A list of 12 car attributes was developed from the initial interviews with consumers and by consulting *Consumer Reports*. (See Case Exhibit 4.2.) The importance of each attribute was measured with a 7-point numerical scale with end points labeled "very important" and "very unimportant." The List of Values (LOV) scale in Case Exhibit 4.3 was used to measure the importance of values. Respondents were asked to rate each of the eight values (we combined fun, enjoyment, and excitement into one value) on a 7-point numerical scale with end points labeled "very important" and "very unimportant."

CASE EXHIBIT 4.1 Issues That Consumers Consider When Buying Luxury Atomobiles

Having a luxury car is a major part of my fun and excitement.[a] (Issue 1)

Owning a luxury car is a part of "being good to myself." (Issue 2)

When I was able to buy my first luxury car, I felt a sense of accomplishment. (Issue 3)

I enjoy giving my friends advice about luxury cars. (Issue 4)

Getting a good deal when I buy a luxury car makes me feel better about myself. (Issue 5)

I seek novelty and I am willing to try new innovations in cars. (Issue 6)

I tend to buy the same brand of the car several times in a row. (Issue 7)

I tend to buy from the same dealer several times in a row. (Issue 8)

I usually use sources of information such as *Consumer Reports* in deciding on a car. (Issue 9)

I usually visit three or more dealerships before I buy a car. (Issue 10)

I would read a brochure or watch a video about defensive driving. (Issue 11)

When buying a new luxury car, my family's opinion is very important to me. (Issue 12)

My family usually accompanies me when I am shopping for a new luxury car. (Issue 13)

I usually rely upon ads and salespersons for information on cars. (Issue 14)

I usually rely upon friends and acquaintances for information on cars. (Issue 15)

When shopping for a car, it is important that the car dealer make me feel at ease. (Issue 16)

Most of my friends drive luxury import cars. (Issue 17)

Most of my friends drive luxury domestic cars. (Issue 18)

I think celebrity endorsers in ads influence people's choices of luxury cars. (Issue 19)

I would not buy a luxury car if I felt that my debt level is higher than usual. (Issue 20)

[a] Note: Subjects' responses were measured with 1 as "strongly agree" and 7 as "strongly disagree."

CASE EXHIBIT 4.2 Car Attributes

Attribute	Code	Attribute	Code
Comfort	Comfort	Low maintenance cost	Lomc
Safety	Safety	Reliability	Rely
Power	Power	Warranty	Warrant
Speed	Speed	Nonpolluting	Nonpol
Styling	Styling	High gas mileage	Gasmle
Durability	Durabil	Speed of repairs	Repairs

CASE EXHIBIT 4.3 List of Values

Value	Code	Value	Code
Fun-Enjoyment-Excitement	Fun	Sense of accomplishment	Accomp
Sense of belonging	Belong	Warm relationship	Warm
Being well respected	Respect	Security	Security
Self-fulfillment	Selfful	Self-respect	Selfres

The Sample

Of the 155 respondents in the sample, 58 (37.4 percent) owned an American luxury car, 38 (24.5 percent) owned a European luxury car, and 59 (38.1 percent) owned a Japanese luxury car. The majority of the sample consisted of older (85 percent were 35 years of age or above), more educated (64 percent were college graduates), and economically well-off (87.2 percent earned $65,000 or more) consumers.

THE CODE BOOK

Case Exhibit 4.4 lists the SPSS variable names and identifies codes for these variables. (Note that this data set is also available in Microsoft Excel.)

CASE EXHIBIT 4.4 **List of Variables and Computer Codes**

ID—Identification number

AGE (categories are 2 = 35 years and under, 3 = 36–45 yrs, 4 = 46–55 yrs, 5 = 56–65 yrs, 6 = 65 + yrs)

SEX (1 = male, 0 = female)

EDUC—Education (1 = less than high school, 2 = high school grad, 3 = some college, 4 = college grad, 5 = graduate degree)

INCOME (1 = less than $35,000, 2 = $35–50,000, 3 = $50–65,000, 4 = $65,000+)

CAR—Type of luxury car (American car, European car, Japanese car)

ISSUES—The sequence of issues listed in Case Exhibit 4.1. (Strongly agree = 1; strongly disagree = 7)

ATTRIBUTES—The sequence of car attributes listed in Case Exhibit 4.2. (Very important to you = 1; very unimportant to you = 7)

VALUES—The sequence of values listed in Case Exhibit 4.3. (Very important = 1; very unimportant = 7)

ADDITIONAL INFORMATION

Several of the questions will require the use of a computerized database. Your instructor will provide information about obtaining the VALUES data set if the material is part of the case assignment.

Questions

1. Is the sampling method adequate? Is the attitude measuring scale sound? Explain.

2. Using the computerized database with a statistical software package, calculate the means of the three automotive groups for the values variables. Do any of the values variables show significant differences between American, Japanese, and European car owners?

3. Are there any significant differences on importance of attributes?

4. Write a short statement interpreting the results of this research.

Advanced Questions

5. Are any of the value scale items highly correlated?

6. Should multivariate analysis be used to understand the data?

Case materials based on research by Ajay Sukhdial and Goutam Chakraborty, Oklahoma State University.

Case 5 Say It Ain't So! Is This the Real Thing?

INTRODUCTION

David Ortega is the lead researcher for an upscale restaurant group hoping to add another chain that would compete directly with the upscale Smith and Wollensky restaurants (http://www.smithandwollensky.com). Smith and Wollensky is part of the Patina Restaurant Group. The average check for a customer at Smith and Wollensky is approximately $80 to $90.[1] Whenever a new venture of this type is planned, one has to wonder whether there are enough customers willing to pay premium prices given the large number of lesser priced alternatives. In fact, Smith and Wollensky is considering opening a lesser priced "Grill" that would be positioned so that the average customer check would be about half that of the original. What is it that people are willing to pay for and what sacrifices can be made to deliver a satisfying if not luxurious experience? How can he create a unique experience at a lower price? These are the questions facing David Ortega.

RESEARCH APPROACH

After considering how to study the issue, David decides a qualitative research approach will be useful. He hopes to develop a deep understanding of how the fine dining experience offers value—and perhaps some insights into what intangibles create value for consumers in general. After considering the different options, he decides on a phenomenological approach. The primary tool of investigation is conversational interviewing. David plans to enter into casual conversations with businesspeople in the lounge of the downtown Ritz Carlton. He begins the conversation by commenting on the wine he is sipping—something like, "It isn't bad, but it's hard to believe they get $15 for a glass of this stuff."

[1]MacNealy, Jeremy (2006), "Smith and Wollensky on the Grill," The Motley Fool, http://www.fool.com/News/mft/2006/mft06040425.htm, accessed November 6, 2008.

RESULTS

Two weeks later, David has completed "conversations" with five consumers. He found them very willing and free to talk about the things they indulge in. He develops a field log of notes from the consumers' comments. The notes are recorded verbatim.[2] The following field notes are highlighted:

Respondent	Date/Time	Text
Joe, wm, 55, attorney	12/5/08 – 10:15 PM	Well, wine doesn't have to be expensive to be good. Beyond some basic price point . . . maybe $14 a bottle . . . I find a lot of good wines. But, the wine has to fit the situation. It has to add something. A fake Rolex will tell time; but a real Rolex tells you about you. I don't mind paying for something that's unique—even though it might not be my cup of tea. Chateau Masur is like that. It's from Lebanon! It isn't always elegant or delicious, but it is always real. You always know it comes from some place very unique and is made under the most trying circumstances.
Sally, hf, 45, medical sales	12/7/08 – 5:45 PM	We pay too much for a lot of stuff though. I like things to be genuine. When you ask for crab you get crab—not Krab with a "K." It's made of fish you know!
		. . .
		I love old neighborhood Italian restaurants. They aren't always expensive. But, they have character. I think that it is very easy to spoil. I might not want a checkered red and white table cloth at home, but the Italian restaurant has to have one. I have to smell the garlic from the parking lot. And, that cheap Chianti, the kind with the basket cradle—it had better be from Italy—it tastes sooo good there. You know, you could pay more, but a nice dinner there with a couple of friends is worth a lot.
		You know, the people who make great wine or who have great restaurants kind of luck into it. I don't think they really ever sent out a survey asking what the restaurant or the wine should be like. I think they said "I am going to make this the way that I want it to be . . ." and it just happens to be right! They are so committed to the product that it works—no matter the price. But commitment like that costs a little more usually—although they aren't in it for the money.
Hebert, wm, 40, oil executive	12/8/08 – 11:00 PM	How old is it? The older it is, the more it is worth—yeah! I like this French wine that has "depuis 1574," maybe its name is Hugel (trying to recall). Imagine the same family running that company for hundreds of years. I like to think about the family in the vineyards—the old man on a tractor with his sons running around the sides. Their kids are hanging around the barn.
		. . .
		You know, you can buy cheap things and get cheated too. We are free to be cheated at any price point! (laughter) I remember bringing home a bottle of "Louisiana Hot Sauce." Man, that stuff didn't have any heat to it at all. When I looked at the bottle, do you know where it was from? . . . Man, it was from Tennessee . . . can you believe that, Louisiana Hot Sauce from Tennessee!! What a scam.
		. . . .
		When I buy something nice, I want it to be real. Burgundy should be from Burgundy. Bordeaux should be from Bordeaux. Champagne should be from Champagne—not Texas or California! (laughter) Because I know in Champagne, they know how to make Champagne—sparkling wine. They have perfected the methods over hundreds of years. A good glass of Champagne is worth what you pay!
Angela, bf, 60, insurance executive	12/9/06 – 6:45 PM	Look at this hotel . . . when you just look at the price you think 'this is crazy!' But, look at the attention to detail. Cleaning the floor is a production. Have you noticed the way they turn down your bed? Taking care of the plants is serious business to these people. I've stayed at a place like this in Florida—I loved it. At first, I couldn't put my finger on it. Then, it hit me. The place smelled like Florida. They have a way of giving everything the smell of sweet grass and citrus. It's terrific. Another one in California smelled of sandalwood and cypress. You have to be willing to pay more for people that care so much about what they do. Maybe that's your wine? Those smells make me think of those special places. When I drink a wine, I think about where it comes from too.
Burt, wm, 35, sales	12/9/06 – 9:30 PM	It's okay for something to be cheap . . . even fake! As long as I know it's fake. I've got three fake Rolexes. This one looks pretty good . . . looks genuine . . . but look at the way the second hand moves . . . it's jumping. A real one wouldn't do that!!
		I ate with this guy the other night who sent back a bottle of wine after ordering it. When the waiter pulled the cork, it didn't have Domaine Mas Blanc written on it—that's the name of the wine. He said, "How do I know it is real?" At first I thought he was crazy but after I looked at my fake Rolex . . . you know, I think he was right. When you spend $100 for a bottle, you want real stuff. But, if you spend $10 for a bottle of wine in a restaurant, who the hell cares? You didn't pay for it to be real . . . one day, when I pony up ten grand for a real Rolex, I'll send back the fakes!

Note: w = white; h = hispanic, f = female, m = male, etc.

[2]For more comments along this same line, see Beverland, M., "The Real Thing: Branding Authenticity in the Luxury Wine Trade," *Journal of Business Research* 59 (February 2006), 251–258; Beverland, M., "Crafting Brand Authenticity: The Case of Luxury Wines," *Journal of Management Studies* 42 (July 2005), 103–129; and Wolff, C., "Blending High Style and Authenticity," *Lodging Hospitality* 61 (November 1, 2005), 72–76.

RESULTS

David decides to use a word count to try to identify the main themes. Hopefully, these themes can help clarify the business problem. Perhaps if the information can't answer the questions above, it will point him in the right direction. Whatever the case, David feels the project has helped him better understand the total value proposition offered by restaurants, wines, hotels, and other products.

Questions:

1. Comment on the research approach. Do you feel it was an appropriate choice?

2. ETHICS David did not inform these respondents that he was doing marketing research during these conversations. Why do you think he withheld this information and was it appropriate to do so?

3. 'NET Using the Internet, try to identify at least three restaurants that Smith and Wollensky competes with and three with whom the new S&W Grill may compete.

4. Try to interpret the discussions above. You may use one of the approaches discussed in the text. What themes should be coded? What themes occur most frequently? Can the different themes be linked together to form a unit of meaning?

5. What is the result of this research? What should David report back to the restaurant group?

Case 6 TABH, INC., Automotive Consulting

(Download the data sets for this case from www.cengage.com/marketing/zikmund or request them from your instructor.)
TABH consulting specializes in research for automobile dealers in the United States, Canada, Mexico, and Europe. Although much of their work is done on a pay-for fee basis with customers such as dealerships and dealership networks selling all major makes of automobiles, they also produce a monthly "white paper" that is sold via their Web site. This off-the-shelf research is purchased by other research firms and by companies within the auto industry itself. This month, they would like to produce a white paper analyzing the viability of college students attending schools located in small college towns as a potentially underserved market segment.

TABH management assigns a junior analyst named Michel Gonzalez to the project. Lacking time for a more comprehensive study, Michel decides to contact the traffic department at Cal Poly University in Pomona, California, and at Central Missouri State University in Warrensburg, Missouri. Michel wishes to obtain data from the students' automobile parking registration records. Although both schools are willing to provide anonymous data records for a limited number of students, Cal Poly offers Michel a chance to visit during the registration period, which just happens to be next week. As a result, not only can Michel get data from students' registration forms, but a small amount of primary data can be obtained by intercepting students near the registration window. In return, Michel is asked to purchase a booth at the Cal Poly career fair.

As a result, Michel obtains some basic information from students. The information results in a small data set consisting of the follow observations for 100 undergraduate college students in Pomona, California:

Variable	Description
Sex	Student's sex dummy coded with 1 = female and 0 = male
Color	Color of a student's car as listed on his or her registration form
Major	Student's major field of study (Business, Liberal Arts (LA), or Engineering (ENG))
Grade	Student's grade record reported as the mode (A, B, or C)
Finance	Whether the student financed the car he or she is driving or paid for it with cash, coded 0 = cash payment and 1 = financed
Residence	Whether the student lives on campus or commutes to school, coded 0 = commute and 1 = on campus
Animal	Michel asks each student to quickly draw a cartoon about the type of car they would like to purchase. Students are told to depict the car as an animal in the cartoon. Although Michel expects to interpret these cartoons more deeply when time allows, the initial coding specifies what type of animal was drawn by each respondent. When Michel was unsure of what animal was drawn, a second researcher was conferred with to determine what animal was depicted. Some students depicted the car as a dog, some as a cat, and some as a mule.

The purpose of the white paper is to offer car dealers considering new locations a comparison of the profile of a small town university with the primary market segments for their particular automobile. For instance, a company specializing in small pickup trucks appeals to a different market segment than does a company specializing in two-door economy sedans. Many small towns currently do not have dealerships, particularly beyond the "Big 3." Although TABH cannot predict with certainty who may purchase the white paper, it particularly wants to appeal to companies with high sales growth in the United States, such as Kia (http://www.kia.com), Hyundai (http://www.hyundai-motor.com), and potentially European auto dealerships currently without significant U.S. distribution, such as Smart (http://www.smart.com), among others. TABH also hopes the white paper may eventually lead to a customized project for one of these companies. Thus, the general research question is:

What are the automobile market segment characteristics of students attending U.S. universities in small towns?

This question can be broken down into a series of more specific questions:

- What segments can be identified based on identifiable characteristics of students?
- How do different segments view a car?
- What types of automobiles would be most in demand?

Questions:

1. What types of tests can be performed using the data that may at least indirectly address the primary research question?
2. What do you think the primary conclusions of the white paper will be based on the data provided?
3. Assuming a small college town lacked an auto dealership (beyond Ford, GM, and Chrysler), what two companies should be most interested in this type of location? Use the Internet if necessary to perform some cursory research on different car companies.
4. What are the weaknesses in basing decisions on this type of research?
5. Are there key issues that may diminish the usefulness of this research?
6. What kinds of themes might emerge from the cartoon drawings?
7. Are there any ethical dilemmas presented in this case?

Case 7 Survey on Americans and Dietary Supplements

The NPR/Kaiser/Kennedy School Poll is a project of National Public Radio, the Henry J. Kaiser Family Foundation, and Harvard University's Kennedy School of Government. These organizations collaborated to conduct a Survey on Americans and Dietary Supplements. The results of this survey are based on telephone interviews conducted between February 19 and February 25, 1999, with 1,200 adults 18 years or older nationwide. Case Exhibits 7.1 through 7.6 summarize some of the results of this survey.

Question

Analyze these data and write up a report on your conclusions.

CASE EXHIBIT 7.1 **Knowledge of and Attitudes about Dietary Supplements by Frequency of Use**

	Total	Frequency of Use		
		Regularly	Sometimes	Hardly Ever/Never
Follow news reports about dietary supplements very/fairly closely	35%	56%	49%	27%
Very/somewhat familiar with supplements	55%	88%	83%	40%
Give supplements to kids (have kids < 18)	18%	42%	40%	8%
Important to have access to supplements	60%	91%	84%	46%
Good for health/well-being	52%	85%	76%	38%
Supplements can help people with at least 4 of 6 illnesses	36%	57%	47%	27%
Supplements are inadequately tested	48%	39%	44%	52%
Many supplements don't do what ads claim	49%	29%	36%	58%
Boosting immune system means:				
Prevents illness	64%	73%	63%	62%
Helps people when sick	43%	48%	45%	41%
People who use supplements are hurt/sick often/sometimes	47%	38%	45%	50%
Know that government doesn't regulate supplements	53%	58%	46%	54%
Should be more government regulation of:				
Safety	59%	55%	55%	62%
Purity/dosage	60%	55%	58%	62%
Ad claims	63%	62%	62%	65%
Extra regulation for supplements produced for children	77%	78%	77%	77%
If government said supplements were ineffective, would continue to use	72%	71%	72%	NA

CASE EXHIBIT 7.2 **Knowledge of and Attitudes about Dietary Supplements by Age**

	Total	Sum				
		18–29	30+	30–49	50–64	65+
Very/somewhat familiar with supplements	55%	63%	53%	58%	57%	37%
Know that government doesn't regulate supplements	53%	45%	56%	58%	57%	47%
Use supplements regularly	18%	16%	19%	15%	24%	22%
Good for health/well-being	52%	56%	51%	53%	54%	43%
Supplements can help people with at least 4 of 6 illnesses	36%	35%	36%	38%	37%	29%
Supplements are inadequately tested	48%	43%	50%	51%	53%	45%
Many supplements don't do what ads claim	49%	44%	50%	50%	56%	44%
Extra regulation for supplements produced for children	77%	82%	76%	79%	73%	70%

CASE EXHIBIT 7.3 **Knowledge of and Attitudes about Dietary Supplements by Education**

	Total	College Graduate	Some College	High School Graduate or Less
Follow news reports about dietary supplements very/fairly closely	35%	46%	39%	30%
Very/somewhat familiar with supplements	55%	64%	64%	49%
Know that government doesn't regulate supplements	53%	67%	56%	46%
Supplements are inadequately tested	48%	62%	49%	43%
Many supplements don't do what ads claim	49%	55%	47%	47%
Boosting immune system means:				
Prevents illness	64%	68%	69%	60%
Helps people when sick	43%	42%	43%	43%
Should be more government regulation of:				
Safety	59%	62%	61%	58%
Purity/dosage	60%	65%	64%	57%
Ad claims	63%	68%	63%	62%
Use supplements regularly	18%	22%	20%	16%
Good for health/well-being	52%	53%	59%	49%
Supplements can help people with at least 4 of 6 illnesses	36%	37%	38%	34%

CASE EXHIBIT 7.4 **Demographic Profile of Regular Users of Dietary Supplements**

This table gives the percent of regular users who are in each category.

Men	46%
Women	55%
18–29	20%
30–49	34%
50–64	25%
65+	19%
Household income:	
<$20K	20%
$20–29.9K	16%
$30–49.9K	15%
$50–74.9K	13%
$75K+	10%
Refused	20%
Don't Know	5%
Education:	
<High-School Graduate	4%
High-School Graduate	27%
Some College	32%
College Graduate	27%
Region:	
East	22%
Midwest	20%
South	32%
West	26%
Urban/rural:	
Urban	31%
Suburban	48%
Rural	21%
Party ID:	
Republican	24%
Democrat	27%
Independent	42%
Think they promote health:	
Yes	85%
No	3%
Belief in their health benefits:	
High	57%
Medium	34%
Low	9%

CASE EXHIBIT 7.5 **Regular Users of Dietary Supplements**

This table gives the percent of each specific group who are regular users.

National	18%
By gender:	
Men	18%
Women	19%
By age:	
18–29	16%
30–49	15%
50–64	24%
65+	22%
By race/ethnicity:	
White (non-Hispanic)	20%
Black (non-Hispanic)	8%
Hispanic	14%
By household income:	
<$20K	20%
$20c29.9K	20%
$30–49.9K	16%
$50–74.9K	17%
$75K+	16%
By education:	
<High-School Graduate	16%
High-School Graduate	17%
Some College	20%
College Graduate	22%
By region:	
East	20%
Midwest	15%
South	17%
West	23%
By urban/rural:	
Urban	18%
Suburban	19%
Rural	18%
By party ID:	
Republican	17%
Democrat	16%
Independent	21%
By think they promote health:	
Yes	30%
No	3%
By belief in their health benefits:	
High	30%
Medium	14%
Low	8%

CASE EXHIBIT 7.6 **Believers in Benefits of Dietary Supplements**

This table gives the percent of each group who believe dietary supplements are good for people's health and well-being.

National	52%
By gender:	
Men	51%
Women	53%
By age:	
18–29	56%
30–49	53%
50–64	54%
65+	43%
By race/ethnicity:	
White (non-Hispanic)	53%
Black (non-Hispanic)	40%
Hispanic	57%
By household income:	
<$20K	54%
$20–29.9K	56%
$30–49.9K	53%
$50–74.9K	58%
$75K+	45%
By education:	
<High-School Graduate	46%
High-School Graduate	50%
Some College	59%
College Graduate	53%
By region:	
East	54%
Midwest	51%
South	49%
West	56%
By urban/rural:	
Urban	49%
Suburban	52%
Rural	56%
By party ID:	
Republican	54%
Democrat	48%
Independent	54%
By use of supplements:	
Regular	85%
Sometimes	76%
Hardly ever/never	38%

NPR/Kaiser/Kennedy School Poll is a project of National Public Radio, the Henry J. Kaiser Foundation, & Harvard University's Kennedy School of Government.

APPENDIX

APPENDIX

Statistical Tables

TABLE A.1 **Area Under the Normal Curve**

z	.00	.01	.02	.03	.04	.05	.06	.07	.08	.09
0.0	.0000	.0040	.0080	.0120	.0160	.0199	.0239	.0279	.0319	.0359
0.1	.0398	.0438	.0478	.0517	.0557	.0596	.0636	.0675	.0714	.0753
0.2	.0793	.0832	.0871	.0910	.0948	.0987	.1026	.1064	.1103	.1141
0.3	.1179	.1217	.1255	.1293	.1331	.1368	.1406	.1443	.1480	.1517
0.4	.1554	.1591	.1628	.1664	.1700	.1736	.1772	.1808	.1844	.1879
0.5	.1915	.1950	.1985	.2019	.2054	.2088	.2123	.2157	.2190	.2224
0.6	.2257	.2291	.2324	.2357	.2389	.2422	.2454	.2486	.2518	.2549
0.7	.2580	.2612	.2642	.2673	.2704	.2734	.2764	.2794	.2823	.2852
0.8	.2881	.2910	.2939	.2967	.2995	.3023	.3051	.3078	.3106	.3133
0.9	.3159	.3186	.3212	.3238	.3264	.3289	.3315	.3340	.3365	.3389
1.0	.3413	.3438	.3461	.3485	.3508	.3531	.3554	.3577	.3599	.3621
1.1	.3643	.3665	.3686	.3708	.3729	.3749	.3770	.3790	.3810	.3830
1.2	.3849	.3869	.3888	.3907	.3925	.3944	.3962	.3980	.3997	.4015
1.3	.4032	.4049	.4066	.4082	.4099	.4115	.4131	.4147	.4162	.4177
1.4	.4192	.4207	.4222	.4236	.4251	.4265	.4279	.4292	.4306	.4319
1.5	.4332	.4345	.4357	.4370	.4382	.4394	.4406	.4418	.4429	.4441
1.6	.4452	.4463	.4474	.4484	.4495	.4505	.4515	.4525	.4535	.4545
1.7	.4554	.4564	.4573	.4582	.4591	.4599	.4608	.4616	.4625	.4633
1.8	.4641	.4649	.4656	.4664	.4671	.4678	.4686	.4693	.4699	.4706
1.9	.4713	.4719	.4726	.4732	.4738	.4744	.4750	.4756	.4761	.4767
2.0	.4772	.4778	.4783	.4788	.4793	.4798	.4803	.4808	.4812	.4817
2.1	.4821	.4826	.4830	.4834	.4838	.4842	.4846	.4850	.4854	.4857
2.2	.4861	.4864	.4868	.4871	.4875	.4878	.4881	.4884	.4887	.4890
2.3	.4893	.4896	.4898	.4901	.4904	.4906	.4909	.4911	.4913	.4916
2.4	.4918	.4920	.4922	.4925	.4927	.4929	.4931	.4932	.4934	.4936
2.5	.4938	.4940	.4941	.4943	.4945	.4946	.4948	.4949	.4951	.4952
2.6	.4953	.4955	.4956	.4957	.4959	.4960	.4961	.4962	.4963	.4964
2.7	.4965	.4966	.4967	.4968	.4969	.4970	.4971	.4972	.4973	.4974
2.8	.4974	.4975	.4976	.4977	.4977	.4978	.4979	.4979	.4980	.4981
2.9	.4981	.4982	.4982	.4983	.4984	.4984	.4985	.4985	.4986	.4986
3.0	.49865	.4987	.4987	.4988	.4988	.4989	.4989	.4989	.4990	.4990
4.0	.49997									

Chaiho Kim, *Statistical Analysis for Induction and Decision*. Copyright © 1973 by The Dryden Press, a division of Holt, Rinehart and Winston, Inc. Reprinted with permission of Holt, Rinehart and Winston.

TABLE A.2 **Distribution of *t* for Given Probability Levels**

d.f.	Level of Significance for One-Tailed Test					
	.10	.05	.025	.01	.005	.0005
	Level of Significance for Two-Tailed Test					
	.20	.10	.05	.02	.01	.001
1	3.078	6.314	12.706	31.821	63.657	636.619
2	1.886	2.920	4.303	6.965	9.925	31.598
3	1.638	2.353	3.182	4.541	5.841	12.941
4	1.533	2.132	2.776	3.747	4.604	8.610
5	1.476	2.015	2.571	3.365	4.032	6.859
6	1.440	1.943	2.447	3.143	3.707	5.959
7	1.415	1.895	2.365	2.998	3.499	5.405
8	1.397	1.860	2.306	2.896	3.355	5.041
9	1.383	1.833	2.262	2.821	3.250	4.781
10	1.372	1.812	2.228	2.764	3.169	4.587
11	1.363	1.796	2.201	2.718	3.106	4.437
12	1.356	1.782	2.179	2.681	3.055	4.318
13	1.350	1.771	2.160	2.650	3.012	4.221
14	1.345	1.761	2.145	2.624	2.977	4.140
15	1.341	1.753	2.131	2.602	2.947	4.073
16	1.337	1.746	2.120	2.583	2.921	4.015
17	1.333	1.740	2.110	2.567	2.898	3.965
18	1.330	1.734	2.101	2.552	2.878	3.922
19	1.328	1.729	2.093	2.539	2.861	3.883
20	1.325	1.725	2.086	2.528	2.845	3.850
21	1.323	1.721	2.080	2.518	2.831	3.819
22	1.321	1.717	2.074	2.508	2.819	3.792
23	1.319	1.714	2.069	2.500	2.807	3.767
24	1.318	1.711	2.064	2.492	2.797	3.745
25	1.316	1.708	2.060	2.485	2.787	3.725
26	1.315	1.706	2.056	2.479	2.779	3.707
27	1.314	1.703	2.052	2.473	2.771	3.690
28	1.313	1.701	2.048	2.467	2.763	3.674
29	1.311	1.699	2.045	2.462	2.756	3.659
30	1.310	1.697	2.042	2.457	2.750	3.646
40	1.303	1.684	2.021	2.423	2.704	3.551
60	1.296	1.671	2.000	2.390	2.660	3.460
120	1.289	1.658	1.980	2.358	2.617	3.373
∞	1.282	1.645	1.960	2.326	2.576	3.291

TABLE A.3 **Chi-Square Distribution**

Degrees of Freedom (d.f.)	Area in Shaded Right Tail (α)		
	.10	.05	.01
1	2.706	3.841	6.635
2	4.605	5.991	9.210
3	6.251	7.815	11.345
4	7.779	9.488	13.277
5	9.236	11.070	15.086
6	10.645	12.592	16.812
7	12.017	14.067	18.475
8	13.362	15.507	20.090
9	14.684	16.919	21.666
10	15.987	18.307	23.209
11	17.275	19.675	24.725
12	18.549	21.026	26.217
13	19.812	22.362	27.688
14	21.064	23.685	29.141
15	22.307	24.996	30.578
16	23.542	26.296	32.000
17	24.769	27.587	33.409
18	25.989	28.869	34.805
19	27.204	30.144	36.191
20	28.412	31.410	37.566
21	29.615	32.671	38.932
22	30.813	33.924	40.289
23	32.007	35.172	41.638
24	33.196	36.415	42.980
25	34.382	37.652	44.314
26	35.563	38.885	45.642
27	36.741	40.113	46.963
28	37.916	41.337	48.278
29	39.087	42.557	49.588
30	40.256	43.773	50.892

Example of how to use this table: In a chi-square distribution with 6 degrees of freedom (*d.f.*), the area to the right of a critical value of 12.59 2—i.e., the α area—is .05.

TABLE A.4 Critical Values of F_{v_1,v_2} for $\alpha = .05$

v_1 = Degrees of Freedom for Numerator

v_2	1	2	3	4	5	6	7	8	9	10	12	15	20	24	30	40	60	120	∞
1	161	200	216	225	230	234	237	239	241	242	244	246	248	249	250	251	252	253	254
2	18.5	19.0	19.2	19.2	19.3	19.3	19.4	19.4	19.4	19.4	19.4	19.4	19.5	19.5	19.5	19.5	19.5	19.5	19.5
3	10.1	9.55	9.28	9.12	9.01	8.94	8.89	8.85	8.81	8.79	8.74	8.70	8.66	8.64	8.62	8.59	8.57	8.55	8.53
4	7.71	6.94	6.59	6.39	6.26	6.16	6.09	6.04	6.00	5.96	5.91	5.86	5.80	5.77	5.75	5.72	5.69	5.66	5.63
5	6.61	5.79	5.41	5.19	5.05	4.95	4.88	4.82	4.77	4.74	4.68	4.62	4.56	4.53	4.50	4.46	4.43	4.40	4.37
6	5.99	5.14	4.76	4.53	4.39	4.28	4.21	4.15	4.10	4.06	4.00	3.94	3.87	3.84	3.81	3.77	3.74	3.70	3.67
7	5.59	4.74	4.35	4.12	3.97	3.87	3.79	3.73	3.68	3.64	3.57	3.51	3.44	3.41	3.38	3.34	3.30	3.27	3.23
8	5.32	4.46	4.07	3.84	3.69	3.58	3.50	3.44	3.39	3.35	3.28	3.22	3.15	3.12	3.08	3.04	3.01	2.97	2.93
9	5.12	4.26	3.86	3.63	3.48	3.37	3.29	3.23	3.18	3.14	3.07	3.01	2.94	2.90	2.86	2.83	2.79	2.75	2.71
10	4.96	4.10	3.71	3.48	3.33	3.22	3.14	3.07	3.02	2.98	2.91	2.85	2.77	2.74	2.70	2.66	2.62	2.58	2.54
11	4.84	3.98	3.59	3.36	3.20	3.09	3.01	2.95	2.90	2.85	2.79	2.72	2.65	2.61	2.57	2.53	2.49	2.45	2.40
12	4.75	3.89	3.49	3.26	3.11	3.00	2.91	2.85	2.80	2.75	2.69	2.62	2.54	2.51	2.47	2.43	2.38	2.34	2.30
13	4.67	3.81	3.41	3.18	3.03	2.92	2.83	2.77	2.71	2.67	2.60	2.53	2.46	2.42	2.38	2.34	2.30	2.25	2.21
14	4.60	3.74	3.34	3.11	2.96	2.85	2.76	2.70	2.65	2.60	2.53	2.46	2.39	2.35	2.31	2.27	2.22	2.18	2.13
15	4.54	3.68	3.29	3.06	2.90	2.79	2.71	2.64	2.59	2.54	2.48	2.40	2.33	2.29	2.25	2.20	2.16	2.11	2.07
16	4.49	3.63	3.24	3.01	2.85	2.74	2.66	2.59	2.54	2.49	2.42	2.35	2.28	2.24	2.19	2.15	2.11	2.06	2.01
17	4.45	3.59	3.20	2.96	2.81	2.70	2.61	2.55	2.49	2.45	2.38	2.31	2.23	2.19	2.15	2.10	2.06	2.01	1.96
18	4.41	3.55	3.16	2.93	2.77	2.66	2.58	2.51	2.46	2.41	2.34	2.27	2.19	2.15	2.11	2.06	2.02	1.97	1.92
19	4.38	3.52	3.13	2.90	2.74	2.63	2.54	2.48	2.42	2.38	2.31	2.23	2.16	2.11	2.07	2.03	1.98	1.93	1.88
20	4.35	3.49	3.10	2.87	2.71	2.60	2.51	2.45	2.39	2.35	2.28	2.20	2.12	2.08	2.04	1.99	1.95	1.90	1.84
21	4.32	3.47	3.07	2.84	2.68	2.57	2.49	2.42	2.37	2.32	2.25	2.18	2.10	2.05	2.01	1.96	1.92	1.87	1.81
22	4.30	3.44	3.05	2.82	2.66	2.55	2.46	2.40	2.34	2.30	2.23	2.15	2.07	2.03	1.98	1.94	1.89	1.84	1.78
23	4.28	3.42	3.03	2.80	2.64	2.53	2.44	2.37	2.32	2.27	2.20	2.13	2.05	2.01	1.96	1.91	1.86	1.81	1.76
24	4.26	3.40	3.01	2.78	2.62	2.51	2.42	2.36	2.30	2.25	2.18	2.11	2.03	1.98	1.94	1.89	1.84	1.79	1.73
25	4.24	3.39	2.99	2.76	2.60	2.49	2.40	2.34	2.28	2.24	2.16	2.09	2.01	1.96	1.92	1.87	1.82	1.77	1.71
30	4.17	3.32	2.92	2.69	2.53	2.42	2.33	2.27	2.21	2.16	2.09	2.01	1.93	1.89	1.84	1.79	1.74	1.68	1.62
40	4.08	3.23	2.84	2.61	2.45	2.34	2.25	2.18	2.12	2.08	2.00	1.92	1.84	1.79	1.74	1.69	1.64	1.58	1.51
60	4.00	3.15	2.76	2.53	2.37	2.25	2.17	2.10	2.04	1.99	1.92	1.84	1.75	1.70	1.65	1.59	1.53	1.47	1.39
120	3.92	3.07	2.68	2.45	2.29	2.18	2.09	2.02	1.96	1.91	1.83	1.75	1.66	1.61	1.55	1.50	1.43	1.35	1.25
∞	3.84	3.00	2.60	2.37	2.21	2.10	2.01	1.94	1.88	1.83	1.75	1.67	1.57	1.52	1.46	1.39	1.32	1.22	1.00

v_2 = Degrees of Freedom for Denominator

TABLE A.5 **Critical Values of F_{v_1,v_2} for $\alpha = .01$**

v_1 = Degrees of Freedom for Numerator

v_2	1	2	3	4	5	6	7	8	9	10	12	15	20	24	30	40	60	120	∞
1	4,052	5,000	5,403	5,625	5,764	5,859	5,928	5,982	6,023	6,056	6,106	6,157	6,209	6,235	6,261	6,287	6,313	6,339	6,366
2	98.5	99.0	99.2	99.2	99.3	99.3	99.4	99.4	99.4	99.4	99.4	99.4	99.4	99.5	99.5	99.5	99.5	99.5	99.5
3	34.1	30.8	29.5	28.7	28.2	27.9	27.7	27.5	27.3	27.2	27.1	26.9	26.7	26.6	26.5	26.4	26.3	26.2	26.1
4	21.2	18.0	16.7	16.0	15.5	15.2	15.0	14.8	14.7	14.5	14.4	14.2	14.0	13.9	13.8	13.7	13.7	13.6	13.5
5	16.3	13.3	12.1	11.4	11.0	10.7	10.5	10.3	10.2	10.1	9.89	9.72	9.55	9.47	9.38	9.29	9.20	9.11	9.02
6	13.7	10.9	9.78	9.15	8.75	8.47	8.26	8.10	7.98	7.87	7.72	7.56	7.40	7.31	7.23	7.14	7.06	6.97	6.88
7	12.2	9.55	8.45	7.85	7.46	7.19	6.99	6.84	6.72	6.62	6.47	6.31	6.16	6.07	5.99	5.91	5.82	5.74	5.65
8	11.3	8.65	7.59	7.01	6.63	6.37	6.18	6.03	5.91	5.81	5.67	5.52	5.36	5.28	5.20	5.12	5.03	4.95	4.86
9	10.6	8.02	6.99	6.42	6.06	5.80	5.61	5.47	5.35	5.26	5.11	4.96	4.81	4.73	4.65	4.57	4.48	4.40	4.31
10	10.0	7.56	6.55	5.99	5.64	5.39	5.20	5.06	4.94	4.85	4.71	4.56	4.41	4.33	4.25	4.17	4.08	4.00	3.91
11	9.65	7.21	6.22	5.67	5.32	5.07	4.89	4.74	4.63	4.54	4.40	4.25	4.10	4.02	3.94	3.86	3.78	3.69	3.60
12	9.33	6.93	5.95	5.41	5.06	4.82	4.64	4.50	4.39	4.30	4.16	4.01	3.86	3.78	3.70	3.62	3.54	3.45	3.36
13	9.07	6.70	5.74	5.21	4.86	4.62	4.44	4.30	4.19	4.10	3.96	3.82	3.66	3.59	3.51	3.43	3.34	3.25	3.17
14	8.86	6.51	5.56	5.04	4.70	4.46	4.28	4.14	4.03	3.94	3.80	3.66	3.51	3.43	3.35	3.27	3.18	3.09	3.00
15	8.68	6.36	5.42	4.89	4.56	4.32	4.14	4.00	3.89	3.80	3.67	3.52	3.37	3.29	3.21	3.13	3.05	2.96	2.87
16	8.53	6.23	5.29	4.77	4.44	4.20	4.03	3.89	3.78	3.69	3.55	3.41	3.26	3.18	3.10	3.02	2.93	2.84	2.75
17	8.40	6.11	5.19	4.67	4.34	4.10	3.93	3.79	3.68	3.59	3.46	3.31	3.16	3.08	3.00	2.92	2.83	2.75	2.65
18	8.29	6.01	5.09	4.58	4.25	4.01	3.84	3.71	3.60	3.51	3.37	3.23	3.08	3.00	2.92	2.84	2.75	2.66	2.57
19	8.19	5.93	5.01	4.50	4.17	3.94	3.77	3.63	3.52	3.43	3.30	3.15	3.00	2,92	2.84	2.76	2.67	2.58	2.49
20	8.10	5.85	4.94	4.43	4.10	3.87	3.70	3.56	3.46	3.37	3.23	3.09	2.94	2.86	2.78	2.69	2.61	2.52	2.42
21	8.02	5.78	4.87	4.37	4.04	3.81	3.64	3.51	3.40	3.31	3.17	3.03	2.88	2.80	2.72	2.64	2.55	2.46	2.36
22	7.96	5.72	4.82	4.31	3.99	3.76	3.59	3.45	3.35	3.26	3.12	2.98	2.83	2.75	2.67	2.58	2.50	2.40	2.31
23	7.88	5.66	4.76	4.26	3.94	3.71	3.54	3.41	3.30	3.21	3.07	2.93	2.78	2.70	2.62	2.54	2.45	2.35	2.26
24	7.82	5.61	4.72	4.22	3.90	3.67	3.50	3.36	3.26	3.17	3.03	2.89	2.74	2.66	2.58	2.49	2.40	2.31	2.26
25	7.77	5.57	4.68	4.18	3.86	3.63	3.46	3.32	3.22	3.13	2.99	2.85	2.70	2.62	2.53	2.45	2.36	2.27	2.17
30	7.58	5.39	4.51	4.02	3.70	3.47	3.30	3.17	3.07	2.98	2.84	2.70	2.55	2.47	2.39	2.30	2.21	2.11	2.01
40	7.31	5.18	4.31	3.83	3.51	3.29	3.12	2.99	2.89	2.80	2.66	2.52	2.37	2.29	2.20	2.11	2.02	1.92	1.80
60	7.08	4.98	4.13	3.65	3.34	3.12	2.95	2.82	2.72	2.63	2.50	2.35	2.20	2.12	2.03	1.94	1.84	1.73	1.60
120	6.85	4.79	3.95	3.48	3.17	2.96	2.79	2.66	2.56	2.47	2.34	2.19	2.03	1.95	1.86	1.76	1.66	1.53	1.38
∞	6.63	4.61	3.78	3.32	3.02	2.80	2.64	2.51	2.41	2.32	2.18	2.04	1.88	1.79	1.70	1.59	1.47	1.32	1.00

v_2 = Degrees of Freedom for Denominator

Maxine Merrington and Catherine M. Thompson, "Tables of the Percentage Points of the Inverted F-Distribution," *Biometrica* Vol. 33, 1943, pp. 73–78. Reprinted with the permission of Biometrica Trustees.

Glossary of Frequently Used Symbols

Greek Letters

α (alpha)	level of significance or probability of a Type I error
β (beta)	probability of a Type II error or slope of the regression line
μ (mu)	population mean
ρ (rho)	population Pearson correlation coefficient
Σ (summation)	take the sum of
π (pi)	population proportion
σ (sigma)	population standard deviation
χ^2	chi-square statistic

English Letters

$d.f.$	number of degrees of freedom
F	F-statistic
n	sample size
p	sample proportion
$Pr(\ )$	probability of the outcome in the parentheses
r	sample Pearson correlation coefficient
r^2	coefficient of determination (squared correlation coefficient)
R^2	coefficient of determination (multiple regression)
S	sample standard deviation (inferential statistics)
$S_{\bar{x}}$	estimated standard error of the mean
S_p	estimated standard error of the proportion
S^2	sample variance (inferential statistics)
t	t-statistic
X	variable or any unspecified observation
$\bar{X}$	sample mean
Y	any unspecified observation on a second variable, usually the dependent variable
$\hat{Y}$	predicted dependent variable score
Z	standardized score (descriptive statistics) or Z-statistic

A

absolute causality Means the cause is necessary and sufficient to bring about the effect.

acquiescence bias A tendency for respondents to agree with all or most questions asked of them in a survey.

administrative error An error caused by the improper administration or execution of the research task.

advocacy research Research undertaken to support a specific claim in a legal action or represent some advocacy group.

aided-recall Asking the respondent to remember something and giving them a clue to help.

analysis of variance (ANOVA) Analysis of the effects of a categorical treatment variable on an a least interval-scaled dependent variable—a hypothesis-testing technique to determine whether statistically significant differences in means occur between two or more groups.

applied marketing research Research conducted to address a specific marketing decision for a specific firm or organization.

artifacts The things that people made and consumed within a culture that signal something meaningful about the behavior taking place at the time of consumption

at-home scanning systems Systems that allow consumer panelists to perform their own scanning after taking home products, using handheld wands that read UPC symbols.

attitude An enduring disposition to consistently respond in a given manner to various aspects of the world; composed of affective, cognitive, and behavioral components.

attribute A single characteristic or fundamental feature of an object, person, situation, or issue.

B

back translation Taking a questionnaire that has previously been translated into another language and having a second, independent translator translate it back to the original language.

backward linkage Implies that later steps influence earlier stages of the research process.

balanced rating scale A fixed-alternative rating scale with an equal number of positive and negative categories; a neutral point or point of indifference is at the center of the scale.

basic experimental design An experimental design in which only one variable is manipulated.

basic marketing research Research conducted without a specific decision in mind that usually does not address the needs of a specific organization. It attempts to expand the limits of marketing knowledge in general and is not aimed at solving a particular pragmatic problem.

behavioral differential A rating scale instrument similar to a semantic differential, developed to measure the behavioral intentions of subjects toward future actions.

between-groups variance The sum of differences between the group mean and the grand mean summed over all groups for a given set of observations.

between-subjects design Each subject receives only one treatment combination.

bivariate statistical analysis Tests of hypotheses involving two variables.

blocking variables A categorical variable included in the statistical analysis of experimental data as a way of statistically controlling or accounting for variance due to that variable.

box and whisker plots Graphic representations of central tendencies, percentiles, variabilities, and the shapes of frequency distributions.

briefing session A training session to ensure that each interviewer is provided with common information.

C

callbacks Attempts to recontact individuals selected for a sample who were not available initially.

cannibalize When consumers choose a new offering as a replacement for another product offered by the same company.

case studies The documented history of a particular person, group, organization, or event.

cata analysis The application of reasoning to understand the data that have been gathered.

categorical variable A variable that indicates membership in some group.

category scale A rating scale that consists of several response categories, often providing respondents with alternatives to indicate positions on a continuum.

causal inference A conclusion that when one thing happens, another specific thing will follow.

causal research Allows causal inferences to be made; seeks to identify cause-and-effect relationships.

cell Refers to a specific treatment combination associated with an experimental group.

census An investigation of all the individual elements that make up a population.

central location interviewing Telephone interviews conducted from a central location allowing firms to hire a staff of professional interviewers and to supervise and control the quality of interviewing more effectively.

central-limit theorem The theory that, as sample size increases, the distribution of sample means of size n, randomly selected, approaches a normal distribution.

check boxes In an Internet questionnaire, small graphic boxes, next to answers, that a respondent clicks on to choose an answer; typically, a check mark or an X appears in the box when the respondent clicks on it.

checklist question A fixed-alternative question that allows the respondent to provide multiple answers to a single question by checking off items.

Chi-square (χ^2) test One of the most basic tests for statistical significance that is particularly appropriate for testing hypotheses about frequencies arranged in a frequency or contingency table.

choice A measurement task that identifies preferences by requiring respondents to choose between two or more alternatives

classificatory variable Another term for a categorical variable because it classifies units into categories.

click-through rate Proportion of people who are exposed to an Internet ad who actually click on its hyperlink to enter the Web site; click-through rates are generally very low.

cluster analysis A multivariate approach for grouping observations based on similarity among measured variables.

cluster sampling An economically efficient sampling technique in which the primary sampling unit is not the individual element in the population but a large cluster of elements; clusters are selected randomly.

code book A book that identifies each variable in a study and gives the variable's description, code name, and position in the data matrix.

codes Rules for interpreting, classifying, and recording data in the coding process; also, the actual numerical or other character symbols assigned to raw data.

coding The process of assigning a numerical score or other character symbol to previously edited data.

coding sheet A book that identifies each variable in a study and gives the variable's description, code name, and position in the data matrix.

coefficient alpha (α) The most commonly applied estimate of a multiple item scale's reliability. It represents the average of all possible split-half reliabilities for a construct.

coefficient of determination (R^2) A measure obtained by squaring the correlation coefficient; the proportion of the total variance of a variable accounted for by another value of another variable.

cohort effect Refers to a change in the dependent variable that occurs because members of one experimental group experienced different historical situations than members of other experimental groups.

communication process The process by which one person or source sends a message to an audience or receiver and then receives feedback about the message.

comparative rating scale Any measure of attitudes that asks respondents to rate a concept in comparison with a benchmark explicitly used as a frame of reference.

completely randomized design An experimental design that uses a random process to assign subjects (test units) to treatment levels to investigate the effects of an experimental variable.

composite measures Assign a value to an observation based on a mathematical derivation of multiple variables.

composite scale A way of representing a latent construct by summing or averaging respondents' reactions to multiple items, each assumed to indicate the latent construct.

computer-assisted telephone interviewing (CATI) Technology that allows answers to telephone interviews to be entered directly into a computer for processing.

concept A generalized idea that represents something of meaning.

concept testing A frequently performed type of exploratory research representing many similar research procedures all having the same purpose: to screen new, revised, or repositioned ideas.

conclusions and recommendations section The part of the body of a report that provides opinions based on the results and suggestions for action.

concomitant variation One of three criteria for causality; occurs when two events "covary," meaning they vary systematically.

conditional causality Means that a cause is necessary but not sufficient to bring about an effect.

confidence interval estimate A specified range of numbers within which a population mean is expected to lie; an estimate of the population mean based on the knowledge that it will be equal to the sample mean plus or minus a small sampling error.

confidence level A percentage or decimal value that tells how confident a researcher can be about being correct; it states the long-run percentage of confidence intervals that will include the true population mean.

confidentiality The information involved in a research will not be shared with others.

conflict of interest Occurs when one researcher works for two competing companies.

confound In an experiment means that there is an alternative explanation beyond the experimental variables for any observed differences in the dependent variable.

constancy of conditions Means that subjects in all experimental groups are exposed to identical conditions except for the differing experimental treatments.

constant Something that does not change; is not useful in addressing research questions.

constant-sum scale A measure of attitudes in which respondents are asked to divide a constant sum to indicate the relative importance of attributes; respondents often sort cards, but the task may also be a rating task.

construct A term used to refer to concepts measured with multiple variables.

construct validity Exists when a measure reliably measures and truthfully represents a unique concept; consists of several components including face validity, convergent validity, criterion validity, and discriminant validity.

consumer panel A longitudinal survey of the same sample of individuals or households to record their attitudes, behavior, or purchasing habits over time.

content analysis The systematic observation and quantitative description of the manifest content of communication.

content providers Parties that furnish information on the World Wide Web.

contingency table A data matrix that displays the frequency of some combination of possible responses to multiple variables; cross-tabulation results.

continuous measures Measures that reflect the intensity of a concept by assigning values that can take on any value along some scale range.

continuous variable A variable that can take on a range of values that correspond to some quantitative amount.

contributory causality Means that a cause need be neither necessary nor sufficient to bring about an effect.

contrived observation Observation in which the investigator creates an artificial environment in order to test a hypothesis.

control group A group of subjects to whom no experimental treatment is administered.

control method of test-marketing A "minimarket test" using forced distribution in a small city; retailers are paid for shelf space so that the test-marketer can be guaranteed distribution.

convenience sampling The sampling procedure of obtaining those people or units that are most conveniently available.

convergent validity Another way of expressing internal consistency; highly reliable scales contain convergent validity.

conversations An informal qualitative data-gathering approach in which the researcher engages a respondent in a discussion of the relevant subject matter.

cookies Small computer files that a content provider can save onto the computer of someone who visits its Web site.

correlation coefficient A statistical measure of the covariation, or association, between two at-least interval variables.

correlation matrix The standard form for reporting correlation coefficients for more than two variables.

correspondence rules Indicate the way that a certain value on a scale corresponds to some true value of a concept.

counterbalancing Attempts to eliminate the confounding effects of order of presentation by requiring that one fourth of the subjects be exposed to treatment A first, one fourth to treatment B first, one fourth to treatment C first, and finally one fourth to treatment D first.

counterbiasing statement An introductory statement or preamble to a potentially embarrassing question that reduces a respondent's reluctance to answer by suggesting that certain behavior is not unusual.

covariance Extent to which two variables are associated systematically with each other.

covariate A continuous variable included in the statistical analysis as a way of statistically controlling for variance due to that variable.

cover letter Letter that accompanies a questionnaire to induce the reader to complete and return the questionnaire.

criterion validity The ability of a measure to correlate with other standard measures of similar constructs or established criteria.

critical values The values that lie exactly on the boundary of the region of rejection.

cross-checks The comparison of data from one source with data from another source to determine the similarity of independent projects.

cross-functional teams Employee teams composed of individuals from various functional areas such as engineering, production, finance, and marketing who share a common purpose.

cross-sectional study A study in which various segments of a population are sampled and data are collected at a single moment in time.

cross-tabulation The appropriate technique for addressing research questions involving relationships among multiple less-than interval variables; results in a combined frequency table displaying one variable in rows and another in columns.

cultural cross-validate To verify that the empirical findings from one culture also exist and behave similarly in another culture.

curb-stoning A form of interviewer cheating in which an interviewer makes up the responses instead of conducting an actual interview.

custom research Research projects that are tailored specifically to a client's unique needs.

customer discovery Involves mining data to look for patterns identifying who is likely to be a valuable customer.

customer relationship management (CRM) Part of the DSS that addresses exchanges between the firm and its customers.

customer-oriented Describes a firm in which all decisions are made with a conscious awareness of their effect on the consumer.

D

data Facts or recorded measures of certain phenomena (things).

data conversion The process of changing the original form of the data to a format suitable to achieve the research objective; also called data transformation.

data entry The activity of transferring data from a research project to computers.

data file The way a data set is stored electronically in spreadsheet-like form in which the rows represent sampling units and the columns represent variables.

data integrity The notion that the data file actually contains the information that the researcher promised the decision maker he or she would obtain, meaning in part that the data have been edited and properly coded so that they are useful to the decision maker.

data mining The use of powerful computers to dig through volumes of data to discover patterns about an organization's customers and products; applies to many different forms of analysis.

data quality The degree to which data represent the true situation.

data reduction technique Multivariate statistical approaches that summarize the information from many variables into a reduced set of variates formed as linear combinations of measured variables.

data transformation Process of changing the data from their original form to a format suitable for performing a data analysis addressing research objectives.

data warehouse The multitiered computer storehouse of current and historical data.

data warehousing The process allowing important day-to-day operational data to be stored and organized for simplified access.

data wholesalers Companies that put together consortia of data sources into packages that are offered to municipal, corporate, and university libraries for a fee.

database A collection of raw data arranged logically and organized in a form that can be stored and processed by a computer.

database marketing The use of customer databases to promote one-to-one relationships with customers and create precisely targeted promotions.

data-processing error A category of administrative error that occurs because of incorrect data entry, incorrect computer programming, or other procedural errors during data analysis.

debriefing Research subjects are fully informed and provided with a chance to ask any questions they may have about the experiment.

decision making The process of developing and deciding among alternative ways of resolving a problem or choosing from among alternative opportunities.

decision statement A written expression of the key question(s) that the research user wishes to answer.

decision support system (DSS) A computer-based system that helps decision makers confront problems through direct interaction with databases and analytical software programs.

degrees of freedom (d.f.) The number of observations minus the number of constraints or assumptions needed to calculate a statistical term.

deliverables The term used often in consulting to describe research objectives to a research client.

demand characteristic Experimental design element or procedure that unintentionally provides subjects with hints about the research hypothesis.

demand effect Occurs when demand characteristics actually affect the dependent variable.

dependence techniques Multivariate statistical techniques that explain or predict one or more dependent variables.

dependent variable A process outcome or a variable that is predicted and/or explained by other variables.

depth interview A one-on-one interview between a professional researcher and a research respondent conducted about some relevant business or social topic.

descriptive analysis The elementary transformation of raw data in a way that describes the basic characteristics such as central tendency, distribution, and variability.

descriptive research Describes characteristics of objects, people, groups, organizations, or environments; tries to "paint a picture" of a given situation.

determinant-choice question A fixed-alternative question that requires the respondent to choose one response from among multiple alternatives.

diagnostic analysis Seeks to diagnose reasons for market outcomes and focuses specifically on the beliefs and feelings consumers have about and toward competing products.

dialog boxes Windows that open on a computer screen to prompt the user to enter information.

direct observation A straightforward attempt to observe and record what naturally occurs; the investigator does not create an artificial situation.

director of marketing research This person provides leadership in research efforts and integrates all staff-level research activities into one effort. The director plans, executes, and controls the firm's marketing research function.

discrete measures Measures that take on only one of a finite number of values.

discriminant analysis A statistical technique for predicting the probability that an object will belong in one of two or more mutually exclusive categories (dependent variable), based on several independent variables.

discriminant validity Represents how unique or distinct is a measure; a scale should not correlate too highly with a measure of a different construct.

discussion guide A focus group outline that includes written introductory comments informing the group about the focus group purpose and rules and then outlines topics or questions to be addressed in the group session.

disguised questions Indirect questions that assume the purpose of the study must be hidden from the respondent.

disproportional stratified sample A stratified sample in which the sample size for each stratum is allocated according to analytical considerations.

do-not-call legislation Restricts any telemarketing effort from calling consumers who either register with a no-call list or who request not to be called.

door-in-the-face compliance technique A two-step process for securing a high response rate. In step 1 an initial request, so large that nearly everyone refuses it, is made. Next, a second request is made for a smaller favor; respondents are expected to comply with this more reasonable request.

door-to-door interviews Personal interviews conducted at respondents' doorsteps in an effort to increase the participation rate in the survey.

double-barreled question A question that may induce bias because it covers two issues at once.

drop-down box In an Internet questionnaire, a space saving device that reveals responses when they are needed but otherwise hides them from view.

drop-off method A survey method that requires the interviewer to travel to the respondent's location to drop off questionnaires that will be picked up later.

dummy coding Numeric "1" or "0" coding where each number represents an alternate response such as "female" or "male."

dummy tables Tables placed in research proposals that are exact representations of the actual tables that will show results in the final report with the exception that the results are hypothetical (fictitious).

dummy variable The way a dichotomous (two group) independent variable is represented in regression analysis by assigning a 0 to one group and a 1 to the other.

E

editing The process of checking the completeness, consistency, and legibility of data and making the data ready for coding and transfer to storage.

effects coding An alternative to dummy coding using the values of -1 and $+1$ to represent two categories of responses.

elaboration analysis An analysis of the basic cross-tabulation for each level of a variable not previously considered, such as subgroups of the sample.

electronic data interchange (EDI) Type of exchange that occurs when one company's computer system is integrated with another company's system.

electronic test-markets A system of test-marketing that measures dependent variables with scanner-based consumer panels and manipulates advertising based on a special delivery system that can swap out one television commercial or advertisement for another.

e-mail surveys Surveys distributed through electronic mail.

empirical testing Means that something has been examined against reality using data.

environmental scanning Entails all information gathering designed to detect changes in the external operating environment of the firm.

error trapping Using software to control the flow of an Internet questionnaire—for example, to prevent respondents from backing up or failing to answer a question.

ethical dilemma Refers to a situation in which one chooses from alternative courses of actions, each with different ethical implications.

ethnography Represents ways of studying cultures through methods that involve becoming highly active within that culture.

experiment A carefully controlled study in which the researcher manipulates a proposed cause and observes any corresponding change in the proposed effect.

experimental condition One of the possible levels of an experimental variable manipulation.

experimental group A group of subjects to whom an experimental treatment is administered.

experimental treatment The term referring to the way an experimental variable is manipulated.

experimental variable Represents the proposed cause and is controlled by the researcher by manipulating it.

exploratory research Conducted to clarify ambiguous situations or discover ideas that may be potential business opportunities.

external data Data created, recorded, or generated by an entity other than the researcher's organization.

external validity Is the accuracy with which experimental results can be generalized beyond the experimental subjects.

extremity bias A category of response bias that results because some individuals tend to use extremes when responding to questions.

eye-tracking monitor A mechanical device used to observe eye movements; some eye monitors use infrared light beams to measure unconscious eye movements.

F

face (content) validity A scale's content logically appears to reflect what was intended to be measured.

factor analysis A prototypical multivariate, interdependence technique that statistically identifies a reduced number of factors from a larger number of measured variables.

factor loading Indicates how strongly a measured variable is correlated with a factor.

factor rotation A mathematical way of simplifying factor analysis results to better identify which variables "load on" which factors; the most common procedure is varimax.

factorial design An experiment that investigates the interaction of two or more independent variables on a single dependent variable.

fax survey A survey that uses fax machines as a way for respondents to receive and return questionnaires.

field A collection of characters that represents a single type of data—usually a variable.

field editing Preliminary editing by a field supervisor on the same day as the interview to catch technical omissions, check legibility of handwriting, and clarify responses that are logically or conceptually inconsistent.

field experiments Research projects involving experimental manipulations that are implemented in a natural environment.

field interviewing service A research supplier that specializes in gathering data.

field notes The researcher's descriptions of what actually happens in the field; these notes then become the text from which meaning is extracted.

fieldworker An individual who is responsible for gathering data in the field.

filter question A question that screens out respondents who are not qualified to answer a second question.

fixed-alternative questions Questions in which respondents are given specific, limited-alternative responses and asked to choose the one closest to their own viewpoint.

focus blog A type of informal, "continuous" focus group established as an Internet blog for the purpose of collecting qualitative data from participant comments.

focus group A small group discussion about some research topic led by a moderator who guides discussion among the participants.

focus group interview An unstructured, free-flowing interview with a small group of around six to ten people. Focus groups are led by a trained moderator who follows a flexible format encouraging dialogue among respondents.

foot-in-the-door compliance technique A technique for obtaining a high response rate, in which compliance with a large or difficult task is induced by first obtaining the respondent's compliance with a smaller request.

forced answering software Software that prevents respondents from continuing with an Internet questionnaire if they fail to answer a question.

forced-choice rating scale A fixed-alternative rating scale that requires respondents to choose one of the fixed alternatives.

forecast analyst Employee who provides technical assistance such as running computer programs and manipulating data to generate a sales forecast.

forward linkage Implies that the earlier stages of the research process influence the later stages.

free-association techniques Record respondents' first (top-of-mind) cognitive reactions to some stimulus.

frequency distribution A set of data organized by summarizing the number of times a particular value of a variable occurs.

frequency table A table showing the different ways respondents answered a question.

frequency-determination question A fixed-alternative question that asks for an answer about general frequency of occurrence.

F-test A procedure used to determine whether there is more variability in the scores of one sample than in the scores of another sample.

F-test (regression) A procedure to determine whether a regression equation or variable explains a significant amount of variance in a dependent variable

funded marketing research Refers to basic research usually performed by academic researchers that is financially supported by some public or private institution as in federal government grants.

funnel technique Asking general questions before specific questions in order to obtain unbiased responses.

G

general linear model (GLM) A way of explaining and predicting a dependent variable based on fluctuations (variation) from its mean. The fluctuations are due to changes in independent variables.

geo-demographics Refers to information describing the demographic profile of consumers in a particular geographic region.

global information system An organized collection of computer hardware, software, data, and personnel designed to capture, store, update, manipulate, analyze, and immediately display information about worldwide business activity.

goodness-of-fit (GOF) A general term representing how well some computed table or matrix of values matches some population or predetermined table or matrix of the same size.

grand mean The mean of a variable over all observations.

graphic aids Pictures or diagrams used to clarify complex points or emphasize a message.

graphic rating scale A measure of attitude that allows respondents to rate an object by choosing any point along a graphic continuum.

grounded theory Represents an inductive investigation in which the researcher poses questions about information provided by respondents or taken from historical records; the researcher asks the questions to himself or herself and repeatedly questions the responses to derive deeper explanations.

H

hawthorne effect People will perform differently from normal when they know they are experimental subjects.

hermeneutic unit Refers to a text passage from a respondent's story that is linked with a key theme from within this story or provided by the researcher.

hermeneutics An approach to understanding phenomenology that relies on analysis of texts through which a person tells a story about him- or herself.

hidden observation Observation in which the subject is unaware that observation is taking place.

histogram A graphical way of showing a frequency distribution in which the height of a bar corresponds to the observed frequency of the category.

history effect Occurs when some change other than the experimental treatment occurs during the course of an experiment that affects the dependent variable.

host Where the content for a particular website physically resides and is accessed.

human subjects review committee Carefully reviews proposed research design to try to make sure that no harm can come to any research participant. Otherwise known as an Institutional Review Board or IRB.

hypothesis A formal statement explaining some outcome.

hypothesis test of a proportion A test that is conceptually similar to the one used when the mean is the characteristic of interest but that differs in the mathematical formulation of the standard error of the proportion.

hypothetical constructs Variables that are not directly observable but are measurable through indirect indicators, such as verbal expression or overt behavior.

I

idealism A term that reflects the degree to which one bases one's morality on moral standards.

image profile A graphic representation of semantic differential data for competing brands, products, or stores to highlight comparisons.

importance-performance analysis Another name for quadrant analysis.

impute To fill in a missing data point through the use of a statistical process providing an educated guess for the missing response based on available information.

independent samples *t*-test A test for hypotheses stating that the mean scores for some interval- or ratio-scaled variable grouped based on some less-than interval classificatory variable.

independent variable A variable that is expected to influence the dependent variable in some way.

index measure An index assigns a value based on how much of the concept being measured is associated with an observation; indexes often are formed by putting several variables together.

index numbers Scores or observations recalibrated to indicate how they relate to a base number.

index of retail saturation A calculation that describes the relationship between retail demand and supply.

information Data formatted (structured) to support decision making or define the relationship between two facts.

information completeness Having the right amount of information.

informed consent When an individual understands what the researcher wants him or her to do and consents to the research study.

in-house editing A rigorous editing job performed by a centralized office staff.

in-house interviewer A fieldworker who is employed by the company conducting the research.

in-house research Research performed by employees of the company that will benefit from the research.

Institutional Review Board Another name for a human subjects review committee.

instrumentation effect A nuisance that occurs when a change in the wording of questions, a change in interviewers, or a change in other procedures causes a change in the dependent variable.

integrated marketing communication Means that all promotional efforts (advertising, public relations, personal selling, event marketing, and so forth) should be coordinated to communicate a consistent image.

integrated marketing mix The effects of various combinations of marketing-mix elements on important outcomes.

interaction effect Differences in dependant variable means due to a specific combination of independent variables.

interactive help desk in an Internet questionnaire, a live, real-time support feature that solves problems or answers questions respondents may encounter in completing the questionnaire.

interactive medium A medium, such as the Internet, that a person can use to communicate with and interact with other users.

interactive survey approaches Communication that allows spontaneous two-way interaction between the interviewer and the respondent.

interdependence techniques Multivariate statistical techniques that give meaning to a set of variables or seek to group things together; no distinction is made between dependent and independent variables.

internal and proprietary data Secondary data that originate inside the organization.

internal consistency Represents a measure's homogeneity or the extent to which each indicator of a concept converges on some common meaning.

internal validity Exists to the extent that an experimental variable is truly responsible for any variance in the dependent variable.

Internet A worldwide network of computers that allows users access to information from distant sources.

Internet survey A self-administered questionnaire posted on a Web site.

interpretation The process of drawing inferences from the analysis results.

interquartile range A measure of variability.

interrogative techniques Asking multiple what, where, who, when, why, and how questions.

interval scales Scales that have both nominal and ordinal properties, but that also capture information about differences in quantities of a concept from one observation to the next.

interviewer bias A response bias that occurs because the presence of the interviewer influences respondents' answers.

interviewer cheating The practice of filling in fake answers or falsifying questionnaires while working as an interviewer.

interviewer error Mistakes made by interviewers failing to record survey responses correctly.

intranet A company's private data network that uses Internet standards and technology.

introduction section The part of the body of a research report that discusses background information and the specific objectives of the research.

inverse (negative) relationship Covariation in which the association between variables is in the opposite direction. As one goes up, the other goes down.

item nonresponse The technical term for an unanswered question on an otherwise complete questionnaire resulting in missing data.

J

judgment (purposive) sampling A nonprobability sampling technique in which an experienced individual selects the sample based on personal judgment about some appropriate characteristic of the sample member.

K

keyword search Takes place as the search engine searches through millions of Web pages for documents containing the keywords.

knowledge A blend of previous experience, insight, and data that forms organizational memory.

knowledge management The process of creating an inclusive, comprehensive, easily accessible organizational memory, which is often called the organization's *intellectual capital*.

L

laboratory experiment The researcher has more complete control over the research setting and extraneous variables.

laddering A particular approach to probing asking respondents to compare differences between brands at different levels that produces distinctions at the attribute level, the benefit level, and the value or motivation level. Laddering is based on the classical repertory grid approach.

Latin square design A balanced, two-way classification scheme that attempts to control or block out the effect of two or more

extraneous factors by restricting randomization with respect to the row and column effects.

leading question A question that suggests or implies certain answers.

Likert scale A measure of attitudes designed to allow respondents to rate how strongly they agree or disagree with carefully constructed statements, ranging from very positive to very negative attitudes toward some object.

list-wise deletion A method of handling missing data in which the entire record for a respondent that has left a response missing is excluded from use in statistical analyses.

literature review A directed search of published works, including periodicals and books, that discusses theory and presents empirical results that are relevant to the topic at hand.

loaded question A question that suggests a socially desirable answer or is emotionally charged.

longitudinal study A survey of respondents at different times, thus allowing analysis of response continuity and changes over time.

M

mail survey A self-administered questionnaire sent to respondents through the mail.

main effect The experimental difference in dependent variable means between the different levels of any single experimental variable.

mall intercept interviews Personal interviews conducted in a shopping mall.

manager of decision support systems Employee who supervises the collection and analysis of sales, inventory, and other periodic customer relationship management (CRM) data.

managerial action standard A specific performance criterion upon which a decision can be based.

manipulation means that the researcher alters the level of the variable in specific increments.

manipulation check A validity test of an experimental manipulation to make sure that the manipulation does produce differences in the independent variable.

marginals Row and column totals in a contingency table, which are shown in its margins.

market intelligence The subset of data and information that actually has some explanatory power enabling effective decisions to be made.

market opportunity A situation that makes some potential competitive advantage possible.

market penetration The percentage of target market customers who purchased the product—often measured early in a test-market.

market problem A situation that makes some significant negative consequence more likely.

market tracking The observation and analysis of trends in industry volume and brand share over time.

market-based analysis A form of data mining that analyzes anonymous point-of-sale transaction databases to identify coinciding purchases or relationships between products purchased and other retail shopping information.

marketing channel A network of interdependent institutions that perform the logistics necessary for consumption to occur.

marketing concept A central idea in modern marketing thinking that focuses on how the firm provides value to customers more than on the physical product or production process.

marketing ethics The application of morals to behavior related to the exchange environment.

marketing metrics Quantitative ways of monitoring and measuring marketing performance.

marketing orientation The corporate culture existing for firms adopting the marketing concept. It emphasizes customer orientation, long-term profitability over short-term profits, and a cross-functional perspective.

marketing research The application of the scientific method in searching for the truth about marketing phenomena. These activities include defining marketing opportunities and problems, generating and evaluating marketing ideas, monitoring performance, and understanding the marketing process.

maturation effects Effects that are a function of time and the naturally occurring events that coincide with growth and experience.

mean A measure of central tendency; the arithmetic average.

measure of association A general term that refers to a number of bivariate statistical techniques used to measure the strength of a relationship between two variables.

measurement The process of describing some property of a phenomenon of interest, usually by assigning numbers in a reliable and valid way.

median A measure of central tendency that is the midpoint; the value below which half the values in a distribution fall.

median split Dividing a data set into two categories by placing respondents below the median in one category and respondents above the median in another.

mixed-mode survey Study that employs any combination of survey methods.

mode A measure of central tendency; the value that occurs most often.

model building The use of secondary data to help specify relationships between two or more variables; can involve the development of descriptive or predictive equations.

moderator A person who leads a focus group interview and insures that everyone gets a chance to speak and contribute to the discussion.

moderator variable A third variable that changes the nature of a relationship between the original independent and dependent variables.

monadic rating scale Any measure of attitudes that asks respondents about a single concept in isolation.

moral standards Principles that reflect beliefs about what is ethical and what is unethical.

mortality effect (sample attrition) Occurs when some subjects withdraw from the experiment before it is completed.

multi-attribute model A model that constructs an attitude score based on the multiplicative sum of beliefs about an option times the evaluation of those belief characteristics.

multicollinearity The extent to which independent variables in a multiple regression analysis are correlated with each other; high multicollinearity can make interpreting parameter estimates difficult or impossible.

multidimensional scaling A statistical technique that measures objects in multidimensional space on the basis of respondents' judgments of the similarity of objects.

multi-level analysis Research studying variables measured at more than one unit of analysis.

multiple regression analysis An analysis of association in which the effects of two or more independent variables on a single, interval-scaled dependent variable are investigated simultaneously.

multiple-grid question Several similar questions arranged in a grid format.

multistage area sampling Sampling that involves using a combination of two or more probability sampling techniques.

multivariate analysis of variance (MANOVA) A multivariate technique that predicts multiple continuous dependent variables with multiple categorical independent variables.

multivariate statistical analysis Statistical analysis involving three or more variables or sets of variables.

mystery shoppers Employees of a research firm that are paid to pretend to be actual shoppers.

N

net promoter score The score based on customer responses to a question asking how likely he or she would be to recommend the company to a friend or colleague.

neural network A form of artificial intelligence in which a computer is programmed to mimic the way that human brains process information.

no contacts People who are not at home or who are otherwise inaccessible on the first and second contact.

nominal scales Represent the most elementary level of measurement in which values are assigned to an object for identification or classification purposes only.

non-forced-choice scale A fixed-alternative rating scale that provides a "no opinion" category or that allows respondents to indicate that they cannot say which alternative is their choice.

noninteractive survey approaches Two-way communication by which respondents give answers to static questions.

nonparametric statistics Appropriate when the variables being analyzed do not conform to any known or continuous distribution.

nonprobability sampling A sampling technique in which units of the sample are selected on the basis of personal judgment or convenience; the probability of any particular member of the population being chosen is unknown.

nonrespondent error Error that the respondent is not responsible for creating, such as when the interviewer marks a response incorrectly.

nonrespondents People who are not contacted or who refuse to cooperate in the research.

nonresponse error The statistical differences between a survey that includes only those who responded and a perfect survey that would also include those who failed to respond.

nonspurious association One of three criteria for causality; means any covariation between a cause and an effect is true and not simply due to some other variable.

normal distribution A symmetrical, bell-shaped distribution that describes the expected probability distribution of many chance occurrences.

numerical scale An attitude rating scale similar to a semantic differential except that it uses numbers, instead of verbal descriptions, as response options to identify response positions.

O

observation The systematic process of recording the behavioral patterns of people, objects, and occurrences as they are witnessed.

observer bias A distortion of measurement resulting from the cognitive behavior or actions of a witnessing observer.

online focus group A qualitative research effort in which a group of individuals provides unstructured comments by entering their remarks into an electronic Internet display board of some type.

online panels Lists of respondents who have agreed to participate in marketing research along with the e-mail contact information for these individuals.

open-ended boxes In an Internet questionnaire, boxes where respondents can type in their own answers to open-ended questions.

open-ended response questions Questions that pose some problem and ask respondents to answer in their own words.

operationalization The process of identifying scale devices that correspond to variance in a concept to be involved in a research process.

opt in To give permission to receive selected e-mail, such as questionnaires, from a company with an Internet presence.

optical scanning system A data processing input device that reads material directly from mark-sensed questionnaires.

oral presentation A spoken summary of the major findings, conclusions, and recommendations, given to clients or line managers to provide them with the opportunity to clarify any ambiguous issues by asking questions.

order bias Bias caused by the influence of earlier questions in a questionnaire or by an answer's position in a set of answers.

ordinal scales Ranking scales allowing things to be arranged based on how much of some concept they possess.

outlier A value that lies outside the normal range of the data.

outside agency An independent research firm contracted by the company that actually will benefit from the research.

P

paired comparison A measurement technique that involves presenting the respondent with two objects and asking the respondent to pick the preferred object; more than two objects may be presented, but comparisons are made in pairs.

paired-samples *t*-test An appropriate test for comparing the scores of two interval variables drawn from related populations.

pair-wise deletion A method of handling missing data in which only the actual variables for a respondent that do not contain information are eliminated from use in statistical analyses.

parametric statistics Involve numbers with known, continuous distributions; when the data are interval- or ratio-scaled and the sample size is large, parametric statistical procedures are appropriate.

partial correlation The correlation between two variables after taking into account the fact that they are correlated with other variables too.

partial least squares (PLS) A multivariate tool that combines a factor analytic and regression approach to provide path estimates to a proposed model but falls short of providing an assessment of fit. PLS is appropriate when the data are insufficient for use in SEM.

participant-observation Ethnographic research approach where the researcher becomes immersed within the culture that he or she is studying and draws data from his or her observations.

percentage distribution A frequency distribution organized into a table (or graph) that summarizes percentage values associated with particular values of a variable.

performance-monitoring research Refers to research that regularly, sometimes routinely, provides feedback for evaluation and control of marketing activity.

personal interview Face-to-face communication in which an interviewer asks a respondent to answer questions.

phenomenology A philosophical approach to studying human experiences based on the idea that human experience itself is inherently subjective and determined by the context in which people live.

picture frustration A version of the TAT using a cartoon drawing in which the respondent suggests a dialogue in which the characters might engage.

piggyback A procedure in which one respondent stimulates thought among the others; as this process continues, increasingly creative insights are possible.

pilot study A small-scale research project that collects data from respondents similar to those to be used in the full study.

pivot question A filter question used to determine which version of a second question will be asked.

placebo A false experimental effect used to create the perception that some effect has been administered.

placebo effect The effect in a dependent variable associated with the psychological impact that goes along with knowledge of some treatment being administered.

plug value An answer that an editor "plugs in" to replace blanks or missing values to permit data analysis; choice of value is based on a predetermined decision rule.

point estimate An estimate of the population mean in the form of a single value, usually the sample mean.

pooled estimate of the standard error An estimate of the standard error for a *t*-test of independent means that assumes the variances of both groups are equal.

population (universe) Any complete group of entities that share some common set of characteristics.

population distribution A frequency distribution of the elements of a population.

population element An individual member of a population.

population parameters Variables in a population or measured characteristics of the population.

pop-up boxes In an Internet questionnaire, boxes that appear at selected points and contain information or instructions for respondents.

predictive analytics a system linking computerized data sources to statistical tools allowing more accurate forecasts of consumers' opinions and actions.

preliminary tabulation A tabulation of the results of a pretest to help determine whether the questionnaire will meet the objectives of the research.

pretest A small-scale study in which the results are only preliminary and intended only to assist in design of a subsequent study.

pretesting Screening procedure that involves a trial run with a group of respondents to iron out fundamental problems in the survey design.

pricing Involves finding the amount of monetary sacrifice that best represents the value customers perceive in a product after considering various market constraints.

primary sampling unit (PSU) A term used to designate a unit selected in the first stage of sampling.

probability The long-run relative frequency with which an event will occur.

probability sampling A sampling technique in which every member of the population has a known, nonzero probability of selection.

probing An interview technique that tries to draw deeper and more elaborate explanations from the discussion.

problem Occurs when there is a difference between the current conditions and a more preferable set of conditions.

problem definition The process of defining and developing a decision statement and the steps involved in translating it into more precise research terminology, including a set of research objectives.

production-oriented Describes a firm that prioritizes efficiency and effectiveness of the production processes in making decisions.

product-oriented Describes a firm that prioritizes decision making in a way that emphasizes technical superiority in the product.

projective technique An indirect means of questioning enabling respondents to project beliefs and feelings onto a third party, an inanimate object, or a task situation.

promotion The communication function of the firm responsible for informing and persuading buyers.

promotion research Investigates the effectiveness of advertising, premiums, coupons, sampling, discounts, public relations, and other sales promotions.

proportion The percentage of elements that meet some criterion.

proportional stratified sample A stratified sample in which the number of sampling units drawn from each stratum is in proportion to the population size of that stratum.

proprietary marketing research The gathering of new data to investigate specific problems.

pseudo-research Conducted not to gather information for marketing decisions but to bolster a point of view and satisfy other needs.

psychogalvanometer A device that measures galvanic skin response, a measure of involuntary changes in the electrical resistance of the skin.

pull technology Consumers request information from a Web page and the browser then determines a response; the consumer is essentially asking for the data.

pupilometer A mechanical device used to observe and record changes in the diameter of a subject's pupils.

push button In a dialog box on an Internet questionnaire, a small outlined area, such as a rectangle or an arrow, that the respondent clicks on to select an option or perform a function, such as submit. See radio button.

push poll Telemarketing under guise of research.

push technology Sends data to a user's computer without a request being made; software is used to guess what information might be interesting to consumers based on the pattern of previous responses.

p-value Probability value, or the observed or computed significance level; p-values are compared to significance levels to test hypotheses.

Q

quadrant analysis An extension of cross-tabulation in which responses to two rating-scale questions are plotted in four quadrants of a two-dimensional table.

qualitative data Data that are not characterized by numbers, and instead are textual, visual, or oral; focus is on stories, visual portrayals, meaningful characterizations, interpretations, and other expressive descriptions.

qualitative marketing research Research that addresses marketing objectives through techniques that allow the researcher to provide elaborate interpretations of market phenomena without depending on numerical measurement; its focus is on discovering true inner meanings and new insights.

quantitative data Represent phenomena by assigning numbers in an ordered and meaningful way.

quantitative marketing research Marketing research that addresses research objectives through empirical assessments that involve numerical measurement and analysis.

quasi-experimental designs Experimental designs that do not involve random allocation of subjects to treatment combinations.

quota sampling A nonprobability sampling procedure that ensures that various subgroups of a population will be represented on pertinent characteristics to the exact extent that the investigator desires.

R

radio boxes A small box character that can be inserted into a word-processing or JavaScript document that allows a respondent to indicate a choice with a check mark or X.

radio button In an Internet questionnaire, a circular icon, resembling a button, that activates one response choice and deactivates others when a respondent clicks on it.

random digit dialing Use of telephone exchanges and a table of random numbers to contact respondents with unlisted phone numbers.

random sampling error A statistical fluctuation that occurs because of chance variation in the elements selected for a sample.

randomization The random assignment of subject and treatments to groups; it is one device for equally distributing the effects of extraneous variables to all conditions.

randomized response questions A research procedure used for dealing with sensitive topics, in which a random procedure determines which of two questions a respondent will be asked to answer.

randomized-block design An extension of the completely randomized design in which a single, categorical extraneous variable that might affect test units' responses to the treatment is identified and the effects of this variable are isolated by being blocked out.

ranking A measurement task that requires respondents to rank order a small number of stores, brands, or objects on the basis of overall preference or some characteristic of the stimulus.

rating A measurement task that requires respondents to estimate the magnitude of a characteristic or quality that a brand, store, or object possesses.

ratio scales Represent the highest form of measurement in that they have all the properties of interval scales with the additional attribute of representing absolute quantities; characterized by a meaningful absolute zero.

raw data The unedited responses from a respondent exactly as indicated by that respondent.

record A collection of related fields that represents the responses from one sampling unit.

refusals People who are unwilling to participate in a research project.

relationship marketing Communicates the idea that a major goal of marketing is to build long-term relationships with the customers contributing to their success.

relativism A term that reflects the degree to which one rejects moral standards in favor of the acceptability of some action. This way of thinking rejects absolute principles in favor of situation-based evaluations.

relevance The characteristics of data reflecting how pertinent these particular facts are to the situation at hand.

reliability An indicator of a measure's internal consistency.

repeated measures Experiments in which an individual subject is exposed to more than one level of an experimental treatment.

replicable Something is intersubjectively certifiable meaning the same conclusion would be reached based on another researcher's interpretation of the research or by independently duplicating the research procedures.

report format The makeup or arrangement of parts necessary to a good research report.

research analyst A person responsible for client contact, project design, preparation of proposals, selection of research suppliers, and supervision of data collection, analysis, and reporting activities.

research assistants Research employees who provide technical assistance with questionnaire design, data analyses, and similar activities.

research design A master plan that specifies the methods and procedures for collecting and analyzing the needed information.

research follow-up Recontacting decision makers and/or clients after they have had a chance to read over a research report in order to determine whether additional information or clarification is necessary.

research generalist An employee who serves as a link between management and research specialists. The research generalist acts as a problem definer, an educator, a liaison, a communicator, and a friendly ear.

research methodology section The part of the body of a report that presents the findings of the project. It includes tables, charts, and an organized narrative.

research objectives The goals to be achieved by conducting research.

research program numerous related studies that come together to address multiple, related research objectives.

research project A single study that addresses one or a small number of research objectives.

research proposal A written statement of the research design.

research questions Express the research objectives in terms of questions that can be addressed by research.

research report An oral presentation or written statement of research results, strategic recommendations, and/or other conclusions to a specific audience.

research suppliers Commercial providers of marketing research services.

researcher-dependent Research in which the researcher must extract meaning from unstructured responses such as text from a recorded interview or a collage representing the meaning of some experience.

respondent error A category of sample bias resulting from some respondent action or inaction such as nonresponse or response bias.

respondents People who verbally answer an interviewer's questions or provide answers to written questions.

response bias A bias that occurs when respondents either consciously or unconsciously tend to answer questions with a certain slant that misrepresents the truth.

response latency The amount of time it takes to make a choice between two alternatives; used as a measure of the strength of preference.

response rate The number of questionnaires returned or completed divided by the number of eligible people who were asked to participate in the survey.

results section The part of the body of a report that presents the findings of the project. It includes tables, charts, and an organized narrative.

reverse coding Means that the value assigned for a response is treated oppositely from the other items.

reverse directory A directory similar to a telephone directory except that listings are by city and street address or by phone number rather than alphabetical by last name.

reverse recoding A method of making sure all the items forming a composite scale are scored in the same direction. negative items can be recoded into the equivalent responses for a non-reverse coded item.

S

sample A subset, or some part, of a larger population.

sample bias A persistent tendency for the results of a sample to deviate in one direction from the true value of the population parameter.

sample distribution A frequency distribution of a sample.

sample selection error An administrative error caused by improper sample design or sampling procedure execution.

sample statistics Variables in a sample or measures computed from sample data.

sample survey A more formal term for a survey.

sampling Involves any procedure that draws conclusions based on measurements of a portion of the population.

sampling distribution A theoretical probability distribution of sample means for all possible samples of a certain size drawn from a particular population.

sampling frame A list of elements from which a sample may be drawn; also called working population.

sampling frame error An error that occurs when certain sample elements are not listed or are not accurately represented in a sampling frame.

sampling unit A single element or group of elements subject to selection in the sample.

scales A device providing a range of values that correspond to different characteristics or amounts of a characteristic exhibited in observing a concept.

scanner data The accumulated records resulting from point of sale data recordings.

scanner-based consumer panel A type of consumer panel in which participants' purchasing habits are recorded with a laser scanner rather than a purchase diary.

scientific method The way researchers go about using knowledge and evidence to reach objective conclusions about the real world.

search engine A computerized directory that allows anyone to search the World Wide Web for information using a keyword search.

secondary data Data that have been previously collected for some purpose other than the one at hand.

secondary sampling unit A term used to designate a unit selected in the second stage of sampling.

self-administered questionnaires Surveys in which the respondent takes the responsibility for reading and answering the questions.

self-selection bias A bias that occurs because people who feel strongly about a subject are more likely to respond to survey questions than people who feel indifferent about it.

semantic differential A measure of attitudes that consists of a series of seven-point rating scales that use bipolar adjectives to anchor the beginning and end of each scale.

sensitivity A measurement instrument's ability to accurately measure variability in stimuli or responses.

significance level A critical probability associated with a statistical hypothesis test that indicates how likely an inference supporting a difference between an observed value and some statistical expectation is true. The acceptable level of Type I error.

simple (bivariate) linear regression A measure of linear association that investigates straight-line relationships between a continuous dependent variable and an independent variable that is usually continuous, but can be a categorical dummy variable.

simple random sampling A sampling procedure that assures each element in the population of an equal chance of being included in the sample.

simple-dichotomy (dichotomous-alternative) question A fixed-alternative question that requires the respondent to choose one of two alternatives.

simulated test-market A research laboratory in which the traditional shopping process is compressed into a short timespan.

single-source data Diverse types of data offered by a single company; usually integrated on the basis of a common variable such as geographic area or store.

site analysis techniques Techniques that use secondary data to select the best location for retail or wholesale operations.

situation analysis The gathering of background information to familiarize researchers and managers with the decision-making environment.

smart agent software Software capable of learning an Internet user's preferences and automatically searching out information in selected Web sites and then distributing it.

snowball sampling A sampling procedure in which initial respondents are selected by probability methods and additional respondents are obtained from information provided by the initial respondents.

social desirability bias Bias in responses caused by respondents' desire, either conscious or unconscious, to gain prestige or appear in a different social role.

sorting A measurement task that presents a respondent with several objects or product concepts and requires the respondent to arrange the objects into piles or classify the product concepts.

split-ballot technique Using two alternative phrasings of the same question for respective halves of a sample to elicit a more accurate total response than would a single phrasing.

split-half method A method for assessing internal consistency by checking the results of one-half of a set of scaled items against the results from the other half.

spyware software placed on a computer without consent or knowledge of the user.

standard deviation A quantitative index of a distribution's spread, or variability; the square root of the variance for a distribution.

standard error of the mean The standard deviation of the sampling distribution.

standardized normal distribution A purely theoretical probability distribution that reflects a specific normal curve for the standardized value, z.

standardized regression coefficient (β) The estimated coefficient indicating the strength of relationship between an independent variable and dependent variable expressed on a standardized scale where higher absolute values indicate stronger relationships (range is from -1 to 1).

standardized research service Companies that develop a unique methodology for investigating a business specialty area.

Stapel scale A measure of attitudes that consists of a single adjective in the center of an even number of numerical values.

statistical base The number of respondents or observations (in a row or column) used as a basis for computing percentages.

statistical power A measure of how much ability exists to find a significant effect using a specific statistical tool. Mathematically, power is a direct function of Type I error rate $(1 - \beta)$

status bar In an Internet questionnaire, a visual indicator that tells the respondent what portion of the survey he or she has completed.

stratified sampling A probability sampling procedure in which simple random subsamples that are more or less equal on some characteristic are drawn from within each stratum of the population.

streaming media Consist of multimedia content such as audio or video that is made available in real time over the Internet or a corporate intranet.

string characters Computer terminology to represent formatting a variable using a series of alphabetic characters (nonnumeric characters) that may form a word.

structural equations modeling (SEM) A multivariate tool that combines an interdependence and dependence technique to allow a researcher to test theory by providing an omnibus assessment of fit centered around a χ^2 goodness of fit test.

structured question A question that imposes a limit on the number of allowable responses.

subjective Results are researcher-dependent, meaning different researchers may reach different conclusions based on the same interview.

subjects The sampling units for an experiment, usually human respondents who provide measures based on the experimental manipulation.

summated scale A scale created by simply summing (adding together) the response to each item making up the composite measure. The scores can be but do not have to be averaged by the number of items making up the composite scale.

supply chain Another term for a channel of distribution, meaning the link between suppliers and customers.

survey A research technique in which a sample is interviewed in some form or the behavior of respondents is observed and described in some way.

symptoms Observable cues that serve as a signal of a problem because they are caused by that problem.

syndicated service A marketing research supplier that provides standardized information for many clients in return for a fee.

systematic error Error resulting from some imperfect aspect of the research design that causes respondent error or from a mistake in the execution of the research.

systematic or nonsampling error Occurs if the sampling units in an experimental cell are somehow different than the units in another cell, and this difference affects the dependent variable.

systematic sampling A sampling procedure in which a starting point is selected by a random process and then every *n*th number on the list is selected.

T

tabulation The orderly arrangement of data in a table or other summary format showing the number of responses to each response category; tallying.

tachistoscope Device that controls the amount of time a subject is exposed to a visual image.

t-distribution A symmetrical, bell-shaped distribution that is contingent on sample size; has a mean of 0 and a standard deviation equal to 1.

telephone interviews Personal interviews conducted by telephone, the mainstay of commercial survey research.

television monitoring Computerized mechanical observation used to obtain television ratings.

temporal sequence One of three criteria for causality; deals with the time order of events—the cause must occur before the effect.

tertiary sampling unit A term used to designate a unit selected in the third stage of sampling.

test of differences An investigation of a hypothesis stating that two (or more) groups differ with respect to measures on a variable.

test tabulation Tallying of a small sample of the total number of replies to a particular question in order to construct coding categories.

test units The subjects or entities whose responses to the experimental treatment are measured or observed.

testing effects A nuisance effect occurring when the initial measurement or test alerts or primes subjects in a way that affects their response to the experimental treatments.

test-market An experiment that is conducted within actual market conditions.

test-market sabotage Intentional attempts to disrupt the results of a test-market being conducted by another firm.

test-retest method Administering the same scale or measure to the same respondents at two separate points in time to test for stability.

thematic apperception test (TAT) A test that presents subjects with an ambiguous picture(s) in which consumers and products are the center of attention; the investigator asks the subject to tell what is happening in the picture(s) now and what might happen next.

themes Identified by the frequency with which the same term (or a synonym) arises in the narrative description.

theory A formal, logical explanation of some events that includes predictions of how things relate to one another.

Thurstone scale An attitude scale in which judges assign scale values to attitudinal statements and subjects are asked to respond to these statements.

time series design Used for an experiment investigating long-term structural changes.

timeliness Means that the data are current enough to still be relevant.

top-box score Proportion of respondents who chose the most positive choice in a multiple choice question.

total quality management A business philosophy that emphasizes market-driven quality as a top organizational priority.

total value management Trying to manage and monitor the entire process by which consumers receive benefits from a company.

tracking study A type of longitudinal study that uses successive samples to compare trends and identify changes in variables such as consumer satisfaction, brand image, or advertising awareness.

t-test A hypothesis test that uses the *t*-distribution. A univariate *t*-test is appropriate when the variable being analyzed is interval or ratio.

type I error An error caused by rejecting the null hypothesis when it is true; has a probability of alpha. Practically, a Type I error occurs when the researcher concludes that a relationship or difference exits in the population when in reality it does not exist.

type II error An error caused by failing to reject the null hypothesis when the alternative hypothesis is true; has a probability of beta. Practically, a Type II error occurs when a researcher concludes that no relationship or difference exists when in fact one does exist.

U

unaided recall Asking respondents to remember something without providing any clue.

unbalanced rating scale A fixed-alternative rating scale that has more response categories at one end than the other resulting in an unequal number of positive and negative categories.

undisguised questions Straightforward questions that assume the respondent is willing to answer.

Uniform Resource Locator (URL) A Web site address that Web browsers recognize.

unit of analysis A study that indicates what or who should provide the data and at what level of aggregation.

univariate statistical analysis Tests of hypotheses involving only one variable.

unobtrusive methods Methods in which research respondents do not have to be disturbed for data to be gathered.

unobtrusive observation no communication with the person being observed is necessary so that he or she is unaware that he or she is an object of research.

unstructured question A question that does not restrict the respondents' answers.

V

validity The accuracy of a measure or the extent to which a score truthfully represents a concept.

value labels Unique labels assigned to each possible numeric code for a response.

variable Anything that varies or changes from one instance to another; can exhibit differences in value, usually in magnitude or strength, or in direction.

variable piping software Software that allows variables to be inserted into an Internet questionnaire as a respondent is completing it.

variance A measure of variability or dispersion. Its square root is the standard deviation.

variate A mathematical way in which a set of variables can be represented with one equation.

verification Quality-control procedures in fieldwork intended to ensure that interviewers are following the sampling procedures and to determine whether interviewers are cheating.

virtual-reality simulated test-market An experiment that attempts to reproduce the atmosphere of an actual retail store with visually compelling images appearing on a computer.

visible observation Observation in which the observer's presence is known to the subject.

voice-pitch analysis A physiological measurement technique that records abnormal frequencies in the voice that are supposed to reflect emotional reactions to various stimuli.

W

welcome screen The first web page in an Internet survey, which introduces the survey and requests that the respondent enter a password or pin.

within-group error or variance The sum of the differences between observed values and the group mean for a given set of observations; also known as total error variance.

within-subjects design Involves repeated measures because with each treatment the same subject is measured.

World Wide Web (WWW) A portion of the Internet that is a system of computer servers that organize information into documents called web pages.

Z

z-test for differences of proportions A technique used to test the hypothesis that proportions are significantly different for two independent samples or groups.

Chapter 1

1 Bennett, J., N. F. Boulette and N. Serena, "GM Slate Sweeping Rebates as Toyota Closes in on #1," *Wall Street Journal* – Eastern Edition, 251 (June 24, 2008), A1–A15; Traeger, C., "What are Automakers Doing for Women? Part I: GM Reaches Out," Edmunds.com (2008),www.edmunds.com/advice/womenfamilies/articles/105204/article.html, accessed June 16, 2008; Traeger, C., "What are Automakers Doing for Women? Part II: Toyota Taking an American Approach to Reaching Women," Edmunds.com (2008), www.edmunds.com/advice/specialreports/articles/106270/article.html, accessed June 12, 2008; *Automative News Europe*, "Industry Would Benefit from More Women Execs," 13 (May 12, 2008), 10.

2 Keyo, Michelle "Web Site of the Week: Jelly Belly: Using Sampling to Build a Customer Database," *Inc. Online* (1996), http://www.inc.com, December 9, 1996.

3 Penn, Catherine, "New Drinks Include a Health Benefit for 05," *Beverage Industry*, 96 (January 2005), 45–54.

4 Jelly Belly Candy Company (March 6, 2008). "April Fools' Day: Bamboozle Someone with New Jelly Belly BeanBoozled Jelly Beans: A Fools Errand and Silly Celebrations." Press release.

5 "U.S. Coffee Makers Perky as Consumption Increases," *Nations Restaurant Business*, 36 (April 22, 2002), 34; "U.S. Specialty Coffee Market in 30 Year Renaissance," http://www.cnn.com, December 15, 2000.

6 "Coffee: Demographics," in *The 2008 Beverage Market Research Handbook*, (Loganville, GA: Richard K. Miller & Associates, 2008), 98–100.

7 Kafka, Peter, "Bean-Counter," *Forbes*, 175 (February 28, 2005), 78–80. www.starbucks.com, accessed Oct. 30, 2008.

8 Garvin, Andrew P., "Evolve Approach to Serve Complex Market," *Marketing News* (September 15, 2005), 22.

9 Thomas, Jerry W., "Skipping MR a Major Error," *Marketing News* (March 4, 2002), 50.

10 Gibson, Lawrence D.,"Quo Vadis Marketing Research?" *Marketing Research*, 12 (Spring 2000), 36–41.

11 Matthew, Arnold,"FDA Delays DTC Draft Guidance to Study How Consumers Use Brief Summaries," *Medical Marketing and Media*, 39 (November 2004), 10.

12 See, for example, Babin, Barry J., J. C. Chebat, and Richard Michon, "Perceived Appropriateness and Its Effect on Quality, Affect and Behavior," *Journal of Retailing and Consumer Services*, 11 (September 2004), 287–298.

13 Sin, Leo Y. M., Alan C. B. Tse, Oliver H. M. Yau, Raymond P. M. Chow, Jenny S. Y. Lee, Lorett B. Y. Lau,"Relationship Marketing Orientation: Scale Development and Cross-Cultural Validation," *Journal of Business Research*, 58 (February 2005), 185–194; Nakata, Cheryl and K. Sivakumar, "Instituting the Marketing Concept in a Multinational Setting: The Role of National Culture," *Journal of the Academy of Marketing Science*, 29 (Summer 2001), 255–275; Day, George,"The Capabilities of Market-Driven Organizations," *Journal of Marketing*, 58 (October 1994), 37–52; Ward, James C., M.D. Hutt and Peter H. Reingen, "Evolving Patterns of Organizational Beliefs in the Formation of Strategy," *Journal of Marketing*, 58 (April 1994), 96–110.

14 Reyes, Sonia, "Ian Friendly: Groove Tube," *Brandweek* (October 16, 2000), M111–M116.

15 Stoll, J. D., "GM Weighs More Layoffs, Sale of Brands," *Wall Street Journal* (July 7, 2008), A1.

16 Gelb, Betsy D. and Gabriel M. Gelb,"What Research Inside the Organization Can Accomplish," *Marketing Research* (December 1991), 44.

17 *Marketing News*,"Burger King Opens Customer Hot Line" (May 28, 1990), 7.

18 *Professional Builder*, "David Weekley Homes Reign in Fort Worth Market," 69 (December, 2004), 31–34.

19 Sharman,G. K.,"Sessions Challenge Status Quo," *Marketing News* (November 10, 1997), p. 18.

20 Schwartz, David, *Concept Testing: How to Test Product Ideas Before You Go to Market* (New York: AMACOM, 1987), p. 91.

21 Wyner, Gordon A., "Biz Problems Can Get Solved With Research," *Marketing News* (September 15, 2005), 33–34.

22 Benezra, Karen, "Fritos Around theWorld," *Brandweek* (March 27, 1994), 32; "Cheetos Make Debut in China But Lose Cheese inTranslation" *USAToday* (September 2, 2004), B-1.

23 See Allenby, Greg M.,Thomas S. Shively,Yang Sha and Mark J. Garratt, "A Choice Model for Packaged Goods: Dealing with Discrete Quantities and Quantity Discounts," *Marketing Science*, 23 (Winter 2004), 14–21.

24 Mohn, N. Carroll, "Pricing Research for Decision Making," *Marketing Research* (Winter 1995), 11–12.

25 See Allenby, Greg M., Thomas S. Shively,Yang Sha and Mark J. Garratt, "A Choice Model for Packaged Goods: Dealing with Discrete Quantities and Quantity Discounts," *Marketing Science*, 23 (Winter 2004), 14–21. Mohn, N. Carroll, "Pricing Research for Decision Making," *Marketing Research* (Winter 1995), 11–12. Ofir, Chezy, "Reexamining Latitude of Price Acceptability and Price Thresholds: Predicting Basic Consumer Reaction to Price," *Journal of Consumer Research*, 30 (March 2004), 612–621.

26 Bonamici, Kate,"Big-Foot Dips Toe in Coffee," *Fortune*, 149 (January 26, 2004), 70.

27 Gardyn, Rebecca, "Same Name, New Number: AT&T's Brand Image Gets a Needed Boost from a Well-Rounded Hero," *American Demographics* (March 2001), 56.

28 Schneider, Lars-Peter and Bettina T. Cornwell, "Cashing in on Crashes via Brand Placement in Computer Games," *International Journal of Advertising*, 24, no. 3 (2005), 321–342.

29 Low, George S., "Correlates of Integrated Marketing Communications," *Journal of Advertising Research* (May 2000).

30 Hein, Kenneth, "Best Buy Calls the 'Odd' Squad: Group of Tech 'Geeks' gets Spotlight in National Branding Spot," *Brandweek*, 45 (October 18, 2004), 11; *DSN Retailing Today*, "Best Buy Turns On the Geek Appeal. (CE & Entertainment)," 42 (February 24, 2004), 22.

31 Garretson, Judith and Scot Burton, "The Role of Spokescharacters as Advertisement and Package Cues in Integrated Marketing Communications," *Journal of Marketing*, 69 (October, 2005), 118–132.

32 Clancy, Kevin J. and Randy L. Stone, "Don't Blame the Metrics," *Harvard Business Review*, 83 (June, 2005), 26–28.

33 Honomichl, Jack, "Growth Stunt," *Marketing News* (June 4, 2001), 144.

34. *Express Magazine*, "You Say Tomato, I say Tomahto," (Spring 2006), 19.

35. Kiley, D. "Jack Daniel's International Appeal," *Businessweek*, October 10, 2007, accessed at http://www.businessweek.com/innovate/content/oct2007/id20071010_651037.htm, September 14, 2008.

Chapter 2

1 Granados, N., A. Gupta and R. J. Kauffman, "Designing Online Selling Mechanisms: Transparency Levels and Prices," *Decision Support Systems*, (2008), forthcoming; Jackson, T. W., "Personalization and CRM," *Journal of Database Marketing & Customer Strategy Management*, 15, no. 1 (2007), 24–36; Beirne, M., "Southwest Airlines Delivers Fare Offers with DING!" *Brandweek* (2006), www.brandweek.com/bw/news/recent_cisplay-jsp?vnu_content_id=1002765480 accessed June 16, 2008.

2 See Albers, Brad, "Home Depot's Special Projects Support Team Powers Information Management for Business Needs," *Journal of Organizational Excellence*, 21 (Winter 2001), 3–15; Songini, Marc L., "Home Depot's Next IT Project: Data Warehouse," *Computerworld*, 36 (October 7, 2002), 1–2.

3 "SAS helps ImpactRX Provide Real Time Marketing Intelligence to Pharma Companies," *Business Wire*, (March 17, 2008). Retrieved July 14, 2008 from ABI/INFORM Dateline database (document ID: 1447327611).

4 LaBahn, Douglass W. and Robert Krapfel, "Early Supplier Involvement in Customer New Product Development: A Contingency Model of Component Supplier Intentions," *Journal of Business Research*, 47 (March 2000), 173–190.

5 Tay, Nicholas S. P. and Robert F. Lusch, "A Preliminary Test of Hunt's General Theory of Competition: Using Artificial Adaptive Agents to Study Complex and Ill-Defined Environments," *Journal of Business Research*, 58 (September 2005), 1155–1168.

6 Knapp, Ellen M., "Knowledge Management," *Business and Economic Review* (July–September 1998), 3–6.

7 Sherman, D. J., D. Berkowitz, and W. E. Soulder, "New Product Development Performance and the Interaction of Cross-Functional Integration and Knowledge Management," *Journal of Product Innovation Management*, 22 (September 2005), 399–411.

8 Chonko, L. B., A. J. Dubinsky, E. Jones, and J. A. Roberts, "Organizational and Individual Learning in the Sales Force: An Agenda for Sales Research," *Journal of Business Research*, 56 (December, 2003), 935–946.

9 Wells, H. G., "*The Brain: Organization of the Modern World*" (1940).

10 "Benefits of RFID Becoming More Visible" *DSN Retailing Today*, (August 8, 2005), 22.

11 Hall, Mark, "Seeding for Data Growth," *Computerworld*, 36 (April 15, 2002), 52.

12 Angwein, J. and K. J. Delaney, "Top Web Sites Build Up Ad Backlog, Raise Rates," *Wall Street Journal* (November 16, 2005), A1.

13 Sellers, J., "Teen Marketing 2.0," *Publishers' Weekly*, 254, no. 35 (2007), 27. www.compete.com, accessed Nov. 29, 2008.

14 *Gale Annual Directory of Databases*, Gale Research Inc.: Detroit.

15 Beasty, C., "Analytics Brought to Bear," *Customer Relationship Management*, 10 (December 2006), 26–29.

16 Geng, X., M. B. Stinchcombe, and A. B. Whinston, "Radically New Product Introduction Using On-Line Auctions," *Journal of Electronic Commerce*, 5 (Spring 2001), 169–189.

17 "A Better Web Through Higher Math," *Business Week Online*, (January 22, 2002), http://www.businessweek.com (accessed November 12, 2005).

18 Jackson, T. W., "Personalisation and CRM," *Database Marketing & Customer Strategy Management*, 15, no. 1 (2007), 24–36.

19 Rangaswamy, Arvind and G. Lilien, "Software Tools for New Product Development," *Journal of Marketing Research*, 34 (February 1997), 177–184.

20 Desouza, Kevin and Yukika Awazu, "Maintaining Knowledge Management Systems: A Strategic Imperative," *Journal of the American Society for Information Science and Technology*, 56 (May 2005), 765–768.

21 Rangaswamy, Arvind and G. Lilien (1997).

22 Close, A. G., A. Dixit and N. Malhotra, "Chalkboards to Cybercourses: The Internet and Marketing Education," *Marketing Education Review*, 15 (Summer 2005), 81–94.

23 Adopted with permission from deJony, Jennifer, "View from the Top," *Technology*, 1 (1995), downloaded from the Internet July 3, 1998.

Chapter 3

1 Haytko, D., "Message from the Guest Editor," *Marketing Education Review*, 18 (Spring 2008), 1; Anwar, A., M. Al-Shami and S. A. Ahmed, "Developing a Market-Oriented MBA Program: Practitioners' Views from GCC Countries," *Journal of International Marketing & Marketing Research*, 31 (October 2006), 129–139.

2 This section is based in part on Richard Draft, *Management* (Hillsdale, IL: Dryden Press, 1994).

3 Zahay, Debra, Abbie Griffin and Elisa Fredericks, "Sources, Uses, and Forms of Data in the New Product Development Process," *Industrial Marketing Management*, 33 (October 2004), 658–666.

4 Hara, Yoshika, "New Industry Awaits Human-Friendly Bipeds—'Personal Robots' get Ready to Walk on the Human Side," *Electronic Engineering Times* (September 16, 2002), 157–159.

5 Bocchi, Joe, Jacqueline K. Eastman, and Cathy Owens Swift, "Retaining the Online Learner: Profile of Students in an Online MBA Program and Implications for Teaching Them," *Journal of Education for Business* (March/April 2004), 245–253.

6 Janoff, Barry, "Brands of the Land," *BrandWeek* (April 20, 2001), 28.

7 Bocchi, Eastman and Swift (2004); Carr, S., "As Distance Education Comes of Age, the Challenge is Keeping the Students," *Chronicle of Higher Education* (2000) 23, A1.; Moskal and Dziuban, "Present and Future Directions for Assessing Cybereducation: The Changing Research Paradigm," in L. R. Vandervert, L. V. Chavinina and R. A. Cornell, Eds., *Cybereducation: The Future of Long-Distance Learning* (2001), New York: P. D. Moskal and C. G. Dziuban, Liebert, 157–184.

8 Thomas, Jerry W., "Skipping MR a Major Error," *Marketing News* (March 4, 2005), 50.

9 A. Einstein and L. Infeld, *The Evolution of Physics* (New York: Simon and Schuster, 1942), p. 95.

10 See Bhardwaj, S., I. Palaparthy and A. Agrawal, "Exploration of Environmental Dimensions of Servicescapes: A Literature Review," *The Icfai Journal of Marketing Management*, 7, no. 1 (2008), 37–48 for a relevant literature review.

11 Perdue, B. C. and J. O. Summers, "Checking the Success of Manipulations in Marketing Experiments," *Journal of Marketing Research*, 23 (November 1986), 317–326.

12 See, for example, Kwok, S. and M. Uncles, "Sales Promotion Effectiveness: The Impact of Consumer Differences at An Ethnic-Group Level," *Journal of Product and Brand Management*, 14, no. 3 (2005), 170–186.

13 Approximate currency rates as of August 2008.

14 Babin, B. J., D. M. Hardesty and T. A. Suter, "Color and Shopping Intentions: The Effect of Price Fairness and Perceived Affect," *Journal of Business Research*, 56 (July 2003), 541–551.

15 Crowley, Michael, "Conservatives (Finally) Rejoice," *New Republic*, 231, (2004) 13–14.

Chapter 4

1 Lanzoni, G. and N. Marcus, "Seeking Market Research/Competitive Intelligence," *LIMRA's Market Facts Quarterly*, 23 no. 1 (2004), 20–23.

2 Russell-Bennett, R., J. R. McColl-Kennedy and L. V. Coote, "Involvement, Satisfaction, and Brand Loyalty in a Small Business Services Setting," *Journal of Business Research*, 60 (December 2007), 1253–1262.

3 Kinnear, Thomas C. and Ann Root, Eds., *Survey of Marketing Research* (Chicago: American Marketing Association, 1994).

4 Henderson, N. R., "The Power of Probing," *Marketing Research*, 19, no. 4 (2007), 38.

5 Schoder, D., "The Flaw in Customer Lifetime Value," *Harvard Business Review*, 85 (December 2007), 26; Ulaga, Wolfgang, Arun Sharma, and R. Krishnan, "Plant Location and Place Marketing: Understanding the Process from the Business Customer's Perspective," *Industrial Marketing Management*, 31 (August 2002), 393–401.

6 Blembach, J. and K. Clancy, "Boy, Oh Boy!" *Adweek*—Southeastern Edition, 21 (September 25, 2000), 16.

7 See Armstrong, J. S., "Why Do We Know? Predicting the Interests and Opinions of the American Consumer," *Journal of Forecasting*, 5 (September 1989), 464.

8 See John, Joby and Mark Needel, "Entry-Level Marketing Research Recruits: What Do Recruiters Need?" *Journal of Marketing Education* (Spring 1989), 68–73.

9 See Izzo, G. Martin and Scott J. Vitell, "Exploring the Effects of Professional Education on Salespeople: The Case of Autonomous Agents," *Journal of Marketing Theory & Practice*, 11 (Fall 2003), 26–38; Loe, Terry and William A. Weeks, "An Empirical Investigation of Efforts to Improve Sales Students' Moral Reasoning," *Journal of Personal Selling and Sales Management*, 20 (Fall 2000), 243–252.

10 Barnett, Tim and Sean Valentino, "Issue Contingencies and Marketers' Recognition of Ethical Issues, Ethical Judgments and Behavioral Intentions," *Journal of Business Research*, 57 (April 2004), 338–346.

11 Robin, D. P., R. E. Reidenbach and B. J. Babin, "The Nature, Measurement and Stability of Ethical Judgements in the Workplace," *Psychological Reports*, 80, (1997), 563–580.

12 Gillin, Donna L., "The Evolution of Privacy Legislation: How Privacy Issues Are Changing Research," *Marketing Research*, 13 (Winter 2001), 6–7.

13 Jarvis, Steve, "CMOR Finds Survey Refusal Rate Still Rising," *Marketing News*, 36 (February 4, 2002), 4.

14 Gillin, Donna (2001).

15 Ahuja, R. D., M. Walker, and R. Tadepalli, "Paternalism, Limited Paternalism and the Pontius Pilate Plight When Researching Children," *Journal of Business Ethics*, 32 (July 2001), 81–92; Clegg, A., "Out of the Mouths of Babes," *Marketing Week*, (June 23, 2005), 43.

16 Spangenberg, E., B. Grohmann and D. E. Sprott, "It's Beginning to Smell (and Sound) a Lot Like Christmas: The Interactive Effects of Ambient Scent and Music in a Retail Setting," *The Journal of Business Research*, 58 (November 2005), 582–589; Michon, Richard, Jean-Charles Chebat and L. W. Turley, "Mall Atmospherics: The Interaction Effects of the Mall Environment on Shopping Behavior," *Journal of Business Research*, 58 (May 2005), 576–583.

17 Mack, Beth, "Online Privacy Critical to Research Success," *Marketing News*, 36 (November 25, 2002), 21.

18 Carrigan, M. and M. Kirkup, "The Ethical Responsibilities of Marketers in Retail Observational Research: Protecting Stakeholders through the 'Ethical Research' Covenant," *International Journal of Retail, Distribution and Consumer Research*, 11 (October 2001), 411–435.

19 Brennan, M., S. Benson and Z. Kearns, "The Effect of Introductions on Telephone Survey Participation Rates," *International Journal of Market Research*, 47, no. 1 (2005), 65–74.

20 *Marketing News*, "Marketers Value Honesty in Marketing Researchers," 29 (June 5, 1995), 27.

Chapter 5

1 Gibson, Lawrence D., "Defining Marketing Problems: Don't Spin Your Wheels Solving the Wrong Puzzle," *Marketing Research*, 10 (Spring 1998), 4–12.

2 Moon, M., J. T. Mentzer and D. E. Thomas, Jr., "Customer Demand Planning at Lucent Technologies: A Case Study in Continuous Improvement through Sales Forecast Auditing," *Industrial Marketing Management*, 29 (January 2000), 19–26.

3 "What's New in Your Industry," *Business China*, 30 (February 16, 2004), 8–9.

4 Waters, C. L., "The United States Launch of Sony PlayStation 2," *Journal of Business Research*, 58 (July 2005), 995–998. Provides a discussion of research issues associated with launching a game console in today's competitive environment.

5 Chapman, Randall G., "Problem Definition in Marketing Research Studies," *Journal of Consumer Marketing*, 6 (Spring 1989), 51–59; Yang, Yoo S., Robert P. Leone and Dala L. Aldaen, "A Market Expansion Ability Approach to Identify Potential Exporters," *Journal of Marketing*, 56 (January 1992), 84–96.

6 Majchrzak, A., L. P. Cooper and O. E. Neece, "Knowedge Reuse for Innovation," *Management Science*, 50 (February 2004), 174–188.

7 Gibson, Lawrence D. (1988).

8 Henderson, N. R., "The Power of Probing," *Marketing Research*, 19 (Winter 2007), 38.

9 Gibson, Lawrence D. (1988).

10 Martin, C. A. and A. Bush, "Psychological Climate, Empowerment, Leadership Style, and Customer-Oriented Selling: An Analysis of the Sales Manager-Salesperson Dyad," *Journal of the Academy of Marketing Science* (2006), 34, 419–438.

11 See for example Marinova, Detelina, J. Ye and J. Singh, "Do Frontline Mechanisms Matter? Impact of Quality and Productivity Orientations on Unit Revenue, Efficiency, and Customer Satisfaction," *Journal of Marketing*, 72 (March 2008), 28–45.

12 Chapman, Randall G. (1989).

13 Holbert, N. B., "Research: The Ways of Academe and Business," *Business Horizons* (February 1976), 38.

14 Honomichl, Jack, "ICR/ International Communications Research," *Marketing News*, 36 (June 11, 2002), 47.

15 Excerpt reprinted with permission from Paul E. Green, Abba M. Krieger and Terry G.Varra,"Evaluating New Products," *Marketing Research: A Magazine of Management and Applications* (Winter 1997), 17–18.

Chapter 6

1 Cassidy, Hilary, "Many Paths to Cool, But Big Gains for All," *Brandweek*, 46 (June 20, 2005), 53.

2 Niemi, Wayne, "Schoenfeld to Leave as Vans CEO; As Its Deal with VF Corp. Closes,The Skate Brand Gains a New President and A New Focus on Apparel," *Footwear News* (July 5, 2004), 2; Montgomery, T., "Vans' Second Life," *OC Metro*, (October 11, 2007), 24.

3 McLaughlin, Lisa, "The New Roll Model," *Time*, 164 (July 26, 2004), 74.

4 *Entertainment Newsweekly*, "Electronic Arts Inc.; EA Brings Entries' Fifth Annual Goofy versus Regular Skateboarding Competition to Skate," (September 26, 2008), 181.

5 Sayre, Shay, *Qualitative Methods for Marketplace Research* (Sage: Thousand Oaks, CA, 2001).

6 Sayre, Shay (2001); Morse, Janice M. and Lyn Richards, *Readme First for a User's Guide to Qualitative Methods* (Sage: Thousand Oaks, CA, 2002).

7 See, for example, May, Carl, "Methodological Pluralism: British Sociology and the Evidence-Based State: A Reply to Payne et al.," *Sociology*, 39 (July 2005), 519–528; Achenbaum, A. A., "When Good Research Goes Bad,"*Marketing Research*, 13 (Winter 2001), 13–15; Wade, K. R., "We Have Come Upon the Enemy: And They are Us," *Marketing Research*, 14 (Summer 2002), 39.

8 Babin, Barry J., William R. Darden and Mitch Griffin, "Work and/ or Fun: Measuring Hedonic and Utilitarian Shopping Value," *Journal of Consumer Research*, 20 (March 1994), 644–656.

9 Stengal, J. R., A. L. Dixon and C. T. Allen, "Listening Begins at Home," *Harvard Business Review* (November 2003), 106–116.

10 Semon, Thomas T., "You Get What You Pay For: It May be Bad MR," *Marketing News*, 36 (April 15, 2002), 7.

11 The NPD process in the Exhibit is similar to that described in Lamb, C., J. Hair and C. McDaniel, *Essentials of Marketing*, 5th Edition (Thompson: Mason, OH, 2005), 297.

12 Hamel, G. and C. K. Prahalad, "Corporate Imagination and Expeditionary Marketing," *Harvard Business Review* (July–August 1991), 85.

13 Martens, Claire, "Sometimes a Great Notion Isn't Yet a Great Product," *Harvard Management Update* (March 2004), 3–4.

14 Thompson, Craig J., "Interpreting Consumers: A Hermeneutical Framework for Deriving Marketing Insights from the Tests of Consumers' Consumption Stories," *Journal of Marketing Research*, 34 (November 1997), 438–455 (see pp. 443–444 for quotation).

15 Thompson (1997). Craig J., "Interpreting Consumers: A Hermeneutical Framework for Deriving Marketing Insights from the Tests of Consumers' Consumption Stories," *Journal of Marketing Research*, 34 (November 1997), 438–455; Woodside, Arch G., H. M. Pattinson and K. E. Miller, "Advancing Hermeneutic Research for Interpreting Interfirm New Product Development," *Journal of Business and Industrial Marketing*, 20 (2005), 364–379.

16 While we refer to a hermeneutic unit as being text-based here for simplicity, they can actually also be developed using pictures, videotapes, or artifacts as well. Software such as ATLAS.ti will allow files containing pictures, videos, and text to be combined into a hermeneutic unit.

17 Morse, Janice M. and Lyn Richards (2002).

18 Winsome, S. J., and P. Johnson, "The Pros and Cons of Data Analysis Software for Qualitative Research," *Journal of Nursing Scholarship*, 32, no. 4 (2000), 393–397.

19 See Feldman, Stephen P., "Playing with the Pieces: Deconstruction and the Loss of Moral Culture," *Journal of Management Studies*, 35 (January 1998), 59–79.

20 "Futurespeak," *American Demographics*, 26 (April 2004), 44.

21 Louella, Miles, "Living their Lives," *Marketing (UK)* (December 11, 2003), 27–28.

22 Reid, D. M., "Changes in Japan's Post-Bubble Business Environment: Implications for Foreign-Affiliated Companies," *Journal of International Marketing*, 7, no. 3 (1999), 38–63.

23 Cutler, I. S., "Avoid Instinktive Marketing," *Upholstery Manufacturing*, 19 (January 2006), 33.

24 Morse, Janice M. and Lyn Richards (2002).

25 Strauss, A. L. and J. Corbin, *Basics of Qualitative Research* (Sage Publications: Newbury Park, CA, 1990).

26 Geiger, S. and D. Turley, "Personal Selling as a Knowledge-Based Activity: Communities of Practice in the Sales Force," *Irish Journal of Management*, 26 (2005), 61–70.

27 Beverland, M., "The Components of Prestige Brands," *Journal of Business Research*, 59 (February 2006), 251–258. Beverland, M., "Brand Value, Convictions, Flexibility and New Zealand Wine," *Business Horizons*, 47 (September/October 2004), 53–61.

28 Harwood, Jonathan, "Philip Morris Develops Smokeless Cigarette," *Marketing Week*, 28 (March 31, 2005), 5.

29 See Palan, K. M. and R. E. Wilkes, "Adolescent-Parent Interaction in Family Decision Making," *Journal of Consumer Research*, 24 (September 1997), 159–170; Haytko, Diana L. and Julie Baker,"It's All at the Mall: Exploring Adolescent Girls' Experiences," Journal of Retailing, 80 (Spring 2004), 67–83.

30 Godes, David and Dina Mayzlin, "Using On-Line Conversations to Study Word-of-Mouth Communications," *Marketing Science*, 23 (2004), 545–560.

31 Babin, Barry J., William R. Darden and James S. Boles, "Salesperson Stereotypes, Consumer Emotions, and Their Impact on Information Processing," *Journal of the Academy of*

Marketing Science, 23 (Spring 1995), 94–105.

32 Murphy, Ian, "Aided by Research, Harley Goes Whole Hog," *Marketing News*, 30 (December 2, 1996), 16–17.

33 Heather, R. P., "Future Focus Groups," *American Demographics* (January 1, 1994), 6.

34 Creamer, Mathew, "Slowly, Marketers Learn How to Let Go and Let Blog," *Advertising Age*, 76 (October 31, 2005), 1–35.

35 Fass, Allison, "Collective Opinion," *Forbes*, 176 (November 28, 2005), 76–79.

36 Godes, David and Dina Mayzlin, "Using On-Line Conversations to Study Word-of-Mouth Communications," *Marketing Science*, 23 (2004), 545–560.

37 Smith, A., R. Bolton and J. Wagner, "A Model of Customer Satisfaction with Service Encounters Involving Failure and Recovery," *Journal of Marketing Research*, 36 (August 1999), 356–372. Bolton, R. and T. M. Bronkhorst, "Quantitative Analysis of Depth Interviews, Psychology & Marketing, 8 (Winter 1991), 275–297.

38 "SPSS Text Mining Reveals Customer Insights As Organizations Worldwide Tap into Unstructured Data," *Business Wire*, (June 16, 2008), accessed through ProQuest, document number 14956884601 on July 14, 2008.

39 Wooliscroft, B., R. D. Tamilia and S. J. Shapiro (2006), A Twenty-First Century Guide to Aldersonian Marketing Thought, Springer, New York, NY.

40 Klahr, S., "Getting' Buggy With It," *Advertising Age's Creativity*, 8 (May 2000), 9.

Chapter 7

1 "Licensed to Snoop," *Human Resources*, (June 2008), 57–58; Marks, P., "Pentagon Sets Its Sights on Social Networking Websites," *New Scientist* (June 9, 2006), http://www.newscientist.com/article/mg19025556.200, accessed August 6, 2008; Lowry, Tom, "Obama's Secret Weapon," *Business Week* (July 7, 2008), 56–57.

2 "Breakfast Sandwich Boom," *Restaurants & Institutions,* 116 (Jan 15, 2006), p. 39.

3 Grow, Brian, "Yes, Ma'am, That Part Is in Stock," *Business Week*, (August 1, 2005), p. 32 "Servigistics Pricing: Maximizing the Profitability of Your Service Network," Servigistics, http://www.servigistics.com, accessed February 7, 2006.

4 Prasso, Sheridan, "Battle for the Face of China," *Fortune*, 152 (December 12, 2005), p. 156–161.

5 Charles, Susan K.,"Custom Content Delivery," *Online*, (March–April 2004),

p. 24–29. Fleming, Lee, "Digital Delivery: Pushing Content to the Desktop," *Digital Information Group*, (January 31, 1997), p. 7; and "How Smart Agents Will Change Selling," *Forbes ASAP*, (August 28, 1995), p. 95.

6 "Seeking New Beer Drinkers in the High Andes," *Global Agenda*, (September 6, 2005), p. 1; and "China Ranked Largest Beer Consumer in 2004," *Kyodo News International*, (December 15, 2005), Knight Ridder Tribune Business News, p. 1.

7 This section is based on Levy, Michael and Barton Weitz, *Retail Management* (Homewood, IL: Richard D. Irwin, 1992), pp. 357–358.

8 Data from the "About Us" section of the Capital One Web site, http://www.capitalone.com, accessed February 9, 2006.

9 Rao, Srikumar S.,"The Hot Zone," *Forbes*, (November 18, 1996).

10 Mehta, N., "Investigating Consumers' Purchase Incidence and Brand Choice Decisions Across Multiple Product Categories: A Theoretical and Empirical Analysis," *Marketing Science*, 26 (Mar/Apr 2007), 457–479.

11 Wasserman, Todd, Gerry Khermouch and Jeff Green, "Mining Everyone's Business," *BrandWeek*, (February 28, 2000), p. 34.

12 "Clients: Case Studies," DataMind, http://www.datamind.com, accessed February 6, 2006.

13 Totty, Michael, "Making Searches Work at Work," *Wall Street Journal*, (December 19, 2005), http://online.wsj.com, accessed February 10, 2006.

14 Weiss, A. M., N. H. Lurie and D. J. MacInnis, "Listening to Strangers: Whose Responses Are Valuable, How Valuable Are They, and Why?" *Journal of Marketing Research*, 45 (August 2008), 425–436.

15 "Hispanic-Owned Businesses: Growth Projections, 2004–2010," HispanicBusiness.com Store, http://www.hbinc.com, accessed February 7, 2006.

16 Neff, Jack,"Wal-Mart Takes Stock in RetailLink System," *Advertising Age*, (May 21, 2001), p. 6.

17 See Federal Grants Wire, "National Trade Data Bank (NTDB)," http://www.federalgrantswire.com, accessed February 6, 2006; and STATUSA, "What Information Is Available under GLOBUS and NTBD?" and "GLOBUS & NTBD," http://www.stat-usa.gov, accessed February 6, 2006.

18 Based on Brown,Warren,"Pain at the Pump Doesn't Faze New-Car Buyers," *Washington Post*, (January 29,2006), http://www.washingtonpost.com, accessed, February 10, 2006; and Halliday, J.,"Prius Prices Outrun Inventory," *Advertising Age,* 79 (June 2, 2008), pp. 3–4.

Chapter 8

1 Darlin, Damon, "The Only Question That Matters," *Business 2.0*, (September 2005), downloaded from InfoTrac at http://web2.infotrac.galegroup.com; Kirkpatrick, David, "Throw It at the Wall and See if It Sticks," *Fortune*, (December 12, 2005), http://web2.infotrac.galegroup.com; and McGregor, Jena, "Would You Recommend Us?" *Business Week*, (January 30, 2006), http://web5.infotrac.galegroup.com.

2 Swientek, B., "Using Consumer Insights to Guide Package Design: Traditional Research Can Give You Answers. But…" *Brand Packaging*, (March 1, 2003), accessed at www.interbrand.com, June 30, 2008.

3 Vascellaro, Jessica E. "Who'll Give Me $50 for This Purse from Nana?" *Wall Street Journal*, (December 28, 2005), http://online.wsj.com; "Survey Reveals Majority of Americans Receive Unwanted Gifts," *Survey.com* news release, (December 19, 2005), http://www.survey.com.

4 Excerpts from Arlen, Michael J., *Thirty Seconds* (New York: Farrar, Straus and Giroux, Inc., 1979, 1980), pp. 185–186. This material first appeared in the *New Yorker*.

5 Tuckel, Peter and Harry O'Neill, "The Vanishing Respondent in Telephone Surveys," a paper presented at the 56th annual conference of the American Association of Public Opinion Research (AAPOR) in Montreal on May 17–20, 2001.

6 Cull, William L., Karen G. O'Connor, Sanford Sharp, and Suk-fong S. Tang, "Response Rates and Response Bias for 50 Surveys of Pediatricians," *Health Services Research*, 40 (February 2005), p. 213.

7 Lee, Eunkyu, Michael Y. Hu and Rex S. Toh, "Respondent Noncooperation in Surveys and Diaries: An Analysis of Item Non-response and Panel Attrition," *International Journal of Market Research*, 46 (Autumn 2004), p. 311.

8 Douglas Aircraft, Consumer Research (undated), p. 13.

9 For an interesting study of extremity bias, see Baumgartner, Hans and Jan-Benedict E. M. Steenkamp, "Response Styles in Marketing Research: A Cross-National Investigation," *Journal of Marketing Research*, (May 2001), pp. 143–156.

10 Raven, G., "Major Holocaust Polls Show Built-In Bias," *Journal of Historical Review*, 15, no. 1 (2008), accessed at http://www.ihr.org/jhr/v15/v15n1p25_Raven.html, August 12, 2008.

11 Turner, Charles F., Maria A. Villarroel, James R. Chromy, Elizabeth Eggleston and Susan M.

Rogers, "Same-Gender Sex among U.S. Adults: Trends across the Twentieth Century and during the 1990s," 70 *Public Opinion Quarterly*, (Fall 2005), pp. 166–196.

12 The term "questionnaire" technically refers only to mail and self-administered surveys, and the term "interview schedule" is used for interviews by telephone or face-to-face. However, we will use "questionnaire" to refer to all three forms of communications in this book.

13 Bright, Beckey, "Nearly Half of Americans Resolve to Get Healthy in 2006, Poll Shows," *Wall Street Journal*, (January 17, 2006), http://online.wsj.com, accessed March 2, 2006.

14 Ohlemacher, Stephen, "Study Finds that Marriage Builds Wealth," *Yahoo! News*, (January 18, 2006), http://news.yahoo.com; Pierret, Charles, "The National Longitudinal Survey of Youth: 1979 Cohort at 25," *Monthly Labor Review*, (February 2005), pp. 3–7.

15 The Bureau of Business Practice, *Profiles in Quality: Blueprints for Action from 50 Leading Companies* (Boston: Allyn and Bacon, 1991), p. 113.

16 Weisberg, Karen "Change Maker," *Food Service Director*, 19 (January 15, 2006), pp. 18-19.

17 Gavin, David A., "Competing on the Eight Dimensions of Quality," *Harvard Business Review*, (November–December 1987), pp. 101–8.

18 Forelle, Charles, "Many Colleges Ignore New SAT Writing Test," *Wall Street Journal*, (December 7, 2005), http://online.wsj.com; "Kaplan's New SAT Survey Results," Kaplan Inc., College Admissions, Kaplan Web site, http://www.kaptest.com, accessed February 14, 2006.

Chapter 9

1 Brady, D., "Showcase Covers Hot Topics," *Marketing Week*, 30 (November 1, 2007), 37–40; Callegaro, M., C. Steeh, T. D. Buskirk, V. Vehovar, V. Kuusela, and L. Piekarski, "Fitting Disposition Codes to Mobile Phone Surveys: Experiences from Studies in Finland, Slovenia and the USA," *Journal of the Royal Statistical Society*, 170, no. 3 (2007), 647–670; Tourangeau, R., "Survey Research and Social Change," *Annual Review of Psychology*, 55 (2004), 775–801.

2 Tourangeau, R. (2004), "Survey Research and Social Change," *Annual Review of Psychology*, 55, 775–801.

3 Warwick, Donald T. and Charles A. Lininger, *The Sample Survey: Theory and Practice* (New York: McGraw-Hill, 1975), p. 2.

4 Lockley, L. C. "Notes on the History of Marketing Research," *Journal of Marketing* (April 1950), pp. 733–736.

5 Hof, Robert D. "The Power of Us," *BusinessWeek* (June 20, 2005), 74–82.

6 For a complete discussion of conducting surveys in Hispanic neighborhoods, see Hernandes, Sigfredo A. and Carol J. Kaufman, "Marketing Research in Hispanic Barrios: A Guide to Survey Research," *Marketing Research* (March 1990), pp. 11–27.

7 Lavrakas, P. J., C. D. Shuttles, C. Steeh and H. Fienberg, "The State of Surveying Cell Phone Numbers in the United States," *Public Opinion Quarterly*, 71, no. 5 (2007), 840–854.

8 Brick, J. M., P. D. Brick, S. Dipko, S. Presser, C. Tucker and Y. Yuan, "Cell Phone Survey Feasibility in the U.S.: Sampling and Calling Cell Numbers Versus Landline Numbers," *Public Opinion Quarterly*, 71 (Spring 2007), 23–39.

9 Curtin, Richard, Stanley Presser and Eleanor Singer, "Changes in Telephone Survey Nonresponse over the Past Quarter Century," *Public Opinion Quarterly* (Spring 2005), downloaded from InfoTrac at http://web3.infotrac.galegroup.com.

10 Cuneo, Alice Z., "Researchers Flail as Public Cuts the Cord," *Advertising Age* (November 15, 2004), 3–52.

11 Hembroff, Larry A. Debra Rusz, Ann Rafferty, Harry McGee and Nathaniel Ehrlich, "The Cost-Effectiveness of Alternative Advance Mailings in a Telephone Survey," *Public Opinion Quarterly*, 69 (Summer 2005), 232–245.

12 Brennan, Mike, Susan Benson and Zane Kearns, "The Effect of Introductions on Telephone Survey Participation Rates," *International Journal of Market Research*, 47, no. 1 (2005), 65–74.

13 Dillman, Don A., *Mail and Internet Surveys: The Tailored Design Method* (New York: John Wiley and Sons, 2000), p. 173.

14 Schaefer, David R. and Don A. Dillman, "Development of a Standard E-Mail Methodology: Results of an Experiment," *Public Opinion Quarterly*, 62, no. 3 (Fall 1998), p. 378.

15 Ibid.

16 For a complete discussion of fax surveys, see the excellent article by Dickson, John P. and Douglas L. Maclachlan, "Fax Surveys: Return Patterns and Comparison with Mail Surveys," *Journal of Marketing Research* (February 1996), pp. 108–113.

17 Merriman, Joyce A., "Your Feedback Is Requested," *American Family Physician* (October 1, 2005), downloaded from InfoTrac at http://web3.infotrac.galegroup.com.

18 Dillmann, Don A., *Mail and Internet Surveys, The Tailored Design Method* (New York: John Wiley and Sons, 2000), pp. 369–372.

19 Göritz, Anja S., "Recruitment for On-Line Access Panels," *International Journal of Market Research*, 46, no. 4 (2004), 411–425.

20 Fricker, Scott, Mirta Galesic, Roger Tourangeau and Ting Yan, "An Experimental Comparison of Web and Telephone Surveys," *Public Opinion Quarterly*, 69 (Fall 2005), 370–392.

21 See Nielsen, Jakob "Keep Online Surveys Short," Alertbox (February 2, 2004), http://www.useit.com; "About Jakob Nielsen," http://www.useit.com, accessed February 21, 2006; and "About Nielsen Norman Group," Nielsen Norman Group, http://www.nngroup.com, accessed February 21, 2006.

22 See Kilbourne, Lawrene, "Avoid the Field of Dreams Fallacy," *Quirk's Marketing Research Review* (January 2005), pp. 70, 72–73.

23 Porter, P. R. and M. E. Whitcomb, "Mixed-Mode Contacts in Internet Surveys: Paper Is Not Necessarily Better," *Public Opinion Quarterly*, 71 (Winter 2007), 635–648.

24 Gruen, T., T. Osmonbekov and A. J. Czaplewski, "eWOM: The Impact of Customer-to-Customer Online Know-How Exchange on Customer Value and Loyalty," *Journal of Business Research*, 59 (April, 2006), 449–456.

25 Mary Lisbeth D'Amico, "Call Security," *Wall Street Journal* (February 13, 2006), http://online.wsj.com.

26 Braunsberger, K., H. Wybenga and R. Gates, "A Comparison of Reliability between Telephone and Web-Based Surveys," *Journal of Business Research*, 60 (July 2007), 758–764.

27 For an interesting empirical study, see Akaah, Ishmael P. and Edward A. Riordan, "The Incidence of Unethical Practices in Marketing Research: An Empirical Investigation," *Journal of the Academy of Marketing Sciences* (Spring 1990), pp. 143–152.

28 Based on "Do-Not-Call List Reduces Telemarketing, Poll Finds," *Wall Street Journal* (January 12, 2006), http://online.wsj.com.

Chapter 10

1 Based on Thomas Mucha, "This Is Your Brain on Advertising," *Business 2.0* (August 2005), 8 (August), 47–49 and Peter Laybourne and David Lewis, "Neuromarketing: The Future of Consumer Research?" *Admap* (May 2005), pp. 28–30.

2 Abrams, Bill, *The Observational Research Handbook* (Chicago: NTC Business Books, 2000), pp. 2, 105.

3 Redmond, E. C. and C. J. Griffith, "A Comparison and Evaluation of Research Methods Used in Consumer Food Safety Studies," *International Journal of Consumer Studies*, 27 (January 2003), 17–33.

4 Adapted with permission from the April 30, 1980 issue of *Advertising Age*. Copyright © 1980 by Crain Communications, Inc.

5 "About Nielsen Media Research," Nielsen Media Research, http://www.nielsenmedia.com, accessed February 24, 2006.

6 "The Portable People Meter System," Arbitron, http://www.arbitron.com, accessed December 17, 2008.

7 "About the PreTesting Company" and "Television," PreTesting Company, http://www.pretesting.com, accessed February 24, 2006.

8 Conley, Lucas, "At 1600 Pennsylvania Avenue, Of Course, It's 'Rush Limbaugh,'" *Fast Company* (February 2005), 91, 29; Dina ElBoghdady, "Advertisers Tune In to New Radio Gauge," *Washington Post* (October 25, 2004), http://www.washingtonpost.com; "iBiquity and Mobiltrak: Bringing Radio into the Digital Age," Bear Stearns Equity Research, February 8, 2005, http://www.bearstearns.com.

9 "Losing Track," Direct, 17 (October 15, 2005), 50–51. See also Steve Johnson, "Who's in Charge of the Web Site Ratings Anyway?" *Chicago Tribune* (February 26, 2006), 1, 18.

10 Kiley, David "Google: Searching for an Edge in Ads," *Business Week* (January 30, 2006), 80–82. infotrac.galegroup.com. See also Pieter Sanders and Bram Lebo, "Click Tracking: A Fool's Paradise?" *Brandweek* 46 (June 6, 2005), 46. Klaassen, A., M. Creamer, A. Hampp and E. Tan "10 Lessons from the Ad Age Digital Marketing Conference," Advertising Age, (3/12/2007), 42.

11 Neff, Jack, "Aging Population Brushes Off Coloring," *Advertising Age*, 76 (July 25, 2005), 3–49.

12 Horovitz, B., "Marketers Take a Close Look at Your Daily Routines," *USA Today* (2007), www.usatoday.com/money/advertising/2007-04-29-watching-marketing_N.htm, accessed August 10, 2008.

13 Starr, R. G. and K. V. Fernandez, "The Mindcam Methodology: Perceiving through the Native's Eye," *Qualitative Market Research: An International Journal*, 10, no. 2 (2007), 168–182.

14 Lee, N. and A. J. Broderick, "The Past, Present and Future of Observational Research in Marketing," *Qualitative Market Research: An International Journal*, 10, no. 2 (2007), 121–129.

15 Stringer, Kortney "Eye-Tracking Technology for Marketers," *Detroit Free Press* (August 1, 2005), downloaded from http://www.highbeam.com/doc/1G1-134701284.html, accessed December 18, 2008,

Hill, D., "Face Value," Marketing Research, 19 (Fall 2007), 9–14.

16 Krugman's, Herbert B. statement as quoted in "Live, Simultaneous Study of Stimulus, Response Is Physiological Measurement's Great Virtue," *Marketing News* (May 15, 1981), pp. 1, 20.

17 Based on "Mazda Turns to Eye-Tracking to Assist Revamp of European Site," *New Media Age* (November 3, 2005), 8; and "Persuasion Is the New Focus," *Revolution* (February 21, 2006), downloaded from the Media Coverage page of the Syzygy Web site, http://www.syzygy.co.uk.

18 Adapted with permission from Bruce Rayner, "Product Development, Now Hear This!" *Electronic Business* (August 1997).

Chapter 11

1 See http://www.law.com and search key terms such as cigarettes, tobacco, Brown and Williamson, and so on for some examples.

2 Doward, J., "Cigarette Giant to Deny Cancer Link," *The Observer* (October 5, 2003), http://www.guardian.co.uk/society/2003/oct/05/smoking.cancercare, accessed August 24, 2008; Seenan, Gerard, "Smoker's Widow Loses Legal Fight," *The Observer* (June 1, 2005). http://www.guardian.co.uk/society/2005/jun/01/smoking.publichealth1, accessed August 24, 2008.

3 See for example, Bolton, L. E., J. B. Cohen and P. N. Bloom, "Does Marketing Products as Remedies Create "Get Out of Jail Free Cards'?" *Journal of Consumer Research* 33 (June 2006), 71–84; Smith, K. H. and M. A. Stutts, "The Influence of Individual Factors on the Effectiveness of Message Content in Antismoking Advertisements Aimed at Adolescents," *The Journal of Consumer Affairs* 40 (2006), 261–293; Zhao, G. and C. Pechmann, "The Impact of Regulatory Focus on Adolescents' Response to Antismoking Advertising Campaigns," *Journal of Marketing Research* 44 (November 2007), 671–687.

4 Babin, Barry J., David M. Hardesty and Tracy A. Suter, "Color and Shopping Intentions: The Intervening Effect of Price Fairness and Perceived Affect," *Journal of Business Research* 56 (July 2003), 541–551.

5 Christie, J., D. Fisher, J. Kozup, S. Smith, S. Burton, and E. Creyer, "The Effects of Bar-Sponsored Alcohol Beverage Promotions Across Binge and Nonbinge Drinkers," *Journal of Public Policy and Marketing* 20 (Fall 2001), 240–253.

6   Shadish, William R., Thomas D. Cook and Donald T. Campbell, *Experimental and Quasi Experimental Designs for Generalized Causal Inference* (Geneva, IL: Houghton Mifflin, 2002).

7   Like Dragnet, the story is true but the brand names are fictitious.

8   Reitter, Robert N., "Comment: American Media and the Smoking-Related Behaviors of Asian Adolescents," *Journal of Advertising Research* 43 (March 2003), 12–13.

9   Lach, Jennifer, "Up in Smoke," *American Demographics,* 22 (March 2000), 26.

10 Mitchell, Vincent-Wayne and Sarah Haggett, "Sun-Sign Astrology in Market Segmentation: An Empirical Investigation," *Journal of Consumer Marketing* 14, no. 2 (1997), 113–131.

11 Roethlisberger, F. J. and W. J. Dickson, *Management and the Worker* (Harvard University Press: Cambridge, MA, 1939).

12 Shiv, Baba, Ziv Carmon and Dan Aneley, "Placebo Effects of Marketing Actions: Consumers May Get What They Pay for," *Journal of Marketing Research* 42 (November 2005), 383–393.

13 Chou, Ya-Lun, *Statistical Analysis with Business and Economics Applications* (Ft. Worth: Holt, Rinehart and Winston, 1975).

14 Peterson, Robert A., "On the Use of Students in Social Science Research: Evidence from a Second Order Meta Analysis," *Journal of Consumer Research* 28 (December 2001), 450–461.

15 Tybout, Alice M. and Gerald Zaltman, "Ethics in Marketing Research: Their Practical Relevance," *Journal of Marketing Research* 21 (November 1974), 357–368.

16 Reprinted with permission from Lee Martin, Geoffrey "Drinkers Get Court Call," *Advertising Age* (May 20, 1991). Copyright © 1991 Crain Communications, Inc.

17 Shadish, William R., Thomas D. Cook, and Donald T. Campbell (2002).

Chapter 12

1   This vignette is drawn from multiple sources: Sampey, Kathleen, "Heineken Test Marketing New Light Beer," *Adweek* 46 (November 7, 2005), 7; Beirne, Mike, "Heineken Green Lights $40M," *Brandweek,* 46, no. 40 (2005), 9; Beirne, Mike, "Brewers Face Hard Questions about Luxury Light Beers," *Brandweek* 46 (November 14, 2005), 7; Sampey, Kathleen, "Heineken Seeks 'Light-Line' Ideas," *Adweek* 46 (November 7, 2005), 7; Allen, M., "Anheuser-Busch Transfers U.S. Import Rights of Grolsch Beer to Rival Miller," *St. Louis Business Journal* (May 14, 2008), 47.

2   Riell, H., "Getting Back to Beer," *Convenience Store Decisions* 19 (February 2008), 14.

3   *Market Testing Consumer Products* (New York: National Industrial Conference Board, 1967), p. 13.

4   Riste, Christine, "La suprématie contée des prospectus," *Libre Service Actualité-LSA* (January 17, 2002), 1751.

5   Babin, B. J. and Adilson Borges, "Product Category and Promotional Theme Congruency: Its Effect on Preference and Retail Store Image," in *Development in Marketing Science,* H. Spotts, Ed., (Academy of Marketing Science, Coral Gables, FL, 2005).

6   Wilson, M., "Solution Makes It Simple," *Chain Store Age* 81 (June 2005), 69.

7   "Jackass 2.5 to Test Market for Online Film Release," CBC News, http://www.cbc.ca/arts/film/story/2007/12/13/jackass-online.html?ref=rss, accessed August 24, 2008.

8   Neff, Jack, "Millstone," *Advertising Age* (June 29, 1998), S16.

9   Ding, Ming and Jehoshua Eliashberg, "Structuring the New Product Development Pipeline," *Management Science* 48 (March 2002), 343–363.

10 Cadbury, N. D., "When, Where, and How to Test Market," *Harvard Business Review* (May–June 1975), 96–105.

11 "Spirit Category Expected to See Robust Growth," *Drug Store News* 27 (May 2, 2005), 60.

12 Neff, Jack, "Average City, USA," *Advertising Age* 72 (July 9, 2001), 12.

13 Neff, Jack (2001).

14 Ramage, Norma, "Testing, Testing 1, 2, 3," *Marketing Magazine* 110 (July 2005), 1196; CNW_Telbec, "Imperial Tobacco Canada Lives Up to Its Corporate Social Responsibility Promise," Groupe CNW (2007), http://www.newswire.ca/fr/releases/archive/September2007/12/c7976.html, accessed November 12, 2008.

15 "How to Open the Northern European Market," U.S. Commercial Service Denmark (2006), http://www.buyusa.gov/denmark, accessed January 22, 2006.

16 Berta, Dina, "Utah City Turns Out to Be Best Test Market for Brazilian Concept," *Nation's Restaurant News* (September 22, 2003), 192.

17 Sally Scanlon, "The True Test," *Sales and Marketing Management* (March 1979), 57.

18 Vence, Deborah L., "Net Serves as Best Tool to Connect with Hispanics," *Marketing News* (September 1, 2005), 29–37.

19 Pollack, Jodham, "Price Issues Dog Frito Olean Tests," *Advertising Age* (November 25, 1996), 4.

20 LaVallee, Andrew, "Road Testing T-Shirts," *Women's Wear Daily* 189 (April 27, 2005), 8.

21 Burke, Raymond R., "Virtual Shopping: Breakthrough in Marketing Research," *Harvard Business Review* (March–April 1996), 120–131.

22 Bell, G. H., "Multivariable Testing: An Illustration," *Circulation Management* 23 (May 2008), 16–18.

23 Winer, B. J., *Statistical Principles in Experimental Design*, 2nd ed. (New York: McGraw-Hill, 1971).

Chapter 13

1   Babin, Barry J. and Jill Attaway, "Atmospheric Affect as a Tool for Creating Value and Gaining Share of Customer," *Journal of Business Research,* 49 (August 2000), 91–99; Verhoef, P. C., "Understanding the Effect of Customer Relationship Management Efforts on Customer Retention and Customer Share Development," *Journal of Marketing* 67 (October 2003), 30–45.

2   Periatt, J. A., S. A. LeMay and S. Chakrabarty, "The Selling Orientation-Customer Orientation (SOCO) Scale: Cross-Validation of the Revised Version," *Journal of Personal Selling and Sales Management,* 24 (Winter 2004), 49–54.

3   Anderson, Barry F., *The Psychology Experiment* (Monterey, CA: Brooks/Cole, 1971), p. 26.

4   Kerlinger, Fred N., *Foundations of Behavioral Research* (New York: Holt, Rinehart and Winston, 1973).

5   Cohen, Jacob, "Things I Have Learned (So Far)," *American Psychologist*, 45 (December 1990), 1304–1312.

6   Arnold, Catherine, "Satisfaction's the Name of the Game," *Marketing News*, 38 (October 15, 2004), 39–45. Also, see http://www.theacsi.org.

7   In more advanced applications such as those involving structural equations analysis, a distinction can be made between reflective composites and formative indexes. See Hair, J. F., W. C. Black, B. J. Babin, R. Anderson and R. Tatham, *Multivariate Data Analysis*, 6th ed. (Upper Saddle River, NJ: Prentice Hall, 2006).

8   Bart, Yakov, Venkatesh Shankar, Fareena Sultan and Glen L. Urban, "Are the Drivers and Role of Online Trust the Same for All Web Sites and Consumers? A Large-Scale Exploratory Study," *Journal of Marketing*, 69 (October 2005), 133–152.

9   Cronbach, Lee J., "My Current Thoughts on Coefficient Alpha and Successor Procedures," *Center for the Study of Evaluation Report*, 64, no. 3 (2004), http://epm.sagepub.com/cgi/content/short/64/3/391, accessed October 25, 2008.

10 Hair et al. (2006).

11 Wells, Chris, "The War of the Razors," *Esquire* (February 1980), 3.

12 Burke Marketing Research, "Rough Commercial Recall Testing," Cincinnati, OH (undated).

13 Hair et al. (2006).

14 Cox, Keith K. and Ben M. Enis, *The Marketing Research Process* (Pacific Palisades, CA: Goodyear, 1972); Kerlinger, Fred N., *Foundations of Behavioral Research,* 3rd ed. (Ft. Worth: Holt, Rinehart and Winston, 1986).

15 Headley, Dean E., Brent D. Bowen and Jacqueline R. Liedtke. This case, originally titled "Navigating through Airline Quality," was reviewed and accepted for publication by the Society for Case Research.

Chapter 14

1   Reichheld, F. F., "The One Number You Need to Grow," *Harvard Business Review* 81 (2003), 46–54; Keiningham, T. L., B. Cooil, T. W. Andreassen and L. Aksoy, "A Longitudinal Examination of the Net Promoter and Firm Revenue Growth," *Journal of Marketing* 71 (2007), 39–51; Grisaffe, D. B., "Questions About the Ultimate Question: Conceptual Considerations in Evaluating Reichheld's Net Promoter Score (NPS)," *Journal of Consumer Satisfaction, Dissatisfaction and Complaining Behavior* 20 (2007), 36–53; Mitchell, A., "The Only Number You Need to Know Does Not Add Up to Much," *Marketing Week* (March 6, 2008), 22–23.

2   Howell, N., "Looking Deeper," *New Media Age* (December 1, 2005), 24–25.

3   Breeden, Richard, "Owners, Executives Cite Small Firms' Advantages," *Wall Street Journal* (January 3, 2006), http://online.wsj.com, accessed August 1, 2006; "Third Annual State of the Union Study for Small and Mid-Sized Business," AllBusiness.com (Winter 2008), News and Press page, http://www.allbusiness.com/economy-economic-indicators/economic-indicators/6598585-1.html, accessed November 14, 2008.

4   Osgood, Charles, George Suci and Percy Tannenbaum, *The Measurement of Meaning* (Urbana: University of Illinois Press, 1957). Seven-point scales were used in the original work; however, subsequent researchers have modified the scale to have five points, nine points, and so on.

5   Menezes, Dennis and Norbert F. Elbert, "Alternative Semantic Scaling Formats for Measuring Store Image: An Evaluation," *Journal of Marketing Research* (February 1979), pp. 80–87.

6   Costanzo, Chris, "How Consumer Research Drives Web Site Design," *American Banker* 170 (April 19, 2005), 74.

7   Peterson, R. A. and W. Wilson, "Measuring Customer Satisfaction: Fact and Artifact," *Journal of the Academy of Marketing Science* 20 (Spring 1992), 61–71; Dawes, J., "Do Data Characteristics Change According to the Number of Scale Points Used? An Experiment Using 5-Point, 7-Point and 10-Point Scales," *International Journal of Market Research* 50, no. 1 (2008), 61–77.

8   See Muk, A., "Consumers' Intentions to Opt in to SMS Advertising," *International Journal of Advertising* 26, no. 2 (2007), 177–198; or Summers, T. A., "Predicting Purchase Intention of a Controversial Luxury Apparel Product," *Journal of Fashion Marketing & Management* 10, no. 4 (2006), 405–419, for examples.

9   Roeder-Johnson Corp., "Technology Still Matters to Start-Ups Say Venture Capitalists and Other Industry Influencers," news release (January 24, 2006), http://finance.yahoo.com, accessed June 30, 2006; and Roeder-Johnson Corp., "Importance of Unique Technology to Start-Up Companies: A Survey," January 2006, downloaded at http://www.roeder-johnson.com, accessed June 30, 2006.

Chapter 15

1   White, Joseph B. "The Price of Safety," *Wall Street Journal* (December 5, 2005), http://online.wsj.com; J.D. Power and Associates, "J.D. Power and Associates Reports: Premium Surround Sound Systems and HD Radio Garner High Consumer Interest Based on Their Market Price, while Consumers Prefer One-Time Fee over the Monthly Fee Associated with Satellite Radio," news release (August 18, 2005), http://www.jdpower.com.

2   Smith, Robert, David Olah, Bruce Hansen and Dan Cumbo, "The Effect of Questionnaire Length on Participant Response Rate: A Case Study in the U.S. Cabinet Industry," *Forest Products Journal* 53 (November–December 2003), 31.

3   "Insurers Question Methods in U.S. Treasury Survey on Terror Backstop," A. M. Best Newswire (April 12, 2005), downloaded from Business & Company Resource Center, http://galenet.galegroup.com.

4   "Mothers Misunderstand Questions on Feeding Questionnaire," *Medical Letter on the CDC and FDA* (September 5, 2004), downloaded from Business & Company Resource Center, http://galenet.galegroup.com.

5   Donahue, Amy K. and Joanne M. Miller, "Citizen Preferences and Paying for Police," *Journal of Urban Affairs* 27, no.4 (2005), 419–35.

6   Nathan Weber, "Research: A Survey Shows How Media Influence Our Decorating and Cooking Choices,"

HFN, the Weekly Newspaper for the Home Furnishing Network (December 5, 2005), downloaded from Business & Company Resource Center, http://galenet.galegroup.com.

7   Roll, Charles W., Jr. and Albert H. Cantril, *Polls: Their Use and Misuse in Politics* (New York: Basic Books, 1972), pp. 106–7.

8   Other product attributes are relative advantage, compatibility, complexity, and communicability.

9   Dawson, L., "Will Feminization Change the Image of the Sales Profession?" *Journal of Personal Selling and Sales Management* 12 (Winter 1992), 21–32.

10 Payne, Stanley L., *The Art of Asking Questions* (Princeton, NJ: Princeton University Press, 1951), pp. 102–3.

11 Dillman, Don A., *Mail and Internet Surveys: The Tailored Design Method* (New York: John Wiley and Sons, 2000), pp. 357–61.

12 Young, Sarah J. and Craig M. Ross, "Web Questionnaires: A Glimpse of Survey Research in the Future," *Parks & Recreation* 35, no. 6 (June 2000), p. 30.

13 Michel, Matt, "Controversy Redux," CASRO Journal, http://www.decisionanalyst.com/publ_art/contredux.htm, downloaded February 8, 2001.

14 Ghaleb Almekhlafi, Abdurrahman, "Preservice Teachers' Attitudes and Perceptions of the Utility of Web-Based Instruction in the United Arab Emirates," *International Journal of Instructional Media* 32, no. 3 (2005): 269–84.

15 Harzing, Anne-Wil, "Does the Use of English-Language Questionnaires in Cross-National Research Obscure National Differences?" *International Journal of Cross Cultural Management* 5, no. 2 (2005): 213–24.

16 Cateora, Philip R., *International Marketing* (Homewood, IL: Richard D. Irwin, 1990), pp. 387–89.

Chapter 16

1   Based on Deborah Ball, "As Chocolate Sags, Cadbury Gambles on a Piece of Gum," *Wall Street Journal* (January 12, 2006), A1; Cadbury Schweppes, "Products: Trident Splash," Gumopolis, http://www.tridentgum.com, accessed March 16, 2006; Cadbury Schweppes, "New Cadbury Schweppes Americas Confectionary Facility Holds Future Gum Innovation: New Jersey Based Science & Technology Center to Meet Demands of Growing Gum Market," news release, http://www.cadburyschweppes.com (February 6, 2006).

2   Kinne, Susan and Tari D. Topolski, "Inclusion of People with Disabilities in Telephone Health Surveillance Surveys," *American Journal of Public*

Health 95, no. 3 (March 2005): 512–517.

3   Brock, Sabra E. "Marketing Research in Asia: Problems, Opportunities, and Lessons," *Marketing Research* (September 1989), p. 47.

4   Rideout, Bruce E., Katherine Hushen, Dawn McGinty, Stephanie Perkins and Jennifer Tate, "Endorsement of the New Ecological Paradigm in Systematic and E-Mail Samples of College Students," *Journal of Environmental Education* 37 (Winter 2005), 3–11.

5   SurveySite, "What We Do: Quantitative Research," http://www.surveysite.com, accessed March 15, 2006.

6   Council of American Survey Research Organizations (CASRO), "Frequently Asked Questions about Conducting Online Research: New Methodologies for Traditional Techniques," (1998), http://www.casro.org.

7   Krosnick, J., "The Distinguishing Characteristics of Frequent Survey Participants," *Proceedings of Midwestern Political Science Association* 1 (2006).

8   Krosnick, J., D. Rivers and N. Norman, "Web Survey Methodologies: A Comparison of Survey Accuracy," *Proceedings of the American Association for Public Opinion Research* 1 (2005).

9   Mellinger, Gloria, "Harris Interactive Inc.," *World Opinion Research Profiles* (July 18, 2000).

10 Ibid.

11 Survey Sampling International, "Internet Sampling Solutions," http://www.ssisamples.com, accessed March 15, 2006.

12 Yeganeh, Hamid, Zhan Su, Elie Virgile and M. Chrysostome, "A Critical Review of Epistemological and Methodological Issues in Cross-Cultural Research," *Journal of Comparative International Management* (December 2004), downloaded from InfoTrac at http://web2.infotrac.galegroup.com.

13 Sigenman, Lee, Steven A.Tuch and Jack K. Martin, "What's in a Name? Preference for 'Black' versus 'African-American' among Americans of African Descent," *Public Opinion Quarterly* 69 (Fall 2005), 429–438.

14 Based on Gene Mueller, "It's Hard to Figure Number of Anglers," *Washington Times* (March 20, 2005), downloaded from InfoTrac at http://web3.infotrac.galegroup.com; Atlantic Coastal Cooperative Statistics Program, "About Us: Committees," http://www.accsp.org, accessed March 16, 2006; Atlantic States Marine Fisheries Commission, "About Us," http://www.asmfc.org, accessed March 16, 2006.

15 Material for this case is from Scientific Telephone Samples User's Manual, Scientific Telephone Samples, Santa Ana, CA.

Chapter 17

1   "Gaming News," *Marketing News*, 42 (February 1, 2008), 39; Hellebusch, S. J., "Know Sample Quantity for Clearer Results," *Marketing News* 40 (September 15, 2006), 23–26; Sheth-Voss, P., "How Big Should Your Sample Be?" *Marketing Research* 20 (Summer 2008), 25–29.

2   Most of the statistical material in this book assumes that the population parameters are unknown, which is the typical situation in most applied research projects.

3   See Jurik, R., M. Moody and J. Seal, "The Mean vs. the Top Box(es) Scores," *Marketing Research* 20 (Summer 2008), 41–42.

4   The reasons for this are related to the concept of degrees of freedom, which will be explained later. At this point, disregard the intuitive notion of division by n, because it produces a biased estimate of the population variance.

5   In practice, most survey researchers will not use this exact formula. A modification of the formula, $Z = (X - \mu)/S$, using the sample standard deviation in an adjusted form, is frequently used.

6   Hayes, William L. *Statistics* (New York: Holt, Rinehart and Winston, 1963), p. 193.

7   Wonnacott, Thomas H. and Ronald J. Wonnacott, *Introductory Statistics* 2nd ed. (New York: Wiley, 1972), p. 125.

8   Note that the derivation of this formula is (1) $E = ZSX$; (2) $E = ZS/\sqrt{n}$; (3) $\sqrt{n}$ ZS/E; (4) (n) = $(ZS/E)2$.

9   Based on Bialik, Carl, "A Survey Probes the Back Seats of Taxis, with Dubious Results," *Wall Street Journal* (January 28, 2005), http://online.wsj.com; and Pointsec Mobile Technologies, "Taxis Hailed as Black Hole for Lost Cell Phones and PDAs, as Confidential Data Gets Taken for a Ride," news release (January 24, 2005), http://www.pointsec.com.

Chapter 18

1   Cowlett, M., "Research Leagues," *Marketing* 35 (September 2007), 37–42; Bond, J., "Mastering the Budget," *Marketing* 19 (October 3, 2007), 19; Furness, V., "Research Comes of Age," *Revolution* 53 (January 2007), 54–57; Serf, B. J., "A Day in the Life of Your Customer," *Medical Marketing and Media* 42 (September 2007), 61–62.

2   Hughes, D., "Study Finds 12,000 Laptops Lost or Stolen Each Week," *Aviation Daily* 373 (July 9, 2008), 6.

3   Sauerbeck, Laura R., Jane C. Khoury, Daniel Woo, Brett M. Kissela, Charles J. Moomaw and Joseph P. Broderick, "Smoking Cessation after Stroke: Education

and Its Effect on Behavior," *Journal of Neuroscience Nursing* 37 (December 2005), 316–319.

4   This section relies heavily on *Interviewer's Manual*, rev. ed. (Ann Arbor, MI: Survey Research Center, Institute for Social Research, University of Michigan, 1976).

5   Ibid., p. 11.

6   Ibid., pp. 11–13. Reprinted by permission.

7   Oliver, Daniel G., Julianne M. Serovich and Tina L. Mason, "Constraints and Opportunities with Interview Transcription: Towards Reflection in Qualitative Research," *Social Forces* 84 (December 2005), 1273–1289.

8   http://www.viewpointlearning.com

9   Serf, B. J., "A Day in the Life of Your Customer," *Medical Marketing and Media* 42 (September 2007), 61–62.

10 Sullivan, E. A., "Qual Research by the Numbers," *Marketing News* 42 (September 1, 2008), 21–24.

11 Ripley, Birch G. "Confessions of an Industrial Marketing Research Executive Interviewer," *Marketing News* (September 10, 1976), p. 20.

12 Based on Susanna Eng and Susan Gardner, "Conducting Surveys on a Shoestring Budget," *American Libraries* 36, no. 2 (February 2005), 38–39.

Chapter 19

1   Hareli, Shiomo, Noga Shomrat and Haum Biger, "The Role of Emotions in Employees' Explanations for Failure in the Workplace," *Journal of Managerial Psychology* 20, no. 8 (2005), 663–680.

2   Braunsberger, Karin, B. R. Buckler and David J. Ortinau, "Categorizing Cognitive Responses: An Empirical Investigation of the Cognitive Intent Congruency Between Independent Raters and Original Subject Raters," *Journal of the Academy of Marketing Science* 33 (Fall 2005), 620–632.

3   These imputation methods are beyond the scope of this text. For more see Hair et al., *Multivariate Data Analysis* (Upper Saddle River, NJ: Prentice Hall, 2006), pp. 39–73, 709–740.

4   Pope, Jeffrey L., *Practical Marketing Research* (New York: AMACOM, 1981), p. 22 © 1998–1999 VNU Business Media Inc. Used with permission.

Chapter 20

1   Dolliver, Mark, "Plow Under Your Hops and Plant Some Vines," *Adweek* 46 (July 25 2005), 36–8.

2   Kasper, R., "Beer Bubbles to Top of the Poll," *Baltimore Sun* (August 6, 2008), http://www.baltimoresun.com, accessed October 3, 2008.

3   Dolliver, Mark (2005).

4   Zhang, Y., X. Guo, R. Saltz, D. Levy, E. Sartinit, J. Niu and R. C.

Ellison, "Secular Trends in Alcohol Consumption over 50 Years: The Framingham Study," *American Journal of Medicine* 121 (August 2008), 695–701.

5   Kirsche, M. L., "Targeting Boomers Could Boost Fizzling Out Beer Sales," *Drug Store News* 27 (June 6, 2005), 81.

6   Longo, Don, "Drink Up," *Progressive Grocer* 84 (October 15 2005), 52–58.

7   Corso, R. A., "The Harris Poll #6," (January 14, 2008), www.harrisinteractive.com, accessed October 6, 2008.

8   Ricklefs, Roger, "Ethics in America," *Wall Street Journal* (October 31–November 3, 1983), 33.

9   See Dubinsky, Alan J., Rajan Nataraajan and Wen-Yeh Huang, "Consumers' Moral Philosophies: Identifying the Idealist and the Relativist," *Journal of Business Research* 58 (December 2005), 1690–1701; Deal, Ken, "Deeper into the Trees," *Marketing Research* 17 (Summer 2005), 38–40.

10 Adapted from Yavas, Ugur and Emin Babakus,"What Do Guests Look for in a Hotel? A Multi-Attribute Approach," *Services Marketing Quarterly* 25, no. 2 (2003), 6–14.

11 http://www.wineinstitute.org/resources/statistics, accessed December 30, 2008; http://winemarketcouncil.com, accessed December 30, 2008.

12 The data analysis tool must be added to the conventional Excel install by unpacking the data tool. This can be done by clicking on tools and then clicking on ad-ins and following the instructions. See http://www.microsoft.com for more instructions on how to accomplish this.

13 Iuso, Bill, "Concept Testing: An Appropriate Approach," *Journal of Marketing Research* 12 (May 1975), 230.

14 Diamon, Sidney, "Market Research Latest Target in Ad Claim," *Advertising Age* (January 25, 1982), 52. Reprinted with permission by Crain Communications, Inc.

15 Adapted with permission from Melvin Prince, *Consumer Research for Management Decisions* (New York: John Wiley and Sons, 1982), pp. 163–166.

Chapter 21

1   Gale Research Database, http://www.gale.cengage.com/.

2   Ziobro, P., "At Domino's, Dough Gets Tighter," *Wall Street Journal* (October 15, 2008), B1.

3   Technically the t-distribution should be used when the population variance is unknown and the standard deviation is estimated from sample data. However, with large samples, the t-distribution approximates the Z-distribution, so the two will generally yield the same result.

4   See a comprehensive statistics text for a more detailed explanation.

5   Cohen, J., "A Power Primer," *Psychological Bulletin* 112, no. 1 (1992), 155–159.

6   A more complex discussion of the differences between parametric and nonparametric statistics appears in Appendix 22A.

7   Kranz, Rick (2004),"Maybach, Rolls Models are Far Below Predictions," 79 Automotive News (10/18).

8   In most cases, low p-values support hypotheses. However, if the hypothesis is that the observations will be equal to the theoretical expectations for a given distribution (this would be the null case), then a high p-value would support the hypothesis. Generally, this is not good form for a hypothesis. Exceptions to this rule exist. One of the most common is when a researcher compares some matrix of values with some alternative matrix of values with a goodness-of-fit test. Particularly in advanced applications (beyond the scope of this book), the researcher may wish to test whether or not the two matrices are the same within sampling error. In this case, the researcher would need an insignificant p-value (above α) to support the hypothesis.

Chapter 22

1   Murphy, Victoria, "The Revolution That Wasn't," *Chain Store Age* 172 (October 27, 2003), 210.

2   Tang, F. F. and X. Xing, "Will the Growth of Multi-Channel Retailing Diminish the Pricing Efficiency of the Web?" *Journal of Retailing* 77 (2001), 319–333.

3   Three nonparametric tests—the Wilcoxon matched-pairs signed ranks test, the Kruskal-Wallis test, and the Mann-Whitney U test can also be used but are not described here. ANOVA for complex experimental designs is covered in an appendix to this chapter.

4   The formula is not shown here but it can be found in most basic statistics books.

5   See, for example, Armstrong-Stassen, M., "Designated Redundant but Escaping Lay-Off: A Special Group of Lay-Off Survivors," *Journal of Occupational and Organizational Psychology* 75 (March 2002), 1–13.

6   This is the "statistical alternative" hypothesis.

7   Sukhdial, Ajay, Damon Aiken and Lynn Kahle, "Are You Old School? A Scale for Measuring Sports Fans' Old-School Orientation," *Journal of Advertising Research* 42 (July/August 2002), 71–81.

Chapter 23

1   Levitsky, David L. and Trisha Youn, "The More Food Young Adults Are

Served, the More They Overeat," *Journal of Nutrition* 134 (October 2004), 2546–2549.

2   Rolls, B. J., L. S. Roe and J. S. Meengs, "Reductions in Portion Size and Energy Density of Foods Are Additive and Lead to Sustained Decreases in Energy Intake," *American Journal of Clinical Nutrition* 83 (January 2006), 11–17.

3   Gray, Stephen, "McDonald's Menu Upgrade Boosts Meal Prices and Results," *Wall Street Journal* (February 18, 2006), A1.

4   For a discussion of the other measures of association, see the appendix to this chapter and Jean Dickinson Gibbons, *Nonparametric Methods for Quantitative Analysis* (New York: Holt, Rinehart and Winston, 1976).

5   Bott, Jennifer P., Daniel J. Svyantek, Scott A. Goodman and David S. Bernal, "Expanding the Performance Domain: Who Says Nice Guys Finish Last?" *International Journal of Organizational Analysis* 11, no. 2 (2003), 137–152.

6   Bagozzi, Richard P., "Salesforce Performance and Satisfaction as a Function of Individual Difference, Interpersonal and Situational Factors," *Journal of Marketing Research* (November 1978), 517–531.

7   Recall that the mean for a standardized variable is equal to 0.

8   For more on this topic, see Hair, J. F., W. C. Black, B. J. Babin, R. Tathum and R. Anderson, *Multivariate Data Analysis* 6th ed. (Upper Saddle River, NJ: Prentice Hall, 2006).

Chapter 24

1   Heesup, H. and K. J. Back, "Investigating the Effects of Consumption Emotions on Customer Satisfaction and Repeat Visit Intentions in the Lodging Industry," *Journal of Hospitality and Leisure Marketing* 15, no. 3 (2006), 30–55.

2   Reynolds, K. E., J. Ganesh and M. Luckett, "Traditional Malls vs. Factory Outlets: Comparing Shopper Typologies and Implications for Retail Strategy," *Journal of Business Research* 55 (September 2002), 687–696.

3   Albert, N., D. Merunka and P. V. Florence, "When Consumers Love Their Brands: Exploring the Concept and Its Dimensions," *Journal of Business Research* 61 (October 2008), 1062–1075.

4   Holak, S. L. and W. Havlena, "Feelings, Fun and Memories: An Examination of the Emotional Components of Nostalgia," *Journal of Business Research* 42, no. 3 (1998), 217–226.

5   When the actual regression model is illustrated as an explanation of the actual dependent variable in

a population, Y_i is used and an error term (e_i) is included because the sample parameters cannot be expected to perfectly predict and explain the actual value of the dependent variable in the population. When we use a regression equation to represent its ability to predict sample values of the dependent variable from the estimated parameter coefficients, $\hat{Y}_i$ is used to represent predicted values of Y_i and no error term is included since the actual amount of error in any given observation is unknown.

6   School enrollment statistics can often be found using the Internet and either searching through government statistics or examining the Web site for the local school district or school board.

7   The constant term has disappeared since it is equal to 0 when the regression coefficients are standardized.

8   See Hair et al. (2006) for more on this topic.

9   Cox, A. D., D. Cox and R. D. Anderson, "Reassessing the Pleasures of Store Shopping," *Journal of Business Research* 58 (March 2005), 250–259.

10 Closs, D. J., M. Swink and A. Nair, "The Role of Information Connectivity in Making Flexible Logistics Programs Successful," *International Journal of Physical Distribution and Logistics Management* 35, no. 4 (2005), 258–277.

11 Morrison, Mark, A. Sweeney and T. Heffernan, "Learning Styles of On-Campus and Off-Campus Marketing Students: The Challenge for Marketing Educators," *Journal of Marketing Education* 25 (December 2003), 208–217.

12 See Hair et al. (2006) for more on this topic.

13 Holak, S. L. and W. Havlena (1998).

Chapter 25

1   Dowling, Mike, "Mr. Dowling's Rosetta Stone Page," http://www.mrdowling.com/604-rosettastone.html, accessed November 2, 2008; "Rosetta Stone," Microsoft Encarta Online Encyclopedia (2008), http://encarta.msn.com, accessed November 2, 2008.

2   Yore, L. D., M. K. Florence, T. W. Pearson and A. J. Weaver, "Written Discourse in Scientific Communities: A Conversation with Two Scientists about Their Views of Science, Use of Language, Role of Writing in Doing Science, and Compatibility between Their Epistemic Views and Language," *International Journal of Science Education* 28 (February 2006), 109–141.

3   Sullivan, E. A., "Twitterpated: Marketers Enamored of Online Communication System," *Marketing News* (October 15, 2008), 8.

4   The original version of this chapter was written by John Bush, Oklahoma State University, and appeared in William G. Zikmund, *Business Research Methods* (Hinsdale, IL: Dryden Press, 1984).

5   Keating, M., "Research Reports: A Valuable Tool for Getting Up to Speed in the Marketplace," *Occupational Hazards* (August 2008), 56D–56F.

6   "A Speech Tip," *Communication Briefings* 14, no. 2 (1995), p. 3.

7   These guidelines, adapted with permission from Marjorie Brody (President, Brody Communications, 1200 Melrose Ave., Melrose Park, PA 19126), appeared in "How to Gesture When Speaking," *Communication Briefings* 14, no. 11 (1995), p. 4.

8   "Tips of the Month," *Communication Briefings* 24, no. 7 (May 2005), p. 1.

9   Based on Bridis, Ted, "Study: Shoppers Naïve about Online Pricing," *Information Week* (June 1, 2005), downloaded from InfoTrac at http://web2.infotrac.galegroup.com; Annenberg Public Policy Center (APPC), "Annenberg Study Shows Americans Vulnerable to Exploitation in the Online and Offline Marketplace," news release (June 1, 2005), http://www.annenbergpublicpolicycenter.org; and Joseph Turow, Lauren Feldman and Kimberly Meltzer, "Open to Exploitation: American Shoppers Online and Offline," APPC report (June 2005), downloaded at http://www.annenbergpublicpolicycenter.org.

INDEX